THE MANAGERIAL AND COST ACCOUNTANT'S HANDBOOK

THE MANAGERIAL AND COST ACCOUNTANT'S HANDBOOK

Edited by

Homer A. Black
Professor of Accounting
Florida State University

James Don Edwards
J. M. Tull Professor
of Accounting
University of Georgia

Dow Jones-Irwin
Homewood, Illinois   60430

ISBN 0-87094-173-9
Library of Congress Catalog Card No. 78–61201

Printed in the United States of America

1 2 3 4 5 6 7 8 9 0 K 6 5 4 3 2 1 0 9

Dedicated to the two Claras—
Clara Black *and* **Clara Edwards**
*whose confidence, patience, support,
and tolerance made this book possible.*

Preface

The executives of businesses—whether engaged in production, distribution, or financing—and the executives of governmental and not-for-profit organizations are faced with increasingly complex and difficult problems in managing the economic enterprises for which they are responsible. Cost accounting information, analyses, and projections, combined with a knowledge of how to employ this information in planning and controlling enterprise operations, are invaluable to today's manager. *The Managerial and Cost Accountant's Handbook* is intended to be a unique, practical quide to both the enterprise manager and those advisers on whom he relies for information and counsel.

The impact of cost accounting information and managerial accounting know-how on the ability of economic enterprises to obtain capital and to employ it effectively and profitably has increased significantly in recent years. Factors causing this increased importance include:

1. The increasing comprehensiveness of public financial reporting requirements, together with growing needs for internal reporting to management.
2. The expanding use of sophisticated management concepts and analytical techniques in planning and controlling economic activity.
3. The accelerating use and capability of high-speed, high capacity data processing systems.
4. The growing demands for more and better information by public agencies such as the Cost Accounting Standards Board, the Departments of Labor and Defense, the Internal Revenue Service, and the Securities and Exchange Commission.

The expanding scope of management's accountability, the intensifying need for more and better cost accounting information, and the availability of improved methods of managerial planning and control, all require new and more comprehensive knowledge on the part of enterprise executives and their professional advisers. In the past it has been necessary for them to spend great amounts of time in reading many different publications in order to gain this knowledge. The objective of *The Managerial and Cost Accountant's Handbook* is to fill a void in accounting literature by providing in one convenient volume practical guidance for solving a wide variety of managerial and cost accounting problems of the modern economic enterprise.

To accomplish this objective, the *Handbook* has used a *team* approach. Most of the chapters are written by a team consisting of an accounting executive from industry or public accounting practice and an accounting educator. The purpose is to provide an accurate, up-to-date compendium of knowledge on managerial and cost accounting policies that have been effective in practice. Chapter authors are individuals who have been significantly involved in formulating and implementing managerial and cost accounting policy, or who have a sound knowledge of modern developments in these areas.

The Editorial Advisory Board is comprised primarily of top-level executives in business and industry, but also includes executives in professional accounting associations and in public accounting.

Part One of the *Handbook* provides a brief but meaningful historical perspective and a review of some basic ideas which have had a lasting influence in the field of cost accounting.

Part Two, Managerial Uses of Cost Accounting Information, and Part Three, Organizational Aspects of Cost Accounting, provide information that is potentially useful to management and accountants in all types of business. Many of the chapters deal extensively with specific managerial problems involved in planning, pricing, negotiating, evaluating, and controlling organizational performance.

Four chapters of Part Four, Common Elements of Cost and Managerial Accounting Methodology, deal primarily with the problems of manufacturers. The other two chapters are relevant for budgeting and reporting cost performance for a wide variety of businesses.

Part Five, Cost Accounting and Control Systems for Manufacturers, deals with both historical and standard cost systems, as well as the use of direct and incremental costing for planning and control purposes.

Part Six, Cost and Managerial Accounting for Other Economic Entities, applies to a wide variety of business enterprises, as well as to government and not-for-profit organizations. Part Seven, Special Methods of Cost Accounting and Control, also has important implications for manufacturers, other business enterprises, government, and not-for-profit organizations.

Part Eight, Emerging Trends and Challenges in Managerial and Cost Accounting, deals with some of the important recent developments and unsettled issues, and outlines some potential solutions to unsolved current problems.

The aim throughout the *Handbook* is to give *practical* guidance based on the experience of those who have faced the problems and found useful solutions to them.

A detailed, comprehensive index has been developed in order to make it easier for the reader to find the particular information which relates to his or her problems.

The Managerial and Cost Accountant's Handbook is up-to-date, theoretically and professionally sound, and practical. It is a relevant, dependable, and useful guide for those who must make decisions relating to the reporting, evaluation, and use of cost and managerial information for economic enterprises.

We particularly wish to acknowledge the significant contributions of the members of the Editorial Advisory Board: Terence E. (Mac) McClary, William M. Young, Jr., Allan H. Seed III, Robert J. Donachie, Robert Morgan, William Buxbaum, Robert K. Mautz, Adolph T. (Bud) Silverstein, Richard I. Polanek, Lloyd H. Chant, and J. O. Edwards; Richard F. Vancil, Harvard University, Editor-in-Chief of the Dow Jones-Irwin Handbook series; and, for her devoted, patient, and excellent secretarial assistance, Isabel L. Barnes.

February 1979   **Homer A. Black**
                                             James Don Edwards

Contributing authors

*Alonzo, Martin V.   (Chapter 19)
Vice President and Controller, AMAX, Inc.

Anderton, F. Norman   (Chapter 32)
Vice President and Treasurer, Vulcan Materials Company

*Baker, Donald W.   (Chapter 2)
Corporate Controller, Southwire Company

*Baskin, Elba F.   (Chapter 24)
Associate Professor, Oklahoma State University

*Baudhuin, Clarence J.   (Chapter 5)
Executive Vice President-Finance and Administration, Chemical Plastics Group, Dart Industries, Inc.

Beard, Larry H.   (Chapter 20)
Associate Professor, College of Business Administration, University of South Carolina

*Beisman, G. H.   (Chapter 26)
Project Manager, Kellogg Corporation

Biagioni, Louis F.   (Chapter 16)
Professor of Accounting, Indiana University

Bonsack, Robert A.   (Chapter 37)
Principal, Peat, Marwick, Mitchell & Co.

*Brown, Michael M.   (Chapter 12)
Manager-Project Management, Industrial Packaging Group, International Paper Company, New York, New York

Bulmash, Gary F.   (Chapter 42)
Assistant Professor, The American University

Carroll, John M.   (Chapter 33)
Vice President Finance, Leach & Garner Company

Coie, Michael J.   (Chapter 29)
Touche Ross & Co.

Deakin, Edward B., III   (Chapter 4)
Associate Professor, The University of Texas at Austin

*DeMoville, Wig B.   (Chapter 41)
Assistant Professor of Accounting, University of Wisconsin-Milwaukee

Dudick, Thomas S.   (Chapter 21)
Manager, Ernst & Ernst

---

* Denotes coauthor

Edwards, J. O. (Chapter 22)
Controller, Exxon Company, USA

*Fella, James** (Chapter 36)
Director of Planning, Celanese Corporation

Fischer, Paul M. (Chapter 28)
Associate Professor, University of Wisconsin-Milwaukee

Frank, Werner G. (Chapter 36)
Professor, University of Wisconsin-Madison

*Franklin, Larry D.** (Chapter 41)
Senior Vice President and Treasurer, Harte-Hanks Communications, Inc.

Freeman, Robert J. (Chapter 30)
The University of Alabama

Fremgen, James M. (Chapter 19)
Professor, Naval Postgraduate School

*Gilley, E. R.** (Chapter 31)
Vice President for Business Affairs, The University of Texas System Cancer Center, M. D. Anderson Hospital

*Grenell, James H.** (Chapter 6)
Vice President and Controller, Honeywell, Inc.

Grinnell, D. Jacque (Chapter 25)
Professor of Accounting, The University of Vermont

Haley, Donald C. (Chapter 39)
Controller, The Standard Oil Company (Ohio)

Harwood, Gordon B. (Chapter 34)
Associate Professor of Accounting, Georgia State University

*Hensold, Harold H., Jr.** (Chapter 30)
Arthur Young & Company

*Holder, William W.** (Chapter 30)
Texas Tech University

*Howard, Edgar N.** (Chapter 4)
General Manager, Management Information Division, Texas Eastern Transmission Corporation

*Ihlanfeldt, William J.** (Chapter 38)
Manager, Accounting Research and Policy, Shell Oil Company

*Jordan, Raymond B.** (Chapter 35)
Administrator-Cost Systems & Studies, General Electric Company

Klink, James J. (Chapter 27)
Partner, Price Waterhouse & Co.

Kollaritsch, Felix P. (Chapter 35)
Chairman and Professor of Accounting, The Ohio State University

Landekich, Stephen (Chapter 23)
Research Director, National Association of Accountants

*Levine, Kenneth C.** (Chapter 34)
Forecasting Manager, Coca-Cola USA

Loschen, Leslie R. (Chapter 5)
Associate Professor of Accounting, University of Southern California

Louderback, Joseph G. (Chapter 8)
Associate Professor, Rensselaer Polytechnic Institute

McClary, Terence E. (Chapter 9)
Vice President-Corporate Financial Administration, General Electric Company

McDonald, Charles L. (Chapter 3)
Associate Professor, School of Accounting, University of Florida

McIntyre, Edward V. (Chapter 38)
Professor of Accounting, Florida State University

Maher, Michael W. (Chapter 18)
Assistant Professor of Accounting, The University of Michigan

Okes, S. R., Jr. (Chapter 26)
Senior Project Manager, Kellogg Corporation

Palmer, John R. (Chapter 7)
President, Twin Cedars Associates, Inc.

* **Parks, Dave** (Chapter 11)
Partner, Arthur Andersen & Co.

* **Plum, Charles W.** (Chapter 39)
Professor of Accounting, Texas A & M University

Powell, Henry D. (Chapter 24)
Manager of Corporation Operations Analysis and Control, Phillips Petroleum Company

Purdy, Charles (Chapter 6)
Associate Professor of Accounting, The University of Minnesota

Rayburn, Frank R. (Chapter 12)
Associate Professor of Accounting, School of Accountancy, The University of Alabama

Rhode, John Grant (Chapter 10)
Lecturer, University of California

Roemmich, Roger A. (Chapter 2)
Assistant Professor, School of Accounting, University of Georgia

* **Rosen, Louis I.** (Chapter 42)
Staff, The Cost Accounting Standards Board

* **Rowan, Thomas F.** (Chapter 37)
Manager, Peat, Marwick, Mitchell & Co.

* **Russell, T. Alan** (Chapter 1)
Controller, Illinois Cereal Mills, Inc.

* **Schek, Leslie G.** (Chapter 20)
Senior Vice President-Administration and Finance, Noxell Corporation

* **Schoonover, John D.** (Chapter 28)
Vice President & Controller, Alcan Aluminum Corporation

Schroeder, Richard G. (Chapter 13)
Associate Professor of Accounting, Texas A & M University

Seiler, Robert E. (Chapter 31)
Professor, University of Houston

* **Shealy, Arthur L., Jr.** (Chapter 3)
Controller, Barnett Banks of Florida, Inc., Jacksonville, Florida

Silverstein, Adolph T. (Chapter 15)
Controller, Fruehauf Corporation

* **Smith, Fulton M., Jr.** (Chapter 10)
Director, Management Advisory Services, Deloitte, Haskins, & Sells

Sollenberger, Harold M. (Chapter 11)
Chairman, Accounting and Financial Administration Department, Michigan State University

Stallman, James C. (Chapter 1)
Associate Professor of Accountancy, University of Missouri, Columbia

* **Stoddart, William** (Chapter 27)
Partner, Price Waterhouse & Co.

Strathdee, Kenneth A. (Chapter 14)
Partner, Management Consulting Services, Coopers & Lybrand

Thiry, Donald L. (Chapter 17)
Partner, Arthur Andersen & Co.

Turney, Peter B. B. (Chapter 40)
Associate Professor of Accounting, Portland State University

* **Vobroucek, Calvin A.** (Chapter 13)
Manager, Profit Planning Accounting, Caterpillar Tractor Co.

* **Wait, Donald J.** (Chapter 25)
Consultant, Product Cost Accounting, General Electric Company

* **Warne, Richard A.** (Chapter 16)
Assistant Corporate Controller, Eli Lilly and Company

* **Watne, Donald A.** (Chapter 40)
Assistant Professor of Accounting, Portland State University

* **Webb, Richard P.** (Chapter 8)
Vice President and Chief Financial Officer, Carrier Corporation

* **Wieland, William H.** (Chapter 5)
Retired Senior Vice President and Comptroller, United California Bank

Williams, Doyle Z. (Chapter 41)
Professor and Chairman, Department of Accounting, University of Southern California

* **Yates, David C.** (Chapter 18)
Assistant Controller, Great Lakes Steel Division, National Steel Corporation

* **Yeargan, Percy B.** (Chapter 32)
Professor of Accounting, School of Business, University of Alabama in Birmingham

* **Zimmer, Robert K.** (Chapter 6)
Professor of Accounting, The University of Minnesota

Contents

PART THREE
ORGANIZATIONAL ASPECTS OF COST ACCOUNTING

Develop the long-range plan. Installing the MIS. The role of the controller in executing the MIS plan: *MIS planning and control "truths." Ongoing controller involvement in MIS.*

**PART FOUR
COMMON ELEMENTS OF COST AND MANAGERIAL ACCOUNTING METHODOLOGY**

level (denominator) should be used? Fixed manufacturing overhead variances: *Volume variance. Spending variance.* Variable manufacturing overhead variances: *An illustration of variances.* Direct costing. The Cost Accounting Standards Board (CASB). The Internal Revenue Service (IRS).

PART FIVE
COST ACCOUNTING AND CONTROL SYSTEMS FOR MANUFACTURERS

Incremental costing: *Types of decision problems. The incremental approach. Other considerations.*

PART SIX
COST AND MANAGERIAL ACCOUNTING FOR OTHER ECONOMIC ENTITIES

Standards. Standards for business line profitability analysis. Standards for cost control. Nonlabor costs. Fitting the pieces together. A conceptual framework. Using the framework for decision making.

Introduction. Cost accounting versus cost finding. Essential fund accounting concepts and terminology: *Types of funds.* Essential cost concepts and terminology: *Variable versus fixed costs. Cost centers and responsibility accounting. Job order versus process costing. Direct and indirect costs.* Cost accounting and cost finding: "Proprietary" activities: *Enterprise Funds. Internal (Intragovernmental) Service Funds.* Cost accounting and cost finding: "General government" activities: *Reconciliation of expenditures, costs, and expenses (costs). Governmental fund distinguishing characteristics. Project-oriented fund costing. Period-oriented fund costing.* Budgeting tools: *Static (fixed) budgeting. Flexible budgeting. Performance budgeting. Zero base budgeting.* Standard costs and variance analysis. Different costs for different purposes.

Nature of not-for-profit organizations. Importance of cost accounting: *Cost accounting methods.* Importance of budgeting. Organizational aspects of control. Hospitals: *Organization. Third-party billing requirements. Revenue centers. Cost centers. Payroll-related costs. Donated services and supplies. Use of statistical allocational bases. Cost finding. Calculation of daily room costs. Cost allocation to type of patient. Budget systems. Capital budgeting.* Private clubs: *Role of cost accounting. Cost centers. Allocation bases. Contribution margin prices. Budgeting. Capital budgeting.* Churches. Voluntary health and welfare organizations: *Cost classifications. Depreciation. Donated materials and services.* Schools and universities: *Cost sharing. Overhead rate for sponsored programs. Cost Accounting Standards Board (CASB).*

PART SEVEN
SPECIAL METHODS OF COST ACCOUNTING AND CONTROL

Introduction. Objectives. Forecasting. Cash collections. Cash disbursements. Investing. Borrowing. Bank relations.

Introduction. Strategic context of capital spending proposals: *The structure of strategy. Strategy and risk. Linking capital investments to strategy.* The capital expenditure proposal: *Developing investment opportunities.*

PART ONE

Cost accounting background and concepts

1
Historical development, uses, and challenges of cost accounting

*James C. Stallman**
T. Alan Russell†

Cost accounting is a discipline in the process of developing. It has both a long and honorable past and a promising future. In its long history cost accounting has surely encompassed many techniques and procedures which, having never been described in written form, have long been forgotten. Others have been documented, but their purposes at the time they were used are unclear as the cultural setting of their use and the motives of their originators are beyond our ability to comprehend fully. Similarly, there will be uses emerging in the future for cost accounting and newly developed procedures to satisfy those uses which we have yet to perceive. It is the purpose of this introductory chapter to sketch a picture of the development of cost accounting, to describe briefly some of the important purposes to which its activity is directed, and to suggest some of the major challenges which lie before it.

Cost accounting as it is presently practiced may be thought of as that portion of the accounting discipline concerned with the development of cost information related to the activities of an economic entity. This cost information may be estimated

* Associate Professor of Accountancy, University of Missouri, Columbia.
† Vice President and Controller, Indiana Telephone Corporation.

future costs developed for planning purposes, or accumulated actual costs directed toward the evaluation of performance. It may emerge somewhat routinely out of a carefully designed system which has been developed to provide information regarding recurring activities, or be the result of a special cost study directed to an objective not considered in the design of the regular system.

Cost accounting comprises all of the methods and procedures used to associate actual costs with the activities for which they were incurred. It includes the recording and the reporting forms and procedures as well as the rules for cost measurement which support them. With regard to cost estimation, cost accounting provides structure to the analysis. It provides a means of visualizing a proposed activity into cost-generating components, and organizing individual cost estimates for those components for aggregation to total cost for the overall activity.

It is important to understand that all of the methods and procedures encompassed by cost accounting exist to serve some particular use or purpose. Often a procedure will be found to serve several purposes; however, it should not be taken for granted that a procedure which appears legitimate for one purpose would necessarily provide useful information for another purpose.

In its present state cost accounting is useful for a variety of purposes. While it might be argued that the sole purpose of cost accounting is to provide cost information for decision making, it is useful to organize the broad variety of decisions which might be based in part on cost accounting information into broad purpose-oriented categories. For example, cost accounting might be thought of as being useful for the following broad purposes:

1. Product or service costing (inventory valuation/income determination)
2. Product pricing
3. Coordination of operations
4. Performance evaluation
5. Decision making

After briefly sketching the historical development of cost accounting we will return to these purposes to try to identify the role played by cost accounting in each. Then we will attempt to suggest some of the major challenges facing our discipline.

HIGHLIGHTS IN THE HISTORICAL DEVELOPMENT OF COST ACCOUNTING

As long as men have accumulated, held, and transferred property, either for business transactions or for the payment of taxes, there has been a need for accurate record keeping. This has been especially true whenever parties acting for their principals desired to show accountability for payments, receipts, or stocks of property held.

Perhaps the earliest preserved records are the clay tablets on which scribes recorded with cuneiform script the commercial transactions of the Babylonian and Sumerian civilizations which flourished in the Mesopotamian Valley several thousand years before the birth of Christ. Among these tablets are examples of receipt and expense records. One Sumerian Wage-List (from about 2350 B.C.) shows the amount of barley paid monthly to 162 workers for 13 months. Other records, almost as old, have been found in Egypt. One is reported to give a statement of receipts and disbursements of the court of King Sebekhotep (about 2000–1900 B.C.) at Thebe (Eldridge, 1954, p. 13).

Such early record keeping was very simple, of course, in effect involving special-purpose modifications of inventory records. But it is evidence of the early attempt to provide a set of records which served the simple objectives of the people involved.

Evidence of a much more extensive and well-organized system has been preserved in a collection of over 1,000 documents from Egypt which have become known as "the Zenon papyri." For the most part, these documents concern the private estate of Apollonious, who was the secretary of finance for Ptolemy Philadelphos. Zenon, who took charge of administering Appollonious' estate in 256 B.C., apparently instituted an accounting system whereby a supervisor in charge of each section of the estate (the farms, vineyards, livestock, grain storage, and so forth) would be held accountable for receipts, expenditures, and stocks of goods under his control (Hain, 1966, p. 700).

In Zenon's system every transaction was recorded, a procedure greatly facilitated by the availability of inexpensive and good quality papyrus writing material. Some of the documents show asset accounts where acquisitions were added and disposals were deducted after every transaction so that a perpetual inventory was maintained. Others show statements prepared only periodically from summaries of daily expenditures. Records show loans of money, seed grain, and breeding stock to the farmers of the estate as well as their subsequent repayment. Some of the accounts are for money, whereas many are in physical quantities of grain, livestock, lighting oil, and so forth. Of course, these accounts were kept separate because it was not until a much later date (about A.D. 630 in the Greek cities) that money was used as a measure of value.

The system seems to have been designed to control the use of the assets of the estate. However, there may have been other purposes. Among the documents were included several monthly, annual, and triennial summaries of transactions. These may have provided the basis for an annual assessment of taxes by the state bank at Philadelphia. H. P. Hain (1966, p. 702) has even speculated that several instances of management action, changes in personnel, discontinuation of existing departments, and so forth, may have occurred as the result of decisions based on these accounting statements.

Early industrial bookkeeping

Accounting historians have produced many scholarly treatises dealing with the development of record-keeping practices and have concluded that the best attained prior to the dark ages came far short of the systematic "double-entry" systems which began to appear in Italy around A.D. 1300. Yet in these primitive beginnings there is evidence of the recognition that systematic record keeping could promote an understanding of the nature and extent of personal wealth, provide evidence of wage payments and tax collections, facilitate credit transactions, and control by statements of accountability the activities of managers, supervisors, and agents of property owners.

In 1075 the Turks captured Jerusalem, and for the next 200 years thousands of men traveled across Europe to the Crusades. The Crusades proved to be a great stimulus to commercial interests which were beginning to develop at that time. Trading routes to the East were reopened and the crusaders returned to Europe with desires for the luxuries they had seen in their travels. Italy naturally became the center of European trade with the East, a trade so profitable that men were willing to risk great quantities of money (often in partnerships) to finance the trading voyages to the East.

As trade grew, the volume of credit transactions increased, and soon many of the largest traders in the Italian cities had developed into merchant-bankers. The first bank of importance, the Casa di San Georgio, was founded during the 12th century in Genoa (ten Have, 1976, p. 31). The development of double-entry bookkeeping in this trading and banking environment is a familiar, although still intriguing, story.

According to O. ten Have (1976, p. 34) the nature of the transactions of the merchant produced a need for recording each transaction twice in order to keep separate accounts for each debtor and creditor, for each type of merchandise, for cash, and for the components of his capital investment.

Systematic double-entry recording is found in the accounting of the bankers Musciatto and Biccio Franzesi in 1299. In books kept by the treasurers (massari) of Genoa (1340) the double-entry technique is extended to include an annual closing and transfer of gains and losses to a capital account for the municipality of Genoa. In the records (1399) of the commercial and banking house of Datini is found a detailed income statement (ten Have, 1976, p. 35). That the double-entry technique was extended and improved over the next hundred years by the large merchant-bankers to record greater volumes of transactions in greater detail is known, although it was the system of a medium-sized merchant which Luca Pacioli chose to describe in the first published description of the double-entry system in 1494.

At the same time trading and banking enterprises were thriving manufacturing operations were beginning to develop, too, bringing new forms of transactions to the accounting system and the need for alterations to accommodate industrial accounts. For example, the books of the Del Bene Company, manufacturers of wool, show the use of two sets of accounts in order to separate its trading activities from its manufacturing activities. By 1368 the company was gathering prime cost data in a separate "book of raw wool purchased," a "laborers wage book," and a "dyers wage book." These books were summarized periodically and their totals carried to the ledger of the company in order to obtain a profit for the period. Although quite crude even in relation to systems in use less than a hundred years later, the records of this firm have been said to hold the origins of industrial accounting (Garner, 1954, p. 15).

Another example of early industrial bookkeeping is found in the accounts of the Medici industrial enterprises. The Medici family, well known for its banking activities and political influence, also was engaged in the production of silk and wool during the 15th and 16th centuries.

The complicated and comprehensive system used by the Medici industrial partnerships underwent many changes through its long use as operations of the business became more complex. By 1441 the firm was using a double-entry system, taking inventories, and drawing up balance sheets. Using an account called "cloth manufactured and sold" to keep track of all the cloth manufactured, the Medici accountants were also able to summarize all the material, wages, and other costs of producing finished cloth.

After 1520 several additional books were used in the Medici system. One, a special wage ledger, seems to have been of particular importance. It is believed to be the first known example of a subsidiary ledger. The wage ledger contained accounts for workmen, cash, general expenses, cost of manufacturing, profit and loss, and a brokerage account, as well as a reciprocal account used to tie this ledger in with the general ledger. Several books of original entry were used along with the ledgers, and the complicated and technical system (by 1556) was capable of producing a great amount of detail relative to the firm's manufacturing costs including, separately, materials costs, labor costs of over a dozen manufacturing processes, and overhead (Garner, 1954, p. 12).

Garner (1954, p. 15) reports the following comment by Raymond De Roover:

> The bookkeeping system of the Medici was entirely adequate for their purpose and fitted perfectly their organization. It provided the means which the management needed to control the

flow of material as well as the movement of funds. It was not yet a cost finding system, but came very close to being one. The account books give enough indication to permit one to assume that the Medici had a good knowledge of their approximate cost.

Although the earliest examples of industrial accounting to be found in existing records are from the textile industry, presumably industrial accounts were appearing in other industries as well. At about the same time as the most detailed cost data were becoming available in the accounts of the Medici industrial firm, we find a very clear example of job order costing in an elementary form among the records of the Plantin publishing house in Antwerp.

During the period from 1563 to 1567, while Christopher Plantin was in partnership with several Antwerp merchants, the books of the business were kept by double entry in the style described by Pacioli. Florence Edler de Roover (1937) has carefully described the use of raw materials (paper), equipment, and manufacturing expense accounts in the Plantin records. For each book Plantin printed, a special account was opened to which the costs of paper used, wages, and other major direct expenses were charged (the paper and expense accounts were credited). When the book came off the press the special account was closed and an account "Books in Stock" was opened.

Although no charges were made for glue, ink, or depreciation, the principal direct charges were clearly being taken into a work-in-process account and then to a finished goods account as the books were completed. It is also of interest that the paper account was a perpetual inventory account with special extension columns for physical quantities on the debit and credit sides, so that the quantity of paper on hand could easily be determined.

Also during the 16th century, industrial accounting of a much different form was being used by the Fuggers in connection with their silver, lead, iron, and copper mining operations in Austria. Accounts were kept for various ores, for mining, foundry, and smelting operations, for general expenses, and for freight and transport costs (Garner, 1954, p. 6). It is interesting that the Fugger's chief accountant, Matthaus Schwarz, after making a thorough study of the Italian double-entry systems in use at that time (about 1500), decided that they were not suitable for his purposes and so designed his own system (ten Have, 1976, p. 47).

Other examples of early attempts at accounting for industrial operations have been cited by accounting historians, but the few noted here should suffice to suggest that early in the development of bookkeeping technique it was recognized that industrial operations required special accounts and procedures which differed from those sufficient for commercial operations. It is interesting, however, that while commercial accounting technique was widely described in published books over the next 250 years, almost no mention was made of special procedures for manufacturing operations. And little evidence of what was practiced by firms in the few emerging industries has been described by the historians. We can be sure, however, that new forms of business coming into existence were creating problems for the accountant and that these problems were being dealt with situation by situation with some degree of effectiveness.

Even during the 18th and most of the 19th centuries as the Industrial Revolution began and picked up momentum, published descriptions of special industrial accounting technique were sparse. From what little was published, however, we can perhaps obtain some insight as to what developments were occurring in practice.

In England in 1697, John Collins wrote a book entitled *The Perfect Method of Merchants Accounts*, in which he used a system of accounts for a cloth dyer as an illustration. In the illustration he described a material inventory account containing both quantities and prices kept on a perpetual basis. As material was used, its cost along with other miscellaneous costs was charged to a dyehouse account which served as a combination work-in-process, finished goods, and profit and loss account (Garner, 1954, p. 33).

James Dobson gives a clear illustration of a set of shoemaker's accounts in a book written in 1750. In the system described, a raw materials account was charged for hides purchased and credited as the hides were cut into shape to produce shoes. Accounts for soles, heels, and upper leather were charged as the hides were cut, and credited as the cut pieces were given out to craftsmen to complete the shoes in their homes. Accounts for each craftsman were charged for the leather given out, as well as cash paid for the work when it was returned. The total was then transferred into finished shoe accounts and allocated among sets of pairs of different sizes (Solomons, 1968, p. 6).

An interesting description of "process" cost accounting is given in a book by Wordhaugh Thompson in 1777. In an example of the manufacture of "thread-hosiery" from flax, he shows the manner by which manufacturing costs can be accumulated process by process through spinning, bleaching, dyeing, weaving, and trimming accounts (Solomons, 1968, p. 7). This "process" cost accounting system, it must be remembered, dealt with processes outside the firm, as the so-called domestic system of manufacture was still in wide use. It should be noted, then, that neither Dobson nor Thompson were describing flows of costs to portray internal transactions between departments or processes within the same firm, but rather were building their costs from a series of transactions with external parties.

In 1788 Robert Hamilton described the use of subsidiary records, advocated separate accounts for different kinds of manufacturing costs, and stressed the importance of structuring the records so as to be able to determine the profit earned on each of the separable activities being performed by the manufacturer (Solomons, 1968, p. 7).

In 1817 Anselme Payen, a Frenchman, described accounting systems appropriate for a carriage factory and a glue factory. Garner notes that these two illustrations are perfect examples of what we now call job-order and process costing. In Payen's systems there were two separate journal-ledger combinations, one for quantities and one for money. In his carriage illustration is found a definite internal transaction transferring labor costs of three completed carriages from the factory to the warehouse. His discussion illustrated several manufacturing cost statements or "abstracts," showed cost per unit computations, prescribed treatment of waste allowances, and described the allocation of joint costs between products (although the method of arriving at the allocated amounts was not explained). Garner (1954, p. 50) suggests that Payen came very close to integrating the cost and financial records.

Also in France, de Cazaux (1824) discussed depreciation expense distribution between the operations which received the benefits from the use of equipment, and M. Godard (1827) advanced thinking on raw materials costing, advocating that it be costed out of inventory at average cost and that detailed perpetual inventory records be kept (Solomons, 1968, p. 15).

Several other discussions of factory accounting prior to 1885 in France, England, and the United States could be mentioned, but space does not permit it. The few discussed should suffice to suggest that, although many emerging problems were being dealt with and progress toward modern cost accounting was being made, the pace of this development was slow. Where a discussion by one author might seem particularly advanced and modern in one area, other parts of it were likely to be retarded or incomplete. It should be noted that prior to 1885 there had been no true integration of factory cost records with the financial accounts and very little thought regarding the systematic application of overhead to manufactured product.

The modernization of cost accounting (1880–1920)

During the last two decades of the 19th century and the first two decades of the 20th, cost accounting developed rapidly in what Solomons (1968) has called a "costing renaissance." Many writers were influential during this period. Some were practicing accountants, but many were engineers. In the remainder of this section only a few of the more notable contributors to cost accounting thought will be mentioned as several developments are described separately. These developments are (1) the application of overhead costs, (2) the integration of factory cost records with financial accounts, and (3) the emergence of standard costing.

One of the prerequisites of accurate product costing is a systematic and detailed methodology for capturing the associated incidence of cost incurrence and production. In 1885 Henry Metcalfe, an American Army Ordnance officer, published his *Cost of Manufactures,* in which he made extensive recommendations on the manner by which detailed records of raw materials and direct labor usage could be associated with production of specific jobs. Two years later Emile Garcke and J. M. Fells, two British industrial executives and accountants, also published a book giving extensive coverage to materials and direct labor costs.

In these two works are found many modern ideas which had never before been recommended concerning the use of special-purpose documents which would serve simultaneously to authorize, initiate, and coordinate the flow of materials and work in the factory, and also to provide evidence with which to associate cost incurrence with that work. For example, Metcalfe recommended using a loose-leaf recording system in which cards would be originated for all materials transactions (both purchase and issuance by order) so that by sorting and summarizing the cards, stores inventory records could be assembled, and by refiling, amounts and costs of material used on each job would be available. He also suggested the use of cards upon which laborers could record the amount of time spent working on various jobs each day. These cards could serve in support of payroll procedures as well as allow labor costs to be associated with specific jobs (Garner, 1954, pp. 92, 110).

Suggestions by Garcke and Fells included issuance of work orders to foremen and materials requisitions to storeskeepers, with duplicates to bookkeepers, whereby exact reconciliation of accounts in the stores ledger with the stores account in the general ledger could be made. With regard to labor costs, they suggested the use of a "time board" by which labor time of individuals could be associated with jobs as well as support payroll preparation. Garcke and Fells are perhaps remembered more for their insistence that the cost records be carefully integrated with the financial accounts and their illustration of how it was to be accomplished (Garner, 1954, pp. 92, 111).

In the treatment of raw materials, refinements as to special stores ledger forms, reconciliations with physical inventory counts, the use of a "bill of materials" for new jobs, and requisition summaries to ease posting, were suggested continuously in subsequent works by various authors, so that by 1925 as Garner (1954, p. 100) states, ". . . the techniques and theories involved in handling and controlling the raw materials of a factory had become fairly well known." Similar refinements for labor costing seemed also to develop as the need arose.

Developments with regard to overhead application to production were subject to considerably more debate. First of all, the matter of which costs were to be included had to be settled. The sharp distinction now made between manufacturing costs as product costs on the one hand, and selling and administrative costs as period costs on the other, was not clearly seen by authors at the turn of the century. To be sure, some saw the distinction that way, but many argued for the inclusion of some elements of selling or administrative costs with overhead. And a vigorous debate developed as to whether or not imputed interest should be included.

There was also the problem of how to determine the overhead rate. Early practice seemed to favor the use of prime cost or labor cost as a basis for overhead application. Gradually, labor hours and then machine-hours were advocated, with Alexander Hamilton Church (1901) clarifying the advantages and deficiencies of each and advancing the novel idea that the factory could be considered as a collection of small production centers so that a more appropriate overhead rate per machine-hour could be developed for each and applied as product passed through it (Solomons, 1968, pp. 25–26). Additional clarifications followed as writers discussed the use of different bases for application of various categories of overhead costs seeming to be more naturally related to material usage, labor cost or time, or machine usage.

Also a topic of debate was the problem of rates fluctuating with production levels. Ideas about setting rates on the basis of full or normal capacity became prevalent, but raised the problem of what to do with idle capacity costs. It was the view of Alexander Hamilton Church that idle capacity costs should be applied to production via a supplementary rate in the same proportions as the normal overhead charges. This novel idea, although it was later discarded, drew attention to the problem of dealing with idle capacity costs and raised the question of whether some portion of manufacturing costs might reasonably be omitted from the computation of product costs. This idea was important later in the development of standard costing.

This development of thought concerning idle capacity was closely related to the question of whether overhead rates should be based on actual costs and determined at year end, or whether they should be predetermined. Serious discussion of this matter began in the 1890s, although predetermined rates had been used in a few firms and advocated by a few authors before then. Predetermination of rates was initially to be based on the previous year's costs, or an average of several previous years' costs. Only later did the orientation shift to budgeted cost estimates. As late as 1910 several noted accounting authorities were still reluctant to give up the notion that the only proper overhead allocation required spreading actual incurred costs over actual production.

Although the British authors, Garcke and Fells, insisted that the integration of the cost and financial records be done in their 1887 publication, many accountants (ironically mostly the English) argued for almost 30 years for keeping the two sets of records separate. They cited several reasons for this separation, including ease of recording, the difference in the nature and purposes of the records, the avoidance of several opportunities for embezzlement, and complications that integration of the records would cause for the auditor. Integration of the cost and financial accounts was much more easily accepted by American authors, and the gradual adoption of integrated systems by firms in this country provided experience which contradicted the arguments of those opposed to the procedure.

According to Solomons (1968, p. 36), a few of the writers of the late 19th century implied the use of cost estimates or norms with which actual manufacturing costs might be compared. However, he gives credit to John Whitmore for the first detailed description of a system of standard costing (1908). Prior to this description, one very notable contribution to the development of standard costing was the novel idea of an American engineer, Percy Longmuir, in 1902. In a discussion involving foundry costs, Longmuir advanced the idea that a comparison of actual costs with standards of what costs ought to be for various manufacturing functions would be valuable for the purpose of controlling costs (Solomons, 1968, p. 36).

After Whitmore, the value of standard costing for control purposes was stressed in the writing of many accountants and engineers. Harrington Emerson, noted American industrial engineer, discussed standard costing very clearly in a series of articles during 1908 and 1909. G. Charter Harrison developed the ideas of Emerson into the first complete standard cost accounting system (for the Boss Manufacturing Co., of Kewanee, Illinois in 1911). According to Solomons (1968, p. 47) articles by Harrison in 1918 "have a sureness of touch and a comprehensiveness in their treatment which shows standard costing to have left the experimental stage and to have attained the status of established practice."

Further developments (1920–1940)

While the development of cost accounting during the last two decades of the 19th century and first two of the 20th was truly remarkable, much work was left undone. Although the best cost accounting was quite good, many improvements would be forthcoming. Refinements in both job order and process costing, accounting for joint and by-products, treatment of scrap and spoilage costs, distribution of overhead costs to and between departments, and standard costs occurred more or less continuously through the next 20 years. Improvements were made both in recording practices and in reporting practices.

Not only were the best practices continually being improved, but also increased use and much wider acceptance of good practices among companies both large and small in a variety of industries increased the importance of these improvements. In addition, many of the new forms of analysis were carried from the manufacturing function to the areas of selling, distribution, and administration.

Several closely related developments of the 20s and 30s seem of such importance as to deserve special attention. Basically they were the result of efforts to increase the value of cost accounting in the uses we characterize as "Coordination of Operations," "Performance Evaluation," and "Decision Making." One of these developments, the development of business budgeting, seems to provide a unifying theme within which to discuss the others: flexible budgeting, break-even analysis, distribution costing, and responsibility accounting.

Writing near the close of the 20-year period being examined, Edwin L. Theiss (1937) traced the development of government budgeting in England and the United States to about 1922 and examined the close relationship of early business budgeting to this development. He also described several other influences or conditions which were present and of importance in stimulating the growth of budgeting as a tool of management. These included the standardization of manufacturing resulting from the "scientific management" movement, the early success of standard costing, industrial expansion and competition, and the endorsement of business budgeting by banks, credit officials, and insurance companies.

Apparently, the governmental budget was originally used in England as early as 1760 to control more effectively the spending of public officials, as well as to limit the power of the king to levy burdensome taxes on his subjects. The budget, which the Chancellor of the Exchequer presented to Parliament at the beginning of each year, included an accounting report of the previous year's governmental expenditures, an estimate of those for the coming year, and a set of recommendations regarding taxing methods. The effectiveness of the budget in making officials more accountable in their administration of public funds was increased greatly in 1800 when the enforcement of the budget was placed in the hands of the Cabinet, and even more so in 1837 by the Reform Acts, "which provided for enforcement of the budget by a truly representative Parliament." At that point the disbursements of public officials "were limited to budget appropriations, and all their incomes were properly accounted for by the annual audit." (Theiss, 1937, p. 44).

Governmental budgeting got its start in this country about 1895, when many municipalities began to take budgeting seriously. Theiss (1937, p. 46) reports that by 1920 practically all American cities and towns had adopted budgeting as part of better city administration. Forty-four states enacted budget laws between 1911 and 1919, and our national budget became a reality when Congress passed the National Budget and Accounting Act in 1921.

Actually, many of the essential ideas underlying budgeting are much older. A. C. Littleton (1954) found evidence of budgeting activity in the organizational procedures of the English manor of the mid-16th century. According to Littleton it was customary to forecast the need for various supplies a year in advance and to estimate the costs for each. In addition, the times of various supply needs were scheduled to provide a basis for cash needs and to determine the times that stated amounts of money should be transferred to specified officers of the estate.

This budgeting process was often quite detailed. For example, the duke and his council planned the menus of all meals for the coming year, allowing extra dishes for special feast days. This detailed plan apparently aided the kitchen supervisors in obtaining and issuing proper amounts of provisions. In addition, the clerks of the kitchen, brewery, granary, and so forth were required to report monthly summaries of purchases, issues, and inventories of supplies on hand to the countinghouse clerks. These reports were prepared under supervision of the controller's clerks, summarized in the countinghouse, examined by the auditor, and presented to the duke and his council for judgment of compliance and to provide for the next year's estimates.

Littleton (1954) also reports that the baker, brewer, and larderer were expected to produce a predetermined amount of bread, beer, and meat out of a given amount of materials. Thus the basic notion of physical production standards was present, even if used more as a check on accountability for amounts of raw and processed supplies than in judging efficient performance. And such predetermined production standards were no doubt also used in the budget estimates for needed kitchen provisions.

L. F. G. DeCazaux devoted a brief chapter of his book, *Elements D'Economie Privee et Publique,* Book II, Chapter III (Paris, 1825) to the preparation of a budget comparing the needs of a farmer for the coming year with the resources available at its beginning. In it, DeCazaux states, "Obviously, it is best to forsee not only all the needs in the greatest detail, but the exact times of those needs, so that one will be able to meet them effectively and on time" (*Journal of Accounting Research,* 1965, pp. 264–65). This modern-sounding purpose was obviously one of the motivating objectives behind the experiments that companies began making in the early 1900s with business budgeting.

Theiss (1937, p. 48) suggests that the earliest experiments with budgeting in the United States after the turn of the century involved fragmentary budgets of the governmental type. A few of the large companies budgeted certain expenses which were considered luxuries, such as advertising, research, and personnel expenses, the purpose being simply to limit the amount of the expenditures. But as production operations began to be standardized by the efficiency engineers and as cost accounting procedures developed to provide adequate cost information, the idea of budgeting production and other costs became possible. Gradually, the role of the budget shifted to aiding management's efforts at planning and coordinating its complex operations, to the evaluation of management effectiveness, and to cost control.

It is difficult to determine when the practice of budgeting by any large number of companies in this country began. However, in an editorial preface to an article published in the *NACA Bulletin* (1926) by Chester E. Weger, Manager of the Budget Department, Henry L. Doherty & Co., the editor noted,

> Henry L. Doherty & Co. was one of the first to see the value of budget planning and to develop it as a definitely dependable instrument of management. The methods of budget procedure and administration as employed throughout the organization have been in the course of development since 1913 and are applied as effective aids to the management in controlling all the operations under their supervision.

From the contents of Weger's article it is apparent that his company's budgeting system was quite well developed at the time of the article. Apparently budgeting was being developed to a sufficient degree in many other companies as accountants working with those budget systems began to describe their procedures in the emerging cost accounting literature. A steady stream of descriptions of budget procedure was forthcoming in the early issues of *NACA Official Publications* (called the *NACA Bulletin* after 1925) in this country, *The Cost Accountant* in England, and *Cost and Management* in Canada during the 1920s.

About 1920, the Metropolitan Insurance Company began to survey budgetary practice and to publish its findings through its Policy Holders Service Department. In 1926 the series of pamphlets which had been developed were assembled and published in book form. According to Theiss (1937, p. 52), this book was widely read and provided valuable information regarding budgeting forms and procedures. The meetings and publications of trade associations also enabled smaller companies to share the experience of those in their industries who had budgetary systems operating successfully.

From these early articles and descriptions of budgeting procedure, it is apparent that in trying to make their budgeting systems more effective several common problems were of concern to these early authors. One major problem related to the difficulty of accurately forecasting sales levels, so that production budgets might be established well enough to serve planning uses before implementation and to provide a basis for control evaluations after implementation. To deal with the effect of the problem on planning and control evaluations, it was suggested that the manufacturing cost budgets be made "flexible" so that costs could be budgeted at various production levels. By studying the behavior of costs as output fluctuated, the budgeter could test the budget plan with reference to expected profits (using "break-even analysis") and could adjust the plan with reference to actual volume after the fact so that control evaluations would be more meaningful.

Actually, recognition of the importance of cost variations due to changes in the level of plant activity came slowly to accountants. Solomons (1968, p. 32) cites Dionysius Lardner, the Irish economist, as one of the first to state clearly the importance of distinguishing between fixed and variable costs for an individual firm. This occurred in 1850 in Lardner's book, *Railway Economy.* The first reference to the fixed-variable cost distinction in a book widely read by accountants seems to have appeared in the first edition of Garcke and Fells' *Factory Accounts* (1887, p. 74). While there may have been some confusion in their association of variable costs only with manufacturing costs, and fixed costs only with administrative expenses, the distinction between cost behavior patterns is clear (Solomons, 1968, p. 34). It is difficult to understand why the importance of the distinction was not acknowledged in the writing of cost authorities in this country, with one exception, until the 1920s.

In a 1903 article in *Engineering Magazine,* Henry Hess illustrated the use of the now familiar break-even chart, which clearly demonstrated the importance of the fixed-variable cost distinction. However almost 20 years passed before another cost accounting authority devoted any great amount of attention to it.

In November 1921, an article by C. B. Williams entitled "Treatment of Costs during Periods of Varying Volumes of Production" was published in *The Journal of Accountancy.* While this article was devoted to justifying the use of "normal" capacity in establishing predetermined overhead rates, the author clearly illustrated the flexible overhead budget when he argued against setting overhead rates on the basis of actual production volume. He carefully showed that because the variable elements of overhead moved in proportion to volume fluctuations, the variable overhead rate would remain the same; but the fixed overhead rate would be distorted by volume changes unless a predetermined "normal" capacity level was used to define the rate. One year later, John H. Williams reexamined the variability of costs, discussed the third category of "semivariable" costs, and explained the use of the "high-low points" method of separating semivariable costs into their fixed and variable components.

By 1923, J. M. Clark had published his book, *The Economics of Overhead Costs,* and in 1924 Urban F. von Rosen provided an excellent brief description of the break-even chart. Beyond this date reference to the distinction between fixed and variable costs was common. Discussions of flexible budgeting became more explicit and comprehensive. Examples which might be cited include articles by Wilmot (1926), Bradley (1927), Ultrich (1929), Kennedy (1930), Brett (1932), and Klein (1936). Similarly, break-even analysis and marginal cost thinking were important, if not dominant, themes in articles by Kemp (1926), Bradley (1927), Rorem (1928), Sanders (1929), Freeman (1929), Burns (1931), and Dohr (1932).

During this period of time the use of flexible budgets and break-even analysis was apparently spreading to moderate-sized and even small companies. In response to an article by Chubbuck (*NACA Bulletin,* 1934) entitled "The Flexible Budget and Standard Costs in a Business of Moderate Size," Raeford Baily wrote a letter to the editor (which was published two months later) stating that his company was not only using the techniques described by Chubbuck, but was also using the related technique of break-even analysis. Mr. Baily was Chief Accountant for Mother's Cake and Cookie Company.

Also during this period, the now familiar techniques for separating fixed and variable components of costs, including the accounts method, the high-low points method, the engineering method, and the scattergraph method, were all discussed. In 1936 the economist Joel Dean surveyed the cost variability literature from 1920 to 1936. He then produced a series of cost behavior studies over the next half dozen years using regression analysis as his basic technique.

But the growing budget literature was not only concerned with this recognition of the importance of cost variability. Many articles appeared in which the budget was discussed as a comprehensive planning and control tool for all parts of the business. Administration of budget procedures was also a major topic in this early budget literature. Representative of this theme were articles by McKinsey (1922), Tobey (1925), Owen (1926), and Fletcher (1928). The importance of the sales budget and the interrelationships between various schedules of the comprehensive budget were emphasized. Especially visible in the literature of that period was concern with the analysis of selling and distribution costs.

Among the early articles on nonmanufacturing costs were two papers which had been presented at the Third Annual Costing Conference in London (July 25, 1924) under the session title "Administrative and Selling Costs, Their Nature and Distribution." These two papers by W. H. Higgenbotham and A. Stewart were published in *The Cost Accountant* (1924) and were reprinted in this country in *NACA Official Publications* less than six months later.

Quickly following were articles by Grover (1925), Crockett (1926), Tyrell (1927), and Hilgert (1927). Emphasis in these articles quickly shifted from cost finding techniques to analysis aiding coordination and control, and to planning uses. Using the marginal cost ideas developing at the same time, some of the analyses were aimed at measuring product or market area profitability and discussed marginal cost pricing (McNiece, 1929, and Freeman, 1929).

The development of distribution costing was a natural extension of the cost finding-standard cost-budgeting development which originally made its greatest strides in the manufacturing areas. Clerical and administrative costs also became subjects for analysis in articles such as Van Vlissingen's 1930 article, "Office Management & Efficiency Standards for Clerical Help." The development of nonmanufacturing cost analysis continued from these beginnings through the 30s and beyond, as did the more general topic of comprehensive budgeting.

Another development in cost accounting thought—closely related to the development of budgeting and the increased use of cost accounting for cost control and cost reduction, coordination, and performance evaluation—concerns the form, content, and procedures of cost reporting. As soon as it was recognized that the effectiveness of cost accounting in these uses depended upon the quality of the communication of cost information between the accountants, engineers, production foremen, sales executives, and other management personnel, attention was drawn to cost reporting policies and practices. Questions such as "To whom should cost reports be directed?", "Which costs should be included?", and "In what form should the costs be reported?" drew significant attention in the 1920s.

Hugo Diemer (1924, p. 3) stated in an article entitled "Methods of Supplying Cost Information to Foremen,"

> Our experience with over 1,000 foremen in 192 separate kinds of industry shows that in not over 10 percent of the cases are cost records brought to the foremen's attention at all. In most of the smaller businesses, the management keeps cost data closely guarded and usually does not want the foremen to know what profit is being made.

Notwithstanding this commentary on the state of cost reporting in the American factory, the thinking of some in the United States and England was well advanced, dealing with the early ideas and practices of "Responsibility Accounting." Representative of this thinking is a statement made by W. H. Higgenbotham after presenting a paper at the Third Annual Costing Conference in London (1924). In his reply to some criticism of the amount of detail into which his company analyzed administrative and selling costs, Mr. Higgenbotham made the following comment:

> We have developed a scheme of charging a man for responsibility for his actions as expressed in terms of cost. He must also be given the opportunity of controlling that cost within certain limits and either a statement of expense which he is prepared to accept and on the basis of which he is prepared to produce must be put before him, or he must himself be put in a position to authorize certain portions of the cost. . . . As regards to the general idea of distributing expenditure and charging it up to disbursements which have been incurred by people who know nothing about it, I am of the opinion that that is entirely wrong and should be restricted as far as possible. (Higgenbotham, 1924, p. 102.)

In his 1926 article, "The Preparation and Administration of Budgets," Chester E. Weger made some very pointed comments concerning the need for participation in preparing budget estimates and the value of establishing responsibility for parts of the budget. He also commented on the need for adjusting the budget to reflect uncontrollable changes in conditions. Thus the seeds had been sown for later development of carefully conceived performance evaluation and control systems based on the assessment of individual managers' decision authority.

One final development beginning in the 1920–40 period which relates closely to those previously discussed is that of direct costing. This distinct form of income computation and presentation, in recent years also called "variable costing," began to receive considerable attention in the accounting literature following two articles which appeared in the *NACA Bulletin* in 1936 and 1937. Weber suggested in his book, *The Evolution of Direct Costing* (1966), that the new form of income computation may well have been tagged with the name "direct costing" because of terminology used in the first of those two articles. In his 1936 article, "What Did We Earn Last Month?", Jonathon N. Harris referred to his proposed system as the "direct cost plan." Harris' article stirred the readers of the *NACA Bulletin* to considerable comment in succeeding issues of that journal.

In 1937 Clem N. Kohl also argued clearly for an income computation which avoided allocations of fixed manufacturing costs to product produced. He believed that by deducting all fixed manufacturing costs in the period incurred, a more understandable income statement would result. He felt that this form of computation would be more meaningful to executives because income would vary directly with sales volume and would not be influenced by production volume. In support of his position, Kohl cited the success his own firm, the Gates Rubber Company, had been having with it since it began using the system in 1919.

Following these two articles, debate concerning the value of the direct costing income computation occurred frequently in the accounting literature. In fact, over the last four decades more has probably been written on direct costing than on any other cost accounting subject. It has been advocated for internal performance reporting for overall company operations, as well as for reporting on product lines, divisions, or other segments of a company. It has also been advocated for external financial reporting. While direct costing has never gained the acceptance of the profession for external reporting, it has been widely adopted for internal use.

Continuing influences

In the previous section the development of a number of procedures was associated with the 1920–40 period. Just as it was noted in that section that several of those procedures actually took root in the thinking and practice of previous decades (or even previous centuries), it should be noted here that their development has continued even to the present day. Discussion and use provided understanding of the value of those procedures and fostered refinement of technique and adaptation for new uses.

Of course there have also been new ideas and procedures whose development can be associated with the last two or three decades. We will not attempt to enumerate them here, as their development is a familiar part of our contemporary literature. At some later time perhaps we will have the required perspective to trace their development and to separate those of lasting value from those whose value was exaggerated during the time they were in vogue.

We should reflect on the historical development of cost accounting a bit longer, however, before we proceed to our discussion of its current uses and the challenges which lie ahead. It is important that we recognize that the development of cost accounting has been, and will continue to be, shaped by a variety of influences, facilitated by a number of organizations, and stimulated by the enthusiasm, the dedication, and the insight of a great many individuals. From the beginning, the development of new techniques, procedures, and forms of analysis and reporting have been motivated by the need for information to plan, coordinate, and control the operations of the business enterprise. As the nature of the operations of those enterprises has changed, so has the need for information. The accelerating growth and complexity of business has created problems, the solutions for which have created demands for new information. Increased mechanization in industry, changing forms of organization, and increased governmental regulation have all had their impact.

Not only has the changing need for information been influential in shaping the development of cost accounting; the increasing ability to generate and use information has also presented opportunities for further development. The influence of advances in other disciplines has also been felt as ideas from such areas as engineering, economics, mathematics, statistics, and social-psychology have been borrowed whenever needed to alter old procedures or to create new ones. Also, of course, the introduction and improvement of the digital computer has greatly increased our ability to process cost information—indeed, it has stimulated us and provided the ability to develop entirely new approaches to solving the problems of business.

USES OF COST ACCOUNTING

We have chosen to discuss the uses of cost accounting under the headings of (1) product or service costing (income determination), (2) product pricing, (3) coordination of operations, (4) performance evaluation, and (5) decision making. Although the uses of cost accounting can be classified in several other ways, this five-purpose classification seems somewhat easier to relate to common discussions of the activities of cost accounting, to the functions performed by the controller and his staff, and to descriptions of the role of cost accounting information in the management of economic entities.

Product or service costing (income determination)

The use of cost accounting to determine product or service costs for financial statement purposes is well known. In this use cost accounting might be thought of as part of financial accounting, an extension aimed at providing reasonable measures of the cost of manufacturing a given product or providing a given service. Since in this use the output of cost accounting is information for published financial statements or the computation of taxable income, cost accounting is greatly influenced by the principles and procedures prescribed by the authority of general acceptance for financial reporting or by regulations of the SEC, the Internal Revenue Service, and various regulatory commissions.

The role of cost accounting in this use is to associate the costs of various inputs to the revenue producing activities of a firm with the resulting revenues. In the case of a manufacturer, this requires the accumulation and application of a wide assortment of manufacturing costs to units of product produced, so that reasonable costs can be assigned to inventory for the balance sheet and to Cost of Goods Sold for the income statement. This is not an easy task, however, as anyone familiar with a complex multiproduct manufacturing operation will testify.

It is not too difficult to associate costs with the various inputs to the manufacturing process. It is considerably more difficult, however, to associate those input costs with the various activities, processes, and departments engaged directly in manufacturing products or providing support services for that manufacturing. It is more difficult still to associate those input costs with final product output. The logical connection between input costs and product output is often tenuous.

Some costs, to be sure, are easily traced by highly visible causal relationships between inputs, activities, and outputs. Others, however, are much less direct in their effect on coincident production. The relationships are more subtle and assumptions and judgments, which are often quite arbitrary, are required to make the cost assignments.

It is the broad financial reporting purpose which tends to dictate the basic recording structure for virtually all cost accounting systems encountered in practice. The objective is to insure that those systems will be compatible with the financial accounting system and that compliance with applicable laws or authoritative pronouncements can be observed. Typically, the entire structure of ledger accounts (and to a great extent the structure of subsidiary records, journals, and source documents) is based on the information needs of this use and the facilitation of the auditing function related to it. This is understandable. It is also a source of difficulty.

The difficulty arises when cost information is needed for other uses. For example, a system designed to efficiently record, classify, summarize, allocate, and apply manufacturing costs to individual products may not be flexible enough to provide unallocated, unsummarized data capable of reclassification in a manner appropriate for evaluating the impact of a particular decision which has recently been made. Such evaluations, although important, often fail to be made for want of appropriate cost information; or perhaps as bad, they are sometimes made by using inappropriate information.

Arbitrary allocations often make common fixed costs appear to be attributable to a particular activity, to be variable with the rate of that activity, and by implication to be controllable by the manager responsible for that activity. These allocations can easily lose their visibility in the process of summarizing or reclassifying such costs in combination with other costs, so that their effect on the data is hidden. The use of such costs in the evaluation of a decision involving an activity may result in misleading assessments of the quality of the procedures used to make the decision, or of the efficiency of the manager in implementing it.

Product pricing

The techniques of cost accounting have been associated with the purpose of product pricing almost from the beginning. In fact, it was reported by Garner (1954, p. 2) that some of the first significant developments in cost accounting in England resulted from the efforts of a small group of woolen workers. Being resentful of the many restrictions of the guild, they moved from the cities into the country to established industrial communities, hoping to be able to sell their products outside the influence of the organized guild. When they found themselves competing not only against the guilds, but also among themselves, they realized the need for carefully prepared cost records upon which to base their pricing decisions.

The problem of determining the "best" prices to attach to the products and services offered for sale by a firm is one of the most difficult of all problems of business. Many factors need to be considered in making pricing decisions, such as the amount of product expected to be demanded by customers at various selling prices, the nature of the competition for sales (including anticipated reactions by existing competitors to price changes and the ease of entry of new competitors), legal considerations, and of course, the expected costs of producing the product. Just how these factors should be considered in a given pricing situation is difficult to say, and the role of cost information in such decisions varies from situation to situation.

At one extreme, cost may seem to play no role at all for an individual firm in setting prices for a product which is sold in a purely competitive market. At the other, cost may be the primary factor in situations where prices must be negotiated by cost-plus contracts or where prices are being regulated by some governmental commission.

In the first instance, because an individual firm's decisions have no appreciable effect on the market, there would be no motivation to price products below the market price and no sales could be made at prices above the market. Thus, considerations of cost would not affect the price at which the product would be sold in the short run for the individual firm. Rather, costs in relation to the going price would be used by the firm to decide whether the product should be produced for sale at all. Of course, collectively such decisions would impact on the supply of the product by the industry and market prices would be affected.

In the second instance, the virtual absence of a competitive market leaves cost to serve as the basis for artificially constructed prices, the equitableness of which depends on the bargaining of contracting parties or the history of perceptions of regulatory commissions.

Between these extremes, the manner in which costs influence prices varies considerably. There are several distinct approaches to the pricing decision in which costs play differing roles. In each, cost considerations seem important.

Occasionally, the short-run incremental costs of producing and selling a product can be estimated with some degree of accuracy and can serve as a minimum value below which prices would clearly be unacceptable. But at what margin above that minimum a price becomes clearly acceptable may be very difficult to assess. A price—which covers incremental cost ever so slightly—may be acceptable in the short-run for a special order when idle capacity is present, but would lead to bankruptcy if used to price all production in the long run if it did not provide a sufficient margin to cover fixed costs.

It is not easy to judge what price will provide a margin sufficient to cover fixed costs in the long run for even a single-product
firm in the face of uncertain demand. For a multiproduct firm,
the pricing of individual products so that their aggregate margin
covers fixed cost may be possible in many ways. The best combination of prices to accomplish the guiding objectives of the firm
is still indeterminate without accurate predictions of demand
at various prices, as well as the individual products' usage requirements of fixed facilities.

At this point full (absorption) cost accounting, with its arbitrary
allocations of costs common to the production of many products,
is sometimes seen as providing a means of judging individual
product prices so that each product covers its "fair share" of
common fixed costs. In the face of competitive markets for multiple products the logic of full cost-based pricing schemes is not
compelling. In light of the tremendous difficulty of multiproduct
pricing, however, some pricing officers have argued that full
cost provides a good basis from which to begin making the kind
of executive judgments necessary to develop acceptable long-
run pricing policies.

Whether better pricing is possible in competitive markets with
reference to full product costs or not, such pricing seems to
be the rule in the area of defense contracting. Considerable
effort is being devoted to standardizing the procedures used
to allocate costs for this purpose.

Another use of cost accounting related to pricing is the justification of price differences for different classes of customers in
defense of proceedings under the Robinson-Patman Act. The
need or desire to justify prices in terms of costs seems to arise
with increased frequency these days, as firms try to defend their
actions in the face of increasing pressure for "social responsibility." But this is not strictly a modern development. Garner (1954,
p. 31) reports the public posting of a cost analysis in justification
of higher bread prices by the Worshipful Company of Bakers
in England back in 1620.

The role of cost accounting in each of these instances is to
provide a measurement system capable of conveying an understanding of the causal relationships between activities performed
and the resulting incurrence of costs. Only through such understanding is it possible to judge the probable profit impact of
various price/volume combinations, to justify price differences

to various customers on the basis of cost differences, or to arrive at an equitable cost basis upon which to construct a "reimbursement of cost" type of artificial price in contract situations or under regulatory authority.

Coordination of operations

By providing a framework of analysis within which to trace the flow of resources within an organization, cost accounting provides a means of coordinating related activities. This coordination can result from the flow of work-related source documents, or from summary analysis signaling the completion of a given transaction or operation and the need to initiate the next. Here cost accounting provides information flow which allows proper sequencing of related activities on a day-to-day basis. Cost accounting assists in increasing the efficiency of overall operations by tracing the flow of responsibility as it is accepted at the start and discharged at the completion of each component activity necessary for the success of those operations. Thus it allows both the coordination of resource flows with work flows and the tracing of accountability for resource use.

The cost accounting framework also provides the opportunity for associating expected resource flows, both their timing and amount, with plans for future operations. Such formalization of operating plans into operating and financial budgets permits a logical testing of the feasibility of those plans in the initial stages of the planning process and points to the need for work force, facility, and other resource acquisitions. The broad plans for future operations are interpreted into the necessary work schedules which detail the manner and timing of activities required to meet the objectives implied in the broad plans. As this is done, the expected relationship between activities and resource requirements which can be established from the experience recorded in the cost accounting system allows parallel scheduling of resource acquisitions.

Performance evaluation

Another general use for cost accounting data and analysis is to provide cost measures which can be used in the evaluation of the economic performance of managers, products, departments, or processes. The need for such evaluations stems from the desire to increase the efficiency of activities directed toward the attainment of an organization's goals. Cost measures the economic sacrifice required to complete some defined sequence of activities. Thus it provides an economic criterion with which to evaluate performance in the completion of desired activities. That is, completion of a given set of activities at a lower cost would be preferred to completion of the same set at higher cost. Or, for a given cost, completion of a greater set of activities would be preferred to completion of a smaller set.

Cost accounting measurements are often used in making such evaluations. The evaluations may compare the actual performance of a single organizational unit on several occasions (we did better this month than last), or may compare the actual performance of several units on one occasion (Process A performed better than Process B). Alternatively, useful comparisons can often be made between actual and expected cost performance (we didn't perform as well as we expected to). This latter form of evaluation is sometimes considered to imply that performance was better or worse than "it should have been." Whether or not such an implied judgment is warranted depends upon the confidence one has that the expected cost performance used as a standard of comparison reflects an attainable performance level in light of the actual conditions in which the performance was accomplished.

Performance evaluation reporting can take many forms and can be directed at many different objects. It can also be made for different reasons. In one instance an evaluation might be made of the profitability of a given product or service. This would likely involve a careful study of the costs attributable to that product or service which might be avoided in the long run through appropriate contractions of operations and facilities if manufacture of the product or provision of the service were discontinued. Such an analysis would attempt to provide an understanding of the factors affecting the level of cost incurred, such as volume of production, quality characteristics of the output, and length of production runs. Together with actual revenue this data might be used to evaluate the actual profit performance of the product. Together with estimates of future prices and volumes, the evaluation of potential future profitability might lead to a decision to discontinue production of the product. Alternatively, the evaluation might be of a decision recently made. It might assess the accuracy of predictions used, the validity of assumptions made, and the effectiveness of implementation procedures selected.

In another instance, cost measurements for a manufacturing process might be compared to expected levels (standards) with the hope that variances could provide clues to the existence and causes of operating difficulties. In other words, the performance evaluation might serve as a diagnostic tool. By monitoring the cost performance of a manufacturing process, management may be alerted to changes in operating conditions which could lead to identification and correction of specific operating problems.

Sometimes where problems cannot be detected soon enough to allow corrective action to reduce their effects, means are available to prevent (or at least reduce) the frequency of their recurrence. If the cost system can provide information which can be used to estimate the cost effect of a particular problem, an efficient combination of preventive and corrective control procedures might be found.

Of course, the same process performance evaluation system could detect uncontrollable changes in conditions affecting costs incurred in the process. In this case knowledge of changed conditions and their influence on costs allows decisions affecting the process to be reevaluated, so that those decisions can be altered if necessary to maintain optimality. For example, the effect of a labor rate restructuring might induce a decision to change material quality specifications in order to reduce labor cost lost on spoiled units, or to substitute machine processing for hand labor.

In still another instance, the performance evaluation may be specifically directed at judging the performance of an individual manager. This is a particularly difficult form of evaluation. It requires a great deal of knowledge about the operations under control of the manager, the nature of costs being incurred as a result of these operations, and the extent of the manager's decision-making authority (to influence the levels of costs incurred). It is also important to recognize and understand the factors beyond the control of the manager which can influence the level of his costs, so that the impact of these uncontrollable factors does not distort the evaluation being made.

Decision making

By our classification of uses, the final use of cost accounting is to provide information for making decisions. Of course, only future costs which are expected to differ between alternative courses of action can be relevant to a given decision. The role of the cost accounting system is to provide a pool of cost data from which to gain an understanding of the various costs which might be affected by a particular decision and the factors influencing those costs.

One of the major problems in this use is that several very different decisions may require cost data regarding the same set of operations. However, because of the nature of the decisions, costs might be used differently for different decisions. That is, a short-run product mix decision for a department may ignore some cost elements that would be relevant to a decision involving replacement of some of the department's equipment. In turn, the equipment replacement decision might ignore some cost elements needed in analyzing the advisability of closing the department altogether. Thus the cost data of the department must be recorded in sufficient detail so that it can be assembled in several meaningful combinations.

Another difficulty is that a given decision might be approached in several different ways, depending on how the decision maker visualizes the interaction of controllable and uncontrollable variables jointly influencing the outcome of the decision. In some cases there may be several well-defined models in common use with which to evaluate the consequences of a decision's alternatives. Choices among the competing models depends on their treatment of variables, judgments of the appropriateness of their underlying assumptions, and so forth. In other cases no existing ready-to-use models may be available, in which case the decision maker is faced with the task of constructing an appropriate model. No decision can be made without an evaluation of the available alternative courses of action. The role of the cost accounting system is to present cost information in a form which allows appropriate judgments of relevant costs for this evaluation process. This requires the cost information to be organized so that it can aid in the predictions required by alternative predefined models. It must also allow the decision maker, faced with constructing his own evaluation model, to interpret the relevance of the various elements of cost which seem to be related to the activities to be influenced by the decision.

Critical demands are placed on the supporting cost system because of these problems, which arise out of the complexity of the contexts within which decisions must be made. The extent to which the cost system should be capable of providing cost data in "ready to use" form for the range of possible decisions which have to be made is, of course, a cost-benefit question. Recurring decisions may justify routine processing and analysis of data in forms which make it quickly available for decision evaluations. Other special one-shot decisions, which cannot always be anticipated, may require extensive special cost studies. In the former case, anticipation of cost information needs may dictate appropriate classifications of the underlying cost data. However, the latter situation may be even more demanding, in that the underlying data must be preserved in a form which allows special purpose analysis to extract the needed information.

The role of cost accounting

As one considers the function performed by cost information in each of the previously described uses, it becomes apparent that the fundamental purpose of cost accounting is to provide a description of the relationships between the cost incurred to obtain resource inputs, the activities or processes performed to alter those inputs, and the resulting product or service outputs from those activities. From the initial collection of input cost data to the eventual reporting of cost information for a specific use, the methods and procedures of cost accounting provide structure to the cost measurement process. The effectiveness of those methods and procedures for a given use depends upon their ability to preserve the essential characteristics of the measured cost data to support analysis and interpretation of the relationships critical to that use.

Internal communication of cost and other associated information descriptive of these relationships may then serve to direct attention to problem areas requiring control effort, or to allow predictions of future costs for planning purposes. They may aid in the appraisal of managerial effectiveness and provide perspective to managers seeking ways to cut costs. They may even serve to motivate individuals in the organization to strive toward the attainment of their organization's goals and to direct their activities in appropriately coordinated patterns to achieve those goals.

External communication of cost information descriptive of the conversion process from input resource to output objective of an economic entity may allow verification of compliance with contractual obligations, observance of applicable laws and regulations, and perhaps satisfaction of social responsibilities. External communication provides, in conjunction with other financial information, a basis for taxation and regulation, and contributes to the information needs of credit grantors and investors. Additionally, if it properly reported to highlight the effects on the cost of output products or services of changes in the cost of productive inputs or changes in the nature of productive activities, cost information may be used to facilitate cost-reimbursement contract negotiations, to support utility rate changes, or to portray the impact of proposals of competing parties in labor negotiations.

THE CHALLENGES OF COST ACCOUNTING

The challenges to be discussed in this final section are actually various aspects of one broad challenge to cost accounting—to accelerate the continued improvement of cost determination and reporting techniques.

For a discipline involved with recording or estimating the costs of performing the various activities required by economic entities, continued improvement of measurement techniques must be emphasized. Determination of costs incurred in producing products or services received much of the attention of early cost accountants. However, we are still making improvements in cost determination procedures and we must continue to do so.

Proper determination of the costs of performing the necessary activities of a business is essential for all of the cost information uses just discussed. It is important to recognize, however, that cost information needs for these varied uses may differ considerably. For example, the usual cost classifications by object of expenditure, by function, and by organizational subunit may vary in importance from use to use. For one purpose costs may be highly aggregated; for another, great detail may be necessary. While allocations of common costs may seem essential for one purpose, they may not be appropriate at all for another.

Thus it is important that we improve our understanding of the characteristics of cost information which are essential, those that are desirable but not essential, and those which are undesirable for each specific use, so that we can design (at least conceptually) ideal single-purpose costing systems. Only by understanding what would constitute an ideal system for each specific use, and by judging the importance of each use for a given organization, can we hope to make reasonable judgments regarding the trade-offs which might be necessary to produce an efficient, effective, practical, multipurpose cost accounting system for that organization. We also need to develop practical methodologies for evaluating these trade-offs or compromises in a cost-benefit sense.

This continued development of cost determination procedures must be broad enough to improve the measurement processes related to all types of costs which might be relevant to the various uses. Historical cost-related procedures need improvement, but in addition effective procedures must be developed to determine, store, and process current replacement cost data. The importance of such data, and other similar information, has been recognized in connection with various uses over the years. By this improvement we must eventually be able to measure with sufficient reliability, objectivity, and with whatever other characteristics seem important, the costs that are relevant for a particular use. In this way we can avoid continually having to use essentially irrelevant cost data by default, just because it is available.

In order to meet this challenge, cost accountants will have to continue being open to the developments in other disciplines which can be adapted to serve our needs, as well as to continue creating new measurement procedures or methods of analysis of our own. In addition, of course, we must be willing to discard existing procedures after they have been improved upon.

For example, by employing the methodologies of the behavioral sciences we may be able to understand the role of cost data in specific decision contexts, thus allowing us to judge the relevance of specific cost presentations to management. We may look to statistics for techniques which might produce better cost predictions, to management science for decision-modeling techniques, and to computer science for efficient simulation procedures. Then we might return to the methodologies of the behavioral sciences in attempting to understand the (possibly undesirable) interaction between cost and other financial presentations used in performance evaluations and those designed to provide information for optimal decisions.

It seems imperative that we gain a better understanding of the behavioral effects of the cost reporting systems we employ so that we can make these systems as effective as possible. Attainment of organizational goals typically requires a good deal of effort on the part of most, if not all, individuals comprising the organization. We must attempt to improve our measurement and reporting systems so that they support and aid the efforts of those individuals by providing motivation in the appropriate direction, and by facilitating the kind of cooperation which is necessary for the close coordination of their efforts toward the attainment of the organization's objectives. This will require considerable care in making performance evaluations truly supportive, not just punitive, and in keeping those performance evaluations consistent with current decision models so that incorrect decisions will not be rewarded by improved performance measures.

Another dimension of this general challenge to cost accounting relates to the need to develop appropriage cost determination and reporting systems for organizations other than the typical manufacturing enterprise. Service-providing organizations of various types often have unique characteristics which make it more difficult to associate costs incurred with service provided. This creates difficulties in situations requiring cost reimbursement as, for example, in Medicare reimbursements to hospitals. It also makes performance evaluation more difficult. Numerous examples related to governmental program evaluation could be cited to illustrate this difficulty. Similar difficulties also exist with service-type activities in manufacturing concerns. It remains a challenge for cost accountants to improve costing systems for these types of activities.

It is somewhat difficult to see what the future holds for cost accounting—to suggest what challenges the discipline will have to face in the years to come. It is certain, however, that just as the nature of business has changed in the past, it will continue to change in the future. New forms of business with new forms of organization will need the planning and coordinating guidance that can come from meaningful analysis of the costs of performing organizational activities. Thus, the role of cost analysis in describing and interpreting the consequences of various sets of past or alternative future activities will continue. However, the forms and procedures of the analysis may well be quite different. The role of the cost analyst in the organization may have changed and the tools and techniques employed may be more sophisticated.

Thus we see the education of the entering professional cost analyst as one of the major challenges to cost accounting. The future cost analyst must be capable of judging the information needs of his organization and assessing the trade-offs which might be necessary to keep his system efficient. This will require the broadest possible education in the goals and techniques of the functional areas of business as well as in the tools of cost analysis. He must be knowledgeable not only in accounting, but also in economics, mathematics, statistics, and in individual and organizational behavior so that he can adapt his systems and procedures to incorporate the most recent advances in those disciplines.

REFERENCES

Baily, Raeford. "Our Open Forum." *NACA Bulletin,* May 1934, pp. 1049–51.

Bradley, Albert. "Financial Control Policies of General Motors Corporation and Their Relationship to Cost Accounting." *NACA Bulletin,* January 1927, pp. 412–33.

Brett, A. C. "Flexibility in Budgeting." *NACA Bulletin,* June 1932, pp. 1406–17.

Burns, Francis. "The Effect of Volume on Profits." *NACA Bulletin,* January 1931, pp. 821–35.

Crockett, Horace G. "Analysis of Selling Costs and Proper Basis of

Salesmen's Compensation." *NACA Bulletin,* December 1, 1926, pp. 228–49.

Dean, Joel. "Statistical Determination of Costs, with Special Reference to Marginal Costs." *Studies in Business Administration,* University of Chicago Press, 1936.

DeCazaux, L. F. G. *Elements D'Economie Privee et Publique,* Book II, Chapter III. Paris, 1825. Translation published in *The Journal of Accounting Research,* Autumn 1965, pp. 264–65.

de Roover, Florence Edler. "Cost Accounting in the Sixteenth Century." *The Accounting Review,* September 1937, pp. 226–37.

Diemer, Hugo. "Methods of Supplying Cost Information to Foremen." *NACA Official Publications,* June 2, 1924.

Dohr, James L. "Budgeting Control and Standard Costs in Industrial Accounting." *The Accounting Review,* March 1932, pp. 31–33.

Eldridge, H. J. *The Evolution of the Science of Bookkeeping.* (Gee & Company, 1954).

Fletcher, F. Richmond. "A Manual for Budget Preparation." *NACA Bulletin,* October 1929, pp. 264–74.

Freeman, E. Stewart. "The Manufacturer's Marketing Cost." *NACA Bulletin,* November 1929, pp. 331–53.

Garner, S. Paul. *Evolution of Cost Accounting to 1925.* University of Alabama Press, 1954.

Grover, A. E. "The Cost of Distribution." *NACA Bulletin,* October 15, 1925, pp. 98–103.

Hain, H. P. "Accounting Control in the Zenon Papyri." *The Accounting Review,* October 1966, pp. 699–703.

Harris, Jonathon N. "What Did We Earn Last Month?" *NACA Bulletin,* January 15, 1936, pp. 501–27.

Hess, Henry. "Manufacturing: Capital, Costs, Profits and Dividends." *Engineering Magazine,* December 1903, p. 367.

Higgenbotham, W. H. "Administration and Selling Costs, Their Nature and Distribution." *The Cost Accountant,* August 1924, pp. 82–102.

Hilgert, J. R. "Methods of Controlling Distribution Costs," *The Accounting Review,* September 1927, pp. 254-62.

Kemp, William S. "Budgets and Predetermination of Costs." *NACA Bulletin,* July 15, 1926, pp. 817–27.

Kennedy, Donald D. "Variability of Overhead Costs." *Journal of Accountancy,* March 1930, pp. 202–12.

Klein, Frank. "Some Developments in Variable Budgeting." *NACA Bulletin,* June 1936, pp. 1155–71.

Kohl, Clem N. "What Is Wrong with Most Profit and Loss Statements?" *NACA Bulletin,* July 1937, pp. 1207–19.

Littleton, A. C. "Old and New in Management and Accounting." *The Accounting Review,* April 1954, pp. 196–200.

McKinsey, J. O. "Relation of Budgetary Control to Cost Accounting." *NACA Official Publications,* January 1922.

McNiece, T. M. "Measurement and Control of Selling and Distribution Costs." *NACA Bulletin,* March 1, 1929, pp. 823–49.

Owen, H. S. "Preparation and Administration of the Budget." *NACA Bulletin,* October 1, 1926, pp. 80–87.

Rorem, C. Rufus. "Differential Costs." *The Accounting Review,* December 1928, pp. 333–41.

Sanders, T. S. "The Uses of Differential Costs." *The Accounting Review,* March 1929, pp. 9–15.

Solomons, David. "The Historical Development of Costing." in Solomons, David, ed. *Studies in Cost Analysis.* Homewood, Ill.: Richard D. Irwin, 1968, pp. 3–49.

ten Have, O. *The History of Accountancy.* (Bay Books, 1976).

Theiss, Edwin L. "The Beginnings of Business Budgeting." *The Accounting Review,* March 1937, pp. 43–55.

Tobey, J. R. "The Preparation and Control of a Budget." *NACA Bulletin,* September 15, 1925, pp. 36–48.

Tyrrell, S. C. "The Recovery of Sales and Distribution Expense in the Cost Figures." *The Cost Accountant,* April 1927, pp. 328–33.

Ultrich, William A. "Manufacturing Expense Analysis, Classification, and Distribution." *NACA Bulletin,* December 1, 1929, pp. 397–418.

Van Vlissingen, Arthur, Jr. "Office Management & Efficiency Standards for Clerical Help." *NACA Bulletin,* October 1930, pp. 161–81.

von Rosen, Urban F. "Operating Ratios and Costs as Guides to Management." *NACA Official Publications,* September 15, 1924.

Weber, Charles. *The Evolution of Direct Costing.* Center for International Education and Research in Accounting, University of Illinois, 1966.

Weger, Chester E. "The Preparation and Administration of Budgets." *NACA Bulletin,* January 2, 1926, pp. 327–40.

Williams, John H. "A Technique for the Chief Executive, A Definite Responsibility—A Definite Procedure—A Definite Measure of Results." *Bulletin of the Taylor Society,* April 1922, pp. 47–68.

Wilmot, Harold. "Modern Developments in Cost Accounting." *The Cost Accountant,* October 1926, pp. 122–27.

2

Concepts of cost

*Roger A. Roemmich**
Donald W. Baker†

COST: A CONCEPTUAL VIEW

The layman generally thinks of cost as the price paid for goods or services acquired from another person. This simple definition is no doubt adequate for the layman. For the business executive, however, cost is a significant item which must be dealt with on a regular basis. Consequently, the business executive must have a much greater depth of understanding with respect to the concepts of cost. The text of this chapter addresses the many concepts of cost and discusses the appropriate uses of those concepts.

In its Accounting Terminology Bulletins, the American Institute of Certified Public Accountants (AICPA) defines cost as "the amount, measured in money, of cash expended or other property transferred, capital stock issued, services performed, or a liability incurred, in consideration of goods or services received or to be received."[1] The committee on Cost Concepts and Standards of the American Accounting Association defined cost as the "foregoing measured in monetary terms, incurred or potentially

---

* Assistant Professor, School of Accounting, University of Georgia.

† Corporate Controller, Southwire Company.

[1] *Accounting Terminology Bulletin No. 4,* July 1957, Prepared by the Committee on Terminology (New York: American Institute of Certified Public Accountants, 1957).

to be incurred, to achieve a specific objective."[2] More recently in *Accounting Research Study No. 3,* "A Tentative Set of Broad Accounting Principles for Business Enterprises," cost is defined as "a foregoing, a sacrifice made to secure benefits, and is measured by an exchange price."[3] In financial accounting the foregoing or sacrifice at date of acquisition is represented by a current or future diminution in cash or other assets. In short, cost is a term used to express the economic sacrifice measured in monetary terms to acquire goods or services. It is important to recognize there are "different cost concepts for different purposes." In other words, there is no unique definition or classification common to all situations. Accountants, engineers, and economists have all developed cost concepts and terminology to suit their particular needs. Cost then must be defined and understood for every application or use. In this sense, cost can be conceptually defined or classified from a natural viewpoint; it can be classified from the standpoint of its relationship to accounting periods; it can be classified and must be understood in terms of its behavior, its relationship to products and departments, as well as in terms of its use for analytical purposes and for planning and control.[4] It is important to have an understanding of these various classifications before entering into a discussion of the concepts of measurement and uses of cost data.

A natural viewpoint

Cost can be classified according to the basic purpose for its incurrence. Examples of this classification are found in the titles assigned in a chart of accounts such as cost of wages and salaries, fringe benefits, utilities, supplies, insurance, taxes, and so forth; in other words, in terms of the goods or services acquired. This classification can be most useful in controlling costs by identifying the reason for incurrence and allowing for consideration of the benefit received.

---

[2] Report of the Committee on Cost Concepts and Standards, *The Accounting Review,* vol. 27, no. 2, p. 176.

[3] Robert T. Sprouse and Maurice Moonitz, "A Tentative Set of Broad Accounting Principles for Business Enterprises," AICPA *Accounting Research Study no. 3* (New York: American Institute of Certified Public Accountants, 1962), p. 8.

[4] Adolph Matz, Othel. J. Curry, Milton F. Usry, *Cost Accounting—Planning and Control* (Cincinnati, Ohio: Southwestern Publishing Company, 1972), p. 44.

Relationship to accounting periods

Cost must be classified and understood with respect to its relationship to accounting periods. Often the terms *cost* and *expense* are used synonymously. Cost, however, is the amount paid for the good or service. Expense, more appropriately, refers to the sacrifice or the foregoing. Cost may be classified as a *capital* expenditure and called an asset. If an expenditure benefits only the current period, it is classified as a revenue expenditure and called an expense. Costs which benefit a future period are also referred to as *unexpired costs* and those which benefit only the current period are referred to as *expired costs.* Thus, cost may be incurred in one period and treated as a capital expenditure to be charged to a future period. Upon expiration, costs originally capitalized become an expense.

Relationship to products

It is important that costs are understood with respect to their relationship to products. When referred to in relation to a product, costs are generally classified as *direct* or *indirect costs.* Further, direct costs may be categorized as direct materials and direct labor. A combination of these two cost classifications results in another classification called *prime costs.* In addition to prime costs, products are generally assigned a proportion of indirect or overhead costs. *Direct materials* include those materials which can be specifically identified with a product, for example, aluminum and copper metal used in the manufacture of electrical transmission wire and cable. To be classified as direct material, it is necessary that the quantity of the material used in the product be measurable with respect to a unit of that product.

Likewise, *direct labor* includes that human effort which can be traced directly to the manufacture of a product. The manufacture of many products has become less labor intensive and more capital intensive through advances in technology which have resulted in a significantly greater amount of automation. Nevertheless, it is important to identify labor costs directly with the product if at all possible. Generally, direct labor is expected to vary with the quantity of product produced, holding the same ratio at all levels of production. In practice, because of automation, labor classified as direct labor may remain the same over a wide range of activity because automation requires a fixed complement of labor to operate a given piece of productive equipment. The cost of this labor remains the same regardless of the level of output in a given time period. It is not uncommon to find labor classified as direct although it can be shown that a major portion of the labor cost is unresponsive to changes in production levels.

Indirect or *overhead costs* include elements of cost which are not directly traceable to a specific product. Included in this indirect cost category are material costs which are necessary for the productive process but are not traceable to the product. Examples of these indirect materials may be certain lubricating and cooling oils, certain types of packaging materials, and other miscellaneous materials. Several types of labor costs also are necessary for the productive process but cannot be traced directly to a unit of product. Costs of this nature include certain wages and salaries such as supervision, material handling, and machine setup wages, as well as janitorial labor, all of which are generally classified as indirect labor.

Additionally, costs other than indirect materials and indirect labor are often incurred which are traceable to the productive process but not to the product. These include such costs as rent, depreciation, real and personal property taxes, general insurance, as well as any other costs not traceable to the product and not in the nature of material or labor. Indirect costs or overhead are assigned to the product through one of many allocation processes. The allocation process should, as much as possible, reflect the causal relationship between the incurrence of the indirect costs and the productive process. Frequently used activity bases for cost allocation or assignment are direct labor hours, direct labor dollars, and machine-hours.

Behavior of costs

Costs may be further classified and understood in terms of their behavior with respect to various factors, such as the level or volume of production. Cost behavior can be classified in three basic categories, that is *variable, semivariable* (sometimes referred to as *mixed* costs), and *fixed* costs. *Variable costs* include those costs which move in direct response to changes in the level or volume of production. Direct material by definition is a complétely variable cost. As discussed previously, direct labor may not be completely variable; rather it may fit along with many other costs into the semivariable classification. Costs in this category have both variable and fixed elements. Examples of these costs are certain costs of utilities which have a flat charge plus a rate per unit for quantities used. Supervision may also fit in this category since a one shift operation may only require one supervisor, but two shifts would require the addition of another supervisor. Several techniques are available for segregating the variable and nonvariable portions of these costs, including such sophisticated techniques as regression analysis and such simple techniques as the high-low method. *Regression analysis* calls for the use of mathematical formulas whereas the *high-low method* simply requires the analyst to identify costs and units with high and low levels of activity and to measure the rate of variability between those levels. Generally, the analyst will ignore any abnormal variations from the trend over the period of time involved.

Departmental relationships

Costs may also be classified according to their departmental relationships. These relationships can best be described in terms of producing and service departments. Costs in *producing departments* may fit into the category of direct or prime costs. On the other hand, costs incurred in *service departments* may more appropriately fit the category of indirect costs, particularly since it will generally be necessary to make some type of allocation of these service department costs to the various producing departments before they can be assigned to the productive process. Additionally, it is often desirable to collect cost data by departments which are the responsibility of various individuals as a means of controlling those costs by charging the individual responsible for the department with the costs incurred in that department. Care must be taken, however, not to hold an individual department supervisor responsible for costs allocated to a department on some arbitrary basis and over which he or she has no control. Assigning costs to products is another important factor in collecting costs by department. It is quite possible that a variety of products may flow through a given productive facility but not follow the same path through all the various operations. It then becomes important to have cost data by departments for purposes of assigning costs to the product according to the departments through which the product passes as it moves toward completion.

Costs for analytical uses

A very important classification of cost is according to various analytical uses of cost data. In reality, this may include several different types of cost.

Out-of-pocket cost is a term generally used to identify cash costs associated with an activity. Noncash costs such as depreciation and certain allocated costs are not included in this definition. It is an important concept to understand in various types of analyses.

Sunk cost is another type of cost important to the decision-making process. Costs of this type are those which represent resources already acquired and will remain unchanged by any choice between alternatives. For example, the depreciation on a piece of production machinery will have no effect on a decision with respect to replacing that machine.

Incremental cost is the additional cost incurred as a result of a change in the actual or planned courses of action. Incremental costs is similar to the economist's concept of *marginal cost,* which the economist defines as the additional costs incurred by producing one more unit of product.

Another concept important to the analytical process is that of *opportunity cost.* This concept is associated with the sacrifice made by deciding to choose one alternative over another. It may be thought of as the amount given up by not choosing the next best alternative.

Imputed costs are costs not actually incurred in an economic transaction but relevant to the decision at hand. Traditional accounting procedures fail to recognize these imputed costs; however, recognition of these economic costs results in better decisions. The most common example of an imputed cost is the inclusion of an "interest cost" when a company uses internally generated funds for a special project. No actual interest payments would be required; but, if the internally generated funds were invested in another manner, interest revenues would have been earned. The revenue foregone represents an opportunity cost of undertaking the special project. Thus, imputed costs are a type of opportunity cost. Imputed costs are very important to small businesses. An owner or manager should deduct from computed profits of his business an amount equivalent to the salary the owner would have earned in his or her profession and the interest which the owner's capital would have earned in an alternative business.

One final concept to understand is that of *differential costs*. Differential costs are the total changes in costs resulting from a given decision. The concept is one of totals rather than individual unit costs and may represent changes up or down.

An important concept associated with these cost classifications, as well as with other classifications, is *relevancy*. In other words, costs must be relevant to a decision. For costs to be relevant, they must be future costs and they must differ between alternatives. Historical costs are not relevant for decision-making purposes, although they may be adequate predictors of future costs, which are relevant. If costs do not meet this relevancy criteria, they need not be considered in any analytical process related to that decision.

Costs for planning and control

One final classification which should be discussed is related to planning and control of an operation. Generally, two types of costs are included in this group: standard costs and budgeted costs.

First, *standard costs* are used extensively in manufacturing entities. For an in-depth discussion of standard costing and its uses, the reader should refer to Part Five of this handbook. However, conceptually, standard costs can be thought of as yardsticks used to measure actual costs as a means of controlling the operation. Analysis of variances from standard is a very useful means of identifying operational problems as well as inefficiencies in acquiring the materials and labor necessary to the manufacturing process.

Several considerations are necessary in a decision to use a standard cost system. They include decisions relative to whether the standards will be used to value inventories. If standard costs are to be used in this manner, they must generally reflect an actual situation and therefore approximate *"actual costs."* Standards may also be set in such a manner as to represent an ideal productive situation but one impossible to obtain. Use of this *"ideal" standard* implies a desire to measure the inefficiency in the operation using an ideal situation as a yardstick, as well as to always maintain a goal toward which to strive. Standards set in this manner seldom are useful for financial reporting purposes. Standards may also be set in such a way as to provide a *bench mark* to compare the change in actual cost of producing over a significant time period. It may well have been profitable to produce a given product years ago, but not in the present market situation. Basic standards such as these provide for no change in the standard cost except as the process itself is changed. Management can always measure the validity of the original decision in changing market conditions.

Standard costs are generally set for material, labor, and overhead and are generally thought of in the sense of unit costs. As one can see, standard costs are very useful in a control process. They can be vital to making pricing decisions, although management must first understand the method by which standards have been set. Generally, standard costs and a good standard cost system will greatly simplify the accounting process.

The second type of costs included in this broad classification is *budgeted costs.* Budgeted costs are predetermined and may be thought of as a plan of action for a period of time. Unlike standard costs, which generally are thought of in terms of units, budgeted costs carry a connotation of *total costs* for a period of time at a given level of operation. Standard costs may be used to develop budgeted costs, but estimated actual costs may work as well in the budgeting process. Although the budgeting process involves a great deal more information other than cost data, it cannot be ignored in discussing the many concepts or classifications of cost.

CONCEPTS OF COST MEASUREMENT AND FLOW

With the conceptual view of cost and the various classifications as presented in the foregoing paragraphs, one can then understand those same concepts and classifications as they are associated with *cost measurement*. The measurement of cost appears to be very simple but requires one to have a thorough conceptual understanding of cost. The first step in measuring is to define the cost object or cost objective. The Cost Accounting Standards Board, formed in 1973 with the responsibility of promulgating cost accounting standards designed to achieve uniformity and consistency in cost accounting principles (followed by defense contractors under Federal contracts), defines a *cost objective* as "a function, organizational subdivision, contract, or other work unit for which cost data are desired and for which provision is made to accumulate and measure the cost of processes, projects, jobs, capitalized projects, and so forth." Once the cost objective has been established, the remaining problems requiring solutions are:

1. The inclusiveness of the definition of cost. This requires the consideration of cost in terms of its relationship to products or departments and its behavior, as well as from a natural viewpoint.
2. The method or methods to be used in allocating common or joint costs. The primary qualities required in any allocation method are that the method be systematic and rational. Again, consideration must be given to the relationship of the cost to products and departments, and most importantly to its behavior.
3. The proper measure in monetary terms when the economic transaction is nonmonetary in nature. This problem brings up the definition of cost as set by the AICPA which said in part that cost is ". . . the amount, measured in money, of cash expended or other property transferred . . . , in consideration of goods or services received or to be received."
4. The appropriate cost measure when all or a portion of the payments are to be deferred on the strength of its economic benefit to some future period. Consideration of its behavior is most important in resolving this problem.
5. The recognition of cost when transactions occur between organizational subunits. In practice, products are often moved from department to department within an organizational subunit and from one organizational subunit to an-

other subunit for processing before the product is available for movement to a customer. This requires consideration of the relationship of cost to products and departments, as well as to organizational subunits.

Inclusiveness of the cost definition

As already discussed under the heading "Relationship to products," conceptually all costs have a direct or otherwise determinable association with the production of a product or the performance of a service. Direct costs are those costs which are traceable directly to the product or service. Indirect or overhead costs, on the other hand, are those costs which are necessary for the productive process but are not directly traceable to the product. For external purposes such as financial and income tax reporting, these indirect costs must be attached to the units of product. For internal purposes such as performance evaluation and decision making, it is frequently desirable to treat indirect costs as period costs when incurred. This concept uses the previously discussed idea that costs must be relevant to a decision before being used in the decision-making process.

Measuring the acquisition cost of an asset

Conceptually, an asset includes all costs incurred to create that asset. This includes the actual cash outlay for the asset, cost of transporting the asset to the location where it is to be used, cost of preparing and installing the asset for use, and all other costs incidental to placing the asset in use by the enterprise. We have previously discussed the concept of capital versus revenue expenditures. If the costs associated with the acquisition of an asset are properly identified and collected, they will be treated as a capital expenditure to be charged to future periods in which a benefit is expected. The process of charging this unexpired cost to a future benefit is generally referred to as depreciation and/or amortization. In practice, certain costs such as sales and use taxes, which theoretically fit the definition of cost to be treated as a capital expenditure, are often actually treated as revenue expenditures and charged to the current period. Advantages of immediately charging such costs to the current period are a reduction of tax liability in the current period and simplification of record keeping.

Measurement of the acquisition cost of an asset can be greatly complicated by nonmonetary transactions. *Accounting Principles Board* (APB) *Opinion No. 29*, "Accounting for Nonmonetary Transactions," provides certain guidelines for approximating the monetary cost of acquiring an asset. Generally, the monetary cost is approximated by attempting to determine the fair value of the asset given up, if determinable. For complex transactions of a nonmonetary nature, the reader should refer to *APB Opinion No. 29*. Determining cost in a nonmonetary transaction can have a significant effect upon financial accounting and disclosure.

During the life of an asset, it often becomes necessary to make additional expenditures to maintain or expand its productivity. These additional expenditures are treated as capital expenditures if they improve the productivity of an asset or extend the asset's life. For example, the modification of a previously purchased computer system which expands the core space would be properly treated as a capital expenditure. Similarly, a major overhaul of a piece of productive equipment which will significantly extend the productive life of the equipment should be treated as a capital expenditure. Conversely, an expenditure to maintain an asset which does not extend its life or expand its productivity is treated as a revenue expenditure. Normal preventive maintenance such as painting, lubrication, and minor repair work are examples of such revenue expenditures. Conceptually, these expenditures simply insure that the productive asset will be useful for the original intended service life or that the original productivity will be realized.

Assignment of costs to plant and equipment

It was pointed out previously that an asset includes all costs necessary to put it into use as desired by the enterprise. Thus, the initial costs assigned to plant and equipment should contain the cost of acquiring the asset and the costs of putting the asset into working condition at the desired location. The cost of a specific asset is definite only when a single asset in the form required by the business is acquired for cash.

A common problem in the determination of the cost of single

items of equipment or single units of plant is the "basket" purchase. A basket purchase occurs when a group of items is purchased without the buyer and seller agreeing upon the portion of the total purchase price attributable to each asset. A reasonable allocation of the total purchase price is important for asset valuation and income determination. Since the single assets may have different useful lives, the amount of depreciation charged to individual years is affected.

One method used to allocate the total cost to individual assets is to obtain the appraised value for each item. Each item is allocated a percentage of the total purchase price equal to the percentage its appraised value represents of total appraised value.

Another method used to allocate the total purchase price is to use the carrying value of assets acquired on the other company's book as a means of approximating the percentage of value each item represents. This approach is based upon the assumption (which may be invalid) that the original cost of these assets will give an adequate approximation of the relative value of the assets.

When plant or equipment is acquired in a nonmonetary exchange, it is very important to base the accounting for this transaction on the nature of the assets exchanged. In *APB No. 29*, "Accounting for Nonmonetary Transactions," the Accounting Principles Board listed two exceptions to the general rule that nonmonetary transactions should be based on the fair values of assets exchanged.

One of these exceptions is the exchange of a productive asset not held for sale in the ordinary course of business for a *similar productive asset* or an equivalent interest in a similar productive asset. This exception is applicable to many exchanges involving plant and equipment. For exchanges involving similar productive assets, the proper accounting treatment is to record the acquired asset at the book value of the asset exchanged unless the evidence suggests a loss on the exchange. If the asset acquired has a fair value lower than the book value of the asset exchanged, the new asset should be recorded at its fair value and a loss on the disposal of the old asset should be recognized.

When exchanges involving plant and equipment *do not qualify as an exchange of similar productive assets*, the transaction should be recorded based upon the fair value of each asset. Gain or loss should be recognized in these transactions.[5]

When the purchaser of plant and equipment incurs transportation costs to place the asset at the desired location, these costs should be capitalized. Sales or use taxes should be capitalized; but, where the income tax law permits, most businesses expense these costs for tax purposes in the period incurred. Another necessary cost which should be capitalized is the cost of modifying the asset for use in a specific business.

Treatment of costs incurred after the initial acquisition of plant and equipment should be based upon whether they qualify as capital improvements or betterments. To qualify as a *capital improvement,* an expenditure must increase the future service potential of an asset. Replacements of entire assets are recorded by retiring the old asset and recording the acquisition of a new asset. Replacement of parts of an asset are normally charged directly against operations since they are considered necessary to achieve the normal service life of the composite asset.

Cost of self-constructed assets

Determination of the cost of self-constructed assets is similar to the costing of manufactured products. Labor and material costs can be directly associated with the constructed asset. The major question is: How much overhead should be assigned to the constructed asset? There are five possible answers to this question. They are:

1. Assign no overhead to constructed facilities. This answer is based upon the logic that overhead costs are a fixed expense related primarily to normal operations. Proponents of this argument contend that assignment of overhead costs to self-constructed assets results in overstatement of income for the period of construction.
2. Assign the incremental overhead costs which result from the construction of plant and equipment to the self-constructed asset. The theoretical basis for this argument is sound, but the discovery or determination of incremental

---

[5] Refer to *APB Opinion No. 29*, par. 22, for the proper treatment of exchanges of nonmonetary assets that include a monetary consideration.

costs is difficult. Identification of incremental variable costs with self-constructed assets is much easier than identification of incremental fixed costs. Another problem in determining incremental costs to be associated with self-constructed facilities occurs when facilities are constructed during periods of slack activity. If overhead costs could be avoided during these periods in the absence of construction the avoidable costs should be assigned to the assets.

3. Capitalize variable overhead costs traceable to self-constructed assets but do not capitalize any fixed overhead. This approach is based upon the premise that assigning fixed overhead costs to self-constructed assets will overstate income in the current period. Another less convincing argument made by proponents of this approach is the direct costing argument that fixed overhead costs are a period cost. This argument seems less appropriate for fixed assets which clearly provide future benefits to the business than for inventory.

4. Assign overhead costs to self-constructed assets on the same basis that overhead is assigned to units of production. This approach represents the normal full-costing approach. It is based upon the premise that future benefits accrue to the business as a result of the construction of plant and equipment. Thus, capitalization of overhead costs results in a better matching of revenues and expenses in both the future and in the current period. Advocates of this approach maintain that when idle capacity exists use of this capacity to construct plant and equipment is a sound economic activity. These advocates see no disadvantage resulting from the increased income reported in the current period as a result of assigning overhead costs to the self-constructed assets. Theoretically, the argument for capitalization is weakened if idle capacity is used for construction. The theoretical objection to assigning full costs to constructed assets under these conditions is that these costs cannot be directly associated with the construction.

5. Assign overhead costs to self-constructed assets only to the extent that these costs would have been assigned to curtailed production. This approach assigns the same amount of overhead to goods produced that would have been assigned to

those goods if production had not been curtailed. It is important to note that this approach does not result in the same amount being charged to current operations that would have been charged without the construction of plant and equipment. The overhead costs assigned to plant and equipment do not represent the opportunity cost of curtailing production to plant and equipment. The opportunity cost is the difference between the total selling price of the units not produced and the out-of-pocket costs necessary to produce and sell those units.

Cost of leased plant and equipment

We have previously noted that an expense is an expired cost. A cost that has not expired is recorded as an asset. A perplexing problem which has confronted the accounting profession in recent years is the proper treatment of leased plant and equipment. The definition of an asset contains two elements which are crucial to determining the proper accounting treatment. These elements are that future benefits must be expected and the entity must own or control the property in order for plant and equipment to constitute an asset. Leased plant and equipment are expected to provide future benefits but they are not owned. This creates a situation where leased plant and equipment are not technically assets due to lack of legal ownership, but are assets in economic substance.

To clarify the proper accounting for leases, several official pronouncements have been released, the most recent of which is *Statement of Financial Accounting Standards No. 13,* "Accounting for Leases." This Standard requires all leases to be classified by the lessee as either *capital* or *operating leases.* If the lease meets *one* of the four criteria listed below, it must be classified as a capital lease and recorded as an asset. The asset's cost then is charged to income over the life of the asset (certain capital leases are amortized over the term of the lease).

1. A "bargain purchase" option is included which allows the lessee to purchase the asset at a price substantially below its fair market value.
2. The lease transfers ownership of the plant and equipment by the end of the term of the lease.

3. The lease term is 75 percent or more of the estimated economic life of the leased property.
4. The present value at the beginning of the lease term of the minimum payments equals or exceeds 90 percent of the fair market value of the leased plant and equipment to the lessor at the inception of the lease.

The cost capitalized for a capital lease is the present value at the beginning of the lease term of the minimum lease payments minus any executory costs to be paid by the lessor (except that if the amount so determined exceeds the fair value of the property, the asset is measured at its fair value). The appropriate discount rate for determining the present value is the marginal or incremental borrowing rate of the lessee unless the lessee can determine the implicit rate computed by the lessor and that rate is less than the lessee's incremental borrowing rate.

A lease of plant and equipment which does not qualify as a capital lease is called an *operating lease.* Plant and equipment leases meeting the criteria of an operating lease are not capitalized. Rental on these leases is charged to expense as it becomes payable. If payments of rent are not on a straight-line basis, rental expense nevertheless is to be recognized on a straight-line basis unless another systematic and rational basis is more representative of the benefits derived from that leased property.

Measuring the cost of inventory

The last several paragraphs have been devoted to discussing the acquisition costs of an asset generally defined as a productive piece of equipment, a building, or a similar type of asset. Another significant type of asset which requires a sound understanding of the concepts of cost measurement and cost assignment is *inventory.*

Periodic versus perpetual inventory procedure

The two basic procedures for accounting for inventory flows are the *periodic* method and the *perpetual* method.

The *periodic* inventory method is used primarily by enterprises in retail or service industries. Under the periodic inventory method, the cost of goods sold is assumed to be the difference between the recorded cost of goods available for sale (beginning inventory plus net purchases) and ending inventory, which is measured periodically by physical count.

Perpetual inventory methods are used primarily by manufacturing firms. Under perpetual methods, determination of the cost of goods sold is made for each transaction at the time the transaction occurs. The amount of cost of goods sold is often the result of several productive processes each of which resulted in the addition of certain costs to the product, resulting in a buildup of the cost of the final finished product. The cost of the finished product is then placed in inventory until sale of that product takes place.

Specific identification

For external reporting purposes, inventory of product costs includes direct product cost as well as allocated overhead cost. Assignment of costs to inventory was a significant reason for earlier discussion of the classification of cost according to products and department. In theory, the determination of which costs are associated with units remaining in ending inventory and which costs are associated with inventory sold during a period should be based on the *specific identification* of costs with an individual unit of inventory or an *assumption* relative to the *flow of costs.* Some accountants argue that the specific identification of units of inventory is theoretically preferable because it facilitates that determination of the "true" or actual historical cost of inventories and results in a matching of revenues resulting from the sale of inventory with costs of acquisition of products in inventory. However, the use of the specific identification method where the units are economically the same opens the door to manipulating reported income and asset valuation by selecting the units sold arbitrarily, on the basis of identified cost. Moreover, specific identification is frequently not practical, especially for units of small value, because record-keeping costs may be prohibitive relative to the advantages of tracing costs to the individual product units. It is advisable to use specific identification only when the benefits accruing from its use exceed the cost. Specific identification is most practical in industries where costs change very rapidly and each unit has a relatively high value. An excellent example is the construction industry.

Cost flow assumptions

When specific identification is not possible, useful, or economically justified, an assumption about the flow of goods is required for costing the ending inventory and determining the cost of goods sold.

Three major cost flow assumptions are (1) First-in, first-out (Fifo); (2) Last-in, first-out (Lifo); and (3) some form of average.

First-in, first-out, or Fifo

Fifo is a commonly used flow assumption based upon the premise that the first goods purchased or produced are normally sold before goods acquired later. Because this assumption is consistent with sound inventory management techniques, it usually provides a good approximation of the actual flow of goods. However, the use of Fifo for income determination results in the matching of earlier and generally lower acquisition costs with later and generally higher revenues during periods of rising prices. (It has the opposite effect during periods of declining prices.) No distinction is made between gains or "inventory profits" resulting from rising prices and gains earned by processing goods. To illustrate, assume an item of inventory was acquired for $70 in 1975. In 1976 when the replacement cost of this item of inventory was $75, it was sold for $80. For financial reporting and income tax purposes, a gain of $10 would be reported; however, the real income from selling this unit of inventory was the difference between the selling price and its replacement cost, or $5. *Real income* is the amount available for distribution to owners without impairing the capital of the firm. Thus, one measure of real income is the selling price of an inventory item minus its replacement cost.

Last-in, first-out, or Lifo

Lifo is a flow assumption based upon the premise that the last units acquired are sold before goods acquired earlier. Lifo does not actually provide a good approximation of the physical unit flows. The use of Lifo in a period of rising prices does tend to match the most recent inventory acquisition costs against sales revenue. This results in income which more nearly approximates real income than that determined under Fifo inventory methods. Since Lifo is acceptable for income tax reporting, it is often used because it lowers income for tax purposes and results in the deferral of taxes on "inventory profits or holding gains" for unsold goods. Inventory profits or holding gains on inventory are the difference between the historical acquisition cost of the inventory and its current replacement cost. These gains are often described as illusory or paper gains because in terms of ability to command goods or services they do not represent gains if the entity must replace the inventory at the new prices. Inventory valued in the financial statements of an enterprise using Lifo is frequently much less than the replacement cost of the inventory. Lifo proponents claim that the advantage for purposes of income determination and the postponement of payment of taxes on the "inventory profits" in unsold goods outweigh the disadvantages of presenting misleading inventory costs in the balance sheet. Double digit inflation in the 1970s has motivated many enterprises to make the change from Fifo to Lifo inventory methods to postpone payment of taxes resulting from holding units of inventory in an inflationary period. Making such changes requires careful consideration by the management of the enterprise since the use of Lifo for tax purposes, unlike certain other tax accounting elections, requires its use for financial reporting purposes. The Internal Revenue Service has been very insistent upon this conformity requirement. The management of enterprises using Lifo must exercise great care to insure that conformity is met to the letter of the law to insure that their Lifo election will not be disallowed for income tax purposes, thereby triggering a potentially large tax payment at an inopportune time. The IRS has allowed certain disclosures, primarily through footnotes to financial statements, which can be used to approximate income of the enterprise had inventory been costed on a Fifo basis. This generally is done through the disclosure of difference between Lifo and Fifo values of inventory. However, no reference can be made to the effect on income with the exception of the initial year in which the election is made. Obviously, for subsequent years, an informed reader can use this information to approximate income assuming the use of Fifo costing methods.

Average costing

Other alternatives to using specific identification methods of assigning costs to Cost of Goods Sold and Ending Inventory include various techniques of average costing. *Year-to-date averaging* may be appropriate if the costs of production or other acquisition have been reasonably stable throughout the year. Conversely, if costs have been unstable during the year, the use of a *moving average* will be more appropriate because the resulting average reflects current conditions more dependably. Regardless of what technique is used, the average should be weighted by using units in Beginning Inventory plus all units purchased or produced during the accounting period.

Allocation of indirect costs

Earlier in this chapter, the relationship of costs to products led to a discussion of the allocation of indirect costs to the productive process. It was also pointed out that for external purposes overhead costs must be allocated to individual product units in a systematic and rational manner. Commonly used activity bases which are used to make these allocations are direct labor hours, direct labor dollars, and machine-hours.

Problems which arise in this allocation procedure generally are associated with the fluctuations in levels of production and in seasonal behavior of indirect costs. The amount of indirect costs assigned to a unit of product generally will be determined by developing an annual rate which will smooth some of the seasonal fluctuations. However, significant fluctuations of the actual level of production from the level anticipated and used for developing the overhead application rate will create differences between the amount of costs incurred and the amount applied on the basis of production. These variances may be *planned,* i.e., by the use of a *normal level* of production concept which would generally be a level of production which tends to smooth the fluctuations over a period defined to be the business cycle for that industry. Generally, this time period will cover several years, giving rise to continual differences. Conceptually, these under or overabsorbed overhead costs should be allocated to inventories and cost of goods sold in order to more closely approximate actual cost flows. In practice, over- or underabsorbed overhead costs are frequently charged totally to Cost of Goods Sold in the current period. The justification for this treatment is based on the assumptions that the relative proportion of inventories in each stage of production is reasonable constant and that differences in income resulting from this approach are relatively insignificant. Other levels of production assumed for overhead rate development will cause similar differences to occur. An in-depth discussion of these methods can be found in Chapter 24.

ALTERNATIVES TO HISTORICAL COST

A fundamental assumption of financial or external accounting practice from the 1930s until the present has been that the monetary unit is stable. With the exception of a couple of years in the mid-40s and early 50s, inflation had been rather mild until the late 60s. The high rates of inflation which have prevailed in the 70s have made this stable dollar assumption less appropriate. Inflation makes the historical cost of assets reported in financial statements less representative of the value of the assets. Although the assets' costs do not purport to represent value, they usually provide a reasonable approximation of the cost of acquiring an equivalent asset in noninflationary times.

A more serious problem which arises from the use of traditional accounting procedures in inflationary times is the matching of historical acquisition costs much below current acquisition costs against revenues in income determination. This matching results in showing the entire difference between selling prices and acquisition cost as income. If the business is going to continue operations, it must acquire inventory at current costs. Thus, the real gain from a sale is the difference between the selling price and the replacement cost of the good. Note that this is true even though the inventory may not be replaced with similar units.

One of the problems which arises as a result of the overstatement of income in inflationary times is creation of an impression among financial statement users that the business is doing better than it is doing. This impression often causes stockholders to expect dividends which would cause an impairment of the business's operations.

Another problem which results from overstatement of income is the payment of taxes on the reported gain. Payment of taxes on the portion of the gain which results from changes in the price level results in the impairment of operating capital, measured in real terms.

Although for many years there has been theoretical discussion of the need for an accounting system which recognizes the impact of inflation, the need for such a system was not officially recognized by policy setting bodies until the early 1970s. In 1973–74 the Financial Accounting Standards Board (FASB) formulated and released an exposure draft which would have required supplementary financial statements based on price-level-adjusted accounting methods. These statements were designed to supplement traditional historical cost statements. The response to this exposure draft was sufficiently unfavorable to cause the FASB to withdraw the exposure draft.

In 1976 the Securities and Exchange Commission issued *Accounting Series Release No. 190,* which requires approximately 1,000 companies to provide supplementary replacement cost information in quarterly 10-K reports and annual financial statements issued for years ending on or after December 31, 1976. (For further details, refer to Chapter 38.)

Replacement cost

The *replacement cost* of an asset is the cost of securing an asset at the current moment in time. There are three common approaches to determination of replacement cost. One approach is to determine the cost of acquiring an asset in the *form* in which the existing asset was originally acquired. This approach is the *current input* approach. Another approach is to attempt to determine the replacement cost for the asset in its current form. A third approach, which is labeled the current output approach, attempts to determine the ultimate value of the asset at disposition.

Many accountants prefer the current input approach to determining replacement cost for two reasons. The current input approach is more objective since it does not require determination of current condition of the asset and because a market price is more easily established for new assets. Note that while the current input price is more objective than the cost of replacing "in kind" it is also probably less relevant or useful for distinguishing between holding gains and real income. Another advantage attached to the use of current input values is that income from continuing operations is not recognized until the asset is sold or scrapped; the use of replacement cost "in kind" would result in recognizing gains resulting since acquisition. For the reasons listed above, the following discussion of replacement costs is based on the current input value approach.

The primary advantages of presenting *supplementary* replacement cost information are:

1. The replacement cost represents the best available approximation of the value of the asset. Matching of the replacement cost against current revenue is useful for assessing the future prospects of a business.

2. Matching of replacement costs against current revenues permits a distinction between holding gains and operating gains. This distinction may be reflected in a better understanding of profitability by financial statement users. Hopefully, this distinction will result in the stockholders forming expectations for dividend payments based on operating gains. Another important advantage which advocates suggest will result from the presentation of replacement cost information is an increased awareness of taxing authorities of the distinction between holding and operating gains. Since holding gains differ among industries and firms, taxation of holding gains—which results in impairment of capital—results in inequities in taxation. Many businesses would prefer a higher rate based on operating gains.

3. The summation of replacement costs provides a more meaningful approximation of the value of the net assets of the firm than is portrayed by historical costs. It should be cautioned that because of the existence of intangible assets such as goodwill and because of interrelationship of assets the

value of a firm may be quite different from the sum of the replacement costs of its assets. Further, it should be remembered that replacement costs normally represent input values rather than exit values.

The primary disadvantage which may result from the use of replacement costs is the loss in objectivity. Unless an asset is in a form or condition identical to assets sold in the market, subjectivity must be introduced in selection of a current replacement cost.

Another problem which may occur when replacement costs are reported is that a firm may have no intention of replacing an asset when it is sold. When this is true, the matching of current revenues with replacement cost will not provide a good representation of future operations. The increased replacement cost in such cases may have made other assets more attractive for use in normal operations.

Price-level adjustments of cost

Price-level-adjusted statements are an attempt to restate accounts to reflect all financial data in dollars of equivalent purchasing power. The underlying principles of price-level accounting are those of historical cost accounting. Price-level adjustment advocates maintain that restatement of nonmonetary assets into units of general purchasing power is necessary to maintain a proper distinction between invested capital and income. There are two types of income recognized under this approach, income from the sale of goods or performance of services (with no distinction between operating gains and holding gains) and income from holding a position in monetary items.

Monetary assets and *liabilities* are defined as those fixed in money by contract or otherwise. *Nonmonetary items* include all other assets and liabilities. Because they are fixed in monetary terms, monetary assets and liabilities do not need to be restated in units of general purchasing power; they are reported at their face values. Price-level gains or losses result from the holding of monetary items in periods of inflation. Those businesses which hold more monetary assets than monetary liabilities have a net monetary asset position. These businesses show price-level losses in periods of inflation. Businesses which have a net monetary liability position show price-level gains in periods of inflation. (In periods of falling prices the effects are the reverse.)

The index used to adjust nonmonetary assets and liabilities is the GNP deflator, which is probably the best index of the general level of prices in the United States. This single index is used for adjusting all nonmonetary items. This points to a major problem associated with price-level statements. The prices of individual assets do not change in the same way that general prices change; it would be purely coincidental for the price of a specific asset to change at the same rate that the general price level changes. Thus, application of a general price-level index to historical costs in a statement of financial position often does not result in a good approximation of the current replacement cost of individual assets. Further, the total price-level adjusted assets may not approximate the total value or replacement cost of the assets.

Although general price-level adjustments are inferior to replacement cost accounting for presentation of current values, these adjustments are more objective than replacement costs. Some advocates of price-level accounting feel that the greater objectivity which results from their approach more than offsets the utility of better approximations of current value which are provided by current replacement costs.

3

Cost components and cost behavior

Charles L. McDonald*
Arthur L. Shealy, Jr.†

The total costs of an entity for a period may be defined as the total deductions from sales revenue; however, such a definition provides little insight into the entity's operations. A useful division of costs distinguishes between manufacturing costs and commercial expenses. _Commercial expenses_ encompass _marketing expenses_—including selling and distribution costs such as advertising, travel expenses, and sales salaries—and _administrative expenses_—such as office salaries, auditing expenses, and legal expenses. _Manufacturing cost,_ also referred to as "production" or "factory" cost, includes each element that enters into the finished product of an entity. The costs of manufacturing are the primary concern of cost accountants due to their importance in (1) determining inventory value and (2) providing a greater ability to plan and control manufacturing costs due to their standardization derived from fairly uniform operations, as contrasted with less routinized processes of marketing and administration.

* Associate Professor, School of Accounting, University of Florida.
† Controller, Barnett Banks of Florida, Inc., Jacksonville, Florida.

COST COMPONENTS

The components of manufacturing costs are direct materials, direct labor, and factory overhead. Materials represent the basic substance of manufacturing; labor processes the materials; and physical plant and other factors permit the application of labor to materials.

Direct materials

The cost of any significant item of material or supplies which forms an integral part of a finished product and can be directly identified with individual products on a consistent basis should be classified as a *direct material* cost. Often direct materials are called raw materials, but one should not be misled as this term is not limited to basic natural resources. The raw material of one firm may be the finished product of another—Goodyear's finished product of a tire can be the raw material of American Motors Corporation. Thus it is difficult to assess the classification of a cost by its physical description; it is the use of the item which dictates its classification.

The ease and feasibility with which materials can be traced to the finished product are important considerations in their classification. A cardinal rule in designing accounting systems is that the benefit derived from an accounting technique must always at least equal the expense of that technique. Screws and glue used in the manufacture of wood furniture or degreasing solution used in a metal-working plant are clearly direct materials of production because of their nature; but because of the minor cost involved and the difficulty and expense of tracing and measuring their consumption, they may be accounted for as *indirect materials*, a part of factory overhead.

Note that despite the description of a raw material as an "integral" part of the finished product, it does not have to be a visible facet of the final product. As long as the use and cost of a material or supply can be specifically related to the quantity of product processed, it should be included in the cost component of direct materials.

Direct labor

The cost of wages paid to skilled and unskilled workers that can be assigned to the particular unit produced, i.e., the labor that is expended directly upon the materials which comprise the final product, is classified as *direct labor*. It must be recognized that the nature of the work is more important than the classification of the worker in distinguishing between direct and indirect labor (to be discussed later). A machinist may spend 90 percent of his time directly producing the product, but the 10 percent of his time spent on clean-up activities should be classified as indirect labor.

As with direct materials, the pragmatic considerations of measurability and materiality arise. While the theoretical classification of fringe benefits is as a direct labor cost and of overtime payments as an indirect labor cost, there is significant variance in practice as to how they are classified.

Factory overhead

The aggregate amount of all the various manufacturing cost items which cannot be considered as direct charges to the products or jobs in the production process due to their heterogenous nature, complexity, or fairly insignificant size is classified as *factory overhead*. It is important to be familiar with the diversity of terms applied to this category of costs: manufacturing expense, factory expense, burden, factory burden, loading, indirect expense, overhead, and manufacturing overhead. A practical means of describing this cost component is that it includes all manufacturing costs except direct materials and direct labor. Two important subcategories of this cost component include indirect materials and indirect labor.

Indirect materials. The cost of materials required to finish an entity's product which is either too small to account for separately—as suggested earlier with respect to glue for wooden furniture—or too complex considering the amount involved, is classified as *indirect materials*. Another class of indirect materials is termed "factory supplies," and includes materials needed to maintain the working area and machinery in a workable and safe condition. Lubricating oils, grease, cleaning rags, and brushes are examples of this second class of indirect materials.

While shipping containers and packing materials should be classified as direct materials, often the method of packing makes this impracticable or their cost may be negligible, leading to an expedient charge to indirect materials. Additional examples of direct materials often charged to indirect materials due to their minor cost are bolts, nuts, rivets, washers, and cotter pins.

Indirect labor. Labor expended which does not directly affect the construction or the composition of the finished product is called *indirect labor.* Typically the compensation of supervisors, timekeepers, truckers, maintenance men, shop clerks, general helpers, and other employees involved in service work is classified as indirect labor.

Other indirect costs. Indirect expenses other than indirect labor and indirect materials include heat and power, depreciation of factory equipment, insurance on factory equipment, machinery repairs and maintenance, rent, small tools, and taxes related to manufacturing.

Relevant terminology

Two useful groupings of cost components are prime costs and conversion costs. *Prime costs* are defined as those costs which are identified directly with the product: They generally consist of direct material and direct labor. *Conversion costs* result from the action performed to transform raw material into finished product. Since direct material is acted upon in the conversion process, it cannot be considered a conversion cost. Labor and overhead costs together are commonly referred to as conversion costs.

The extent to which costs can be classified is evidenced by the Cost Accounting Standards Board Disclosure Statement (required by Public Law 91–379) which specifically requests the classification of 36 specific costs which are commonly classified differently by varied companies, for example, cash discounts on purchases, freight in, health insurance, pension costs, contract administration, and rework costs.

To illustrate how costs are classified, consider the suggested classification of the accompanying cost items, including designation of their direct versus indirect nature.

Classification symbols

DM = Direct Materials	DL = Direct Labor
MO = Manufacturing Overhead	
D = Direct	I = Indirect

Examples   **Examples**

DM;D Cement for a roadbuilder   *MO;I* Depreciation-factory
MO;I Fuel for factory machinery   *MO;I* Idle time for direct laborers
DL;D Payroll fringe benefits to direct *MO;I* Supervisory salaries
       laborers
MO;I Floor cleaner for the factory building *MO;I* Insurance of equipment
DM;D Wheat for a flour mill   *MO;I* Salaries of janitors
DL;D Wages of a machine operator

COST BEHAVIOR

A useful tool for managerial analysis and decision making is the behavior pattern of costs. The behavior pattern of costs describes how certain costs fluctuate in relation to some activity. Costs may behave differently in relation to different activities; therefore, when referring to the behavior of a certain cost it must be clear upon what activity the analysis is based.

Commonly the activity used in describing the behavior pattern of a given category of cost is some measure of volume. For example, the behavior pattern of selling costs is often described in relation to the volume of sales. On the other hand, the behavior of various manufacturing costs is often described in relation to the volume of production.

There are two basic behavior patterns of costs: *variable* and *fixed.* Unfortunately, not all costs fall clearly into either the variable or the fixed categories. As will be discussed later, some costs exhibit partly fixed and partly variable patterns, while other costs exhibit a variation of the fixed behavior pattern.

Variable costs

A cost exhibits a variable behavior pattern if its total amount changes proportionately with changes in the activity measure. Consider sales commissions as an example of a variable cost. If a firm pays its sales personnel a commission of 5 percent of sales, then sales of $100,000 would result in the incurrence of commissions of $5,000, while sales of $500,000 would cause com-

EXHIBIT 1
Variable behavior pattern of sales commission

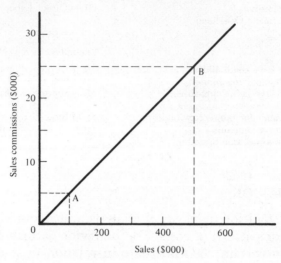

missions to be $25,000. Exhibit 1 illustrates the behavior of the sales commissions.

In Exhibit 1, point A represents sales of $100,000 and sales commission expense of $5,000. Point B represents sales of $500,000 and sales commission expense of $25,000.

In dealing with variable costs a distinction must be drawn between *total* variable costs and *per unit* variable costs. In the

EXHIBIT 2
Graph of variable cost per unit

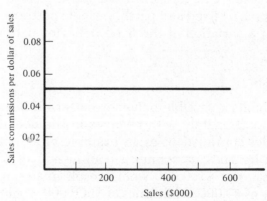

above example of the sales commissions only total sales commissions fluctuate proportionately with sales. Per unit sales commissions remain constant, that is, sales commissions are $0.05 for each $1.00 of sales (Exhibit 2). This illustrates a characteristic of variable costs: total variable costs fluctuate proportionately with the activity while per unit variable costs remain constant.

Additional examples of variable costs include direct materials, direct labor, and fuel for productive machinery. Depreciation of machinery is a variable cost if the units-of-production depreciation method is used—that is (Historical cost − Salvage value) ÷ (Number of units produced over life) × Number of units produced during the current period.

Fixed costs

A cost exhibits a *fixed* behavior pattern if its total amount remains constant for a given period of time as the measure of activity fluctuates. For example, consider a manufacturing firm that rents its facilities for $50,000 per year even though the value of output might fluctuate considerably from year to year. Of course, there is some maximum amount of output that the facilities are capable of producing without expanding the facilities. This idea introduces the concept of relevant range. The *relevant range* is the range of activity over which the fixed cost remains constant. Relevant range is normally defined in terms of a time dimension and a level of output. For example, during the next year output is expected not to reach 30,000 units of production, the capacity of the $50,000 per year manufacturing facilities. Exhibit 3 illustrates the concepts of fixed cost and relevant range for this manufacturer.

It is important to note that, although most costs vary to some degree in total, a variation in *direct proportion to output* is required to constitute a *variable cost*.

As an example of a cost that varies, but is not a variable cost, when a taxicab company is considering the operating expenses of an automobile over its useful life, it is reasonable to state that its total tire cost will exceed the cost of four tires. However, the cost of the fifth tire is not uniformly incurred per mile driven, unless all tires are automatically rotated at a certain mileage level. In contrast, gasoline expense (given a fixed price of $0.65

74

EXHIBIT 3
Behavior pattern of manufacturing rental cost
over relevant range

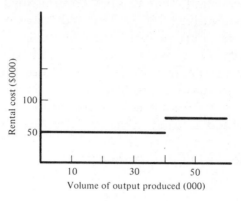

per gallon and usage of 10 miles per gallon, for example) will
vary directly with miles driven; for 10,000 miles of driving, gasoline costs will total $650. However, the total tire cost does not
vary directly with miles driven. The total tire expense at 10,000
miles may be $200 (four tires at $50 each), or perhaps $250
(five tires), depending on how quickly the tires wear out. The
tire cost would behave as a step cost (to be discussed).

Exhibit 3 demonstrates that rental cost is fixed at $50,000
per year for the relevant range of zero to 30,000 units of output
for a time horizon of one year. For a volume over 30,000 units
the firm would have to rent additional facilities and the fixed
cost would increase to $75,000 per year; however, this level of
output would be outside of the relevant range. Although it might
be expected that production will reach 40,000 within three years,
for current planning purposes the rental cost of manufacturing
facilities is strictly fixed. This example again illustrates two important characteristics of fixed costs: they are constant for some
period of time over a relevant range of activity.

As is the case with variable costs, a distinction must be drawn
between *total fixed cost* and *fixed cost per unit*. While total fixed
cost remains constant, fixed cost per unit varies inversely with
fluctuations in activity. This is a characteristic of fixed costs. This
can be illustrated utilizing the rental cost of manufacturing activities with fluctuating production (Exhibit 4). At a production
level of 10,000 units, the cost of rent per unit of output will

EXHIBIT 4
Fixed cost per unit graph

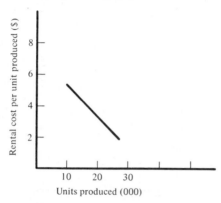

be $5, while at 25,000 units of output the unit cost drops to $2.

Other examples of fixed costs include administrative salaries, property taxes, and insurance. Depreciation on a straight-line basis is also a fixed cost:

$$\text{Annual depreciation} = \frac{\text{Historical cost} - \text{Salvage value}}{\text{Number of years of useful life}}$$

Semivariable costs

Semivariable costs are those costs that do not fall entirely into either the variable or the fixed category, but exhibit characteristics of both. In other words, semivariable costs have a fixed portion and a variable portion. An example of a semivariable cost is a rental agreement for a building that consists of $1,000 per month plus 0.5 percent of sales. Exhibit 5 illustrates the behavior pattern of this semivariable cost.

As Exhibit 5 illustrates, the rental cost if sales for the month are $400,000 is $3,000 ($1,000 + 0.005 × $400,000). This type of rental agreement is very common for shopping centers.

Semifixed (step) costs

A *semifixed cost* is another form of cost that does not fall entirely into either the variable or the fixed category. A semifixed

76

EXHIBIT 5
Semivariable rent expense

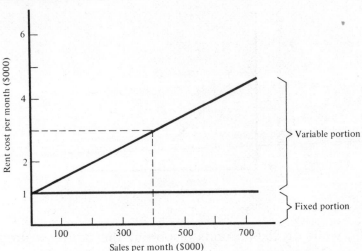

cost is constant for a given amount of activity and then increases
in a fixed amount at a higher activity level.

Consider the cost of assembly line supervision. Assume that
each supervisor costs $2,000 per month and can supervise 25
assembly line workers. As long as no more than 25 workers are
employed the cost of supervision remains constant at $2,000
per month. At this level of activity supervision cost exhibits the
behavior pattern of fixed costs. But as soon as the 26th worker
is employed the cost of supervision increases by $2,000 per
month to $4,000. The cost of supervision remains fixed at $4,000
if no more than 50 workers, but at least 26 workers, are employed. Exhibit 6 illustrates the behavior pattern of this semifixed
cost.

Exhibits 5 and 6 illustrate the difference between semivariable
and semifixed costs. Semivariable costs increase continuously,
while semifixed costs increase in steps that cover some range
of activity. Returning to the tire example for the taxicab company, the cost of tires at purchase is for four tires per cab and
the fixed cost of tires for the company jumps four tires at a
time as demand for cabs increases and additional cars are purchased. Or, on the basis of use, four tires may yield a fixed expense for 10,000 miles (4 × $50 per tire = $200) and then two

EXHIBIT 6
Semifixed supervision costs

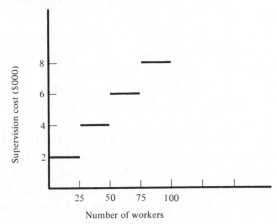

tires may need replacement. The company's tire cost jumps to six tires (6 × $50 = $300).

In analyzing the behavior pattern of costs, a very important consideration is the *length of the time span* involved. As the time span is lengthened costs that are considered fixed may become variable. For example, a manufacturing firm that has several plants would consider the costs of the plants to be fixed in the short run. But as the time span is lengthened, at some point the costs could be considered semifixed, because with sufficient time, management could acquire or dispose of plants. On the other hand, as the time span is shortened costs that are considered variable may become fixed. In a time span of a day or a week, for instance, legal or operating characteristics may prohibit certain costs from being eliminated even if activity is significantly reduced (a six-month lease must be honored). Therefore, in analyzing cost behavior patterns it is critical to keep in mind what time span is involved.

Distinction between physical behavior of costs and cost behavior caused by management policy

In classifying costs according to their behavior, it is important to distinguish those with undeniable physical behavior and those costs with behavior *set by management*. For example, a unit of product such as a bag of flour requires physical inputs, such as wheat, in set proportion to units of output. The amount of raw materials for the unit of product physically varies with production. In contrast, management may dictate variable cost behavior through policy decisions. For example, a firm may always spend 5 percent of sales revenue on advertising. There is no physical necessity that for every $1 of flour sold, $0.05 is paid for advertising.

The importance of recognizing cost items with *discretionary behavior* is that this behavior is controllable and can be altered to impact the cost-volume-profit (C-V-P) analysis of a firm. For example, the advertising spending policy could be altered to a fixed cost of $10,000. The impact of fixed and variable cost behavior of C-V-P analysis is discussed in the next section.

COST-VOLUME-PROFIT ANALYSIS

Cost behavior patterns combined with the revenue behavior patterns provide the basis for a very useful tool for decision making, commonly referred to as *cost-volume-profit* (C-V-P) *analysis* or *break-even analysis*. C-V-P analysis concerns the relationship between changes in volume and changes in profit. C-V-P may also be used to assess the effects on profit of changes in fixed costs, changes in variable costs, or changes in revenue.

There are three approaches to C-V-P analysis: the *C-V-P graph* or *break-even chart*, the use of *cost and revenue equations*, and the use of the concept of *contribution margin*. These three approaches to C-V-P analysis will be discussed in this section, employing the following example to illustrate the concepts involved.

Ace Manufacturing Company manufactures tennis rackets and sells them to wholesale dealers. The accounting staff has determined that Ace's fixed costs for the operating range of 40,000–80,000 rackets are $320,000 per year. This range is the volume that Ace normally produces during a year. The variable costs consisting of direct materials, direct labor, and variable factory overhead amount to $12 per racket. Ace sells the tennis rackets to the wholesale dealers for $20 each.

The C-V-P graph (break-even chart)

Using the information in the above example we may construct the graphs in Exhibit 7A, 7B, 7C, and 7D.

The fixed cost graph is constructed to illustrate that the relevant range for Ace is 40,000 to 80,000 rackets. At volumes less than 40,000 or greater than 80,000 the cost and revenue relationship will change. For convenience the fixed cost line is drawn to the axis representing zero units. But keep in mind that fixed costs are $320,000 only for the relevant range. The same caution

EXHIBIT 7

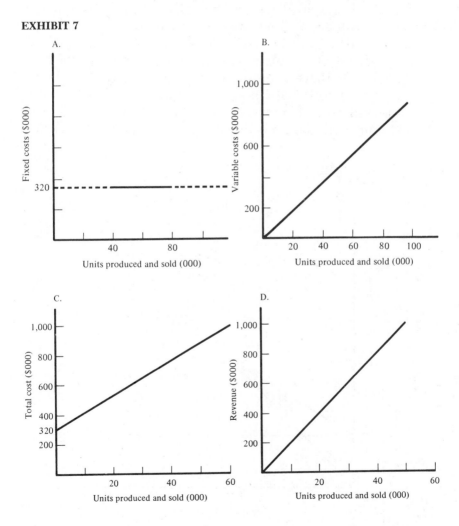

is true for variable costs, total costs, and revenue. This holds due to varied economies of scale at different output levels and the relationship between price and demand, as developed in the economics literature.

Exhibit 7C for total costs represents the combination of Exhibit 7A and 7B, that is, fixed costs plus variable costs equal total costs.

The three graphs in Exhibit 7A, 7C, and 7D may be combined into a single graph. The single graph is the cost-volume-profit graph and is presented in Exhibit 8.

The C-V-P graph illustrates the relationship between Ace's costs and revenues as the volume changes. Notice that revenue at sales of 40,000 units is equal to 40,000 × $20, or $800,000. Since total cost of production at that level of sales is $800,000, at 40,000 units there is no profit or loss; this is the break-even point. At volumes of less than 40,000 units total costs exceed revenue and a loss is incurred, while at volumes greater than 40,000 units revenue exceeds total costs and a profit is earned.

EXHIBIT 8
C-V-P graph

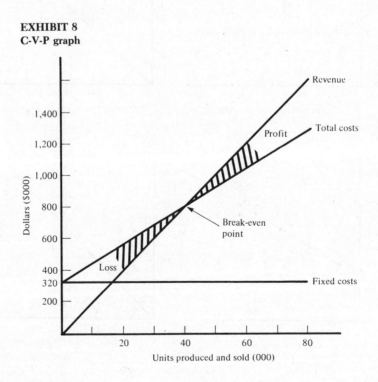

Use of equations for C-V-P analysis

The C-V-P graph in Exhibit 8 is a convenient visual representation of C-V-P relationships. But for purposes of answering detailed questions such as what volume is required to produce a profit of $24,000, the use of C-V-P equations is more convenient. C-V-P equations may be derived by considering the relationships of an income statement. An income statement has the following relationships:

$$\text{Revenue} - \text{Expenses} = \text{Net income}$$

This relationship may be expanded to include the notion of variable and fixed costs. The following equation is the result.

$$\text{Revenue} - \text{Variable expenses} - \text{Fixed expenses} = \text{Net income}$$

This equation may then be used to answer the question of what volume is required to earn a profit of $24,000.

Let X represent the number of units. Then our equation becomes the following:

$$\$20X - \$12X - \$320,000 = \$24,000 \tag{1}$$

To obtain the desired answer the equation is simply solved for X.

$$\$20X - \$12X = \$320,000 + \$24,000 \tag{2}$$

$$\$8X = \$344,000 \tag{3}$$
$$X = 43,000 \text{ units}$$

At 43,000 units, revenue equals $20 × 43,000, or $860,000, and variable expenses are $12 × 43,000, or $516,000. Therefore,

$$\text{Revenue} - \text{Variable expenses} - \text{Fixed expenses} = \text{Net income}$$
$$\$860,000 - \$516,000 - \$320,000 = \$24,000$$

To answer this same question using the C-V-P graph, lines would have to be carefully drawn and the chance of error is much greater. The use of a C-V-P equation is not only more convenient but also more accurate.

Contribution margin

In the preceding section in solving the equation for the desired level of profit an intermediate step produced equation (3). The left side of equation (3) represents the difference between sales price per unit and variable expense per unit. This difference is called the *contribution margin*. The contribution margin represents each sales unit's contribution to covering fixed expenses and earning a profit. In the Ace Manufacturing Company example the contribution margin of $8 per unit can be used to answer a number of different questions concerning the relationship between changes in volume and changes in profit. Consider the following questions:

1. What is Ace's break-even point?

$$\text{Break-even volume} = \frac{\text{Fixed expenses}}{\text{Contribution margin per unit}}$$

$$\text{Break-even volume} = \frac{\$320,000}{\$8}$$

$$\text{Break-even volume} = 40,000 \text{ units}$$

Alternatively, break-even in dollars may be obtained by utilizing the contribution margin percentage:

$$\frac{\text{Contribution margin per unit}}{\text{Sales price per unit}} = \frac{8}{20} = 40 \text{ percent}$$

$$\text{Break-even sales volume} = \frac{\text{Fixed expenses}}{\text{Contribution margin percentage}}$$

$$\frac{\$320,000}{40 \text{ percent}} = \$800,000 \text{ (that is, 40,000 units} \times \$20 \text{ selling price)}$$

The contribution margin percentage is useful when unit selling price is not provided.

2. What happens to profits if sales are increased from 50,000 to 60,000 units?

$$\begin{aligned}\text{Increase in profits}\\ \text{(or decrease in loss)}\end{aligned} = \text{Increase in units} \times \text{Contribution margin}$$
$$= 10,000 \times \$8$$
$$= \$80,000 \text{ increase in profit}$$

The effect of changes in costs

Occasionally either fixed costs or variable costs, or both, may change. These costs may increase because of inflation, inefficiencies, or numerous other factors. Fixed and variable costs may also decline because of improved efficiencies or other factors. The effect of a change in variable costs is to change both the contribution margin and the break-even point. In the Ace Manufacturing Company example, if variable expenses per unit increase from $12 to $15 the contribution margin decreases from $8 to $5. The new break-even point may be computed as follows:

$$\text{Break-even volume} = \frac{\text{Fixed expenses}}{\text{Contribution margin}}$$

$$\text{Break-even volume} = \frac{\$320,000}{\$5}$$

$$\text{Break-even volume} = 64,000 \text{ units}$$

As this example demonstrates, a change in variable costs may have a significant effect on break-even volume and profits.

A change in fixed costs changes the break-even volume but not the contribution margin. For example, assume that in addition to the increase in variable costs, fixed costs increased by $15,000. The effect of this change on the break-even point may be computed as follows:

$$\text{Change in break-even point} = \frac{\text{Change in fixed expenses}}{\text{Contribution margin}}$$

$$\text{Change in break-even point} = \frac{\$15,000}{\$5}$$

$$\text{Change in break-even point} = 3,000 \text{ unit increase}$$

In addition to changing the break-even point, a change in fixed costs has a corresponding effect on profits and losses.

Profit-volume graph

A convenient device for illustrating the contribution margin and the effect on profits of changing volumes is the *profit-volume graph*. Exhibit 9 presents a profit-volume graph for Ace Manufacturing Company using the original assumptions.

The vertical axis of the profit-volume graph represents profit and the horizontal axis represents volume of sales. In Exhibit 9

84

EXHIBIT 9
Profit-volume graph

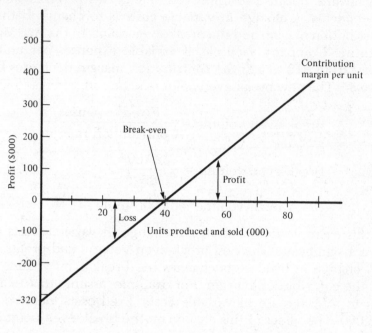

volume is presented as the number of units sold. Sales dollars may also be used as a measure of volume. Notice that the contribution margin line starts at $320,000. This is the amount of fixed costs and at zero volume a loss of $320,000 would be incurred. The contribution margin line intersects the horizontal axis, indicating zero profit, at the break-even point of 40,000 units.

The profit-volume graph may also be used to illustrate the effects on profits of changes in fixed and variable costs. We previously assumed that fixed costs increased by $15,000 and variable costs increased by $3 per unit. The effects of these changes are illustrated in Exhibit 10.

Exhibit 10 illustrates that the increases in the costs increased the break-even point. In addition to this, the slope of the new contribution margin line indicates that profits will increase at a slower rate with increases in volume because of the lower contribution margin per unit.

EXHIBIT 10
Profit-volume graph of effects of changes in costs

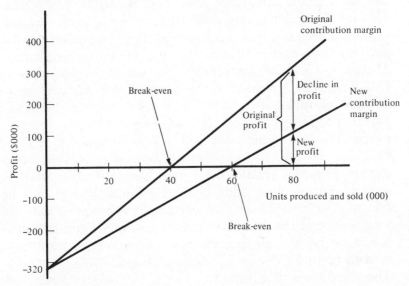

The impact of changes in costs and selling price on the break-even point can be summarized as follows:

1. An increase in selling price per unit decreases the break-even point.
2. An increase in fixed costs increases the break-even point.
3. An increase in variable cost per unit decreases the contribution margin and hence increases the break-even point.

Assumptions of cost-volume-profit analysis

Cost-volume-profit analysis as previously described is derived from the economic model of the firm. C-V-P, or break-even analysis, as used by accountants employs several assumptions that simplify the economic model and make the model more practical to apply. To fully understand C-V-P analysis the user should be aware of the assumptions and the possible effects if significant deviations from these assumptions occur. The assumptions may be categorized into six areas, which are enumerated and discussed below.

1. A necessary assumption for C-V-P analysis is that all costs can be divided into their *fixed* and *variable components*. This involves identifying costs that are completely variable or completely fixed, and separating those costs that contain both variable and fixed elements into their components.

2. The second area of assumptions implicit in the accountant's C-V-P analysis is related to the concept of a *relevant range*. A basic assumption of C-V-P analysis is that the behavior patterns of revenues and costs are linear over the relevant range. The economic model of a firm assumes that these behavior patterns are curvilinear. Within a relevant range the curvilinear relationships may be approximated by straight lines. As an additional consideration, the cost involved in estimating the exact shape of the behavior patterns would exceed the benefits in most cases. An additional assumption related to the relevant range is that fixed costs remain constant over the relevant range.

3. The third area of assumptions of C-V-P analysis concerns the *relationship between the behavior patterns and volume*. A basic assumption is that the only thing affecting revenues and costs is volume. Revenues and costs are affected by other things, such as inflation, and to this extent C-V-P analysis is an oversimplification of the real world. Another assumption in this area is that variable costs do vary in proportion to volume. An additional assumption is that both revenues and costs are comparable in relation to some common measure of volume.

4. A single C-V-P analysis assumes that the *behavior patterns* of revenue and costs are *static*. That is, selling prices and cost prices are unchanged. In addition, it is assumed that efficiency and productivity do not change during the C-V-P analysis. When prices change or efficiency and productivity change the usual approach is simply to perform another C-V-P analysis employing the new prices and new efficiency and productivity factors.

5. A basic assumption of C-V-P analysis is that for multiproduct firms the *sales mix remains constant* over the relevant range. Since different products may have different contribution margins, a firm may reach its goals in terms of sales dollars, but encounter a different profit figure than was anticipated,

depending on the sales mix. Higher than expected sales of a product with a lower contribution margin would lead to smaller profits associated with a given level of total sales.

6. The final assumption is related to the fact that the number of units produced is rarely equal to the number of units sold. C-V-P analysis assumes that this difference, and therefore changes in inventories, are insignificant. If this is not a valid assumption in a particular instance, the effect on profits depends on the inventory costing method employed by the firm.

CONCLUSION

Cost behavior and C-V-P analysis are intuitively appealing in that increased costs should lead to a requirement that sales levels be increased to maintain the current profits, just as decreased selling prices force the volume of sales to be increased to maintain the total revenue level of a firm. The model facilitates quantification of the impact of economic changes and policy decisions on the profit picture of a firm. C-V-P analysis is especially useful in the setting of company goals and the formulation of budgets.

PART
TWO

*Managerial uses of cost
accounting information*

4

Budgeting

Edward B. Deakin, III*
Edgar N. Howard†

A budget represents a comprehensive plan through which all levels of management indicate in a formal manner their expectations of the future and the way that future conditions will impact on the organization. A formal budget may be considered as a representation of the financial impact on the business likely to be realized from operating conditions in the coming fiscal period. As such, the budget reflects the strategy that management anticipates taking to meet the conditions in the coming period and to attain the long-range goals and objectives of the organization. Once the plan has been formalized it may be defined as an *operational budget,* which is used to coordinate activities during the budget period, and to motivate persons at all levels of the organization to meet the stated plans. Periodically and at the end of the period, an evaluation is customarily made which compares actual performance with the levels of performance anticipated in the budget.

---

* Associate Professor, The University of Texas at Austin.

† General Manager, Management Information Division, Texas Eastern Transmission Corporation.

ORGANIZATIONAL CONTEXT
OF BUDGETING

The progress of an organization plan may be viewed as consisting of three phases which are developed by Welsch:

    I.   The substantive plan

    II. Strategic long-range profit plans, and

    III. Tactical short range (annual) profit plan.[1]

The substantive plan is established by company management and includes a statement (whether formal or informal) of the broad objectives of the enterprise towards which management action is ultimately directed, and the specific enterprise goals which operationalize the broader objectives and which can provide the basis for measurable standards. The substantive plan also includes consideration of the strategies which have been adopted to attain the specific goals and broad objectives of the enterprise.[2] The broad objectives are designed to provide an ethical and philosophical statement within which the company may be expected to operate. The specific enterprise goals are designed to set forth the relative emphasis to be placed on such objectives as profitability desired, products and services to be offered, geographic areas to be served, and the share of the market to be obtained for the company's major product lines. Strategies would be stated in more specific terms and adapted to the needs of each company. Specific measures of performance, price markups and profit margins, quality specifications, and the allocation of financial and physical resources would be incorporated into the planned strategies for attaining company goals and objectives.

While the statement of goals, objectives, and strategies is a necessary condition for guidance of the organization, it is important to detail the steps that are to be taken over the next several

---

[1] Glenn A. Welsch, *Budgeting: Profit Planning and Control* (Englewood Cliffs, N.J.: Prentice-Hall, 1976), pp. 60–84.

[2] Statement of broad organization goals and the operationalization thereof is generally considered a part of the overall management process. A classic discussion of organization goal setting is provided by J. G. March and H. A. Simon in *Organizations,* (New York: John Wiley and Sons, 1958). Their analysis is considered the foundation of contemporary organization theory.

years to attain the company objectives. These steps may be expressed in terms of a long-range or strategic plan. Because the long-range plans look into the intermediate and distant future, it is usually only realistic to state these plans in rather broad terms. Strategic plans would include long-range forecasts of sales and production levels, aggregate cost levels, and a projection of cash flows to meet the projected sales and production levels. These strategic plans would include consideration of the major capital investments required to maintain present facilities, increase capacity, or diversify to other products and/or processes.

Although the strategic plans provide more specific statements of activity levels (sales volumes, costs, and cash flow projections) over the long run, the planning process also requires the more specific statements contained in the operating or period budget. The tactical profit plan indicates the sales levels, production and cost levels, income, and cash flows that are anticipated for the coming (annual) period. In addition, these data are used to construct a budgeted statement of financial position (balance sheet) to indicate exactly what resources are expected to be available to the company for subsequent periods' operations as well as to point out needs for additional financing or the commitment of additional assets to expand the company's investment.

This discussion is designed to focus on the development of the tactical budget plan; to indicate the use of the tactical budget as a planning, control and performance evaluation tool; and to relate the behavioral considerations which have been considered important in budget preparation and use.

The tactical budget and its relationship with other plans, accounting reports, and the management decision-making process may be diagrammed as in Exhibit 1. On the left side are the organization goals, strategies, and objectives that set the long-term operating plan for the company. The tactical budget is derived from the long-range budget in consideration of conditions that are likely to hold during the coming period. The anticipated conditions are based on forecasts and include a reflection of individual management members' views about the near-term prospects for various facets of company operations. The individual's relationship to the budget is diagrammed on the right side of Exhibit 1. The individual manager's beliefs about the coming

94

EXHIBIT 1
The organizational and individual context of the tactical budget

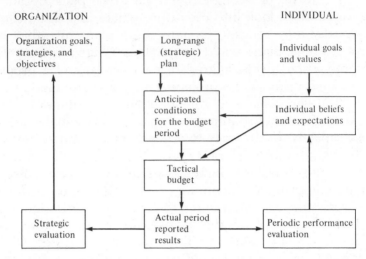

ORGANIZATION   INDIVIDUAL

period are affected by a number of factors including the individual's established goals and values.[3]

HUMAN FACTORS IN BUDGETING

The importance of human factors in budget preparation arises not only because human estimates of an unknown future are required to develop the budget, but also because the budget is compared with actual events that occur during the period to arrive at a measure of individual performance. Therefore, the person preparing the budget estimate may have a predisposition to develop an estimate which will not be too difficult to meet during the budget period. When using a budget for performance evaluation purposes, therefore, care must be taken to assure that the results of the evaluation will induce the manager to continue to provide the best estimates of future condi-

---

[3] A more comprehensive discussion of the behavioral effects of individuals and budget plans is presented by Don T. DeCoster in "An Intuitive Framework for Empirical Research in Participative Budgeting," in Gary John Previts, ed., *Accounting Research Convocation,* University of Alabama, 1976. A more general discussion of accounting and human behavior is available in Anthony Hopwood, *Accounting and Human Behavior* (Englewood Cliffs: N.J.: Prentice-Hall, 1974).

tions and not just the type of estimate that will make the manager's evaluation look good.

In addition to the individual periodic performance evaluation resulting from the use of budgets, management may use budgeted and actual results to evaluate company progress towards the organization goals, strategies, and objectives. If it appears that these goals are not compatible with the observed operating results, then changes may be in order.

Preparation of the budget and the enactment of the technical steps required to construct a comprehensive tactical budget plan must therefore be viewed in the context of the effect of people on the budget, and of the effect which the budget will have on people. Ideally, the budget will motivate people to attain better results than expected and will provide coordination among organization subunits that will serve to maximize organization performance.

THE BUDGET PERIOD

Preparation of the tactical budget should be undertaken prior to the start of the period for which the budget is considered applicable (the budget period), and the resulting budget should be used throughout that period. The typical budget period is one year. If the fiscal and calendar years are identical, then a schedule of required events leading up to distribution of the budget throughout the organization might call for a preliminary budget period (for example, October). The information gathered from such preliminary planning would include forecasts of product demand, sales prices, production activity, and various expense levels.

These preliminary data would be formalized into a preliminary set of budgeted statements for presentation during the early part of November. After reviewing the entire set of preliminary statements, adjustments may be made to reflect needed coordination, or items which were not evident at the time of preliminary data gathering.

The results of this review would be used to prepare a revised set of budgeted statements. The revised statements would also be reviewed and adjustments made where necessary.

During the last month of the year, a set of budgeted financial statements would be distributed as the official budget plans for the coming year. These plans would not be revised unless extraordinary events during the period made the budget seriously out of line with the actual environment.

An alternative method calls for continual revision of the budget on a roll-forward basis. That is, a budget for the coming year is prepared in a manner similar to that outlined for an annual budget period. This would, for example, be a one-year budget for the calendar year. Then, during the first quarter of the budget period, the budget planning and preparation process is carried out again although in a less formal manner. The results of this step would be the preparation of a new estimate or forecast which would reflect anticipated operations for the year starting April 1. The process would be carried out in the second quarter resulting in a yearly forecast for the year beginning July 1, and so on for the remainder of the year.

While the system seems to entail a great deal of effort with the preparation of yearly budgets which seem to be discarded after the first quarter of the budget period, the method does take advantage of any changes in operating conditions that arise subsequent to the preparation of the annual budget. Moreover, the budget is really not discarded, but an updated forecast is prepared which better reflects operating results. A one-year period is usually required to account for seasonal factors.

Whether the budget is prepared for an entire year or the roll-forward approach is used, the basic steps to be followed are identical. We begin the presentation of these steps with an overview of the components of the tactical budget and then turn to a detailed discussion and illustration of the budget preparation procedures.

COMPONENTS OF THE TACTICAL BUDGET

The tactical budget plan consists of relatively detailed schedules listing various components which, when taken together, will appear as a comprehensive set of projected financial statements. Attention is usually first directed towards preparation of the anticipated income statement. This task is generally subdivided into the following elements:

1. Sales forecast.
2. Production plan.
3. Operating expense budget.
4. Other income and expense budgets.

The *sales forecast* is considered the most critical of the income statement elements because both the production plan and the operating expense budgets are considered to be highly dependent upon the level of sales and the amount of sales revenue obtained. Moreover, the financial position of the company at the end of the budget period will, to a great extent, depend upon the volume of sales and the prices obtained for the goods or services sold.

The *production plan* provides a basis for planning to meet the quantities of goods expected to be sold, as well as to maintain the optimal inventory level during the period. The production plan incorporates consideration of the sales volume and the likely mix of styles, colors, or other characteristics of the anticipated merchandise to be sold. The production plan provides vital feedback to management in that the ability to attain a given sales level is limited by the ability to maintain required production. If the indicated sales level is in excess of the ability to produce, then it is necessary to adjust the sales forecast to reflect capacity constraints.

The *operating expense budget* will include all anticipated costs to market the goods produced and to administer the operations of the company. Many of these costs will be committed prior to the start of the budget period. Building costs, administrative salaries, and similar items are generally considered fixed costs. The operating expense budget may be used to review the levels of these fixed costs prior to extending commitments for the following year or other long-run periods. Other operating costs (e.g., sales commissions, shipping supplies, and collection costs) may vary closely with the changes in sales volume and/or sales revenue. Once the sales forecast is prepared, these variable cost items may be estimated based on the anticipated sales level.

In addition to consideration of the components of operating income, attention is also directed toward *other revenues and expenses* that may be anticipated during the period. These items are generally obtained through discussion with higher level management, since the generation of nonoperating income and expense items usually results from specific policy decisions. Sales of plant or other long-term assets, changes in financing arrangements, and investment in income producing securities will give rise to income effects that fall into this category. Pending events such as contingencies may also impact on the income statement and should be evaluated as part of the budgeting process.

The elements of the income statement budget are combined to produce projected sales revenues, cost of goods sold, operating expenses, and nonoperating income and expense, which together provide a *budgeted income statement.*

The budgeted net income becomes an important component of the *financial position budget.* This phase of the budget process focuses on the major asset and liability balances that are anticipated for the end of the budget period. There are two major components of the financial position plan:

1. Cash flow budget.
2. Projected statement of financial position.

These two statements are closely related. The *cash flow budget* would include the cash from operations as well as forecasted sources and uses of cash for operating and nonoperating purposes. Cash requirements for current assets, such as receivables and inventories, would tend to follow from the projected sales and production levels estimated in the income statement phase of the budget process. However, expected amounts for long-term assets would be dependent upon capital investment decisions, while asset balances in short-term investment accounts would be dependent upon management decisions with respect to dividend levels, the need for asset reserves, and similar factors. On the liability side, decisions with respect to financing requirements, debt service, and the different stockholder accounts would need to be made to derive the estimated balances in each of these accounts.

The process of deriving the estimated cash flows and the projected statement of financial position requires intensive involvement of senior management. Estimates contained in these budgeted statements are based on management's expectations of how the current period will fit into the long-run profit plan and how the anticipated events of the current period will lead to the attainment of the company's strategies, goals, and objectives.

BUDGET PREPARATION PROCEDURES

The detailed procedures used in the preparation of the budget begin with preparation of the sales forecast. This is followed by the production plan and a subsequent development of the operating expense budget. Other income and expense budgets are then prepared. Using the results of these budgets, a projected statement of sources and uses of cash can be developed. Almost simultaneously with the development of the cash flow statement,

EXHIBIT 2
Projected starting balance sheet for the budget period

HYPOTHETICAL MANUFACTURING COMPANY
Projected Balance Sheet
December 31, 19A
(prepared on September 30, 19A data)
(thousands of dollars)

Assets

Current Assets:
Cash	$ 150	
Accounts receivable (net)	220	
Inventories	615	
Other current assets	23	
Total Current Assets		$1,008
Long-term Assets:		
Property, plant, and equipment	$2,475	
Less: Accumulated depreciation	850	
Total Long-Term Assets		1,625
Total Assets		$2,633

Liabilities and Shareholders' Equity

Current Liabilities:
Accounts payable	$ 140	
Taxes and other payables	217	
Current portion of long term debt	85	
Total current liabilities		$ 442
Long-term Liabilities (net of current portion included above)		469
Deferred taxes		67
Total Liabilities		$ 978
Shareholders' Equity:		
Common stock	$ 350	
Retained earnings	1,305	
Total Shareholders' Equity		1,655
Total Liabilities and Shareholders' Equity		$2,633

the projected balance sheet can be constructed. Each of these steps is detailed in the following sections of this chapter.

The start of the budget preparation process takes place prior to the end of the year before the budget period. Because of this, it is necessary to estimate the company's financial position at the beginning of the budget period. Usually, this is accomplished by taking the latest available balance sheet (a calendar year company may use the September 30 balance sheet) and projecting from that an estimated year-end balance sheet. For illustrative purposes, a projected balance sheet for the year end, prepared as of September 30, is given in Exhibit 2.

With this preliminary information, as well as with a knowledge of the company's operations and the different product lines, it is possible to begin the budget preparation process. The first step in this process is preparation of the sales forecast and the estimated revenues from sales.

SALES FORECAST

Obtaining the sales forecast is perhaps the most difficult aspect of the budgeting process, because the subjectivity in sales forecasting is quite high. A number of different techniques have been devised to attempt to minimize the subjectivity and to provide estimates from different sources and using different approaches. If the different estimates are reasonably close, then one tends to have greater confidence in the results. However, large variations are not uncommon when comparing sales forecasts by using different methods. Obviously, management evaluation and discussion is necessary to integrate the different sales forecasts and derive that forecast which is considered to represent the expectations for the coming period.

Forecasting techniques may be divided into three broad categories:

1. *Ad hoc* estimates.
2. Trend analysis.
3. Econometric techniques.

Ad hoc estimates

The most common type of forecast is the *ad hoc* estimate made by a single individual or group of individuals. The simplest estimate would be an answer to the question: "What do you expect the sales to equal during the budget period?" The usefulness of that answer would depend upon the qualifications of the person or group making the forecast, the biases that may be evident in the reply, and the real ability to make any estimate about future sales levels.

With respect to competence, it is likely that an experienced manager will have a better background to draw on for making forecasts of sales than a casual observer. In many cases, a group of managers and sales personnel confer to prepare estimates for the budget period. The use of group forecasting is often superior to individual forecasts because different group members may draw on different areas of expertise which may impact on the sales level. Thus, use of an economist as a group member may provide some different insights into sales expectations than those obtainable from a salesperson in a district office.

The relationship between the individual and the budget as shown in Exhibit 1 gives rise to inherent opportunities for bias. A person likely to be evaluated in a manner that punishes underattainment of the sales forecast but does reward overattainment will be biased towards underestimating future sales levels. On the other hand, members of a selling staff seem to be overly optimistic and tend to overestimate future sales. The extent of the impact of these biases on the forecast is difficult to measure and may vary from one budget period to the next. Groups may also exhibit bias, so that a group must be chosen carefully to help reduce the potential effects of biased estimates.

The *Delphi technique* has been employed to enhance group forecasting and to reduce the effects of bias. With this method, members of the forecasting group prepare individual forecasts and submit them to the group anonymously. Each group member obtains a copy of all of the submitted forecasts, but is unaware of the source of any of the other members' forecasts. In this way, differences between individual forecasts can be addressed and hopefully reconciled, without involving the personalities or positions of the person making the forecast. After the differences are discussed, each member of the group prepares a new forecast and distributes it anonymously to the other members of the group. These forecasts are then discussed in the same manner as before. The process is repeated until the forecasts converge on a single best estimate of the coming year's sales level.

Of course, sales forecasts are bound to be more accurate in a situation where the product has relatively stable demands and a well-defined competitive situation. Public utilities have, for the most part, been better able to forecast sales than have cyclical businesses such as paper products or machinery manufacturers.

The Hypothetical Manufacturing Company surveyed its sales staff and estimated sales for the coming year totaling 7,100 units at $800 each. However, discussion with the staff economist indicated that in view of current economic conditions, it was not reasonable to anticipate such a strong sales performance. The economist estimated that total sales would not exceed 5,400 units at the $800 price. These data were presented to management as part of the sales forecasting process.

In a situation where there are diverse estimates of future sales levels, management will be likely to seek other estimates. For this reason, the trend analysis and econometric techniques may be relevant. Discussion of each of these methods follows.

Trend analysis

The analysis of trends in data can extend from a relatively simple extrapolation from a graphed set of data points to a highly sophisticated analysis of times series data.[4] Because of the complexity of the topic, this chapter presents only a brief survey of the alternative methods.

Trend analysis techniques are characterized by the data employed in the analysis. The methods use only past observations of the data series to be forecasted over time. No other data are included in the analysis. Logically, this methodology is justified on the grounds that since all factors which affect the data series (e.g., sales) are reflected in the actual past observations of the series, then the past data contain the best reflection of available information. Use of this approach is also relatively economical in that it is only necessary to have a list of past sales data—no other sets of data have to be gathered.

The simplest approach to trend analysis is to prepare a graph which scales the sales levels on the vertical axis and includes

---

[4] For reference, see Charles R. Nelson, *Applied Time Series Analysis for Managerial Forecasting* (San Francisco: Holden Day, Inc., 1973).

the time periods on the horizontal axis. The resulting *scattergraph* is then inspected visually. One can plot the next point in the series by visual methods if the series is fairly stable.

For example, if unit sales over the past five years were 4,700 units in Year 1, and 5,300, 4,900, 5,800, and 6,300 in Years 2 through 5, respectively, a plot of the sales values by year would appear as in Exhibit 3. A best fitting straight line is drawn by visual methods. A line similar to the dotted line in Exhibit 3 would be a likely choice. The point where the projected line crosses a line drawn perpendicular to the next year's mark on the horizontal axis would be the projected sales level for that year. This point would correspond to the + mark on the graph in Exhibit 3. Tracing from the + point back to the vertical axis indicates a projected sales level of 6,600 for the coming year.

Of course, the results of use of this method are highly dependent on the ability to draw a straight line that best fits the data. Divergent answers are possible, and become more likely as the plotted sales data fluctuate.

Another approach is to enter the past sales data into a regres-

EXHIBIT 3
Graph of past and projected sales volume

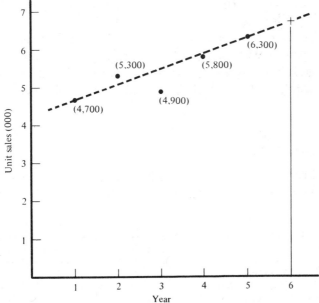

sion analysis program to obtain a statistical estimate of the projected sales value. A simple linear equation of the form

Next year's sales $(Y) = a + b$ [Year number (X)]

where a represents the intersection of the best fitting straight line with the vertical axis and b represents the increment in sales each year, can be used to prepare the forecast. Many hand calculators have preprogrammed regression capabilities, as do computer systems and programmable calculators.[5] Use of any of these methods requires entering the past sales values as the Y variable and the year number (starting with 1 and following sequentially). When these instructions were followed using a hand calculator, an estimate of 4,290 was obtained for a and 370 for b. To obtain the forecast, these estimates were substituted in the equation as:

$$Y = 4{,}290 + (6) \times (\$370)$$
$$= 6{,}510$$

for the estimated sales level.

Other forecasting techniques based on trend analysis are more complex and require long series of past data to derive a suitable solution. The class of forecasting techniques called Box-Jenkins models requires approximately 50 past observations to be used successfully. Generally, when these models are used in accounting applications, monthly data are required so that the required number of observations may be obtained. A discussion of these techniques is beyond the scope of this chapter. Further reference may be obtained from Nelson and also from Mabert and Radcliffe.[6]

Econometric techniques

In addition to the models which attempt to forecast based on past observations of the data series itself, there are a number

---

[5] The calculations may be done by hand as well. A presentation of the use of the technique in a cost analysis setting is available in John J. W. Neuner and Edward B. Deakin, *Cost Accounting: Principles and Practice,* 9th ed. (Homewood, Ill.: Richard D. Irwin, 1977), pp. 434–37.

[6] V. A. Mabert and R. C. Radcliffe, "A Forecasting Methodology," *The Accounting Review,* January 1974, pp. 61–75.

of models which can be employed to relate the sales forecast to other relevant variables. An equation can be formed which states that the predicted sales for the coming period is some weighted sum of predictor variables such as economic indicators, reports of consumer confidence indexes, back order volume, and other relevant predictors which may come from inside the company or from external sources. The use of these models is advocated because so many relevant predictors can be included in preparing a forecast. By manipulating the assumed values of the predictors, it is possible to examine a variety of "what if" conditions and relate them to the sales forecast. However, the task of predicting is shifted from a direct prediction of sales volumes to a prediction of some other variables. When employing this method, therefore, it is usually worthwhile to obtain the assistance of a specialist in economic forecasting.

CHOOSING THE SALES FORECAST

In the above discussion we indicated that four forecasts were derived from different sources as follows:

	Units
Ad hoc forecasts:	
Sales Staff	7,100
Economist	5,400
Trend analysis:	
Scattergram	6,600
Linear regression	6,510

In an actual application, there would probably be other forecasts derived from the use of econometric models or group efforts at forecasting. Once all of the forecast data have been assembled, it is usually the practice to present the forecasts to management. Management can then review the different forecasts, reconcile differences in light of the alternatives, confer with different persons who had a hand in the forecasting, and finally derive a single estimate of sales for the coming year. The estimate will then be used to derive the remaining components of the master budget.

For purposes of the example, we have assumed that management has weighted each of the four forecasts equally and derived an estimated sales level of 6,400 units as rounded to the nearest 100. The unit sales estimates may be converted to dollars by multiplying by the unit price of $800.

The next step in the budgeting process is to use the sales forecast to derive production estimates and a projected income statement.

THE PRODUCTION BUDGET

Once the anticipated sales level has been ascertained, it is possible to estimate the production levels required. Production is required not only to meet the sales demand, but also to insure that inventory levels are sufficient for efficient operations at the activity level expected during the budget period. It is necessary, therefore, to determine the required inventory level for the end of the budget period. Once this is done, the production budget becomes a simple exercise. The production level may be computed as:

Production = Budgeted sales for the period
+ Required ending inventory − Beginning inventory

This equation simply determines production as equal to the sales demand plus or minus an inventory volume adjustment. One may also view the equation as indicating that production is undertaken to meet sales and required ending inventory levels and that some of the units demanded will come from beginning inventory, with the remainder to be provided by current period production.

Of course, the production budget must be determined in terms of units rather than in dollars. For this reason, it is necessary to look beyond the financial accounting data to the underlying quantitative unit measures of inventories and sales.

Measurement of the number of units included in the sales forecast would probably be obtained as a part of the forecasting process. The inventory levels in terms of numbers of units would have to be estimated and reflected in the projected balance sheet (Exhibit 2) for the end of the current year (and start of the budget period).

In the illustrative example in this chapter, it is assumed that upon investigation it is learned that projected sales amount to

6,400 units and there are 900 units in the beginning inventory of finished goods. The required ending inventory is determined after consultation with operating management. For these purposes, it is assumed that the required ending inventory level amounts to 1,000 units.

With this information, the projected level of production is computed as follows:

$$\text{Production} = \underset{\text{(sales)}}{6{,}400 \text{ units}} + \underset{\substack{\text{(required} \\ \text{ending} \\ \text{inventory)}}}{1{,}000 \text{ units}} - \underset{\substack{\text{(beginning} \\ \text{inventory)}}}{900 \text{ units}}$$

$$= 6{,}500 \text{ units}$$

The production budget is then reviewed with management of the production facilities to ascertain whether the budgeted levels of production can be reached, and to determine the likely costs that would be incurred during the coming period at that level of activity. Analysis of the costs of production leads to the budgeted cost of goods sold statement, which is subsequently integrated into the budgeted income statement. In addition, the desired inventory level is converted to a dollar cost associated with the units included therein, and the result is included on the budgeted balance sheet.

The production budget may be expressed in a more formal schedule similar to that shown in Exhibit 4. If there are a number of different items to be produced, separate columns may be

EXHIBIT 4
Budgeted production schedule

HYPOTHETICAL MANUFACTURING COMPANY
Budgeted Production Schedule
For the Budget Year Ending December 31, 19B
(prepared on September 30, 19A)

	Units
Estimated sales	6,400
Plus:	
Required ending inventory	1,000
Units required	7,400
Less:	
Beginning inventory	900
Budgeted production	6,500

used to show the required production levels for each of the items.

Budgeted income statement

Once the sales and production budgets have been prepared and reviewed by management to coordinate the efforts of both the sales and the production groups and to assure the feasibility of these budgets, the next step is to prepare the budgeted income statement. This process is often accomplished in two steps, usually simultaneously: (1) the budgeted cost of goods manufactured and sold, and (2) budgeted selling, general, and administrative expenses. When these budgets are consolidated with the sales and production budgets, it is possible to prepare the complete budgeted income statement. In this discussion, preparation of the budgeted cost of goods manufactured and sold statement is examined, followed by a discussion of the remainder of the operating expense budget items.

Budgeted cost of goods manufactured and sold

Construction of a schedule of budgeted costs of goods to be manufactured and sold during the budget period may be carried out by simply itemizing the anticipated manufacturing costs expected at the budgeted production level. When a standard cost system is in use (Chapter 23), the setting of standards and the budgeting of costs and expenses may be carried out simultaneously.

Manufacturing costs may be subdivided into the major components: direct materials, direct labor, and manufacturing overhead. Each of these components is considered in turn for budgeting purposes.

First, the direct materials budget requires consideration of the materials needs during the period. The needs would include materials required for production as well as the inventory of materials necessary to carry on an efficient manufacturing process. The materials needs are considered to be met by drawing materials from inventory or by purchasing materials. The basic equality:

$$\underset{\substack{\text{Materials used} \\ \text{in production}}}{} + \underset{\substack{\text{Required ending} \\ \text{materials inventory}}}{} = \underset{\substack{\text{Materials to} \\ \text{be purchased} \\ + \text{Beginning materials} \\ \text{inventory}}}{}$$

can be used to formulate required materials purchases, usage, and ending inventories in both unit and dollar terms. If any three of the terms are known, it is possible to compute the remaining term in the equation. Normally, the materials to be used in production are derived from engineering analyses of the production budget. The beginning materials inventory can be derived from the projected balance sheet (shown in Exhibit 2), and the required ending inventory may be estimated through discussions with production management and with other management personnel.

Thus, the usual form of the equation will be designed to solve for required materials purchases and will appear as follows:

$$\underset{\substack{\text{Materials} \\ \text{to be} \\ \text{purchased}}}{} = \underset{\substack{\text{Materials} \\ \text{used in} \\ \text{production}}}{} + \underset{\substack{\text{Desired ending} \\ \text{materials} \\ \text{inventory}}}{} - \underset{\substack{\text{Beginning} \\ \text{materials} \\ \text{inventory}}}{}$$

The materials purchased together with the other materials data are entered in the first part of a pro forma standard cost of goods manufactured and sold statement.

Following the example in this chapter, we assume that the production for the coming period will require two types of materials as input: Material R and Material S. For each unit to be produced, three units of R and five units of S are required. The beginning materials inventory consists of 2,200 units of R and 4,000 units of S. The required ending inventory has been determined by management to equal 1,300 units of R and 4,600 units of S. The standard cost for each unit of R is $10 and the standard cost of each unit of S is $30. These costs are expected to remain constant during the coming budget period.

Computation of the required materials purchases in units would be as follows:

$$R = 6{,}500 \times 3 + 1{,}300 - 2{,}200$$
$$R = 18{,}600 \text{ units}$$

$$S = 6{,}500 \times 5 + 4{,}600 - 4{,}000$$
$$S = 33{,}100$$

EXHIBIT 5
Budgeted statement of cost of goods manufactured and sold

HYPOTHETICAL MANUFACTURING COMPANY
Budgeted Statement of Cost of Goods Manufactured and Sold
For the Budget Year Ending December 31, 19B
(prepared as of September 30, 19A)
(thousands of dollars)

Direct materials costs:		
Beginning inventory	$ 142	
(2,200 R @ $10 + 4,000 S @ $30)		
Purchases	1,179	
(18,600 R @ $10 + 33,100 S @ $30)		
Materials available for manufacturing	$1,321	
Less: Ending inventory	151	
(1,300 R @ $10 + 4,600 S @ $30)		
Total direct materials costs		$1,170
Direct labor		949
Manufacturing overhead (see schedule)		1,131
Total cost of manufacturing		$3,250
Add: Work in process, beginning inventory		32
Deduct: Work in process, required ending inventory		(97)
Cost of goods manufactured		$3,185
Add: Finished goods, beginning inventory		441
Deduct: Finished goods, required ending inventory		(490)
Cost of Goods Manufactured and Sold		$3,136

In dollar terms, this would amount to purchases of $186,000 for R and $993,000 for S.

These data on materials purchases, inventory levels, and materials required for production of 6,500 units may be presented formally for budget purposes as part of a budgeted cost of goods manufactured and sold statement. The level of detail required would depend upon management specifications. The data from this example have been used to prepare the direct materials cost portion of the budgeted statement of cost of goods manufactured and sold, which is shown in Exhibit 5.

Budgeting direct labor costs

The direct labor component of the statement in Exhibit 5 would be based on the estimated direct labor required to produce the 6,500 units called for in the production budget. These estimates are often obtained from engineering and production management personnel.

For purposes of the example, it is assumed that the direct labor costs are based on a standard of $146 per unit produced.

The result of multiplying $146 times the 6,500 units is the direct labor cost of $949,000 shown in Exhibit 5.

Budgeted overhead cost estimation

Budgeting overhead costs requires consideration of a variety of costs and the way those costs relate to changes in production levels. (See Chapter 3 for a discussion of cost behavior.) A schedule can be prepared to list the elements which comprise manufacturing overhead for the company. Each of the items on the list may be reviewed in terms of the cost levels last year and the expected cost levels for the coming year. Those costs that are expected to change with changes in production must be reviewed in terms of the anticipated production level for the coming year. Those that are expected to remain fixed relative to production must still be reviewed to make certain that external price changes have been incorporated into the budget, as well as to reflect any changes in plant facilities, operations, or other elements that could change the level of these fixed cost items.

An example of a schedule of overhead costs that would support the budgeted statement of cost of goods manufactured and sold is shown in Exhibit 6.

EXHIBIT 6
Schedule of manufacturing overhead costs

HYPOTHETICAL MANUFACTURING COMPANY
Schedule of Budgeted Manufacturing Overhead
For the Budget Year Ending December 31, 19B
(prepared as of September 30, 19A)
(thousands of dollars)

Budgeted production level	6,500 units
Indirect materials and supplies	$ 18
Supervisory labor	195
Personnel services	273
Heat, light, and power	29
Depreciation of building and equipment	236
Insurance	42
Computer services	71
Maintenance and repairs	84
Property taxes	117
Other indirect labor	37
Materials handling	29
Total Budgeted Manufacturing Overhead	$1,131

Computing the budgeted cost of goods sold

After the manufacturing overhead schedule has been pre-pared, the total is included in the cost of manufacturing. The three components of manufacturing cost (direct materials, direct labor, and manufacturing overhead) are summed to obtain the budgeted total manufacturing cost. Add to this the estimated beginning work-in-process inventory and deduct the required ending work-in-process inventory. The result is the cost of goods manufactured during the period. To this is added the estimated beginning inventory of finished goods, while the required ending inventory is deducted. The result is the cost of goods manufac-tured and sold as budgeted for the coming period. Note that the desired inventory levels for work in process and for finished goods were required at this point. The required work-in-process ending inventory would be obtained from consultation with management, while the required ending inventory of finished goods was obtained in terms of units as a part of the production budget. The units from the production budget would be multi-plied by the unit cost obtained as the cost of goods manufactured during the period. In the example, 6,500 units were manufac-tured at a cost of goods manufactured of $3,185,000, or $490 per unit. There were 1,000 units desired as ending finished goods inventory, which at $490 per unit yields the $490,000 shown in Exhibit 5 for required ending inventory of finished goods.

The resulting cost of goods manufactured and sold will be used in the determination of budgeted income.

Determining budgeted selling, general, and administrative expenses

Budgeting selling, general, and administrative expenses are usually obtained through a review of past cost data and through analysis of the relationship between past costs and revenue dol-lars as well as through discussions with management and those responsible for each function. The discussions with management should be designed to determine whether changes have taken place that would modify any of the past relationships. For exam-ple, a new sales incentive program may serve to increase the selling expense as a percentage of sales dollars. Consolidation

EXHIBIT 7
Schedule of budgeted selling, general, and administrative expenses

HYPOTHETICAL MANUFACTURING COMPANY
Schedule of Budgeted Selling, General, and
Administrative Expenses
For the Budget Year Ending December 31, 19B
(prepared as of September 30, 19A)
(thousands of dollars)

Selling expenses:

Sales salaries	$105	
Sales commissions	255	
Travel	31	
Marketing and advertising	297	
Other selling	47	
Total Selling Expenses		$ 735
General and administrative expenses:		
Administrative salaries	$154	
Legal and accounting staff	241	
Data processing services	103	
Outside professional services	39	
Depreciation—Building, furniture and equipment	94	
Insurance	26	
Taxes—Other than income	160	
Total general and administrative		817
Total Budgeted Selling, General, and Administrative Expenses		$1,552

of management functions may reduce the total administrative costs, while acquisition of new equipment and retirement of old equipment may change the total depreciation charges and may effect cost savings in other cost categories.

When these potential effects have been evaluated, a schedule of selling, general, and administrative expenses for the budget period may be prepared. The schedule may be as detailed as required for the coordination, performance evaluation, and control purposes derived from the budget process. An example of a schedule of selling, general and administrative expenses is shown in Exhibit 7. These data are used to prepare the budgeted income statement, and are also important in the estimation of budgeted cash flows.

THE BUDGETED INCOME STATEMENT

Preparation of the budgeted income statement requires gathering the data which has been prepared in the sales budget,

EXHIBIT 8
The budgeted income statement

HYPOTHETICAL MANUFACTURING COMPANY
Budgeted Income Statement
For the Budget Year Ending December 31, 19B
(prepared as of September 30, 19A)
(thousands of dollars)

Budgeted revenues:

Sales (6,500 units @ $800)	$5,200	
Other	85	
Total Revenues		$5,285
Budgeted expenses:		
Cost of goods manufactured and sold (per Exhibit 5)	$3,136	
Selling, general, and administrative expenses (per Exhibit 7)	1,552	
Other expenses	71	
Total Budgeted Expenses		4,759
Budgeted net income before taxes		$ 526
Federal and other income taxes:		
Currently payable	$ 238	
Additions to deferred tax liability	14	
Total Federal and Other Income Tax		252
Budgeted Net Income after Taxes		$ 274

the cost of goods manufactured and sold budget, and the budgeted selling, general, and administrative expenses. In addition, data on potential sources of other income and expense must be obtained by discussions with top management responsible for nonoperating income and expense decisions. In addition, the statements prepared up to this point should be reviewed with the tax staff of the company to evaluate the likely tax liability and the tax expense to be reported in the financial statements. Any deferred taxes should also be reviewed at this time.

Gathering the data from Exhibits 5 and 7 and the budgeted sales of 6,500 units at $800 provides the first portion of the illustrated budgeted income statement in Exhibit 8. The data on other income and expense, as well as the tax data, are presumed to have been obtained in consultation with the appropriate management personnel. The result of this information is the budgeted net income. This data is then used to prepare a budgeted statement of financial position, as well as a budgeted statement of sources and uses of cash.

THE BUDGETED STATEMENT
OF FINANCIAL POSITION

An enterprise can view each of its financial position statements as individual steps that reflect the company's progress towards long-run goals and objectives. The position anticipated at the end of the period may be viewed as where the company hopes to be in terms of its long-range plans. The income statement and related schedules tell part of the story. However, other management decisions need to be made concerning the structure of assets and equities. Viewing the present balance sheet and the budgeted income statement alone will not tell the full story. These documents may be taken together with plans for changes in assets and equities that will lead to the next step in the long-range plan. A budgeted balance sheet may be used to establish where management hopes that next step will be located.

Preparation of the budgeted balance sheet begins with the projected balance sheet for the beginning of the budget period (from Exhibit 2). Each item on that balance sheet is reviewed to determine the changes that will be expected to take place over the budget period.

Many of the account balances on the budgeted financial position statement will have been derived as a part of other aspects of the budget process. For example, the inventory accounts for the end of the year were required to produce the budgeted statement of cost of goods manufactured and sold. Changes in the deferred tax account would have been discussed as part of the preparation of the budgeted income statement. Likewise, acquisitions and dispositions of fixed assets and acquisitions of new assets would probably be considered while reviewing the other income and other expense categories, as well as while preparing the estimated overhead expenses, the selling, general, and administrative expenses, and the cash budget. Changes in long-term debt can also affect expense through changes in interest obligations. It is often helpful to enter those items that have been determined through other phases of the budget process into a skeleton budgeted balance sheet.

Determination of the remaining items can be accomplished through consultation with management. By reviewing the data accumulated to this point in the budgeting process, management's attention can be focused on those facets of operations that require special attention. Information such as the cash requirements and availability and accounts receivable balances may be obtained at this time. Likewise, any additional revisions considered in the property, plant, and equipment account may be made in view of the other budget data. A projected permissible level for the liability accounts may also be determined at this time. Finally, attention may be directed towards the shareholders' equity accounts and level of dividends (whether by contract as with preferred shares, or though the policy of the board of directors). Proposals for changes in dividend policy may be initiated after viewing the results of all budget plans for the period.

The data from Exhibits 2, 5, 6, 7, and 8 have been drawn together to prepare the budgeted balance sheet in Exhibit 9. The references for data from these other schedules and statements are shown on Exhibit 9 in the appropriate places. Those account balances that require management review and determination have also been indicated.

A review of the budgeted balance sheet may indicate areas that are in need of some rethinking. For example, when the data from the capital budget are included in the balance sheet,

EXHIBIT 9
Budgeted balance sheet

HYPOTHETICAL MANUFACTURING COMPANY
Budgeted Balance Sheet
For the Budget Year Ending December 31, 19B
(prepared September 30, 19A)
(thousands of dollars)

Assets

Current Assets:

Cash (cash budget)		$ 180
Accounts receivable (from estimates of credit and sales management together with treasurer's assessment)		235
Inventories:		
Materials (Exhibit 5)	$ 151	
Work in Process (Exhibit 5)	97	
Finished goods (Exhibit 5 and the production budget)	490	738
Other current assets (per management)		23
Total Current Assets		$1,176

EXHIBIT 9 (*continued*)

Long-Term Assets:

Property plant and equipment:

Beginning balance (Exhibit 2)	$2,475	
Net additions (capital budget)	311	$2,786

Accumulated depreciation:

Beginning balance (Exhibit 2)	$ 850	

Current charges:

Manufacturing (Exhibit 6)	236	
General and administrative (Exhibit 7)	94	
Less: Depreciation applicable to retired assets (per management)	(31)	(1,149)
Total Property Plant and Equipment		1,637
Total Assets		$2,813

Liabilities and Shareholders' Equity

Current Liabilities:

Accounts payable (consultation with treasurer and purchasing)	$ 155	
Taxes and other payables (per management)	317	
Current portion of long-term debt (per treasurer)	48	
Total Current Liabilities		$ 520
Long-term liabilities (net current portion included above) (management and treasurer evaluations of new debt and reductions)		423
Deferred taxes (beginning balance plus Exhibit 8)		81
Total Liabilities		$1,024

Shareholders' equity:

Common stock (beginning balance plus management evaluations of changes		$ 350

Retained earnings:

Beginning balance (Exhibit 2)	$1,305	
Add: Budgeted net income (Exhibit 8)	274	
Less: Budgeted dividends per management	(140)	1,439
Total Shareholders' Equity		1,789
Total Liabilities and Shareholders' Equity ..		$2,813

it may become evident that the level of expenditures on new projects may need to be revised because of the funds available for such purposes. Decisions to obtain new financing may also need rethinking in light of the projected financial position and the resultant liquidity and debt/equity ratios.

Once the budgeted statement of financial position has been prepared and the expected adjustments to all of the categories of assets and liabilities have been made, a cash budget may be prepared for the year. Of course, the availability of cash must be kept in mind as the various budgets are prepared.

THE CASH BUDGET

The cash budget is one aspect of cash planning that is conducted to assure company solvency and to take advantage of any fluctuations in levels of cash resulting from seasonal or longer term factors. Cash planning is discussed in more detail in Chapter 32. Our attention is directed towards preparation of a cash budget on a one-year basis.

Preparation of the cash budget requires that all revenues, expenses, and other transactions be considered in terms of their effects on cash. The budgeted cash receipts are computed by taking the collections on accounts receivable (rather than sales), and adding other collections of cash anticipated through sale of assets, financing, or other cash generating activities. Disbursements are computed by considering the cash required for materials purchases, other expenses related to manufacturing, and other operations, as well as the cash required to pay federal income taxes and stockholder dividends. In addition, the cash disbursements necessary for repayment of debt or to be incurred for the acquisition of assets must also be incorporated in the cash budget. Management estimates of the cash balance required for operating purposes are also necessary for preparation of the cash budget.

When this phase of the budgeting process is reached, many of the required inputs for the cash budget will have already been obtained. It is usually expedient to assemble the available data into the cash budget and then obtain any additional information that may be required.

An example of a cash budget based on the data used in this discussion has been prepared in Exhibit 10. The source of each of the data items is indicated. Certain of the data items require further elaboration. These are discussed below.

The budgeted cash from sales was computed by taking the gross sales, deducting the end-of-period accounts receivable, and adding the beginning accounts receivable. A deduction would also be made to reflect any anticipated uncollectible accounts.

EXHIBIT 10
The cash budget

HYPOTHETICAL MANUFACTURING COMPANY
Cash Budget
For the Budget Year Ending December 31, 19B
(prepared as of September 30, 19A)
(thousands of dollars)

Cash balance beginning of period (per Exhibit 2)...............		$ 150
Receipts:		
Collections on accounts (Exhibits 2 and 9)	$5,185	
Other receipts:		
Other revenue (per management discussion for Exhibit 8)	85	
Sales of assets (per management)...........................	25	
Total Receipts..		5,295
Disbursements:		
Payments for accounts payable (Exhibits 2, 5, and 9)	$1,164	
Direct labor (Exhibit 5)	949	
Manufacturing overhead requiring cash (Exhibit 6) less		
noncash depreciation charges............................	895	
Selling general and administrative expenses (Exhibit 7)		
less noncash charges (depreciation).......................	1,458	
Other expenses (Exhibit 8)	71	
Required payments for federal income taxes (per discussion		
with tax staff)	185	
Dividends and other distributions to shareholders (from		
management as presented for Exhibit 8)...................	140	
Reduction in long-term debt (Exhibit 8)	83	
Acquisition of new assets (from the capital investment		
budget)...	320	
Total Disbursements		(5,265)
Budgeted Ending Cash Balance (ties in with Exhibit 9)		$ 180

This computation resulted in the estimated cash receipts from sales of $5,185,000 ($5,200,000 + $220,000 − $235,000).

Budgeted cash required for purchases would include the aggregate purchases included in the budgeted cost of goods manufactured and sold statement (Exhibit 5), adjusted for the net increase in the accounts payable liability. The computation was: $1,164,000 = $1,179,000 + $140,000 − $155,000.

The manufacturing expenses have been included on the assumption that there are no significant accrued liabilities that would affect these items. Had there been accrued payrolls or other accruals, it would be necessary to adjust the amounts in Exhibits 5 and 6 to reflect the cash payments required during the budget period. The manufacturing overhead requiring cash was determined by subtracting the $236,000 in depreciation from the total budgeted manufacturing overhead of $1,131,000 shown in Exhibit 6. The resulting $895,000 is entered in the cash budget.

A similar adjustment was made to reflect the cash expenditures for selling, general, and administrative expenses ($1,-458,000 = $1,552,000 − $94,000).

The final item on the cash budget is the cash balance required for operation of the company. This amount is computed by taking the beginning balance from Exhibit 2, adding the budgeted receipts, and deducting the budgeted disbursements. Should the cash balance appear out of line, portions of the budget must be revised. Typical methods used to accomplish this are through adjustments to liability accounts, by changes in the assumed financing arrangements, or through revisions in the amount of temporary investments in marketable securities. In many cases the amount of cash budgeted for the end of the period will be such that management may consider additional ventures because of cash availability. The resulting desired end-of-period cash balance should also be reflected in the cash balance stated on the budgeted balance sheet.

SUMMARY

The budgeting process is undertaken for purposes of planning, performance evaluation, coordination, and control of operations. At the end of the budget period, actual events must be compared to budgeted plans to determine the cause of variances (See Chapters 19 and 24). Investigation of these variances from budget may lead to better performance in the future or to better budgetary planning, or both.

In addition, by laying out company plans for the coming year in a formal budget plan, management is given important information on the decisions that need to be made to meet current and long-run goals and objectives. The comprehensive budget enables each member of the management team to see how the individual pieces of the company fit together into a complete picture. Moreover, the budget may be used to motivate personnel to attain the stated budget levels of activity at the planned cost amounts.

5

Cost as a means
of controlling operations

Leslie R. Loschen*
Clarence J. Baudhuin†
William H. Wieland‡

MANAGEMENT PHILOSOPHY OF CONTROL

Cost analysis, based upon a knowledge of the cost structure and of cost behavior patterns, can be helpful to any management, regardless of whether the organization is centralized or decentralized. Historically, cost accounting developed to serve the needs of financial reporting; that is, costs were accumulated for the purpose of *product costing,* to enable inventory to be valued and income to be measured. The second, more recent, purpose of cost accounting is that of *cost control.* The cost control purpose requires that some standard of comparison be available, either informal or formal. A formal standard may be in the form of a budget, and/or it may be in the form of a standard cost accounting system. Whereas a fixed (static) budget is sufficient for product costing purposes, it is likely to be unsatisfactory and inappropriate for cost control purposes whenever the actual attained activity level varies significantly from the level for which the fixed budget was prepared. For this reason, flexible budgets (with

---
* Associate Professor of Accounting, University of Southern California.

† Executive Vice President–Finance and Administration, Chemical Plastics Group, Dart Industries, Inc.

‡ Retired Senior Vice President and Comptroller, United California Bank.

or without a standard cost accounting system) are essential for meaningful cost control. (See Chapter 4.)

Actual costs may be compared to a fixed budget to obtain a measure of the spending variance, but such a variance is neither a measure of *effectiveness* nor a measure of *efficiency*. *Effectiveness* can probably best be measured as the difference between the quantity actually produced and the quantity planned for; this quantity might be valued at the standard (or normal) contribution per unit. On the other hand, *efficiency* can be measured only by comparing actual costs incurred (inputs) with the standard allowable costs of the good output (that is, the flexible budget for the actual good output).

Obviously, costs do not control operations; *people* control costs of operations. Also, it should be remembered that the controller does not control costs or people, except in his own department. The control of costs must be exercised by line management; the controller assists line management by collecting, analyzing, and reporting cost information to management. Behavioral considerations are highly important in controlling costs and in using costs as a means of controlling operations; they are discussed in Chapter 10. It should be mentioned here that the key to control of operations is motivation of people, so this must be kept in mind at all times when considering costs as a means of controlling operations. In addition, the principle of "management by exception" is applicable; i.e., the attention of management should be directed to the exceptional performance, whether it is favorable or unfavorable, in order that management's time is most economically employed.

Perhaps because cost accounting originated as a means of product costing, most people probably think in terms of the cost of a physical product and as a result perceive of costs as being useful principally in a manufacturing concern. A subtle psychological change results when costs are interpreted as the *cost of doing something,* the cost of an activity which results in production of a product in some firms, whereas in other firms or in other departments the activity is that of providing a service. When costs are viewed as costs of doing something, it becomes much easier to utilize them in controlling operations because it is obvious that *people* are responsible for doing things, and that cost control can be achieved only through motivation of people. Costs are fixed or variable, direct or indirect, controllable or noncontrollable because people made them that way by their decisions.

Before any cost control system can be designed and used for the development and growth of an operation, management goals and objectives must be defined. A careful evaluation of these goals and objectives is then necessary to determine that management's need for information is being recognized.

Some of the specific needs or control objectives which such a system must satisfy are: strategic planning, profit planning, costing products, product pricing, product profitability measurement, make-or-buy decisions, product mix and volume decisions, breakeven analysis, capital investment evaluation, and preparation of reports for custodial accounting.

In summary, for effective cost control the management reporting system must reflect how the company is operating in order to enable management to plan how the company *should be* operating. This approach creates a basis for variance analysis and can reflect problems developing before problems show up on the income statement, some time after the end of the accounting period.

CONTROLLABILITY OF COSTS

Although it is common to speak of controllable and noncontrollable costs, ultimately there are no noncontrollable costs. All costs are (or were) controllable by someone at some time. The two determinants of controllability of costs are:

1. Level of management responsibility.
2. Time span covered.

Level of responsibility

Responsibility for incurring, and therefore for controlling, costs can be traced to successive levels of the management hierarchy. The higher one goes in the organization chart, the more the costs that can be controlled. To accomplish performance measurement, the design of the chart of accounts must follow the organization chart. Management must be involved in setting the responsibility structure through a thorough review of the organization chart. If the organization should be changed, such changes should be made and reflected in the chart of accounts. The chart of accounts must reflect the needs of the operation in controlling costs by responsibility.

Development of the chart of accounts must be one of the first steps taken to provide the cost information necessary to control operations. It must accommodate the accumulation of data from all segments of the business in the smallest units or segments which can be economically determined. These segments can then be rearranged to form all kinds of meaningful information patterns. The chart of accounts is the vehicle for accumulating costs, expenses, and information to satisfy the needs for management information. This information must be gathered so that costs and expenses are gathered by responsibility.

If the chart is to be effective, it must be designed so that all members of the management team can understand and use the

EXHIBIT 1
X chart

	11	15	16	20	33	34	71	72	34	35	36	37	38	51	52	53	54	55	56	61	62	63	65	68	69	81	83	84	99
RENT (560-569)																													
561 - RENTAL - BUILDING					X																								
Monrovia Warehouse						X																							
Western Region Sales Office																							X						
562 - RENTAL - EQUIPMENT																													
OFFICE EQUIPMENT																													
Typewriter						X			X	X	X	X		X	X		X	X					X		X	X			X
Adding Machine-Calculator						X						X				X													
Duplicating Equipment						X											X						X						
Postage Meter						X											X						X						
Mailing Scales																	X												
Paper Cutter																	X												
Dictation Equipment								X																					
P.A. System																	X												
Bottled Water Cooler						X																							
Computer System																X													
Unit Record Equipment																X													
WAREHOUSE																													
Fork Lift Truck							X																						
Lease Rental																													
Mileage Charge																													
Personal Property Tax																													
LEASED FLEET																													
Leased Trucks								X																					

section that applies to their areas of responsibility. Titles must be descriptive and numeric codes should be understandable so that all levels of management, and particularly the front line supervisor, can properly code expense items. If this is done a supervisor can relate to the charges on the cost report, and in the case of a questionable charge he can trace it back to the responsible person.

To use the chart properly as a means of gathering costs, there should be definition of the types of costs to be charged to an account. A very effective method of providing definitions in a simple manner is the "X" Chart shown in Exhibit 1. This form shows the account number, the items that can be charged to that account, and the department that has a budget for that account.

The chart of accounts must be flexible. Organizations are constantly changing and the different information requirements must be reflected. A chart of accounts must be changed as the organization changes to reflect properly the information needed by management to guide and control the operation.

Time span

The second determinant of controllability is the span of time covered. Variable direct costs of production are the result of decisions on current production levels and respond quickly to changes in volume. Some fixed costs are discretionary and result from management decisions on the short-run current budget, and other fixed costs are committed by past decisions which have a long-term effect. In addition to the above examples of costs which result from operations, the costs of capital expenditures and major projects have an important time dimension and are therefore controllable only over a relatively long time span. (See Chapter 33 for an example.)

Time span is also a factor in allocating and controlling the costs of service departments. For example, a service department such as factory power will have committed costs based on a maximum standby capacity requested by the user departments; such committed costs are not controllable in the short run. In addition, some power department costs are variable as a result of the level of usage in the current period.

CONTROL TECHNIQUES

Control implies the existence of (1) a plan or standard and (2) an authority who has the power to effect corrective action. Accordingly, all of the techniques described will provide a base of measurement and a means of informing the appropriate persons in a timely and meaningful manner.

The use of costs to control manufacturing activities is based on a long historical background. Of equal if not greater importance, however, is the use of costs to control other business activities. Only in relatively recent times has serious attention been focused on applying cost control techniques to such business activities as services, marketing, projects, and administration. The following descriptions outline the techniques found to be the most useful in controlling the business activities mentioned.

Effective employment of these techniques has been enhanced by developments in recent decades of (1) industrial engineering advancements applicable particularly to nonmanufacturing activities and (2) computer-based systems which permit large volumes of data to be analyzed and reported in a short period of time at a justifiable expense.

CONTROL TECHNIQUES—MANUFACTURING

As mentioned previously, cost accounting in a manufacturing environment is well established and has long been considered essential to effective management.

The use of costs to control manufacturing operations requires some sort of norm or standard against which actual results may be compared. Historical costs may be useful in operations which are simple and not subject to change. However, in the more realistic environment of complex operations and rapid changes, historical costs have major disadvantages: (1) they incorporate inefficiencies which exist in the current operation and (2) they portray the past and thus do not represent what should be expected in the future.

Direct labor and materials

In the case of direct labor and materials used in the manufacturing process, a system of standard costing is considered to be the most effective method of providing a means of control.

A comprehensive discussion of standard cost systems may be found in Chapters 23 and 24 but the essence of such a system is the quantity of labor and material at predetermined prices needed to manufacture one unit of product under average or normal conditions.

Practical considerations may limit the amount of detail which can be included in a standard costs system, but from a standpoint of control greater detail is more likely to produce better results. In this regard, computerized systems can provide volumes of data which would be almost unthinkable under a manual system.

As indicated earlier, control implies the existence of (1) a standard against which measurement can be made and (2) an authority capable of providing corrective action.

The development of standards is primarily the responsibility of the industrial engineer. However, the cost accountant should work very closely with the engineer to assure that the resulting standard costs are both accurate and useful for control purposes.

The cost accountant's primary responsibility is to provide useful information to the proper levels of management. This seemingly simple step is one which requires very careful consideration. Timing is particularly important, as is the matching of the level of detail with the level of management.

The key to control is the *effective handling of variances* from standard. In reporting to a production supervisor, for example, variances should be reported in as much detail as the system affords and should consist of the following major groupings:

Direct labor—quantity.

Direct labor—price.

Direct material—quantity.

Variances from standard price for direct materials should be charged or credited to the purchasing department.

Promptness in reporting is particularly important at the lower levels of management. Production supervisors should be informed of variances as soon as practical, probably daily in most cases, so that problems may be identified and if possible corrected at the production level.

Promptness in reporting to higher levels of management is also important, but care should be taken not to sacrifice quality in one's eagerness to impress senior management. Time should be taken to isolate the important variances and to identify the reasons, so that management's efforts can be concentrated on significant problems.

Variances of direct labor costs from standard can, of course, be attributed to a number of causes. Here again it is important to take the time to make the reporting system responsive to the needs of those receiving the reports. Rather than yielding to the temptation of merely listing all the possible causes of labor variances, care should be taken to group the variances into meaningful and useful categories. For example, variances could be grouped according to organizational units having responsibility for corrective action, as in the following list of causes of direct labor performance variances:

Materials:
  Poor quality
  Improper specifications
  Insufficient quantities
Engineering:
  Changed method, standard not adjusted
  New machine, standard not changed
Maintenance and support:
  Machine problems
  Materials not received on schedule
  Power outage
Personnel:
  Insufficient personnel with needed skills
  Inadequate training
  Deliberate work slow down
Supervision:
  Inefficient flow of materials
  Improper manning
  Efforts of workers below/above standard
  Absence from work station in excess of standard allowance

Attributing variances, particularly unfavorable ones, to other departments can result in sensitive situations. It is therefore imperative that the type of reporting suggested above be supported by prompt and cooperative action by those involved.

Direct material usage variances could have a similar list of causes and consequently present a similar set of problems and opportunities to the cost accountant and all levels of management.

Factory overhead

Factory overhead differs substantially from direct labor and materials, and the differences suggest that the same control techniques cannot be used effectively in both cases. Direct labor and materials exhibit a preciseness which has resulted in their being classed as engineered costs. This preciseness is lacking in factory overhead. Costs related to overhead tend to be semifixed, whereas direct labor and materials costs move with changes in volume. Overhead costs are common costs which are incurred for the benefit of more than one production area. Further, overhead costs often result from factors outside the control of the overhead department.

Factory overhead could be controlled by a fixed budget, but in many cases portions of overhead costs vary with levels of production. On the other hand, standard overhead costs per unit would not be satisfactory for control purposes, because low volumes of production would likely cause unfavorable variances and high volumes would probably cause favorable variances. The point is that in a complex environment, variances from either a fixed budget or a standard cost per unit would be of little value in terms of control and would not be very useful in identifying problems in need of corrective action.

A flexible (semivariable) budget is likely to be a very good choice as the most effective control technique for factory overhead. Of course, if production volume is stable or if production fluctuations have little influence on overhead costs, then a fixed budget can be both simple and effective.

Flexible budgets are more difficult and costly to develop and administer than are fixed budgets. The effort and expense may, however, be well justified if the operational environment is a complex one, particularly where overhead is a significant part of total cost of production.

One of the principal difficulties associated with flexible budgets is the selection of activity indices. There is an assumed causal relationship between activity and cost. Unfortunately, the activities which cause the costs to be incurred are often too complex to measure; so as a practical solution a single indicator which correlates closely with overhead costs is used to represent the activity. This area is one of many in which the cost accountant would be well advised to work closely with an industrial engineer.

CONTROL TECHNIQUES—SERVICES

As anyone familiar with the national economy is aware, manufacturing constitutes a relatively small part of business activities; services make up a much larger portion of gross national product. Yet cost accounting and control techniques tend to focus on manufacturing—partly because of historical factors (that is, an early need) and partly because the cost of services yields reluctantly to precise measurement.

In recent decades, however, the management of service businesses—such as retail stores, financial institutions, hospitals, and restaurants—have developed techniques for improved cost controls over their operations. These same techniques are also used for clerical and other support services in manufacturing companies. For the purpose of applying control techniques, the various types of services are divided into two principal categories:

1. Uniform (homogeneous) services.
2. Diversified (heterogeneous) services.

Uniform services

Uniform services are defined as those services which are performed by repetitively following an established routine. Included would be such services as billing, preparing a payroll, processing accounts receivable or payable, collecting loan payments, cooking a hamburger, preparing an insurance policy, and checking out a grocery customer. Although the tasks performed are not precisely the same each time, they are sufficiently homogeneous to permit usable standards to be set.

It is not necessary that the worker perform only one task. A variety of tasks may be performed in random sequence without invalidating the concept of uniform services. For example, a bank teller may within a short period of time (*a*) cash a check, (*b*) accept and process a deposit, and (*c*) post interest to a savings account. Standards can be established for performing these and related services, resulting in a means of control where workers are performing a variety of tasks. This technique is particularly applicable to groups of workers.

Uniform services closely parallel direct factory production operations. Standards may be set not only in terms of time required but also as to the level of skill needed. Thus standard costs may be established which will permit evaluation of (*a*) performance efficiency and (*b*) utilization of personnel at the proper compensation level.

There are several methods which can be used to develop standards for performing uniform services, ranging from estimates by work supervisors to detailed studies by engineers.

Work sampling is a technique which occupies a middle ground between the extremes of supervisors' estimates and engineers' detailed studies. In the hands of a skilled person, it can be developed into a very useful and practical method for determining the time needed to perform repetitive tasks.

The setting of standards involves selection of activity indices which correlate closely with the cost of the operation. These indices could include such items as the number of bills prepared, employees paid, loans serviced, hamburgers cooked, policies prepared, and grocery items sold.

Whatever approach is taken, the cost accountant will need to work very closely with an industrial engineer who is particularly skilled in the field of work measurement applicable to clerical and other nonmanufacturing services.

In reporting the results for any period (usually a month), an integrated computerized system is very helpful. For example, in a commercial bank the computer system which processes checks deposited can count the number of checks and deposits and automatically feed this information into the work measurement system.

Variances from standard can be handled in much the same manner as in the case of direct labor and material in a manufacturing operation. Frequency of reporting, however, is likely to be different in that a manufacturing operation benefits from frequent reports but a service operation usually is not amenable to frequent fine tuning.

However, there are cases where services, even though uniform, are not performed in sufficient volume to warrant formal cost standards. In these situations controls often can be developed by use of competitive comparisons such as open market prices or comparing costs of similar functions at different locations within the company.

Diversified services

In every organization there are a number of services performed which vary only slightly with changes in the volume of general activity. Broadly speaking, these services tend to be administrative in nature and range from senior management to some of the lowest level positions, such as night watchman or window cleaner.

The costs of administrative services are among the most difficult to control. These services are usually diversified and do not lend themselves well to cost-benefit analyses. Left unchecked, administrative payrolls have a very strong tendency to rise regardless of the direction taken by the rest of the organization.

Control is usually exercised through use of a fixed budget. The size of the budget is sometimes related to some financial goal (e.g., administrative services as a percentage of anticipated sales), but management often determines the amounts by subjective judgment. These costs have been classified as "discretionary" costs, because they are incurred as a result of management's discretion, usually for a short-term planning horizon.

CONTROL TECHNIQUES—PROJECTS

The success of many commercial companies is dependent not only on efficient sales and production organizations but also on their ability to develop new and improved products and services. The development process is usually in the form of *projects,* some of which are continuous and some discrete.

Projects also are an important means by which government and other noncommercial organizations achieve their aims and accomplish tasks assigned to them.

As with administrative services costs, control is related to appropriations rather than to expenditures. However, it is important to recognize that success of a project will finally be measured in terms of future results (profitability in the case of commercial ventures) and not by the degree of compliance with a financial budget.

Allocations of funds to projects represent faith in the ability of those involved in the activity, particularly in the case of research projects. But faith cannot be entirely boundless, and there must be a means of measuring progress.

Overall cost control can be, and often is, achieved by limiting total project allocations to a percentage of sales or some other criterion which management believes represents the proper amount to be spent.

From the cost accountant's viewpoint, the most difficult part is the design of a system which effectively controls costs during the life of the project. Unfortunately, projects are seldom timed to fall neatly within accounting periods. The usual approach is to provide justification for approval of a project, submit and evaluate progress reports, adjust allocations as necessary, and conduct an after-the-fact evaluation as a guide for future projects. For very large projects a system such as PERT (Program Evaluation and Review Technique) might be justified.

The entire subject of project administration is very complex and is receiving increasing attention. Cost control is only one aspect of the problem but it represents an opportunity for the cost accountant to make a substantial contribution.

PERFORMANCE REPORTS

Accounting reports are normally issued on a monthly basis and can generally be put into a standard format. *Cost control reports* have different formats and the content will vary between companies due to the type of company, management style, management expertise, and product. However, even the best designed cost control report issued only on a monthly basis can be ineffective. Monthly reports are historical, in that they are not issued until after the month-end. At that time no correction can be made for last month's performance, and since half of the current month usually has passed before the report is issued, a correction, if possible, may not take effect until the following month. In addition, it will be difficult and time consuming for a manager to supply a detailed explanation of what happened in the first week of last month when it is now the middle of the current month. For this reason, daily and weekly reports can be more vital than monthly reports. Daily and weekly reports need not be lengthy and complicated to be effective. In preparing these reports, which may be considered "flash reports," the important element is that they provide information that will be an indicator of the business trend for the period. In addition to content, it is extremely important that all managers receiving reports understand the factors that affect the results shown and that they have the responsibility, authority, and ability to take action in their respective areas.

The frequency of issuance of performance reports, and the amount of detail contained in them, are functions of:

1. The level of management to whom the report is addressed.
2. The nature of the costs whose performance is being measured.

Level of management

For the board of directors and top management, quarterly reports are usually sufficient, and a summary rather than details is appropriate. Of course, individual management style and preferences must be considered; for example, the press has sometimes characterized President Jimmy Carter as a "detail man." Operating management, however, must have timely reports in sufficient detail to enable them to take prompt corrective action. Costs cannot be controlled *after* they are incurred, so the management information system must provide data as early as possible so that action can be taken prior to incurrence of the costs.

Opinions differ as to the propriety and usefulness of including costs which are not controllable by the level of management to whom the report is addressed. Some authorities believe that allocated costs may be included in a performance report for information purposes, even though control of such costs can be exercised only at a higher level of management, with the *caveat* that the noncontrollable costs should be clearly separated from those that are controllable. Others oppose the inclusion of noncontrollable costs as unnecessary detail, or in some cases as undesirable disclosure of competitive information.

In addition, we discuss a few of the formula pricing applications in some detail. We will cover the following:

1. Cost-plus pricing.
2. Rate of return pricing.

Cost-plus pricing

Shillinglaw has stated that there are four steps in the process of cost-based formula pricing, as follows:[6]

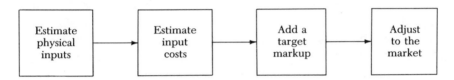

The cost-plus pricing procedure depends heavily on cost but cannot completely ignore the demand element discussed in previous sections. A percentage markup on full cost is set, which varies by industry and by product line. The markup appears to be related to the rate of turnover of the products in the industry and the risk involved in handling the product or service. If all competitors use essentially the same formula, the derived price should tend to be competitive.

For many merchandise retailers, price determination is merely accomplished by reference to catalog price schedules. The price lists are developed not on the basis of how price will affect demand, but on standard markups. The automobile parts wholesaler will have price catalogs for his retail buyers, his customers that are going to resell the merchandise (auto dealers and service stations), and possibly for trucking firms and government or public sector buyers. The markup rates no doubt will be different in each case.

The very large number of different products sold by the parts wholesaler requires the use of catalog pricing. Other retailers, such as the furniture retailer, may not be faced with complex products but with fewer products. This retailer generally sets a standard markup. A piece of furniture that costs $100 would

---

[6] Shillinglaw, *Managerial Cost Accounting*, pp. 548–50.

have a standard markup of say 80 percent applied thus setting the target price at $180.

Cost-plus pricing is also common in the service area. Professional organizations often set hourly rates based on the average hourly salary to the employee. For instance, a CPA firm might price its professional services at three times the average hourly costs. If first year assistants in the firm were paid an average rate of $6 per hour, the firm would price its assistants at $18 to the client.

In most situations the "plus" part of the formula is determined by someone else. Standard markups in the trade set at least a bench mark for the person setting price. In other areas price catalogs are available. Still others are given suggested list prices (auto dealers). The net effect of the standard markup is to make pricing simple, but it also limits price competition.

If the company wants to deviate from the standard markups, what are the major considerations?

1. What will happen to the *demand* for the firm's products and services?
2. How will the competition react to the firm's price changes? Will they change their prices?
3. How will the price changes affect net profit?

Rate of return pricing

One of the ways that the markup percentage on cost can be developed is to base it on a desired return on investment. A firm develops a desired return on investment and sets the price of its products to yield the return desired. The Subcommittee on Antitrust and Monopoly (Washington, D.C.: Government Printing Office, 1963) argued that more powerful firms are more likely to be target pricers than less powerful concerns. A firm using target pricing must be able to set price. Consequently, the products must be differentiated and have limited competition.

Pricing goals of large industrial corporations. A number of studies have been conducted to determine the pricing goals of large industrial corporations. Most of the corporations studied would be considered price leaders in an oligopoly market. The

TABLE 6
Pricing goals of large industrial corporations

Company	Principal pricing goal (percent)*	Collateral pricing goals
General Motors	20	Maintaining market share
U.S. Steel	8	Target market share; stable price; stable margin
Alcoa	10	"Promotive" policy on new products; price stabilization
Exxon (Standard Oil of New Jersey)	12	Maintaining market share; price stabilization
Du Pont	20	Charging what traffic will bear over long run; maximum return for new products—"life cycle" pricing

* Return on investment after taxes.
  Source: Lanzillotti [specific target rates for Exxon (Standard Oil of New Jersey) and Du Pont based on interviews by Lanzillotti; rate for General Motors based on testimony by company officials in *Hearings on Administered Prices*] as quoted by Kanerscher, p. 244.

TABLE 7
Target rates of return (after taxes), selected firms

	Target return on investment (percent)	Actual return on investment, 1947–55 (percent)
General Electric	20	21.4
General Motors	20	26.0
Sears Roebuck	10–15	5.4
U.S. Steel	8	10.3

Source: Lanzillotti, as quoted by Kanerscher, p. 244.

TABLE 8
Comparison of target with actual returns, 1953–1968

Rate of return	General Motors	U.S. Steel	Alcoa	Exxon (Standard Oil of N. Jersey)	Du Pont	Weighted average	Unweighted average*
Target	20.0%	8.0%	10.0%	12.0%	20.0%	14.6%	14.0%
Actual	20.2%	8.4%	9.5%	12.6%	22.2%	15.1%	15.1%
Deviation†	0.2	0.4	−0.5	0.6	2.2	0.5	1.1

* 1954–68 figures are 14.0 for target, 14.9 for actual, and 0.9 for deviation.
  † In percentage points.
  Source: Actual rate of return from Federal Trade Commission, special tabulation. Last column computed by Kanerscher from FTC data.

purpose of including these data here is to show the effectiveness of this pricing procedure in large companies. In Tables 6 and 7, Kanerscher cites Lanzillotti's findings.[7]

How to calculate the target rate of return on investment. The following is a step-by-step development of how a firm might use the target rate of return to determine the price of its products or services. We first assume that there is only one product or service to be sold.

Step I. Capital investment. The first step is to determine the investment required to produce and sell the product or service. The valuation of this investment is generally on the historical cost basis, but more appropriately should be done on a current value basis. The main question is how much investment value is utilized to produce the product.

In a one-product corporation, we need either the market value of total assets or the market value of the residual owners' equity. For example, XYZ Corporation has the following historical cost balance sheet:

XYZ CORPORATION
Balance Sheet
December 31, 1977

Current assets	$ 100	Current liabilities	$	50
		Long-term debt		200
Fixed assets	900	Owners' equity		750
	$1,000			$1,000

The XYZ Corporation has an established market for its stock. The 500 shares outstanding have a market value of $2 per share. The value of the stockholders' investment is 500 × $2 or $1,000. The creditors have $50 + $200 or $250 investment. The market value of the total assets can then be stated as the combination of the stockholders' value of $1,000 plus the creditors $250 or a total of $1,250.

If the company does not have an established market for its stock, the alternative would be to attempt to determine the market value of the assets. The current value of owners' equity could then be determined by subtracting total liabilities from

---

[7] David R. Kanerscher, "The Return of Target Pricing?" *The Journal of Business,* April 1975 (Chicago: University of Chicago Press, 1975), p. 244. © 1975 by The University of Chicago.

total assets. Estimates of the replacement cost of the assets adjusted for their present age and condition may be feasible.

Step. II. Target profit. The company should establish a target return on investment. The investment base may be either the assets employed or owners' equity. Depending upon choice, the desired rate of return will differ. Since debt typically carries an interest cost below the rate of return earned by the assets acquired via the use of debt, the rate of return on owners' equity exceeds the rate of return on assets. In the single-product company, there is no problem in associating the debt with the assets employed, and we can use owners' equity as the investment base.

The rate would also depend upon what management felt would be a reasonable expectation for the investment and risk. If relatively risk free investments paid 8 percent, the desired return would likely be greater than 8 percent. What the return ultimately will be is beyond the scope of this chapter. *Let us assume that the company established an after-tax rate of 10 percent on owners' equity.*

The target profit would be calculated as follows:

Value of investment (Step I)	$1,000
Target return (Step II)	10%
Target profit after tax	$ 100

Step III. Pro forma income statement. In Step II we calculated the desired profit after tax. The next step is to establish the relationships that exist in the income statement. How does cost behave in relation to revenue? and so on. To accomplish this, prior income statements must be studied and the cost behavior patterns analyzed. We briefly discussed this in the preceding section.

Direct material	$ 1.60 per unit
Direct labor	2.20 per unit
Variable manufacturing overhead	1.20 per unit
Direct selling	0.11 per unit
Fixed manufacturing overhead	$220.00 annually
Fixed selling	$ 42.00 annually
Fixed administrative cost	$ 88.00 annually
Interest 7% on long-term debt	$ 14.00 annually

Assume 200 units and tax rate of 50%

Net profit after tax	$100	
Tax 50%	100	
Net profit before tax		$ 200

Add: Costs

Direct material ($1.60 × 200)	$320	
Direct labor ($2.20 × 200)	440	
Variable manufacturing overhead ($1.20 × 200)	240	
Direct selling ($0.11 × 200)	22	
Fixed manufacturing overhead	220	
Fixed selling	42	
Fixed administrative cost	88	
Interest ($200 × 0.07)	14	
Total costs		$1,386
Desired Revenues = Net profit + Costs =		$1,586

Step IV. Price determination. The price of the product is calculated by dividing the desired revenue by the standard or planned volume of sales.

$$\text{Target selling price} = \$1,586/200 = \$7.93$$

Step V. Adjust to the market. Except for the estimated annual output of 200 units, the preceding steps have ignored demand. Some assessment of the price-volume relationship must be made, and the target price and volume may need to be adjusted. Is the target price in line with competing products and previous prices charged? What is the potential total demand? What share of the total market are we shooting for? Is it realistic? Is more or less promotional effort desirable?

Rate of return pricing of multiple products. To use rate of return pricing for more than one product, one must determine the investment value utilized by each product. Here, use of asset values will prove easier than the use of owners' equity. Nevertheless, if a number of products make use of the same facilities, only an arbitrary allocation can be made, perhaps on the basis of time utilized. The bases used might well be the same as those used to allocate the fixed production costs to each product.

The variable production costs should be less troublesome. They can usually be traced directly to the product produced. However, the variable cost per unit will likely be different for each product line, and total cost will be different for each product mix.

Having determined the investment base and production costs by product line, the steps outlined above can be performed for each product. Because we have several products, there are several estimated annual volumes as well as arbitrary investment and fixed cost allocations. As a result, the final step, adjust to the market, is critical. The problem is that of what mix of products and selling prices best satisfies the objective of a desired after tax of return on total investment. Some products may be priced above their target price and others below in order to meet the objective.

REFERENCES

Abramovitz and others. *The Allocation of Economic Resources.* California: Stanford University Press, 1958.

AMA Management Report No. 66. *Pricing: The Critical Decision.* New York: American Management Association, Inc. 1961.

American Economic Association. *Readings in Price Theory.* Chicago: Richard D. Irwin, Inc., 1952.

Amey, L. R., and Egginton, D. A. *Management Accounting.* London: Longman Group Limited, 1973. (Chapter 9, How Much to Produce: Price-Output Decisions.)

Beckwith, Burnham P. *Marginal-Cost Price-Output Control.* New York: Columbia University Press, 1955.

Bierman, Harold Jr. *Topics in Cost Accounting and Decisions.* New York: McGraw-Hill Book Company, 1963.

Churchill, William L. *Pricing For Profit.* New York: The Macmillan Company, 1932.

Churchman, Ackoff and Arnoff. *Introduction to Operations Research.* New York: John Wiley & Sons, Inc., 1957. (Chapter 19, Competitive Bidding Models.)

Committee on Price Determination. *Cost Behavior and Price Policy.* New York: National Bureau of Economic Research, 1943.

De Coster, Donald, and Schafer, Eldon. *Management Accounting.* New York: Wiley/Hamilton, 1976. (Chapter 6, Revenue & Pricing Decisions.)

Fitzpatrick, Albert Arthur. *Pricing Methods of Industry.* Boulder, Colo.: Pruett Press, Inc., 1964.

Fremgen, James M. *Accounting for Managerial Analysis*. 3d Ed. Homewood, Ill.: Richard D. Irwin, Inc., 1976. (Chapter 17, The Role of Costs in Pricing Decisions.)

Gisser, Micha. *Introduction to Price Theory*. Penn.: International Textbook Company, 1966.

Haynes, W. Warren. *Pricing Decisions in Small Business*. Kentucky: University of Kentucky Press, 1962.

Kaplan, Dirlam, and Lanzillotti. *Pricing in Big Business*. Washington, D.C.: The Brookings Institution, 1958.

Lere, John. *Pricing Techniques for the Financial Executive*. New York: John Wiley and Sons, 1974.

Oxenfeldt, Alfred R. *Executive Action in Marketing*. Belmont, Calif.: Wadsworth Publishing Company, Inc., 1966.

————. *Industrial Pricing and Market Practices*. New York: Prentice-Hall, Inc., 1951.

————. *Pricing For Marketing Executives*. Belmont, Calif.: Wadsworth Publication Company, Inc., 1961.

Rossell, James H., and Frasure, William W. *Managerial Accounting*. Columbus, Ohio: Charles E. Merrill Books, Inc., 1964. (Chapter 15, Cost-Volume-Profit Relationships.)

Shillinglaw, Gordon. *Managerial Cost Accounting*. 4th Ed. Homewood, Ill.: Richard D. Irwin, Inc., 1977.

Articles

Areeda, Phillip, and Turner, Donald F. "Predatory Pricing and Related Practices Under Section 2 of the Sherman Act." *Harvard Law Review*, vol. 88, no. 4, February 1975, pp. 697–733.

————. "Scherer on Predatory Pricing: A Reply." *Harvard Law Review* vol. 89, March 1976, pp. 891–903.

Attunsi, Emil. "Some Interpretations of Sequential Bid Pricing Strategies." *Management Science*, vol. 20, no. 11, July 1974, pp. 1424–27.

Baker, Raymond. "A Decision Model in Consumer Pricing Research." *Journal of Marketing Research*, vol. 9, August 1972, pp. 287–98.

Bell, Albert L. "Flexible Budgets and Marginal Cost Pricing." *Management Accounting*, vol. 58, January 1977, pp. 34–37.

Berman, George R. "Constructing and Using a Company Cost Index." *The Business Quarterly*, Summer 1976, pp. 50–53.

Betley, A. J. "Contribution Pricing." *Managment Accounting*, vol. 54, March 1973, pp. 29–30.

Boyle, Stanley E., and Hogurty, Thomas F. "Pricing Behavior in the American Automobile Industry." *The Journal of Industrial Economics,* vol. 24, December 1975, pp. 81–95.

Brooks, Douglas G. "Cost Oriented Pricing: A Realistic Solution to a Complicated Problem." *The Journal of Marketing,* April 1975, pp. 72–74.

Carr, Arthur V. "The Role of Cost in Pricing." *Management Accounting,* November 1974, pp. 15–18.

Cox, Eli P. "A Case for Price Discrimination." *MSU Business Topics,* Summer 1975, pp. 39–46.

Darden, Bill R. "An Operational Approach to Product Pricing." *Journal of Marketing,* vol. 32, April 1968, pp. 29–33.

Davis, K. Roscoe, and Simmons, L. F. "Exploring Market Pricing Strategies Via Dynamic Programming." *Decision Sciences,* vol. 7, no. 2, April 1976, pp. 281–93.

Deakin, Michael. "Pricing for Return on Investment." *Management Accounting,* December 1975, pp. 43–46.

Dean, Joel. "Pricing Policies for New Products." *Harvard Business Review,* November–December 1976, pp. 141–53.

"FTC to Put More Muscle into Robinson-Patman Act," *Merchandising.* vol. 1, April 7, 1976, p. 7.

Franklin, Peter J. "The Normal Cost Theory of Price and the Internal Rate of Return Method of Investment Appraisal: An Integration." *Journal of Business Finance and Accounting,* vol. 4, Spring 1977, pp. 61–81.

Fuss, Norman H. Jr. "Pricing in an Unsettled Economy." *S.A.M. Advanced Management Journal,* Spring 1975, pp. 27–36.

"Goodbye Robinson-Patman, Hello Predatory Pricing?" *Progressive Grocer,* November 1975, p. 33.

Guiltinan, Joseph P. "Risk-Aversion Pricing Policies: Problems and Alternatives." *The Journal of Marketing,* vol. 40, January 1976, pp. 10–15.

Hancock, Keith. "The Relation between Changes in Costs and Changes in Product Prices in Australian Manufacturing Industries 1949–50 to 1967–68," *The Economic Record,* March 1976, pp. 53–65.

"Helping in Pricing Decisions," *CPA Journal,* vol. 47, April 1977, p. 96.

Jensen, Daniel. "Hartley's Demand-Price Analysis in a Case of Joint Production: A Comment." *Accounting Review,* October 1973, pp. 768–70.

———. "The Role of Cost in Pricing Joint Products: A Case of Production in Fixed Proportion." *The Accounting Review,* vol. 49, July 1974, pp. 465–76.

Jones, D. Frank. "A Survey Technique to Measure Demand under Various Pricing Strategies." *Applied Marketing,* July 1975, pp. 75–77.

Kamerschen, David R. "The Return of Target Pricing," *The Journal of Business,* April 1975, pp. 242–52.

Kortanek, K. O., Soden, J. V., and Sodaro, D. "Profit Analyses and Sequential Bid Pricing Models." *Management Science,* vol. 20, no. 3, November 1973, pp. 396–417.

Low, David W. "Optimal Dynamic Pricing Policies for an M/M/s Queue." *Operations Research,* May–June 1974, pp. 545–61.

Mailandt, P. "Alternatives to Transfer Pricing." *Business Horizons,* vol. 19[18], p. 81–86.

McKeown, J. C. "Comparative Application of Market and Cost Based Accounting Models." *Journal of Accounting Research,* vol. 11, Spring 1973, pp. 62–99.

McManus, George J. "Pricing Process: Facts or Flip of a Coin." *Iron Age,* April 28, 1975, pp. 32–34.

McManus, J. "Cost and Competition are the Price Fixers." *Iron Age,* vol. 219, January 17, 1977, pp. 19–21.

Mepham, M. J. "Applying the Limiting-Factor Rate to Cost-Plus Pricing." *Management Accounting,* October 1975, pp. 321–23.

Mogenroth, W. M. "Simulation: A Method for Understanding Price Determinants." *Journal of Market Research,* vol. 1, August 1964, pp. 17–26.

Osborne, D. K. "On the Rationality of Limit Pricing." *Journal of Industrial Economics,* Summer 1973, pp. 71–80.

Ornstein, S. I. "Empirical Uses of Price Cost Margin." *Journal of Industrial Economics,* vol. 24, December 1975, pp. 105–17.

Pedder-Smith, D. W. "Price, Cost and Product Size." *Management Accounting,* April 1976, pp. 136–37.

"Pricing for Future Doesn't Have to Be Hit-or-Miss." *Iron Age,* August 16, 1976, pp. 24–26.

"Pricing Strategy in an Inflation Economy." *Business Week,* April 6, 1974, pp. 43–49.

Ripley, Frank C., and Segal, Lydia. "Price Determination in 395 Manufacturing Industries." *The Review of Economics and Statistics,* vol. 60, August 1973, pp. 263–71.

Robinson, Bruce, and Lakhanis, Chet. "Dynamic Price Models for New-

Product Planning." *Management Science,* vol. 21, no. 10, June 1975, pp. 1113–22.

Scherer, F. M. "Predatory Pricing and the Sherman Act: A Comment." *The Harvard Law Review,* vol. 89, March 1976, pp. 869–90.

Shinkai, Y. "Business Pricing Policies in Japanese Manufacturing Industries," *Journal of Industrial Economics,* vol. 22, June 1974, pp. 255–64.

Struszheim, Donald H., and Struszheim, Mahlon R. "An Econometric Analysis of the Determination of Prices in Manufacturing Industries." *The Review of Economics and Statistics,* vol. 58, July 1975, pp. 191–201.

Wells, M. C. "Justifying Price Discrimination." *The Australian Accountant,* July 1976, pp. 338–42.

Werner, Ray O. "Legal Developments in Marketing." *Journal of Marketing,* July 1976, pp. 92–105.

Woodside, Arch G., and Sims, J. Taylor. "Retail Experiment in Pricing a New Product." *Journal of Retailing,* vol. 50, Fall 1974, pp. 56–65.

7

Costs in labor negotiations

*John R. Palmer**

The use of cost accounting information in labor negotiations has grown steadily since the 1940s to a point where costs play some role in the union contract negotiations of the vast majority of major American companies. Perhaps more important, a recent broad-based study by this author[1] indicated that companies which brought extensive cost accounting information to the contract bargaining table, and allowed the union negotiators reasonable access to that information, were likely to have a better company-union relationship and smoother labor negotiations.

Modern negotiations concern the levels at which three cost factors—wages, fringe benefits, and quality of working conditions—should be set within the particular union contract period. Since these items comprise the labor expense of a company, they have a direct bearing on its profits, ability to compete, and even its survival. As such, the computations required to ascertain the costs of labor contract terms and new proposals and their impact on profitability, breakeven points, marketing, and financial planning, have become an important part of labor

* President, Twin Cedars Associates, Inc.

[1] John R. Palmer, *The Use of Accounting Information in Labor Negotiations*, (New York: National Association of Accountants, 1977), p. 38.

negotiations. The accountant, as the expert in these areas and the keeper of the company quantitative data, has developed a labor negotiations role.

Once the labor negotiation is viewed as a joint decision-making process between the agents of capital and labor, it becomes axiomatic that the optimal decision should be based on the best available data. Negotiators have been known to use information such as: census wage and hour data, sales, earnings, division and plant breakouts, all internal costs, expenses of each item of the current contract, variances from anticipated contract costs, cost of each demand of the new contract including individual fringe items, roll-up,[2] costs of existing work rules or changes in them, strike costs, various ratios using labor as a percent of other inputs, competitive company figures, area industry figures, productivity figures, rates of inflation, product price increases, and cost of living.

CURRENT ACCOUNTING PARTICIPATION IN LABOR NEGOTIATIONS

Corporate practice today varies widely in the role allotted to accounting in labor negotiations. A small number of firms has seen fit to make an accountant a full-fledged member of their contract negotiating team. An equally small number has regrettably avoided any cost involvement in negotiating their contracts, but simply arrived at contract terms based on the muscle of management and the corresponding strength and tenacity of the union, with strikes and lockouts as common results.

Among firms with some labor negotiations role for cost accounting, the specific activities being pursued include: preparation of "fact books" containing in-depth cost information that the negotiators can take to the bargaining table for reference; creation of "cost manuals" with all present and potential items stated in cents per hour, breakdowns of employment costs per operating hour of the facility covered by the bargaining, compiling basic economic data and payroll data for the facility, computing cost variations from the basic industry pattern, and computerization of all data related to the labor contract.

---

[2] *Roll-up* is the cost increase automatically created in certain wage-related fringe benefits by any increase in hourly wages themselves.

The specific activity levels for accountants themselves include: full negotiating team participation especially at smaller companies and divisions; direct participation on a limited basis for cost items only; direct back-up for the negotiator possibly from an adjoining room; or most frequently, participation only in preparation of materials and data prior to the actual bargaining.

Lack of company internal coordination influences this role because often no system exists for industrial relations department negotiators to gain access to needed information in accounting areas. This can result in duplicate work being done by the industrial relations people, who in effect create their own specialized accounting department. Also, the labor negotiators themselves sometimes have accounting backgrounds, although no longer working in accounting roles.

DATA AVAILABILITY VERSUS DATA NEEDS
AT THE BARGAINING TABLE

The vast majority of industrial relations managers enter into negotiations with all current contract items completely costed, while most others have at least partial costing of significant items. A group comprising possibly ten percent have no cost figures on their existing contracts, and essentially "fly blind" as to even this starting point for new bargaining.

Beyond the standard contract items, some managers secure supplementary information on costs involving human resources, work rules, incentive plans, and actuarial studies. Variances from anticipated contract costs are used to make estimated costs on the new contract more accurate and to get "credit" in the bargaining for any unanticipated overage on the old contract.

Virtually all of the companies that enter negotiations with current contract items costed also cost all new union demands prior to final bargaining. Some only work on key items or "reasonable" demands, and one company that carries on continuous bargaining does this costing on an ongoing basis. The companies that prepare no cost figures on their existing contract are also unlikely to do so on new contract items.

The value of "second-guessing" union demands and attempting to assign costs to them prior to bargaining is somewhat controversial. Some industrial relations managers regard this possibly useless work as a small price to pay for being better prepared, while others see no value in working on any item that is not a known, concrete demand.

Among these anticipated costs that are sometimes calculated are strike costs that will result if agreement cannot be reached, and work rules changes desired by management, and their impact percent per hour by product line on profit margins.

Only about half of all industrial relations executives claimed to have access to the output of their company's long-range planning department and took those plans into consideration in negotiating the terms of labor contracts. Some managers admitted to having access to the long-range plans, but not using them. Others did their own long-range planning outside of the official company plans.

Good points were made by negotiators who said that top management reviewed the settlement and could factor in their long-range plans or that the plan was useless in labor negotiations since the union had no commitment to work within it.

Overall, most industrial relations executives feel that they have access to all the accounting data within their firm that they need. Yet, many feel that data exists in the accounting, controller's or treasurer's area that could be useful in labor negotiations, but is not made available for that purpose.

The reasons for this nonavailability of useful accounting data varied. Insufficient efforts to locate the data and make it available were admitted to by some industrial relations managers. Other factors mentioned were "old line" negotiators who would not use the material, "unresponsive" accounting departments, and poor communications systems.

MANAGEMENT NEGOTIATOR'S COMMAND
OF ACCOUNTING DATA

The opinions of the other parties to labor negotiations provide an interesting cross-check on the extent of management's command of company accounting data.

Among union officials, fewer than half saw the company negotiator as really well prepared with accounting figures on the company's costs, profits, break-even points, productivity, and so forth. The majority of the union negotiators suffered from a general or partial lack of this material. It was noted, however, that the situation appeared to be improving.

Labor mediators, with their continual exposure to negotiations, had even less regard for the level of the management negotiator's knowledge of company accounting data.

The union negotiators were seen as sometimes having a better grasp of company data than the management negotiators. This handicap creates a situation where the company negotiator has only a sketchy idea of his bargaining objectives and can respond to the union's demand for "more" only by taking the position of "less."

FACTORS INFLUENCING THE USE OF ACCOUNTING DATA IN THE NEGOTIATIONS PROCESS

Certain key factors exist that strongly influence the use of accounting data in negotiations at particular companies.

Accounting data is far less likely to be used by management in companies where labor negotiations are regarded as having little real importance to the company's operations. A low level of union organization of a company's work force is likely to create this situation, since the cost of the union contract relative to other labor costs will be minimal. Thus, special systems or data availability will not be worthwhile.

Even some heavily unionized companies give labor negotiations a low priority if they are in nonlabor-intensive industries. Accounting data here, too, will be less likely to get into the low-priority labor negotiations of a company that is highly capital intensive, such as an oil company. Such companies are likely to use industry or area wage figures as the basis for their labor contract rates, rather than company data.

Companies whose labor negotiations follow a strict industry bargaining pattern are also less likely to introduce any significant amount of accounting data into their negotiations process. In such a situation, the likelihood is that only the industry leaders truly negotiate the contract, and all others merely fall in line.

Companies who bargain their union contract as part of an industry association are also less likely to use much accounting data in their negotiations. Such companies are in reality competitors, other than in their labor negotiations. Under these circumstances, no member is likely to want to disclose any of his costs to his competitors.

Small local bargaining is also likely to have a low level of accounting input. However, the reason here is a lack of sophistication and understanding on the part of both labor and management negotiators.

THE ACCOUNTANT'S IDEAL ROLE IN THE LABOR NEGOTIATIONS PROCESS

Based upon the thinking of labor mediators, union negotiators, and industrial relations managers, an ideal practical role can be formulated for the accountant, at least in the eyes of the principal negotiations participants.

In general, the cost accountant should not have any direct participation in the bargaining, according to their thinking. He is seen primarily as a specialist serving on a subcommittee, not being trained or psychologically oriented to engage in active bargaining. As an amateur at the bargaining table who does not understand the negotiations process, the accountant could harm negotiations by losing sight of the fact that accounting data is not the only factor to be considered in negotiating labor contracts.

The role the accountant should play is advisory, providing back-up data needed at the bargaining table and by top management to knowledgeably negotiate and make decisions on the labor contract. The accountant has a responsibility to get into the system usable cost information, based upon which others can create bargaining strategy.

The area of *initiative* is a sensitive one in that there is one school of thought that the accountant should provide information only on an "as requested" basis, but on a much shorter lead time than is presently required. The contrasting opinion holds that the accountant should actually provide many data inputs for negotiations automatically without any request necessary from the industrial relations department. This initiative may help particularly where the negotiators may be unaware of the existence within the company of potentially valuable bargaining back-up data.

Virtually all parties to labor negotiations see the accountant's role therein growing exponentially as fringe benefits become more sophisticated under laws such as ERISA. Those companies where an accounting function has grown within the industrial relations department are simply experiencing the reaction to a lack of initiative by cost accountants. Accountants may need to do a "selling job" within the company to achieve their proper labor negotiations role. Also, accounting systems must be altered where necessary to make them generate the information needed in labor negotiations.

USE OF AND ACCESS TO CORPORATE ACCOUNTING INFORMATION BY LABOR UNIONS

Much debate has been occasioned over the subject of providing corporate accounting data to the union negotiators. Certainly, well reasoned arguments can be made for giving the union broad access to the company's data, for withholding any information that will not directly advance the company's bargaining position, and for positions between these two extremes.

The union's desire for and trust in management accounting data have been major factors in this debate. It has been indicated that a substantial number of unions request and receive little or no company data. However, the majority of union negotiators admit definite interest in such information as: earnings by bargaining unit, profit percentages, worker census, wage rates, fringe benefits, total costs, pension data, insurance costs, layoffs, production levels, expansion, economic conditions, area wages, safety figures, and cost of living information. Fringe benefit costs are the most strongly desired.

Most union negotiators complain of not receiving this desired company data, or about the way it is presented by the company. Selectivity is a particularly common practice, whereby companies provide any information that aids their bargaining position, even up to opening the books in a very poor profit year. Clarity, format, usefulness, and reliability are also criticized.

Union officials would react more favorably to company accounting data and put more trust in it if it were independently audited, provided on an ongoing basis rather than only at contract bargaining time, and provided equally in successful and in poverty years of the company.

Union negotiators also complain of: failure to meet even limited NLRB disclosure requirements, lack of data comparability, lack of data broken down by bargaining unit, lack of timeliness of the information given, overstated costs, unrealistic standard costs, contingency reserves used to hide profits, lack of broken-out labor costs, buried figures of conglomerates, accounting changes, highly inexact productivity data, double bookkeeping for taxes versus financial reporting figures, and lack of sophistication.

QUANTITATIVE RESEARCH
BY LABOR UNIONS

Most union negotiators get considerable information about company profits, sales, and so forth, from sources outside the company. In some closely regulated industries such as trucking and airlines, the responsible government agencies (ICC, CAB, and others) collect and make publicly available such detailed corporate accounting data that further union research or even company disclosure becomes virtually immaterial.

Other sources for outside data open to the union include Dun & Bradstreet, Standard & Poor's, and Moody's reports; industry publications, economic services, the AFL–CIO Industrial Union Department research, Wage and Price Board data, BLS publications, and SEC filings. The recent SEC requirement that companies provide an accounting breakout of individual lines of business was greeted by unions as a chance to get closer to bargaining-unit type data, but the experience thus far is that the new reporting is still too broad to be of use.

MANAGEMENT DISCLOSURE OF
ACCOUNTING DATA TO
UNION BARGAINERS

Confirming the union officials' complaints of little or no access to company accounting information, most industrial relations managers admit that they have given out little or no information, or only enough to comply with NLRB law. In particular, data related to profit figures and division breakdowns is withheld. Most managers do provide equal access (be that great or small) to data for all unions bargained with unless the data requested by the unions varies, in which event most supply no more than what is asked for. Other guidelines for data dissemination include: need to know, ability to understand, local policy, and level of cooperation.

On the subject of *selectivity* in management's data disclosure, most industrial relations men claimed to provide the same amount and type of data to the unions whether the company is prospering or languishing. Those managers who admit to providing data selectively defend their practice by showing that broad disclosure in very successful years would only make the union bargain harder, while allowing broad disclosure in bad years would lower expectations and smooth the bargaining process. However, the point cannot be ignored that selectivity in disclosure makes for disbelief or disinterest by the union in the data when it is presented.

The motivation for data disclosure policies shows a minority of industrial relations managers acting solely to smooth the bargaining process. The majority, to a greater or lesser extent, are motivated by NLRB legal requirements to disclose financial information.

TIMING OF MANAGEMENT
DATA DISCLOSURE

Despite the strong union preference for ongoing disclosure of financial information, the majority of industrial relations executives make no effort to supply data to the union at any time other than contract negotiation. The emphasis, as in so many other details, is on the easiest approach, the greatest convenience, and the interest level of the industrial relations men, rather than on the interest of the union bargainer or on the attainment of smooth bargaining.

Labor mediators reported the same lack of ongoing information disclosure discussed by union and management people. However, they recognized the possible beginning of a trend toward life-of-the-contract bargaining, whereby continuing contact and information supplied between the union and management might improve industrial relations and lessen union suspicion of data provided to them.

EFFECTS OF BROAD DATA DISCLOSURE
ON NEGOTIATIONS

Industrial relations managers have long felt that increased union access to corporate data would result in more successful negotiation for wages and benefits by the union, which might be detrimental to the corporation. Most union officials admit the basic truth of this position, but tend to mitigate it by stating that the greater data access would enable them to bargain more intelligently, more realistically, and take more of a "common goal" approach with possible reduction in the number of strikes.

Additionally, most industrial relations managers have felt that the union negotiator would be unlikely to alter his bargaining position or soften his demands based on corporate quantitative information showing inability or limited ability to pay. Most union negotiators claim to have softened demands in bargaining based on quantitative information provided them in the following situations: where corporate books were opened, where the problem shown was ongoing rather than cyclical, where the politics *vis-à-vis* the rank and file allowed, and where poor management was not being subsidized. Most union officials claim that they would show a company more cooperation in bargaining in response to that company's broadening its management data disclosure to them—a *quid pro quo* approach. Also, almost all union officials agreed that the success, profitability, and growth of a company are properly union, as well as management, concerns.

The union/management relationship vis-à-vis union access to management accounting data

A comparison of the company/union relationship with the company's management data disclosure policy perhaps gives the clearest picture of the value of providing this access to the union. The accompanying matrix is based upon results of this author's earlier study of the subject. It shows the level of company/union relationship as rated by the corporate industrial relations manager (good through poor) compared with corporate accounting data disclosure by management (heavy through little or none).

Corporate accounting data disclosure by management	Company/union relationship			
	Good	Average	Mixed	Poor
Heavy	15	0	0	0
Moderate	34	1	2	0
By law	2	1	0	1
Little or none	9	9	5	1

While this data may not be considered qualitatively conclusive, its results strongly recommend a corporate policy of management accounting data disclosure to union bargainers.

TYPES OF INFORMATION SYSTEMS FOR VARIOUS TYPES OF LABOR NEGOTIATIONS

The schematic diagrams in Exhibits 1, 2, and 3 depict some possible information systems for the three principal types of labor negotiations—national bargaining, association bargaining, and local bargaining. They combine the approaches of many companies and may suggest some new ideas to managers and firms lacking such an organized technique in handling labor negotiations information.

1. National collective bargaining

National collective bargaining (Exhibit 1) involves a company-wide effort at one company. Accounting and personnel departments collect information at the individual plant and operating division levels. Personnel collects census and wage and hour data which it provides to the accounting department for use in various cost calculations. It also provides data to the labor relations department, either directly or through the computer.

The accounting department collects most other operating information that is quantifiable and assembles it in a book for the labor relations department, or puts it on the computer to

EXHIBIT 1
National collective bargaining

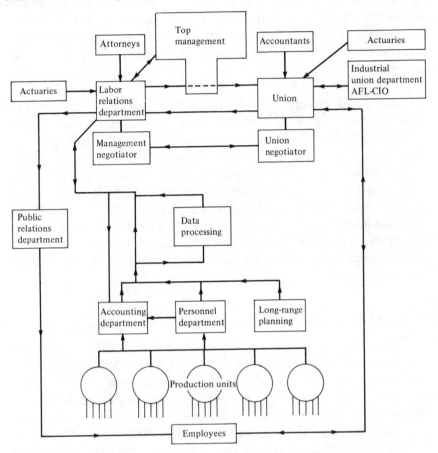

which labor relations has easy access. The long-range planning people make certain that the labor relations department has a copy of the long-range plan so that an effort can be made to keep the settlement within the projected parameters. The computer is an optional tool for central storage, easy availability, and orderly dissemination of the various data used in labor negotiations.

The labor relations department is the hub of the bargaining wheel. Information arrives from other departments, from outside attorneys, and from actuaries. Information flow with accounting and top management is likely to be two-way, in that various questions and information are required to elicit the needed answers and decisions. Information may be provided to the public relations department for dissemination to the workers, possibly helping to keep their expectations from becoming unrealistic and maintaining a good rapport that can be valuable at contract time.

Before and during actual bargaining, a flow of information exists between labor relations and the union and between the actual negotiators. Top management can act as a filter to prevent data that might be competitively damaging from being divulged.

The union has various data sources other than management, including the Industrial Union Department of the AFL–CIO, outside actuaries, and accountants. The union also maintains communication with employees in order to learn about the plant and company conditions and to keep them informed as to progress in bargaining, so that any necessary rank-and-file ratification can be secured.

2. Association collective bargaining

Association collective bargaining (Exhibit 2) differs from national collective bargaining in that it involves several companies that have chosen to band together to negotiate with a union for their labor contract. The benefit of this approach is that, as competitors, the companies will have the same labor costs and contract terms, with no one being at a disadvantage to the other. In this way the union cannot use whipsaw tactics to gain higher wages among the competitors by playing one against the other. The disadvantage is that the operating problems and accounting data of any one company are merged into the overall negotiations effort and have little bearing on the outcome.

From the point of view of an information system, the overriding factor is that as competitors the companies are unwilling to divulge substantial internal data to one another. Thus, all representatives in the joint bargaining team bring to the table a viewpoint based upon knowledge of their company's operations and the data they could assemble, but the planning of a joint position is not likely to include heavy consideration of accounting information.

EXHIBIT 2
Association collective bargaining

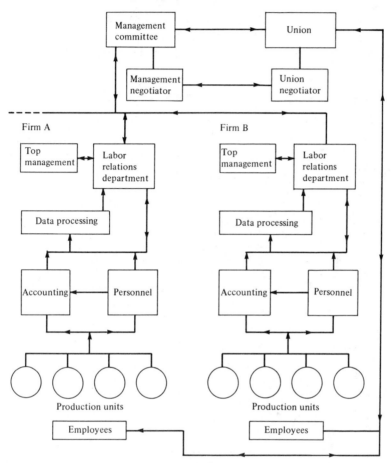

The information system works for each firm much as it did
in national bargaining for a single company, with the same departments making the same contributions. Each firm sends its
representative, usually its manager of labor relations, to the joint
bargaining table (or votes to elect representatives if the association is very large).

The information provided to the union is much more limited
in joint bargaining because of the competitors' unwillingness
to reveal internal data from their firms. Only a general statement
of industry conditions is presented to the union, and individual

representatives try to influence this broad picture so that it includes special situations at their firms.

Under these circumstances, the union has no specific data to work with and must simply adjust its demands to the "average" conditions presented by the joint committee.

3. Local unit collective bargaining

Collective bargaining at the local unit of a firm (Exhibit 3) presents a situation slightly different from the first two cases. In most instances, a mix of a certain amount of local autonomy and a certain amount of central control is involved.

EXHIBIT 3
Local unit collective bargaining

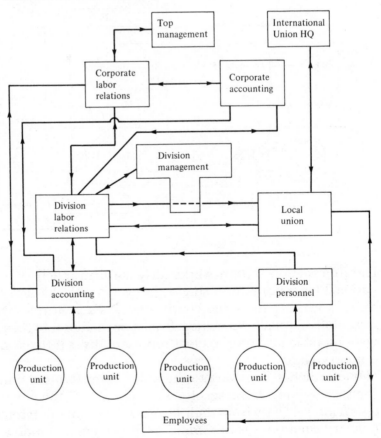

Division personnel and accounting departments collect data from the production units and provide it to the division labor relations department. This data also goes to corporate headquarters where the corporate accounting and labor relations departments become involved, perhaps consulting top management if major issues are involved.

The headquarters managers interact with their division counterparts to varying extents at this point. Broad parameters may be set, with local people handling all actual bargaining. Central corporate people may come to the bargaining table or be in charge there, or division management may have total control, including a filter on what information is provided to the union. In the latter instance, labor negotiations would be treated as just another aspect of managing the division, with division management taking total control and responsibility.

Another possibility is having headquarters managers on call or restricting division authority to certain items such as wages and work rules, with a central control on fringe programs.

The union, too, has varying degrees of control at the local versus the national level. To some extent, management's approach can influence the union's approach. More often, the importance or anticipated difficulty of the settlement determines the international union's level of participation.

The amount of information provided to the union in local unit bargaining is sometimes much less than in national bargaining because no publicly reported figures exist. However, sometimes the level of information exchange is higher because of the close relationship of the local parties.

8

Costs for managerial purposes versus financial and income tax purposes

Joseph G. Louderback*
Richard P. Webb†

The purpose of this chapter is to highlight the major areas in which cost reporting for financial accounting and for income tax purposes differs from cost reporting for managerial use. Other chapters in this book provide detailed discussions and analyses of particular points developed in this chapter and those chapters should be consulted for greater depth of analysis. This chapter points out some of the problems that are encountered when cost data developed for financial reporting and tax accounting are used for managerial purposes, and serves as an overview of the more significant differences among the three orientations of accounting information.

DIFFERING OBJECTIVES AND ENVIRONMENTS OF REPORTING

The treatment of costs (and revenues) for financial reporting, tax accounting, and managerial use differs for two principal reasons. One is that the *objectives* of each type of accounting are different, the other that the *environments* are different.

---

* Associate Professor, Rensselaer Polytechnic Institute.
† Vice President and Chief Financial Officer, Carrier Corporation.

Financial accounting

Financial accounting is concerned with the needs of persons outside the firm, primarily, but not exclusively, current and prospective creditors and stockholders and their representatives, security analysts. Investors make decisions about the relative desirability of firms based on assessments of the potential risks and returns. Risk and return are related to earning power and financial strength. These factors are reflected, however imperfectly, in the income statement and balance sheet. Consequently, the major concerns of financial accounting have been the related topics of asset valuation and income determination.

It is a commonplace that the income of a firm cannot be definitely determined until the end of its life. Periodic income measurement and asset valuation are tentative and are based on a number of assumptions and conventions that are employed to implement the more basic concepts and principles, like the matching concept. These assumptions and conventions form the bases of alternative acceptable methods of treating various transactions and events. Thus, inventory and related cost of sales can be determined by first-in-first-out, last-in-first-out, weighted average, and so on. The acceptability of alternative methods stems from accountants' inability to *know* that one method is clearly superior to another.

Although alternative accounting methods are available, they are limited. The broad framework of acceptable alternatives has been, and continues to be, set out by the Financial Accounting Standards Board and its predecessors, and by the Securities and Exchange Commission. The general ground rules under which financial reporting is carried out are imposed by these external agencies, giving managements relatively limited choices. The environment of financial reporting is not one of wide management discretion.

Tax accounting

It is difficult to speak of objectives of *tax accounting*. Tax accounting is governed by tax law, which can be said to have objectives like securing a steady stream of receipts for the government and promoting certain types of behavior. Firms have objectives in selecting methods to be used for tax accounting, but these are not objectives in the sense in which we speak of objectives of financial accounting. The users of tax returns do not have the same types of objectives as investors. They are concerned with whether the return conforms to tax law, but not with the relative desirability of investing in a firm.

Tax accounting is extremely important for many managerial purposes, more important than financial accounting. The reason is that cash flow is an important aspect of many managerial decisions and income taxes are a cash flow. Hence, the method used to report a transaction for tax purposes is more relevant than the one used for financial reporting purposes.

Tax accounting and financial reporting are not the same: A few items, like receipts of rent, *must* be treated one way for tax purposes, another way for financial reporting purposes. More common are items, like depreciation expense, that may be treated in different ways for financial and tax purposes. For the most part, tax law permits firms to use the same method for tax accounting that they use for financial reporting. The issue of tax deferral, which arises when items are reported as expenses in different periods for financial and tax purposes, is not germane to this chapter. Therefore, financial reporting and tax accounting will be treated as one topic throughout this chapter to promote clarity and brevity.

Managerial accounting

The objective of *managerial accounting* is to provide information that managers can use in fulfilling their functions. Managers, unlike investors, are not usually concerned with an entire firm, but with some part of it. The informational requirements of managers vary as do their responsibilities. A manager engaged in planning routine operations does not need the same information as one who is making a major investing decision or evaluating the performance of a division. Reports to managers are usually special-purpose, in contrast to the general-purpose reports published for external use. Reports to managers do not have to conform to generally accepted accounting principles and can therefore treat costs, and revenues, in ways that are unacceptable for financial reporting and tax accounting.

Informational requirements vary not only among managers, but also among situations encountered by the same manager. The information needed for short-term planning is not necessarily the same as that needed for making particular decisions, or for controlling operations. In some cases the information routinely developed for financial-tax purposes will also serve the needs of managers, but in many cases it will not. Because information is a costly commodity, it is only recently that managers have been able to obtain information other than that provided by the accounting system for financial-tax purposes. The advent of computers with their powers of multiple classification and rapid retrieval of information has hastened the development of managerial accounting. One example is classification. For managerial use the same revenue and cost data might be classified by geographical area, by class of customer, by product or product line, or some combination of the preceding.

In sum, managerial accounting is designed to meet the needs of managers who have the responsibility of both day-to-day operations and of special decisions relating to a part of the firm. The managers of a firm require information related to their specific activities. Stockholders and creditors of a firm require information related to the whole of the firm. Their decisions—buy, sell, or hold the stock, lend money or decline to—relate to the entire firm and are made at less frequent intervals than those of managers.

COSTS FOR FINANCIAL-TAX PURPOSES

Determination of periodic income

The central concern in financial and tax accounting is the *determination of periodic income.* Determining income requires the disposition of incurred costs into two types: expired and unexpired. Expired costs are expenses and appear on the income statement; unexpired costs are deferred to future periods and appear on the balance sheet. The criterion for classifying a cost as expired or unexpired is whether it is expected to have future benefits to the firm. A cost that can be expected to provide future benefits that are reasonably measurable is considered to be unexpired, and one that has given up its benefits, or whose future benefits are not readily measurable, is considered to have expired.

The first point about income determination is that financial-tax accounting are almost solely concerned with incurred, historical costs. A few exceptions, like estimated product warranty costs, occur in financial accounting, but rarely do such exceptions occur in tax accounting. It is true that current accounting practice requires predictions: Useful lives of assets and expected salvage value are obvious examples. But the costs that are both expensed and deferred have already been incurred for the overwhelming proportion of cases. (The fact that replacement cost data must now be reported to the SEC will be discussed later.)

Expense recognition

The basic rule for expense recognition is the *matching* concept. Ideally, all costs would be determined to have expired, to have yielded their benefits, in the earning of particular revenues. The relationship would be causal: The expiration of the benefits would "cause" the revenues to be earned. In practice there are few costs that satisfy the ideal and so two other principles are employed. One is to associate the expiration of a cost with all of the revenues of a particular period in an *indirect* fashion; the other is to *arbitrarily expense* a particular cost in the period in which it was incurred.

The most common examples of costs that are directly matched with particular revenues are the costs directly related to a particular sale of product. The cost of the units themselves, sales commissions, and shipping costs can be directly related to the individual sale, provided that we make a few simplifying assumptions. The major assumption is that we know the cost of the units, which we usually don't, but deal with through the adoption of cost flow assumptions like first-in-first-out or last-in-first-out.

Lacking the ability to match expenses directly with revenues, the accountant must determine whether the benefits of a cost can be associated with particular accounting periods. In theory, a cost should be allocated to periods on the basis of the pattern of expiration of benefits, but this is rarely possible. In practice, firms adopt some rational and systemic method of allocating a cost to the periods in which benefits are expected to be received. The method reflects an *assumed pattern of benefits.* Straight-line depreciation assumes a relatively level pattern of benefits; accelerated depreciation methods assume a declining pattern.

Finally, some costs are *expensed as incurred* for one of two reasons. First, there may be no evidence that any future benefits can be expected at the end of the accounting period, such as would be the case with clerical salaries or consumed postage and office supplies. Second, there may be expected future benefits, but their measurability is so conjectural that objectivity and conservatism dictate that the costs be expensed. Such costs as advertising and consulting fees may be expected to benefit future periods, but are usually expensed when incurred. Research and development costs are now immediately expensed on these grounds.

Much of the process of expense recognition is *allocation,* the dividing up of a whole among a number of parts. Costs that are expensed as incurred are being allocated to a single period. Costs that clearly benefit more than one period are allocated among those periods. Even costs directly associated with revenues are allocated; inventory accounting requires the adoption of some method for determining which units have been sold, and which are still on hand. If units have been acquired at different prices the expense (cost of sales) and the asset (inventory) will be different under different cost flow assumptions. These allocations are necessary under current financial and tax accounting, but are generally not helpful for mangerial purposes.

Expense classification

Expired costs—expenses—are also classified on income statements. Two general schemes are used, object and function. An *object* classification is based on the types of inputs of the expenses, such as salaries, depreciation, taxes, utilities, and so on. A *functional* classification is based on the *output* or activity of business that is benefited, such as cost of sales, selling expenses, general administrative expenses, and financing expenses. Classifying expenses by function is not usually as relevant for managerial purposes as are other classifications that we discuss later.

The preceding general discussion applies to any type of firm:

service, merchandising, or manufacturing. The most interesting, and most difficult, problems in income determination relate to manufacturing because the calculation of cost of sales and inventory are much more complicated for manufacturers than for other firms.

Manufacturing costs

Both financial and tax accounting require that the cost per unit of manufactured goods include nearly all manufacturing costs. The major exception is that a firm using standard costs may expense variances in the period incurred, provided that the standard costs reflect current production conditions. The principal difference between the cost per unit of a merchandiser and that of a manufacturer is the inclusion of conversion costs (labor and overhead) by the latter. Conversion costs include fixed costs, costs that do not change in proportion to changes in production. This costing method is called *absorption costing* or *full costing*.

A merchandising firm has relatively little difficulty in determining its inventory cost because the cost consists almost solely of the purchase price of the goods. The cost flow assumption is therefore the primary determinant of the amounts to be expensed and deferred. The manufacturing firm must also adopt a cost flow assumption and has an additional problem in determining an appropriate cost per unit because of the requirement that fixed overhead be included in the cost of product. It is fixed overhead that creates the most difficulties. Variable costs of production like materials, direct labor, and variable overhead are analogous to the purchase price incurred by merchandising firms.[1] Variable production costs increase when additional units are produced, just as inventory of a merchandising firm increases when goods are purchased.

Costs that are *joint,* or *common,* to both manufacturing and other functions are allocated to those functions according to some formula. Formulas are usually related to relative use by the various functions. Thus, if 80 percent of the floor space of

---

[1] The existence of guaranteed annual employment agreements and other constraints on layoffs makes a good many labor costs fixed rather than variable. However, most firms can adjust production within relatively wide limits and maintain constant per unit labor costs.

a building is used for manufacturing and 20 percent for general administration, the costs associated with the building like depreciation and property taxes could be allocated 80–20. At this stage there could be two allocations, one of costs to periods, the other to various functional areas of business for each period.

Two additional allocations of manufacturing costs could be made. Once total manufacturing costs are determined, there can be an allocation to different *products* or product lines and finally to *individual units* of product. These allocations are usually accomplished by the employment of overhead rates, either plant-wide or departmental. Fixed manufacturing costs are generally allocated to products and to units of product on the basis of relative labor or machine time. The selection of the basis depends on the characteristics of the manufacturing process. If the process is labor-intensive, labor time is used; if capital-intensive, machine time is used.

The appropriateness of allocations, like those of fixed overhead to units of product, for financial-tax purposes is not at issue here. It may seem reasonable to allocate fixed overhead to units of product because fixed overhead is incurred to provide the capacity to manufacture. The emphasis on periodic income determination, and the resulting need for unit cost data, requires that some assumption be made about the "benefit-per-unit" of total fixed manufacturing costs.

Relevance of financial-tax information for managerial use

Because financial-tax reporting is required for nearly all firms, the cost accounting system must be geared to produce the information needed to comply with generally accepted accounting principles and tax law. There is no requirement that the accounting system also produce information relevant for managerial use and so there can be tendencies to use the information for financial-tax purposes for managerial use as well. The remainder of the chapter is devoted to the analysis of information to be used for specific managerial purposes.

COSTS FOR MANAGERIAL USES

The basic principle of cost classification and analysis for managerial uses is *relevance* to the intended purpose for which the information is being prepared. There are no hard-and-fast rules for treating costs; the specific situation governs the type of cost information to be employed. In general, managerial uses of cost information are enhanced by the avoidance of allocations, including calculations of full cost per unit. The distinction between expired and unexpired costs is also less relevant for managerial uses than for financial-tax purposes. Historical costs are not used exclusively for managerial purposes; expected costs are generally more important.

The phrase "different costs for different purposes" describes the analysis of cost data for managerial purposes. Not only will the treatment of particular costs vary from the financial-tax treatment, but it will also vary among different managerial uses. A given element of cost could be treated one way for one managerial purpose, another way for a different purpose, and ignored for a third use. The need is to tailor the cost information to the particular circumstances.

Any well-managed firm has an information system that provides data that are not available from the financial-tax accounting system. A good deal of information needed for routine, recurring managerial uses can be readily provided by such a system. However, some information is required only at infrequent intervals and must be developed more or less from scratch.

The different purposes for which different costs are required can be identified broadly with activities of managers. Although there is disagreement regarding what these activities are, it seems reasonable to use the categories of planning, decision making, and control and performance evaluation. The discussion is arranged under these headings.

Planning

The planning process takes many forms in a modern, well-run business. There will be analyses of cost-volume-profit relationships for single products or departments; expense budgets for manufacturing, marketing, and other functional areas; comprehensive budgets including projections of cash flow and pro forma balance sheets; and long-term financial planning.

For planning purposes the relevant costs are *future costs*. Managers are concerned with what to expect, not with what has already happened. Historical costs are important only insofar as they can be used to predict future levels of costs. Cost classifications for planning purposes do not parallel those for financial-tax purposes: Functional and object classifications of cost are of secondary importance in planning.

For budgeting and profit planning a classification of costs by *behavior* is important. Costs should be analyzed in regard to whether they are likely to be fixed in total amount over the planning period, or whether they will vary with some measure of volume like sales or production.

The technique known as flexible budgeting (see Chapter 18) is used when the firm, or one of its segments, has both fixed and variable costs. For example, manufacturing overhead might be analyzed as in the accompanying table.

Cost element	Fixed amount per month	Variable amount per unit produced
Indirect labor	$ 84,000	$0.15
Supplies and indirect material	14,000	0.03
Depreciation	22,000	—
Other (detailed)	44,000	0.26
Totals	$164,000	$0.44

A flexible budget formula for total manufacturing overhead per month would be

Total manufacturing overhead = $164,000 + ($0.44 × P)

where P = production in units for the month.

A major reason for separating costs into fixed and variable components is to determine contribution margin. *Contribution margin* is selling price minus variable cost per unit. Contribution margin can also be expressed as a percentage of selling price. Exhibit 1 shows two income statements, one prepared using the traditional financial accounting classifications, the other using the contribution margin format in which costs are classified by behavior.

This simplified example, which could relate to a single product, product line, or the firm as a whole, highlights the importance of a behavioral classification of costs for planning and other

EXHIBIT 1
Alternative income statement formats

Financial accounting format

Sales		$3,200,000
Cost of goods sold		1,400,000
Gross profit		$1,800,000
Selling expenses	$850,000	
Administrative expenses	740,000	1,590,000
Profit before taxes		$ 210,000
Income taxes		120,000
Net income		$ 90,000

Contribution margin format

Sales		$3,200,000
Variable costs:		
Cost of sales	$800,000	
Selling expenses	200,000	
Administrative expenses	80,000	1,080,000
Contribution margin		$2,120,000
Fixed costs:		
Cost of sales	$600,000	
Selling expenses	650,000	
Administrative expenses	660,000	1,910,000
Profit before taxes		$ 210,000
Income taxes		120,000
Net income		$ 90,000

managerial purposes. Using the contribution margin format a manager can determine the effects on planned profits of increases or decreases in volume, or of actions like advertising campaigns expected to lead to increased sales. For example, contribution margin is 66.25 percent of sales ($2,120,000/$3,-200,000). If the manager is considering a promotional campaign that would add $200,000 to selling expenses, the minimum increase in sales that would justify the campaign would be about $302,000 ($200,000/66.25 percent). Any lesser increase in expected sales would make the campaign a losing proposition.

The financial-tax format, with its functional classification of costs, cannot be used in such planning activities without modifications designed to determine contribution margin per unit of product or per sales dollar, information that is already captured by the contribution margin format.

However, cost-volume-profit analysis for a manufacturing firm involves a critical assumption that the firm's beginning and ending inventories are equal, or that the firm uses direct (variable) costing. For financial-tax purposes direct costing is not acceptable. Nor is it likely that a firm's inventories will be perfectly stable. Accordingly, if absorption costing is used for internal purposes as well as for external reporting, both pretax and aftertax profits will be affected not only by sales, but also by production. It is possible to remove the effects of production from the periodic income figure used for planning purposes. Isolating the effects of production may give managers a better picture of the average long-term profitability of a product line because in the long run sales and production will generally be about the same.

The following data will be used to illustrate the technique.

Selling price of product		$10.00
Variable costs:		
Production	$5.00	
Selling and administrative	0.50	5.50
Contribution margin		$ 4.50
Fixed costs per year:		
Production	$1,200,000	
Selling and administrative	550,000	

The firm uses a standard fixed cost of $2 per unit for inventory determination purposes, based on normal production of 600,000

EXHIBIT 2
Income statements

	Production 550,000 units	Production 580,000 units
Sales 550,000 × $10	$5,500,000	$5,500,000
Cost of sales:		
Beginning inventory	$ 140,000	$ 140,000
Production costs		
Variable @ $5/unit	2,750,000	2,900,000
Fixed	1,200,000	1,200,000
Cost of goods available for sale	$4,090,000	$4,240,000
Ending inventory @ $7/unit	140,000	350,000
Cost of goods sold	$3,950,000	$3,890,000
Gross profit	$1,550,000	$1,610,000
Selling and administrative expenses:		
Variable 550,000 × $0.50	$ 275,000	$ 275,000
Fixed	550,000	550,000
Total	$ 825,000	$ 825,000
Pretax profit	$ 725,000	$ 785,000
Income tax at 45%	326,250	353,250
Net income	$ 398,750	$ 431,750

units and $1.2 million budgeted fixed production costs. The tax rate, for simplicity, is assumed to be a flat 45 percent and the beginning inventory is assumed to be 20,000 units.

Exhibit 2 shows income statements for two situations: one in which sales and production are both 550,000 units; another in which sales are 550,000 units, but production is 580,000 units. As production increases, so does net income because of the higher fixed costs being deferred in inventory.

The difference in net incomes of $33,000 ($431,750 − $398,750) is caused by the after tax effect of the change in fixed costs included in inventory. This difference would be highlighted if variable costing were used. If absorption costing is used internally, the effects of production and sales being different can be calculated using the following formula.

Difference in income = (Change in units in inventory ×
Fixed cost per unit) × (1 − Tax rate)

In the example given, the change in units is 30,000 and the results are:

Difference in income = (30,000 × $2) × 55% = $33,000

The merits of variable costing and absorption costing are treated extensively in Chapter 25. The concern here is to show the differing treatment of fixed costs that managements might adopt in profit planning and evaluation. Eliminating the effects on profits caused by differences between production and sales can be helpful in analyzing the long-term profitability of a product or line.

Other planning activities. Besides profit planning, comprehensive budgeting is employed by most firms. Included in a comprehensive budget will be budgets for production, purchases of raw materials, and cash flows. Cash budgeting is the most important of these planning activities. The matching concept is of little significance for cash budgeting. The important consideration in cash budgeting is the timing of the expenditure that is related to the individual cost. (The time of collecting receivables is likewise more important than the time of making sales.) The expenditure may precede or succeed the incurrence of the cost and its expensing for financial-tax purposes.

Depreciation expense is not in itself significant for cash budgeting, but the expenditure required to obtain fixed assets is extremely important. The book treatment of depreciation is not relevant, but the tax treatment is. The tax treatment of depreciation will affect the tax payment, which is an element of cash flow. The tax expense shown in published income statements is a mixture of required payments and of deferrals required by generally accepted accounting principles for financial reporting.

In one sense, tax accounting is more important for managerial purposes than financial accounting. The impact on cash flow is limited to tax payments, which are governed by the procedures and methods used for tax purposes. The impact on tax expense reported on the income statement, of differences between treatment for financial reporting purposes and tax purposes is not of particular importance for managerial purposes.

Decision making

It is in decision making that the greatest divergence between classifications and interpretations of costs used in financial-tax accounting and in managerial accounting is found. Many costs that are recorded and used in financial reporting are ignored for decision making, and some costs that are not recorded at all for financial purposes are used in making decisions.

The emphasis in decision making, as in planning in general, is on the future. Revenues and costs are not important *per se;* the critical factor in decision making is *expected cash flows.*[2] (This important point is treated fully in Chapter 33.) In the present chapter we shall limit attention to decisions that do not require capital investment. In such cases it is *usually* reasonable to assume that cash flows are equivalent to revenues and costs and therefore we shall deal with revenues and costs rather than cash flows.

Because decisions involve actions to be taken, the historical cost data already accumulated in the records are of no direct help to the manager. The role of historical costs is limited to their usefulness in predicting future costs. In some types of decisions, especially ones involving the consideration of existing courses of action, like continuing to sell a product or dropping it, or continuing to buy a component or starting to make it, historical costs will prove useful in predicting some of the future costs. However, because any decision involves a choice among alternative courses of action, some of the cost data will have to be developed from scratch. These data consist of the cost information related to actions that the firm is not currently taking. Thus, if a firm is now buying a component for a product and is considering manufacturing the component, there are not likely to be any historical data available regarding the costs to make the component.

Decision making involves the following steps:

1. Identifying feasible alternatives. It is generally impossible to identify all possible alternatives. Even if it were possible to do so, the cost of seeking out all possible courses of action could well be greater than the potential benefits. Additionally, some known alternatives can be ruled out as a matter of company policy or because of external factors. Some firms will not sell their products under "house brands," some will not lay off large numbers of workers, and some will not

---

[2] The impact of a decision on book profit may be significant and may make a good economic decision seem unwise. An example appears later in this chapter.

produce particular types of products even though they have the ability to do so.

2. Determining the expected relevant revenues and costs involved for each feasible alternative. This process may involve the use of probabilistic estimates and statistical techniques. An important component of this step is the identification and estimation of side effects that can accompany a particular decision. For example, the use of excess capacity to make a product to be sold under a private brand might lead to reduced sales at normal selling prices if the ultimate consumers become aware that the less expensive private brand is essentially the same as the higher-priced product.

3. Selecting the alternative that is expected to produce the highest total income (cash flow) for the firm.

Differential costs and sunk costs. A *differential cost* is one that will differ among alternative courses of action.[3] It will take on one value under one alternative, another value under a different alternative. Differential costs are relevant for decision making. Differential costs are always *expected costs,* not historical costs, although in many cases historical costs can be good predictors of future costs. For example, a decision to increase production requires an estimation of the total cost to produce at the higher level and at the lower level. The difference between these two costs is the differential cost. Variable cost per unit may be expected to be about the same as it was in the past and would therefore be one of the components of total differential cost.

A *sunk cost* is one that has either (*a*) already been incurred, or (*b*) is yet to be incurred, but will be the same no matter which alternative course of action is chosen. Sunk costs, also called *unavoidable costs,* are irrelevant for decision-making purposes precisely because they cannot be changed. Nothing can be done to increase or decrease them and their amounts are common to all alternatives. The most prevalent example of a sunk cost is the book value of an existing asset, whether it be inventory, machinery, copyright, or investment in securities.

---

[3] Differential costs are also incremental costs. The term incremental suggests an increase. The term differential is more general because it comprises both increases and decreases.

Aside from possible tax effects of gains or losses on sales of any asset, the book value is irrelevant to an analysis of using or disposing of the asset. The tax effect is relevant because it is, or shortly will be, a cash flow, but the tax effect depends on the tax basis, not the book value. If the tax basis and book value are the same, the amount is relevant only because it is the tax basis.

The term *out-of-pocket costs* is sometimes used to refer to differential costs. Out-of-pocket costs are those that require cash disbursements either in the period incurred or shortly thereafter. However, out-of-pocket costs are not necessarily differential. Expenditures that are required because of commitments like employment contracts are unavoidable. The cash outflows will occur regardless of the courses of action selected by the firm's managers.

The determination that a particular cost is relevant or irrelevant must be made with careful attention to the surrounding circumstances. A given cost could well be relevant in one situation, yet irrelevant in a situation only slightly different.

The emphasis on future costs is illustrated in the following examples. A firm has 1,000 units of product on hand that have a total historical cost of $7,000, of which $4,000 was variable production cost and $3,000 was allocated fixed production costs.

First, assume that the units cannot be sold as was anticipated prior to production. They can be sold as scrap for $1,500 or modified at a cost of $3,000 and sold for $4,000. The only relevant items are the expected revenues and costs; the original costs are irrelevant because they are sunk. The accompanying analysis shows that the units should be sold as scrap because to do so would result in $500 greater profit than if they are modified and sold.

	Sell as scrap	Modify and sell
Revenue	$1,500	$4,000
Incremental costs	0	3,000
Incremental profit	$1,500	$1,000

If the original cost were included in the analysis the results would be the same. The advantage of selling as scrap would still be

$500 over modifying and selling the units. The sunk costs would be included under both alternatives and would therefore not affect the relative profitability of the two possible actions.

Consider a different situation. Suppose now that the same units could be sold as part of a special order at $4.20 apiece. The regular selling price is $10 and the special order would not affect total sales at the $10 price. The critical question now is the amount of cost that would have to be incurred to replace the units. If the units are sold for $4.20, another 1,000 will have to be produced to meet sales at the $10 price. The $4 per unit variable production cost is not relevant except insofar as it can be used to predict the differential cost of producing an additional 1,000 units. Suppose that variable production costs are expected to be $4.50 during the coming period. The firm will have to incur $4,500 to produce the units for sale at the $10 price and will receive only $4,200 from the special order. The order should not be accepted.

The example above assumed that variable production costs were the only differential costs. This is sometimes not the case, most frequently when the firm experiences step-variable costs. *Step-variable* costs are those that jump from one level to another at a particular threshold of volume. For example, a firm might have to hire an additional supervisor if production goes above 10,000 units, and another if production exceeds 11,500 units. In analyzing differential costs it is necessary to consider whether higher (or lower) production will take the firm past a threshold of step-variable costs.

Opportunity costs.   Most resources that a firm controls are scarce and many have more than one potential use. Raw materials can usually be sold as is or used to make products. Space can be used for manufacturing or warehousing or leased to another party. Investments in securities can be sold or held. When a scarce resource has more than one use, it has an opportunity cost. Its *opportunity cost* is the value of its being employed in the best alternative way, a way not currently used. Opportunity costs are often market values. The opportunity cost of a share of stock owned by a firm is its resale price; of a warehouse, its rental value.

Opportunity costs are important in evaluating alternative

courses of action. The objective in decision making is the selection of the best alternative use of resources and this is promoted by the determination of opportunity costs. However, precisely because opportunity costs relate to actions not being taken, but to opportunities, they are usually not recorded for financial-tax purposes.[4] There are usually no clues to the existence of opportunities in historical records and hence they are sometimes overlooked.

Perhaps the most important reason for paying attention to opportunity costs is that many actions taken will be profitable, but not as profitable as others might have been. The historical records will normally show that a profit was earned because a firm acted in a particular way. What is not shown is whether the firm would have been better off acting differently.

The consequences of failing to consider opportunity costs can be illustrated by the following example. A firm makes three products using a single type of machine. The machinery has 1,000 available hours per month and fixed costs associated with it are $10,000 per month. The firm uses a $10 fixed overhead rate per hour for product costing purposes. Data on the three products are given below.

	A	B	C
Selling price	$10	$12	$15
Variable cost	6	7	8
Contribution margin	$ 4	$ 5	$ 7
Machine time required, per unit, in hours	0.10	0.12	0.20

An analysis of profitability of the products that considered only the contribution margins of the three products would rank the products C, B, A. However, if the firm is able to sell as much of any product as it can produce, Product B should be chosen because it contributes more profit per machine-hour than either of the others. The appropriate analysis is on the following page.

---

[4] One exception to the rule that opportunity costs are not recorded for financial-tax purposes is the use of lower of cost or market for inventory determination. The net realizable value of a unit is generally its opportunity cost. This value is the "ceiling" on market that is used in applying the lower-of-cost-or-market rule.

	A	B	C
Contribution margin per unit	$ 4	$ 5	$ 7
Divided by required time	0.10	0.12	0.20
Equals contribution per machine per hour	$40	$41.67	$35

The $41.67 contribution margin per hour that can be generated in making Product B is the opportunity cost of using the machinery for some other purpose. The fixed overhead rate of $10 per hour does not represent the cost of using the machinery. The opportunity cost is the appropriate measure of cost because it is the sacrifice required in using the machinery for some purpose other than producing Product B. If the firm cannot sell its entire output of Product B but can sell all of Product A, the opportunity cost is $40 per hour, the contribution margin that could be earned producing Product A.

Joint processes and joint costs.   A joint process is one that produces two or more products in relatively fixed proportions. The processing of beef yields various types of meat, hides, bones, and by-products. The costs incurred in operating the joint process, whether fixed or variable with the quantity of raw material processed, are joint costs. Joint costs are not associated with any one joint product, but with the entire output of the joint process. Because they are not incremental with regard to any single product, they are irrelevant in decisions regarding the individual products. The most common such decision is whether to sell the joint product at split-off, the point at which it emerges from the joint process as a single product, or to process it further.

The other major decision involved with joint processes is whether they should be operated at all. For these decisions, some of the costs of operating the joint process are relevant. The cost of raw materials, variable conversion costs, and some fixed costs could be avoided if the process were not operated. Therefore, these costs, irrelevant with regard to individual products, are relevant to the decision whether to operate the joint process at all. The classification of a cost as relevant or irrelevant depends on the decision being made.

Two general rules regarding decisions about joint products can be set down. Individual products should be processed beyond the split-off point so long as the incremental revenues exceed the incremental costs. The joint process should be operated so long as the total revenues from the most profitable disposals of the joint products exceed the total incremental costs of joint processing and of further processing of individual products.

No reasonably straightforward allocation method will satisfy the requirements of both product costing and decision making. However, if the manager examines all of the available alternatives, and if the allocated joint cost is the same for each alternative, the allocations will do no harm. The alternative that shows the highest book profit or lowest book loss will also be the best alternative if no allocations are made.

For financial-tax purposes an allocation method should result in products being carried in inventory at less than their net realizable values. The reason is that if they are carried at net realizable values, profit will be recognized at the production stage rather than at the point of sale. If there are by-products of the joint process—products with relatively low values in comparison with the major products—they are sometimes carried at net realizable value because the amounts are immaterial.

When there are markets for products at their split-off points, the *relative market values* of different products are frequently used as the basis for allocating joint costs. Another method that results in satisfactory allocations is called the *constant gross profit rate* method. This method values all products at their net realizable values less the normal profit margin on the joint production as a whole. Both methods are illustrated in the following example. Data for the illustration are in the accompanying table.

	Products	
	A	B
Sales value at split-off	$ 6,000	$12,000
Sales value after further processing	14,000	18,000
Incremental further processing costs	4,000	8,000

Total costs of operating the joint process are $15,000, of which $8,000 is incremental.

First, the decision regarding further processing should be made only on the basis of the additional revenues and additional costs associated with further processing. Product A should be processed further and Product B should not, as shown.

	A	B
Sales value after further processing	$14,000	$18,000
Less additional processing costs	4,000	8,000
Incremental profit	$10,000	$10,000
Less sales value at split-off	6,000	12,000
Advantage (disadvantage) of further processing	$ 4,000	$ (2,000)

The joint process should be operated because the incremental costs of $8,000 are less than the net revenues of $22,000 ($10,000 + $12,000) of the best actions with regard to the joint products. The joint costs would be allocated as shown using the relative split-off values.

Product	Split-off value	Fraction of total	Total joint cost	=	Allocated joint cost
A	$ 6,000	⅓	$15,000		$ 5,000
B	12,000	⅔	15,000		10,000
	$18,000				

An income statement using these allocations would appear as shown.

	A	B	Total
Sales	$14,000	$12,000	$26,000
Additional processing costs	$ 4,000	0	$ 4,000
Allocated joint costs	5,000	$10,000	15,000
Total costs	$ 9,000	$10,000	$19,000
Profit	$ 5,000	$ 2,000	$ 7,000

This allocation scheme does no harm for managerial purposes so long as it is used consistently. The allocated costs would then be the same under any alternative courses of action, which is tantamount to ignoring them. However, it is possible to show losses because not only the incremental, but also the unavoidable joint costs are included in the allocation and an unwise decision to discontinue the joint process in the short run might be made.

Sometimes there are products that do not have split-off values. In such cases, the constant gross profit rate method of allocation can be used. The method can also be used when there are split-off values. Essentially, the method requires that joint costs be so allocated that all products show the same gross profit rate. In the case described above, the allocation would be made after the most profitable processing plans had been determined, and would appear as shown.

	A	B	Total
Sales	$14,000	$12,000	$26,000
Gross profit	3,770	3,230	7,000
Total costs	$10,230	$ 8,770	$19,000
Incremental processing costs	4,000	0	4,000
Joint cost	$ 6,230	$ 8,770	$15,000

Gross profit rate = $7,000/$26,000 = 26.9%

Gross profit for Product A = $14,000 × 26.9% = $3,770 (rounded)

Gross profit for Product B = $12,000 × 26.9% = $3,230 (rounded)

Both of the allocation methods illustrated will comply with financial accounting requirements that inventory valuation not exceed net realizable value, but both are irrelevant for managerial purposes. For planning, control, and decision making the joint cost allocations should be avoided.

Evaluations of segment profitability

The principles of incremental and sunk costs can be of use in evaluating the profitability of a segment of the firm, such as a product, product line, class of customer, or geographical area. In general such evaluations are of two types: long-term and short-term. A segment that may be marginally profitable in the short run should normally be continued unless some better use of the facilities is available (opportunity cost of operating the segment). But, such a segment may be a candidate for long-term phasing out as the unavoidable, committed costs associated with it come up for renewal.

When a segment shares fixed resources with other segments,

joint costs are present. Some costs that are direct to the segment, traceable or separable costs, are sunk and unavoidable. All of these costs are irrelevant in short-term analyses. Separable costs are usually relevant in long-term analyses.

Costs will be classified differently depending on the particular segment being evaluated. Many of the fixed costs associated with a factory that makes several products will be joint with respect to the products, but separable with respect to geographical area. Costs associated with the functions of a product line manager are separable with respect to the product line, but joint with respect to geographical area or class of customer.

If a segment employs capital in the form of receivables, inventory, or fixed assets, it could be charged with return on the invested capital. This charge is an imputed cost; it is not incurred either by the segment or by the firm, but is an opportunity cost. If capital investment does not produce a minimum required rate of return, it should be shifted into areas where the potential return is higher. There is little difficulty in applying this principle to receivables and inventory, but some problems arise in regard to fixed assets. This problem is discussed in a later section. For now, we shall limit the application to investment in current, liquid assets.

Exhibit 3 shows income statements by product. The state-

EXHIBIT 3
Product line income statements (thousands of dollars)

		Products	
	Total	A	B
Sales	$3,900	$1,300	$2,600
Variable costs:			
Cost of sales	$1,050	$ 430	620
Selling and administrative	790	350	440
Total variable costs	$1,840	$ 780	$1,060
Contribution margin	$2,060	$ 520	$1,540
Direct, avoidable fixed costs			
(itemized)	560	150	410
Short-run product margin	$1,400	$ 370	$1,030
Direct, committed fixed costs			
(itemized)	855	215	640
Long-run product margin	$ 545	$ 155	$ 390
Imputed interest on receivables			
and inventory........................	170	55	115
Product profit	$ 375	$ 100	$ 275
Joint costs (itemized)	280		
Profit	$ 95		

ments highlight short- and long-term product margins. They do not show allocated costs for individual products; only the total amount of joint costs is shown in the total column.

Effect of financial accounting methods on decisions

At the beginning of the section on decision making we said that it was usually reasonable to use revenues and expenses rather than cash flows in the evaluation of decisions that do not entail additional capital investment. Financial accounting methods will sometimes produce misleading results because of a lack of correspondence between profits and cash flows. The principal source of difficulty is the use of absorption costing for financial-tax purposes.

The following illustration highlights the potential difficulty. The firm whose partial income statements are shown below uses standard costs for financial and tax purposes. It has been approached by another firm that would like to buy 10,000 units of its product at $12, which is above the current and expected variable production cost of $10. The special order would not reduce sales at the regular $20 price and the firm would fill the order from inventory rather than by increasing production.

	Without special offer	With special offer
Sales 100,000 units at $20	$2,000,000	
100,000 × $20 + 10,000 × $12		$2,120,000
Standard cost of sales 100,000 × $15	1,500,000	
110,000 × $15		1,650,000
Standard gross profit	$ 500,000	$ 470,000

There would be no difference in overapplied or underapplied overhead in the two situations because production does not change. The $30,000 difference in gross profit is the $3 "loss" per unit based on total standard cost including $5 in applied fixed costs for the 10,000 units sold.

The firm will have to replace the sold units at some time in the future. An increase in production of 10,000 units above the number originally budgeted for the coming period would result in the absorption of another $50,000 in fixed overhead ($5 × 10,000 units). Therefore, the following period's income statement will show $50,000 more income than it would have if the offer had not been accepted and 10,000 fewer units had been produced. Thus, an examination of budgeted results for the two-year period as a whole would show that the decision is wise, but the financial reporting results would not.

Similarly, a wise decision to make a component instead of buying it could also lead to lower book profits for the product of which the component is a part. Suppose that a firm is currently paying $11 for a component that could be made for variable costs of $8 and incremental fixed costs of $40,000 per year. Annual use of the component is 20,000 units. To make the component would require the use of machinery that is currently underutilized. For financial reporting purposes the depreciation charged to the making of the component would be $30,000. The effects of the decision on cash flows and on costs allocated to the product would be as follows.

	Cash flow	Book costs
Variable costs 20,000 × $8	$160,000	$160,000
Incremental fixed costs	40,000	40,000
Allocated depreciation	0	30,000
Totals	$200,000	$230,000

The cash flow associated with purchasing the component outside is $220,000 per year (20,000 × $11). The decision to make the component is wise, but the costs charged to the product would be $10,000 higher than before. The $30,000 depreciation would increase the book profits and reduce the inventoriable cost of other products for which it is used so that an internal shift in profitability would appear to have occurred.

Such problems can be severe if performance evaluation is based on book profits of products and if one manager is responsible for the product that uses the component, while other managers are responsible for the products that will benefit from reduced allocations of depreciation. In such cases a transfer price for use of the machinery could be negotiated among the managers involved. The price would have to be less than $20,000 per year in this case, to induce the manager to make the component instead of continuing to buy it outside.

Control and performance evaluation

The *control* process is directed towards determining whether operations have gone according to plan and if they have not, whether steps can be taken to bring future operations more in line with plans. The most widely used accounting procedures involved in the control process are *budgets* and *standard costs*, which serve as bases for comparison with actual costs. These comparisons are used to determine whether investigations should be made, which in turn might indicate the need for some corrective actions.

Performance evaluation is an implicit part of the control process. *People* are responsible for executing plans, and evaluations of the extent to which control has been good or bad are implicitly evaluations of the performance of people.

The basic principle of control, from the viewpoint of the use of accounting data, is *responsibility*. The information given to managers should be such that they can use it to improve their performance, evaluate the performance of their subordinates, and assist their subordinates in improving their performance. Accordingly, control reports should indicate clearly the manager's performance in those areas for which he is responsible and in which he has the authority to act. Additionally, the criteria by which superiors evaluate the performance of their subordinates should not encourage the latter to take actions that are undesirable for the firm.

The problem of a particular performance measure encouraging undesirable actions can be illustrated by a few examples. If a production manager is evaluated on the basis of unit costs, he can lower his unit costs simply by producing more units. If profits are the sole measure for evaluating the manager of a profit center, misleading results in the short-term can be achieved through the postponement of expenditures for maintenance or employee training and development. Accordingly, several measures of performance should normally be used in order that concentration on one measure does not produce undesirable behavior.

In modern business firms it is virtually impossible to isolate the responsibilities and performance of individual managers. The operations of a modern firm are complex and interdependent;

each manager's performance is affected by the performance of others. The best sales manager cannot continually increase sales of shoddy products, nor can an excellent production manager accomplish much if the firm's equipment is obsolete and cannot be replaced because of poor access to capital markets. Although it is unrealistic to expect to eliminate all traces of interdependency from control and performance evaluation reports, it can be held within reasonable limits by the judicious application of the principles of *controllability* and *responsibility.*

Responsibility accounting

Once the responsibilities of managers have been reasonably well set forth the focus is on identifying the costs that the managers are responsible for controlling. If a manager cannot control a particular cost there is serious doubt whether the cost should be reported to him. If noncontrollable costs are reported, they should be explicitly identified and separated from controllable costs.

Methods used for product costing purposes for financial-tax reporting are not likely to be helpful in control and performance evaluation. The major reason is that product costing requires the determination of unit costs at relatively low levels in the firm's organizational structure, such as small production departments. But the farther down one goes in the organization, the less one finds that a manager or supervisor can control. For example, the manager of a production department is probably not responsible for wage rates; therefore, the relevant information for him is not total labor cost, but total labor hours. The practice of reporting labor use at standard wage rates, rather than actual rates, at the departmental level overcomes this problem.

Additionally, the manager of an operating department is not responsible for the costs incurred by service departments like maintenance, factory accounting, and other general services. These costs are commonly allocated to individual operating departments on some basis like relative use of the service. In some cases the operating department manager is able to control the amount of the service for which the costs will be allocated, but not the level of costs. For example, operating managers will make use of maintenance services that may be provided by a separate maintenance department. Each operating manager can usually determine how much of the service he wishes to use, but he cannot control the level of costs incurred by the maintenance department. In other cases managers will be charged with shares of service department costs even though they cannot determine how much service will be provided. Charges for allocated shares of cafeteria, personnel, accounting, and general factory administration will not usually reflect requested use of the services, but will be determined by the relative shares of the operating departments on some basis such as number of employees, or volumes of particular types of transactions.

If costs of service departments and other joint costs are to be allocated, the allocations should bear some reasonable relationship to the operating department's use of the service. Additionally, the amount allocated should be based on budgeted or standard costs rather than actual costs of the service department so that the costs of inefficiencies are not passed on from service departments to operating departments. Finally, the amounts allocated to particular departments should not be influenced by the activities of other operating departments.

If costs are allocated simply on the basis of relative use of the service, the amounts allocated to each operating department will depend on the use made of the service by all of the other departments. An example is shown below. In both periods, operating department A used the same amounts of the service, but was charged different amounts because of the different amounts that department B used. The total service department cost being allocated is $4,000 in both periods.

	Period 1 departments		Period 2 departments	
	A	B	A	B
Use of service, in hours	1,000	1,000	1,000	500
Allocated cost	$2,000	$2,000	$2,667	$1,333

A method of allocation that is reasonable from the standpoints of both product costing and responsibility accounting is to charge operating departments a set amount per unit of the service used, based on budget variable costs of providing the service plus a flat amount per period reflecting the expected relative long-term use of the service. The flat amount should be based on the budgeted fixed costs of the service department. Basing this part of the allocation on expected long-term use of the service recognizes that the service department's fixed costs are incurred primarily to provide the capacity to render the service, and that the capacity of the service department is planned by reference to the expected use of the service in future periods.

A report that uses the principles so far discussed appears in Exhibit 4. The allocated, noncontrollable costs are shown

EXHIBIT 4
Sample control report

Month of May, 19XX

Department Machining   Manager R. James
Date received 6/8/19XX   Date returned 6/13/19XX

	Budgeted	*Actual*	*Variance*
Production in units		9,000	
Controllable costs:			
Materials......................	$18,000	$18,800	$ 800 U*
Direct labor....................	27,000	27,600	600 U*
Indirect labor	1,200	1,160	40
Supplies	800	680	120
Maintenance	750	820	70 U
Total controllable costs........	$47,750	$49,060	$1,310 U
Noncontrollable costs:			
Depreciation	$ 1,300	$ 1,300	0
Building services	600	600	0
Other allocated costs............	2,100	2,100	0
Total noncontrollable costs	$ 4,000	$ 4,000	
Total costs	$51,750	$53,060	$1,310

Note: "U" denotes unfavorable variances.

Comments and explanations *Faulty materials resulted in waste and extra labor

time.

separately from the controllable costs. Their presence on the report serves to remind the manager of the benefits he receives.

The major problems associated with control and performance evaluation are *behavioral*. It is important that managers trust the system and that the information provided by the system encourages managers to work in the firm's best interests. In general, as we have said, allocations are not conducive to desirable behavioral effects. However, allocations or transfer prices can be employed to help in achieving desired objectives.

A firm might have a new computer that top management believes should be used for particular purposes by operating managers. If the operating managers are reluctant to use the computer, top management might set a very low transfer price on its use. The low price would be more likely to stimulate the desired use than a price designed to allocate fully the costs of operating the computer. Similarly, a service that is being overused could be given a relatively high transfer price to discourage its use. A decision to increase the transfer price would have to be based on careful analysis designed to determine the extent to which use of the service is unnecessary, or costlier than alternative means. When a transfer price is used, the amount of allocations to operating departments for managerial reporting purposes could be more or less than the actual cost incurred by the service department. For financial-tax purposes the usual practice is to allocate all service department costs to individual products. Hence, a supplemental allocation would have to be made for product costing purposes.

Imputed costs

The use of an imputed charge for interest or return on investment was illustrated earlier in connection with analyzing the profitability of product lines. Imputed costs can also be used for evaluating the performance of managers who have control over revenues, expenses, and investment in assets.

The most common use of imputed costs is in the *residual income method* of evaluating divisional performance. The division is charged with a dollar amount that is based on the invested capital and the minimum satisfactory rate of return. For example, if a division has an operating profit of $200,000, investment of $800,000, and the minimum satisfactory return on investment is 15 percent, residual income would be $80,000, calculated as follows.

Operating profit		$200,000
Investment	$800,000	
Minimum ROI	15%	
Minimum satisfactory dollar return		120,000
Residual income		$ 80,000

Residual income is an alternative to ROI in evaluating the performance of divisions.

Balance sheets

Just as costs that are to be shown as expenses on income statements can vary between financial-tax accounting and managerial accounting, so too can costs shown on balance sheets. In the calculation of residual income or return on investment the basis used to determine the amount invested could be original cost or market resale price. Each of these bases of measuring the investment would serve different purposes. Market resale price is the opportunity cost of assets, and if a segment does not have a satisfactory return on the market value of its assets, it should probably be disposed of in the near future.

Replacement cost is an indication of the amount required to keep the segment's operations at their current level. Return on investment based on replacement cost indicates the profitability of entering the line of business that the segment is now in. Hence, if the return is unsatisfactory, the segment may well be a candidate for gradual phasing out. The application of capital budgeting techniques would show that replacing the existing assets would be a poor decision unless better operating results could be expected in the future.

Original cost and original cost less accumulated depreciation are the most widely used bases of measuring investment, at least partly because the information is readily available in the accounting records. The use of original cost does not provide good information when segments have assets of widely varying ages, but it does avoid the problem that depreciated cost is influenced by the depreciation method used. If one segment uses straight line depreciation and another an accelerated method, comparisons of return on investment are made difficult. Most firms will therefore use uniform depreciation methods among their various segments.

RECENT DEVELOPMENTS

The Securities and Exchange Commission and the Financial Accounting Standards Board have recently promulgated reporting requirements that reflect principles employed in managerial accounting. These requirements are interesting in their own right, and have been advocated on grounds other than their applications in managerial accounting. Although it is early to tell, the results of their being used for financial reporting might well be to provide to outsiders some of the types of information now used by managers.

Forecasts

The SEC now permits the inclusion of forecasts in company filings. The publication of forecasts, like that of replacement cost data, has not been universally supported and the desirability of publishing forecasts is not established. In the past, some forecasting has been done by company officials in the form of statements to security analysts and stockholders. These forecasts have typically been limited to figures like sales and earnings per share. So far as the authors of this chapter are concerned, the publishing of forecasts is a step toward bringing financial and managerial accounting closer together.

For most managerial purposes forecasted costs (and revenues) are more important than historical costs. Cost-volume-profit analysis and comprehensive budgeting are forecasting techniques that rely on assumptions about future levels of sales and future relationships of costs to sales. Managers must make assumptions, or sets of assumptions, about the factors that influence sales and costs. Analyses of economic indicators, market shares, and other factors are made explicit in formulating profit plans and budgets. The manager seeks a reasonable basis for his forecasts and probably works with ranges rather than single point estimates, or presents "most likely," "optimistic," and "pessimistic" forecasts.

Whether investors can make intelligent use of forecasts is a critical question in deciding whether they should be published. The answer depends partly on whether investors can make use of the same information that managers use. Investors do not make the same kinds of decisions as managers, but it is arguable that they can employ the same kinds of information.

Segment reporting

Both the SEC and FASB have published reporting requirements for segments of a business. The SEC is, at this writing, moving to amend its requirements to coincide with those of *Statement of Financial Accounting Standards No. 14.* The FASB requires that the following be disclosed, among other things: segment revenues, both outside and intracompany; operating profit by segment; and identifiable assets for each segment. Both operating profit and identifiable assets contain some allocations. Expenses and assets common to two or more segments are to be allocated to those segments on some "reasonable basis." General corporate assets and expenses are not to be allocated.

Firms may also present profit contribution before operating profit. Profit contribution is the excess of revenues over direct, separable costs without allocations of joint costs. Pretax profit would result from deducting allocated corporate expenses from operating profit. Contribution to profit is an important figure for managerial purposes, while operating profit or pretax profit after allocated costs is not so important. Nor are allocations of joint assets helpful in evaluating the profitability of a segment. Both the allocated expenses and allocated assets will change from year to year if they are based on relative shares of revenue or some other factor that itself changes.

Because the requirements relate only to large segments of a firm, relatively few allocations may be needed. Very large segments are most likely to be more or less self-contained, and the fact that no general corporate expenses or assets are to be allocated to them may result in the information being fairly allocation-free for many firms.

Replacement costs

For decision-making purposes the manager should use *expected costs* of taking various actions, rather than historical costs. Although current replacement costs are not necessarily equal to future costs, they are likely to be closer than historical costs. For purposes of evaluating the performance of a segment of the firm, the current costs to replace assets can provide a better picture than historical costs. The SEC now requires the disclosure of current replacement cost information and the FASB has been studying the whole problem of accounting during periods of price and price-level changes.

The reporting of current replacement costs is not altogether new. The lower of cost or market rule for inventories requires the use of replacement cost, subject to the "floor" and "ceiling" on market value. The Lifo inventory method is often supported by arguments that cost of goods sold is based on an approximation of current replacement cost, matching current costs with current revenues.

The use of replacement costs does present some problems, one of the most serious of which is how to interpret the term "replacement." There are several possible ways to define and determine replacement costs. For managerial purposes interest should be concentrated on the costs that would be expected to be incurred if replacement is made in the most favorable way. This might mean that assets of types entirely different from those currently being used would be acquired. Considerable savings in operating costs, exclusive of depreciation, might be expected to result. The SEC allows these expected cost savings to be reported, provided that they are separately disclosed. However, many firms will report replacement cost data, both for assets and depreciation, as if similar assets were to be acquired and will not adjust operating expenses to reflect expected savings.

The lack of uniformity of the application of the SEC requirements makes it problematical whether investors can effectively use the information now being provided. Further refining of the requirements might enable investors to make better evaluations of the potential profitability of the firm than is possible with only historical data, but the costs of providing more refined data and other related problems may be considerable. (For more detailed information on this point see Chapter 38.)

SUMMARY

Cost reporting for financial-tax purposes and for managerial purposes differ in several respects. Historical costs are used for financial-tax purposes; expected costs, for managerial use. Financial-tax requirements include the use of absorption costing and allocation of fixed costs to periods of time, product lines, and units of product. Managers make less use of allocated costs because their total amounts do not change when activity changes and because they are not generally controllable by the segments to which they are allocated.

This chapter is a general survey of the principal differences. Detailed attention to specific managerial uses of cost data is found in other chapters, some of which are referenced in this chapter.

PART
THREE

*Organizational aspects
of cost accounting*

9

Responsibility accounting: Profit centers and cost centers

Terence E. McClary*

Delegation of responsibility and authority to accomplish defined parts of a total task is a management concept that has been utilized successfully to cope with the complexities associated with increasingly larger organizations. Along with responsibility and authority, there is usually a degree of accountability; and, to this end, systems must be established to report accomplishments by responsibility so that performance can be measured. Thus, a system of accounting and reporting by responsibility defines the term "Responsibility Accounting."

In the business enterprise, responsibility accounting is the mechanism through which managers communicate with subordinates in order to maintain control over the segments of the business for which they are responsible. This mechanism is represented by an accounting system that is designed to control expenditures by directly relating the reporting of expenditures to the individuals in the company organization who are responsible for their control. The business segments are classified as *cost centers*, if responsibility is for cost control alone, or as *profit centers*, if the degree of responsibility and control that can be exercised encompasses all activities involved in the production and sale of products, systems, or services.

* Vice President–Corporate Financial Administration, General Electric Company.

The role of the financial executive in support of the responsibility accounting system is to implement an effective communication mechanism that will function as an integral part of the total financial reporting system. In this regard, there are certain key principles which should be applied to ensure an effective responsibility accounting system. These principles will be developed in later portions of this chapter. Even with these principles, responsibility accounting remains more of a general concept than a precise technique, and the particular systems that have been developed to serve the responsibility accounting purpose are as varied and as unique as the complexity and diversity of large business enterprises would suggest. Each particular responsibility accounting system represents the effort of the financial function to modify traditional accounting practices to emphasize information useful to operating management and to deemphasize the traditional accounting and bookkeeping data not pertinent for operating decisions.

To some extent, the concept of responsibility accounting has applicability to any organizational format; however, the primary emphasis in this discussion will be on its use in multiproduct business corporations where the authority for operation of business segments has been delegated and the need exists to monitor performance of these segments on a regular basis. The process of delegation has been labeled "decentralization." This organizational structure is quite different from the corporate entity that merely manages a "portfolio" of several business activities comprising the corporate whole, wherein control and performance monitoring of the separate business activities is not an ongoing activity.

RESPONSIBILITY ACCOUNTING CONCEPT

That a simple and straightforward system is necessary to effectively manage and control large multiproduct business enterprises is an accepted fact of modern corporate survival. In response to this need, management systems have been developed which rest on three principal elements: *delegating* to successively lower organizational levels the responsibility for specific goals which are necessary to achieve the objectives of the corporation; *motivation* of management in charge of each operating unit to perform in accordance with the established goals; and, lastly, *measurement* of the progress of management efforts towards achieving the specified goals. In this respect, responsibility accounting is not a conceptual island unto itself but is part of the total management system. Therefore, the system must be directly linked to the organization structure of the business and to other financial planning, measuring, and reporting systems in use.

Responsibility accounting and the organization structure

Three fundamental steps must be taken in order to have an effective responsibility accounting system that will meet the needs of a decentralized organization:

1. Responsibility for all revenues and costs must be assigned to individuals in the organization.
2. A structure of accounting for revenues and costs must be put in place which will capture and accumulate these items according to the organizational responsibilities as assigned.
3. A system for comparing accumulated revenues and costs with relevant targets by responsibility centers must be designed and implemented.

In theory, these steps could be taken in the order listed and it might appear possible to assign each task to a specific functional manager. In practice, the steps are interrelated and the implementation of each step will have a bearing on what can be done in the other steps. Consequently, the development of a complete responsibility accounting system must be an iterative process involving all interested parties in the organization. In this regard, the assignment of responsibilities should parallel closely the organization structure. A responsibility accounting system which might appear conceptually sound but which does not reflect the realities of the organization structure is likely to be ineffective.

The need to parallel the organization in a responsibility reporting system does not necessarily mean, however, that the responsibility and reporting system should match exactly the existing organizational arrangement. It is essential to understand first how the business really operates and which responsibilities the managers actually control. Lines and boxes on charts, even written position descriptions, may not reflect the real organizational responsibilities. If this is the case, responsibilities will require clearer definition or, in some instances, realignment before a meaningful responsibility accounting system can be implemented as an effective management tool. As a caution, if responsibilities are unclear, reporting of performance will not, in itself, serve to make them clear. The discipline of structuring an appropriate responsibility reporting system should be viewed by general management as an opportunity to sharpen organizational responsibilities with a view towards enhancing control and accountability.

Although responsibility for cost control should be assigned specifically to organizational units capable of controlling costs, this is easier in concept than in practice because many costs are separately or jointly controlled, either by separate organizations at the same level or to varying degrees by higher organization levels. Special arrangements for assigning responsibility will be necessary in these instances. Generally, costs can be assigned to organizational units based on the degree of control. In other situations, the solution may not be so readily apparent.

For example, in many large enterprises various organizational units provide services or products to other units. The responsibility accounting system must charge these services or products to the benefiting units on some rational basis. The nature of transfer pricing is a complex subject which is beyond the scope of this chapter. However, the reader should be aware that numerous methods are available to solve situations that may arise. These methods include transfer of goods or services at the market price, at cost, at cost plus a negotiated fee, or at a predetermined standard price for the measurement period. Depending upon the desired objective, then, there is an ample supply of methods, one of which will be suitable to the situation. Whatever pricing methodology is selected to transfer services or goods to other units, the responsibility accounting system should consider costs to be controllable on the basis transferred.

As another example, it may be necessary to allocate or assess certain costs from one unit to other units when it is not practical to keep an accounting of specific services performed for each unit. Such a need may arise, for example, when the true profitability of operating segments is required for pricing or market strategy purposes. In these instances it is imperative that corporate staff costs be included in the business results. Although these practices are essentially at variance with the responsibility accounting concept, it is possible to segregate responsibility reports into controllable and noncontrollable cost elements. Moreover, the component which incurs costs that are assessed out to other components can still be held accountable for the total costs it incurs before such assessments.

The process of determining which costs are properly controlled by various organizational units and the matching of these costs with the existing, or a revised, organization structure is, by far, the most difficult and the most critical aspect of implementing an effective responsibility reporting system. The experience of numerous companies, large and small, proves that it can be done in a workable fashion, however, and the evidence is that the process is worth the effort.

Integration with other financial systems

The financial reporting systems of a business may be viewed as existing to accomplish three main objectives or purposes as they relate to revenues and costs.

1. The calculation and reporting of operating costs and revenues—financial accounting.
2. The provision of information for managerial planning and decision making.
3. The control of operations.

Responsibility accounting relates primarily to the third major objective—*control*—and is a fundamental concept in providing financial information for this purpose. Under the responsibility accounting concept, a first principle of reporting information for control purposes is that revenues and costs must be *classified according to responsibility.* Other classifications of cost, such as aggregating total research and development costs for annual operating report purposes, are relevant to the requirements served by these other objectives.

A second principle of primary importance in reporting financial information for control purposes is that reported revenues and/or costs should be *compared with predetermined budgets.* In this regard, it is essential that budgets be established on a basis consistent with that which will be used in accumulating and reporting actual revenues and costs. Line management must be able to focus clearly on those elements necessary for their own success, which presumably will contribute to corporate success. Thus, the responsibility accounting system and the annual budgeting system, especially, must be linked closely together.

In practice, three separate financial recording and reporting systems are not established to serve each of the three main objectives. Rather, one flexible system is devised to serve each major purpose and, frequently, other purposes as well. Thus, the responsibility accounting system does not function apart from other financial systems. Classifications of cost by responsibility are necessarily integrated with the other classifications (for example, compensation, materials, supplies, services) that are needed for external financial reporting or for product cost determinations. This, of course, requires systems integration, but the essential responsibility accounting element that must be reflected in such integrated systems is the need to collect and report costs according to where they will be controlled, not according to how they may eventually need to be reported for other purposes.

In any business organization there are additional goals and related performance measures that are not directly measurable through the financial systems. These goals, such as human resource development, are properly includable in the total responsibility concept. However, accomplishments that are measurable by the financial accumulating and reporting systems will represent the more effective responsibility performance measures, since they are quantifiable. Goals that are not quantifiable are likely to be less effective, precisely because success or failure in attaining them cannot be measured. Also, the financial reporting system generally provides information in a timely manner which may not be the case when reports are required for less exacting measures of performance.

As to timeliness of reports, it should be noted that a financial system geared only to reporting monthly operating results and annual budgets will normally not permit timely implementation of contingency plans or other corrective action. An effective responsibility reporting system will also require weekly or daily reporting of some elements or activities. One such element that readily comes to mind is cash. The effective management of cash is a major concern of today's corporate management, and the total financial system must be tailored to accomplish this as well as other elements of sound business management if the operations control—inherent in the concept of responsibility accounting—is to be accomplished.

Thus, responsibility accounting is not only based on the organization structure; it should contribute to its refinement. In addition, it should be integrated with other financial systems in a way that permits control of performance through measurement by responsibility.

PROFIT CENTER RESPONSIBILITY ACCOUNTING

The complexity of most business entities usually increases faster than the size and diversity of the organization. These complexities emerge as the firm moves from single-product, single-plant, to multiproduct, multiplant stature. For the diversified firm, the dimensions of managerial control usually span a wide range of alternatives. The broadening of the required managerial perspective is the result of limitations placed on singular actions that will not apply "across-the-board" to a diverse organization, for a number of reasons such as:

Product cycles—short versus long cycle

Market segments—consumer versus original equipment manufacturers

Economies served—domestic versus international

Product resource requirements—labor intensive versus material intensive

Product and market constraints—regulated versus nonregulated

Business objectives—harvest/divest versus invest/grow

Competition—many/few, large/small

Each of these issues and more must be addressed if the total business activity is to be successful; and it is apparent that a single manager may find it difficult to focus on this diversity on a day-by-day basis without some loss of control. Thus, the need arises to decentralize the business and delegate responsibility.

However, if the decentralization process is not to result in loss of overall control at the corporate level, there must be an assignment of objectives and goals to operating segments and a reservation of certain authority by corporate management. Implementation of a responsibility accounting system should help retain overall control at the corporate level.

Once a multiproduct-multiplant business has been decentralized into separate business segments with a manager in charge of operations for each segment, the first requisite for responsibility accounting—*assignment of responsibility*—has already been met. The appropriate measures placed on these business segments ordinarily pertain to the accomplishment of profit objectives; for this reason, the segments are referred to as profit centers.

Profit center managers are also, of necessity, responsible for costs incurred by all organizational units within the segment; however, insofar as revenues are also their responsibility, the appropriate measurement of their performance properly focuses on profitability. These profitability measures can be expressed in many ways, including net income dollars, percent net to sales, percent return on investment, or residual income (dollar return after a capital charge).

In the decentralized company, then, the measurement of profitability at the segment level is the primary means of controlling operations. In this regard, certain questions can be raised as to how well managerial performance can be measured by profit performance. Should allocations of corporate costs be included in the profitability measure? How should the relationships among segments be considered? These questions are particularly relevant if these relationships place constraints on operating freedom. At this point it is essential to recognize that measurement of managerial performance through a profitability measure can be distinguished from a determination of the precise profitability of a business segment. Although similar in scope and often confused with each other, these two concepts are different. For example, it may be decided, for reasons of simplicity or management philosophy, to measure the performance of a segment manager without including corporate costs. These corporate costs could encompass corporate support overheads as well as income taxes, corporate research and development, and interest charges for capital employed in the business segment. On the other hand, to determine the profitability of the business segment, these corporate costs would be relevant. On balance, however, it can be argued that profitability measurements are complicated rather than simplified if corporate costs are excluded from profit center results. For example, the profit center manager may need cumbersome analyses or consultations with corporate personnel to ensure that decisions affecting business profitability are made correctly. In addition, the profit center manager's performance might be misjudged if capital is tied up in idle facilities without an associated interest charge.

Similarly, issues can be raised with respect to the appropriate *level* of profitability of a business segment, apart from the issue of what should be included in the profit calculation. For example, artificially high profits can be achieved by ignoring longer range business needs by failing to reinvest in facilities or by reducing research and development spending. Thus, while segregating revenues and costs of a separate operating segment and measuring performance in terms of profitability is the essence of a profit center concept, it is also true that many judgmental issues are associated with establishing a properly balanced measure and with interpreting the extent to which the measure can be utilized in the decision-making process. Relating this concept, for a moment, back to the need to establish performance measures in the form of budgets, it is evident that exceeding the budgeted profit by a substantial margin *may* be as indicative of a poor performance as is a significant shortfall. In this regard, the budget itself can serve as an equalizer for judging performance of managers in different businesses with different basic profitability outlooks—whatever the reason.

Reporting of profit center results is illustrated in Exhibits 1 and 2. The format of the statement in Exhibit 2 can be contrasted with the more traditional statement of operations in Exhibit 1, in which cost of sales is deducted from sales billed to reflect a gross margin, and selling and administrative expense is then deducted to arrive at income from sales. The statement in Exhibit 2 is in the *responsibility format,* which includes the profit

EXHIBIT 1

"A" COMPANY
Summary of Financial Operations
Year Ended September 30, 19XX
(amounts in millions)

	Actual	Budget	Percent of variance from budget
Sales of products and services	$15.5	$16.0	(3)%
Materials engineering and production costs	10.9	10.9	0
Gross margin	$ 4.6	$ 5.1	(10)
Selling, general, and administrative expenses	3.5	3.5	0
Operating margin	$ 1.1	$ 1.6	(31)
Other income	0	0.2	(U)
Earnings before taxes	$ 1.1	$ 1.8	(39)
Provision for taxes	(0.5)	(0.8)	(37)
Net earnings	$ 0.6	$ 1.0	(40)
Return on average investment	6.3%	10.0%	
Percent net income/Net sales billed	3.9%	6.3%	
Residual income	$ 0.1	$ 0.5	

Over/(under) budget.
U = unfavorable amount.

center as well as cost center concepts. Although this type of statement might be used for external reporting purposes, it is unlikely that it would have meaning to external statement users who have no role to play in control of costs. For internal use, however, it provides a tie in between cost center responsibility accounting within the segment and profit center responsibility accounting for the total segment. A review of these two statements indicates the advantage of the responsibility statement in that the following issues can be immediately raised for further analysis.

1. Marketing expense was 9 percent below budget. Is this the reason for failure to achieve the budgeted sales?
2. Why was manufacturing operating cost over budget when volume was less than budget?
3. Why were financial costs and corporate assessments over budget?

The information shown on Exhibit 1 is not in the proper format for the profit center manager to generate these questions.

EXHIBIT 2

"A" COMPANY
Summary of Financial Operations
Year Ended September 30, 19XX
(amounts in millions)

	Actual	*Budget*	*Percent of variance from budget*
Sales of products and services	$15.5	$16.0	(3)%
Direct material—in sales	3.1	3.2	(3)
Contributed value	$12.4	$12.8	(3)
Operating costs:			
Engineering	$ 1.8	$ 1.9	(5)
Manufacturing	6.0	5.8	3
Marketing	2.0	2.2	(9)
Finance	0.6	0.5	20
Relations	0.3	0.3	0
Administration	0.2	0.2	0
	$10.9	$10.9	0
Corporate assessments	0.4	0.3	33
	11.3	$11.2	1
Income from sales	1.1	$ 1.6	(31)
Other income	0	0.2	(U)
Taxes	(0.5)	(0.8)	(37)
Net income	$ 0.6	$ 1.0	(40)
Return on average investment	6.3%	10.0%	
Percent net income/Net sales billed	3.9%	6.3%	
Residual income	$ 0.1	$ 0.5	

Over/(under) budget.
U = unfavorable amount.

Returning for a moment to the second principal element of management systems, *motivation,* we can envision instances in which reporting for profit centers can be utilized as a measure of performance even though a fully decentralized delegation of authority does not exist. For example, a plant manager may not have responsiblity for marketing; but, nevertheless, he can be measured as if his plant were a profit center by establishing standard transfer prices for his output or for products sold from his plant.[1] In these cases, we would expect the stronger and more relevant motivation of profitability to provide more successful control than a cost center basis. Similarly, a service center such as a computer operation may be measured on a profit basis

---

[1] Masculine pronouns are being used for succinctness and are intended to refer to both females and males.

using, for example, prices as if the services had been purchased outside. The term *profit center* is usually used when profitability is determined for these segments although there is no delegation of complete responsibility for the operations of the segment. In these instances the concept is not profit center responsibility accounting, but rather the accumulation of financial information to serve the motivational aspects attendant to the management system concept. Nevertheless, such techniques do fall within the scope of the responsibility accounting process and, because the important elements of modern management systems are delegation, motivation, and measurement rather than an exact determination of profitability, such techniques are in wide use. Managerial style and motivational considerations will, of course, determine when and under what circumstances use of these techniques is desirable.

COST CENTER RESPONSIBILITY ACCOUNTING

Once a system of decentralized profit centers has been established, the profit center executive can implement control procedures to ensure that his own objectives are realized. If we assume here that further decentralization into lower tier profit centers is not an alternative, then lower tier managers can be held primarily responsible for control of costs only.

The responsibility accounting concept can then be used to achieve effective cost control. To institute such a system, all controllable costs are assigned to managers in the organization according to responsibility. Additionally, subdivisions of the major responsibilities are made according to the actual organization and responsibility within the business. Then, systems for accumulating and reporting can be designed. Since the accumulation system exists to support the reporting system, it is appropriate to consider, first, the nature of the reports which might be produced for various cost centers in line with the responsibility accounting concept.

Reporting system

The reporting system is characterized by two basic types of reports:

1. Each level of management receives a report detailing only those expenditures which he has been assigned to control and which he has elected not to redelegate. The report compares these expenditures individually and in total to a budget classified in the fashion that the manager requires.
2. Each manager also receives a report which lists the total expenditures which were delegated to each manager reporting to him as well as the total of the costs he, himself, controls. These, likewise, are compared to budget. Of course, first level management receives only the first report since they have not redelegated, or cannot redelegate, control of costs to any lower level.

Thus, there are but two types of reports: those which detail expenditures, and those which list the performance of reporting managers.

To illustrate this report structure, consider the simplified manufacturing organization shown on Exhibit 3. Exhibits 4 and 5 illustrate representative responsibilitiy reports which would be used for the various cost centers in this organization. In the interest of simplicity of illustration, only selected costs are shown on these reports.

Exhibit 4 is a report for one of the first-line manufacturing operations headed by a foreman, or unit manager. The following features of this report are significant:

First—There is a minimum of items on the report.

EXHIBIT 3

"A" Company manufacturing organization

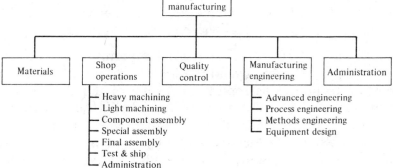

EXHIBIT 4
A.

"A" COMPANY
Operating Costs—Heavy Machining Operation
April 19XX

Expenditures:	Current month		Year-to-date	
	Amount	Variance	Amount	Variance
Compensation and benefits				
Direct employees	$22,600	$(1,800)	$ 85,000	$(5,050)
Indirect employees	14,200	1,600	51,000	2,600
Total	36,800	(200)	136,000	(2,450)
Scrap losses	2,200	150	6,800	450
Maintenance	6,500	1,800	21,200	300
Supplies services	300	(50)	1,050	(200)
Total expenditures	$45,800	$1,700	$165,050	$(1,900)

Over/(under) budget.

B.   **Cost trend**

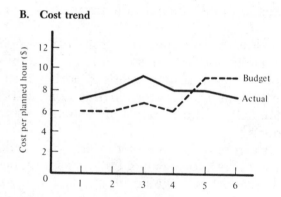

Second—The items on the report are those selected as appropriate to this particular unit.

Third—All costs incurred in this unit are shown and totaled.

Fourth—In addition to comparing actual expenditures with target, there is a trend line, also compared to target.

Exhibit 5 illustrates a report that the Superintendent, or Manager—Shop Operations, would receive. He has six unit managers reporting to him. This report is a listing of the expenditures for his six managers plus another line labeled Administration. The latter is to recognize that there are some activities in his subsection which the Manager-Shop Operations has elected to control. For these administrative expenditures, he would receive

EXHIBIT 5

"A" COMPANY
Operating Costs—Shop Operations
April 19XX

Responsibility:	Current month		Year-to-date	
	Amount	Variance	Amount	Variance
Heavy machining	$ 45,800	$ 1,700	$ 165,050	$(1,900)
Light machining	28,100	(1,500)	101,550	(1,760)
Component assembly......	52,200	(1,600)	220,600	2,200
Special assembly	53,100	2,400	229,100	(6,000)
Final assembly	20,600	(1,600)	80,450	(4,200)
Test and ship	55,000	1,500	251,000	5,050
Administration	18,200	(200)	71,300	2,100
Total	$273,000	$ 700	$1,119,050	$(4,510)

Over/(under) budget.

an additional report similar in general form to the report illustrated for the heavy machining operation. Note that all expenditures are, of course, compared to budget.

At this second level, then, there is no reporting of details, by type of expense. The Manager-Shop Operations has, instead, delegated to his six unit managers and to himself responsibility for control of separate parts of the total. Naturally, he would confer with a particular unit manager if, in total, that unit manager was out of line with budget. At that time a review of detailed expenditures might be undertaken.

A similar report would be furnished to the Manager of Manufacturing (and so on up the line), which would show the total performance of each subsection as well as administrative expense controlled by himself.

These reports represent the basic reporting structure that is required if costs are being controlled in accordance with the concept of delegated responsibility. Reports which cross-add similar categories of expenditures (such as shop supplies) across the lower levels of management are not needed for the purpose of cost control because the higher level manager does not control these expenses himself. He delegates their control to those managers reporting to him. Cross-added reports, however, may occasionally be needed for other reasons. Such reports might, for example, facilitate forecasting or be needed for planning changes in operations, such as reducing or increasing shifts due to overtime costs.

Ordinarily it is not necessary or desirable for a manager to receive copies of reports sent to managers reporting to him since he is holding them responsible for their total performance. This is true whether the reporting manager is receiving a report which details specific items of cost or one which only lists the performance of a still lower tier of management.

It would be well to emphasize that these monthly responsibility reports used in the control of costs may not provide all the information needed to manage a business. Managers also need what might be called *information reports*, which give them data needed to perform their other control functions. These reports might include items such as inventory levels, scrap and rework costs, number of direct labor employees, overhead rates, and so forth. The information provided on such reports can be tailored to the needs of each manager and such reports can be issued weekly if this is the requirement, or on whatever periodic basis is needed.

Accumulation system

Practically all cost reporting systems make use of two basic classifications, that is, by *type of expenditure* and by *function*. The cost accumulation system which supports the responsibility reporting structure represents a change in emphasis of the two classifications. With many older organizations, where there was a lack of clear-cut authority and responsibility for costs, emphasis was placed on accumulation of costs by type of expenditure within certain overall groupings. These groupings, such as manufacturing costs, engineering costs, and commercial and administrative costs, represented an effort to develop the cost of the function rather than the cost which that functional manager controls, as in responsibility accounting. On the old basis, for example, it would have been reasonable to include in manufacturing a fair proportion of costs associated with such items as payroll preparation or employee relations. Under responsibility accounting, however, these two activities are the responsibility of the financial and employee relations functions, respectively, and ordinarily remain in those functions. The costs assigned to Manufacturing are only those which they are responsible for controlling.

Having first classified all costs according to responsibility, the next job is to provide an accumulation of cost elements that are relevant to each responsible manager. The relevant elements will be different for different kinds of activities, and in this respect the accumulation system is not merely one set of common accounts—but rather subdivisions of costs tailored to the needs of the particular manager.

In summary, responsibility accounting requires directing the account structure towards the accumulation of costs by actual responsibility as a prime classification, and subdividing this according to responsibility assignments down to the first line of responsibility for management of costs. The further classification of costs by type of expenditures, insofar as control is involved, is merely a subdivision of these responsibility areas to serve as a tool in analyzing and controlling the costs in each responsibility center.

Other considerations

Although the general principle upon which responsibility accounting and reporting rests is quite simple, i.e., costs should be accumulated and reported to those managers who have been assigned responsibility for their control—there are a number of practical problems in establishing such a system. Perhaps the most fundamental problem is that of deciding whether responsibility for control rests where costs are *incurred* or where they are *authorized.*

In defining the general principles of responsibility accounting, it has been assumed that each manager has a specific job to do and that either he, himself, decides to perform any given activity, or he is required to do so by the needs of the business. He then proceeds to incur the costs and can be held fully responsible for them. In actual practice, however, there are many areas in which the work to be done by one manager may result from the decision of another manager to whom he does not report. In this case, the first manager will incur the cost but someone else has made the decision that the cost should be incurred. The first manager can only control the unit-cost level. A more significant control decision might have been made by the manager authorizing the expenditure in the first place. Examples of such situations would be a centralized graphic reproduction operation or a centralized tool room. In the graphics operation, the manager in charge can make decisions related to the most economical method of reproducing documents; however, other managers will control the volume of work he must produce. If costs are not charged back to the requester, there is a lack of control over the amount of work that is requested. However, by charging costs back to the requester, there may be loss of efficiency and control of costs in the reproduction operation.

The decision in these situations is a matter for action in each specific area. If arbitrary rules are adopted, the objective of responsibility reporting—current cost control—may be hindered. The decision in any particular case must be made according to what action will provide the best motivation for cost control. Nevertheless, the initial emphasis in responsibility reporting is, and should be, on control by the same individual who incurs the cost. The burden of proof should be on the assertion that better control is obtained by charging other people with costs which they do not directly incur. This is particularly true in cases where it is difficult to develop a proper predetermined value at which to bill the individual who does not incur the cost.

Other areas which frequently require careful consideration in developing a responsibility reporting system include:

Facility costs.   Should such costs as depreciation and heat, light, and power be considered the responsibility of one particular manager, or should they be charged to all using components?

Customer warranty costs.   Should the costs of satisfying customer complaints be (a) assigned in total to some function such as Marketing or Engineering, (b) analyzed for distribution to the various functions, or (c) retained at the top level because these costs cannot be assigned to individual functions?

Labor-related costs.   Should labor-related costs such as pension benefits be charged to the component where the labor is incurred on the premise that these costs follow the labor costs, or should there be an accumulation at some higher level on the basis that the lower level manager can do nothing to control the actual cost level? Also, incorporating these items in lower level reports may tend to complicate these reports and obscure the full impact of the items on the business.

Manager's salaries and expenses. Are these costs properly included in the manager's own report or are they controlled by the next higher level?

These grey areas result from two general conditions: (1) the conflict with other purposes for which information may be accumulated and (2) the inherent uncertainty and shared responsibility for some costs. The solution to the first condition lies in designing a total system of accumulating and reporting which aims to provide both responsibility accounting for cost control and information for other needs, without subordinating one to the other or unnecessarily mixing the separate needs in individual reports. With respect to the second condition, it has already been noted that while special arrangements may be needed in some cases, costs can generally be assigned based on the preponderance of control. An effective business enterprise must be an operating entity, not an accumulation of separate pieces. In order to make it operate, reasonable segregation of responsibility for performing a job and controlling costs must be assigned.

Thus, budgeting, accounting, and reporting of costs by responsibility cost centers is both a useful tool for planning and controlling costs to an established target and a way of looking at operations which should introduce more evaluation of worth versus costs into the planning activity.

REPORTING INTEGRATION

Integration of the responsibility reporting system with the informational needs of the business involves a reclassification and resummarization of costs and expenses. Exhibit 6 shows a simplified summary of costs for both control and informational purposes. Note the following:

1. For cost control purposes, a departmental cost summary can show the total of all controllable costs, categorized by each major responsibility function.
2. Costs that are controllable by other means can also be shown on the department cost summary.

EXHIBIT 6
"A" COMPANY

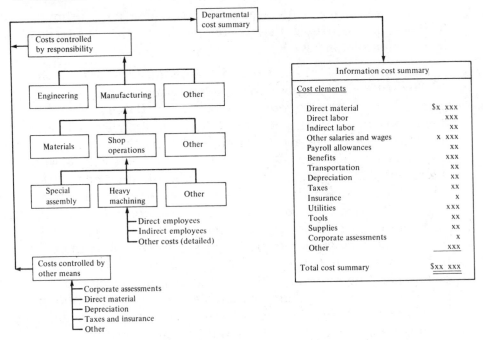

3. An informational cost summary used for other business purposes can be derived from the same cost elements and could show the elements of cost categorized by major item.

Note that similar cost summaries could be prepared for cost centers at any reporting level inasmuch as all controllable costs are accumulated in detail at the controlling levels and selected costs controlled by other means can also be assigned to various levels in the organization. For example, appropriate portions of depreciation, taxes, and insurance could be assigned to the manufacturing section based on inventory levels and plant and equipment records.

In summary, Exhibit 6 demonstrates the difference between detailed reporting of cost elements for information purposes and the reporting of costs by cost center for measurement and control purposes. From this, it is clear that responsibility accounting requires careful integration with the existing financial system

so that the same cost information serves each reporting requirement equally well.

ROLES OF OPERATING AND
FINANCIAL EXECUTIVES

A discussion of responsibility accounting would not be complete without describing the principal roles that the operating
and financial executives must take in establishing an effective
system. Although the points that will be discussed here may
be inferred from the previous material, it is the managers who
"make things happen." For this reason, a summary and reempha-
sis of their respective roles is required.

Operating executive

To implement a responsibility system, the operating executive
has three principal responsibilities. First, he should organize the
business in a fashion that will allow as much *responsibility* as
possible to be *delineated among the organizational units*. The
emphasis here is on delineation of responsibility, which does
not imply that he must delegate fully that responsibility. Imprecise delineation of responsibility will not only serve to make
the measurements unclear, but will more importantly result in
inefficiency of action. Informational systems can easily be designed to provide an upper-echelon manager with all the relevant business facts; but when a changed course of action is required, it is the corporation which has well-defined centers of
responsibility that can respond to those changes quickly, efficiently, and through a minimum of organizational channels.

A second major responsibility of the executive is to have a
*working knowledge of the implications of various financial
measures* that are associated with the delegation of responsibility.
The imposition of singular, and single-minded, goals may result
in misdirected performance. For example, with respect to profit
center measurements, focusing on a single measure—such as
return on sales—could work to exclude other desirable goals—
such as market share growth, total profits, and so forth. Similarly,
reliance on return on investment as a single measure could well
result in a manager receiving high marks for short-range achieve-

ments at the expense of longer term business viability because decisions to invest in added facilities were postponed or eliminated, or expensive leasing arrangements were selected. Therefore, with respect to performance measures, the executive must strike a balance among the many available measures that will best serve the overall corporate objectives. He cannot do this properly if the implications of the measures are not understood.

Finally, the executive must *establish goals that are achievable*. While this may appear to be self-serving, it is important that the motivational aspects of goals and objectives be realized, otherwise performance is likely to be less than expected. Although teamwork is desirable and face-to-face discussions should be held, it is not essential that agreement be reached on the targets but it is essential that the performing manager know what his target is. In many instances, it may be appropriate to challenge line management with a goal beyond what they believe is achievable, or at least beyond what they will admit is achievable. In this regard, however, the manager setting the goals must recognize that he, perhaps as much as anyone, is also responsible for the success or failure in achieving the targets.

Financial executive

Turning to the role of the financial executive, we find two principal responsibilities. First is the need to *establish systems that will report the required data accurately and in a timely manner*. Second, the financial executive *serves as an advisor to operating management*. Although providing accurate and timely data is not a very glamorous feat, nevertheless, the failure to do so is one of the major shortcomings of weak financial systems and does have significant consequences for the business. Inaccurate reports of cost and performance data will surely lead to erroneous decisions, and failure to provide timely reports may prevent decisions from being made at the time they are needed. In some instances, even what appears to be relatively timely information loses its impact because a one- or two-week delay may result in operating management refocusing on current and future problems, and they will be reluctant to review critically what they consider a "stale" report. Furthermore, the situation compounds itself as each hierarchy of management usually requires consolidated reports from the next lower tier. In some businesses this situation is tolerated because management is too sympathetic with the excuse that continual changes to the reporting system or to the organizational structure are at fault, when in fact the real problem is lack of system flexibility.

With respect to the second, and equally important responsibility, that of advising management, the financial executive must guide and assist the executive function in establishing goals that are truly meaningful for the particular business and ones which will motivate line management in the right direction. He must also be prepared to provide the required data, as well as trend charts and concise but perceptive analyses of selected items that may require specific management attention. In this respect, the role of the financial executive begins rather than ends with the establishment of the system. It should be recognized that the advice and counsel, provided by interpreting the reported results, may be more essential to managing the business than the numbers themselves. For example, a monthly review and estimate of operations might be provided to management which would include current month and year-to-date actual results for key items compared with budget, latest estimate, and prior year, along with budgeted and estimated amounts for the next month and total year. Significant variances can be highlighted by showing a schedule of sources of the variances, such as cost, price, volume, product mix, and timing, and then providing comments regarding the reasons for the variances.

CONCLUSION

The previous material has defined responsibility accounting and has provided an insight into the reasons for its development. Also, the inherent advantages of increased control of operations, as well as the mechanics required for implementation of the concept, were covered. Knowing that a little knowledge can be misleading, some additional perspective is in order on two possible pitfalls that should be avoided.

First, the system will not work if management is "sold" on the idea because of a promise that it will solve all control and measurement problems. Responsibility accounting must be viewed as a tool and a guide to be used in establishing goals and measuring results as part of an effective management control system. It cannot be viewed as a panacea for supplanting management judgment. Real world problems of cost transfers and allocations are just too complex and judgmental to expect a degree of precision that would obviate the need for judgment when a final assessment of performance is made.

Second, responsibility accounting serves the management system and is not a free standing financial system. Therefore, it cannot be implemented without the full support and leadership of operating management, as well as the cooperation of all levels of employees. Only limited success will result if a financial manager decides, on his own, to improve control with a responsibility accounting system.

10
Cost accounting and organizational behavior

John Grant Rhode*
Fulton M. Smith, Jr.†

INTRODUCTION

The issue of how cost accounting systems affect organizational behavior is a critical one for anyone interested in the determinants of organizational effectiveness. It is especially important to accountants and psychologists who are interested in understanding individual behavior in organizations. Because cost accounting systems are such an important part of complex organizations it is impossible to explain much of the behavior that takes place in organizations without examining them as information and control systems. Moreover, since effective information systems are essential for organizations to function at optimal levels, individuals interested in organizational behavior need to consider seriously the impact of these systems on behavior (Lawler and Rhode, 1976).

Knowledge of how information and control systems affect behavior is also important for those who design and implement cost accounting systems. Their whole purpose is to develop systems that will influence behavior so as to make it more effective.

* Lecturer, University of California.
† Director, Management Advisory Services, Deloitte Haskins & Sells.

Who is included in this large and somewhat diverse group? Most prominent are accountants who develop the financial information systems, budget, and standard costs systems. Also in this group are the management scientists who specialize in developing computer-based management information systems. In addition, industrial engineers who develop standards and measurement systems need to understand the effects of information and control systems on behavior.

Operating managers also should be aware of how information and control systems affect behavior. They need to know how to use the systems in order to influence the behavior of their subordinates. There is evidence that the impact of a particular information system is strongly influenced by the way line managers utilize the information the system produces. Good management practice must involve the utilization of information and control system data to influence behavior. It is unrealistic to expect managers to know instinctively how best to use the various information and control systems that exist in an organization to influence behavior. They need to be trained to respond properly to the information received.

There has been an increasing recognition during recent years that behavioral science knowledge and research should be used to understand how control systems should and do operate. Writers in the fields of accounting, industrial engineering, and systems design have called for the increased use of behavioral science knowledge in their fields. This call has been heard perhaps most clearly, loudly, and consistently in the field of accounting.

In 1967, Roy and MacNeill recommended that "the common body of knowledge for beginning CPAs include fundamental training in both psychology and sociology with emphasis upon those parts of both subjects focused upon the behavior of formal organizations (p. 234)." Two important behavioral phenomena, communication and decision making, are emphasized. Once it is decided that a control system is created to influence behavior, then study of human behavior must be part of the study of information and control systems.

Unfortunately, until recent years limited information was available on how information and control systems affect behavior. Consequently, those people who designed control systems had to rely on untested and often invalid assumptions about the nature of human behavior. This situation has now changed sufficiently so that a chapter on information and control systems could be written. Hopefully, this is a first step in the direction of providing a better indication of the relationship between information (or cost accounting) systems and organizational behavior.

THE ROLE OF INFORMATION AND CONTROL SYSTEMS IN ORGANIZATIONS

Information systems and organizational effectiveness

The literature concerned with accounting systems is full of many anecdotes documenting the ineffectiveness and negative effects of information and control systems in organizations. For example, Dearden (1960, 1961) described managers who were reluctant to replace equipment, even when it was in the company's economic interest, because of the heavy book losses that would be reflected in their current performance reports. In a similar vein, Beyer (1963) noted a case of managers scheduling work on old equipment with low unit depreciation charges even though new equipment had lower variable costs. By trying to reduce the total costs reported on their performance reports, the managers increased the company's total processing costs. In a classic article, Jasinski (1956) has described how one company's production measures caused maintenance problems. As one foreman described the situation:

> We really can't stop to have our machines repaired. In fact, one of our machines is off right now, but we'll have to gimmick something immediately and keep the machine going because at the end of the month, as it is now, we simply can't have a machine down. We've got to get those pieces out. Many times we run a machine right to the ground at the end of the month trying to get pieces out, and we have to spend extra time at the beginning of the month trying to repair the machine (Jasinski, 1956, p. 107).

The many cases of control systems causing dysfunctional behavior raises some crucial issues about the general effectiveness of information and control systems. Probably the most important question is whether the kind of breakdowns described occur frequently. The answer seems to be yes. A large body of research suggests that information and control systems often fail to accomplish their purpose. The systems are often fed invalid data by the members of organizations and they often cause other dysfunctional behavior. Why does this happen? Can information systems be designed to be more effective? This chapter will explore these issues. But before we can deal with them, we need to understand why organizations create information and control systems, the different types of systems, and the characteristics that all systems share.

Need for information and control systems

One reason for information and control systems is the difficulty of coordinating and controlling the activities of members of organizations. A group of people constitute an organization only if there is some coordination among the activities they perform; some type of control is an inevitable result of the need to coordinate activities. The coordination and order created out of the diverse interests and potentially different behaviors of members of organizations is largely a function of control (Tannenbaum, 1968). Control of an organization and coordination of its activities are impossible without information about what is occurring in that organization; thus information systems are developed.

Small organizations typically do not have extensive formalized information and control systems. Managers responsible for coordination and control often observe personally all the activities of their employees. As a result, these managers feel little need for a formal information system. For example, some small organizations may have a manager who represents the only information and control system in that organization. However, large organizations, with substantial specialization of function, usually contain a number of formal information and control systems.

It is not accidental that control systems seem to be more prominent and better developed in large organizations where there is a division of labor and specialization of function. These are the organizations that most need control systems because they have the most severe coordination and information processing problems. They are usually so large physically that no one can personally observe and control all the activities. Consequently, they are in danger of having their operating "parts" fly off in different directions. General Creighton Abrams made this point clearly in his testimony on a dysfunctional system:

> Rules have been our way of life out there. If I or any other commander picks and chooses among the rules, it will unravel in a way that you will never be able to control. A lot of these rules looked silly to many of the men. In a military, in a purely military sense, they appear silly, but they must be—if you are going to hold it together—they must be followed (*Time*, 1972, p. 14).

Abram's statement agrees with a study (Haire, 1959) that pointed out that large organizations frequently have proportionately more people involved in "holding the organization together" than do small organizations, because they have the greatest need to be held together.

Complex organizations usually have two major elements to their control system: *internal control* and *budgetary control.* It is not sufficient for an organization simply to measure its gains or losses in financial terms. There must also be a safeguarding of the assets or resources of the enterprise. Thus, internal control procedures are established to insure that all cash received is properly credited to the organization, that cash disbursed represents payment for necessary and expected expenditures, and that inventory and other assets owned and controlled by the organization are safe from theft and are properly used. The system that facilitates such safeguarding of cash and other assets is the *internal control system*—an extension of the financial reporting system and an integral component of the total information processing system. The need for a strong internal control system was well articulated by Carmichael (1970) in a series of hypotheses frequently held by accountants who design, operate, and audit internal control systems. These hypotheses maintain that individuals have inherent mental, moral, and physical weaknesses, that the threat of prompt exposure will deter an individual from committing fraud, and that an individual who is independent will recognize and report irregularities. In sum, these human weaknesses make an extensive internal control system necessary.

Together with the internal control system, the *budget* is one of the most critical financial documents available to managers in large organizations. Indeed, one of the most extensively researched areas in accounting is the budget and its effect on people and enterprises.

The traditional, or scientific management, view of employees as inefficient beings whose work activities must be closely controlled forms the basis for most of the logic defending the need for budgets. The primary concern of scientific management is to promote efficiency and thereby generate higher profits. Moreover, until Argyris' (1951) classic study, *The Impact of Budgets on People*, not much attention was paid to the negative behavioral side effects of budgets; much of the literature emphasized how the budget could help management make higher profits.

Characteristics of control systems

In some ways many of the cost accounting systems that operate in organizations seem to have little in common. Since organizations differ widely in their goals, structure, resources, and management styles, so will the details of their cost accounting systems differ. As we have noted, the systems differ widely in the kinds of information they deal with and in the audience they are intended for. Yet, they do have two important characteristics in common:

First they all *collect, store, and transmit information* in the form of abstract measures of reality.

a. Usually they deal with information about the condition of the organization in the form of measures that are quantitative (for example, the cost and quantity of production) and that can be understood only by trained personnel.

b. The collected abstract information is stored and transmitted in a specific form and with a specific frequency. For example, a company makes quarterly profit reports based on a particular set of accounting practices regarding its methods of treating inventory and depreciation.

c. The summarized information is distributed to a specific, usually predetermined, group of people. The group may or may not include all the members of the organization. Some information is given to only a few people in the organization, while other information is more public (for example, earnings reports for corporations).

Second, all cost accounting systems try to accomplish the same thing—*influence behavior*. The crucial aspect of any control system is its effect on behavior. As Anthony (1965) has noted, the central function of a management control system, therefore, must be motivation. The system needs to be designed in a way that assists, guides, and motivates management to make decisions and act in ways that are consistent with the overall objectives of the organization. Financial control systems provide clear examples of systems that are created to influence behavior. Different systems are intended to influence different groups of individuals, but they all are intended to influence behavior.

Information and control systems typically try to influence behavior by specifying what kind of behavior is appropriate and by providing some means of gathering information about the adequacy of the behavior that takes place. Management uses this information for several purposes: to coordinate the activities of different parts of the organization; as a basis for taking corrective action when problems exist; and to reward and punish the behavior of members of the organization.

As Argyris (1957) clearly stated, implicit in the design of any control system is a set of assumptions about what causes human behavior. Traditional reward-based control systems assume that:

a. Man is rational and motivated to maximize his economic gain.
b. Man is not a social animal.
c. Man can be treated in a standardized manner.
d. Man needs to be stimulated by management if he is to work.

This set of assumptions about human behavior does not, of course, fit with what is known. It is precisely because people don't fit these assumptions that control systems often lead to dysfunctional behavior. Fortunately, a body of literature exists that can help us make valid assumptions about the causes of human behavior. From this knowledge it is often possible to predict how individuals will react to information and control systems.

DYSFUNCTIONAL EFFECTS OF COST ACCOUNTING SYSTEMS

There is little question that information and control systems often produce dysfunctional behavior. Numerous studies have documented the kinds of dysfunctional behavior that typically occur. Four types have received the most attention: rigid bureaucratic behavior, strategic behavior, the production of invalid information, and resistance. We will discuss these in turn and then try to specify when control systems are likely to produce these behaviors.

Rigid bureaucratic behavior

Control systems can cause employees to behave in ways that look good in terms of the control system measures but that are dysfunctional so far as the generally agreed upon goals of the organization are concerned. This phenomenon, referred to as *rigid bureaucratic behavior,* has been described by a number of authors (see Merton, 1940; Selznick, 1949; and Gouldner, 1954). It comes about because certain conditions lead people to act in whatever ways will help them look good on the measures that are taken by control systems. In many cases this is a functional outcome, but in others it is not. In some cases it results in rigid, inflexible, dysfunctional behavior because that is what is required by the system. There are a number of examples of this phenomenon in the social science literature.

Blau (1955) analyzed the operation of a department in the public employment agency of a state government. The agency's "major responsibility is to serve workers seeking employment and employers seeking workers" (p. 19). The tasks performed by the department included interviewing clients, helping them to fill out application forms, counseling them, and referring them to jobs. The organization saw these activities as instrumental to the accomplishment of its objectives, and instituted a control system to be sure they were done. To evaluate the individual interviewers, managers kept statistical records of such things as how many interviews a particular interviewer conducted. The effect of this control system was to motivate the employees to perform those kinds of behavior that were measured by the system (for example, interviewing). Unfortunately, this did not always contribute to the organizational goal of placing workers in jobs. As Blau points out:

> An instrument intended to further the achievement of organizational objectives, statistical records constrained interviewers to think of maximizing the indices as their major goal, sometimes at the expense of these very objectives. They avoided operations which would take up time without helping them to improve their record, such as interviewing clients for whom application forms had to be made out, and wasted their own and the public's time on activities intended only to raise the figures on their record. Their concentration upon this goal, since it was important for their ratings, made them unresponsive to requests from clients that would interfere with its attainment (p. 43).[1]

Babchuk and Goode (1951) have provided an interesting case study that highlights how control systems, when combined with rewards, can cause employees to behave dysfunctionally. They studied a selling unit in a department store where a pay incentive plan was introduced to pay employees on the basis of sales volume. Total sales initially increased but the pay plan was not functional as far as the long-term goals of the organization were concerned. There was considerable "sales grabbing" and "tying up the trade" as well as a general neglect of such unrewarded and unmeasured functions as stock work and arranging merchandise for displays.

It is possible to cite a number of other examples of situations where employees in large organizations respond to control systems with rigid control-system-oriented behavior that is dysfunctional from the point of view of the organization. In fact, the negative connotation that has become attached to the initially neutral term, bureaucracy, stems from just this kind of behavior. Each of us has probably had many experiences where people representing formal organizations have dealt with us in ways that all the parties acknowledged were dysfunctional for both the organization and ourselves.

The views of a number of sociologists about the bureaucratic behavior phenomenon have been summarized by March and

---

[1] Material reprinted from *Dynamics of Bureaucracy* by P. M. Blau by permission of the University of Chicago Press. © 1955 by The University of Chicago. All rights reserved.

Simon (1958). Merton's (1940) model shows that rigidity stems from the emphasis on reliability and from the need to defend individual actions. However, Merton does not explain why *not all* individuals respond this way to the emphasis on reliability, nor does he say anything about the conditions that favor people responding this way. Clearly, not everyone responds to control systems with rigid behavior all the time. People are often willing to break the rules to get things done. Frank (1959), in discussing Soviet management practices, has noted that managers often violate some standards and even laws in order to keep their organizations functioning effectively. This occurs so much that it has become socially legitimate. It is also interesting that one form of labor bargaining is a work-to-rules action. What this means is that, unlike normal times, the employees follow the rules closely, observing the letter of the law, and as a result the organization functions much less effectively. It is also obvious that organizations differ widely in the degree to which the members rigidly respond to the rules and measures set up by the control system (Burns and Stalker, 1961). Part of the explanation for this difference rests in the nature of the control systems that are used in different organizations, and part of it rests in the nature of the individuals that work in different organizations.

Strategic behavior

In addition to producing the kind of long-term rigid bureaucratic behavior that has been described so far, information systems can cause employees to engage in what Cammann (1974, 1977) has called *strategic or defensive behavior*. Strategic behavior involves actions designed solely to influence information system results so that they will look good or acceptable for a certain time period. This kind of behavior does not involve feeding false data to the systems; rather, it usually involves altering behaviors for a period of time to make the control system measures look acceptable. In this respect it is like the kind of rigid bureaucratic behavior that has been discussed so far. Like bureaucratic behavior it also is not always dysfunctional for the organization. However, unlike bureaucratic behavior it only involves a short-term behavior change. For example, if a manager needs to buy a piece of equipment and it's near the end of a budget period, he or she may make a strategic choice. If money is left in the budget, he or she probably will buy the equipment to use up the budget. On the other hand, if the budget has been spent, the purchase probably will be deferred until the next budget period to keep from overspending the budget. From the point of view of organizational effectiveness, it probably won't make much difference if the equipment is bought at the beginning of one period or the end of another, and in either case valid data are being reported. Still, the budget system is clearly influencing the behavior of the manager in the sense that the manager is behaving in a strategic way in order to look good on the information system measures.

An interesting example of managers engaging in strategic behavior to keep their facility open occurred in a gold mine. In this particular company, mines were shut down after the yield per ton of ore dropped below a certain level. One old marginal mine managed to stay open for several extra years because of the strategic behavior of its management. It happened that the mine contained a very rich pocket of ore. Instead of mining this all at once the management used it as its reserve. Every time the yield of the ore it was mining fell below an acceptable level, it would mix in a little high grade ore so that the mine would remain open. This was dysfunctional as far as the company was concerned, since maximum cost effectiveness would have been achieved by mining all the high grade ore and then closing the mine.

There are numerous other examples of strategic behavior in the literature where employees develop JIC (just in case) and CYA (cover your ass) files in order to defend any decisions they have made. Jasinski (1956) and Hopwood (1972, 1973, 1974*a*, *b*) have written about how control systems have led to dysfunctional maintenance and production schedules. Thus, the evidence is overwhelming that strategic behavior is fostered by information and control systems.

Invalid data reporting

All control systems need valid data about what is occurring in the organization to be effective, yet behavioral science research shows that often false data are obtained (see Wilensky,

1967). As Argyris (1964, 1971) points out, control systems tend to be effective and to produce valid information only for the unimportant and programmed problems.

Evidence suggests that control systems produce two kinds of *invalid data:* invalid data about what can be done and invalid data about what has been done. The first kind of invalid data, of course, makes planning difficult, while the second makes the control of day-to-day activities difficult. The research on budgets and on piece-rate payment systems provides a number of good examples of situations where organizations are given invalid data about what is possible. Much of the available research data is from case studies and thus it is difficult to establish how widespread the production of invalid data is. To understand how and why invalid data are reported, it is worth reviewing a few of the case studies that have illustrated this phenomenon.

Whyte (1955) has provided some graphic case examples of how individuals distort the data that are fed into production measuring systems. Most of Whyte's examples are cases where individuals under pay incentive systems distort data about the kind of production possible on a given job.

Gardner (1964) has also pointed out that employees often give invalid data in industry, and provided an example of how it can occur:

> In one case, a group, who worked together in assembling a complicated and large-sized steel framework, worked out a system to be used only when the rate setter was present. They found that by tightening certain bolts first, the frame would be slightly sprung and all the other bolts would bind and be very difficult to tighten. When the rate setter was not present, they followed a different sequence and the work went much faster (pp. 164–165).

Argyris (1951,1964), Hofstede (1967), Hopwood (1973), and others have pointed out that employees also often provide misleading data when they are asked to give budgetary estimates. Not surprisingly, they tend to ask for much larger amounts than they need. On the other hand, in instances where a low budget estimate is needed in order to get a budget or project approved (for example, under some program planning and budgeting systems, Lyden and Miller, 1968), a low estimate is submitted. Managers submit their requests because they realize that their budget request will be cut, and to play the game they must come in with a high initial budget figure. The bargaining process they go through is not too dissimilar from the one that goes on between the time-study man and the blue collar employee. Both the time-study man and the manager try to get valid data about what is possible in the future, and the employees who are subject to the control system often give invalid data and try to get as favorable a standard, or budget, as they can. Budget setting sessions can degenerate into a game of seeing how much slack can be placed in the budget by the subordinate and how little slack is allowed by the superior. As Schiff and Lewin (1970) have cogently stated, slack in budgets—the process of underestimating revenues and overstating costs—exists because many managers prefer to operate in a slack environment. It makes sense for managers to opt for slack since the negative sanctions for missing a tight budget are likely to have more impact than the rewards for making a tight budget (Onsi, 1973).

How frequently do employees consciously provide invalid data when standards and budgets are being set? It is impossible to come up with any hard figures, but the research on standard setting suggests that it happens much of the time (Lawler, 1971). There is less evidence on how often it occurs in budget setting, but what data there are suggest that it happens much of the time there, too. In this situation as in the standard setting situation there is usually low trust, and as a study by Mellinger (1956) shows, when there is low trust, people are likely to conceal data or to communicate invalid data (see also Rosen and Tesser, 1970).

Roethlisberger and Dickson (1939), in their classic study of the Bank Wiring Room, point out how employees can manage the kind of production reports that go outside their work group. In the Bank Wiring Room the employees were on a pay incentive plan and they wanted to show a consistent daily production figure. They did this by not reporting what they produced on some days and on other days reporting things as having been produced that were never produced. Similar examples have been cited by others who have looked at the way employees react to financial incentive systems (Whyte, 1955; Lawler, 1971).

There are also data that suggest that employees will consciously feed invalid information into management information systems (Argyris, 1971; Mumford and Banks, 1967; Pettigrew,

1970, 1972, 1973). One reason for such falsification seems to be to cover up errors or poor performance. Employees also feed invalid data to the management information systems to make the system look bad and to discourage people from using it. Invalid data are also sometimes fed into a control system simply because control systems occasionally demand data that simply are not, and cannot be, collected. Faced with this situation an employee may choose to estimate the data rather than admit that it does not exist, or give up on the system. This would seem to be a particular problem where computer-based management information systems are being installed. They often call for historical cost, production, and other data that simply are not available (Argyris, 1971).

Resistance

Every discussion of the behavioral problems associated with control systems points out that they often meet strong resistance from the people who are subject to them. Rarely, however, do these discussions show that control systems can also fulfill some important needs people have because they provide feedback and structure, and that for this reason many people want a control system. Virtually every author who discusses control systems tends to explain the resistance to them in terms of their being perceived as a threat to the need satisfaction of employees (Argyris, 1971; Caplan, 1971; Mumford and Banks, 1967; Pettigrew, 1970; and Whisler, 1970 a, 1970 b. They then go on to emphasize how control systems can threaten the satisfaction of a number of different needs. Lawler (1971) and Whyte (1955) have shown how the imposition of a pay incentive, performance measurement system can threaten the satisfaction of social, esteem, and security needs. Argyris (1951) and others have shown how budgets can do the same thing. Along similar lines, Argyris (1971), Gibson and Nolan (1974), Mumford and Banks (1967), and Whisler (1970 b) have pointed out how computer-based management information systems can threaten the satisfaction of social, security, esteem, autonomy, and self-realization needs. Pettigrew (1970, 1972) has pointed out that control systems also often significantly change the power and status relationships in an organization.

The questions that remain concern why control systems are generally seen as such significant threats to the satisfaction of so many needs, and why they significantly change the power relationships in organizations. There are a number of reasons, the most significant of which will be discussed next.

Control systems can automate expertise. Control systems can automate or computerize jobs that presently are considered to require expertise (Carroll, 1967; Pettigrew, 1970, 1973; and Gibson and Nolan, 1974). The effect of this can be to make superfluous a skill that a person has developed and has been respected for having. This phenomenon seems to occur most frequently when management information systems (MIS) are installed. Such systems can have a tremendous impact on the nature of middle- and lower-level management jobs. For example, they can make costing, purchasing, and production decisions that previously were the essence of many management jobs. Because of this, Leavitt and Whisler (1958) have pointed out that the potential is present for the elimination of many management jobs. This has not happened, and it may not ever happen, but there is still the potential for automating or computerizing many jobs. Even if systems don't lead to the elimination of managerial jobs, they may make managerial jobs less desirable because they lead to a "rationalization" and "depersonalization" of managerial work (Carroll, 1967).

The elimination and depersonalization of jobs certainly are not restricted to managerial jobs. Pettigrew (1973) has provided an example of how stock order clerks saw computerization as potentially making unnecessary the skills they had developed to do their jobs. It didn't turn out that way, but the point is that they feared it would happen. A study of the impact of computerization on white collar jobs in a bank also found that computerization was seen as making useless the expertise that was required to do some jobs (Mumford and Banks, 1967). A crucial factor in understanding the impact of computerized information systems seems to be the stage of their development. Gibson and Nolan (1974) have suggested that there are four stages. During the first stage (installation) computers have a tendency to produce strong job displacement anxieties. This problem is particularly likely to occur at the lower levels of organizations. It is only when the systems reach stage four (maturity) that they are likely to be in a position to displace middle-level managers. At this point they are devoted to applications touching on critical business operations and the head of the system is a member of top management.

To the extent that control systems can automate, standardize, and rigidify work, people will see them as threatening their need satisfaction in a number of areas. Particularly relevant would appear to be satisfaction in the status, autonomy, and security need areas: security, because the person may feel more expendable; status, because what the person is respected for can become valueless; and autonomy, because the new system may seriously restrict the person's freedom to perform the job (Argyris, 1971).

Control systems can create new experts and give them power. Pettigrew (1970, 1973) gives an excellent example of how the installation of a computerized MIS created a new power elite in one organization. There was considerable jockeying for position within the organization and some groups' power and status were reduced. The individuals who ended up in control of the system, however, gained in power; they not only didn't resist the system, they pushed for its expansion and development into a stage four system. In another report, Pettigrew (1972) stresses how information can be a source of power in an organization and how the individuals who run Management Information Systems (MIS) can find themselves in the sometimes powerful and satisfying role of gatekeeper even though they are in staff positions. This is particularly likely to occur as the systems approach stage four.

It is probably safe to assume that no matter what control system is involved, there is some group that will gain as a result of its installation and another that will lose. In the case of budgets the winners typically are the accountants that run them, in the case of incentive systems it is the time-study experts, and in the case of MIS it is the computer experts and staff people who run them. These people favor installation of the system because the system helps them. However, there are usually others who lose power to these people. They typically see their power, status, and job security threatened as a result of the new control system, and resist it.

Control systems have the potential to measure individual performance more accurately and completely. Certain kinds of control systems can increase the validity of performance measurement in an organization by improving both the accuracy of the performance data collected and its inclusiveness. For example, moving from a simple superior's rating of performance to a performance evaluation system based on both quantitative responsibility accounting data and production data can increase the accuracy of the available performance data. Some employees welcome this since it reflects positively on their performance and increases their own position in the organization. Others feel that such objective data will put them in a less favorable light than they are in presently. In fact, they might see the installation of such an objective evaluation system as threatening their job security, their status, and their power in the organization. Thus, while one group will favor better measurement, another group is likely to resist it.

Argyris (1971) has talked about how an MIS can lead to leadership based more on competence than on power. In many ways this point is similar to the one being made here. Both are pointing out that with better performance data the highest level of need satisfaction is more likely to go to the more competent. This is a positive outcome for some, but it may be resisted by those who doubt their own competence but have achieved reasonably satisfactory positions in organizations.

Control systems can change the social structure of an organization. Changes in a control system can produce major changes in the social relationships in an organization (Mumford and Banks, 1967). They can break up social groups, pit one friend against another, create new social groups, and, as was pointed out earlier, by creating new experts they can change the status and power of organization members. This is dramatically illustrated in studies where pay incentive plans, work measurement systems, and computerized MIS have been installed or altered. Changes in these control systems almost always have a strong impact on the social relationships in the organization. Some people have less opportunity to form friendships after the changes have been made, others have more. Some people end up pitted in a competitive way against people with whom they formerly had cooperative relationships. Because of the potential impact of control systems on social need satisfaction, it is not surprising that some employees see control systems as threats to their social need satisfaction and for that reason resist the installation of such systems.

Control systems can reduce opportunities for intrinsic need satisfaction. Information systems can help provide feedback about performance, thus they can help create opportunities for psychological success and intrinsic satisfaction. However, they can also reduce the opportunities available for experiencing psychological success if, as often happens, they reduce the amount of autonomy employees have by specifying in considerable detail how jobs have to be done. This has already happened in many jobs where incentive pay and budget systems are in effect, and it appears to be about to happen in many jobs because of the installation of automated information systems. If, as Carroll (1967) says, real time decisions will soon be made by centralized management information systems, then it certainly appears that many lower level jobs in organizations will lose their autonomy.

The fact that control systems can provide feedback may not compensate for the fact that they may decrease autonomy, since this often is enough to prevent people from experiencing intrinsic satisfaction from task accomplishment. Naturally, when people see that the control system will reduce their autonomy and thereby their opportunities for experiencing psychological success and intrinsic satisfaction, they will resist the system if they value these feelings.

CAUSES OF DYSFUNCTIONAL BEHAVIOR

So far we have discussed four kinds of dysfunctional behavior that information systems can produce: rigid bureaucratic behavior, strategic behavior, invalid data reporting, and resistance. Now we need to consider in detail when control systems are likely to lead to these kinds of behavior. Dysfunctional behavior is not a necessary result of the existence of an information and control system; it only occurs when the system has characteristics that produce dysfunctional behavior.

Characteristics of sensor measures

As far as producing dysfunctional behavior, the *completeness of measures* is a mixed picture. Complete measures seem to produce less rigid bureaucratic behavior and less strategic behavior, but typically produce more resistance and perhaps more invalid data than incomplete measures. Let us look at each of these in turn so that we can understand the mixed impact of completeness.

By definition, rigid bureaucratic behavior should not exist when complete measures are used. It results when people perform only a limited part of their job because that is all that is measured. Several examples were given at the beginning of this chapter. The study by Babchuk and Goode (1951) provides a good example of a control system that failed to measure all the necessary or relevant behavior, while the study by Blau (1955) shows what can occur when systems measure activities rather than results. Another example is the case of a trailer company that decided to measure their salespeople on how many trailers they sold. The result was a dramatic increase in trailer sales, a number of sales to poor credit risks, and a sales lot full of overpriced trade-ins. The dysfunctional behavior in all of these examples occurred for one simple reason: an incomplete measure of individual performance was used. It was incomplete either because it measured only activities and not results, or because it measured only some of the results necessary for organizational effectiveness.

Completeness leads to resistance because it often is a threat to individual need satisfaction. As was noted earlier, the use of better performance measures can make some individuals look better and others worse. It can also reduce the autonomy of individuals by making it impossible for them to ignore performing well in unmeasured areas.

The installation of an MIS or a budgeting system can, for example, measure an aspect of a manager's performance that has not been measured before. Again, some managers might want this while others resist it. Specifically, those managers who see themselves as doing poorly in the area about to be measured would be expected to resist the installation of the new control system. Other managers might also resist it because it would restrict their freedom to perform. The more that is measured, the less freedom there is to disregard certain aspects of performance in order to do well in those areas that are measured.

Completeness is unlikely to have a strong impact on the tendency of individuals to produce invalid data. There are situations where it might, however. As has been mentioned, when more complete measures are generated individuals often find performing well more difficult because they have to be concerned about more performance areas. They can no longer ignore unmeasured X to look good on measured Y. This pressure for performance can force individuals to provide false data and lead them to resist information and control systems.

Objectivity is also a mixed blessing as far as dysfunctional behavior is concerned. It can lead to rigid bureaucratic behavior because it can make it obvious that measures are not complete. One of the advantages of subjective measures (like a superior global performance rating) is that they can potentially include everything. When measures are objective, it is clear what they include and what they don't include. This is fine if the measures are complete; it is not fine if they are incomplete. Objectivity can encourage strategic behavior in the same way. Strategic behavior is only effective if there are clear ways to influence measures.

It is difficult to say whether objective or subjective measures are likely to be resisted more. When superior-subordinate trust is low, subjective ones probably will be resisted more for obvious reasons. Individuals do not like to be measured by systems they cannot trust. Some individuals, however, may resist objective measures because they often allow for better measurement and for potentially embarrassing comparisons among individuals. Individuals who will not look good on objective measures resist them because they have little to gain and much to lose from better measures. Thus, both objective and subjective measures are resisted, but usually for different reasons.

Individuals provide invalid data to both objective and subjective measurement systems. Earlier in this chapter, there were a number of examples of how employees provide false data to their bosses and to time-study experts. A clear example of workers providing false data to an objective system occurred recently in an automobile plant. A telemetric system was set up to count the number of parts that went through a certain machine. At the end of one week, the production engineers found that the system showed the employees had produced almost twice as many finished products as they had received parts for. It seems that the workers found out how to fool the counter and decided to see how many parts they could run up.

Overall, employees probably are more likely to try to distort subjective measures than objective ones. For one thing, providing false data to subjective measures is easier and the possible repercussions are less serious. Also, it seems to be true that biasing is most likely to occur where there is uncertainty (March and Simon, 1958; Pettigrew, 1970). This means that a manager is more likely to report that morale is high when it is low and that a group of subordinates is working well when they are working poorly, than he or she is to report false data about whether the budget was made. Or in the case of a commander in Vietnam, he was more likely to report invalid data on enemy casualties than his own. One implication of this, of course, is that organizations need to mistrust measures of subjective dimensions, particularly when the sensor is the person responsible for the measure and extrinsic rewards are involved.

Uninfluenceable measures tend to produce invalid data and resistance but not rigid bureaucratic behavior or strategic behavior because, if measures are truly uninfluenceable, these behaviors will not accomplish their objective—making the person look good on the measures. Uninfluenceable measures are resisted because, when individuals cannot influence measures, they don't get valid feedback on their performance and they are unable to influence the kind of extrinsic rewards they receive.

Individuals seem to feel justified in feeding systems invalid data when they are being evaluated and measured based on measures they cannot influence by normal job performance. The unfairness of the situation the organization has placed them in seems to justify their presenting false data. Of course, in some cases when individuals cannot influence the measures by normal job behavior, they cannot do it by presenting false data either. Corporate profits sometimes fit into this category. They are often influenced by factors beyond the control of most employees and, because of the way they are audited, they are difficult to falsify.

There are, of course, famous cases (Yale Express, Penn Central, Equity Funding) where the top officers of the companies have presented false data and for a while have even influenced profits in the direction they wanted. These are the exceptions rather than the rule, however.

Nature of standards

When standards are seen as unreasonably difficult, they tend to produce rigid bureaucratic behavior, strategic behavior, invalid data, and considerable resistance. A clear illustration of this point is provided by Berliner's (1961) description of the situation faced by plant managers in the Soviet Union. The managers are typically placed on a production-based pay incentive plan and are assigned unreasonably high production goals on the assumption that this is best for the overall economy.

It is not difficult to understand why individuals often resort to rigid bureaucratic behavior, strategic behavior, and reporting invalid data when they are faced with unreasonable standards. These are the only ways they can achieve the standards. Unreasonable standards also provide psychological justification for reporting invalid data: "If they are going to do that to me then I can deal with them dishonestly."

Standards set by others are less likely to be understood and more likely to be seen as unreasonable and difficult to achieve. Because of this they tend to cause more dysfunctional behavior than participatively set goals. Participation in setting standards reduces dysfunctional behavior because it reduces the chance that too difficult, poorly understood standards will be set. When people participate, they simply don't allow this to happen. The major reason that employees are not allowed to participate in the standard setting process seems to be the fear that they will try to have standards set too low. This may happen in some instances, but it happens anyway as is illustrated by the studies of piece rate situations cited earlier. Further, there are studies that suggest that it may not happen when the standards are set by the employees. For example, Gillespie (1948) has reported on a favorable situation where workers were allowed to participate in setting rates.

Much of the literature on the effects of participation suggests that under certain conditions participation can reduce the amount of resistance toward change. In the classic study on this topic, Coch and French (1948) found that participation reduced the motivational and morale problems associated with a change in work procedures. Mann and Williams (1960) found in a company they studied that resistance to the introduction of a computer was greatly reduced by participation. This firm had managers meet and discuss the changes for several years before they took place. Somewhat similar results have been found in a recent study of a Danish bank (Winther, 1974). Seventy-eight percent of the employees in the study felt that the new system was better for the employees.

Miller (1960) and Mumford and Banks (1967) have reported on studies where participation was not used in the installation of a control system and where resistance was high. They concluded that participation probably would not have reduced resistance. Others (for example, Strauss, 1963) have seriously questioned the value of participation in reducing resistance to change, and some earlier studies have shown (French, Israel, and As, 1960) that participation does not always reduce resistance to change. As we mentioned earlier, one reason for this seems to be that certain individuals are not comfortable with participation and do not respond to it favorably (Vroom, 1960). It also seems that participation is effective only when it involves areas or topics on which employees feel there should be participation.

Finally, it seems that participation in something like standard-setting is likely to be effective if it is part of an overall strategy of participative management and employee-management trust. When it isn't, employees seem to use participation to get slack standards set and to manipulate management (Hopwood, 1973).

A number of explanations have been offered in the literature for why participation reduces resistance under some conditions, but three of the reasons seem to be the most valid. The first is that with participation individuals have a chance to shape the nature of the change being instituted. Presumably because the individuals will be motivated to protect their need satisfaction, they will influence the change in ways that will make it less threatening than a change designed by someone else might be. Thus, because of participation the change may actually be less

threatening to the satisfaction of their needs, and for this reason
be resisted less. This explanation is directly relevant to the issue
of standard setting, since participation should reduce the likelihood that unreasonable standards will be set.

The second reason is suggested by a number of studies that
have pointed out that some of the resistance to control systems
is irrational (Mumford and Banks, 1967; Pettigrew, 1970, 1973).
It is irrational in the sense that it is based on misinformation.
Most major organizational changes tend to produce a tremendous number of rumors. Not infrequently these rumors have
only a small basis in fact and make the change look worse than
it is. This is not surprising since it follows from some of the
early research on rumors. Rumors are particularly likely to occur
on important topics where there is ambiguity about what is occurring (Allport and Postman, 1947). Control systems certainly
are important, and when there is little participation there is
often a great deal of ambiguity about what is going on. People
also tend to spread rumors to make them fit their own organization of the world. They elaborate on facts, make inferences,
and so on, until the rumor no longer resembles the fact that
started the rumor. In situations where people are anxious because a major change is anticipated they often fit the rumor
to their anxieties, and as a result the rumor paints a much more
threatening picture than the real one. This leads to resistance
because people see the control system as threatening their need
satisfaction.

One obvious way to reduce resistance based on erroneous
information is to communicate valid information. This often is
done by organizations on a top-down, one-way basis. Unfortunately people don't always hear or believe one-way communications and even if they do, the communications may not answer
the questions they are concerned about. The obvious point is
that good communication in sensitive areas must be two way,
hence the relevance of participation to the issue of communication and resistance to change. One thing participation encourages is good communication. Thus, where participation takes
place one would expect people to be better informed about
the nature of any change. In some cases, this should lead to
less resistance to change because the valid picture is less threatening than the invalid one. If, however, the valid picture is a

threatening one, then obviously, participation will not eliminate resistance and may increase it.

Earlier it was suggested that participation can lead to employees feeling that decisions are theirs. This sense of ownership is the third reason why participation may reduce resistance. When decisions are theirs, people's self-esteem and feelings of competence get tied to their success. Thus, not only are people unlikely to resist changes which are associated with decisions they make, they are motivated to carry them out.

The three explanations we have given for the fact that participation can reduce resistance to standards and control systems are not mutually exclusive; all can and probably do operate at the same time. Also, they probably are not equally powerful. There is relatively little data to indicate how important the various explanations are and how often they operate to reduce resistance, but it is still possible to speculate a little about their relative potency. Probably the major reason participation reduces resistance is that it allows individuals to shape the change to better fit their needs. Probably less important is the fact that with participation the change is owned by the people, and least important is the informational effect. If the information effect were strong, it would seem that better communications alone should be able to reduce resistance, yet there is little evidence of this. Power equalization seems to be necessary for resistance to be significantly lowered. There are no strong, data-based reasons for stating that ownership of the change is a less important factor than restructuring the change to better fit the needs of the people. It does seem, however, that the latter is more likely to occur and to make a concrete, easily noticeable difference.

Source of discrimination

It is not clear who should act as the discriminator to minimize dysfunctional behavior. A brief review of the impact of having different individuals serve as the discriminator will illustrate this point.

If the discrimination function is performed by someone other than the person being evaluated, the control system is more likely to be adhered to and thus there is a greater potential for rigid bureaucratic behavior. Once an outsider becomes involved, there is the possibility that rewards can be given on the basis of how the person performs the behavior measured by the control system. The rewards may be formal (e.g., pay, promotion) or they may simply be approval or disapproval as shown by the discriminator. Once valued rewards become involved, the person's behavior is going to be influenced by what he or she feels must be done to obtain them. The person may develop the idea that rewards depend on the control system measures if someone with reward power acts as the discriminator. Based on this reasoning, if the discriminator function is performed by a person's superior, the chances of rigid adherence to the system will be greater than if it is performed by a staff person, some other outside agent who lacks reward power, or the person performing the job.

The more the individual whose behavior is being measured acts as discriminator and sensor for his or her own behavior, the greater the possibility there is for invalid data. If the individual reports the data and compares them to the standard, it is easier for him or her to distort them. Whether the individual will distort data under these conditions is influenced by how the data will be used, who receives them, and the relationship between the individual and the organization. As was noted in the discussion of standard setting, individuals don't always try to cheat the organization. However, they are particularly likely to produce invalid data when extrinsic or monetary rewards are involved.

If the individual acts as the discriminator, there is usually less resistance to the control system than if another person acts as the discriminator. There are two reasons for this. First, if the individual acts as the discriminator, then he or she will receive performance feedback, and people want to receive feedback about their performance. Second, when people act as discriminators, they may feel that they can control the data that are passed on to their superiors or to the rest of the system. This can be important if the individuals feel that the system is likely to produce data that will threaten their need satisfaction. If the individual acts as the discriminator, there is the possibility of distorting or withholding negative data. This may allow the individual to avoid many of the negative repercussions that might come from a control system. A control system that has an outside agent acting as the discriminator makes such distortion more difficult, and thus the person is likely to see it as potentially more threatening to his or her need satisfaction. If performance is poor under these conditions, there is little the performer can do to prevent this information from being passed on to the rest of the organization.

In summary, having the individual act as the discriminator tends to reduce rigid bureaucratic behavior and resistance. However, when extrinsic or monetary rewards are involved, it can increase the tendency for invalid data to be produced. This suggests the advisability of having the individual be one of several persons who act as the discriminator in most situations. A good joint process developed by the person and whoever else is involved should lead to the lowest overall level of dysfunctional behavior.

Recipients of communication and source of motivation

The amount of bureaucratic behavior, strategic behavior, resistance, and invalid information present in an organization are all influenced by who receives information from the control system. When information goes to someone (a superior) who either has or potentially has the power to give extrinsic rewards, rigid bureaucratic behavior, strategic behavior, and invalid data are much more likely to be present. The reason for this is that when extrinsic rewards are involved, employees become concerned about looking good on performance measures. Behaving in a rigid bureaucratic or strategic manner and giving invalid data are ways to look good, as has been shown in a number of studies (Argyris, 1951; Dalton, 1959; Stedry, 1960; Becker and Green, 1962; and Tannenbaum, 1968). It occurs because in some situations individuals perceive that the only way (or best way) to receive the rewards they want is to distort the data used to evaluate them. In these situations, people tend to withhold and distort data that go to individuals who can give them rewards. For example, Read (1959) has documented the tendency of subordinates to withhold information from their superiors. According to his study, managers tend to withhold information about such issues as fights with other units, unforeseen costs, rapid changes in production, insufficient equipment, and so on. Read also reports that the tendency to restrict information was most severe among managers who would be classified as being high upward mobiles.

Two recent studies have shown that when superiors use information to create pressure for better performance and to punish poor performance, it is particularly likely to produce dysfunctional behavior (Cammann, 1974*b*; Hopwood, 1972, 1973, 1974*a*). In his research, Hopwood has distinguished three distinct ways superiors use budgetary information for appraising the performance of their subordinates.

1. **Budget Constrained style**
   . . . performance is primarily evaluated upon the basis of ability to continually meet the budget on a short-term basis. This criterion of performance is stressed at the expense of other valued and important criteria and the manager will receive unfavorable feedback from his superior if, for instance, his actual costs exceed the budgeted costs, regardless of other considerations.

2. **Profit Conscious style**
   . . . performance is evaluated on the basis of ability to increase the general effectiveness of [the] unit's operations in relation to the long-term purposes of the organization. For instance, at the cost center level, one important aspect of this ability concerns the attention which [is devoted] to reducing long-run costs. For this purpose, however, the budgetary information has to be used with great care in a rather flexible manner.

3. **Nonaccounting style**
   The budgetary information plays a relatively unimportant part in the . . . evaluation of . . . performance (Hopwood, 1973, p. 85).

Hopwood's research shows that:

While both the Budget Constrained and Profit Conscious styles result in a concern with costs, only the Profit Conscious supervisor achieves this concern without the costly dysfunctional decision making and manipulation of the data. [There were] decisions taken in Budget Constrained departments which resulted in higher processing costs, less innovative behavior and a poorer quality service to the customer, and where the manipulation of the data reduced their usefulness for analytical purposes (Hopwood, 1972, p. 176).

This did not tend to happen in all situations. He also reports that tensions and mistrust are much higher when the Budget Constrained style is used.

Another study has shown that the leadership styles of managers seem to be influenced by the kind of budget pressure they are under from their superiors (DeCoster and Fertakis, 1968). The negative effects of control system pressures are emphasized by Carmichael (1970), who notes how it may actually motivate embezzlement (the ultimate form of invalid data!).

A further danger created by the idea that strong punishment-oriented internal control systems are necessary because employees are immoral, dishonest, or prone to fraud is that the supposition may become a self-fulfilling prophecy. If employees are treated as if they are dishonest and must be constantly watched, they may become motivated to challenge the system and do whatever they can to work around the tight internal control. This may also be counter-productive because the employees are pitted against the organization. McGregor (1967) has concluded that pressure for accountability can easily provide some justification for dishonest behavior. He stated that:

> One fundamental reason control systems often fail and sometimes boomerang is that those who design them fail to understand that an important aspect of human behavior in an organizational setting is that noncompliance tends to appear in the presence of a perceived threat (p. 8).

It is not hard to see why people present invalid data when the information goes to individuals involved in giving extrinsic rewards. They have something to gain. It is not as clear why this happens even when such obvious extrinsic rewards as pay are not directly on the line, but behavior is influenced by expectations about what will happen. Any time information goes to someone else there is the potential that it will be used for reward and punishment purposes.

The amount of resistance to information and control systems is also strongly influenced by who receives information about the results of the discrimination. It has already been stressed that individuals are more likely to accept control systems if they receive the feedback from them. If they act as the discriminator, they will get the feedback directly, but even if someone else acts as the discriminator, they can still give the employees feedback and reduce their tendency to resist. If individuals do get the feedback their need to know can be satisfied by the control system, provided that the data are presented in meaningful terms. Naturally, if the installation of a control system offers people something they value (for example, feedback about performance), they are less likely to resist its installation than if it offers nothing of value. If social comparison theory and psychological success theory are correct and people do value feedback about their performance, then control systems that provide it should be resisted less than those that do not.

Likert (1961, 1967) has pointed out that the amount of resistance to a control system is very much determined by who gets the information. He correctly notes that when the data go to the individual's superior or to others in the organization, resistance to the system is likely to be increased. It is particularly likely to be high if the information is used to determine the level of reward an individual will receive. When rewards are involved, there is the greatest threat to a person's need satisfaction level. However, if the control system does not provide performance data to the superior or to higher levels in the organization, the system may fail to fulfill some of its most important functions, for example, providing higher levels with the information they need to coordinate and plan the future activities of the organization. Likert, recognizing this dilemma, suggests that superiors be given data only on the performance of the group of people who report to them. Thus, no data on an individual's performance is passed on to a superior; such data go only to the individual, and superiors receive combined data on the performance of all their subordinates.

Likert suggests that a similar pattern could be followed up the hierarchy so that no superior would receive individual data on the performance of his or her subordinates. This should reduce many people's resistance to control systems. However, it also would prevent the use of control system data to reward and punish on an individual basis and this could damage extrinsic motivation. Some sort of individual performance measures are needed to produce extrinsic motivation, unless the organization decides to use a group or company-wide incentive plan. It is also important to note that some people prefer to have their rewards based on their performance (Lawler, 1966) because they feel it allows them to control the rewards they receive and to receive a high level of rewards. They, of course, are likely to resist the kind of approach Likert suggests. Finally, group performance data cannot be used for individual problem solving and career development unless, of course, the individual is willing to share the uncombined data with his or her superior. Thus, Likert's approach should reduce resistance to control systems among some individuals, but with significant costs.

There is evidence that frequently a majority of the workers in an organization prefer to work where pay is based on performance (Lawler, 1971). When asked why they prefer this type of pay system, many of them talk in terms of the kind of control it gives them (Viteles, 1953; Whyte, 1955). Evidence also suggests that the reason many employees do not favor pay incentive plans is that they don't trust management to administer them fairly. It is not that they don't like the control it could give them; rather, they seem to believe that because of the way the plan would be run, it would not give them that control. Thus, it appears that control systems tied into reward systems may, under certain conditions, be sought by most employees rather than resisted by them.

Speed and frequency of communication

It is doubtful that either speed of communication or frequency of communication influence the frequency with which rigid bureaucratic behavior, strategic behavior, or the reporting of invalid data occur. One qualification is probably necessary here, however. When communications are too infrequent they can produce strategic behavior if they are used for reward purposes.

Ironically, if communication is very slow and the frequency very inappropriate, it may, under some conditions, decrease the frequency of dysfunctional behavior. The reason for this is that when communication is poor, there is less potential for using the results to give rewards and punishments, and less reason for individuals to behave dysfunctionally.

Frequent rapid communications can lead to reduction in the resistance to information and control systems under certain conditions. As has been stressed, many individuals want valid feedback on their performance and they want it when it is useful to them. An information system that measures their performance quickly and at appropriate time intervals can fulfill this need. Thus, rather than resisting it, they want it.

Type of activity

The more important an organization considers an activity the more likely measures of it are to be distorted. This relates to Argyris' (1964, 1971) point that organizations have their greatest difficulty gathering data when important issues are involved. It also follows from the fact that organizationally important activities are more likely to make a difference in a person's rewards, and there is greater pressure to look good on those particular measures. This pressure may be generated internally by the person or externally by the organization's reward system. In short, measures of important dimensions are more likely to be distorted because they can make a difference to a person, and, therefore, according to motivation theory, there should be more motivation present to distort the measures. The same line of reasoning led to the prediction that important activities are more likely to produce rigid bureaucratic behavior and strategic behavior.

Because they are more likely to be used for reward and punishment purposes, measures of important activities will be resisted by some and supported by others. Those who feel they will gain in terms of extrinsic rewards will, of course, be inclined to support them. Measures of important activities may be sought for other reasons as well. As has been continually stressed, people want feedback on their activities. They particularly want it on the important activities. Thus, an information and control system that gives people information on how they perform an important activity is likely to be welcomed rather than resisted.

Conclusion

A summary of the major causes of dysfunctional behavior as delineated by Lawler and Rhode (1976) is presented in Exhibit 1. As you can see by looking at the last four columns, the same characteristic that tends to cause one kind of dysfunctional behavior sometimes tends to reduce another. This conflict was

EXHIBIT 1.
Characteristics of control systems that produce dysfunctional behavior

		All dysfunctional behaviors	Bureaucratic behavior	Strategic behavior	Invalid data	Resistance
Characteristics of sensor	a.	Incomplete	Incomplete	—	—	Complete
	b.	Subjective	Objective	Objective	Subjective	Subjective
	c.	Uninfluenceable	Influenceable	—	Uninfluenceable	Uninfluenceable
Nature of standard	d.	Set by others without participation	Set by others	Set by others	Set by others	Set by others
	e.	Very difficult	Very difficult	Very difficult	Very difficult	Very difficult
Source of discrimination	f.	Superior or Other	Superior/Other	Superior/Other	Self	Superior/Other
Recipients of communication	g.	Superior or Other	Superior/Other	Superior/Other	Self	Superior/Other
Speed of communication	h.	Fast	Fast	Fast	Fast	Slow
Frequency of communication	i.	Frequency inappropriate	Frequent	Too infrequent	Frequent	Too infrequent
Type of activity	j.	Important	Important	Important	Important	—

Source: E. E. Lawler, III and J. G. Rhode, *Information and Control in Organizations* (Pacific Palisades, Calif.: Goodyear, 1976).

taken into account in producing an overall summary of the characteristics that produce the greatest amount of dysfunctional behavior. The first column in Exhibit 1 considers the effects of a certain characteristic and reveals decisions on what characteristics are likely to produce the greatest amount of dysfunctional behavior. For example, sensors that are incomplete, subjective, and uninfluenceable are likely to produce more dysfunctional behavior than ones that are complete, objective, and easy to influence. Completeness and objectivity can, in fact, lead to resistance, but they tend to strongly reduce bureaucratic behavior; thus, the conclusion is that overall they lead to less dysfunctional behavior. In sum, the effects on organizational behavior caused by cost accounting, or information and control systems, are direct and pervasive. A knowledge of these effects is necessary to avoid dysfunctional results and to achieve employee motivation toward desired organizational goals.

REFERENCES

Allport, G. W., and Postman, L. *The Psychology of Rumor.* New York: Holt, 1947.

Anthony, R. N. *Planning and Control Systems: A Framework for Analysis.* Boston: Division of Research, Graduate School of Business Administration, Harvard University, 1965.

Argyris, Chris. *The Impact of Budgets on People.* New York: Controllership Foundation, 1951.

_____. *Personality and Organization.* New York: Harper, 1957.

_____. *Integrating the Individual and the Organization.* New York: Wiley, 1964.

_____. "Management Information Systems: the Challenge to Rationality and Emotionality." *Management Science,* vol. 17, 1971, pp. 275–92.

Babchuk, N., and Goode, W. J. "Work Incentives in a Self-Determined Group," *American Social Review,* vol. 16, 1951, pp. 679–87.

Becker, Selwyn, and Green, D. "Budgeting and Employee Behavior." *The Journal of Business,* vol. 35, 1962, pp. 392–402.

Berliner, Joseph S. "The Situation of Plant Managers" in A. Inkeles, and K. Geiger, eds., *Soviet Society: A Book of Readings.* Boston: Houghton Mifflin, 1961.

Beyer, R. *Profitability Accounting for Planning and Control.* New York: Ronald, 1963.

Blau, P. M. *The Dynamics of Bureaucracy.* Chicago: University of Chicago Press, 1955.

Burns, Thomas J., and Stalker, G. M. *The Management of Innovation.* London: Tavistock, 1961.

Cammann, C. "Can Accounting Systems Produce Change?" Presented at the APA Convention, 1974*a*.

_____. "Effects of the Use of Control Systems." *Accounting, Organizations and Society,* vol. 2, 1977, pp. 301–14.

_____. *The Impact of a Feedback System on Managerial Attitudes and Performance.* Unpublished Ph.D. thesis, Yale University, 1974*b*.

_____, and Nadler, D. "Fit Control Systems to Your Managerial Style." *Harvard Business Review,* vol. 54, 1976, pp. 65–72.

Caplan, Edwin H. *Management Accounting and Behavioral Sciences.* Reading, Mass.: Addison-Wesley, 1971.

Carmichael, D. R. "Behavioral Hypotheses of Internal Control." *The Accounting Review,* vol. 45(2), 1970, pp. 235–45.

Carroll, D. C. "Implications of On-Line, Real-Time Systems for Managerial Decision-Making." in C. A. Meyers, ed., *The Impact of Computers on Management.* Cambridge: MIT Press, 1967, pp. 140–66.

Coch, L., and French, J. R. P. Jr. "Overcoming Resistance to Change." *Human Relations,* vol. 1, 1948, pp. 512–32.

Dalton, M. *Men Who Manage.* New York: Wiley, 1959.

Dearden, J. "Problems of Decentralized Profit Responsibility." *Harvard Business Review,* vol. 38, 1960, pp. 79–86.

_____. "Problems in Decentralized Financial Control." *Harvard Business Review,* vol. 39, 1961, pp. 72–80.

DeCoster, D. T., and Fertakis, J. P. "Budget Induced Pressure and Its Relationship to Supervisory Behavior." *Journal of Accounting Research,* vol. 6, 1968, pp. 237–46.

Frank, A. G. "Goal Ambiguity and Conflicting Standards: An Approach to the Study of Organization." *Human Organization,* vol. 17, 1959, pp. 8–13.

French, J. R. P. Jr., Israel, J., and As, D. "An Experiment on Participation in a Norwegian Factory." *Human Relations,* vol. 13, 1960, pp. 3–19.

Gardner, B. B., and Moore, D. G. *Human Relations in Industry,* 4th ed. Homewood, Ill.: Irwin, 1964.

Gibson, C. F., and Nolan, R. L. "Managing the Four Stages of EDP Growth." *Harvard Business Review,* vol. 74, 1974, pp. 76–88.

Gillespie, J. J. *Free Expression in Industry.* London: Pilot Press, 1948.

Gouldner, A. W. *Patterns of Industrial Bureaucracy.* Glencoe, Ill.: Free Press, 1954.

Haire, M. "Biological Models and Empirical Histories of Growth of Organizations" in M. Haire, ed., *Modern Organization Theory.* New York: Wiley, 1959, pp. 272–306.

Hofstede, G. H. *The Game of Budget Control.* Assen, Netherlands: Van Gorcum, 1967.

Hopwood, A. G. "An Empirical Study of the Role of Accounting Data in Performance Evaluation." *Empirical Research in Accounting: Selected Studies, 1972.* Supplement to vol. 10, *Journal of Accounting Research.*

Hopwood, A. G. *An Accounting System and Managerial Behavior.* Lexington, Mass.: Lexington Books, 1973.

―――. "Leadership Climate and the Use of Accounting Data in Performance Evaluation." *The Accounting Review,* vol. 49, 1974a, pp. 485–95.

―――. *Accounting and Human Behavior.* London: Haymarket Publishing, 1974b.

Jasinki, F. J. "Use and Misuse of Efficiency Controls." *Harvard Business Review,* vol. 34, 1956, pp. 105–12.

Lawler, E. E. "Managers' Attitudes Toward How Their Pay Is and Should Be Determined." *Journal of Applied Psychology,* vol. 50, 1966, pp. 273–79.

―――. *Pay and Organizational Effectiveness: A Psychological View.* New York: McGraw-Hill, 1971.

Lawler, E. E., III, and Rhode, J. G. *Information and Control in Organizations.* Pacific Palisades, Calif.: Goodyear, 1976.

Leavitt, H. J., and Whisler, T. C. "Management in the 1980s." *Harvard Business Review,* vol. 36, 1958, pp. 41–48.

Likert, R. *New Patterns of Management.* New York: McGraw-Hill, 1961.

―――. *The Human Organization.* New York: McGraw-Hill, 1967.

Lyden, F. J., and Miller, E. G., eds. *Planning, Programming and Budgeting: A Systems Approach to Management.* Chicago: Markham, 1968.

Mann, F. C., and Williams, L. K. "Observations on the Dynamics of a Change to Electronic Data Processing Equipment." *Administrative Science Quarterly,* vol. 5, 1960, pp. 217–66.

March, J. G., and Simon, H. A. *Organizations.* New York: Wiley, 1958.

McGregor, Douglas. *The Professional Manager.* New York: McGraw-Hill, 1967.

Mellinger, G. D. "Interpersonal Trust as a Factor in Communication." *Journal of Abnormal and Social Psychology,* vol. 52, 1956, pp. 304–09.

Merton, R. K. "Bureaucratic Structure and Personality." *Social Forces,* vol. 18, 1940, pp. 560–68.

Miller, B. *Gaining Acceptance for Major Methods Changes.* Research Study No. 44. New York: American Management Association, 1960.

Mumford, E., and Banks, O. *The Computer and the Clerk.* London: Routledge and Kegan Paul, 1967.

Onsi, M. "Behavioral Variables Affecting Budgetary Slack." *The Accounting Review,* vol. 48, 1973, pp. 535–48.

Pettigrew, A. *A Behavioral Analysis of an Innovative Decision.* Published Ph.D. dissertation, University of Manchester, 1970.

———. "Information Control as a Power Resource." *Sociology,* vol. 6, 1972, pp. 187–204.

———. *The Politics of Organization Decision-Making.* London: Tavistock, 1973.

Read, W. *Factors Affecting Upward Communication at Middle Management Levels in Industrial Organizations.* Unpublished doctoral dissertation, Ann Arbor: University of Michigan, 1959.

Roethlisberger, F. J., and Dickson, W. J. *Management and the Worker.* Cambridge: Harvard University Press, 1939.

Rosen, S., and Tesser, A. "On Reluctance to Communicate Undesirable Information: The Mum Affect." *Sociometry,* vol. 33, 1970, pp. 253–63.

Roy, R. H., and MacNeill, J. H. *Horizons for a Profession: The Common Body of Knowledge for Certified Public Accountants.* New York: American Institute of Certified Public Accountants, 1967.

Schiff, M., and Lewin, A. Y. "The Impact of People on Budgets." *The Accounting Review,* vol. 45, 1970, pp. 259–68.

Selznick, P. *TVA and the Grass Roots.* Berkeley: University of California Press, 1949.

Stedry, A. *Budget Control and Cost Behavior.* Englewood Cliffs, N.J.: Prentice-Hall, 1960.

Strauss, G. "Some Notes on Power-Equalization." in H. J. Leavitt, ed. *The Social Science of Organizations.* Englewood Cliffs, N.J.: Prentice-Hall, 1963.

Tannenbaum, A. S. *Control in Organizations.* New York: McGraw-Hill, 1968. *Time.* vol. 99 (26), 1972, p. 14.

Viteles, M. S. *Motivation and Morale in Industry.* New York: Norton, 1953.

Vroom, V. H. *Some Personality Determinants of the Effects of Participation.* Englewood Cliffs, N.J.: Prentice-Hall, 1960.

Whisler, T. L. *The Impact of Computers on Organizations.* New York: Praeger, 1970a.

———. *Information Technology and Organizational Change.* Belmont, Calif.: Wadsworth, 1970b.

Whyte, W. F., ed. *Money and Motivation: An Analysis of Incentives in Industry.* New York: Harper, 1955.

Wilensky, H. L. *Organizational Intelligence.* New York: Basic Books, 1967.

Winther, E. "The Study of a Computer System and Work Design in a Danish Bank." Paper presented at ALTOR conference, Hindas, Sweden, 1974.

11

Cost accounting and the management information system

Harold M. Sollenberger*
Dave Parks†

INTRODUCTION

The purpose of this chapter is to discuss the controller's role in a new environment of sophisticated accounting, operating, and management information systems. The focus is on management information and how traditional accounting systems can be integrated into a much broader information network. The analysis is aimed at companies that have had computer systems experience and are considering substantial information system changes or additions.

Most mature, medium-to-large size companies have had accounting transaction and basic operating systems in place for many years. Through the experience gained with these basic systems, operating management has typically identified numerous enhancements that they would like, and executive management has identified the need for better decision-making data. Most of the time the fundamental accounting needs are met, but more operating and management data are required. Soon it becomes evident that the basic transaction systems must

---
* Chairman, Accounting & Financial Administration Department, Michigan State University.
† Partner, Arthur Andersen & Co.

change to meet these requirements. This chapter talks about how to build a systems structure that will meet the needs of operating, accounting, and executive management. The system builds upon the fundamental transaction systems and filters and summarizes the same basic data for management reporting. The chapter also describes the required management information system structure and how to develop a plan to implement the components of that structure. It discusses the hardware and software advances that make this possible in today's computer environment, but it is a practical approach that salvages as much as possible of the basic transaction systems that are in place.

This chapter is directed at the controller, not the data processing manager. It is recognized that the controller may no longer have direct responsibility for data processing but typically still has a strong influence on system requirements. The controller must ensure that the new systems meet accounting needs as well as provide better operating and management information.

The discussion is organized as follows: The first section focuses on the evolution of information systems from basic, stand-alone accounting applications to an integrated MIS structure. This discussion examines historical, transaction-oriented systems and their place in the current environment. The forces that push a company toward consideration of new information systems are also presented.

Next, the structure inherent in an MIS and its major component systems are discussed. This section explains system integration and the flow of data into and through the transaction system and on to managerial planning and control systems.

Then, the topic of a long range system plan (LRSP), which is the key to a successful management information system structure, is addressed. The LRSP process is explained and its ability to enable the achievement of an MIS structure is shown. The remaining steps of the system development sequence are also outlined.

Finally, the controller's new responsibilities are pinpointed. The controller must be a catalyst who can understand the relationship between the information available and the ability to serve the firm's decision makers. The emphasis here is on mechanisms whereby the controller can influence system development.

THE EVOLUTION OF MANAGEMENT INFORMATION SYSTEMS

Many articles have attempted to define, in great detail, what a management information system is and what it does for a corporation; that is not the intent here. A management information system is a structure of all the systems in place to support management, accounting, and operating requirements, rather than a single comprehensive system.

Transaction-oriented systems

For most companies, the applications that reduced clerical costs came first, such as payroll, billing, inventory records, and sales analysis. Then came more complex applications which were of a clerical nature but were costly to coordinate or execute in a timely manner with manual techniques. Purchasing, production scheduling, order entry, product costing, budgeting, and responsibility reporting are examples of such application areas.

The majority of these early data processing systems were transaction-oriented and directly operations or accounting related. For example, the order entry system (for accounting use) became a common early application of unit record equipment. Accounting rules were the basis for systems design and dominated the resulting EDP systems, often because the systems department reported to the controller. In response, nonaccounting users developed their own (formal or informal) information systems for operating data and adapted available accounting data for their needs as well as possible. Only some information needs of operating managers were met directly, and then only after accounting systems were in place.

The initial EDP applications could be characterized as follows:

1. Stand alone applications. A specific problem was solved, then another, and another. As an example, the payroll system was designed with its own inputs and outputs. Later, as productivity monitoring systems were implemented, they too were designed with separate input forms to record time. Typically, the two systems reported on different time frames (i.e., calendar months versus weeks); they included different scopes, like productive time versus paid time; and it was difficult to reconcile one system to the other.

2. Multiple inputs of the same data for multiple purposes. Data capture was designed and executed for each application. The data files were integral parts of application programs. A new input document was created for each system. For example, a payroll time card, production output card, productivity measurement, and personnel data might all need similar data but require separate input forms.

3. High transaction volume with heavy clerical activity. Common initial applications were intended to eliminate groups of clerical personnel and to avoid huge increases in personnel as business volume grew. EDP justification was based solely on cost savings. Each system was aimed at a specific bottleneck.

4. Accounting data were the primary interfaces. Regardless of the user's purpose or functional role or need, the accounting data were the common denominator in the flow of information. For example, sales analysis operated off the sales accounting system based on accrual accounting rules.

5. Management decision information not included. Management was forced to rely on historical accounting data to try to make timely decisions, rather than current or forecast data. Different managers often had different data from independent sources.

6. Typically the EDP staff was greatly influenced by a queue of work requests for maintenance or "patches." The systems people were knowledgeable in the details but had little opportunity to see the big picture.

If these systems were related at all, the link was often a manual step. The accounting transaction system might have interfaced only with the general ledger system. Little data flowed automatically from one application to another. Few links existed between accounting and operating systems.

The current environment—Why and where to from here?

Again, organization and evolution of the information systems function has followed many courses and stages. Often the accounting area had primary responsibility for systems and procedures work, then unit record equipment, and then the first computer center. The growth in nonaccounting applications, the integration of data processing into the actual operating activities, and the increase in technically oriented personnel in EDP operations have all combined to reduce the strength of the natural ties between data handling and the traditional accounting or controllership functions. The result is the creation of a separate information systems function either inside or outside of the controller's responsibility but certainly less accounting dominated.

Meanwhile, the improving state of equipment development and systems experience has created new approaches to MIS planning and design. Technical hardware developments, like cheaper, faster, and more versatile processors and mini computer networks, have enabled system designers of many companies to place data entry and query functions closer to systems users. Software developments, such as data base software, have further increased system designer's freedom and flexibility. But the knowledge and experience that most companies have gained from their first attempts at system design are what make better utilization of upgraded equipment more likely. Company managers with system experience know, for example, what functions and features need to be added to transaction processing. They have an idea of management information requirements, and they have a better understanding of how to collect and integrate data. Managers have also learned to work with on-line as well as batch systems and have gained some skills in systems project management.

The impetus for systems change may come from management demands for "higher quality information," the obsolescence of existing hardware, or the final realization that it is cheaper to redesign systems than to patch them again. Tremendous opportunities exist for the firm that is willing to seriously examine its present status, plan its long-range systems needs, and integrate and prioritize the design and implementation steps. It is clear that to capitalize on the advantages of the current environment takes very serious planning, deep executive management commitment to determine MIS requirements, and finally a thoroughly integrated approach to accounting, operating, and management systems. Certainly, the traditional accounting systems can be converted to the new hardware; however, the same limitations would exist, and the degree of improvement is only slight when compared to the potential betterment.

Firms continue to experience growth in demands for computer resources. The data processing function is now nearly unequalled in the manner it permeates the entire organization with services and day-to-day usage. An important result is that accounting managers are now primarily the clients of the EDP department instead of the managers of it. As a result, the controller can now separate the issues of managerial uses of accounting data and the data handling needs of the accounting function itself. However, the controller's responsibility for providing analytical accounting data for decision making remains.

STRUCTURE OF MANAGEMENT INFORMATION SYSTEMS

The concept of management information systems is not a single application or reporting system which satisfies all management reporting requirements. Rather, it is an integrated structure of systems which reports appropriately summarized and filtered data to each level of management. Some of this reporting is manually prepared, while some is computerized or mechanized. This concept of a management information structure is illustrated in Exhibit 1. This exhibit is a portion of the management information systems structure developed for an electric utility company. It shows how the foundation for the MIS structure is the typical transaction systems which collect, validate, update, and maintain data on basic business events. Above the basic transaction systems resides middle level or operational management reporting. This operational reporting would include the transmission of data to both first line supervision and successively higher management levels. Above the management control systems are systems which help plan operations activities as well as more long-term strategic planning. The reporting for both types of planning is aimed at both executive management and operating managers.

An example may help illustrate this concept. The order-entry systems is a transaction system which probably includes recording requests for service from the utility's customers and the

EXHIBIT 1
Detail of information requirements planning chart for electric utilities

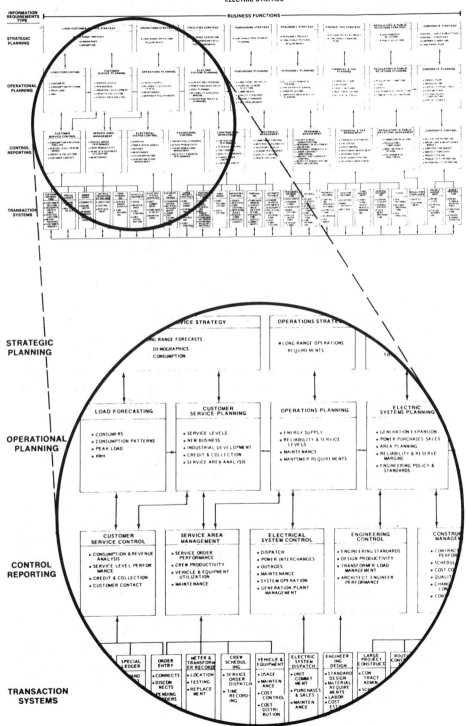

scheduling of those orders for service routing or crew scheduling. When the actual order is executed, the time taken to perform the work is recorded. It is then used at the more comprehensive management control reporting level by department management, possibly to monitor crew productivity. This same data regarding the original order goes into a data base for service area analysis or the projection of service level requirements for the next year. Thus the data are reused in the operational planning segment. The same data would be further utilized in strategic planning, where they may support a corporate model forecast of long-term service level requirements.

This concept of management information reporting can be better understood by a discussion of three of its features: integrated reporting of information, the integrated approach for collecting data, and the integration of systems.

Integrated management reporting

As we stated earlier, a characteristic of the early transaction systems was that they handled or processed the high volume, routine, repetitive transactions of the business. It was also mentioned that most of the interfaces or integration of these applications came in the accounting area, to ensure the integrity of the financial records. In contrast, a MIS entails more than recording cost for the accounting archives. It performs such things as integrating cost and budget data on a responsibility basis with operational and planning data. In this way, cost data become an integral part of the management philosophy of the company. Therefore, one of the most distinguishing characteristics of the management information system is realized: data reporting requirements at all levels of management are identified; and the basic transactions or events which occur in a company are summarized, filtered, and reported at the appropriate levels. This results in the reporting of cost data on a responsibility basis which allows individual managers to take action to bring costs back into control.

A situation where cost data integration might be useful could occur in the utility industry through relating costs to work actually performed. Rather than collecting and reporting historical cost by an accounting category, such as natural expense breakdowns of labor, materials, and so forth, the cost of performing customer service calls is reported in the form of expected versus actual cost per call. This necessitates collecting all costs of performing customer service, including labor, materials, and an appropriately sophisticated allocation of overhead expenses. The overall approach helps operating management evaluate the effectiveness of personnel. This evaluation measures productivity by reporting expected service times against actual times to perform house calls. The effectiveness of management personnel is also gauged by reporting anticipated utilization of crews versus actual utilization. Utilization is defined here as the ratio of workers' time spent actually performing tasks to their total time, including nonproductive time that is spent in waiting, training, or some other indirect activity. This often means recording costs at a point in the expenditure cycle before checks are written. Costs can also enter the system when purchase orders are cut or when materials are received. Therefore, costs are recorded on an incurred basis rather than a paid basis. The keys here are putting costs in a perspective that is meaningful to the operating management and reporting costs on a timely basis.

Integrated data collection

Although we have noted that an MIS still should perform transaction processing, one of the distinctions of the integrated management information system structure is that the basic data are usable beyond existing transaction systems. Because a data item may be reported at all levels of the organization, all common data output must come from the same source transaction. The advantages of this approach are obvious. Operating personnel need not enter the same data more than once for use in different systems. This can result in significant labor cost savings through less duplicate data recording. Another advantage is that the integrity of the data that are reported at all levels is increased. Therefore, the productivity variance that the first line supervisor is looking at will be traced all the way to a report a vice president will see when comparing the work done to the work budgeted. When questions are asked at the top of the organization, the answers can be found by the people at lower levels, since information used by everyone emanates from the same source. However, this concept requires a reorientation of system designers' thinking. Formerly, in the primarily transaction-oriented systems, whenever an additional new system was designed, an input form was developed to record the data required by that application. But using an integrated approach to data collection requires that the systems designer identify all of the data requirements from an organizational unit at one point in time. This includes accounting transactions, operating data, and all management information. The approach then is to design a data collection package that captures all of the data from that individual or team. The data are then entered or read by the machine, validation is performed, errors are corrected, and the data elements are spun off to the appropriate transaction systems. This approach is quite different from the traditional input form for each transaction system. The package concept usually makes more sense to the operating and production people as opposed to a series of dissimilar forms for different systems. Distributed processing techniques add much to this approach by allowing errors to be corrected closer to the source of the transaction, where a more informed decision can be made regarding corrections.

A possible application of this approach in the utility industry might be data collection for a work crew in the service department. The information required to plan, control, and manage this work includes the type of jobs done, the time taken per job, the materials used on the job, and data regarding equipment usage. New data collection techniques would require the design of a carefully planned package that would be completed either by the worker or his crew foreman. These forms would record all necessary data on a daily basis at the central location where the crew reports to work. This may be distinct from the host computer at central headquarters. This concept is illustrated in Exhibit 2. After the data are entered and validated, they would be transmitted in batches to the host computer where they would update many of the files. Thus there would be valid data transmitted to the materials and supplies application, the payroll application, the detail work measurement application, the work load scheduling application, and eventually into the management responsibility report. All of these data, which reside in each of these files and are used for many applications, would

EXHIBIT 2

Flow of information through transaction systems to integrated management reporting

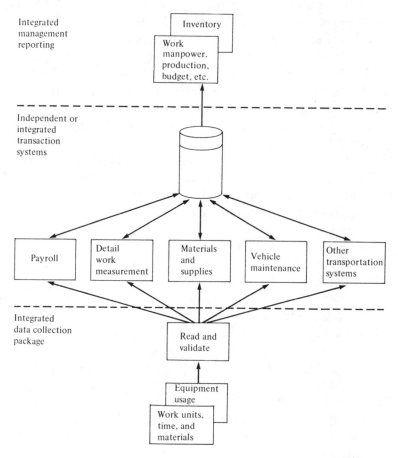

be consistent. If the data entry and validation are done on an intelligent terminal or a mini-processor in a distant location, the same data could be used to update algorithms for a daily scheduling system.

Integrated systems

The key components in a Management Information System structure are the integrated data collection and the integrated operational and management reporting which have just been discussed. An additional concept that is not a requirement, but is often useful, is integrated systems. As companies redo their transaction systems, quite often they combine systems like payroll and personnel into a single application. This typically has many advantages if the company must redo existing transaction systems. However, the point to be made is that it may not be necessary for a successful MIS structure. Most companies cannot afford to redo all of their fundamental systems at once; but, by careful planning and perhaps some extra processing, many existing transaction systems can be changed to support an MIS structure. This usually means that the data collection programs read the new integrated package and spin-off data to the existing transaction systems in the format they are accustomed to. All of the additional data required to support the integrated reporting must then be passed to new maintenance programs. The integrated reporting also often requires the traditional files to be processed separately before preparation of the integrated reports. These are data processing considerations and need not be discussed here. The point is that an MIS structure can often be built upon existing transaction systems and doesn't always require modern integrated applications.

To understand and to take full advantage of all existing transaction systems require a long range plan for the development of an integrated system. These transaction applications, such as payroll or work measurement, were typically developed at different points in time. Now, these applications are being redone and integrated into a management information structure. The optimal way to achieve such an MIS that can reach its information supplying potential is first to develop the concepts of the overall systems structure, then to formulate a long range system plan, and finally to develop and execute each of the individual projects. Just how one goes about developing such a structure is the topic of the next section.

DEVELOPING THE MIS

The essential ingredient: LRSP

To build the MIS structure explained above requires extensive company resources, a firm commitment from management, and a major planning effort. The long-range systems plan is the first step in this process, since it defines the general path toward the initially unrefined target of an MIS suited for the company. The goal here is not to design a system that will never need modification. There are many tools which can increase the flexibility of systems with respect to maintenance and changing of applications after they are installed and running. Rather, it is important at this time for the system's designer to determine a general conceptual outline of the structure.

The approach to this systems planning process can include several different methodologies, but the basic concept is similar in each. The success of such an undertaking requires personnel on the project team who have prior experience in the development of applications in that industry. Analysts who understand the company's business and their current systems can help management define their key control factors and management information system needs.

The concepts of the long-term approach are quite straightforward. First, perform a review and conduct interviews with management and define the outline of the structure. Second, take an inventory of current systems and match it against the structure to see where you stand right now. The third step is to develop a plan to get from the current system to the desired structure as defined in the first step. There are different approaches that can be used, but one that has been used successfully many times is depicted in Exhibit 3. The following is a description of the major steps in this system planning methodology.

The LRSP in detail

Organization and administration. One of the most important aspects of organization in a Systems Planning engagement is the need for senior management to review and approve the systems plans and to participate in their development. This objective can usually be achieved through the establishment of a Steering Committee of top management representatives from the various functional areas of the company. The involvement of senior management is a prerequisite for success in the development of the plan. The establishment of a Steering Committee

EXHIBIT 3

Long-range systems planning procedures chart

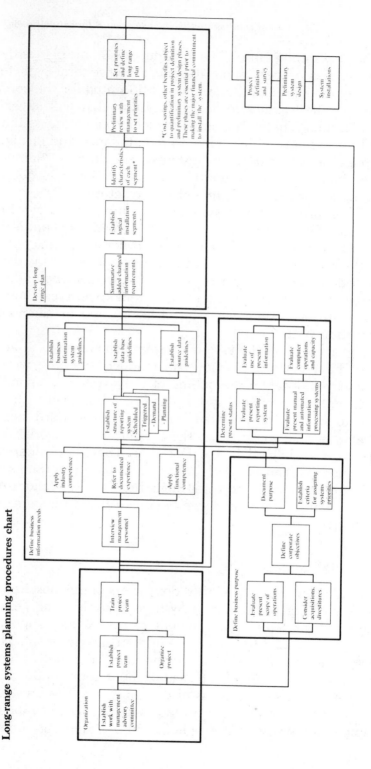

can be a very effective means of achieving needed management involvement in the data processing systems effort. In short, the Committee is responsible for insuring that the Systems Plan is responsive to the company's requirements. They can meet their responsibility by:

Defining corporate objectives for systems projects undertaken.

Insuring that functional executives contribute to the development of the plan as required.

Evaluating proposed systems projects and making selections from alternatives available.

Establishing priorities among approved systems projects.

Approving a schedule of systems effort and assignment of personnel to tasks.

This team should be capable of creating the proper atmosphere so that support for the plan is developed among key management personnel.

Proper project leadership is important. Assuring that the project team has the proper blend of skills and securing the commitment and involvement of executive management are two primary tasks in the Organization section of the project. Other tasks include the traditional project control techniques, like completing a detailed work program and timetable and establishing the mechanism for measuring work performed against the timetable, to assist in keeping all project objectives on schedule.

Document business objectives and their impact on the long-range systems plan. The first important step in the development of the Systems Plan is to become familiar with the business environment in which the company operates as well as with the characteristics and goals of the company staff (operating philosophies, policies, and assumptions). This knowledge will help identify the impact these factors will have on the Systems Plan and help achieve the following objectives:

1. To identify the characteristics of the external environment that significantly affect the company, for example, government policies, trends in key geographic markets, and so forth.

2. To identify characteristics of the industry and company that

impact systems requirements, for example, cost center structure, goals, financial performance, and so forth.
3. To identify present long-range business plans and objectives regarding projected growth rate and areas of growth, changes in direction, key assumptions that must be monitored, and their impact on the Systems Plan.
4. To review the existing system development plan regarding computer applications, personnel, and hardware.

The output of this study is the documentation of basic corporate objectives, the key factors which must be controlled to insure the achievement of these objectives, and the impact of these factors on the Systems Plan. The documentation should identify the main business assumptions on which the Plan will be based, indicate the key issues or systems which need particular examination, and broadly identify all areas which will be studied as candidates for systems development.

Define business information needs and related systems features. This segment identifies the specific information required by management to run the business effectively and to support the achievement of the business objectives. Information needs are approached from the top down within the organization. The work done in this segment is perhaps the most important of all tasks to be performed because the subsequent specification of systems projects will be based on information needs and related systems features defined here. Clearly, it is impractical to cover every information requirement in a company; however, a reasonably detailed layout is needed.

If information systems are to be considered as central management tools, their purpose should be to provide critical data necessary for key decisions which contribute to the earnings and/or general operating improvement of the company . As such, the task is to assist management in identifying the ingredients that are critical to the success of the company. The development of the key success factors results from close contact with functional management to obtain details of the operations, present information sources, methods for measuring performance, and various problems and opportunities facing the company.

Typically, this segment of the planning process is accomplished by many interviews with key management personnel.

The objective of these interviews is to identify all of the information and reporting necessary to assist the management of these operating areas in the operation, planning, control, and management of their areas of responsibility. When the analysis is approached from the top down, the results identify the comprehensive set of information needs. Included would be those systems that need to be developed on a corporate basis as well as those that would relate typically only to a local area. This work often results in the identification of the major functions and features required for mechanization as well as major enhancements to existing systems. It also would include those key reports required for the operation and management of each area.

In order to better understand the operation, data should be obtained on key volumes, necessary service levels, timing requirements, and other pertinent constraints and characteristics. Careful analysis of the data collected will provide the broad definition of the proposed reporting systems. This effort should result in an inventory of major reports and should also include a narrative that generally describes the uses of the information, the expected resultant actions, and the media and format of key reports.

After the management, operations, and accounting reports are identified, the next step is to outline the concepts of the data collection process for each area. At this point it means identifying all of the major transactions and types of data that must be collected, as well as collection frequencies and volumes. This will serve as the basis for designing the integrated data collection approach described earlier as a key component of a successful MIS structure.

In performing the analysis of information needs, it is helpful to recognize the hierarchy of systems requirements and their interrelationships. This is important for two major reasons. First, some systems are necessary building blocks to the effective design and implementation of other systems. Second, this hierarchy facilitates the evaluation of the implementation priorities in terms of the impact on cost or profit performance of a particular system to be implemented.

Determine the present status of systems. Determining present status involves documenting the operational, accounting, and management systems that currently exist or that are under development in the company. The work done here will establish that some requirements are computerized, while some are operating on a manual or partially mechanized basis, and that others have not been identified previously as systems requirements. The systems that have been automated must be carefully examined to determine their adequacy. This evaluation should consider the content of the existing systems as well as the general design approach and the necessary controls that will insure reliability, accuracy, and efficiency of the processing system. The present systems may meet management needs; however, they may not be efficient or cost effective; they may be inflexible in terms of data extraction, summarization, and reporting capabilities; or they may be difficult to maintain. In evaluating current systems, another important consideration is whether anticipated future volume levels can be accommodated.

Also during this segment, the present status of the systems development function and computer operations is assessed on an overall basis. The project team should evaluate these activities to determine how effectively they can meet management's objectives of quality, usefulness, service levels, and cost. In addition to reviewing the current state of computer operations, a review must be made to determine the impact of future anticipated volume levels with respect to work loads, hardware adequacy, manpower requirements, and cost of operations.

Develop the long-range plan

All data must now be summarized and organized in a format which specifies systems development efforts to be undertaken by the company over the next three to five years. The systems plan should present a logical approach to systems development and installation based on priority setting criteria approved by the Systems Steering Committee in the first segment and on prerequisite system requirements. The plan will also broadly outline the personnel, computer hardware and software, and dollars required for implementation and indicate the timeframe in which these resources must be available. Typically, this plan is published in two volumes. The first gives a management summary and outlines the objectives of the systems plan, the basis for establishing development priorities, and the organization of the detailed plan. Usually, the plan is summarized in terms of the short- and long-term action required, the resources required by time periods, any organizational changes to be considered, and the implementation approach of the plan. The implementation approach would specify any commitments management has to make and the applicable dates. The other document is the detailed systems plan, which specifies reports, files, and data collection systems.

A key step in the development of the systems plan is a clear explanation to members of the Systems Steering Committee to assure a level of understanding among these members and a firm basis for their approval of the plan and its concepts. This commitment must be communicated to the entire organization to enable the plan to receive the support necessary for execution. This top executive commitment is especially necessary if the plan includes the development of integrated data collection schemes and data bases or systems, both of which imply a shared responsibility for data handling.

Installing the MIS

The controller's continuing interest in building the MIS structure is probably one of monitoring the execution of each project identified in the long-range systems plan. The controller should participate as part of the Steering Committee to monitor progress. As such, familiarity with the basic methodology that is used by data processing management to plan and control the development and installation of each component of the MIS is needed. There are many different detailed methodologies that are in use for installating systems, but they all contain certain fundamental steps that are required to accomplish the job. Each approach may have more or fewer checkpoints, a different scope for each phase, or use different names for the phases. For this discussion these differences are not important. It is not the intent here to discuss any of this in detail; rather, it is to outline briefly the major tasks that must be accomplished to develop and implement a major system. Exhibit 4 is a graphical representation of a methodology that has been used successfully to install hundreds of major systems. In addition to the LRSP step which has already been discussed, this approach includes three major phases: (1) project definition, (2) preliminary systems design, and (3) systems installation.

EXHIBIT 4
Overall planning chart for business systems

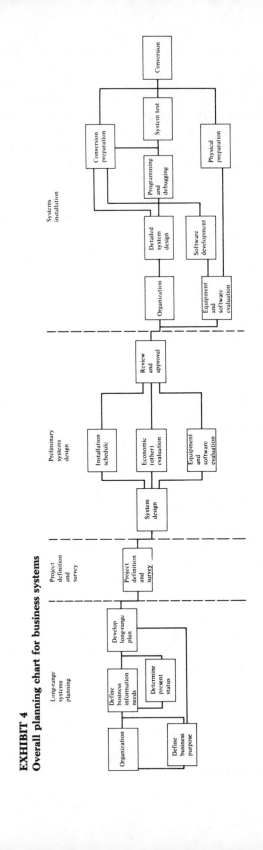

The primary purpose of the project definition phase is to reconfirm the scope and objectives of the system that were outlined in the related segment of the LRSP. Typically, this means discussions with the user departments who will operate the system, as well as with appropriate management personnel who will use management summary information developed by the system. Another primary purpose of this phase is to set the stage for the next phase, which should be the key phase from the controller's standpoint.

This next phase is the preliminary system design. The objective of this work is to define the system and to develop a cost/benefit analysis for management. This usually starts with a definition of the functions and features of the system from a business standpoint. This effort is typically done in sufficient detail to communicate to user and management personnel how the system will operate. Next, a level of data processing design work is done to estimate effectively the effort required to implement the system. Finally, a cost/benefit analysis is prepared to demonstrate to management the benefits and savings that will result from the system as well as the one-time development cost and the continuing operating cost. Typically it is not until this point in the process that installation cost can be determined with any degree of accuracy. At the conclusion of this phase, the company's management has an opportunity to make an informed decision regarding the implementation of the system.

Assuming that management is convinced of the merits of the system, the next major step is the detailed data processing design, programming, testing, and conversion activities. Although this is primarily a data processing effort, the controller and other members of the Steering Committee would be close to the conversion and user training activities included in this phase. In addition, there are usually post conversion follow-up activities including, perhaps, an operations audit to determine if the system is meeting the stated objectives and operating within the cost guidelines.

THE ROLE OF THE CONTROLLER IN EXECUTING THE MIS PLAN

The role that the controller should play in system development and use can be simply stated:

Active involvement is critical and means leadership and participation.

The controller's formal MIS responsibilities may have changed, but the task remains to be a key mover and shaper of information systems. Involvement is a shopworn term, but it is essential.

Three major activities stand out as key involvement areas:

1. *Long range systems planning.* Whose problem areas are most critical to the company, and where should resources be committed? What EDP capabilities should be expanded, contracted, or developed? The common answers to these questions are developed by the Steering Committee. The controller can and should direct their progress along the LRSP lines discussed above.

2. *Project management.* Only users can determine and design applications that will meet the decision needs of the managers affected. Participation in preliminary studies, system specifications, documentation and training, and implementation and follow-up activities are all necessary if the results are to meet the user's needs and expectations. A key element is direct management of the project itself. Others are participation in project reviews at critical decision points and managerial inputs regarding content, controls, and cost/benefit criteria.

3. *User/EDP operations relationships.* Ongoing EDP activities are vital to nearly every organizational unit. The highly technical EDP environment creates a need for communication and service links between the EDP center and the EDP user. Quality of data services, charges for services, improvements in applications, and resolution of problems are all factors that need user involvement in EDP activities on a regular basis.

MIS planning and control "truths"

The traditional management theme of planning and control is replayed. Experience has provided numerous guidelines. Controllers have a responsibility to incorporate these lessons, where appropriate, into a constructive planning and control system of MIS. A few "truths" dominate, including:

1. The starting point for extensive MIS development is the long-range systems plan explained earlier. But, the LRSP must be "do-able," lend itself to updating, and express the management's agreed upon priorities or else it loses its effectiveness.

2. The need exists for experienced management. Experience here implies EDP and general company management training that will allow MIS managers to match management's information needs and goals with EDP resources and plans. Fortunately, there is emerging a new generation of EDP managers who have technical knowledge and managerial experience. They have also witnessed the evolution of systems management and have a much clearer picture of the MIS management task.

3. Systems and computer operations are support functions with an objective of customer satisfaction. Actions must be taken directly and indirectly to avoid the natural erection of barriers between the MIS function and other parts of the firm. Physical, organizational, and attitudinal factors are all potential aids or stumbling blocks.

4. Responsibility assignments must be specified. Many management problems that have arisen in MIS work can be traced to broken responsibility links. At each developmental stage and in each step of information processing, clear job assignments are necessary as well as the definition of responsibility for time deadlines, incurring cost, and assessing the return on the system both before and after installation.

5. A philosophy of control needs to permeate the systems organization. While systems grow more complex, the need for controls grow at much faster rates. Controls are expensive and often include overhead, both of which reduce the efficiency of a system. Obviously, trade-offs are made, but controls and control itself must be weighed properly in these decisions.

6. Economic analysis must be applied to each systems decision. The difficulty is that most current systems work is aimed at qualitative improvements with benefits that are not readily measurable. Clearly, incremental costs and revenues are the key elements, but neither are easily measurable. Application of proven management accounting techniques is essential.

7. Organization location should be appropriate to give proper management exposure, decision authority, and service level control. The MIS unit does not have to report to the president, be under the controller's responsibility, nor be centralized or divisionalized. But the MIS executive must have a strong voice in EDP capabilities and firmwide systems planning and operation (hopefully with the executive management support cited earlier).

Many other factors could be cited; however, those already noted have clearly emerged as important to successful management. They have also remained valid over the past ten years—a period which has seen the significant maturing of systems management.

Ongoing controller involvement in MIS

As was cited earlier, the controller has historically been the primary mover in information systems development. Technological advances, organizational restructuring, and a multitude of other reasons have caused the MIS function to appear in many different places among firms. The controller may or may not have direct responsibility for MIS management. If not, a special problem of maintaining good relationships between the controller's office and the MIS staff undoubtedly exists. The well-being of the firm's decision makers requires cooperation and understanding between these two groups.

The controller has many formal and informal roles to play in the firm's MIS. Most of these have been identified and discussed. They include a diverse set of tasks:

1. The controller can generate executive-level management interest in and support for the development of a long-range systems plan.
2. Executive-level management's willingness to study ongoing MIS needs and priorities often depends on a few key active individuals. The controller should be the most active.
3. By providing leadership and/or manpower in the actual development and updating of the long-range plan, the controller can mold the direction and content of the LRSP.
4. Participation in the priority setting process and in commit-

ments to implement the LRSP means action, manpower, and budget support.

5. Willingness to provide leadership and/or manpower in systems projects which impact accounting in any manner is a key indicator of MIS commitment.

6. The careful selection of MIS management to assure that MIS knowledge and managerial experience are both present will produce a match of MIS management needs and managerial skills.

7. In an appropriate manner, the controller should apply to the MIS function budgetary and analytical controls that automatically start responsibility accounting in action.

8. Supporting the declaration that the MIS function is a service unit places emphasis on the need to be management supportive and customer oriented.

9. Reinforcing the deep commitment to control by requiring control checks in newly developed systems and reviews of controls in existing systems places the controller in the traditional namesake role.

10. The controller should be sure that the accounting staff has a sufficient level of EDP training to be effective in dealing with the systems staff.

11. The controller should develop corporate criteria for cost/benefit analysis applicable to systems work and other areas (including, perhaps, budget charges to users for EDP services used).

12. The controller's information needs now reverse the roles of user and provider of systems resources for the controller. Accounting is now one of a large set of system resource consumers.

13. Because of the firmwide accounting system ties, the controller can aid in building links between the MIS organization (both systems development and the EDP center managers), users of systems services, and the controller's personnel.

In summary, leadership and participation stand out as the keys to the controller's management information systems responsibilities. Much emphasis has been put on the long-range systems plan. This LRSP is a necessity if the management is to have an organized, coordinated, and prioritized MIS development program. The controller has a vital role to play in building and executing this plan.

The controller's MIS role will continue to evolve over time. It is clear that the MIS function will continue to grow as a major factor and force within most organizations. For a firm to have successful MIS, it must have active and cooperative systems and controllership functions. The controller has a parallel responsibility for planning and control activities. Improvement in a management information system can be defined as improvement in the quality of decision making.

12

Measuring and using return on investment information

*Frank R. Rayburn**
Michael M. Brown†

INTRODUCTION

Most financial control systems emphasize the importance of some form of return on investment (ROI). Alfred P. Sloan evaluated the principle of ROI as follows:

> I am not going to say that rate of return is a magic word for every occasion in business. There are times when you have to spend money just to stay in business, regardless of the visible rate of return. Competition is the final price determinant and competitive prices may result in profits which force you to accept a rate of return less than you hoped for, or for that matter to accept temporary losses. And, in times of inflation, the rate-of-return concept comes up against the problem of assets undervalued in terms of replacement. Nevertheless, no other financial principle with which I am acquainted serves better than rate of return as an objective aid to business judgment.[1]

---

* Associate Professor of Accounting, School of Accountancy, The University of Alabama.

† Manager-Project Management, Industrial Packaging Group, International Paper Corp., New York, N.Y.

[1] Alfred P. Sloan, Jr., *My Years with General Motors* (Garden City, N.Y.: Doubleday & Co., 1964), p. 140.

Although expressing some reservations about the concept, David Solomons said "it is widely regarded as a simple and effective measure of the efficiency with which a division or other profit-earning segment of the business is using the capital entrusted to it."[2]

J. Fred Weston stated "ROI is useful in providing information on every element of the balance sheet and income statement as a basis for further analysis."[3]

In a survey of 3,525 companies, Mauriel and Anthony found that 92.36 percent of responding firms who had investment centers used ROI as a measure of performance.[4]

From a random sample of 250 firms selected from Dun and Bradstreet's *Reference Book of Corporate Managements*, Fremgen determined that 49 percent of all respondents computed ROI as an input to capital budgeting decisions.[5]

Thus, there is ample evidence that return on investment is a generally accepted and widely used financial ratio.

Measurement of ROI and applications of ROI are addressed in this chapter.

MEASUREMENT OF RETURN ON INVESTMENT

Du Pont formula

E. I. du Pont de Nemours & Company generally are credited with development of the ROI concept as an operating tool. In the du Pont system, ROI is the product of profit margin (earnings as a percent of sales) and asset turnover. Thus, ROI is influenced by every item on the balance sheet and the income statement. Exhibit 1 depicts the relationship of the factors affecting ROI.

Asset turnover indicates the ability of a company or operating unit to convert the assets of the firm into sales, and *profit margin*

[2] David Solomons, *Divisional Performance: Measurement and Control* (Homewood, Ill.: Richard D. Irwin, 1965), p. 125.

[3] J. Fred Weston, "ROI Planning and Control," *Business Horizons* (August 1972), p. 42.

[4] John J. Mauriel and Robert N. Anthony, "Misevaluation of Investment Center Performance," *Harvard Business Review* (March–April 1966), p. 101.

[5] James M. Fremgen, "Capital Budgeting Practices: A Survey," *Management Accounting* (May 1973), p. 20.

EXHIBIT 1
Relationship of factors affecting return on investment

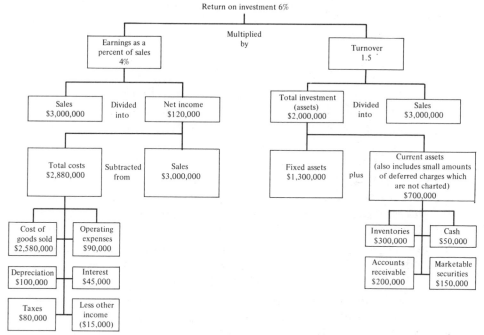

Source: J. Fred Weston and Eugene F. Brigham, *Managerial Finance* (New York: Holt, Rinehart and Winston, 1969), p. 75.

indicates the unit's ability to convert these sales into profits. The product of these two indicators reveals the ability of an operating unit to turn assets into profits (ROI).

These relationships are reflected by the following equation:

$$\text{ROI} = \frac{\text{Sales}}{\text{Total investment}} \times \frac{\text{Earnings}}{\text{Sales}}$$

To illustrate, assume total investment of $100, sales of $200 and earnings of $18:

$$\text{ROI} = \frac{200}{100} \times \frac{18}{200} = \frac{18}{100} = 18 \text{ percent}$$

ROI, asset turnover, and profit margin form the first level of an evaluation of an ongoing business unit's performance. The next level or phase of analysis requires breaking these three basic financial indicators into the balance sheet and income statement items of which they are comprised. This analysis is discussed in more detail later.

EARNINGS

For ROI to be useful, earnings must be clearly defined and understood. The matching principle of financial accounting is explicit but somewhat imprecise. Within the framework of the matching concept, there are several factors which may cause incomparability of earnings. Most notable of these factors are revenue, depreciation, and inventory valuation.

In addition to the need to define the components of earnings, the purpose of the ROI measure should be considered. For example, if the manager of a firm segment (any business unit of a firm that has the characteristics of an investment center) is being evaluated, earnings controllable by the manager (controllable operating profit as illustrated in Exhibit 2) would be appropriate. As demonstrated, this figure excludes both nonoperating gains and/or losses and other noncontrollable items. In addition, interest on the controllable investment is excluded as this is a financing charge and should not be included in measuring operating results. If the division manager has the ability to influence income taxes, appropriate income taxes could be deducted from controllable operating profit.

On the other hand, if the success of the division is to be evaluated as a business unit of the firm, the appropriate figure from Exhibit 2 would be net residual income after taxes plus interest on the total investment.

Revenue

Sales made to external parties, domestic or export, can typically be traced directly to a business segment. In a multidivision firm, however, intracompany sales can be sizeable. Of course, these sales can also be traced to a business segment. In reporting revenue, however, it may be desirable to report intracompany sales as a separate item for two reasons which are interrelated: (1) so that management can see the interdependence among

EXHIBIT 2
A form of divisional income statement

	$	$
Sales to outside customers	xxx	
Transfers to other divisions at market value	xxx	
Variable charges to other divisions for		
transfers not priced at market value	xxx	
		xxx
Less:		
Variable cost of goods sold and		
transferred	xxx	
Variable divisional expenses......................................	xxx	
		xxx
Variable profit		xxx
Add (deduct):		
Fixed charges made to (by) other divisions		
for transfers not priced at market value		xxx
		xxx
Less:		
Controllable divisional overhead	xxx	
Depreciation on controllable fixed assets	xxx	
Property taxes and insurance on		
controllable fixed assets..	xxx	xxx
Controllable operating profit		xxx
Add (deduct):		
Nonoperating gains and losses		xxx
		xxx
Less:		
Interest on controllable investment		xxx
Controllable residual income before taxes		xxx
Less:		
Noncontrollable divisional overhead	xxx	
Incremental central expenses		
chargeable to division	xxx	
Interest on noncontrollable investment	xxx	xxx
Net residual income before taxes		xxx
Less:		
Taxes on income		xxx
Net residual income after taxes		xxx

Source: David Solomons, *Divisional Performance: Measurement and Control* (Homewood, Ill.: Richard D. Irwin, 1965), p. 82.

the divisions of the company, and (2) so that the impact of transfer prices on income can be considered. The transfer pricing problem will not be discussed here, but it is important to note that a decision to transfer products at market prices will impact income quite differently than a decision to transfer goods at cost or some other price.

It should also be noted that whereas transfer prices affect the revenue of the selling unit, they affect the cost of goods sold of the buying unit.

Depreciation

The theory of depreciation accounting is well known and thoroughly covered in the accounting literature. The purpose here is not to recount theory but to point out that different depreciation methods are appropriate and acceptable, and further that periodic earnings are directly affected by the depreciation method used. If ROI is to be used in a comparative sense, either on an interfirm basis or on a time series basis for the same firm or division, depreciation charges should be analyzed to ensure that they relate to the life expectancy of the assets and, moreover, that the assumed rate of usage (accelerated or straight-line depreciation) is appropriate and comparable.

This statement is not intended to constrain selection of the most favorable depreciation methods for tax purposes. Rather, it is to recognize that depreciation methods used for tax purposes might be inappropriate for performance evaluation.

Inventory valuation

Under the last-in, first-out (Lifo) inventory valuation method, the most recently incurred costs flow through the income statement as cost of goods sold and the earlier costs are deferred in the inventory accounts. When using the first-in, first-out (Fifo) method, the earlier costs flow through the income statement as cost of goods sold and the later, more recent costs are deferred in the inventory accounts.

Traditionally, two arguments have come forth in support of Lifo: (1) In periods of rising prices, Lifo results in a lower periodic income, thereby deferring the income tax liability and increasing cash flow; and (2) Lifo results in the matching of current costs with current revenue, which yields an income figure practically devoid of holding gains if inventory quantities remain constant, or increase. While one could make a strong case for the theoretical issue, the practical tax benefit cannot be overlooked.

Where profit is used to measure performance of a business segment, however, Lifo has certain deficiencies: (1) In periods of fluctuating prices, income is subject to manipulation; i.e., a division can decide to replace or not to replace low-cost inventories; and (2) the tax issue may prove dysfunctional in that "a division may be discouraged from doing what it ought to be encouraged to do, namely, to cut its investment in inventory to the minimum amount consistent with fully efficient operations."[6] The income manipulation problem follows from the fact that, in periods of rising prices, a decision not to replace part or all of a Lifo layer will flow old, lower costs through the income statement, thus increasing income and the tax liability. The ability to manipulate income under Lifo is not only theoretically possible but also has been observed in practice. In some firms, however, monthly Lifo inventory levels are budgeted and the Lifo adjustment is made only at year-end at the corporate level, thus minimizing the opportunity for divisional manipulation of income. Additionally, the use of a "Reserve for Replacement of Lifo Inventory" account would thwart attempts to manipulate income to improve short-run ROI.

There is another way to have the best of both worlds. If Lifo is desirable for tax purposes, divisional income could be computed on a Fifo basis with an adjustment made to Lifo basis at the statement date for external purposes. The use of Fifo is recommended for performance evaluation purposes, because it tends to minimize a segment's ability to manipulate income by merely deciding to replace or not to replace low-cost inventories. At the same time, management is motivated to optimize its investment in inventory.

INVESTMENT

There are two aspects of investment that appear critical: (1) definition of the investment base and (2) measurement of the investment base.

Definition of investment base

If ROI is to be a useful statistic, the investment base must be clearly defined. The following four alternatives have been suggested by Horngren:

1. *Total assets available.* This base includes all business assets, regardless of their individual purpose.

---

[6] Solomons, *Divisional Performance,* pp. 99–100.

2. *Total assets employed.* This base excludes excess or idle assets, such as vacant land or construction in progress.
3. *Net working capital plus other assets.* This base is really the same as (1), except that current liabilities are deducted from the total assets available. In a sense, this represents an exclusion of that portion of current assets that is supplied by short-term creditors. The main justification for this base is that the manager often does have direct influence over the amount of short-term credit that he utilizes. An able manager should maximize the use of such credit, within some overall constraints to prevent endangering the company's credit standing.
4. *Stockholders' equity.* This base centers attention on the rate of return that will be earned by the business owners.[7]

The use of stockholders' equity as an investment base confounds the operating and financing decisions within the firm. Return on stockholders' equity is critical to the firm and the stockholders, but is inappropriate as a measure of operating performance. To illustrate, consider the following example which has been extracted from Horngren:[8]

($000)	*(1)* Assets	*(2)* Lia-bilities	*(3)* Stock-holders' equity	*(4)* Income before interest	*(5)* 8% interest	*(6)* Net income*	*(4) ÷ (1)* Return on investment* Assets	*(6) ÷ (3)* Stock-holders' equity
Company A ...	$1,000	$500	$ 500	$200	$40	$160	20%	32%
Company B ...	1,000	—	1,000	200	—	200	20	20

* Income taxes ignored here for simplicity.

If return on stockholders' equity is used to measure the performance of the managers of Company A and Company B, the performance of the manager of Company A would appear superior when, in fact, there is no difference in the operating results of the two companies. The increase in return on stockholders' equity for Company A is the product of a financing decision,

---

[7] Charles T. Horngren, *Cost Accounting: A Managerial Emphasis,* 4th ed. (Englewood Cliffs, N.J.: Prentice-Hall, 1977), p. 715.
[8] Ibid.

not an operating decision. Specifically, one half of Company A's assets are provided from debt capital at a cost of 8 percent, which in turn has earned 20 percent or a net return of 12 percent on debt equity. Trading on the equity is a critical management decision, but the results of financing decisions should not be commingled with the results of operating decisions when evaluating operating managers.

Thus, for measuring the performance of managers of a business segment, either total assets, total assets employed, or net working capital plus other assets should almost always be preferred over stockholders' equity.

If the segment manager controls both the acquisition and the use of assets without regard to their financing, total assets is perhaps the best base. If, in addition to the authority to control the acquisition and use of assets, the manager has direct influence over the use of short-term trade credit and bank loans, then net working capital plus other assets would be better. If the manager either has no direct control over the acquisition of assets or is forced by top management to carry excess assets, then total assets employed would be superior.

NAA Research Report #35 reported that total assets available was most often used as the investment base.[9] A later study by Mauriel and Anthony found that total assets available was most often used, with net working capital plus other assets a close second.[10]

Centrally controlled or shared items

So far, we have assumed an environment where all assets and liabilities (current) are controlled by and directly traceable to specific divisions. In many cases this assumption does not hold.

In multidivision firms it is common practice for cash, accounts receivable, and perhaps trade payables to be centrally administered. Where this condition prevails, part of the corporate cash balance should be allocated in computing division investment on the grounds that the corporate cash balance could be reduced if a division was eliminated. Traditionally, many firms have allo-

---

[9] National Association of Accountants, *Return on Capital as a Guide to Managerial Decisions: Research Report 35* (New York, 1959), p. 8.

[10] Mauriel and Anthony, "Misevaluation of Investment Center Performance," pp. 101–2.

cated cash on the relative proportion of sales or cost of sales. This would be appropriate only if there is a direct and definable relationship between cash needs of a division and its sales or cost of sales. Another approach has been to exclude cash from the division investment base on the presumption that current liabilities would offset the cash investment. A better procedure would be to analyze the cash flows of each division so that a reasonable estimate of the real cash investment can be made.

Centrally administered receivables and payables can readily be identified with specific divisions and should be included in the investment base.

Regarding centrally controlled fixed assets, there are two basic classifications: (1) centrally held and centrally used assets, such as corporate office buildings, and (2) shared assets, such as research and development centers and sales offices.

Arguments have been set forth in opposition to allocation of centrally held and centrally used assets on the grounds that such allocations are arbitrary and meaningless. We concur with the grounds stated, but since ROI is a relative financial ratio we are indifferent about the allocation of these assets. Consistency is more relevant, and so long as actual ROI is computed on the same basis as targeted ROI we find little support for either allocation or nonallocation.

For shared assets, a predetermined allocation base related to proportional usage, either in terms of physical space or services rendered, is appropriate.

Measurement of the investment base

Having defined the investment base, the firm then must determine how the assets in the investment base should be measured. The measurement problem relates primarily to nonmonetary items, as monetary assets and liabilities are stated in terms of historical cost, current value, and units of general purchasing power (assuming a viable going concern). Some practical measurement alternatives for nonmonetary items are historical cost, replacement cost, and general price-level adjusted cost.

Historical cost. Mauriel and Anthony reported that only 2.8 percent of the firms responding to their questionnaire used some measurement base other than historical cost. Another way of stating this is that 97.2 percent of firms used historical cost.[11] Where historical cost is used, one must go further and choose either gross book value or net book value.

Gross book value. Mauriel and Anthony found that 18.5 percent of the firms studied used gross book value.[12] A strong argument for this basis was espoused by E. I. du Pont deNemours & Company, whose position is explained in the following quotation:

> Gross operating investment represents all the plant, tools, equipment, and working capital made available to operating management for its use; no deduction is made for liabilities or for accumulated depreciation and obsolescence. Since plant facilities are maintained in virtually top condition during their working life, we believe it would be inappropriate to consider that operating management was responsible for earning a return on only the net operating investment. Furthermore, if depreciable assets were stated at net depreciated values, earnings in each succeeding period would be related to an ever-decreasing investment; even with stable earnings, return on investment would continually rise, so that comparative return on investment ratios would fail to reveal the extent or trend of management performance. Relating earnings to investment that is stable and uniformly compiled provides a sound basis for comparing the profitability of assets employed as between years and between investments.[13]

Recent research by Williamson reveals the following:

> . . . it appears that the accounting rate of return computed using gross assets is a more useful management tool than the rate computed using net assets because the former rate is not affected by changes in expansion rates. Changes over time in the accounting rate of return based on gross assets indicate that changes in the average time-adjusted rate have occurred, whereas changes in the rate based on net assets may mean only that the division's expansion rate has changed. The rate based on gross assets is thus useful in making period-to-period comparisons of a particular segment's profitability.[14]

---

[11] Ibid.

[12] Ibid.

[13] Solomons, *Divisional Performance,* pp. 134–35, as modified by E. I. du Pont letter dated August 8, 1978.

[14] Robert W. Williamson, "Measuring Divisional Profitability," *Management Accounting* (January 1975), pp 41–42.

On the other hand, Dearden has pointed out the following deficiencies of gross book value:

> If gross book value is used, it is possible for a manager to increase his investment return by scrapping perfectly useful assets that are not contributing profits equal to the division's objective. (When an asset is scrapped, the fixed-assets account is reduced by the original cost of the asset.) If composite depreciation is used (and most large companies use composite depreciation) the division will not even show a capital loss from disposition. This occurs because, under composite depreciation, assets are considered to be fully depreciated when they are retired.
>
> The theory is that the depreciation rates are based on the average life of a group of assets. Some will last longer than the average; others, shorter. No gain or loss is taken, therefore, when an individual asset is retired. Even if unit depreciation is used, the loss will be less than the reduction in the investment base where assets have been depreciated. This means that the impact of scrapping a fixed asset can be favorable to the division's ROI even where such action is clearly detrimental to the company.
>
> In addition to encouraging the disposition of perfectly good assets, the use of gross book value will have an inconsistent effect on the investment base when equipment is replaced. The gross book value will increase only by the difference between the cost of the new equipment and the original cost of the old. The investment of the company, however, is equal to the cost of the new equipment minus the salvage value of the old equipment. In most cases, the salvage value will be far below the original cost. Thus, replacement investments that are far below the company's cutoff rate could improve the division's rate of return.[15]

Net book value. Over 73 percent of firms use net book value as the basis for plant and equipment in computing ROI.[16] The problems with net book value can best be illustrated with the one-asset case. To illustrate, let us use an example of a business segment formed by a large manufacturing company in 1971 with an investment in plant of $6 million. The following simplifying assumptions apply:

---

[15] John Dearden, "The Case Against ROI Control," *Harvard Business Review* (May–June 1969), p. 127. Copyright © 1969 by the President and Fellows of Harvard College; all rights reserved.

[16] Mauriel and Anthony, "Misevaluation of Investment Center Performance," pp. 101–2.

The plant and equipment have an expected life of ten years, and straight-line depreciation is used.

During this ten-year period, the $6 million investment represents the only assets employed.

The assets last ten years as predicted and have zero salvage value at that time.

A segment net after-tax profit of $375,000 annually remains constant throughout the ten-year period.

As Exhibit 3 shows, ROI computed on net book value is 6.6 percent in Year One and increases at an increasing rate each

EXHIBIT 3
Calculation of book ROI
($000)

	1971	1972	1973	1974	1975	1976	1977	1980
1. Profit	$ 375	$ 375	$ 375	$ 375	$ 375	$ 375	$ 375	$375
2. Investment base* ..	$5,700	$5,100	$4,500	$3,900	$3,300	$2,700	$2,100	$300
3. Book ROI (1 ÷ 2) ..	6.6%	7.4%	8.3%	9.6%	11.4%	13.9%	17.9%	125%

* Average of beginning and end-of-year book value of assets.

year with an ROI of 125 percent in the tenth year. The true rate of return for this investment is 10 percent on a discounted cash-flow basis.[17]

Although the above is a one-asset case, the results are confirmed for the multi-asset case by logic and by Williamson's study which concluded that ROI based on net book value is inversely related to the rate of expansion of the asset base, in addition to being related to earnings performance. Specifically, as the rate of expansion of the asset base increases, ROI will decrease, and vice versa.

Research has indicated, however, that the assumption of an ever-decreasing fixed asset base or an ever-increasing fixed asset base does not always hold. If the business has reached a stable size such that the fixed asset valuation is reasonably constant, or if the fixed asset base is expanding at a fairly constant rate, a constant rate of return ensues whether the assets are valued at gross or net book value, though its absolute value will differ in the two cases.

---

[17] Adapted from Mauriel and Anthony, "Misevaluation of Investment Center Performance," p. 103.

Replacement cost. Because of the physical nature of fixed assets, in periods of rising prices, *ceteris paribus,* profits tend to rise faster than the asset base. Thus, ROI tends to rise in a period of rising prices. The problem is that profit and capital required to generate profit are measured in dollars of different purchasing power. Thus, ROI is directly affected by not only its operating performance, but also the aging schedule of asset acquisitions. Specifically, business segments with older asset mixes would tend to have higher ROI's than those whose asset base had been acquired more recently.

Ideally, the measurement basis for evaluating performance should be uniform. For example, suppose Division A acquired fixed assets in 1970 at a cost of $100 and that Division B acquired assets on 1/1/77 at a cost of $100. Further, assume profit for each division for 1977 of $10. Using historical cost, each division generates a return of 10 percent. Is this realistic? Only if the assets of Division A could have been acquired on 1/1/77 at $100. Suppose for illustrative purposes that the replacement cost of Division A's assets on 1/1/77 was $125. Which division performed better in 1977? Division B's return of 10 percent would be superior to Division A's ROI of 8 percent.

The basic arguments raised in opposition to replacement cost involve implementation. It has been suggested that the objective of approximating the current cost to obtain similar assets that would produce the same expected operating cash flows as the existing asset is either unattainable or too subjective and too costly to justify the increased accuracy.

Since *Accounting Series Release No. 190* requires replacement cost data for inventories and plant and equipment for certain large firms, information is readily available for these firms. Furthermore, this process should help determine the cost of generating such data for all firms.

To summarize, it may well be that even an approximation of replacement cost is preferred over historical cost. To implement replacement costs would require a major psychological adjustment, however. Managements would probably find that returns so computed would be considerably lower than the numbers to which they have been accustomed.

General price-level adjusted cost. As indicated earlier, periods of monetary instability result in assets carried in the accounts

EXHIBIT 4
Comparison—1967

	Division A		Division B	
	Gross book value	*General price level adjusted*	*Gross book value*	*General price level adjusted*
Asset base	$100	$107.20*	$100	$102.50†
Profit	$ 10	$ 9.28	$ 10	$ 9.75
ROI................	10%	8.66%	10%	9.51%

* To restate 1965 dollars to 12/31/67 dollars, the GNP Implicit Price Deflator suggests a conversion factor of 1.072.

† To restate 1/1/67 dollars to 12/31/67 dollars, the GNP Implicit Price Deflator suggests a conversion factor of 1.025.

being measured by dollars of different purchasing power. One solution is to restate historical cost data by the use of price indices which measure the change in the ability of the monetary unit (the dollar) to command goods and services. This adjustment corrects only for changes in the value of money and restates assets on a common dollar basis.

General price-level adjusted data is not an attempt to determine current value or replacement cost. The subjectivity associated with replacement cost is removed because historical cost is the basis for price-level adjustments. To illustrate, assume that Division A acquired fixed assets at a cost of $100 on 1/1/65 and Division B purchased fixed assets at a cost of $100 on 1/1/67. In both cases, assume a ten-year useful life, straight-line depreciation, and accounting income of $10 annually. For a comparison of 1967 ROI using gross book value and general price-level adjusted data, see Exhibit 4.

Note that on the basis of historical cost, ROI is the same for both divisions, whereas on a price-level adjusted basis Division B yields a higher return.

General price-level adjusted data is not a surrogate for replacement cost, but it does adjust for changes in the value of the dollar. Current knowledge suggests that few companies use price-level adjusted data to compute ROI.

In the first part of this chapter, the measurement of ROI was discussed with considerable emphasis on some of the problems that must be addressed by the firm which uses ROI as a measure of performance. The next section deals with the application of ROI.

APPLICATION OF RETURN ON INVESTMENT

While there are other uses of ROI (such as pricing and inventory strategy), the concept has been applied most widely to two broad areas: (1) performance evaluation of an entire company or of business units within the firm, and (2) evaluation of capital investment opportunities.

Performance evaluation

The problems associated with evaluating the strengths and weaknesses of an ongoing business differ in perspective from the problems associated with evaluating an investment decision. While both types of evaluation concern themselves with future performance, the analysis of an ongoing business also concerns itself heavily with past performance and existing trends. This historical perspective, combined with the availability of data on actual performance, allows the evaluation of an ongoing business to be based on a wide array of financial indicators.

Most financial control systems emphasize the importance of some form of return on investment (ROI) as a basic indicator of business performance. Any evaluation of a business decision must eventually indicate how that decision will impact ROI.

After ROI, two indicators of particular importance are profit margin and asset or capital turnover. The product of these two indicators forms a company's ROI. Asset turnover indicates the ability of a company or operating unit to convert the assets its shareholders own into sales, and profit margin indicates the unit's ability to convert these sales into profits. Combining these indicators reveals the ability of an operating unit to turn assets into profits (ROI).

ROI, profit margin, and asset turnover form the first level of an evaluation of an ongoing unit's performance. The next level or phase of analysis requires breaking these three basic financial indicators into the balance sheet and income statement items of which they are comprised.

Evaluation of profit margin requires a close analysis of the factors affecting both sales and net income. One technique for analyzing the sales portion of the ratio is to perform a variance analysis. Such an analysis breaks any change in sales into its price, volume, and mix components. This breakdown clearly enlarges management's understanding of changes in the total sales figure.

If further evaluation of total sales is required, a sensitivity analysis of the price/volume relationship can be constructed (through market studies or the judgment of sales personnel). This sensitivity analysis reveals the price elasticity of the product lines involved. An understanding of this elasticity allows management to evaluate whether, in fact, it has effectively used the pricing mechanism to maximize sales.

As previously noted, another factor to be considered in management's analysis of the profit margin indicator is *mix*. Mix not only affects the sales portion of profit margin, but it also alters the net income portion of the ratio. Thus, product mix plays an important role in any analysis of the profit margin indicator and must be considered when attempting to evaluate changes in an operating unit's margin.

Further ratio analysis of the profit margin indicator requires closer examination of total cost and its components. Ratios and indicators used in this type of analysis normally express some cost category as a percent of sales. Indicators that are rising, or are higher than the industry norm, indicate areas requiring management's attention.

Clearly, trend analysis is an important tool at this stage of the analysis. Plotting movement in each cost category as a percent of sales and comparing these trends against movements in industry cost factors help indicate where an operating unit is losing competitive cost advantages.

The other contributor to ROI, asset turnover, can be analyzed by developing ratios from the balance sheet. Current assets can be analyzed by using inventory turnover and the average collection period. Inventory turnover indicates whether excessive inventory levels are being maintained for the level of sales activity. Average collection period indicates how well the operating unit has been able to turn its receivables into cash.

Finally, fixed asset turnover indicates how well the unit is using its plant and equipment capacity. A low or declining turnover shows that the unit is maintaining too large a production capacity for the sales level being generated.

Using all these indicators in the analysis of an ongoing business permits a broad evaluation of its strengths and weaknesses. By identifying particular points of weakness, management can turn to the operating and marketing statistics that find their financial expression in that particular indicator. It is at this point in the analysis that management must turn from financial indicators to marketing and production statistics.

For example, the formal vehicle by which International Paper Company (IPCO) monitors the performance of the company's operating units is the monthly Performance Review Management Summary (PRMS). Weekly earnings forecasts and other formal and informal reports are also used by management, but the PRMS lies at the heart of the company's performance evaluation system.

The PRMS is a monthly summary of an operating unit's historical results as well as a projection of the unit's results for the year. It is designed to communicate to management each unit's current and near-term problems and opportunities.

While a variety of statistical data is provided by this report, it focuses on the following financial indicators:

$$\text{Profit margin} = \frac{\text{Net earnings}}{\text{Net sales}} \times 100$$

$$\text{Capital employed} = \text{Net working capital} + \text{Other assets}$$

$$\text{Asset turnover} = \frac{\text{Net sales}}{\text{Average total capital employed}}$$

$$\text{Net earnings per share} =$$
$$\frac{\text{Net earnings} - \text{Preferred stock dividends}}{\text{Average number of shares of common stock outstanding}}$$

$$\text{Return on investment} =$$
$$\frac{\text{Net earnings (annualized)} + \text{Pretax interest (annualized)}}{\text{Average capital employed}} \times 100$$

$$\text{Return on share owners' equity} =$$
$$\frac{\text{Net earnings (annualized)}}{\text{Number of shares} \times \text{Assigned value per share}} \times 100$$

As noted in the preceding discussion on the analysis of operating unit performance, three of these indicators (ROI, profit margin, and asset turnover) are particularly important. In the PRMS, actual results for these indicators are compared to budget, forecast, and the preceding year's actual performance. These comparisons are made for the month being reported and for year-to-date totals (See Exhibit 5).

Two additional indicators reported in the PRMS, earnings per share (EPS) and return on share owners' equity (ROE), play an important role in the monitoring of monthly operating unit performance. Basically, operating unit EPS and ROE are used as a quick check against the company's EPS and ROE. This comparison indicates whether a particular unit is supporting the company's earnings performance (has an EPS above the company's EPS), or is hindering the company's performance. One important question is whether the unit is able to cover its share of the company's current dividend rate per share.

Since individuals do not directly invest in the company's operating units, some artificial method of assigning shares and equity must be used. At International Paper, units are assigned a portion of the company's shares at the beginning of each year. This portion is based on the unit's budgeted capital employed for the coming year. Once this assignment is made, the unit's number of shares does not vary throughout the year.

Shareowners' equity, however, is assigned on a monthly basis. The company's total equity is computed each month and assigned to the units on a per share basis. Thus an operating unit's number of assigned shares will remain constant each month, but its assigned equity will vary as the company's equity varies.

From an operating manager's standpoint, ROI, profit margin, and asset turnover are the most critical financial indicators in management's monthly performance review. Normally, however, attention does not focus directly on these indicators. Instead, discussion is focused on the operating statistics that give rise to these indicators. For example, the earnings contribution of an operating unit and its level of sales normally receive first attention. Falling sales and earnings are clearly going to face some hard questioning even if the relationship between them, as expressed in the profit margin, is improving.

Thus the importance of financial ratios as monthly perfor-

EXHIBIT 5

-- Performance Review Management Summary (Detail)

_____ 1977

SALES

						1976		
	1 9 7 7							
Actual	Forecast	% Diff. Actual Vs. Fore-cast	Budget	% Actual B/(W) Than Budget	Actual	% Actual B/(W) Than 1976	$ Thousands	
							January	
							February	
							March	
							April	
							May	
							June	
							July	
							August	
							September	
							October	
							November	
							December	
							Yr-End Adj	
							YTD___Mos	
F							YEAR	

NET EARNINGS

	1 9 7 7						1976	
Actual	Forecast	% Diff. Actual Vs. Fore-cast	Budget	% Actual B/(W) Than Budget	Actual	% Actual B/(W) Than 1976		
F								

FINANCIAL INDICATORS

MONTH						YEAR TO DATE		
1977			1976		1977			1976
Actual	Forecast	Budget	Actual		Actual	Forecast	Budget	Actual
%	%	%	%	Profit Margin	%	%	%	%
a	a	a	a	Asset Turnover	a	a	a	a
b	b	b	b	Capital Employed	c	c	c	c
				Common Shares Assigned				
a	a	a	a	Net Earnings/Share	a	a	a	a
%	%	%	%	Return on Investment (d)	%	%	%	%
%	%	%	%	Return on Share Owners Equity (e)	%	%	%	%
				Number of Employees				

a Annualized.
b At end of prior month.
c Average of Year to end of prior month.

(d) $\frac{\text{Net Earnings (Annualized)} + \text{Pretax Interest (Annualized)}}{\text{Capital Employed}} \times 100$ (e) $\frac{\text{Net Earnings (Annualized)}}{\text{Number of Shares X Assigned Value per Share}} \times 100$

SALES BY MARKET SEGMENT

MONTH				YEAR TO DATE			
1977			1976	1977			1976
Actual	Forecast	Budget	Actual	Actual	Forecast	Budget	Actual

Form 040 (Rev. 1/77)

mance indicators is somewhat secondary to other absolute figures. There are several reasons for this, but two reasons in particular should be mentioned.

Normally, at IPCO, changes in the month-to-month level of asset turnover are dictated by changes in the absolute level of sales. With an asset base as large as International Paper's, significant changes in assets (as a percent of the total asset base) do not normally occur from month to month. Thus, explanations addressed to changes in the absolute sales level do, in fact, explain changes in the capital turnover rate.

Profit margin is normally used as a measure of a unit's cost effectiveness. A decline in profit margin indicates that costs are not changing proportionately to sales. To explain changes in a unit's profit margin requires an examination of individual cost factors. These cost items are so extensive in a corporation the size of International Paper that the profit margin indicator carries very little useful information for the operating manager.

To better manage these costs and allow management to effectively go below the profit margin level, International Paper employs an elaborate standard cost system. This system achieves two goals that make it a more effective tool for evaluating operating performance.

First, the standard cost system allows management to quickly isolate those cost factors requiring their attention. In essence, the standard cost system is one large exception-reporting system. As a result, management can focus on just those items causing significant cost variances. This, in turn, allows them to effectively address those items that ultimately cause undesirable changes in profit margin.

The second characteristic of the standard cost system that makes it such an important management guide is its hierarchical structure of cost summaries. Cost information is initially input to the system at levels far too detailed for most reviews by management. However, cost variances computed at this highly detailed level are summarized in stages that gradually decrease the level of detail. As a result, management can not only focus on those factors adversely affecting the profit margin indicator, but they can do so at whatever level of detail they choose.

Return on investment, like other ratios or index numbers, is not a perfect measure of operating performance and must be interpreted in conjunction with other factors. Some aspects of the problem are as follows:

1. Realistic ROI levels should be budgeted for each operating unit; company-wide ROI targets are useful only as a measure of company-wide performance and generally are not useful in evaluating the performance of individual operating units. Performance should be judged by variance from the targeted return and not by the absolute level of return.
2. In addition to looking at variance from targeted ROI for a given period, ROI should be evaluated over time. To facilitate this analysis, management should concentrate on percentage improvement instead of looking at absolute changes.
3. If ROI is to be used to compare performance of business units or business unit managers, great care must be taken to insure comparability of items included in ROI. As noted earlier in this chapter, distortions can result from several factors: inventory valuation methods, depreciation methods, capitalization versus expense policy, age of plant, and so forth.
4. If ROI is to be used effectively, management at all levels must understand the basis for the computation and why that basis is appropriate.

It is also important to remember that ROI is a quantitative measure of performance. As such, it is a very strong management tool, but qualitative factors should also be considered in analyzing the performance of a business unit manager. Some qualitative elements to be evaluated are quality of the products, employee relations, public relations, customer relations, product development, and intrafirm relations.

Capital investment decisions

NAA Research Report # 35 states:

> Evaluation of capital investment proposals raises problems which are distinctly different from the measurement of past performance. In reviewing past performance, the amounts of capital employed and of income realized have been established by historical events and the figures have been recorded in the accounts. On the other hand, in looking toward the future there are alternative

EXHIBIT 6
Return on investment method

Amount invested	$20,000
Annual aftertax cash flow	6,200
Less: Annual depreciation ($20,000/5)	4,000
Annual net income	$ 2,200
Return on original investment	
($2,200/$20,000)	11%
Return on average investment	
($2,200/$10,000)	22%

courses of action from which to choose and comparative evaluation of these alternatives in financial terms is the heart of the problem of decision making in the broad field of capital budgeting. Return on capital, determined from estimates of future costs and revenues for each project, is a useful tool for this purpose.[18]

The ROI model, when used to evaluate capital investment proposals, also is referred to as the accrual accounting model, the financial statement model, the unadjusted rate-of-return model, and the book-value model. In its simplest form the computation is as follows:

$$\frac{\text{Average annual net income (savings)}}{\text{Average investment}} = \text{Rate of return}$$

Sometimes the denominator is the original investment rather than average investment.

Recent research revealed that ROI was computed as an input to capital investment decisions by 49 percent of all responding firms and by 60 percent of firms with capital budgets in excess of $100 million. This study found further that ROI was the most important method used by 22 percent of all firms and by 31 percent of those firms with capital budgets greater than $100 million.[19]

The popularity of this method probably stems from its simplicity, familiarity, and usefulness in post audits. The method is simple to apply as illustrated in Exhibit 6. This case assumes consideration of a proposal to invest $20,000 in a depreciable asset with an expected useful life of five years, straight-line deprecia-

---

[18] National Association of Accountants, *Research Report 35*, p. 49.
[19] Fremgen, "Capital Budgeting Practices: A Survey," p. 20.

tion, no salvage value, and projected average annual net income of $2,200. As shown, the return computed on the original investment is 11 percent and when computed on average investment is 22 percent. The basic decision criterion would be to establish an acceptable return based on either the original or the average investment; compare the projected return with the hurdle rate; and make a decision.

The familiarity aspect mentioned above relates to the fact that even though projected data is used, the investment and net income figures are determined in accordance with accrual basis accounting principles. It is also this foundation that facilitates post audits of capital expenditures. To the extent that accounting data can be traced to specific investments, the data regularly accumulated by the accounting information system can be used to follow up on the results of investment decisions.

The basic weakness of the accounting rate-of-return model is that it is based on annual averages, which ignores the problem of uneven income streams and the time value of money.

CONCLUSION

It would be naive to suggest that return on investment has no limitations. The problems of defining the components of ROI have, therefore, been reviewed. On the other hand, if ROI is understood and properly implemented, it can be the single most useful financial ratio available to management.

The primary advantages of ROI have been discussed at length in the literature and are recounted here as follows:

1. ROI is a comprehensive and generally accepted measure of overall performance. ROI is impacted by any activity within the firm that affects either a balance sheet item or an income statement item. Thus, segment managers are motivated to consider the impact of all operating decisions on ROI. If each business segment maximizes return on investment, the ROI for the company as a whole should be maximized. ROI is a means of achieving goal congruence between business segments and the company.
2. ROI is a common denominator which provides for meaningful comparisons of intrafirm as well as interfirm activities.

Similarly, comparisons of alternative investment proposals are facilitated.

3. ROI provides an incentive to use existing assets to the fullest and to acquire additional assets only when they offer potential for maintaining or increasing an acceptable rate of return. ROI also makes it possible to measure the success of a division's capital investment activities. Where accounting data can be traced to specific capital projects, actual ROI can be compared with the projected return. If accounting data are accumulated by divisions and not by capital projects, by including new investments in the investment base, divisional ROI will be reduced when actual profits fail to meet projections.

4. ROI is easily understood and interpreted. For example, a division or a proposed capital investment which generates an after-tax return of 2.8 percent is earning less than the return afforded by risk-free government bonds. With respect to the division, something clearly is wrong and attention is required. For the proposed investment, the decision should be not to invest. Likewise, divisions or capital proposals projecting after-tax returns of 18 percent are earning a return greater than could be realized from almost any alternative investment opportunity.

13

Transfer pricing

Richard G. Schroeder*
Calvin A. Vobroucek†

Decentralization, the segmentation of a large enterprise into smaller entities, has become a fact of corporate life during the past three decades. The companies which have undertaken decentralization have claimed the following benefits:

1. The individual enterprise becomes more efficient because it adapts faster to supply and demand factors.
2. Management is closer to the operations of the entity and is therefore in a better position to make decisions.
3. The burden of decision making is more widely distributed, thereby allowing more time for managers to examine relevant information.
4. The freedom to make decisions increases the individual manager's incentive.
5. The distribution of decision making allows for more and better training of managers.
6. Less red tape in the decision process allows for faster decisions.

---

* Associate Professor of Accounting, Texas A & M University.

† Manager, Profit Planning Accounting, Caterpillar Tractor Co.

PROFIT CENTERS

The decentralization of a firm is most frequently accomplished through the establishment of profit centers. A *profit center* is a segment of a business which is responsible for the costs it incurs as well as the revenues it generates. The establishment of profit centers in a decentralized environment implies that the managers of these segments are free to make all decisions affecting that segment. For example, the manager of a segment should be able to purchase raw materials from an outside supplier rather than another segment of the firm if they can be acquired more economically outside the total company.

Economic efficiency is the utilization of resources to achieve the maximum possible benefit. Inefficient operations cause waste and can ultimately result in an enterprise being unable to compete effectively in the marketplace. If a segment is to be economically efficient it should follow the same patterns of behavior found in independent entities competing against each other. Generally this goal will be accomplished when the individual components attempt to maximize their individual segmented profits. The efficient profit center should have the following characteristics:

1. *Operational independence.* The manager of the division should have control over its operations and be free to make decisions concerning such questions as the volume of production, methods of operation, and product mix.
2. *Access to sources and markets.* The manager should be free to buy and sell in alternative markets, both inside and outside the company. Where freedom to trade is absent, the buyer and seller may have little incentive to reach decisions.
3. *Separable costs and revenues.* The profit center should be able to identify all costs and to measure a realistic price for its end product.
4. *Management intent.* A profit center should be established only when the overall goal of management is profits for the segment. This distinguishes a *profit center* from a *service center.*[1]

---

[1] Joel Dean, "Decentralization and Intercompany Pricing," *Harvard Business Review* (July–August 1955), pp. 65–75.

Exhibit 1 illustrates how one corporation, Sun Oil Company, has decentralized.

In summary, the modern complex business organization will undoubtedly function more efficiently when it is subdivided into a number of independent units which operate as economic entities. The attempt of each subunit to maximize its own profits should result in a high degree of efficiency and productivity, and should encompass the same advantages found by individual independent entities operating in a competitive economy.

OBJECTIVES OF TRANSFER PRICING SYSTEMS

The decentralization of firms and the establishment of profit centers have created the need for an internal price system to assist in resource allocation and to motivate managers. Such a system should influence the individual units to promote the welfare of the corporate group as a whole. Transfer pricing arose from this need to establish *goal congruence* between units.

Transfer pricing systems have four primary objectives:

First, they assist top management in *appraising and guiding divisional performance.* Management needs to be informed of each division's performance. When information about revenues and expenses is available for individual segments, it is possible to evaluate the relative performance of each division as well as its total contribution to the firm over a span of time.

Second, transfer pricing systems provide *day-to-day guidance for the manager* whose performance is being evaluated. The manager will be aware of the performance evaluation criteria and be able to take action as the facts indicate and circumstances warrant.

Third, transfer pricing systems allow *autonomy in decision making.* Many of the benefits to be derived from decentralization are based upon the premise that the freedom of managers to make decisions causes them to have greater incentive, which provides the basis for improved performance.

Finally, transfer pricing systems *help to satisfy domestic and foreign tax authorities.* In an effective transfer pricing system there should be an awareness of the legal implications of antitrust, dumping, and customs regulations. For example, custom

EXHIBIT 1
Primary operating units of Sun Company

Sun Company

- **Administrative Services Group**
  Provides financial, legal, management, employee and public relations services to operating units and parent company

- **Great Canadian Oil Sands Limited**
  Operates mining and processing facilities in Alberta, Canada, to produce synthetic crude from oil sands

- **Sperry-Sun, Inc.**
  Manufactures and markets instruments and tools; provides specialized services worldwide to oil, mining and other industries and government agencies

- **Sun Enterprises Group**
  Implements Sun's long-term expansion strategies in nonenergy related areas; supervises wholly owned subsidiaries; oversees minority positions in operating companies

- **Sun Gas Company**
  Operates all Sun domestic properties related primarily to gas production; markets natural gas, unprocessed and processed natural gas liquids, all LPG

- **Sun International, Inc.**
  Trades crude oil and products worldwide; manages overseas marketing subsidiaries; owns and operates marine terminalling facilities

- **Sunmark Exploration Company**
  Engages in worldwide (except Canada) exploration and production; markets earth science and land management services

- **Sunmark Industries**
  Markets gasoline, distillates and related petroleum and automotive products and services in U.S.

- **Sunoco Energy Development Co.**
  Manages and identifies development opportunities for coal, uranium, synthetic fuels and geothermal sources in continental U.S., including Alaska

- **Sun Company Limited**
  Explores for and produces crude oil and natural gas in Canada; refines crude production; distributes and markets products and services to wholesale and retail customers

- **Sun Petroleum Products Company**
  Operates six refineries, engages in marketing fuels, lubricants, chemicals and specialty products to U.S. industrial and wholesale customers

- **Sun Pipe Line Company**
  Owns and operates domestic pipelines transporting crude oil and petroleum products; provides crude oil gathering services.

- **Sun Production Company**
  Develops, produces and markets petroleum from principally oil related domestic properties; acquires crude oil and related natural gas reserves; provides technical and other contract services

- **Sun Shipbuilding and Dry Dock Company**
  Engages in shipbuilding and repair and construction and repair of other types of floating structures

Source: 1977 Sun Company Annual Report.

duties are levied on import prices, but may be adjusted upward if the authorities rule that the transfer prices are not a fair representation of value.

ELEMENTS OF AN EFFECTIVE TRANSFER PRICING SYSTEM

In establishing the transfer pricing system, several questions need to be answered:

1. Is the transfer pricing system consistent with overall corporate objectives? The system should be designed to insure that divisional management and top management would make the same decision if all of the information available is known to all parties.
2. Is the transfer pricing system fair to all concerned parties? The system must not favor one manager or component over another, because inequities in the system will be rapidly detected and cause the system to break down.
3. Is the transfer pricing system designed to minimize the conflict between buying and selling units? Conflict over transfer pricing is inevitable, but techniques should be developed which minimize internal bickering. A transfer pricing system which makes good business sense will usually meet these objectives.
4. Is the transfer pricing system long range in scope, or does the system suboptimize by pursuing only short range objectives?

There are a number of characteristics which an effective transfer pricing system should have. Business International Corporation has provided the following checklist of these characteristics:

1. Be as simple as reasonably possible.
2. Offer flexibility where and when it may be needed.
3. Facilitate speed and minimize delays: offer a fast response to changing business conditions country by country around the world.
4. Minimize duplication and paperwork.
5. Reflect the true profit contributions of all concerned (including, for example, reducing the denominator in an ROI for-

mula of a product division if the profit is credited to a marketing unit).

6. Act as an incentive to keep costs down—worldwide.

7. Maximize profits and sensibly minimize taxes.

8. Put profits in locations where they can best be used (e.g., to build up new business).

9. Foster cooperation across divisional and country lines.

10. Effectively motivate managers worldwide to maximize total-company profits.

11. Involve—really involve—all relevant units in the corporation that are affected by pricing decisions.

12. Facilitate assessment or calculation of what is going on—where, and on which products, the company is really making its profits.

13. Tell top management what is really going on. While this may seem very basic, in some cases it appears that top management is not fully and truly informed as to sales and profit contribution and the role that transfer pricing plays in determining those contributions.

14. Help the company plan for worldwide product potential, either product-by-product or product group-by-product group.

15. Be believable, both internally and externally.

16. Be acceptable as reasonable and fair internally, and defensible externally.[2]

CALCULATING THE TRANSFER PRICE FOR TANGIBLE PRODUCTS

A horizontally integrated company will frequently establish profit centers by product lines, and most of its revenues will be the result of external transactions. On the other hand, the vertically integrated company is often structured along the lines of components for a final end-product. In such cases the prices paid to suppliers, as well as sales prices to users, must be generated internally. The creation of internal prices is of paramount importance, because a small difference in the unit price of a transferred product can have a large impact upon the reported

---

[2] *Setting Intercorporate Pricing Policies.* Business International Corporation, New York, (November 1973), p. 12.

profit of the profit center. A number of methods exist for pricing internal transfers for tangible salable products.[3]

Market-based prices

A market-based price is established by the open market. It is the price at which a product could be sold externally. Market-based prices may be established by examining competitor prices or through bids. Entering transactions at market price has the advantage of utilizing objective data to produce information regarding the efficiency of the profit center. This price is similar to the price which would be charged in an "arm's-length" transaction.

In effect, the market price establishes the ceiling for a recorded price. Market prices may be adjusted downward to take into consideration such factors as volume and the degree of marketing effort required under the circumstances. Situations which require such adjustments will result in *negotiated prices*, which are discussed below.

In many cases the establishment of a market price is difficult. If no market exists for a product in a particular stage of completion, market prices may be established arbitrarily, and thereby lose much of their usefulness. Additionally, management must attempt to consider the impact the profit center might have on an established market. The entry of a new company in the market place would undoubtedly have an impact upon prices, and the extent of that impact should be assessed.

There are three methods which may be used to set market-based transfer prices: (1) the price may be *negotiated* between the buyer and the seller; (2) a *discount* may be taken from list price, or (3) the division which ultimately sells the product may be considered an *agent*.

A *negotiated price* will frequently create a buyer-seller situation. Such a situation is similar to dealing with independent firms; the negotiating parties are motivated to obtain reasonable prices. However, the process of negotiating may become an end in itself (or a management game), and result in executives spending a disproportionate amount of time on negotiations.

---

[3] For a further discussion of alternative transfer price policies see Paul W. Cook, Jr., "Decentralization and the Transfer Price Problem," *The Journal of Business* (April 1955), pp. 87–94.

In a system of *discounts* from list transfer prices, pricing is accomplished by working backward from market price. First, the market price is determined; then a discount is applied to the market price. Each division is allowed profits on the basis of the ultimate selling price. The key factor in discount systems is the establishment of the discount percentage, which should reflect the historical relationship between prices and profit. Rates may be set before, or determined on the basis of, individual transactions.

Finally, a transfer pricing system may consider the *seller as an agent.* In such a system the ultimate market price is reduced by a commission to the seller. While this procedure may serve to motivate producing divisions, it does not provide a sufficient incentive to the ultimate seller.

Cost-based transfers

The first problem encountered in using cost-based systems is determining a definition of *cost.* Cost-based systems may utilize full cost, standard cost, marginal cost, or opportunity cost.

Full-cost transfers. Full-cost transfers are based upon the actual costs incurred by the producing department. Transfers at full cost require the receiving department to absorb the inefficiences of the other divisions, and may have the effect of lessening motivation to control total cost. On the other hand, it may sometimes be necessary to increase costs for long-run profitability, but when managers are evaluated solely on the basis of costs they may not recognize the necessity to make the required changes on a timely basis.

Standard cost transfers. A transfer at standard cost charges out the product at a predetermined conception of what costs ought to be under certain circumstances. This method has the advantage of eliminating the cost of inefficiencies from the transfer price, but can cause problems when special orders or special packaging, for which there is no established standard, are involved. A standard cost is set at some predetermined level of efficient operation, and meeting the standard will generally require lengthy production runs with predetermined specifications. The *acquiring department* may wish a slight alteration in specifications or an individualization of orders for a special promotion. However, the *producing department* will be hesitant to comply with such requests, as they will undoubtedly result in increased costs and cause the producing department to exceed its standard costs. The use of standard costs can thereby have the effect of causing suboptimization of the total corporate goal structure.

Direct cost systems transfer products at the costs of direct material, direct labor, and variable overhead incurred in the production of the product. The method has the advantage of setting prices which are independent of production levels, but does not result in all costs being charged against the product, because fixed costs are not included in the calculation.

Marginal cost systems. Marginal cost systems transfer products at the incremental cost of producing additional volume. These systems require the calculation of costs at various levels of operations. The acquiring manager will generally purchase additional products as long as their marginal cost is less than the marginal revenue which can be received from the sale of these products, less any additional processing or selling costs. The marginal cost and revenue curves are generally depicted as shown in Exhibit 2. These curves depict the economic theory that increases in sales volume require a lower per unit price, whereas increases in production will initially result in a lower

EXHIBIT 2
Marginal unit cost and unit revenue

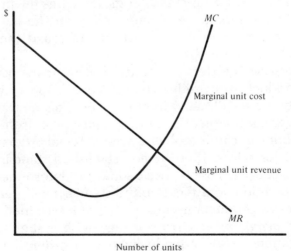

Number of units

per unit cost. But once the optimum production level is achieved, increases in production will cause an increase in per unit costs.

There is an inherent difficulty in the use of marginal costs for interdivisional transfers. Such cost calculations are generally not available and surrogates for marginal cost must be used. One approach is to use the techniques of cost-volume-profit analysis, but some authors advocate simply using variable or direct cost in place of marginal cost.

Opportunity cost. An opportunity cost-based transfer pricing system charges the product with the profits foregone by the total firm if the goods are transferred internally. These profits may be computed on the basis of lost contribution margin when an external market exists for the product. This method is not applicable where there is no external market for the product.

Dictated prices

Arguments over the merits of a particular transfer pricing system are not uncommon. Corporations frequently employ a dictated pricing scheme to minimize the possibility of interdivisional arguments on transfer pricing. Dictated prices may be arbitrarily set by a pricing authority (or czar), or they may be set at a certain percentage of the standard manufacturing cost. For example,

$$\text{Price} = 115\% \text{ of standard cost}$$

Negotiated prices

A negotiated transfer price system requires the divisions to deal with each other in the same manner as they deal with external suppliers and purchasers. Such systems have the advantage of requiring managers to be sensitive to market requirements and responsive to competitive alternatives.

On the other hand, a negotiated transfer pricing system can have undesirable effects. It may accentuate personality conflict between managers, and when there is ego involvement gaining the upper hand may become more important than company profitability. Additionally, it can become time consuming and cause wide variations in reported divisional profitability.

A negotiated transfer pricing system will work best when

there are outside markets for the intermediate product, market information is freely available to all parties, and there is complete freedom to deal with outsiders if a negotiated settlement cannot be reached. When any of these conditions is violated the negotiated transfer pricing system is likely to break down and result in inefficiencies.

AN EXAMPLE OF ALTERNATIVE TRANSFER PRICING TECHNIQUES

The Blue Division of the Walther Corporation makes Product T. This product is manufactured from raw materials acquired externally. Product T may either be sold externally or transferred internally to the Red Division of the Walther Corportation. The Red Division currently uses the entire output from the Blue Division but wishes to increase purchases by 1,000 units. The following information is available with which to compute the transfer price under each of the previously discussed alternatives.

Product T

Actual manufacturing costs per unit (last year):

Direct materials	$3.10
Direct labor	3.70
Variable overhead	1.95
Fixed overhead	1.00
Total	$9.75

The plant is operating at full capacity for a single shift and can manufacture 5,000 units.

Standard manufacturing costs per unit:

Direct materials	$ 3.00
Direct labor	4.00
Variable overhead	2.00
Fixed overhead	1.00
Total	$10.00

Current market price = $11 per unit:

$$\text{Market price} \times \text{Units transferred}$$
$$\$11 \times 1{,}000 = \$11{,}000$$

Full cost:

$$\text{Actual cost per unit} \times \text{Units transferred}$$
$$\$9.75 \times 1{,}000 = \$9{,}750$$

Standard cost:

$$\text{Standard cost per unit} \times \text{Units transferred}$$
$$\$10 \times 1{,}000 = \$10{,}000$$

Direct cost:

$$\text{Direct cost of material, labor, and overhead} \times \text{Units transferred}$$
$$\$8.75 \times 1{,}000 = \$8{,}750$$

Marginal cost:

In order to produce 1,000 more units a second shift must be started, since the Blue Division is operating at 100 percent capacity on the first shift. Assume that starting a second shift will increase fixed costs by 50 percent. Fixed costs are now $5,000 (5,000 units × $1) so that fixed costs in the second shift will be $2,500. The marginal cost of production could then be calculated:

Material	$ 3.00
Direct labor	4.00
Variable overhead	2.00
Fixed overhead	2.50*
Total	$11.50

* $2,500 ÷ 1,000 units.

Opportunity cost:

$$\text{Lost contribution margin} \times \text{Units}$$
$$(\$11 - \$10) \times 1{,}000 = \$1{,}000$$

Dictated price:

Assume the dictated price is 110 percent of Standard cost × Units
$$(1.10 \times \$10) \times 1{,}000 = \$11{,}000$$

Negotiated price:

The negotiated price would be set by the parties; however, negotiated prices frequently use the market price as a starting point and then take into consideration the saving by avoiding unnecessary selling and advertising expenses. Assume that the parties agreed that the market price of $11 included $0.50 of selling and advertising expenses. The negotiated price would then be computed:

$$\text{Negotiated price} \times \text{Units transferred}$$
$$\$10.50 \times 1{,}000 = \$10{,}500$$

TRANSFER PRICING FOR INTANGIBLE ITEMS

In some cases a transfer pricing mechanism will be needed where one organizational unit licenses another to sell a product under a patent or royalty rate. The transfer pricing of such intangibles involves some problems not associated with tangible products. Since the actual cost of many intangibles is frequently unknown, and may in many cases be arbitrarily assigned, the *cost-plus approach* is inapplicable. Generally, the most meaningful valuation procedure for intangibles is market value, and the transfer pricing mechanism can be established as a percentage of sales which reflects value.

EXTERNAL CONSTRAINTS ON TRANSFER PRICING

As noted previously, the transfer pricing system adopted by a particular company should be designed to encourage all parties to act in the best interest of the organization as a whole; however, there may be some external constraints which limit the effectiveness of the system. Several of these constraints which have been alluded to previously are: competitor activity, tax considerations, and antidumping and antitrust laws.

A transfer pricing scheme which fails to consider competitor prices may be less than optimal. If the transfer price is set at a level which requires sales at noncompetitive prices, the result will be lost sales. A system should be developed which sets prices at a level that is profitable to the total corporation and competitive in the market place.

Taxes have an impact on transfer pricing in two main areas: (1) income taxes on profits, and (2) customs duties. Section 482 of the Internal Revenue Code allows the IRS to allocate income and expenses among affiliated companies in order to more clearly reflect the net income of the group and to prevent evasion of taxes. Accordingly, care should be exercised in developing an internal pricing mechanism which recognizes the impact of this section of the Internal Revenue Code.

A divisionalized company that operates internationally must deal with the dual impact of customs duties and foreign income taxes. It should also be noted that the impacts of customs duties and foreign income taxes are in direct conflict, because a relatively lower export price will cause higher reported profits, and vice versa. A company must carefully examine the tax and customs regulations of a particular country before attempting to set an export price.

Antitrust and antidumping regulations are based upon similar considerations, but impact on different markets. In both cases the company must be certain that its transfer pricing mechanism does not result in an ultimate sales price which may cause antitrust action in domestic markets, or antidumping duties in foreign markets.

JOURNALIZING TRANSFER PRICES

In most cases the cost of a product transferred from one division of a firm to another will be in excess of the inventory cost of that item. Some companies may choose to record the transfers at cost and report on divisional profits separately from the formal accounting records. In such cases the only entry necessary is to transfer the cost of the inventory from one division to another on the total corporate books in the following manner:

```
Division B Inventory ....................................  60,000
    Division A Inventory ................................          60,000
```

To record the transfer of 5,000 units of inventory at $12 from Division A to Division B.

On the other hand, other companies may incorporate the transfer pricing system into the formal accounting records. This necessitates the recording of a "profit" by the "selling division;" this profit, however, must later be eliminated when the company's financial statements are issued.

Assume that the Moody Corporation has two divisions, X and Y. Division X transfers 3,000 units to Division Y. This transfer is recorded at the market price of $4 per unit and the cost per unit is $3. Entries at the time of the transfer are:

```
X Books:
Accounts Receivable from Y ............................  12,000
Cost of Goods Sold ....................................   9,000
    Sales ................................................          12,000
    Inventory ...........................................           9,000
Y Books:
Inventory .............................................  12,000
    Accounts Payable to X ..............................          12,000
```

Assume that the Moody Corporation had to prepare consolidated financial statements before any settlement and prior to the use of any inventory. It would then be necessary to eliminate the intercompany payables (a company cannot owe itself), and eliminate the intercompany profit (a company cannot report a profit by selling to itself). These eliminations would be made on consolidated working papers as follows:

```
Accounts Payable to X .................................... 12,000
    Accounts Receivable from Y ..........................          12,000

Sales...................................................... 12,000
    Inventory of Y........................................           3,000
    Cost of Goods Sold ...................................           9,000
```

OTHER USES OF TRANSFER PRICING

The previous sections have outlined the internal uses of transfer pricing for a business organization. Essentially, a transfer pricing mechanism is designed to aid in the evaluation of a decentralized organization by encouraging wise decisions by managers and by measuring managerial performance. However, our ever-changing economic environment has resulted in the incorporation of transfer pricing into other situations. Several of these areas are discussed below.[4]

The evaluation of a company for sale. In recent years many companies have acquired or disposed of *segments* of their organizations. When such segments are engaged primarily in sales to affiliates, it becomes difficult to evaluate segment profitability. A purchaser will wish to review the existing transfer pricing scheme to determine the adequacy of reported earnings.

Minority interests. When less than 100 percent of a company is acquired by a parent, the surviving interest is termed a minority interest. The transfer pricing scheme will affect the reported interests of these investors, and care must be taken to ensure that the rights of the minority are not violated.

Segmental reporting. There has been increased emphasis upon segmental reporting for *diversified companies.* Segment and product-line reporting is now required by the Securities

---

[4] For a further discussion of these factors see Itzhak Sharav, "Transfer Pricing—Diversity of Goals and Practices," *The Journal of Accountancy* (April 1974), pp. 56–62.

and Exchange Commissions, and the FASB has recently issued *Standard No. 14* on segmental reporting. When segments deal extensively with each other, the transfer pricing mechanism will have an impact upon segmental reporting.

Tax implications.   Many diversified companies elect to report separately for income tax purposes, and certain types of segments may be eligible for special tax considerations under the Internal Revenue Code. The IRS may review the transfer pricing system to ensure that it is appropriate and not designed purely to avoid higher taxes.

PART
FOUR

*Common elements
of cost and managerial
accounting methodology*

14

Accounting for production materials

*Kenneth A. Strathdee**

In many industries production materials represent a majority of the cost of a manufactured product and in most industries production materials are at least a significant portion of product costs. In either case, cost of production materials requires management attention if profits are to be planned, realized, and then reported with a reasonable degree of accuracy. The purpose of this chapter is to offer to the reader for consideration appropriate accounting methodologies for the typically important accounting activities associated with production material which could lead to a more efficient and effective cost accounting system. For this purpose, a *production material* is defined as being a prime cost material which could be introduced into the product build-up process at any point from initial fabrication to final assembly and pack. It could, as well, be a purchased material requiring no further individual processing other than inclusion in a subassembly or final assembly of a product.

The typically important activities to be considered in the development or maintenance of an efficient and effective cost accounting system for production materials include:

---

* Partner, Management Consulting Services, Coopers & Lybrand.

Production material cost planning
Purchased materials price accounting
Freight cost accounting
Materials receipt accounting
Materials usage accounting
Salvage, rework, and discards accounting
Surplus, excess, and obsolete materials accounting

In the balance of this chapter each of these accounting activities will be discussed in sufficient detail to acquaint the reader with a related accounting methodologies which the author has employed in the design and installation of cost management systems. The chapter will conclude with a summarization of the methodologies of concern with respect to providing for a more efficient and effective accounting of production materials.

PRODUCTION MATERIAL COST PLANNING

The accounting cycle for production materials usually begins with the development of the profit plan. Sales forecasts, cost bills of materials, inventory investment objectives, and projected material cost prices are synthesized to produce the production material cost section of the profit plan.

For the most part, the product of planning as it pertains to production material accounting is the documentation of material costs to be incurred and material inventory investment to be made by time period, in relation to a planned level of sales and production. This plan usually forms the basis by which to account for actual material costs incurred and investments made, and to monitor and report operating performance. Exhibit 1 depicts a typical report format used internally to report operating performance to plan.

An in-depth discussion of standard costing and reporting was not intended for this chapter. That will be done in other chapters of this book. The intention in depicting on Exhibit 1 the operation of a standard cost system was to demonstrate the multidimensional reporting of production material costs that can and should occur in an accounting system. The report shows standard costs, such as production material purchased and used, being reported by "plan to actual" and "standard to actual." The report

EXHIBIT 1

\multicolumn{7}{c}{XYZ COMPANY Profit Plan Performance Report For Period Ending _____}						

\multicolumn{3}{c}{*This period*}		\multicolumn{3}{c}{*Year-to-date*}	
Plan	*Actual*	*Variance*	*Item*	*Plan*	*Actual*	*Variance*

			Sales
			Standard cost of sales
			  (detail)
			Standard gross margin
			Standard cost variances directly
			  assignable
			  (detail)
			Actual contribution margin
			Less other expenses—Not
			  directly assignable
			  (detail)
			Net income			

			Return on investment Total investment			

			Key investment categories:
			  Inventories:
			    Raw material
			    Work-in-process
			    Finished goods
			  Other key items			

format also provides for inventory investment to be measured by the same dimensions. Obviously, other key elements of total investment could also be included in the report format as appropriate.

Furthermore, profit plan performance reporting should be supported with narrative reports describing the reasons for variances from the plan and from standard costs, and the corrective action which either is contemplated or has been taken. The day-to-day management decision-making process relies to a great degree on the validity of such plans and standard costs. Unplanned conditions which arise or abnormal costs which are experienced, such as a production material shortage in the market place resulting in higher than normal purchase prices, should be reported. They are necessary in understanding results and in testing the ongoing validity of plans and standards.

Where a company is organized by product line it is often appropriate to plan and account for results by product line. Then, the profit plan performance report package includes reports by product line. Where the company consists of multidivision operations, results might also be reported by division. In either case, the reporting format similar to that shown as Exhibit 1 could be appropriate. However, it usually happens that where a more detailed reporting of costs occurs, such as by product line or by division, greater reliance has to be placed on cost allocation techniques. This may not always be desirable, particularly when the allocation techniques employed are by necessity arbitrary. For example, it could happen that there is common usage among product lines for a specific production material, and precise accounting of resulting purchases of the common material by product line might not be practical. Consequently, it would be difficult to avoid use of an arbitrary allocation when accounting for related purchase price variances by product line. The problem is often similarly experienced with joint process costs. Accounting and reporting of costs like this are best treated in total by requiring that income by product line or division be reported only to the point beyond which arbitrary allocation techniques would have to be employed. Then performance of a product line or division would be evaluated on the basis of its contribution to the recovery of such costs and, of course, the realization of the profit objective. Exhibit 2 shows a report format which appro-

EXHIBIT 2

<table>
<tr><td colspan="7" align="center">XYZ COMPANY
Profit Plan Performance Report
(by product lines or division)
For Period Ending _____</td></tr>
<tr><td colspan="3" align="center">This period</td><td></td><td colspan="3" align="center">Year-to-date</td></tr>
<tr><td>Plan</td><td>Actual</td><td>Variance</td><td>Item</td><td>Plan</td><td>Actual</td><td>Variance</td></tr>
<tr><td></td><td></td><td></td><td>Sales
Standard cost of sales
(detail)
Standard gross margin
Standard cost variances
directly assignable
(detail)
Actual contribution margin</td><td></td><td></td><td></td></tr>
</table>

priately addresses these accounting issues and information needs when reporting results by product line or by division.

Where neither profit planning nor standard costs exists, current results are usually measured against results of a previous period, such as last month or last year to date. If the mix of products remains relatively constant, such reporting for line items as production material costs could be meaningful. If the mix fluctuates and the individual products have varied prime cost content, the report recipient is forced at best to rely on a mixture of experienced judgment and "gut feel" to assess the significance of reported results. There can be little justification for an accounting system or report structure that requires that type of interpretation of results by the report recipients.

The ABC technique

For some time it has been recognized by those charged with designing and operating cost accounting systems that in order to be effective in planning, accounting, reporting, and controlling results some technique had to be employed that made efficient use of time being made available for these activities. From this need emerged a technique which, in essence, places emphasis on the high usage-valued items—and consequently the important items—and on items about whose demand or cost little is known—the exceptions. Somewhat less emphasis is placed on the remaining items with a minimum, but nevertheless practical, risk to desired results. The ABC technique is a readily recognized label for this approach. There are other labels. The basic concept of the ABC technique is often portrayed in a table and/or graph which summarizes the results of a proportional value analysis of a population of items to be managed. For our purposes the technique can be demonstrated in Exhibit 3 for a population of production materials used by the XYZ Company. The exhibit shows, with regard to production materials, that the XYZ Company could provide coverage for 80 percent of its annual usage value of all production materials by initiating rigorous planning, accounting, reporting, and control activities for the "A" item materials, which represent 10 percent of the total materials. The graph depicts that any attempts at generally expanding this coverage by including more of the lower usage value materials would result in a rapidly increasing number of items, with

370

a disproportionately lower increase in usage value coverage. This is important to recognize because it follows that, as the population of "A" item materials increases, there would (without staff increases) be less time available to spend managing the individual items in the category. If the population of "A" item materials continued to increase to the point where all production materials are treated as important items, it could probably be found, as my experience has shown, that some materials are far undercontrolled and others are greatly overcontrolled in relation to their cost or potential impact on the company. Finally, as noted ear-

EXHIBIT 3
Proportional value analysis summary for XYZ Company (10,000 production materials)

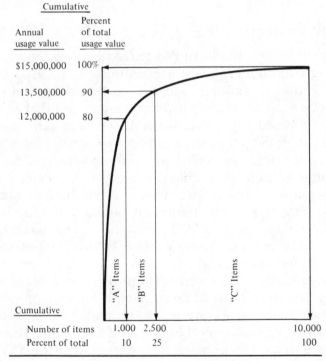

Classification	Number of items	Percent of total	Total annual usage value	Percent of total
A	1,000	10%	$12,000,000	80%
B	1,500	15	1,500,000	10
C	7,500	75	1,500,000	10
	10,000	100%	$15,000,000	100%

lier, it should be kept in mind that the rules should be relaxed where an individual material should be managed or accounted for on an exception basis, for whatever reason.

The cost planning process

Effectiveness in profit planning is often inhibited by the sheer number of products which can be anticipated for production and sale during the period being planned. Although data processing technology has advanced to the stage where large quantities of data can be economically processed in short periods of time, the problem most often is one where the raw data is simply not available for such processing. Some product lines are too complex to permit forecasts of all products to be developed individually. In other instances, variations of products or permutations of a product content are so voluminous that it becomes an almost impossible task for accounting to establish, and then maintain, a cost for each end product. Without an alternative approach, profit planning is often forsaken or plans are grossly misstated.

The flow chart shown as Exhibit 4 portrays the essential features of the planning cycle as it pertains to production material costs. It depicts, first, that the net of available inventory and individual product forecasts are exploded by using corresponding bills of material to arrive at gross requirements. Then gross requirements by item are matched against on-hand inventory balances and the inventory investment guidelines to determine the net requirements which will have to be provided during the planning period. Finally, the net requirements are extended by the cost bills of material to arrive at planned production costs. The process is straightforward; given sales forecasts, on-hand inventory, production, and cost bills of material and an adequate data processing facility, the results in terms of profit data should come off without much of a hitch. However, more often than not, the sales department simply cannot provide a forecast for every item it plans to sell, and the accounting department does not have a current cost bill of material for every product in the forecast. When these shortcomings in data requirements occur there is significant risk that, without a compensating provision, results will be considered incomplete and subse-

EXHIBIT 4
The profit planning cycle for production material costs

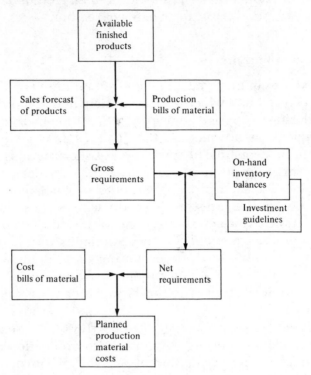

quent tracking of performance to plan will be inconclusive and somewhat meaningless.

For the purpose of making adequate provision for production materials when not all product sales to be experienced are forecast, or when cost bills of materials do not exist for all products to be sold, three alternative steps to the flow process shown in Exhibit 4 could be taken.

1. Request the sales department to forecast the remaining sales in total by product grouping or product line. Care must be taken to ensure that products that represent a significant portion of sales are not included in this category.

2. Construct a product cost that is representative of each group forecast. Typically, the approach here might be one in which the group can be made to identify with an adjusted cost

bill of material for an existing product. Alternatively, a cost bill of material could be constructed by using historical cost ratios of production materials to other costs for a related or similar product line.

3. Consulting with materials management, make provision for that portion of production material cost that would probably be satisfied out of existing inventories.

Essentially, this cost planning process gives recognition to the fact that a certain number of products, usually a small minority of the total number, represent a great majority of sales and cost dollars of a product line. It usually follows, then, that the potential for a significant over- or understatement of sales and costs in profit plans is minimized, by giving the greatest amount of time and attention to the development of accurate forecasts of sales and production to the development of cost bills of material for these products. The approach can usually be made flexible enough so that appropriate treatment can be given to the individual exception—the currently unimportant item which should be treated as important, or vice versa, for whatever reason.

Cost bill of material

The principal document used to account for the standard, estimated, or historical costs of production materials, as well as other cost items, is the *cost bill of material*. This might otherwise be called the product cost record. This document plays a significant role in the accounting aspects of the planning process, and also can be used to estimate the cost of new products or orders, often employing a "same as except for these items" approach. It can serve as a basis for production performance reporting, such as would pertain to material usage and scrap. It can also be used to cost the use and movement of inventory through the various stages of product buildup. The cost bill of material is, in itself, merely a dollarized version of the bill of material used by the materials management activity in providing for, and in managing the flow of, inventory into the production process. With its dollarization a detail accounting using standard, estimated, or historical cost of production materials, labor, and overhead in a product is made possible. Sometimes, as a result of attempts at simplification of accounting and the related paperwork systems, a cost bill of material can be a summary of two or more levels of bills of material. The summarization is done to avoid accounting for costs at product buildup levels where production costs are considered insignificant or, perhaps, not controllable.

Oftentimes, the construction of necessary cost bills of material can be a very time-consuming and expensive process. Once such bills of material are constructed, however, the benefits to be gained from their use in profit planning as well as in control and performance evaluation will far outweigh such expense. To ensure that cost bills will be effectively used, it is important

EXHIBIT 5

COST BIL

Item number and description: _____

Operation or component		Standard Labor							Standard pro	
Department number	Description	Hours per/M	Labor rate	Efficiency factor	U/M	Unit cost	Standard content	Scrap	Samples
	Material component: (detail)								
	Labor component: (detail)								
	Cost summary: Total material, labor, and overhead								
	Summary of cost sources: Raw material inventory Work-in-process Current labor pool Current overhead absorbed Total								

that user needs—relative to data content—be carefully identified and provided for. Here again, the data processing industry has performed a great assist in standardizing bill-of-material formats. However, the potential user must recognize that each user company is different, if only because the people that make up the organization of the potential user are different, often with different management styles or methods of approach to problem solutions.

The essential features of a cost bill of material are displayed in Exhibit 5. The cost bill should be thought of as an amalgam of three major sources of necessary information: the production

OF MATERIAL

Date of issue _____

duction material					*Cost summary*								
	Factors			*Freight cost absorbed*	*Material over-head absorbed*	*Total prime cost*		*Overhead absorbed*				*Total cost*	
								Variable		*Fixed*			
Usage	*Freight*	*Over-head*				*Labor*	*Ma-terial*	*Rate*	*Amount*	*Rate*	*Amount*	*By line*	*Cumu-lative*

bill of material, the routing or process sheet, and the master record of cost standards or rates. The production bill of material is the source of the information needed to identify and account for the usage of production materials at all stages of development; the routing or process sheet is the source of the related labor and equipment data; and the master record of cost standards or rates provides information concerning the unit costs.

In reviewing Exhibit 5, or in contemplating structuring or restructuring a cost bill of material to meet production material accounting requirements for such purposes as planning, control, performance evaluation and reporting, attention should be focused on the following desirable features, which are sometimes overlooked:

1. *Approved alternatives to standard materials should be identified if substitutions should be necessary.* By incorporating into the cost bill of material an approved substitute for use when the standard material is in an out-of-stock condition, the material substitution cost variance can then be more readily identified and accounted for as part of routine variance analysis activity. The practice of identifying standard material substitutions for planning and production purposes is often followed by materials management and quality assurance.

2. *Provide for anticipated variances from established standards through use of performance factors, such as a material usage factor and a labor efficiency factor.* Employing such factors permits recognition of a temporary condition adversely impacting performance in relation to otherwise sound cost standards. Such conditions might include use of a substitute material, introduction of a new production crew such as on a second shift, or start-up of new equipment. All of these examples could result in higher than normal costs of production materials. Such variances might best be treated as standard until normal conditions resume. When normal conditions are resumed, the factor would be deleted from the cost bill of material.

3. *When they represent a significant portion of the requirements of a production run, standard sample requirements, such as those required for product quality assurance, should be established as a direct product cost and clearly distinguished on the cost bill from any provision for standard yield loss.* This will

permit such growing costs of business to be more clearly and accurately recognized by product, thereby making the planning and accounting for such costs more meaningful.

4. *The material, labor, and overhead elements of a product or component cost should be accounted for separately and cumulatively in total by line item on the cost bill.* Besides promoting a better understanding of the true composition of the production cost of a product or of the cost content of inventory, established product costs can be more easily modified when universal modifications are appropriate. This may occur in planning when inflation factoring or providing for an imminent wage increase is appropriate.

5. *When production material-related overhead is significant, a provision should be made in the cost bill for recording and accumulating the absorption of such overhead separately as the materials are committed to and processed in production.* This should result in more accurate distribution of costs to products. It should also permit management to make decisions related to materials, such as make or buy, more readily and from a more informed position.

6. *Provide for the summarization of cost of the sources of materials input, such as from raw material or work-in-process inventories.* Where appropriate, this information could be helpful in making financial projections about the movement of inventory if a production plan should be implemented. Such information might also be used for inventory usage accounting when the bill of material serves as the basis of issues of standard requirements for a production run.

The preceding six considerations are offered not necessarily as being exhaustive or universally feasible, but more to demonstrate the kind of thinking that should be employed in the construction of cost bills of materials for production material accounting purposes.

PURCHASED MATERIALS
PRICE ACCOUNTING

Purchase price standards are important in (*a*) establishing product costs for profit planning or product price estimating,

(b) monitoring the effectiveness of the purchasing activity, and (c) improving the efficiency of activities concerned with accounting for the investment in, and movement of, inventory in the normal course of business. The price standards used in accounting for production materials often are the prices established as part of the annual planning process, as part of a standard cost system, or as part of the cost data required for a product cost estimate. Generally, the establishment of the price standards results in the application of a combination of knowledge and understanding of economic trends, projection of requirements, and commitments from vendors. In companies where purchase prices paid are monitored by using the ABC technique discussed earlier, great attention is given to maintaining on a current basis the price standards of those few materials which represent a great majority of purchased dollars. The price standards of the remaining purchased materials might then be updated individually once a year, or by group or family of common materials periodically by factoring established prices, as appropriate.

The volatility of purchase prices for materials has caused some companies to resort to the use of two sets of price standards for accounting and reporting purposes: a frozen and a current set of standards. The frozen set remains constant during the year unless interim changes to the profit plan are permitted. Frozen standards are typically used for reporting purposes external to the reporting unit and for intercompany transactions in instances where business relations are maintained at arms' length. In reporting, frozen standards are used to simplify tracking and reporting of performance to committed profit plans between the reporting unit and headquarters. The current set of standards is used by accounting for purposes of internal control and performance monitoring and reporting.

When the price standards used in cost bills of material in accounting for the movement of inventory of production materials are changed during a fiscal year, an inventory valuation account can be used to address the impact that such a change will have on the value of other identical inventory acquired at a different price. In so doing, when a change is implemented it will be necessary to determine the amount of the change in the value of the material other than that purchased under the new price. The amount of the change is then recorded in the

EXHIBIT 6
Technique for accounting for interim price changes

Facts:
1. On-hand inventory = 3,000 at $10 each = $30,000.
2. Latest purchase = 3,000 at $12 each = $36,000.
3. Cost bill for purchased item changed from $10 each to $12.
4. Production issue = 3,500 at $12 each = $42,000.
5. Inventory turnover = four turns per year.
6. Amortization calculation = 3,000 × $2 ÷ 3 = $2,000.

Raw Material Inventory		Work-in-Process Inventory		Cost of Goods Manufactured	
(1) $30,000	$42,000 (4)	(4) $42,000			$2,000 (6)
(2) 36,000					
(3) 6,000					

Inventory Valuation		Accounts Payable	
(6) $2,000	$6,000 (3)		$36,000 (2)

valuation account and a provision is made for its amortization on the basis of the normal turnover of such inventory. As an example, if it can be demonstrated that the inventory turns four times per year, then the amount entered into the valuation account should be amortized over a three-month period. Where multiple entries have been made to the valuation account, a schedule of amortization should be maintained to simplify journal entries affecting the account balance.

An example of the technique for accounting for interim production material price changes can be found in Exhibit 6.

FREIGHT COST ACCOUNTING

In some instances freight costs are not, as a practice of vendors, included in the price of purchased materials. In such cases consideration should be given to adopting a freight cost absorption technique which, through freight cost absorption factors, permits assignment of freight costs to materials on the basis of a cost relationship which exists between the cost of the material or class of material purchased and the freight cost that can be anticipated with the acquisition of such materials. Such freight cost factors could be developed either by using a forecast of purchases and related freight costs, or by using historical purchase and freight cost data. This technique would be particularly appropriate in companies where freight costs are significant and where any of the following conditions prevail:

1. Freight costs are classified as a general overhead item and are absorbed by application of a general overhead recovery rate to total costs, and the labor and material cost mixes in a product are significantly different among products of a product line.
2. Freight costs incurred are significantly different among purchased materials.
3. Freight costs can be significantly different with each purchase because of the quantity purchased, or because of the mix of purchases included in the delivery.

Once the freight factors have been established, their application in accounting for production materials can be rather simple. First, the factor should be included as a separate cost item in the production material section of the cost bill of material. Then, when invoiced for a purchase of production materials, the appropriate freight factor can be identified for application to the purchased value of the item. The accounting transactions required can be rather easily depicted by using the following two journal entry formats:

At the time a freight invoice is recorded:

Dr. Freight Cost xxx
Cr.   Accounts Payable   xxx

At the time a purchase invoice is recorded:

Dr. Production Material
          Inventory xxx
Cr.   Accounts Payable   xxx
Cr.   Freight Cost Absorbed   xxx

The latter transaction depicts either of two conditions:

1. The standard cost of the material, including a standard provision for absorption of freight, was entered into inventory;
2. If an actual cost system existed, the actual cost of the material was entered into inventory, along with a standard provision for the absorption of freight.

The freight absorption variances (freight cost less freight cost absorbed) should be frequently reviewed to evaluate the adequacy of established absorption factors. If the variance is significant and remains significant over time, the factors should be changed to reflect more accurately the ratio of freight costs to materials purchase costs. However, such changes should be subject to the same rules as those pertaining to the frequency of change of other cost standards used in the accounting system.

Generally, the establishment of the freight absorption factor can be considered a responsibility of the purchasing department. Also, the freight cost on purchases and freight cost absorbed accounts would be treated as operating accounts of the purchasing department.

MATERIALS RECEIPT ACCOUNTING

To help ensure that good accounting practice exists for the purchase and receipt of production material either a purchase order, a blanket order release, or a warehouse transfer order for materials held in outside warehouses should be prepared and issued to initiate the receipt of required materials. The purchase order or release and the warehouse release form, at a minimum, should provide for recording at the time of their preparation the chart of accounts number to be charged, the quantity required, and the order due date and delivery point. The purchase order form should also provide for recording unit price and freight cost responsibility.

For purposes of cash and inventory management, all significant purchases of production materials generally should be subject to the review and approval of an authority higher than the person who makes the purchase. Planned purchases of major materials should include in the review process additional levels of authority in both materials management and finance before any commitment is made to a vendor. The review process, itself, should be structured in a manner whereby it becomes more rigorous as the value of the purchase increases. Moreover, the ABC technique previously discussed could be appropriately employed in defining a review policy that would help ensure that a majority of management attention in reviewing planned purchase commitments would be directed at those purchases which represent a great majority of purchase dollars.

A method of streamlining the approval policy suggested above may be applied to regular, recurring procurement for replenishment of inventory. An ever-increasing number of companies employ automated replenishment systems which utilize time-phased material requirements planning, or reorder point planning techniques, to purchase production materials for their standard product lines. These replenishment systems are necessarily based on either statistical or judgmental demand forecasts. In either case, an essential component of the forecasting system would be the review and approval of the forecast itself. Then proper design of the review and approval cycle in the replenishment system, utilizing exception reporting techniques, would considerably reduce the managerial effort in reviewing individual purchase orders.

When it is necessary to issue an oral order to a vendor, care should be taken to make certain that the vendor understands that an oral order is only tentative until such time as it is confirmed by the receipt of a signed purchase order. The vendor, or the outside warehouse activity, should be further instructed that any communications relative to the movement and delivery of, and billing for, the ordered materials should include a reference to the purchase or warehouse order number.

Internal distribution of copies of the purchase or warehouse delivery order should include copies to those responsible for quality assurance, receiving, inventory control, and inventory accounting for the following purposes:

1. Receipt by quality assurance of a copy of a purchase order for production materials should be used to trigger the scheduling of necessary inspection and test procedures and to prepare and distribute inspection and test notifications to receiving, inventory control, and accounting.
2. The receiving department should attach the notification to their copy of the related purchase order as notice that the material must be routed to quality assurance at the time of receipt.
3. The copy distributed to inventory control serves as notice that the purchased material must pass through quality assur-

ance before it can be considered as on-hand and available material.

4. The inventory accounting section of accounting should attach their copy of the inspection and test notification to their copy of the purchase order as notice that the eventual receipt must be considered as quarantined inventory, subject to the approval of quality assurance. For purposes of accounting for the inventory and liability, when the receipt does occur, it should be charged to a special inventory account for quarantined inventory and remain there until notification is received from quality assurance that the material has passed inspection and is available for use. The actual entry reducing the quarantined inventory account and charging the regular inventory account would probably best occur at the time the material is received and reported as such by the stores activity.

If the same practice is followed by inventory control, and it should be, then it can be considered as a step taken that should help minimize the risk of potential problems in reconciling on-hand balances with perpetual records when physical inventories are taken, or in reconciling accounting ledgers and perpetual record balances. The accounting transactions required when a quarantined inventory account is used can be depicted by using the following two journal entry formats:

At the time the inventory receipt is recorded:

Dr. Quarantined Incoming Inventory xxx
Cr.   Accounts Payable   xxx

At the time stores reports receipt of approved inventory:

Dr. Production Material Inventory xxx
Cr.   Quarantined Incoming Inventory   xxx

Although it is not often used, a quarantined inventory account gives management an opportunity to evaluate the amount of capital invested in inventory that is tied up in quality assurance programs. Such information might serve as a basis for reviewing quality assurance policies and practices or evaluating the adequacy of their operating budgets.

When it is necessary to return production materials to a vendor for whatever reason, a *debit memorandum* should be used to officially communicate the rejection of the receipt to the vendor. The debit memorandum can also be used to nullify any official internal communications previously distributed pertaining to the pending receipt. In instances where materials to be returned have been recorded as a value on accounting records or where the amount of a previously recorded invoice is to be adjusted, the debit memorandum can be used as a basis for reversing or correcting such recordings. Because the debit memorandum often can be the basis for significant adjustments to accounting records, it should be prepared and issued only by the accounting department. The preparation of a debit memorandum for production materials should be initiated only after the receipt of a request for a debit memorandum has been duly authorized and issued by materials management. The use of the debit memorandum formalizes accounting transactions with vendors in particular, and helps to ensure that those transactions which have occurred or should occur will be properly accounted for.

Finally, it should be a policy of accounting that all production material receipts will be properly documented at the time of receipt with a *receiving report*. The receiving report should be prenumbered serially and used in sequence, thereby better enabling the accounting department to account for all receipts. To ensure that an accurate accounting of receipts does occur, a receiving report log of serial numbers available and issued to the receiving department should be maintained by accounting for purposes of logging in receiving reports used, and detecting reports used but not returned to the accounting department. Also, to further ensure that all production materials received have been entered in the accounting system, accounting should maintain a receiving report record of receiving reports matched to related purchase orders, and recorded by vendor pending receipt of the vendor's invoice. This record will serve as a basis for preparing the unrecorded liability entry at the end of a fiscal period for production materials received but not otherwise recorded. This record procedure can be particularly helpful in overcoming the problem of accounting for materials received from vendors with slow billing practices.

MATERIALS USAGE ACCOUNTING

There are many different methods employed in industry in controlling inventory and in accounting for the usage of production materials. Because information needs of inventory control and accounting so closely parallel one another with respect to usage and balance on hand information, it is logical to think in terms of needs related to both systems in assessing an existing system or in developing an improved system. Similarly, since both the inventory control and accounting systems utilize common transaction documents, they should be designed to be fully integrated with one another. For this reason, many companies find it most economical to design or modify and implement inventory management and production accounting systems as a single project.

Although both the inventory management and accounting systems should be fully consistent with one another, the application of these systems can vary by company. Two main approaches are used:

(1) Some companies will buy all of their production materials for a specific customer order only at the time when that order is received from the customer. Then the purchases made for the customer's order are charged specifically to the order at time of receipt.

(2) Other companies employ some form of forecasting to anticipate customer requirements. These requirements are then exploded by using standard product bills of materials to determine production material requirements. Purchase orders for high usage-value production materials are issued in sequence with anticipated needs by stage of product buildup and within established inventory investment guidelines. Receipts of these materials, which account for the bulk of total production material costs, are scheduled close to the time of anticipated use. These items are generally issued from stores only at the time required, and then only in exact quantities to meet scheduled production requirements. Requisitions for issues in excess of these standard requirements normally require manager-level approval. This immediately calls attention to the fact that

scheduled requirements are being exceeded or that scrap is excessive. To permit attention at all levels to be concentrated on the high usage-value materials, the low usage-value materials are then issued in bulk to a production line to satisfy requirements over a period of time, rather than being issued to satisfy requirements of a specific order. When warranted an individual material could, on an exception basis, be issued to production by employing either method as needs dictate.

Although the first approach to accounting and control of production materials is relatively simple from a systems standpoint, it generally results in exceptionally high investment in inventories and long product-delivery lead times. The second approach will usually involve high one-time systems development costs and higher ongoing systems operating costs. However, more often than not, the latter approach can be cost justified not only in terms of lower inventory investment and better service to customers, but also in terms of more timely and more accurate cost information for use in profit planning, cost control, and performance reporting and evaluation. Consequently, the tendency is increasingly toward systems designed along the latter approach, employing forecasts and bills of material to determine and account for production material requirements.

When product bills of material are used to issue high usage-value materials to production, a copy of the bill should be prepared as a form for use as an issue slip. Space should be provided to permit stores to acknowledge that standard quantities of each line item were issued to meet requirements of the production schedule. The accounting department then merely has to reference and extend a cost bill of material to relieve materials inventory and charge work-in-process. As noted earlier, excess inventory requirements should be accounted for as an excess issue and reported on a withdrawal slip designed solely to report such usage to inventory control and accounting. In accounting, the excess issue slip would be extended by established costs of the material issued and charged as excess usage. Conversely, unused materials returned to stores would be recorded on a material return slip and accounted for in a material return account. Of course, material returns should be subject to the same scrutiny for cause from managers as an excess issue. The return could mean that scheduled production has not been met or that the standard provision for usage is, in itself, excessive.

Typically, low usage-value materials impede the overall effectiveness of materials management and accounting efforts simply because they represent a relatively large number of items requiring a great deal of paperwork to account for usage. Because of this, it has been found expedient to issue these materials in bulk to production to cover usage requirements for a period of time, rather than for the manufacture of a particular job order or product. This greatly reduces material handling and paperwork requirements. However, it does require use of special accounting technique in accounting for usage for the low usage-valued items. There are a number of approaches employed, but in essence they fall into two categories:

1. Cost of low usage-valued items is treated as overhead cost at the time of payment for a purchase, or when a bulk issue is made, and absorbed into work-in-process inventories much like other operating overhead expenses.
2. Standard usage is considered actual usage. The amount to be relieved from inventory is determined by extending reported good production by the standard content of low usage-valued items in the goods produced.

If the latter approach is used, consideration should be given to maintaining a separate inventory account for low usage-value materials and to summarizing their standard cost separately on the cost bill of material. This would then permit periodic testing of the validity of established usage standards by periodically comparing a physical inventory to the book inventory for this type of material.

Finally, there are some high usage-value materials that are best treated for purposes of usage accounting as an *exception*. This requires structuring an accounting methodology that best satisfies the need for producing accurate and timely information in an efficient manner. For example, in a fabricating operation coil steel typically is a high usage-value material. However, very often such operations are not equipped with a convenient facility for weighing the coil to determine usage after each order. In such instances where it is also impractical to weigh-count scrap or waste, it may be more practical to account for material usage on a process basis and to account for excess scrap and waste as an expense of the operation, which is allocated back to the product on some appropriate basis. When such an approach is used the material content of total good production is compared to the total quantity issued to determine total scrap and waste. Obviously, when the results indicate that intolerable scrap and waste is being experienced, more exacting methods might have to be employed to localize the problem for corrective action. Such actions might include weigh-counting of scrap and waste or the unused material, such as the coil, after each future run until the problem has been localized.

SALVAGE, REWORK, AND DISCARDS ACCOUNTING

Distinct definitions need to be adopted for discussing the methodology to employ in accounting for production materials in product salvage, rework, or discard activities.

Salvage applies to activities performed on unacceptable product or production material which cannot be reworked to make it acceptable for its original purpose. Consequently, the product or production material being salvaged will be broken down so that usable components or elements can be extracted for reuse in other production.

Rework applies to activities which require additional production material and/or labor to restore a product or production material to a normal, acceptable condition.

Discard applies to activities performed on an unacceptable product or material which results in its being totally scrapped or destroyed.

To help exercise an appropriate degree of control over salvage, rework, and discard activities, consideration should be given to employing an authorization procedure for such work. First, the department requesting the salvage, rework, or discard action should be required to complete a *disposition* or *discrepancy statement*, which identifies and states the value of the product or production material involved, the reason for the action to be taken, and the costs to be incurred. The authorization to proceed should be approved by production, materials, and engineering management and reviewed by accounting as to financial feasibility before any work is performed. When appropriate, a specific work order number should then be assigned for purposes of reporting and accumulating any production material or other costs incurred, and for evaluating the actual results of a specific salvage, rework, or discard activity.

The following considerations should be given to improving accounting for *salvage:*

1. Where total salvage activities are significant, a salvage department or cost center should be established. Process cost techniques should be employed to accumulate the cost of materials for salvage and the salvage costs incurred. When the activities are not significant, an indirect cost account to accumulate salvage costs in individual departments which perform salvage work would be adequate.
2. Salvaged materials should be returned to stores for reissue to production. Salvage credit should be initiated by accounting only when a receipt of salvaged materials is acknowledged by the stores activity.
3. A salvage income account should be used to record the value of salvaged materials and to offset the recording of materials received for salvage and the subsequent cost.

In salvage and rework, the size of the order and the work to be performed often dictate the cost accounting technique to be employed. Process cost accounting techniques are probably best employed, because salvage quantities are relatively small and the work site is usually improvised in a manner whereby a number of materials can be salvaged simultaneously (and often by the same employees). In rework, however the quantities are usually larger and the material to be reworked is usually injected into the normal production process for reworking. Rework costs, then, can be more naturally collected by job order and results can be more accurately measured against rework budgets. Key points to consider with regard to accounting for *rework* of production materials are:

1. The department or cost center assigned to perform rework should be required to report by rework order the actual rework costs incurred, by item, for production material and other costs, together with a report of the quantity of re-

worked product or production material made acceptable. This accounting is perhaps best performed if a rework report is provided the department for this purpose. The form should be constructed in a manner that permits the performing department to identify readily the actual cost incurred in rework operations. This is a particularly useful requirement when the reporting department is responsible for creating the need for rework and when the established rework budget is included in the rework report at the time of issue. Then a ready comparison of actual to budget can be made by the performing department as the actual costs are being reported.

2. When it is necessary to remove product or production material from inventory for reworking and combine it with a normal production run at the point where the necessary reworking must begin, the identity of the material being reworked is often lost. When this occurs, the difference of the value of the withdrawn inventory and the estimated cost of the material to be reworked from the point of rework is charged directly to a rework cost account. The reworked material would then be treated and valued as normal production at the time it is completed, along with the other production with which it was necessarily combined. This accounting practice could be followed in most situations where it would be impractical, if not impossible, to identify actual rework costs.

Discards of production materials generally result in the incurrence of some indirect labor cost in handling, and no additional material costs. If the labor required is significant, a separate indirect labor account is employed. Otherwise, the normal material handling account for a department or cost center should be adequate in accounting for the cost associated with the discard of production materials.

SURPLUS, EXCESS, AND OBSOLETE MATERIALS ACCOUNTING

Often in a production environment materials accumulate in excess of current or long-range needs. When these materials involve stocks of active items which may be depleted through normal usage over a relatively long period of time, they are generally deemed *surplus.* If the items are inactive or slow moving to the point where they may cover several years' needs, the quantities beyond current requirements are designated as *excess.* Materials in these categories may be reclassified as non-current inventories, or may require an allowance for obsolescence. When the materials relate only to items which are no longer usable on current products they are *obsolete.* Items may move from one of these categories to another, and indeed, items which currently are surplus or excess should be thought of as potentially obsolete, to stimulate the disposition of this stock at minimum cost.

The two major costs associated with these inventory categories are (1) the cost of holding these materials in stock and (2) the decline in value of the materials, often to a value considerably lower than that paid for the materials when they were acquired. These costs tend to grow with the passage of time; therefore, it is essential that materials in these categories be reviewed regularly and that decisions regarding their disposition be made promptly. It is also important to separate the accounting and disposition aspects of this decision. Although it may be appropriate from an accounting standpoint to establish an allowance to cover excess or surplus materials which may ultimately become obsolete, or which may eventually be disposed of at less than cost, it may not be beneficial to dispose physically of all of the materials immediately. This is especially true in the case of spare parts inventories where stock must be maintained for possible future service needs.

There are two vital ingredients for a program directed at effective accounting for and disposition of surplus, excess, and obsolete materials: (1) a sound inventory management system which facilitates the identification of potentially surplus, excess, or obsolete items, and (2) a task force charged with the responsibility of making and executing the necessary accounting and disposition decisions. An effective system is probably the easier of the two to obtain. Many inventory management systems report as exceptions inventories in excess of requirements to meet open sales orders or long-range forecasted production. All active materials items with stock on hand in excess of a given number of months' coverage are flagged for review. If the reports are stratified by the value of the excess inventory, the most significant items can then be acted upon quickly.

An active *task force,* composed of capable individuals from accounting, purchasing, engineering, and production, is an equally important component of a successful program. This task force should meet regularly to review the excess inventory reports and to make decisions concerning the accounting and physical disposition of the surplus, excess, and obsolete materials. In this process, the task force should be guided by established financial policy and accounting requirements related to declaration and disposition of these materials. The alternative disposition actions (e.g., modification of the part, making a close-out run, return to the vendor, scrap) should be identified and assigned priorities as to their economic implications. The responsibility for carrying out the most desirable alternative within a specified time period should be assigned to one of the members of the task force. The assignment of responsibility for action, and the establishment of a target action date, will strongly reduce the probability that action will not be taken.

Another way to enhance the prospects of a successful inventory disposition program is to establish a series of accounts which reflect the performance of the task force. When materials are designated for disposition, their written down value may be transferred into a special inventory account assigned to the task force. The balance of the original value is accounted for according to established financial policies. If the task force disposes of the materials at some value above that at which it is being carried, the increase in value is reflected as a profit for the task force. Costs associated with the disposal effort, such as special advertising, promotion, and trips to potential customers, may similarly be charged in the task force's statement. While this approach is generally applicable only when the disposal activity is significant, it can be expected to improve materially the performance of a disposition program when it is utilized.

SUMMARY

This chapter has offered the reader accounting methodologies to consider for typically important concerns associated with production material costs. If applied, the results could mean a more accurate and effective cost system and more efficient accounting activities. The methodologies discussed included the following:

1. The accounting cycle for production materials begins with the *profit plan* which defines costs to be incurred and inventories to be maintained by planning period, using forecasts and established costs. The accounting system accounts for and reports results in relation to the plan and to the established costs used in planning. Reports should include variance analyses, which enable management to take and monitor corrective action and to evaluate the adequacy of existing plans and standards. Where standards do not exist, comparisions to historical data can be meaningful provided that the mix of product activity is comparable.

2. The application of the *ABC technique* in accounting for production materials will help focus attention on important material cost items and thereby aid in the development of more accurate total production material costs with little, if any, increase in the operating cost of the related accounting system. Although the technique minimizes the amount of attention directed at remaining production materials, it should not be interpreted as promoting inadequate control over such material. Oftentimes, the technique when applied results in control being applied at minimal cost where it previously was nonexistent. Furthermore, when warranted the ABC classification could be abandoned for an individual material that might be better managed on an exception basis.

3. The *cost bill of material* is a key document in planning, accounting, and control of production materials. Careful thought must be given to the format to help insure that certain cost information important in the management and operation of a business has not been overlooked. Its structure might include authorized substitutions; identification of sample requirements separately from other yield loss data; use of temporary performance factors; identification of the material, labor, and overhead cost elements individually and cumulatively by line item; application of production material overhead recovery factors; and a summary of the inventory account sources of production materials for inventory accounting purposes.

4. Two sets of standards could be used to account for the purchase price of materials where the volatility of such prices in the market place impede effectiveness in accounting and control. A *frozen set of price standards* would be maintained for purposes of reporting external to the reporting unit. A *current set of price standards* would be maintained for internal reporting and for performance evaluation purposes.

When cost bills of material standards need to be changed during the year, consideration should be given to use of an inventory valuation account to adjust results for the impact that changes will have on the value of other identical inventory acquired at different prices, and whose movement in the production process will be accounted for by the changed cost bills of material.

5. *Freight cost absorption factors* can be useful in providing for freight costs in developing the total cost of production materials. When freight costs are significant, a freight factor is a valid consideration for improved cost accounting. This would be particularly appropriate when freight costs are being treated as overhead and applied on the basis of total costs and there is a significant difference in the labor and material cost mix among products, when freight costs can be significantly different among purchased materials, and when freight cost incurred can be influenced by the size and mix of purchased materials shipped by the vendor.

6. A *purchase order, blanket order release,* or *warehouse transfer order* should be used to initiate necessary activities for the receipt of all required production materials. In controlling the use of available cash and the size of investment in materials inventories, the ABC technique could be effectively employed to help define a potential-purchase-commitment review policy that directs a majority of management attention to those potential purchases which would require the majority of available purchase dollars. Once a purchase order is authorized, it should be confirmed with a vendor by using a normal purchase order, which contains all the necessary accounting information to be used by the vendor in subsequent communications. This helps to ensure an accurate recording of materials at time of the delivery receipt and accounting for the payment. To minimize inventory reconciliation problems, special inventory accounts should

be employed to account for inventory that is quarantined at time of receipt pending quality approval.

7. Where accounting communications are necessary internally between departments—or externally with vendors—relative to such matters as rejected materials being returned to vendors or invoices being adjusted for vendor errors, a *debit memorandum* should be used to help clarify communications and to document any related actions or required accounting transactions.

8. Because key information needs of materials management and accounting closely parallel one another and dictate the development of a common data base, any program to bring about improvements in accounting for production materials would logically include the common problems and solutions applicable to both activities. Current systems of material management are employing bills of material as a basis of planning, issuing, and controlling production materials. Costed bills of material can be used to account for the movement and standard use of production materials through the production process. Both systems concentrate on the high usage-value production materials, with the result that management attention is focused on the most significant aspect of the cost of, and the investment in, production materials. Less time-demanding, but effective, techniques of accounting and control are then employed for the remaining materials.

9. Effective accounting and control over *salvage, rework,* and *discard activities* should feature authorization procedures which define the value of the material to be salvaged, reworked, or discarded, the reason for the work, and the estimate of the costs to be incurred. The estimate should serve as a basis for deciding whether or not the work should be performed, and as a budget for the subsequent work if approved. Typically, in accounting for actual cost of salvage and rework, process costing techniques are usually most appropriate for salvage operations, and job costing techniques for rework operations.

10. Effectiveness of a program directed at accounting for and disposition of *surplus, excess,* and *obsolete materials* depends on a sound inventory management system which facilitates identifying them, and an action-oriented task force which recommends and directs necessary activities related to disposing of

them. The key objective of the program is to minimize inventory holding costs, declines in realizable value, and disposition costs. The success of the program and the performance of the task force can be enhanced by accounting for and reporting the disposal revenues and operating expenses of the task force much like those of a profit center.

15

Accounting for production labor

*Adolph T. Silverstein**

DEFINITION OF PRODUCTION LABOR

The most important consideration in establishing a system of accounting for production labor is *consistency in defining labor*—that is, what time expended is direct labor and what time is indirect labor. Consistency is also required in classifying the fringe costs associated with direct labor. Consistency of classification within a plant is essential, and it is desirable throughout a given corporation.

The major comparisons of plant or departmental performance are usually based on efficiency. Efficiency is a ratio of measured work performance (usually in standard hours) to the related hours paid. The method of measuring efficiency will be discussed later in this chapter.

It has been a long-standing and widespread industry practice to use *direct labor dollars* as the basis for allocating overhead dollars to units of product. As manufacturing processes have become more sophisticated and more mechanized, the labor content of the product expressed in dollars—and even more so in hours—has been decreasing steadily. Concomitantly, overhead costs, particularly depreciation and those fringe benefits

* Controller, Fruehauf Corporation.

accounted for as overhead, have been climbing steadily. As a result, we are allocating more and more burden dollars on the basis of a decreasing number of standard labor hours, which were never measured with precision to begin with. At the end of World War II typical burden rates were 100 percent of labor, with many more plants below 100 percent than over 100 percent. Now 150 percent is a far more typical number. As the burden rate rises past 200 percent, consideration of using a different basis of allocation is suggested.

There is not a universally accepted definition of *direct labor.* My definition would be the labor performed by employees whose efforts result in a change in the physical characteristics of a product during a manufacturing operation. Some would go beyond this definition to include set-up time, inspection, material handling, and occasionally even supervision. If these items are not considered to be direct labor, their cost would be treated as indirect labor, a component of overhead. In a related vein, certain costs associated with direct labor, however it is defined, can be treated either as components of the cost of a direct labor hour or as elements of burden. The varying treatments result in a different split between labor content and overhead content of the end product; however, if the underlying allocation assumptions are proper, the total product cost should be identical.

In determining what should be included in a standard hour, let us consider the three primary purposes to be served by this measurement: product cost, efficiency, and interplant/intercompany product cost comparisons.

MEASURING AND REPORTING EFFICIENCY

Efficiency is a most important measurement of plant and departmental performance. In order to make valid comparisons, the methodology followed by the organizational units being compared must be the same. The customary system encountered is a standard cost system wherein routing sheets are used to develop a time allowance for each department that works on a given unit of production. The routing sheets are prepared in industrial engineering departments and, ideally, should contain standards based on precise time studies of each operation. In practice, however, unless the production is highly standardized,

EXHIBIT 1

GROUP OPERATION	DAILY STD HRS	DAILY ACT HRS	DAILY EFF	ACCUM THIS MO STD HRS	ACCUM THIS MO ACT HRS	ACCUM THIS MO EFF	ACCUM LAST MO STD HRS	ACCUM LAST MO ACT HRS	ACCUM LAST MO EFF
BLDG 4 MISC PARTS — 12 PRESS SHOP PARTS	649.9	557.6	116.6	9,481.4	9,556.8	99.2	10,008.5	10,087.5	99.2
21-1 MISC PARTS + ASSY	4.3	32.0	13.4	342.8	344.0	99.7	342.8	376.0	91.2
21-2 COUPLERS	22.6	32.0	70.6	313.2	536.7	58.4	313.2	568.7	55.1
31 PAINT	166.6	162.0	102.8	2,130.0	2,182.7	97.6	2,272.0	2,323.9	97.8
TOTAL	843.4	783.6	107.6	12,267.4	12,620.2	97.2	12,936.5	13,356.1	96.9
NARROW — 23 WELDING	380.2	362.0	105.0	5,955.1	5,902.5	100.9	6,282.1	6,244.0	100.6
23-1 BRAKE,WIRE+ U/C	275.6	269.2	102.4	4,089.0	3,992.0	102.4	4,283.9	4,176.9	102.6
23-2 FLOORING	223.8	204.0	109.7	3,948.3	3,334.5	100.4	3,557.8	3,524.2	100.4
23-3 BRAKE + WIRE	76.0	96.0	79.2	1,666.1	1,668.4	99.9	1,770.2	1,772.4	99.9
FRAMES — 23-4 CHASSIS LINE FRAM	105.3	104.0	101.3	1,749.7	1,775.2	98.6	1,829.5	1,854.2	98.7
TOTAL	1,060.9	1,035.2	102.5	16,808.2	16,673.5	100.8	17,703.5	17,571.7	100.8
DUMP — 24 SET + T/M CONVEY	197.8	260.0	76.1	3,353.4	3,466.6	96.7	3,565.2	3,703.3	96.3
UNITS — 24-1 FINAL WELD TMBLER	247.5	265.4	93.3	3,468.5	3,500.8	99.1	3,653.0	3,728.7	98.0
24-2 FINAL ASSY	294.2	304.0	96.8	3,981.9	4,111.5	95.8	4,248.1	4,391.4	96.7
TOTAL	739.5	829.4	89.2	10,803.5	11,078.9	97.5	11,466.3	11,823.4	97.0
TOTAL BLDG. # 4	2,643.8	2,648.2	99.8	39,879.1	40,372.6	96.7	42,106.3	42,751.2	98.4
BLDG 6 PARTS — 12-2 YODERS	.0	.0	**	39.2	.0	**	39.2	.0	**
13 DOOR DEPARTMENT	38.0	83.5	45.5	537.4	888.7	60.5	557.4	936.7	59.5
21 AXLE ASM + PARTS	126.9	126.0	100.7	1,837.2	1,827.5	100.5	1,963.9	1,947.5	100.8
TOTAL	164.9	209.5	78.7	2,413.8	2,716.2	88.9	2,560.5	2,884.2	88.8
WAREHSE VANS — 28-1 SIDE PANEL ASSY	11.7	16.0	73.1	109.9	146.7	74.9	113.9	153.4	74.3
28-2 CHASSIS ASSY	12.0	16.0	75.0	127.8	156.7	81.6	161.5	202.7	79.7
28-3 WAREHSE FINAL ASM	23.7	32.0	74.1	147.1	180.0	81.7	147.1	180.0	81.7
TOTAL				384.8	483.4	79.6	422.5	536.1	78.8
CARYALL DROP FME UNITS — 29 WELDING	210.2	210.0	100.0	3,401.0	3,384.5	100.5	3,532.8	3,519.5	100.4
29-1 BRAKE,WIRE + U/C	74.7	75.0	99.6	1,166.0	1,160.5	100.5	1,227.2	1,221.5	100.5
29-2 FLOORING	19.0	19.0	100.0	210.0	210.2	99.9	217.5	218.2	99.7
29-3 TELE. FRAME	27.0	26.9	100.4	279.0	274.6	101.6	306.0	301.6	101.5
TOTAL	330.9	331.1	99.9	5,056.0	5,029.8	100.5	5,283.5	5,260.8	100.4
TOTAL BLDG.# 8	519.5	572.6	90.7	7,854.6	8,229.4	95.4	8,266.5	8,681.1	95.2
MISC — 12-1 MACHINE SHOP	.0	.0	**	3.9	35.5	11.0	3.9	35.5	11.0
MISC — 48-3 SHIPPING	26.9	24.0	112.1	294.4	290.0	101.5	322.0	314.0	102.5
TOTAL	26.9	24.0	112.1	298.3	325.5	91.6	325.9	349.5	93.2
TOTAL ALL GROUPS	3,190.2	3,244.8	98.3	48,032.0	48,927.5	99.2	50,698.7	51,781.8	97.9

there is a tendency to use certain "bench mark" standards. The standard hours set for different types of product are increased or decreased from the bench marks on the basis of an estimate by the industrial engineering department.

Efficiency reports (Exhibit 1) are generally prepared on a daily basis, showing the results for the day as well as the month to date. The month-to-date information is generally included for the current month and the preceding month. Efficiency is expressed as a percentage, usually to the first decimal place. Notice that the report also shows standard hours earned and actual hours paid for the periods.

In order to generate the efficiency report, production has to be reported on a daily basis and the related standard hours earned must be developed and summarized by department. The actual hours paid for the day are then summarized by department. The hours paid are then adjusted to exclude the various "lost time" categories which include, but are not limited to, holidays, vacation, paid personal leave, jury duty, and time transferred to another department. The ratio of the standard hours earned to the net actual hours worked is the efficiency percentage.

PROBLEMS IN SETTING LABOR STANDARDS

This all seems very straightforward, but what are the real life problems? The key determination in setting standards involves a definition of a *standard hour.* In a typical situation, a union contract will call for eight hours of pay with the workers allowed a 15-minute break in the morning and a 15-minute break in the afternoon. Is the standard hour based on the work that can be performed in seven and one-half hours or eight hours? It would seem that the basis should be seven and one-half hours with the extra 30 minutes alternatively treated as a component of the cost per standard hour or as an element of burden. Why? Envision a simple case where the time study allowance to do a job is 30 minutes; in seven and one-half hours, 15 pieces should be produced. If the eight-hour base is used, the standard time allowance would be 32 (480 minutes divided by 15 pieces) and the accuracy of the time standards would be weakened, since inaccuracy would result for any time period other than the normal (eight hour) day.

Another problem involves *transfer time*. There is a natural motivation for a foreman to transfer time to another function or department. Since an effective transfer reduces the denominator, it automatically improves efficiency—the yardstick by which the foreman is customarily measured. Tracing transferred time to its ultimate destination used to be laborious and time consuming. By the time the transferee department was aware of the charge, the efficiency report had often been published. In today's computer generation this should not be possible— transferred time should be accepted by the transferee, if the transfer was proper, prior to issuance of the daily efficiency report. Beware also of the transfer of direct labor time to maintenance labor and material handling.

Another term that is often discussed in connection with direct labor is a *line-balance factor*. The line-balance factor arises when you have different items to be produced on a common assembly line. In a given situation, ten items may pass through in an hour, eight of which require four men to work on them, and two of which require only three men. For the two units that require only three men, what do you do with the other man for 2/10 of an hour? It obviously would not pay to reassign him, so most companies facing this problem generate a line balance factor. This is virtually the only time allowance which should be permitted to creep into the standard hours earned. It is derived by an analysis of anticipated product mix over a fairly long period of time. Obviously, the key to minimizing the line-balance factor lies in scheduling. The more like items that can be grouped for consecutive production, the lower the line-balance factor required. The alternatives are to permit the foreman to charge this time to a "lost time" account, an element of overhead, or to ignore it entirely with the effect of reducing departmental and plant efficiency. The latter alternative distorts performance evaluation. The difficulty in developing a line-balance factor is that the foreman who squeaks the loudest will too often get the highest factor.

The treatment accorded *set-up costs* should be determined by the characteristics of the item being produced. If relatively little set-up is involved or the amount of set-up is a relatively constant percentage of the cost of all products, the most convenient approach is to charge all set-up labor directly to an overhead account. If a given set-up is expensive and not relatively consistent among the various products, the set-up time and a standard product run size should be estimated. The set-up time per piece should then be included as a separate item in the standard time for the operation. A variance account should be charged for the actual set-up labor paid and credited with the set-up time earned, based on the standard time allowance for the production achieved. Any net variance should be charged to income as incurred; if the variance is significant, an analysis should be made to determine if the cause is poor performance or run size. Since the foreman customarily cannot control run size, the set-up time variance should not affect his reported efficiency. The set-up problem is generally much more severe in a parts operation than in an assembly operation.

Inspection labor is generally treated as an element of overhead cost, primarily because of the difficulty in identifying inspection labor with a specific unit of production. Notable exceptions involve products with very little tolerance which therefore require a high level of inspection, e.g., aircraft and high technology items produced under government contracts. In these situations, one often encounters inspection being treated as a separate category of direct labor, applied on a percentage basis. If this is done, there will normally be a variance between inspection labor paid and inspection labor applied. This variance should also be charged to income as incurred.

With respect to *material handling,* it seems odd that the labor used to move a piece of raw material to a work station is performed by a material handler whose wages are charged to overhead, while the wages of the man who lifts the piece of raw material and places it in a machine is direct labor. Nonetheless, that is the treatment accorded in virtually all industries.

Supervision, at any level, should never be considered an element of standard direct labor. The plant that makes a proposal to the contrary often would propose to include the supervisory time in the standard while charging supervisory wages to overhead. This blatant inconsistency is not good accounting. If plant management makes this type of recommendation, I would be conerned about the ability of the plant to meet its time standards.

Thus far our comments have been directed to assembly operations, or operations where the end product is the output of a single department. Another area where problems tend to be generated involve *parts fabrication* where the parts ultimately are being used in the assembly process. If, within the same plant, parts are fabricated as well as assembled, there is a tendency for over-reporting of the parts production. The easiest way to avoid this problem is to have the parts department(s) earn standard hours based on finished end units, not finished parts. This assumes that the float of parts in process is always relatively constant. One must be careful that he can be comfortable with this assumption.

The parts fabrication department should also receive hour credit for parts shipped to other plants or sold for service parts. If parts hours earned are not accounted for as I suggest, the controller should watch carefully for a buildup of parts-labor dollars. This could indicate either of two conditions, both highly unsatisfactory. One, production is being over-reported and/or scrap is not being properly reported, or alternatively, there may be excess parts around the premises. If scrap is not being properly reported, there well may be a bigger problem with respect to the material value associated with those parts as compared to the labor and burden value.

The assembly department(s) should, wherever possible, earn standard hours based on products being finished. There should be relatively little change in the float of line labor in process unless there is a very sharp swing in volume of production and/ or in product mix.

Within a corporation, *interplant performance comparisons* generally start at the *"plant contribution"* level, but plant managers tend to discuss *efficiency percentages* and *burden rates*. The validity of the comparisons are highly dependent upon similar classification of costs. If like products are built in more than one plant, the standard hours allowed should be identical except for differences caused by characteristics of the individual plants, primarily tooling, layout, and size of run. Intercompany comparisons of standard hours, efficiency, and burden rates tend to be performed by all levels of management. However, in most cases the individuals performing the comparisons are well aware of the idiosyncrasies of their own operation but relatively unaware of the practices of the operation being compared.

PROBLEMS IN MEASURING
ACTUAL LABOR COSTS

The foregoing discussion addresses a standard cost environment in which a major objective is the ability to compare the standard and actual hours required to build like objects. We stress that comparability dictates consistent treatment of like elements of cost, and also comparable volumes, tooling, and equipment. The standard cost system is generally used in manufacturing assembly operations, whereas an actual job cost system is more often encountered in service or repair operations. In an actual cost environment, the primary function with respect to quantity is determining the actual hours spent by each laborer on each job. This is generally accomplished through some form of time card reporting by each individual which identifies his time spent with a work order or job number. The time is usually kept by the employee and its accuracy reviewed by a timekeeper. The ratio of employees to timekeepers can be much higher than the ratio of employees to foremen. In an actual cost environment, the problems that tend to arise include time switching and excess hours on a given job, as well as the traditional lost time categories.

In order to manage an operation using a system of actual direct hours, it is necessary to set some form of target for each job. If the job involves work from more than one department, the time allowance for each department is given separately. The actual hours paid are then accumulated by department and compared to the allowance for the work produced. A problem occurs when, in a department or plant, hours in excess of the time allowance are accumulated. There is a tendency for the foreman to shift some of the excess actual hours to a different job, which is the main reason the timekeeper should be independent of the foreman. The time shifting practice, if undetected, takes away the ability of management to control what is going on on the shop floor and, in the worst case, could result in serious legal problems where a customer is billed on a time basis for time not spent on his job.

When time switching occurs, it is very difficult for management to know the status of any given job. A buildup of hours in process can readily occur and since the floor is hopefully never clear of production, this excess can go undetected until the next physical inventory is taken. Another problem in a job cost environment plagued with time switching is the unreliability of historical data as a basis for pricing proposals for new jobs of a similar nature.

Cost factors

Whether actual or standard measures of quantity are used for direct labor, it is customary to use a standard rate or group of standard rates to account for the cost. If a group of rates is used, it generally reflects different skills, not the effect of a different mix in seniority. As we will discuss later, the fewer labor rates employed, the easier the application.

There is no question that the wage payment is the major element of standard or actual cost per hour (see Exhibit 2). Notice that the direct wage payment is only 68 percent of the total standard cost.

The *efficiency factor* is that cost associated with all scheduled breaks and the anticipated failure to achieve 100 percent efficiency based on the standard time allowances. This factor may vary from plant to plant or even between operations. It is vital to have this factor included in product cost if prices are to be established based on cost. Establishing the proper efficiency fac-

EXHIBIT 2

COMPANY NAME
Type of Plant
Cost of Standard Hour
Inventory Year 11/1/78–10/31/79

Wage payment	$ 6.75
Efficiency factor	1.10
Social security taxes (employer's share)	0.64
Shift premium	0.07
Overtime premium	0.05
Vacation	0.39
Holiday	0.34
Pensions	0.28
COLA	0.38
Total	$10.00

tor requires a great deal of subjective judgment. Too high a factor causes noncompetitive pricing; too low a factor might result in unrecovered costs.

There are many other cost factors which are also properly included in the cost of a standard hour. Each of the other cost factors has its own peculiarities. Typical is the *vacation allowance*—in a given example no vacation allowance is payable unless a minimum of 500 hours are worked. Does this mean that the first 500 hours have no vacation cost associated with them? Obviously not. An assumption must be made as to the standard hours that will be earned by the work force. The actual hours to be worked must be projected and since the vacation allowances also tend to vary with seniority, an assumption must be made also as to seniority mix. These factors are used to project a total cost of vacations, which is then divided by the anticipated standard hours to be earned to develop a vacation rate per standard hour.

A balance sheet account should be charged with vacation payments made and credited with the standard allowance per hour earned. Until year-end, the net difference should be deferred; at year-end, it should be closed out to the income statement. In the example, the credit should be based on 39¢ per *standard* hour, not an amount per actual hour. If in the course of a year there is a major shift in the level of production, the allowance factor should be reevaluated.

Pension costs are generally stated in terms of either cost per hour or defined benefit. If the pension agreement calls for a stipulated cost per hour, the only adjustment required is to convert from actual hours to standard hours. The factor used would normally be developed from the efficiency factor previously discussed. If the pension plan provides defined benefits, the anticipated cost should be spread over the anticipated standard hours to be worked during the year. It should be noted that often the pension year also differs from the firm's fiscal year.

Holiday pay is also quite straightforward, as the holidays are generally defined in the union contract. The anticipated annual holiday expense is calculated and the total cost is spread over the anticipated standard hours to be earned with the accounting the same as is accorded vacation pay.

The basic *social security tax* is applicable to the first $17,700 of wages earned (although it is scheduled for increases in future years). How should the labor hours be handled after an employee earns $17,700? The recommended treatment is to set a rate based on the anticipated social security taxes and level of activity each year. The accounting, again, is the same as is accorded vacation pay.

Overtime and shift premium, as well as hospitalization and dental insurance premiums, can be handled in either of two ways. One can attempt to predict the total premium per year and develop an allocation factor as with social security taxes. Alternatively, the premium can be charged to overhead as incurred. The practical result should be the same in either case. It should be emphasized that we are talking about the premium pay associated with overtime, not the standard rate.

Cost of Living Allowance (COLA) is generally included in the standard costing rate based on a projected average rate for the year, although in some instances standard costing rates are changed quarterly in respect of COLA.

The *wage rates* paid in manufacturing operations are generally established annually, particularly in a union environment. The financial statement year-end usually does not coincide with the union contract payment anniversary date. In such a case, a decision has to be made as to the treatment of rate changes. Is it preferable to change the standard in mid-year and if so, how is it handled? If there is a single plant-wide wage rate, it is an easy matter to determine the number of hours included in inventory by merely dividing the dollars of inventory by the appropriate rate. Once the hours are known, the change in the standard rate would give rise to a new dollar amount in inventory. This difference can either be credited to income (assuming a rate increase) or deferred until the book to physical inventory adjustment is computed and recorded. The latter treatment is generally recommended, for this tends to create a cushion for any material shortages that may be disclosed by the physical inventory. The ease of handling is one reason why a single plant-wide labor rate should be used wherever possible.

Physical inventory

In conclusion, the only time one can be comfortable with the dollars of direct labor in process carried in the financial statements is after a physical inventory is taken. It is customary to take a physical inventory at a manufacturing plant once a year. In terms of accounting for direct labor in process, it is necessary that the different pay points be recognized when the physical inventory is taken. Unless one department does extensive work on the product, the pay point is set on a departmental basis; that is, no hours are earned until all the labor in a department has been accomplished. If work in process is extensive, accumulating the quantity of hours in process can be burdensome. The physical inventory date is a natural date to change costing rates, although fiscal year-end or date of contractual rate change could be used. Care should be taken lest the increase in inventory value attributable to inflation obliterate a loss in quantity of hours in process which could indicate a deficient reporting system.

I wish to repeat the need for the chief accounting officer to monitor the amount of labor in process. This one statistic is the best early warning signal that something may be going wrong with the internal reporting and accounting. Significant fluctuations, *up* or *down*, should be investigated immediately. Do *not* accept the pat answer that the change is due to a change in rate of production, but rather attempt to quantify the change in production level and relate it to the change in labor hours in process.

16

Accounting for production overhead

Louis F. Biagioni*
Richard A. Warne†

BASIC COST CONCEPTS

For manufacturing enterprises, costs may be classified in a number of different ways. Some of the more common groupings of manufacturing costs include

1. Manufacturing costs/nonmanufacturing costs.
2. Product costs/period or nonproduct costs.
3. Service department costs/producing department costs.
4. Fixed costs/variable costs.

If we focus on the first grouping, we find that there are further subdivisions. For example, manufacturing costs may be classified as (1) direct materials, (2) direct labor, and (3) manufacturing overhead. Elements of nonmanufacturing costs include (1) selling or marketing, (2) general and administrative, (3) research and development, and (4) financial costs. Financial costs represent the interest costs applicable to the acquisition of debt funds.

The accounting treatment of manufacturing and nonmanufacturing costs follows a specified procedure. According to *generally accepted accounting principles* (GAAP) manufacturing costs are

---

* Professor of Accounting, Indiana University.
† Assistant Corporate Controller, Eli Lilly and Company.

EXHIBIT 1
Basic flow of costs for manufacturing enterprises

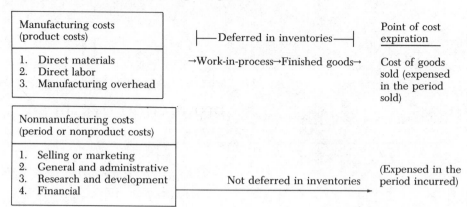

charged to the products produced and these costs are expensed in the accounting period in which the products are sold. Non-manufacturing costs, on the other hand, are not charged to the products but instead are expensed directly in the period in which the costs are incurred. This basic treatment of costs is illustrated in Exhibit 1.

From this illustration, we can see that manufacturing costs are charged first to an inventory account entitled *Work-in-Process* and then transferred to another inventory account entitled *Finished Goods.* It is not until the goods are sold that the manufacturing costs find their way to the income statement. On the other hand, nonmanufacturing costs are carried directly to the income statement in the period incurred.[1] Because manufacturing overhead costs are an element of manufacturing costs, the expensing of these overhead costs is a function of sales, not a function of time. If products are produced and sold in the same accounting period, then there is no difference in the final disposition of manufacturing overhead costs. However, when

---

[1] There are some exceptions to this statement. GAAP recognizes the deferral of some nonmanufacturing costs which clearly can be shown to benefit several fiscal periods. For example, insurance premiums paid in advance for several fiscal periods are deferred in a prepaid asset category and expensed with the passage of time. However, such costs, if not associated with the manufacturing process, are deferred as prepaid expenses or deferred charges, not as inventory.

the accounting periods are different for production and sales, then it becomes important to understand the GAAP treatment of manufacturing overhead costs and the impact that such treatment has on the financial statements.

DEFINITION OF
MANUFACTURING OVERHEAD

There are two characteristics which distinguish manufacturing overhead costs from other manufacturing costs: (1) they are not readily or directly traceable to the finished product, and (2) an increase or decrease in production volume does not necessarily lead to a proportionate change in cost. Manufacturing overhead costs are all manufacturing costs other than direct materials and direct labor. They include all the *indirect* costs incurred in the manufacturing process. Examples of manufacturing overhead costs are such items as indirect materials, indirect labor, factory building occupancy costs, depreciation on machinery and equipment, utilities (water, heat, power), waste treatment costs, social security taxes paid on factory payrolls, fringe benefits, and compensation insurance on factory payrolls. Indirect materials include such items as grease, oil, cleaning compounds, and uniforms for employees. Indirect labor includes salaries and wages of foremen, inspectors, janitors, storekeepers, and factory supervisors.

Any attempt to develop an all-inclusive list of specific account titles for the manufacturing overhead area would be futile. Such a list of subsidiary accounts would become obsolete periodically as different accounts were developed through either aggregation of several existing accounts, or disaggregation of an existing account. For a comprehensive discussion of manufacturing versus nonmanufacturing costs and a further list of types of manufacturing overhead, the U.S. Internal Revenue Service Regulations on this subject may be helpful. (See Regulations 1.471–11.)

Manufacturing overhead costs are referred to as *indirect* manufacturing costs because they are *not directly* traceable to specific products. The incurrence of these cost items benefits all production. They are traceable to products only on an "indirect" basis, as contrasted to direct materials and direct labor, which can be traced specifically or directly to the finished product.

MANUFACTURING COST
ACCOUNTING CYCLE

The manufacturing cost accounting cycle is the process which transforms the basic manufacturing costs into product, or inventory, costs. The cycle is well defined and standardized. The basic elements of manufacturing costs flow from one set of ledger accounts to another in a systematic manner.

The basic flow of manufacturing costs is depicted through the accompanying flowchart. This flowchart is a schematic description of the cost flow process for a manufacturing enterprise. This basic flow does not change; only the amounts and rate of absorption of costs will differ from company to company and from time to time. Referring to Exhibit 2, the dotted lines extending from "Materials and Supplies" and "Factory Payroll" to "Manufacturing Overhead" represent the indirect materials (supplies) and indirect labor incurred. These are items of overhead and thus should not be charged *directly* to the "Work in Process" account. They enter the "Work in Process" account via Manufacturing Overhead.

A question which remains open in the cost accounting cycle is the amount, or more specifically the *rate*, that should be used in assigning the manufacturing overhead. The amount or rate can be different depending on the volume or activity level which is chosen when establishing the predetermined overhead rate. More will be said on this point in a later section of this chapter.

OBJECTIVES OF
MANUFACTURING OVERHEAD

When discussing the area of manufacturing overhead costs, at least three objectives should be kept in mind. These three objectives may be classified into a *primary* and a *secondary* level. Each objective is not necessarily independent of the others; they are interrelated. These objectives are:

Primary level objectives
1. The *accounting* objective of income determination and inventory valuation.
2. The *managerial* objective of profit planning and cost control.

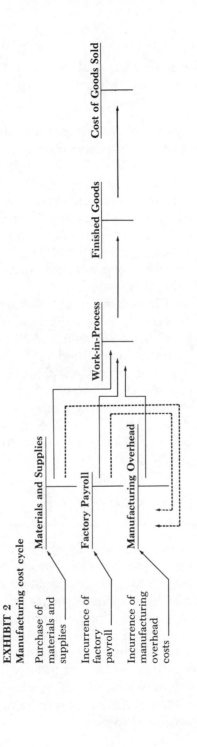

EXHIBIT 2
Manufacturing cost cycle

Secondary level objective

3. The *auditing and systems* objective of traceability of costs in order to maintain integrity of reporting and to satisfy the attestation function.

As we shall see in the next section of this discussion, manufacturing overhead costs are introduced into the accounting system via a *predetermined* manufacturing overhead rate. The peculiarities associated with the development of a manufacturing overhead rate are such that no one method may completely satisfy the first two primary level objectives. Therefore, an enterprise may decide to select a particular option (method) to satisfy the income determination objective for external reporting purposes, and then use some other option (method) to satisfy internal or managerial reporting purposes.

An important feature which should be kept in mind throughout our discussion is that whatever method of overhead costing is used, an adequate documentation and record-keeping system must be developed and maintained. This feature is necessary in order to maintain the integrity and reliability of the costing system and to facilitate the periodic review which is made of the accounting records by both the internal and external auditors. Documentation is also of use in controlling costs, to help trace costs assigned to final products back to their initial point of incurrence.

PREDETERMINED MANUFACTURING OVERHEAD RATES

A manufacturing enterprise may choose to allocate its actual manufacturing overhead costs to its products by waiting until the end of the fiscal year. In such a situation, the enterprise will accumulate all of the manufacturing overhead costs which have actually been incurred. Then, selecting some basis of allocation, these actual overhead costs will be assigned to the various products manufactured during the fiscal period. Such an approach is procedurally very simple to apply. However, as the following discussion indicates, manufacturing enterprises do not generally follow such a procedure, favoring instead an approach of using a predetermined rate.

First, it is neither practical nor expedient to wait until the end of the accounting period to determine the amount of manufacturing overhead that should be charged to production. As work is completed, the total manufacturing costs applicable to this work should be transferred to *Finished Goods* and then on to *Cost of Goods Sold*. Without the use of a predetermined rate, costing of production and sales could not be effected until the end of the accounting period. The use of a predetermined overhead rate permits management to prepare interim financial reports.

Second, there are a number of cost items that reflect a seasonal pattern. Under such circumstances, the increase or decrease in cost arises because of the particular season and it is not attributable to volume movements. The cost of heat during the winter months is an example of a seasonal cost. The calculation of a predetermined rate based on an estimate of *annual* manufacturing overhead averages out the effect of these seasonal fluctuations. A predetermined rate charges each stage of production throughout the year with an "average" amount of such seasonal overhead costs. In addition to seasonal items there are other items, such as maintenance costs, which may be incurred at specific times during the year; a plant-wide shut down for maintenance would be an example. The use of a predetermined manufacturing overhead rate permits such a cost to be annualized rather than to be charged entirely to the products produced during the month in which the maintenance costs were incurred.

Third, in order to maintain an element of cost control, some predetermined standard or estimate should exist against which actual costs can be compared. This objective cannot be accomplished without a predetermined overhead rate. A predetermined overhead rate permits management to evaluate cost differences arising from either *spending* or *volume* reasons. More will be said about these differences, or variances, in a later section.

JOURNAL ENTRY TREATMENT

When a company uses a predetermined manufacturing overhead rate, it is advisable to establish *separate* ledger accounts to record *actual* manufacturing overhead costs and *applied* manufacturing overhead costs. In addition, it is advisable to establish these separate ledger accounts for *each* production department.

As a company incurs actual manufacturing overhead costs the journal entry to record the transactions is:

```
Actual Manufacturing Overhead  ............................... XX
    Cash, Accounts Payable, etc.  ..............................      XX
```

The credit portion of this entry would vary depending upon the transaction.

After a company has established its predetermined manufacturing overhead rate, it uses this rate to charge (or apply) overhead costs to the product. The journal entry to record *applied* manufacturing overhead costs is:

```
Work-in-Process  .................................... XX
Applied Manufacturing Overhead  ...........................      XX
```

The amount of overhead to be charged to the production account "Work in Process" is determined by multiplying the predetermined overhead rate times the number of actual "base units" utilized during a given period. For example, if the "base unit" is measured in direct labor hours and the predetermined rate per direct labor hour is $2.00, the following entry would result when 2,100 direct labor hours are incurred:

```
Work-in-Process  .......................................... 4,200
    Applied Manufacturing Overhead  ......................      4,200
```

At the end of a given accounting period (usually at the end of the fiscal year, although the procedure can be done monthly), the actual and applied overhead accounts are closed. The difference between the dollar balances in these two accounts is called over- or underapplied overhead. The disposition of this over- or underapplied overhead may be treated in several ways. To illustrate, assume the following end-of-period account balances:

Actual Manufacturing Overhead	Applied Manufacturing Overhead
105,000	100,000

If we are dealing with interim statements, the underapplied overhead of $5,000 ($105,000—$100,000) is generally carried forward on the balance sheet. Underapplied overhead will appear as a deferred charge; overapplied overhead will be classified as a deferred credit. A company may wish to analyze any interim differences that arise from under- or overapplied overhead; however, this analysis can be accomplished without closing out the actual and applied overhead accounts.

If we are dealing with year-end financial statements, we must dispose of the over- or underapplied overhead. Two assumptions can be made relative to the difference which exists between the actual and applied overhead: (1) that the predetermined rate was in error, or (2) that the rate was correct. If it is assumed that the rate was in error, then the accounts which have been affected by the rate must be corrected. This approach would require that an adjustment (correction) be made to the three accounts affected: work in process, finished goods, and cost of goods sold. The adjustment can be made to these accounts based on the relative amount of applied overhead costs in each account. For example, assume that upon analysis it is determined that the amount of applied overhead costs in each account is:

Work-in-process	$ 5,000	5%
Finished goods	10,000	10
Cost of goods sold	85,000	85
Total applied overhead	$100,000	100%

The journal entry to "correct" the amount of overhead costs in each of the three accounts affected would be:

Applied Manufacturing Overhead	100,000	
Work-in-Process (5% × $5,000)	250	
Finished Goods (10% × $5,000)	500	
Cost of Goods Sold (85% × $5,000)	4,250	
Actual Manufacturing Overhead		105,000

This treatment assumes that the predetermined rate was, in some sense, incorrect.

Another treatment for the disposition of the over- or underapplied overhead is to close the difference directly to the cost of goods sold account. This treatment can be justified at the expediency level when the majority of the production for the year has been sold. In such a case, it may be argued that the time and cost of making adjustments to all accounts involved is not worth the benefit of the results.

Closing the difference directly to an income statement account, such as cost of goods sold, can also be supported at the theoretical level. Such support is predicated on the following assumptions:

1. The rate is "correct."
2. The differences are due to inefficiencies or efficiencies of operations, and hence should be recorded in the current period rather than deferring some of the differences to the future in inventories (that is, work in process and finished goods).

Referring to the illustration above, the journal entry to dispose of the $5,000 underapplied overhead directly to the income statement would be:

```
Applied Manufacturing Overhead ....................... 100,000
Cost of Goods Sold...................................   5,000
    Actual Manufacturing Overhead ....................          105,000
```

An analysis of the $5,000 underapplied overhead would reveal to management how much of this difference (variance) is attributable to prices (*spending variance*) and how much is due to volume or activity (*volume variance*). A measure of these dimensions is important to management in evaluating the current period's performance. How these two variances are calculated and how they can aid management are discussed later in this chapter.

VARIABILITY OF MANUFACTURING OVERHEAD COSTS

The variability of manufacturing overhead costs becomes important for both primary level objectives. The concept of cost variability deserves a great deal of emphasis because an understanding of how various items of manufacturing overhead costs behave, and the rate and level of behavior, is important to aid management in the planning and control of operations. In addition, cost behavior (variability) is also important in calculating the predetermined overhead rate used for product costing (external reporting) purposes.

Three classifications of cost behavior are: (1) fixed costs, (2) variable costs, and (3) mixed costs. *Fixed costs* are defined as those costs that do not vary in total with volume or activity. *Variable costs*, in total, fluctuate proportionately with some factor of production or activity. *Mixed costs* are those costs that are partially variable and partially fixed; they contain a mixture of fixed and variable costs. These costs are sometimes referred to as "semivariable" or "semifixed" costs. Technically, these terms are misnomers. These costs contain a *mixture* of both fixed and variable costs and are thereby more appropriately termed "mixed costs." For purposes of calculating and using a manufacturing overhead rate, these mixed costs should be separated into their fixed and variable components. Note that the definitions of "fixed," "variable," and "mixed" costs represent behavior over a reasonably expected range of production. This range is referred to as the "relevant range." The behavior patterns of both the fixed and variable elements of costs may be different if production is expected to fall outside of this relevant range of activity.

INVERSE RELATIONSHIP OF UNIT AND TOTAL COST BEHAVIOR

A basic and important relationship of cost behavior exists between unit and total cost behavior. An understanding of this relationship is fundamental to an understanding of the overhead costs charged to products, as well as an analysis of variances which are generated periodically by the accounting system.

When estimating the variability of *total* manufacturing overhead costs, we find that the relationship for fixed and variable costs follows the patterns illustrated in Exhibit 3.

EXHIBIT 3
Total fixed and variable overhead costs

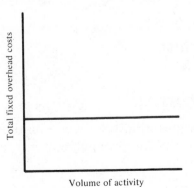

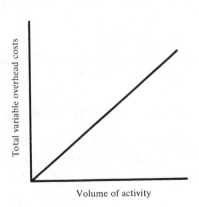

EXHIBIT 4
Unit fixed and variable overhead costs

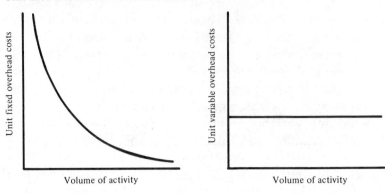

When viewing the *unit* or *average* fixed and variable costs, we find the variability of these costs to have an inverse relationship as compared to the total cost functions. In other words, unit variable costs remain constant per unit over different volume/activity levels, while unit fixed costs vary over different volume/activity levels (see Exhibit 4).

FOUR CATEGORIES OF MANUFACTURING COSTS

When calculating the predetermined manufacturing overhead rate, a separate calculation should be made for the fixed and variable components of overhead costs. Such a separation highlights the impact which each of these costs has on product costing. Accordingly, when one thinks of manufacturing costs, four categories should come to mind:

1. Direct materials.
2. Direct labor.
3. Variable manufacturing overhead.
4. Fixed manufacturing overhead.

PROCESS VERSUS JOB ORDER COSTING

The previous discussion did not distinguish between methods of accumulating manufacturing costs for product costing purposes.

Basically, there are two systems of manufacturing cost accumulation: (1) the job order cost system and (2) the process cost system. Under each of these systems, manufacturing overhead costs are accumulated by *cost centers* (operating departments) and then distributed to the products via an overhead rate. Therefore, whether an enterprise has a job order or process cost system is immaterial as far as the accumulation of manufacturing overhead costs is concerned. In both systems some identification of cost or responsibility centers must be established. These centers become the locus for the accumulation and distribution of overhead costs to the products. Consequently, one of the first tasks which an enterprise must accomplish to handle manufacturing overhead costs is to establish cost centers. These cost centers become the vehicle for transferring manufacturing overhead costs to the products. Throughout most of the discussion in this chapter, these cost centers are referred to as *production departments*. However, it should be recognized that several cost centers may be established in one production department for cost control purposes as well as product costing purposes.

DEPARTMENTAL OVERHEAD RATES

Generally, in manufacturing companies, overhead rates are established on a departmental basis. An alternative to departmental rates is the establishment of a plant-wide rate or a rate that would include a number of separate departments. Such aggregate or plant-wide rates are not recommended since they tend to lead to an inequitable distribution of overhead costs to products. Whenever more than one operating department exists, it is not logical to assume that each department contributes the same amount of effort and in the same proportion as every other department when producing output. Each department will have its own cost characteristics. For example, one department may be completely mechanized, whereas another department may be primarily manual. Not all operating departments are comparable, and therefore their costs should not be pooled together in some grand average, or plant-wide, rate. Departmentalization is necessary to meet the objective of assigning manufacturing overhead costs to products according to the efforts expended on each product.

Not only are departmental overhead rates preferable to plant-wide rates for product costing purposes; they are also useful for cost control purposes. Each department may be viewed as a responsibility center which should be required individually to account for its costs. As noted above, there may be situations where management identifies several cost responsibility centers within one department. In such cases costs may be accumulated and reported by these cost centers for cost control purposes, while the departmental level may be used to establish a manufacturing overhead rate that will be used for product costing purposes.

SERVICE DEPARTMENT COST ALLOCATIONS

Categorization of operations for manufacturing enterprises can be simply illustrated.

As shown in Exhibit 5, manufacturing operations are composed basically of two types of activities—those related to the actual processing or *producing* of the finished units, and those activities which service the *producing* functions of the enterprise. Although the service department operations are not directly involved in the processing of finished units, they provide assistance to the producing departments in the performance of their functions. Therefore, the costs of such service operations are manufacturing costs and should eventually find their way into product costs. Examples of service departments are: (1) maintenance and repair, (2) power, (3) engineering, (4) waste treatment, and (5) general factory administration.

EXHIBIT 5

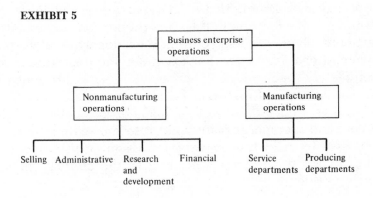

Costs applicable to service departments should be allocated among the processing departments on a basis which management believes is feasible and equitable. Consequently, the total dollar amount of manufacturing overhead assigned to a processing department includes not only the items of overhead directly incurred in the processing department (such as depreciation, indirect labor, and payroll taxes), but also the share of service department costs that have been apportioned to it.

When apportioning service department costs to producing departments a question arises as to the reciprocal service relationships that exist between service departments. This reciprocal service relationship signifies that in addition to servicing producing departments, service departments also service other service departments. For example, the maintenance department will service the power plant, and the power plant will service the maintenance department. Additionally, they both serve producing departments. When such reciprocal relationships exist, a fundamental question of apportionment arises—should the cost apportionment recognize this reciprocal service relationship? At the theoretical level, the answer seems to be yes. However, at the practical level, a reciprocal cost allocation scheme may not always be advisable for the improved accuracy of costing may not justify the cost of the system. The decision should consider at least two criteria: (1) What is the objective intended? and (2) Is the additional cost of using a reciprocal cost apportionment system worth the benefits derived? If the objective intended by management is to deal with decisions on pricing, for example, then reciprocal allocations of service department costs may be useful. In all instances, if decisions are not sensitive to the use of reciprocal reallocations compared to simpler methods, then the additional costs of reciprocal reallocations may not be justified.

Methodologically, the use of *simultaneous equations* or linear algebra may be used to effect reallocation of costs on a reciprocal basis. A detailed discussion and illustration of this methodology may be found in an article by Williams and Griffin entitled "Matrix Theory and Cost Allocation" (*The Accounting Review*, July 1964, pp. 671–78.)

In addition to the reciprocal method of reapportionment, there are two other methods in common use: (1) the direct

EXHIBIT 6
Step method of reapportionment

			Service departments		Producing departments		
Cost item	Basis of distribution	Total	Building and grounds	Factory administration	Cutting	Assembly	Finishing
Supervision	Actual salaries per department	$123,000	$ 22,000	$ 37,000	$ 24,000	$ 19,000	$ 21,000
Indirect labor	Actual per department	226,000	48,000	56,000	37,000	38,000	47,000
Supplies	Actual requisitions per department	22,800	1,500	8,200	4,500	4,900	3,700
Employee benefits	Payroll per department	35,400	7,200	9,100	6,300	5,900	6,900
Payroll taxes	Payroll per department	28,700	6,400	7,200	4,800	4,700	5,600
Insurance, machinery	Value of machinery	2,200	500	600	400	300	400
Insurance, buildings	Value of buildings	5,700	1,200	1,300	1,100	900	1,200
Property taxes, machinery	Value of machinery	1,300	200	200	300	300	300
Property taxes, buildings	Value of buildings	2,300	300	300	500	600	600
Depreciation, machinery	Actual machinery per department	32,000	9,500	7,000	5,000	6,000	4,500
Depreciation, buildings	Square feet per department	18,400	3,000	4,000	3,500	4,200	3,700
Heat	Floor space	3,800	800	700	900	800	600
Light	KWH per department	1,400	200	300	200	300	400
			$100,800				
		$503,000	(100,800)				
Square footage occupied				15,120	25,200	30,240	30,240
				$147,020			
				(147,020)			
Direct labor hours					36,755	51,457	58,808
A. Total manufacturing overhead costs per department					$150,455	$167,597	$184,948
					÷	÷	÷
B. Activity level for predetermined rate (DLH)					25,000 DLH	20,000 DLH	15,000 DLH
Manufacturing overhead rate per department (A ÷ B)					$6.02	$8.38	$12.33

method and (2) the step method. The *direct method* treats service departments as if they service only producing departments, and not other service departments. Therefore, service department costs are allocated *directly* and only to producing departments on some rational, consistent, and equitable basis.

The *step method* recognizes service rendered to other service departments, but does not get involved in a reciprocal reallocation of costs between service departments. In essence, the step method ranks the service departments by the amount of service each generates, starting with the highest and proceeding to the lowest. This ranking may be somewhat difficult to achieve when looking at the service itself; however, the ranking problem can be simplified by using dollar value as the measure of rank. Therefore, the service department with the highest dollar cost incurrence is assumed to render the greatest amount of service, and thus it is apportioned first. This apportionment is made to all remaining service departments which utilize the service, as well as to the producing departments. This system of sequential reapportionment is continued until all service department costs have been allocated to the producing departments. An illustration of the step method of apportionment appears in Exhibit 6.

The step method illustrated in Exhibit 6 recognizes the interrelationship of service departments; however, it does not encompass the full extent of reciprocal relationships among the service departments. Generally, the step method suffices in most practical situations.

In large and complex companies, mixtures of the above methods may be used. Sometimes service department costs may be allocated directly to products through the work-in-process account rather than by allocation through producing departments. Such might be the case of a testing or quality control department or a waste treatment department where costs, while not directly incurred on the product itself, can nevertheless be attributed directly to specific products.

DETERMINATION OF MANUFACTURING OVERHEAD RATES

In order to calculate the manufacturing overhead rates to be used in each department (cost center), three decision questions must be answered:

1. What *base* is to be used to calculate the manufacturing overhead rate in each department?
2. What measurement techniques are available to determine the *cost behavior patterns* of the manufacturing overhead costs in each department?
3. What *activity level* (denominator) is to be used in each department?

Each of these questions addresses a separate and distinct characteristic of the manufacturing overhead rate. In an earlier section, the *concept* of the variability of cost behavior was discussed. The decision questions above address the issue of the *determination* of the cost behavior, i.e., what techniques are available which may be used to determine the *level and rate* of cost incurrence in each department.

In an earlier section, it was recommended that the manufacturing overhead rate to be used in applying overhead costs to production should be broken down into a separate fixed and variable overhead rate. The following discussion is predicated on this separation.

What base should be used?

A predetermined manufacturing overhead rate may be stated in terms of a number of different activity bases. The activity base which is selected should be the one which corresponds most closely to the incurrence of the manufacturing overhead costs. Some of the more common activity bases that are used to apply manufacturing overhead costs to production are:

1. Direct labor hours
2. Direct labor cost
3. Direct materials cost
4. Prime costs (Direct materials + Direct labor)
5. Machine hours
6. Units of output
7. Number of job orders or batches processed.

In an attempt to select a base to be used, observation, common sense, and the use of statistical methods of measurement will be helpful. Management should consider each processing center to determine if there is some rather obvious relationship which is apparent. For example, if a processing center is composed primarily of machines with very little, if any, manual operations, then the use of machine hours might seem more appropriate as a base of allocation. If a company is producing only one product, then the use of a "units of output" may be an appropriate base. Generally, a company is producing more than one product and hence some common denominator measure is needed. In such situations, the use of a *resource input* measure is preferable to an output measure; for example, direct labor hours or machine hours would be preferable to units of product produced.

The objective of selecting an activity base is to select one which management can assume is causally related to changes in manufacturing overhead costs. Generally, manufacturing overhead costs are more causally dependent upon inputs than outputs. For example, indirect labor costs are usually related to the amount of direct labor hours worked and power costs are usually related to the amount of machine hours used. Granted that these costs are a function of output—as more output is produced more of these costs are incurred—these costs are more directly or causally related to the input index rather than the output index.

It is essential that management attempt to relate the incurrence of manufacturing overhead costs with causality. This will require the exercise of managerial judgment by those managers who are familiar with the productive process being studied. An obvious example of causality would be to relate labor-related overhead expenses (social security taxes, fringe benefits, factory supervision) to products on the basis of direct labor hours or direct labor dollars. Similarly, warehousing costs might use direct materials costs as a base. If both of these costs are major cost elements in a department, prime costs might be an appropriate base for the entire department. If the department also has a high equipment cost content (such as a stamping department, or a foundry which has people using heavy equipment), a unit of output (tons of iron, square feet of plywood) may be appropriate.

In some instances it may be desirable to segregate a department into more than one cost center in order to achieve a more realistic allocation of costs. Such a segregation could separate those costs which follow materials from those which follow labor or machinery. It is important to determine causality, for if causality cannot be determined, management may have to revert to some arbitrary selection of a base with the resultant loss in the usefulness of costs for appraising performance, pricing, and other purposes.

What are some measurement techniques?

In the process of selecting a reasonable base to apply manufacturing overhead costs, there are several techniques which may be used to identify and measure the variability patterns of overhead costs. These methods may be broadly classified into five categories:

1. Inspection of accounts.
2. Interpolation method.
3. Scattergraph method.
4. Regression analysis.
5. Engineering studies.

Two NAA publications that deal with this subject matter are *Research Series No. 16,* entitled "The Variation of Costs with Volume," and *Accounting Practice Report No. 10,* entitled "Separating and Using Costs As Fixed and Variable."

Inspection of accounts. In determining the variability of costs, the inspection of accounts method is the simplest and least time consuming. It involves a review of the chart of accounts and selection of accounts believed to be fixed, variable, or mixed.

Inspection of the chart of accounts will generally reveal some accounts that contain costs commonly known to be fixed. Real estate property taxes and most rental payments are examples of fixed commitments that are not readily changed.

Likewise, certain items of cost generally are regarded as variable. For example, when power costs are based on a flat rate, the variability of such an item becomes apparent. However, the number of cost items that reveal themselves as wholly variable by mere inspection of accounts is rather limited. Very few costs can be assumed to be in this category. More definite investigations of cost behavior should be pursued to determine if there is truly a variable element inherent in the cost item.

In many cases, discussion with individuals directly responsible for cost incurrence will reveal items of cost that are readily identifiable as fixed or variable. These individuals are most familiar with the cost under their control and thus can provide much useful evidence as to the variability of costs growing out of their methods of managing the cost.

Interpolation method. Basically, the *interpolation method* (sometimes called the "high and low points method") consists of estimating costs at two levels of operations and then interpolating between these two volume levels in order to determine the degree of variability applicable to the cost item being investigated. The variability of cost is obtained by dividing the change in volume into the change in cost for the two levels selected.

If there is no significant difference in cost between volume levels, the cost item is assumed to represent a fixed pattern. If there is a proportionate increase in both volume and cost at different levels, the cost item is assumed to represent a wholly variable pattern. In those cases where the cost item takes on the nature of a mixed cost, the interpolation method also permits the measurement of its fixed and variable portions. For mixed costs, determination of the portion that is fixed and that which is variable requires multiplication of the variable rate times the number of hours (or other unit of volume measurement) for a particular volume, and subtraction of this product from the total cost at that same volume level. The residual represents the fixed cost element.

To illustrate, suppose that a company shows the following cost and activity data for six recent periods of time:

Period	Power cost	Activity level measured in machine hours
1	$950	1,250
2	920	1,000
3	890	750
4	900	875
5	935	1,100
6	925	1,050

From these data, we can select two activity levels (usually the high and low activity levels) and interpolate the cost difference between these two points as follows:

Period	Activity level	Power cost
1	1,250	$950
3	750	890
Difference.....................	500	$ 60

1. Divide the difference in activity level into the difference in cost to determine the variable rate: $60 ÷ 500 hours = $0.12 per hour.
2. Multiply the variable rate times the number of hours at any of the activity levels and subtract this product from the total cost at that level in order to calculate the fixed portion of the cost; for example:
   a. $0.12 × 1,250 hours = $150
   b. $950 − $150 = $800
3. The power cost in this illustration is composed of a fixed portion of $800 plus a variable rate of 12¢ per machine hours worked.

Although this method is simple and easy to apply, caution must be exercised that the volume levels used are not distorted by any abnormal costs incurred during the periods selected. To overcome such distortion, the high and low points may be based on averages of several points revolving around these levels. Another note of caution should be exercised when interpolating between two points, namely, that the patterns which exist between these points will be ignored. It is quite possible that a pattern may exist which would be hidden if the interpolation method is used. For this reason, it may be advisable to prepare a graphic analysis of the cost-volume data to ascertain the general trend indicative of the cost data. For example, the true cost pattern may be one representing a discontinuous or step fixed cost, and analysis of the cost pattern by means of the interpolation method will assume a continuous pattern. Graphic analysis, representing the cost-volume data over a number of observations, would disclose the discontinuous nature of the cost. Referring to Exhibit 7, if we assume that the solid lines (AB and CD) represent the actual cost behavior, the use of the interpolation method would result in a function (behavior) which is represented by the broken line (EF).

EXHIBIT 7
Discontinuous (step) fixed cost function

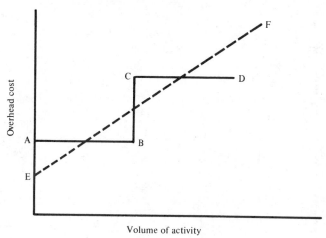

Volume of activity

Scattergraph method.   The *scattergraph method* accumulates historical cost-volume data over a period of time. After sufficient observations have been plotted, the cost-volume relationship can be determined by examining the dispersion of the plotted points on the scattergraph. If there is any definite relationship between volume and cost, the majority of the plotted points will cluster around a line. A line of correlation is then visually fitted through the points indicating the average pattern of the past cost-volume relationships.

If the cost function contains both a fixed and variable component, the fixed and variable elements are determined in the following manner:

1. The point at which the correlation line intersects the cost axis represents the fixed component. (See Exhibit 8.)
2. The variable component may be interpolated between two levels on the correlation line by dividing the difference in volume into the cost difference at the two levels.

The total amount of cost for any particular volume level can be estimated by referring to that level on the scattergraph and extending a perpendicular from that point to the correlation line, and then reading horizontally from there to the cost indicated on the vertical axis. See Exhibit 8 for an illustration of a

EXHIBIT 8
Scattergraph

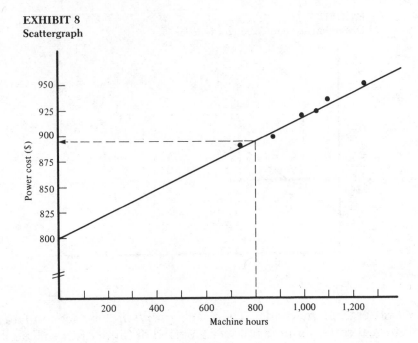

scattergraph using the data on power costs for six periods, as discussed above in the section on the interpolation method.

The preparation of a scattergraph is relatively simple. It provides visual evidence of the presence or absence of an obvious relationship, the character of that relationship (continuous, discontinuous, curvilinear), and the closeness of the relationship.

Regression analysis. The method of *least squares*, also referred to as *regression analysis*, is a more refined method of fitting a line to cost-volume data. Regression analysis has the advantage of objectivity and theoretical accuracy and is, therefore, a more accurate approach to the development of a cost line than a line visually fitted as with the scattergraph.

Either a linear or curvilinear equation may be selected for the method of least squares. A first-degree equation will be selected if the cost function is determined to be linear. In this connection, preliminary plotting of a scattergraph would help to determine the form of equation which is suitable for the data. The linear equation measures the relationship between two variables, an *independent variable* (X) and a *dependent variable* (Y). The independent variable (X) is activity or volume and the dependent variable (Y) is cost. Basically, this equation states that total cost (Y) depends upon the level of activity (X) achieved. The equation for total cost is expressed as follows:

$$Y = a + b X$$

Y represents the dependent variable, in this case total cost; a represents a constant value, in this case the fixed component (if any) of the cost; b represents the slope of the correlation line, in this case the variable rate of the cost item; and X represents the independent variable, in this case volume. Thus, the term bX represents total variable cost at the volume X.

To determine the values of a and b, the following equations are used:

$$\Sigma Y = na + b(\Sigma X)$$
$$\Sigma XY = a(\Sigma X) + b(\Sigma X^2)$$

where n = number of paired observations
  X = independent variable (volume)
  Y = dependent variable (cost)
  ΣX = sum of the given Xs
  ΣY = sum of the given Ys
  ΣX^2 = sum of the squares of the given Xs
  ΣXY = sum of the products of the given Xs and Ys

To illustrate the least squares method, let us assume that the following data have been accumulated for a particular manufacturing overhead cost item in a producing department where the activity level is measured in *units of output*. Again, the objective is to determine the variability of the cost, or, the values of a and b. (This illustration is adapted from *NAA Accounting Practice Report Number 10*, "Separating and Using Costs as Fixed and Variable," June 1960.)

Month	Units of output (X)	Total cost (Y)	XY	X^2
January	22	$ 23	506	484
February	23	25	575	529
March	19	20	380	361
April	12	20	240	144
May	12	20	240	144
June	9	15	135	81
July	7	14	98	49
August	11	14	154	121
September	14	16	224	196
Total (Σ)	129	167	2,552	2,109

$$\Sigma\,Y = na + b\,(\Sigma\,X) \text{ or}$$
$$167 = 9\,a + 129\,b \tag{1}$$

$$\Sigma\,XY = a(\Sigma\,X) + b\,(\Sigma\,X^2) \text{ or} \tag{2}$$
$$2{,}552 = 129\,a + 2{,}109\,b$$

Solution:

Eliminate a as follows:
Multiply Equation (2) by 3
   $387\,a + 6{,}327\,b = 7{,}656$
Multiply Equation (1) by 43
   $387\,a + 5{,}547\,b = 7{,}181$
Subtract (1) from (2)
(2) $387\,a + 6{,}327\,b = 7{,}656$
(1) $387\,a + 5{,}547\,b = 7{,}181$
        $780\,b = 475$
         $b = 0.609$
Substituting 0.609 for b in (1)
(1) $9\,a + 129(0.609) = 167$
    $9\,a + 78.561 = 167$
    $9\,a = 167 - 78.561$ or 88.439
     $a = 9.82$
Therefore:
   Fixed expense = \$9.82
   Variable expense = \$0.609 per unit

Regression analysis, or the method of least squares, has an advantage over the scattergraph method by not relying on visual perception for the development of the correlation line. This method results in one definite correlation line through a given set of plotted points which provides the best available estimate of the true relationship.

Engineering studies. The *industrial engineering approach* to cost determination is an attempt to calculate what costs "should be" by analysis of the physical input factors necessary for performance at various operating levels. The methods discussed above rely on historical data to determine the variability of costs, whereas the engineering approach examines input-output relationships in an attempt to achieve the most efficient means of production.

In the absence of the availability of past cost-volume data, the engineering method provides a possible approach for the projection of cost behavior. Even in situations where past data are available, the engineering method can be used to check upon the reasonableness of historical data. Cost estimates that are based solely on past data would perpetuate any inefficiencies in cost that previously existed. Engineering studies can be used to detect any such inefficiencies. Conversely, historical cost data can be used as a check on the reasonableness of the engineering estimates. Also, engineering studies can be used for forecasting cost behavior when there will be changes in the state of technology. Of the several methods discussed for quantifying cost data, engineering studies are conceivably the most expensive.

No matter which method is chosen, it should be remembered that the variable and fixed cost relationships apply only over an expected range of production. This range might be, for example, from 60 percent to 80 percent of capacity. If variability of costs outside the expected range needs to be considered, cost behavior should be restudied to incorporate the new range.

What activity level (denominator) should be used?

If manufacturing overhead costs were all variable, then the *capacity (denominator) level* selected for determining the applied rate would have no effect on the manufacturing overhead rate. This is the case because if a cost, in total, fluctuates proportionately with increases or decreases in the activity level, then on a unit basis such a cost does not change. This point was discussed in the earlier section on the inverse relationship between total and unit costs. It will be recalled that in that section we saw that on a unit basis variable costs are constant. Therefore, for all practical purposes, the level of capacity chosen would not affect the predetermined manufacturing overhead rate if all manufacturing overhead costs were variable.

Unfortunately, not all manufacturing overhead costs are variable in nature. Some overhead costs are fixed. It is because of the fixed element that the capacity level selected for rate determination purposes is so important. When we deal with the fixed element of manufacturing overhead costs, the predetermined overhead rate is a function of the denominator (capacity level) selected. To illustrate, assume that a production center estimated that its total fixed manufacturing overhead costs for the upcoming year will be $100,000. It now must determine what capacity level it will use to absorb these fixed overhead costs into production. If it selects 10,000 productive hours, the predetermined overhead rate will be $10 per productive hour. If it selects 8,000 productive hours, the predetermined overhead rate will be $12.50 per productive hour. If it selects some other capacity level it will get still another rate, and so on.

Because different capacity levels will lead to different fixed manufacturing overhead rates, it becomes important that management understand the implications of selecting one capacity level over another. Unfortunately, there is no one best capacity level—what is "best" depends on the objective management has in mind. *NAA Research Report No. 39* entitled "Accounting For Costs of Capacity" addresses this point well.

The range of absorbing fixed manufacturing overhead costs into production may be from zero to 100 percent of actual fixed overhead costs. The zero end of this scale is the result of the use of "direct costing." This method of product costing will be discussed briefly in a later section. The absorption of 100 percent of actual costs is the result of using an "expected actual capacity" level for predetermining the overhead rate and then calculating a "supplemental rate" at the end of each month. The "supplemental rate" is determined by taking the under- or overapplied manufacturing overhead and dividing it by the *actual* activity level recorded during the month.[2] This supplemental rate is then added to, or subtracted from, the predetermined rate and the output is costed at this combined rate.

To illustrate, assume that a company has a predetermined fixed overhead rate of $1.75 per direct labor hour (DLH); at the end of a month the *actual* DLH = 2,170 and the *actual* fixed manufacturing overhead costs = $4,123. The amount of fixed manufacturing overhead costs applied to production would be $3,797.50 (2,170DLH × $1.75); the difference between the *applied* and *actual* fixed manufacturing overhead costs is $325.50 ($4,123 − $3,797.50); the supplemental rate would be $0.15 ($325.50 ÷ 2,170 DLH). Therefore, an adjustment would be made to the manufacturing overhead charged to production

---

[2] The under- or overapplied manufacturing overhead is the difference between the actual manufacturing overhead costs incurred and the manufacturing overhead costs applied (charged) to production. If the amount applied is greater than the actual costs, then we have *overapplied* overhead. If the amount applied is less than the actual costs, then we have *underapplied* overhead.

of this month for $0.15 per DLH. This procedure, in fact, makes the cost accounting system an *actual cost* system.

A "supplemental rate" can be used for variable as well as fixed manufacturing overhead costs, although the discussion above illustrated fixed overhead costs only.

The *capacity (activity) levels* which have been generally used and accepted in practice include:

1. Expected actual capacity.
2. Normal or average capacity.
3. Practical capacity.

The first two capacity measures are based on a company's *capacity to sell.* The third measure is based on a company's *capacity to manufacture.* Assuming that for a given company, for a given period, there is a difference between these three capacity levels, then the fixed portion of the manufacturing overhead rate will be different depending on which capacity level is selected as the denominator. This difference will lead to a different product cost and a different measure of idle capacity.

Practical capacity represents the full utilization of resources in a production department under attainable operating conditions. It is not theoretical or ideal capacity. Practical capacity takes into consideration allowances for predictable and unavoidable operating interruptions such as maintenance, repairs, setups, and other delays. Also, the number of shifts and the length of the working week to be included in this measure are determined by management policy. (*NAA Research Report No. 39* has an extended discussion of capacity costs.) Once this level of practical capacity is calculated, the measure of *idle capacity* is the difference between the capacity *actually* achieved during a given period and the practical capacity level. The use of the practical capacity method permits management to separate the costs of capacity between (1) used capacity and (2) unused, or idle, capacity. Such a separation brings to the attention of management the cost of capacity which is *not* currently being employed.

Normal capacity represents an estimate of productive use based on a forecast of sales over several future years. This measure of capacity would be an *average* of the sales forecasts over several years; it is sometimes referred to as "average capacity" instead of "normal capacity." This average measure is based on the assumption that a company is in a cyclical industry. Furthermore, it is assumed that the cycles are recurrent and reasonably predictable. Under these circumstances, a company's product cost would fluctuate with the cycle if an expected *annual* capacity measure is used. To overcome this cyclical movement in product cost, a company may wish to use some averaging technique over the forecasted cycle period. In essence, this approach would tend to smooth out unit product costs over the cycle.

Expected actual capacity represents the scheduled production which is derived from the forecast of sales for each year. This measure of capacity is made for each coming year. Advocates of this measure of capacity are of the opinion that the cost of any idle capacity should be included in the current cost of production. They recognize that an enterprise may intentionally overbuild capacity on the assumption that the cost of excess capacity is less than the risk (cost) of not having enough capacity to meet demand. Therefore, they argue that the product should bear this cost of idle capacity. By using an annual expected actual capacity level derived from the demand for products, the company will effectively be absorbing into inventory the cost of its used and unused (idle) capacity.

FIXED MANUFACTURING OVERHEAD VARIANCES

At the end of an accounting period, a reconciliation must be made between the *applied* fixed overhead costs and the *actual* costs. This difference is called the over- or underapplied overhead. In the analysis of this difference, two causes may be isolated: (1) differences due to volume or activity, and (2) differences due to spending. These differences are generally referred to as a *volume variance* and a *spending variance*.

Volume variance

The relationship of fixed manufacturing overhead costs and the activity (denominator) level selected may be illustrated through the use of a two-dimensional graph. Referring to Exhibit

EXHIBIT 9
Fixed manufacturing overhead variances

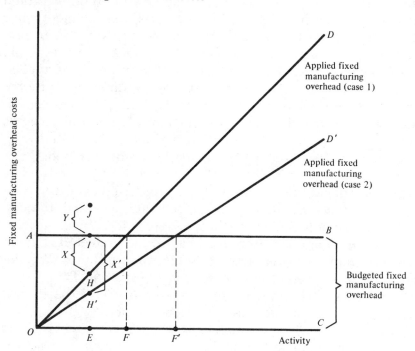

9, the horizontal axis measures activity level and the vertical axis measures fixed manufacturing overhead costs. The formula for the determination of the applied fixed manufacturing overhead rate is:

$$R = \frac{BFOH}{A}$$

where

R = predetermined fixed manufacturing overhead rate.
$BFOH$ = budgeted fixed overhead costs.
A = activity level selected.

For a particular year, the budgeted fixed manufacturing overhead costs for a given plan of operations will be estimated. This budgeted cost represents the amount of fixed cost incurrence planned by management for the upcoming year. This amount does not change for rate determination purposes. Therefore, the budgeted fixed overhead costs may be plotted on the graph as line *AB*. For product costing purposes, management must decide how it wishes to apply this budgeted fixed cost to production by selecting a volume or activity level. On the graph, if volume level *F* is selected then line *OD* represents the applied fixed overhead line. The slope of this line is determined by the activity level selected. This activity level, as discussed earlier, may be (1) expected actual, (2) normal, or (3) practical capacity. However, only one of these levels may be selected and once it is selected the slope of the applied line is determined.

Once the level is selected, the applied fixed overhead rate is calculated and this rate is used to charge fixed overhead costs to the products. At the end of the accounting period, the cost of idle capacity (volume variance) is determined by comparing the amount of applied fixed overhead to the budgeted amount. On the graph, if actual activity is *OE*, then distance *X* (point *H* minus *I*) represents the *cost of idle capacity*. This cost of idle capacity is the amount of budgeted fixed overhead costs which are not absorbed (charged) to inventory.

Conceptually, the absorption of fixed manufacturing overhead costs may be depicted as in Exhibit 9. However, it must be remembered that the slope of line *OD* is determined by the activity (denominator) level selected in arriving at the applied rate. If management selects a different level of activity, the slope of the applied overhead line will be different; however, the budgeted fixed overhead costs may remain the same (*OA*). The selection of a different activity level will result in a different measure of idle capacity. Referring to Exhibit 9, if the activity level selected is *F'* then the applied fixed overhead line is *OD'*. Since the budgeted fixed overhead costs remain the same (*OA*), and the actual activity level achieved for a given period would be the same (*OE*), then the *cost of idle capacity* would be the distance *X'* (point *H'* minus *I*).

Invariably, the question is asked: Which measure of idle capacity is correct? Procedurally, they are all correct. There is no one activity level which is considered "correct" in some generally accepted accounting sense. A more appropriate question to be asked is: Which capacity (activity) level should management select in establishing its predetermined fixed overhead rate? Unfortunately, the answer to this question depends on management's objectives. Management must think through the consequences of each activity level and select the one which satisfies their objectives. For financial reporting purposes, the accounting profession does require that consistency be applied when there are several acceptable alternatives available.

At this point a digression may be in order. The use of the term *idle capacity* (or idle capacity variance) is a misnomer unless the *practical capacity* concept is used to measure the denominator in the overhead rate equation: $R = (BFOH/A)$. Only when practical capacity is used can it be said that the unabsorbed fixed manufacturing overhead is, in some sense, a cost of idle capacity. This seems to be the only rational context within which the term "idle capacity" makes any sense. For a given producing department, in a given period of time, with a given mix of resources, there is a *measurable* practical capacity of operations. The costs of providing and maintaining this total capacity are called "capacity costs," and these are generally fixed in nature. The optimum use of these capacity costs will occur when the total amount of productive capacity is utilized. If some of this capacity is not used in a given period, then the proportion of capacity costs assigned to this unused capacity may be called "idle capacity cost."

If some measure of capacity other than practical capacity is used to determine the fixed manufacturing overhead rate, then any unused or overused capacity should be called under- or overabsorbed (applied) fixed manufacturing overhead costs. The use of the term "idle capacity cost" in such a context, it seems, is inappropriate.

Spending variance

In addition to the volume variance, there may be a *spending variance* associated with the fixed manufacturing overhead costs. This spending variance is the difference between the budgeted and the actual fixed overhead costs. This difference comes about because of the increases or decreases in cost of the resource factors. This spending variance is not a function of volume, but rather a function of price. It measures whether a production department *spent* more or less than the budget anticipated. In

Exhibit 9, if actual spending for activity *OE* were at level *J,* then the spending variance would be the distance *Y* (point *J* minus *I*). This would be true regardless of the volume level selected in determining the applied fixed manufacturing overhead rate. In other words, the spending variance is the same for both Cases 1 and 2 depicted in Exhibit 9.

VARIABLE MANUFACTURING OVERHEAD VARIANCES

As with the fixed manufacturing overhead costs, a reconciliation must be made of the variable overhead costs at the end of the accounting period. Differences which result in the *variable* overhead area are the result of *spending (price) only.* There is no volume variance associated with variable manufacturing overhead costs. It is not necessary to reach some predetermined level of activity in order to fully absorb variable overhead costs. By definition, if there is no activity, there would be no variable overhead costs incurred. As the production department commences operations, the amount of variable overhead—both budgeted and applied—increases by the same amount with the increase in activity. Because the amounts of variable overhead budgeted and applied will be equal at all levels of activity, there is no possibility of having a volume variance. The only variance that might exist is if the prices paid for the variable overhead resource factors are different from those planned (budgeted).[3] The spending variance is the difference between the actual variable manufacturing overhead costs incurred and the budgeted variable manufacturing overhead costs for the actual level of activity achieved.

An illustration of variances

To illustrate the discussion above, assume the following annual data for a production department:

---

[3] There is another variance which might exist if a standard cost system is in use; this variance is called an "efficiency variance." See Chapter 24 of this handbook which discusses "Variances from Standard."

Budgeted data:
Fixed overhead (total) $12,000
Variable overhead rate .... $1 per DLH
Practical capacity 10,000DLH
Average capacity 9,000DLH
Expected actual capacity 8,000DLH
Actual data:
Fixed overhead (total) $12,750
Variable overhead (total) .... $ 8,900
Actual capacity used 8,500DLH

The computation of the *spending variance* would be made by comparing the actual overhead costs (both fixed and variable) to the budgeted overhead costs at the *actual* level of capacity used.

	Fixed	*Variable*	*Total*
Actual costs.....................	$12,750	$8,900	$21,650
Budgeted costs at			
8,500 actual DLH	12,000		
(8,500DLH × $1)		8,500 }	20,500
Spending variance...........	$ 750	$ 400	$ 1,150

The computation of the *volume variance* will depend upon the level of capacity used to establish the predetermined fixed overhead rate. The volume variance is the difference between the budgeted fixed overhead costs and the applied fixed overhead costs. The applied fixed overhead rate is different for each capacity level, as follows:

Practical capacity .... $12,000 ÷ 10,000DLH = $1.20
Average capacity............................ $12,000 ÷ 9,000DLH = $1.33
Expected actual capacity .... $12,000 ÷ 8,000DLH = $1.50

Since the fixed overhead applied rate is different when using different capacity levels, it follows that the volume variance will also be different when different capacity levels are used. The volume variance for each capacity level in the data assumed is as follows:

	Budgeted fixed overhead	*Applied fixed overhead**	*Volume variance†*
Practical capacity	$12,000	$10,200	$1,800
Average capacity	12,000	11,305	695
Expected actual capacity	12,000	12,750	(750)

  * 8500 DLH × $1.20 = $10,200
   8500 DLH × 1.33 = 11,305
   8500 DLH × 1.50 = 12,750
  † Subtract applied overhead from budgeted overhead.

EXHIBIT 10
Impact of different capacity levels on variances

	Capacity measures					
	Variable overhead variances			Fixed overhead variances		
	Practical	Average	Expected actual	Practical	Average	Expected actual
Applied overhead rate	$1.00	$1.00	$1.00	$1.20	$1.33	$1.50
Amount charged to inventory	$8,500	$8,500	$8,500	$10,200	$11,305	$12,750
Volume variance	None	None	None	$1,800	$695	($750)*
Spending variance	$400	$400	$400	$750	$750	$750

* This volume variance is a credit balance; it is sometimes called a *favorable variance*. What it represents is the fact that the company overabsorbed its fixed manufacturing overhead into production, i.e., it charged (applied) more fixed overhead to production than was budgeted for the period.

The impact which the data above have on various elements of the cost accounting system is summarized in Exhibit 10. Note that differences appear only in the fixed overhead area and these differences are a direct result of the different capacity levels that are used.

DIRECT COSTING

In an earlier section, a comment was made that under a costing procedure called "direct costing" there would not be any fixed manufacturing overhead costs charged to products. Direct costing is a procedure which expenses all fixed manufacturing costs in the period of incurrence. These fixed manufacturing costs are not charged to production, and thus there are never any fixed costs in inventory. Proponents of this theory of product costing are of the opinion that the fixed costs are a function of time, and hence should be expensed with the passage of time and not deferred in inventories. In other words, a given amount of fixed manufacturing costs will be incurred regardless of the level of activity achieved, and therefore such costs are not a function of the amount of production incurred during the period but rather a function of the passage of time. Presently, direct costing is not a generally accepted accounting principle; therefore, its application is not acceptable for financial reporting purposes. It may be used for internal purposes if managment desires. A more elaborate discussion of direct costing appears in Chapter 25 of this handbook.

THE COST ACCOUNTING STANDARDS
BOARD (CASB)

The Cost Accounting Standards Board (CASB) came into existence by the passage of the Defense Production Act Amendments of 1970 (Public Law 91–379). The CASB is directed by this law to develop accounting standards which will lead to uniformity and consistency in the cost accounting principles used by defense prime contractors and subcontractors. The rules developed by the CASB apply to virtually all companies having negotiated contracts in excess of $100,000 with the Federal Government. A number of Standards have been passed to date. Any company which has negotiated contracts with the Federal Government should become familiar with the CASB requirements. A detailed discussion of the CASB and its pronouncements appears in Chapter 42 of this handbook.

THE INTERNAL REVENUE SERVICE (IRS)

Although the IRS follows the general methods of accounting for manufacturing overhead costs as described in this chapter, there may be some unique features which are advocated by this IRS. Hence, it would be worthwhile to become familiar with the appropriate regulations that apply to manufacturing overhead costs. Especially note Regulation 1.471–11.

REFERENCES

Dopuch, Nicholas; Birnberg, Jacob G.; and Demski, Joel. *Cost Accounting.* 2d ed. New York: Harcourt Brace Jovanovich, 1974.

Horngren, Charles T. *Cost Accounting: A Managerial Emphasis,* 4th ed. Englewood Cliffs, N.J.: Prentice-Hall, 1977.

Matz, Adolf, and Usry, Milton F. *Cost Accounting: Planning and Control.* 6th ed. Cincinnati, Ohio: South-Western Publishing Co., 1976.

National Association of Accountants. *Research Report No. 39,* "Accounting for Costs of Capacity." New York, 1963.

National Association of Accountants. *Research Series No. 16,* "The Variation of Costs with Volume." New York, 1949.

National Association of Accountants. *Accounting Practice Report No. 10,* "Separating and Using Costs as Fixed and Variable." New York, 1960.

U.S. Internal Revenue Service Regulations. Regulations 1.471–11.

Williams, Thomas H., and Griffin, Charles H.; "Matrix Theory and Cost Allocation." *The Accounting Review,* July 1964, pp. 671–78.

17

Accounting for work-in-process and finished goods inventories

Donald L. Thiry

INTRODUCTION

Inventory valuation is the monetary measurement of inventory quantities using specific unit costs. Generally, inventory valuation can be accomplished in one of two ways:

1. Take and value an ending physical inventory. The change in the inventory amount since the last physical inventory plus the sum of additions and deletions to the inventory will equal cost of sales.
2. Begin with a known inventory amount for a period and value material movements between transfer points to arrive at an ending valuation and also cost of sales. The ending valuation forms the known starting point for the next period. Physical inventories are only needed to check the process to make certain it is operating effectively.

Inventory valuation is required to accomplish the following:

Interim financial reporting.
Outside financial reporting.

* Partner, Arthur Andersen & Co.

Short term and annual planning of profitability and cost requirements.

Government contract reporting.

For most manufacturing companies, the credibility of interim financial reports is dependent upon the credibility of interim inventory valuations and cost of sales calculations. Inventory valuation is not normally a service industry consideration, with the exception of the requirement for valuing unbilled professional services in a professional services firm or large supplies inventories in a regulated industry such as a utility or an airline.

Different companies may use a variety of inventory accounts to meet their interim and outside financial reporting requirements. Work-in-process and finished goods inventory categories are discussed in this chapter. They may be segregated into subcategories or called by different names for financial or management reporting purposes.

Finished goods are finished items ready for sale or top level assemblies which are combined in various manners just prior to shipment. In reality, the finished goods inventory account can be considered a special category of the stores inventory account. Work-in-process is material, labor, and usually overhead associated with items which are "in production."

There may be instances, particularly in certain process industries, where only one of the major inventory accounts includes significant inventory value. In these instances what is known as a *"four wall" inventory* approach may be used, meaning the use of one account. Where the stores inventory is relieved only when parent item production is reported (and consequently there is no material cost in the work-in-process inventory) a modified four wall concept using two accounts is appropriate. Either approach cuts down the source reporting required. The difficulty with these approaches is the reduction in the opportunities to identify variances. Normally under a computerized inventory system these shortcuts are not necessary or appropriate.

Improper inventory valuation can lead to major book-to-physical inventory adjustments, changes in cost of sales, and changes in profit or loss. Some of these adjustments are closely related to systems inadequacies and others relate to management action or inaction. Following is a summary of some of the problems leading to "inventory busts":

Not accounting for all movements, not reconciling inventory volumes from period to period, and not providing adequate audit trails.

Inconsistencies between input and output units or unit costs.

Failure to recognize cut-off and timing problems, particularly when using unit cost methods such as Fifo and weighted average.

Failure to provide adequately for scrap, yield, and material use variances.

Failure to recognize properly and account for direct labor and related overhead variances.

Failure to identify adequately obsolete items.

Improper joint or by-product costing.

GENERAL INVENTORY
VALUATION CONSIDERATIONS

Inventory valuation accounting is normally accomplished by one of two basic accounting approaches, regardless of the cost collection systems (job, process, or assembly) or the management reporting approach. They are:

1. Pricing out the effect of inventory movements along with the beginning inventory to arrive at an ending inventory valuation for each inventory account and for cost charges to the profit and loss statement. This approach is preferred, since it will provide the best data for cost control purposes and it applies to both job cost and process cost systems. Inventory movement and valuation information can be obtained as a by-product of the cost control and responsibility reporting system, or from a separate work-in-process reporting system. Where the data for inventory valuation journal entries come from will depend upon the company environment and the cost control and management reporting systems in place. It may be practical to support the "book balances" by valuing ending on-hand inventory quantities.

Valuing individual ending inventory items may not, of course, be practical except as a result of physical inventory counts or where stock status reporting can be tied directly to accounting balances.

2. Obtaining the ending inventory valuation by costing physical inventory count. Purchases or issues, direct production labor, and overhead absorbed during the period are charged directly to cost of sales. Cost of sales and the inventory value on the balance sheet are then adjusted to reflect the new inventory balance determined using the physical inventory. This is often referred to as the *"disappearance" method.* This method, of course, requires period-end physical inventory counts. It is often used by new or unsophisticated companies. It is also used by companies with relatively sophisticted systems for specific process type cost centers that are not material from an overall cost standpoint.

Inventory costing alternatives

The use of *engineered standards* or *good estimates* is the preferred method of costing units of product in most situations for two basic reasons:

1. Standards or estimates provide a relatively stable base from which variances can be measured. Standards normally provide the best basis for cost control. If standards undergo frequent changes, a *baseline* type standard will be required to measure the overall impact and trend of cumulative changes.
2. From a mechanical viewpoint, standards are easier to handle than actual costs. There is more assurance that (*a*) account input and output will be valued at the same unit cost; (*b*) the impact of unit cost changes are more easily identified, and (*c*) timing problems such as partial job completions can be accommodated.

The use of *actual weighted average* unit costs is acceptable (and could be required in some government contract environments and for cost-plus type work). The use of the weighted average method has three disadvantages, however:

1. Significant errors can build up in inventory accounts when using average costs in fast turnover situations where issues from an account are made using an old average because the most current receipt into the account has not yet been processed.
2. A problem occurs in a job cost collection environment when partial job completions must be costed. The new average obviously has not yet been calculated.
3. Average costs can provide accurate inventory valuation if input and output units and costs can be kept consistent. Obtaining and analyzing cost control information, however, is difficult when averages are used. Historically, bad practices and methods are reflected in the averages to which new actual costs are compared and therefore costs used for planning and control purposes reflect the past rather than the future.

In most situations *actual Fifo* or *Lifo* costing is difficult to accomplish in that the quantities must be maintained at each cost level for each stock keeping unit. Fifo and Lifo costing is also the most susceptible to unit costing errors caused by improper transaction sequence, input timing, and cutoff problems. For example, the costing of receipts prior to recording the vendor's invoice is difficult unless the purchase order price can be used and relied upon to reflect accurately the price that will be invoiced. As with average costs in a job environment, partial unit completions on a job cannot be costed except at an estimate which has to be adjusted later to actual.

Accounting for all inventory movement

One of the most common inventory valuation problems results from price or unit inconsistencies when adding to or relieving amounts from inventory accounts. Some examples of inconsistent treatment are as follows:

1. Violating the rule that all material movements must be accounted for. Those which are commonly missed relate to:
   a. Scrap.
   b. Spare parts sold.
   c. Excess issues (material usage in excess of requirements).

    d. Materials required for rework.

    e. Items transferred to an account for rework.

    f. Outside processing.

    g. Engineering use.

    h. Marketing use.

2. The use of inaccurate conversion ratios between input units of measure and output units of measure (i.e., buying in pounds and charging to work in process in feet).

3. Relieving items from an account at a previous average, Fifo, or Lifo value before the transaction which will update those unit costs has been posted. For example, issuing from a stores account before the vendor receipt for input to that account has been processed.

4. Issuing components based on the number of units started on a job and then relieving that job based on the number of units completed without accounting for material, labor, and overhead related to uncompleted units.

5. The use of alternative materials or alternative methods where the relief from work-in-process is based on the material shown on the standard bill of materials.

6. Improper use of "dummy" or "blanket" work orders in a job cost situation. It is fairly typical to see blanket work orders set up in a job cost environment to cover special situations or cost centers where it is not practical to charge directly to jobs. This occurs where a process type cost center such as chemical cleaning, heat treating, or grinding is interspersed with assembly cost centers. Actual costs are charged to the dummy job and in effect relieved to actual jobs at a standard. If the dummy job is not closed or reviewed periodically, variances build up.

In general, the problems related to issuing and receiving at the same values require that the effects on system requirements of transaction timing, unit costing, units of measure, and reporting of all nonproductive movements be understood clearly.

Variance recognition

By definition a *variance from standard* represents a cost over or under the cost of producing a normal quantity, of normal quality, under normal working conditions. Variances should therefore be recognized immediately on the profit and loss statements.

Where it is known that standards have been in error but not changed on a timely basis, it may be appropriate to allocate a portion of some variances to ending inventory amounts. This situation might occur where "normal conditions" are changing rapidly or where standards are set as production targets—as opposed to basing them on "normal conditions."

Some companies charge variances to manufacturing overhead pools and thus to inventory as part of the overhead rate. This is not normally desirable in that the variances become hidden and costs may be incorrectly capitalized.

Variances should be recognized as soon as practical. Variances buried in extremely long jobs which are only recognized as the result of job closing or a physical inventory count distort interim financial results and cannot be used to trigger management corrective action. Long jobs can often be broken up into smaller jobs or lots to obtain meaningful reporting on a more timely basis. In job cost environments where production is reported by operation, it is usually possible to recognize costs and variances as operations are completed—as opposed to waiting for job completion.

Stock status valuation

It is normally practical to value *finished goods* accounts by costing all receipts from production and shipments to customers, and applying these amounts to an opening balance to arrive at an ending balance. Where practical and when transaction timing differences between costed material movements and stock status reporting can be overcome, it is desirable to reconcile the ending inventory valuation to a period-end costed stock status report. This cross check may catch miscellaneous material movements which have not been properly recorded in the books. For example, an issue from stores to cover part shortages due to scrap loss on the floor may be recorded as a reduction for stock status purposes, but the proper journal entry may not have been recorded.

Work-in-process may be more difficult to value and reconcile for the following reasons:

1. Issues to work-in-process may be made from uncontrolled storage areas and therefore dependent on strict paperwork discipline. If some stores areas are uncontrolled, a company may elect to explode standard usage based on completed production, which would leave usage variances undetected either in stores or in work-in-process. This is due to the differences between the quantity actually issued and the exploded quantity, or due to timing differences between issue time and relief based on the explosion. (If a physical inventory is taken in-between the two occurrences, the materials will not be physically present in stores and will not be included in work-in-process because the explosion has not taken place.)

2. Shop floor control systems may not yet be developed to the point where work-in-process can be identified with an operation or cost center by accurate counts. Therefore, variances will build up in work-in-process until lots close or accurate count points are reached.

It may be practical to take a physical inventory of work-in-process, or in some cases ignore work-in-process. These situations would occur in process flow cost collection situations where there is little work-in-process at the end of any given period or when the work-in-process is relatively easy to count. These approaches can also be useful in assembly-line situations if the material stocking the line can be accounted for.

Good inventory valuation reporting requires, then, that it be possible to start with beginning inventory balances and adjust these balances for current period movements to arrive at ending balances. Detail transactions should be printed or available for review in some manner (microfiche, inquiry, etc.). Movements out of inventory accounts (i.e., moved to cost of sales, capital asset accounts, or expensed) should be available for review and reconciliation. Where practical, physical inventory counts and priced status reports are used to reconcile quantities to book amounts. Cycle counting of store items can be used to check physical balances on an ongoing basis.

Timing of reporting

Inventory transactions are often recorded for accounting purposes in a specific time period because they carry a date identifying them with that accounting period. The transaction may not, however, be recorded for stock status reporting purposes until the following accounting period due to a delay in transaction processing or to errors corrected in the following accounting period.

General ledger entries are normally recorded by accumulating priced inventory movements applicable to the accounting period, regardless of when they hit the stock status reporting. The result of accounting period versus stock status inconsistencies is that costed stock status reports and listings of jobs in process will not be consistent with what is reported for inventory valuation purposes in an inventory account. The cost system should be able to recognize the transactions required to print a report showing reconciling movements.

WORK-IN-PROCESS
INVENTORY ACCOUNTING

Considerations relative to the valuation of work-in-process are highly dependent upon the company environment, products, and on management reporting subsystems related to inventory control and shop floor control.

There are various types of cost collection systems that can be defined for various types of industries or parts of an industry:

Process cost collection system.   A system where costs are accumulated by or charged to cost centers, processes, or departments over a period of time.

Job cost collection system.   A system where costs are charged to specific jobs or lots produced irrespective of the time required for production.

Hybrid cost collection system.   A combination or variation of the collection systems described above, either because of capabilities to measure input, or the presence of product or process characteristics such that the control of costs, or reporting of output, must be modified.

Systems considerations can differ greatly from one department to the next as well as between companies. For example, a company may have a machine shop department using job cost collection procedures with control by operation, and several assembly and test departments using completed job cost collection procedures with control by completed job. (These cost collection approaches are discussed separately later in this chapter.) The company may also have plating, grinding, and chemical cleaning departments using process cost collection procedures for labor control. The effect is that a company's system may have to embrace a variety of system alternatives in order to meet all of the conditions which exist.

The potential to violate the input/output consistency rule is probably higher in work-in-process than in other inventory accounts. It is affected by quantity as well as unit of measure and rate changes. In addition, the potential for inaccurate source reporting is higher than in other accounts since a large number of individuals are involved in reporting labor, scrap, production, and so forth, versus a relatively small number of individuals reporting material movements in and out of storerooms.

Valuing work-in-process inventory where the work-in-process account is insignificant at the end of any accounting period is relatively simple. This is often the case in process situations such as an assembly line, where it is practical to set a fixed inventory level for the line or essentially clean off the line at the end of each period.

Conversely, the most difficult work-in-process valuation situations arise where there are a number of large custom jobs being built and the jobs are open for relatively long periods of time. Typically it is difficult with this type of job to define a unit of production other than the completion of the entire job.

There are almost as many systems variations possible as there are companies to apply them. The best way to identify the appropriate cost collection systems approach for the situation at hand is to get a picture of the cost flow in terms of input requirements, measuring points, processes involved and production reporting. This is accomplished by reviewing the situation and:

a. Identifying the physical transfer points and potential variances.

b. Developing a cost flow schematic that presents the actual situation. (See Cost Flow example, Exhibit 1.)

c. Identifying the journal entries required to record the costs. (See Work-In-Process Journal Entries, Exhibit 2.)

d. Verifying the cost flow by building a simple model using units and amounts to trace all entries through "T" accounts to model financial statements. Verify that the costed ending inventory units are equal to the ending inventory account balances.

Work-in-process cost flow example

Plastics, Inc. produces extruded plastic sheet and formed products such as buckets, covers, and automotive interior components. They have an extrusion process and subsequent job operations to form, trim, grind, and finish parts. The trimmed edges and uneven sheets from the extrusion process and trim scrap from forming is broken up and reground. Bad pieces are reported as scrap upon inspection and are reclaimed by regrinding them for use as raw material. A scrap credit is allowed in costing the original product for scrap pieces and trim. Production counts or weights are taken before all operations and as the finished product is transferred to finished goods inventory.

Further discussion of inventory valuation can be divided into considerations relative to work-in-process costing for: (*a*) job cost collection systems, (*b*) process cost collection systems, and (*c*) hybrid systems (an example is a job-operation cost system). Each section covers peculiar valuation considerations for that environment, appropriate journal entries necessary to measure the cost flow in terms of money, and the use of typical source reporting information as a basis for making those entries.

Accounting for inventories in a job cost collection systems environment

In an environment calling for a job cost collection system labor, material, and overhead are charged to work orders or jobs. Jobs may be of short, intermediate, or long duration but there are normally no logical points during the life of the job where accurate production counts can be made. Therefore,

EXHIBIT 1
Plastics, Inc. work-in-process cost flow

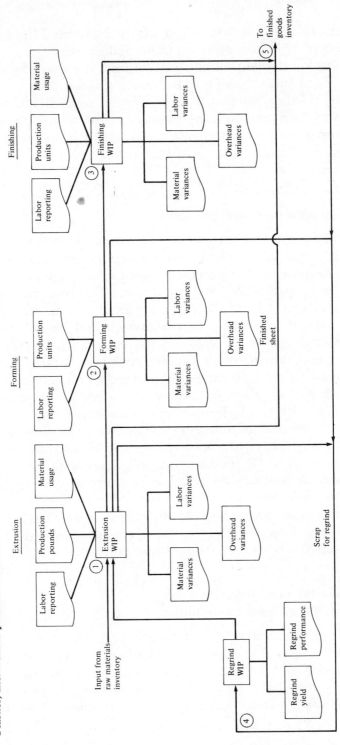

① Sheet plastic is made from polyvinyl and/or regrind.
② Sheet plastic is formed as a job.
③ Product is trimmed, ground, and polished.
④ Scrap trim and sheet is sent to regrinding.
⑤ Sheet and finished products flow to finished goods inventory.

EXHIBIT 2
Work-in-process journal entries, Plastics, Inc.

Event	Source document	Stores	Regrind: Inventory	Regrind: Scrap credit	WIP: Extrusion	WIP: Forming	WIP: Finishing	Finished goods	Variance: Material	Variance: Labor	Variance: Overhead	Clearing: Payroll	Clearing: Overhead
Material input	Materials usage	−			+				①+				
Regrind input	Materials usage	−			+				①+				
Production reporting—Extrusion	Production report		+	−	−	+		+	①+	①+	①+		
Production reporting—Forming	Production report		+	−		−	+		①+	①+	①+		
Production reporting—Finishing	Production report		+	−			−	+	①+	①+	①+		
Labor reporting	Labor tickets		+		+	+	+			②+		−	
Overhead absorption	Labor summary				+	+	+				③+		−
Regrind generated	Weigh ticket	+	−						④+				

① Scrap variance.
② Efficiency variance.
③ Overhead volume.
④ Regrind yield.

work-in-process is valued based on the beginning balance plus additions of labor, material, and overhead, less the value of completed units. Most of the variances which occur, such as material usage, labor efficiency, and scrapped production, are not recognized until the job is completed. Those that can be recognized, such as scrapped production, should be booked and charged to cost of sales when they become known. Recognized variances may, however, be accumulated by jobs on a memo basis so that complete job cost information is available for management and variances can be related to an end product where appropriate.

Standard costs in this type of environment are often based on historical cost and may be little more than estimates. The controls available in this system are highly dependent upon the accuracy of recording job openings and completions and the period of time jobs remain open.

Where jobs are large and of long duration, procedures should be established to review progress and make estimates of the cost at completion. If cost at completion compared to the last estimate exceeds an acceptable range, write-offs should be taken on a current basis. This is a common practice for government contractors and in the construction industry. Control approaches related to packaging work in controllable units are appropriate.

Exhibit 3 is a summary of the economic events, transaction sources, and journal entries resulting in the valuation of work-in-process where a completed job cost collection system is used.

A trial balance of all of the charges accumulated on open jobs is normally prepared periodically to substantiate the work-in-process balance recorded in the company's books as a result of costed material movements. Where job volume is high and there is a high degree of confidence that all material movements are properly accounted for, it may be appropriate to arrive at the book balance at the end of a period by listing only exception jobs, with a sum for all others. *Exception jobs* would include those:

a. That are open past their completion date.
b. That have passed the point where a certain percentage of units started have been completed.
c. On which a certain percentage of the standard labor or material has been expended.

EXHIBIT 3
Job cost collection system

Event	Source	Entry	Comments
1. Material moved from stores to work-in-process.			
a. Initial issue	Bill of material, pick list generated from bill of material, or requisitions based on analysis of plans and specifications.	Cr.—Stores Dr.—WIP	The initial issue may be time phased so that material arrives on the job at various periods of time. The entire bill of material need not be issued prior to release of a job to the floor, but items shorted from an issue must be accounted for.
b. Short fills	Transaction generated by receipt in stores of items shorted on initial issues.	Cr.—Stores Dr.—WIP	A separate manual or mechanized system is required to keep track of the items shorted on jobs and the receipt of those items so they can be issued to the floor and identified as short fills as opposed to subsequent issues.
c. Subsequent issues	Material requisitions	Cr.—Stores Dr.—Material variance	All subsequent issues to jobs can be considered as material variances assuming that the initial issues and short fills were made correctly. Material variances should be recognized and charged to cost of sales at the time of the issues, but they can also be accumulated on a memo basis against the job for reporting and control purposes.
d. Return to stores	Credit material requisition	Dr.—Stores Cr.—Material variance	Occasionally more material is issued to the floor than is required. This material may have been charged off as a subsequent issue on a previous job or maybe material left over from previous jobs due to items started but not completed. Since normally the returned material will have already been written off to a variance, the return to stores would be treated as a favorable variance.

Exhibit 3 (*continued*)

Event	Source	Entry	Comments
2. Labor	Time cards charging jobs	Dr.—WIP Cr.—Labor clearing account	Cost centers or operations, as well as jobs, may be charged so that more complete analysis can be made of actual costs when jobs are closed. Labor variances are not normally recognized until the job is completed.
3. Overhead applied	Journal entry	Dr.—WIP Cr.—Manuf. overhead	Overhead is normally charged as a percentage of actual labor, but material and machine rates are sometimes used also. When overhead is charged as a percentage of actual labor, it will be charged on that portion of labor which will eventually be written off as a variance when the job closes. This creates an overhead variance in work-in-process at the end of a period.
4. Completed production	A material movement transaction transferring units out of work-in-process to finished goods.	Dr.—Finished goods Cr.—WIP	Completed production is moved out of WIP at standard, or where standards are not available, at some sort of estimate.
5. Job closing	Notification of job closing, along with the number of units started and those which have been completed and transferred to finished goods as part of 4 above.		
a. Units started but never completed	Journal entry based on units started vs. those completed.	Dr.—Production reporting variance Cr.—WIP	The cost of uncompleted units will include material and, where definable, some factor for labor and overhead.

b. Write-off of the
job balance . . . .   Job records showing the total amount of input to the job and deductions for completed units or variances recorded.

Dr.—Overhead
        variances
Dr.—Labor
        variance
Cr.—WIP

The amount remaining in the job after all units completed have been transferred to finished goods and an accounting has been made for those units started but never completed. This amount generally relates to the labor variance and overhead attributable to the labor variance.

The variance amounts are the result of a combination of: labor efficiency; rework done and changed to the regular job number; labor rate and labor mix variances; and inaccurate standards.

Normally it is not meaningful to attempt to identify exception jobs based on total cost charged relative to total standard cost. Normally significant material amounts are charged to the job when it is released and after that point it may change little. Exceptions should be identified based on excess material and excess labor charges separately.

Valuation of work-in-process in a process cost collection environment

The process environment may fit the entire work-in-process inventory of a company, or it may only apply to certain cost centers or departments. In either case, there are three preliminary questions to be asked relative to valuing work-in-process in a process situation:

1. Is the dollar amount of work-in-process significant at the end of the accounting period? Quite frequently work-in-process amounts are small, particularly where the inventory is contained within a single flow (i.e., a single series of operations) without any staging points. Significance may depend on the ending balance relative to the total amount of inventory which has passed through work-in-process during the accounting period, or on the relationship of the inventory to the net profit. If any potential inventory writedown would have a large effect on the reported net profit, management would surely want more effort extended to ensure that the inventory is accurate.
2. Can work-in-process or the flow into and out of work-in-process be physically measured fairly easily at period-end using some form of instrumentation?
3. Can quantities in work-in-process be estimated fairly accurately by assessing whether the capacity of the process is either completely full or empty? This may be possible in a process involving a liquid product where the content of tanks and piping systems is well established by an engineering analysis.

If work-in-process is insignificant or easily determined, valuation is very simple.

Problems arise in valuing work-in-process when work-in-process is significant, physical measurement is difficult, and any of the following conditions exist:

a. Input to work-in-process is calculated based on an explosion of production output. This occurs where input is not metered or charged in some manner to a production job, lot, or batch.

b. There are staging points in the process and the product characteristics and instrumentation are such that staged amounts are difficult to count.

c. Yield loss is significant throughout the process and it is difficult to record the loss until a lot or batch is completed, or at least until it moves through a count point.

d. Instrumentation is inaccurate.

e. Set-up costs are significant and difficult to identify with specific products. Many process systems use production jobs, lots, or batches to control the properties or quality of the output. When a job is completed a costly set-up for the next job may be required. If significant, set-up may be treated as a direct cost and included in the standard unit cost rather than charging it to manufacturing overhead.

f. There are a large number of orders in process and physical control over usage on particular production orders is difficult. Examples could include the conversion of wood to wood products, like cabinets or mill work, and the conversion of paper in roll form to a large variety of sizes, shapes, and colors of products such as school tablets, notebook fillers, and pads.

Exhibit 4 is a summary of the economic events, transaction sources, and journal entries resulting in the valuation of work-in-process where a process cost collection system is used.

Valuation of inventories in a hybrid cost collection system

Many companies use a hybrid job/process cost system where material is controlled by job (or lot) and labor is controlled on an operational basis.

Labor variances are generated as the job or lot moves from operation to operation (or cost center to cost center). Variances identified at the completion of an operation should be charged directly to cost of sales. It may be appropriate in some situations,

EXHIBIT 4
Process cost collection system

Event	Source	Entry	Comments
1. Material input to work-in-process from stores			
a. Measured in	Instrumentation, a pick list, or a material requisition	*Dr.*—WIP *Cr.*—Stores	
b. Input exploded from production counts	Production counts	*Dr.*—Finished goods *Cr.*—Stores	Material is never actually recorded in WIP except where it moves from one operation to the next with a count point between. In that case the debit would be to work-in-process. Period-end WIP in a given operation must be estimated or, if insignificant, ignored.
2. Labor	Time cards or journal entries charging labor costs to processes or operations.	*Dr.*—Machine or operation cost pool *Cr.*—Labor clearing *Dr./Cr.*—Labor variance if standard labor instead of machine manning is used.	The machine or operation cost pool is charged to WIP based on standard labor hours or as part of a machine rate. The latter method is used where labor costs are insignificant relative to the total cost of the operations cost pool.
3. Overhead			
a. Process or operation-related costs		*Dr.*—A machine or an operation cost pool *Cr.*—Payables, allowance for depreciation, etc.	These costs relate directly to a machine or operation and are charged to the production or operation cost pool which will subsequently be absorbed into work-in-process on the basis of machine usage or operation reports.

b. General manufacturing overhead ....

Dr.—WIP
Cr.—Manufacturing overhead pool

These costs are typically absorbed into product cost on some overall basis, such as direct labor or total direct costs.

4. Machine usage .... Time required to complete job or batch per the standard process sheet or based on the actual time to flow through a process

Dr.—WIP
Cr.—Machine or operation cost pool

5. Completed production .... Production count

Dr.—Finished goods
Cr.—WIP
Dr./Cr.—Yield and mix variances

468

however, to accumulate the variances for the complete job on a memo basis so that they can be associated with a specific end product.

Material may be "kitted," as is often the case in the completed job system, or it may be issued directly to operations for use as needed. Material would be issued to a specific job or lot control number. Material variances are recognized based on either issues subsequent to the issue of a complete bill of materials or as the job is closed.

Exhibit 5 is a summary of the economic events, transaction sources, and journal entries resulting in the valuation of work-in-process where a hybrid cost collection system is used. Material is controlled by job and labor is controlled on an operational basis. These entries and transaction sources will vary by company environment as the types of products, production processes, and types of variances identified are different.

Some type of trial balance of all jobs is normally prepared or available at the end of an accounting period to substantiate the book work-in-process balance. If volumes are high, and they often are in this environment, consideration must be given to printing only exception jobs or categories of jobs. It must be possible to obtain a trial balance if required.

Exception jobs might include those:

Where the completion date is approaching or has passed.
Where there is a potential count problem. In-process units differ significantly from standard units.
Variances recognized on the job exceed some limit.

The hybrid system normally includes the use of standard parts, or routers or process sheets, and requires a manual or mechanized shop floor control system to control the flow of work through the shop.

Accounting for items awaiting rework

Items awaiting rework are segregated in a separate inventory account or location so that the additional costs can be reported. The easiest ways to handle this are: (1) write off all inputs to a rework account and value the account at zero even though the individual item carries the normal standard cost, or, (2) value the units at the normal item standard and provide an overall allowance for rework to be performed. The allowance would be based on the historical costs incurred for rework.

Valuing rework at zero or full cost is not practical, however, where the value of material awaiting rework is high or the cost to rework is definable and relatively high compared to the cost of a good item. In these situations rework would be valued at the standard cost of the completed items less the estimated cost to rework.

Inventory at outside processors

Inventory at outside processors may be valued and accounted for in several ways. One way is to sell material to a vendor and buy back completed items. If there is no obligation to buy the material back, there is no valuation problem. If there is, the commitment should be covered through the purchasing system.

Often the purchasing or billing system is used as a means of control over outside processing. The purchasing system is often used where purchased materials are sent directly to the outside processor by the vendors. When the material is received from the outside processor, quantities are checked and normal receiving paperwork is prepared. Receivers are matched and costed, using both vendor and outside processor billings in the same manner as normal accounts payable items. Care must be taken to see that receivers are valued at the sum of the material vendor's price plus outside processing, not one or the other.

If items are sent outside during normal processing, the shipment to the outside processor might be controlled and documented by the shipping function on bills of lading or normal shipping advices and treated as no-charge billings. This paperwork would have to be distributed to purchasing and inventory control functions for control and valuation purposes. The value of materials in the hands of outside parties is usually segregated in a separate account to facilitate reconciliation of shipment inventories and to trigger confirmation of accounts held by outside parties.

Work can be sent to outside vendors on a production job number. This is convenient because outside processing jobs can easily be segregated and valued in much the same manner as regular production jobs. The separate job approach is not convenient

EXHIBIT 5
Hybrid cost collection system

Event	Source	Entry	Comments
1. Material movement from stores to work-in-process			
a. Initial issues	Bill of material or a pick list generated from the bill of materials. Material may be delivered to various operations or may be "kitted" and delivered to the first operation.	Cr.—Stores Dr.—WIP	The entire bill of materials need not be "kitted" prior to release to the floor. Items shorted on the bill of materials must be accounted for. Kitting may result in materials from one job being borrowed for another job, leading to concealment of material variances.
b. Short fills	Receipt in stores of items shorted on job	Cr.—Stores Dr.—WIP	A mechanized or manual system is required to account for issuing of short fills to the floor without treating them as a loss.
c. Subsequent issues	Material requisitions	Cr.—Stores Dr.—Material variance	Issues to operations subsequent to the original bill of material requirements (which may include scrap allowances) as the result of requirements for rework or material loss. These items would be identified immediately as a material variance.
d. Return to stores	Credit material requisition	Dr.—Stores Cr.—Material variance	Occasionally more material is issued to the floor than is required. This material may have been charged off as a subsequent issue on a previous job or may be material left over from previous jobs due to items started but not completed. Since normally the returned material will have already been written off to a variance, the return to stores would be treated as a favorable variance.
e. Losses at a given operation	Production reports	Cr.—WIP Dr.—Material variance	Where the number of items starting through an operation is reconciled to good and bad completed items, material usage variance (or scrap)

	Source	Entry	Explanation
			can be calculated at each operation. (See Scrap Variance Reporting in the Cost Control Section of this chapter.) The labor and overhead associated with that scrap must either be consistently recorded as a labor inefficiency variance or included as part of the scrap loss variance.
2. Labor charges	Time card charges for the above operations (or to both operations and jobs).	Dr.—WIP Cr.—Labor clearing Dr./Cr.—Labor variance	Labor is charged to a specific operation for working on a specific part number. Based on the standard in the routing for the part, standard labor is charged to WIP, actual labor is relieved from the labor clearing account, and the labor variance is recorded.
			The labor variance may be the result of an inaccurate standard, labor efficiency, alternative methods, or labor mix. The labor variance is recognized immediately but may be accumulated over an entire job on a memo basis so as to provide a means for associating the variance with a specific end product.
3. Overhead charged to work-in-process	Journal entry	Dr.—WIP Cr.—Mfg. overhead	Overhead is often charged as a percentage of actual labor but material and machine overhead rates can be used. Overhead is applied to the standard (labor, material, or machine time) so that no overhead would be accumulated on variances as is the case in completed job systems.
4. Completed production a. Movement to the next operation	Production counts	Cr./Dr.—WIP variance	As noted in 1 above, material variances may be recorded based on good production counts at the beginning of an operation and at the completion of the operation.
b. Movement to stores	Production counts	Cr.—WIP Dr.—Stores or finished goods	Work-in-process is cleared for the standard cost of the items produced at the point the items are moved to stores or finished goods. This clears all of the charges against a job out of work-in-process.

472

where outside processing is one in a series of in-house operations. The job would have to be closed and a new one opened or the system would have to be able to handle nesting of jobs within jobs. Where the outside processing is consistently a separate operation within a series of operations, the router or process sheet should indicate which operations are done outside.

Rules must be established as to part identification prior and subsequent to outside processing to insure proper inventory control and costing. The outside processing step may be specified as a normal or alternate routing operation whereby the part number designation does not change after outside processing is completed. The sub-contracted operation could be first, last, or an intermediate operation on a manufacturing routing. In this case the part must be retrieved to work-in-process (unless it is the last operation). If the part returns to stock, the part numbers must change or physically different units may be commingled in inventory.

Positive job counts should be made prior to, and subsequent to, the outside operation by someone in the shipping and receiving function. It should be possible to summarize in the accounting system the value of inventory at all outside processing operations.

Inventory at separate plant locations

Different plant locations may have different costs for the same item. Each plant can maintain its own standards; then an interplant transfer standard and a variance is recorded upon transfer between plants or when the item is sent to a selling division. If each plant sells its own products, each would have a separate gross profit percentage.

For interplant transfers, the plants would maintain a special interplant transfer standard, which is used only when transferring between inventory locations, in addition to the intraplant transfer standard. The following is an example.

	Plant A	Plant B
Current cost	$5.00	$6.00
Intraplant accounting transfer cost	5.75	6.00
Interplant transfer cost	6.00	6.00
Plant transfer variance	0.25	0

FINISHED GOODS INVENTORY

Considerations related to valuation of various finished goods inventory accounts are separated from work-in-process considerations primarily because:

1. Finished goods inventory valuation is normally an integral part of the systems which maintain inventory quantities (see discussion of stock status reporting in the General Inventory Valuation Considerations section). Typically, the inventory quantity input from work-in-process and the output cost of sales to and from the stock status, along with the beginning inventory balance, is costed at the standard product cost to provide a value for the finished goods inventory. There is a good deal of similarity among various companies in this area, whereas there is not in accounting for work-in-process.

2. The valuation of finished goods inventory accounts is often more precise than the valuation of work-in-process. In an environment requiring job/lot controls, unless a comprehensive shop floor control system is in place, the exact location and stage of completion of a particular item in work in process is difficult to determine. Many variances will be left in jobs until they are closed. In a process control environment where work-in-process is significant, accurate measuring devices may not be available.

Current and accounting transfer standards

It is important to know the most current product cost for planning and control purposes. It is usually not appropriate to cost inventory transfers at the most current cost unless all on-hand quantities are recosted and the books are adjusted for each change. Using the most current standard could approach a Lifo cost policy and would probably violate the principle of consistency between account input and output. Accounting accuracy, planning, and cost control objectives can best be met when transactions are costed at the accounting transfer standard.

Finished goods inventory should be valued and reported at both the current and accounting transfer cost each period, so that management can determine if the inventory should be revalued to account properly for the change in standards.

The lower of cost or market

The most common situation in which cost versus market valuation occurs is where a company produces commodity-type materials or products. Commodity examples include steel, wheat, milk, semiconductors, and oil. Consideration should be given to maintaining special market value data in the same format as used for costing so that this data can be updated with market prices as of a given date. Inventory can then be valued at the accounting standard as well as at market value. Gains or losses recognized from commodity revaluation should be recognized in separate accounts as nonoperating gains and/or losses.

Valuation of joint products

Joint production is defined as production where two or more products automatically result from the same process. For example, in oil refining, gasoline and kerosene are produced in the same process. Both are desirable products to have in the output, therefore they are joint products.

Unit costs of joint products are meaningless for determining product line profitability. Management decisions must be made based on total cost and profit of all related joint products. Unit costs are established for joint products *only* because inventories must be valued. Product line profitability, where joint products span lines, is also misleading. The key consideration in costing joint products is to do it in such a manner as not to mislead management into wanting to change production and sales of a single joint product.

Joint products may be costed in several ways. The preferred way is the market price or the modified market price method.

1. Market price method. A method calculated by allocating joint costs to all related joint products as a percentage of selling price, and then adding the unique costs of completing any given joint product.

2. Modified market price method. This is an extension of the above where unique distribution costs are subtracted from total revenue prior to establishing the cost percentage in order to keep profits from being distorted by sales mix and unique distribution costs. The disadvantage of using it is that the unique distribution costs of products must be determined.

These calculations provide acceptable inventory valuation amounts without distorting management information. Note that these methods do not preclude the use of standards. The calculations described above are merely used to set the standard.

The costing problem is more complex for joint products which can be produced in a variable array. The most obvious example is the number of alternatives which exist for processing crude oil. It is difficult to value an intermediate level of refined petroleum when management has a wide latitude in determining the ultimate array of products to be produced from it. Management must make a decision based on the total revenue anticipated less the cost to complete the processing. No consideration should be given to the allocation of the unit cost up to the point where the production decision must be made.

A less preferred method is the use of an *average cost based on a common unit of measure.* This method will distort product profitability where sales are generated with significant differences in selling prices per unit of measure. The only advantage of the average method is its ease of calculation.

More sophisticated allocation techniques, though frequently used for valuation in certain industries, are not discussed in this chapter.

Valuation of by-products

By-product treatment is generally given to joint products with relatively low sales revenues. *By-products* are typically defined as products of minor importance resulting incidentally from the manufacture of one or more major products. Traditionally, by-products are accounted for by subtracting net by-product revenue from joint production costs. *Net by-product revenue* is the selling price less unique costs to complete and sell. The calculation of net by-product revenue is used to inform management that the unique costs to complete a by-product do not exceed revenue. Where the modified market price method is used for joint products, the same calculation can be used for by-products.

By-products are valued for inventory purposes in one of the

following manners: (*a*) no value; (*b*) unique cost; (*c*) selling price; and (*d*) selling price less unique cost.

The best method is the one which has the least effect on net profit in a given situation. The use of selling price less unique costs is useful in that this is the same as the by-product revenue which will be netted against joint costs when the item is sold.

CONCLUSION

Since inventory valuation is basic to credible financial statements and effective financial planning, executives at all levels should understand its impact upon work-in-progress and finished goods inventories.

18

Flexible budgeting

Michael W. Maher *
David C. Yates †

How often have you heard managers complain that they were being held responsible for something beyond their control? A manager of a maintenance department in a manufacturing firm recently complained that he lost his bonus because costs were 10 percent higher than budget. "Why didn't they look at the fact that demand for maintenance services also increased 10 percent because of increased production and some rush orders? If you ask me, I did pretty well to keep costs as low as I did. Next year I'll keep my costs down by not responding to demands for our services."

The other side of this coin emerges frequently, too. "Our sales dropped last year, but our overhead costs continued at the old level," one executive reported. "I know those aren't all fixed costs, but I don't know how to control those people to make sure that when production and sales drop, overhead costs go down, too."

In this chapter, we discuss a means for monitoring costs which adjusts the budget for variation in external factors beyond the control of operating personnel. This approach, known as *flexible*

---
* Assistant Professor of Accounting, The University of Michigan.

† Assistant Controller, Great Lakes Steel Division, National Steel Corporation.

budgeting, overcomes some of the problems noted above. In contrast to a *static budget,* which sets the budget at a fixed sum for some period of time, the flexible budget allows the budget amount to vary as the level of activity varies. In this way, operating personnel are held accountable only for activities within their control.

In the first part of this chapter we discuss the concept of *flexible budgeting,* with reference to situations where it may be appropriately used. In the next section we discuss some of the *technical issues* that are encountered in flexible budgeting. In the third section we address some of the *behavioral problems* related to flexible budgeting. Finally, we discuss *methods for performance reporting* that we have found useful. Throughout the chapter, we focus on application problems encountered in using flexible budgeting.

THE CONCEPT OF FLEXIBLE BUDGETING

The *budget* is a managerial tool which translates the goals and objectives of the organization into a financial plan of action. It is a blueprint for operations, much like the architect's blueprint for construction of a building. After selecting the best alternatives with respect to products, pricing, capacity, and so forth, the budgeting process requires management to translate these alternatives into an integrated plan of action. This forces management to make sure that all alternatives are compatible with each other, and with the organization's overall strategy for achieving its goals. When complete, the budget presents a comprehensive picture of the expected operations, much like an architect's blueprint presents a comprehensive picture of a planned building.

When used as blueprints for planning, budgets are normally static. That is, they are developed for the level of activity that is *anticipated.* Some sensitivity analysis is often done to see how the budget is affected if costs or sales are somewhat higher, or lower, than expected. However, it would be quite costly to develop a budget for every conceivable level of activity in the organization. Consequently, planning budgets are typically static.

When used as tools for control and performance evaluation,

EXHIBIT 1

	Original plan	Flexible budget	Actual results
Activity level	100,000 units	80,000 units	80,000 units
Costs	$2,500,000	$2,100,000	$2,350,000

Difference due
to change in
activity $400,000 $250,000
                                    under   over

Difference
attributable to
the department $250,000
                                              over

however, budgets should be flexible. In this way, the budget is constructed to recognize that costs *should be* different from the plan if the level of activity is different from the plan. The comparison of the planning and control budgets is demonstrated in the following example.

Example: Studies of past cost behavior in the machining department of the Greater Manufacturing Company indicated that the department should incur fixed costs of $500,000 per year and variable costs of $20 per unit produced. For planning purposes, 100,000 units are budgeted as the expected activity level for 1978. Budgeted costs for the machining department are $2,500,000 [$500,000 + ($20 × 100,000 units)].

Suppose actual costs are $2,350,000 for 1978. A superficial analysis indicates that a good job of cost control was accomplished in the machining department, because costs were $150,000 lower than budgeted. But suppose a more in-depth examination reveals that the activity level was only 80,000 units actually produced, instead of the 100,000 units originally planned. According to the flexible budget concept, budgeted costs for control and performance evaluation would be $2,100,000 [$500,000 + ($20 × 80,000 units)]. Now it is clear that while costs are lower than planned, they are $250,000 higher than they should be, *considering the level of activity in the department.*

These comparisons between the original plan, the flexible budget, and the actual costs and activity for the period are summarized in Exhibit 1.

EXHIBIT 2

Original plan .... $E(C) = \$500,000 + [\$20 \times E(A)]$
$= \$500,000 + \$20 \times 100,000$
$= \$2,500,000.$

Flexible budget .... $E(C) = \$500,000 + (\$20 \times A)$
$= \$500,000 + (\$20 \times 80,000)$
$= \$2,100,000.$

Actual results .... $C = \$2,350,000$

The comparison between the two approaches to budgeting can be summarized by the following formulas.

Static (planning) budget:
$$E(c) = f[E(A)]. \qquad (1)$$

Flexible (control) budget:
$$E(c) = f(A). \qquad (2)$$

Actual results:
$$C = f(A). \qquad (3)$$

$E(c)$ refers to *expected costs* during the period.
C refers to actual *costs* that were incurred during the period.
$E(A)$ refers to the *expected activity* level during the period.
A refers to the *actual level of activity* that occurred during the period.
$f(\ )$ refers to a functional relationship between the activity level and costs.

Exhibit 2 shows how these formulas can be applied to the data for Greater Manufacturing Company. Of course, fixed costs are assumed not to change with variations in activity level.

DIFFICULTIES IN APPLYING THE CONCEPT OF FLEXIBLE BUDGETING

The concept demonstrated above is a relatively simple one and we wonder why its application is not more widespread.[1]

---

[1] A recent survey of 53 large business firms indicated that only 30 use flexible budgeting in performance evaluation. See E. Imhoff, "On the Dissemination of Managerial Accounting," *Proceedings of the Mid Atlantic AAA Meetings,* George Washington University, March 1977.

Although the flexible budgeting notion is widely used in budgeting direct labor and direct material costs, accountants have encountered major obstacles in applying flexible budgeting to manufacturing overhead and to nonmanufacturing costs. A moment's reflection reveals that this may be due to the nature of overhead costs. The variability of direct labor and direct materials usually can be traced directly to variations in activity levels (usually, production). However, directly tracing variations in overhead costs to changes in activity levels is nearly impossible. Manufacturing overhead typically varies with a large number of activities, including labor hours, machine time, order deadlines, size of orders, and many others. Further, many overhead cost items vary with activities in different time periods. For example, repairs and maintenance are often scheduled when the production rate is low, yet there is general agreement that high production creates the need for high repairs and maintenance. In addition, variations due to changes in activity levels are frequently masked by changes in costs because of changing wage rates, property taxes, insurance rates, utility rates, and so forth.

These obstacles led accountants to treat overhead costs as mostly fixed. Operating managers soon learned to earn their budget by maximizing production. In industries having strong demand for services, this concentration on maximizing production may be desirable. But for industries operating below capacity, such as the American steel industry, maximizing production may lead to unnecessary production and inventory costs. Therefore, operating personnel often need to be shown how it is possible to reduce production and still make a profit.

This dictum that a profit should be budgeted in bad times as well as good is central to the need for flexible budgeting. If we assume that the planning budget is developed to provide a profit, what happens if the demand for the organization's product is severely reduced? The static budget would not demonstrate how to earn a profit in the face of reduced market demand and production levels. However, the flexible budget shows how the reduced activity level *should* have an impact on costs. This enables management to control costs despite an unexpected change in production activity.

Applications of flexible budgeting methods have also been limited in nonmanufacturing settings, particularly in government. This comes as no surprise considering the parallels that have been drawn between overhead, service, and government by such observers of management as Peter Drucker in *Management: Tasks, Responsibilities, Practices.*[2]

Applications of flexible budgeting to nonmanufacturing settings requires the ability and determination to identify key operating variables, to measure activities, and to establish a relation between costs and activities that makes sense. As with manufacturing overhead, these relations are very difficult to define and measure. Consequently, operating personnel have often treated costs as fixed.

In summary, the flexible budget recognizes that "nothing ever goes as planned." It also forces operating managers to recognize that they cannot earn their budget by maximizing production. Instead, their budget is based on activity levels required to satisfy external market demands for the organization's product. Flexible budgeting encourages the smart operating manager to be sensitive to changes in activity levels, and to manage costs for the appropriate activity level.

TECHNICAL ISSUES IN FLEXIBLE BUDGETING

Flexible budgeting requires the capability and determination to identify the components of the $C = f(A)$ relation that we discussed earlier. In this section we discuss some of the problems that are frequently confronted in the installation and use of flexible budgeting. These include

1. Determining which activities cause costs to fluctuate.
2. Identifying which costs fluctuate with activities.
3. Relating costs to activities in the same time period.
4. Determining the functional relations between costs and activity levels.
5. Determining the range over which relationships between costs and activities are valid.

---

[2] Peter Drucker, *Management: Tasks, Responsibilities, Practices,* (New York: Harper & Row, 1973).

Activity levels: Causes of cost fluctuations

A cost should be related to the activity which causes it to fluctuate. Common measures of these activities include units of output, labor time, machine time, volume of materials handled, and so forth. Examples of activities that typically cause cost fluctuation are shown in Exhibit 3.

EXHIBIT 3

Cost	Activity base
1. Indirect materials	1. Direct materials used; production level.
2. Supervision	2. Number of employees; production level; direct labor employed.
3. Material-handling labor	3. Units of material handled; number of times units are handled; distance travelled; obstacles encountered.
4. Billing	4. Invoices processed.
5. Payroll	5. Time cards processed; number of changes in personnel status.
6. Mailing	6. Pieces mailed.
7. Equipment repairs and depreciation	7. Volume of activity; rate of activity.
8. Employee training	8. Number of new employees; number of employees in new positions; number of employees.

One approach is to identify budgeted cost items from the chart of accounts and judgmentally identify the activity measures that are expected to cause the cost to fluctuate. This judgmental approach can be verified through statistical techniques, such as regression analysis.[3] Observations of work processes can also be used to verify one's judgment.

Perhaps the most important step is to verify with operating personnel one's judgment of what makes certain cost items fluctuate. No one in the organization is likely to understand cost behavior better than the operating personnel who are continu-

---

[3] There are a number of excellent books on regression analysis. Two books which provide comprehensive treatment of the subject are J. Kmenta, *Elements of Econometrics*, Macmillan, 1971, and R. Pindyck & D. Rubinfield, *Econometric Models and Economic Forecasts* (New York: McGraw-Hill, 1976).

ally involved with the activities that cause costs to occur. Of course, they must not be made to feel that they have anything to lose by providing inside information about their operations. Operating personnel have little incentive to provide accurate information about their operations in the first place. Further, they will be even more reluctant to provide information if they believe it will be used against them (for example, by tightening standards).

In budgeting overhead costs, we often find that costs fluctuate more closely with inputs than with outputs. For example, materials-handling labor costs depend on the quantity of materials handled, rather than on the yield from production. This presents a problem if the budget for materials-handling costs depends on the yield of materials rather than on the number of items handled. If production is very inefficient, actual materials used will probably exceed the budget. Consequently, we expect labor costs for handling materials to be higher. Thus the flexible budget for materials-handling labor costs should be based on materials handled, which is an input to production, rather than on production output.

A second problem is whether actual or standard activity should be the basis for the flexible budget. For example, should budgeted materials-handling costs be based on *actual* materials handled, or should costs be budgeted on the basis of *standard* materials handled? Basing the budget for materials handling costs on standard materials used violates the premise of flexible budgeting. The activity level, which is materials used in this case, is beyond the control of the individuals responsible for the cost of handling materials. Thus, assuming that materials handlers are not responsible for overages in the use of materials, the budget should be based on the *actual, not the standard,* level of activity.

Of course, responsibility should be placed for inefficiencies in production that result in the overuse of materials. In fact, those responsible for the overuse of materials should also be held responsible for the resulting budgeted increase in materials handling costs.

An example is presented in Exhibit 4. Because of inefficiencies in production, an excess of 200 pounds of material, at a standard cost of $2 per pound, results in an unfavorable materials usage

EXHIBIT 4

Budgeted output	1,000 units
Budgeted materials per unit of output.................................	10 pounds at $2 per pound (standard) = $20 per unit.
Budgeted materials-handling labor cost per pound	$0.10
Actual output	900 units
Standard materials used (10 pounds per unit)	9,000 pounds
Actual materials used	9,200 pounds
Materials used in excess of standard	200 pounds
Total material cost based on standard cost per pound and total pounds used	$18,400
Actual materials handling cost	$ 950
Variances charged to production:	
Materials usage	$ 400 (unfavorable)
Materials handling cost	$ 20 (unfavorable)
Variance charged to materials handling	$ 30 (unfavorable)

variance of $400. The flexible budget for materials handling is based on 9,200 pounds of materials handled; thus the budget allowance for materials handling is $920 ($0.10 per pound times 9,200 pounds). Production is charged for a $20 ($0.10 per pound times 200 pounds use overage) unfavorable variance in materials handling costs.

The use of multiple measures of activity, as we suggest, makes the system more expensive. Common sense dictates that there is a limit to the extent of detailed analysis of cost fluctuations. The incremental costs of developing and maintaining a very detailed system should always be compared with the incremental benefits from the system.

Which costs fluctuate with activity?

Many cost items are not directly related to an independent variable, such as volume of production. Advertising, for example, is not *caused* by sales. Research and training costs are not directly caused by volume of output. In fact, the relationship between the independent activity and these costs could be reversed. For example, sales are usually assumed to be *caused* by advertising, not the other way around.

Costs like these are frequently called *discretionary costs.* Discretionary costs are budgeted by management in light of some desired goals. A target level of sales indicates a desired level of advertising expenditures to achieve the sales level. Unlike direct manufacturing costs, these costs are not subject to ordinary predetermined relationships in which expected costs are functionally related to activity levels. While we may be sure what material costs *should be,* given some level of output, we are never as sure what the level of advertising, research, or training costs *should be.*

There are many items in addition to those mentioned earlier, such as advertising and research, which are somewhat discretionary. Examples include certain sales travel allowances, repairs and maintenance (especially to buildings and grounds), management consulting fees, certain types of fringe benefits, some clerical costs, expenditures for employee recreation, and charitable donations.

In flexible budgeting it is advisable to leave out costs that are purely at the discretion of management. They are not directly dependent on activity levels; thus, there is no reason for these costs to vary directly with variations in activity. We recommend that these costs be budgeted separately in a discretionary expense budget.

Time lags

In estimating cost-activity relationships, it is important to recognize that costs and activities may not fluctuate in the same time period. For example, equipment maintenance may be linked to equipment usage. However, high equipment usage now may result in high maintenance several periods hence. On the other hand, high sales now may be the result of high advertising costs several periods in the past.

Functional relations between costs and activity levels

Costs seldom vary with activities in an easy-to-estimate linear fashion. Instead, costs often vary as a step function or in a curvilinear manner. One relationship between costs and activity may hold at 95–105 percent of capacity, while another may hold at the 70–80 percent level.

These relations are difficult to determine at any time. Further, they are constantly changing over time. Many of us have had the experience of being evaluated on a performance standard developed in the past that is no longer appropriate.

In light of these difficulties, we recommend that the following procedures be followed.

1. Recognize that the relation developed is subject to error.
2. Actively solicit input from operating managers and others who are in a position to observe the relationship between costs and activity levels. As we mentioned earlier, the best way to obtain this input is to assure operating managers that they have nothing to lose (and perhaps something to gain) from better measurement of controllable operating variables.
3. List the costs to be analyzed in some order of priority. At the top should be the costs that vary most directly with activity and are easiest to analyze. Indirect materials and supplies are overhead items that are frequently top priority.
4. Relying on past experience and existing data, establish a relationship between the cost and activity levels. If possible, use several different sources of information to estimate the relationship. An approach that has worked well for us is to inspect visually the relationship from a plot of the data, like that in Exhibit 5. This could be supplemented with statistical analysis, such as regression, in complex cases when several

EXHIBIT 5

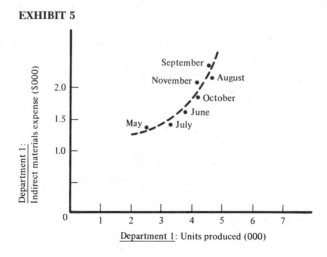

types of activities cause a cost to fluctuate. However, a simple visual plot is an excellent aid in understanding cost behavior.

5. Verify the relationship with operating personnel. Find out whether conditions are changing and whether the data used to make the estimate are valid.

6. To the extent possible, verify the relationship with experience in comparable divisions and/or companies. This provides an external check on what the relationship *should be.* Sources of data on other companies include trade journals, consultants, and employees who were hired from other companies. Obviously, interdivisional and interorganizational comparisons are only as valid as the similarity of the units being compared.

7. Determine what changes are expected for the budget period. Will new equipment replace old? How will that affect the estimate? What price changes are anticipated?

8. Armed with this information, you are in a position to estimate the relationship between costs and activity levels. Of course, the amount of time and effort spent on each step should be based on your priority list. Top priority items may get considerable attention, while those at the bottom of the list may be virtually ignored.

Over time it is easy to develop some shortcuts. Some relationships are stable and can be budgeted with ease. For example, the ratio of supervisors to line personnel may remain approximately the same over time (as a step function). It may be necessary only to determine supervisors' salary changes from period to period.

On the other hand, some costs may require special attention in every budget period. For example, past experience with repairs and volume may not indicate what current repairs should be for current volume.

Summary

We have mentioned several technical problems in estimating cost-activity relationships. These include, but are not limited to, the following.

1. Determining what activity *causes* costs.
2. Determining which costs are really caused by the activity

and which activities are caused by output. For example, many costs and activities are really at management's discretion rather than directly traceable to production.
3. Matching the time period of the activity to the time period in which the cost was incurred.
4. Estimating the relationship between the activity and costs.
5. Determining the range over which the estimated relationships are valid.

It is impossible to solve all of these problems. For some costs, it may be impossible to solve any! While we recognize that no system is perfect, the success of a flexible budgeting system is directly related to the resolution of these problems.

BEHAVIORAL ISSUES IN FLEXIBLE BUDGETING

Earlier we drew the analogy between an architect and an accountant. Both architects and accountants are concerned with designing structures and systems which are meant to serve human needs. Sometimes we accountants, like architects, can become so involved in the technical niceties of the systems we are designing, that we overlook the people who will be using them. In short, accountants, like architects, should not look upon human beings as unsolicited intruders on magnificent technical systems. It should not be forgotten that these technical systems have no meaning by themselves. Rather, they are designed to serve managers, employees, and outsiders in making decisions and evaluating performance.

In this section, we address some of the behavioral issues frequently encountered in developing and using flexible budgets. We do not attempt the ambitious and foreboding task of addressing all behavioral issues that arise in using budgets. Rather, we merely wish to create a sensitivity to frequent behavioral problems. Specifically, we address the following issues:

1. *Understandable.* Are the budget and performance reports understandable to both operating personnel and top management?
2. *Acceptance.* Are the principles and concepts underlying flexible budgeting accepted by operating personnel? Do attitudes about the budget have to be changed?

3. *Information.* Do operating personnel believe they have nothing to lose by providing information about their operations? Do they understand the benefits they will derive by using a flexible budgeting system?

4. *Participation.* Do operating personnel have a chance to participate in the budgeting process? Are their ideas used in developing budgets and standards? Is the budget developed from the bottom up in the organization, or is it imposed from the top down?

5. *Rewards.* Are performance measures tied to rewards? Are there payoffs to employees who meet standards or make the budget? Are there penalties for those who don't? If there is a link between performance and rewards, has it been communicated to employees?

6. *Controllable.* Are employees being evaluated on activities they can control and influence?

It has been our experience that seemingly good ideas have not been effective because they have been resisted by the people who have had to implement them. Unless the behavioral issues that follow are dealt with, no budgeting system, flexible or other, will be effective.

Understandable

The system must be understandable to the operating personnel who use it. Consequently, when a department works on several products *input measures* of activity, like machine time or labor time, are often used instead of *output measures* such as equivalent units of production. In some organizations, especially service providers such as CPA and law firms, an input measure like labor time is used as the basic measure of output. There is no universal rule that applies, however. The best approach is to determine how operating personnel measure how much work they are doing.

Acceptance

Most new systems meet with considerable resistance in the best of circumstances. Employees see them as being burdensome and requiring additional work, at the least. Often new budgeting systems are also seen as attempts by top management to get additional work out of them. For effective implementation, employees must be convinced that they have more to gain from the system than they have to lose. In the case of flexible budgeting, this may not be a major problem. In particular, employees who are averse to risk often prefer flexible budgets to static budgets. The following example demonstrates this.

Let's assume that the manager of the Repairs Department is given a budget of $100,000 for December. It turns out that machine time is low in December, and repairs can be easily scheduled without overtime. As a result, the manager spends only $90,000 of the budget. However, suppose production increases during the month of January, and department personnel are working overtime to make the necessary repairs. Expenditures for the Repairs Department are $110,000 in January.

Let's assume the manager of the Repairs Department believes performance is evaluated on the basis of meeting the budget. Thus, the manager's bonus, raises, promotions, and job could depend on meeting the budget. A manager who is averse to risk will prefer a system which adjusts the budget down to $90,000 in December, and up to $110,000 in January, to reflect the changing levels of production, even though the average results for the two months are the same. Further, most operating personnel would see the flexible budget as more equitable in the situation described.

The flexible budgeting approach should help make a profit when sales are low, as well as when sales are high. However, operating personnel may have to change their attitude and approach substantially. For example, operating managers often focus on production, assuming that whatever is produced will be sold. This attitude can result in needless costs if overtime is used or if repairs are required on an emergency basis in an effort to turn out as much product as possible.

Reducing allowances for costs like overtime and repairs when sales are down can help operating personnel to change their thinking and focus on reducing unnecessary costs. On the other hand, when sales are high and full capacity production is required, the flexible budget allows more liberal spending for items like repairs and overtime, so production is not needlessly cut back in an effort to cut costs.

In summary, there is a *trade-off between cost control and production.* Operating personnel should place relatively more emphasis on getting out the product when sales are high, and relatively more emphasis on cost control when sales are low. A properly designed flexible budget will incorporate this trade-off and help operating personnel adjust their emphasis to reflect changes in sales. This helps companies make money (or at least reduce losses) when times are bad as well as when times are good.

Information

Earlier in this chapter, we indicated the importance of getting unbiased information from operating personnel to make cost estimates and predictions. We stated that data from operating personnel are normally superior to historical data from the accounting records for determining current relationships between costs and activities. It is even more important to get information from operating personnel to assess the effects of proposed changes in production methods on cost relationships.

Unfortunately, many managers and accountants have had difficulty in obtaining unbiased information from operating personnel. Often it is not in operating personnel's best self-interest to provide unbiased information. For example, past experience with accounting and budgeting personnel may have resulted in tightening a standard which they thought was appropriate. Thus, they may overstate the expected cost of activities to build some slack into the system.

It is nearly impossible to verify these stated relationships before the fact. After-the-fact verifications are difficult because the data indicate what costs were for a level of activity, not what they should have been. For these reasons, it is important for accounting and budgeting personnel to develop a high level of credibility with operating personnel. Operating personnel must be assured (through experience) that any information they provide will be used to improve methods of evaluating performance and providing rewards, and that it will not always be used against them. They should be made aware that the information they provide will be combined with information from other sources, such as engineering studies, interdivisional comparisons, and intercompany comparisons, which help validate the information they provide. However, operating personnel should have the opportunity to critique other sources of information about operations.

In summary, operating personnel are an excellent source of information—if they don't believe it will be used against them. There are no guaranteed ways of assuring them that such is the case. However, an environment in which considerable trust exists between managers, operating personnel, and accounting personnel is conducive to a free flow of information.

Participation

The issues previously discussed—understandability, acceptance, and availability of trustworthy information—generally require participation by operating personnel in the development and use of the budget. Operating personnel are the best source of information for developing the budget. They see changes in cost relationships before these changes are reflected in the accounting records, and they are in the best position to explain the cause of variations from budget. These reasons alone indicate the need for participation by operating personnel in the budgeting process.

In addition, there is a substantial body of literature indicating that participating in setting budgets may increase motivation. These results are far from conclusive; however, it is becoming popular to involve lower level employees through management-by-objectives and bottoms-up-budgeting. Thus, employee participation may increase employee motivation as well as provide a valuable source of information.

A word of caution is in order before accepting the notion that participation is helpful in developing and using budgets. First, much depends on the existing relationships and lines of communication between operating personnel, accounting personnel, and management. Where there is a tradition of distrust and closed lines of communication, the introduction of an open system of communication, requiring trust and participation, may evoke suspicion. Second, the participation must be real; it must not be a facade. The value of participation in improving information flows and job performance lies in active participation, in which operating personnel have real input. Pseudo-participation in which operating personnel have no real input will be counter-productive.

In short, there are many organizations in which a free flow of trustworthy information simply is not available, and participation would be looked upon with suspicion. While the payoff from a flexible budgeting system is lower in these organizations, it is not negated. Accountants and budgeting personnel will be required to rely more heavily on other sources of information.

Rewards

It is possible that performance measures affect workers' job performance independent of rewards. Workers may perform better if they are being evaluated than if they are not being evaluated, even if their evaluation is not tied to rewards. However, performance evaluation is more likely to affect performance if it is tied to rewards for good performance and penalties for poor performance. Flexible budgeting is more likely to serve as a motivating tool if it is tied to rewards and penalties.

Of course, these rewards can take many forms. Just meeting the standard can be a rewarding experience, in itself. Feelings of self-satisfaction can come from good performance. If these feelings are reinforced with praise from superiors, then employees are likely to be motivated to work harder. This is an inexpensive way to provide employees with internal rewards for their performance.

Of course, there are many visible rewards that are provided by the organization as well. These include merit pay raises, promotions, bonuses, vacation time, expense accounts, secretarial and clerical support, rights to the executive cafeteria, and so forth.

In general, we assume that employees analyze their opportunities for rewards as shown in Exhibit 6. The employee has the greatest control over effort.[4] Effort may be seen as leading to performance, although other factors, like ability, also affect job performance. Performance may be seen as leading to rewards,

---

[4] Effort is defined here to include the *direction* of effort as well as the amount of effort. Greater performance may result from "working smart" then from "working hard."

EXHIBIT 6

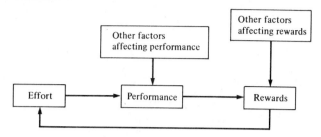

although other factors, like length of time on the job, also affect rewards.

The greatest motivating force is to insure that the employee sees a direct linkage between effort, performance, and rewards, and to insure that the rewards are those desired. Any breaks in the linkage, as evidenced by the employee who says "No matter how hard I work, I can't seem to do a good job," will thwart the motivating potential of performance measures and rewards.

To be effective, the relation between performance and rewards must be communicated to workers. We presume that workers are motivated when they see some payoff for their performance. Consequently, they must be informed of the relation between performance and rewards. Many employees may be under the impression that promotions and merit pay raises are related to the length of time on the job, rather than to their performance. "As long as I do enough so I'm not fired, I'll get my raises and promotions just like everyone else," is a common statement. An excellent way of nipping in the bud the idea that length of time on the job, not performance (as long as performance is above minimum acceptable level) is important, is to reward some workers more than others. A promotion of one high performing individual faster than a colleague who is not performing well is a clear signal of the importance of performance for rewards, *if* the reasons for the promotion are communicated.

In short, some workers are highly motivated and perform well regardless of performance evaluation methods. However, we assume that most workers look at the relation between effort, performance, and rewards, and are motivated to put forth effort to the extent that they see a benefit. Thus, employees are generally motivated to work harder if their performance is evaluated and rewarded (or penalized).

Flexible budgeting is an important tool in this scenario because it is a measure of performance that takes into account variations beyond the worker's control. Thus, the worker is not rewarded when external uncontrollables are better than expected, nor penalized when they are worse than expected.

Controllable

The linkage between effort (E), performance (P), and rewards (R) will be clear only if the employees' performance is evaluated on the basis of activities they control. Thus, rewards tied to corporate net income are not likely to motivate department managers, because there are so many factors outside of their control that affect corporate net income. On the other hand, basing rewards on an evaluation of departmental activities under a manager's control reinforces the $E \rightarrow P \rightarrow R$ relation and is much more likely to motivate employees.

Flexible budgeting is a helpful tool for evaluating performance on the basis of activities that employees can control. The principle of flexible budgeting is that a change in external factors is incorporated into the budget. For example, if production levels drop below budgeted levels because of an unexpected market decline, operating personnel are expected to reduce production costs accordingly; however, they are not held responsible for declines in plant or corporate net income because of the market decline.

Summary

Flexible budgeting has a number of major behavioral benefits. It can be used to communicate clear performance signals up and down the organization. Because it isolates the performance of an organizational unit, employee, or group of employees, it makes that unit responsible for only the activities it controls. This should increase acceptance of the entire budgeting scheme by employees, because they know that they are not held responsible for activities outside of their control. Further, this reinforces the $E \rightarrow P \rightarrow R$ relation because rewards can be tied directly to those activities on which employees have a major impact.

The topics we have discussed barely scratch the surface of behavioral issues to be faced when using any performance evaluation method, such as flexible budgeting, as a control tool. Nevertheless, we hope that the situations described have created a sensitivity to the impact of technical accounting and budgeting tools on the people involved. As we noted earlier, we must not view people as *intruders on* our systems, but as *users of* our systems.

PERFORMANCE REPORTING WITH FLEXIBLE BUDGETING

We noted earlier that flexible budgeting is only one dimension of budgeting: *budgeting for control.* In addition, *planning budgets* are developed which are typically static. Thus, performance should demonstrate the relation between the initial (planning) budget, the flexible (control) budget, and actual, as shown in Exhibits 7, 8, and 9.

The performance report in Exhibit 8 isolates major causes of the deviation from plan. Decreases in selling price account for $1,800,000 unfavorable variance, offset by a $90,000 reduction in sales commission, for a net effect of $1,710,000, unfavorable. The decline in sales volume reduced revenue by $1,200,000, offset by a reduction of $800,000 in standard cost of sales and a $60,000 reduction in sales commissions. Production declines resulted in $500,000 unfavorable manufacturing volume variance. These volume variances net to $840,000 unfavorable. On the other hand, operating personnel could be credited for favorable variances totaling $1,050,000.

Exhibit 8 demonstrates the effect of each variance category on the planned income statement. The flexible budget column shows the results of operations if there had been no input variances, while the column labeled "budget, adjusted for selling price variances" shows operating results if there had been no input *nor* volume variances. Management often is less concerned about the impact of each variance on the income statement than about the source of the total variance. If so, the information contained in the report in Exhibit 8 can be simplified as shown

498

EXHIBIT 7

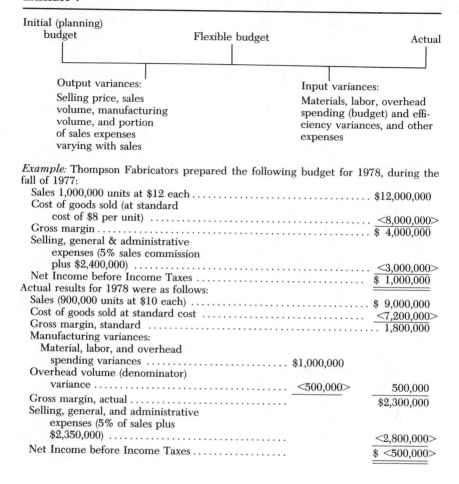

Initial (planning) budget — Flexible budget — Actual

Output variances:
Selling price, sales volume, manufacturing volume, and portion of sales expenses varying with sales

Input variances:
Materials, labor, overhead spending (budget) and efficiency variances, and other expenses

Example: Thompson Fabricators prepared the following budget for 1978, during the fall of 1977:

Sales 1,000,000 units at $12 each	$12,000,000
Cost of goods sold (at standard cost of $8 per unit)	<8,000,000>
Gross margin	$ 4,000,000
Selling, general & administrative expenses (5% sales commission plus $2,400,000)	<3,000,000>
Net Income before Income Taxes	$ 1,000,000

Actual results for 1978 were as follows:

Sales (900,000 units at $10 each)		$ 9,000,000
Cost of goods sold at standard cost		<7,200,000>
Gross margin, standard		1,800,000
Manufacturing variances:		
Material, labor, and overhead spending variances	$1,000,000	
Overhead volume (denominator) variance	<500,000>	500,000
Gross margin, actual		$2,300,000
Selling, general, and administrative expenses (5% of sales plus $2,350,000)		<2,800,000>
Net Income before Income Taxes		$ <500,000>

in Exhibit 9. Additional information can be provided by showing an explanation for each variance and the department or division assigned responsibility for it.

The chart in Exhibit 9 lends itself to hierarchical reporting, as well. Some variation of the tree presented in Exhibit 9 may be sufficient for top management and the board of directors. A marketing vice president would want more detailed branches extending from the gross margin and SGA branches, while production managers would prefer more data on manufacturing variances. At each lower level in the organization, the tree becomes more and more detailed. Maximum flexibility in reporting

EXHIBIT 8

THOMPSON FABRICATORS
Operating Performance Report
(in $000)

	Initial (planning) budget	Output variances			Input variances		
		Selling price variances	Budget, adjusted for selling price variances	Volume (activity) variances	Flexible budget	Spending and efficiency variances	Actual
Sales	$12,000	$<1,800>*	$10,200	$<1,200>*	$ 9,000	–	$9,000
Cost of sales at standard cost	<8,000>	–	<8,000>	800†	<7,200>	–	<7,200>
Gross margin, after standard cost of sales	$ 4,000	$<1,800>*	$ 2,200	$ <400>*	$ 1,800	–	$1,800
Manufacturing variances	–	–	–	<500>*	<500>	1,000†	500
Gross margin, actual	$ 4,000	$<1,800>*	$ 2,200	$ <900>*	$ 1,300	$1,000†	$2,300
Selling, general & admin. exp.	<3,000>	90 †	<2,910>	60 †	<2,850>	50†	<2,800>
Net Income before Income Taxes	$ 1,000	$<1,710>*	$ <710>	$ <840>*	$<1,550>	$1,050†	$ <500>

* = unfavorable variance.
† = favorable variance.

EXHIBIT 9
Summary of variances, Thompson Fabricators ($000)

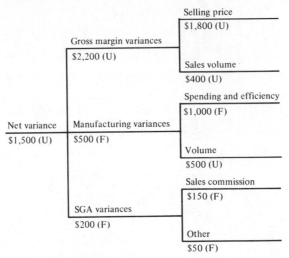

U = unfavorable variance.
F = favorable variance.

variances is thus achieved by using a simple format like that presented in Exhibit 9.

SUMMARY

In this chapter, we have discussed the concept of flexible budgeting and technical and behavioral difficulties in applying the concept, and we have presented some ways to report performance by using flexible budgeting.

The concept of flexible budgeting is relatively simple. We recognize that the budget developed for planning purposes may not suffice as a control tool. For control purposes, the flexible budget is developed taking into account external factors which have affected sales and production volume. Thus, operating personnel are allowed a budget based on actual volume rather than on planned volume.

While the concept of flexible budgeting is simple, the application is difficult. To develop a budget which varies with volume, budgeting personnel must know which costs *should* vary with volume, as well as *how* these costs should vary. Overhead costs cause particular problems because a causal relationship between activity and costs is often difficult to find and measure for a short time period. Many costs are discretionary, while others may seem to vary inversely with volume (for example, repairs and maintenance).

We have argued that flexible budgeting is primarily a tool for performance evaluation and control. Thus, the acid test of its benefits lies in its impact on people and their use of it. Although flexible budgets have a multidimensional impact on individuals, we believe that particular attention should be paid to their impact on the following perceived relation between effort (including both direction and amount of effort), performance, and rewards:

$$E(\text{effort}) \rightarrow P(\text{performance}) \rightarrow R(\text{rewards})$$

Using the flexible budget to isolate those things which are controllable by employees strengthens the belief that *their* efforts and actions have an impact on performance.

Finally, use of a flexible budget requires performance reporting which isolates the source of variances and demonstrates their impact on the original plan. Firms that use flexible budgets sometimes compare only the flexible budget with actual results. We recommend reporting the initial plan, or static budget, as well.

Despite the technical difficulty of relating costs to volume, many firms have found that the benefits in employee performance evaluation, control, and motivation outweigh the costs of implementing and using the system.

19

Structure and content of cost reports

*James M. Fremgen**
Martin V. Alonzo†

No matter how well designed and carefully implemented a cost accounting system may be, it will be ineffectual unless it results in the preparation of reliable, timely, and understandable reports containing information relevant to the needs of the people to whom the reports are addressed. Good reports are the absolutely essential media by which raw cost data are transformed into useful information and communicated to those who need it. Thus, cost reports are properly regarded as the crucial final step in any cost accounting system. Unfortunately, there are no simple reporting rules that are applicable in all cases. To a large extent, the structure and content of cost reports are matters that must be determined by each individual organization to suit its own particular needs. However, it is possible to identify some general guidelines that should be helpful in the design and preparation of reports.

The primary consideration in the design of the format and in the selection of the content of a report is the *purpose* for which the report will be used. Of course, a single report may serve two or more purposes. In general, however, it is both

* Professor, Naval Postgraduate School.

† Vice President and Controller, AMAX, Inc.

valid and useful to classify cost reports in the following three broad categories:

1. *Product or project costing reports,* designed to answer the question, "What did it cost?" These have also been described as scorekeeping reports.
2. *Control reports,* designed to answer the question, "How well did we do in relation to some established standard of performance?" These have been referred to as attention-directing reports.
3. *Special reports for decision making,* designed to answer the question, "What are the consequences of the alternative choices?" These are problem solving reports.

Much of the discussion in this chapter is developed around these three types of reports.

A very important secondary consideration in the design of reports is the *audience,* or intended users of the reports. The level of detail contained in a report depends largely upon the particular persons expected to use it. For example, it is commonly assumed that outside parties are interested in less detail than the management of an organization. Similarly, top management may not want as much detail about specific operations as the lower managers who have direct responsibility for those operations. The frequency and promptness of reports also depend upon the audience, as well as upon the purposes for which the reports are prepared. Control reports, for example, are usually submitted more frequently and more promptly to first-line managers than to their superiors in top management. Further, there is usually a relationship between the frequency and the timing of reports. A daily report of labor costs to a department supervisor, for example, should be submitted at the beginning of the very next day. A monthly report of total department costs to the plant manager, on the other hand, can usually be deferred for several days after the end of the month without causing problems. Similarly, a special report analyzing the cost effects of alternative decisions would seldom have a tight deadline. While significant decisions must be made on a timely basis, they are rarely forced into a tight schedule on short notice. Indeed, it is usually essential that time be allowed for adequate analysis to support cost reports for decision making. Without such analysis, the reports will be less reliable, if not altogether useless.

The remainder of this chapter discusses cost reports in the three basic categories described above—product costing reports, control reports, and special reports for decision making. Several illustrations of report content and format are presented. These may not be interpreted as standard report forms, of course. They are simply models that may provide guidance in the design of forms in a particular organization. Within an organization there are substantial advantages to standardized report forms. Among different organizations, however, standardization is unimportant—except when reports are distributed to outsiders who are likely to make comparisons among the firms.

PRODUCT COSTING REPORTS

Among the most familiar of cost reports are those that indicate the actual costs incurred to produce some product or group of products or to complete some other project. Such reports are essentially historical statements of what some specified output did cost. As such, they are useful for purposes of preparing financial statements in which the cost of inventory on hand and the cost of goods sold must be reported. In addition, they may be used for pricing contracts for custom-made products for which no market price is available. An important example of this latter use is in the pricing of negotiated defense procurement contracts. Of course, reports of actual costs may also be used by management for purposes of evaluating cost performance. This use implies the existence of some standard or criterion against which actual costs may be compared. Thus, it transforms the reports into control reports. These are discussed in the following section.

Statement of cost of goods manufactured and sold

Probably the most common example of a product costing report is the statement of cost of good manufactured and sold, which supports the income statement of a manufacturing firm. An illustration of this statement appears in Exhibit 1. The format of the statement in this exhibit is not standard, of course; and

EXHIBIT 1
Statement of cost of goods manufactured and sold

Current production costs:		
Direct materials	$15,000,000	
Direct labor	20,000,000	
Manufacturing overhead applied	12,000,000	$47,000,000
Add inventory of work in process,		
January 1, 19xx		3,000,000
		$50,000,000
Deduct inventory of work in process,		
December 31, 19xx		2,000,000
Cost of goods manufactured		$48,000,000
Add inventory of finished goods,		
January 1, 19xx		6,000,000
Cost of goods available for sale		$54,000,000
Deduct inventory of finished goods,		
December 31, 19xx		9,000,000
Cost of goods sold (normal)		$45,000,000
Add underapplied manufacturing overhead		1,000,000
Cost of goods sold (actual)		$46,000,000

different arrangements are often encountered. The format illustrated here does clearly show the total new manufacturing costs charged to production during the period and then explains how changes in inventories combine with those current costs to determine the cost of goods finished during the period, as well as the cost of the goods actually sold.

Cost classifications

The statement in Exhibit 1 classifies manufacturing costs in the three familiar categories, direct materials, direct labor, and overhead. While this classification scheme is conventional, it is not necessarily the only one that might be used. Cost classifications should meet management's needs for information. These needs may vary considerably among organizations. Even within a single organization, they may vary with the levels of management to which reports are directed and with the purposes for which the reports will be used.

To begin with, further breakdowns of the three basic cost categories are possible. As an example of such a breakdown, the Department of Defense requires contractors to subclassify direct materials into purchased parts, subcontract items, raw materials, standard commerical items, and internal transfers. Direct labor is subdivided into engineering and manufacturing labor. Overhead is broken down into costs associated with materials, engineering, and manufacturing. This fairly extensive set of cost classifications is based upon the government's concern for identifying and controlling costs on contracts whose prices will be based on those costs. A firm that sells its products to commercial customers at established market prices might perceive no similar need for so many cost classifications. In addition, the detailed breakdowns of costs may depend upon the level of management to which reports are directed. For example, top management may be satisfied with the three major categories of direct materials, direct labor, and overhead. Department management, on the other hand, may find it useful to have further breakdowns by types of materials, classes of labor, and individual items of overhead.

Companies using direct costing (see Chapter 25) must subclassify manufacturing costs separately as variable and fixed, for only the variable costs are included in the cost of goods manufactured and sold. Other firms may also elect to use this classification of costs, even though it is not essential to their cost accounting system. And, of course, costs may be classified according to the departments or cost centers in which they were incurred.

Unit cost data

The statement of cost of goods manufactured and sold is a summary report of manufacturing costs for a period. As such, it normally includes no details regarding individual products; nor does it indicate physical data on the numbers of units of products manufactured or their unit costs. Naturally, management is interested in production costs by products and in unit costs as well as totals. Further, unit cost data by products are essential to support the inventory values and the cost of goods sold reported in published financial statements. Hence, product costing reports must be sufficiently comprehensive to show total costs charged to specific products, quantities of those products, and the resultant unit costs. Usually, such reports are prepared for discrete batches of production in a job order cost accounting system and for the total production of a single department during some time period in a process cost accounting system. Both of these types of systems are discussed below.

Job order cost reports

Reports of product costs in job order systems are usually in the form of job order cost sheets for individual orders and summaries of those sheets for reporting periods. Each job order cost sheet should include at least the following data: total materials costs by major categories, direct labor costs by departments in which they were incurred, overhead applied by departments, units produced on the job, and total unit cost. Obviously, management will want certain other information on the job cost sheet, such as the purpose of the units produced on the job (for a customer or for stock) and the dates on which the job was started and completed. Moreover, considerable expansion of the cost data may be desirable. For example, labor costs may be subclassified by specific functions within departments; and unit costs may be broken down by cost categories.

Job order cost sheets are the primary product costing reports in this system. They will typically be reviewed by production managers and by marketing managers when goods are produced to customers' orders or when prices are based on unit costs. Top management, however, is more likely to want summaries of job order cost sheets for reporting periods, except in unusual cases in which special attention to individual jobs is warranted. Such summaries may show nothing more than total costs and unit costs by products. Alternatively, management may wish to see breakdowns by departments as well.

Process cost reports

In the typical process cost accounting system, costs are initially accumulated within departments, processes, or costs centers for specified periods of time. These costs are then allocated among the units of product produced in the departments during the periods. Separate identification of direct materials, direct labor, and manufacturing overhead is typical; and further breakdowns may be made as desired. Presentation of units of production during each period is commonly complicated by the facts that equivalent units are used to determine unit costs and that different quantities of equivalent units may be applicable to direct materials, to direct labor, and to overhead. Moreover, these equivalent units are probably not the same number of units completed and transferred out of the department during the period.

Thus, a complete presentation of equivalent units pertinent to each category of cost, to units completed, and to units still in process at the end of the period would be fairly complicated and might be more confusing than helpful to the readers of the report. Consequently, the most useful process cost report would seem to be one that shows only full (not equivalent) units of production along with total costs and unit costs by cost element. An example of such a report appears in Exhibit 2. The important features of this illustration are the data that it contains, not the arrangement of those data. The report accounts fully for all units put into production and for all costs charged to the department. It provides the information that would be required for summary journal entries charging costs to the department during the period and crediting the department for the

EXHIBIT 2
Process cost accounting report

	Total costs	Unit cost
Unit production statistics:		
In process at beginning of month	8,000	
Started into production during month	42,000	
	50,000	
Completed and transferred out	38,000	
Loss or shrinkage in processing	2,000	
In process at end of month	10,000	
	50,000	
Costs		
In process at beginning of month	$ 43,800	
Costs incurred currently:		
Direct materials	249,600	$ 6.40
Direct labor	200,200	5.20
Manufacturing overhead	150,150	3.90
	$643,750	$15.50
Completed and transferred out	$589,000	$15.50
In process at end of month	54,750	
	$643,750	

cost of completed production. It does not show any equivalent units, however, and, therefore, does not explain exactly how the unit costs were computed. As a practical matter, equivalent units are not likely to be of particular interest to management; and there is little practical alternative to reliance on the accuracy of the cost accountant's computation of unit costs or, indeed, of total costs. If questions are raised about the cost report, the underlying computations should be available on work sheets.

CONTROL REPORTS

In general, control reports present a comparison of actual costs with some standard or criterion for what costs should be. Unlike simple product costing reports, control reports present a critical view of cost performance. Thus, they provide the reader some basis for making a qualitative judgment about that performance. This is not to say that a comparison of actual costs with some standard for costs automatically indicates whether management's performance was good or bad. It does, however, provide a logical frame of reference within which management may make that judgment. There are four essential characteristics of a good control report, as follows:

1. The report should deal only with costs incurred in a single, defined responsibility center.
2. The report should distinguish clearly between costs which are controllable in that responsibility center and those costs which are uncontrollable there.
3. Reasonable and useful criteria must be used for purposes of comparison with actual costs.
4. The report should highlight variances between actual costs and the established criteria.

Each of these basic characteristics is discussed below.

Identification of the responsibility center

In product costing reports, the emphasis is on what was produced or accomplished as a consequence of the incurrence of costs. In control reports, the emphasis is on the manager(s) responsible for incurring the costs. Ultimately, cost control rests upon the personal responsibility of some manager. Systems and procedures facilitate control, but only people can actually control costs. Thus, control reports should focus on the points at which responsibility for cost control lies. These are called responsibility centers. A *responsibility center* is any segment of an organization for which a single manager or management group is clearly responsible. Responsibility centers frequently coincide with departments or other organizational units, but they may be product lines, sales territories, or any other segment for which distinct management responsibility has been established. In the typical medium-size or large organization, responsibility centers form a pyramid; and responsibility for costs cumulates as the level of management rises and narrows toward the top. For example, a factory department foreman is responsible for those costs directly traceable to his department. The factory superintendent is responsible for all such costs in all of the factory's departments, as well as for other factory costs not directly traceable to any single department. The vice president for manufacturing is then responsible for the total costs of all factories and for indirect manufacturing costs incurred in the corporate office. Finally, top management is responsible for all costs, manufacturing and others.

The nature of the responsibility for cost control is not the same at each successive higher level of responsibility. At the lowest level, the responsibility is direct and immediate. That manager should be able to take specific actions to control costs. At higher levels, cost control is implemented indirectly through supervision of lower-level managers and through the established management control system. It is difficult to reflect these differences in responsibility explicitly in the formats of cost reports, but the readers of those reports must understand exactly how each responsible manager can and does control the costs included in the reports.

Controllable and uncontrollable costs

Since the focus of control reports is on responsible personnel, it is essential that a clear distinction be made between costs controllable at the particular level of responsibility and costs that cannot be controlled at that level. Failure to make this distinction clearly may result in the reader of the report inferring responsibility for control of costs where no such responsibility actually lies. In practice, the distinction between controllable and uncontrollable costs at some level of responsibility is not always unambiguous. For example, a factory department foreman may be held responsible for the cost of raw materials used— to the extent that cost is determined by the quantities used. He or she would normally have no control over materials prices, however. Hence, if materials costs are included in the control report as controllable costs, it would be preferable if only budgeted or standard prices were used along with actual usage. If the company employs a standard cost system, such presentation should cause no difficulties. In other cases, however, it might require a discrimination between actual and standard prices that is not regularly incorporated in the cost accounting system.

An even more complex example of a cost whose controllability is not obvious is the repair and maintenance of equipment in a factory department. In most cases, the department foreman would have had no responsibility for the acquisition of the equipment. Thus, it might be argued that he or she should not be held responsible for controlling the basic maintenance costs that are required periodically, regardless of the amount of use of the equipment. However, if the foreman is considered responsible for the rate of utilization of the equipment and for the care with which it is used, all repair and maintenance cost in excess of the "basic" maintenance might be treated as a controllable cost. There may be problems in deciding what really constitutes "basic" maintenance, of course. And the difficulties are further compounded if the maintenance work is done by another department, whose prices and efficiency are beyond the control of the department foreman. Perhaps the best compromise in such a case would be to treat the fixed maintenance costs as uncontrollable at the department level and the variable costs as controllable. Further, if there is a standard or budgeted rate for variable maintenance cost, only that rate should be charged to the using department. Any differences between actual and budgeted rates would then be reported as variances in the maintenance department.

Separate reporting of variable and fixed costs.   In a company that uses direct costing, separate identification of variable and fixed costs is essential to the cost accounting system. Hence, separate reporting of these two classes of costs in control reports is a natural extension of that system. Even in a company that uses absorption costing, however, separate reporting of variable and fixed costs is possible. More importantly, it is useful to management. Knowing how costs behave as volume changes is essential for planning and control, even if it has no bearing on the method of costing inventories. Moreover, cost-volume relationships and cost controllability are often significantly related. There is a general tendency for variable costs to be controllable at relatively low levels of responsibility. Some fixed costs may also be controllable at lower levels, of course, but many of them can be controlled only by top management actions.

Allocations of uncontrollable costs. As was noted earlier, there are certain costs that are directly traceable to a particular organizational unit, and yet cannot be controlled by that unit's manager. Property taxes and insurance on equipment used exclusively in one department are examples. There are also indirect costs that benefit all departments but are not controllable by any department manager. For purposes of product costing, such indirect costs are commonly allocated among the departments on some rational basis. Nevertheless, the fact remains that the amounts of such costs are not affected by the operations of any single department. Should allocations of such indirect costs be included in control reports? The simple logic of cost control suggests that the answer to this question should be "No." The costs cannot be controlled by the department manager, and they would not be changed if the department were discontinued. There should be no question about the irrelevance of such indirect cost allocations for purposes of cost control. Nevertheless, some firms apparently believe that these allocations serve a useful educational purpose. That is, they help to remind the department manager that he or she is a part of a larger organization and is dependent upon other parts of it for certain important services. Hopefully, this awareness will develop a broader perspective in the department manager and help prepare him or her for higher management responsibilities later. Whether allocations really have this educational value and whether alternative methods would have the same effect are certainly arguable. The critical requirement is that, if allocated shares of indirect costs are included in control reports, they be clearly identified as such and the readers of the reports be fully informed as to the nature of the allocations and the fact that the department managers have no control over those costs.

Cost classifications in the report. The arrangement and identification of costs in Exhibit 3 illustrate the recommendations discussed above. The important features of this illustration are the cost classifications presented. The comparison of actual costs with the budget is included because it is typical of control reports, but it is not pertinent to the present discussion. (A more expansive version of this report format appears in Exhibit 4.) Inclusion of the operating volume in the report makes the separate identification of variable costs more meaningful. Actual and budgeted variable cost rates might also be included if management wanted them. Of course, each of the basic cost classifications would be broken down into as many distinct cost items as were considered appropriate in the particular organization.

The major distinction between cost classifications in Exhibit 3 is that between controllable and uncontrollable costs. This is appropriate in a control report, for the focus is on cost controllability. All other cost classifications are secondary here. The separate reporting of variable and fixed costs, for example, is very useful but not absolutely essential. Since cost controllability is the primary concern of the reader of this report, one might argue that the uncontrollable costs should not be included at all. Excluding them would certainly not impair the report as an indicator of cost performance by the responsible manager. Indeed, inclusion of the uncontrollable costs—and, particularly, inclusion of any variances for uncontrollable cost items—might

EXHIBIT 3
Cost classifications in control reports

	Actual costs	Budgeted costs	Variance
Operating volume:			
Direct labor hours			
Costs controllable by department manager:			
Variable costs			
Fixed costs			
Total controllable costs			
Costs uncontrollable in the department:			
Costs directly chargeable to department ...			
Allocated share of indirect costs			
Total uncontrollable costs			
Total costs................................			

cause some confusion if the true nature of these costs and any variances is not made very clear. (A method of handling variances from uncontrollable costs is illustrated in Exhibit 4.) Finally, it would be quite unusual if the "total costs" line were not included at the bottom of the report; but a very logical argument can be made to omit it. From the point of view of responsibility for cost control, the sum of controllable and uncontrollable costs is not really significant.

Criteria for comparison of actual costs

Control implies the existence of some predetermined criterion, norm, or standard for the quantity subject to control. Hence, cost control is meaningful only in relation to some criterion for what costs should be. This criterion may be external to the organizational unit whose costs are being reported, or it may be internal to that unit. Common examples of external criteria are cost performance in other departments within the same firm and costs incurred in other firms—perhaps the average costs for all firms in an industry. As a general rule, such external criteria are not very satisfactory bases for evaluating actual cost performance. Circumstances differ among departments of the same firm and differ even more among firms. Moreover, differences in accounting principles applied and changes in prices over time make interfirm comparisons extremely questionable. Even within a firm, differences in basic operations, in labor and equipment employed, and in locations tend to invalidate direct comparisons of costs among departments. Consequently, internal criteria are normally more appropriate and useful for management's appraisal of cost performance.

The two principal types of internal criteria are past cost performance in the same department and budgeted or standard costs for the department. Past cost data have the advantage of being readily available in prior periods' reports. Their use as a criterion for current cost performance, however, implies that past cost performance was good and that there have been no changes in circumstances that would make past costs irrelevant to current operations. Clearly, management cannot simply assume that past performance was satisfactory. Some evidence to that effect is needed, and such evidence would imply the existence of other criteria against which past costs could be evaluated. Similarly, changing circumstances mean that criteria must be changed to conform to them. Hence, as a practical matter, budgeted costs or standard costs are the most useful criteria for comparison with actual costs. Budgets and standards are never perfect, of course; and changes in conditions may invalidate what were once good budgets or standards. Nevertheless, budgets and standards focus on what costs should be in the particular department during the period in question. Further, it is often possible to make adjustments to them as circumstances change (e.g., to reflect price increases).

Variances in the report

Control reporting is based largely on the principle of management by exception. Management is most keenly interested in exceptions, or deviations from what conditions should be. With regard to costs, exceptions are usually called *variances.* Thus, variances are the most critical bits of information in control reports. They should be highlighted so that they are immediately apparent to the reader. There are many ways of doing this. Several are described and illustrated in the following paragraphs.

Tabular reports.   Undoubtedly, the most familiar type of accounting report for any purpose is the tabular report. This is simply a listing of pertinent financial quantities in some logical order, usually with one or more totals and frequently with some comparative data. The balance sheet, income statement, and statement of changes in financial position in the annual report are probably the most familiar examples of tabular reports. The illustration in Exhibit 3 was a tabular report. It was a very abbreviated example, of course. It did identify variances of actual costs from the budget, but it did not necessarily highlight those variances that constituted truly significant exceptions warranting management's attention. As was observed in the preceding section, budgets or standards are never perfect criteria for comparison with actual costs. Some variance may be expected for almost every cost item. Yet, not every variance is an exception worthy of management's attention. Thus, some predetermined threshold of materiality should be established to discriminate between significant and insignificant variances. Such a threshold might be expressed as a percentage of budgeted or standard cost (particularly in the case of a variable cost) or as an absolute dollar amount (particularly in the case of a fixed cost). Of course, the same percentage relationship is not necessarily appropriate for every variable cost item. What is a reasonable range within which a variance may occur before it is considered significant is a question that can be answered only for each different cost item in each firm. Exhibit 4 is an example of a tabular report that compares actual costs with the budget, identifies all variances between the two, and also separately details those variances that exceed some established threshold of materiality.

EXHIBIT 4
Departmental overhead cost variance report

	Actual cost	Budgeted cost	Total variance	Significant variances
Operating volume:				
Direct labor hours	90,000	90,000		
Costs controllable by department manager:				
Variable costs:				
Indirect materials	$ 18,600	$ 18,000	$ 600	
Repairs	66,800	72,000	(5,200)	
Labor-related costs	151,200	144,000	7,200	
Power	40,400	36,000	4,400	$ 4,400
	$277,000	$270,000	$ 7,000	$ 4,400
Fixed costs:				
Indirect labor	$ 88,000	$ 80,000	$ 8,000	$ 8,000
Labor-related costs	22,000	20,000	2,000	2,000
Heat and light	17,500	15,000	2,500	
	$127,500	$115,000	$12,500	$10,000
Total controllable costs	$404,500	$385,000	$19,500	$14,400
Costs uncontrollable in the department:				
Costs directly chargeable to department:				
Maintenance	$ 98,000	$100,000	$ (2,000)	
Supervision	42,000	40,000	2,000	
Depreciation	200,000	200,000		
Taxes and insurance	63,000	60,000	3,000	
	$403,000	$400,000	$ 3,000	
Allocated share of indirect costs:				
Plant supervision	$ 30,000	$ 30,000		
Plant occupancy	90,000	90,000		
Production control	15,000	15,000		
	$135,000	$135,000		
Total uncontrollable costs	$538,000	$535,000		
Total costs	$942,500	$920,000		

Thus, management's attention is drawn quickly to the three cost items for which significant variances are listed in the fourth column. This is not to say that all of the other cost data presented are of no interest. The reader can derive whatever information he or she wishes from the report. However, the critical variances that exceed predefined limits of tolerance stand out clearly in the report.

Note particularly the shaded areas in the lower right hand portion of Exhibit 4. This report is so structured that there can be no variances at all between the actual and budgeted allocations of indirect costs. Differences between actual and budgeted amounts of these allocated cost items should be reported only in the department(s) or cost center(s) in which they are originally incurred. The actual amounts allocated to other departments, then, should be exactly the same as the budgeted allocations. The manager of the department for which Exhibit 4 was prepared can do nothing whatever to control these indirect costs, and there is no reason to include any variances for them in this report of his or her department's performance. Similarly, the report format is designed to preclude any variance for the uncontrollable costs from being shown as significant. If the department manager cannot control a cost, then any difference between its actual and budgeted amounts is not significant at his or her level of responsibility.

Graphic reports. Another convenient device for highlighting variances in control reports is to present those reports in graphic format. Graphs can show relationships between actual and budgeted quantities very quickly and can be constructed so as to bring the reader's attention directly to the significant variances. They are not as good as tabular reports, however, in depicting precise dollar amounts. On the other hand, they are definitely better than tabular reports in depicting trends in key relationships over time. Exhibit 5 is an example of a graphic report of variances. It is a plot of actual materials usage in a department in relation to standard usage during one week. In this case, variances of up to 5 percent above or below standard usage have been determined to be normal and not worthy of management's attention. Accordingly, a range of 5 percent on each side of standard cost is shaded on the graph to indicate an area of acceptable performance. Only the actual materials usage that falls out-

EXHIBIT 5
Materials usage report (for week of October 10–14, 19xx)

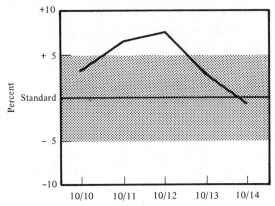

side of the shaded area is brought to the attention of the reader. Of course, the tolerable range may be set at whatever percentage (or other) relationship to standard management has decided is appropriate. Moreover, it need not be symmetrical, as is the one in Exhibit 5. The percentage variance above standard considered significant might be either more or less than the percentage variance below standard that is regarded as significant. In this particular illustration, it is quickly apparent that materials usage was out of control on October 11 and 12 but was brought back into the acceptable range of performance on the next day and then down to a very satisfactory level on the 14th.

As noted above, one of the advantages of the graphic format is that it facilitates comparisons of actual and planned, or standard, performance over time as well as at a single date. Such comparisons may be very useful to management, as long as the time period presented is not so long as to invalidate the basis for comparison. For example, if the materials usage report in Exhibit 5 were for five years instead of five days, both the standard usage and the tolerable range of variances might have changed because of technological developments or new operating practices.

An illustration of a graphic control report that would be particularly useful in evaluating performance on a major project is shown in Exhibit 6. This report compares the actual costs in-

EXHIBIT 6
Project cost/schedule report (as of November 30, 19xx)

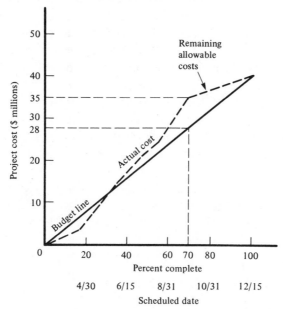

curred to date with the budgeted costs, and also the actual percentage of completion with the scheduled completion. To begin with, the budget line shows the expected costs at various stages of completion of the project. It also shows that total costs were initially budgeted at $40 million and that completion of the project was scheduled for December 15. On the horizontal axis of the graph, percentages of project completion are related to scheduled dates. The report reveals that actual cost was below the budgeted amount at the early stages of the project, but that costs have since increased significantly and now exceed the budget for the actual stage of completion. As of November 30, the date of the report, the project is 70 percent complete, and cumulative actual costs amount to $35 million. The graph then permits the following comparisons of actual and planned performances: The actual costs of $35 million exceed the budgeted costs of $28 million for the actual percentage of completion. According to the budget, total costs of $35 million should not have been incurred until the project was about 88 percent complete, and it is now only 70 percent finished. Finally, the 70 percent completion point was planned for some time prior to October 31, and it has been reached more than a month late. The dashed line connecting the total actual costs to date with the total budgeted costs at 100 percent completion (remaining allowable costs) indicates the reduced rate of spending that would be necessary if the project were yet to be completed within its budget. In this illustration, of course, management might well interpret that line as actually indicative of how improbable completion at the budgeted amount is. Obviously, management will need further information to determine why costs are over the budget and why the project is behind schedule. This single report, however, briefly and simply depicts the project's status. With this information in hand, management can decide how much further, if at all, it wishes to pursue this particular project's performance.

SPECIAL REPORTS FOR DECISION MAKING

Special reports for management's use in considering decision alternatives may be among the most important products of the cost accountant. They are not prepared regularly or frequently, but they may significantly influence the way in which crucial and costly decisions are made. Unfortunately, they are the most difficult type of report for which to specify structure and content. Both depend upon the nature of the decision at hand and also upon the preferences of management. Cost data relevant to decision making cannot be identified in advance of the decision problem and reported in a routine format. The exact dimensions of each different decision problem determine the relevant data. And different managers may prefer to see those relevant data arrayed in different formats. There is no reason not to honor such preferences, for decision reports are entirely for the benefit of the individual firm's management. To the extent that management does not express any preference in regard to format, the accountant has the opportunity of demonstrating his own ability at creating useful report forms. The best general guidance here is to present reports that highlight the major cost items that will be affected by the decision and that clearly show the net financial effect of the decision.

Report format

In general, reports for decision making may take either of two basic formats. They may present the complete expected results of operations, both with and without implementation of the proposed decision. Alternatively, they may present only those financial variables that will be different depending upon how the decision is made. These two alternatives may best be visualized by means of an illustration. The parts plant of a small electrical equipment manufacturer currently makes general-purpose components from the basic parts. Recently, one of its principal suppliers has advised the company that it could provide partially assembled subcomponents rather than unassembled parts. Such an arrangement would, of course, increase the company's materials costs; but it would also reduce labor and other processing costs. The decision is whether to continue to purchase parts and manufacture components, or to purchase partially assembled subcomponents and finish them in the plant. Following is a summary of the parts plant's monthly costs under the present method of operation:

Direct materials		$100,000
Direct labor		300,000
Manufacturing overhead:		
Supervision	$25,000	
Labor-related costs	65,000	
Supplies	15,000	
Repair and maintenance	25,000	
Power and light	5,000	
Taxes and insurance	5,000	
Depreciation	20,000	160,000
		$560,000

If the subcomponents were purchased, direct materials costs would increase by $140,000. However, direct labor would be reduced by $90,000, and the following decreases would occur in manufacturing overhead costs:

Supervision	$ 5,000
Labor-related costs	19,000
Supplies	3,000
Power and light	1,000

The financial effects of the decision proposed here may be presented in either of two ways. One way is to compare the

EXHIBIT 7
Gross comparison of decision alternatives

	Present operations: Manufacture subcomponents	Proposed operations: Purchase subcomponents	Difference
Direct materials costs	$100,000	$240,000	$140,000
Direct labor costs	300,000	210,000	(90,000)
Manufacturing overhead:			
Supervision	25,000	20,000	(5,000)
Labor-related costs	65,000	46,000	(19,000)
Supplies	15,000	12,000	(3,000)
Repair and maintenance	25,000	25,000	
Power and light	5,000	4,000	(1,000)
Taxes and insurance	5,000	5,000	
Depreciation	20,000	20,000	
Total operating costs	$560,000	$582,000	$ 22,000

total costs of the parts plant under the present operations with the total costs of operations if partially assembled subcomponents are purchased. This method may be referred to as a *gross comparison* of the alternative. It is illustrated in Exhibit 7. The report presented here shows that purchasing the subcomponents would cost more than continuing to manufacture them. Thus, it would be an unprofitable decision. Total operating costs would be increased by $22,000, and profit would be reduced by that amount.

The second method of presenting the costs relevant to this decision is to show only those amounts of costs that will be different depending upon how the decision is made. This may be called an *incremental analysis* of the decision. It is illustrated in Exhibit 8. Essentially, this report contains only the differences in costs that are shown in the last column of Exhibit 7. Thus, it presents exactly the same net result as the previous illustration; but it is more compact and focuses management's attention only on the things that will change if the decision to purchase the subcomponents is made. The gross comparison of the alternatives includes cost items that will not be affected by the decision. For example, it lists the costs of repair and maintenance, taxes and insurance, and depreciation, even though these three items will be exactly the same no matter which alternative is chosen. Similarly, it includes the total costs of the other items, including

EXHIBIT 8
Incremental analysis of decision

Increase in direct materials costs		$140,000
Less decreases in operating costs:		
Direct labor	$90,000	
Supervision.................................	5,000	
Labor-related costs..........................	19,000	
Supplies	3,000	
Power and light	1,000	118,000
Net increase in production costs		$ 22,000

those portions that will not be changed by the decision. Thus, some managers may prefer the incremental analysis for its direct and exclusive attention to the relevant decision variables. Others may choose the gross comparison because it permits them to evaluate the relevant variables (the differences) in relation to present operations. For example, the net increase in costs is approximately 4 percent of the total present costs. Further, management may prefer one format for certain types of decisions and the other for other decisions. For example, the gross comparison of the alternatives might be useful in comparing major operating alternatives, such as the total operating costs of two potential new plant sites, when only one will be chosen. On the other hand, the incremental analysis may be preferred for decisions that would involve only small changes in current operations (e.g., make or buy choices, such as the one illustrated here). In any case, the choice of formats of decision reports is one for management to make in each organization and, perhaps, in each different decision situation.

Inclusion of underlying computations

A question that might arise in connection with special reports for decision making is whether they should include only the financial results of the analysis, or also include the underlying data and computations that led to the results. Probably the best guidance here is to limit the formal report to the final financial figures and to keep well-organized and clearly labeled working papers in the event that management wishes to examine them. Presumably, managers will not ordinarily be interested in the underlying analysis, unless they have some reason to question the results. If the mechanics of the computations are included in the report, they are more likely to distract the reader than to provide information that will really help in making the decision. For example, a report summarizing the results of an analysis of a proposed capital investment (see Chapter 33) should include both the estimated cash flows and their present values or the internal rate of return. However, there is no need for it to detail the mechanics of discounting that led to those present value figures or to the rate of return.

CONCLUSION

The main theme of this chapter has been that cost reports must be designed with the purposes of their users in mind. Management needs cost information for various purposes. Reports should be so structured as to present the relevant information in a format that is readily comprehensible in terms of the particular purposes of the individual reports. Product costing reports should focus on the costs charged to production and/or to individual products. Control reports should emphasize significant variances between actual costs and predefined criteria for costs within designated responsibility centers. Reports for decision making should direct management's attention to the financial implications of proposed decisions. Finally, all cost reports should be both clear and concise. It is very important to keep in mind that to be concise is to be both complete and brief. Brevity alone is not desirable if important facts are omitted or obscured. Nor is completeness a justification for a tediously long report. A multipage computer printout may contain all of the information management needs for some purpose. It is not an effective report, however, until management actually reads it. Few managers have the time to dig out the relevant facts from such a printout. Not every report can be complete on a single sheet of paper, but most reports can be. It is a good target to aim for.

PART
FIVE

*Cost accounting and
control systems for
manufacturers*

20

Historical cost systems: Job order and process

Larry H. Beard*
Leslie G. Schek†

BENEFITS OF COST ACCOUNTING SYSTEMS

Cost accounting systems utilizing actual or historical cost data are usually classified as "job order" or "process." They differ from financial accounting systems primarily in scope and emphasis. Each cost system utilized within an organization is a component of the overall accounting system; each is specifically designed to provide a greater amount of information regarding the cost of a given product or service. Job order and process cost systems are expansions of financial accounting systems to generate additional information. Therefore, this additional information must survive a rigorous cost/benefit analysis in order to ensure that the costs incurred in implementing and maintaining the expanded system are outweighed by the benefits.

The *benefits* which may be derived from job order and process cost information are threefold:

1. An improved capability to measure and evaluate the historical performance of operating divisions, product lines, functional departments, and management personnel within the

* Associate Professor, College of Business Administration, University of South Carolina.

† Senior Vice President—Administration and Finance, Noxell Corporation.

organization (the stewardship and accountability function).
2. An ability to control current operations by detecting and analyzing deviations from historical trends in cost patterns.
3. An enhanced ability to plan for and to implement future activities of the organization.

Although historical quantities and prices for units, activities, departments, and/or cost elements may be integral components of a cost accounting data base, the benefits are obtained only by using the information to make better decisions regarding current or future evaluation, control, or planning activities.

JOB ORDER VERSUS PROCESS COST SYSTEMS

Product costs may be obtained by either job order or process costing procedures. In *job order* shops, costs are accumulated by individual jobs, and unit costs may be determined by dividing the number of units into the total costs assigned to the job. *Cost centers* (i.e., the smallest activity or area in which costs are assigned) or *time periods* may be employed to accumulate costs to be allocated to jobs; but they are at best secondary considerations. *Process costing* collects costs incurred within a given cost center for a certain period of time. Unit costs are computed by dividing the total costs by the units passing through the cost center during the time period.

Job order costing is generally used where the products or services are expected to be unique or dissimilar, while *process costing* procedures are more frequently found in organizations where products or services are homogeneous. Nevertheless, either job order costing or process costing may be used in virtually any situation if appropriate jobs, cost centers, and/or time periods are defined, and under appropriate conditions the two costing approaches may be used at various stages in the manufacture of a single product.

Job order and process costing systems provide information not only about the costs of individual jobs, units, and cost centers; they also provide specific data regarding the cost elements contained within, or consumed by, the products or services. Previous chapters have described accounting procedures for the cost elements of direct material, direct labor, and overhead; therefore, we will point out only that the direct material and direct labor elements are traceable directly to the product or service. All other items are considered to be overhead, and they are usually estimated and applied to the jobs or cost centers to reflect the total costs incurred. Actual overhead costs are sometimes accumulated in a cost center and assigned directly to the product or service under a process costing procedure. When estimated costs are applied, the over- or underapplied variances may either be deferred or charged to income, depending upon the cause of the variance.

Job order and process cost systems are applicable to manufacturing, merchandising, and service organizations; however, cost accounting techniques are illustrated more completely by manufacturers since these companies utilize raw material, work-in-process, and finished goods inventory accounts.

Assembly cost systems employ preassembled parts and subassemblies in the production process instead of, or in addition to, raw materials. They require a relatively small conceptual modification of basic job order or process costing procedures. Assembly cost systems will not be discussed specifically, but one may readily visualize how the quantity and cost of these preassembled components and transferred subassemblies may be substituted for the quantity and cost of raw material inputs in subsequent explanations.

OVERHEAD APPLIED IS AN ESTIMATE

The actual amount of direct material and direct labor consumed in the production of a product or service can normally be determined at the time of usage. Direct material requisitions, excess material requisitions, job or departmental time tickets, time cards, and various other documents furnish this information. The actual overhead, however, is not usually known until after the financial records have been summarized for the period. In order to charge overhead costs to job sheets or cost centers, even though the actual overhead dollars may as yet not have been ascertained, an estimated overhead application rate is calculated.

The total overhead costs must be estimated prior to the beginning of a given accounting period. The overhead elements might include such items as utilities, depreciation, property taxes, indirect materials and labor, as well as many others. This estimate of costs will become the numerator of the overhead application ratio. The denominator or base of the ratio must also be carefully selected and estimated. Any measurable variable may be chosen for the base since its function is exclusively to facilitate the assignment of overhead costs to the jobs or cost centers in the forthcoming period. Examples of variables which have proven effective are direct labor dollars, direct labor hours, machine hours, units produced, consumed or extracted, or customers serviced.

The primary factor that should be considered in the selection of a base variable or denominator for the overhead application ratio is whether the variable can predict changes in overhead cost incurrence. Ideally a cause and effect relationship will exist between increases or decreases in the actual activity of the base variable and corresponding changes in total overhead costs; however, a clear cause and effect relationship is usually difficult to discern. In order to determine the most appropriate base variable, various techniques such as scatter diagrams or alternative types of trend analyses may facilitate the selection process, but certain general guidelines may also aid in a manager's selection. Direct labor costs may be a valid predictor if a significant proportion of overhead costs are payroll-related fringe benefits or if the more highly paid direct labor employees utilize the expensive equipment which generates a major portion of overhead. Direct labor hours are usually a good predictive variable if overhead is sensitive to the amount of time that direct labor employees spend on a product, and machine-hours may be effective if the operation is highly mechanized with overhead costs consisting primarily of items such as depreciation, power, taxes, or equipment maintenance and rental fees. Guidelines for selecting other base variables may be posited by examining the underlying relationships that exist in individual circumstances.

When the base variable has been chosen, the estimate of the volume anticipated is made. The result of the ratio shown below is the overhead application rate for the period covered by the estimate.

$$\frac{\text{Estimated overhead dollars}}{\text{Estimated activity of base variable}} = \frac{\text{Overhead}}{\text{application}}\ \text{rate}$$

Assume that on December 31 a company projects that it will incur $100,000 in factory overhead during the next year. Also assume that direct labor dollars have been chosen as the base for applying factory overhead to units of product, and that $200,000 of direct labor will be required to maintain the level of production expected. The overhead application rate is therefore $.50 per direct labor dollar ($100,000/$200,000). The rate of $0.50 will be utilized to estimate the overhead element in either jobs or cost centers during the subsequent period. Once the rate has been computed, the estimates of total overhead dollars and direct labor dollars (base variable) are not utilized. Their function has been completed in generating the rate itself. The overhead applied to each job or cost center will be the product of the estimated overhead rate multiplied by the *actual* direct labor dollars (base variable) expended. If, at the end of the following period, the company determines that the estimated overhead which has been applied to the jobs or activities is not equal to the actual overhead incurred, the records must be corrected. The variance may be caused by either actual expenses or actual units of activity differing from the estimates used to calculate the application rate. A discussion of how this adjustment is made will be reserved for a later section of this chapter. At this point it is conceptually sufficient to recognize that the estimated overhead dollars included in the cost of jobs or cost centers ultimately must be increased or decreased to correspond with the actual overhead.

JOB ORDER SYSTEMS

The primary document utilized in most job order costing procedures is the *job cost sheet* (see Exhibit 1). When updated for the amounts of direct material, direct labor, and overhead applied to the activity, the job cost sheets reflect perpetual inventories of work-in-process and finished goods, as well as the costs and quantities of goods sold. Since a separate cost sheet is prepared for each job, the cost sheets representing those jobs started but not finished are the work-in-process inventory. When a job is completed, the appropriate cost sheet could be placed in a second group of cost sheets representing finished goods inventory, or the costs could be posted to the finished goods perpetual

EXHIBIT 1
Job cost sheet

| Customer _____ | Job no. _____ |

Job description _____   Product _____

_____   Quantity _____

Remarks _____   Date started _____

_____   Date completed _____

| Date | Materials | | Labor | | Overhead applied | |
	Requisition #	Amount	Ticket #	Amount	Dept. rate	Amount
	Material total	$	Labor total	$	O/H total	$

records. As individual jobs are sold, a third group would reflect the cost of goods sold amount. The customer designation on the job cost sheet may be the name of the specific customer who has placed an order, or it may denote that the product is being produced for stock or inventory to be sold at a later date. Since several jobs may be in progress at the same time, space is usually provided for the product description and special remarks or comments that may be necessary.

As materials are requisitioned for the job and direct labor is expended, the actual amounts are recorded on the cost sheet in the material and labor columns. Remember that the overhead applied is an estimate, and it is normally added to the overhead column by using the overhead application rate. The overhead computations are entered either at the end of a cost center operation when the job has been completed, or at the end of a fiscal period when work-in-process inventory costs are needed for financial accounting and cost control purposes.

Cost flows in job order systems

To simplify the discussion on cost flows, the assumption is made that only one job will be in production. Multiple job orders increase the transactions and accounts required, but each job is handled conceptually in the same manner. Exhibit 2 depicts the four major control accounts through which the costs flow. The first three—materials, work-in-process, and finished goods— are the inventory accounts utilized by a manufacturer. A service organization may have a work-in-process (or equivalent) account for incomplete projects supported by hours incurred and valued at billable rates for "percentage of completion" contracts, or by direct cost plus overhead if a "completed project" method is utilized.

The balance in the materials control account equals the sum of the individual balances in the subsidiary material and preassembled component accounts. When materials or preassembled components are purchased, the subsidiary accounts are increased, and this results in an increase in the control account for materials. As direct materials are requisitioned for production, the material subsidiary accounts are decreased, and the work-in-process account is increased.

```
Material #2 .................................................. XXX
       Accounts payable ...................................          XXX
    Purchase of Material #2.

Work-in-Process, Job #1 ..................................... XXX
       Material #3 ..........................................          XXX
    Direct materials requisitioned by the factory.
```

In addition to direct materials, the work-in-process account is increased by two other cost elements—labor and overhead—

EXHIBIT 2
Cost flows in job order systems

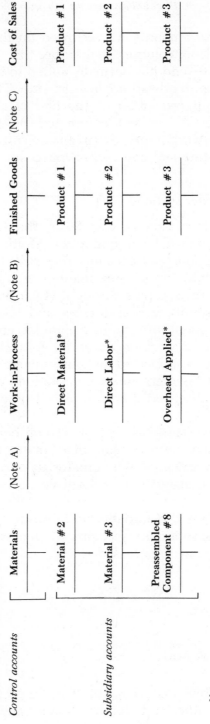

Control accounts

Materials	(Note A) →	Work-in-Process	(Note B) →	Finished Goods	(Note C) →	Cost of Sales
		Direct Material*		Product #1		Product #1
		Direct Labor*		Product #2		Product #2
		Overhead Applied*		Product #3		Product #3

Subsidiary accounts

Material #2
Material #3
Preassembled Component #8

Notes:
  A. Cost flow assumptions for materials consumed may be specific identification, weighted-average, Fifo, or Lifo.
  B. Cost flow assumptions will be specific identification for the job, but within each job the cost flow assumption will be a function of the cost flow incorporated from materials inventory requisitions and prior department cost transfers.
  C. Cost flow assumptions will be the cost of completed jobs, or if the product went into stock, any cost flow assumption indicated in Note A can be used to trace the costs through finished goods inventories and cost of sales.
* Job cost sheet data.

which are not in inventory prior to their being placed into production. A sample journal entry for direct labor follows:

```
Work-in-Process, Job #1 ................................. XXX
    Accrued Wages ......................................        XXX
    Direct labor consumed by the factory.
```

In an earlier discussion on overhead, it was stated that only an estimate of manufacturing overhead is available prior to the end of a period when the actual amount is determined, and an overhead application rate permits the overhead cost element to be estimated. Therefore, when the operation or job is completed or at the end of a period, the work-in-process account is increased by the following entry:

```
Work in Process, Job #1 ................................. XXX
    Overhead Applied ...................................        XXX
    To apply overhead to production.
```

The general ledger control account for work-in-process is usually increased by summary entries at the end of the period merely by adding the individual columns for the current period additions to direct materials, direct labor, and overhead applied from the job cost sheets.

When the jobs are completed, work-in-process is decreased and the finished goods account is increased. The cost of goods sold account is increased as jobs are sold and products are shipped from stock, and finished goods inventory is decreased. Either the finished goods inventory or cost of sales accounts may have subsidiary accounts classified by product categories or items if the information is beneficial. The following journal entries show the completion of a job and the shipment of merchandise.

```
Finished Goods ......................................... XXX
    Work-in-Process....................................        XXX
    Completion of a job.

Cost of Sales .......................................... XXX
    Finished Goods ....................................        XXX
    Sale of merchandise.
```

A service organization would close out its job in process at the time a fee is billed.

```
Cost of Services ....................................... XXX
    Work-in-Process....................................        XXX
    Billing of fee.
```

PROCESS COST SYSTEMS

One of the major differences between job order and process cost systems pertains to the necessity of coordinating cost flows with the flow of physical units. In job order costing, costs are accumulated by job, and since the costs attach to the job itself as the units move through the various cost centers in the factory, no additional effort is required to insure that the cost flows conform to the physical flow of units. The costs for the job always conceptually reside in the cost center in which the job can be found. In process cost systems the flow of physical units may proceed through several cost centers during a period, while the costs are accumulated by cost centers that originally provided the material, labor, or overhead. It is this disparity between physical unit flows and cost accumulation which must be reconciled by the process cost system.

In order to permit the costs retained by the cost centers to "catch up" with the physical units at the end of the period, four major questions must be answered:

1. How many physical units were completed by the cost center during the period, and how many are still in process?
2. What were the total costs incurred by the cost center during the period?
3. What was the cost per unit of each cost element in the cost center?
4. How much of the total costs that have been incurred by the cost center during the period should be transferred forward to the next cost center, and how much should be retained?

Process costing and physical units

The number of units that are completed and sent to the next cost center over a period of time is not an accurate measure of production; two other factors must be considered. If any units were in process when the period began, this beginning inventory would require less effort to complete than if no work had been done in the preceding period. Also materials, labor, and overhead may have been added to units that have not been completed at the end of the current period. This situation results in measuring productive activity by using the concept of *equivalent production units*. This is a common denominator which is divided into costs incurred in the process, in order to calculate the unit cost of each completed unit.

The concept behind an equivalent production unit (EPU) is that it takes the same amount of a cost element to start and finish one unit as it takes to do one third of the work on three units. For example, if one unit is in process in a cost center when a period begins, and it was one-half completed in the prior period, only one half of the effort is required during the current period to complete the unit. If one quarter of the work on another unit had been performed when the period ended, the equivalent of one quarter of a unit would have been completed. If one unit were *both started and finished* in a cost center during a period, one EPU of work would have been performed. Therefore, in this example one may conclude that the cost center finished and transferred two actual units during the period, worked on three different units, but produced only one and three-quarters equivalent production units. The foregoing information is calculated as follows:

	Physical units	Percentage completed during the period	EPUs
Beginning inventory units	1	50%	.5
Units started and finished	1	100	1
Ending inventory units	1	25	.25
Total EPUs			1.75

The essential concept that should emerge from the previous discussion is that equivalent production units are not physical units; they are abstract representations utilized to facilitate performance evaluation and product costing activities. One should also recognize that two critical assumptions are incorporated within the prior EPU calculations. The first assumption is that the physical units (and subsequently the cost flow) are on a first-in, first-out basis. The second assumption is that each of the cost elements is added evenly or uniformly as the units progress through the productive processes of the cost center. If either of these assumptions is changed, different EPU computations will be required.

ILLUSTRATION OF UNIT
COST COMPUTATIONS

To illustrate how varying these two assumptions will affect both EPU and cost computations, the following data will be utilized in all computations to illustrate process costing procedures. The hypothetical product will be manufactured from direct material, direct labor, manufacturing overhead, and prior department costs. The prior departments costs are assumed to be added to production at the beginning of processing; direct labor and manufacturing overhead (i.e., conversion costs) are added evenly throughout production; and additional direct material is added at the end of the production process in Cost Center No. 2. In this manner a variety of variations can be illustrated to show how computations are made when the cost elements enter the productive process at different times. The following actual units were worked on in Cost Center No. 2 during the month of August:

	Units	Percent completed
Beginning inventory, work-in-process	40,000	50
Units started and finished in August	80,000	100
Ending inventory, work-in-process	20,000	25

Two cost flow assumptions will be described for the process costing examples—Fifo and weighted average. The selection of either cost flow assumption by management is related to the usefulness of inter-period changes in unit cost information. If management desires to use unit cost information pertaining to specific time periods, Fifo would probably be the most beneficial. If longer term trends are preferred, the weighted-average assumption could be used to smooth out interperiod fluctuations in unit costs.

Fifo EPUs

Exhibit 3 incorporates the *Fifo flow* assumption and Exhibit 4 reflects a weighted-average approach.

In Exhibit 3 the actual number of physical units worked on is shown in Column 1. These units may be partially completed

EXHIBIT 3
Cost Center No. 2, August Fifo computations for EPUs

	(1) Actual units	(2) Material EPUs	(3) Conversion cost EPUs	(4) Prior department EPUs
1. Beginning inventory	40,000	40,000	20,000	–0–
2. Started and finished	80,000	80,000	80,000	80,000
3. Total finished	120,000	120,000	100,000	80,000
4. Ending inventory	20,000	–0–	5,000	20,000
5. Total units	140,000	120,000	105,000	100,000

or totally started and finished during August, but they are the total physical units that Cost Center No. 2 is accountable for at the end of August. Notice in all columns that the Beginning inventory units plus the Started and finished units equal the Total finished units, and the Total finished and Ending inventory units equal the Total units for which the cost center is accountable. Also notice that the units "started" during the period may be computed by adding the actual units which were Started and finished and the actual units "started and not finished" (i.e., Ending inventory) for the period. The first step in the computation should be to determine the actual number of physical units in Column 1, since the EPUs in the remaining columns are a function of Column 1 units and the two assumptions stated earlier—*physical unit flow* and the *specific timing* as to when the cost elements were added to production.

The *equivalent production units for materials* under Fifo are computed as follows. The beginning inventory material EPUs in Exhibit 3 are 40,000 for August, because even though the units were started in the prior month of July, material was added only at the end of processing, which occurred in August. Therefore, 40,000 full "doses" or portions of material were added this month to the inventory that was in process at the beginning of the period. Since 80,000 units were both started and finished in August, 80,000 EPUs of material were added. The total units finished and transferred to the next cost center for material EPUs were 120,000. No material has been added to the 20,000 units in ending inventory because the work-in-process has not been completed, and material is added only as the last step in

Cost Center No. 2. The total material EPUs that Cost Center No. 2 must account for are 120,000.

Conversion cost EPUs in Column 3 of Exhibit 3 include direct labor and overhead since both are added concurrently. Separate columns could be included for each conversion cost element, but the computations based on the illustration assumptions would result in identical EPU quantities. Taking into account that one half of the work had been completed in July on the 40,000 units in beginning inventory, only the second half of direct labor and overhead must be added to complete these units (20,000 EPUs). Conversion cost EPUs for ending inventory are 5,000 due to the 20,000 actual units being 25 percent completed.

Prior department EPUs are units that were transferred into Cost Center No. 2 from prior cost centers, and they are the result of material, labor, and overhead applied in earlier operations. If Cost Center No. 2 performed the initial operations on a unit or component, no prior department EPUs would have been transferred in, and the column could be disregarded. No prior department EPUs were needed to complete the units in beginning inventory because all 40,000 units were added last month by Cost Center No. 2 when processing was started. During August, 80,000 units were started and finished, and 20,000 units were added to this month's ending inventory; this results in Cost Center No. 2 being responsible for 100,000 prior department EPUs for the month.

Weighted-average EPUs

Exhibit 4 indicates the EPU computation that would have resulted if Cost Center No. 2 had utilized a *weighted-average flow* assumption.

Note the difference in EPUs computed under the weighted-average method and the Fifo method. This difference is attributable exclusively to the *beginning inventory quantities*. Under the weighted-average method all beginning inventory EPUs are combined whether placed into production in the current period or in the previous period, since the costs for the current period will be added to the costs for the previous period to compute the weighted-average cost per EPU of output.

EXHIBIT 4
Cost Center No. 2, August weighted-average computations for EPUs

	(1) Actual units	(2) Material EPUs	(3) Conversion cost EPUs	(4) Prior department EPUs
1. Beginning inventory	40,000	40,000	40,000	40,000
2. Started and finished	80,000	80,000	80,000	80,000
3. Total finished	120,000	120,000	120,000	120,000
4. Ending inventory	20,000	–0–	5,000	20,000
5. Total units	140,000	120,000	125,000	140,000

$$\frac{\text{Current period cost} + \text{Prior period cost}}{\text{Current period EPUs} + \text{Prior period EPUs}} = \text{Weighted-Average Unit Cost}$$

Therefore, while the Fifo method strictly observes the EPUs consumed in *this cost center for this period,* the weighed average approach combines the current period EPUs and costs with the EPUs produced and costs incurred in the previous period and carried over as beginning inventory.

Computing total costs for a process cost center

The journal entries which record the dollars and cost elements placed into production in a process cost system are almost identical to those shown previously in the job cost discussion. The primary difference is that the *debits to work-in-process are for the respective cost centers* instead of for specific jobs. The following journal entries illustrate this distinction; observe their similarity to the earlier job cost entries:

Work-in-Process,
Cost Center No. 2 XXX
    Material No. 3 XXX
Direct materials requisitioned by the factory using specific
identification, weighted average, Lifo, or Fifo cost
assumptions.

Work-in-Process,
Cost Center No. 2 XXX
    Accrued Wages XXX
Direct labor consumed by the factory.

Work-in-Process,
Cost Center No. 2 XXX
    Factory Overhead Applied XXX
Overhead is added to production.

In addition to the three entries for direct material, direct labor, and factory overhead there may be another entry required in process costing which represents the prior department costs that are transferred into production. The method used to determine the appropriate dollar amounts to be transferred into the cost center will be described shortly; however, a pro forma entry showing costs being transferred from Cost Center No. 1 into Cost Center No. 2 follows:

```
Work-in-Process,
  Cost Center No. 2. ........................................ XXX
      Work-in-Process,
      Cost Center No. 1 ....................................          XXX
      To transfer costs to the following cost center.
```

Conceptually, it is in this manner that the cost flows "catch up" with the physical unit flows through the factory.

The succeeding information will be employed in computing the costs under both Fifo and weighted-average assumptions. The examples include the EPU quantities obtained in Exhibits 3 and 4.

```
Beginning inventory costs:
  Prior department costs .................................... $ 70,400
  Direct material costs .....................................        0
  Conversion costs .........................................   43,200
                                                                        $113,600
Current period costs:
  Prior department costs .................................... $185,600
  Direct material costs .....................................  180,000
  Conversion costs .........................................  229,950
                                                                        595,550
Total Costs, Cost Center No. 2                                          $709,150
```

Fifo process costing

The following format is shown in two segments. The first segment, Exhibit 5, displays the technique for obtaining the *costs per equivalent production unit*. Exhibit 6 indicates how the cost per EPU is combined with the EPU quantities to determine how much of the *total cost is transferred* to the next cost center or to finished goods inventory.

The costs listed in Column A are accumulated from the journal entries shown earlier as material, labor, factory overhead,

EXHIBIT 5
Abbreviated cost summary (Fifo)

	(A) Cost	(B) EPUs	(C) Cost/EPU
Total costs accountable for:			
Beginning inventory	$113,600	—	—
Prior department costs	185,600	100,000	$1.856
Direct material	180,000	120,000	$1.500
Conversion costs	229,950	105,000	$2.190
Total	$709,150		

and prior department costs were placed into production. The total cost of $709,150 is the amount Cost Center No. 2 must account for during the month of August. Total EPUs listed in Column B for the various cost elements are carried forward from Exhibit 3. In order to obtain the costs per EPU listed in Column C, the total cost for each element is divided by the total EPUs for that element.

For the purposes of this example, it is unnecessary to compute the beginning inventory cost per EPU. Under the Fifo concept, the units in beginning work-in-process are assumed to be completed before units that are started later. If any units were both started and finished during the period, the units in beginning inventory that were started last period must have been completed, and therefore all beginning inventory costs (in this instance $113,600) will be included in the total costs transferred to the next department. This transfer may be observed in Exhibit 6. Nevertheless, the cost per EPU for the beginning inventory elements will normally be available by reference to the prior period computations of ending inventory costs.

The Fifo cost flow procedure in process costing is frequently referred to as "modified Fifo"; this distinction refers to the manner in which cost centers treat the costs that are transferred in from prior departments. For example, assume that Cost Center No. 2 utilizes a Fifo system for its materials inventory and adds a material with two different costs into the process. A strict interpretation of Fifo costing would require Cost Center No. 3 to maintain separate "layers" of inventory for the different batches received from the prior department. However, the record-keeping burden that would be encountered to follow the costs through multiple processes normally precludes this more

EXHIBIT 6
Cost summary* (Fifo)

	(A) Cost	(B) EPUs		(C) Cost/EPU
Total costs accountable for:				
Beginning inventory	$113,600	—		—
Prior department costs	185,600	100,000		$1.856
Direct material	180,000	120,000 (1)		$1.500
Conversion costs	229,950	105,000		$2.190
Total	$709,150			
Costs transferred out:				
Beginning inventory	$113,600	—		—
Prior department costs	148,480	80,000		$1.856
Direct material	180,000	120,000 (2)		$1.500
Conversion costs	219,000	100,000		$2.190
Total	$661,080			
Ending inventory costs:				
Prior department costs	$ 37,120	20,000		$1.856
Direct material	0	0 (3)		$1.500
Conversion costs	10,950	5,000		$2.190
Total	48,070			
Total Costs	$709,150			

* The authors wish to acknowledge Donald L. Kyle who developed the specific format for the Process Cost Summary presented in this chapter.
Notes from Exhibit 3: (1) Row 5; (2) Row 3; (3) Row 4.

rigorous treatment, and prior department costs are averaged together by the subsequent cost center to obtain a weighted-average unit cost for goods transferred in during the period.

The completed cost summary separates the total cost of $709,150 into the costs that are to be transferred into the next department or finished goods and the costs that are to remain in the ending work-in-process inventory of this department. The journal entry to transfer the completed amount into Cost Center No. 3 is as follows:

```
Work-in-Process,
  Cost Center No. 3 .................................... 661,080
    Work-in-Process,
      Cost Center No. 2 ...............................         661,080
    To transfer the completed costs into the next cost center.
```

The residual amount, $48,070, is not transferred and becomes the cost of the ending inventory in Cost Center No. 2. The total cost figures for each cost element transferred out or in ending inventory result from multiplying the various costs per EPU from Column C by the corresponding EPUs in Column B.

Weighted-average process costing

The computations under the weighted average cost flow assumption are very similar to those followed under the Fifo assumption. The major procedural difference pertains to consolidating the production costs of the unfinished units from the previous period with the costs of production from the current period. Refer to the beginning inventory EPUs in Exhibit 4 to review that the EPUs from last period's unfinished units were also carried forward into the current period's totals. Merging these prior and current period EPUs and costs results in a weighted average cost per EPU. Notice in Exhibit 7 that the

EXHIBIT 7
Cost Summary (weighted average)

	(A) Cost	(B) EPU	(C) Cost/EPU
Total costs accountable for:			
Prior department costs:			
Prior period .... $ 70,400			
Current period.............. 185,600	$256,000	140,000 (1)	$1.8285
Direct material:			
Prior period .... $ 0			
Current period.............. 180,000	180,000	120,000 (2)	$1.5000
Conversion costs:			
Prior period .... $ 43,200			
Current period.............. 229,950	273,150	125,000 (3)	$2.1852
Total	$709,150		
Costs transferred out:			
Prior department costs.....................	$219,420	120,000 ⎤	$1.8285
Material costs	180,000	120,000 ⎬ (4)	$1.5000
Conversion costs	262,224	120,000 ⎦	$2.1852
Total	$661,644		
Ending inventory costs:			
Prior department costs.....................	$ 36,570	20,000 ⎤	$1.8285
Material costs	0	0 ⎬ (5)	$1.5000
Conversion costs	10,926	5,000 ⎦	$2.1852
Total	$ 47,496		
Total cost	$709,140*		

* There is a $10 rounding error in the computations. This amount should be included in the costs transferred out so that future costs will not be distorted.

Notes from Exhibit 4: (1) Column 4, Row 5; (2) Column 2, Row 5; (3) Column 3, Row 5; (4) Row 3; (5) Row 4.

separate Beginning Inventory category has been deleted, but the cost for each beginning inventory element has been added to the production costs for the current period.

The journal entry to transfer the costs for completed units into Cost Center No. 3 under the weighted-average cost flow assumption is as follows:

```
Work-in-Process,
Cost Center No. 3 ..................................... 661,654
    Work-in-Process,
    Cost Center No. 2 ...............................       661,654
    To transfer the completed costs into the next cost center.
```

As indicated in the introductory remarks concerning process costing, a primary objective of the procedures discussed is to reconcile the flow of costs with the flow of physical units. At the end of each period, the costs must be transferred forward by each successive cost center so that the appropriate costs may "catch up" with their physical unit counterparts. These explanations have described how one cost center in a given month would treat its costing requirements under either of two cost flow assumptions; however, it should be emphasized that each cost center in the productive process would have to perform these computations sequentially in order to include the costs transferred in from previous operations.

Finished goods inventory accounts will normally be supported by perpetual records by item. The units and costs transferred from the last operation would normally be the cost of the goods manufactured during the period. Cost flow assumptions such as weighted average, Fifo, or Lifo would be utilized to determine the cost of units sold or withdrawn from finished goods inventory and to value the units remaining in finished goods inventory.

Reconciling actual and estimated overhead

As indicated in a previous section of this chapter, an estimated overhead cost is normally applied in job order and process costing systems by an overhead application rate, since the actual overhead is not known until the end of the period when the accounting records are summarized. In process costing, the overhead element is usually applied only at the end of the period;

however, in many instances the duration of the time period desired for product costing and control information is not the same as the time period that is satisfactory for financial reporting. Where the periods are equal and actual overhead costs can be obtained on a timely basis, the application of estimated overhead to each cost center's production is unnecessary, and using actual overhead is preferable. In job order costing the overhead element is applied when each job is completed or at the end of the cost period if jobs are still in process, but the demand for timely product cost information precludes waiting for actual overhead costs by the majority of companies.

Cost systems that apply estimated overhead to production accumulate actual overhead during the period by a comparatively independent and seemingly unrelated recording process. As invoices for items such as utilities and taxes are received, or as depreciation, expired insurance, indirect materials, indirect labor, and others are determined, these costs are debited to an overhead cost subsidiary ledger. Exhibit 8 shows several typi-

EXHIBIT 8
Manufacturing overhead accounts (actual costs)

Mfg. Overhead Control (9XX)

XXX

Cost Center No. 1 (910)   Cost Center No. 2 (920)

XX   XX

Lights (126)   Power (128)   Taxes (140)

XX   XX   XX

Subsidiary accounts

Depreciation (170)   Indirect Material (180)   Indirect Labor (190)

XX   XX   XX

Chart-of-account code examples:

Manufacturing overhead	9XX–XXX
Cost Center No. 1	910–XXX
Cost Center No. 2	920–XXX
Functional expenses	
Lights	XXX–126
Power	XXX–128

cal manufacturing overhead subsidiary accounts and Departmental and Manufacturing Overhead Control accounts. At the end of the accounting period, the subsidiary accounts equal the control account, which then contains the *total actual overhead* incurred during the period. Comparable results are usually obtained by using accounting coding systems employing cost center and functional expense fields (three digits for cost center and three digits for expense description resulting in a six digit chart-of-accounts code).

When estimated overhead was added to the work-in-process account during the period (that is, for individual jobs in job order costing or to cost centers in process costing), an applied overhead account was credited for the same amount. Therefore, an Overhead Applied Control account contains the *total estimated overhead applied* to production.

If the Overhead Applied Control account (credit balance) is greater than the Manufacturing Overhead Control account (debit balance), the difference is referred to as *overapplied* or *overabsorbed* overhead. If the applied overhead is less than the actual overhead, the difference is said to be *underapplied* or *underabsorbed* overhead. Underapplied overhead means that the overhead application rate was too low for the level of activity encountered during the period, and the work-in-process, finished goods, and cost of sales accounts should be increased to reflect the actual overhead incurred. Overapplied overhead indicates that the rate was too high for the level of activity, and the accounts should be reduced by the amount of the difference. If the under- or overapplied overhead is immaterial, the amount may be closed to cost of goods sold, but if the amount is material, the balance should be allocated to the appropriate accounts so that the financial records will reflect actual costs.

For example, assume that at the end of an accounting period a company has underapplied overhead of $10,000. Also assume that the accounting records show that the following amounts of applied overhead remain in the accounts at the end of the period: work-in-process, $30,000; finished goods, $70,000; cost of sales, $100,000. The journal entry to adjust the under-applied overhead would be as follows:

```
Work-in-Process (30,000/200,000 × $10,000) .................. 1,500
Finished Goods (70,000/200,000 × $10,000) .................. 3,500
```

```
Cost of Sales (100,000/200,000 × $10,000) . . . . . . . . . . . . . . . . . . . 5,000
    Overhead Applied Control . . . . . . . . . . . . . . . . . . . . . . . . . . . .        10,000
```

Notice that the costs of each of the three accounts are increased by adjusting the Overhead Applied Control account to equal the actual overhead incurred. If an overapplied balance had existed, the entry would have been reversed, and work-in-process, finished goods, and cost of sales would have been reduced. Ultimately the two overhead control accounts are closed into each other to effect a zero beginning balance for the next period.

In certain instances the company may experience unusual circumstances that would distort the cost information if underapplied or overapplied overhead were allocated to inventories and cost of sales. Imagine that some severe economic condition occurred, a strike halted production in the factory, or production was temporarily interrupted for an unexpected reason. The fixed overhead costs would continue to be incurred, but it would normally be considered inappropriate for the full amount of these costs to be absorbed by production for the period. In such cases an "equitable" portion of these fixed costs may be charged directly to the income statement accounts as an adjustment reflecting the abnormal conditions of the reporting period.

SUMMARY

Job order and process cost systems are expansions of the financial accounting system in order to provide information which will facilitate evaluation, control, or planning activities within an organization. Merely accumulating historical cost data for financial statements is seldom a sufficient economic justification for implementing a cost system; the results must be used in current or future decision making for the major benefits to accrue. The information output should be continually monitored to insure that it is (1) considered to be useful by management, (2) reasonably accurate and timely, and (3) of greater value than the costs incurred in maintaining the system.

This chapter has presented an overview of the two basic cost accounting systems as well as pointing out that, depending on the specific needs of the organization, the systems may be combined or used in conjunction with one another. In addition, cost systems may be modified—as in the cases of joint costing or direct costing environments—or further expanded by overlaying standard or predetermined costs onto the basic job order or process system.

In many instances actual overhead costs cannot be obtained on a basis that is timely enough to permit effective control or pricing decisions to be made; therefore, the overhead cost element is often estimated and included in the cost objective by utilizing an overhead application rate. At the end of the financial accounting period when actual cost data are available, the appropriate inventory and cost accounts must be adjusted to reflect actual costs.

In job order cost systems perpetual inventory records for work-in-process and/or finished goods are usually maintained on job cost sheets. A separate job sheet is prepared as each batch or job is placed into production or as each project is started. The cost of the job is then incremented as direct materials and direct labor are added. Overhead is added to the job to obtain cost data for work-in-process inventories at the end of an accounting period or when the job has completed appropriate operations or departments.

Process cost systems accumulate cost data in cost centers instead of individual jobs, and the crucial problem normally involves how the costs retained in the cost centers will "catch up" with the physical units that may have moved through several departments or activities. This situation is resolved by developing a cost per equivalent production unit, determining how many EPUs have been completed within each cost center during the period, and then sequentially transferring an appropriate dollar amount to subsequent cost centers. Since costs are transferred separately from the flow of physical units, process cost systems require an explicit selection of a cost flow assumption for work-in-process inventories. Examples of Fifo and weighted-average methods have been illustrated.

In conclusion, it should be reiterated that job order or process cost systems provide additional information at an additional cost, and although the value of additional information is extremely difficult to quantify, every reasonable effort should be made to ensure that the value of the information exceeds the cost. Perhaps the most effective way to fully utilize cost data, and the projections inherent in the system, is to integrate the output into the budgeting system of the organization. Only by integrating information concerning capacity and expected activity levels, unit costs, and material and labor requirements with sales estimates, cash flow projections, purchasing requirements, and other planning activities can the full potential of a cost accounting system be realized.

21

Year-end "physical to book" discrepancies: Accountability for losses and waste

*Thomas S. Dudick**

Many books and papers have been published on the subject of better control of operations through more informative reporting to management. Much of this deals with format, that is, reporting by responsibility, profitability by product line, and marginal contribution. These topics are important, but it is quite surprising how many writers and speakers overlook proper inventory accountability and valuation as a necessary ingredient of accurate reporting. The problem of accountability for waste and spoilage (called scrap by some) is often brushed over lightly as if it were merely a problem of proper reporting. While it is true that proper reporting of production losses is important to good inventory accountability, there are factors other than losses in production that affect inventory accuracy. Because of this, the first part of the chapter will deal with inventory accountability as it relates to the year-end physical versus book problems. The second part will cover the subject of waste and spoilage.

YEAR-END PHYSICAL INVENTORY TO BOOK DISCREPANCIES

There seems to be a general lack of awareness of the many hundreds of manufacturing companies which, at year end, find

---

* Manager, Ernst & Ernst.

that an eleven months' profit has seriously deteriorated because of a large difference between "physical" and "book". For example:

> $5 million inventory shortage at ABC Corporation; several lawsuits in the offing.

Only the inventory shortages that result in lawsuits make the headlines. These represent only the tip of the iceberg. The average executive is not aware of the many occurrences because there is no tabulation available. In fact, the embarrassment to the financial executive tends toward suppression rather than publicizing the occurrence. Most times the shortages are not real losses—the discrepancy being the result of a poor cost system that underrelieves inventories during the year, requiring adjustment at year-end.

This raises several questions:

1. Why is correct inventory valuation so important?
2. How do the discrepancies occur?
3. What is the solution?

Why is proper inventory valuation so important?

Good inventory accountability is necessary to assure correct reporting of profits during the interim periods as well as at year end for three reasons:

1. There is nothing more disconcerting to the general manager responsible for the profit goals of his operation than to go along for 11 months of the year under the illusion that he is meeting his business plan—only to find in the twelfth month that a large inventory difference between physical and book wipes out a large part of the profit. Often when this happens a promising career can be demolished overnight. This can happen not only to the financial executive, but to the general manager of the operation as well.

   Often, a defensive stance is taken, wherein it is argued that the discrepancy between physical and book is only one half of one percent of throughput (flow of production). The implied question is, "How much more accuracy can you expect with the massive movement of material and parts that takes place in the course of a year?"

While it seems logical to equate the magnitude of the discrepancy with the volume of throughput, the more frequently used measure in the real world of business is the impact on profits. The difference is demonstrated in the two illustrations below:

	Company A	Company B
Annual throughput	$10,000,000	$10,000,000
(Factory cost of production)		
Inventory discrepancy	$ 100,000	$ 100,000
Percent to throughput	1%	1%
Pretax profit	$ 1,000,000	$ 200,000
Percent discrepancy to profit	10%	50%

Obviously, a more unfavorable reaction can be expected from Company B's management and stockholders than from Company A's even though the amount of inventory discrepancy and throughput are exactly the same.

2. Another reason for the need for proper inventory accountability is the requirement for quarterly submissions to the Securities and Exchange Commission. A company whose inventory is overstated on its books may show overstated profits in the first three quarters and a relatively poor performance for the fourth quarter after adjusting to the physical. This does not represent acceptable reporting.

3. Stock analysts who make recommendations to their clients on the basis of reported earnings can be greatly misled by incorrect profits resulting from overstated earnings. This can work to the detriment of a company seeking to raise capital.

How does it happen?

There are a number of ways in which inventory discrepancies occur. The case studies which follow are illustrative of the more typical occurrences.

Company A

This company had one inventory pool on the books. There was no breakdown among raw material, work-in-process, and finished goods.

Input into inventory was based on the actual cost of material purchased and the actual direct labor as recorded on the payroll. Overhead was applied on the basis of a predetermined overhead rate on direct labor.

Output. Relief to inventory was determined on the basis of "standard" costs that were applied to shipments. These were developed to approximate actual costs. As the rate of cost escalation accelerated during the year, the standards used for costing sales fell far short of actual costs. As a result, the book inventory was substantially higher than the value of the physical inventory— resulting in a substantial reduction in profits that were reported in the earlier months.

Company B

This company did not have a formal standards program.

Input. In an attempt to approximate a standard cost system, actual labor costs were factored by estimated efficiency factors. Material input was therefore considered to be based on standard prices.

Output. To arrive at the cost of sales, an historically experienced percentage was applied to each month's sales. As in the case of Company A, the basis of output was not consistent with input. The percentage applied to sales was 51%. Because the mix of products changed during the year to include more of the high material content items, the actual cost of sales turned out to be 57%. Because of this underrelief of 6% there was an inventory discrepancy of approximately a million dollars.

In both Company A and Company B, the solution was to establish uniform standards that would be used for both input and output.

Company C

Because of a defect in a newly launched product, customers were authorized to return the product for replacement of the defective part. As the returns began accumulating, paperwork fell behind. The controller therefore resorted to a physical inventory each month as a means of accounting for the backlog of returned products. This resulted in an overstatement of inventory since most of the items were still the property of the customers.

Company D

A certain amount of rework is characteristic of many products. In doing rework, it is important to monitor carefully the production count to assure that double-counting is avoided—once when the original work is done and again when the defect is corrected.

Company D made a product that was subject to about 10 percent rework. Its controls to assure accurate counting were somewhat weak. As a result, double-counting caused an inventory buildup on the books that was unknown until the book and physical inventories were compared at year-end.

Company E

Company E did have a formalized standard cost system. The same standards used for costing individual operations added up to the total standard product costs used for arriving at cost of sales. However, because losses in production were not fully accounted for, this company found at year-end that it had an inventory shortage between physical and book amounting to $465, 000.

Reporting production losses through direct paper work is easier said than done. Frequently, such losses occur because material thickness and widths (particularly in metal stamping) exceed the specifications called for. In plastics molding, mold wear can result in use of more material than called for. Since the end product in this company has an average factory cost of only $.25 per unit, this is certainly not enough to warrant an expensive monitoring procedure to assure that all losses are correctly and fully accounted for. The solution is to report the good finished components and subassemblies only when accepted into stock, thus automatically excluding waste and spoilage. This approach, which is applicable to many companies, will be discussed later.

The experience of Companies A, B, C, D, and E are illustrative of circumstances that can cause a large inventory discrepancy. The number and variety of such occurrences are almost limitless. Positive steps that give consideration to the variations in cost flow must be taken to minimize the potential causes of discrepancies.

Variations in cost flow

The nature of the inventory accounting procedures is dependent on the type of cost flow. Cost flow, in turn, should be based on the actual production flow of the product being manufactured.

A custom product is an entity unto itself—production flow being patterned around making specific products for specific customers. The flow of material, labor, and overhead is directed toward satisfying the requirements for making that specific product. When completed, it is shipped to the customer out of work-in-process rather than out of a finished goods warehouse. In a number of instances, companies make custom products from standard components that are interchangeable. Thus, the production flow for the components can be quite similar to the flow in making standard products for stock, while the assembly of the finished unit can be quite similar to that of custom products.

A standard product is usually built to stock and sold out of finished goods. The production flow can be pictured as a steady stream of material, labor, and overhead flowing into work-in-process through the various operations. From work-in-process, the flow is through the finished goods inventory, from which shipments are made.

Job costing

The job costing system generally utilizes two basic inventory accounts:

1. Raw material.
2. Work-in-process (jobs in process).

While purchases are normally directed into the raw material inventory account and then issued to jobs as needed, this is not always the case; material purchased specifically for a job can bypass the raw material inventory account. Direct labor is charged directly against the job on which the work is performed.

Inventory accountability under job costing is relatively simple—as each job is completed, all accumulated costs that were charged to that job are cleared out of inventory, leaving no unaccounted for residual quantities. If relief is made at the standard cost of the finished job (or estimated cost), the resulting residual quantity represents a variance. This would be cleared out of work-in-process as a separate step.

There are disadvantages to the job costing method, however, because such a system requires substantially more work than a process cost system. As an example, a company with annual sales of less than $10,000,000 could have as many as 500 jobs in process. There is also a tendency in job shops to "borrow" from one job to meet priority requirements of another. When such borrowing is done without paperwork documentation, the accuracy of the inventory value carried on the books becomes questionable. While process costing is simpler and therefore less costly, it cannot be substituted for job costing when customized production and costing are required.

The type of product or service dictates the type of cost system required. When the product or service is unique and its specific cost must be known, then the job cost system is mandatory. In a process-type business in which standardized products are built to stock, rather than to a customer's order, a standard cost process flow type of system is more suitable.

Standard costing in a process flow

In a process (repetitive) type business, three basic inventory accounts are required:

1. Raw material.
2. Work-in-process.
3. Finished goods.

Many companies that have greatly improved the credibility of their financial statements through better inventory accountability are still vulnerable to year-end discrepancies because of incipient problems that are not reflected in the paperwork that documents the various transactions affecting the inventory. Examples are: overreporting of production, excessive use of material that is unreported, and rejects that are not completely accounted for.

As will be illustrated later, the work-in-process account should be broken down further to identify those items that are being *stored in a controlled stockroom* and those that make up the *floor work-in-process.* Accounting systems rarely recognize this breakdown in work-in-process, and thereby miss an opportunity for better accountability of inventory.

Most of the foregoing problems that result in underrelief of inventory in a process flow system occur in work-in-process. Efforts to correct the reporting frequently become highly frustrating exercises because the cost of the cure often far exceeds the benefits. This is particularly true when low unit values are involved.

What is the solution?

True accountability of inventory requires two steps: (1) accountability for the physical units, and (2) assigning dollar values to the physical units accounted for.

The accounting department rarely has the tools necessary for good physical accountability; this capability is possessed by the production and inventory control group whose major responsibility is to:

a. Issue requisitions for purchase of material.
b. Issue shop orders for production of components and subassemblies as well as the finished product.
c. Maintain perpetual records of items in inventory.

With the introduction of the computer in maintaining perpetual records of all stockroom inventories and, in many cases, status reports of floor inventories, it behooves the accountant to make better use of the same paperwork that is used for moving material into and out of the various stores accounts.

The big "hangup" of many accounting departments lies in the work-in-process inventory. The accountant looks upon this as a single pool of costs. The production and inventory control group, on the other hand, identifies work-in-process in at least two segments—finished parts in work-in-process inventory that contains two or more controlled areas: components (manufactured and purchased parts); subassemblies; and unpacked goods (finished goods that have not yet been packed).

The components and subassembly stockrooms are usually enclosed areas, while the unpacked goods are in an open area located at the end of the production line. Although the latter

EXHIBIT 1
Production flow

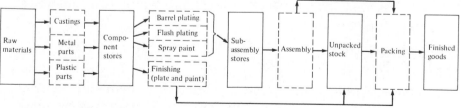

Solid lines: Controlled stores.
Dotted lines: Floor work-in-process (float).

area is not enclosed, it is closely controlled as are the other two.

Receipts into all three areas are based on counts of items that have been inspected and accepted by the inspector. The smaller items are weighed and scale-counted through use of conversion factors. The larger items are accounted for individually.

The tickets representing receipts into stock and issues out of stock are sequentially numbered. Each day's receipts and issues are batched and forwarded to the data processing department for processing. The preprinted numbers are listed sequentially for both the receipts and issues to determine if any tickets are missing. In the event that there is a gap, the issuer of the ticket is asked for an accounting. It is usually found that missing numbers are tickets that were voided and thrown out. Insistence on full accountability serves as a disciplinary reminder to all new personnel that every transaction must be documented.

The quantities received into each of the controlled areas as well as the quantities issued out of these areas are used as the basis for adjusting the "on hand" figures on the perpetual inventory status report for each stockroom (same procedure followed for raw material and finished goods). The same paperwork used for adjusting the perpetual inventories should be the basis for input into inventory on the books. Before discussing accountability for the floor work-in-process, let us cover cycle counting—the assurance that the units in stock are correct.

Importance of cycle counts

No perpetual inventory can be run "ad infinitum" without regular verification. The preferred method is to use *cycle counting*—so named because of the systematic selection of items to be counted. There are two basic considerations for effective cycle counting:

1. Proper cutoffs.
2. Frequency of counting.

Proper cutoffs. Any paperwork that documents the transactions affecting the perpetual inventory will usually lag by a day or more. The reason for such lag is that the documents must be reviewed, accounted for in numerical sequence, batched, and then processed before the perpetual records correctly reflect the status of the items covered by the paperwork.

All such delayed transactions must be accounted for when the physical units counted are compared with the balances shown on the inventory status report. This reconciliation is just as important as making the physical count.

Determination of frequency of counting. The proper selection and categorization of items to be counted is important in assuring accuracy of stockroom inventories. The first step is to list each item in inventory sequentially, by dollar value.

Categorizing the inventory

The next step is to break the inventory into four categories identified as A, B, C, and D. This must be done on a judgmental basis, keeping in mind the following guidelines:

The A and B items, taken together, should account for approximately 80 percent of the value. The B items ideally should be roughly half of the A items in dollar value.

As between C and D items, the categorization should leave between 50 percent and 60 percent of the total items and approximately 10 percent of the total dollar value in the D classification. The following figures illustrate the desired breakdown into four categories:

	Number of items	Percent of total items	Percent of total value
A items	1,350	7.4%	48%
B items	2,300	12.6	26
C items	3,200	17.5	16
D items	11,400	62.5	10
Total	18,250	100.0%	100%

Cycle counting schedule

Once the categories have been determined, a frequency for counting must be established. A sugested schedule is shown below:

A items	Every 2 months
B items	Every 3 months
C items	Every 6 months
D items	Every 12 months

Since the A and B items account for 74 percent of the total inventory value and require counting only 20 percent of the total number of items, cycle counts for these two categories are scheduled more frequently. The D items, which represent over 60 percent of the total number of items in inventory but only 10 percent of the total value, can safely be scheduled for counting once a year.

Over and above verification through cycle counting, there is an automatic verification opportunity for each item in which an issue depletes the supply. In some instances, negative quantities will appear on the inventory status report (perpetual). This can be the result of a misidentification of a part number. When negative balances are found, they should never be automatically adjusted to zero because this is tantamount to a writeup of inventory. Every effort should be made to determine the reason for the error.

Overview of cycle counting requirements

Cycle counting is a full-time job. It must be taken seriously and cannot be treated as "fill-in" work when time allows. This program can require as many as 150 items to be counted each work day. Because of this large number, it will be necessary for the computer to provide the daily listing of the items to be counted. This listing should also provide space for the inventory control clerk to show the actual number in stock as well as the cutoff reconciliation quantities.

Accounting for floor work-in-process

Once the stockroom work-in-process inventories are accounted for, only the *floor inventories* remain to be discussed. These are the raw materials that have not yet been processed but are lying around the work places awaiting processing. Floor work-in-process will also include items that have been partially processed, as well as those awaiting acceptance into stockrooms.

If the floor work-in-process is in the nature of "pipeline stock" it is possible that it can be properly accounted for by carrying a fixed dollar value on the books. If there are "expansion points" at which fluctuations in amount of floor inventories occur, it may be necessary to take physical inventories at such points and to adjust the fixed value carried on the books.

Some production and inventory control departments account for floor work-in-process through shop orders which utilize "travelers" or shop orders to identify the production at each point of the process, as well as the number of units that have been lost through defective workmanship or materials. Where such information exists, the balances on the travelers or shop orders can be costed to arrive at the value of the floor work-in-process.

Some accountants monitor floor inventories by attempting to account for movement from cost center to cost center. While this method seems to be theoretically proper, it can result in a fictitious buildup on the books with a resulting discrepancy at year end when the book value is compared with the physical value.

The weakness in this method is that production figures on an operation-by-operation basis, even if correct, would result in input into inventory of costs that would be too high because of losses in later operations.

If such losses were removed from the inventory, the net result would be approximately correct. However, in the real world, reporting of production losses is one of the weak links in inventory accountability. It is a rare company that can boast of reliability in reporting of such losses—leaving as the most practical alternative, the acceptance into inventory of only the costs of those items that are physically received into the various stockrooms. Although the author favors this method, he recognizes that there must be accountability for losses and waste to facilitate corrective action. This will be covered in the section that follows.

ACCOUNTABILITY FOR LOSSES AND WASTE

Too often the accounting system, which admittedly has an important mission in reporting the financial condition of the business to the owners, results in a paperwork routine that fully occupies too many financial groups to the extent that the more pertinent day-to-day controls are never properly implemented. While the financial executive's responsibilities in making up payrolls, billing customers, paying suppliers, monitoring inventories, controlling capital acquisitions, preparing budgets, and summarizing expenditures are not to be dismissed lightly, he must, in spite of these demands, find a way to implement timely cost controls, one of which includes production losses and waste. He must enlist the aid of other members in the organization: production control in preparing information needed for measurement of material utilization, and the quality group for reporting and control of production losses. Most companies have substantial amounts of good basic information already available, which needs only to be correlated and recast into meaningful and actionable reports.

The phraseology "accounting for losses and waste," taken alone, is somewhat misleading because it implies that losses and waste are known as soon as incurred. *Losses* refers to units (usually fabricated components) that are not of acceptable quality and cannot be reworked. *Waste* refers to material that is used in excess of the quantities specified in the production standard allowances. In the case of metal stamping, excess usage of material could be caused by using metal strip that is on the high side of the dimensional specifications called for in the production standards. In molding, waste can result from worn molds.

The reason that losses and waste cannot be properly accounted for in many instances is that screening of production does not take place immediately after fabrication. This is frequently done just before acceptance into a controlled stock area and after a wheel-abrading, tumbling, or cleaning operation has been performed. Some parts—foundry castings, for instance—can have hidden defects under the surface that are not evident until the boring or grinding operation takes place.

By the nature of his position, the financial executive is looked upon by his fellow managers as the logical one to act as catalyst in the assembly, interpretation, and distribution of this information. This section will discuss the types of analysis which could be made and reports that are necessary in order to control losses and waste more effectively.

Control of material losses

Material is probably the most difficult element of manufacturing cost to account for. Actual usage is not known in many instances until an inventory is taken. Taking inventories can be expensive and time consuming. This undoubtedly is one of the reasons accountability on a more frequent basis is lacking. It is not sufficient to report material (and labor) efficiencies once a month or after the completion of a job. Management must have this information on a more timely and more frequent basis.

Although material accountability presents some real problems, the case for control is not hopeless. It will be found that although many items of material need to be accounted for, a small number of items will usually make up a large percentage of the total. Even if an inventory is required in order to properly report material usage on a more frequent basis, the inventory need only cover the few items. This is the *selective control* technique.

Selective control technique for material control

One company effected substantially better material control through use of this technique. An analysis showed that 87 different material items were used in normal production and that 14 of these accounted for 52 percent of the value. Although fuller than 52 percent coverage would have been desirable (27 items were required for 85 percent coverage), it was felt in the interest of economy and speed that only 14 items would be controlled at the outset. Arrangements were made with the factory to take an inventory of the 14 key items each Friday shortly before close of work. The stockroom would also furnish the financial group with figures showing the number of the items issued and returned to stock. These were furnished daily, along with the number of units that were produced and accepted by the stockroom. Receipt of these figures on a daily basis permitted cursory checks to be made to detect unusually low or unusually high activity, a circumstance that resulted in the financial group becoming more production oriented through questions which arose and which required answers by production personnel. Daily receipt of production and issue figures facilitated the accumulation of the figures during the week, so the final day's production and issues needed only to be added to the prior four days' totals. As soon as the inventory information was available, each item was summarized and the material utilization percentage was determined, as illustrated in Exhibit 2.

The beginning inventory is always the same as the preceding

EXHIBIT 2
Weekly material utilization report (figures are in units)

Part number	Beginning inventory	Issues to floor	Returns	Ending inventory	Material usage	Production	Utilization percent
135812	98,156			2,926	95,230	82,812	87%
138819	98,000	18,045		26,000	90,045	82,812	92
144404	5,400	96,750		10,750	91,400	82,812	90
211362	3,500	63,500			67,000	51,891	77
223414	860	252,695	3,010	8,624	241,921	252,190	104
201134	8,000	378,510	6,000	3,080	377,430	252,170	67
199966	15,530	133,000		7,224	141,306	101,527	72
211633	14,217	33,400		26,307	21,310	19,683	92
198986	8,820	69,000	11,000		66,820	24,066	36
253007	1,550	35,650	21,130	3,000	13,070	5,689	44
244031	3,640	10,500	2,860	3,920	7,360	5,689	77
22306	2,000	8,150		1,000	9,150	5,689	62
23364	15,754	88,540	6,653	12,507	85,134	65,482	77
19966	5,370	104,275	6,900	19,800	82,945	65,482	79

Week ended

week's ending inventory—unless an error is found. Issues to the floor are added to the beginning inventory to determine the total amount of material available. This figure is reduced by returns to stock, which sometimes are high because they represent rejects due to poor workmanship by a preceding department. The adjusted amount is then reduced by the ending inventory to arrive at the amount of material usage. This, divided into the output or production, results in a material utilization percentage.

Part 198986 is illustrative of the use to which this type of control may be put. The beginning inventory amounts to 8,820 units; 69,000 units were issued to cover the next two weeks' production requirements. The 11,000 returns to stock represented defective parts which were returned to stock. The entire amount of material available, less returns, was used in the production of 24,066 finished parts—a material utilization of only 36 percent. Investigation into this low percentage revealed that the quality of the parts which were issued from stock was generally poor. Only 11,000 were returned to stock, although more should have been returned, because of a rush order which had to be filled for a customer requiring immediate delivery. As a result of poorly fitting parts, over 66,000 had to be used to make 24,000 finished units. The financial group, as a result of this experience, began to watch for large returns to stock as a clue to repetition of this type of low utilization. To prevent similar problems in the future, rush production of parts such as 198986 was minimized by maintaining a min-max inventory in stock sufficient to take care of two or three weeks' production requirements. When issues would be made to the floor in the future, there was greater assurance that the parts would not be defective because adequate lead times were provided all departments to eliminate waste due to haste.

Through inspection of the utilization figures, trends were carefully watched to determine what could be done to improve utilization. This report also provided a weekly analysis of inventory of the 14 dominant items. If an inventory remained too high and was untouched for four weeks in a row, questions were asked, and frequently it was possible to obtain orders to reduce the inventory to tolerable limits. This eliminated later obsolescence and consequent write-offs.

Maintaining this type of report in units rather than in dollars eliminates a great deal of work in dollarizing the figures. Since the 14 items represented over half the value of all materials used, there was no need to incur additional cost to reconfirm this fact each week.

It is not always necessary to account for inventory changes in order to obtain effective control. When the flow of the product and its components can be monitored so that "unaccounted-for disappearance" is not an important factor, an *analysis of spoilage* provides adequate control. This type of control is usually more economical than the weekly material utilization report. It is also more timely because spoilage information can be provided hourly if need be.

One of the companies whose material cost control procedures were studied prepares a daily spoilage report which shows the number of each unit rejected (minor items omitted). If the defect can be reworked, the spoilage quantity is adjusted and the re-work cost noted. This report is issued each morning for the preceding day, with a short statement explaining major causes of an unusually high spoilage rate.

The information appearing on the daily report is summarized on a weekly basis by type of unit and type of defect causing the rejection. Dollar values are then assigned and a listing is made in order of dollar magnitude of spoilage, with the highest cost items appearing at the top of the list. A specimen copy of this report is shown in Exhibit 3.

EXHIBIT 3
Weekly spoilage report (dollar value of rejects)

		Week ended _____			
Part number	*Used on product no.*	*Week's scheduled production*	*No. of rejects*	*Type of defect*	*Total cost*
603.......... 78396		300	19	116	$ 625
301.......... 69842		150	9	43	531
673.......... 39461		75	8	52	503
498.......... 21312		890	150	14	342
306.......... 14398		250	14	16	221
403.......... 31982		600	32	6	114
106.......... 21699		300	25	55	98
198.......... 4443		250	8	62	42
					$2,476
		This week's annualized total			$123,863
		Prior week's annualized total			$114,132

The part number rejected is shown as well as the final product in which the part is used. The week's scheduled production is shown in order that a determination might be made as to the magnitude of rejects. While a "Percent Rejects to Week's Scheduled Production" might be useful for this purpose, it was decided that every additional column adds to the complexity of the report and to the preparation time. The next to the last column shows the reject code, while the last column shows the dollar cost of the rejects. The total week's rejects of $2,476 is annualized to emphasize the magnitude of spoilage over a year's time. The prior week's annualized total is also shown for comparative purposes.

The report is closed out at the close of business on Tuesday and issued Wednesday morning. In a weekly meeting held on Wednesday shortly after distribution of the report, the quality assurance group and production foremen discuss the causes of spoilage and suggest remedies. Primary emphasis would be placed on the first three items, which account for 70 percent of the rejects. If time permits, the fourth item, which accounts for another 10 percent, would be discussed. When appropriate, other parties such as the purchasing agent or material control supervisor are called in. The purchasing agent might be called in on a discussion of quality of parts or other materials being purchased, while the material control supervisor might be called in on a discussion dealing with defects due to rough handling of parts or improper storage. Actual participation by these parties has a more salutary effect than a telephoned complaint delivered in haste and received in haste. The purpose of the midweek meeting is to permit action to be taken in the same week as the decisions and recommendations are made. The results are carefully reviewed in the following week's meeting to determine if the problems have been corrected.

Another company which assembles components that, once assembled, cannot be taken apart for repair, summarizes weekly spoilage in units on a cumulative basis. The figures correspond with the sequence of operations, and are illustrated in Exhibit 4. At Assembly Operation 1, there were 100 units started but one was rejected, showing 99.0 percent good. Operation 2 shows 99 starts with one rejected. Operation 3, with 98 starts because two had already been rejected, resulted in three rejects or 96.9 percent good units. Operations 4 and 5 follow the same pattern.

EXHIBIT 4
Weekly spoilage report (units scrapped)

			Week ended _____		
Assembly operations	Number of starts	Good units	Percent good to starts	Cumulative percent good	Rejects
1 100		99	99.0%	99.0%	1
2 99		98	99.0	98.0	1
3 98		95	96.9	95.0	3
4 95		75	78.9	74.9	20
5 75		65	86.7	65.0	10

The cumulative "percent good" shows the cumulative effect of losses all along the line. While this figure is readily apparent from looking at the column headed "Good Units" and relating this to 100 starts at Operation 1, it is not always possible in actual practice to determine this figure in this manner. The reason is that all units started in each operation are not always completely processed and forwarded to the next operation in the same week. The illustration in Exhibit 5 would be more typical.

The significance of the cumulative percentage of rejects is that it highlights the total impact of accumulated spoilage. It appraises the overall effect of the rejects rather than looking at only a segment at a time. Referring again to Exhibit 4, it should be little consolation to management to see that Operations 1, 2, and 3 are running better than 90 percent when only 65 percent of all units started are good.

This type of control highlights such losses without requiring

EXHIBIT 5*

Assembly operations	Number of starts	Good units	Percent good to starts	Cumulative percent good	Rejects
1 145		145	100.0%	100.0%	—
2 140		134	95.7	95.7	6
3 42		41	97.6	93.4	1
4 41		36	87.8	82.0	5

* The cumulative percent good would be calculated as follows:
100.0% in Operation 1 multiplied by 95.7% in Operation 2 = 95.7%
95.7% in Operation 2 multiplied by 97.6% in Operation 3 = 93.4%
93.4% in Operation 3 multiplied by 87.8% in Operation 4 = 82.0%

time-consuming cost calculations. While application of costs to the units would better equate for relative values, it is questionable that the additional information obtained would justify the delay in issuance of the report.

Inventory discrepancies not always due to unreported losses and waste

Although unreported losses and waste are a factor that must be considered when there is a difference between physical and book inventories, this is not necessarily the predominant factor. Inconsistency in valuation of input versus output is probably a larger factor. This would include instances in which partial and completed production are costed at values that are not consistent with the costs assigned to finished products shipped to customers. The earlier examples of Companies A, B, C, D, and E cite specific company experiences in such valuation inconsistencies.

Like many occurrences in the dynamics of modern business, accountability for losses and waste are so intertwined with other factors affecting inventory that it is frequently very difficult and economically impractical to sort out the factors and evaluate them individually.

22

Accounting for joint and by-product costs

*J. O. Edwards**

A manufacturing operation often produces two or more products from a single raw material. By the nature of the process, one product frequently cannot be manufactured without producing one or more additional products, although the mix of product quantities may be variable. Examples of such operations include petroleum refining, meat packing, chemicals, lumber processing, mining, and canning. Multiple products which are produced from a single raw material and which have significant sales values are called *joint products.* Those products whose production is incidental to that of the major products and whose sales value is relatively small in comparison to the major products are referred to as *by-products.*

At some point in the manufacturing process, the joint products become identifiable as separate and distinct products, some of which may be finished goods, whereas others may require additional processing. For accounting purposes, this point is commonly defined as the *split-off point.* Costs incurred prior to this stage in the process are called *joint costs* and are allocated to the joint products by one or more of the methods described in this chapter. Additional processing costs incurred after the

---

* Controller, Exxon Company, USA.

split-off are usually traceable to a particular product and are appropriately assigned to that product.

Generally there is no attempt to allocate actual costs to by-products. Instead, these products are usually valued at their net realizable value, with a corresponding reduction in the costs allocated to the joint products. This chapter will discuss the various methods of gathering and allocating costs to multiple products as well as the usefulness and limitations of such procedures.

COST COLLECTION

Costs must be collected and identified before any allocation can be made to specific products. These costs are generally segregated and controlled by areas of managerial responsibility rather than by product. These areas of responsibility, commonly called cost centers, are normally departmental units within the production process or within service or administrative functions.

Within each cost center, expenses can be further identified by character of expense such as materials, salaries and wages, supplies, and so forth. Although cost centers are covered in considerable detail in Chapter 9, some mention is appropriate here since they are a necessary part of accumulating costs to be allocated to joint products.

Generally, expenses are accumulated and controlled within one of the following three basic cost center categories:

1. *Process cost centers*—Containing expenses incurred in the direct operation of the processing function.
2. *Service and utility cost centers*—Containing the expenses incurred in providing operating services and utilities to other cost centers.
3. *Burden (overhead) cost centers*—Containing the expenses associated with administrative, accounting, technical, and mechanical support not directly related to process or service/utility cost centers.

Cost control within any cost center is maintained through reconciliation of forecasted direct costs and production volumes with actual results over a given period of time. Results of a current period may also be compared to those of prior periods. Managers of service/utility and burden cost centers are held accountable for centers under their control in a manner similar to that by which process cost center managers are held responsible for their directly incurred costs. This accountability reduces the possibility that process center managers could suffer from distributed costs that are inflated by inadequate cost control.

Service and utility costs are often distributed to other centers based on some measure of consumption, such as pounds of steam, kilowatt hours, or computer hours. The determination of appropriate bases for burden cost distribution is more difficult. Usually an indirect relationship must be established (for example, warehousing and purchasing overhead distributed on some combination of factors relating to materials issued, such as dollar value or quantities withdrawn). The primary consideration is that the distribution bases be reasonable and appropriate to the specific fact situation. Furthermore, it is important that the bases not vary so much over time that comparability of total costs distributed to cost centers from period to period becomes misleading.

Burden cost centers may cycle (receive and distribute) costs with service and utility cost centers. *Cycling,* as used here, refers to the interchange of services between cost centers. For example, an employee relations department uses electricity and accounting services. It also provides services to personnel of the accounting and electrical departments. This interchange of services leads to the use of simultaneous equations to allocate costs.

After the cycling of costs among service/utility and burden centers, the final distribution of all expenses to process centers can be made. The process costs, including cycled costs, are then assigned to joint products under various joint cost allocation methods.

ALLOCATING COSTS TO JOINT PRODUCTS

The meat packing industry is often thought of as presenting typical joint product costing problems. In order to produce a sirloin steak, a steer must be slaughtered, which in turn provides the sirloin as well as a variety of other products ranging from hide and trimmings to other cuts of meat. The problems associated with allocating the raw material costs (the steer plus acquisition costs) and the various subsequent processing costs (equipment, salaries, materials, etc.) among the meat, hide, and

EXHIBIT 1
Base case data used in Examples 1 through 4

	$1,000 joint costs	
	Product A	Product B
Pounds produced	400	600
Sales price per pound	$0.75	$ 2.00
Total sales value	$ 300	$1,200

trimmings demonstrate that the allocation of joint and by-product costs is often a difficult and arbitrary procedure.

There are three generally used methods of allocating joint product costs, with several possible variations and combinations of each. One method allocates costs to products in proportion to their *relative sales values* while a second allocates costs in proportion to some *physical measure* of the joint products (e.g., weight, volume, number of units, etc.). The third is a *replacement method* which represents an opportunity cost approach that is used by manufacturers with the ability to alter their product mix; in other words, to produce one product at the expense of another. The first two methods are demonstrated using the base case data shown in Exhibit 1.

Relative sales value method

This method, which is also referred to as the Sales Realization Method, the Federal Trade Method, and the Joint Product Method, is based on the assumption that product costs should bear a relationship to a product's earning power; that is, joint costs should be allocated to joint products in proportion to their ability to absorb those costs. Inherent in this approach is the assumption that all products earn the same profit percentage. Application of this method to the data in Exhibit 1 produces the following product costs:

Example 1

Product A

$$\frac{\$300}{\$300 + \$1,200} \times \$1,000 = \$200 \ (\$0.50/\text{lb.})$$

Product B

$$\frac{\$1,200}{\$300 + \$1,200} \times \$1,000 = \$800 \ (\$1.33/\text{lb.})$$

For simplicity, this example assumes that a process has only one split-off point and that there is a market value for the joint products at that point. However, the joint products of some manufacturing processes are not saleable at that point and, therefore, require further processing. In such cases, manufacturers using the Relative Sales Value Method have at least two alternatives for determining a value to be used in allocating costs to joint products at this point. First, an estimated sales value at the split-off point can be calculated by reducing the product's ultimate sales value by the costs of processing the product beyond the split-off. For example, assume for a moment that Products A and B in Exhibit 1 are not saleable at the split-off point and must incur additional processing costs of $150 and $250 to achieve sales values of $650 and $1,750, respectively.

	Product A	Product B
Ultimate sales value	$650	$1,750
Less: Costs beyond split-off	150	250
Computed sales value at split-off	$500	$1,500

The joint product costs of $1,000 would then be allocated as follows:

Example 2

Product A

$$\frac{\$500}{\$500 + \$1,500} \times \$1,000 = \$250 \ (\$0.63/\text{lb.})$$

Product B

$$\frac{\$1,500}{\$500 + \$1,500} \times \$1,000 = \$750 \ (\$1.25/\text{lb.})$$

A second choice would be to allocate total costs, including those for additional processing, to the finished joint products, without regard to the split-off point. Although this approach does not make the normal distinction between joint and additional processing costs, it is often used by industries with a continuous process multiproduct operation, such as petroleum refining, where process complexities, large numbers of products, and a lack of clearly defined split-off points make it impractical from a cost/benefit standpoint to differentiate such costs.

The Relative Sales Value Method is generally viewed by business and government as a reasonable basis for determining product costs for financial statement purposes. It should be recognized, however, that sales values are normally established by the market, not by costs of production. A problem arises when the price of an individual product changes significantly, thus altering the proportion of costs allocated to the joint products without any variations in production volumes or costs. For example, a fluctuation in the world market price for gold would cause a mining company to adjust the portion of joint costs allocated to its other products such as silver, although production volumes and costs for these minerals are unchanged. Accordingly, there are limitations on the usefulness of this method for making operating decisions, such as whether or not to process a joint product beyond a split-off point.

Physical basis method

The Physical Basis Method allocates joint costs to products in proportion to some form of physical measure—in this example, the weight of the products. Applying this method to the data in Exhibit 1, product costs would be determined as follows:

Example 3

Product A

$$\frac{400 \text{ lbs.}}{400 \text{ lbs.} + 600 \text{ lbs.}} \times \$1,000 = \$400 \ (\$1/\text{lb.})$$

Product B

$$\frac{600 \text{ lbs.}}{400 \text{ lbs.} + 600 \text{ lbs.}} \times \$1,000 = \$600 \ (\$1/\text{lb.})$$

For simplicity, the example again assumes that a process has only one split-off point. However, it should be recognized that joint cost methods are similarly applied to processes with several such points. The joint costs calculated at one split-off are further allocated at a subsequent point. For example, assume that the 400 pounds of Product A (at $1/lb.) is further processed into 300 pounds of Product A_1 and 100 pounds of Product A_2 at an additional processing cost of $200 ($0.50/lb.). As shown in Example 4, the total costs allocated to Products A_1 and A_2 are as follows:

Example 4

Product A_1

$$\frac{300 \text{ lbs.}}{300 \text{ lbs.} + 100 \text{ lbs.}} \times (\$400 + \$200) = \$450 \ (\$1.50/\text{lb.})$$

Product A_2

$$\frac{100 \text{ lbs.}}{300 \text{ lbs.} + 100 \text{ lbs.}} \times (\$400 + \$200) = \$150 \ (\$1.50/\text{lb.})$$

The Physical Basis Method assumes that each product receives similar benefits from the production process and thus should be allocated the same unit cost. This assumption appears reasonable for a manufacturer whose various products have a relatively small difference in unit price. However, as shown below, a large difference in unit price, such as that between Product A and B in Exhibit 1, may result in one product continually showing a loss while another may boast a high margin.

	Product A	Product B
Sales	$ 300	$1,200
Less: Costs (from Example 3)	400	600
Gross margin	$(100)	$ 600
Gross margin percentages	(33⅓%)	50%

Obviously, due to the sometimes arbitrary assumptions of this method, such a variance in profits may or may not be reflective of a product's true contribution to the profitability of an operation. Accordingly, costs determined by this method should not normally be the sole support for decisions to produce or not produce a product.

Replacement method

A rather specialized joint costing approach—called the replacement method—has application to those industries (such as petroleum refining, petrochemicals, and lumber) that by the nature of their processes have the ability to alter their product mix. For example, a petroleum refiner, through various conversion processes, has flexibility to vary the mix of its products (usually gasoline and distillates) produced from crude oil. The replacement method assumes that the manufacturer processes most of its raw materials into one or more major (prime) products, and that all other (nonprime) products are made by reducing the volume of prime products. In short, the replacement cost assigned to nonprime products is equated to the average cost of replacing the prime products' volumes, plus the net effect of any operations added or saved as a result of making these nonprime products. When production capacity limits the ability to replace products, the sales values of the prime products are used in the place of costs when pricing nonprime products.

EXHIBIT 2
Illustration of replacement method of costing joint products

A. Diagram of actual operation

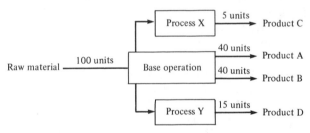

B. Theoretical conversion of actual operation to
process all raw material into Products A and B

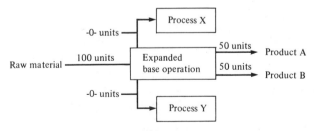

Note: Production of Products C and D stops. Operating costs for Process X and Y are saved, but additional operating costs are incurred to convert their raw material into Products A and B.

580

The costs of prime products are determined by a combined effort of cost and engineering analysis. The engineering effort consists of identifying the physical process steps and marginal costs involved in converting one product into another. Once this engineering model has been established, accounting methods can be applied to estimate the effect on product costs of altering the product mix. For illustration purposes, assume that a manufacturer produces Products A through D, with Products A and B being the prime products (Exhibit 2). In replacement costing, the first step is to simplify the actual operation so that only prime products are produced. As shown at the bottom of Exhibit 2, Process X and Y are theoretically shut down so that all of the raw materials will pass through the base operation to produce Products A and B, using the base operation unit cost per barrel and yield pattern for these prime products. Next, an assumption must be made of the cost per unit of some process or processes within the overall operation that is capable of converting Product B into Product A. Using this assumed conversion cost (determined by engineering analysis), a replacement cost can then be calculated for Products A and B by the method shown in Exhibit 3.

EXHIBIT 3
Calculation of costing products A and B

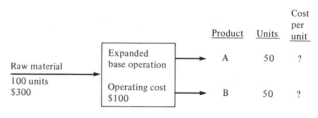

		Product	Units	Cost per unit
Raw material 100 units $300	Expanded base operation	A	50	?
	Operating cost $100	B	50	?

Calculation	*Cost*
Cost of raw material	$300
Operating cost	100
Cost of Products A and B	$400

Let:
X = Cost of Product B
$1/Unit = Cost of converting Product B into Product A based on engineering analysis

Then:

$50 (X + \$1) + 50X = \$400$
Product B Cost, $X = \$350/100 = \$3.50/Unit$
Product A Cost $= \$3.50 + \$1.00 = \$4.50/Unit$

The costs of the nonprime products can now be determined by using the prime product replacement costs. Exhibit 4, which illustrates the cost calculation for Product C, shows that the costs of replacing Products A and B are credited for operating costs that were saved, and charged for processing costs that were added to produce Product C. Costs for Product D would be calculated in a similar manner.

EXHIBIT 4
Calculation of costing product C

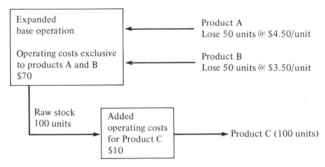

			Dollars
Calculation		*Dollars*	*per unit*
Cost of replacing Product A (50 × $4.50)		$225	
Cost of replacing Product B (50 × $3.50)		175	
Credit for saved operations		(70)	
Product C raw stock cost		$330	
Charge for added operating costs		10	
Final total cost of Product C		$340	$3.40

Like the other joint costing methods discussed earlier, the replacement method can be used to cost products for financial statement purposes. Normally, the product costs applied to volumes and the resulting total dollars will be reasonably close to the actual dollars spent for a given time period. Any balance of unallocated costs can be ratioed up or down so that the calculated production cost will equal the dollars spent.

In addition to its usefulness for determining costs of goods sold and inventory values, the replacement method can provide input that is useful when making choices among processing alternatives (products) due to its consideration of opportunity costs.

USE OF JOINT COSTS

Current accounting literature stresses that joint product costing methods are used as tools for calculating inventory values. This point of view is silent as to whether the primary thrust of joint costing is toward providing the most meaningful presentation of inventory costs in the balance sheet or toward the most meaningful statement of the cost of goods sold for purposes of income determination. The emergence of the income statement in recent years as the most widely used financial statement and the increasing emphasis on the importance of net income suggest that joint costing should be perceived primarily as a tool for income determination, with inventory valuation being a secondary objective. Recognition of this principle is important since the underlying concepts often provide guidance for application of specific procedures, especially in the absence of rules which adequately address unique problems. In the case of joint costing, the guiding concept should be the *matching principle*— the idea of providing the most meaningful matching of costs with the resultant revenues from the sale of the joint products. Proper valuation of products remaining in inventory at the end of the accounting period logically follows.

The usefulness of a particular joint product costing method is a function of the reasonableness of the cost allocation process. A reasonable method that can be consistently applied in a uniform manner can provide satisfactory product costs for financial statement purposes. Absolute accuracy is not expected as it is well recognized that financial position and results of operations for any given period are reasonable estimates rather than precise measurements. Material distortion will not occur if products are consistently valued over a period of time by using the same reasonable method.

Although a joint product costing method may be suitable for financial statement purposes, the arbitrary assumptions underlying joint costing preclude product costs from being used for cost control purposes (a function of the cost center), or from being the sole support for pricing products or choosing among production alternatives. In the short run, a product's price is determined by the marketplace rather than on a cost-justified basis using the methods discussed in this chapter. Over a longer term basis, product costs may be an aid to a manufacturer in evaluating cost efficiencies that are required to assure that product prices adequately recover costs. A user of a joint cost method who understands its limitations can use it as a bench mark when making an operating or pricing decision. Joint product costs are often only indicators that further analysis is necessary. This analysis is often performed by using incremental or other cost concepts discussed in other chapters of this handbook.

In some industries, such as meat packing and mining, the joint cost allocation process is so subjective that many companies do not allocate joint costs at all, but instead value their inventories at sales or net realizable value (selling price less selling and distribution costs). It should be recognized that this would result in profits being recognized prior to the sales transaction. Although this procedure is inconsistent with the realization principle discussed in *Accounting Principles Board Statement No. 4,*[1] the Statement also points out that there are exceptions to the principle due to difficulties in determining costs of products on hand. Using net realizable values as a measure of the costs of goods sold is not inconsistent with generally accepted accounting principles, assuming that any resultant distortion of the financial statements is not material. To alleviate the inconsistency with *APB Statement No. 4,* many firms choose to reduce the net realizable value of their inventory by an estimated profit margin, which is in effect an application of the relative sales value method.

ALLOCATING COSTS TO BY-PRODUCTS

By-products are those goods produced in the manufacturing process which result incidentally from the production of the major product and whose relative sales value is significantly smaller than that of the joint products. The distinction between by-products and joint products is often difficult to make. Market differences between geographical areas may, for instance, cause a particular product to be considered a by-product by one com-

---

[1] Accounting Principles Board, APB Statement No. 4: "Basic Concepts and Accounting Principles Underlying Financial Statements of Business Enterprises" (New York: American Institute of Certified Public Accountants, 1970), paragraph 152. Copyright © 1970 by the American Institute of Certified Public Accountants, Inc.

pany and a joint product by another. Technological changes over a period of time may also affect a particular product's status as a joint or by-product. The National Accounting Association Research Report on Costing Joint Products describes by-products as follows:

1. Aggregate value of a by-product is low in comparison with the value of the related major product. This may be the result of either low unit value for the by-product or a small output of the by-product.

2. By-products are incidental and sometimes undesired items which unavoidably accompany production of products which are the major objectives of a manufacturing process.[2]

There may also be difficulties in differentiating between by-products and scrap, but the classification is not material for financial statement purposes since the accounting treatment for by-products and scrap is similar; i.e., cost is equal to realization value.

Generally, there is no attempt to assign actual costs to by-products since these products are only incidental to the manufacture of the main products. Instead, by-products are usually valued at net realizable value (sales value less disposal costs). Additional processing costs incurred after the split-off point are charged against the by-product revenue. If a market value is not available for a by-product, the market value of an equivalent product may be used. For example, a lumber producer may burn a by-product to generate heat. The value of this by-product can be determined by equating the heat supplied by the by-product to that of fuel oil or natural gas, which have established market values.

There are three basic income statement approaches to accounting for by-products:

1. The net realizable value of by-product production is subtracted from the cost of the main product.

2. The net revenue from by-product sales is treated as other income.

3. The net revenue from by-product sales is subtracted from the cost of the main product.

---

[2] "Costing Joint Products," *NAA Research Report 31*, (April 1957), p. 7–11.

Assume the following:

	Main product		By-product	
	Units	*$*	*Units*	*$*
Beginning inventory	—	—	—	—
Production	5,000	75,000	600	1,200
Sales.......................	4,000	100,000	400	800
Ending inventory	1,000	—	200	400
Sales value	$25 per unit		$2 per unit	
Costs of disposal	—	—	$0.25 per unit	

Net revenue of by-product:
By-product sales (400 units) $800
Costs of disposal (400 units × $0.25) 100
    Net revenue $700

Net realizable value of by-product production:
By-product production (600 units) $1,200
Costs of disposal (600 units × $0.25) 150
    Net value $1,050

EXHIBIT 5

	Methods of accounting for by-products		
	(1)	*(2)*	*(3)*
Sales—Main product	$100,000	$100,000	$100,000
Net revenue—by-product	—	700	—
Total Revenue	100,000	100,700	100,000
Cost of sales:			
Production—Main product	75,000	75,000	75,000
Net realizable value—			
By-product production	(1,050)		
Restated cost of production	73,950		
Net revenue of by-product			(700)
Ending inventory—Main product	(14,790)*	(15,000)	(15,000)
Cost of sales	59,160	60,000	59,300
Gross margin	$ 40,840	$ 40,700	$ 40,700

* Restated cost of production	$73,950	
Ending inventory of main product as percentage of total production (1,000 Units ÷ 5,000 Units)	×0.20	
Ending inventory	$14,790	

Using this data, the three methods of accounting for by-products are illustrated in Exhibit 5.

In Exhibit 5, the $140 variance in profits ($40,840 less $40,700) is reflected in the inventory values of the main and by-products, as follows:

	Main product	By-product	Total
Method 1	$14,790	$350*	$15,140
Methods 2 and 3	15,000	—	15,000
Difference	$ (210)	$350	$ 140

* 200 units × ($2.00 sales value − $0.25 cost of disposal) = $350

Method 1 allows the most meaningful matching of revenues and costs because the production and ending inventory costs of the main product are immediately reduced by the net realizable value of the resultant by-products. Thus, the delay between production and sales does not affect periodic income. Also, under this method the balance sheet reflects a by-product inventory at its net realizable value.

SUMMARY

Many manufacturers, by the nature of their processes, produce multiple products from a single raw material. Joint costs are the common costs shared by these products until they become identifiable as separate and distinct products. Those products with a significant sales value are called joint products, while those with a minor value are called by-products. The net realizable value of a by-product is generally subtracted from the cost of the joint (major) products.

Joint costs must be identified before any allocation can be made to specific products. Costs are generally segregated and controlled by areas of managerial responsibility, commonly called cost centers. There are various techniques of allocating expenses among cost centers before any attempt is made to allocate costs to products.

There are three generally used methods of allocating joint costs, with numerous variations of each. Of these three, the physical basis method and relative sales value method can be applied to almost any type of multiproduct manufacturing operation. Respectively, these methods allocate joint costs to products in proportion to a unit of physical measure or to sales value. The replacement cost method, on the other hand, uses an opportunity cost approach to costing products and can be used only by manufacturers with the ability to alter their product mix. All three approaches have merit for costing products for financial

statement purposes. However, the arbitrary assumptions underlying these methods may limit their use for managerial decision
making.

REFERENCES

Crowningshield, Gerald R., and Gorman, Kenneth A. *Cost Accounting: Principles and Managerial Applications.* Boston: Houghton-Mifflin Company, 1974.

Financial Accounting Standards Board. *Tentative Conclusions on Objectives of Financial Statements of Business Enterprises.* Stamford, Conn. December 1976.

Horngren, Charles T. *Cost Accounting: A Managerial Emphasis,* 4th ed. New York: Prentice Hall, Inc., 1977.

Irving, Robert H., Jr., and Draper, Verden R. *Accounting Practices in the Petroleum Industry.* New York: The Ronald Press Company, 1958.

Jensen, Daniel L. "The Role of Cost in Pricing Joint Products: A Case of Production in Fixed Proportions." *The Accounting Review,* July 1974, pp. 465–84.

Louderback, Joseph G. "Another Approach to Allocating Joint Costs: A Comment." *The Accounting Review,* July 1976, pp. 683–85.

Moriarity, Shane. "Another Approach to Allocating Joint Costs." *The Accounting Review,* October 1975, pp. 791–95.

Porter, Stanley P. *Petroleum Accounting Practices.* New York: McGraw-Hill, 1965.

Schmeltz, William F. "Accounting and Management Control Practices in Petroleum Refining." Ph.D. dissertation, Western Reserve University, 1966.

23

Setting standards and reporting standard costs

Stephen Landekich*

Principal notions and terms

All cost accounting is concerned, in one way or another, with relationships between assets and costs. Assets are financial representations of economic resources held by an enterprise. Costs are financial representations of the use of economic resources by an enterprise.

Historical cost accounting states assets in terms of *past* costs. It is focused on costs incurred, also called *actual* costs. Actual costs are determined from accounting records of past transactions or events as they actually occurred.

Standard cost accounting states costs in terms of *future* assets. It is focused on costs to be incurred. Standard costs are *predetermined*, that is, set in advance of transactions or events to which they apply.

Standard cost accounting provides advance information, which is not available from historical cost accounting. Each standard is designed to yield a bench mark—a point of reference in measuring performance. As the historical data on actual performance become available, only the deviations from standards,

---

* Research Director, National Association of Accountants.

called *variances*, require analysis, so as to decide whether or not any corrective action is needed.

Standard costs add a new dimension to cost accounting, which increases its usefulness for planning (budgeting) and managerial decision making. Standard costs are particularly suited for the application of management-by-exception methods in monitoring business activities. Standard costs also provide a reliable and efficient alternative to historical costs for many cost accounting and financial reporting purposes. For example, companies often use standard costs as a base to value inventories. On the other hand, the extra costs incurred, for standard setting and revising in particular, must be taken into account in evaluating the overall effectiveness of standard costing.

In standard costing, the term *standard* is used in reference to numerical expressions adopted by business enterprises to serve as relatively stable *predetermined* measures for the specified processes or organizational units. Standards relate resources (costs) to products or organizational units or other cost objectives, such as contracts, projects, and job orders. Standards are set to reflect the cost-objective relationships which will prevail in the foreseeable future.

Standards for variable costs relate these costs, directly or indirectly, to the units of output (products or services). In principle, standards for variable costs are constructed (set) from a rigorous analysis of every component (operation). Standards for direct variable costs set in physical terms are called *quantity (time) standards*. They are usually stated also in dollar amounts as *cost standards*. To determine the amount of cost from a physical standard, the physical standard is multiplied by the *standard price* (for material) or *standard rate* (for labor).

The cost-objective (input-output) relationship is stated *directly* for each of the two main input elements—labor and material. A direct standard is sometimes set for energy as well. Other variable costs are related to the output *indirectly* by constructing one single standard for all of them as a group (cost category). Such a standard is not set per unit of output; it is set (computed) per unit of labor, machine time, or in reference to some other activity or control unit.

In practice, some costs which do not originate from the process are added to indirect cost standards constructed from the standard-setting analysis. Such costs, known as *overhead* or *burden*, are derived from the total amounts set by *budgeting* procedures. Hence, the budgeted overhead allocated to a process or organizational unit becomes a component of its standard cost structure, usually called the *overhead standard rate*.

The overhead standard rate is either fixed or it varies, in part at least, with the changing levels of activity (volume). The respective budgeting procedures are called *fixed budgeting* and *flexible budgeting*.

As to the items to be included in direct or indirect standards, standard costing follows the methods and procedures adopted by the enterprise for its historical cost accounting. Standard costing is consistent with job order or process costing, direct or absorption costing, responsibility accounting, and so forth. Any disagreements would tend to introduce unwarranted complexities and to detract from the usefulness of standard costing. For example, the actual and standard performance figures would not be fully comparable.

A special type of discrepancy is sometimes introduced intentionally by setting budgeted amounts above or below the corresponding standard costs. For example, management may decide that relatively high ("tight") standards will motivate the production people to reach such an aspiration level of performance, while at the same time leaving the budgeted amounts at the past (average) performance level.

Applicability of standards and standard costs

In general. In the basic sense of a predetermined relationship between efforts and the corresponding results, the notion of a standard or a set of standards underlies all goal-oriented (purposive) activities—business activities in particular. People do not engage in an ongoing (continuing) business unless and until they have determined, in sufficient detail and to their satisfaction, the expected cost-objective relationship.

Production. In a broad sense, production is any business activity that takes place as a process designed to transform a set of inputs (resources) into a set of outputs (products and services). An input-output model of production is given below:

Input (resource) → Transformation → Output (products, services)

This model covers all types of production, because it is stated in general terms only. In practice, the distinction between the input and the transformation process is not always delineated in a clear-cut manner. Labor, material, and energy are basic inputs. Plant (office) and facilities make up the process.

Basic inputs.   Standard costs for labor and material are set on the basis of the respective physical standards expressing materials (quantity) and labor (time, usually hours) per unit of product or service:

$$\text{Quantity (time)} \times \text{Price (rate)} = \text{Standard cost}$$

Setting physical standards.   Production of a single product or service can always be stated in terms of physical standards for basic inputs, provided that there also exists some quantitatively (numerically) determinable measure for the unit of product or service. When one single set of inputs is used to produce two or more products or services, it may not be feasible or practicable to segregate the respective quantities of labor and materials in order to set physical standards per unit of each individual product or service. It is possible sometimes to determine at least some material and to use this as the basis for all materials. Similarly, a direct labor measure is generally used as the basis for all labor and related costs. Problems of this type are usually resolved in accordance with the company policy governing joint-product costing.

Determining units of output.   A difficult and often intractable problem arises when there is no satisfactory unit measure for products or services. A surrogate measure can occasionally be selected or constructed analytically. More often than not, however, such procedures yield physical standards of questionable usefulness. The use of some partial simile, regardless of its scientific aura, may turn into an expensive folly. Although the standard derived in such a way may have been introduced only as a partial aid in understanding the process, its limitations are likely to be forgotten or neglected by management. As a consequence, the people whose performance is so measured will give priority to the respective efforts. A partial measure thus becomes a major goal or *the* goal, to the detriment of the other goals that are, taken together, probably more important than the goal represented by the standard.

Process stability. Standards are not going to be meaningful, no matter how they are set, unless they reflect well-defined and stable relationships between the resources to be used and the objectives to be accomplished. The critical task for the analysis involved in both the measuring of inputs and the determination of units of output is to take into account the relevant operational and behavioral properties of the process. In particular, there must be some assurance that current conditions will continue to obtain, if only to the degree which justifies the effort involved in setting standards.

Input-output stability. We can often make good use of our past observations, supplemented perhaps by testing and simulation, to determine whether the input-output relationship is sufficiently stable under current conditions. On this basis we may assume that, if everything else remains as before, the transformation process will retain its current properties.

The linear assumption. One simplifying assumption is widely adopted in theory and practice: the linearity of the input-output relationship over a relevant range of change in the size of production. For example, a 10 percent increase in the input will raise the output in the same proportion, i.e., by 10 percent. We infer, therefore, that moderate fluctuations in the size (scale) of operations will not require revision of the standards for direct labor and direct materials. The same inference is applicable to all the standards for indirect costs that are set on the basis of the direct labor standard or the direct material standard, provided that there is a stable relationship between these cost categories and the respective basic standards. In other words, this reasoning applies to all variable costs of production.

Process costs. Most process costs represent fixed overhead—they do not vary with the number of units produced. They can be determined with respect to a period of time rather than in terms of the size of production, i.e., they remain fixed regardless of changes in the size (volume) of production. It is often both feasible and desirable to identify certain process cost elements which are subject to change whenever the volume of production moves beyond a certain range. Hence, a distinction is usually made between fixed and semivariable overhead costs. As a corollary, we have fixed and flexible overhead rates.

Manufacturing enterprises. Standards are applicable to all of the main business operations in a manufacturing enterprise. Each of these operations is, or should be, organized and monitored in reference to some measures which could be used to develop standards. Most commonly, however, standards are used only for factory operations.

Factory operations. Standards are applicable to all types or systems of factory operations. Only exceptionally are these operations run as custom shop operations, where almost no processing patterns are ever repeated. In those cases, standards may not be sufficiently effective. There is an observed tendency in company practice, however, to use standards for all factory operations, or not to use standards at all, regardless of their suitability to individual processes or shops. It is usually more economical (effective) to set uniform standard-costing policies in terms of the overall company preferences. In order for a large system to perform in an optimal (the "best possible") manner, often the participating subsystems must be required to adopt some suboptimal policies.

Manufacturing costs. The use of standards and standard costs does not necessarily mean that standards are set for all the input elements or, if set, that standards are incorporated into the double-entry system of accounting. When not incorporated, the standards may be used for operational control and standard costs may be used for cost control, planning, pricing, budgeting, and so forth, but they are not ordinarily used for inventory pricing.

Partial versus complete application. Partial applications of standard costs are frequently found in practice. As a matter of fact, the use of predetermined burden rates in historical cost systems is referred to as standard costing, though such rates actually represent budgeted costs, that is, budget allowances rather than standard based costs. Historically, this practice of applying standard costing only to the manufacturing overhead preceded the use of standard costs for direct materials and direct labor.

It is also true that the cost accountant must usually set the standard for the factory overhead cost, while standards for direct materials and direct labor are primarily set by industrial engineers and managers of production and purchasing functions.

Some manufacturers use standards costs for labor and overhead, but not for material; they often refer to labor and overhead as *conversion costs*. A complete standard costing system covers, as a rule, the complete production cycle—from raw materials to finished products.

Financial statements. In addition to applications in cost accounting, standard costs are applicable to financial (external) reporting. When standard costing is used consistently, either as full absorption costing or as direct costing (adjusted, of course, to include all manufacturing costs), business enterprises may price materials, work-in-process, and finished-goods inventories on a standard cost basis:

> Standard costs are acceptable if adjusted at reasonable intervals to reflect current conditions so that at the balance-sheet date standard costs reasonably approximate costs computed under one of the recognized bases. (Footnote to *ARB No. 43*, Ch. 4, Statement 4, AICPA, 1953.)

Defense contracts. Standard costs are acceptable, provided that they meet the specified criteria, for use in negotiated national defense contracts which are subject to cost accounting standards promulgated by the Cost Accounting Standards Board (CASB). Recognizing the complexity of applications in business practice, the Board will cover standard costing in phases. The use of standard costs for direct material and direct labor is already covered by the Cost Accounting Standard (CAS) issued as Part 407 on April 1, 1974. The use of standard costs for service centers and the use of standard costs for overhead represent two other phases that are still under consideration.

Design and implementation

It is essential to have the intended standard cost system fully designed and thoroughly examined (pretested) well in advance of implementation. The implementation may be scheduled as a gradual application, from the partial to the complete, or the system may initially be implemented as a complete application in one cost center only. No matter how it is scheduled or carried out, the implementation should not take place while any of the design work involved is still in process. The system is not ready for implementation until all of its parts become fully operational and interlocked.

Preliminary work. The development of a standard cost system is ordinarily preceded by several preliminary phases, such as:

1. The feasibility phase—to see whether standard costing is applicable in principle, to determine the extent of the intended application both with respect to the operations to be covered and the degree of completeness of the system, to outline a suitable design, and to indicate the changes to be made in the company functions affected by standard costing.
2. The methodology phase—to explore various applicable approaches and methods in order to select and agree on those that meet the company objectives.
3. The proposal phase—to develop the design in full and get it approved.
4. The experimental phase—to test for completeness and quality, to give all concerned the opportunity to get acquainted with the system as a whole and how it relates to their respective functions and jobs, and to make concluding revisions in the design.
5. The implementation program phase—to prepare detail forms and instructions, to develop schedules and make assignments for participation in standard setting, and to determine the respective responsibilities and delegate the authority to interpret the system and resolve possible implementation problems.

Feasibility. Applicability of standards and standard costs is covered in the preceding section of this chapter, although in general terms only. In terms of a company's needs and conditions, standard costing should be considered applicable only to the extent to which the expected benefits exceed the corresponding incremental costs. Hence, the major task of a feasibility study is to establish the basic cost-benefit relationship and then select an optimal combination of the alternatives with respect to the features of the standard cost system and the related objectives. The overall usefulness of a standard cost system is largely determined by the proper matching of the system properties with the requirements of the particular company. The system has to be tailor-made.

Methodology. Wherever several methods appear equally suitable, the choice should be made in accordance with the preferences of the people involved. In addition to the analysis in terms of comparable costs and benefits, the alternative methods should be examined with respect to their quality attributes, such as (*a*) the behavioral impact on the company people; (*b*) uniformity with respect to the methods employed in the historical cost accounting system, budgeting, and other company activities, as well as with respect to industry practice and practice prevailing in business enterprises in general; and (*c*) the cost of revisions in order to adapt the system to various contingent changes in the company organizational structure, in the external circumstances affecting the activities covered by standards, and so forth.

Design. It is necessary to have all the parts interlocked as they relate to one another. But it is not sufficient to have it done mechanically, in terms of the flow of data, information feedback provisions, and so on. The design should show that all of this will work in the desired direction, to converge toward a common goal. For example, it is not sufficient to use an efficient method for setting standards; it should also be shown that the method is efficient for variance analysis and other direct or indirect uses of the method. This quality is sometimes called effectiveness.

Effectiveness. The notion of effectiveness can be contrasted with the notion of "different costs for different purposes" which is so frequently emphasized in cost accounting theory and practice. At times it is even interpreted to imply that a multiple-purpose cost is somehow suspect. To the contrary, the goal is to find suitable multipurpose costs wherever it is not necessary to develop specific costs for individual purposes. For example, a standard which approximates subsequent performance more closely than a standard set at any other level is not only efficient in a statistical sense (it minimizes variances), but it also results in more reliable (efficient) standards for most of the other purposes as well.

Forms. The principle of effectiveness is especially applicable to the forms designed for standard costing purposes. One single form, if skillfully designed, serves a variety of purposes. In general, a form should carry spaces for entering data pertaining to several successive phases in the production process. Not all of these spaces will be used in every case. A well-designed form also groups and/or segregates data in a manner suitable for direct transcription into the cost accounting records. For example, a special-purchase order is the only form needed for special-purchase materials, provided that it contains spaces for all of the required data.

Instructions.   In large companies, policies and procedures are set forth in considerable detail, since they apply throughout the company. As to the cost accounting function, the relevant policies and procedures are organized in the form of the company's cost accounting manual. The implementation of a standard cost system should be accompanied by a careful review of the manual in order to remove any remaining inconsistencies. Standard costing is usually covered in a separate section of the manual.

Setting standards

A special package of policies and instructions is prepared for use in setting standards. It is recognized in practice that standards are the outcomes obtained from a complex set of interconnected problem solutions and decisions on a multitude of technological, organizational, and behavioral factors. It is also recognized that the people assigned to the task of setting standards hold differing views of the issues involved. They are often selected on this basis, so as to make sure that proper attention will be given to conflicting considerations. The policies and instructions are designed to establish a common frame of reference, rather than to serve as substitutes for the judgment to be exercised by the participants in arriving at a consensus. In other words, they are designed basically to serve as a communication device in relating various aspects of standard-setting to the overall company objectives.

Prime responsibility.   The task of setting standards is primarily the responsibility of the respective production and purchasing departments. Most of the work is done by the nonaccounting personnel—industrial engineers and production control experts in particular.

Participation by accountants.   Cost accountants are active participants in practically all the phases of standard-setting. Their work includes analyses of both the historical and projected data, and assistance to those who are less familiar with the intricacies of the standard cost system and cost classification in general. In addition, the plant controller's office usually coordinates standard-setting with the other parts of the system implementation. The plant controller also interprets the applicable policies and procedures, and reviews the results.

Methods of obtaining data

In general, data are obtainable: (1) by means of estimates and guesses, (2) by observation, laboratory experimentation, engineering, and other analytical (work study) measurements, and (3) by a knowledge of relationships (patterns, trends, etc.) acquired from company records on past performance or derived mathematically (statistically) from sampling, and so forth. In many cases, these methods are alternative ways of looking at one single problem, while in some other cases the problems may be resolved by using the most readily obtainable data only.

Data sources

Modern production management subscribes to the view that every operation should have its counterpart in data form. The documentation appears in various forms and under various names, but it is the content (purpose) that counts. To illustrate: blueprints are drawn up in total detail, describing both products and processes. The project or job requirements are organized in the bill of materials for further and more detailed accounting by parts. Route sheets (operations sheets) specify the equipment, which provides a basis for specifications of all materials, components, and subassemblies. Precedence diagrams are drawn for line balancing. The order of assembly is depicted on sequence charts or "Gozinto" (goes into) charts, and so forth.

To summarize: in a well-managed company, most of the data for standard costing—setting standards in particular—will have been available by the time the implementation gets underway. Many companies also regularly monitor performance, and the data needed for labor standards will also be available from the engineering and work studies (method study, method measurement, and other types of studies).

SETTING PRODUCTION STANDARDS

Levels of performance

Standards are set in accordance with the company management position regarding the basic policy issue: What constitutes the *target level of performance* for standard-setting purposes? The decisions regarding various aspects of design and implementation will necessarily indicate the managerial preferences and they will thus set implicitly a policy for standard-setting. Nonetheless, many companies set an explicit guideline as part of their policies and instructions prepared for the use in setting standards.

The *tightness* with which standards are set differs markedly among users of standard costs. While the variations are not precisely distinguishable in practice, several distinct types of standards can be identified as the main alternatives:

1. The historical or average past performance standards.
2. The average expected performance standards.
3. The currently attainable good performance or realistic standards.
4. The ideal, scientific, theoretical, or perfection standards.

Past performance standards.   It is generally conceded that historical standards are not consistent with the intended role of standard costing, particularly with respect to managerial control objectives. Standards should be goal oriented. The past is not a suitable criterion of what the costs should be in the future. The average past performance data tend to bury the very inefficiencies that the implementation of standard costing is designed to ferret out and eliminate. On the other hand, past performance standards have several desirable attributes; they are (*a*) readily comprehensible, (*b*) easy to develop and implement, (*c*) quite useful for some decisions, and (*d*) might represent the best information available, as well.

Expected performance standards.   The implementation of a standard cost system encompasses numerous steps toward more efficient performance. It is reasonable to expect that additional benefits will accrue through the subsequent use of information provided by the standard cost system. The expected-performance approach takes into account the anticipated favorable impact of the actions which will be taken in the course of, or as a result of, the establishment and use of standard costing. Altogether, this seems to be a practicable approach, provided that it is not used to promote some short-term schemes, known occasionally as cost-reduction drives.

Currently attainable standards. These standards do not purport to do away with all inefficiencies, but they give some recognition to the potential increases in performance. Such standards are centered on various practicable improvements and they thus include a degree of challenge to the performers. Some maintain, however, that currently attainable standards will not sufficiently motivate workers to do the best possible job.

Ideal standards. These standards represent the best performance under optimal conditions. The aim is to determine what could be done. Only the irreducible allowances, if any, are recognized. The thinking in favor of setting ideal standards tends to focus on their advantages in terms of the positive behavioral impact on workers. This thinking is based on the assumption that standards will be adopted ("internalized") as the goals toward which to work. There is some evidence that standards may have varying effects on motivation, but there is no conclusive evidence that ideal standards are generally producing favorable motivational effects. To the contrary, some findings from behavioral studies indicate that motivation is reduced rather than increased by the use of ideal standards. Much depends, of course, on the way in which they are used.

Applications in practice. It may be concluded from the evidence available that attainable standards are, generally speaking, at least equal to ideal standards in terms of the prospective behavioral impact. Attainable standards are preferable in all other respects, which is apparently recognized in current practice.

Some companies refer to the level of performance in general terms only. One company, for example, defines its standard costs as "predetermined costs that are arrived at by a process of scientific fact-finding using past history and controlled experiment." Other companies are specific with respect to the level of performance to be used in setting standards. To illustrate company reasoning in favor of attainable standards, let us see in a simplified version how a company interprets "attainable":

. . . as possible of accomplishment with a reasonable degree of efficient performance. Thus the standard does not cover inefficiencies which are due to low or unbalanced volume, inadequate supply of labor or material, construction work, . . . This type has been selected because within its scope all the requirements of effective management can be met.

Standards for materials

Material-quantity standards. Physical standards are set for all direct materials. In general, direct materials are those inputs that are used for, and identified with, specified saleable (end) products. This does not necessarily mean that all direct materials must actually (physically) be incorporated in the end product. On the other hand, some physical inputs of minor importance are not considered direct materials for standard-setting purposes.

It is good practice to have inventory records, materials requisitions, bills of materials, route sheets, production work orders, standard cost sheets (registers), and so forth, organized in such a manner that each item is referred to in consistent terms. Only one code number is established for an item, though the item may be used for different purposes and in more than one location. The physical standard is usually determined in reference to the unit of quantity measure which is applicable to the production use of the item. This unit of measure might not be identical to the units of measure used to purchase and store the item. For example, the material billed per pound or square foot may be delivered in rolls, drums, pieces, or sheets varying in thickness, size, and so forth, while still another unit of measure is used in processing. For such materials, it is necessary to establish standardized conversion ratios, multiples, etc., so that materials requisitions correspond to the units of measure used for inventory records, though a different measure may be used in the respective bills of materials.

A *bill of materials* is made out for each product, operation, or assembly (called "line assembly" when the operation is performed without the aid of a machine tool). The bill of materials identifies the product by its number and description, including size and weight. All specifications are set per unit of product, which is often assigned a serial number in sequence, or the quantities may be calculated on the basis of some other standardized measure, such as lot size (10 units, 50 units, and so forth). Each item of materials listed on a bill of materials is identified by its code number, description, and standard quantity. The form may include columns for material-price standards and standard costs, in which case the total standard cost of direct materials can be shown, as well.

When the physical standard is determined for a standard lot size, the calculation may be based on the average number of all units to be produced in order to obtain the specified number of good quality products. That is, the material-quantity standard provides an allowance for the defective units of product. The more common practice—especially when material-quantity standards are stated per unit of product—is to show this allowance separately or let it be reported as a variance. Such an allowance is sometimes part of a scrap or spoilage allowance which covers other similar losses as calculated for individual inputs.

Allowances incorporated in material-quantity standards are needed to convert the engineering or laboratory calculations into attainable standards. These calculations often include some irreducible losses, while the allowances for other types of losses are calculated separately—either to be added to the engineering standards or to be shown separately, usually as indirect costs. When the allowances are included in material-quantity standards, the excess materials requisitions indicate that the usage is over-and-above the attainable level. Past performance records are often taken into account with respect to the allowances considered to be unavoidable. The nature and relative size of material losses in manufacturing depends, of course, on the kind of materials used and on the type of processing and material handling involved. Several typical losses are listed below:

1. Processing allowance or yield—these losses are often incorporated in the engineering or laboratory calculations. For example, in a casting process, the base metal is retrieved, while alloys and core materials are nonrecoverable; hence, the material-quantity standards for alloys and core materials are adjusted accordingly. In chemical and similar formula recipes there are losses due to leakage, evaporation, and so forth.

2. Material shrinkage allowance—unavoidable losses in yard-age, etc., mostly inherent in the nature of the material or process.
3. Scrap allowance—small residual pieces left over from pro-cessing of metals, lumber, cloth, etc., such as turnings, chips, butt ends cut off, damaged ends of felt rolls, breakage, and trimmings. The pieces without any value represent waste.
4. Spoilage allowance—imperfections in materials and prod-ucts.

Material-price standards. These standards are set with re-spect to all of the materials covered by the material-quantity standards. In setting material-price standards, there are three main steps to complete: (1) estimate purchase prices, (2) compute acquisition costs, and (3) include operational and other costs which are directly assignable to materials.

Purchase prices. Many materials in a large company are not purchased from outside sources, but are supplied by other plants or other departments (cost centers) of the same plant. The re-spective prices are readily obtainable, since they are set at stan-dard costs or on some comparable basis. It is almost equally easy to obtain current and projected prices of materials regularly purchased on the basis of a long-term firm contract, or to esti-mate prices for commodities with relatively stable or predictable prices. In some cases, the company may engage in hedging, so as to minimize the financial effect of commodity price fluc-tuations.

With respect to materials subject to wide price fluctuations, management must estimate the anticipated price changes in terms of both size and timing, so that a weighted-average cost can be computed. The amounts of scheduled individual pur-chases are usually obtainable from the data prepared by the purchasing function for budgeting and cash-flow planning pur-poses.

In setting material-price standards, the purchase price is com-puted generally for purchases made in accordance with the com-pany's inventory control policies regarding the most economical order size and/or frequency of ordering. It is also assumed that buying, shipping, and warehousing will take place under the most favorable terms and conditions that are currently available.

Acquisition costs. The acquisition cost is computed by applying various adjustments designed to reflect terms of purchase other than the purchase price, and thus increase the accuracy with respect to the cost of material. Another purpose is to establish comparable cost data for standard-setting purposes. Companies often use the lowest obtainable acquisition cost of an item as the basis for the material-price standard, regardless of occasional variations due to differing order sizes, suppliers, and so forth. This also means that warehouse buys, quantity extras, and similar bargains are ignored unless they are regularly available. A few specific examples are listed below; they indicate adjustments which are usually applied to the invoice price in order to compute the acquisition cost:

1. All freight-in (from supplier's plant) charges are added, unless they have already been included in the invoice price.
2. Price is adjusted for federal excise tax and other costs specific to the material purchased, such as special set-ups, packaging, and nonreturnable containers.
3. Trade discounts are taken into account, but no adjustments are made to reflect cash or special discounts.
4. Excluded from the invoice price are all extra charges which are not regularly required for the material in question.

Allowances for assignable costs. It may be argued in principle that a material-price standard should reflect all the variable costs directly associated with an item for which the standard is set. These costs include receiving, testing, and losses due to breakage. In practice, however, the advantages may not warrant the required effort, except for large companies. In any event, the losses incurred during receiving and inventory handling should not be included in the material-quantity standards.

Standards for labor

Labor-time standards. These standards are set for all the labor required by work orders prepared for specific products, operations or assemblies. It is customary to designate certain functions or occupations as direct labor: production workers, machine operators, line-assembly operators, and so forth. Labor-time standards may also be set for *indirect labor,* which is defined as the work performed in the factory by an hourly employee whose function or occupation is not classified as direct labor. Indirect labor is also performed by the direct-labor employees, such as handling material, sweeping, tool or die changes, and bringing defective work up to inspection requirements. On the other hand, all the productive employees in a factory or machine shop which produces one single product may qualify as direct labor, including the foreman. But this is not standard practice.

In setting labor-time standards, basic calculations are derived from work studies or MTM (Methods-Time Measurement) or

EXHIBIT 1
Labor-time standard versus work conditions

Good conditions	*Hours*	*Poor conditions*
	6	Instructions are not clear and have to be repeated
		Tools are scattered and difficult to locate
	5	Materials are not in proper places; substitutes are not available
	4	Starting job, including time lost because another job was not completed on schedule
Time receiving supervisor's instructions		Performing job, including time lost because of:
Time getting tools which are readily available	3	Substitution of material required getting new tool, and required extra operations
Time starting job		
Time performing job without interruption due to lack of tools, materials, etc.	2	Improper workmanship, required part of job being done over
		Improper scheduling, required additional set-up
	1	
		Time after completing job, including waiting time because next job is not available
Time after completing job until next job is started		Time lost due to injury because of improper safety conditions
Personal time	0	Personal time

from test run results and/or are compiled from analyses of the past performance records. Allowances for nonproductive time are then added to provide for (1) the time used by the workers to attend to their personal needs, and for other personal factors, including fatigue, and (2) the time lost due to the nature of the production process and the prevailing working conditions, such as delays in getting materials delivered or machines repaired. Special allowances are made, of course, for the "learning curve" effects where appropriate.

For machine operators the set-up time is determined separately from the operating time. The operating time may be equal to the machine run time, but in many instances a machine can now operate without substantial labor participation and direct labor time may be required only at certain time intervals. The time required to set up and tear down a fixture is usually allowed on the basis of a complete set-up, though it often involves changing of some tools only (a partial set-up).

The labor-time standards are set for individual operations required to produce a product or part. A list of these operations with the respective labor-time standards, in hours, is known under various names. Sometimes it is simply called the operations list or labor-time standards list. The rates and total labor cost may also be added, in which case the list shows the total direct-labor standard cost.

If the operations are performed by one or more machines, the operations (route) list identifies the machine or machines and lists machine hours as well as labor hours for each of the listed operations. When the labor hours are equal to the machine hours, only the labor hours need to be listed. They are usually listed as hours per machine set-up, showing both the set-up and run time standards.

All the quantity and time standards are usually shown on a production work order. A production work order contains a listing of material-quantity standards, together with the standard processing requirements in terms of labor time, machine time, or tools. These data may be supplemented by the respective prices (rates), in which case the production work order shows the total direct cost of the product.

Labor-rate standards. In setting these standards, there are two main tasks to accomplish: (1) to identify for each labor-time standard the applicable wage rate or rates, and (2) to decide on the level at which the standards are to be set, that is, whether the standards will be equal to the wage rates or they will be set higher in order to cover some or all of the fringe benefits. Both tasks appear to be quite simple. Moreover, all the required data are readily obtainable from the company records.

In many companies, the task of determining the wage rates applicable to various jobs and operations can become difficult and time-consuming due to the diversity of the payment plans. The problem is usually simplified considerably by identifying average rates applicable to the main types of work performed by the direct labor employees. Another, even simpler, alternative is to compute average rates by departments or to compute a single average rate for the plant as a whole. In some companies, the top wage rate identified with the job is used rather than the average wage rate.

As to the inclusion of fringe benefits, the usual procedure would make good sense—to segregate the variable from the fixed—and to include the variable portion of fringe benefits. Some companies find it more convenient to exclude all fringe benefits—to treat them as indirect costs. Other companies include those fringe benefits that tend to vary in amount with the wage rate differentials, or those fringe benefits that can be readily computed in dollars (cents) per direct-labor hour.

Revision of standards

Regular updating.   Many companies maintain a regular schedule of updating their standard costs once a year. They rarely make partial interim revisions, except for major changes, such as a new union contract.

Basic versus current standards.   These terms are commonly used to refer to the two extremes when revising standard costs. Basic standard costs remain unchanged for several years, as a rule. Current standard costs are promptly revised in response to any significant change in the cost level or in the method of production.

Standards for manufacturing overhead

What constitutes manufacturing overhead.   In the total spectrum of cost and expenses, manufacturing overhead covers the area between direct costs and general expenses. Both boundaries are subject to the continuing dispute over some items with dual attributes. Let us, therefore, explore these two contiguous areas along the boundaries to see whether we can identify the items that belong to manufacturing overhead.

Direct versus indirect costs. Many overhead items have something in common with direct costs—they are variable. The variable overhead items are often called *indirect costs.* Direct costs vary with the number of units produced; indirect costs do not.

In setting standards for indirect costs we have the additional task to select an appropriate base for each category (pool) of indirect costs or, alternatively, to form these pools in such a way that all the included indirect costs are related to the same base, such as labor hours, machine-hours, direct-material or direct-labor costs. (This is yet another good reason for the use of the term *burden* for indirect costs and for manufacturing overhead in general.)

Cost versus expenses. In accordance with our introductory definitions, let us state that production costs represent resources which are being transformed into assets—work-in-process and finished goods inventories. From the production point of view, any other use of company resources is an expense or an investment, not a manufacturing cost. Alternatively, we can say that all overhead items which are reflected in the inventories belong to manufacturing overhead.

The above reasoning establishes a clear-cut criterion serviceable as a definite guide for any company. But this leaves us without a general criterion, since companies do not follow any uniform inventory policy. In order to establish a general criterion for the purposes of our discussion, we have to select one of the numerous varieties, preferably a commonly used one.

Inventoriable costs. To identify common practice in inventory measurement, we will refer to the findings of a research study (Stephen Landekich, "Cost Allocations to Inventory," *Management Accounting,* March 1973) which served as a basis for *Statement No. 6,* "Guidelines for Inventory Measurement," issued on November 16, 1973, by the NAA Committee on Management Accounting Practices (MAP).

The findings show that, out of 1,200 responses by manufacturing firms which were included in the tabulation, 671 (56 percent) firms do not allocate—while 529 (44 percent) do allocate—all expenditures indirectly related to production (at least on a broad-brush basis) in preparation of their financial statements. For purposes of management (internal) reporting, 691 (58 percent) do not allocate and 494 (42 percent) do allocate those expenditures.

Clearly, there is no uniformity in practice. Let us assume that all overhead costs incurred by or directly associated with a plant (factory) represent inventoriable costs—manufacturing overhead.

Material and labor overhead. Not all of the costs that vary directly with the output are included in standards for direct material and direct labor. They are left out and treated as indirect costs for a variety of reasons: to set tighter standards, for variance analysis and management control reasons, for convenience and/or efficiency reasons, to retain comparability or uniformity among direct standards, and so forth.

Examples: Instead of setting separate allowances for inventory losses and production related losses, a common allowance for the specified materials losses is included in the material overhead. The uniformity reason is especially applicable to the labor-time standards; they are used as a common medium of overhead allocation.

In setting standards for the material and labor overhead items, there is no problem with respect to the selection of appropriate allocation bases. Some of these standards could even be computed directly per unit of product.

Homogeneous overhead. The Cost Accounting Standards Board uses the concept of homogeneity to define the "production unit" level at which it is appropriate (for government contracting) to account for standard costs of direct material and direct labor. A *production unit* is:

> A grouping of activities which either uses homogeneous inputs for direct material and direct labor or yields homogeneous outputs such that the costs or statistics related to these homogeneous inputs or outputs are appropriate as bases for allocating variances. [CAS 407.30(a)(7)]

In setting standards for indirect costs applicable to homogeneous sets of inputs or outputs, the procedure could be basically

EXHIBIT 2

Standard Cost Card

Product A

Bill of materials No. _____
Work order No. _____

Product: _____
No. _____ Description: _____

Lot size (units): _____
Total cost ($): _____

Operation or item		Material		Labor		Overhead				Total ($) per unit
Cost center	Description	Quantity	Cost	Hours	Cost	Base	Units	Rate	Cost	
	Total ($) per unit of product									

Standard Cost Card

Product B

Product: _____
Issue date: _____

Batch quantity _____
Cost per batch $ _____

Direct cost per unit $ _____
Total cost per unit $ _____

Department	Code	Description	Unit of Measure	Quantity or Base	Price or Rate	Material		Labor		Overhead	
Department A											
				Total ($)							
Department B											
				Total ($)							
Other											
				Total ($)							
Total standard costs per batch											

of the type used for material and labor overhead. In some cases, however, there will be problems with respect to selecting the appropriate allocation base and/or establishing a practical method for distribution to several cost objectives when they are not treated as a homogeneous set.

Semivariable and fixed overhead. Setting standards for direct costs and variable overhead sets the stage for a higher level of accuracy and efficiency in determining budget allowances for the semivariable and fixed overhead. Considerations with respect to the choice of appropriate activity levels are similar to those used to determine levels of performance. In principle, one common approach—reflecting the basic management philosophy—should be used consistently for standard-setting, budgeting, reporting, and all other purposes.

In determining the activity level for computation of fixed manufacturing overhead, the costs resulting from the ownership of facilities represent a key element. The basic problem is to decide on the policy with respect to *idle capacity*. The NAA Committee on Management Accounting Practices (*Statement No. 6*) states that the portion of these costs that relates to the facilities which are not being utilized to the extent of their normal capabilities should not be treated as an inventoriable cost; that is, it is an *expense* rather than a part of manufacturing overhead. On the other hand, any material amount of reduction in manufacturing overhead (the favorable volume variance) which results from abnormal utilization of facilities should be taken into account to avoid stating the inventory in excess of the costs assigned to the inventory.

All the budget allowances for manufacturing overhead are incorporated in the calculations of total standard costs. They are usually shown on a form known as the standard cost sheet or card or register. Two alternative designs are presented in Exhibit 2.

REPORTING STANDARD COSTS

Performance reporting

Control features of standard costing. For the purpose of monitoring production performance, standard costing offers several significant advantages to company management at all levels:

1. In the course of standard setting, all the cost elements are under scrutiny in reference to the respective objectives (outputs). This brings into focus the cost-benefit responsibilities and helps clarify any related ambiguities in the organizational structure.
2. Control factors and degrees of controllability are taken into account when standards are constructed. (A direct cost remains directly responsive to changes in the output only under conditions of direct control.)
3. Standard costs reflect basic performance control levels and thus provide reliable criteria for performance reporting in terms of deviations (variances).
4. Variance reporting highlights significant control problems.
5. Standard costing information makes budget control more effective.

Reporting structure. Standard costing does not require that changes be made in the structure of performance reporting. Nevertheless, the implementation of a standard cost system is often accompanied by some changes which result from the analytical work needed to design a standard cost system. Those changes are made as improvements, not to accommodate standard costing as such.

Reporting format. Companies which use standard costing extend their historical cost reporting format to include standard cost data and variances. An example:

Product A, Dept. A

	Actual	*Standard*	*Variance*
Direct material	$46,000	$42,000	$4,000 Unfavorable (U)
Direct labor	19,000	20,000	1,000 Favorable (F)
Total direct costs	$65,000	$62,000	$3,000 Unfavorable (U)

The total variance shown above is composed of one favorable variance and one unfavorable variance. This breakdown is more informative than the variance shown in the total amount; we can see that the total is the net result (a net variance), since the favorable direct-labor variance offsets partly the cost effect of the unfavorable direct-material variance.

Let us suppose that no further decomposition is needed for the labor variance. It is the company policy not to investigate the causes of variation unless the relative size of the variance is in excess of the predetermined control limit. We assume for this example that the control limit for favorable labor variances is 6 percent of the standard for direct labor.

The relative size of the material variance indicates, however, that the process (either the purchase or the use of material, or both) is not under control. In order to identify the specific (assignable) cause in the course of variance analysis, let us first determine whether it is a problem of price or quantity, or both.

Variance decomposition. Continuing with the same example, we proceed by getting the relevant standard costs from the standard cost card and the relevant historical costs from the material requisition and purchase price files. Let us assume the following data for the material in question:

Standard ..... 21 yards	$2.00 per yard	$42 per unit	$42,000 per batch
Actual .... 20 yards	2.30 per yard	46 per unit	46,000 per batch

We have here a favorable material-quantity variance of $2 per unit (1 yard at $2), or $2,000 per batch. We also have an unfavorable material-price variance of $6 per unit ($0.30 × 20 yards), or $6,000 per batch.

Computation of variances. *Material-quantity variances,* as well as *labor-time variances,* are also called usage variances and efficiency variances. They represent physical variances, of course, but they are usually reported in dollars at *standard* prices or rates and for the total quantity rather than per unit of product. *Material-price* and *labor-rate variances* are usually computed for *actual* quantity or time amounts.

Analytical significance. It can be seen from the above that the unfavorable direct-material variance of $4,000 is a net variance resulting from the unfavorable price variance of $6,000, which is partially offset by the favorable quantity variance of $2,000. Companies usually decompose material variances even when they are not particularly high in their composite amounts. With respect to labor variances, the problem is not so important under ordinary circumstances, since the labor-rate variances are either negligible or they represent known variances; that is, there is no need to investigate and analyze them.

Some companies isolate immediately, as they occur, all the unusual variances attributable to the known and nonrepetitive causes. This procedure excludes such variances from the regular variance reporting. For example, purchases have to be made occasionally, under special circumstances, at exceedingly high prices. Hence, the respective material-price variances will be treated as known variances.

Overhead variances. The variable overhead rates are not directly variable with the production volume. Moreover, the actual spending can differ from the budgeted spending at any level of activity. Consequently, *variable overhead variances* usually are composed of *volume variances* and *spending variances.* The same applies to *fixed overhead,* or to the fixed portion of the single overhead rates. Since the fixed overhead rate remains unchanged regardless of fluctuations in the production volume, it is likely that the volume variance for fixed overhead will be relatively higher than for variable overhead.

The *composite (net) overhead variance* is the difference between the amounts applied to (absorbed by) products in calculating the total standard costs, on one side, and the actual overhead, on the other side. In other words, the composite (net) overhead variance indicates that the actual overhead amount was either overabsorbed or underabsorbed, which is comparable in meaning to the distinction between favorable (overabsorbed, overapplied) and unfavorable (underabsorbed, underapplied) direct cost variances.

Inventory reporting

Complete application. As defined before, a complete standard cost system covers the complete production cycle—from raw materials to finished products. As a result, all the inventories are stated at standard costs. Inventory cost can be determined at standard costs for financial reporting purposes as well, provided that the standard costs meet the applicable financial reporting standards. For example, in compliance with the lower of cost or market principle, the net realizable value will have to be used where applicable.

Many companies use two or more alternative methods of inventory valuation. For example, one company states in its financial statements for 1976 that the inventory cost is determined "using either average or standard factory costs, which approximate actual costs, excluding certain fixed expenses such as depreciation and property taxes."

Isolation of variances. In a complete application, all the variances are isolated (entered in separate variance accounts) before the charges are entered in the inventory accounts. Alternatively, the material variance account, for example, could be charged with the actual cost and credited at the standard cost.

It is customary to establish four variance accounts: *Material-Price Variance, Material-Quantity Variance, Labor Variance,* and *Overhead Variance.* Practice varies mostly with respect to the point at which material variances are isolated. Some companies carry raw material at actual cost. In such a system, the material variance account is used to incorporate both the price and the quantity components of the variance. But the practice of costing materials at standard price on receipt has prevailed for a long time. For example, the NAA research conducted in 1947–48 showed that 51 participating companies used the following three methods: (1) materials costed at standard price on receipt (36 companies), (2) materials costed at standard price on issue (12 companies), and (3) materials costed at standard price on completion of manufacturing process (3 companies). For a detailed discussion, see pp. 56–57 in *Standard Costs and Variance Analysis,* National Association of Accountants, New York, 1974.

Disposition of variances. The variance accounts serve as a repository for the respective amounts which subsequently—in the financial statements—are reported as period income or expense, or are allocated among inventories and cost of goods sold, or are incorporated in cost of goods sold. Provided that the variance accounts do not contain amounts generated by abnormal efficiencies or inefficiencies, it would seem preferable to allocate them among inventories and cost of goods sold.

On the other hand, in order to allocate the year-end amounts on a reasonable basis, considerable effort is required. This additional work does not seem to be warranted, under ordinary circumstances, in terms of the practical advantages, if any. Hence, the equally defensible and more practicable methods of reporting the year-end variance amounts as period income or expense or cost of goods sold adjustments are quite common in practice.

Reporting for budgeting and pricing

Budgeting. To obtain the information usable for budgeting purposes, standard costs for direct material and direct labor are grouped (aggregated) in accordance with the budget structure. It is important to show separately the material supplied (produced) by a company plant. The material purchased from outside sources differs in many relevant respects from the material which contains the value added by conversion within the company or division. The most obvious difference is in terms of cash flows involved. The same applies to the other interdepartmental or interplant charges for products and services.

Beginning inventories will have to be revalued for budgeting purposes by incorporating changes (revisions) in standard costs. Some companies make these adjustments as part of the year-end closing inventory valuation. In cases where standards are tighter than expected actual performance, the anticipated net debit (unfavorable) variances must be taken into account.

Pricing. Companies selling standardized products manufactured for stock usually need costs for periodic price adjustments. Standard costs and variance reports provide valuable information, though the standard cost data usually are adjusted—not only for past variances but also for the anticipated ones. Companies pricing on a bid basis construct their estimates from the standard cost data. Very few, if any, companies make no use of the standard cost information in setting or revising prices for their products and services.

Transfer pricing. Standard costs are frequently used in transfer pricing. In many cases, standard costing is introduced in the service departments mainly for the purpose of providing a uniform basis for interdepartmental charges for services to the producing departments.

24

Analyzing variances
from standard

*Henry D. Powell**
Elba F. Baskin†

In the past few years the theory and application of control systems have made tremendous advances and now there is a more definitive literature dealing with investigative strategies utilizing probability theory, including Bayesian statistical techniques and strategies for evaluating variances resulting from multiple sources. However, it is doubtful that these rather elaborate techniques have found their way into practice. There are several reasons for this conclusion. There is, of course, always resistance to change; and, admittedly, the current literature has not to date empirically demonstrated the value of the techniques in terms of cost versus benefit. Another more basic reason is that present applications of the cost control concept are after the fact rather than immediate (real-time) applications. Thus, those persons in an organization's hierarchy who deal with accounting control systems must rely on employees in achieving the goals or standards developed in the planning process. Therefore, the accounting control system is basically an after-the-fact monitor of the performance of subordinates. In today's complex organiza-

---

* Manager of Corporation Operations Analysis and Control, Phillips Petroleum Company.

† Associate Professor, Oklahoma State University.

tional environments, this is indeed a demanding role for accounting control systems.

This chapter's purpose is to discuss some of the control processes which have found wide use among various organizations. Where appropriate, extensions suggested by the literature on the theory of control systems will be examined. Specifically, this chapter will examine the traditional two factor variance models for computing variances from standard for materials, labor, and overhead costs and will examine such techniques as percentage and probabilistic models for assessing the significance of variances.

RESPONSIBILITY CENTERS

A *responsibility center* is defined as an organizational unit for which some designated person has overall authority for activities within the unit. The designated person could have individual responsibility for revenues, costs, profits, or profits in relation to capital employed (return on investment.) Many of the concepts and techniques discussed in this chapter could be utilized in analyzing the activities of these various types of responsibility centers. However, this chapter will be primarily oriented to a discussion of the concepts and techniques utilized in examining the activities of an organizational unit which is responsible for manufacturing costs. To facilitate the discussion, a continuing example will be used. The basic data for this example are presented in Exhibits 1 and 2.

Exhibit 1 is an income statement for the unit in the example on an actual and planned basis. Cost control systems need not articulate with traditional financial accounting systems. In fact, articulation may lead to inappropriate decisions by the head of a responsibility center since financial accounting requires allocation of nonvariable or fixed costs for inventory purposes. However, many managerial units are required to indicate the impact of their activities on the overall net income of the firm. Therefore, many firm managements do choose to tie financial and cost control systems together.

In Exhibit 1 the assumption is that the responsibility center head is only responsible for manufacturing costs, although revenues and other expenses are also shown. Income taxes are omit-

EXHIBIT 1

RESPONSIBILITY COST CENTER Y
Income Statement
For the Month of January, 19X2

	Actual	Planned	Variance*
Revenue	$40,000	$35,000	$5,000 F
Cost of goods sold:			
Direct materials	$10,020	$ 9,600	$ 420 U
Direct labor	6,000	4,800	1,200 U
Factory overhead	13,000	10,400	2,600 U
Total Cost of Goods Sold	$29,020	$24,800	$4,220 U
Gross profit	$10,980	$10,200	$ 780 F
Administrative and selling expenses	$ 5,000	$ 4,000	$1,000 U
Net Income	$ 5,980	$ 6,200	$ 220 U

    * U = Unfavorable
    F = Favorable

Additional information

	Units		Prices per unit	
	Actual	Planned	Actual	Planned
Sales	800	700	$50.00	$50.00
Production	800	800		$31.00
Direct materials purchased:				
Material A	2,600	—	$ 1.90	—
Material B	2,800	—	$ 3.10	—
Direct materials used:				
Material A	2,500	2,400	—	$ 2.00
Material B	1,700	1,600	—	$ 3.00
Direct labor used	1,500	1,600	$ 4.00	$ 3.00
Factory overhead:				
Variable	—	—		$ 2.00
Nonvariable	—	—		$ 4.50

ted, although in some situations a responsibility center head could have an impact on taxes. For example, a responsibility center head with the authority to purchase and dispose of assets could affect taxes through the investment tax credit. Exhibit 1 also indicates the basic information from which the statements were developed.

Exhibit 2 presents a standard cost sheet or card. Standards are defined as expected levels of performance in terms of price and quantity or usage. Exhibit 2 is related to Exhibit 1 in that the numbers for the manufacturing cost of goods sold in the planned columns of Exhibit 1 are either the same as those in Exhibit 2 or derived from the data in Exhibit 2. For example, the planned or expected wage rate for direct labor of $3.00 in the additional data is, of course, the standard price indicated

EXHIBIT 2

STANDARD COST SHEET FOR ___ ONE ___ UNIT OF PRODUCT ___ X ___ IN
RESPONSIBILITY COST CENTER ___ Y ___

Date of Standard December 1, 19X1

Materials:

Item*	Standard quantity	Standard unit price		Totals
Material A	3	$2.00/piece	$6.00	
Material B	2	$3.00/piece	6.00	
		Total Materials Cost		$12.00

Direct labor:

Task number	Standard hours	Standard rate per hour		
1	2	$3.00	$6.00	
		Total Direct Labor Cost		$6.00

Factory overhead:†

Variable component:

	Standard hours	Rate per direct labor hour		
	2	$2.00	$4.00	

Nonvariable component

	2	4.50	9.00	
		Total Factory Overhead		$13.00
		Total Manufacturing Cost		$31.00

* Material codes are typically used, such as Material A is the type of material coded 3217.
 † Total estimated variable cost for the fiscal year is $48,000, with the volume for inventory valuation purposes established at practical capacity of 24,000 direct labor hours (2,000 DLH per month). This produces a variable rate per DLH of $2.
 Total estimated nonvariable cost for the fiscal year is $108,000, with the volume for inventory valuation purposes established at practical capacity of 24,000 direct labor hours (2,000 DLH per month). This produces a nonvariable rate per DLH of $4.50.

in Exhibit 2. A further discussion of the development of the standard cost sheet is presented in the following sections.

TRADITIONAL TWO-FACTOR VARIANCE MODEL

In accounting control systems the net *accounting variance* is defined as the difference between the actual cost of an item and its corresponding standard or planned cost. Traditionally, this accounitng variance is broken down into subcomponents based on two factors, *price* and *quantity*. Once this breakdown is complete, the significance of the variance can be assessed and a decision can be made as to whether or not to investigate.

Standard cost sheet

The traditional two-factor variance model requires two inputs, the actual manufacturing costs incurred during a period and the standard or planned manufacturing costs. The actual manufacturing costs are accumulated by using the normal accounting data accumulation methods for materials, labor, and manufacturing overhead. Standards are usually developed through engineering, marketing, or cost studies. Exhibit 2 is an example of the standards established for a given unit or batch of output on a standard cost sheet or card.

Three points need to be emphasized concerning Exhibit 2:

1. The standard cost for materials, labor, and overhead is a function of a standard price per unit of input multiplied by the standard units of input required to produce a unit or batch of product.

2. The standard inputs for materials are assumed to be in terms of fixed proportions. For example, the standard cost sheet in Exhibit 2 shows that three units of Material A in combination with two units of Material B are necessary to produce one unit of Product X. The fixed proportions assumption concerning the production of Product X suggests that a comparable material might be substituted for Material A. But this substitution would require three units of the material and, in combination with two units of Material B, would produce one unit of Product X. Production processes can possess a variable proportions characteristic. However, under the variable proportions characteristic it is possible that the mix between basic manufacturing elements may vary in such a way that the output produced can differ from that suggested by the standard mix and standard output and still retain the quality specifications for the final product. Thus, in Exhibit 2, the proportions of Materials A and B might be varied from those indicated and the output, but not quality, of Product X might be different. Therefore, production processes exhibiting variable proportions characteristics introduce the need for further analysis of quantity variances into mix and yield components.[1]

---

[1] Mix and yield components are discussed in more detail later in this chapter.

EXHIBIT 3
Cost behavior patterns for variable factory overhead

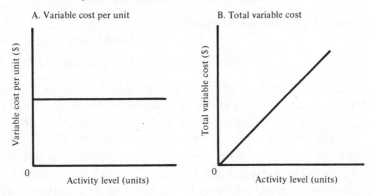

A. Variable cost per unit

B. Total variable cost

3. Overhead is composed of both variable and nonvariable components. The variable component possesses the following dimensions:

  a. The variable rate per direct labor hour (application or activity base) is constant over the relevant or assumed level of activity.

  b. The total variable cost, which is the product of the total standard cost per unit of output multiplied by the number of units of production, varies in a linear fashion with production over the assumed level of activity.[2] Panels A and B of Exhibit 3 provide a graphic depiction of these dimensions.

The variable overhead rate of $2 shown in Exhibit 2 is calculated by estimating the total variable cost for the period, $48,000, and dividing it by the anticipated activity base of 24,000 direct labor hours. The variable overhead rate of $2 is constant over the relevant range of activity.

Nonvariable overhead or burden application rates are developed to allocate the nonvariable component of overhead to units of inventory. Inventory valuation is, of course, necessary for financial reporting in computing gross profit and net income.

---

[2] It should be noted that one can convert from output to standard inputs by examining the standard cost sheet. For example, for one unit of output five units of input are needed. Thus, for 10 units of output 50 units of input would be required.

However, from a control system viewpoint, it is not always useful. The basic formula utilized for this allocation process is:

Nonvariable Overhead Application Rate

$$= \frac{\text{Total nonvariable overhead cost}}{\text{Anticipated activity or application base}}$$

In the example in Exhibit 2 the nonvariable overhead rate of $4.50 is computed by dividing the estimated total overhead costs for the period, $108,000, by the anticipated activity of 24,000 direct labor hours. The total nonvariable overhead cost of $108,000 is constant over the relevant range of activity. The numerator of the formula can be either actual or estimated overhead costs; however, estimated overhead costs are generally the more appropriate measure to allow for the financial reporting objective of valuing inventory prior to knowing actual costs. The denominator presents two selection problems:

First, a measure must be selected, such as direct labor hours, direct labor cost, machine hours, units of production, or some other basis reflecting a judgmental process with all the inherent risks of poor estimates.

Second, a level of activity must be selected. The levels of activity that are generally suggested are:

1. *Actual activity,* which uses actual production levels and can be computed only near the end or after the end of a period, which creates an obvious disadvantage.
2. *Expected activity,* which requires the prediction of the demand level for the next accounting period.
3. *Normal activity,* which requires the prediction of the demand level over a length of time that considers seasonal, cyclical, and trend factors. Basically, this is practical capacity adjusted for elements outside the manufacturing function, such as market demand.
4. *Ideal, or theoretical capacity,* which looks to the expected production capacity without regard for demand and assumes that ideal operating conditions will obtain.
5. *Practical capacity,* which is equal to ideal capacity less estimated delays due to such items as normal maintenance, relief time, predicted breakdowns and so on. This is very similar to normal activity as described above.

The control systems area itself does not produce the criteria for selecting of any one of the above levels of activity; therefore, managerial judgment must be employed. For example, generally accepted financial accounting principles suggest that actual costs must be used when valuing inventory.[3] Standard costs are acceptable if "adjusted at reasonable intervals to reflect current conditions . . ."[4] so that at the balance-sheet date standard costs reasonably approximate costs computed under one of the recognized bases. Therefore, management might use expected activity as the level of activity so that end-of-period inventory adjustments for overhead variances would be minimized.

Normal capacity is frequently used where a firm uses a cost-plus pricing procedure. This procedure implies both equity and a decision-making criterion. The equitable implication is that a product should not cost more to produce in any one accounting period just because production is lower, while the decision-making criterion suggests that the seller is selling the capacity of the firm to produce and implies that demand is equal to or greater than production capacity. However, since pricing decisions are based on demand and cost considerations, this argument may be circular in nature. One study employing a nonrandom survey technique of the bases firms used in applying non-variable manufacturing overhead indicated that of 84 firms, 63 percent used actual activity, 18 percent used expected activity, 5 percent used normal activity, 1 percent used ideal capacity, and 13 percent used practical capacity. While these percentages may not be representative of current practice, they probably are indicative of the wide divergence in the selection and use of a level of activity[5] for applying nonvariable manufacturing overhead.

Variance calculations for materials

After standards have been established, the control process consists of accumulating actual costs for comparison with stan-

---

[3] Commerce Clearing House, Inc., *Professional Standards—Current Text*, as of July 1, 1977, Par. 5121.04–.05.

[4] Ibid., Par. 5121.06.

[5] Charles R. Purdy, "Industry Patterns of Capacity or Volume Choice: Their Existence and Rationale," *Journal of Accounting Research* (Autumn 1965), pp. 228–41.

dards and analyzing the net variance. Exhibit 1 indicates that the total net unfavorable manufacturing variance to be analyzed is $4,220. This net variance is analyzed by the major manufacturing elements: direct materials, direct labor, and manufacturing overhead or burden. For each of these elements, the net variance is reduced to two components based on price and quantity or usage factors.

In the materials area, this would be analyzed as follows:

Inputs at actual prices	Inputs at standard prices	Standard inputs at standard prices
Actual materials used × actual materials price	Actual materials used × standard materials price	Standard inputs of material for output achieved × standard materials price

Difference equals materials Price variance   Difference equals materials Quantity variance

By utilizing the data presented in Exhibits 1 and 2, the above calculation process may be used to break down the net direct materials variance of $420 shown in the Exhibit 1 income statement. The additional information section of Exhibit 1 shows that 2,500 pieces of Material A costing $1.90 per piece were used in the production of 800 units of Product X. The standard cost sheet in Exhibit 2 shows that three pieces of Material A at a per piece cost of $2 were expected to produce one unit of Product X. Thus, 800 units of Product X would call for 2,400 pieces of Material A.[6] These data and the calculation format produce a favorable materials price variance of $250 and an unfavorable usage variance of $200 as shown below.

Inputs at actual prices	Inputs at standard prices	Standard inputs at standard prices
Actual materials used × actual materials price	Actual materials used × standard materials price	Standard inputs of material for output achieved × standard materials price
2,500 × $1.90 = $4,750	2,500 × $2 = $5,000	2,400 × $2 = $4,800

2,500 pieces × −$0.10   100 pieces × $2
Price variance, − $250   Quantity variance, $200

---

[6] This standard input of Material A, 2,400 pieces, is computed as the 800 units of output multiplied by the expected usage per unit of three pieces.

The analysis of the variance for Material B would follow the same format and would produce an unfavorable price variance of $170 and an unfavorable quantity variance of $300. The price variance is an unfavorable variance when actual cost exceeds standard cost, and a favorable variance when actual cost is less than standard. Potential causes of a price variance are efficient or inefficient decisions in selecting suppliers, purchase of materials which differ in quality from that assumed when the standard was established, purchasing at less than optimum quantities, rush orders, or changing market conditions which may call for a revision in the standard. As with the price variance, the quantity variance is unfavorable when actual materials usage exceeds standard inputs or favorable when actual usage is less than standard usage. Potential causes of a quantity variance are that the quality of materials was different from that implied by the standard, thus increasing or reducing scrap, or that the production process has been changed enough that the standard needs revision. Errors in setting production volume due to changes in the sales forecast are another potential cause.

The example above computes the price variance on the basis of materials used rather than materials purchased. This procedure is appropriate under several circumstances. If management chooses to have control systems tie in with financial reporting, then this computation procedure provides for easier articulation. If the responsibility center head has little or no impact on purchasing, basing the materials price variance on usage rather than purchases may also be appropriate.

However, basing materials price variances on purchases also seems to have advantages. First, it is a doubtful assumption that persons responsible for production have little impact on purchasing. Production scheduling can create the need for rush orders and higher prices than expected. Second, price variances based on purchase quantities produce a better measure of the variance than that produced by basing the variance on usage. That is, the price variance occurs on every unit purchased. Waiting until the material is used delays the measurement of the variance by the control system and then only part of the variance is recognized. Finally, recognizing price variances on purchases enables raw materials inventory to be recorded at standard costs, which may reduce the paperwork associated with inventory records.

Variance calculations for direct labor

Variance analysis for labor proceeds along the same lines as described for materials. The calculation process can be characterized as:

Inputs at actual prices	Inputs at standard prices	Standard inputs at standard prices
Actual labor hours × actual labor wage rates	Actual labor hours × standard labor wage rates	Standard input of labor for output achieved × standard labor wage rates
1,500 hours × $4/hour = $6,000	1,500 hours × $3/hour = $4,500	1,600 hours × $3/hour = $4,800

1,500 hours × $1/hour	−100 hours × $3/hour
Wage rate variance, $1,500	Labor usage variance, −$300

Continuing the example shown in Exhibits 1 and 2 where 800 units of Product X were produced, the additional data indicates that this production employed 1,500 direct labor hours at an actual wage rate of $4 per hour. Further, the standard cost sheet in Exhibit 2 indicates that each unit of output requires two direct labor hours of input at a standard wage rate of $3 per hour. Utilizing these numbers, the net labor variance of $1,200 shown in the Exhibit 1 income statement is broken down into a wage *rate variance* of $1,500 and a *usage variance* of $300. The negative sign indicates a favorable variance. For the wage rate variance, actual wage rates were greater than standard, and for the usage variance actual hours were less than that expected for the output achieved.

Potential causes for a wage rate variance are changes in labor markets resulting in wage rates different from standard. If permanent, this will lead to a revision in standards. Other causes are the substitution of labor of a different quality or skill such that wage rates differ from standard, or overtime wage or shift differentials being different than expected. Usage or efficiency variances may be caused by the substitution of labor of a different quality such that labor time is affected by idle time caused by various work situations, or by production processes or methods that differ from those expected when the standards were established.

Variance calculations for factory overhead

The two factor model for analyzing the net overhead variance of $2,600 shown in the income statement of Exhibit 1 requires a division into two components labeled the *controllable variance* and the *noncontrollable* or *volume variance.* As mentioned earlier, the volume variance computations are due to the demands for inventory valuation and will not produce useful results for control purposes. However, a more useful analysis which surrogates the volume variance will be suggested.

The *net overhead variance* is merely the difference between actual overhead and applied overhead. Accounting data gathering techniques accumulate *total actual overhead* costs in a control account and appropriate subsidiary records. *Applied overhead* is that amount of overhead allocated into the initial work-in-process inventory accounts. Total applied overhead is a function of the variable and nonvariable standard overhead rates developed prior to an accounting period and the activity levels occurring in an accounting period. For example, the applied or planned overhead in the income statement of Exhibit 1 is computed utilizing the overhead standards in Exhibit 2 as follows.

Applied overhead = (Nonvariable   overhead   rate + Variable overhead rate) × the standard application units for the actual output achieved.

Applied overhead = ($4.50 + $2.00) × 1,600DLH (direct labor hours)

Applied overhead = ($6.50) × 1,600DLH

Applied overhead = $10,400

The standard application units for the actual output achieved, 1,600 direct labor hours, is computed by multiplying the actual production of Product X, 800 units, by the application units per unit of output, two direct labor hours, indicated on the standard cost sheet of Exhibit 2.

In order to determine the controllable and volume variances, a *flexible budget* is needed. A flexible budget allows management to ask what overhead costs should have been given the level of activity attained in the current period. For example, the flexible budget from the data in Exhibits 1 and 2 would be:

Flexible budget = Total planned nonvariable overhead + (Planned variable overhead per unit × the standard application units for the actual output achieved)

Flexible budget = $9,000 + ($2.00 × 1,600DLH)

Flexible budget = $9,000 + $3,200

Flexible budget = $12,200

The total nonvariable overhead of $9,000 is the total estimated nonvariable overhead of $108,000 in Exhibit 2 divided by the assumed 12 months in the period. The $3,200 amount is the estimated total variable cost for the production level achieved.

Three items should be noted about the flexible budget. First, it is *total planned nonvariable overhead,* not the nonvariable overhead per unit, that is desired. Second, the planned variable overhead per unit when multiplied by the standard application units produces the budgeted *total* variable overhead *for the output achieved.* Finally, the standard application units for the actual output achieved is the same level of activity used to apply overhead into work-in-process and is computed as indicated in the discussion above concerning applied overhead.

At this point, the controllable and noncontrollable, or volume, variances can be computed. The *controllable variance* is defined as total actual overhead minus the amount of overhead determined by the flexible budget, or:

Controllable variance = total actual overhead − flexible budget amount

Controllable variance = $13,000 − $12,200

Controllable variance = $800

In the example, actual overhead exceeds the budgeted overhead, thus the controllable variance is unfavorable. Causes for controllable variances range from price changes on both nonvariable and variable factors to usage different from that expected on the inputs needed to achieve the actual production levels. The price changes are generally called *spending variances.* An example of a specific spending variance would be price changes on insurance policies covering plant and equipment. One should also note that this specific example suggests that many items in the so-called controllable variance are only controllable when the decision to acquire the inputs is made. By referring to the additional data in Exhibit 1, an example of *usage differences* can be noted. In the example, direct labor hours were utilized as the overhead application base. For the production level achieved of 800 units of Product X, management expected 1,600 direct labor hours to be used. However, only 1,500 direct labor hours were used. Thus, certain efficiences were realized. However, since the controllable variance in the example was unfavorable, spending inefficiences must have offset this efficiency in usage.

The *noncontrollable* or *volume variance* is defined as the flexible budget amount minus the total applied overhead or:

Volume variance = Flexible budget amount − Total applied overhead
Volume variance = \$12,200 − \$10,400
Volume variance = \$1,800

In the example, budgeted overhead exceeds applied overhead, thus the variance is unfavorable and implies inefficiency. However, this is most misleading. By referring to the data in Exhibit 1, one finds that management expected Responsibility Center Y to produce 800 units of Product X and, in fact, the production level achieved was 800 units. As indicated earlier, the volume variance is not useful for control purposes and arises because of the necessity to determine inventory values for financial reporting purposes. In fact, a more direct measure concerning performance evaluation as to volume is available—the difference between the expected and actual levels of production.

In evaluating performance in the overhead area, management should be concerned with *effectiveness* and *efficiency*. In determining effectiveness, management asks the question of whether actual levels of activity achieved equal expected levels. Here a comparison of *actual quantities* with *standard quantities* is appropriate. Thus, the volume variance is generally either redundant or useless for control purposes. In determining efficiency, management asks the question of whether, given activity levels attained, input factors were acquired and used in the expected fashion. The controllable overhead variance when properly evaluated is appropriate in addressing this issue.

Exhibit 4 indicates a reporting framework for factory over-

EXHIBIT 4
Reporting framework for factory overhead

ANALYSIS OF FACTORY OVERHEAD
For the Month of January, 19X2

Responsibility center ___Y___

Category	Practical capacity Expected capacity	2,000DLH 1,600DLH	Actual output in input terms	800 units of product 1,600DLH	Explanation
	Flexible budget	Actual cost	Expected cost	Variance*	
Variable:					
Indirect materials	$1.00V	$ 1,800	$ 1,600	$200 U	
Indirect labor	0.75V	600	1,200	600 F	
Other	0.25V	1,200	400	800 U	
	$2.00V				
Nonvariable:					
Indirect materials	$1,000	$ 1,000	$ 1,000	—	
Depreciation	4,000	4,000	4,000	—	
Insurance	2,000	2,200	2,000	200 U	
Other	2,000	2,200	2,000	200 U	
Totals	$9,000	$13,000	$12,200	$800 U	
Applied overhead: $6.50 × 1,600DLH		10,400			
Net Variance		$ 2,600 U			

*U = Unfavorable.
F = Favorable.

head for the responsibility center in the example used throughout this chapter. In Exhibit 4, several characteristics of the assumed situation should be noted.

1. Costs are divided into variable and nonvariable components. This division should be a natural outcome of the planning process where cost behavior patterns should be examined. The column labeled Flexible budget indicates for the variable category that one merely needs a volume measure, V, to determine the expected cost for a particular level of activity. For example, the flexible budget for indirect labor is $0.75V. Given the standard inputs for the output achieved of 1,600 direct labor hours (DLH), the total expected cost for this category is $0.75 (1,600 DLH) or $1,200.

2. The category of indirect materials is listed in both the variable and nonvariable sections of the report because this cost consists of both components. An alternative presentation may be necessary since most accounting systems do not accumulate actual costs along variable and nonvariable dimensions. That is, only one category of indirect materials would be listed with the flexible budget written as $1,000 + $1V or $2,600, and then compared with the actual indirect materials cost of $2,800.

3. In the nonvariable category, the flexible budget amounts would equal the expected cost. One should also note that the total flexible budget amounts for all categories, $9,000, is merely the annual amount of $108,000 divided by 12 months.

4. The Explanation column is blank, implying that the significance of the variances has not been assessed; therefore, no investigation into specific causes has been undertaken. The actual overhead of $13,000 is shown in the Actual Cost column of Exhibit 4 and is accumulated by the accounting system. The applied overhead is the sum of the nonvariable and variable overhead rates of $4.50 and $2.00 (which are found on the standard cost sheet in Exhibit 2) multiplied by the standard inputs for the output achieved of 1,600 direct labor hours. The unfavorable net overhead variance is $2,600, which is the amount for this category indicated in the income statement of Exhibit 1.

EXHIBIT 5
Summary of variance analysis results

	Net variance	Price or spending	Quantity or usage
Direct materials:			
Material A	$ −50	$−250	$ 200
Material B	470	170	300
Total materials variance	$ 420	$− 80	$ 500
Direct labor	1,200	1,500	−300
Factory overhead	2,600	800	1,800
Total manufacturing variance	$4,220	$2,220	$2,000

Summary of two-factor variance analysis

This section on the two-factor variance model for materials, direct labor, and factory overhead provided a detailed path of the process of breaking net variances into subcomponents on price and usage. Exhibit 5 provides a summary of these price and usage components for the example utilized in this chapter.

CALCULATIONS OF MIX AND YIELD VARIANCES

A production process may exhibit a variable proportions characteristic, such that the persons responsible for the production of a product may vary the actual proportion of inputs of both material and work effort from that implied by the standard values. In such cases the price variance is unaffected, but the quantity variance can be further divided into *mix* and *yield* components. Exhibit 6 displays the materials section of a standard cost sheet for which a variable proportions characteristic will be assumed.

The standard cost sheet indicates that the standard inputs are four pounds of Material C and six pounds of Material D, or a total of ten pounds of input. The standard mix is 40 percent (4 lbs./10 lbs.) of Material C and 60 percent of Material D. The production process utilizing these inputs produces eight pounds of the output, Product Z. This loss from ten pounds of raw material to eight pounds of finished product is due to the physical characteristics of the production process. Specific causes might be evaporation, or the input might be mixed in such a way that a residue or other scrap materials are lost.

Further assumptions needed to demonstrate the calculation procedures for the materials mix and yield variances are that

EXHIBIT 6
Materials section of a standard cost sheet

Standard cost sheet for <u>8 lbs</u> of <u>Product Z</u>			
Date of standard <u>December 1, 19xx</u>			
Item	*Standard quantity*	*Standard unit price*	*Total*
Material C	4 lbs.	$3/lb.	$12
Material D	6	2/lb.	12
	10 lbs.		$24

800 pounds of Product Z are actually produced and that 300 pounds of Material C and 510 pounds of Material D were acquired and used to produce this output. Assume that inputs were acquired at the standard unit price indicated on the standard cost sheet. Thus, price variances will be equal to zero. Finally, the standard cost sheet indicates that the per unit cost of inputs in the standard mix is $2.40 ($24.00 total material cost divided by 10 lbs. of input in the standard mix) and that the per unit cost in the standard mix based on output is $3.00 ($24.00 total material cost divided by 8 lbs of output of Product Z).

The traditional quantity variance for materials is calculated as before:

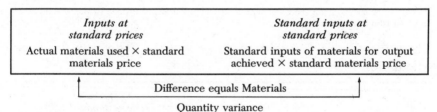

Inputs at standard prices	*Standard inputs at standard prices*
Actual materials used × standard materials price	Standard inputs of materials for output achieved × standard materials price

Difference equals Materials

Quantity variance

Thus, the materials quantity variance in the assumed case is:

Material	*Actual materials used*	*Standard inputs for output achievement*	*Difference*	*Standard input prices*	*Quantity variance*
C	300 lbs.	400*	−100	$3	$−300
D	510	600*	−90	$2	−180
	810 lbs.	1,000†			$−480

* Standard mix multiplied by standard inputs for output achieved: Material C, 40 percent × 1,000 pounds; Material D, 60 percent × 1,000 pounds.
† The output achieved is 800 pounds of Product Z. The standard cost sheet in Exhibit 6 indicates 10 pounds of input in the standard mix to produce 8 pounds of output. Thus, to produce 800 pounds of output, the production process called for 1,000 pounds of inputs in the standard mix of 40 percent to 60 percent. That is, the process normally suffers a 20 percent loss on inputs.

The above calculations indicate a favorable quantity variance of $480. Since price variances are zero by assumption, an alternative calculation proves the accuracy of the above calculation. Actual materials cost is actual materials purchased and used multiplied by actual prices (assumed equal to standards) or:

$$
\begin{aligned}
\text{Material C: } & 300 \text{ lbs.} \times \$3/\text{lb} = \$ \ \ 900 \\
\text{Material D: } & 510 \text{ lbs.} \times \$2/\text{lb} = \underline{1,020} \\
& \phantom{510 \text{ lbs.} \times \$2/\text{lb} =} \$1,920
\end{aligned}
$$

The standard cost of production is 800 pounds of output multiplied by the standard cost of output based on the standard mix of $3, or $2,400.[7] The difference between $1,920 and $2,400 is, of course, $−480.

The total quantity variance of $480 can be divided into a mix and yield variance. The calculation process for the yield variance is:

Materials	Actual units of input	Standard units in standard mix for output achieved	Difference	Standard price per input unit in standard mix*	Yield variance
C	300	400	−100	$2.40	$−240
D	510	600	−90	2.40	−216
	810	1,000	−190	2.40	$−456

* From the standard cost sheet (the total materials cost of $24.00 divided by the total inputs in the standard mix of 10 pounds).

Thus, the favorable yield variance is $456. The mix variance calculation is:

Material	Actual units of input	Standard units in standard mix for output achieved	Difference	Difference between standard unit price and standard price per input unit in standard mix*	Mix variance
C	300	400	−100	$0.60	$−60
D	510	600	−90	−0.40	+36
	810	1,000			$−24

* From the standard cost sheet:
Material C: $3.00/lb. − $2.40/lb. = $0.60
Material D: $2.00/lb. − $2.40/lb. = −0.40

---

[7] Alternatively one can calculate the amount applied into production on the basis of standard inputs for outputs achieved. In this assumed case, 1,000 pounds of input multiplied by $2.40 per input also equals $2,400.

Thus, the favorable mix variance is $24. The sum of the mix and yield variances should equal the traditional quantity variance of $480.[8]

The mix and yield variances possess a straightforward interpretation. In the assumed case, the standard mix was varied by substituting the lower cost input, Material D, for the higher cost input. The *yield variance* indicates that if the standard mix had been maintained and 190 fewer pounds of input utilized, savings would have been $456 due to an improved yield. That is, in the standard mix, the production process would require 1,000 pounds of input to produce 800 pounds of output. By varying the mix, yield was improved. The *mix variance* indicates that the substitution of the lower cost input for the higher cost input produced a savings of $24. These are general conclusions from the example. In real-world situations assessment and investigation of such variances would, of course, be necessary.

THE VARIANCE ASSESSMENT PROCESS

In the preceding section of this chapter the computation techniques for computing variances from standard were detailed. This section will examine techniques for assessing the significance of variances so that decisions may be made concerning whether to determine the actual causes of variances. The analysis will first present an example to indicate the interdependent and complex nature of the variables affecting the assessment process. Next, a formal model of the assessment process will be developed. Finally, alternative rule-of-thumb models which surrogate the formal model will be introduced and examined.

Variables affecting the assessment process: An example

In examining the variables that affect the assessment process, it will be useful to work from a specific example but one that has general applicability. In this example, the firm assumes a certain demand for its output and instantaneous supply for its inputs used to produce the output. The only decision facing

---

[8] $-456 + $-24 = $-480.

the firm is the quantity of inventory to hold. Under these circumstances, a simple economic order quantity (EOQ) model is appropriate for use. That is, the firm would minimize its total inventory cost defined as follows:

$$TC = PD + (D/q)\ C_o + (q/2)\ C_h$$

where:

TC = total inventory costs
D = demand for final output
P = cost of acquiring one unit that is independent of ordering cost
q = order quantity
D/q = number of orders
C_o = cost of placing an order
$q/2$ = average inventory on hand at any point in time
C_h = cost per unit of holding average inventory over time.

All the above parameters such as demand, D, and cost functions, C_o and C_h, are initially assumed to be known with certainty. Utilizing suitable mathematical techniques, the optimal inventory ordering quantity is:

$$q^* = \sqrt{\frac{2 C_o D}{C_h}}$$

where:

$$q^* = \text{optimal order quantity}$$

and the remaining variables are defined as above.

The above decision concerning the optimal order quantity was derived under an assumption of certainty. However, usually this decision concerning the optimal order quantity is made in an environment characterized by uncertainty. In essence, the decision rule concerning order quantity is derived assuming all future events are known but in reality is utilized in an environment where these events are unknown. Therefore, the exact values assigned to these future events may be characterized as "standards." That is, these standards are management's predictions of the average future performance. This model, then, provides a framework within which one can examine the variables affecting the variance assessment process.

For example, the order cost, C_o, is a standard. The actual value measured by the accounting system for C_o is $C_o{}^a$. Thus, the variance is $C_o{}^a - C_o$. The potential causes of this variance are:

1. A failure to achieve the standard because of inaccurate managerial assessment of the real situation. These failures reflect either human or mechanical actions, are controllable, and can be remedied.
2. The accounting system incorrectly measured the actual value, $C_o{}^a$. This also is generally due to human error, is controllable, and can be suppressed at some cost.
3. The value for the parameter or standard, C_o, was incorrectly established. This error may be controllable if it is due to human error in prediction. But the error may be due to changing environmental conditions, and while it is also error in prediction, it may be noncontrollable. If it is a noncontrollable situation or a genuine change in the environment, an adjustment in the standard should be made changing the optimal decisions or order quantity levels.
4. The model utilized is incorrect in some aspect. This is a most typical situation since models are generally simpler than the complex environment they are attempting to surrogate. A "better" model may be developed if the cost savings can justify the development.
5. The variance may be due to random causes. A standard is an average of expected performance. Therefore, not all variances are assumed by management to be critical. That is, even though a cause may be found, the variance is anticipated within the tolerance limit established by management. By definition, the random variance possesses no significance and management would choose not to determine its cause.

From the above points, one may note that management wishes to distinguish between an *in control* and *out of control process*. That is, when the variances are random, management does not wish to investigate to determine specific causes. But when the variances are nonrandom and potentially controllable, management will wish to investigate.

The investigation decision: A formal approach

The determination of whether a process is in or out of control may be introduced in a formal framework. Exhibit 7 portrays a characterization of the decision to investigate.[9]

EXHIBIT 7
A model for the investigation process

Possible states for the production process / Possible actions by management	Investigate A_1	Do not investigate A_2	Probabilities of states occurring
In control	(1) C_1	(2) 0	$1 - P$
Out of control	(3) $C_1 + C_2$	(4) V	P

Exhibit 7 shows that two possible states of the production process exist, *in control* or *out of control*. The probabilities of these states occurring are $1 - P$ for the in control state and P for the out of control state. Management has two choices to pursue: it may investigate and determine the cause of the variance, as denoted by A_1, or it may choose not to investigate, as denoted by A_2. The cell in the matrix labeled (2) produces a zero outcome. That is, if the production process is in control and management chooses not to investigate then no benefits or costs result above those already realized. All other cell outcomes are measured relative to cell (2). In cell (1), the production process is in control. Thus, if management chooses to investigate it will incur the investigation costs, C_1, and zero benefits. In cell (3), the production process is out of control and it will cost C_2 dollars to bring it into control. Management chooses to investigate at a cost of C_1 dollars. Finally, cell (4) indicates that the

---

[9] This development process follows that found in H. Bierman, Jr., L. E. Fouraker, and R. K. Jaedicke, "A Use of Probability and Statistics in Performance Evaluation," *The Accounting Review* (July 1961), pp. 409–17.

production process is out of control and management chooses not to investigate. The size of the variance from standard, V, will be assumed to represent the opportunity cost for this outcome.[10]

From the situation in Exhibit 7, one can determine the expected value of a particular action by management. The expected value of an action is the payoff outcome associated with the action and a particular state multiplied by the probability that the state will occur. That is,

Expected value $(investigate) = C_1 (1 - P) + (C_1 + C_2) (P)$
Expected value $(A_1) = C_1 (1 - P) + (C_1 + C_2) (P)$

In a similar fashion, the expected value for the action *do not investigate* is:

Expected value $(do\ not\ investigate) = 0(1 - P) + V(P)$
Expected value $(A_2) = V(P)$

One may determine a critical probability by determining the indifference point between the two actions. When the expected values of the two actions are equal, the critical probability is:

Expected value $(A_1) = $ Expected value (A_2)

Substituting for the expected values of each action and solving for P:

$$C_1 (1 - P) + (C_1 + C_2) (P) = V(P)$$
$$C_1 - PC_1 + PC_1 + PC_2 = PV$$
$$C_1 + PC_2 = PV$$
$$C_1 = PV - PC_2$$
$$C_1 = P(V - C_2)$$
$$P^* = C_1 / (V - C_2)$$

P^*, the *critical probability*, is the probability of the production process being out of control. The above formula is intuitive in that when the cost of investigation, C_1, is equal to zero, the critical probability is also zero. That is, any time that management believes the system is out of control, it should investigate since investigation is costless. Thus, the interpretation of the

---

[10] Technically, one may need to introduce discounting techniques if this out of control situation will obtain over a prolonged period of time.

critical probability when investigation costs are positive is that investigation is desirable only when the probability of being out of control exceeds the critical probability. In most real world cases, information concerning the size of investigation and other costs and the benefits to be gained by investigation is not exact. Therefore, managerial judgment is employed in deciding on a particular investigation strategy.

Surrogates of the formal model

While the formal model presented above is useful in understanding the issues involved and in assessing and investigating a variance from standard, this approach is not widely used in industry. Two rule-of-thumb models which have found wide use and which are surrogates of the formal model are the percentage model and the quality control model.[11]

The percentage model. The *percentage model* develops an actual percentage by dividing the variance from standard by the standard. If this actual percentage is greater than, or equal to, some standard percentage, investigation is required. Thus, any variance which produces a percentage *greater than* or *equal to* the standard percentage is an indication of an out-of-control process and investigation would result to determine specific causes. If the actual percentage is *less than* the standard percentage the probability of an out-of-control situation is zero. In essence, the standard percentage defines the random element that management is willing to tolerate.

The worth of the percentage model is its ease of calculation and understanding. There is a cost involved in its use, since many investigations may lead to a finding that the production process is in control.

Percentage standards should be different depending on the critical nature of the production process and on the organizational level in the firm. That is, percentage standards would be established at a higher level if one is examining variances at the individual employee level than if one is examining variances at the departmental level. More variation is expected at

---

[11] A third model suggests the use of the absolute numerical size of the variance. This approach is most useful where no variances, or very small variances, from standard can be tolerated. For example, if precious metals were used in the manufacturing process the absolute size approach might be utilized.

the individual level than at the departmental level. Departmental variances are aggregates of individual levels and, as one aggregates across individuals, variation is reduced such that lower percentage standards are established for the department.

The quality control model. The *quality control model* is a statistical model which may be used in defining the limits of the random element of a variance which management is willing to tolerate. Since the quality control model is based on probability and statistical theory, care should be taken in its application. For example, standards are a product of a price and quantity. Quality control models assume certain (generally normal) distributions for the price and the quantity components. But the product of price multiplied by quantity may not conform to this distributional assumption. Therefore, applications of quality control should be applied to each component *separately* rather than jointly.

The basis of quality control is the *control chart.* Exhibit 8 presents a typical example of a control chart for a labor time situation. The standard specifies that 15 minutes of labor time are needed to produce one unit of output. However, the *upper control limit* of 20 minutes of labor time and the *lower control limit* of 10 minutes of labor time define the random variation

EXHIBIT 8
A control chart example

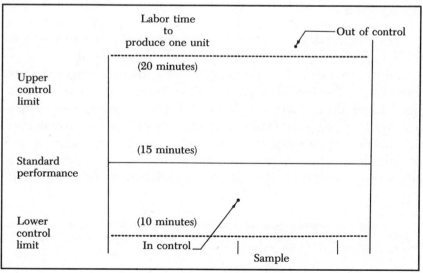

which is acceptable to management. If a sample of performance were drawn which falls outside these control limits, the process would be considered out of control and investigation would be in order. Likewise investigation is indicated if there is a "run" of observations either above or below the standard performance.

The establishment of the upper and lower control limits may be based on subjective judgment or historical data, and generally the basis for this establishment is the normal distribution. That is, the means of repeated samples from a process are distributed according to a normal distribution. Thus, statistical tables may be utilized in determining the probabilities associated with the upper and lower control limits.[12]

Because of the normal probability assumption underlying the quality control model, applications appear appropriate in the materials price, labor time, and overhead areas. Due to labor contracts, the distribution of labor wage rates may not conform to the assumption of the quality control model. In the materials quantity area, problems with the distribution assumption may also exist. If the production process is characterized by fixed proportions, then an upper control limit for materials usage may exist, but no lower control limit. Presumably in a process characterized by variable proportions, quality control charts for materials usage could be developed and would be related to the mix of materials actually utilized.

SUMMARY

This chapter introduces the basic computational procedures for calculating variances from standards for materials, direct labor, and overhead. The potential causes for such variances are mentioned. The usefulness of certain overhead variances is questioned and alternatives are described. The process of determining whether variances from standard should be investigated to determine actual causes is discussed in both a conceptual and pragmatic manner. Alternative models for this investigation decision are described and their relative effectiveness is examined.

---

[12] For a specific example of the application of the quality control model, see Charles T. Horngren, *Cost Accounting: A Managerial Emphasis* 3d ed. (Englewood Cliffs, N.J.: Prentice-Hall, Inc., 1972), pp. 858–63.

25

Direct and incremental costing

D. Jacque Grinnell*
Donald J. Wait†

In recent years, the increased emphasis on the importance of determining cost behavior patterns has had a significant impact on the development of management planning, decision making, and control techniques. The development of direct costing and incremental costing represents two especially noteworthy examples. The first part of this chapter deals with the use of direct costing for the purpose of facilitating routine planning and control; the second part is concerned with the use of incremental costing as a basis for analyzing special decision-making situations.

DIRECT COSTING

Direct costing (also called variable costing, marginal costing, and contribution accounting) may be described as that type of product costing which assigns to units produced—as inventoriable costs—only *variable manufacturing* costs. Fixed manufacturing costs, together with all nonmanufacturing costs, are expensed in the period in which they are incurred. Fixed manufacturing costs are viewed as being associated with the passage of time as opposed to actual production.

---

* Professor of Accounting, The University of Vermont.

† Consultant, Product Cost Accounting, General Electric Company.

In contrast, *absorption* (or full or conventional) *costing* may be described as that type of product costing which assigns relevant manufacturing costs to units produced—as inventoriable costs—without regard to their variability with respect to volume; nonmanufacturing costs are expensed in the period in which they are incurred. Under absorption costing, fixed manufacturing costs are viewed as being necessary to production in general, and therefore assignable to individual units of production. As a result of the differing treatment of fixed manufacturing costs, net income and inventory values may differ between the two approaches. Both direct costing and absorption costing are adaptable to job order and process cost situations as well as to standard and nonstandard systems.

The merits of direct costing versus absorption costing is a subject of continuing controversy among accountants, educators, and management. In large part, this controversy concerns the applicability of direct costing for external reporting purposes. At the present time, the public accounting profession does not consider direct costing to be an acceptable concept for external reporting purposes. In addition, the Securities and Exchange Commission refuses to accept financial reports based on the direct costing method. Further, the Internal Revenue Service expressly prohibits its use for income tax purposes. Nevertheless, direct costing has proven to be a useful tool for internal management planning and control in many companies. If direct costing is employed for internal use, relatively simple periodic adjustments are required to convert net income and inventory to an absorption costing basis to meet external financial reporting and income tax requirements. With this conversion, however, a semantic question arises as to whether or not direct costing technically is the accounting method in use; the adjusted information to be published externally is obviously reported and recognized internally as well.

Comparing direct and absorption costing results

Under absorption costing, a cost is *inventoriable* if it is associated with the manufacturing process and is not abnormal. Under direct costing, a cost is inventoriable if it is associated with the manufacturing process *and* is variable in nature; inventoriable costs include prime costs (direct material and direct labor) plus variable manufacturing overhead costs. A fundamental difference, therefore, between direct and absorption costing concerns the accounting treatment of fixed manufacturing overhead costs. Such costs are treated as product costs under absorption costing and as period costs under direct costing. The term "variable costing" might better be used in place of the more common term "direct costing" since the approach is not differentiated from absorption costing on the basis of direct (traceable) and indirect (non-traceable) manufacturing costs. Rather, it is differentiated from absorption costing in terms of variable and fixed manufacturing cost behavior.

A second fundamental difference between direct and absorption costing relates to the format of the income statement associated with each of the two approaches. The income statement

EXHIBIT 1
Cost flows under absorption costing

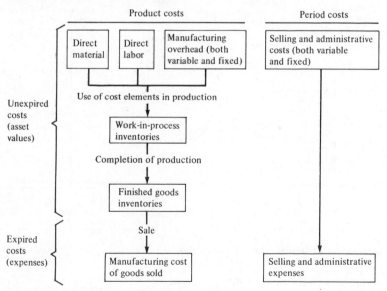

Income statement format under absorption costing

Revenues.	$X
Less: Manufacturing cost of goods sold	X
Gross margin (or gross profit).	$X
Less: Selling and administrative expenses	X
Operating income	$X

format under absorption costing generally depicts expenses categorized as manufacturing (cost of goods sold) and nonmanufacturing (selling and administrative); gross margin (or gross profit) appears as a key line item in the statement. The direct costing format reflects a classification of expenses into variable and fixed behavior categories; the format is highlighted by contribution margin (or marginal income) which appears as a key line item in the statement.The cost flow patterns, together with the basic income statement formats, under absorption costing and direct costing are presented in Exhibits 1 and 2.

Due to the difference in accounting for fixed manufacturing overhead costs, the timing of the release of such costs to the income statement is necessarily affected. Consequently, the ab-

EXHIBIT 2
Cost flows under direct costing

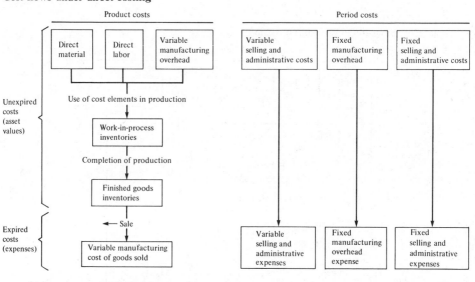

Income statement format under direct costing

Revenues. . . . . $X
Less: Variable manufacturing cost of goods sold X
Variable manufacturing margin . . . . $X
Less: Variable selling and administrative expenses. X
Contribution margin (or marginal income). . . . . $X
Less: Fixed expenses:
      Fixed manufacturing overhead . . . . $X
      Fixed selling and administrative X   X
Operating income . . . . $X

sorption and direct costing approaches may result in significantly different income figures in the short run. This phenomenon is reflected in the simplified example in Exhibit 3 which compares direct costing results for two consecutive years with results obtained under three different absorption costing assumptions. Based on the Exhibit 3 illustration, a number of important observations may be made.

Relationship of income to revenue and cost trends. Since sales *increase* and total costs *decrease* from Year 1 to Year 2 in the example, the initial reaction might be that income also should increase from Year 1 to Year 2. While this is the case with the direct costing system, it is not the case using an absorption costing system. In fact, profits decrease in the example from Year 1 to Year 2 under absorption costing.

Relationship of income to inventory changes. Any difference between an absorption costing income figure and the direct costing income figure for a given period may be explained in terms of the *change* (from the beginning to the end of the period) in fixed manufacturing overhead lodged in inventory under absorption costing. For example, when inventory is being built-up (Year 1), additional fixed manufacturing costs are being held back in inventory thereby increasing absorption costing income above direct costing income. Conversely, when inventory is being liquidated (Year 2), additional fixed manufacturing costs are released to the absorption costing income statement thereby decreasing absorption costing income below direct costing income. Three generalizations may be drawn from the results provided by the Exhibit 3 illustration:

1. When production exceeds sales (an inventory buildup), then absorption costing income exceeds direct costing income. This situation is exemplified by the Year 1 results. Note that Year 1 income under each of the three absorption costing assumptions ($2,700, $2,800, and $2,700, respectively) shown in Part B of Exhibit 3 is greater than Year 1 direct costing income ($1,800) shown in Part C(1).

2. When production is less than sales (an inventory liquidation), then absorption costing income is less than direct costing income. This situation is exemplified by the Year 2 results. Note that Year 2 income under each of the three absorption

costing assumptions ($2,100, $2,000, and $2,100, respectively) shown in Part B is less than Year 2 direct costing income ($3,000) shown in Part C(1).

3. When production equals sales (no change in the level of inventory), then absorption costing income equals direct costing income. This situation is exemplified by the *combined* results for Years 1 and 2. Note that total income for Years 1 and 2 together under each of the three absorption costing assumptions ($4,800 in each case) shown in Part B agrees with the combined Year 1 and 2 direct costing income ($4,800) shown in Part C(1).

While the relationships described in 1, 2, and 3 above represent useful generalizations, they are not always valid. Exceptions may occur in situations where an actual system based on Fifo or average costing is employed, since beginning and ending inventories are valued using different unit costs.

Income differences within absorption costing. Absorption costing income is affected by whether an *actual* cost system or a *standard* cost system is employed. For example, compare the results shown in Part B(1) of Exhibit 3 with those in Part B(2). In addition, income results under a *standard* absorption costing system are affected by the standard production capacity level used to "normalize" unit fixed manufacturing overhead cost. For example, compare the two standard costing results shown in Parts B(2) and B(3).

Role of the volume variance. While the volume variance is unique to an absorption costing system where overhead is charged to inventory on a standard production capacity basis, and is inherent in the calculation of gross margin, it does not explain the difference in income between absorption and direct costing. The difference between absorption and direct costing income is due to differences between production and sales levels, whereas the volume variance occurs as a result of differences between actual production and standard production levels.

Short-run versus long-run differences. While absorption costing and direct costing income may differ significantly over short periods of time if inventory levels change, the two costing methods will produce similar results over extended periods of time. However, unless inventories are completely depleted, the aggregate income for all accounting periods reported under absorption costing will exceed the aggregate income under direct costing by the amount of fixed manufacturing overhead costs still lodged in inventory.

In short, it may be stated that, under pure direct costing, income is solely a function of sales and is independent of inventory changes. In contrast, under absorption costing, income is a function of sales, production, and the capacity level chosen to unitize fixed manufacturing overhead costs.

Modified direct costing. It is possible to obtain most of the benefits of the direct costing concept by a compromise method. This method involves carrying inventory at a variable manufacturing cost value and making a periodic adjustment to place fixed manufacturing costs in ending inventory. Consequently, when this inventory adjustment for fixed costs is reflected in the direct costing income statement, the adjusted income figure will be the same as that obtained under an actual absorption costing system, or under standard overhead costing if actual production and standard production capacity are equal. An example of this modified direct costing approach is shown in Part C(2) of Exhibit 3. It may be observed that the adjusted income and inventory values agree with the actual absorption costing results depicted in Part B(1). The adjustment to place fixed costs in inventory may be included in period costs on the income statement or, as in Exhibit 3, shown separately with an identification such as "Net change in fixed costs in inventory."

It is clearly a matter of semantics whether this modified approach is properly referred to as direct costing. Nevertheless, when this modification is employed, it is ordinarily labeled as direct costing even though it is not a pure direct costing system. The principal difference between modified direct costing and absorption costing, then, concerns the format of the income statement. In the modified direct costing statement, the contribution from sales can be compared to the fixed costs incurred during the period and, in addition, the amount of fixed costs deferred in inventory can be discerned—information which is not available with an absorption costing statement.

Arguments can be made in support of either the direct costing income or absorption income, but it seems impossible to prove one correct and the other incorrect. Either may be viewed as

EXHIBIT 3
Absorption costing versus direct costing

A. Basic data

	Year 1	Year 2
Production units	1,000	900
Sales units	900	1,000
Unit selling price	$15	$15
Unit variable manufacturing cost	$ 3	$ 3
Fixed manufacturing cost per year	$ 9,000	$ 9,000
Total manufacturing cost per year	$3(1,000) + $9,000 = $12,000	$3(900) + $9,000 = $11,700
Total unit manufacturing cost	$12,000 ÷ 1,000 = $12	$11,700 ÷ 900 = $13

B. Results under absorption costing

1. *Actual cost system:*

	Year 1	Year 2
Revenues	$15(900) $13,500	$15(1,000) $15,000
Less: Cost of goods sold	$12(900) 10,800	$12(100) + $13(900) 12,900
Gross margin	$ 2,700	$ 2,100
Ending inventory	$12(100) $ 1,200	$ 0

2. *Standard cost system* (assuming standard production capacity = 900 units per year):

	Year 1	Year 2
Revenues	$15(900) $13,500	$15(1,000) $15,000
Less: Standard cost of goods sold	$13(900) 11,700	$13(1,000) 13,000
Standard gross margin	$ 1,800	$ 2,000
Volume variance adjustment	$12,000 − $13(1,000) 1,000 Favorable	$11,700 − $13(900) 0
Gross margin	$ 2,800	$ 2,000
Ending inventory	$13(100) $ 1,300	$ 0

Year 1

3. Standard cost system (assuming standard production capacity = 1000 units per year):

	Year 1		Year 1	
Revenues	$15(900)	$13,500	$15(1,000)	$15,000
Less: standard cost of goods sold	$12(900)	10,800	$12(1,000)	12,000
Standard gross margin		$ 2,700		$ 3,000
Volume variance adjustment	$12,000 − $12(1,000)	0	$11,700 − $12(900)	900 Unfavorable
Gross margin		$ 2,700		$ 2,100
Ending inventory	$12(100)	$ 1,200		$ 0

C. Results under direct costing

1. *Pure direct costing system:*

	Year 1		Year 1	
Revenues	$15(900)	$13,500	$15(1,000)	$15,000
Less: Variable cost of goods sold	$ 3(900)	2,700	$ 3(1,000)	3,000
Contribution margin		$10,800		$12,000
Less: Fixed manufacturing expense		9,000		9,000
Income		$ 1,800		$ 3,000
Ending inventory	$ 3(100)	$ 300		$ 0

2. *Modified direct costing system:*

	Year 1		Year 1	
Income (as above)		$ 1,800		$ 3,000
Net change in fixed costs in inventory	$ 9(100)	900	$ 9(−100)	− 900
Adjusted income		2,700		2,100
Ending inventory—Adjusted	$12(100)	$ 1,200		$ 0

a distortion from the standpoint of the other. In reality, these two methods reflect different allocations of income to periods based on different concepts. As noted previously, however, direct costing does not have general acceptance as an income concept for external reporting. Its value to management, insofar as income accounting is concerned, lies in the greater insight into the nature of operations provided by the direct costing income statement with its emphasis on contribution margin, not in whether the final income for a period is different from absorption costing.

Exhibit 4 provides a more detailed and comprehensive illustration of the application of standard direct costing, together with a comparison of the direct costing income result with one ob-

---

EXHIBIT 4

Situation: Company X produces Product A. Standard variable manufacturing costs are $11 per unit for direct material, $5 per unit for direct labor, and $4 per unit for variable manufacturing overhead. Budgeted fixed manufacturing overhead costs are $30,000 per year. For purposes of unitizing fixed manufacturing overhead costs for absorption costing, normal production activity has been established at an annual level of 5,000 units (therefore, the standard fixed manufacturing overhead cost per unit is $6). Variable selling and administrative expenses are budgeted at a rate of $2 per unit sold; budgeted fixed selling and administrative expenses are $26,000 per year. All variances are treated as period costs.

Actual results for 19X1 were as follows:

Selling price per unit of Product A	$ 40
Beginning inventory of Product A	500 units
Production of Product A	5,500 units
Sales of Product A	5,200 units
Ending inventory of Product A	800 units
Costs incurred:	
Direct material	$62,500
Direct labor	29,000
Variable manufacturing overhead	22,500
Fixed manufacturing overhead	31,000
Variable selling and administrative	11,000
Fixed selling and administrative	26,400

Analysis of cost variances (U = Unfavorable, F = Favorable):
Variable cost budget variances:

Direct material: $62,500 − (5,500 × $11)	=	$2,000 U
Direct labor: $29,000 − (5,500 × $5)	=	1,500 U
Variable manufacturing overhead: $22,500 − (5,500 × $4)	=	500 U
Variable selling and administrative: $11,000 − (5,200 × $2)	=	600 U

Fixed cost budget variances:

Fixed manufacturing overhead: $31,000 − $30,000	=	$1,000 U
Fixed selling and administrative: $26,400 − $26,000	=	400 U

Fixed manufacturing overhead volume variance (absorption costing only):
$$\$30,000 - (5,500 \times \$6) = \$3,000 \text{ F}$$

EXHIBIT 4 (*continued*)

Presentation of direct costing results:

Revenue (5,200 × $40)		$208,000
Less variable expenses at standard:		
Variable manufacturing cost of goods sold (5,200 × $20)	$104,000	
Variable selling and administrative expense (5,200 × $2)	10,400	
Total variable expense at standard		114,400
Contribution margin (before variable cost variances)		$ 93,600
Adjustment for variable cost variances:		
Direct material variance	$ 2,000 U	
Direct labor variance	1,500 U	
Variable manufacturing overhead variance	500 U	
Variable selling and administrative variance	600 U	
Total variance		4,600 U
Adjusted contribution margin		$ 89,000
Less fixed expenses (actual):		
Fixed manufacturing overhead	$ 31,000	
Fixed selling and administrative	26,400	
Total fixed expense		57,400
Operating income		$ 31,600

Presentation of absorption costing results:

Revenues (5,200 × $40)		$208,000
Less standard manufacturing cost of goods sold (5,200 × $26)		135,200
Gross margin (before manufacturing cost variances)		$ 72,800
Adjustment for manufacturing cost variances:		
Direct material variance	$ 2,000 U	
Direct labor variance	1,500 U	
Variable manufacturing overhead variance	500 U	
Fixed manufacturing overhead budget variance	1,000 U	
Fixed manufacturing overhead volume variance	3,000 F	
Total variance		2,000 U
Adjusted gross margin		$ 70,800
Less selling and administrative expense (actual)		37,400
Operating income		$ 33,400

Reconciliation of results:

Operating income—Absorption costing	$33,400
Operating income—Direct costing	31,600
Difference to be explained	$ 1,800

Alternative explanations of difference:
1. The $1,800 difference in operating income in favor of absorption costing may be explained in terms of the buildup of fixed manufacturing overhead in inventory under absorption costing: 300 unit increase in inventory × $6 per unit for fixed manufacturing overhead = $1,800.
2. The difference may also be explained by comparing the total amounts of fixed manufacturing overhead in the two income statements:

Fixed manufacturing overhead in direct costing statement		$31,000
Fixed manufacturing overhead in absorption costing statement:		
As part of standard manufacturing cost of goods sold (5,200 × $6)	$31,200	
Fixed manufacturing overhead budget variance	1,000 U	
Fixed manufacturing overhead volume variance	3,000 F	
Total		29,200
Difference		$ 1,800

tained by using standard absorption costing. It may be noted that the direct costing income statement depicted in Exhibit 4 could be slightly modified, without disturbing the basic contribution margin format, to provide the absorption costing income result; the modification entails the insertion of a $1,800 adjustment factor into the direct costing statement, either as a direct reduction of fixed manufacturing overhead expense or as a separate line item, to allow for the buildup of fixed manufacturing overhead in inventory.

Direct costing as a planning and decision-making tool

The importance of cost behavior knowledge to effective management planning and control is well established. The usefulness of direct costing may be attributed primarily to the fact that it recognizes and preserves these behavior patterns. The variable and fixed components of all costs (manufacturing, selling, and administrative) are formally segregated in the accounts. That is, the concept of cost variability is applied to historical cost data within the formal accounting system. As a result, actual income statements are developed along cost behavior lines. Fixed costs are deducted from contribution margin, instead of being mingled with the cost of goods sold and inventory where the amounts of such costs tend to become obscured from view.

Thus, for planning and decision-making purposes, direct costing provides historical cost-volume-profit information in a routine manner to facilitate management forecasts and projections. More specifically, a direct costing system:

1. Facilitates routine profit planning by providing historical information which serves as a basis for estimating the cost and profit effects of changes in product prices, volume, and/ or mix. The establishment of a satisfactory combination of price, volume, and mix is, of course, necessary to the development of a profit plan for achieving an adequate profit and return on investment.
2. Assists in the identification and selection of the more profitable products or product lines, customers, sales territories, or other business segments. This information is particularly crucial in situations where existing facilities limit present business volume.

3. Since direct costing constitutes a concept of product cost which corresponds closely with current out-of-pocket expenditures necessary to manufacture goods, it facilitates incremental analyses for special decision making. Examples include pricing special orders (computing minimum selling prices in short-run), make or buy decisions, and decisions concerning expansion or contraction of facilities.

Direct costing as a control tool

For control purposes, actual direct costing results may be compared to plans without adjustment to provide comparable cost-volume-profit data. Exhibit 5, based upon the situation described in Exhibit 4, provides an illustrative format for comparing budgeted income with actual results for a company which employs standard and direct costing. The total variance from budgeted income may be explained in terms of a contribution margin variance, variable cost variances, and fixed cost variances. As shown in Exhibit 5, the variance in contribution margin (before variable cost variances) may be further analyzed in terms of a selling price variance and a sales volume variance. In multiproduct situations, sales volume variances also may be subdivided into sales mix and sales quantity components, if desired.

The fixed expenses shown in Exhibit 5 might be further subdivided as committed and discretionary (or managed or programmed) to assist management in recognizing other cost characteristics useful to control. The Exhibit 5 format could also be extended to report results by major segments (product lines, sales territories, or customer classification) of the company. When the purpose is to evaluate segments of the business, fixed expenses may be divided between those specifically identified with the segment in question and those which are common or joint to a number of segments. A discussion of segment analysis is provided in Chapter 39.

Specific attributes of direct costing which facilitate control include the following:

1. It meshes with, and supports, other proven tools and concepts of cost control such as standards, flexible budgets, and responsibility accounting.
2. It provides contribution margin figures which facilitate

EXHIBIT 5

Situation: Company X employs standard costs and direct costing for planning and control purposes. Budgeted revenues for Product A for 19X1 were set at $195,000, based upon an estimated sales volume of 5,000 units and an estimated selling price of $39 per unit. Information concerning standard variable costs, budgeted fixed costs, and actual results for 19X1 are provided in Exhibit 4.

Comparison of planned and actual results:

	19X1 planned (5,000 units)	19X1 actual (5,200 units)	Variance
Revenues	$195,000	$208,000	
Less variable expenses at standard:			
Variable manufacturing cost of goods sold ($20/unit)	$100,000	104,000	
Variable selling and administrative expenses ($2/unit)	10,000	10,400	
Total variable expense at standard	$110,000	$114,400	
Contribution margin (before variable cost variances)	$ 85,000	$ 93,600	$8,600 F*
Less variable cost variances (all unfavorable):			
Direct material variance		$ 2,000	
Direct labor variance		1,500	
Variable manufacturing overhead variance		500	
Variable selling and administrative variance		600	
Total variance		$ 4,600	4,600 U†
Contribution margin (after variable cost variances)	$ 85,000	$ 89,000	
Less fixed expenses:			
Fixed manufacturing overhead	$ 30,000	$ 31,000	
Fixed selling and administrative	26,000	26,400	
Total fixed expense	$ 56,000	$ 57,400	1,400 U‡
Operating income	$ 29,000	$ 31,600	$2,600 F

* This favorable contribution margin variance of $8,600 is subject to further analysis in terms of a selling price component and a sales volume component:

Selling price variance = Actual units sold (Actual selling price—Budgeted selling price)
   = 5,200 ($40 −$39) = $5,200 F

Sales volume variance = Budgeted contribution margin/unit (Actual units sold—Budgeted units to be sold)
   = ($39 − $22) (5,200 − 5,000)
   = $3,400 F

† Total variable cost variance.
‡ Total fixed cost budget variance.

short-run performance evaluation of profit centers without having the results obscured by subjective assignments of joint or common costs. Further, the impact of fixed costs on profits is emphasized since the total amount of such costs for the period appears on the income statement. The use of pure direct costing would avoid entirely the troublesome problem of unitizing fixed manufacturing costs for income determination and inventory valuation purposes and the misleading inferences which may be drawn from such unitization. Ultimately, however, fixed manufacturing costs must be allocated between the income statement and inventory to convert the financial statements to an absorption costing basis for external financial reporting and income tax purposes.

3. Income under pure direct costing is sensitive only to changes in sales. Other things being equal (selling prices, product mix, unit variable costs, and fixed costs), profits move in the same direction as sales volume if pure direct costing is used. Under pure direct costing, changes in inventory levels do not influence the profit calculation. Under absorption costing, however, fixed manufacturing costs are inventoriable and, as a result, the amount of such costs charged against revenue may differ from the amount actually incurred during the period. Thus, producing goods for inventory tends to increase profits, while reducing inventory tends to decrease profits. Therefore, under absorption costing, production scheduling can influence short-run profits. Pure direct costing eliminates the manipulative possibility of improving short-run profits through inventory buildups. It would appear that the preferable accounting approach is the one that does not encourage decisions that are counter to overall and long-run company goals. However, from a practical standpoint, the influence of inventory changes on profits cannot be avoided, since eventually an adjustment for fixed manufacturing costs in inventory must be made to convert income to an absorption costing basis for external reporting and tax purposes.

Implementing direct costing

The practical application of direct costing depends on a reliable separation of variable and fixed costs. The adoption of direct costing, therefore, requires the ability to realistically identify and separate actual costs into variable and fixed categories. The behavior of costs as variable and fixed depends, of course, on the length of time in question and the magnitude of change in volume of activity. Since direct costing is designed primarily as a tool for current planning and control, cost behavior should be determined within the context of the short-run over a limited range of activity changes. Further, some cost elements are not inherently variable or fixed in nature, but acquire behavioral characteristics as a result of management decision. For example, a decision to keep equipment and a labor force in a state of readiness to serve without regard to immediate production volume may cause certain costs to be viewed as fixed as opposed to variable.

If individual costs were either perfectly variable or perfectly fixed in nature, little difficulty would be experienced in classifying costs. However, many types of overhead costs do not fit cleanly into either category, possessing both fixed and variable attributes. Three basic approaches exist for segregating manufacturing costs into variable and fixed costs for the purpose of employing direct costing. These three approaches, beginning with the simplest but least accurate, are:

1. Consider only prime costs (direct material and direct labor) as variable, with all manufacturing overhead considered as fixed and, therefore, noninventoriable. This approach interprets the term "direct costing" literally at its face meaning.

2. In addition to prime costs, treat as entirely variable those overhead costs that are largely variable in nature. Overhead costs that are largely fixed in nature are considered as entirely fixed.

3. Overhead costs are identified as variable, fixed, and semivariable. In turn, semivariable costs are further subdivided into their variable and fixed components. Subsequently, prime costs, purely variable overhead costs, and the variable portions of semivariable costs are considered as product costs. This approach, while the most accurate, is also the most costly to implement. In most cases, it is impossible to determine with absolute precision that portion of an *actual* semivariable cost which is variable and that portion which is fixed. Fortunately, this problem is negated in situations where standard costs and flexible overhead budgets are also employed, since *standard* variable manufacturing overhead costs may be used for product costing purposes. Chapter 3 provides a detailed discussion of methods for determining cost behavior patterns.

Should direct costing be employed?

Direct costing has sometimes been criticized as a method which tend to undervalue inventory since only variable costs are considered as product costs for inventory valuation purposes. However, a debate of the merits of direct costing versus absorption costing predicated on whether the incurrence of fixed manufacturing overhead costs adds value to inventory is fruitless since neither product costing method is intended as a valuation process. The primary question involves the matching of revenues and costs for product costing purposes. Absorption costing employs a long-run concept of product cost for costing manufactured products. Direct costing is intended to match short-run costs (variable costs) against short-run revenues without arbitrary allocation of fixed costs to units and periods.

Direct costing has also been criticized as a method which provides a potential for underpricing by emphasizing variable unit cost information for price-setting purposes. Certainly, fixed costs, together with volume estimates, must be considered in generating full cost information for long-run target pricing purposes. In the case of direct costing, long-run target pricing to cover all costs, including both fixed manufacturing and nonmanufacturing costs, can be accomplished by using markup percentages tied to variable costs as opposed to percentages tied to "full" manufacturing costs. Direct costing does offer the advantage of providing variable cost data for use in setting short-run or minimum prices on special orders. An elaboration on the use of cost information for pricing purposes can be found in Chapter 6.

The usefulness of determining cost behavior patterns for profit planning and control is unquestioned. The classification of costs between variable and fixed must be made in order to have adequate cost information available to meet the needs of management, but these needs may or may not include using this classification for inventory valuation and income measurement purposes. It should be noted that many companies developed and used cost behavior information long before the upsurge of direct costing. Other companies may not have utilized cost behavior information prior to adopting direct costing. In implementing direct costing for internal use, they are required to determine cost behavior patterns that should have been identified much earlier. Consequently, because cost behavior information is useful for many purposes other than inventory valuation and income measurement, undue credit for its usefulness may sometimes be attributed to direct costing, rather than to the segregation of costs that is required to implement direct costing. In short, the use of cost behavior information to analyze operations in terms of contribution margin does not depend upon any particular method of inventory valuation. Rather, direct costing merely extends the use of cost variability knowledge with the premise that only variable manufacturing costs should be included in inventory.

In summary, the primary benefits of direct costing derive from the fact that actual cost data is formally recorded in the accounts in a manner useful to the needs of management. The use of direct costing forces the identification of cost behavior patterns if they have not been previously determined. The historical cost behavior and profit information generated by direct costing provides input to management for planning, forecasting, and decision-making purposes. For control purposes, management's ability to compare results with budgets is enhanced since both planned and actual results focus on the behavior of costs.

INCREMENTAL COSTING

Cost accounting for manufacturers serves three broad purposes, each requiring a different orientation and approach toward the accumulation of cost information. First, to meet external financial reporting and income tax requirements, costing for inventory valuation and income determination reflects the use of a full (absorption) cost concept. In this context, the appropriate costing unit is the product, which is assigned costs equal to its own direct costs plus an equitable portion of related indirect costs. Second, to meet the requirements of management for routine planning and control information, the use of a responsibility cost concept is employed. In this context, the appropriate costing unit is the responsibility center, which is assigned direct and controllable costs; subjective assignments of indirect and uncontrollable costs are avoided. The use of standard costs, flexible budgets, and contribution accounting through direct costing represent valuable aids to the fulfillment of routine planning and control.

Third, management requires cost information for making special nonroutine decisions. In this case, the appropriate costing unit may best be described as the project or "decision-making unit." Depending on the nature of the decision, the appropriate costing unit might be, for example, a product, department, sales territory, customer, or machine. It is within this decision-making context that the concept of incremental (or differential) cost is particularly useful.

While full cost and responsibility cost information is generated on a routine basis by the company's cost accounting system, incremental cost information is not. It must be developed through special studies according to the needs of the specific decision problem at hand, utilizing information generated by the routine cost accounting system and/or other sources.

Like direct costing, incremental costing places emphasis on cost behavior patterns. Unlike direct costing, however, which focuses on past (or historical) costs, incremental costing is oriented toward the future. That is, incremental costing is concerned with the *expected* cost effects of alternative decision choices. Direct costing information may, of course, represent useful input to incremental cost analyses. Nevertheless, historical cost information, although often providing the best available basis for predicting future costs, is in itself irrelevant.

Types of decision problems

The decision-making process basically may be viewed as one of choosing among alternative proposals, each having its own investment requirements together with resulting revenue and cost flows. Ideally, the goal of business decisions is to select from among courses of action those that will maximize the company's total income and return on investment. The purpose of incremental analysis is to aid management in the analysis of the profit effects of alternative decision choices.

The types of alternative choice problems which lend themselves to incremental analysis are many and varied. In some cases, the analysis requires consideration of both revenue and cost effects. Examples include those concerned with whether to:

1. Accept or reject special orders.
2. Add (expand)/drop (curtail) business segments (products or product lines, sales territories, and customer groups).
3. Sell or process further (degree of processing).
4. Spend additional amounts for sales promotion.

In other cases, only an analysis of costs is required since revenues will be unaffected by the decision choice. A common example is that concerned with whether to make or buy raw materials or component parts.

It should be noted that many types of decision problems also require consideration of the additional investment (capital expenditure) effect, as well as cost and/or revenue effects. Common examples include those concerned with equipment replacement and facilities expansion. In such cases, the profit effects of decision alternatives must be evaluated in relation to any associated investment in assets in order to make reasoned decisions. The discussion in this chapter is limited to analyzing revenue and cost effects of decision alternatives. The additional aspect of considering revenue and cost flows when capital expenditures are involved is taken up in Chapter 33. In situations where the amount of uncertainty and required investment are the same among, or unaffected by, a set of mutually-exclusive alternatives, the quantitative analysis should be based on a comparison of the amounts of expected additional income associated with each alternative. Other factors being the same (that is, qualitative considerations), the alternative which is expected to make the largest addition to, or smallest reduction in, income should be selected.

It is apparent that the term "incremental costing" inadequately describes the total quantitative analysis process, since many types of decision problems require consideration of revenue effects as well as cost effects. The complete approach might better be described as incremental revenue and cost analysis, incremental profit analysis, or merely incremental analysis. This discussion does, however, concentrate on incremental costs because they involve the most difficult problems of understanding.

The incremental approach

Incremental analysis involves a *comparison* of the expected *changes* in revenues and costs associated with each course of action encompassed by a decision problem. The types of special nonroutine decision problems are many, with each having its own unique aspects and complications. While this discussion cannot cover the specifics of all situations that might arise, there are certain basic ideas or principles of incremental analysis that may be extended to a variety of alternative choice problems.

The costs and revenues which are relevant to problems of alternative choice are called incremental (or differential) costs and revenues. For decision-making purposes, an *incremental cost (revenue)* may be defined as the *expected change* in a cost (revenue) associated with a contemplated change in the level or nature of operations resulting from a decision choice. That is, an incremental cost (revenue) is represented by the expected *increase* or *decrease* in a total cost (revenue) item resulting from a proposed variation in operations.

Future and differential costs. Thus, for purposes of comparing alternative choices, the relevant costs are represented by anticipated *future* costs which *differ* among alternatives. There are two important aspects of this working definition which merit comment. First, the relevant costs are future in nature. Past costs are, in themselves, irrelevant; they cannot be altered by current decisions. Historical cost data may, of course, serve as a useful basis for predicting future cost levels. Second, relevant costs are differential in nature; it is the changes in cost levels that are important. If the level of a cost is unaffected by the decision, then it is irrelevant to the decision.

While in comparing alternatives it does no harm to include items of cost that do not differ among alternatives, the relevant costs are limited to those that do differ among mutually-exclusive alternatives. Therefore, incremental analysis permits those cost elements which do not differ to be excluded, thus reducing the analysis to focus on those items which are affected.

Exhibit 6 provides an example of an incremental analysis which compares the alternatives of accepting or rejecting a special order at a price below normal. The incremental costs and revenues are shown in the third column. Based on the quantita-

666

EXHIBIT 6

Situation: Company X has an annual manufacturing capacity for Product A of 10,000 units. It presently manufactures and sells approximately 7,000 units per year; the unit selling price is $15.

The company has the opportunity to manufacture an additional 2,000 units for sale to a well-known chain at $10 per unit, f.o.b. factory. Regular sales commissions (5 percent of selling price) would be paid to the company's sales personnel for the contract. The contract would have no effect on the company's other sales.

Analysis:

	Without special order (7,000 units)	With special order (9,000 units)	Incremental revenues and costs (2,000 units)
Sales	$105,000	$125,000	$20,000
Variable costs:			
Raw material*	$ 28,000	$ 34,200	$ 6,200
Direct labor ($3 per unit)	21,000	27,000	6,000
Variable manufacturing overhead ($1 per unit)	7,000	9,000	2,000
Shipping ($0.25 per unit)	1,750	1,750	—
Commissions (5% of sales)	5,250	6,250	1,000
Total variable costs	$ 63,000	$ 78,200	$15,200
Contribution margin	$ 42,000	$ 46,800	$ 4,800
Fixed costs:			
Manufacturing	$ 15,000	$ 15,000	—
Selling	5,000	5,000	—
Administration	10,000	10,000	—
Total fixed costs	$ 30,000	$ 30,000	—
Operating income	$ 12,000	$ 16,800	$ 4,800

* Raw material purchases subject to quantity discounts:

7,000 units at $4.00 = $28,000
9,000 units at $3.80 = $34,200

tive analysis, the special order should be accepted since a positive profit increment is expected. It may be noted that the contribution margin format is employed in the analysis, thereby providing insight into the behavior of costs.

In conducting an incremental analysis, it should not be presumed that additional variable costs associated with a decision alternative will necessarily increase at a constant or uniform rate. For example, in the Exhibit 6 situation, the purchase of additional raw material for the special order results in a price break (quantity discount) on total raw material needs. In other situations, the use of additional labor hours may result in the incurrence of an overtime or shift premium at some point, causing labor costs to increase at an increased rate (see Exhibit 7 illustration).

EXHIBIT 7

Situation: Company X presently manufactures, to an intermediate stage of completion, 10,000 units of Product A. The product in this form is sold for $15 per unit. The company is considering further processing of this product to its final completion. In final form the product can be sold for $18 per unit.

Analysis:

Incremental revenue: 10,000 units × ($18 − $15)		$30,000
Incremental costs:		
Incremental variable costs:		
Raw material	$ 0	
Direct labor (4,000 additional hrs. at $3)	12,000	
Overtime premium (1,000 hrs. at $1.50)*	1,500	
Variable manufacturing overhead (4,000 hrs. at $1)	4,000	
Sales commissions ($30,000 × 6%)	1,800	
Total variable	$19,300	
Incremental fixed costs:		
Manufacturing supervision	$ 3,500	
Other (heat, light, insurance, etc.)	500	
Total fixed..	$ 4,000	
Total incremental costs		23,300
Incremental profits.......................................		$ 6,700

* It is anticipated that 1,000 of the 4,000 additional direct labor hours will require the payment of an overtime premium.

Incremental variable and fixed costs. While true in some cases (such as in the situation depicted by Exhibit 6), it should not be concluded that incremental costs in general are comprised only of changes in variable costs. In some cases, a decision alternative may require the incurrence of additional fixed costs as well as, or instead of, variable costs. A fixed cost remains fixed only within a certain presumed range of activity. If a proposed decision will result in a change in activity to a level outside that range, total fixed costs will increase or decrease. Fixed costs should be considered in the analysis whenever they are expected to change as a result of the contemplated decision. It should be noted that the method by which fixed costs are applied or assigned to manufactured goods for product costing purposes should not be considered in incremental analysis. Such a method only serves as a basis for spreading total fixed manufacturing costs over all production but does not measure the incremental change in total fixed costs resulting from a particular decision choice. The use of unitized fixed cost information should be avoided in incremental analyses, since such costs may be incorrectly interpreted as behaving in a manner similar to that of variable costs. Exhibit 7 provides an example of an incremental analysis associated with a decision problem concerning whether to sell a product at an intermediate stage of production—or process further. The example shows a comparison of the additional revenues to be obtained against additional variable and fixed costs to be incurred as a result of further processing. It is assumed that no additional investment in facilities is required in order to process further.

Out-of-pocket and opportunity costs. To this point, the incremental variable and fixed costs which have been discussed may be viewed as out-of-pocket costs; that is, they represent the additional cash outlays or expenditures associated with a particular decision alternative. In many situations, however, opportunity costs as well as out-of-pocket costs may require consideration. For decision-making purposes, an *opportunity cost* may be defined as the maximum addition to profits that is foregone as a result of using existing resources or capacity for a particular purpose. That is, the opportunity cost of making a particular decision choice is represented by the contribution to profits associated with the next best alternative. For example, in Exhibit 6, if the capacity utilized for the special order would not otherwise be idle but would be used for some other purpose, the contribution to profit associated with that other purpose should be considered as an additional cost of the special order. Similarly, in Exhibit 7, if the existing capacity required to accommodate additional processing has alternative uses, then the opportunity cost associated with the next best alternative use should be added to the incremental out-of-pocket costs of further processing.

It should be noted that opportunity costs exist only in situations where alternative uses of limited resources or capacity exist. If, for example in Exhibits 6 or 7, the capacity needed for the purpose at hand would otherwise remain idle, then no opportunity cost exists. It should also be noted that opportunity costs, as such, need to be considered only in situations where *all* alternative choices concerning use of existing resources or capacity are not formally listed and compared in the analysis. For example, in Exhibit 7, all other alternative uses of available capacity along with the "further processing" alternative could be listed and formally compared with one another to determine which alternative provides the greatest expected incremental contribution to profits. Only when one or more alternatives are ex-

EXHIBIT 8

Situation: Company X has the opportunity to purchase, from an outside supplier, a component part which it presently manufactures. Annual requirements for the part are 10,000 units. Facilities presently used for manufacturing the part could be rented out for $20,000 per year. If not rented out, the facilities would remain idle since no other feasible opportunities currently exist.

Analysis:
Cost of manufacturing:
Out-of-pocket costs:
Variable:

Raw material (10,000 units × $3)	$ 30,000	
Direct labor (10,000 units × $4)	40,000	
Variable overhead (10,000 units × $1)	10,000	
Total	$ 80,000	
Fixed overhead that can be avoided by not manufacturing	25,000	
Total out-of-pocket costs	$105,000	
Opportunity cost (rental income foregone)	20,000	
Total relevant cost of manufacturing		$125,000
Cost of purchasing:		
Variable costs:		
Invoice price (10,000 units × $11)	$110,000	
Shipping (10,000 units × $0.60)	6,000	
Total		116,000
Difference in favor of purchasing		$ 9,000

cluded from the list of alternatives formally being compared, is it necessary to consider the contribution to profit associated with the best of the excluded alternatives as an opportunity cost to be assigned to each of the included alternatives. Exhibit 8 provides an example of an incremental analysis for a make-or-buy decision. In the example, it may be seen that rental income foregone is considered as an opportunity cost of the "make" choice. Alternatively, rental income could have been considered as a revenue factor associated with the "buy" choice.

Other considerations

The previous discussion has focused on the identification of relevant costs and revenues for purposes of analyzing decision problems. In many instances, other factors also represent important considerations in the analysis.

Capital budgeting implications. In the examples cited earlier, no additional investment is presumed to be required in order to implement the decision choice. However, if current capacity is not available to accommodate a decision choice, additional capital expenditure may be required. Further, a decision requiring additional investment generally influences operating levels, together with revenue and cost flows, over an extended period of time. In such instances, the return on incremental investment and the time value of money are important factors to be considered in arriving at a decision. These factors are considered as part of the capital budgeting process described in Chapter 33.

The problem of uncertainty. Since decision making is necessarily future-oriented, the estimation of incremental costs and revenues associated with decision alternatives is not certain. The forecasting of these incremental values frequently is the most difficult and agonizing aspect of the decision analysis. Instead of using single-value estimates, the use of probability theory and expected values provides a basis for formal and explicit recognition of uncertainty in the analysis. While managers may not find it easy to develop estimates in the form of probability distributions, such estimates can greatly improve the validity of the analysis. Chapter 34 provides a discussion of this subject.

Qualitative considerations. Incremental analysis focuses on the quantitative aspects of the decision problem. In many instances, qualitative factors must also be considered. For example, the future effect on the long-run price structure of other products may be an important consideration in the decision to accept or reject a special order. Similarly, in evaluating make-or-buy proposals, the reputation and dependability of outside suppliers, the quality of purchased products, and the possibility of future price changes may represent important qualitative considerations. While a decision analysis should seek to quantify as many factors as possible, nonquantifiable factors remain. These qualitative factors may well be more important to a decision than the measured dollar benefits or costs.

PART
SIX

*Cost and managerial
accounting for other
economic entities*

26

Cost accounting for construction contracts

S. R. Okes, Jr.*
G. H. Beisman†

INTRODUCTION

In general, accounting addresses itself to a wide spectrum of business needs. It maintains a financial record of business transactions, and it also prepares reports on the assets, the liabilities, and the operating results of an enterprise. *Construction cost accounting*, however, focuses on the operating results of a construction organization. As a construction contractor knows, construction costs must be determined continually and compared with the cost budget for the work. Thus, cost accounting becomes the heart of the contractor's cost control program.

Cost accounting for construction is an especially important topic since the construction industry comprises the largest single segment of the American economy. Including the suppliers and manufacturers directly dependent upon the construction industry, over 10 percent of the 1975 Gross National Product was directed into construction. During 1975, for example, over 5 million people were directly employed in the construction industry, or 1 worker out of every 17 in the labor force.

If the primary divisions of the construction industry were es-

---

* Senior Project Manager, Kellogg Corporation.
† Project Manager, Kellogg Corporation.

tablished according to the physical types of construction provided, construction would be divided into three major groups. These would be building construction, highway and heavy construction, and industrial and commercial construction. Or, if the industry were divided according to the contractual arrangements utilized, there would be four principal divisions: design/build contracts, construction management contracts, prime contractor arrangements, and specialty trades contracts. Contracts within these categories are defined according to whether they are fixed price, cost-plus, or a combination of arrangements. Each physical type of construction and each type of contractual arrangement requires the development and maintenance of a different cost accounting system.

The large number and small average size of construction organizations present an additional complication in the development of cost accounting systems for construction. According to the 1972 *Census of Construction Industries,* approximately 438,000 organizations completed $156 billion of construction in 1972. Yet, 19 percent of these companies reported receipts of $25,000 or less, and only 6 percent reported receipts of $1 million or more. Consequently, the average size of a construction organization is very small, with few organizations completing as much as 1 percent of the total construction. Cost accounting needs, however, remain constant.

The construction industry is also unique because of the relatively rapid operation of the cycle from completion of work to receipt of payment. This means that the capital requirements for operation of a construction organization will be substantially lower than those, for example, of a retailing establishment with the same business volume. Any construction cost accounting system must, therefore, place varying emphases on the organization of cost components according to the components' variabilities.

This diversity and low capital requirement of the construction industry lead to another characteristic of cost accounting for construction: the subdivisions, in great detail, of specific cost categories. Therefore, detailed record keeping is necessary throughout the cost development cycle. To be effective, the construction cost accounting system must not only be very carefully planned, but must also be comprehended and accepted by everyone in a construction organization. For example, the units of work selected for measurement must be understood, maintained, and carefully reported by the field level personnel. Then the work item *costs* must be reported to the accounting department with the same accuracy as the *units* were reported. Finally, the reported raw cost data must be quickly processed and reviewed so that any necessary corrective management actions may be taken. The manager must first review the cost information to determine where there are deviations from the budget. Then the manager must determine whether the reported variances are significant and, if they are, find the cause or causes of the variations from the budget. Appropriate action can then be taken.

Cost control during construction requires careful project preplanning, and construction should be completed according to a preplanned system. By regularly and continuously reviewing the actual project performance relative to the planned performance, any cost overruns may be isolated and the causes corrected before disastrous overruns are experienced. The cost accounting system uses management tools, including time and motion studies, production rate analyses, schedule development analyses, labor and equipment reports, and general cost analyses.

These considerations determine what appropriate cost information is required for a typical construction project. The most elementary cost accounting system for a construction project will recognize that the most variable of construction costs is the labor component. Therefore, once the planned budget is distributed among the appropriate cost categories, ordinarily the labor cost component need be the only cost component observed in detail and in great frequency. The remaining project costs might be accumulated under the category of "other" construction costs. If the project is either small or of short duration, it may not even be necessary to maintain a detailed in-progress analysis of quantities. These generalizations apply to a relatively small contractor or, perhaps, a specialty contractor. The owner of the construction organization might well be the field manager of his organization's activities as well as the individual monitoring the project costs.

The next level of complexity in cost information will come when the contractor begins to maintain specific accounts for those cost components other than labor and to maintain careful records of completed work quantities. After labor, ordinarily the next cost component needing control will be either materials or equipment, depending on the nature of the specific construction project. If the construction work is principally building construction, it may be necessary to control the materials as carefully as labor. Most important, this level of complexity is distinguished from the elemental level by the keeping of detailed quantity information. Thus, unit cost information may be developed, a factor speeding the detection of substantial variances from planned production rates.

Finally, the most detailed level of cost accounting systems will include careful analyses of labor, equipment, job materials, permanent materials, subcontracts, quantities, and cost projections to completion.

Under this detailed cost structure, virtually any construction project can be monitored, from building construction to sophisticated nuclear power plants. Also, the data reduction can be accomplished by any combination of tools from simple hand computations to elaborate computer systems. The key element in a detailed cost accounting information system is that field reporting of quantities and costs must be completed quickly and accurately, and that the office accounting procedures must effectively utilize this field information. Detailed projections of cost to completion, for example, will enable the contractor both to control on-project costs efficiently and to generate projections of financial data that are essential to the market development efforts. The carefully designed and effectively used cost accounting system will, consequently, provide three principal types of information:

Historical information. This information will be organized according to the labor cost components, the remaining cost components, and the work quantities completed. Historical data is especially valuable, for example, in the development of cost estimates for similar future construction projects.

Comparative information. This information compares the current status of a project with the planned status of that project. There are four key types of information in this category:

1. Actual unit costs compared to budget unit allowances.
2. Actual progress compared with the expected progress of a project.

3. The actual cash status of a project should be developed and this information should be compared with the planned cash status.
4. The project's profit position and the planned profit position should be compared.

Projections. Utilizing the comparative information generated above, it is then possible to predict the project final cost position. Information developed will consist of estimates of the project's final profit position, as well as analyses of intermediate positions and the impacts on an organization's total financial position.

RESOURCES OF COST CONTROL

For cost accounting to be responsive to the needs of management, it must be structured to show job expenditures accurately, and simultaneously to enable management to manage these expenditures properly. The critical elements of project control are *cost* and *time.* Proper job cost accounting must address both of these needs. Medium to large projects usually break their field resources into labor, equipment, job materials, permanent materials, and subcontracts. Therefore, the cost accounting system should show these categories of job resources. (Smaller projects may account for only "labor" and "other"; however, this discussion will direct itself towards cost accounting for larger projects.)

Definitions of the five basic resources of costs used on construction projects are as follows:

Labor. This cost includes the direct compensation of both hourly paid and salaried employees. The individuals are those employed on the project, as contrasted to those employed in the home office.

Equipment. These costs are divided into two principal subcategories:

1. *Equipment ownership expense:* the cost of depreciation, replacement cost escalation, interest on investment, insurance, and storage. Charges for rental or lease of equipment would also be included in this subcategory.
2. *Equipment operating expense:* the costs of field repairs, shop repairs, overhauls, replacement tires and tracks, and other

major component parts, whether performed by the contractor on the job or by an outside repair service. Also included are the costs of fuel, oil, grease, and expendable parts and supplies.

Job materials. The cost of all materials that do not become a part of the completed work. Examples of direct expense materials would be form lumber, scaffolding, and curing compound. Nondirect expenses in this category would be the cost of services and supplies for the project, that is, electric power, drinking water, safety clothing, and office supplies. Also included would be payroll taxes and insurance, fringe benefits, and project bond.

Permanent materials. The cost of all materials that are physically incorporated into the constructed project. Examples are the cost of concrete, steel, lumber (if incorporated into the project), and brick.

Subcontracts. Normally subcontracts are written for those persons or firms who perform a service on the project site. This separates them from materialmen or suppliers who, while they may come onto the job site, perform no work thereon.

COST CENTERS

Project accounting requires the establishment of cost centers in order to segregate the costs into meaningful categories. Two major cost centers are used: Direct Costs and Indirect Costs. Into the first category, direct costs, would go all the costs required to complete the project that are identifiable with specific items of work. Project indirect costs, on the other hand, cannot be identified with a specific work item. They, in effect, are distributable costs which apply to numerous items of work.

On large projects the indirect costs may be further distributed among the following categories:

a. General and administrative expenses.
b. General operations.
c. Equipment and plant.
d. Plant, buildings, and facilities.
e. Insurance, taxes, and bonds.

Two additional categories are usually carried as indirect costs: (1) contract adjustments, to include all change orders, force account work, backcharges and outside work (that are not specifically connected with the project), and (2) job margin or profit. This last category becomes important to show properly on a project-by-project basis when reporting for federal income tax purposes, whether using the accrual or the completed contract method of accounting.

BUDGETS

To monitor costs properly, an effective distribution of the project budget must be made. A "chart of accounts" should be developed to show the various activities of work to be performed. These activities should be subdivided into the smallest identifiable and measurable parts that are significant from a cost standpoint. Costs are budgeted against these activities, which are then

EXHIBIT 1
Control budget

		TYPICAL CONSTRUCTION CO.				
	CONTROL BUDGET REPORT	—BY OPERATION				
DEPT – EXCAVATION & GRADING						
OPERATION	LABOR	EQUIPMENT	JOB MATL	PERM MATL	SUB CONTR	TOTAL
110 ACCES ROAD NO 1						
1 . EXCAVATION & HAULING	3791	4922	1260	1100	400	11473
19800 P 20000 CY	.191	.249	.064	.056	.020	.579
2 FINE GRADING	400	1100				1500
2000.00 LY	.200	.550				.750
3 SURFACING	500	1800	180	1600		4080
10000 SY	.050	.180	.018	.160		.408
4 DUMP ROYALTY					20000	20000
20000 DOLS					1.000	1.000
110 ITEM TOTAL	4691	7822	1440	2700	20400	37053
19800 P 20000 CY	.237	.395	.073	.136	1.030	1.871
111 ACCES ROAD NO 2						
1 LOAD & HAUL FILL	1600	2500	200		5100	9400
15000 CY	.107	.167	.013		.340	.627
2 COMPACTION	450	1400			300	2150
19725 P 15000 CY	.023	.071			.015	.109
3 . FINE GRADING	340	700	100			1140
1500.00 LY	.227	.467	.067			.760
4 SURFACING	400	1350				1750
7500.00 SY	.053	.180				.233
111 ITEM TOTAL	2790	5950	300		5400	14440
1500.00 LY	1.860	3.967	.200		3.600	9.627
112 REMOVE OVERBURDEN						
1 . EXCAVATE AND HAUL	140000	210000	21000		20000	391000
1000000 CY	.140	.210	.021		.020	.391
2 SUBCONTRACT ACCNT TEST						
7000.00 DOLS						
112 ITEM TOTAL	140000	210000	21000		20000	391000
1000000 CY	.140	.210	.021		.020	.391
GRP–EXCAVATIONS	147481	223772	22740	2700	45800	442493
DEPARTMENT TOTAL	147481	223772	22740	2700	45800	442493
		CONTROL BUDGET				

distributed to the resources that will go into completing each activity. One or more of the resources of labor, equipment, job materials, permanent materials, or subcontracts should apply to each activity. Activities should be assigned units of measure (cubic yards, square feet, man-months, percent, and so forth). To complete the budget, the quantities of work should then be listed for each activity. There may be instances where the quantity of work to be performed is not significant; this is then treated as a "lump sum" item.

The example in Exhibit 1 shows a cost budget. All of the elements necessary to monitor cost and time properly are now present. During construction, actual costs and quantities of work completed to date should be reported. The budget is corrected to reflect the revised total quantity only when the quantities of work change to a degree that is significant compared to that originally estimated.

GENERAL ACCOUNTING PROCEDURES

The question of *centralized* or *decentralized* accounting usually arises when construction companies are forming or revising their accounting procedures. In answering this question, it is important to remember that an accounting system should be adopted that will accommodate both centralized and decentralized accounting without making basic changes in procedures or forms. A construction firm that performs all of its work within a fairly small geographical area and whose jobs are of relatively small dollar amount and short duration would use centralized accounting in the home office. Even in this instance, however, some accounting functions will be performed in the field, including material receiving, timekeeping, and payroll check writing for field terminations. As the size and duration of the jobs increase, more and more of the accounting functions should be moved to the jobsite.

Complete job accounting, in addition to materials receipt and minimal paycheck writing, would include payrolls; approval and payment for all materials, subcontracts and other job-incurred expenses; progress payment requests to the owner; other outside billings; maintenance of general ledgers and subsidiary cost ledgers; and preparation of financial statements to include balance sheet, profit and loss statements, schedules of accounts receivable and payable, schedules of equipment, and project detailed cost and revenue reports. In addition, cost reestimates and cash flow projections may be required.

A discussion of the cost accounting procedures that specifically apply to manual cost accounting on construction projects follows.

General ledger

The general ledger is established to record cash receipts and disbursements, purchases, contract and other income (billed and accrued), and contract costs. An example of the general ledger chart of accounts for a medium-sized general contractor is shown in Exhibit 2. From the general ledger, the balance sheet and profit and loss statement are produced.

Subsidiary ledger

Subsidiary cost ledgers are utilized to record all of the project direct and indirect costs, broken down by the various cost categories established for the project. While the double-entry method of accounting is used for the general ledger, the subsidiary ledger requires only a single entry, as all entries are either expenses or income. As an example, the direct cost subsidiary ledger code for concrete materials would, with numerous other codes, fall under the general ledger account for *project direct costs*. When costing to the subsidiary ledger, the code can be flagged with a L, E, J, P, or S, to further define the expense as labor, equipment, job materials, permanent materials, or subcontracts. This is done so that costs can be properly distributed by the appropriate resource on the detailed costs reports. Expenses posted to the general and subsidiary ledgers would come from the check voucher for all general accounts, from the weekly labor distribution work sheets, and from a journal entry work sheet for all transactions not covered by the writing of a check (check vouchers).

Cash journal

A cash journal is the form used to record all cash receipts and expenditures, except individual payroll checks. In the case

682

EXHIBIT 2
General ledger chart of accounts

SECTION ONE - ASSETS

CURRENT ASSETS:

Cash:
- 111 General Account
- 112 Payroll Account
- 113 Savings Account
- 121 Petty Cash

Accounts Receivable:
- 131 Accounts Receivable - Officers & Employees
- 132 Accounts Receivable - Trade
- 133 Accounts Receivable - Projects
- 134 Pay Estimates Receivable
- 135 Pay Estimates Retained
- 136 Extra Work
- 137 Unbilled Work
- 138 Payroll Deductions
- 139 Accrued Interest

Notes Receivable:
- 155 Notes Receivable

Recoverable Income Taxes:
- 160 Recoverable Income Taxes

Securities:
- 165 Securities

Prepaid Expenses:
- 171 Prepaid Insurance
- 172 Insurance Deposit
- 173 Prepaid Surety Bond
- 174 Plan Deposits
- 175 Prepaid Rent
- 176 Telephone Deposit
- 177 Airline Deposits

Investment in Projects:
- 181 Advances
- 182 Rentals
- 183 Undistributed Share of Profits

INVESTMENTS AND OTHER ASSETS:

Investments:
- 201 Advances To Affiliates
- 202 Notes Receivable - Officers and Employees
- 203 Cash Value of Life Insurance
- 204 Sundry Accounts and Deposits
- 205 Organizational Expense

PROPERTY AND EQUIPMENT AT COST:

Property and Equipment at Cost:
- 301 Land
- 302 Improvements
- 303 Buildings
- 304 Accumulated Depreciation - Buildings
- 305 Construction Equipment
- 306 Accumulated Depreciation - Equipment
- 307 Automobiles and Trucks
- 308 Accumulated Depreciation - Autos & Trucks
- 309 Plant
- 310 Accumulated Depreciation - Plant
- 311 Office Furniture and Fixtures
- 312 Accumulated Depreciation - Office Furniture & Fixtures

DEFERRED CHARGES:
- 321 Project Control Deferred Charges

SUSPENSE:
- 331 Suspense Account

SECTION TWO - LIABILITIES AND SHAREHOLDERS' EQUITY

CURRENT LIABILITIES:

Notes Payable:
- 401 Notes Payable - Bank
- 402 Notes Payable - Trade
- 403 Notes Payable - Individuals

Accounts Payable:
- 411 Accounts Payable - Officers and Employees
- 412 Accounts Payable - Trade
- 413 Accounts Payable - Projects
- 414 Accounts Payable - Subcontractors Current Estimate
- 415 Accounts Payable - Subcontractors Retainage
- 416 Payrolls Payable
- 417 Vacation Reserve
- 418 Insurance Premiums Payable
- 419 Income Premiums Payable
- 420 Federal Unemployment Tax
- 421 State Withholding Tax
- 422 State Unemployment Tax
- 423 Local Occupation Tax
- 424 Personal Property Tax
- 425 Miscellaneous Tax
- 426 Sales Tax
- 427 Union Fringe Benefits
- 428 Union Funds
- 429 Workmans Compensation
- 430 Dividends Payable

Accrued Expenses:
- 461 Interest Earned and Accrued
- 462 Insurance Premiums Earned and Accrued
- 463 Investment Credit
- 464 Reserve for Contract Claims and Losses

Income Tax Payable:
- 481 Federal Income Tax - Accrued
- 482 State Income Tax - Accrued
- 483 Other Income Tax - Accrued

Deferred Credits:
- 491 Project Control Deferred Credits

LONG-TERM LIABILITIES

SHAREHOLDERS' EQUITY:
- 501 Common Stock
- 502 Treasury Stock
- 511 Additional Paid in Capital
- 521 Retained Earnings
- 531 Profit and Loss
- 541 Surplus - Earned
- 542 Surplus - Paid In

EXHIBIT 2 *(continued)*

SECTION THREE - REVENUE

REVENUE:

601	Construction Revenue
611	Consulting Services
621	Sale of Property and Equipment
631	Rentals
641	Dividends
651	Interest, Discounts & Exchange Earned
661	Miscellaneous Income

SECTION FOUR - EXPENDITURES

EXPENDITURES:

Administrative Salaries:

701	Salaries - Officers
702	Salaries - Employees
703	Salaries - Holding

Administrative Expense:

711	Prospective Work
712	Engineering Expense
713	Professional Services
714	Rent
715	Heat and Air Conditioning
716	Janitor and Yard Service
717	Water
718	Light and Power
719	Maintenance of Building
720	Telephone and Telegraph
721	Postage
722	Stationery, Printing & Supplies
723	Sundries
724	Computer Services
725	Permits and Licenses
726	Business Permits
727	Office Service and Repairs
728	Agency Services
729	Travel Expense
730	Personnel Expense
731	Employment Expense
732	Employee Moving Expense
733	Photos and Reports
734	Books and Manuals
735	Publications and Subscriptions
736	Automobile Expense
737	Banquets and Christmas Expense
738	Coffee Shop
739	Safe Deposit Box
740	Legal Expense
741	Audit Service
742	Public Relations
743	Donations
744	Advertisements
745	Entertainment
746	Membership and Dues
747	Interest Expense
748	Freight
749	Building Depreciation Expense
750	Equipment Depreciation Expense
751	Automobile and Truck Depreciation Expense
752	Plant Depreciation Expense
753	Office Furniture & Fixture Depreciation Expense
754	Miscellaneous Single Charge Items
755	Amortization

Insurance, Taxes, and Bonds:

771	All Risk
772	Automobile and Truck (Owned)
773	Automobile and Truck (Non-Owned)
774	P.L. and P.D.
775	Fire
776	Surety Bond Premiums
777	Excess Liability
778	Accidental Death - Employee Benefit
779	Accidental Death - Employer Benefit
780	Insurance - General
781	Group Life Insurance and L.T.D.
782	Group Medical, Surgical & Hospitalization
783	Life Insurance on Individuals
784	Workmans Compensation
785	Pension Expense
786	Retirement Trust

801	F.I.C.A.
802	Federal Unemployment Tax
803	State Unemployment Tax
804	Local Occupation Tax
805	Personal Property Tax
806	Miscellaneous Taxes
807	Sales Tax
808	Union Fringe Benefits
809	Union Funds
810	Federal Income Tax
811	State Income Tax

PROJECT CONTROL ACCOUNTS

900	Project Direct Cost - Labor, Equipment (EOE) Job Materials, Permanent Materials, and Subcontracts
910	Project Indirect Cost - Equipment, Equipment Rentals, and Freight
920	Project Indirect Cost - Plant, Buildings and Facilities
930	Project Indirect Cost - Equipment and Plant Salvage
940	Project Indirect Cost - Administrative Salaries and Expense, Insurance, Taxes and Bonds, and General Operations
950	Project Indirect Cost - Equipment Maintenance and Operation
960	Project Change Orders
961	Project Force Account Work
962	Project Quantity Adjustments
963	Project Backcharge to Subcontractors
964	Project Recovery from Subcontractors
965	Project Backcharge to Vendors
966	Project Recovery from Vendors
967	Project Outside Work
968	Project Recovery Outside Work

of payroll checks, the payroll will serve as the cash disbursement record. The cash journal for double-entry accounting can be established with only three headings: General Bank Account, Payroll Bank Account, and General Ledger. The General Ledger column should have a space for the account code number in addition to the usual debit and credit columns. Posting to the General Ledger should be made, on a monthly basis, at a minimum. Some companies also use the Cash Journal to control their accounts payable.

At the back of the Cash Journal, a section entitled "Accounts Payable" can be inserted. The purpose of this section is to record invoices, or known expenses, which apply for cost purposes to the current period, but which are due and payable in a subsequent calendar accounting period. This will allow the cost reports to reflect an accurate picture of the cost of work performed to date. When payment is made, offsetting entries must be made to clear the accounts payable section.

Journal entry form

A standard journal entry form should be used, showing account numbers and debit and credit columns for general and subsidiary ledger accounts. This form is used for all accruals, deferrals and other transactions not covered by the writing of a check.

Payroll journal entry form

A standard journal entry form should be used to summarize all payroll-related expenses which can be derived from: (*a*) payroll distributions, (*b*) craft fringe benefits, (*c*) workers compensation, and (*d*) payroll taxes and insurance.

Cost ledgers

The cost ledger is established to show all the project costs defined in the chart of accounts. In this case, only the amount and code number (flagged for L, E, J, P, or S) need be shown under the general cost categories of direct and indirect work. (See earlier discussion under "Cost Centers.") Posting should be from the check vouchers, payroll journal, and the journal entry forms.

Bank accounts and check writing

Usually a general bank account and a payroll bank account are established at a local bank convenient to the work. Funds are advanced to the project from the home office, sometimes from a special account entitled a "control account." Each pay period, funds to cover the payroll are transferred from the general account to the payroll account. A sample of a general bank account check is shown in Exhibit 3 which includes a two-part voucher form allowing for simultaneous cost coding to the General Ledger and Subsidiary Ledger accounts. The first copy of the check voucher should be filed in the vendor's alphabetical file, together with the supporting documents such as the invoice, receiving and inspection report, and purchase order. The second copy of the voucher check should be filed in a numerical file and used for posting to the Cash Journal and Cost Ledgers. As a minimum, two people in the field should be required to sign all general account checks. One signature is usually sufficient on payroll checks.

Detailed cost reports

These reports are prepared monthly to cover all costs paid for or accrued during that period. The various cost accounts, as discussed under "Cost Centers," are listed with space to show the cost resources, L, E, J, P, and S, that are applicable to that cost account. The report should provide for recording costs for the period, costs to date, and projected costs to completion. An example of a detailed cost report is shown in Exhibit 4. Detailed Cost Reports can also be used on a weekly basis to reflect only labor and the appropriate quantity of work performed. These weekly labor cost reports are very beneficial; they can provide management with timely information on what is usually the most difficult of all costs to control, *labor.*

EXHIBIT 3
General bank account check

TYPICAL CONSTRUCTION CO.

OOI $\frac{22-00}{2000}$

DATE

PAY

$

TO THE
ORDER
OF

BY

STATEMENT OF ACCOUNT•DETACH BEFORE DEPOSITING   GROSS   DISCOUNT   NET

VOUCHER
OOI

PAID
TO

CHECKED BY

ENTERED BY

APPROVED BY

STATEMENT OF ACCOUNT   GROSS   DISCOUNT   NET

SUMMARY OF ITEMS

VOUCHER
OOI

GENERAL LEDGER				COST DETAILS					
ACCOUNT	DEBIT	P.	CREDIT	CODE	P	AMOUNT	CODE	P	AMOUNT

NET

APPROVED   DATE

ROUTING — ALPHABETICAL

GENERAL LEDGER				COST DETAILS					
ACCOUNT	DEBIT	P.	CREDIT	CODE	P	AMOUNT	CODE	P	AMOUNT

APPROVED   DATE

ROUTING — NUMERICAL

TYPICAL CONSTRUCTION CO.

DEPT – EXCAVATION & GRADING OPER. ACTIVE TODATE–EXCLUDING COMPLETED OPER

OPERATION	PCT CMP	WORK QUANTITY CURRENT	WORK QUANTITY TODATE	CURRENT BUDGET	CURRENT COST	CURRENT SAVING	TO-DATE BUDGET	TO-DATE COST	TO-DATE SAVING	TOTAL BUDGET	PROJECTED COST	PROJECTED SAVING	T R
110 ACCES ROAD NO 1													
1. EXCAVATION & HAULING													
LABOR				957	876	81	2872	2575	297	3791	3400	391	I —
EQUIPMENT				1243	1186	57	3729	3530	199	4922	4660	262	
JOB MATERIALS				318	331	13—	955	969	14—	1260	1279	19—	*
PERM MATERIALS				278	283	5—	833	893	60—	1100	1179	79—	*
SUB CONTRACT				101	100	1	303	300	3	400	396	4	
OPN TOTAL	75	5000.00	15000	2897	2776	121	8692	8268	424	11473	10914E	559	
19800.OOP 20000.00 CY					.555	.024		.551	.028	.579	.551	.028	
2 FINE GRADING													
LABOR				100	117	17—	300	333	33—	400	444	44—	I —
EQUIPMENT				275	240	35	825	710	115	1100	947	153	+
OPN TOTAL	75	500.00	1500.00	375	357	18	1125	1043	82	1500	1750M	250—	I —
2000.00 LY					.714	.036		.695	.055	.750	.875	.125—	
3 SURFACING													
LABOR				125	168	43—	375	443	68—	500	568	68—	I +
EQUIPMENT				450	500	50—	1350	1350		1800	1800		
JOB MATERIALS				45	30	15	135	111	24	180	156	24	I —
PERM MATERIALS				400	400		1200	1140	60	1600	1540	60	I —
OPN TOTAL	75	2500.00	7500.00	1020	1098	78—	3060	3044	16	4080	4064L	16	
10000.00 SY					.439	.031—		.406	.002	.408	.406	.002	
4 DUMP ROYALTY													
S SUB CONTRACT				100	100		300	300		20000	20000		
S OPN TOTAL	2	100.00	300.00	100	100		300	300		20000	20000		
20000.00 DOLS					1.000			1.000		1.000	1.000		
110 TOTAL ITEM	75	5000.00	15000	4392	4330	62	13177	12654	523	37053	36727	326	
19800.00 P 20000.00 CY					.866	1.005		.844	.028	1.871	1.855	.016	
ADJUSTED UNIT COSTS	36	2346.89	7041.07		1.845	.026		1.797	.074				

INPUT REQUIRED FOR COST ACCOUNTING

All the cost information required for a proper accounting system can be obtained from three sources: (1) Payrolls; (2) Job Cost Journals for receipts and earnings, accrued costs and earnings, backcharges, and commitments; and (3) Progress Reports showing quantities of work completed (in units of measure or percent). Depending on the size of the project, this cost information may be taken directly from the check vouchers when a general and a subsidiary cost ledger are kept, or it may be obtained from work sheet entries.

Progress reporting in job cost accounting is needed to provide a means of projecting the total cost of an operation or activity to completion. If, for example, 100 cubic yards of concrete were required for a particular footing and the costs to date were $125 for labor and $750 for permanent materials (concrete), based on 25 cubic yards placed, then the unit labor cost to date would be $5/cu. yd. and the unit material cost $30/cu. yd. Projecting these units to completion, the total cost of labor would be $500 and materials $3,000 to place 100 cubic yards of concrete. If, for example, the budgeted costs for labor and materials were $450 and $2,950 or $4.50/cu. yd. labor and $29.50/cu. yd. materials, it is clear that the budget is not being met. Management, then, based on comparative costs to date, can take corrective action early in the life of that particular operation to meet the budgeted costs. In this example, the total budgeted cost is $3,400 ($450 + $2,950) and the projected total cost is $3,500, an overrun of $100. If, by improved utilization of labor, the unit labor cost can be cut to $3 per cubic yard for the remaining work while the cost of the concrete remains unchanged, the final cost at completion will be:

Labor:	$5/cu. yd. × 25 cu. yd.	$ 125
	$3/cu. yd. × 75 cu. yd.	225
Materials:	$30/cu. yd. × 100 cu. yd.	3,000
Total projected cost		$3,350
Original budget		3,400
Projected cost underrun		$ 50

The concept of unit costs (or percentages) completed for the various activities of work at any one time allows project management to determine what the final cost of that operation will be if no changes are made (assuming a straight-line projection for the cost of work-in-process). This gives project management the opportunity to change their operations where needed in order to meet budgeted costs.

EMPLOYMENT AND PAYROLL PROCEDURES

As stated earlier, accounting for labor is extremely important. This one resource is the most variable, and the bottom line profitability of a construction company is usually determined by how well labor is managed.

It is desirable for one person on a project, a payroll clerk or office manager, to be responsible for employment and payroll procedures. If employment is handled through the main office and personnel are dispatched to the field jobs, an individual equivalent to a payroll clerk or office manager would be the responsible home office dispatcher.

The following general employment and payroll procedures will ordinarily apply to a construction project.

Hiring. Project management should first determine that there is a need for a specific number of men, within certain job classifications, to perform the scheduled work. Since construction work is performed according to trade classifications, it is the nature of this work that people trained in certain skills are hired for a particular task and then terminated once that task is completed. For example, a pipefitter would not perform carpenter's work. Only recently, since the nonunion or merit shop construction contractors have emerged as a force in the industry, have there been craftsmen working in several trade classifications. Individuals are obtained for a construction project through several methods: rehire of previous employees, personal references by presently employed foremen, union hall referrals, use of hiring agencies, and by advertising in local papers and trade journals.

Each project should have a supply of job application forms so that those people seeking employment will have the opportunity to submit their applications and be judged on their individual capabilities, even if no jobs are open at the time. Employment regulations vary from state to state, that is, "Right to Work states," minority hiring quotas, and so forth, and construction contractors should thoroughly familiarize themselves with the specific conditions under which they will be hiring.

Employment record. When first reporting for work, the new employee should be required to complete specific company forms. Mandatory are: The Federal Form W–4, "Employee's Withholding Allowance Certificate," and, in some states, a similar tax withholding form. It is important to *see* the individual's Social Security card to be certain of his social security number and the proper spelling of his name.[1]

An employment record should be completed. Lengths and formats vary; but at the minimum they should (in addition to the information on Form W–4), show the employee's phone number, date and place of birth, age, nationality, citizenship, employment position, date of hire, rate of pay, and a statement by the employee about his physical health. Any subsequent changes should be corrected on the appropriate records.

Safety rules. Each new employee should be provided with a list of the company's safety rules and any safety regulations that apply specifically to his or her project. It is advisable to have the employee sign a short statement acknowledging that he has read and understands the safety rules. This should be accomplished before the employee begins work.

Tools and clothing issue report. This form can be easily developed for each job to show those items of safety, wearing apparel, and special tools that are issued to each employee. When these items wear out or are damaged, the employee should return the old issue to obtain a new replacement. Here, again, the employee should sign for receipt of these items.

Foreman's daily time and equipment card. Refer to Exhibits 5 and 8 for examples of Foreman's Time Cards, Labor Distribution Work Sheets, and Weekly Payroll. Every foreman is required to complete for each shift a time report covering all the men and equipment under his supervision, including himself. He should enter the name of the man and his badge number (if assigned) and the hours worked, distributed to those activities previously established for cost control purposes. The total number of hours worked is shown, including overtime or bonus time

---

[1] Masculine pronouns are being used for succinctness and are intended to refer to both females and males.

EXHIBIT 5
Labor cost forms

TYPICAL CONSTRUCTION CO.

FOREMAN'S DAILY REPORT   DATE: _____

FOREMAN: _____   JOB NAME: _____   JOB NO. _____

LOCATION: _____   FROM STAT. _____   TO STAT. _____

LOCATION: _____   FROM STAT. _____   TO STAT. _____

SOIL TYPE: _____

OPERATION: DRAG ☐   BKHOE ☐   SPECIFICATION   RATE   COST CODE

LABOR DISTRIBUTION SUMMARY

SHIFT NO. _____   WEEK ENDING _____

DAY	ACCT. NO.	ACCT. NO.	ACCT. NO.	ACCT. NO.	ACCT. NO.	ACCT. NO.	ACCT. NO.
MON.							
TUE.							
WED.							
THURS.							
FRI.							
SAT.							
SUN.							
TOTAL							

	ACCT. NO.	ACCT. NO.	ACCT. NO.	ACCT. NO.	ACCT. NO.	ACCT. NO.	ACCT. NO.
MON.							
TUE.							
WED.							
THURS							
FRI.							
SAT.							
SUN.							
TOTAL							
MON.							
TUE.							
WED.							
THUR							
FRI.							
SAT.							
SUN.							
TOTAL							
MON.							
TUE							
WED.							
THUR							
FRI.							
SAT.							
SUN.							
TOTAL							

CERTIFIED TRANSCRIPT OF LABOR PAYROLL

PAYROLL NO. _____   SHEET NO. ___ OF ___
PROJECT NO. _____
STATE OF _____   COUNTY _____
PAYROLL WEEK ENDING _____

CONTRACTOR _____
ADDRESS _____
TYPE _____

NAME   LABOR POSITION   HOURS WORKED EACH DAY   S M T W T F S hours if worked. For mechanics, the foreman may also distribute the hours for each man by the equipment on which he worked.

The time cards should be collected daily; applying the hourly rate of pay, the total pay is computed in the office. The wages chargeable to each activity should then be calculated. Finally, the numbers should be "squared" to insure that the totals for the "amount" columns equal the totals distributed to the cost accounts for the work activities.

Labor distribution work sheet. After the Foreman's Daily Time Card has been balanced for wages earned, and checked for proper coding (usually an engineering function), all wages chargeable for the day are posted to the Labor Distribution Work sheet (see Exhibit 5). At the close of each week, the totals for each account are posted on a backup sheet to the Payroll Journal Entry Form and, at the close of the month, to the General and Subsidiary Ledgers.

Weekly payroll. In preparation for writing the payroll checks, which are issued weekly for hourly paid employees, a payroll summary or certified transcript of labor payroll is completed. This payroll shows, for each employee, the total hours worked each day for the week, straight time and bonus time, rates of pay deductions (federal, state, and other), and net pay. The checks can then be written. A number of "peg board" systems are in use that allow, when writing the pay check, simultaneous recording on the employee's "Earnings Record" and the "Payroll Journal." When computerized payrolls are used many of the above steps can be automatically completed; however, the basic information provided by the foreman in the field remains the same.

Earnings record. An earnings record should be completed for each new employee when hired. The basic information will be obtained from the employee's Employment Record. As noted earlier, the basic payroll information will be recorded on the earnings record at the same time the payroll check is written. These earnings records will be used to monitor the level of withholding for FICA, FUT, and SUT, and must be totaled periodically to prepare the various state and federal tax forms.

Payroll journal. This form, using typical "peg board systems," will be completed as the payroll checks are written. After all checks are written the payroll journals are totaled to make certain that all items on the checks match exactly those on the weekly payroll form and thus, that the payroll journals will be in balance.

Payroll taxes, insurance, and fringe benefits.   The amount of employee and employer contributions for FICA tax is established by law and is changing yearly. Federal and State Unemployment Tax contributions, made solely by the employer, also change from year to year. Other contributions made by the employer, based on wages or hours worked by his employees, include Workers' Compensation and, depending upon labor or company agreements, contributions to health insurance plans, benefit plans, and union fringe benefit plans.

Termination.   A termination slip should always be used when an employee is terminated. It should show the date and reason for termination and whether the employee is eligible for rehire. A copy should be given to the employee. The importance of noting the reason for termination is that in many states when the employee voluntarily quits his job, or is terminated for cause, his unemployment benefits either do not start until after a waiting period or are at a reduced level.

PURCHASING PROCEDURE

The responsibility for jobsite purchasing is usually delegated by the project manager to the office manager. On large projects, or where many purchases must be made, an on-site purchasing agent may be needed. For smaller projects, the purchasing function may be performed in the home office, with the field only identifying specific needs as they arise.

Purchasing, from a control-accounting standpoint, is usually accomplished through the following steps:

1. Request for bid.
2. Bid evaluation.
3. Requisition to purchasing.
4. Purchase order.

Request for bid.   This is a formal request usually sent to selected vendors. It should contain a complete and detailed description of what is to be quoted (the inclusion of plans and specifications may be appropriate), and the terms and conditions on which the bid is to be based should be completely detailed. Delivery method, date, and other appropriate shipping instructions should be shown.

Bid evaluation. Where the contractor is performing work for an owner on a cost reimbursable basis, it is necessary that the contractor formally evaluate bids and show the reason for his selection of a particular vendor. Occasionally, the owner may require his concurrence with the contractor's selection prior to issuance of the purchase order. Reasons for selection should be shown; they can include lowest price, early delivery, better quality, only available source, and others.

Requisition to purchasing. This form is designed for the use of the personnel in the field. It is prepared by the superintendent or foreman responsible for the work where the materials are to be used. The materials usually requested in this manner are expendables. The formal requests for bid and bid comparison may be bypassed, since the person responsible for purchasing usually knows the best source for these materials. The individual preparing the request should keep a copy with the original, which is then reviewed and approved by the project manager or his designated representative prior to purchase.

Purchase order. A growing number of construction companies now write a purchase order to cover *every* item of material or equipment purchased for the project. (See example shown in Exhibit 6.) The informal procedures of the past, where many verbal orders were placed, do not give management the controls needed in today's competitive markets. Specifically, a purchase order should accomplish the following:

a. Clearly spell out what is being bought.

b. List the terms and conditions under which the order is placed. This can be accomplished through boiler plate language printed on the back side of the purchase order. Specific guarantees and warranties should always be written out.

c. Show the f.o.b. origin point. This becomes important as "FOB manufacturer's plant, freight allowed to jobsite" means the product is still in the care and custody of the supplier until it reaches the job and any damages en route must be remedied by the seller. If the f.o.b. point is the

EXHIBIT 6
Purchase order form

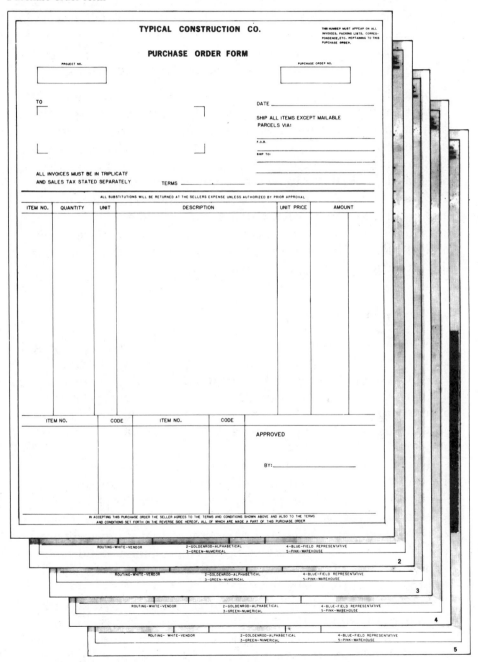

manufacturer's plant, the buyer pays, or has to collect from others, for damages which may occur en route to the job.

d. The delivery date, method of shipment, and delivery address.

e. Discounts, if any, and payment terms.

f. Formal purchase orders *prevent* unauthorized buying.

In addition to the above, purchase order forms may be coded so that the cost of the materials is distributed according to the project chart of accounts. Also, this coding will assist in determining the amount of money committed, but not actually paid, when lengthy time periods elapse between the issuance of a purchase order and the final receipt and payment for all materials ordered. Purchase orders should be numbered and should include an original and three copies with distribution as follows: The original goes to the vendor, the duplicate is retained for the office alphabetical file, the triplicate is placed in the numerical file, and the quadruplicate goes to the warehouse.

WAREHOUSING PROCEDURE

Warehousing procedures may differ considerably, depending on the sizes of the projects, the nature of the work, and the flow of materials required. Project management will designate the personnel and provide the facilities for handling and storing property to prevent waste, damage, and pilferage. The following procedures would apply for a medium-sized construction project.

Receiving and inspection report. It is the responsibility of the warehouseman to check and record all deliveries received. He must satisfy himself as to the quantity and quality of materials received and see that all items are properly stored. The report should include an original and one copy so that the warehouseman can retain a copy in his files. Spaces for notation of shortages, damaged material, and location of the stored material should be provided on the form.

Warehouse requisition. This form is used to record all withdrawals from warehouse stock and must show the description of the materials requisitioned and where the materials are to be used. When the materials are issued by the warehouseman, the authorized person receiving the materials should sign the form acknowledging receipt. If an item which is out of stock appears on the requisition, a description of the item requisitioned and the quantity required should be reported immediately to purchasing.

Tools and clothing issue report. This form was discussed earlier under "Employment and payroll procedures."

Delivery records. The purpose of this form is to provide a record of equipment and materials delivered to third parties, i.e., subcontractors and other contractors. The warehouseman should check each month with the office manager to be certain that all deliveries to third parties have been billed or otherwise reconciled.

Inventory control. This form is used to maintain inventory control over those items which are normally stocked and requisitioned on a repetitive basis. A minimum stock level should be established to ensure timely reordering. Typical items over which inventory control should be exercised are explosives, fuel, oil, nails, and form lumber, to name a few.

SUBCONTRACT PROCEDURE

Subcontract quotations are usually received by the general contractor during the bidding stages of the project. In many cases, these quotes are taken over the phone and it is important for the person taking the quote to insure that it is clear to both parties exactly what is included in the work to be subcontracted and what, if any, services are furnished the subcontractor by the general contractor.

The successful general contractor should, upon being notified of his low bid, set out to evaluate his subcontractor bids. Careful consideration should be given to the sub's past performance on work of a similar nature, his financial strength, insurance coverage, and bonding capacity. The decision of whether or not to subcontract work or perform it with one's own forces is a management decision and depends upon many factors; however, for the successful subcontractors selected, a formal subcontract should be entered into between the parties. Numerous standard subcontract agreements are available for this purpose and it is sufficient in this discussion to state that the importance

EXHIBIT 7
Subcontractor's Receipt and Release

Subcontract No. _____

For and in consideration of a payment in the amount of _____
_____Dollars ($ _____)
to be made to the undersigned by _____
_____, being full and final payment due the undersigned under the certain
Subcontract No._____, dated _____ by and between the
undersigned and_____
_____, covering the performance of work or the furnishing of services
therein described under a prime contract dated _____ between
_____ , and _____
_____ , as Owner, the undersigned does hereby:

    1.   Certify that the undersigned has paid in full for all labor, materials, tools, plant, equipment and services used or furnished in connection with the performance of said subcontract, and that there are no outstanding claims, demands or lien rights against the undersigned or the premises thereby affected arising out of said subcontract or the work performed thereunder on the part of any materialman, laborer or other person, and agreed to indemnify and hold harmless the said_____
and the Owner named in said subcontract, their successors and assigns from any mechanic's or materialman's lien arising out of or in any way connected with said subcontract or the work performed thereunder.

    2.   Release and discharge the said _____
_____ and the said Owner, their successors and assigns of and from any and all claims, demands or causes of action of whatsoever nature which the undersigned has or might in the future assert against them arising out of or in connection with the said subcontract or the work performed thereunder.

    In Witness Whereof _____
_____ , the aforesaid Subcontractor, has caused this Receipt and Release to be executed this_____day of _____ , 19___, by
_____ (a partner) (its designated and authorized officer or representative), acting in its behalf.

Witness:

_____

_____   By _____
                                              (Signature)

_____

                                              (Title or Authority)

of a well drafted subcontract spelling out in detail the work to be performed, payment procedures, and responsibilities and obligations of both parties cannot be overemphasized.

The work in some subcontracts is of such a short duration that only a final payment is required. However, most subcontract work extends over a period of time such that progress payments become necessary. Procedures for adding extra work to the subcontract must be provided for, as well as backcharges to the subcontractor for services provided him. Progress payments should also reflect retainage on work performed to date if this is required in the subcontract.

As a general rule, progress payments are submitted at the end of the month, and since payments to the subcontractors are not made until the following month, shortly after the general contractor receives his progress payment, payments due subcontractors should be accrued at the end of each month. Posting to the General Ledger and Subsidiary Ledger (for detailed project costs) is accomplished from journal entry work sheets which allocate, by cost code, the subcontracted work performed during the month.

Upon satisfactory completion of the work a final payment, including retainage, will be due the subcontractor. In order for the general contractor to protect himself and the owner from any backcharges, lien claim, or other claims by the subcontractor, a "Subcontractor's Receipt and Release" is used. An example of this form is shown in Exhibit 7. Many owners require a release from all subcontractors before they will make final payment to the general contractor. The use of this release form will usually allow the general contractor to receive his final payment from the owner covering his retention prior to, or concurrently with, the general contractor's final payments to his subcontractors.

EQUIPMENT COST ACCOUNTING

Expenses related to the ownership, rental, maintenance, and repair of construction equipment will usually be a major part of the cost of a project. Even in the case of building construction, equipment costs can be substantial. Where a project relies heavily on the use of equipment, the equipment costs may well exceed the labor component of the project's cost. Consider, for

700

EXHIBIT 8
Combined labor and equipment reporting form

TYPICAL CONSTRUCTION CO.

FOREMAN'S DAILY REPORT　　　　　　DATE: _____

FOREMAN: _____　JOB NAME: _____　JOB NO. _____

LOCATION: _____　FROM STAT. _____　TO STAT. _____

LOCATION: _____　FROM STAT. _____　TO STAT. _____

SOIL TYPE: _____

OPERATION: DRAG ☐　BKHOE ☐

NO.	EMPLOYEE	CLASSIFICATION	RATE	COST CODE								TOT. HRS.
		P/S										
		P/S										
		P/S										
		P/S										
		P/S										
		P/S										
		P/S										
		P/S										
		P/S										
		P/S										
		P/S										
		P/S										
		P/S										
		P/S										

EQUIPMENT		IDLE HOURS	DOWN TIME							TOTAL HOURS
NO.	DESCRIPTION									

P—PREMIUM TIME
S—STRAIGHT TIME

example, a major highway construction project where the contractor's cost accounting system may need to be as elaborate for equipment as it is for labor.

To insure that the appropriate job cost charges are made, equipment use time must be reported as conscientiously as labor time. Likewise, actual equipment costs must be carefully recorded. Time or use reports must be prepared in the field by each project for each piece of equipment on that project. As in labor cost accounting these field reports provide the basis for equipment cost control. The reporting form used may be similar to the labor cost reporting form; in fact, the reporting form could well be a part of the daily foreman's report. (See Exhibit 8.)

If total equipment costs are to be segregated according to the individual units, or according to groups of equipment, a separate field report should be prepared for labor expended on maintenance and repair of the equipment. This field report may take the form of a specific condition report for each unit of equipment serviced and repaired, or it may take the form of a daily mechanic's time card. (See Exhibit 9.) If individual reporting by mechanics is used, as above, then the cost trail for actual equipment expenses will be clearly separate from the equipment reporting for project item progress. Thus, accurate evaluations of both equipment costs and project item costs are possible.

For equipment repair, whether the equipment is owned or rented or whether repairs are accomplished by the construction contractor's work force or by outside repair forces, an "Equipment Work Order" should be prepared whenever equipment repairs are considered necessary for a specific unit. (See Exhibit 10.) The purpose of this work order is to document any work accomplished on a unit other than fuel, oil, grease, and normal maintenance. With this form as the basic document, it is then possible for the office force to accurately code equipment charges including, for example, suppliers' invoices.

The final significant record to be maintained for equipment cost accounting is a basic "Equipment History Report." Equipment histories can be kept by unit in detail, and should include complete information on repairs, frequency of repairs, machine availability, and utilization. Whether this information is kept

EXHIBIT 9
Mechanic's daily time card

TYPICAL CONSTRUCTION CO.		
MECHANIC'S DAILY TIME CARD		
EQUIPMENT REPAIR & MAINTENANCE		
UNIT NO.	REPAIR	HOURS
	SERVICING	
	OTHER	
	TOTAL HOURS	
	MECHANIC	

EXHIBIT 10
Equipment work order

TYPICAL CONSTRUCTION CO.			
EQUIPMENT WORK ORDER		W.O. NO. _____	
		METER READING: _____	
PROJECT NO. EQUIPMENT NO.		S/N	
EQUIPMENT DESCRIPTION:			
DATE REPAIR STARTED: DATE REPAIR COMPLETE:			
PART NO.	PART DESCRIPTION	VENDOR	COST

COMMENTS: (WARRANTY, REASON FOR REPAIR, ETC.)

EXHIBIT 11
Summary equipment history report

TYPICAL CONSTRUCTION CO.

EQUIPMENT HISTORY REPORT

NAME _____

ADDRESS _____

UNIT NO. _____ SERIAL NO. _____

PURCHASED FROM _____ DATE _____

ADDRESS _____ WARRANTY _____

ORIGINAL ENGINE   ENGINE REPLACEMENT   TRANSMISSION   FINAL DRIVE

MAKE _____

MODEL _____

SERIAL _____

CAPACITIES

COOLING SYSTEM _____ GAL.   HYDRAULIC SYSTEM _____ GAL.   TANDEM DRIVES _____ GAL.

ENGINE CRANKCASE _____ QTS.   OIL CLUTCH _____ QTS.   GEAR HOUSINGS _____ QTS.

TRANSMISSION _____ GAL.   DIFFERENTIAL _____ QTS.

TORQUE CONVERTER _____ QTS.   FINAL DRIVES _____ GAL.

CABLE SPECIFICATIONS

HOIST: LENGTH _____ DIA. & TYPE _____

HOIST: LENGTH _____ DIA. & TYPE _____

HOIST: LENGTH _____ DIA. & TYPE _____

TIRES

SIZE _____ FRONT _____ BACK _____ PRESSURE _____ FRONT _____ BACK _____

G.E.T. PART NUMBERS

CUTTING EDGES   BITS   BUCKETS   RIPPERS

CENTER _____ END _____ TIP _____ TIP _____

ROUTER _____ ADAPTER _____ PROTECTOR _____

ENDS _____ OVERLAY _____

FILTER PART NUMBERS

CRANKCASE _____ STEERING CLUTCH _____ HYDRAULIC SYSTEM _____

FUEL _____ TORQUE DIVIDER _____ AIR CLEANERS _____

TRANSMISSION _____ FINAL DRIVE _____

MAINTENANCE AND REPAIR COST RECORD

FOR (MONTH)	SERVICE METER READING (WHEN PERFORMED)	DESCRIPTION	TOTAL COST

MONTHLY MACHINE AVAILABILITY

DATE	HOURS WORKED	HOURS AVAILABLE FOR WORK	POSSIBLE WORKING HOURS	STANDBY HOURS	WAIT FOR REPAIR HOURS	AVAILABILITY %	UTILIZATION %
JAN.							
FEB.							
MAR.							
APR.							
MAY							
JUNE							
JULY							
AUG.							
SEPT.							
OCT.							
NOV.							
DEC.							

NOTE: HOURS AVAILABLE INCLUDES TIME TO PERFORM PREVENTIVE MAINTENANCE.

AVAILABILITY = HOURS WORKED
POSSIBLE WORKING HOURS
MINUS WAIT FOR REPAIR HOURS
MINUS STANDBY HOURS

UTILIZATION = HOURS AVAILABLE
HOURS WORKED

MULTIPLY RESULTS BY 100 TO GET % FIGURE

in detail folders and summarized manually, or summarized and presented through computer utilization, the basic records should be retained by equipment unit. (See Exhibit 11.)

Effective utilization of the available equipment cost data frequently requires substantial arithmetic computation. Therefore, the use of computer analyses simplifies enormously the summarization and analysis of equipment charge and cost data. For example, computer analyses of actual equipment costs substantially help in finding the optimum trade-in time for equipment units.

Although equipment expenses consist of the two groupings of (1) ownership and rental expense and (2) operating expense, specific job item cost charges should be made on the basis of a single estimated use rate. All actual equipment costs, then, should be accumulated in an equipment account that is subdivided according to the categories in ownership and operation. To match the direct job cost charges, appropriate clearing accounts should be established to accumulate the credits resulting from this dual practice. Periodically, depending on the relative job cost importance of the equipment accounting, the total direct job operational equipment charges should be compared with the actual total costs accumulated in the equipment cost account. The total project item equipment charges should nearly match the actual equipment costs accumulated over periods encompassing the useful lives of the equipment. Also, as the equipment costs are accumulated in the equipment cost account, it is ordinarily desirable to develop specific maintenance and repair cost information relating to each unit of equipment, or according to particular groupings of equipment.

Thus, for example, the job cost charges on a short-term project using all new equipment may be substantially above the actual equipment costs accumulated because the new equipment did not need significant repairs. Conversely, the job cost charges for a short-term project using old, heavily used equipment might be well under the actual equipment costs accumulated; major repairs might have been necessary. In these examples, the only relatively accurate way to determine job item costs would be to assess a reasonable charge for equipment against each item according to the equipment time worked on that item. Corrections to direct job charges could be made after examination of the actual equipment costs accumulated over, perhaps, a three-month period.

To illustrate the elements of the basic accounting procedures, the following example is provided:

A 3.5 cubic yard capacity rubber-tired front-end loader is used on several projects, as is a 30-ton self-propelled hydraulic crane. The front-end loader has a job charge rate of $20 per hour, while the hydrocrane has a job charge rate of $22 per hour. Over a six-month period, the hydraulic crane is charged 1,000 hours, while the front end loader is charged 750 hours. Each unit is used on three projects, and four projects are charged. The project costs charged are shown in the accompanying table.

Project and unit	Hours used	Charge	Total
1 Front-end loader	250	$ 5,000	
Total			$ 5,000
2 Front-end loader	400	8,000	
Hydraulic crane	455	10,010	
Total			18,010
3 Front-end loader	100	$ 2,000	
Hydraulic crane	410	9,020	
Total			11,020
4 Hydraulic crane	135	$ 2,970	
Total			2,970
Total project charge			$37,000

The matching holding account would show the credit, then, of $37,000.

The actual equipment costs for the same six-month period might have consisted of the following:

Ownership expenses		
Front-end loader	$5,800	
Hydraulic crane	9,800	
Total		$15,600
Repairs		
Front-end loader	$6,800	
Hydraulic crane	8,000	
Total		14,800
Operation (excluding operator labor)		
Front-end loader	$3,800	
Hydraulic crane	4,500	
Total		8,300
Total cost of equipment		$38,700

Examination of this actual cost data reveals that the hourly cost of the front-end loader was $21.87 per hour, while the hydraulic crane cost was $22.30 per hour. Suppose, however, that significant repairs were made on the front-end loader while it was on Project No. 3 and that these repairs would not be needed again for an additional 1,250 hours. Charging Project No. 3 for these costs would seriously distort the project cost reports. By using the estimated use rates for project charges, the projects have only been charged their proper shares of the total repair costs.

The method outlined in this example applies whether the actual equipment costs are accumulated at the job level or under a home office general and administrative account, as a construction contractor with many short-term projects would find necessary. Also, substantial appropriate variations in these methods are used. For example, the small building and industrial contractor may consider equipment costs a part of his general and administrative expenses, to be charged to his projects only as percentages of the projects' costs. Or, a large industrial contractor on a long-term project with limited equipment use may accumulate equipment costs in his field overhead accounts. Rather than providing job item equipment charges, he may maintain accounts, for example, covering "equipment ownership expenses" and "equipment operating expenses." In either example, costs can be compiled by unit or groups of units, if desired; usually, they are not compiled when these or similar alternative methods are used.

The majority of shop repairs of equipment can be coded to specific units of equipment by utilization of a shop equipment work order, and maintenance of an equipment repair facility is an integral part of many contractors' operations. Although this expense is a generalized overhead cost, the facilities, personnel, and record keeping enable the costs to be clearly categorized as equipment expenses; yet these costs can rarely be specifically assigned at the time of expenditure commitment to any particular unit of equipment. These expenses include the following:

1. Labor—Management. These would include the labor expenses of shop foremen and general master mechanics.
2. Labor—Other. Remaining shop personnel.
3. Labor benefits. This includes benefits plus the relevant labor taxes.

4. Equipment expense. Actual cost of equipment used in the repair operations.
5. Small tools and supplies. These include expendable tools, equipment and miscellaneous supplies.
6. Allocated organization overhead expenses. These would include appropriate allocation of expenses encountered by the contractor's organization for services used by the shop facility and would include administrative costs, office allowances, and telephone.

Assuming that individual unit equipment costs or costs for groups of equipment are being maintained, these shop overhead equipment expenses should be charged to the specific units, or groups of units, according to a rational formula. Ordinarily, these expenses are charged on the basis of the encountered maintenance and repair costs per unit. Depreciation expenses alone are not desirable bases for distribution of these costs because of the increasing emphasis on rental and lease equipment arrangements.

Finally, in addition to the specific operating expenses detailed above, construction equipment costs include the "total annual ownership expense," as defined by the Associated General Contractors of America. According to the Seventh Edition (1974) of their *Manual*, "The total annual ownership expense is the sum of the percentages of depreciation, replacement cost escalation, the interest on investment, and taxes, insurance and storage, expressed as a percentage of the acquisition cost of each unit of equipment." Although depreciation expenses comprise the largest single area in the ownership expense of equipment, the remaining costs of owning construction equipment will ordinarily exceed 50 percent of the new acquisition costs of the equipment. With depreciation, the method used to accumulate the actual equipment costs will depend largely on tax considerations, not a cost accounting function. Since the useful life of a unit of construction equipment is ordinarily a function of the usage conditions and the number of hours of usage, the principal accounting consideration in establishing a useful depreciated life for construction equipment must consider the usage of an equipment unit. The remaining components of the ownership cost of equipment will ordinarily be a specific function of the value of that equipment, and may well have been included in the shop overhead charges discussed above, particularly the allocated organizational overhead items. In any case, the importance of establishing reasonable depreciation rates is considerable. The most important consideration is that these rates be established after a careful analysis of the planned and actual operating conditions and consequent probable hourly lives of the specific units.

OVERHEAD

Usually, the typical construction project is one of several which a particular contractor might have underway at any given time. Each of these jobs will have a discrete number of specific work items, all supervised and directed by a suitable form of jobsite management structure. Then the contractor's home office will perform a number of specific functions that directly serve the completion of a particular project, or of the several projects underway.

Certain of the costs necessary to complete the project are clearly identifiable with specific work items at each level in the construction contractor's cost hierarchy. These project level costs are referred to as "direct" costs. The remaining costs incurred in completing a project, although clearly necessary for completion of the project, are referred to as "overhead" costs. The key element is that a "direct cost" is one that is clearly identifiable with a particular work item. The distinction between indirect, overhead, and General and Administrative (G&A) costs is less clear. To clarify the situation, it may be desirable for the home office to refer to all those costs incurred at the field level as "field direct and indirect costs." Then, any home office charge clearly identified with a particular project or easily distributed among specific projects can be referred to as an "office overhead" cost. The remaining costs necessary for the operation of the construction organization can be considered, then, "G&A expenses." This terminology is suggested. To effectively control the final cost of a construction project, all these overhead expenses must not only be controlled within themselves, but, also, they must be distributed to the specific work items and the specific construction projects underway.

While a bid is being prepared, the contractor must understand that there are overhead expenses that will be incurred by his organization as a result of undertaking the work. At the same time, he should understand that there will be certain expenses of his operation continuing—whether or not that construction work does start. These distributable expenses must be tentatively allocated when submitting a proposal.

Also, the field indirect costs and a portion of the home office overhead ordinarily are functions of either time or direct labor payroll—once specific one-time costs related to contract volume are considered. These include, for example, bond expenses and gross receipts taxes. Thus, control of both time and labor will affect the field indirect and office overhead expenses. Because few construction projects are completed without extra work being required or claims filed, the construction contractor must develop a rational method for distributing these overhead expenses. Accurate distribution will simplify resolution of extra work and claim negotiations.

Ordinarily, field indirect and overhead expenses are charged to specific projects as they occur. This is desirable because the field indirect expenses are incurred at the field level and are, from the home office point of view, a cost of the project. Likewise, office overhead expenses are clearly related to the expenses incurred at the field level and are identifiable with those expenses. However, the G&A expenses will be distributed to the specific projects according to an organization's tax policies. The tax considerations may override the desirability of obtaining a totally accurate rendition of all of the costs attributable to a construction project.

At the very small contractors' level, the distribution of these overhead costs is relatively simple. He need only tabulate the costs not clearly identifiable with his projects and distribute them to the projects by, probably, a percent allocation. As the construction contractor becomes larger and his projects more complex, the distribution of these overhead expenses becomes increasingly complex.

To obtain total item costs, the distribution of the direct cost components and the field indirect costs must be made to the specific work items. When the home office charges, consisting principally of the G&A expenses, are distributed to the individual work items, they should be clearly identified as a specific cost component to separate job progress measurement from a construction contractor's organizational arrangements. In fact, for financial reporting, it may well be desirable for the contractor to state his field "profits" separately for each project and to tabulate the undistributed overhead costs as a distinct presentation. In preparing a bid proposal, this procedure is virtually essential. Individual unit item costs can be examined and compared with previous jobs up through the level of total field costs. At that point, the planned allocation of overhead, G&A, and profit should be made to determine the total project bid; these selling prices should not be confused with item cost control information.

The methods of distributing overhead costs will vary according to the construction contractor, the type of project or projects to be constructed, and the nature of the expenses to be distributed. In any construction project, certain major costs are encountered immediately upon starting. These include bond and the construction of temporary facilities, for example. For these costs, the key management consideration is to know whether they are what was expected and whether they were incurred at the proper time. Therefore, an accurate preplanning job is essential; a time scale budget clearly shows when and how much to expect in terms of these one-time charges. Separate tabulation of the indirect, the overhead, and the G&A will remove any distortion potentially created by distributing these costs when they occur. The alternative procedure is to distribute these costs to the project as the construction proceeds. This may accurately portray the theoretical costs of the work, but will be of no value in developing reasonable cash flow projections and predictions.

Allocation of the field indirect, the home office overhead, and the G&A expenses is ordinarily done on the basis of item or project total cost. This method may be criticized as inaccurate for a project where a major portion of the cost is in expensive material items, as in electrical construction. The argument is that the material and subcontract items do not require a large overhead expenditure to control. Likewise, if the distribution is made on the basis of field direct labor, then the overhead allocation may be distorted by comparing two projects: one of relatively short duration but with very high direct labor; the other of longer duration but with a very high subcontract percentage. Logically, a different method of allocation of these overhead expenses should be used for each project, even for each work item in each project. However, the resulting complexity of this type of system would overwhelm all but the most sophisticated construction contractor. The important element is to recognize that, in total, a construction contractor has costs which are necessary to maintain his business operation and which vary as a percentage of the project work underway according to the actual construction volume. In submitting proposals for new work, the contractor must balance this understanding against the acknowledged desirability of maintaining a work force when total construction volume is low.

COMPUTER COST ACCOUNTING

The primary purpose of the accounting function is to provide the management of a construction organization with the data necessary for that management to make operational judgments. Consequently, an enormous amount of arithmetic computation is necessary, even to consolidate and present the simplest of summaries. As mechanical means of computation have been developed, they have been utilized in construction cost accounting. The progression was from simple calculators to expensive accounting machines, and now to computers. These detailed data processing techniques and systems are in use throughout the construction industry. The use of this equipment has made possible not only the mechanization of the accounting function, but also expansion of computers into the planning and estimating function of construction.

Significant in utilization of computers in the construction industry has been the delay in their acceptance and utilization by the industry relative to other areas of the society. As noted in the Introduction, the Construction Industry consists primarily of construction contractors whose annual volumes do not closely approach $1 million; small construction volume does not justify the high cost of purchasing and installing sophisticated equipment. Likewise, this fragmentation of the construction industry has tended to develop a high degree of individualism in construction management attitudes. Under these circumstances there can only result a frequent distrust, perhaps even contempt, for a tool that appears to usurp the contractor's decision-making authority and responsibility.

Also, only recently has the mechanical development of computer systems suitable for the very large amount of data handling necessary in construction cost accounting been developed to the degree of mechanical reliability that economically justifies their installation by construction contractors. The physical environment of small contractors and the field offices utilized by large contractors are ordinarily not suitable for equipment highly sensitive to rapid variations in temperature and humidity or to dusty conditions. Computers until recently were, by necessity, housed in air conditioned, humidity controlled environments. As the mechanical reliability of these systems has increased, there have been marked increases in the number of installations by construction contractors. This increased mechanical reliability, together with the increased cost of labor in developing the minimal necessary accounting information, has led to substantially increased computer utilization by the construction industry.

Of the three general areas of the typical construction contractor—estimating, planning and scheduling, and project operations—project operations concerns itself with construction cost accounting and was the first area in which mechanization of repetitive computational tasks was attempted. In particular, computerized labor control and accounting has most frequently been used by construction contractors.

The advantages of computer utilization by the construction contractor in accomplishing the cost accounting function are substantial. First, the accuracy of calculations is higher and the speed is faster than any manual system, limited only by the quality of the available data and the sophistication of the computer program. Thus, substantial duplication of work can be avoided. Second, detailed data analyses that were never previously possible under manual systems, or only most torturously so, can be accomplished. Implicit in these advantages is the obvious statement that reports needed by management can be made available without the long delays that customarily destroyed their usefulness, before the advent of computerized record keeping in construction cost accounting.

A key element to remember, however, is that those contractors using computerized construction cost accounting, either from service bureaus, time sharing, or owned equipment, have rarely reported a reduction in the cost of their construction cost accounting operations. Rather, they have reported substantially improved report quality and timing, enough so that substantial savings in the total operation of their organizations are usually possible by computerization. Any construction contractor considering computerization should not, therefore, look to a reduction in the cost of his accounting operations. Nor can anyone advising a contractor on whether or not to computerize his cost accounting system say that installation of computers is justified or not justified merely on the basis of the contractor's annual construction volume; the diversity of the construction industry precludes that judgment.

For the contractor considering computerization of at least his cost accounting functions, there are three principal routes he can take to computerization, none of which are exclusive of the others:

1. Service bureau utilization.
2. Time-sharing equipment.
3. In-house computers.

The first of these alternatives relies on the facilities of an organization outside the contractor's to accomplish the actual computation and preparation of reports. Ordinarily, this organization will have a relatively large computer and a series of available programs (software) suitable for analysis of a contractor's data with very little modification. This service bureau should assist the contractor in the design of the cost control system to be used, together with development of the reporting forms and procedures. The key element in dealing with a service bureau is that the contractor know and remember what specific reports and information he needs and must have.

The second alternative assumes that the construction contractor will utilize the computational capacities of very large computers that may be accessed over commercial telephone lines. The distinction between this approach and the first one is principally that the service bureau is organized to provide a wide range of computer-related services, while the "time sharing" operation may simply be engaged in selling computer time that is not being utilized in ordinary business activities. Banks, for example, frequently have available and do sell substantial blocks of computer time for use by construction contractors and other business activities. To utilize these facilities, the construction contractor may find it necessary to install communications facilities and input-output equipment at his office, or he may be required to prepare his data (keypunching, time sheets, and so forth) and deliver it to the computer facility.

Finally, a construction contractor may elect to purchase his own facilities, perhaps after utilizing one of the above concepts first. At this point, the contractor working together with his accountants and engineers will decide on the specific configuration of equipment and the necessary software. His key objective, again, must be to know what reports and analyses he needs if he is to improve the quality of his decision making.

Although construction contractors whose first computer use is in their accounting system ordinarily have payroll applications immediately in mind, a first step into more effective computer utilization is to the area of equipment cost accounting. Construction cost accounting is principally a matter of analyzing extremely large quantities of data; equipment cost accounting using computers can effectively analyze additional large amounts of data. In fact, the basic reporting for equipment costs will very closely resemble that for labor. For example, the following daily information would ordinarily be furnished:

Project identification.
Unit equipment identification.
Hours worked, together with the distribution of hours.
Hours idle.
Downtime.

This information permits charging cost items to specific projects. As noted in the discussion of equipment cost accounting, the actual equipment costs can be gathered according to type of expenditure, type of unit, or specific units. The principal limitation in development of this information is the difficulty in gathering meaningful field information. If this information is gathered conscientiously, detailed equipment cost reports can be prepared which clearly point to the exact timing of needed overhauls or the most advantageous time for equipment trade-ins. In any case, a detailed equipment cost system will pinpoint large downtime for repair, as well as unusual amounts of idle time.

Likewise, the remaining areas of cost factors, including materials, subcontracts, and overhead costs, can be effectively controlled. This final step in computerization will lead directly to the preparation of most of the needed cost and financial reports and to the maintenance of the cost accounting system.

REFERENCES

Associated General Contractors of America, *Contractors' Equipment Manual.* (7th ed.) Washington, D.C., 1974.

Bonny, J. B., and Frein, J. P., eds. *Handbook of Construction Management and Organization.* New York: Van Nostrand Reinhold Co., 1973.

Clough, R. H. *Construction Contracting.* New York: John Wiley and Sons, Inc., 1960.

Coombs, W. E., and Palmer, W. J. *Construction Accounting and Financial Management.* (2d ed.) New York: McGraw-Hill Book Co., 1977.

Gray, J., and Johnston, K. S. *Accounting and Management Action.* New York: McGraw-Hill Book Co., 1973.

U.S. Bureau of the Census. *Statistical Abstract of the United States: 1976.* (97th ed.) Washington, D.C., 1976.

27

Cost accounting for land and real estate development

James J. Klink*
William Stoddart†

This chapter includes accounting for costs of all types of land and real estate developments including preacquisition, acquisition, improvement, development, and construction costs, as well as carrying costs, selling and rental costs, and initial rental operations. Thus, this chapter covers accounting for all real estate up to the point of sale or to the point of normal operations for income-producing properties; it is not intended to cover subsequent accounting for operations of income-producing properties such as apartment buildings, office buildings, shopping centers, and so forth. The following are the major topics considered in this chapter:

Accounting for costs
Allocation of costs
Net realizable value

In addition selected reference sources are included at the end of the chapter.

---
* Partner, Price Waterhouse & Co.
† Partner, Price Waterhouse & Co.

RECENT EVENTS IN THE REAL
ESTATE INDUSTRY

During the last two decades the real estate industry has undergone substantial growth and change. In 1976, real estate was the third largest industry in the United States. The industry comprised approximately 350,000 construction firms and 150,000 real estate service and financing establishments. These 500,000 establishments employed approximately 4.5 million workers and accounted for $200 billion (approximately 15 percent) of the gross national product. Traditionally, this industry has been dominated by the small private builder. However, some 300 of *Fortune's* "500" companies have been involved in real estate investment or development.

The significant growth of real estate investment trusts, along with the significant expansion of the economy in the late 1960s and early 1970s, resulted in excessive funds available for development and construction. The pressure to invest these funds aided in the rapid expansion of the real estate industry. Large-scale developments, including new towns, planned unit developments, resorts, and the like, which were previously considered too high an investment risk by many developers, were undertaken. The result—overbuilding—occurred in a number of geographic areas.

During the early 1970s, inflation was occurring at a level unprecedented during peacetime in the United States. Significant shortages of construction materials (lumber, concrete, and steel) developed and the money supply decreased, causing interest rates to soar. Gasoline and other energy sources became critically short and more expensive. During the same period the activities of the ecological interest groups, both public and governmental, resulted in substantial delays for many developments. Sales decreased significantly as buyers were unable to get financing. Contractors found that they were no longer able to fulfill their long-term contracts or commitments. By 1974 the culmination of these factors brought the real estate industry almost to a stop. The number of foreclosures and bankruptcy petitions was on the rise.

Although interest rates in 1976 and 1977 have been reduced somewhat, the high cost of construction and development, coupled with onerous governmental zoning and environmental regulations, continued to hamper the recovery of the real estate industry. Further, financial institutions established more conservative lending policies. The rapid growth and changing environment of the real estate industry have caused the developer and accountant significant problems.

INTRODUCTION TO COST ACCOUNTING

Little authoritative literature exists regarding the principles of accounting for costs of real estate developments, except for retail land operations. The AICPA *Industry Accounting Guide,* "Accounting for Retail Land Sales," sets forth certain broad guidelines concerning cost capitalization and allocation methods. This section will summarize and discuss certain of the more significant alternative methods of cost capitalization and allocation and methods of determining net realizable value which are currently being utilized for land and real estate developments.

Industry characteristics

The cost accounting problems which the real estate developer encounters can be best illustrated by considering the peculiar characteristics of this industry. Certain of these peculiar characteristics are (*a*) the extended business cycle, (*b*) the nature of the common costs, and (*c*) the materiality of transactions.

Business cycle. It is not uncommon for a large real estate development to have a business operating cycle (the average time intervening between the acquisition of materials or real estate and the final cash realization) which spans a number of years and may include several economic cycles. It is difficult to develop a complete master plan with a high degree of certainty for a real estate development which requires a development period of a number of years. Master plans for such developments are often revised numerous times before the project is completed.

Common costs. Costs incurred are frequently large in dollar amount and may benefit more than one project within a development. For example, sewage treatment facilities and amenities may benefit all or a major portion of the total development. This communal benefit, coupled with the heterogeneity of development projects, must be weighed in the selection of capitalization and allocation methods.

Materiality of transactions. Frequently, individual real estate transactions are relatively large, ranging from hundreds of thousands to millions of dollars.

Pervasive measurement principles

Costs incurred in real estate operations range from "brick and mortar" costs which are clearly capitalizable to general administrative costs which are not capitalizable. There is a broad range of costs between these two extremes which often are difficult to classify, and therefore judgmental decisions must be made as to whether such costs should be capitalized. *Accounting Principles Board Statement No. 4,* "Basic Concepts and Accounting Principles," sets forth certain pervasive measurement principles concerning the accounting for costs. The *Statement* in paragraph 147 states that:

> Income determination in accounting is the process of identifying, measuring, and relating revenue and expenses of an enterprise for an accounting period. . . . Expenses are determined by applying the expense recognition principles on the basis of relationships between acquisition costs and either the independently determined revenue or accounting periods. To apply expense recognition principles, costs are analyzed to see whether they can be associated with revenue on the basis of cause and effect. If not, systematic and rational allocation is attempted. If neither cause and effect associations nor systematic and rational allocations can be made, costs are recognized as expenses in the period incurred or in which a loss is discerned.[1]

Iodifying convention—conservatism

Further, the *Statement* in paragraph 171 states that:

> Historically, managers, investors, and accountants have generally preferred that possible errors in measurement be in the direction

---

[1] Copyright © (1970) by the American Institute of Certified Public Accountants,

of understatement rather than overstatement of net income and net assets. This has led to the convention of conservatism, which is expressed in rules . . . such as the rules that inventory should be measured at the lower of cost and market. . . .

Recent developments

The Accounting Standards Division of the AICPA issued Statement of Position 78–3 in June 1978 on accounting for costs to sell and rent and initial operations of real estate projects. The AICPA Real Estate Accounting Committee is currently studying cost accounting in two distinct projects that may result in the issuance of Statements of Position:

1. Accounting for allowances for losses on real estate
2. Accounting for real estate acquisition, development, and construction costs

The Accounting Standards Division of the AICPA issued an Exposure Draft on the first of these projects in May 1976, and a new draft has been sent to the FASB in June 1978 for their consideration. The principal matters pertaining to these subjects are set forth in this chapter.

CAPITALIZATION OF COSTS

A research study by the Canadian Institute of Chartered Accountants, entitled "Accounting for Real Estate Development Operations," sets forth the general premise that "land development costs are those costs that are directly attributable to the development of land and to its ownership during the period of the development." Additionally, the AICPA *Industry Accounting Guide,* "Accounting for Retail Land Sales," states in paragraph 51:

> Costs directly related to inventories of unimproved land or to construction required to bring land and improvements to a saleable condition are properly capitalizable until a saleable condition is reached. Those costs would include interest, real estate taxes and other direct costs incurred during the inventory and improvement periods.

While the propriety of capitalizing certain costs is obvious, other costs are treated inconsistently in practice within the real estate industry.

This section discusses the capitalization of costs categorized as follows:

1. Preacquisition costs.
2. Land acquisition costs.
3. Land improvement, development, and construction costs.
4. Interest costs.
5. Other carrying costs.
6. Overhead costs.
7. General and administrative expenses.
8. Amenities.
9. Selling and rental costs.
10. Initial rental operations.

Preacquisition costs

There are currently no specific prescribed guidelines with respect to costs incurred prior to the acquisition of real estate. Preacquisition costs could include legal, architectural, and other professional fees; salaries, environmental studies, appraisals, marketing and feasibility studies, soil tests, and so forth. Some developers expense such costs while others capitalize them. Many believe that such costs incurred prior to either acquiring the property or obtaining an option to acquire the property are exploratory and thus tantamount to research costs. They believe that accounting in this area should be guided by *Statement of Financial Accounting Standards No. 2,* which requires that research costs be expensed as incurred and not deferred to future periods. Therefore, expensing such costs is clearly the most appropriate treatment under the circumstances, as the future benefits are at best uncertain.

A few developers follow a less desirable course of deferring or capitalizing preacquisition costs in the belief that the incurrence of such costs indicates an implied commitment to acquire the property. Such costs, however, should only be deferred if they are identifiable with a specific property and the acquisition is probable. If negotiations to acquire the property are not successful or development planning is suspended, deferred preacquisition costs should be charged off to current period expense. If significant preacquisition costs are deferred, disclosure should be made in the financial statements of the accounting policy and the amount of such costs included on the balance sheet.

Land acquisition costs

Costs directly related to the acquisition of land are properly capitalizable. They include option fees, purchase costs, transfer costs, title insurance, legal and other professional fees, surveys, appraisals, and real estate commissions. Commitment and other financing fees may also be capitalized, but frequently such costs are expensed. The purchase cost may be required to be increased or decreased for imputation of interest on mortgage notes payable, assumed or issued in connection with the purchase, as required under AICPA *Accounting Principles Board Opinion No. 21*, "Interest on Receivables and Payables."

As set forth in the first paragraph of *APB 21,*

> the use of an interest rate that varies from prevailing interest rates warrants evaluation of whether the face amount and the stated interest rate of a note or obligation provide reliable evidence for properly recording the exchange and subsequent related interest.

If imputation from the stated rate to an appropriate rate is necessary, the mortgage note payable should be adjusted to its present value (with a corresponding adjustment to acquisition cost) by discounting all future payments on the note using an imputed rate of interest at the prevailing rate available for similar financing with independent financial institutions.

Land improvement, development, and construction costs

Costs directly related to improvements of the land are properly capitalizable by the developer and may include the following:

> Land planning costs, including marketing and feasibility studies, direct salaries, legal and other professional fees, zoning costs, soil tests, architectural and engineering studies, ap-

praisals, environmental studies, and other costs directly related to site preparation and the overall design and development of the project.

Onsite and offsite improvements, including demolition costs, streets, traffic controls, sidewalks, street lighting, sewer and water facilities, utilities, parking lots, landscaping, and related costs such as permits and inspection fees.

Construction costs, including engineering and architectural fees, onsite material and labor, direct supervision, permits, and inspection fees.

Project overhead and supervision, such as field office costs.

Recreation facilities such as golf courses, clubhouses, swimming pools, and tennis courts (see separate section on "Amenities").

Sales center and models, including furnishings (see separate section on "Selling and Rental Costs").

General and administrative costs not directly identified with the project should be accounted for as period costs and expensed as incurred.

Construction activity on a project may be suspended before a project is completed for reasons such as insufficient sales or rental demand. These conditions may be indicative of an impairment of the value of a project that is other than temporary. See section on "Net realizable value."

Interest costs

A disagreement exists as to the proper accounting treatment of interest costs incurred in connection with land or development and construction of real estate held for either sale or investment. Proponents of capitalization argue that such interest costs are a necessary cost of the asset, the same as "brick and mortar" costs. Proponents of charging off interest costs as a period cost argue that interest is solely a financing cost, a cost which varies directly with the capability of a company to finance the development and construction through equity funds.

The alternative approaches are recognized in the AICPA *Industry Accounting Guide*, "Accounting for Retail Land Sales," which states in paragraph 51 that:

Interest is properly capitalizable if it results from (*a*) loans for which unimproved land or construction in progress is pledged as collateral or (*b*) other loans if the proceeds are used for improvements or for acquiring unimproved land. Interest not meeting the above criteria . . . should be treated as expenses of the period in which incurred.

Paragraph 40 of the *Guide* recognized that certain companies expense interest, stating that, "Interest and project carrying costs incurred prior to sale on some projects may have already been charged to expense and would therefore not be included in cost of sales at the time the sale is recorded."

The question of capitalization of interest is currently on the agenda of the Financial Accounting Standards Board, but until the matter is resolved by the Board it is generally acceptable to capitalize or expense interest costs.

SEC reporting companies. In November 1974, the SEC issued *Accounting Series Release No. 163*, "Capitalization of Interest by Companies Other Than Public Utilities." The release prohibits SEC reporting companies from adopting a policy of capitalizing interest in financial statements filed with the SEC for periods ending after June 21, 1974, unless the company had previously publicly disclosed an accounting policy of capitalizing interest costs (except for transactions covered by the AICPA *Industry Accounting Guide,* "Accounting for Retail Land Sales").

Survey of practices. A 1977 survey of accounting and reporting practices of real estate developers prepared by Price Waterhouse & Co. reported the following results regarding policies of capitalizing interest for 95 of 100 companies surveyed:

Interest capitalized:
On all real estate 84
On properties under development
and construction, but not
undeveloped land 8
92
Interest not capitalized 3
95

It was not determinable whether the other five companies not disclosing capitalization policies capitalized or expensed interest. The practice of capitalizing interest is clearly predominant.

Methods of interest capitalization. There are three primary methods of capitalizing interest used in practice by the real estate industry. The predominant method is the *specific identification method.* In accordance with the specific identification method, interest on all debt directly related to the properties would be capitalized.

The other two methods of capitalizing interest as used in the real estate industry, but to a far lesser degree, involve an allocation of all interest expense to all assets as follows:

a. Interest cost of specific identified debt is capitalized to the specific asset, and the remaining general interest cost for the period is allocated to all assets based upon the weighted-average of the asset carrying values, net of specific identified debt, with the portion allocated to land or development and construction in progress being capitalized.

b. Total interest costs for the period are allocated to all assets based upon the weighted-average of the gross asset carrying values during the period. The portion of interest allocated to land or development and construction in progress is capitalized.

These methods would also be considered acceptable.

When to stop capitalization of interest. The point at which capitalization of interest should stop is not clearly defined in authoritative literature, except for retail land companies. According to the *Retail Land Accounting Guide,* the point at which capitalization should stop is "saleable condition." The determination of saleable condition can be particularly difficult for some projects. In the case of bulk land, interest is frequently capitalized to the date of sale and, as a result, such practice is considered acceptable.

With respect to projects under development and construction, it is believed that it would usually be most appropriate to stop capitalizing interest at the stage that construction is substantially completed. Capitalization beyond such stage is clearly less desirable and under some circumstances may not be appropriate, such as where sales are extremely slow due to adverse market conditions. With respect to investment properties held for rental, see the section on "Initial Rental Operations."

The 1977 survey cited previously indicated that of 100 companies surveyed, 51 companies disclosed the point to which interest costs in connection with construction and development were capitalized as follows:

Completion of construction	26
Date of sale	10
Certain percentage of occupancy or period of time after occupancy begins	8
Date rental or sales operations begin	5
Commencement of construction	2
	51

Although many companies have a policy of discontinuing capitalization of interest when the capitalization of such costs would result in a carrying cost in excess of net realizable value, another appropriate method would be to continue capitalization of such costs and provide any required adjustment to net realizable value through the use of a valuation reserve (see separate section on "Net Realizable Value").

Disclosure of interest capitalization.   Disclosure in notes to financial statements should include capitalization policies for interest. If interest is capitalized, disclosure should also include the point to which costs are capitalized and the method of determining the interest capitalized.

In addition, SEC reporting companies that capitalize interest are required by the aforementioned *ASR No. 163* to disclose the following:

1. Amount of interest capitalized—present on face of income statement.
2. The reason for the policy of interest capitalization and the way in which the amount of interest capitalized is determined.
3. The effect on net income, for each period for which an income statement is presented, of following a policy of capitalizing interest as compared to a policy of charging interest to expense as incurred.

This information is required only for SEC reporting companies but is considered good disclosure for non-SEC reporting companies as well.

Other carrying costs

Although some developers expense other carrying costs such as real estate taxes and insurance, most developers follow a practice of capitalizing such costs. The aforementioned 1977 survey disclosed that 83 percent of the companies surveyed capitalize property taxes. Although such carrying costs directly identified with the property may be capitalized, there is ample support for expensing such costs as well. Capitalization of other carrying costs should cease at the same time that interest capitalization ceases.

Overhead costs

It is generally accepted in practice to capitalize overhead costs directly related to development and construction of real estate projects. The principal problem is in defining and identifying overhead costs to be capitalized. It would be appropriate to consider the following points before electing to capitalize:

1. Specific information should be available (such as timecards) to support the allocation of overhead costs to specific projects.
2. The overhead costs incurred should be incremental costs; that is, in the absence of the project or projects under development or construction, these costs would not be incurred.
3. The impact of capitalization of such overhead costs on the results of operations should be consistent with the pervasive principle of matching costs with related revenue.
4. The principle of conservatism should be considered.

Overhead costs directly associated with the project which should be considered for capitalization include, for example, direct and indirect salaries of a field office, utilities, and insurance.

General and administrative expenses

Real estate developers incur various types of general and administrative expenses, including officers' salaries, accounting and legal fees, and various office expenses. Certain of these expenses may be closely associated with individual projects, while others are of a more general nature. For example, a developer may open a field office on a project site and staff such a field office with administrative personnel, such as a field accountant. The expenses associated with this field office are directly associated with the project and are therefore considered overhead. On the other hand, the developer may have a number of expenses associated with general office operations which benefit numerous projects and for which specifically identifiable allocations are not reasonable or possible. These administrative costs that are not directly identified with a specific project should be charged to current operations.

Amenities

Real estate developments often include amenities such as golf courses, utilities, clubhouses, swimming pools, and tennis courts. The accounting for the costs of these amenities should be based upon management's intended disposition:

1. Amenities sold with sales units—costs should be included in project costs and allocated to cost of sales upon the sale of the related units.
2. Amenities to be sold separately—costs should be capitalized to the extent of the present value of anticipated proceeds on the sale. Costs, including expected operating losses prior to sale, in excess of anticipated proceeds should be allocated to cost of sales upon the sale of the related units.
3. Amenities to be retained by developer—the portion of the costs incurred in developing amenities that are not expected to provide a return sufficient to recover costs of both operation and construction should be allocated to cost of sales upon the sale of the related units (after giving effect to the present value of amounts obtainable from operations, future sales, recovery, or salvage).

Selling and rental costs

The AICPA issued in June 1978 Statement of Position 78–3 on real estate start-up costs including costs to sell and rent real estate projects and initial rental operations of real estate projects. The Statement is effective for costs incurred in fiscal years beginning after June 30, 1978. It should be noted that the Statement applies only to real estate activities and further does not modify the accounting methods for retail land companies as prescribed in the AICPA Accounting Guide "Accounting for Retail Land Sales."

In the absence of contrary evidence, the owner's representation that the project is held for sale or held for rental should govern the accounting to be followed. In rare situations where a portion of the project is held for sale and a portion is held for rental, the costs of the project should be allocated to the separate portions and each portion should be accounted for on a separate project basis. The following paragraphs summarize the AICPA position and, therefore, the appropriate accounting to be followed.

Selling costs

The following considerations enter into determination of the appropriate accounting for project selling costs:

Project costs. Costs incurred to sell real estate projects should be accounted for in the same manner as, and classified with, construction costs of the project when they meet both of the following criteria:

a. The costs incurred are for (1) tangible assets which are used throughout the selling period or (2) services performed to obtain regulatory approval for sales.
b. The costs are reasonably expected to be recovered from sales of the project or incidental operations.

Cost of model units and related furnishings, sales facilities, certain legal fees and similar costs, and semipermanent signs would meet the criteria.

Prepaid expenses. Costs, other than project costs, incurred to sell real estate projects should be accounted for and classified as prepaid expenses when they are incurred for goods or services before the related goods are used or before the services are performed.

Examples of prepaid expenses are expenditures for future advertising, selling brochures, and commission advances.

Certain prepaid expenses (for example, sales commissions), identifiable with specific future revenue, should be charged to operations in the period in which the related sales revenue is earned. Other prepaid expenses, not identifiable with specific future revenues, should be charged to expense during the period of expected benefit.

Period costs. Costs that are incurred to sell real estate projects but which do not meet the criteria for project costs or prepaid expenses should be charged to expense as incurred. Examples of expenditures that are period costs are those incurred for media advertising, sales salaries and overhead, and "grand openings."

Rental costs

The following considerations enter into the determination of the appropriate accounting for project rental costs.

Chargeable to future periods. Costs incurred to rent real estate projects should be charged to future periods when they are prepaid expenses (see above) or when they are associated with future revenue and their recovery is reasonably expected.

Examples of costs that meet the criteria for deferral are expenditures for model units and related furnishings, rental facilities, semipermanent signs, and brochures.

Deferred rental costs that can be directly related to specific leases should be amortized over the term of the related lease. Deferred rental costs that cannot be directly related to specific leases should be amortized to expense over the period of expected benefit. Estimated unrecoverable deferred rental costs should be written off when it is probable the lease will be terminated.

Period costs. Costs that are incurred to rent real estate projects which do not meet the above criteria should be charged to expense as incurred. Examples of expenditures that are period costs are media advertising, rental salaries and overhead, and "grand openings."

Initial rental operations

Generally, established industrial and commercial companies have expensed initial operating and start-up costs in the period incurred. However, in an attempt to achieve a better matching of costs and revenue, certain real estate companies have previously deferred start-up costs and initial operating losses. The accounting treatment has often varied depending on the purpose and amount of the expenditures as well as the anticipated future benefits and revenue. Typically, the deferral of such costs and losses has stopped when a specific event takes place (for example the initiation of an active sales program, attainment of a certain level of occupancy, or expiration of a predetermined period of time). Of course, start-up and preoperating costs which are not expected to be recovered from future revenue should not be deferred.

Recent developments. The aforementioned AICPA Exposure Draft of a proposed Statement of Position on accounting for selling and rental costs also covers accounting for initial rental operations of real estate projects and will significantly change present practices of certain developers. The Statement is effective for projects becoming substantially complete in fiscal years beginning after June 30, 1978. As set forth in the Statement of Position, certain costs incurred during construction before a rental project is capable of producing revenue should be capitalized. That practice is supported by ample precedents; but, once major construction activity is completed and the project is capable of producing revenue, the accounting for costs and revenue should reflect the change in status of the project.

As defined in the Statement of Position, a rental project is "substantially completed and held available for occupancy" if it meets both of the following conditions:

a. Construction has reached the stage at which the builder originally intended to cease major construction activity.
b. Units are being or have been offered for rental.

The Statement of Position concludes that at that stage a change in the status of the rental project has taken place and the owner's principal activities are substantially different from those during the construction stage.

Accounting for initial operations of a rental project that is substantially completed and held available for occupancy should be as follows:

1. Rental revenue should be recorded in income as earned.
2. Operating costs should be charged to expense currently.
3. Amortization of deferred rental costs should commence.
4. Full depreciation of rental property should commence.
5. Carrying costs (interest, property taxes, etc.) should be charged to expense as accrued.

ALLOCATION OF COSTS

Costs to be allocated

Regardless of the size of a real estate development, the capitalizable costs can be summarized as follows:

1. Common to the entire development.
2. Common to only certain segments or projects within the development.
3. Related directly to construction of buildings being sold.
4. Related directly to the individual sales transaction.

The first two types of costs must be allocated in an appropriate manner to individual sales transactions. The last two types should be specifically charged to the property being sold since they are directly related.

Methods of cost allocation

With respect to allocation of capitalized costs, the only specific source in accounting literature is the AICPA Accounting Guide, "Accounting for Retail Land Sales," which describes four methods frequently used in practice:

1. Area method.
2. Value method.

3. Specific identification method.
4. Hybrid method (involving elements of two or more of the other methods).

The Guide states that "Any reasonable method, consistently applied, that will fairly match costs with related revenues may be used." However, the Guide further states that the value method is preferable as it is less likely to result in deferral of losses.

The method used to allocate costs should accomplish the objective of matching costs with related revenue. The aforementioned 1977 survey of accounting and reporting practices of real estate developers prepared by Price Waterhouse & Co. reported that 49 of 100 companies surveyed disclosed their cost allocation accounting policies as follows:

Method	Number of companies
Value	24
Area	20
Specific identification	9
Hybrid	7
	60

Note: Eleven of the 49 companies indicated that they used different cost allocation methods depending upon the nature or size of the project.

Because of the varying practices, the method of allocating cost to unit sales should be disclosed in an accounting policy footnote to the financial statements.

Value method. As indicated in the survey results above, the value method is predominantly used in practice. Under this method, the allocation of costs is based on relative values such as estimated selling prices or appraised values. Although the aforementioned retail land sales guide states that the value method may be applied using values either "gross or net after estimated future improvement costs," in developments which contain multiple forms of development, common costs are normally allocated based on estimated selling prices, net of direct construction and selling costs. This approach is usually the most appropriate as it is less likely to result in deferral of losses.

The following is an illustration of the use of the value method to allocate common costs for a condominium project which consists of three buildings, each being defined as an individual "project" for accounting purposes.

	Project		
	A	*B*	*C*
Number of units	75	75	100
Estimated sales value	$2,600,000	$3,200,000	$4,200,000
Less: Direct construction and selling costs	1,800,000	2,300,000	3,500,000
Sales value net of direct costs (aggregate of $2,400,000)	$ 800,000	$ 900,000	$ 700,000
Allocation of common costs aggregating $1,500,000:			
1,500,000 × 800,000/2,400,000	500,000		
1,500,000 × 900,000/2,400,000		562,500	
1,500,000 × 700,000/2,400,000			437,500
Gross profit.................	$ 300,000	$ 337,500	$ 262,500
Percent of sales	11.5%	10.5%	6.2%
Had the value method been applied based on gross sales value, the results would have been:			
Allocation of common costs	$ 390,000	$ 480,000	$ 630,000
Gross profit	410,000	420,000	70,000
Percent of sales	15.8%	13.1%	1.7%

Area method. This method of cost allocation is based upon square footage, acreage, frontage, and so on. Often the use of this method will not result in a logical allocation of costs. When negotiating the purchase price for a large tract of land, the purchaser considers the overall utility of the tract, recognizing that various parcels contained in the tract are more valuable than others. For example, parcels which are on a lake front are usually more valuable than those farther back from the lake. In such a situation, if a simple average based on square footage or acreage were used to allocate costs to individual parcels, certain parcels could be assigned costs in excess of their net realizable value. Generally, the use of the area method should be limited to those situations where each individual parcel is estimated to have approximately the same relative value. Under such circumstances, the cost allocations as determined by either the area or value methods would be approximately the same.

Specific identification method. This method of cost allocation is based on determining actual costs applicable to each parcel of land. This method is rarely used for land costs as it is usually not appropriate; however, it is frequently appropriate for direct construction costs because such costs are directly related to the property being sold.

NET REALIZABLE VALUE

On May 25, 1976, the AICPA issued for public comment an Exposure Draft of a proposed Statement of Position entitled "Valuation of Real Estate and Loans and Receivables Collateralized by Real Estate." The proposed statement concluded that real estate inventory should not be carried at an amount in excess of its estimated net realizable value determined by an evaluation of the recoverability of the individual property. Net realizable value should be based on estimated selling price plus other estimated revenue from the property during the expected holding period, reduced by (1) the estimated cost to complete or improve such property to the condition used in determining the estimated selling price, (2) the estimated costs to dispose of the property, and (3) the estimated costs to hold the property to the expected point of sale, including future interest, property taxes, legal fees, and other direct holding costs. Estimated interest holding costs should be based on the higher of (a) the average cost of all capital (debt and equity) or (b) the entity's accounting policy for capitalizing interest.

In January 1978 the AICPA prepared a new Exposure Draft on the same subject matter which is similar to the 1976 Exposure Draft. The draft has been forwarded to the Financial Accounting Standards Board (FASB) to see if they might place the subject on their agenda. The AICPA has approved the new draft for issuance pending the decision of the FASB on its disposition.

Until a position paper is issued the following guidelines are appropriate.

General principles

Real estate held for sale, or for development and sale, should be included in the balance sheet at the lower of cost or market.

This principle is one of long standing; however, the decline in values in the mid-1970s has brought the application of this general principle sharply into focus for many companies.

Accounting Research Bulletin No. 43, Chapter 4, "Inventory Pricing," states that "the term market means current replacement cost (by purchase or by production . . .) except that:

1. Market should not exceed the net realizable value (that is estimated selling price in the ordinary course of business less reasonably predictable costs of completion and disposal), and
2. Market should not be less than net realizable value reduced by an allowance for an approximately normal profit margin."

Major questions about the applicability and the application of the above principles are:

1. What types of real estate should be regarded as inventory and what should be regarded as long-term investment?
2. Should the principle of lower of cost or net realizable value be applied to individual items or groups of items?
3. Should cost of completion include the cost (especially interest cost) to carry the inventory to date of sale?

Inventory versus long-term investment

It is generally agreed that real estate held for sale, or for development and sale, falls in the category of inventory. Thus the inventory guidelines would cover such properties as land (including raw land and land under development), condominiums and single-family housing, as well as income properties held for sale. Raw land should generally be included because such land will in time become inventory. On the other hand, inventories would not include:

a. Income properties held for long-term investment.
b. Real property used in the business (for example, a company's headquarters office building).
c. Land held for development or construction of property described in (a) and (b).

It would not be appropriate for income properties to be declared to be held for investment solely to avoid losses which otherwise would be required to be recorded under rules for inventories.

In the evaluation of real estate held for sale or for development, the following factors should be evaluated:

1. The company's financial ability to hold or to develop the properties in question.
2. The company's intent with respect to the properties, including information as to its past practices and experience.
3. The company's intent with respect to the timing of development and sale.
4. Appraisals of the property prepared either by independent appraisers or by the company staff.

Individual item or group basis

As a general rule, because of the relatively low volume and the significance of individual sales transactions in the real estate industry, the lower-of-cost-or-market test should be applied to each individual sales unit, except where the units are relatively homogeneous—such as units in a condominium project. In this case, the test may be applied on a project-by-project basis. In situations where the developer uses the value method to allocate costs to individual units, net realizable value as determined either on a project-by-project basis or on an individual unit basis should be approximately the same.

The *group convention* was principally established for a manufacturing concern, but for the group convention to be appropriate there must be a high volume of transactions with each individual component of the group having approximately the same rate of turnover. Since this condition is not usually present in the real estate industry, the group convention is not usually appropriate.

Determination of net realizable value

In the application of the general principle of lower-of-cost-or-market, the term *market* generally means estimated net realizable value (that is, estimated selling price in the ordinary course of business less costs of completion and disposal); and market, as previously discussed, should usually be applied on an item-by-item basis rather than a group basis.

Selling price. The selling price should usually be determined on the basis of sale in the ordinary course of business, which would allow a reasonable time to find a willing purchaser under normal market conditions, exclusive of any adjustment for estimated inflation. If, however, the intention is to dispose of the property on an immediate sale basis or if the owner does not have the financial ability to hold the property, the estimated selling price should be determined on an immediate liquidation basis.

The method used to determine selling prices will vary depending on the nature of the property. Selling prices on bulk undeveloped land should ordinarily be based on comparable sales prices, allowing a reasonable time to find a purchaser. Certain future events, such as prospective scientific developments, possible future legislation, and the like, should not be factored into the determination of the estimated selling prices except to the extent that such events are being recognized currently in the marketplace. Possible future zoning should not be considered unless it is reasonably certain that it can be obtained.

In determining selling prices for property under development, such as retail lots, single-family homes, and condominiums, current sales prices should be used. Where experience is lacking or where there has been relatively low sales volume, selling prices of comparable transactions in the local area should be used. Although selling prices should not be adjusted for inflation, it would be appropriate in the case of long-term developments where significant development work remains to be completed (e.g., certain retail land developments and new communities) to adjust selling prices for the effect of inflation reflected in costs to complete. This would only be appropriate when there is reasonable assurance that cost increases can be recovered in sales prices on a dollar-for-dollar basis.

Income properties are usually valued on the basis of their estimated future net cash flow and a capitalization rate which may vary with the type of project and the money market. When using such a valuation process to determine estimated selling prices, pro forma operating costs should be based on current costs rather than historical averages. For example, future net cash flow should be adjusted to reflect recent increases in utility costs.

Cost of completion (inclusion of interest and property taxes). Total cost of completion of properties being evaluated should include all additional costs to be incurred up to the estimated date of disposal. Such costs should include the effects of inflation and should be determined on a basis consistent with the determination of costs previously capitalized or included in inventory. For example, if, as a matter of accounting policy, interest and property taxes are not capitalized, future interest and property taxes need not be included in the calculation. On the other hand, if costs of interest and property taxes have been inventoried or capitalized, then costs of interest and property taxes to estimated date of disposal should be included in the estimated cost of completion. This latter method is consistent with the aforementioned proposed Statement of Position of the AICPA. The AICPA has also tentatively concluded that holding period costs should be included in the computation even when the accounting policy is to expense such costs, but in such cases the interest cost is to be based on the average cost of all capital including debt and equity. In view of this tentative position, this method should also be considered acceptable.

Costs of disposal. Such costs should include marketing, selling, advertising, points, fees, and commissions.

Reversal of write-downs. Write-downs to net realizable value frequently result because of a series of estimates, as opposed to known losses, caused by specific sales commitments and the like. If based on estimates, the reduction in carrying value may be treated as a valuation reserve which should be adjusted periodically based on a relatively complete reevaluation.

Examples of application to bulk land. Assume that a real estate developer, having a policy of capitalizing interest, owns 3,000 acres of bulk land, development of which had been contemplated in the future. To date no commitment for development has been made, although there are a number of possible alternatives for development. The book value per acre is $1,500.

As to these facts, apply several possible sets of additional facts and consider valuation under the principles in this chapter.

1. 140 of the 3,000 acres have recently been sold in bulk for $1,500 per acre; the 140 acres are reasonably typical of the

remaining acreage in character and value. In this situation, it is recognized that the 3,000 acres may not, or even probably will not, be sold immediately or even within a year. *Conclusion:* In this situation (ignoring sales commission for the moment), the sale may be reasonable evidence of "replacement cost" and no reserve or write-down is required; no consideration is required for future interest cost to hold the property as long as current values are used.

As to sales commissions, it will generally be necessary to consider selling cost as a reduction of "replacement cost" when (1) it is expected that the property will be sold for the "replacement cost" of $1,500 *and* the selling costs will be incurred, or (2) the property is held for sale.

2. If the sale in (1) above was not part of the parcel owned but was comparable to the parcel owned, the conclusion should be the same.

3. If no sales occurred but competent appraisal techniques lead to the conclusion that (*a*) comparable sales can be made but only after three years and (*b*) no current sales are possible except at clearly distressed prices and there is no expectation of making sales in this manner, the indication is that the sales price of $1,500 (and thus "replacement cost") is available after three years. The conclusion is that a reserve is required for the excess of (*a*) current net book value ($1,500) plus all future costs (including interest) less (*b*) sales price of $1,500 per acre. (Note—Appraisal techniques frequently result in deduction of interest based on a risk rate of return during the three years in arriving at the sale prices; if so, this interest should be added back before making the preceding calculation, which includes the developer's future interest cost.)

Financial statement disclosures

Since alternative methods are in use, the accounting policy with respect to the carrying value should be disclosed, together with the methods of determining market or net realizable value. In addition, summarized information or explanations with respect to significant inventory write-downs should be disclosed in the footnotes as they are generally important and unusual items.

REFERENCES

"Accounting for Condominium Sales." Price Waterhouse & Co., July 1975.

Accounting Principles Board *Opinion No. 21.* "Interest on Receivables and Payables." New York: AICPA, August 1971.

AICPA. "Accounting for Retail Land Sales." An AICPA Industry Accounting Guide. New York, 1973.

———. "Audits of Construction Contractors." An AICPA Industry Audit Guide. New York, 1965.

———. Statement of Position. "Accounting for Costs to Sell and Rent, and Initial Rental Operations of, Real Estate Projects." New York, June 30, 1978.

———. Exposure Draft. "Valuation of Certain Real Estate and Loans and Receivables Collateralized by Real Estate." New York, May 25, 1976.

———. Statement of Position. "Accounting Practices of Real Estate Investment Trusts." New York, June 27, 1975.

Aronsohn, A. "The Real Estate Limited Partnership and Other Joint Ventures." *Real Estate Review,* Spring 1971.

The Canadian Institute of Chartered Accountants. "Accounting for Real Estate Development Operations." A research study. 1971.

FASB *Statement of Financial Accounting Standards No. 15.* "Accounting by Debtors and Creditors for Troubled Debt Restructurings." Stamford, Conn., June 1977.

Harris, Edward C., and Klink, James J. "Accounting and Reporting for Real Estate Developments." *The Modern Accountant's Handbook.* Edited by James D. Edwards and Homer A. Black. Homewood, Ill.: Dow Jones-Irwin, 1976. Chap. 41.

"1977 Survey of Accounting and Reporting Practices of Real Estate Developers." New York, Price Waterhouse & Co. 1977.

Securities and Exchange Commission *Accounting Series Release No. 163.* "Capitalization of Interest by Companies Other Than Public Utilities." November, 14, 1974.

———. *Accounting Series Release No. 190.* "Current Replacement Cost Information." March 23, 1976.

28

Cost accounting
for distribution

*Paul M. Fischer**
John D. Schoonover†

Distribution costs are accounting for an increasing share of many firms' expenditures. As products tend to become more standardized, market differentiation is accomplished through differences in distribution. Improved customer service is being increasingly included in a firm's total competitive marketing strategy.

Accounting procedures have been slow to acknowledge the importance of distribution costs. For external reporting purposes, distribution costs are scattered around the income statement in such accounts as freight, warehousing, selling, general, or administrative expenses. Internally, budgets fragmentize costs among many responsibilities and merely treat the costs as part of overhead. This chapter will describe accounting methods that recognize the importance of distribution costs and that will make planning and control of such costs possible.

Though unique types of analyses are required, many firms have found that cost analysis and control may be applied to distribution costs. The benefits of doing so are numerous.

First, substantial savings are possible by attempting to make distribution functions more cost efficient. The potential savings

* Associate Professor, University of Wisconsin–Milwaukee.
† Vice President & Controller, Alcan Aluminum Corporation.

are likely to be no less than those secured by applying accounting controls to production functions.

Second, once the cost components and behavior of various distribution functions are known, the same information may be used to attach the cost of service provided by the functions to various sales segments. Such cost attachment is a primary ingredient of the segmental analysis required for marketing analysis. Most firms are able to attach production costs to segments in order to compute segment gross profit. They are, however, often unable to attach distribution costs to arrive at a truer measure of the segment's profitability. There is an obvious need to attach distribution costs to sales segments, since distribution costs tend to vary more among segments than do production costs.

Third, a firm will desire to have a knowledge of distribution costs if it is charged with price discrimination under the Robinson-Patman Act. One possible defense to a charge of discriminatory pricing (a different price to different customers for the same product) is the ability to demonstrate that the price difference is no greater than the differential costs between the customers. Since the product must be the same, the cost differences by definition involve distribution costs.

A first step in the analysis of distribution costs is to understand that there are two distinct types of such costs, each requiring unique analysis:

1. *Order filling costs,* generally characterized in the literature as *physical distribution costs.* Broadly defined, these costs include inventory warehousing, transportation, and order processing. These costs bear resemblances to production costs; they are often repetitive and standardized and lend themselves to existing cost accounting procedures. The accountant should have two concerns in controlling physical distribution costs:

   a. Subject to a concern for customer service, the total cost of providing physical distribution services is to be minimized.

   b. There must be control over the use of services by sales segments.

2. *Order getting,* or *promotional costs.* The most common examples are sales force compensation, advertising, and sales promotion. Such costs represent the efforts made to generate

sales. The objective is really not to minimize these costs, but rather to maximize results per dollar of expenditure. All too often these costs are budgeted without a direct consideration of resulting benefits. The most needed tool to direct promotion efforts is segmental profitability analysis. By directing efforts at the most profitable segment, results should be maximized. Various promotional efforts should be measured by their impact on the relevant segment's profit performance. Where efforts, such as advertising, have a synergistic and indirect effect on sales, financial measures must be supplemented by methods which assess the attainment of communication goals. It is common to measure advertising success in terms of the increase in brand awareness of potential buyers.

PHYSICAL DISTRIBUTION: A TOTAL SYSTEMS APPROACH

The first step in controlling the cost and use of physical distribution costs is to identify and measure costs by functional cost centers. Cost control cannot proceed only by minimizing the cost of each function. The interrelationship of costs between functions must be explicitly considered in order to avoid suboptimization. Finally, the physical distribution system has an effect on profitability to the degree that it defines customer service. The optimal level of service must be defined, and then cost must be minimized for the service level chosen.

Functional cost control

It is unusual for a firm to have cost accumulation techniques built into the accounting system for physical distribution costs such as exist for production costs. Frequently, the analysis of these costs is included only indirectly in a study of general overhead. Where physical distribution costs are analyzed, it is often done crudely, such as by comparing actual current cost to previous periods (which may perpetuate inefficiency) or by comparing costs over time as a percent of sales (which implies some inherent justification for a linear physical distribution cost-revenue relationship). The first and crucial step in controlling physical distribution costs is to *define functional cost centers* in the manner used for production costs. Once they are defined, responsibility accounting concepts are applicable. Cost centers might in general fall in the categories of transportation, inventory, warehousing, and order processing. The unique aspects of each area will be discussed in following sections.

A cost center theory, rather than a profit center theory, is usually most appropriate for physical distribution functions. Clearly the total set of physical distribution activities has an impact on revenue and thus profit, and the impact should be considered in the design and revision of the system. However, the impact of each function is obscure and abstract on an ongoing, operating basis. To use a profit center concept, a complete set of arbitrary transfer prices would be needed. The use of such prices and the "profit" they produce would tend to frustrate functional center managers who envision their responsibility as limited to cost control and defined measures of service provided. Functional cost control requires that costs specifically controlled by a center be identified and that their behavior with respect to activity be analyzed. Some of the costs of each function will vary with activity levels. The challenge is to find a factor of variability which reasonably explains their behavior. Examples might include the dollar value of a unit for inventory costs, labor to pick and pack orders, additional packaging materials (such as pallets and strapping), and cwt-miles for transportation. There may be justification for using multiple factors of variability within a cost center if a better explanation of behavior results. Behavior may be found by using time study techniques where operations are repetitive, and similar in nature to labor and material cost for production processes. In other cases, statistical techniques may be employed in a manner similar to that used to study the behavior of variable overhead in the production process. Generally, techniques already in use for production costs will work if added effort is made to isolate factors of variability. Well-defined factors will allow the use of standard cost techniques as the variable costs are isolated.

Factors of variability should only be used to explain variable cost behavior. They should not be used to give a false appearance of behavior by being used to allocate fixed costs. Fixed costs should be attached to cost centers as lump sums. Preferably only fixed costs specifically controllable to the center should be attached. These costs are often termed *programmed* or *discretionary fixed costs.* If noncontrollable fixed costs are allocated to a center, it should be made clear that they are not specific and that, at best, the functional center may have some indirect influence over them.

The end result of cost analysis by function should be a statement of cost behavior of the function in this form:

Function cost = Fixed cost + Variable cost × Factor of variability.

The foregoing is easily expanded to multiple factors of variability. Generally, ease of application requires a linear cost assumption, though the design stage of the physical distribution system itself could certainly consider nonlinear cost behavior.

The choice of a factor of variability should be based primarily upon its power to explain cost behavior, but it should also consider the following uses of the factor outside of the specific cost center:

1. Costs should be in a form that allows cost comparisons to be made between functions so that the total cost of physical distribution may be quantified and minimized. For example, if a proposal to cut inventory through the use of a shipment of surplus stocks from a more distant location is considered, the information concerning inventory cost savings should be available to compare with the higher transportation costs.
2. Costs should be in a form that is usable for attaching the cost of a function to the sales segments consuming the services. This is crucial for defining the profitability of segments and for controlling the use of service by the sales segments.
3. The suitability of the factors of variability should be considered with regard to a cost defense under the Robinson-Patman Act. Generally, a factor on which decisions are based should be acceptable. It is also believed that before-the-fact consideration of cost differences in setting differential prices between customers will serve as a better defense than an after-the-fact study.

Cost center management: Unique problems

Cost behavior within a function may at first appear to be more theoretical than real—especially with respect to labor. Frequently, past management practice leads to the attitude that labor cost is relatively inflexible in the short run. For example, staff changes in clerical and warehouse operations may not be implemented immediately. Yet upon reflection, staff level adjustments are no less difficult than in the production process, where the concept of labor as a variable cost is readily accepted. The key to labor control is *scheduling*. A functional manager should be aware of any flexibility available in work assignments. Where necessary, unneeded labor time should be assigned to semiproductive tasks. For example, warehouse labor might be used for light maintenance, or clerical help might be used for low priority filing. The important thing is to "smoke out" idle time so that trends indicating staff level adjustment are spotted. It is also important to capture idle time costs so that the functional manager will be aware of these costs and be able to reassess staffing decisions, realign work activities among employees, or develop other work activities to utilize the idle time. There may also be opportunities to make labor cost more variable by using piece rates, overtime, part-time workers, or outside contractors.

A second major concern is the control of functional costs in conjunction with control of the assets used. The need for control is particularly obvious in the areas of inventory and transportation. The planning and control model should encourage trade-offs between labor and capital equipment, which are only possible if the investment in functional center assets is explicitly considered. The most common means of considering investment is the use of return on investment analysis. However, this approach is only applicable for profit centers, where a measure of profits is available to compare to asset investment. In order to include asset investment in a cost center it may be necessary to levy a cost of capital charge for the use funds invested in assets. This charge is usually a cost of capital rate multiplied by the recorded value of the assets used. This means that the capital charge becomes a cost of the center with a prominence equal to that of other incurred costs. The cost of capital charge to a center has both a fixed and variable component. For example, the capital charge for a warehouse might be fixed and unrelated to volume, whereas the charge for inventory is variable. This allows investment in assets to be incorporated into the flexible budget. The charge for the use of assets has a positive side benefit—it permits comparison of the use of leased versus owned assets. For example, if a truck is leased, the charge made by the lessor includes depreciation and an interest charge for the funds invested. If the truck were purchased, the cost center using the truck would be charged for depreciation and a cost of capital charge.

The practical problems involved in implementing a cost of capital charge include the determination of the rate to be used and the asset value to which the rate is to be applied. The *cost of capital* may be computed by using any of several alternative methods described in the finance literature. Generally, the charge is based on a long-run concept covering the use of both equity and debt funds. Some firms which wish to avoid arguments as to the relevant long-run rate have resorted to using a rate which reflects the incremental borrowing rate. Such a rate, while having theoretical shortcomings, is easy to defend to functional center managers. It is particularly convenient to use for assets such as inventory and motor vehicles where short-term borrowing is commonly used.

The *asset value* to which the rate is to be applied is typically *recorded book value*. There are no problems with this procedure for current assets, such as inventory, where book values are close to market values (except where Lifo is used). However, where older assets, such as a warehouse, are involved, it is likely that current value is far in excess of depreciated historical cost. Where this difference exists, opportunity cost theory would dictate that the cost of capital charge be based on a measure of current value. Where the difference between historical and current cost is significant and the current value is reasonably realizable through sale or rental of the asset, better analysis of alternative cost models will result from applying the cost of capital charge to current asset value. Where the Lifo inventory method is used, it is imperative that the capital charge for inventory be based on current, and not recorded, cost if the use of inventory is to be considered rationally.

The accounting system for cost control

The accounting system must provide the information needed for control of costs within functions and control of the use of

750

physical distribution costs by sales segments. This may be accomplished by using the model shown in Exhibit 1. The model requires that source documents be carefully coded to allow sales to be attached to desired sales segments, and that expenses be coded to allow attachment to the proper functional cost centers. A complete set of standard budgeted costs must also be included in the data base for all cost centers. The data base flows sales revenue to the sales segments used for analytical purposes and to accounts required for external accounting. Actual expenses are charged to the cost centers responsible, as well as being recorded in natural accounts for external reporting. The data base credits each cost center with the standard cost of the actual service provided. This includes a charge per unit of service for variable costs and a flat charge for budgeted fixed costs. A comparison of actual and budgeted standard cost is then possible within cost centers. As in the production sector, variances may be of a spending or a usage variety. The standard costs credited to cost centers are charged to the sales segments to which they attach. Variable costs are charged according to actual use, while fixed costs are charged in total. Since many fixed costs are com-

EXHIBIT 1
An operational system for cost and revenue flows

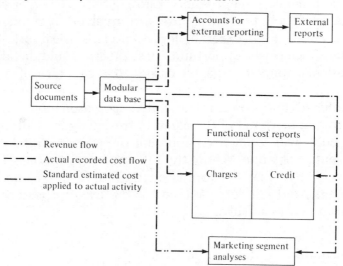

Source: Frank H. Mossman, William J. E. Crissy, and Paul M. Fischer, *Financial Dimensions of Marketing Management* (New York: Wiley-Hamilton, 1978), p. 38.

mon to several segments, fixed costs are only attached to the relevant aggregation of subsegments. A type of variance analysis is possible for sales segments' usage of variable costs. The actual versus budgeted use of these costs may be analyzed on the basis of standard cost of service. This results in a *use of service* variance, but does not charge using segments with the difference between the actual and standard budgeted cost of service.

Concept of trade-offs

The literature in the field of physical distribution management emphasizes the need to consider cost trade-offs in planning functional costs. Typically, three levels of trade-offs are considered:

1. Cost trade-offs within a function, designed to reduce the total cost of the function.
2. Cost trade-offs between functions, designed to lower the total cost of physical distribution.
3. Cost trade-offs between sales revenue and the cost of total physical distribution service.

Level one analysis. A properly designed cost system will make available the cost components needed for cost minimization within a function. For decisions covering future periods, capital budgeting analysis is used. The only other needed information is cost estimates for changes under analysis. Firms which have well-developed functional cost centers will likely already be making level one trade-offs. A constraint must be placed on trade-offs made by the function's manager. There may be no change which has repercussions on the cost of other functions or on customer service unless there is consultation with higher management. If this is not done, suboptimization is likely to occur, meaning that savings in one function are more than offset by higher costs in another function or by a loss in sales revenue.

Level two analysis. The concept of "total systems managements" or "continuous costing" suggests that the total cost of physical distribution be minimized, subject to maintaining a given level of customer service. This suggests that costs in one or more functions may be increased if to do so would decrease costs in other areas by more than an offsetting amount. For example, Exhibit 2 contains a graphic example of the lowering

752

EXHIBIT 2
Using total cost analysis to determine least-cost solution to the number of
regional depots required

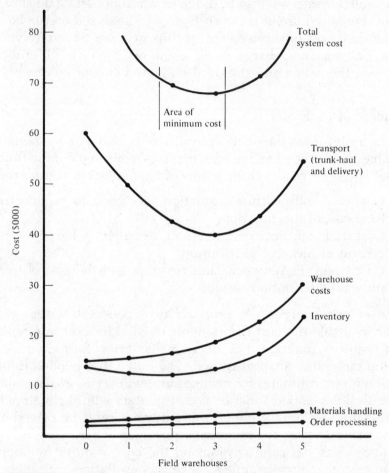

Adapted from Martin Christopher, *Total Distribution: A Framework for Analysis,
Costing, and Control* (London: Gower Press, Ltd., 1971), p. 28.

of total cost caused by an increase in the number of warehouses.
A total systems approach to cost minimization requires that the
cost behavior of each function be analyzed in a way that allows
it to be combined with the cost functions of other cost centers.
A desire to minimize the total systems cost requires that costs
external to the firm be considered. Payments made to outside
parties, such as public carriers or public warehouses, must be

included in the total cost function. These costs are readily available; this relieves the purchasing firm from an analysis of cost behavior. The total systems approach must also consider costs necessary to deliver goods to the purchaser which are borne by the purchaser. Though not recorded in the accounts of the seller, these costs must be considered. For example, it might lower total cost to the customer to reduce customer-paid freight through an increase in the number of field warehouses. This would allow a higher billed f.o.b. cost to the customer which, when combined with a lower freight cost, would lower the total cost of the product to the buyer.

Even at the second trade-off level there is a constraint on actions which may be taken by physical distribution management. No change may be made, without consulting a higher level of management, which would change the level of customer service. To allow otherwise would still allow suboptimization to the degree that total systems cost savings are more than offset by a decrease in revenue.

Level three analysis. The third trade-off level analyzes the impact of changes in the total physical distribution system on corporate profits. This is the level that explores the interface between the cost of customer service and its impact on demand. Optimization at this level requires close cooperation between physical distribution and sales management. Exhibit 3 is a chart depicting the normal physical distribution cost/revenue function. The chart depicts the response of cost and revenue to different service levels, with service levels expressed in percentages. The cost function is that of increasing and then decreasing marginal cost. The demand effect is typically viewed as an *S* curve. The response of demand with respect to service is not great at very high or low levels of service, but is significant between the extremes. To achieve the optimum level of service, market testing and or simulation techniques may be used to estimate the cost/revenue curve.

In testing customer service levels there must be consideration of the many ways in which a well-defined physical distribution system can help to generate sales. Some of them are as follows:

1. *Minimize out-of-stock occurrences.* This reduces lost sales from the inability to fill an order immediately.

754

EXHIBIT 3

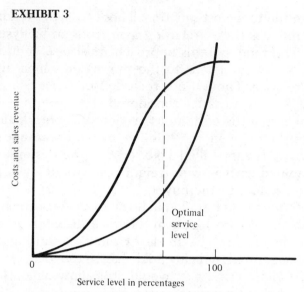

Service level in percentages

Source: Maureen Guirdham, *Marketing: The Management of Distribution Channels* (Oxford: Pergamon Press, 1972), p. 183.

2. *Reduce customer inventory requirements.* By reducing the customer's inventory costs and capital requirements, the total cost to the customer of selling the product is reduced. Thus, a competitive advantage is secured for the supplier.

3. *Solidify supplier-customer relationships.* This is accomplished by integrating physical distribution services with the characteristics of the customer.

4. *Increase delivery discounts.* It may be possible to share cost savings with customers.

5. *Enable expanded market coverage.* More efficient physical distribution operations may permit the firm to compete more effectively in distant markets.

6. *Allow greater concentration on demand creation.* Under a well-organized system, sales personnel can concentrate on demand creation rather than having their attention diverted to expediting orders.

One of the most difficult aspects of the third level of trade-offs is measuring the cost of customer reprisals against poor service. The total loss of profits through lost future sales cannot be measured with accuracy.

Christopher has advocated a method called "Analysis by Distribution Mission to Aid the Process of Making Level Three Trade-Offs." He describes the process as follows:

> A distribution mission is a set of goals to be achieved by the system within a specific product/market context, the initial aim of the distribution planner being to specify closely the exact nature of the distribution mission(s) in which the company is involved. Such a statement of mission could be expressed in terms of the nature of the market to be served, by which products and within what constraints of service and cost. A mission, by its very nature, cuts across traditional company lines. The successful achievement of the mission goals involves inputs from a large number of functional areas and activity centres within the firm.[1]

It is suggested that distribution missions be defined and that alternate means of achieving each mission be considered. Cost-benefit analysis using profit contribution techniques is then applied to each alternative. This approach uses the techniques of the Planning, Programming, Budgeting System (PPBS) and has the advantage of applying profit contribution analysis to missions involving several functions.

Efforts to achieve an optimum level of customer service are of little value if the customer service policy is not controlled in terms of both cost and quality of service. The modular data base previously discussed makes cost control operational. However, added methods are needed to audit the actual versus planned levels of customer services. Nonfinancial measures must be used to measure actual performance. Included in the measures might be the following elements of customer service:

1. *Order processing time.* Elapsed time from receipt of the customer's order until it is ready for assembly.
2. *Order assembly time.* Time required to prepare the order for shipment.
3. *Delivery time.* Time in transit to the customer.
4. *Inventory reliability.* Stock-outs, back orders, percent of demand filled, omission rate, percent of orders shipped complete, etc.
5. *Order-size constraint.* Minimum order size and minimum frequency allowed.

---

[1] Martin Christopher, *Total Distribution: A Framework for Analysis, Costing, and Control* (London: Gower Press Ltd., 1971), p. 60.

6. *Consolidation allowed.* Ability to consolidate items from several locations into a single shipment.
7. *Consistency.* Range of variation in each of the preceding elements.

Cost analysis by functions

The design of the physical distribution system requires consideration of alternative cost structures. Often alternatives involve trade-offs between variable and fixed costs. Once in place, the cost behavior of the system must be available by function. It is not unusual to find a need for multiple factors of variability for a given function. However, it is desirable to use as few factors as possible in order to simplify cost control within the function and to attach the costs to sales segments.

Inventory

Cost analysis of inventory requires consideration of three basic costs: the *cost of holding inventory,* the *cost of ordering* or *production setup,* and the *cost of an outage.* Not all of the costs needed for analysis are recorded. For example, the cost of holding inventory includes interest on funds used, obsolescence, and spoilage. Outage costs may include lost profit on current and future business.

Short-run analysis accepts the other components of the physical distribution system, such as warehouse locations and transportation methods, and balances the cost of ordering for purchased goods or the cost of setup for manufactured goods with the holding costs. Typically, the analysis assumes level daily customer demand, and if demand is level it never allows a stock outage. The lack of a planned outage is based on assumed exorbitant cost. *Economic order quantity* analysis (EOQ) is used to balance ordering and holding costs. EOQ uses the following terms:

a = ordering or setup cost per order. It is to be only the incremental variable cost and is assumed to be constant per order regardless of the order size.

S = annual sales rate in units.

i = interest cost per unit, including a return on capital charge and a risk factor for obsolescence, loss, damage, and shrinkage.

The formula which finds the most economic lot or order size is then:

$$EOQ = \sqrt{\frac{2\,aS}{i}}$$

The EOQ is the quantity to be ordered; the next concern is when to order. The *"reorder point"* is the level of remaining units to be on hand when a replenishment order is placed. It is calculated by multiplying daily demand times the days of lead time between placing the order and receipt of the units. If, for example, the EOQ was 1,000 units, daily demand was 50, and the lead time 5 days, 1,000 units would be ordered when existing stock reach 250 units (5 days × 50 units per day). Providing there is no increase in the lead time or daily demand, there will be no outage. Where outage cost is low and inventory carrying cost is very high, a planned outage may be incorporated into the EOQ model. It is expressed as:[2]

$$\text{Stock-out modifier} = \frac{O}{i+O}$$

The term O is the average cost of a stock-out of one unit for a year. Notice that as O becomes very large the modifer becomes equal to one. The stockout modifier is multiplied by the EOQ derived using the previous formula to arrive at a modified EOQ. Thus, for example, if the basic EOQ was 1,000 units and the modifier was .9, the modified EOQ would be 900 units. The actual instances where the modifier would be significant will be rare; it is seldom used due to the usual desire to not sacrifice customer service with planned outages.

Short-run inventory management based on EOQ theory must consider the problem of unplanned stockouts caused by daily demand exceeding the average during the lead time and by a longer than planned lead time. The increase in the inventory level used to accommodate these events is termed a *"safety stock."* The most common concern in carrying a safety stock is to accommodate above-average demand during the lead time. There are several alternative methods available:

---

[2] Nicholas Dopuch, Jacob G. Birnberg, and Joel Demski, *Cost Accounting* (New York: Harcourt Brace Jovanovich, Inc., 1974), p. 273.

1. Carry a safety stock able to meet maximum expected demand during the lead time.
2. Use statistical analysis and carry sufficient units to meet a given service objective, such as ability to meet 90 percent of possible demand.
3. Combine cost/benefit analysis with a statistical study to find the safety stock which will provide the lowest total cost of outages and holding cost.[3] The basic approach is to consider the combined probabilistic costs at incremental levels of safety stocks.

Similar analysis is used where there is a need to consider longer than planned lead times. An added possibility is to use a computer simulation using Monte Carlo analysis to consider the interactions of varying demand and lead times.

EOQ analysis will result in the dual factors of variability of orders placed and inventory level. Control of costs requires auditing of adherence to EOQ procedures and a comparison of actual and budget cost based on orders placed and inventory level. The two factors of variability will also be used to charge sales segments for inventory.

Longer run cost analysis must consider trade-offs between inventory and other functional costs. This includes a consideration of the interface between inventory levels and transportation methods. For example, the use of air freight might substantially lessen the need for inventory. The effect of multiple warehouses on inventory level also needs to be considered. Present research indicates that the total base inventory does not increase substantially with more locations, but that total safety stocks increase at a decreasing rate.[4]

Transportation

In the short run, control and costing procedures depend on whether common carriers are used or transportation is self-provided. The use of common carriers has the advantage of making predetermined rates available for costing each shipment, thus

---

[3] For further understanding see Edward W. SunyKay, *Physical Distribution Management* (New York: Macmillan, 1973), p. 228.

[4] Ibid., pp. 213–16.

simplifying analysis by sales segments. Control is limited to auditing of freight bills. There are professional independent freight auditors that generally retain 50 percent of the billing errors found. A similar audit function might be used internally. An advantage of using internal auditors is that the audit could be made prior to payment rather than after the transaction, where a refund must be obtained. This places the firm in a better bargaining position. Some firms employ management by exception, by paying the predetermined published rate and making the carrier justify any variance.

Where transportation is self-provided there are two accounting models that might be used. If the service provided is also available from common carriers, a profit center concept may be used. The transportation function is given credit for, and sales segments are charged, the common carrier rates. The rates credited to transportation are compared to incurred costs to compute a profit or loss. Where the profit center model is not practicable, cost center accounting is used. In either method costs should be budgeted and controlled. This requires knowledge of cost behavior. However, the cost function is not needed for charging sales segments if the profit center concept is used.

An efficient method of gaining an understanding of cost behavior for transportation is to study Interstate Commerce Commission (ICC) accounting methods. They have four identifiable direct cost centers: line haul costs, terminal costs, pick up and delivery costs, and billing and collecting costs. A service unit is used to measure the cost of each center. Generally, a fully allocated cost approach is used by the ICC, but the service unit could be costed at only variable cost for budgeting purposes. Following is a brief description of methods used by each direct cost center:

Line haul costs. Time-related costs, such as driver's wages, are analyzed as a function of vehicle hours, while mileage-related costs, such as fuel, are analyzed using vehicle miles. The total variable cost combining these variables is converted to a cost recovery factor quoted per cwt.-mile. This approach assumes an average load factor. However, adjustments are possible for varying loads.

Pick-up and delivery costs. There are also time- and distance-related service units. Costs for a given delivery area are constructed using the service units, which are converted to cost per cwt. Again, a given mix of time and distance factors is assumed.

Terminal platform costs. Total labor and equipment costs are divided by cwt. handled to arrive at a cost per cwt. The average may be adjusted for different weight categories.

Billing and collection costs. A broad average cost per shipment is used. In assigning the cost per cwt. a decreasing cost function is used.

Combining the cost elements, cost for any shipment may be calculated using the equation:

$$\text{Cost} = a + bx$$

where

a = costs nonvariable with distance, quoted per cwt.
b = costs related to distance, quoted per cwt.-mile
x = distance in miles

The model has the advantage of developing detailed cost functions within centers and then using the cost functions to build a simple rate that combines all costs for a given shipment. It would be hoped that the concession to accuracy caused by mix differences is offset by operating convenience.

Warehousing

Warehousing includes space- and labor-related costs. Typically, the cost of owned or leased space is a fixed cost for a given amount of space, and once the firm is committed to given space, the cost is not a function of volume. However, a bit longer run-opportunity concept would hold that the rental value of space is a function of square footage, and thus a space cost per square foot occupied is defensible. Where adjustments of space by virture of rental alternatives exist, a variable charge for space occupied is recommended.

The labor steps involved in warehousing include receiving, transferring, selecting, and shipping goods. Generally, the functions are repetitive enough to allow standard cost techniques to be applied. The factors of variability, such as weight or cubic content, will tend to be product related and will be divided into classes to reflect unique product features. Where standards for warehousing become intricate, a summary variable cost, such as through-put, reflecting general cost variability, might be utilized to charge sales segments. As was true of transportation, an average mix of the detailed cost factors must be assumed and some accuracy is forfeited.

Order processing

Order processing functions include order processing, invoicing, billing, and all other paperwork functions necessary to serve the customer. Knowledge of order processing functions also provides the information needed to monitor other physical distribution functions. Of all areas, this is the one most likely to be treated as overhead and to avoid close scrutiny. Application of precise standards is difficult due to the wide range of activities performed. It is possible, however, to use a subrogate activity which is familiar, such as preparation of an invoice. The basic work measurement unit might be stated as an "invoice equivalent." All other operations would then be stated in terms of an invoice equivalent based on comparative work requirements. For example, billing might be a 0.5 invoice equivalent while a credit memo might be a 1.2 invoice equivalent. Such a procedure does allow staffing adjustments based on anticipated workload and allows a measure of staffing efficiency for past periods. A workload measure is also a convenient method of charging sales segments for services received.

PROMOTIONAL COSTS

Promotional costs are costs of the set of activities which directly or indirectly influence demand to produce a sale. Such activities are viewed as creating a sale, as compared to production and physical distribution costs which are triggered by a sale. The usual costs would include personal selling, media advertising, and other special activities such as catalogs, conventions, point of purchase displays, contests, and trading stamps. Some costs currently treated as offsets to sales should also be recorded and analyzed as promotional costs; these include "cents-off" packages and coupons. Such formalized price concessions are a part of the total promotional mix. Planning and control of promotional costs is unique from other areas. The intent should not be to minimize cost, but rather to maximize the results of a given dollar of expenditure. The process for accomplishing this is less well defined and more abstract than processes to which an accountant is accustomed. There are three goals in analyzing promotional activities:

1. Total efforts must be directed towards segments with the greatest potential.
2. The promotional mix, or the set of activities to be used in a segment, must be decided upon.
3. The optimum level of expenditure within each segment must be determined.

Direction of efforts

Promotional decision making relies on a well-designed system of marketing segment analysis. Since efforts should maximize profits and not just revenue, the segment analysis should analyze segments in terms of a relevant measure of profit contribution. The very design of the set of customer or product segments should be based on promotional decision-making needs. There is little hope of correlating most specific promotional activities to segment results. Rather, segment results measure the successful interaction of the set of promotional efforts used.

Marketing research methods should be used to predict demand by segments. The accounting information system can then be used to reduce projected revenue to a measure of projected profit contribution. The cost system can attach budgeted production and physical distribution costs to projected sales by using a modular data base.

Designing the promotional mix

In designing the promotional mix, the most efficient proportions of the various elements of personal selling, advertising, and other promotional efforts should be sought. The various elements are essentially alternative means of communication designed to influence the potential buyer. Most commonly, no one element is used exclusively, but the elements are combined in such a way as to be interdependent in producing the ultimate sale. Writers in the area of promotion urge that rather than focus only on the desired end-sales result, the total promotional effort be subdivided into component tasks or goals, each of which would be concerned with a phase of the total communication task. Typically, a sale is thought of as being made in stages. As an example, a National Industrial Conference Board study lists five stages in which a sale might be thought to occur:[5]

1. Creation of awareness of the product in the mind of the potential buyer.
2. Nurturing an acceptance of the product.
3. Establishing a preference for the product.
4. Arousing an intent to buy the product.
5. Provoking the sale.

Each type of promotional effort should properly be thought of in terms of its influence at each stage. Objectives should be set in terms of the specific influence desired, and results should be judged accordingly.

Determining the amount of promotional expenditures

In theory, the amount of total promotional expenditures should be budgeted such that expenditures are made until marginal revenue equals marginal cost. This would mean that promotion would proceed to the point where the cost of promotion involved in selling the last unit would be equal to the profit contribution of the unit. In practice, marginal cost and revenue techniques are modified to become incremental analysis. An attempt is made to distribute promotional expenditures among sales segments to create the maximum return per dollar of expenditure. The profit contribution potential of relevant sales segments is defined and the information system is used to estimate the effects of shifts in the direction of efforts among segments, as well as changes in the total amount of expenditure.

---

[5] Harry Dean Wolfe, James K. Brown, and G. Clark Thompson, *Measuring Advertising Results: Business Policy Study 102* (New York: National Industrial Conference Board Inc., 1962), p. 7.

Frequently, firms have directed efforts towards maximizing sales, an approach which ignores production and physical distribution costs. Other firms have focused on gross profit, an approach which considers the production cost of goods sold but still ignores physical distribution costs. The real measure of a segment's impact on corporate profits is its profit contribution, or the excess of revenue over the sum of variable and directly attachable fixed costs. It is this measure of contribution upon which marketing efforts should focus.

Exhibit 4 is an example of a model used to maximize the profitability of promotional expenditures. Each of three segments is studied for its performance during a past period. The same analysis could be used on a pro forma basis. In each seg-

EXHIBIT 4

Segmental profitability analysis by product lines of the XYZ Company (for the quarter ending December 31, 19xx)

Product lines	A	B	C
1. Gross sales	$40,000	$35,000	$50,000
2. Less standard variable costs:			
Production	20,000	7,000	25,000
Physical distribution	5,000	3,000	10,000
3. Variable standard profit contribution	$15,000	$25,000	$15,000
4. Less programmed costs:			
Production costs	2,000	5,000	1,000
Physical distribution costs	1,000	2,000	2,000
5. Profit contribution	$12,000	$18,000	$12,000
6. Less promotional costs:			
Advertising	5,000	2,000	4,000
Direct selling	4,000	10,000	8,000
Price promotions	500	1,000	1,000
7. Gross marketing segment earnings	$ 2,500	$ 5,000	$ (1,000)
8. Average promotional profitability index (item 3 divided by item 6)	1.58	1.92	1.15
9. Incremental variable standard profit contribution*	$ 5,000	$ (5,000)	$10,000
10. Incremental specific promotional expense†	$ 2,000	$ (2,000)	$ 5,000
11. Incremental promotional profitability index (item 10 divided by item 11)	2.5	(2.5)	2

* The incremental variable standard profit contribution is the change in the variable standard profit contribution from the same quarter of the previous year to the quarter being analyzed.

† The increment of promotional expense is the change in promotional expenses from the same quarter of the previous year to the quarter being analyzed.

ment, standard variable costs of production and physical distribution are deducted from revenue to produce the variable standard profit contribution. Programmed or controllable fixed costs of production and physical distribution are deducted next to arrive at profit contribution. This reflects the potential impact of a segment on corporate profits, and is the target at which promotional efforts are directed. Deducting the promotion costs needed to secure the profit contribution produces the gross marketing segment earnings, which is the net profit impact of a segment.

In the short run, the programmed production and physical distribution costs are given, or at least are not affected by changes in promotional efforts. Therefore, the relevant variable which will respond to changes in promotional effort is the variable standard profit contribution. An overall measure of the return on promotional costs is computed by using the average promotional profitability index (item 8). However, it is incremental performance rather than average performance which is to be adjusted. Thus, an incremental promotional profitability index (item 11) is constructed. In this example, it analyzes the result of a change in promotional expenditure from last period to the current period. A similar index could be used on a pro forma basis to analyze alternative expenditures and direction of efforts. The end result of the analysis should be to equalize the incremental index among segments. This will mean that efforts are redirected from less profitable to more profitable segments. The techniques of contribution analysis can, of course, be used only to adjust total promotional efforts; the components of the promotional mix are assumed to be given.

The problem of lagged advertising results

Matching results with advertising expenditures may be particularly difficult for a consumers goods manufacturer, since much of the advertising to consumers is often of an indirect action variety. The results may be lagged, meaning that the ultimate sale occurs in a later period. The results may also be cumulative, meaning that current efforts combined with later efforts produce a sale in the later period. Only limited research has been conducted to measure the lag, and results are too inconclusive to provide guidance in measuring the lag for a given firm. However, some consideration of the lag phenomenon is necessary if accounting comparisons of segment contribution and promotional efforts are to be meaningful.

As a minimum, it may be feasible for a company to incorporate a lag, recognizing the delay due to the distribution channel-revenue circuit. This gives no consideration to the lag between the communication of the advertising message to a consumer and his purchase. It would consider only the time period between a consumer purchase and the impact of the purchase on the manufacturer. This can be done by correlating retail movement with factory sales. Thus, for example, if a 30-day lag were found to exist for the period December through February, advertising would be matched with January through March sales.

The accounting system can also consider the lag by choosing a proper reporting period. Generally, promotional efforts produce sales at a decreasing rate over an extended period of time. An attempt might be made to identify the period of greatest return. To identify this period, the firm might choose the period producing the greatest correlation between retail sales and advertising efforts.

Finally, when a major portion of the effects of an advertising expenditure are expected to occur beyond the reporting period, the timing of their projected effect should be specified in the budgeting process. Subsequent analyses would then distribute the costs in accord with the timing of these expected effects. This will report promotional performance in relation to promotional management's own plans. The concern is that promotional management will have confidence in the feedback process and will be willing to be measured by it.

Control of salesmen

Direct selling time is the most flexible and most easily shifted promotional activity. This feature should be capitalized upon by directing salesmen's efforts to the most profitable products and customers on a frequently recurring basis. Salesmen should be given the tools and taught to understand profitability analysis of customers and products. Motivation to understand the measurement process and to use it is accomplished by basing commissions or bonuses on the profit contribution of sales made. There is little justification for continuing to base compensation on sales revenue or gross profit when they are not the relevant measures of impact on corporate profits.

Control of salesmen's expenses is a tender topic since there is always a possibility of justifying higher expenses with greater sales. Rather than actually attempting to minimize costs and disgruntle the sales staff, two alternatives are possible:

1. The salesman should see that his time is expensive and scarce. This can be accomplished by computing the cost per sales call, or where call time varies, a cost per call hour. Since face-to-face selling time is a fraction (under 50 percent) of most salesmen's total time, the quoted cost will be high. Comparing the cost incurred in terms of call time to the profit contribution will help insure a judicious allocation of time.
2. Subtracting all the expenses, or perhaps only the controllable expenses, of a salesman in measuring the profit contribution of sales and in turn basing commissions on the resulting contribution will reward efforts to minimize costs.

COST DEFENSE UNDER THE ROBINSON-PATMAN ACT

The Robinson-Patman Act controls discriminatory pricing of similar products to different customers where the customers share a common position in the channel of distribution. This means that differing functional discounts for retailers, wholesalers, and distributors are not challenged by the act. Subsection 2(*a*) of the Robinson-Patman Act deals with price discrimination. The subsection states:

> That it shall be unlawful for any person engaged in commerce, in the course of such commerce, either directly or indirectly, to discriminate in price between different purchasers or commodities of like grade or quantity, where either or any of the purchases involved in such discrimination are in commerce, where such commodities are sold to use, for consumption or resale within the United States or any territory thereof or the District of Colum-

bia or in any insular possession or other place under the jurisdiction of the United States, and where the effect of such discrimination may be substantially to lessen competition or tend to create a monopoly, or to injure, destroy, or prevent competition with any person who either grants or knowingly receives the benefit of such discrimination, or with the customers of either of them.

Since the subsection, in effect, prohibits differing prices to competing buyers for like products, it is frequently interpreted as prohibiting quantity discounts. The act allows five types of defenses:

1. The action was not in interstate commerce.
2. The pricing practices do not tend to have a substantially undesirable effect on or among competitors.
3. The action involves the nonrepetitive sales of distress merchandise.
4. The action is the result of a good faith effort to meet competition. This applies only to a particular act and not to a pricing system.
5. The cost defense proviso states:

   Provided: That nothing herein contained shall prevent differentials which make only due allowance for differences in the cost of manufacture, sale, or delivery resulting from the differing methods or quantities in which such commodities are to such purchases sold or delivered.

   The burden of proof under the cost defense proviso is on the accused.

The Federal Trade Commission (FTC) has not offered much guidance to a firm constructing a cost defense. This is because many price discrimination cases are resolved prior to the public hearing stage, and thus the defense is not of public record. Further, where a case is of public record the FTC refuses to accord prior cases the status of precedent, but rather has decided each case on its own merit.

A firm desiring to charge different prices to competing buyers should be prepared to demonstrate that the prices are cost justifiable. The FTC is more likely to accept a study made in advance of setting prices than a study made after the alleged violation. Very likely a hearing will be avoided and the prices will not be challenged where an adequate cost study exists. Firms which have not had adequate cost documentation have often chosen to avoid a formal hearing by agreeing to a consent order and ending their existing pricing. They have, however, been able to design a new plan of price differences based on a cost study. The FTC has given approval to such cost-justified cost differentials as a part of the consent procedure.

Past cases of record contain some useful help to firms making a cost defense in that the following general principles exist:

1. Generally, the study must focus on specific products. A grouping of products has been accepted only where the seller has little control over the mix of products purchased, as would be true for replacement parts.
2. Technically, the FTC can require cost justification by individual customer; however, grouping of customers is allowed. Where grouping does occur, the firm may have to demonstrate that the set of customers is homogeneous. It also appears that the study must be designed to allow the calculation of costs of serving individual customers if the FTC desires to do so.
3. Cost studies include only physical distribution and promotional cost differences since similar products are involved.
4. Most cost defenses have been in the nature of full cost allocations, which include an allocation of fixed costs. Fixed costs, when included, must be spread over all customers receiving the benefit. A firm may not exclude allocation of a cost to a customer on the basis that the customer does not directly affect the cost if the customer in any way benefits from the cost. However, a fixed cost may be excluded entirely from consideration of all customers. A firm making such an omission need only show that including the costs would not lessen the cost justification.
5. The allocation of costs as a percent of sales was often used for promotional costs. This is termed "bootstrapping" by the FTC and is not usually accepted.
6. In attempting to cost justify prices by demonstrating a difference in selling costs, a firm runs the risk of admitting violations of other sections of the Robinson-Patman Act:

    a. Differences in service provided may be viewed as "indirect price discrimination," since section 2(*e*) prohibits services which are not available to all purchasers on "proportionally equal terms."

b. Section 2(a) prohibits allowances or discounts in lieu of services except where the services are actually performed by the buyer. Thus, for example, an allowance for advertising is permitted where the purchaser does provide for the service, but an allowance based on a lower commission cost is not allowed since the purchaser would not provide a service in exchange. This renders differential commission rates to customers useless as a cost justification.

Constructing cost justification

Where a firm desires to use volume or quantity discounts, it should be prepared to cost justify its price policy. Analysis of cost justification should be viewed as defining the available range of defensible price differences. The price differences actually used are based on an economic consideration of the response of demand to price; however, the differences must fall within the range of justification. This suggests that a cost justification study should afford the maximum possible cost differences.

The modular data base typically attaches only variable costs and specific fixed costs to separate customers. This will offer some cost differentials, but not the maximum available. It is suggested that for functional physical distribution costs, all fixed costs of the function be allocated to segments by using the factors of variability already in use for variable costs. This will serve to increase differences in costs between customers receiving differing services.

Allocation of promotional costs to customers will require a special study which will basically allocate common costs to benefiting customers. Since the choice of an allocation method is at best arbitrary, the method chosen should be based on its defensibility and its lack of conflict with other subsections of the Robinson-Patman Act. The following guidelines are offered for personal selling costs:

1. For each salesman, a well documented study must be made of the average time spent per call for each customer discount classification.

2. The salary, commission, and expenses of each salesman should be provided. Thus, the average cost per call per salesman must be used.

3. The number of calls made to each class of customer by each salesman must be recorded. A customer cost is equal to the number of calls times the average cost per call in the territory.

4. Commissions can be charged directly or can be considered salary and allocated as such depending on the facts of the case. The commissions cannot, however, involve differential rates.

5. Sales managers and supervisors may use their own estimates to divide their time among supervision and administration of territories and direct selling. The time spent in direct selling is handled as it is for salesmen. However, the time spent in supervision tends to be allocated in proportion to the other personal selling costs assigned to the customer classifications.

6. Occupancy costs tend to be allocated on the same basis as the salaries of those occupying the space.

Media advertising has been allocated quite simply in cases of record. Where a customer class buys unbranded or privately branded merchandise, it is not charged for advertising. Other customers tend to receive an allocation according to sales made to them. Though this is a form of "bootstrapping," it has not been objected to. Expenditures for cooperative advertising cannot be allocated unless offered to all customers on proportionally equal terms. Remaining promotional costs may be specifically attached—as for example, cents-off packages and coupons costs— or may be allocated where in common in a manner similar to media costs.

29

Cost accounting for financial enterprises

*Michael J. Coie**

A SPECIAL CASE OF COST ACCOUNTING

Cost accounting for financial institutions (commercial banks, mutual savings banks, savings and loan associations, and credit unions) represents a special case in the theory and practice of cost accounting. It is special in the sense that much of the effort, literature, and, at times, controversy surrounding the value and techniques of cost accounting has little, if any, relevance to financial institutions. Briefly stated, cost accounting is usually addressed in terms of its role in relation to the needs of an organization for accounting information for reporting to outside third parties, sometimes called fiduciary or regulatory reporting, and to support management's needs, often called management or internal accounting requirements. Most effort in cost accounting to support external reporting focuses on inventory valuation. Gordon Shillinglaw says, for example,

> Cost accounting's value to financial (external) reporting is in providing the data used to distinguish between those factory costs that are to be charged against current revenues as expenses, and those that are to be assigned to the company produced goods and services in the end of period inventories.[1]

* Touche Ross & Co.

[1] Gordon Shillinglaw, *Cost Accounting: Analysis and Control,* 3rd ed. (Homewood, Ill.: Richard D. Irwin, Inc., 1972), p. 12.

The theory and mechanics of cost accounting for inventory valuation do not affect financial institutions, because, with minor exceptions, financial institutions do not have inventories comparable to manufacturing, distribution, or most other industries.

Cost accounting within financial institutions can focus on satisfying management needs for information without concern for the requirement for product costing for inventory valuation and the associated determination of income. While removing inventory valuation and income determination from the requirements of cost accounting for financial institutions avoids some complexities, it also creates some unique requirements in the design and use of costing systems.

REQUIREMENTS FOR MANAGEMENT INFORMATION

To help provide a perspective of the need for cost accounting in financial institutions, it is useful to understand some fundamental changes which are occurring in this industry. From approximately World War II until the early 1960s, management of financial institutions faced a relatively predictable environment with slowly increasing interest rates, stable deposit sources, and steadily increasing demand for credit.

Up until the 1960s, management was primarily concerned with managing the assets of the institutions to maximize income with little or no need for cost information. The conventional wisdom was that any increase in yields would result in increased profits, because margins (price or income minus cost) were constant, ignoring differences in risk. This belief was probably more right than wrong at the time, because management could adjust to gradually increasing interest rates, and the second major cost element, labor, was managed through controlling wages at a relatively low rate and by utilizing a large clerical force which was readily available. However, during the 1970s and continuing today management's need for information has expanded dramatically.

First, the record growth in financial institutions, measured by assets, has been phenomenal. Using commercial banks as an example, growth in financial institutions since 1963 can be seen from Table 1.

TABLE 1
Principal assets and liabilities for all commercial banks

		Assets Billions of dollars		
		1963	1973	Compound growth
Loans		$156	$495	12.2%
Securities..........................		98	189	6.8
All other assets.....................		59	151	9.8
Total Assets.....................		$313	$835	10.3%
	Liabilities and Capital			
Demand deposits.....................		$164	$310	6.6%
Time deposits.......................		112	372	12.8
Other liabilities		11	95	24.1
Capital		26	58	8.4
Total Liabilities and Capital		$313	$835	10.3%

Source: Federal Reserve Bulletin.

While growth of this magnitude creates many new management requirements by itself, several fundamental changes have also occurred during this period of growth. Funds available to support the growth in loans (12 percent) did not come from the system's traditional inexpensive source of funds, demand deposits, which grew only about 6.5 percent. Obviously, the funds came from time deposits (13 percent growth) and other liabilities (24 percent growth), which include certificates of deposit, Fed Funds purchased, debentures, and other "new" sources of funds, each with a different cost and availability. Savings banks, savings and loan associations, and credit unions all experienced a similar change in the availability and cost of their deposits as the traditional "passbook" accounts became one, rather than the only, source of funds.

The second fundamental change which has occurred in the financial industry, and in turn has changed management's need for information, is the volatility of interest rates and the interest rate structure itself. As shown in Exhibit 1, movements of 276 basis points in commercial loan rates between 1970 and 1972, and then an opposite movement of 472 basis points between 1972 and 1974, are anything but a steady, predictable change in interest rates. Three-month Treasury bills also show a similar pattern of volatility. During the period since 1960, the traditional interest rate structure of long-term rates exceeding short-term

EXHIBIT 1
Average annual rates

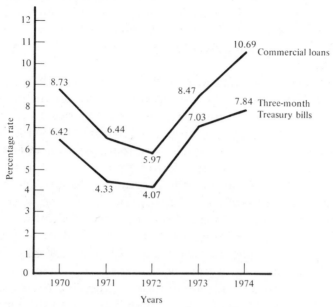

Source: Federal Reserve Bulletin.

rates was often reversed, most noticeably in 1966, 1969, 1973, and 1974. This change in rate structure had dramatic effects on financial institutions, particularly savings banks and savings and loan associations, which normally have the majority of their loans in long-term real estate mortgages.

The third major change impacting management's information needs arose through an explosion of products (loan types and services), markets, and business ventures in response to regulatory changes and perceived customer needs. Subsidiaries formed by commercial banks after passage of the Bank Holding Company Act of 1969 represented new, although related, businesses to manage. Variable rate mortgages, limited consumer lending, and operations under service corporations all resulted in new management requirements for savings banks and savings and loan associations. Negotiable orders of withdrawal, electronic funds transfer systems, and Eurocurrency borrowings are further examples of new products and sources of funds.

Finally, management of financial institutions faces an escalation of costs other than interest. Financial institutions have found themselves caught in the general inflationary push of salary costs, and at the same time have added higher priced middle management to deal with the increasingly complex issues facing the institutions. Other nonsalary costs have also become material cost elements.

These changes—dramatic growth; fundamental changes in the sources, stability and cost of funds; diversification and proliferation of service and product offering; and the rapid increase in noninterest costs—have created a need for new management information. In financial institutions, management needs information to assist in the evaluation of product and business line profitability. Management needs information to support business planning and cost control. In short, management of financial institutions needs the information of a cost accounting system.

An important contribution of cost accounting for financial institutions is providing a conceptual basis for cost classification to aid the various requirements of management. As previously discussed, conventions and techniques for costing to support the periodic determination of cost of goods sold and ending inventories is not an issue in financial institutions. Therefore, management's needs for information to support pricing and profitability analysis, cost control, and planning are the three major requirements of cost accounting in financial institutions.

COST FOR PRICING AND PROFITABILITY ANALYSIS

The central requirement in costing for pricing and profitability analysis is the identification of business line or service costs in relation to changes in volume or activity. While management needs to know the current financial status of various service offerings, they are usually as concerned with what the results will be if changes are made, particularly with respect to increases or decreases in volume or activity. Developing a costing framework for such analysis can be accomplished through a two-step process:

1. Isolating costs which can be attributed to each business line or service from costs which cannot be directly attributed to them.

2. Categorizing costs which are identifiable with business lines or services into their variability with respect to changes in volume or activity.

Isolating product-specific costs from all other costs is usually fairly straightforward. These costs may be thought of as being incurred to support the financial institution itself rather than to support a particular business line or service offering. Examples of such costs are the salaries of the Chairman of the Board and the President, institutional advertising, and public relations.

Classification of product-specific costs in relation to volume or activity changes involves various techniques to isolate the degree of variability of these costs. For example, one technique is to use statistical regression analysis with historical costs and volume or activity levels. Exhibit 2 shows the relationship between dollars paid to proof operators and the volume of checks processed on one day each month during a six-month period during which there were no equipment changes or salary increases, which would distort the data. The dots on Exhibit 2 represent a scatter chart of the individual cost observations. Each point represents the cost of proof department operators for a day and the checks that were processed on one day during that month. The line shown was simply positioned by eye to help identify any abnormal situations. In practice some mathematical

EXHIBIT 2

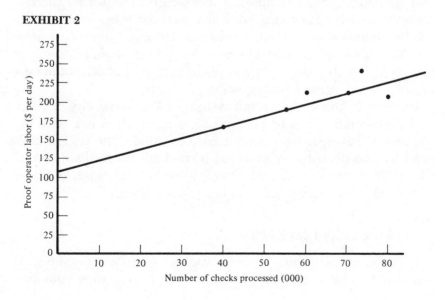

technique, such as the method of least squares, is used to position this line and develop the formula to express the relationship between the cost element and volume.

Another technique for establishing the degree of cost variability for business line costs is through "product" analysis. In this case, factors for each labor and nonlabor cost of a business line "product" are developed through industrial engineering standards, judgmental evaluations, or predetermined factors. (Development and use of standards are discussed later.) The end item of "product" analysis is usually a narrative or flow-chart description of each business line in terms of the elements of cost associated with it.

A useful division in classifying product-specific costs which do not vary directly with volume changes is to separate those costs which represent a practical capacity to serve from those costs which are incurred because of a specific management decision. *Capacity costs,* often called commitment or standby costs, represent costs which will not change over some wide range of volume or activity, and include elements such as space costs, basic equipment costs, and costs of product line supervisors or officers. *Decision costs,* often called programmed costs, are incurred in response to a decision rather than to a change in volume or activity. A product line research project, promotion, and advertising are examples of these costs. The terms *specific standby and programmed costs* are used for those costs which can be identified with a business line or service. *General standby and programmed costs* are the terms used to indicate costs which do not vary with changes in volume or activity but cannot meaningfully be identified with specific products.

Implicit in this classification system of the variability of costs and their relationship to business lines or services is a time dimension. That is, some relevant period, usually the period covered by the decision, is assumed in making these distinctions. The time dimension of cost classification is important, because significant changes can and do occur over time.

CONTRIBUTION CONCEPT

Classifying costs into variable, specific standby, specific programmed, general standby, and general programmed provides a basis for analyzing pricing and profitability issues. While business line or service profitability implies product line revenue less product line cost, the interpretation of cost may range from incremental cost to what is traditionally referred to as full cost. To meet varying needs, the suggested cost classification system provides a means for the measurement of business line profitability at various levels within this range. Exhibit 3 represents the financial results of an escrow business line of a savings and loan association. Three different calculations of profitability can be made with costs classified as shown.

First, revenue less directly variable costs shows that, on a *marginal cost* basis, this product line has a contribution margin of $65,000 or 23.6 percent; thus:

$$\$275,000 - \$210,000 \div \$275,000 = 23.6\%.$$

This rate and amount are often useful in analyzing short-term alternatives.

The second level of profitability calculation is reached by the further deduction of the escrow specific standby and programmed costs—those that do not vary with volume or activity but are specifically identifiable with the individual business line. This measure of profitability is appropriate in analyzing the contribution of a product line to the total institution, in this case at a rate of 7.5 percent:

$$\$275,000 - \$254,500 \div \$275,000 = 7.5\%.$$

The final level of profitability is measured after provision for general standby and programmed costs which do not vary with volume and cannot be directly identified with a specific business

EXHIBIT 3
Anytown Savings and Loan Association, escrow business line

Fee income		$275,000	
Variable costs			
Labor	$175,000		
Other	35,000		
Specific standby	11,500		
Specific programmed	33,000	254,500	
Contribution			$20,500
General standby	$ 15,000		
General programmed	8,000	$ 23,000	
Product line income (loss)			<$ 2,500>

line. This *full cost* measure is useful in evaluating long-term strategies. The example in Exhibit 3 shows that the business line is not profitable according to this measure.

This cost classification system also allows for the calculation of "break-even" values, which is often useful in analyzing business line profitability. Break-even in the escrow example is approximately $286,000 under the full cost analysis and approximately $188,600 under the incremental cost analysis, as shown in Exhibit 4.

EXHIBIT 4
Break-even analysis

Fee income		100%		
Variable costs as a percentage of fee income		76.4%		
Contribution margin ratio		23.6%		
Specific standby and programmed costs	÷	Contribution margin ratio	=	Incremental break-even
$44,500	÷	23.6%	=	$188,559
Specific and general standby and programmed costs	÷	Contribution margin ratio	=	Full cost break-even
$67,500	÷	23.6%	=	$286,017

In addition, by separating programmed costs from standby costs, the options available for impacting costs which do not vary with volume are more readily apparent to management.

STANDARDS

Standards are used in cost accounting systems for financial institutions to support business line profitability analysis and as a tool in operating cost control. It is important to note that standards (standard costs) are not used in the accounting systems of financial institutions in a manner comparable to other industries. Recording of costs at standard and booking variances from them into the accounting system is not appropriate, because accounting records are maintained by so-called natural classification, such as salaries, interest on deposits, and occupancy, not by inventory or activity classification.

STANDARDS FOR BUSINESS LINE
PROFITABILITY ANALYSIS

It is not economically practical to attempt to record actual costs by business line in most financial institutions. For example, it is often the case that a single person or classification of people will work on several different business lines during a day, week, or month, and often in increments of only a few minutes each time. While it is theoretically possible to track labor time through a labor distribution system to account for these small increments of time, it is impractical to do so because of the time and expense involved. Nonlabor variable costs present similar difficulties.

In addition to mechanical and cost problems associated with computing "actual" business line costs directly, "actual" costs may not be the most useful measure of business line costs. This seemingly inconsistent situation arises because during any reporting period it is possible, perhaps likely, that there are aberrations in actual costs incurred arising from unusual labor inefficiencies or efficiencies, equipment malfunctions, special purchasing opportunities, or a host of other similar conditions. The ability to analyze business line costs as previously discussed using the escrow example requires cost data that is not distorted by unusual situations. Properly developed standard costs provide this information.

Developing standards for business line planning can be accomplished in a variety of ways, ranging from detailed work measurement and analysis to judgmental standards developed through the collective experiences of officers and employees of the institution. While cost and effort vary widely among alternative approaches, experience seems to indicate that, regardless of the method used to originally establish standards, adequate accuracy can be accomplished by instituting a defined plan of standards maintenance. The important steps are to collect actual results for comparison with standards, and to calculate variances. These variances can be analyzed to establish whether the standards should be modified, or whether the operations can be improved or actual costs incurred can be reduced. By establishing a strong standards maintenance program, it is possible to develop standards without having to undertake a prohibitively expensive or time-consuming project, and without sacrificing the usefulness or accuracy of the standards.

While standards are the single most important element in developing the ability to report on business line or service profitability, other tasks are required to actually have this capability.

EXHIBIT 5

BUSINESS LINE STANDARD COST DEVELOPMENT OPERATIONS WRITE-UP								

Division _____ Function: _____

Section _____   Operation No. _____

Date _____   Operation: _____

Sheet ___ of ___ Sheet(s)

	Operation / Transport / Inspection / Delay / Storage	Distance in Feet	Quantity	Time	ANALYSIS WHY? What?	Where?	When?	Who?	How?
—1	O⇨□D▽								
—2	O⇨□D▽								
—3	O⇨□D▽								
—4	O⇨□D▽								
—5	O⇨□D▽								
—6	O⇨□D▽								
—7	O⇨□D▽								
—8	O⇨□D▽								
—9	O⇨□D▽								
—10	O⇨□D▽								
—11	O⇨□D▽								
—12	O⇨□D▽								
—13	O⇨□D▽								
—14	O⇨□D▽								
—15	O⇨□D▽								
—16	O⇨□D▽								
—17	O⇨□D▽								
—18	O⇨□D▽								
—19	O⇨□D▽								
—20	O⇨□D▽								

Operator: _____ Supervisor: _____ Analyst: _____

Remarks:

The following is a step-by-step technique for establishing business line standards for financial institutions:

1. Define the functional activities which must be performed in processing a business line transaction throughout its life.
2. Define the detailed operations performed in each function and determine the frequency of occurrence. Exhibit 5 is a sample form which can be used to document the operations through either analysis or judgment.
3. Determine the standard time of each operation using work measurement techniques, predetermined standards, work sampling, or some other technique.
4. Determine the standard variable costs other than labor for each operation through analysis, judgment, or a combination of both.
5. Determine the standard dollars per time unit using wage and/or salary analysis.
6. Extend standard time and standard dollars and add to other variable costs to determine the standard cost per operation.
7. Determine those control factors which will be used to determine the frequency of occurrence of each function.
8. Extend the standard cost per operation and the frequency of operation per function, and summarize them to determine the standard cost per function.
9. Measure (or plan) the frequency of control factors during a period.
10. Determine the frequency of functions.
11. Extend the standard cost of the functions and the frequency of functions to determine the standard cost per business line.

Exhibit 6 shows these steps as a schematic.

Exhibit 7 is an example of a standard cost buildup for a business line, using this step-by-step technique. The business line is Direct Automobile Installment Consumer Loans. The following paragraph describes the meaning and use of the various elements of this example, and references at what point the elements are developed according to the step-by-step technique already described.

In Exhibit 7, each of the activities listed under the "items" column refers to the functional activities shown as Step 1 of

784

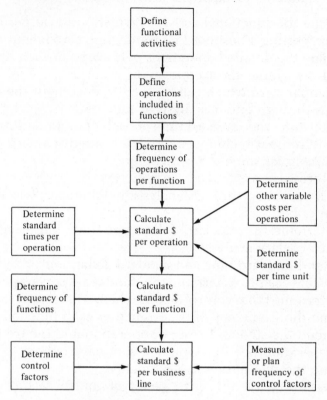

the technique listing. The items under "Operation Standard Dollars" include the variable labor and nonlabor costs at standard developed during Steps 3, 4, and 5 and calculated as Step 6. The values shown under the column "Operation Frequency" are developed as Step 7. These factors are used to express the number of times per function in relation to the control factor, which is used as the count point. For example, the frequency of occurrence of the function "preliminary screening" is shown as 1.15 times in relation to the control factor "open account," meaning that for each opened account, the standard is for 1.15 applications to have been screened. The column "Function Standard Dollars" is the sum of the products of the individual standard dollars and the operational frequency factors for all

EXHIBIT 7
Business line standard costs, example of buildup: Direct automobile installment consumer loans

Items	Operation standard (dollars)	Operation frequency	Function standard (dollars)	Function frequency	Business line standard (dollars)
Preliminary screening	$0.66910	1.15			
Review application	0.14220	1.15			
Credit check	0.85320	1.10			
Credit review	0.71100	1.10			
Closing	0.70610	1.00			
Set up	1.34949	1.00			
Prepare coupon book	0.97675	0.90			
Send envelopes	0.33316	0.85			
Open account			$5.87144	1.00	
# opened (control factor)					$5.87144
Payments	$0.11850	1.00			
Solicitations	0.21470	0.05			
Inquiry	0.07110	0.16			
Payoff inquiry	0.23700	0.083			
Followup	0.17850	0.083			
Account maintenance			$0.17511	1.00	
Accounts outstanding (control factor)					0.17511
Delinquents	$1.44860	0.02			
Collection	2.84400	0.005			
Followup	0.09480	0.02			
Credit administration			$0.04509	1.00	
Accounts outstanding (control factor)					0.04509
Close file	$0.64140	1.00			
Review credit	0.14220	1.00			
Close accounts			$0.78360	1.00	
# closed (control factor)					0.78360
Solicitation	$0.19100	1.00			
Inquiries	0.07110	0.083			
Followup			$0.19690	1.00	
# closed (control factor)					0.19690
Business line standard					$7.07214

steps within each functional control point, shown as part of Step 11. The column "Function Frequency" is developed during Step 10 and identifies the number of times each function occurs during one cycle of the business line standard. The final column is the summation of Function Standards and represents the standard variable cost of the business line, shown as Step 11 in the list of techniques for developing the standard costs.

Not shown is the treatment of standby and programmed costs, both specific and general. These costs are not converted to a standard based on per unit activity, because they are not directly inpacted by activity or volume changes over the relevant time frame. Evaluating contribution margin at different levels of volume or activity, as previously discussed, is the primary thrust of business line or service profitability analysis, which means that standby and programmed costs should not be unitized. Remember, variable costs are fixed per unit, and standard and programmed costs are variable per unit.

STANDARDS FOR COST CONTROL

The second major use of standards within cost accounting systems for financial institutions is to support operating cost control. While unusual or abnormal cost situations are to be compen-

EXHIBIT 8
Performance report, automobile installment loan department (labor analysis)

Cost incurred:
Variable:

Labor—hours 640	$3,040		
Supplies & other—units 55	200		
Total variable		$3,240	
Specific standby	300		
Specific programmed	100		
Total specific standby and programmed		$400	
General standby	250		
General programmed	300		
Total general standby and programmed		$550	

Labor Performance:

Control factor:	Activity	Hours earned	Dollars earned
Accounts opened	50	56.7	$ 269
Accounts outstanding	5,000	232.3	1,103
Accounts closed	40	8.3	39
		297.3	1,411
Personal time		120.0	570
Nonstandard time		60.0	285
Total time accounted for		477.3	$2,266
Percentage of time at standard	87.4%		
Percentage performance	74.6%		
Percentage efficiency	64.6%		

sated for in business-line profitability analysis, these situations are to be highlighted for cost control. Whether standards are developed as "ideal," "practical," "attainable," or "expected," the critical element is to capture and report variances—both favorable and unfavorable—to the various organizational units responsible for cost management.

The standards for cost control utilize the same values as developed for the business line analysis already discussed. That is, each of the factors already developed should be grouped into the responsibility centers where the costs are being incurred. Remaining tasks not previously covered by business line standards can be developed in the same manner as previously discussed.

Exhibit 8 is a sample report for cost control using the automobile installment loan department as an example. The top section presents actual incurred costs. The lower section shows the labor performance factors for the reporting period. Nonlabor analysis is described later. The work performed (units of control factors) is recorded through a departmental statistics report.

While only three control factor activities are reported, the calculation of earned hours is actually performed as follows by using the five functional standards shown in Exhibit 7:

Control factor	Activity	Hours earned
Accounts opened	50	56.7
Accounts outstanding		
Maintenance	5,000	184.7
Credit administration	5,000	47.6
Accounts closed		
Close accounts	40	6.6
Follow-up	40	1.7

In this example, the conversion of the standards expressed in dollar terms into standards expressed in hours is based on a standard cost per labor hour of $4.75. At this standard dollar rate, the standard of $0.17511 per account outstanding for maintenance translates into 2.2 minutes per account; thus:

$$(\$0.17511 \div \$0.079 \text{ cost/minute} = 2.2 \text{ minutes}).$$

In this example, nonlabor costs of $0.50 are included in the functional standard for accounts opened and are discussed later.

In addition to earned time for standard work, an allowance is made for so-called personal time to reflect lunch period and breaks given to each employee. "Nonstandard" time is charged whenever time is spent on functions or tasks which are outside of the work standards system.

The information on the lower portion of the report, percentage of time at standard, percentage performance, and percentage efficiency, are three measures of performance which are often used in responsibility center reporting within financial institutions.

Percentage of time at standard is the ratio of earned hours less nonstandard time to all other earned hours; thus:

$$(417.3 \div 477.3 = 87.4\%)$$

and is a measure of the degree to which each responsibility center's activity is controlled by standards. Such a measure is useful, because nonstandard time is normal in most financial institution responsibility centers due to the practical limitations of establishing and maintaining standards for 100 percent of the tasks and functions performed in each responsibility center. A ratio of 85 percent or more of a responsibility center's time covered by standard is normally considered acceptable for control purposes.

Percentage performance is total "earned" time, including nonstandard and personal time, in relation to hours paid; thus:

$$(477.3 \div 640 = 74.6\%).$$

This is considered to be gross measure of responsibility center productivity in terms of time "worked" in relation to time paid.

Percentage efficiency is hours earned on standard tasks as a percentage of total hours paid less nonstandard time and personal time

$$(297.3 \div 460 = 64.6\%).$$

This measure is intended to show the effectiveness of work on tasks covered by standards.

A word of caution is required in dealing with "normal" efficiency and performance ratios and the meaning and use of standards for responsibility center reporting. Most labor operations in financial institutions do not involve completely interchangeable resources and work tasks which can be turned on and off like a faucet. There is a high degree of salaried labor in financial institutions, which means that minor or normal fluctuations in volume or activity are not met with immediate hiring or firing of workers. Therefore, many managers use responsibility center reporting against standard to track changes over time rather than as absolute measures of good or bad performance for any single reporting period. In addition, the existence of standards does aid in staff planning, and of course is critical for business line profitability analysis, as previously discussed.

NONLABOR COSTS

Nonlabor variable costs can best be controlled through flexible budgets. Again, the values developed for business line profitability analysis should be used and grouped by responsibility center for management control. Continuing the same example of the automobile installment loan department, Exhibit 8, the standard for nonlabor variable costs is $0.50 per new account, which includes supplies, forms, postage, and the like. This standard cost is included in the functional standard cost of $5.87144 and was established during Step 4 in the business line step-by-step technique outline. (Earned labor hours already discussed are based on the labor portion of the functional cost, $5.37144.) Nonlabor costs are actually included in five of the eight items under opening an account, but are shown as a single cost for ease of presentation.

As shown in Exhibit 9, the budget for these costs was $250 at the actual volume of 50 new accounts opened, established

EXHIBIT 9
Performance report, automobile installment loan department (nonlabor analysis)

	Amount incurred	Amount earned	Difference
Supplies and other	$200	$250	$50 Good
Analysis of variance			
Spending variance	$0.136/unit × 55 units =		75 Good
Volume variance	$0.50 × 5 units =		25 Bad
			$50 Good
Specific standby and programmed		No variance	
General standby and programmed		No variance	

through the responsibility center's variable budgeting system for nonlabor costs. The two-level variance analysis shown in the sample report indicates a favorable spending variance of $75 resulting from an actual cost of $0.364 per unit rather than the standard of $0.50 per unit for the 55 units consumed. The volume variance is an unfavorable $25 arising from the use of 5 units more than standard at the standard cost of $0.50 per unit. Where warranted by the magnitude of the nonlabor costs or shared responsibilities, calculation of the joint spending and volume variance separately may be appropriate.

Cost control for standby and programmed costs does not involve flexible budgets, because again these costs vary as a result of management decision, not because of changes in activity or volume. Variances, which are not shown in this example, arise whenever there is a difference between the actual costs incurred and the final budget.

FITTING THE PIECES TOGETHER

The final element of an effective cost accounting system for financial institutions is a management reporting system to tie together the various concepts and control elements into an effective reporting system for the total institution. The following describes such a system, using a commercial bank as an example of financial institutions. Other financial institutions will have somewhat different elements within their systems, but the concepts are the same.

A CONCEPTUAL FRAMEWORK

A conceptual framework for integrating cost accounting concepts and systems into an overall reporting and planning tool for management can be built around the three basic functions performed by a commercial bank.

First, a bank *uses money* for investments. Uses include cash, the investment portfolio, real estate loans, installment loans, Federal Funds sold, and other items. To a great extent uses represent the asset side of the balance sheet.

The second basic function of a commercial bank is *performing services* for which it may or may not be reimbursed. Examples of services are trust operations, correspondent bank services, safe deposit boxes, cash management services, and others.

EXHIBIT 10
Schematic of conceptual framework for reporting with a cost accounting system

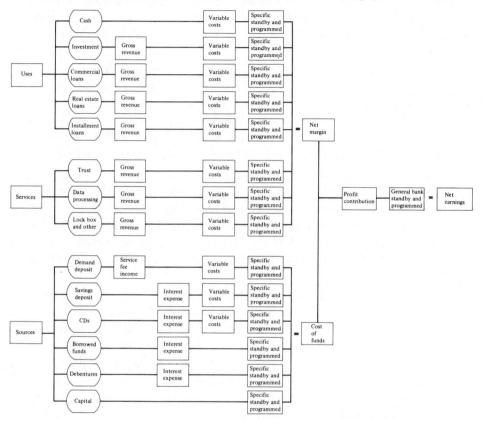

Third, a bank *obtains money* from depositors. Sources include demand deposits, time deposits, Federal Funds purchased, borrowed funds, and capital and stockholders equity.

Within these three functions, the cost concepts already discussed provide a structure for information which is shown schematically in Exhibit 10.

USING THE FRAMEWORK FOR DECISION MAKING

The value of this conceptual structure is that it provides a practical framework for linking the information available in the cost accounting system with management's need to deal with business options and strategies. Critical interrelationships can be evaluated within the framework and the effect on net margins and cost of funds can be quantified. For example, consider how this structure can be used to assist in evaluating the possible impact of a management problem, such as "What happens if new certificates of deposit are issued?" First, this structure shows that additional interest expense and variable costs will be incurred. Specific standby and programmed costs will not necessarily change. Thus the institution's cost of funds will be affected through the issuance of new CDs, and the cost system can quantify the specific amounts.

Other sources of funds might be impacted by the new CD issue. Existing customers who purchase CDs may tend to reduce demand and savings deposits. Rates paid for other sources of funds might also be affected. A new net cost of funds can be estimated which represents the composite net effect of the new CD issue.

The conceptual framework shows that the next area for analysis is to determine alternative uses of funds. Gross revenues and variable costs will be affected throughout the whole funds use structure for each alternative considered. Alternative uses should include all appropriate legal and regulatory constraints, as well as the factors usually considered in asset management, such as risk, market potential, liquidity policies, and organizational profitability objectives.

The final analysis encouraged within this conceptual framework is to determine the change in profit contribution and net earnings resulting from the analysis of the new cost of funds, and the revised net margin of uses and services. Note that within this conceptual framework, specific uses of funds are not allocated to specific sources. This means that the cost of a specific source of funds is not assigned to a specific use. It can be argued that such an allocation might be useful in some cases, for example in a matched foreign exchange purchase and sale, but these appear to be an exception. Normally, sources of funds are not earmarked to uses in practice.

Many enhancements can be made to this simplified conceptual framework. Refinements can be made in the classifications of sources and uses of funds and types of individual services. Specific definitions can be made of the interrelationships among sources, uses, and services. Many elements of this structure can be automated, resulting in an ability to expand the breadth of the structure. However, the fundamental value of the structure will remain as the tool to integrate the information available through the institution's cost accounting system with the needs of management to view the institution as a total entity.

CONCLUSION

Cost accounting in financial institutions represents a special case in the general body of knowledge and practice of cost accounting. The substantial knowledge and experience which support the application of cost accounting for inventory valuation and periodic determination of income does not apply to financial institutions, because they do not have inventories in the traditional sense. While this situation simplifies the requirements for cost accounting in financial institutions in some ways, the absence of a "natural" production or distribution system complicates the design and operation of cost accounting systems for this industry.

Financial institutions have experienced dramatic changes in the recent past and fundamental changes are continuing to occur. Management of financial institutions has a need for the information which can be supplied by cost accounting systems to support business line or service profitability analysis, and operational planning and cost control. In addition, the framework provided by cost accounting systems in terms of defining and capturing costs to support decision making offers a vehicle for management to analyze the complex business line and service interrelationships which exist in financial institutions.

30

Cost accounting and analysis in state and local governments

Robert J. Freeman*
Harold H. Hensold, Jr.†
William W. Holder‡

INTRODUCTION

Cost accounting and analysis have only recently become widely recognized as being at least as important in government as in private industry. Cost accounting techniques have been used for many years in selected governmental activities, such as in utilities and other business type activities. But many governmental activities are conducted and evaluated without the benefit of substantial cost accounting, analysis, or understanding.

While many "business-type" or "proprietary" activities of governments (for example, utilities) are accounted for in a manner paralleling that of similar private business enterprises, this is not true of the "general government" accounting of state and local governments. General government activities (for example, administration, police and fire protection, and education) typically are financed at least partially by taxes or other financial resources restricted for specified purposes, and are controlled through the annual budgetary (appropriations) process. Therefore, general government activities are accounted for through

* The University of Alabama.
† Arthur Young & Company.
‡ Texas Tech University.

a series of distinct *fund* accounting entities in order to control and demonstrate compliance with the numerous legal and budgetary provisions within which governments must function. Since legal restrictions and budgets typically are couched in terms of financial resource inflows or sources ("revenues") and outflows or uses ("expenditures"), financial accounting data routinely assembled for general government activities reflect the beginning balances, sources, uses, and ending balances of the financial resources of each fund. Such data is similar to that presented in the Statement of Changes in Financial Position of business enterprises (sources, uses, and balances of working capital), and is often referred to as "fund flow" information.

Government accounting systems must produce information pertaining to financial resource flows and status, and legal compliance, of each general government fund. Such information is mandatory, not optional, since the most fundamental responsibilities of the governmental accountant are to assure and demonstrate compliance with legal and administrative provisions with respect to the manner in which government financial resources may be secured and expended, and to report properly the fund balances available at year end.

If efficient and effective use is to be made of the limited tax dollars available to finance the increasing types and levels of services demanded by citizens, however, financial accounting data must be recognized as insufficient for management and evaluation purposes. Indeed, it may soon be viewed as necessary, but not sufficient, for external financial reporting purposes.

New York City, for example, though the most publicized, is certainly not the only city in the United States facing problems in applying the proceeds of an eroding tax base and decreasing federal funds to cover both the multiplicity of existing activities and programs and new ones demanded by citizens. Many states face similar problems. Understandable, timely, and relevant planning and performance evaluation information is needed so that governmental managers and officials, as well as citizens, can judge the results of various programs and the efficiency and economy with which operations are conducted. The initial step in any such cost/benefit analysis is *cost accounting* and/or *cost finding.*

Conceptually, the purpose of governmental cost accounting

does not differ substantially from that in profit-seeking organizations. In both, the tools of cost accounting and analysis are used to evaluate the allocation of scarce resources by attempting to relate the total or incremental costs (direct and indirect, fixed or variable) of an operation, function, or program to the activity being conducted. This is done in four steps:

1. *Cost identification,* in which specific costs that can be traced to the project are accumulated in the accounts and isolated.
2. *Activity identification,* in which some meaningful measure or indicator of productivity is developed for the project.
3. Cost and activity *data accumulation* through the accounting system and related records.
4. *Evaluation* of the relationship existing between the inputs and outputs thus isolated.

This chapter discusses and illustrates several areas within government where the application of cost accounting and analysis techniques may be beneficial, with emphasis on those that traditionally have *not* been subjected to such accounting and analysis techniques. More specifically, this chapter discusses the unique aspects of contemporary governmental financial accounting that affect governmental cost accounting and cost finding, how available data must in some instances be converted from one measurement basis (expenditures) to another measurement basis (costs or expenses), and how the total cost incurred by an organization or for an activity can be computed. By relating this cost, where practicable, to the quantity of goods produced or services rendered, a productivity measure that establishes a quantitative link between the expenditure (input) of financial resources, their conversion into productive resources and/or goods and services, and the resultant output of goods and services can be constructed. This allows comparisons between different public and private means of providing goods and services. More importantly, perhaps, it helps a governmental organization avoid evaluating a program based on urgency or expediency alone, while relegating cost aspects to a low level of significance. These techniques also make it possible to determine total costs incurred for operations and programs without regard to either funding source or operating unit. Cost information can also be employed in such managerial planning and evaluative techniques as zero base budgeting, performance budgeting, and planning, programming, and budgeting systems.

This chapter also presents some of the applications of cost accounting and cost finding tools to specific situations. While no listing of specific cost analysis techniques and applications in government can be complete, the concepts and tools discussed and illustrated can be tailored to any number of governmental activities. Some of the more obvious and useful applications are flexible budgeting; variance analysis; standard costing and efficiency analysis; incremental analysis; fee determination (establishing user charges, determining assessments for special projects, or calculating reimbursable costs under contracts or grants); capitalization and analyses of construction projects; and determining total and/or unit costs of activities, programs, or projects. The topic coverage is designed to be suggestive rather than exhaustive, and to encourage practitioners to exercise ingenuity in developing applications of cost accounting and cost finding tools and analyses to governmental operations.

COST ACCOUNTING VERSUS COST FINDING

The National Committee (now Council) on Governmental Accounting (NCGA) defines *cost accounting* as:

> That method of accounting which provides for assembling and recording all the elements of costs incurred to accomplish a purpose, to carry on an activity or operation, or to complete a unit of work or a specific job.[1]

For purposes of this discussion, as in practice generally, cost determination is considered at two distinct levels: (1) cost accounting and (2) cost finding.

Cost accounting is the continuous process of analyzing, classifying, recording, and summarizing cost data within the confines and controls of a formal cost accounting system and reporting them to users on a regular basis. Cost accounting may be accomplished through a *job-order* system where projects are readily identified by individual units or batches (a specific construction

---

[1] National Committee on Governmental Accounting, *Governmental Accounting, Auditing, and Financial Reporting* (Chicago: Municipal Finance Officers Association, 1968), p. 157.

project), or through a *process* costing system (gallons of water processed). These are the types of cost accounting systems used in the usual corporate situation where direct labor, materials, and overhead can be specifically assigned to separate cost centers, and total product cost can be determined as a function of general ledger accounting and the normal recurring record-keeping function.

Cost finding, on the other hand, is a less formal method of cost determination or estimation on an irregular basis. There may be no formal accounting entries during the year to record costs incurred in specific cost accounts. Instead, cost finding usually involves taking available fund financial accounting data and recasting and adjusting it to derive the cost data or estimate needed. For example, hospitals make extensive use of cost finding to determine the total and unit costs of various types of services, such as laboratory and surgical procedures. Data for budgeting, budgetary control, and budgetary reporting are accumulated in responsibility costing centers, which are categorized as "revenue producing" or "nonrevenue producing." At the end of the accounting period all costs of nonrevenue producing departments are distributed (allocated) to all other departments served, both revenue producing and nonrevenue producing, with all costs ultimately being charged to revenue producing cost centers. This cost finding procedure, taking place outside of the general ledger but using such data as a starting point, allows all costs to be assigned to a function or activity without necessitating numerous allocations in the formal account structure and financial accounting system. The end result is a compilation of all pertinent costs for a department, that can then be compared with its productive activity to determine unit costs.

Cost finding for most business-type activities of state and local governments, like that for hospitals, is a relatively straightforward *reclassification* process. In both cases the financial accounting system routinely records revenues earned and expenses or costs incurred, as in business enterprises, and cost finding primarily involves reclassifying such data from one classification (for example, responsibility center) to another classification (for example, function or activity). This may be accomplished manually by means of relatively simple work sheet techniques, or by utilizing a reclassification subroutine in computerized systems.

Cost finding is more complex where general government activities are involved. Here it must be viewed as a two-step process of both (1) *converting* data on one measurement basis (expenditures) to another measurement basis (expenses or costs), and (2) *reclassifying* such derived data from one classification (for example, responsibility center) to another classification (for example, function or activity). Further, data from several funds may need to be converted, reclassified, and aggregated, since a general government function or activity may be financed and accounted for through several fund accounting entities.

Both cost accounting and cost finding—and both approaches to cost finding—are discussed and illustrated later in this chapter. An understanding of certain basic state and local government fund accounting concepts and terminology is essential to understanding these subsequent discussions and illustrations and applying them in practice.

ESSENTIAL FUND ACCOUNTING CONCEPTS AND TERMINOLOGY[2]

Two basic or fundamental categories of funds are utilized in state and local government financial accounting:

1. **Proprietary funds.** Sometimes referred to as "income-determination," "nonexpendable," or "commercial-type," these funds are used to account for a government's ongoing organizations and activities which are similar to those often found in the private sector (Enterprise and Internal Service Funds).

All assets, liabilities, equities, revenues, expenses, and transfers relating to the government's business and quasi-business activities—where *net income and capital maintenance are measured*—are accounted for through proprietary funds. The generally accepted accounting principles here are those applicable to similar businesses in the private sector; and the measurement focus is upon determination of *net income, financial position, and changes in financial position.*

2. **Governmental funds.** Often called "source and disposition," "expendable," or "government-type," these are the funds through which most governmental functions typically are financed. The acquisition, use, and balances of the government's expendable

---

[2] This section is based on the National Council on Governmental Accounting, *GAAFR Restatement*, "Principles," Exposure Draft (Chicago: Municipal Finance Officers Association (February 1978), pp. 10–15.

financial resources and the related current liabilities—except those accounted for in proprietary funds—are accounted for through governmental funds (General, Special Revenue, Capital Projects, Debt Service, and Special Assessment Funds).

Governmental funds are, in essence, accounting segregations of financial resources. Expendable assets are assigned to the various governmental funds according to the purposes for which they may or must be used; the associated current liabilities "follow" the assets; and the difference between governmental fund assets and liabilities, the fund equity, is referred to as "Fund Balance."

The governmental fund measurement focus is upon determination of *financial position and changes in financial position* (sources, uses, and balances of financial resources), rather than upon net income determination. The Statement of Revenues, Expenditures, and Changes in Fund Balance is the primary governmental fund operating statement. It may be supported or supplemented by more detailed schedules of revenues, expenditures, transfers, and other changes in fund balance.

Another category of funds, the fiduciary (Trust and Agency) funds, are used to account for assets held by a governmental unit as a trustee or agent for individuals, private organizations, and/or other governmental purposes, and are of limited concern from a cost accounting standpoint.

Accountability for, and control of, the government's *general* fixed assets and *general* long-term debt are accomplished through a third category of accounting entities, the "account groups."

3. Account groups. Groups of accounts used to establish accounting control and accountability for the government's general fixed assets and the unmatured principal of its general obligation long-term debt. (General Fixed Assets and General Long-Term Debt Account Groups.)

The government's general fixed assets—all fixed assets except those accounted for in proprietary or trust funds—are not financial resources available for expenditure. The unmatured principal of its general obligation long-term debt—its long-term liabilities other than those accounted for in proprietary funds, Special Assessment Funds, or Trust Funds—does not require an appropriation or expenditure (use of financial resources) during the current accounting period. Hence, neither is accounted for in the governmental funds, but in self-balancing account groups. These account groups are not funds—they do not reflect available financial resources and related liabilities—but are accounting records of the general fixed assets and general long-term debt, respectively, and certain associated information.

From a cost accounting and cost finding perspective, the salient points here are that:

Proprietary fund accounting in government parallels commercial accounting. The organization entity corresponds to the accounting entity; all assets and liabilities of the proprietary activity, both current and noncurrent or fixed, are accounted for in the proprietary fund accounts; and data on revenues earned and expenses incurred (costs) are routinely captured in the financial accounting system. Thus, cost accounting systems may readily be established under general ledger control; and if cost-finding is necessary it involves only data reclassification, not data conversion from one measurement basis to another.

Governmental fund accounting entities contain, with minor exceptions, only current asset and current liability accounts; the fund equity (balance) might well be called "working capital;" and the results of governmental fund financial operations are routinely measured in terms of sources of working capital ("revenues") and uses of working capital ("expenditures"). "Expenditure" data reflect current liabilities incurred during a period, whether or not paid by period end, for (*a*) current operation, (*b*) capital outlay, and (*c*) maturing general long-term debt principal and interest. Expenditure data do not include depreciation or amortization.

The General Fixed Assets and *General Long-Term Debt* Account Groups record the "general government" fixed assets and long-term debt, neither of which is recorded in the governmental funds.

The National Council on Governmental Accounting (NCGA) recommends five types of governmental funds and two types of proprietary funds to be utilized in state and local government accounting. (Fiduciary funds are subclassified as either proprietary or governmental from an accounting measurement standpoint.) Specifically, the third NCGA principle is:

Types of funds

The following types of funds should be used by state and local governments:

Government funds

1. *The General Fund*—to account for all unrestricted resources except those required to be accounted for in another fund.
2. *Special Revenue Funds*—to account for the proceeds of specific revenue sources (other than special assessments, expendable trust, or for major capital projects) that are restricted by law or administrative action to expenditure for specified purposes.
3. *Capital Projects Funds*—to account for financial resources segregated for the acquisition of major capital facilities (other than those financed by Special Assessment and Enterprise funds).
4. *Debt Service Funds*—to account for the accumulation of resources for, and the payment of interest and principal on, general long-term debt.
5. *Special Assessment Funds*—to account for the financing of public improvements or services deemed to benefit the properties against which special assessments are levied.

Proprietary funds

6. *Enterprise Funds*—to account for operations that are financed and operated in a manner similar to private business enterprises—where the stated intent is that the costs (expenses, including depreciation) of providing goods or services to the general public on a continuing basis be financed or recovered primarily through user charges—or where periodic determination of revenues earned, expenses incurred, and/or net income is deemed appropriate for capital maintenance, public policy, management control, accountability, or other purposes.
7. *Internal Service Funds*—to account for the financing of goods or services provided by one department or agency to other departments or agencies of the governmental unit, or to other governmental units, on a cost-reimbursement basis.

Fiduciary funds

8. *Trust and Agency Funds*—to account for assets held by a governmental unit as trustee or agent for individuals, private organizations, and/or other governmental units. These include (*a*) Expendable Trust Funds, (*b*) Nonexpendable Trust Funds, (*c*) Pension Trust Funds, and (*d*) Agency Funds.

Exhibits 1 and 2 summarize the nature and primary accounting measurements of state and local government funds and nonfund

EXHIBIT 1
Overview of municipal funds and nonfund account groups

*Municipal
fund and nonfund types*

	Unrestricted	General	"Period-oriented"	*Expendable [governmental] funds*
		Special Revenue*		
	Resources *restricted* as to use.			
"General government" accounting entities		Capital Projects Debt Service Special Assessment Expendable Trust* Agency	"Project or purpose-oriented"	"Funds flow" accounting $(CA - CL = WC = FB)$
	Accountability for "general government *non*current assets and liabilities	General Fixed Assets General Long-Term Debt		*Nonfund account groups* (List and contra)
Other accounting entities	Self-sustaining business and quasi-business activities and trusts.	Enterprise Intragovernmental [Internal] Service Nonexpendable Trust		*Nonexpendable [proprietary] funds* "Business-type" accounting $(A = L + GE)$

* Special Revenue Fund resources may be restricted to use for capital projects; similarly, Expendable Trust Fund resources may be available for expenditure for certain operating purposes.

Source: "Report of the Committee on Nonprofit Organizations, 1973–74," American Accounting Association, *Accounting Review,* Supplement to vol. 50, 1975, p. 10.

Legend: CA = Current assets
CL = Current liabilities
WC = Working capital
FB = Fund balance
A = Assets (*all* related)
L = Liabilities (*all* related)
GE = Government equity

account groups. Exhibit 3 contrasts key differences between proprietary fund and governmental fund accounting. Inasmuch as governmental cost accounting and cost finding typically involve activities financed and accounted for through proprietary funds or governmental funds—and since, in any event, trust funds

EXHIBIT 2
"General government" accounting entities and equations

	Assets & Contra	= Liabilities	+	Fund balances (Assets & Contra)
Expendable funds:				
Fund 1	CA	= CL		+ FB
Fund 2	CA	= CL		+ FB
Fund n	CA	= CL		+ FB
Nonfund account groups:				
General fixed assets	FA	=		Investment in fixed assets*
General long-term debt	Amount(s) available and that must be provided in the future to retire NCL*	= NCL		
Arithmatic summation	ΣCA + ΣFA + ΣNCL*	= ΣCL + ΣNCL +	ΣFB	+ ΣFA*

* Contra or offset accounts.
Source: Adapted from "Report of the Committee on Not-For-Profit Organizations, 1972–73," American Accounting Association, *Accounting Review*, Supplement of volume 49, 1974, p. 229.

Legend: CA = Current assets
 CL = Current liabilities
 FB = Fund balance (CA-CL = Working capital)
 FA = Fixed assets (General fixed assets)
 NCL = Noncurrent liabilities (General long-term debt)

are accounted for in the same manner as either proprietary funds or governmental funds, depending on their nature and the appropriate accounting measurement objectives in the circumstances—fiduciary funds are not considered further in this chapter.

ESSENTIAL COST CONCEPTS AND TERMINOLOGY

The three components involved in product cost or service expense determination are:

1. *Direct labor*—labor costs directly traceable to the production of the good or service (for example, garbage collector's wages).

EXHIBIT 3
Accounting for service activities

Attribute	Governmental (expendable) fund	Proprietary (nonexpendable) fund
1. Example	General Fund	Enterprise Fund
2. Accounting basis	Modified accrual [Sources ("revenues") and uses ("expenditures") and balances of current financial resources.]	Accrual [Revenues earned, expenses incurred, and net income determination.]
3. Fixed asset accounting	Capitalized in the General Fixed Asset Account Group. Depreciation not recognized in fund accounts.	Capitalized in the Enterprise Fund. Depreciation expense is recognized in the fund accounts.
4. Long-term debt	Carried in the General Long-Term Debt Account Group. Recorded as governmental fund expenditure upon maturity.	Recorded in Enterprise Fund. Interest recognized as expense.
5. Treatment of "costs"	Expenditure accounting— expenditures recorded at time current liabilities are incurred. No assignment of resources expended to periods benefited.	Expenses allocated to periods benefited so as to judge ability of revenue produced to cover costs incurred, that is, for determining periodic net income.
6. Accounting emphasis	Legal (fund and budgetary) compliance; stewardship; acquisition, expenditure and balances of financial resources. Working capital model is employed.	Legal compliance; stewardship; efficiency, economy, and responsibility. Normal profit and loss accounting model is employed.

2. *Direct materials*—cost of materials used directly in production of the good or service (for example, brick used in building construction).
3. *Overhead*—indirect labor, indirect materials and all other costs (for example, supervision, depreciation, rent) reasonably associated with the production of the goods or services.

In most cases, accounting records exist for the first two categories. For example, ledger accounts exist to record items such as salaries and materials. Often, however, total overhead cost must be accumulated from numerous accounts and must then be allocated among various activities. For example, the cost of utilities for a building used by many departments must be equitably spread or applied so that each beneficiary of the service is charged a fair share. Cost finding techniques are appropriate in such situations.

The amount recorded in the accounts (even after adjustment for accruals and deferrals) may not properly reflect the cost (expense) of the item or activity in question, however. For activities financed through *proprietary* funds, this may result from the fact that pension costs are borne by the General or another expendable fund, for example, or because an enterprise or intragovernmental service function utilizes part of a building accounted for in the General Fixed Assets accounts. Again, and more significantly, the accounts for *general* government activities financed through governmental funds reflect expenditures— for current operations, capital outlay, and debt service—rather than expenses, though they may be improperly titled "expense" accounts. These must be converted from an expenditure basis to an expense basis if "full cost" is to be determined.

Variable versus fixed costs

Costs may be classified as *variable* or *fixed.* Variable costs change with fluctuations in the activity of the cost allocation base, while fixed costs remain constant in total over a relevant range of activity. Between the two extremes, some costs are semifixed. Semifixed costs increase in steps; that is, they are fixed over certain activity level ranges but increase to another fixed level when activity reaches a certain point. An example of step costs is supervision, where more foremen are needed as activity increases. Other costs are classified as semivariable; that is, they increase with activity to a specified point and remain fixed above that activity level (social security costs, for example).

Variable costs increase a specified amount for each unit of activity added; although *unit* variable costs remain constant, *total* variable costs increase. Fixed costs, on the other hand, do not change in *total* with an increase in activity over the relevant range, but *unit* fixed costs decrease as units of activity are added (rent, for example).

Some accountants contend that only *variable* costs should be inventoried as product costs or considered in determining program or service cost, and that fixed costs should be considered period expenses. This "variable costing"' approach has not gained general acceptance for external reporting purposes in either business or government. Although it is used for internal purposes in some business costing systems, it is not commonly encountered in government costing. Thus, "direct labor" typically includes both fixed and variable direct labor costs, with indirect labor being considered overhead. Likewise, "direct materials" typically includes all directly related material costs, with abnormal spoilage and other costs charged to "overhead."

Separating costs as between fixed and variable is essential to flexible budgeting and standard costing, and is useful in many types of analyses in government, e.g., zero base budgeting. Flexible budgeting, zero base budgeting, and standard costing are discussed later in this chapter.

When repetitive operations are involved, it is often desirable for both planning and evaluation purposes to determine the relationship between the fixed and variable costs that persists over time. A stable, ongoing relationship between cost and the independent variable can be used to estimate cost by use of regression analysis. [Regression analysis is the measurement of the average amount of change in one variable that is associated with unit changes in the amount of one or more other variable(s).] For example, one can calculate a predicted cost of gasoline based on the miles a truck is driven. Although a discussion of the methodology of regression analysis is beyond the scope of this chapter,[3] the technique is a useful tool in cost accounting. With the widespread availability of computers today, a manager can easily use it to assist in the task of prediction, decision making, and feedback of results.

Cost centers and responsibility accounting

A cost center is the smallest segment of activity or area of responsibility for which costs can reasonably be accumulated. The costs may be accumulated by project, location, work order, or some other grouping.

Because of their similarity to profit-oriented businesses, the accounts of proprietary funds (such as an Enterprise Fund) usu-

---

[3] An explanation of the use of regression analysis in decision making is provided in William A. Spurr and Charles P. Bonini, *Statistical Analysis for Business Decisions* rev. ed. (Homewood, Ill.: Richard D. Irwin, Inc., 1973).

ally contain all costs readily traceable to established cost centers. As noted earlier, any adjustments necessary to determine full costs usually are minor, and typically are obvious to the practitioner (pension costs borne by the General Fund). Thus, cost accounting systems are readily installed in proprietary funds.

The expenditure accounts of governmental funds are usually classified by responsibility center (organizational unit and/or subunit) and by object or category of expenditure (personnel, capital outlay). Considerable effort may be required to determine the cost or expense of a given activity or function—since a given department may be financed from several governmental funds, a given activity may involve several departments, and the available data reflect expenditures (rather than costs or expenses). Thus, cost finding, using the available data as a beginning point, often is more feasible than cost accounting for determining the cost of products or activities financed and accounted for through governmental funds.

Job order versus process costing

The identification of cost centers is essential to the development of any cost accounting system or cost-finding methodology. The appropriate approach to cost data accumulation for a cost center depends on the nature of the activity involved.

One of two widely used approaches, referred to as "job order" and "process" costing, respectively, will fit most cost center activity patterns. In some cases, however, a hybrid system, employing elements of both types of systems, may be required to accomplish the cost determination objectives.

The *job order* approach is appropriate where the goods produced or services performed are of a *heterogeneous* nature and are separate, discrete activities. The job order approach in government is typified by cost accounting systems for construction projects and vehicle repair, though it also has application in personal service activities such as building inspection and social welfare case work.

The *process* costing approach, on the other hand, is used where many units of a *homogeneous* good or service are produced in or provided by a cost center which is characterized by a pattern of routine, repetitive activities, perhaps in mechanized work situations. Water purification and distribution systems, sewage collection and disposal, and garbage removal and disposal activities commonly fit this activity costing pattern, as do cashiering, accounting and data processing, and similar activities.

Direct and indirect costs

In practice, some costs are readily charged directly to the job or process cost center involved, while others must be recorded initially in clearing or suspense accounts and later distributed to various jobs or processes on some systematic and rational basis. In a motor pool, for example, the direct costs of operating each piece of transportation equipment are gathered on an individual equipment record. The costs of gasoline, oil, tires, and repairs are directly traceable to each vehicle. On the other hand, overhead expenses connected with operating the motor pool may first be compiled in separate expense accounts and subsequently distributed to all pieces of equipment on some systematic and rational basis. Expense items in this category include the salaries of the superintendent or foreman, depreciation of facilities, and the costs of supplies, such as small tools or grease.

The basis used for distributing overhead costs should bear a logical relationship to the activity being considered. (A common method of allocation in a motor pool is in direct proportion to the number of direct labor hours spent in repairing or maintaining each vehicle.) When overhead is thus applied, each individual equipment record shows the applicable share of overhead, and the total cost of operating each vehicle is available. By dividing total costs by the number of miles driven, a unit cost of operation is determined. These unit costs provide an indicator of the efficiency of vehicle operation, both in total and for individual vehicles, thus facilitating such decisions as vehicle replacement timing and type of vehicle to be acquired.

In other instances even more extensive use of expense allocation may be required. Even if expenses can be charged directly to specific activities, they are sometimes recorded in a clearing account in order that total expenses may be computed before being distributed to various accounts. For example, it may be desirable to know individual vehicle expenses, to allocate vehicle expenses among the various departments for whose benefit the motor pool is operated, and to know the total motor pool expenses for a particular period. (Cost data for vehicles used by individual departments are necessary so that proper amounts may be charged to each user department.) It is necessary to know the total expenses incurred by the motor pool to insure that total charges will cover total costs and to evaluate the efficiency of the motor pool operation. One approach here is to first record costs in separate labor, materials, and overhead clearing accounts, and then transfer them from these accounts to the specific motor pool vehicle and other expense accounts. Thus, after several clearing accounts are used to accumulate total operating costs, the accounts are cleared periodically by charging the proper job or activity accounts and crediting the clearing account. Charges to jobs and activities may be made on the basis of the actual cost of materials, labor, and overhead chargeable to each job or activity, on the basis of predetermined rates, or on a combination of both approaches.

COST ACCOUNTING AND COST FINDING: "PROPRIETARY" ACTIVITIES

State and local government business and quasi-business activities that are financed and accounted for through proprietary funds are accounted for in essentially the same manner as private businesses. Thus, the experienced commercial accounting practitioner is on familiar ground. The fund accounting entity encompasses and corresponds to the organizational entity; all assets, liabilities, equities, revenues, and expenses (and net income) of the proprietary activity should be accounted for in the proprietary fund accounts in conformity with generally accepted accounting principles applicable to privately owned business enterprises; and job order and process cost accounting systems similar to those of commercial establishments are readily implemented under general ledger control.

Where cost accounting systems have not been installed, or where different data (for example, reimbursable cost under an intergovernmental grant or contract) are needed than that routinely accumulated in the proprietary fund cost accounting system, cost finding is usually a relatively simple reclassification process. Where cost accounting systems have *not* been installed, it involves recasting the existing expense data (salaries and wages, materials, etc.) from the financial accounting system into appropriate cost accounting categories. Where cost accounting systems *have* been installed, the existing cost accounting data is reclassified as between "allowable" (reimbursable) and "unallowable" (not reimbursable), and any overhead or profit allowances are added, to determine the proper charge or reimbursement under the provisions of the grant or contract.

Most cost-finding exercises related to proprietary fund activities thus are reasonably straightforward and involve relatively basic analyses and columnar worksheet techniques. Such complications as are encountered typically result from deficiencies in the financial and/or cost accounting system in use, or from complexities (or vagaries) in grant or contract provisions.

Enterprise Funds

Self-supporting activities through which the government renders services to the general public on a user-charge basis should be accounted for through Enterprise Funds in the same manner as similar privately owned businesses. Traditionally, a "primary revenues" test has been applied in determining whether a given activity should be considered a proprietary or general government activity. If most of the activity costs is expected to be recouped annually through user charges, enterprise (proprietary) accounting is deemed appropriate; if not, general government accounting is called for. A secondary "revenue bonds" test has also been applied; that is, most activities for which revenue bonds (to be serviced from user charges) have been issued should be accounted for as enterprises.

Most public utilities (for example, electricity, water and sewage, gas) operated by municipal governments meet these tests, as do many hospitals. Among the other types of activities that may be financed and accounted for through Enterprise Funds are airports, docks and wharf facilities, transportation systems, off-street parking lots and garages, public housing, golf courses, swimming pools, garbage collection and disposal, and parks.

Note that both legislative *intent* for an activity to be self-supporting and the *ability* to finance the operation primarily through user charges are implicit in the above enterprise criteria. Thus, a given type of activity might properly be accounted for as an enterprise by one government and as a general government activity in another.

Furthermore, the term "self-supporting" has been interpreted differently by accountants and auditors in various governments. Some have considered the term to imply that all (full) costs, including depreciation, should be considered in applying the primary revenues test, and have employed enterprise accounting sparingly. Others have interpreted "self-supporting" as meaning that only "out-of-pocket" operating and debt service costs are relevant in applying the primary revenues test, and account for many activities (for example, bridges and toll roads) as enterprises. Too, in some cases (for example, public transit systems), operations are subsidized by local or intergovernmental grants. Some have included these in applying the primary revenues tests and others have excluded them. Still further, user charges may in some situations comprise well over half of the costs in one year and significantly less than half in another. Yet a given activity obviously should be consistently accounted for as either an enterprise or a general government function by a governmental unit, not one way one year and another way the next.

In view of the difficulties in interpreting and applying these criteria in practice, the NCGA has proposed to modify and restate the Enterprise Fund criteria:

> *Enterprise Funds*—to account for operations [1] that are financed and operated in a manner *similar to private business* enterprises—where the stated *intent* is that the *costs* (*expenses, including depreciation*) of providing goods or services to the *general public* on a *continuing basis* be financed or recovered *primarily* through *user charges—or* [2] where periodic determination of revenues earned, expenses incurred, and/or net income is deemed appropriate for capital maintenance, public policy, management control, accountability, or other purposes.[4]

The first part of these proposed criteria may be described as "mandatory"—that is, those government activities that meet it

---

[4] National Council on Governmental Accounting, *GAAFR Restatement*, "Principles," Exposure Draft (Chicago: Municipal Finance Officers Association, February 1978), p. 14.

must be accounted for as enterprises. Note that it refers to intent to finance or recover *full costs* (expenses, including depreciation) through user charges, thus hopefully resolving the issue of what "self-supporting" means. The second part of the proposed criteria *permits* state and local governments to account for activities that do *not* meet the "mandatory" criteria as enterprises.

The question of whether a given activity should be, and is, accounted for as an enterprise or as a general government function for financial accounting purposes clearly should be of at least as much concern to the cost accountant as to the financial accountant and auditor. If the activity is accounted for in an Enterprise Fund, the cost accountant's task involves only traditional cost accounting and/or relatively modest cost-finding efforts. But if the activity is accounted for as a general government function: (1) the related fixed assets will be carried in the General Fixed Assets Account Group, perhaps at original cost without regard to depreciation; (2) the related long-term debt principal will be carried in the General Long-Term Debt Account Group; (3) the related debt will be serviced through a Debt Service (governmental) Fund; and (4) the related revenues and *expenditures* (*not* expenses or costs) will be accounted for through one or more governmental funds, probably the General Fund and/or one or more Special Revenue Funds. Cost accounting *per se* usually is impractical in this instance, and cost finding is more complex than in proprietary fund situations.

The government cost accountant obviously will prefer that major business-type activities of state and local governments be accounted for through Enterprise (or Intragovernmental/Internal Service) Funds rather than as general government functions. Too, many state and local government activities now accounted for as general government functions should be, or may be, accounted for through Enterprise Funds. Thus, the governmental cost accountant may find it appropriate to take the initiative in assuring that significant enterprise-type activities are financed and accounted for through Enterprise Funds.

Even though an activity is accounted for through an Enterprise Fund, the cost accountant must be sensitive to the possibility that some costs are not properly accounted for and must be adjusted in deriving "full cost" data. A fairly common example of this, noted earlier, is that fringe benefit costs (for example, social security taxes, pension costs, hospitalization insurance) for all government personnel may be financed from the General Fund or another governmental fund. Obviously, these costs should be properly computed and attributed to enterprise personnel costs in determining enterprise activity costs. Likewise, payments made from the Enterprise Fund to other funds of the state or local government and charged to enterprise expense may more appropriately be viewed as interfund *transfers*. For example, where "payments in lieu of taxes" are made from an Enterprise Fund to the General Fund, careful analysis may indicate that a portion of such payments is more properly considered a transfer. Thus, although Enterprise Fund accounting should parallel that for similar privately owned businesses, the prudent cost accountant reviews the financial accounting data both for omissions and for instances where form may have prevailed over substance in the financial accounting process.

Internal (Intragovernmental) Service Funds

Internal (Intragovernmental) Service Funds (IGS Funds) may be established by state and local governments to account for the financing of goods or services provided by one department or agency to other departments or agencies of the governmental unit, or to other governments, on a cost-reimbursement basis. Such funds are, in essence, "internal enterprise funds" designed to account for such activities as in-house quasi-business operations, and to assure that the costs of the goods and services provided to other departments or governments are properly charged to the departments, programs, and activities served. This, in turn, assures that such costs are borne equitably among the various funds through which the other departments or agencies are financed, or by other governmental units.

Among the types of governmental activities that may be accounted for through IGS Funds are vehicle fleets (motor pools), central service shops or garages, gasoline service stations, central printing and duplication services, data processing, janitorial services, carpentry and electrical services, central purchasing and stores departments, telephone services, and municipal buildings. Not all such activities are accounted for through IGS Funds, however. Unless the appropriate officials specify that a given activity is to be organized, managed, and accounted for as an IGS Fund, it is likely to be considered (and accounted for as) a general government activity.

In practice, some IGS Funds are extremely simple conduit devices serving essentially as clearing accounts—for janitorial, data processing, or telephone service costs. (Where simple cash disbursement and allocation activities may be more efficiently accounted for through clearing accounts in the General Fund—for example, telephone charges in Centrex Systems—IGS Funds should be abolished.) On the other hand, some are complex operations (motor pools and central repair and service shops), and many fall between these extremes (carpentry and electrical services). Utilizing IGS Funds should be considered wherever significant functions are served centrally and costs should be allocated equitably among departments.

Even where activities are financed and accounted for through IGS Funds, the governmental cost accountant should be sensitive to the possibility that the same types of omissions and form over substance defects discussed under "Enterprise Funds" may be present in IGS Fund financial accounting data. Furthermore, several unique features of IGS Fund financial accounting may impact upon cost accounting or cost finding for internal service activities.

Only those fixed assets expected to be replaced through IGS Fund finances are capitalized in IGS Fund accounts. Thus, a city shop may be expected to recoup all material, labor, and equipment costs, but not the costs of the building in which it is housed. In this case the building would be accounted for in the General Fixed Assets Account Group rather than in the IGS Fund since its depreciation would not be considered an expense (reimbursable cost) properly chargeable to departments served through the city shop. To determine the cost of the city shop operations from a "full costing" standpoint, however, it would be necessary to compute depreciation on the building being utilized, based on the general fixed-asset records, and add it to the expenses accounted for in the IGS Fund accounts.

Likewise, general obligation long-term debt may have been issued to finance buildings or equipment utilized in IGS Fund activities. The proceeds of such debt issues, whether deposited directly to the IGS Fund or invested in fixed assets that are transferred to the IGS Fund, commonly are viewed as general government capital contributions to the IGS Fund. The debt is rarely serviced through the IGS Fund. Rather, it is recorded in the General Long-Term Debt Account Group and serviced from general government resources through a Debt Service Fund; and interest expense is not considered an IGS Fund expense (reimbursable cost) to be charged to departments served through the internal service activity. To determine the "full cost" of the IGS Fund activity, however, the interest expense should be added to the expenses accounted for through the IGS Fund.

As noted earlier, proprietary fund financial accounting systems are far more conducive to efficient and effective cost accounting and cost finding than are general government (governmental funds and nonfund account groups) accounting systems. Even where there are differences between "costs" accounted for in the IGS Fund accounts and "full costs," the cost determination process may involve, for example, 90 percent routine cost accounting procedures and 10 percent relatively simple cost-finding procedures. Governmental cost accountants thus prefer that significant intragovernmental activities financed on a cost-reimbursement basis be accounted for through IGS Funds, and may find it appropriate to take the initiative to assure that such activities are financed and accounted for through IGS Funds.

Finally, some governments have expanded the use of IGS Funds beyond the NCGA financial accounting definition in order to establish cost accounting and management systems for major centralized facilities and services *not* financed on a user-charge basis. For example, space in municipal office buildings traditionally has been a "free good" to tenant departments, whereas the cost of space rented from private landlords often is charged against the budgetary appropriations of the occupant departments. This obviously causes difficulties in departmental (and program, activity, and so forth) budgeting, cost accumulation, and cost comparison and evaluation. Further, many believe it causes occupants of "free space" to attempt to keep it, or obtain more, even when other departments might need it more or better utilize it.

Thus, some governments have established "quasi-lessor" IGS Funds to account for all government-owned office buildings. The building accounts are moved from the General Fixed Assets Account Group to the IGS Fund, operating capital is contributed to the IGS Fund, and building-related costs (repairs and maintenance, utilities, janitorial services) are financed and accounted for through the IGS Fund. In this manner, occupancy costs (including depreciation) may readily be determined and attributed to user departments in a systematic and rational manner—whether or not all costs are funded, and regardless of whether departments are actually billed for occupancy costs.

Proponents of this approach note that it provides "full cost" data; that if full costs are not funded that fact is made apparent by the net loss reported in the IGS Fund; that the approach is workable whether current funding comes from the general administrative budget or from departmental billings; that the cost data is useful in budget comparisons and hearings, in forcing department heads to justify their "free space" usage, and for cost comparison and evaluation purposes; that better management control over the entire building operation can be achieved in this manner; and that its value has been demonstrated in instances where the legislative body ultimately required departments to include rental requests in their budgets and pay rentals to the "landlord" IGS Fund. Opponents contend that the approach is merely a "shell game;" that it is just so many journal entries and budgetary accounting transfers; and that sound building management and costing can be accomplished as well, and with less bookkeeping complication, by other means.

This illustration of expanding the IGS Fund concept is not intended to be presented in either an advocacy or adversary manner. The approach is neither panacea nor poison, but might prove to be either in a given situation. The illustration is intended, however, to stimulate the practitioner's thinking beyond taking the usual financial model as a "given," to considering nontraditional ways of accomplishing costing objectives.

COST ACCOUNTING AND COST FINDING: "GENERAL GOVERNMENT" ACTIVITIES

"General government" activities, as noted earlier, are financed through one or more governmental funds and are accounted for on a "funds flow" or "sources, uses, and balances of fund financial resources" basis. "General government" fixed assets are not accounted for in the governmental funds, but in a nonfund accounting entity, the General Fixed Assets Account Group. "General government" long-term debt is not accounted for in the governmental funds, but in a nonfund accounting entity, the General Long-Term Debt Account Group. "General government" activities include general administration, police and fire protection, courts, corrections, inspection (building, plumbing, elevator), civil defense, welfare, public works (street maintenance and cleaning), library services, and all other activities not financed and accounted for through proprietary (or fiduciary) funds.

Reconciliation of expenditures, costs, and expenses (costs)

Cost, in the conventional accounting sense, is the amount of financial resources—measured in money—used to obtain facilities, goods, or services. In profit-oriented organizations, and in proprietary funds of governments, that part of cost which is associated with the revenues earned during a given period of time is treated as an *expense* in the process of determining periodic net income. The "costs" of goods or services financed through governmental (expendable) funds, however, are measured in terms of *expenditures*—current liabilities incurred for current operations, capital outlay, and debt service—rather than in terms of expenses. Further, a single activity may be financed from more than one governmental fund, and a single governmental fund may finance several different activities. Thus, data on the cost of goods or services produced or provided is not routinely accumulated in the governmental fund accounts. Instead, it must be (1) accumulated in a separate series of cost accounts, related to or reconcilable with the expenditure accounting system, or (2) derived from analysis of the expenditure data and supplemental records—that is, by cost finding.

The object of cost accounting systems or cost finding techniques for activities or projects that are financed and accounted for through one or more governmental (expendable) fund entities is to convert the conventional fund accounting "resource flow" measurements (expenditures) to measures of total costs

EXHIBIT 4
Reconciliation of expenditures and costs or expenses (activity financed through expendable fund)

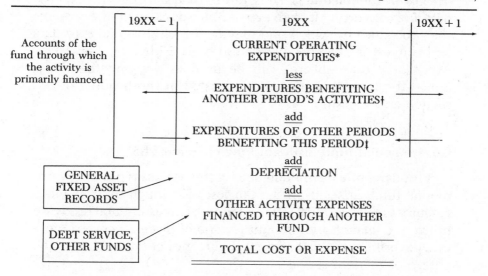

* Excludes debt principal retirement and capital outlay expenditures.

† For example, prepaid insurance and inventory adjustments where expenditures are recorded on a "purchases" basis and other accrual and deferral adjustments for items reflected in the Expenditures account for the period that are applicable to previous or future periods.

‡ Adjustments for items such as those in note 2 that are reflected in the Expenditures account in a previous or future period but are applicable to 19XX.

Source: Edward S. Lynn and Robert J. Freeman, *Fund Accounting: Theory and Practice* (Englewood Cliffs, N.J.: Prentice-Hall, Inc., 1974), p. 647.

of providing goods or services, or of reimbursable or other costs in some instances, during a specific time period.

This conversion process usually is not difficult, assuming that the financial accounting system in place accumulates data for GAAP reporting or data that is readily convertible to a GAAP basis. A general model illustrating the relationship of current expenditures and total activity expenses or product costs is presented in Exhibit 4.

The observant practitioner will note that the process of converting expenditure data to a cost or expense basis, as set forth in Exhibit 4, is merely the reverse of the process typically used in converting net income data (revenues and expenses) to a working capital basis in preparing the Statement of Changes in Financial Position for a commercial organization or a proprietary fund of a governmental unit. That is, rather than starting with expense data and converting it to an expenditure basis, Exhibit 4 presents the procedure by which one may begin with expenditure data and convert it to a cost or expense basis. Either type of data—expense or expenditure—can be used in deriving the other; hence the term "reconciliation" is used in the heading of this section and in Exhibit 4.

Governmental fund distinguishing characteristics

A fundamental distinction among the various types of governmental funds arises from the purposes for which their financial resources may—or must—be expended. Governmental funds are utilized to finance and account for one of three aspects of "general government" fiscal affairs: (1) current operations, (2) capital outlay, or (3) debt service.

General government current operations and debt service typically are financed, budgeted, and evaluated on an annual basis. Hence, the accounting and financial reporting for governmental funds related to current operations and debt service is *period-oriented;* that is, the focus is upon budgeted and actual fiscal operations of each year and the financial position of such funds at year end.

Capital outlay projects, on the other hand, often span more than one fiscal year. The financial accounting and reporting for governmental funds through which major capital outlay projects are financed thus are said to be *project-oriented,* inasmuch as they must reflect *total project* fiscal operations and balances as well as the fiscal operations and balances of the interim years over which the project extends.

These distinctions among governmental funds are important to governmental cost accounting, cost finding, and cost analysis:

1. They relate to the types of activities financed through the governmental funds and the type of financial accounting data present (and absent) in accounting systems that accumulate data that conform to GAAP.
2. They differ as to the extent to which cost accounting systems may readily be implemented under general ledger control,

EXHIBIT 5
Distinguishing characteristics of governmental funds

Used to finance and account for "general government"	Types of governmental funds	Financial accounting and reporting focus (orientation)
Current operations	*The General Fund*—all externally unrestricted resources except those required to be accounted for in another fund.	
	Special Revenue Funds—the proceeds of specific revenue sources (other than special assessments, expendable trusts, or for major capital projects) that are restricted by law or administrative action to expenditure for specified purposes.	Period oriented
Debt service	*Debt Service Funds*—the accumulation of resources for, and the payment of, interest and principal on, general obligation long-term debt (other than special assessment and enterprise debt).	
Capital outlay	*Capital Projects Funds*—financing resources segregated for the acquisition of major capital facilities (other than those financed by Special Assessment and Enterprise Funds).	Project oriented
	Special Assessment Funds—the financing of public improvements or services deemed to benefit the properties against which special assessments are levied.	

and the types of cost accounting systems that might be employed.

3. They differ as to the extent to which cost finding is more feasible than cost accounting.

These distinctions are summarized in Exhibit 5.

Project-oriented fund costing

Capital projects funds are used to account for the acquisition of major general government capital facilities, such as buildings (for example, civic centers), dams, and new street systems. Such projects are typically financed primarily from intergovernmental grants and/or issuance of general government bonds or similar long-term debt securities, though some financing is commonly derived through transfer of resources from other funds (for example, the General or Special Revenue Funds) to the Capital Projects Fund for the project(s). Since indenture and similar provisions of debt issues, reimbursable cost and other grant stipulations, and/or local ordinance requirements must be observed (and hence must be controlled and accounted for) a separate Capital Projects Fund usually is employed for each major project. However, where several projects are financed through a single bond issue, grant, or other source, that is, where a series of fixed asset acquisitions is viewed as one project by all concerned—several projects may be financed and accounted for through a single Capital Projects Fund. Expenditures for the various subprojects should be separated in the accounts where several projects are accounted for through a single Capital Projects Fund.

Special Assessment Funds are used to account for public improvement projects which are deemed to be of primary benefit to the owners of the improved property or abutting property. Typical special assessment projects involve improvements in certain subdivisions or sections of a community—paving streets that previously were unpaved, installing sanitary sewage systems to replace septic tanks, constructing neighborhood sidewalks, or installing new street-lighting systems in a subdivision. Typically, (1) the costs of such improvements are initially financed from interfund loans or special debt issues; (2) the costs of the projects are assessed against the landowners, often with the option of payment (with interest) over a period of several years; and (3) the special assessment principal and interest collections are structured to be sufficient to repay the initial financing debt principal and interest. The governmental unit typically acts dually as general contractor and financier in special assessment situations. It is not uncommon for the government to pay part of the project costs, however, to the extent that the general community interest is deemed to benefit from the improvements.

A Special Assessment Fund thus may be viewed as a Capital Projects-Debt Service Fund combination for a special assessment project. Our concern here is restricted to its "capital projects" component.

Both Capital Projects Funds and the "capital projects component" of Special Assessment Funds are, in essence, job order cost accounting systems for the related projects. To the extent that a project is let by bid to private contractors on a "turnkey" basis—and project quality and costs are controlled through detailed specifications and engineering, architect, and other supervision and inspections—project cost accounting involves only the tabulation of the costs of the project. On the other hand, the governmental unit may construct the facility with its own labor force and equipment. In this case, job order cost accounting systems such as those employed by private contractors are appropriate.

This is not to say that the data accumulated in the accounts of Capital Projects or Special Assessment Funds necessarily reflect the "full cost" of the project. They may or may not. Among the types of discrepancies between the data in the accounts and "full cost" that may be encountered are:

1. Materials and supplies may have been charged as expenditures when purchased rather than only upon use, and significant amounts may remain unused upon completion of the project.
2. Abnormal spoilage or waste may have occurred, without these costs having been separated from the "normal and necessary" costs that should be considered "full cost" and capitalized in the General Fixed Asset Account Group.
3. To the extent that the government used its own labor force and equipment in the construction of the project, (*a*) personnel costs may reflect only direct salaries and wages, exclusive of payroll taxes, unemployment and health insurance premiums, and pension plan costs; (*b*) depreciation of government vehicles may not be included in "full costs," for example, where the vehicles are not accounted for through an IGS Fund; and (*c*) other costs may require similar "expenditure-to-expense" conversion adjustments.
4. Cost data in Capital Projects Funds accounts may reflect "reimbursable costs"; and, to the extent that "reimbursable" and "full" costs differ, may require analysis and conversion to "full cost."

Thus, in Capital Projects and Special Assessment Funds, as in proprietary funds, cost finding techniques often prove necessary in determining "full cost."

Finally, note that proper cost determination is important in Capital Projects and Special Assessment Funds for three reasons:

1. To determine reimbursable project costs under grant provisions or costs to be assessed against certain property owners.
2. To control and demonstrate compliance with bond indentures and grantor restrictions.
3. To determine the amount at which the project should be capitalized in the General Fixed Assets accounts.

Thus, both present period costing and the ability to determine costs in future periods are involved, since the amount capitalized in the General Fixed Assets accounts will determine future depreciation calculations in cost finding, where the asset acquired will be used in providing goods or services in future periods.

Period-oriented fund costing

The *operating expenditures* for most general government functions—police and fire protection, the judiciary and penal system, education, protective inspection, sanitation, highway and street repair, traffic control, welfare, and the myriad of other functions performed by state and local governments—typically are financed and accounted for through the General and Special Revenue Funds. Debt service—principal and interest payments and fiscal charges on general government long-term bonds, notes, and other indebtedness—is accounted for through one or more Debt Service Funds. These types of funds—the General, Special Revenue, and Debt Service Funds—are the *period-oriented* funds.

Cost finding, as opposed to cost accounting, is used almost exclusively in period-oriented fund cost determination. The steps involved in the usual cost finding process are:

1. **Activity identification.** The function, program, or activity for which costs are determined should be carefully identified and defined, together with the departments or other responsibility centers involved in the function, program, or activity.
2. **Funding identification.** The one or more governmental funds through which the function, program, or activity are financed and accounted for must be carefully identified. Care should be taken to assure that all funds are included and that

the pertinent expenditure data is extracted and (assuming manual methods) entered on the worksheet. Where materials are accounted for on a purchases basis, or where significant prepayments are charged as current expenditures, appropriate adjustments to the fund accounting data should be made.

3. Fixed asset identification. The fixed assets utilized in the function, program, or activity must be identified—a simple task where proper General Fixed Asset Account Group records are maintained—and depreciation expense should be calculated. The full cost of fixed assets utilized that are properly accounted for through an IGS Fund should already be included in the governmental fund expenditure data.

4. Interest charge determination. To the extent that general fixed assets utilized by the function, program, or activity being costed were acquired through long-term borrowing, it may be appropriate to attribute an appropriate amount of interest expense to the function, program, or activity. The propriety of such interest charges is debatable, as is the method by which interest should be calculated, if an interest charge is deemed appropriate.

5. Expenditure-to-expense conversion. Following the procedures outlined above and summarized in Exhibit 4, the cost or expense data should be derived.

The cost finding approach described here can be applied to virtually any function, program, or activity for which cost data is deemed relevant for performance evaluation, "do-or-contract" decisions, or other purposes. It is especially appropriate in the following situations:

a. Where activities that might be accounted for through proprietary funds are being accounted for through governmental funds.

b. Where there is a choice between performing an activity "in house" or contracting for its performance with private vendors or contractors (for example, garbage collection and disposal, street sweeping and repair, and data processing).

Controversial and problem areas

One of the most controversial aspects of cost finding is the propriety of attributing interest costs to specific general government activities. To the extent that depreciation charges are included as an element of full cost, some contend that all relevant capital costs have been included—that interest is a cost of borrowing rather than saving for an asset, and is a period cost rather than an activity cost. Further, situations where two fixed assets were acquired, one through available financial resources and the other through borrowing, are not uncommon. Some contend that to charge one with interest costs but not charge interest costs to the other is unfair and misleading. Others note that, since interest rates fluctuate through time, assets costing the same (or for which the same amounts were borrowed, but at different times) will be assigned different interest costs. Still others contend that interest is a proper charge, but should be charged uniformly at an average "cost of capital" rate so that "costs" will not be distorted by whether an asset was acquired through borrowing or from available resources, or by when it was acquired. The practitioner must carefully weigh the pros and cons of computing interest charges, and the manner in which they are to be computed—if they are to be computed—in a given cost finding situation.

Most of the controversies and problems that may be encountered in period-oriented fund cost finding have been discussed earlier (e.g., inadequate financial accounting systems, the possibility that all personnel costs are not reflected in the accounts of the fund through which an activity is primarily financed and accounted for, and the fact that inventories and prepayments may be either charged as expenditures in the period of liability incurrence or prorated over the periods benefited). Two areas deserving further attention, however, are pension costs and encumbrances.

Pension costs. The manner in which pension costs are recorded and reflected for financial accounting and reporting purposes varies widely among state and local governments. Some reflect pension costs on an *actuarial* (accrual) basis, whether or not such costs are funded. Others follow one of several *cash basis* approaches (terminal funding, pay-as-you-go, or reporting the amount funded as pension costs), or a *modified accrual* method under which pension costs are recorded to the extent that fund current liabilities for pension plan funding are recognized. Furthermore, in some jurisdictions all recognized pension costs are recorded in a single fund (for example, the General Fund), notwithstanding the fact that payroll expenditures may be made from many funds. Still further, in some cases governments manage their own pension plans and funds; and a single governmental unit may have several pension funds (for example, Policemen's Pension Fund and Firemen's Pension Fund). In other cases, local governments participate in statewide plans administered by the state government. Thus, the pension expenditure data in the financial accounting records of period-oriented governmental funds may not accurately reflect pension cost, and may require adjustment in the cost determination process.

Encumbrances. "Encumbrances" represent the expenditures which are estimated to result upon delivery of goods of services that have been ordered. Encumbrances often are recorded during the year in period-oriented governmental funds as a budget control device—that is, to assure that expenditures do not exceed appropriations. The encumbrance accounting procedure involves two steps:

1. When an order is placed, record the encumbrance (*a*) in the general ledger Encumbrance account as a debit and in the Reserve for Encumbrances account as a credit, and (*b*) in the expenditure subsidiary ledger, thus reducing the unencumbered appropriations available for subsequent commitment or obligation.
2. When the goods or services are received, reverse the encumbrance entry and record the actual expenditure and liability.

In some governments the encumbrances outstanding at year end are reversed from the accounts at year end and are not reported in the financial statements. In other governments, encumbrances outstanding at year end are reported with expenditures, under one of two common approaches:

1. Encumbrances outstanding at the end of the prior year are treated as reductions of current period expenditures—that is, the "expenditures" data in the accounts reflect all expenditures of the current year, less encumbrances outstanding at the beginning of the year, plus encumbrances outstanding at the end of the year.

2. Encumbrances outstanding at the end of the prior year are added to expenditures of that year, and the expenditures that resulted this year are included again in current year expenditures data.

Note that the "expenditures" data do not reflect actual expenditures in either case, and that the latter case results in double-counting. (Encumbrances outstanding at the end of the prior year are reported both *with* expenditures in the prior year and *as* expenditures in the current year.) Thus, the expenditure data in period-oriented governmental fund accounts may require careful analysis and adjustment during the cost determination process.

BUDGETING TOOLS

Government budgets typically are developed for each fund to cover all activities financed and accounted for through the fund entity. For example, the General Fund budget typically covers an extremely wide range of activities. Four types of budgeting warrant consideration: (1) static (fixed), (2) flexible, (3) performance, and (4) zero base.

Static (fixed) budgeting

The traditional line-item or object-of-expenditure budget is generally prepared on a *static* (or fixed) level of expenditure basis. That is, a specific maximum expenditure amount is authorized for an estimated level of activity, and operating results are compared with this predetermined plan regardless of changes in actual activity levels attained as compared with the original estimate. If expenditures have not exceeded the specific dollar amount authorized, the budget constraints have been observed, even though the quantity and/or quality of goods or services provided may have been more or less than the amount estimated. Since there is no profit measurement or similar index by which to evaluate performance in government, a special effort must be made to measure, control, and evaluate efficiency and effectiveness.

The legal budget typically approved by the legislative body is a static or fixed budget. Some legislatures are adopting other budgeting approaches, however; and government managers may find other budget approaches useful for managerial control purposes regardless of the legal budget approach.

Flexible budgeting

The *flexible budget* is a planning and evaluation alternative to the traditional fixed or static budget. Expenditures authorized by flexible budgets vary in total according to either production or delivery levels of the goods or services. Thus, the flexible budget is designed for various levels of activity, rather than for a single level, and facilitates evaluation of performance by displaying *what costs should have been,* based on predetermined cost behavior patterns for the actual activity levels achieved.

The most common use of flexible budgeting in governmental accounting to date has been in proprietary funds. The desire of legislatures to maintain control over the absolute levels of expenditures, coupled with the relative ease of fixed budget preparation and understanding, has perpetuated the use of fixed budgets in most governmental (expendable) funds. While compliance with the legally adopted budget is necessary, flexible budgeting techniques can also be used for managerial purposes to analyze the economic impact of activity variations, price changes, and performance attainment.

The following steps are necessary to use flexible budgeting in a governmental fund environment:

1. A budget is prepared on the basis of expenditure estimates and a measure of activity. The fixed budget allocations for the year's expenditures is the starting point. If all programs or activity expenditures are variable, the total allocation is divided by the total units of activity expected to attain an estimated unit expenditure. If both fixed and variable expenditures are involved, the fixed and variable components are considered separately.
2. The flexible budget technique is applied to the activity level achieved in a specific budget period; that is, the activity units achieved are multiplied by the expected unit expenditures to determine what the total expenditures for the period should have been.

3. Actual expenditures incurred are compared with the flexible budget for the activity level achieved in order to identify expenditure variances.

A simple example of the above technique assumes that all costs are variable and involves an appropriation of $30,000 for a municipal waterworks. The expected level of activity is 6,000 million gallons produced, giving an expected unit expenditure of $5 per million gallons. If the activity level rises to 6,500 million gallons with total expenditures incurred of $31,200, a static budget shows only that total expenditures exceeded those estimated. Application of flexible budget techniques will show, however, that the department has operated efficiently and lowered the unit expenditures to $4.80 per million gallons. At this level of activity, expenditures would have been $32,500, given the standard expenditure per million gallons (6,500 units produced multiplied by $5 unit expenditure). On the other hand, if expenditures remained within the $30,000 appropriated, but the activity level dropped to 5,000 million gallons, the use of flexible budgeting would show that expenditures should have been only $25,000 (5,000 units actually produced multiplied by $5 unit expenditure), and thus reveal the lack of efficiency in the department's operations. Exhibit 6 illustrates a simple application of the flexible budget. By techniques to be discussed later, these budget variances can be isolated on the basis of the underlying causes and the need for corrective action can be determined.

The key to the use of flexible budgets in governmental (expendable) funds is the identification of the activity base and the related expenditures per unit represented by the approved

EXHIBIT 6
Simple flexible budget application*—Governmental fund activity

	Case A	Case B
Activity level achieved	6,500	5,000
Actual expenditures	$31,200	$30,000
Projected expenditures per flexible budget formula	$32,500	$25,000
Unit expenditure	$ 4.80	$ 6.00

$$* \text{Budget formula} = \frac{\text{Amount appropriated} - \$30,000}{\text{Activity level predicted} - 6,000} = \$5 \text{ unit expenditure (per million gallons)}$$

Note: All expenditures are assumed to be variable in this example. Where both fixed and variable expenditures are involved, this approach is applied only to the variable component.

legal budget. Determination of the common activity base will vary according to each activity or functional objective, and in many cases more than one denominator may be necessary.

Performance budgeting

Flexible budgeting techniques may already be in use in municipalities which employ a performance budgeting system in addition to, or in lieu of, a line-item, object-of-expenditure budget. The NCGA defines a *performance budget* as "A budget wherein expenditures are based primarily upon measurable performance of activities and work programs."[5] Performance budgeting is, in essence, merely applying flexible budgeting in governmental fund planning and control.

The performance budget approach focuses on measuring the performance of activities and emphasizes evaluation of the efficiency with which an activity is performed. Its primary tools are either *cost or expenditure accounting* and *work measurement.* The steps involved are:

1. Classifying budgetary accounts by function and activity.
2. Measuring existing activities to determine maximum (or reasonable) efficiency levels and establishing unit activity and expenditure standards.
3. Basing the budget of the succeeding period upon unit expenditure standards multiplied by the expected number of units of activity estimated to be required in that period.

Although the above represents an oversimplification of the manner in which performance budgets operate, it does emphasize the role of cost or expenditure accounting in providing the estimates of effort and accomplishment in quantitative terms and in filling the need to measure accomplishments (output) as well as costs or expenditures (input).

One criticism leveled at performance budgets is that functions and activities sometimes have been costed and measured in great detail without sufficient consideration being given to the necessity or desirability of the functions and activities themselves.

---

[5] National Committee on Governmental Accounting, *Governmental Accounting and Financial Reporting,* p. 166.

The extension of cost finding and evaluation techniques one step further helps to avoid this problem. The extension is called *zero base budgeting.*

Zero base budgeting

Zero base budgeting is a relatively new management tool for planning and control of activities and for effective allocation of resources to activities judged to be of greatest benefit to the entity. The technique utilizes incremental cost-benefit analysis and project accountability to measure the productivity and the effectiveness of implementation of activity plans. Zero base budgeting is, in essence, a "management by objectives" budgeting approach.

Basically, zero-base budgeting is centered around the creation and evaluation of "decision-packages." Each of these packages, which are self-contained modules giving detailed descriptions of the various departmental and program funding requests, contains:

1. A statement of the purpose and benefits of the activity under consideration.
2. An evaluation of the consequences of not performing the activity.
3. Definitive specification of objective performance measurements or indicators to be employed in evaluating subsequent performance.
4. Identification of alternative methods of accomplishing the objectives of the program or function.
5. An explicit statement of the benefits, costs, expenses and/ or expenditures of each proposed alternative method.

In determining the budget, administrators rank the packages in order of desirability. A further benefit of the zero base approach is the performance measure or indicator by which the program or activity can be monitored and evaluated on the basis of the established criteria.

In some activities within the government setting output can be related to inputs; in some they cannot. Zero base budgeting is more effective in the second category of service or support-type tasks, where output measurement is not feasible, while flexible budgets and variance analysis are more useful where a unit of output can be determined.

The evolution of both performance budgeting systems and zero base budgeting has been in answer to the need to assess an entity's performance. Although such techniques are an improvement over previous methods, the use of flexible budgeting and variance analysis in conjunction with such systems will expand their usefulness and set the stage for the application of other logically related accounting control and evaluation techniques.

STANDARD COSTS AND VARIANCE ANALYSIS

A *unit cost standard* is the cost necessary to perform a unit or work of acceptable quality in an efficient manner. Unit cost standards should be carefully developed by studying the necessary operations and the trend of unit costs over a period of time, eliminating from consideration costs resulting from abnormal conditions. A set of standards outlines how a task should be accomplished and how much it should cost. It provides a target that will help gauge performance. However, the use of poor or inappropriate standards may result in misleading analyses and erroneous performance evaluation. Thus, it is essential that the standards established be both representative of efficient levels of performance and realistically attainable if subsequent analytical endeavors are to be meaningful.

Variance analysis is the process of determining the nature, magnitude, and cause(s) of differences between planned and actual performance, or costs of performance. The combination of standard costs and flexible budgeting techniques provides a powerful tool for post-event evaluation by management.

Such techniques are relatively easy to apply in proprietary funds, but can be extended to more innovative applications without unreasonable difficulty. For example, standard costing and flexible budgeting can be applied to General Fund activities such as fire and police departments. A fire control activity is a difficult functional area in which to apply these management techniques, as little influence can be exerted over the level of activity. However, the tools provide guidance for evaluating the performance of the division's duties, the level of resources devoted to the program, and changes in the mix, level, and frequency of fires fought. Standard costing can also be used to analyze the economic impact of activity variations, price changes, and performance attainment. Such insight into program efficiency and effectiveness cannot be achieved by using variances derived from a static, single-level budget.

In a fire department, for example, the first step in applying the technique is to determine a standard unit cost by dividing the estimated man-hours (the denominator that seems most applicable) to be expended in fighting fires into the budget allocation for fire-fighting operations. The expected number and types of fires and the related man-hours to be used may be developed from historical data.

To perform the most realistic and meaningful cost analysis from a managerial point of view, one should compare the actual performance with a budget based on the actual level of activity achieved instead of the forecast activity level. Thus, standards are applied to the activity level achieved to provide a flexible budget total (standard unit expenditures × man-hours expended = total expenditures forecast based on activity level achieved). This direct comparison of activity level achieved to expenditures makes the flexible budget a powerful managerial tool. It allows management to gauge what expenditures should have been to produce the output achieved. In contrast, a static budget ignores the expenditure/activity relationship and allows comparison only of planned versus actual expenditures—a measure of limited meaning and usefulness in future planning.

Total expenditures should be classified into their fixed and variable components. Variable expenditures are expected to change in proportion to changes in activity levels. Fixed expenditures are expected to remain constant as activity levels vary.

In order to provide information on the *total expense* incurred, however, expenditure data must be converted to expense data, as discussed earlier, so that depreciation and other expenses not included in current expenditures data are properly included in the analysis.

The actual expenses incurred for the period should be compared with the predicted costs and any significant variances should be analyzed. Exhibit 7 displays the computation and composition of a three-variance analysis of the total variance. A full

EXHIBIT 7
Total cost variance analysis*

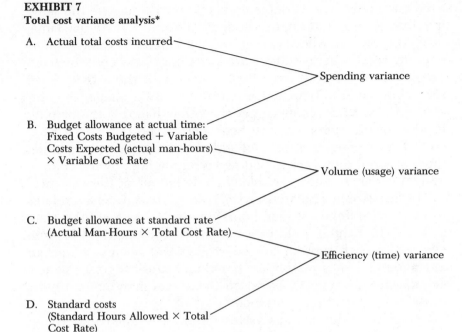

A. Actual total costs incurred

Spending variance

B. Budget allowance at actual time:
Fixed Costs Budgeted + Variable
Costs Expected (actual man-hours)
× Variable Cost Rate

Volume (usage) variance

C. Budget allowance at standard rate
(Actual Man-Hours × Total Cost Rate)

Efficiency (time) variance

D. Standard costs
(Standard Hours Allowed × Total
Cost Rate)

  * Each variance may be favorable or unfavorable.

understanding of cost variations is important for effective operations analyses, and the type of information needed is not provided by the total variance alone. Subdivision of the total variance is necessary to pinpoint the underlying causes of such deviation, and to allow operational courses of corrective action to be identified and taken. Management cannot determine what measures of control are needed until additional detailed variance analysis is performed.

The *spending variance* compares the actual costs of the period with those predicted for the activity level achieved. Fixed costs are assumed to be the same as budgeted for this analysis, since they are not expected to vary with different activity levels. The variable costs are extensions of the variable cost rate applied to the activity level achieved. This spending variance shows only the impact of deviations in actual spending as compared with expected spending at the level of activity achieved.

The second variance, the *volume (usage) variance*, relates to fixed costs only. The variable costs involved would be the same in either B, in Exhibit 6, the Budget Allowance at Actual Time, or C, the Budget Allowance at Standard Rate. The total difference in fixed costs results from spreading fixed costs over an activity level different from that predicted. If the activity level rises above that anticipated, each unit bears a smaller amount of fixed cost than planned. On the other hand, if the activity level is lower, each unit must bear a larger portion of the fixed cost. The economic impact of utilizing facilities or personnel more or less intensely than planned is highlighted by the volume (usage) variance, since variable costs do not affect this variance.

The last variance isolated, the *efficiency (time) variance,* relates to the total number of man-hours needed to perform the tasks at hand. In Exhibit 7, D represents the cost standard of time allowed, if each type of fire controlled had been assigned an average number of man-hours based on historical performance. Comparing this with C, based on the actual man-hours, results in the efficiency (time) variance.

Typically, additional analysis is required to elicit underlying causes of the variances isolated. Variances may be further subclassified or isolated for each line item classification within the cost center, rather than using the total figures as was done in Exhibit 7. *Unfavorable or favorable variances show deviations from the standard, and thus are only a starting point for further managerial analysis.* Spending variances may have been due to a faster rate of inflation than anticipated, and thus were not controllable. *Efficiency (time) variances* may be due to the fires being more severe or complicated than expected, consequently requiring additional resources to control. Until management investigates the reasons underlying the variations, it is impossible to determine if corrective strategies are needed. Control action may not be necessary if the variance is the result of factors that could not be avoided. Analysis may show that, although an unfavorable variance existed, performance was better than could normally be expected, given the circumstances. For example, if inflation caused a 10 percent rise in prices, but spending was only 5 percent over budget, the employee responsible perhaps should be commended for a job well done rather than chastised for overspending.

Management must make these detailed investigations and

analyses before reacting to the information provided by the variances. Budgeting tools such as variance analysis and flexible budgeting provide a dynamic basis for comparing actual performance with planned activity, but much of their potential usefulness is stifled if management does not complete the necessary analysis. Properly used, these techniques provide for early detection of trends of expenses and related economic consequences, and provide relevant and useful information for future planning and budgeting. This type of information cannot be attained through use of a fixed budget, which provides data only as to whether or not costs exceeded the amount authorized and gives no indication as to the productivity or efficiency with which resources were used to produce the outputs of goods or services.

DIFFERENT COSTS FOR DIFFERENT PURPOSES

Situations frequently arise in governmental operations whereby nonroutine decisions require specialized cost information that is not maintained in the formal accounts nor obtained in recurring cost finding routines. Such special-purpose data usually is too expensive to maintain on a routine basis, and is therefore derived on an "as needed" basis. If the governmental entity makes use of computers, future needs can sometimes be anticipated and coded for later retrieval. Further, generalized audit software packages that enable a relatively inexperienced programmer to call forth data as needed are readily available.

These software packages are information retrieval systems that can extract required information from computerized records with a minimum of technical knowledge on the part of the user. The user simply states his data requirements in the software's designed language, which corresponds closely to the way he would express them in English. The package is designed to read the instructions, restructure existing files into the format necessary for the instructions to be carried out, and generate a corresponding program, usually in the COBOL programming language. The COBOL program is then compiled into machine language and executed by the machine. The governmental entity's auditor can often provide more information on how these software packages can be used to supplement the regular data processing programs in satisfying management's needs for specialized information. Most national accounting firms and several federal and state audit agencies have generalized audit software packages, which are generally available to clients and others on a case-by-case basis.

It is important in decision making to determine just what information is relevant to the problem at hand, for the choice of data may alter the decision maker's selection of a course of action. For example, *current replacement costs* are more relevant than historical costs when one plans to replace an asset. *Opportunity costs*—the benefits foregone by using resources for one purpose rather than another—often are relevant in choosing among alternative actions, such as when deciding whether to use a building or to sell it and either build another elsewhere or use the sale proceeds for other purposes. *Differential or incremental costs* are the total increases or decreases in "out-of-pocket" costs involved in changing the level or type of activity. *Marginal cost* is the short-run cost change per unit of increasing or decreasing the level of an existing activity. Such short-run information should be evaluated carefully before using it for decision making, however, as short-run costs often become long-run costs through ongoing programs or projects. Thus, although the cost of paving a mile of street is a relevant figure, the estimated cost of future maintenance and repair is equally important in the decision process.

Finally, as noted earlier, another cost measurement important to governmental entities is *reimbursable costs*—the costs to be reimbursed under terms of a grant or contract. These are usually defined in much detail, and it may be necessary to establish separate special-purpose cost records if the stipulated costs differ materially from full costs. Both sets of records are relevant, however, and one should not supplant the other.

CONCLUSION

The cost of rendering governmental services has increased dramatically in recent years as a result of several factors, including both inflationary trends and citizen demands for increased levels of service. Further, this phenomenon has often been coupled with a stagnant or slowly growing revenue base. In this environment, control of programs and related costs has become crucial to successful governmental operations.

The preceding discussion was designed to illustrate selected applications of cost accounting and cost finding techniques in the government environment to aid in the evaluation and control of expenditures and programs. Practitioners should view the methods presented as illustrative rather than exhaustive, and should undertake innovative applications of them as needs and circumstances dictate.

The keys to successful cost analysis in government remain much the same as in the private, profit-seeking sector. Perhaps the most fundamental concept to be addressed involves the relationship of costs and activity. Practitioners should understand the underlying causal components of cost variations and related performance levels. Indeed, even fixed costs can be subjected to analysis at various levels of activity to determine optimal staffing and capacity levels for given ranges of activities. Unit costing, flexible budgeting, and variance analysis seem to hold much promise for fruitful cost analyses.

For costs in areas of governmental endeavor not already using other adequate control measures, in particular, the concept of zero base budgeting offers a great deal as a control and evaluation device. Indeed, recent professional literature is replete with examples of the applications and desirability of such budgeting systems.

Practitioners should attempt to match the appropriate cost accounting tool to each situation encountered. A contingency approach to the solution of problems of governmental expenditures and programs thus is advocated—whereby analytical and evaluative tools are selected and developed in response to the needs and demands of the governmental operations from the range of cost accounting techniques that may fruitfully be applied in a governmental environment.

31

Cost accounting in not-for-profit organizations

Robert E. Seiler[*]
E. R. Gilley[†]

NATURE OF NOT-FOR-PROFIT ORGANIZATIONS

There is no precise universally accepted definition of not-for-profit organizations that separate them from profit-oriented organizations. A church may be considered a not-for-profit organization, but there are many which are operated for profit. *Purpose* is the single criterion which is used in this chapter to identify the types of organizations considered to be not-for-profit. These organizations, accordingly, include all which utilize their entire resources to provide a socially desirable service, with no profit objective. They are considered not-for-profit because their purpose is service to a broad group of citizens.

The objective of the not-for-profit organization cannot be to widen the spread between inputs and outputs, a difference which is commonly called profit. Their objective is to provide maximum service with a given amount of resources, or to provide a given amount of service with a minimum amount of resources. Utilizing the service criterion, not-for-profit organizations include hospitals, private clubs, schools and universities, governmental units,

---
[*] Professor, University of Houston.

[†] Vice President for Business Affairs, The University of Texas System Cancer Center, M. D. Anderson Hospital.

churches, and social welfare organizations. Cost accounting for governmental units is discussed in a separate section of this handbook; the other forms are covered in this section.

Not-for-profit organizations frequently budget their activities so that they will have an excess of revenue over expenses. However, in order to be a truly not-for-profit organization these planned excesses must be used to implement and/or expand the services which they provide. Excesses of revenue over expenses are sometimes the only means available to not-for-profit organizations to finance the replacement of worn facilities or the acquisition of equipment which makes additional services possible.

IMPORTANCE OF COST ACCOUNTING

The absence of a profit measure makes the accumulation and analysis of cost information critical in not-for-profit organizations. While the efficiency of profit-oriented businesses may be measured by their ability to earn profits, the efficiency of not-for-profit organizations can be measured only by the amount and quality of services which they are able to provide with the resources they expend. Furthermore, the outputs of the not-for-profit organization must be measured in units of service, a difficult measurement at best. Even when service outputs are in some way measurable the multiple objectives which usually exist in this type of organization prevent the service outputs from being a clear measure of the effectiveness of the organization.

Cost data provide the basis for comparing resource expenditures with the benefits, however measured, of the organization's activities. Cost data also become the basis for pricing the various services which the organization provides. In not-for-profit organizations there are usually no inventories to which costs are assigned, since services cannot in most cases be stored and later distributed. Service organizations are in general highly labor intensive, and cost accumulation, analysis, and assignment to segments of the organization assumes major importance in their financial affairs.

The uses of cost information in not-for-profit organizations may be summarized as follows:

1.   As one of the basic elements in the measure of effectiveness.
2.   For expense control.

3. For preparation of operating budgets.
4. For establishing prices for services rendered.

Cost accounting methods

Not-for-profit organizations have trailed profit-oriented organizations in the development of cost accounting systems, primarily because of the absence of an inventoriable product. Early forms of accounting for not-for-profit organizations had as their primary consideration the control of expenditures and not the measurement of effectiveness. Furthermore, the absence of accrual accounting in many not-for-profit organizations led naturally to systems of cost analysis that were "statistical" in nature and were not tied to the basic double-entry accounting records. Without the discipline of this debit-credit framework the danger was compounded that the resulting statistics would be incomplete or inaccurate. Care must always be exercised to insure that statistics are properly prepared when the underlying data are not a part of the formal accounting records.

The normal job order, process, and estimated cost accumulation systems found in manufacturing organizations are rarely encountered in not-for-profit organizations, primarily because the latter are service oriented. Even standard costs are rarely used, although standards are utilized for administrative costs in some profit-oriented organizations. The absence of standard costs for office, clerical, or service activities in not-for-profit organizations is due in part to the inability to measure the organization's effectiveness, which contributes to a weakening in the emphasis on operating efficiency.

The objective of the costing process in not-for-profit organizations is to match, in the best possible way, the costs incurred with the various services which are rendered. For example, a hospital provides facilities for a number of services, such as X ray, operating rooms, pharmacy, and laboratory. The costs must be accumulated so that they are equitably assigned to each service which is provided to the hospital's patients. This assignment may be made in relatively direct fashion for some costs, but there are many indirect costs which must be allocated. The process of allocation of costs to revenue centers is basic to not-for-profit organizations and is called *cost finding*. This process may be compared to full absorption costing in a manufacturing company, where all overhead is ultimately assigned to products.

The process of cost finding may be summarized as follows:

1. Costs which are directly associated with revenue centers are so recorded in the accounts.
2. Indirect or unassociated costs are recorded in general operating accounts.
3. Operating statistics are gathered to be used as a basis for prorating indirect costs to revenue centers.
4. Indirect costs are prorated by using the appropriate operating statistics.

Cost finding methods and procedures are discussed more fully in a later section of this chapter. The proration bases or statistics which are used for various not-for-profit organizations are illustrated there.

IMPORTANCE OF BUDGETING

While many profit-oriented businesses operate without a budgetary planning system, a not-for-profit organization must have a budgetary plan for its continued financial health. Maintaining a close match between *revenues* and *expenses* is the essence of the control process in not-for-profit organizations, and a coordinated revenue and *cost expenditure* program is a basic financial tool. Without a budget the price to be charged for services could not be set properly and the *expenditures* could not be kept in line with the revenues.

Not only are financial amounts budgeted, but it is also necessary to budget the operating activities which are gathered as statistics for cost allocation purposes. Unless the costs and the activities which are used as allocation bases are planned in advance, the price structure may be insufficient to keep the organization financially sound. While the organization is not operating to earn profits, neither can it afford to incur losses. The constraints under which these organizations operate which make them not-for-profit entities also force them to utilize operating budgets to the fullest extent possible.

ORGANIZATIONAL ASPECTS OF CONTROL

The organization of a not-for-profit entity should be built around the services which are rendered. This arrangement permits a matching of the revenue gathering activity and expense incurrence with individual responsibility. The application of traditional responsibility accounting systems to not-for-profit organizations is desirable, and this type of reporting requires a sound organization and clearly assigned responsibilities.

Most not-for-profit organizations are controlled from the top with some kind of board. The hospital board, school board, club board, or church board are examples. In most cases these boards are composed of either professional people (in the area in which services are being rendered), or concerned citizens with little administrative experience. The absence of profit as a measure of effectiveness and the service orientation of the organization make the board's policy-making activities difficult, and frequently insufficient attention is given to the financial control aspects at this level.

The chief administrator is in many cases also a professional in the area. Although the number of top administrators who are chosen because of administrative skills rather than professional or technical skills is increasing, there still exists a tendency in not-for-profit organizations to move successful technical persons into administrative positions.

The controller in not-for-profit organizations is usually more than just the chief accountant. This person usually has responsibility for all aspects of the management control and financial control system. Because of the technical orientation of the board and the top administrator, the controller is frequently left with full responsibility for the administrative control function. In larger organizations the controller has a technical staff of accountants, auditors, EDP personnel, and similarly trained persons.

To the fullest extent possible the control system should accumulate financial data utilizing two principal account classifications: one should be structured in terms of *programs* or *services,* and the other in terms of *organizational responsibility.* As expenditures are incurred they are coded or recorded so that they are assigned simultaneously to both program and responsibility areas. These data may then be summarized or aggregated to reflect the cost of service elements, service subcategories, and service categories, at the same time that they reflect the budgetary or fiscal performance in each responsibility area.

HOSPITALS

Health care is the second largest industry in the United States, preceded only by the construction industry. The services demanded of and available from hospitals are increasing in both number and complexity. The one most significant factor affecting hospital cost accounting is the third-party reimbursement system. Whereas most commercial businesses are paid directly by their customers, hospitals must bill governmental agencies, Blue Cross plans, or commercial insurers for the majority of their revenues. Many billings are on a retrospective, or historical, cost basis, although some are on a negotiated rate basis. The costing system for hospitals is therefore the primary vehicle for pricing the various services performed. Full costing, with allocated general costs, is usually undertaken for this purpose.

Organization

The organization of a hospital almost always separates the nursing services, medical services, general services, and administrative services. A partial organizational framework is illustrated in Exhibit 1.

EXHIBIT 1

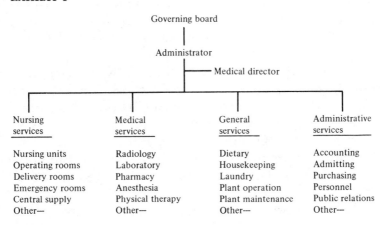

In larger hospitals the organizational subdivisions may be quite numerous. Accounting, for example, may be further divided into payroll, accounts receivable, accounts payable, budgeting, billing, general accounting, inventory, and property accounting. *The Chart of Accounts for Hospitals* published by the American Hospital Association provides a comprehensive organizational framework with a corresponding coding and cost assignment system.

Third-party billing requirements

The costing system employed by most hospitals is based upon the third-party billing requirements to which the hospital is subject. These requirements are so pervasive that the entire cost system is in many cases determined by the reimbursement provisions of Medicare, Blue Cross, and other commercial insurance companies.

Medicare provisions state that hospitals will be reimbursed for the reasonable cost of services furnished. Reimbursable costs must be established on an historical basis, although interim payments are made on an approximation basis. At the end of the cost reporting period a final settlement is made.

Hospitals must submit cost finding schedules to support the settlement computations. The direct costs must be shown by revenue centers, the indirect costs must be allocated to revenue centers, and total costs must be segregated between inpatients, outpatients, and other classifications. The publications of the Department of Health, Education, and Welfare which cover reimbursable costs are entitled (1) *Principles of Reimbursement for Providers Costs and for Services by Hospital-Based Physicians* and (2) *Provider Reimbursement Manual.*

The Medicare program was authorized by the Health Insurance Act, Social Security Amendment of 1965. The program is administered by the Department of Health, Education, and Welfare, but this department has established *intermediaries* which deal directly with the hospitals. The Blue Cross Association is the principal intermediary, and in the normal course of events this or another similar intermediary is the sole contact with a hospital for Medicare services.

The Medicare program calls for periodic examinations of the financial and statistical records of hospitals to ascertain that reimbursable costs are properly calculated. The responsibility for this examination falls upon the intermediary, who may use its own personnel or may utilize CPAs for the necessary audits.

A hospital may apportion cost to Medicare and non-Medicare activities on either (1) the *departmental method* or (2) the *combination method.* The departmental method is applied by calculating for each revenue-producing center a ratio of Medicare Service to non-Medicare service. The reimbursable costs associated with that revenue center are then apportioned on this ratio.

The combination method requires that an average per diem cost of *routine* daily care be computed. This rate is then applied to all Medicare days of coverage. Ancillary or nonroutine services are calculated in the same way as for the departmental method described above. The Medicare billing is the sum of the combination method for routine services plus the ratio apportionment for ancillary services.

Care must always be exercised to prevent costs or revenues from noncovered activities from entering into third party billings. Barber, beauty, and flower shop costs are examples of activities which are clearly not covered, even though they may be billable to patients.

Revenue centers

The beginning point in hospital accounting systems is the establishment of revenue centers. They are important because they determine how the cost centers will be established. Revenues are recorded in a manner that permits identification with the organizational unit which produced the revenue. They are further subdivided according to the type of patient (in patient, out patient, and so forth), by the third-party billing arrangement, or in any other manner deemed appropriate for that particular hospital. The selection of appropriate revenue centers is critical, for these centers become the basis for establishing pricing structures and preparing patient charges.

Revenue centers are very numerous in hospitals, and the separation of (1) daily patient service, (2) professional services, and (3) other nursing services is necessary. The following partial listing indicates the divisions frequently used in revenue center arrangements:

Daily patient service	Professional services	Other nursing services
Pediatric	Operating room	Laboratory
Intensive care	Recovery room	Blood bank
Psychiatric	Delivery room	Electrocardiology
Obstetric	Central supply	Radiology
Newborn	Intravenous therapy	Pharmacy
Other	Emergency room	Physical therapy
	Other	Clinics
		Other

Cost centers

Cost centers are established so that they parallel the revenue centers, that is, for each revenue center there will be at least one related cost center. However, there are usually many more cost centers, since costs are not always directly assignable to revenue centers at the time incurred. For example, Nursing Division Administration cannot be assigned directly to all the revenue centers in which nurses work, nor can such costs as patient food services, elevator operation, hospital security, or chaplaincy services.

The number of cost centers is very large in even medium-sized hospitals, numbering into the hundreds in most cases. These cost centers follow organizational lines and are the basis for budgetary planning, but at the same time they follow operational lines so that they may be used to allocate costs to revenue centers for "full-cost" determination of each service provided.

A cost center need not be a separate responsibility center nor a separate revenue center. Cost centers should be established for any activity within the hospital's operations to which a significant amount of costs can be traced. The cost center may exist primarily for budgetary purposes, providing a logical activity for planning costs or for matching actual costs against plan for control purposes. It may, on the other hand, be established for pricing purposes, providing a logical costing activity for allocation to revenue producing centers. In many cases one responsibility center will have a number of cost centers within it.

Payroll-related costs

Basic cost recording is by natural classification, and wages is one of the natural elements. Thus wage costs are recorded by cost centers, with a breakdown into subclassifications as may be needed. Wages of nurses, for example, would be charged to the various cost centers, broken down by the job categories of nurses.

Salaries and wages of persons who work in more than one cost center should be divided on the basis of hours spent in each center. This requires recording the time spent in each area. Payroll-related costs such as social security and group health insurance costs are normally not recorded directly as charges to cost centers. They are ultimately allocated to cost centers, but direct charging to such centers requires an excessive amount of bookkeeping and the added accuracy is not sufficient to offset the cost.

Donated services and supplies

Hospitals frequently receive the services of both professional and nonprofessional persons who work without monetary compensation. These services should not be recorded as a cost unless (1) there is an employee-employer relationship and (2) there is an objective basis for determining the amount which would have been paid if the service had been acquired at full cost. When these conditions are met, which is relatively rare, the cost is recorded with an offsetting credit to a nonoperating revenue of some kind. Services of a nonessential nature such as is provided by guilds, service organizations, or auxiliaries should not be recorded in the cost accounts.

Supplies which would otherwise be purchased should be recorded as charges at the fair market value of the supplies with an offsetting credit to Donated Commodities.

Use of statistical allocation bases

After all costs and expenses have been accumulated in the various cost centers, statistical bases for allocation can be developed. These bases are necessary for developing "full costs," which serve two major purposes: (1) to determine patient charges for services or for third-party reimbursement and (2) to provide a basis for the control of the various expenses through either budgeting techniques or comparisons with historical data. The importance of these statistics cannot be overemphasized, and internal control procedures, adequate records, and managerial policies must be established to insure the availability of reliable statistical data.

The classification of expense data in dollar terms and the statistical units which measure services must be carefully coordinated. Many cost centers are associated with revenue-producing activities which provide a variety of services involving different degrees of complexity. Consequently, a mere count of the incidence of services provided is inadequate to determine a reliable statistical base for pricing services. An X-ray of a fracture in a patient's forearm, for example, will differ in terms of the technician's time, the materials consumed, the equipment and facilities usage, and the time of the radiologist from those same costs for an X-ray series of the lower intestinal tract. For this reason a weighting system which classifies the various services provided according to their degree of complexity will be necessary if an accurate statistical base is to be available. As a further example, consider an expense center that provides to patients three classes of services, the first of which is approximately twice as complex as the second (in terms of time, materials, and other costs) and four times as complex as the third. In order to establish a statistical base, a count of the number of units of the first service classification would be made; to it would be added twice the number of instances of the second service classification and four times the number of the third. This would give a weighted statistical base for determining the cost of a "unit," and therefore a fair billing rate for each type of service.

Some of the bases used for allocation of cost center totals to revenue producing centers are shown below. Obviously, statistics on each of these bases would be required to facilitate the allocation process.

Cost	Basis
General building and plant	Square footage
Employee benefits	Salaries and wages
Housekeeping	Square footage
Laundry	Pounds or pieces
Dietary	Meals served
Nursing administrative	Hours (or salary dollars) of nurses
Central supply	Dollar amount of requisitions
Pharmacy	Dollar amount of requisitions
Medical records	Percent of utilization
General administrative salaries	Total expenses including salaries

Cost finding

Cost finding is the process of assigning or allocating indirect cost center totals to revenue producing centers in order to arrive at "full cost" for the services. It is a process performed apart from the general record-keeping process; the final full costs are not entered in the accounting records, although a cost report is prepared to reflect the computations. The cost center structure and adequate statistical basis for the allocations are prerequisites for an acceptable cost finding procedure.

The *step-down* or *pyramiding* process is the method most commonly used in cost finding calculations. A second method called the *double-distribution* method is sometimes used because of its greater accuracy.

Step-down method. The step-down method is essentially one of allocating the costs of each nonrevenue cost center to other centers, but never allocating an amount to a center which has already been allocated. One method is to list the cost centers to which costs are *to be allocated* in the left hand column, and the cost centers *from* which costs are to be allocated across the top. In the illustrative costing finding work sheet in Exhibit 2 note that the adjusted balances from the ledger accounts are in the first money column, and that Columns 2 through 15 are used to allocate cost centers in succession. The final totals in the last column represent the full costs of the revenue producing centers.

Each cost center is allocated on the basis of an activity to which it relates. The cost finding statistics which support the work sheet in Exhibit 2 are shown in Exhibit 3. These statistics are reported along with the cost allocation data as a supporting schedule.

Many hospitals have activities which are not subject to reimbursement by third party insurers. Research and teaching activities are examples of this type of activity. Cost centers for these nonreimbursable activities must be established and indirect costs must be allocated to them in the same way as is done for revenue producing centers. In this way they carry a full share of the indirect costs of the hospital.

Double distribution method. The double distribution method is more accurate than the step-down technique because

852

EXHIBIT 2
Cost-finding work sheet, step-down method

	(1) Adjusted Balances	(2) Depreciation	(3) Employee Benefits	(4) Subtotals	(5) F & A Services	(6) Plant O & M
Depreciation	$ 50,000	$ 50,000				
Employee benefits	48,240		$ 48,240			
Fiscal and administrative services	97,000	$ 900	$ 7,920	$105,820	$105,820	
Plant operation and maintenance	63,000	2,500	2,250	67,750	$ 9,993	$ 77,743
Housekeeping	31,000	200	2,070	33,270	4,907	$ 334
Laundry	24,000	1,400	1,530	26,930	3,972	2,335
Dietary	86,000	4,200	4,140	94,340	13,915	7,006
Nursing service — adm. office	9,000	200	720	9,920	1,463	334
Central supply	19,000	1,600	900	21,500	3,171	2,669
Pharmacy	25,000	500	1,260	26,760	3,947	834
Medical records	10,000	400	720	11,120	1,640	667
Cost of meals sold						
Operating rooms	18,000	3,000	1,080	22,080	3,257	5,004
Laboratory	30,000	800	1,800	32,600	4,808	1,334
Radiology	40,000	1,400	2,520	43,920	6,478	2,335
Cost of drugs sold						
Nursing units — adult & pediatric	218,000	29,000	17,640	264,640	39,037	48,386
Newborn nursery	27,000	1,400	2,160	30,560	4,508	2,335
Outpatient clinic	15,000	1,500	810	17,310	2,553	2,502
Emergency rooms	13,000	1,000	720	14,720	2,171	1,668
Cafeteria sales	(17,000)			(17,000)		
Totals	$806,240	$ 50,000	$ 48,240	$806,240	$105,820	$ 77,743

Reprinted from L. V. Seawell, *Introduction to Hospital Accounting* (Chicago: Hospital Financial Management Association, 1977).

it recognizes that nonrevenue producing departments provide services to each other. The nonrevenue producing cost centers are not closed after their initial allocation, and they remain open to receive cost allocations from other cost centers. As a result a second round of allocations is necessary, and this second round follows exactly the same procedure as the step-down method.

(7) Hskpg.	(8) Laundry	(9) Dietary	(10) Nursing Adm. Off.	(11) Central Supply	(12) Pharmacy	(13) Medical Records	(14) Subtotals	(15) Net Cost of Meals Sold	(16) Total Costs
$ 38,511									
$ 1,162	$ 34,399								
3,486	$ 200	$118,947							
166	40		$ 11,923						
1,328	6,000		$ 720	$ 35,388					
415	30				$ 31,986				
332	20					$ 13,779			
		$ 27,000					$ 27,000	$ 27,000	
2,490	6,500		896	$ 4,320	$ 2,668		47,215	$ 609	$ 47,824
664	70				552		40,028	516	40,544
1,162	400				644		54,939	709	55,648
					18,400		18,400		18,400
24,069	16,739	91,947	9,211	29,493	7,422	$ 10,610	541,554	6,952	$548,506
1,162	2,200		440	405	460	1,102	43,172	557	43,729
1,245	800		304	180	736	1,378	27,008	348	27,356
830	1,400		352	990	1,104	689	23,924	309	24,233
							(17,000)	17,000	
$ 38,511	$ 34,399	$118,947	$ 11,923	$ 35,388	$ 31,986	$ 13,779	$806,240	$ 27,000	$806,240

After a cost center is closed and its cost is allocated in the second round, it does not receive further allocations from other cost centers.

The double distribution method is shown in Exhibit 4. Note that the three illustrative nonrevenue centers—laundry, records, and pharmacy—are each allocated a second time. The sequence

EXHIBIT 3

Cost-finding statistics to support cost-finding work sheet

Allocation bases	(1) Depreci- ation Square Feet	(2) Employee Benefits Payroll Dollars	(3) F & A Services Accum. Expenses	(4) Plant O & M Square Feet
Fiscal and administrative services	900	$ 88,000		
Plant operation and maintenance	2,500	25,000	$ 67,750	
Housekeeping	200	23,000	33,270	200
Laundry	1,400	17,000	26,930	1,400
Dietary	4,200	46,000	94,340	4,200
Nursing services — administrative office	200	8,000	9,920	200
Central supply	1,600	10,000	21,500	1,600
Pharmacy	500	14,000	26,760	500
Medical records	400	8,000	11,120	400
Cost of meals sold				
Operating rooms	3,000	12,000	22,080	3,000
Laboratory	800	20,000	32,600	800
Radiology	1,400	28,000	43,920	1,400
Cost of drugs sold				
Nursing units — adult and pediatric	29,000	196,000	264,640	29,000
Newborn nursery	1,400	24,000	30,560	1,400
Outpatient clinic	1,500	9,000	17,310	1,500
Emergency room	1,000	8,000	14,720	1,000
Totals	50,000	$536,000	$717,420	46,600
Accumulated expenses per Worksheet B	$ 50,000	$ 48,240	$105,820	$ 77,743
Unit cost multiplier (line 25/line 23)	1.00	.09	.1475	1.668
Worksheet B column number	2	3	5	6

Source: L. V. Seawell, *Introduction to Hospital Accounting* (Chicago: Hospital Financial Management Association, 1977).

(5) Hskpg. Square Feet	(6) Laundry Pounds	(7) Dietary Meals Served	(8) Nursing Adm. Off. Hours	(9) Central Supply Priced Req.	(10) Pharmacy Priced Reg.	(11) Medical Records Estimated Time	(12) Net Cost of Meals Sold Accum. Expenses
1,400							
4,200	2,000						
200	400						
1,600	60,000		9,000				
500	300						
400	200						
		18,000					
3,000	65,000		11,200	$ 9,600	$ 2,900		$ 47,215
800	700				600		40,028
1,400	4,000				700		54,939
					20,000		
29,000	167,400	61,300	115,137	65,540	8,067	77%	541,554
1,400	22,000		5,500	900	500	8	43,172
1,500	8,000		3,800	400	800	10	27,008
1,000	14,000		4,400	2,200	1,200	5	23,924
46,400	344,000	79,300	149,037	$ 78,640	$ 34,767	100%	$777,840
$ 38,511	$ 34,399	$118,947	$ 11,923	$ 35,388	$ 31,986	$ 13,779	$ 10,000
.83	.10	1.50	.08	.45	.92		.0129
7	8	9	10	11	12	13	15

EXHIBIT 4
Cost-finding work sheet, double distribution method

	(1) Unassigned Expenses	(2) Nonrevenue Dept. 1
Trial balance, December 31, 1977	$ 80,000	$100,000
Allocation of unassigned expenses	−80,000	+10,000
Subtotals	$ −0−	110,000
Initial allocation of Department 1		−110,000
Subtotals		−0−
Initial allocation of Department 2		+ 9,350
Subtotals		9,350
Initial allocation of Department 3		−0−
Subtotals		9,350
Final allocation of Department 1		− 9,350
Subtotals		$ −0−
Final allocation of Department 2		
Subtotals		
Final allocation of Department 3		
Full cost totals		

Adapted from L. V. Seawell, *Introduction to Hospital Accounting* (Chicago: Hospital Financial Management Association, 1977).

| (3) | (4) | (5) | (6) | (7) | (8) |
| Producing Departments | | Revenue Producing Departments | | | |
Dept. 2	Dept. 3	Dept. A	Dept. B	Dept. C	Total
$ 60,000	$ 40,000	$200,000	$250,000	$150,000	$880,000
+ 6,000	+ 4,000	+20,000	+25,000	+15,000	-0-
66,000	44,000	220,000	275,000	165,000	880,000
+27,500	+16,500	+33,000	+22,000	+11,000	-0-
93,500	60,500	253,000	297,000	176,000	880,000
-93,500	+18,700	+37,400	-0-	+28,050	-0-
-0-	79,200	290,400	297,000	204,050	880,000
+15,840	-79,200	+27,720	+35,640	-0-	-0-
15,840	-0-	318,120	332,640	204,050	880,000
+ 2,337	+ 1,403	+ 2,805	+ 1,870	+ 935	-0-
18,177	1,403	320,925	334,510	204,985	880,000
-18,177	+ 4,309	+ 8,079	-0-	+ 6,059	-0-
$ -0-	5,442	329,004	334,510	211,044	880,000
	- 5,442	+ 2,381	+ 3,061	-0-	-0-
	$ -0-	$331,385	$337,571	$211,044	$880,000

of closing the cost centers in both the step-down and the double distribution methods must be based upon a careful determination of which centers provide the most service to other departments. Those providing the least service to other nonrevenue centers would be closed last.

Calculation of daily room costs

The methodology used to establish per diem room rates requires that values be assigned to the various types of accommodation, such as private, semiprivate, and ward. The weights begin with a unit value of 1.0 which is assigned to private accommodations. Semiprivate might then be assigned a value of 0.8 and ward beds 0.6, or whatever the relative valuation is determined to be for that hospital. The calculation is completed by multiplying the percentage of occupancy by the assigned weight, and multiplying this product by the number of beds in that category. The calculations are illustrated below.

Room type	(1) Occupancy rate	(2) Number of beds	(3) Weight	Product of (1) × (2) × (3)
Private	0.86	6	1.0	5.160
Semiprivate	0.91	12	0.8	8.736
Ward	0.72	5	0.6	2.160
Total daily weight				16.056

The daily weight would be multiplied by 365 days to determine an annual statistic which can then be used to calculate the daily cost of the three room categories. Using the dollar amount shown in Exhibit 5, which allocated $548,506 to inpatients who used adult and pediatric nursing units, the cost of the three room categories would be as follows:

$$16.056 \times 365 = 5,860.44 \text{ (annual statistic)}$$
$$\$548,506 \div 5860.44 = \$93.59 \text{ daily private room cost}$$
$$\$93.59 \times 0.8 = \$74.87 \text{ daily semiprivate room cost}$$
$$\$93.59 \times 0.6 = \$56.15 \text{ daily ward room cost}$$

Cost allocation to type of patient

After costs have been fully allocated to revenue producing centers a final costing process must be completed to allocate these full costs to the various types of patients served. The four patient categories are inpatients, newborns, outpatients, and emergency. A ratio of costs to charges is computed for this purpose, and the total gross revenues from each of these categories is necessary in order to make the computation.

The calculation is illustrated in Exhibit 5. Each revenue producing center is listed on the work sheet, and a ratio or cost converter is calculated for each center. This cost converter ratio is then multiplied by the revenues from each patient category to assign costs by type of patient. The final amounts provide a basis for cost reimbursement by governmental, health insurance, and other third party agencies.

Budget systems

The cost finding procedures described above form the basis for budgeting as well as rate setting and third party reimbursement. A budget is much more than a forecast of income and expenses because it comprises a comprehensive plan of operations expressed in monetary terms. It is through the budget that the hospital administration is in a position to request legislative appropriations in the case of governmental units, to set fund raising goals for charitable institutions, and to receive trust funds when part of a foundation. If third party reimbursement is to be based on budgeted rather than actual expenditures, as proposed by Blue Cross, the control of costs and expenses becomes of paramount importance.

The responsibility for and the authority over the budget is usually assigned to the hospital administrator by the Board of Trustees. Generally, the actual preparation of the budget and the control over budget expenditures are delegated to the chief financial officer, who may have the title of Controller, Vice President for Business Affairs, Office Manager, or some similar designation. Often a Budget Committee is established which has as members representatives from the professional staff, personnel, purchasing, plant maintenance, administration, and finance.

Before the actual budget preparation is begun it is helpful to prepare written instructions regarding the procedure to be followed, accompanied by illustrative forms and calculations. These written instructions should be disseminated to all person-

EXHIBIT 5

Calculation and application of a cost converter ratio

	Total Costs	Gross Revenues	Cost Converter	Inpatients	
				Revenues	Allocated Costs
Department:					
Operating rooms	$ 47,824	$ 42,909	1.114545	$ 42,265	$ 47,106
Laboratory	40,544	72,346	.560418	64,822	36,328
Radiology	55,648	95,261	.584164	70,779	41,346
Cost of drugs sold	18,400	29,408	.625680	24,526	15,346
Nursing units — adult and pediatric	548,506	581,221	.943713	581,221	548,506
Newborn nursery	43,729	36,382	1.201941		
Outpatient clinic	27,356	15,290	1.789143		
Emergency rooms	24,233	21,028	1.152416		
Totals	$806,240	$ 893,845		$ 783,613	$ 688,632

	Gross Revenues	Allocated Costs	Net
Type of Patient:			
Inpatients	$783,613	$ 688,632	$ 94,981
Newborn	38,938	45,198	(6,260)
Outpatients	49,310	47,579	1,731
Emergency	21,984	24,831	(2,847)
Totals	$893,845	$ 806,240	$ 87,605

Source: L. V. Seawell, *Introduction to Hospital Accounting* (Chicago: Hospital Financial Management Association, 1977).

Newborn		Outpatients		Emergency	
Revenues	Allocated Costs	Revenues	Allocated Costs	Revenues	Allocated Costs
		$ 644	$ 718		
$ 1,266	$ 709	6,258	3,507		
1,143	668	23,339	13,634		
147	92	3,779	2,364	$ 956	$ 598
36,382	43,729				
		15,290	27,356		
				21,028	24,233
$ 38,938	$ 45,198	$ 49,310	$47,579	$ 21,984	$ 24,831

nel who will be involved in the actual budget preparation or in the execution of the budget.

The hospital budget should be prepared to conform to established cost finding procedures. In addition, detailed cost center budgets should be prepared including anticipated costs and the statistics used for allocations.

Historical cost and expense data must be adjusted for budget purposes to reflect expected changes in capacity, changes in usage, and changes in costs.

One of the important results obtained from effective budgeting is that planning for the future is facilitated. The budget should indicate areas of over- and undercapacity and should facilitate the planning of remedial action. The diversion of resources—such as rooms, beds, equipment, and personnel—from underutilized to overutilized or critical areas produces both cost savings and more complete services to the community.

Capital budgeting

The rapid technological changes that are occurring have often rendered equipment and facilities obsolete long before the end of their useful lives. There is a strong tendency to acquire the latest and most modern equipment in order to provide the best possible medical care. This tendency is heightened by the fact that physicians refer patients partly on the basis of the availability of the most up-to-date equipment and facilities, and by the desire of the medical staff to have the most modern and effective equipment available. For these reasons the technique of cost-benefit analysis is especially useful in hospitals.

A cost-benefit analysis for the acquisition of a major new item of medical equipment is complicated by the fact that the benefit is difficult to quantify in monetary terms. The *cost* of the equipment can be measured with some accuracy, in terms of initial cash outlay as well as annual operating costs. The *benefit* part of the analysis is more difficult and requires the estimates of members of the professional staff and referring physicians. From the point of view of the hospital, consideration must be given to the likelihood that the investment will increase overall capacity utilization and thus reduce overall patient costs. This determination must be based on the estimate of professionals concerning need for the equipment in the community and the likelihood of increased utility. From the point of view of the professional staff and referring physicians, the benefits must be analyzed in terms of enhanced diagnostic and/or treatment ability and the resulting increase in the quality of medical care.

PRIVATE CLUBS

Private clubs are dependent for revenues entirely on member-users of the services which they provide, are less subject to governmental or other regulatory supervision, and exist almost exclusively to provide services to their members. Many private clubs also provide community services and engage in charitable or philanthropic activities. In addition, a large number of private clubs are affiliated with a larger special interest, religious, or fraternal organization. In all cases, however, the services provided are for the exclusive benefit of members and the revenues are normally received exclusively from members.

Private clubs include such diverse groups as local socioliterary reading groups, large metropolitan country clubs, yacht clubs, athletic clubs, and business clubs. They are characterized by the payment by members for the general privilege of belonging to the club, either through an initiation fee or the payment of periodic dues, or both. Members are usually assessed additional fees which are used for specific purposes, such as the construction of new or expanded facilities, the acquisition of new equipment, or the reduction of a burdensome debt or deficit.

Role of cost accounting

The revenues derived from each source are dependent upon the price quality relationship of the services and facilities offered. Private clubs compete with one another in any metropolitan area, and those which survive are those that do the best job of providing quality services and facilities at the best prices. This rationale applies at every prestige or status level. Therefore, cost accounting, which forms the basis for budgeting, pricing, and control, is essential to the continued viable existence of every private club.

An important characteristic of private clubs is that they provide services for which no direct charge is made. Even though the swimming pool incurs continuing costs for utilities, maintenance, and safety, the members and guests use the pool without individual charge. Costs directly incurred by specific facilities such as the swimming pool and the tennis courts, which produce no direct revenue, must be allocated to those facilities which do. In addition the costs of general housekeeping, grounds keeping, and building maintenance must be allocated. This allocation must be carefully handled, since the ardent golfer who shuns the general facilities of the club and the social lion whose primary interest is the club bar are often not pleased to support those facilities in which they have no interest.

Cost centers

All cost centers must be identified so that the direct costs incurred by each center can be accumulated in the accounts. Some of these cost centers will also be revenue centers. The golf course, dining room, bar, catering service, pro shop, and vending machines should be established as separate centers. Even though leased operations, such as the pro shop and vending machines, do not normally incur direct costs, they should be identified as cost centers in order to receive allocations of costs from other cost centers. Cost centers which normally do not generate revenues include administration, swimming pools, tennis courts, gardens, general grounds, general buildings, and roads of general use. The specific identification of such cost centers provides a basis for budgeting and operating control.

Allocation bases

Statistical bases for the allocation of the costs of nonrevenue cost centers to revenue centers must be accumulated. Electricity, for example, may be allocated on the basis of the wattage requirements of electrical devices used in the various cost or revenue centers, multiplied by the average number of hours these devices are in use. Swimming pool lights may only be in use on the average of three hours per day, while the purification system is in operation 24 hours per day. Thus, use of weighted time-usage data can provide an equitable basis for the allocation of electric expense. Administrative expense might be allocated on the basis of total other expenses incurred by, and allocated to, each cost center.

As in hospital cost accounting a pyramiding technique may be used to allocate costs to other cost centers, and subsequently to revenue cost centers. For a country club the apex of the pyramid might be utilities, followed by administration, grounds keeping, housekeeping, building maintenance, equipment maintenance, swimming pool, tennis courts, and playground, in that order. The accumulated direct and allocated costs of these non-revenue cost centers are then allocated to the revenue producing centers. Total revenue received should not be used as a basis for the allocation of costs because the production of revenue depends on providing quality services at commensurate and competitive prices. For this reason a more suitable allocation base would be the total of other costs. Utilizing this allocation basis, if the dining facility decided to upgrade the quality of meals by hiring a top chef and using the highest quality foodstuffs, general allocations would be increased in recognition of the fact that an increased overall cost consumption has occurred. On the other hand, the dining room would not be charged with more allocated costs if it increased its revenues simply by providing a more desirable cost-quality relationship or by providing better service.

Contribution margin prices

The allocation methodology discussed above is based on the premise that the revenue producing centers should produce enough revenue to cover their direct costs and a fair share of indirect costs. An alternative to the above philosophy is the *contribution margin* approach, in which each revenue center is charged with only its direct costs and an appropriate allocation of utilities, taxes, and insurance. Pricing is then determined by using only these direct costs, so that the total of all of the contribution margins will be sufficient for the coverage of all costs. This method places a heavier emphasis on direct costs and can lead to a general discontent of members fostered by the feeling that the users of revenue producing facilities are "carrying" the general membership. However, fewer allocations are required and the resulting accounting effort is reduced when the contribution method is used.

Budgeting

Budgeting for country clubs requires careful estimation of the expected revenues from the various sources at the prices established for the coming period. Income from investment funds and members dues are reasonably predictable and form the foundation for budgeting costs of general club operations. A frequently followed method is to budget the basic costs of providing the general club facilities which are available to all members from these sources. These include housekeeping, groundskeeping, security, building maintenance, and road maintenance.

The revenue producing centers are in a position, after general costs are covered, to be able to cover their own costs. Excesses, or profits, are generally budgeted to be returned to the members in some form, such as parties, balls, expansion or remodeling, specially priced meals or drinks, and reductions in green fees during certain periods. Through such returns as these to members the membership can be maintained at a desired level and member participation enhanced. This facet of the general budget deserves careful attention.

Many private clubs, especially country clubs and yacht clubs, sponsor invitational events which attract large numbers of the general public. These events incur many additional costs and usually are designed to produce additional revenues. Separate budgets for these events should be prepared in order to maximize the potential return to the club. In some cases several separate budgets for various segments which are involved in the event are prepared. An invitational golf tournament, for example, might involve separate budgets for dining room, bar, and general entrance fees.

Capital budgeting

Capital budgeting for a country club represents a problem because it is difficult to determine the revenue effects. Where the capital expenditures are cost effective the usual discounted future cash flow techniques can be used. Discounting, using the marginal interest rate available for investment funds, often provides a reasonable approximation of the cost reduction benefit of a capital expenditure. For example, if the capital expenditure being considered is the installation of an underground automatic fairway watering system, the savings in labor through reduction in personnel or overtime pay and in water consumption can be projected over the life of the equipment. The discounted savings in net cash outflow can then be compared to the acquisition and installation cost of the equipment. If the discounted cash flow is positive, the capital expenditure can be considered worthwhile.

Other non–cost-effective capital expenditures must be evaluated in terms of the benefit to the general membership. Capital expenditures for facilities which are to be available for general member use without specific charge are impossible to quantify, except in terms of initial cost and projected operating costs. The benefit to be derived can only be considered in terms of the desires or acceptance of the membership.

CHURCHES

A good church cost system should be sufficiently comprehensive to

1. Aid in planning future church activities.
2. Report actual progress with the planned church program.
3. Provide an historical record.

Establishing the church program for the coming year is the first step and must precede establishing the cost accounts. The actual cost records to be used must be arranged to provide cost data for the various programs and activities which will require resources. Thus, activities such as evangelism, stewardship, education, property, and general ministry would constitute major cost categories, with separate cost accounts for such natural cost elements as supplies, equipment, postage, and salaries shown for each of the major categories.

Church budgets follow two basic patterns: (1) the unified budget approach and (2) the multipurpose or duplex budget. When the unified budget is used all funds and expenditures pass through a single set of accounts. When a duplex system is used current funds are budgeted, controlled, and disbursed separately from those special funds which may be received for building programs or benevolences. Separate accounting records and even control over disbursements by different individuals may be applied to the separate funds when the duplex method is used.

Monthly or periodic reports which match actual expenditures against the original approved program should be prepared periodically. Care must be exercised to insure that each expenditure is charged against the correct program category, for the approved church program establishes the maximum which may be spent for that program activity without proper approval for a budget adjustment. Prorations of general church expenses to the various program categories serves little purpose in church cost accounting since these costs are usually fixed, and "full costing" of each program category is unnecessary.

VOLUNTARY HEALTH AND WELFARE ORGANIZATIONS

Health and welfare organizations are formed for the purpose of performing voluntary services for various segments of society. They derive their revenue primarily from voluntary contributions by the general public, and expend these funds for general or specific purposes connected with health, welfare, or community services. The organization is subject to the restrictions placed on it either by the community in which it operates or by the individuals who finance its programs. The system of accounts and cost allocations of the organization must give recognition to these restrictions, and for this reason fund accounting similar to that used by governmental organizations is employed.

Cost classifications

The basic cost and expense classifications should be established to measure the resources applied to each separate program which the organization undertakes. Separate accounting should therefore be made of the costs incurred for fund raising and administration so that they do not obscure the amount of resources applied to the basic purposes of the organization. Separate accounts for salaries, supplies, postage, medicines, and other object classifications should be established under each of the program categories.

Allocation to program accounts is frequently necessary to reflect the full cost of each program. Salaries of persons who perform more than one type of service, rental of space used for several programs, management costs, and fund raising expenses are examples of costs which must frequently be allocated.

A study of the organization's activities may be made at the beginning of the year to establish allocation methods and bases. The past year's operations may provide valuable data for setting percentages or ratios to allocate costs to each program, but periodic review of these bases should be undertaken to insure that they continue to represent present conditions. Such studies are necessary to allocate employee salary costs, postage, supplies, automobile costs, telephone, occupancy costs, and equipment depreciation.

Depreciation

Many arguments have been presented that depreciation for voluntary health and welfare organizations is not necessary. These arguments are primarily based on the premise that (1) depreciation is a tax shield, and these organizations are not subject to tax, and (2) funds are not retained for asset replacement in these organizations in the same way as they are in profit-oriented business which follow the going-concern concept. The arguments thus hold that asset replacement in voluntary health and welfare organizations is a funding decision and depreciation need not be reflected in the cost records each period.

The American Institute of CPAs has recommended that depreciation be recorded, as have many other professional groups. The costs incurred for each program during a given period of time are best reflected when the assets consumed in undertaking that program are reflected, and this would include normal depreciation charges.

Donated materials and services

Donated materials of significant amounts should be recorded at their fair market value when received. This process is necessary if the accounts are to reflect the costs of resources applied to each program. However, if the nature of the materials is such that a value is not available or cannot be substantiated, there may be reason not to record them. This is especially true when the materials are given away, as is sometimes the case with used clothing. Free use of facilities or other assets useful in fulfilling the organization's purpose should be recorded at its fair market value.

Donated services are more difficult to value than are donated materials. Ascertaining the value of services is further complicated because there is frequently no control over the amount or quality of the donated services. A value should be placed on donated services and a cost recorded only when the following conditions are met:

1. The service donated is a normal part of the program or supporting services.
2. The organization exercises control over the employment and duties of the donor.
3. The organization has a clearly measurable basis for the amount.

The services of volunteer workers who provide unskilled and nonprofessional duties normally are not recorded as contributions and thus are not given a cost in the accounts.

SCHOOLS AND UNIVERSITIES

Fund accounting, as described in another section of this handbook devoted to governmental accounting, is generally applicable to schools and universities. The funds usually found in an educational institution include (1) current funds, (2) loan funds, (3) endowment funds, (4) annuity and life income funds, (5) plant funds, and (6) agency funds. Schools and universities have cost accounting complexities not normally found in governmental organizations, however, because they engage in sponsored programs of research, instruction, and public service which require special cost apportionments. Sponsors of these special programs include governmental agencies, foundations, corporations, and individual donors. Almost without exception these donors require some cost sharing by the educational institution, and justification of the indirect costs included in the sponsored project cost proposal are necessary.

Cost sharing

Educational institutions are normally required to share in the costs of governmental grants. This policy is also enforced by some private foundations. Each governmental agency or private foundation has its own regulations governing how much and what type of cost sharing must be provided by the educational institution. Governmental agencies follow the guidelines in the *Office of Management and Budget Circular No. A–100* entitled "Cost Sharing on Research Supported by Federal Agencies." This document states that in general the costs to be borne by the educational institution should be at least 1 percent of the total project cost. Cost sharing is accomplished by contributing to the project for either direct or indirect costs from nonfederal funding sources.

Each project should be accounted for as a separate activity. The conditions and stipulations of this type of grant or contract require that the funds be expended only for approved activities or equipment, and thus expenditures for each grant must be segregated from costs of other grants. Cost participation by the educational institution may be accomplished on an individual contract basis, or there may be an institutional agreement permitting cost sharing on all contracts with a particular funding agency to be aggregated.

Overhead rate for sponsored programs

Sponsored projects have both direct and indirect costs, which are set out in the proposal. Direct costs include salaries and wages of those working directly on the project, equipment and material expenditures, and other identifiable costs directly associated with the project. Indirect costs are not listed in proposals by item and amount, but include an allotted share of administrative costs, facilities costs for such operations as the library or purchasing department, utilities, and other general costs.

Indirect costs applicable to any given contract are difficult if not impossible to determine, but if not covered by the sponsoring agency these costs will drain funds away from the educational institution's principal activities. For this reason an overhead rate is calculated and is used in proposals to funding agencies to indicate the overhead or indirect costs which are expected to be covered in the contract and how much of these indirect costs will be covered as a part of the institution's cost sharing arrangement.

The overhead rate is normally stated as a percentage of salaries and wages. Its calculation is completed by determining the total cost of space, administration, utilities, and service operations of the institution which are incurred for research, and dividing this sum by the total wages and salaries paid by the institution for research. When proposals are submitted for funding, the overhead rate is applied to the total salaries and wages appearing on the research proposal as direct costs. Cost sharing is indicated at this point in whatever way the institution elects. The calculation which could be applied to research overhead is made as follows:

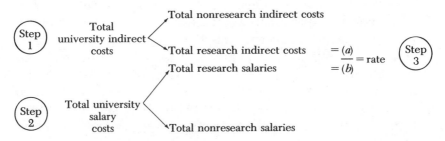

If the project is a special instructional contract instead of a research contract another overhead calculation would be necessary. This calculation would require that a relationship between *instructional costs* and *instructional salaries* be calculated, similar to the research cost–research salary ratio illustrated in the diagram. However, there are limits on the reimbursement of indirect instructional costs, such as the 8 percent maximum of HEW.

A step-down method similar to that used by hospitals may be used in making the calculation to determine the research overhead rate. The first step is to determine the total costs for each principal activity or cost center in the educational institution. These are then divided between the portion applicable

EXHIBIT 6
Nonsalary cost allocations to research and nonresearch activities

Cost center	Allocation base
Physical plant maintenance	Square footage
Occupancy costs	Square footage
Research administration	100% to research
Student services	0 to research
Academic administration	Percent of salaries paid for research
Library	Ratio of graduate students and faculty to undergraduate
General administration	Ratio of total research administration costs to total other costs

to research and the portion not applicable to research. Governmental agencies permit variations in allocations, just as private manufacturing companies permit variations in establishing their overhead application rates.

The centers and bases of allocation to research and nonresearch activities may be accomplished as shown in Exhibit 6.

Application of these ratios provides the total research costs incurred by the institution. Salaries paid for research are taken from payroll data. The services of each individual must be analyzed to obtain these data, and in many universities each faculty or staff person is assigned a fraction of his effort for research and another fraction for instruction. Thus, a professor may be assigned ⅓ time to research and ⅔ time to instruction.

The *Office of Management and Budget (OMB) Circular No. A–88* stipulates that the overhead rate must be audited by and negotiated with a cognizant federal agency. Acceptable procedures by which the indirect costs are to be allocated are described in *OMB Circular No. A–21.*

Cost Accounting Standards Board (CASB)

Schools and universities are included in the institutions subject to pronouncements of the CASB if they have sponsored projects of a "national defense" nature from governmental agencies in excess of $100,000 annually. They are therefore subject to (1) disclosure in writing of their cost accounting practices and (2) agreement to price adjustments for failure to follow standards set by the board.

PART
SEVEN

*Special methods of cost
accounting and control*

32

Cash management

*F. Norman Anderton**
Percy B. Yeargan†

INTRODUCTION

Over the past few years, businesses have been placing an increasing emphasis on the efficient use of cash. With the growth in the size of businesses and the increase in the rate of inflation, the amount of money required to operate a business has increased substantially. Furthermore, businesses have decentralized and the locations where they receive cash have scattered over a wide geographical area, resulting in larger amounts of cash being tied up in the process of collection.

It has become recognized that cash is a resource which should and can be managed like other assets of a business enterprise. Since one can measure it precisely, its effective management can be more controlled and its measurement more exact than the management and measurement of other assets. Each corporate treasurer has some type of cash management system; the degree of sophistication varies among companies of different size. Each system should seek to achieve the goal of effective and profitable use of corporate cash.

The purpose of this chapter is to describe the state of the

---

* Vice President and Treasurer, Vulcan Materials Company.
† Professor of Accounting, School of Business, University of Alabama in Birmingham.

art of cash management in order to compare one's cash activity with the description. One may decide to modify the existing system in a way to better accomplish its objectives.

First, the objectives of such a system will be presented and then the tools—sometimes referred to as the elements of cash management—which one may use to accomplish those objectives will be reviewed. These tools are forecasting, cash collection management, cash disbursement management, investing, borrowing, and bank relations. They may occur in various orders or groupings, but the order outlined here appears to be a logical way of discussing the various aspects of cash management.

OBJECTIVES

The first objective is the *optimum productive use of all company cash*. The optimum may be somewhat less than the maximum because of certain decisions to act in a manner which will not maximize the return or minimize the cost. Further explanation is presented under the topic of bank relations.

The second objective is to *coordinate the cash requirements* of each division, subsidiary, or branch with the total corporate financial plan. The term "division" is used in this chapter to include a division, subsidiary, branch, or any other autonomous part of the company. Each division has a role in the total plan for sources and uses of cash; consequently, each one must be coordinated with the others. The cash surplus created by one division must be readily available to meet the cash deficiency of another.

Most companies experience fluctuations in cash balances because of the seasonal nature of the business or nonoperating demands on cash at particular times. The third objective, therefore, is to *anticipate cash surpluses and cash deficiencies*—in order that the surpluses may be used most effectively and the deficiencies provided for—before the need actually occurs.

The fourth objective is to *minimize dependence on outside sources of financing*. It would be most unusual, probably indicating too much cash, for a company to be in the position of not needing, at least occasionally, an outside source of funds. It is very likely that some companies could reduce the need for outside funds by more efficient cash management procedures.

The fifth objective is very closely related to the preceding one. It is to *minimize interest payments and service charges.* Banks should receive compensation for the services which they render; this thought will be discussed in more detail under the topic of bank relations. However, it is a valid objective for the treasurer to strive to minimize these costs.

As the last objective, the treasurer should seek to *maintain a consistent and equitable policy in the company's relationships with banks.* The best bank relationship is one that is mutually beneficial for both the bank and the company, and one that will stand the test of time.

Certainly, the *cost* of the cash management system must be considered. As with other costs to be incurred, the system should be more beneficial to the company than it costs. The system should be such that it takes a minimum amount of management time, and the time spent by management should be productive. One must keep in mind that certain costs, such as bank charges and brokerage fees, are very visible but that certain other costs, such as the treasurer's time, are not as visible. They must, therefore, be taken into account in the overall evaluation of a plan.

FORECASTING

The first and most basic step is to determine the amount and the time of cash receipts and disbursements. Without such information a cash manager is not able to plan cash requirements, to anticipate short-term borrowing needs, or to foresee short-term investment possibilities.

Cash forecasts of one year or less are referred to as *short-term.* Those of more than one year—usually three or five years—are referred to as *long-term.*

It is usually desirable to prepare three types of budgets for periods of one year or longer. These are the operating budget, the capital budget, and the cash budget. Each has an impact on the other so that they must be prepared concurrently. Short-term cash forecasts—for a month or a quarter—emphasize the changes in timing of cash receipts and disbursements from that reflected in the yearly budget.

Most cash managers find that one year is the optimum length of time for the short-term cash budget. For some, the time may be less than one year. The decision may be made by formal sensitivity analysis or intuitively by the cash manager. The question to be decided is, does the addition of an extra time period have a significant effect on the decisions to be made at the front of the budgeted period? If not, then the addition may not be warranted. A very practical reason for forecasting for one year is that many other reports are for a year. Transferability of information from one to the other and comparison of one with the other are certainly facilitated.

There is a great variety in the length of time periods into which the annual budget is divided. Determining factors seem to be the preciseness with which the decision maker plans to work and the variability of the flows of cash. A smooth, repetitive pattern of cash receipts allows a much longer time period than an irregular, widely varying pattern of cash receipts allows. The period is also affected by the system's flexibility in dealing with daily fluctuations.

One possible combination of time periods is a daily forecast for at least a week, weekly forecasts for the remainder of the month, followed by monthly forecasts for the remainder of the quarter, and quarterly forecasts for the remainder of the year. One should select the combination of short time periods that serves his needs. The forecasts must be continually updated with new information from reliable sources.

In addition to deciding the time period to be used in the cash budget, one must select a *projection format.* The two most commonly used methods are the *direct forecast* of cash receipts and cash disbursements and the *adjusted earnings,* or *balance sheet,* approach. Usually the cash receipts and disbursements method is best for very short periods, with the balance sheet method reserved for periods of at least three months or longer. Other methods are used, of course, but these are the most frequently mentioned ones by writers on this topic.

Each division of the company should furnish its budget information to the corporate office, where it will be reviewed for reasonableness and combined with the budget information from all other divisions. The corporate treasurer is frequently the one responsible for preparing the cash budgets. The responsibility may be divided, of course, between the treasurer and other corporate officials. The controller is usually the one responsible for the capital and operating budgets.

The lack of attention paid to forecasting by the division employees and the unpredictable fluctuations of activities in certain industries are frequently mentioned as problems in forecasting. Close supervision of the division employees and clear, specific instructions to those employees are ways of overcoming these problems. It has long been recognized that complete support by top management and an educational effort by the treasurer and his staff will cure many such problems.[1]

The budgets referred to above must be presented to the board of directors for approval, preferably before the beginning of the year being budgeted. When the budgets are approved, they should then be developed into the formal budget plan of the year. Although a cash budget will be presented to the board of directors, it may be desirable to revise it after year-end balances are known.

CASH COLLECTIONS

In a centralized cash management program, the corporate treasurer must have the authority and the responsibility to do certain things in order to coordinate the collection and disbursement of cash and to achieve optimum productive use of all available cash. He must arrange for the establishment of all bank accounts and any subsequent changes in bank accounts. He must be responsible for maintaining relationships with banks. He must authorize the establishment of petty cash funds and the transfer of funds between banks, and arrange for short-term loans. Additionally, he must keep control records and issue status reports and forecasts.

The rapid transfer of cash receipts to a central depository account requires a network of banks, each of which has been selected because it offers rapid collection of receipts and rapid transfer to the central depository bank. The bank which serves each division must be able to handle the volume of cash transac-

---

[1] Masculine pronouns are being used for succinctness and are intended to refer to both females and males.

tions which the division will generate, and also be able and willing to perform certain other services for the division and its employees.

The treasurer should select a bank and designate it as the one to take cash receipts, either by deposit from division employees or by a lock box, or by both. Exhibits 1 and 2 illustrate the concept of concentration of funds from the divisions to the central depository bank.

The bank should offer the range of services which the treasurer desires as a part of his system. Banks vary considerably in the amount of service offered to customers. Some provide very little in addition to regular deposit and check paying services. Others are very aggressive in offering consultation services on a complete range of cash management techniques.

In the cash collections area, these latter banks will assist in determining locations of depository banks and lock boxes. They offer depository transfer check systems for division deposits.

EXHIBIT 1
Depository banks

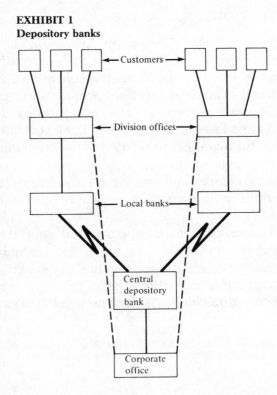

EXHIBIT 2
Lock box system

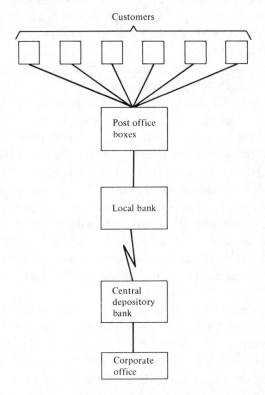

They also offer wire transfer systems of bank wire, TWX, Telex, and the Federal Reserve wire. These possibilities give the treasurer the ability to move cash into the central depository account as rapidly as he considers desirable, usually on a daily basis. One must also consider the cost of these services. The rapid collection and transfer is more expensive than the slower system. Lock boxes do create some problems. One is the inability to review customer checks before deposit, along with the risk of depositing checks marked "paid in full." Also, some customers may be unhappy when their own floats are reduced.

One must have an understanding of the internal float reduction in the system when he finally selects a bank. The bank which receives a check for deposit will convert the item to available funds either on an item-by-item basis or by applying a float factor. This factor will be determined by arbitrarily selecting a number of days, an average time for the bank as a whole, or an average for the account. One also should understand whether the bank clears its checks through the Federal Reserve System or a direct-send network.

To control and manage cash one must have a method of recording all the information which is sent to the treasurer's office concerning the collection and transfer of cash on a daily basis. One possible form of recording this data is shown in Exhibit 3.

Each day the person responsible for recording the data as it comes in by telephone will first record the beginning balance of cash by division and by bank. Each division will call to give this person the amount of its deposit for the day. The bank which has a lock box agreement will call to give the amounts of deposits for the day. Each report will be assigned a number, closely monitored for control purposes, and each call will be confirmed by a written report which will be compared with the daily information recorded at the time the telephone report was received.

Once this daily deposit information has been received over the telephone the treasurer, or an individual under his direction, makes a decision of the amount to be transferred to the corporate concentration account. His criteria for determining the ending balance must be well established and must be such that the relations with the depository banks may be maintained. He instructs the bank of the amount to wire-transfer to the corporate concentration account.

It is entirely possible that the treasurer may establish a standing order for the depository bank to transfer all available funds over a predetermined minimum balance to the corporate concentration account. If this is the case, the bank notifies the treasurer of the amount which it has transferred to the concentration account.

Once all the deposit information and the transfer information is known, the treasurer knows the status of his concentration account. It is necessary for him to know the amount of the disbursements for the day. This topic will be developed in the next section of this chapter; therefore, for the present purpose, assume that it is known. By adding the deposit transfers and

EXHIBIT 3

DIV	BANK	(1) BEGINNING BALANCE	DEPOSITS DATE	DEP. NO.	(2) AMOUNT	(3) CASH AVAILABLE	TRANSFERS TO TREASURY ACCOUNT TRF. NO.	(4) AMOUNT	(5) ENDING BALANCE
HQ	Bank QA	10,500.00	5/11		250.00	10	QA		10,250.00
	Bank QB	55,000.00	5/11	89	6,000.00	61	QB		61,000.00
A	Bank AA	800.00	5/11	92	154,900.00	155	AA 02	155,000.00	700.00
B	Bank BA	1,240.00	5/11	98	430,000.00	431	BA 83	431,000.00	240.00
C	Bank CA	13,700.00	5/11	90	320,000.00	334	CA 63	30,000.00	303,700.00
	Bank CB	1,150.00	5/11	96	970,000.00	971	CB 74	971,000.00	150.00
	Bank CC	2,180.00	5/11	93	150,000.00	152	CC 81	150,000.00	2,180.00
D	Bank DA	3,615.00	5/11	87	765,400.00	847	DA 75	760,000.00	9,015.00
E	Bank EA	5,160.00	5/11	92	75,150.00	77	EA 84	76,000.00	1,310.00
	Bank FA	4,240.00	5/11	90	176,800.00	175	FA 80	170,000.00	55,000.00
F	Bank FB	1,310.00	5/11	88	62,300.00	63	FB 79	55,000.00	5,610.00
	Bank FC	877.00	5/11	95	212,800.00	213	FC 78	213,000.00	677.00
	Bank FD	37,600.00	5/11	57	153,450.00	221	FD 76	190,000.00	31,050.00
G	Bank GA	14,680.00	5/11	90	139,800.00	154	GA 88	140,000.00	14,480.00
	Bank GB	1,670.00	5/11	102	306,360.00	307	GB 86	306,000.00	1,670.00
TOTAL		281,024.00	PLUS		3,902,910.00	MINUS		3,600,000.00	583,754.00

TREASURY ACCOUNT			TRANSFERS FROM CORPORATE DISBURSEMENT ACCOUNT		
BALANCE FROM PREVIOUS REPORT	1,203,790.00	CD	TRF. NO.		AMOUNT
LESS: TRANSFERS TO DISBURSEMENT ACCOUNTS	1,357,265.00	21	34	1,806.301	
		22	45	700,000	
SUB-TOTAL	(153,475.00)	23			
PLUS: MASTER-NOTE LOAN	200,000.00	CHARGE	CORPORATE DISBURSEMENT		
ENDING BALANCE ON 5/11/78	46,525.00	ACCOUNT #00-	$		AND
PLUS: TRANSFERS FROM DEPOSITORY ACCOUNTS	3,600,000.00	TRANSFER BY WIRE TO			
BALANCE AVAILABLE	3,646,525.00				
NOTES:		ATTENTION OF			
		FOR THE CREDIT OF			

TREASURER'S CASH JOURNAL   DATE 5/11/78

EXHIBIT 4

CASH REPORT			
DIVISION _____ G _____		_5/1x/78_ DATE PREPARED	

WEEKLY		MONTH END ONLY	
DEPOSITS TO CORPORATE DEPOSITORY ACCOUNTS		**DISBURSEMENT ACCOUNT**	
MONTH TO DATE – PREVIOUS REPORT	431,x00.00	BALANCE AT BEGINNING OF MONTH	
DEPOSITS SINCE LAST REPORT:		PLUS: TRANSFERS FROM CORP. OFFICE	
SATURDAY 5/6	—0—	SUB-TOTAL	
MONDAY 5/8	110,370.00	LESS: DISBURSEMENTS THIS MONTH	
TUESDAY 5/9	9x,000.00	BALANCE AT MONTH END	
WEDNESDAY 5/10	431,3x0.00	**IMPREST AND OTHER BANK ACCOUNTS**	
THURSDAY 5/11	347,850.00		
FRIDAY 5/1x	306,360.00	NAME OF BANK	
TOTAL MONTH TO DATE	1,719,150.00		

FOUR WEEKS' DISBURSEMENTS – IN THOUSANDS

CURRENT WEEK – ITEMS OVER $200,000		
DAY / CITY MAILED TO	AMOUNT	
5/10 Pitsburg, Pa	x68	
5/1x Denver Colo	x17	
5/1x Chicago, Ill	3x0	

SUBSIDIARY BANK ACCOUNTS		
SUBSIDIARY	NAME OF BANK	

TOTAL – CURRENT WEEK – 5/1x	1,865
TOTAL – WEEK ENDING – 5/19	470
TOTAL – WEEK ENDING – 5/x6	x50
TOTAL – WEEK ENDING – 6/x	350

NEXT FOUR WEEKS' DEPOSITS – IN THOUSANDS

WEEK ENDING – 5/19	770	
WEEK ENDING – 5/x6	4x5	**PETTY CASH FUNDS**
		BRANCH
WEEK ENDING – 6/x	xx5	SUBSIDIARIES
WEEK ENDING – 6/9	900	TOTAL DIVISION

MAIL THIS REPORT AT THE CLOSE OF BUSINESS EACH FRIDAY TO: TREASURER.

SIGNATURE – DIVISION CONTROLLER OR DELEGATE

subtracting the disbursement transfers, the current balance of the concentration account is known.

If the balance is an overdraft, one must take action to cover it. One would be well advised to have made arrangements for the concentration bank to create a loan automatically by the use of a bank master note, or to have made some similar arrangements. This topic will be developed more fully in the last section of this chapter. If the balance is more than the minimum balance for this account, a decision must be made about the proper investment of the excess. Most companies develop a set of "Criteria for Investment," which sets forth the type and quality of investments which can be made. This topic will also be developed more fully in a subsequent part of this chapter. If these criteria have been well described, the persons involved in the day-to-day recording of receipts and transfers will be able to make routine decisions about investments.

The treasurer's cash journal may serve as a source of entries to the various cash accounts, but there must be careful comparisons made of figures that come in on subsequent reports. In transmitting information by telephone, errors are bound to happen. It is very desirable to have specific procedures established to correct errors with subsequent reports, rather than attempting to correct errors by changing reports previously filed.

Each division should prepare a weekly cash report at the end of each week. Exhibit 4 illustrates such a report showing the possibility of obtaining, in addition to a recap of the week's cash activities, estimates from the division of the receipts and disbursements by weeks for the next four weeks. One will note the possibility of obtaining information about large disbursements which will help in anticipating cash needs.

CASH DISBURSEMENTS

Efficient disbursement is an integral part of any effective cash management system. Just as corporate treasurers are interested in speeding up cash collections, they must also be concerned about effective control over disbursements. This control means that the system should provide for payment of payables at the last possible moment to take advantage of all available discounts and to take advantage of all desirable time lags between delivery of the check to the payee and the payment of the check by the issuer.

There are two principal ways to organize the disbursements part of cash management. They are to centralize, to the extent reasonable and practical, the management of the company's payables or to use a decentralized disbursing plan whereby checks are written on bank accounts maintained at division locations.

After discussion of the features of each of these a combination of the two, which seems to give the main advantages of each, will be presented. There are important objectives which the cash manager should strive to accomplish, which will lead to the most suitable disbursement method. Good relations must be maintained with suppliers by making payments correctly and timely. Missing discounts is costly, but late payments may be even more costly. The disbursement system should be operated in the most economical manner that is consistent with other corporate objectives. Disbursement information which is both accurate and timely should be provided. Daily, weekly, and monthly status reports and disbursement forecasts are vital to an effective system. The balance of cash on hand should be kept to the minimum amount which will cover requirements and compensate the bank for credit and services. The corporate reputation is to be maintained but, at the same time, the system should provide the longest float possible, consistent with the foregoing objectives.

It is very apparent that some of these objectives conflict with others. Each cash manager is faced with determining which of these are the overriding objectives and with reconciling the conflicting ones to the extent possible.

If the decentralized plan is adopted, the cash manager will probably set up bank accounts which are especially designed to control the working funds of the divisions, instead of dual-purpose or general accounts. These may be the imprest account, the zero balance account, or the automatic balance account.

The *imprest account* is established at a division's local bank. A balance equal to the needs for a certain time period is established. The fund is replenished when properly approved expenditure documents are submitted to the corporate headquarters. This method allows the division to operate autonomously, but it requires at least as many bank accounts as divisions. It also requires larger cash balances than other alternatives require.

If the *zero balance account system* is selected, an account is established in a bank at the division's location. There is an understanding, usually a written agreement, with the bank that the account is to be maintained with a zero balance. Each day the company deposits with the division's bank an amount equal to the checks presented for payment that day. This deposit may be made from a different account maintained by the company in the same bank, or by wire transfer from another bank. This method allows the division to handle its own disbursements and does not require cash balances to be maintained. The bank must be compensated for rendering this service by payment of a fee or by maintaining a balance in other accounts.

The *automatic balance account* is an arrangement with the bank to receive deposits from the division, to pay checks written by the division, and to monitor the balance in the account. The agreement usually provides for the bank to transfer the excess over a maximum balance to the corporate treasury bank. Conversely, when the balance falls below the minimum account balance, the bank notifies the cash manager who transfers by bank wire a sufficient amount to bring the account back to the agreed minimum.

If *centralized disbursements* are adopted, the divisions authorize payments and send these approved vouchers to corporate headquarters. The payments are made by the corporate office personnel with no further involvement of the division employees. This method allows the greatest degree of concentration of cash, but it also brings with it problems of processing all the disbursements of the corporation. It also adds to the total processing time, which could become critical in achieving payments by discount or due dates.

A system which adopts the best features of decentralization and centralization is both practical and desirable. If the division employees have been well-schooled in the corporate philosophy of cash management and cash control, they can and will do an effective job of managing the payments of regular, routine payables. The disbursement account on which each division writes its checks should be one which is maintained in the corporate treasury bank for that purpose. Therefore, the treasurer opens a zero balance disbursing account for each division in his central concentration bank. As was discussed earlier in connection with Exhibit 3, the bank informs the cash manager each day of the amount of checks presented for payment. By prior agreement, the bank transfers this amount automatically from the concentration account to the various disbursing accounts. The bank also furnishes in writing to the cash manager the amount transferred to each disbursement account. This method requires fewer bank accounts, which is an advantage that is discussed more in the section on bank relations. It also increases the cash manager's opportunity to manage the cash more effectively.

Two other possibilities should be considered by cash managers: remote disbursing and payable-through drafts.

Some banks are aggressively seeking corporate *remote disbursing* business. These banks emphasize the advantage of a longer float time by recommending that zero balance disbursing accounts be established in affiliate banks located in smaller, remote towns where direct-send and intracity clearings are not likely and where Federal Reserve clearings are delivered only one time per day. The bank agrees to notify the cash manager before noon each business day of the dollar amount to by paid that day and agrees that the amount to be paid may be covered by closing time that day.

One must consider the total impact such arrangements will have on the company's total banking relationship and corporate image. It does usually entail adding another bank, which must be compensated in some manner for this service. Employees may have problems in cashing payroll checks drawn on a remote bank; however, there are ways to overcome this problem. Before establishing a remote disbursing system one should consider the Federal Reserve's attitude toward this arrangement. Since the Fed guarantees collection after the second day, the actual float time may be less than that claimed by the bank in espousing its virtues.

The *payable-through draft system* is designed to give the issuer an additional advantage over the advantages of the zero balance account. When the drafts are presented to the bank named as the payable-through bank, it gives the issuer the opportunity to accept or reject the draft before the draft is paid. Otherwise, the PTD is processed just as a check is processed. The opportunity of review before payment is one which should be

considered carefully. It gives the corporate headquarters personnel an opportunity to control even more closely the disbursements made by the divisions. For general disbursements the
draft method is burdensome; it is usually reserved for special-
purpose payments where cash payments are required at time
of purchase.

The cash disbursement system which is selected by the cash
manager should include reports from the bank which provide
the needed information to manage cash effectively. The degree
of detail is almost limitless. More and more banks have available
computer programs which give them the capability of preparing
such reports as frequently and in as much detail as is useful.

INVESTING

Full utilization of cash includes investing surplus cash. Each
cash manager must develop a workable definition of *surplus*
cash to be able to accomplish this objective. Some cash managers
seem to define the term as any excess over the minimum cash
balance to cover the current day's operation and small contingencies. Others add to that definition the compensating balance
which must be held in the bank to compensate it for services
and for lines of credit.

A set of criteria as to amount and quality for investing surplus
cash may be developed by the cash manager, and it may or
may not be subject to approval by officers of the company or
the board of directors. At the other extreme, the criteria may
be established by official resolution of the board and may direct
very specifically the activities of the money manager in this
area. Most lists of criteria include quality of the credit instrument, liquidity or marketability, safety from market price fluctuations, and income or yield criteria. Each cash manager must
put these in the order which fits his particular situation and
add others to these four as he sees fit. He must, of course, take
into consideration the size of his company and the risk it is
willing to assume.

It is very desirable for specific instructions to be provided
so that the person who must make decisions on a day-to-day
basis is able to operate within such guidelines. When the treasurer's cash journal, which was illustrated in Exhibit 3, indicates

excess cash, it is time to make a decision as to where it should be invested and for how long.

As an illustration of such instructions, the criteria in Table 1 are presented as possible ones for a conservative company with net worth of $200 million to $300 million.

All investments of this nature should be in marketable securities which have *price stability*. The cash manager will ordinarily seek to avoid risk as to principal value when investing for this purpose. It is for this reason that most cash managers think of

TABLE 1
Criteria for type of investment

1. Direct obligations of the U.S. government	No limit
2. Obligations of U.S. government agencies........................	No limit
3. Bankers' acceptances of top 100 banks in the United States or top 25 banks in the world	$5,000,000
4. Negotiable certificates of deposit	
a. Top 10 banks in the United States	5,000,000
b. Banks in the United States ranked 11–30th	2,000,000
5. Commercial paper	
a. Rated A–1 by S&P and P–1 by Moody's	4,000,000
b. Rated A–2 by S&P and P–2 by Moody's	1,000,000
c. Rated A–3 by S&P as collateral for a repurchase agreement *only*	2,000,000
6. Corporate bonds, within 90 days of maturity	
a. Rated AA or better by S&P or Moody's	3,000,000
b. Rated A by S&P or Moody's	2,000,000
7. Municipal notes	
a. Rated MIG–1	3,000,000
b. Rated MIG–2	1,000,000
8. Municipal bonds, expected to be held to maturity rated AA or better by S&P and Moody's	3,000,000
9. Nonnegotiable CDs and master note participations in company's line banks, provided these other tests are met:	1,500,000 or 3% of equity, whichever is less

   a. Minimum equity, $50,000,000
   b. 3 year ratios:

(1) Earnings/equity (min.)	12%
(2) Loans/deposits (max.)	70%
(3) Provisions for losses/loans (max.)	1%
(4) Reserve for losses/loans (min.)	1%
(5) Earnings/assets (min.).....................	0.7%
(6) Equity/assets (min.)	5%

   c. Maturity date, not to exceed 90 days
   d. Must meet all ratio tests for last three years except (2) and (4), which are based on most current year.

direct obligations of the Federal Government or repurchase agreements when investing for this purpose.

One is also concerned with the *marketability* of the securities. Although maturities are selected to coincide with forecasted needs, one should be in a position to sell the securities if the cash position dictates. Therefore, it is important to be able to call on the investment banker to repurchase or to be able to liquidate in the secondary market.

Yield is usually listed last among the criteria, although there seems to be more interest in short-term investments when short-term interest rates are high, relatively speaking. It is valid advice to the cash manager to seek the highest yield, but only after quality, liquidity, and safety criteria have been satisfied.

Money market instruments do differ in yield because supply and demand fluctuations affect their prices. For this reason, among others, the responsibility of managing the short-term investment portfolio is frequently vested in one person in the organization who has experience and expertise in this area. This person must have data furnished by others in the company concerning maturity dates of large obligations and payments of dividends, income taxes, and capital expenditures in order that investment maturity dates coincide with payment dates.

The one who is responsible for the management of the portfolio has several sources of help in making decisions. Specialists in investment houses and in commercial banks are always available to furnish information as to what is available and the ratings of the issuers. A cash manager who is managing a portfolio of any size will find it very desirable to have at least one investment banking connection which has access to the money market. In order to have access to a wider range of investment opportunities and to realize the highest available yield, it is desirable to deal with more than one investment banker, but to limit the number to the extent that there will be a genuine interest in serving the company.

In addition to investment bankers who actually deal in short-term investments, it is helpful in a larger money market to have a commercial banking connection which is able to perform many services needed in expediting investments. In order to consummate transactions rapidly, it is desirable to have an agreement with such a bank to buy, sell, and hold securities for the company through its custody department. With the proper agreement, the cash manager may call the bank and instruct it to accept and pay for certain securities, charge the company's account, and hold the securities for safekeeping. Even when the purchase is handled separately the bank will still perform the other functions enumerated. Naturally, these instructions should be confirmed in writing for the records of both the bank and the company.

If a need for cash arises before maturity of the instrument, the manager sells the security through the investment banker and asks the custody bank to deliver the security to the buyer upon payment and to credit the company's account. If the need for cash does not arise before the maturity date, the bank may be instructed (usually in the agreement) to take the proceeds upon maturity, credit the company's account, and deliver the instrument to the proper party. These activities could be carried out without a banking connection in a large money market, but they are much easier if such a connection is available.

BORROWING

In the discussion of the day-to-day receipt and disbursement of cash, it was indicated that when transfers to disbursement accounts deplete the concentration bank account, the account can be returned to a minimum balance through the creation of a loan by adding to the master note. This arrangement is a continuing one but is, naturally, subject to a maximum limit.

When seasonal operations result in this maximum limit being reached, other arrangements must be made by the treasurer. He must consider the amount of cash he needs and the length of time before he can repay it. The length of borrowings usually is referred to as short-term, intermediate-term, or long-term. Short-term is most frequently one year or less in length. Long-term is considered to be ten years or more. Intermediate term is in between the two and is frequently five to eight years. Short-term needs are financed with short-term loans.

The ways one may arrange short-term financing are almost limitless. Only bank loans and commercial paper will be considered here. The treasurer should have already established lines of credit at a sufficient number of banks so that the only thing he needs to decide at this time is which bank to use for this loan. If the lending bank is a local bank, the treasurer sends a signed note and a deposit slip to the bank, which returns the receipted duplicate slip to the treasurer to acknowledge deposit. However, if the bank is not the concentration bank, the funds must be transferred to the concentration bank to meet that day's needs of the system.

If the bank is other than a local bank, the lending bank may be requested to transfer funds by wire to the concentration bank, and a note and appropriate letter of transmittal is sent to the lending bank to confirm the transaction. With good forecasting the money manager can send the note ahead of the date the cash will be needed.

A source of funds for larger companies with high credit rating is the *commercial paper market.* If the company is likely to issue unsecured promissory notes in the money market, prior arrangements should be made to handle the transaction with an investment banker which maintains an active market for commercial paper and is in position to sell the company's paper with an acceptable maturity date. The investment banker can give immediate quotes as to interest rate, depending on the company's credit ratings. If this source of financing is used the company should have its paper rated by Moody's and Standard and Poor's rating services.

To expedite such transactions, it is suggested that the company arrange with a commercial bank in a money market city to act for the company by issuing the notes and taking delivery of the funds. This bank would be the same one used for performing similar services in connection with investments, as explained in that section. The proceeds may be transmitted by this bank by wire transfer to the concentration bank, which should notify the treasurer when the deposit is received. The transaction will, of course, be confirmed in writing to the investment banker and the agent bank. The arrangements with the agent bank will most likely include provisions for the bank to handle payment at maturity upon presentation of the notes, with funds transferred to it by the company.

The amount of the note, the interest, and the maturity date should be recorded on a schedule such as Exhibit 5. The information is necessary in planning for payments on maturity and in making the adjustments for prepaid and accrued interest for the monthly financial statements. It is also very useful when

EXHIBIT 5

SHORT TERM LOANS OUTSTANDING

CREDIT	LENDER CONTACT		LENDER
5 MM	Master Note		Bank QB

REFERENCE		DUE	RATE	PRINCIPAL				INTEREST			
NO.	DATE	DATE	%	LOAN	PAYMENTS	BALANCE	DAYS	ACCRUED PREPAID	PAID WRITE-OFF	BALANCE
1	Aug		7¾							1,019 √
2				100 000		100 000	1	21 23		1,040 3
3				600 000	100 000	600 000	1	127 38		1,167 76
4					600 000	—				
5				1000 000		1000 000				
6						1000 000				
7						1000 000	3	636 00		1,800 25
8					1000 000	—				
9										
10									1,019 √	785 60
11				200 000		200 000	1	43 46		829 06
12					200 000	—				

investments are made to schedule the repayment to match maturities of drafts.

If the forecast indicates that short-term borrowing is not the answer, the treasurer should update the five-year forecast to determine the extent and length of the expected cash deficiency. He must make plans for obtaining the necessary funds by intermediate-term or long-term borrowing or by issuing additional equity shares. A prudent cash manager will not use short-term debt to meet long-term needs. This practice is extremely dangerous.

BANK RELATIONS

The relationship which a money manager establishes with the banks with which he deals is certainly the cornerstone of his cash management plan. Most bankers prefer that their customers have large deposit balances. Conversely, money managers strive to maintain minimum balances in their accounts. It is the successful compromise of this basic conflict that makes this part of the plan very significant.

The number of banks with which a company should do business is to some extent a function of the size of the company. It seems, however, that the nature of the business and the geographical dispersion of the operations play a much larger role in determining the number of banks. The number must be large enough to accomplish all phases of the cash management plan—not only cash gathering but also investing and lending.

The treasurer must evaluate the banks which are available to serve his company's needs. He should consider financial condition, lending limits, responsiveness to credit needs, prices of services, and ability of the bank's personnel in areas where he will need service, plus a friendly and cooperative attitude. For instance, some banks are more efficient in lock box operations than others and certain ones are more experienced in foreign exchange, or specialized types of financing. The final decision between two or more banks considered equal is likely to be based on an evaluation of the management of the bank and its availability for advice and counsel.

The treasurer should be aware that adding another bank is not likely to increase the sales of the company. At the same time, he must be aware that business considerations may require doing some business with a bank that would not otherwise be considered as fulfilling the specific objectives of the cash management system. Sometimes the business consideration can be satisfied by doing something other than opening an account, such as purchasing a certificate of deposit from the bank. At maturity the relationship may be terminated very quietly. Tax deposits offer another opportunity other than the establishment of an account for favoring a bank which does not fit into the efficient network of banks.

If the bank is to be used for limited services, such as payroll accounts only, the bank may be compensated by fees and no balances will be maintained except for the few days it takes the payroll checks to clear.

If the bank is to provide a full line of services, it is very desirable for the treasurer to discuss, at least annually, the services which he expects to use and the manner in which the bank will be compensated. Discussing in advance the line of credit which is desired and the manner of calculating the charges which the bank will make is likely to create better working relations. The charges which are frequently mentioned, 10 percent + 20 percent, meaning 10 percent of the line plus 20 percent of the average borrowing, are frequently negotiable. Lines of credit and compensating balances are usually negotiated for a period of a year.

The method of calculating the average borrowing may be daily, monthly, or some other method. It is much better to know how this average is calculated. It is desirable, also, to have a definite understanding as to whether or not balances may be double counted. If balances are counted for both the line of credit and for service charges, a smaller average balance will satisfy the requirements.

The cash manager has much more leeway in his day-to-day operations if the averages are annual averages. This method gives him the opportunity to keep balances low when he is in a net borrowing position. When he is in a net lending position, he may build up his averages by large balances. This ability makes his daily operations easier and it is also less expensive. A comparison of requirements with actual averages to date, as illustrated in Exhibit 6, is quite helpful in this regard.

EXHIBIT 6

ABC COMPANY
Bank Balances and Bank Borrowing Position
May, 1978
(000 omitted)

			Collected bank balances					Bank borrowing			
			Average requirement year to date					Current month		Year to date	
Bank	Credit line	Compensating balance terms*	Credit line	For services	Minimum	Actual average year to date	Under	Highest amount	Ending balance	Highest amount	Average amount
QA	5,000	15	750	780	780	850	70	2,500	—	3,000	600
QB	1,000	10 + 10	100	109	109	100	[9]				
CA	2,000	10 + 10	200	184	200	216	16			1,500	300
DA	500	10/20	50	102	102	90	[12]				
FA	—		50	50	50	55	5				
	8,500		1,100	1,225	1,241	1,311	70	2,500		4,500	900

* Compensation balance terms:
  15% = 15% of credit line
  10 + 10 = 10% of credit line plus 10% of average borrowing
  10/20 = 10% of credit line or 20% of average borrowing, whichever is greater.

900

To assess the service being rendered by the banks, the treasurer should request monthly account analysis reports, such as Exhibit 7. This information is useful in evaluating the services being provided by the bank and also in comparing prices which banks charge for services.

It is very helpful in bank relations for the treasurer to have personal contact with the officers with whom he deals in his major banks at least once each year; more frequent contact is desirable. This contact helps the treasurer evaluate the services being provided by the banks; it also provides a channel of communication between the company and the bank, which keeps

EXHIBIT 7

```
                          ACCOUNT ANALYSIS

    The bank                          Prepared for: ABC company
                                      For month ended: May 31, 1978


    Balances:
        Average daily ledger balance                    $  620, 000
        Less: Average daily uncollected funds              454, 460
        Average daily collected balances                   165, 540
        Less: Reserve requirement 12%                       19, 865
        Investable/loanable balance                        145, 675

    Bank earnings
        Earnings at 5 3/4 %
        Return on investable/loanable balance           $    698. 03

    Bank charges:
```

Service	#Items	Price per item	Service charge
Items deposited	1202	$ .05	60.10
Checks paid	840	.12	100. 80
Wire transfers	21	3.00	63.00
Account Maintenance			10.
Lock box, variable	415	.25	103.75
Lock box, fixed			120.
Stop payments	4	3.00	12.00
Total bank charges			$ 469. 65

```
    Balance requirements to support banking services (@ 6 %)  $   93,930
    Balance available to support credit or other services      $   51, 745
    Additional balance needed to support banking services      $      —
```

the bank updated on operating plans and future projects. It also fosters a closeness in the relationship, which helps in day-to-day operations, as well as in making decisions concerning future money management plans. A proper relationship will ensure that neither party is ever shocked by a request or response by the other. Each party is essential to the other and should be respected for its position.

33
Capital budgeting

*John M. Carroll**

INTRODUCTION

The conceptual influences shaping the theory and practice of capital budgeting are to be found in the fields of accounting principles, financial analysis, and strategic planning.

The matching concept of Generally Accepted Accounting Principles (GAAP) holds that expenditures should be related to associated revenues for financial reporting. Consequently, expenditures for assets which have an economic life extending beyond one year are initially capitalized and then amortized or depreciated over their revenue-generating life. It is to this group of expenditures that capital budgeting techniques are applied by most companies. Revenues and expenses are accounted for by the operations budget, and working capital by the finance budget.

However, another GAAP concept in conflict with the foregoing is the conservative concept. This concept holds that where the economic outcome is highly uncertain then the particular expenditure should be charged against income during the period in which it is made. Thus, expenditures for research and development, sales promotion, methods and functions efficiency which

---

* Vice President Finance, Leach & Garner Company.

could result in benefits extending beyond one year are charged against income when incurred. Frequently if these items can be fitted into the operating budget of a company on the basis of being "affordable" they escape any rigorous scrutiny. In a business world increasingly beset by uncertainties, it is this problem which, perhaps, most confounds the readers and framers of financial reports.

The discipline of financial analysis does not differentiate between spending proposals on the basis of GAAP. In a theoretical economic sense spending on a research project does not differ from the purchase of a machine tool. Even assumed differences in certainty of commercial purposes and outcome become blurred in advanced and specialized technical economies. The fields of communications, nuclear engineering, and electronics, for instance, are marked by high changeovers in technology which make obsolete certain production techniques and equipment with each advance. Even more basic industries such as steel and glass are vulnerable to materials substitution. Financial analysis and the parent field of microeconomics provide the measurement methodology to evaluate different proposals on a common basis.

Thus the techniques described here are applicable to an examination of, and selection among, a broader range of expenditures than just those capitalized on the balance sheet.

This section is concerned with the process of resource allocation in general, but recognizes that most corporations view the techniques as applicable to capitalized expenditures.

The need to place in a strategic setting a proposed capital expenditure will be reviewed first: a necessary starting point to understand the business purpose of the investment and the conditions under which the investment will be made. Second, the process of proposal development will be described, focusing on the elements needed to evaluate a given proposal. Third, the various techniques used to measure, rank, and select among alternative spending proposals will be examined. Every business is to a greater or lesser extent resource limited, so ways must be found to optimize the direction of these resources. Fourth, attention will be given to measurement techniques which recognize the essential ingredient of uncertainty in capital spending.

Before proceeding, however, it is necessary to eliminate a

class of capital spending decisions which are unrelated to the subject of economic analysis. These relate to the fundamental policies of a business. In the past these have been largely implicit, but increasingly the need is for corporations to state clearly their policy with regard to government compliance in the areas of occupational safety, environmental control, and employment programs. Other noneconomic policies relate to the culture of the firm and include such items as office furnishings, building architecture, and employee recreational facilities. "Economic" justifications of these expenditures on some assumed productivity improvement are usually contrivances. Thus, the subsequent analysis deals only with spending decisions which are concerned with financial returns.

STRATEGIC CONTEXT OF CAPITAL SPENDING PROPOSALS

The problem of deciding whether or not a piece of equipment should be purchased, a research and development project undertaken, or a stack-scrubber installed cannot be determined unless referenced to a predetermined strategy.

The definitions of strategy vary but all have a common focus concerned with the long-term decision-making process which concentrates management's energy and corporate resources on the external environment.

The fact that the particular expenditure will be "profitable" is not, of itself, sufficient reason to proceed, for random investments could dissipate a corporation's energy and result in the business becoming unmanageable. Furthermore, a single action or investment might display a greater return than another, but it could be that these individual actions are components of separate and larger strategies. The allocation of resources to the former could be suboptimal in the broader context. Suppose, for instance, a business has a stated top-priority strategy for market penetration within its industry, and another less important strategy of backward integration. Equipment needed to provide capacity in support of the former strategy would have to be viewed in the context of the total strategy, not as a direct comparison with another piece of equipment needed to produce a previously purchased component.

It is not proposed to deal with the subject of strategic planning in any comprehensive manner within the scope of this book. The aim here is to place capital spending proposals in their strategic context for two reasons: (1) to identify interdependent investments, and (2) to help determine the differing levels of risk associated with different strategies.

The structure of strategy

As was stated earlier, strategy is concerned with the long-term decision-making process which concentrates management energy and corporate resources on the external environment. The range of corporate action can be classified into two sets of *generic strategies* which describe both business unit and corporate strategy. The various operational actions are the tactical activities concerned with the most appropriate method of strategy execution, and as such derive their reason for being from the parent strategy.

As most capital spending decisions are tactical in nature, such as the selection of a machine or building, it is necessary to understand and place the tactical choices in their broader strategic framework. This framework is shown in Exhibit 1 and described below.

EXHIBIT 1
The structure of corporate and business unit strategy

Structure	Example
Business unit strategy	
Generic strategy	New products/new markets
Specific strategy	Mini-computer into OEM
Tactical programs	Engineering development program
Financial	Tooling request
Corporate strategy	
Generic strategy	Diversification
Specific strategy	Acquisition of McDonalds Hamburgers
Tactical program	Investment analysis research
Financial	Consultants fees

This example is based on IBM; it is, of course, fictional.

1. Business unit strategy

Business unit defined. Every corporation is made up of one or more fundamental business units which may or may not conform to that business's organization chart. In order to classify a business unit's strategic strategy it is axiomatic, but frequently not obvious, that the business units of the company be first identified. A strategic business unit is externally oriented and distinguishable from other business activities of the corporation with respect to the following variables:

a. Pricing: Can the price of the business unit's products be set independently?

b. Competitors and customers: Does the business unit share a common set of customers and competitors with another business unit?

c. Quality: Will the quality of its product or service affect sales elsewhere in the organization?

d. Substitutability: Can the products of one business unit be substituted for those of another?

It is necessary to labor on this analysis even if for no other reason than to distinguish between supply points in an organization and the parts of the business serving a market need. For instance, the spending proposals of the Saginaw Gear Division of General Motors can best be understood in the context of the automobile or truck strategies it is supporting.

Generic business unit strategies. While specific classification systems vary, all hold that business unit action can be categorized and that such categories can help explain the risks inherent in the business proposal. One such system is shown in Exhibit 4.

2. Corporate strategy. Corporate strategies are not merely the sum total of various business unit strategies but reflect choices concerning growth and renewal, financial structure, and external relationships.

Growth and renewal. The selection of investments to shape the growth and renewal of the organization is the prerogative of corporate management. Exhibit 2 gives examples of such strategies.

The primary thrust of these decisions is concerned with the deployment of corporate assets to reshape the character and sources of corporate revenues and profits.

Financial structure. The financial structure of the firm is not generally considered a business unit choice. However, in some

EXHIBIT 2
Corporate growth and renewal strategies

Strategy	Purpose	Risk
Conglomeration (industry diversification)	Financial leverage Balanced cash flows	Unfamiliar with business in short term Long-term financial risk lower
Agglomeration (linked industries)	Technology synergy Concentration corporation energy	Low risk
Maturity adjustment (revectoring assets, etc.)	Counterbalance aging process	Problem of going against cultural grain
Excess resource exploitation (exploit surplus raw material)	Increased ROI	Risk from unfamiliar industry
Economic balance (flat or counter-balancing business cycles)	Reduce fluctuations in revenue/earnings	Reduces risk if business understood
International market development	Domestic operating leverage	Broadens competitive base
Multinational corporation	International operations (manufacturing/marketing/ engineering)	Greatly increased
Horizontal interaction (extend company's product/service range)	Broad synergistic opportunities	New business may be more difficult than first appears

cases such as a real estate subsidiary it should be included in the investment and performance measurement.

External relationships. The final corporate decisions are concerned with external relationships.

The latter two decision sets are not the subject of this section. Further, growth and renewal strategies reflect in business units and it is these which affect risk and capital spending.

Strategy and risk

The degree of risk in the execution of a business unit strategy is affected by the environment of that business. This environment is marked by two major characteristics, industry maturity and competitive position. Where a business unit stands in this

EXHIBIT 3
Strategic options/risk matrix

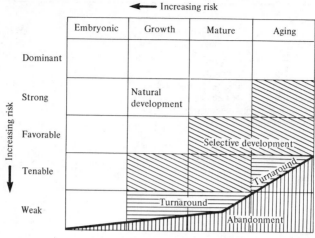

Source: Arthur D. Little Inc.

matrix affects the strategic options available to the business. Exhibit 3 shows this relationship and, as a general statement, the associated risk.

Risks are greater in an embryonic phase because the basis of competition is usually yet to be defined. Technologies are imperfect, changing barriers to entry are fewer, and customer relationships are fickle. Competitive position also helps define risk. Needless to say, the more vulnerable a business unit to competition, the greater the risk in executing strategy.

Furthermore, certain strategies are appropriate to a given phase of industry maturity. For instance, it is more appropriate and less risky to exploit an existing product in existing markets than to develop an overseas business or to seek backward integration opportunities in an embryonic industry. Exhibit 4 depicts the normative period of strategy execution.

Influencing this risk is management experience. A management team which has handled equivalent situations must be considered as better able to reduce the inherent risks than one not so experienced.

Thus, the first step in evaluating a particular capital-spending proposal is to reference that proposal to the business unit and strategy which it supports in order to come to terms with the risk it implies.

EXHIBIT 4
Natural period of strategy execution (of business units of a corporation)

Strategy	Industry/maturity characterization		
	Embryonic	*Growth*	*Mature*
I. Initial Market Development			
L. Market Penetration			
U. Maintenance			
T. Same Products/ New Markets			
P. New Products/ Same Markets			
O. New Products/ New Markets			
A. Backward Integration			
G. Forward Integration			
F. Export/ Same Products			
J. Licensing Abroad			
C. Development of Overseas Facilities			
B. Development of Overseas Business			

Linking capital investments to strategy

A simple technique for ensuring that all capital expenditure proposals relate to business unit strategies is the coding structure shown in Exhibit 5 below.

Incidentally, this linking concept is a major element in the successful design of a zero-base budgeting system. The objectives

EXHIBIT 5
Coding structure for capital spending proposals

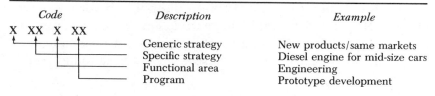

Code	Description	Example
X XX X XX	Generic strategy	New products/same markets
	Specific strategy	Diesel engine for mid-size cars
	Functional area	Engineering
	Program	Prototype development

are also the same in that they seek to explain spending proposals on a rational basis, highlighting the strategic need and the inherent risks of the proposals.

THE CAPITAL EXPENDITURE PROPOSAL

It is frequently the case in the application of capital budgeting procedures that the measurement techniques, discussed in the next section, overwhelm and mask the quality of the proposal itself. The preparer forgets that unless the proposal is well documented, quantified, and reasoned in comparison with alternative approaches, measurement is futile. Indeed, given the propensity for the managerial mind to shape the numbers to fit a need, it is often thought that the greatest benefit to be derived in capital budgeting results from a rigorous preparation of the proposal.

The major components of the capital expenditure proposal are developing investment opportunities, structuring decision alternatives, and projection of the economic implications for each alternative.

Developing investment opportunities

Defining the strategic environment of the business helps in the process of identifying the scope of investment opportunities for the business. But good investment opportunities are difficult to generate and only result from substantial expenditures of time and money. Market research, technical development, and business reputation must be put on the line just to identify the opportunities. It is often the case in mature businesses, no matter how strong, that this *entrepreneurial drive* diminishes, particularly regarding business reputation. Maintenance strategies often dominate and opportunities are not sought to regenerate the business.

Timing is also of the essence in developing investment opportunities. Many companies wait until the demand on a particular plant has exceeded capacity before reacting. Similarly, the demand for a business's products often disappear before management feels a need to seek alternative sources of revenue. In the case of the former, long capital equipment lead times can result in the capacity being available after the demand peaks.

At a minimum, market share can be irretrievably lost if a competitor can supply his product to meet market need. In the latter case, capital resources can be depleted to the point of limiting the company's ability to react.

The recent emergence in many organizations of strategic planning techniques has resulted from the need to create an investment and *divestment* consciousness among the professional managers of the business. The aim is to optimize the use of the company's resources. Some businesses have established corporate development groups to further stimulate the search for investment opportunities. Investment opportunities result from either internal or external development. Included in the former are three general types: the improvement of the base business, spin-offs from existing products or technologies, and only occasionally the creation of a new business unrelated to the traditional activities of the business. External development is accomplished by acquisitions. This is frequently the method for entering entirely new businesses. Furthermore, entry into a mature or even growth industry can be particularly difficult via internal development. Gaining market position can be expensive when the competition is entrenched.

There is no blueprint for identifying investment opportunities. Strategic planning and corporate development can help establish an environment in which managers at all levels become aware of the need to allocate effectively the resources at their disposal.

Tactical alternatives

The identification of investment opportunities is the first step. The second, requiring equal creativity, is the formulation of the tactical alternatives. An effective capital budgeting system must recognize that a particular strategy can be executed in a number of different ways; there is no one and only right way of doing things. Evaluation of these tactical alternatives is accomplished using the same measurement techniques described later, for selecting between different investment proposals. Some of the general tactical alternatives classifications are:

1. **Make or buy.** Should, for example, a new piece of equipment be purchased or built by the company's own tooling department?

2. **Roll out or saturation coverage.** The introduction of a new product can be accomplished by either a limited launching, say within a geographic area, or full coverage of the market.
3. **Base case and increment comparison.** All investment proposals should be measured against a "do nothing" option.
4. **Level of effort.** The "gold plating" criticism is often justified where managers are over cautious in, say, selling the performance specifications for a product.

A technique for ensuring consideration of tactical alternatives is a minimum/maximum/desirable analysis for each proposal submitted. This technique focuses on the least amount of investment which could be made, compared with the maximum and the desirable investment. Of course, benefits are most likely to reflect these changes in investment levels, but not necessarily proportionately.

This technique assists in capital rationing (described later) when a project need not be rejected completely because of the high initial investment. A lower investment (and return) option could be accepted as a suboptimal alternative. This is especially important when the proposal is a component of an overall strategic package.

The objective of framing tactical alternatives is to avoid the "all or nothing" syndrome which often characterizes capital budgeting systems.

Estimates of each investment's alternative cash flow

The third and equally demanding task in preparing the capital investment proposal is the estimation of the economic implications (cash flows) for the project. It is conceptually unnecessary to distinguish between different types of cash flow; the timing of the flows is the critical variable. Nevertheless, it will aid an analysis to consider (1) the amount and timing of investments expenditures, (2) the amount and timing of operating cash flows, (3) the economic life of the assets involved and their residual values, and (4) the implications of federal taxes on investment. Finally, (5) related conceptual costing issues will be discussed, hopefully to clarify some of the common misunderstandings regarding cash flows.

1. Investment outlays. In calculating the investment in a particular proposal, full investment costs should be considered—unencumbered by Internal Revenue Service (IRS) or Financial Accounting Standards Board (FASB) pronouncements. The challenge is to identify, measure, and provide documentation for the costs related to the project, many of which are hidden or sometimes ignored as not being "capital" expenditures. For instance, take the case of a company which is considering the building of a bulk handling and storage facility for processing minerals which were previously purchased and warehoused in bags. The expenditures in Exhibit 6 were related to the project.

In this example, which is based on an actual experience, 70.5 percent of the net investment outlays relate to purchased hardware (equipment and installation costs). The balance is comprised of a variety of items which can often be ignored and result in a misleading judgment on the investment viability. These hidden costs include:

Engineering studies. Few businesses are large enough to carry their own specialized engineers for every function, and so require the use of outside technical expertise to assist in concept and detailed design work. These costs can run to 5–10 percent of a project's cost.

Working capital. Often forgotten is the significant investment in working capital to support a particular system. In this example the increases resulted from increasing inventories as a result of bulk mineral deliveries (benefits are discussed later), increasing the average amount of minerals held. In other cases, significant investments in receivables can result as can reductions in working capital from an increase in trade credit.

Start-up costs. Start-up costs can be both obvious and hidden.

EXHIBIT 6
Investment outlays

	$ thousands	*Percent/total*
Engineering studies	$ 50	0.5%
Equipment and installation	7,050	70.5
Working capital	2,000	20.0
Start-up costs	1,000	10.0
Use of own equipment	200	2.0
	$10,300	103.0%
Obsolete equipment	(300)	(3.0)
	$10,000	100.0%

For instance, the costs of training work crews to handle the new system are readily estimable. However, the costs of lost production time during systems transition because of equipment breakdowns are often forgotten. Careful planning can help reduce the costs, but it is a delusion to think they can be eliminated.

Use of own equipment. The new investment can sometimes incorporate equipment used elsewhere in the business. This should also be regarded as a cost of the project. The method of imputing this cost, however, is not always obvious and will be discussed in Item 3, Economic life and residual value.

Obsolete equipment. The new systems equipment can replace existing equipment, thus reducing the total investment.

Having calculated the investment outlays for the project it is then necessary to estimate the timing of these expenditures. As will be demonstrated (in the later section on Measurement and Selection of Investment Proposals), the specific timing of cash inflows and outflows can greatly affect the project investment returns. Exhibit 7 shows the timing of cash flows related to the investment outlays in Exhibit 6.

This time spreading of the investment outlays is self-evident for the most part. However, three points should be noted. First, year zero expenditures reflect initial outlays. Each yearly expenditure is assumed for analytical convenience to be at year-end. Second, working capital investment follows the build up in operations. Indeed, in some cases there is actually a subsequent liquidation of working capital over the term of the project whenever volumes decline. Third, there is no substitute for clear thinking in coordinating the cash flow analysis with the technical

EXHIBIT 7
Timing of investment cash flows

	Year				
	(0)	(1)	(2)	(3)	(4)
Engineering studies	$ 50				
Equipment installation	150	$3,000	$3,900		
Working capital			500	$1,300	$200
Start-up costs			1,000		
Use of own equipment		200			
Obsolete equipment			(300)		
	$200	$3,200	$5,100	$1,300	$200

project control. The timing of start-up, equipment transfers, and sale should be obtained from the technical analysis.

2. Operations cash flow. In estimating operating cash flows the challenge is shaped by three general types of investment opportunities: (*a*) cost reduction, (*b*) expansion, and (*c*) mixed cost reduction/expansion.

The approach and problem areas in developing the operating cash flows are peculiar to these three categories.

Cost reduction investments. The first is an investment designed to reduce costs. In this event the benefits are reduced outflows such as lower labor, material, or other types of costs. Cost reduction investments can of course, result in increased costs of one type. The overall objective is to lower more costs sufficiently to justify the investment. If this sounds gratuitous it is not always the case in practice. How many executives have been sold computers as a labor saving device! The problem arises because the new equipment has obvious and necessary additional costs associated with the venture, but the benefits (in the form of reducing costs elsewhere) are often less visible. The often stubborn refusal of costs to decline is justified by a variety of "soft" or difficult to measure rationalizations—the computer gives better and faster management information. The claim itself may be difficult to verify but the value of that benefit can be even harder. The challenge with cost reduction investments is to identify the savings but not to delude oneself as to their magnitude.

Expansion investments. The second general type of investment opportunity is one for expansion. Here the benefits are more readily quantified in the expanded potential for product shipment. But while in the case of cost reduction opportunities the intangibles are internal, here the difficulties are external. Our enquiries here are concerned with market analysis, focusing on market growth rates, segment, customers, distribution of markets, and competitor reaction. The latter is particularly difficult to assess but very important to the decision. It is often likely that competitors will respond strongly to increased quantities of the company's product entering the market place, particularly if that means loss of market share. They will respond by a combination of emphasizing their own strengths and the other company's weaknesses. This could result in increased selling and promotion costs on the project. Furthermore, if the competition becomes particularly intense, prices can be cut and the investment may not earn an adequate return. The consideration of externally-oriented investment proposals must therefore take full cognizance of the strategic environment of the business.

Measuring the costs associated with the expansion also requires caution. On the one hand, costs should not be included unless they really are a result of the expansion and not a result of additional spreading of existing overhead (see discussion of incremental cost). On the other hand, full implications of expansion should be measured. For instance, 12 additional machines can mean an addition to the plant, carpark, or even cafeteria.

Mixed cost reduction/expansion investments. The data problems are generally the same for this type of investment as for cost reduction investments. In this case, the scale of operation can provide cost reduction opportunities not previously available. Greater raw material price breaks or more efficient labor utilization can be obtained. Furthermore, the administrative gains from sophisticated control systems can be obtainable at higher levels. These benefits accrue not just to the expansion volume increment but to base business itself. The added complexity is to identify and quantify these synergistic benefits.

To continue the example described before, the operating cash flows are similar to the cost reduction model. The investment is being considered to replace an existing work method and the benefits are expected to lower overall operating costs. Exhibit 8 shows the type and amount of these savings.

The principal benefits result from reduction in material costs from elimination of bagging charges, reduction in freight costs, and volume discounts on bulk purchases. Labor costs are reduced as a consequence of the need for fewer warehousing and material handling personnel. However, the more sophisticated equipment requires increases in maintenance crews and supplies which become even more expensive the older the equipment becomes.

3. Economic life and residual value. Two additional and important variables in the description of the capital expenditure proposal are the economic life and the residual value of the assets.

EXHIBIT 8
Operating cash flows ($000)

							Year				
	(2)	(3)	(4)	(5)	(6)	(7)	(8)	(9)	(10)	(11)
Bag charges and freight ...	$1,300	$ 1,800	$ 1,850	$ 1,850	$ 1,850	$ 1,850	$ 1,850	$ 1,850	$ 1,850	$ 1,850
Bulk purchases	5,900	8,200	8,300	8,300	8,300	8,300	8,300	8,300	8,300	8,300
Direct labor increases	(100)	(140)	(140)	(140)	(140)	(200)	(200)	(200)	(200)	(200)
Direct labor decreases....	400	500	500	500	500	500	500	500	500	500
Maintenance supplies	(50)	(50)	(50)	(50)	(50)	(100)	(100)	(100)	(100)	(100)
	$7,450	$10,310	$10,460	$10,460	$10,460	$10,350	$10,350	$10,350	$10,350	$10,350

Economic life. Economic life is defined by Gordon Shillinglaw as "the time interval that is expected to elapse between the time of acquisition and the time at which the combined forces of obsolescence and deterioration will justify retirement of the asset."[1] Behind this seemingly straightforward statement, however, are a host of complex practical problems of measurement. These vary by circumstance but include the following:

a. The deterioration basis life cycle.

Where the asset is a replacement for existing equipment, historical data can provide useful guides to the deterioration cycle. Even where no historical data exists, engineering estimates can provide an adequate approximation. This point can be theoretically described as the juncture where the present value (described later) of replacement cash flows exceeds the present value of continuing support for the existing system. In practice this means that maintenance costs have increased and output has dropped to where replacement is necessary.

b. The obsolescence basis life cycle.

Much more difficult to assess is the impact of technological obsolescence. High technology industries are characterized by rapid lowering of per unit production costs. Each new breakthrough obsoletes existing production equipment because it cannot compete on a productivity basis. Historical experience serves as an imperfect guide to this problem because of the geometric rate of technological advance; the first two generations of computers took thirty years to develop while the third and fourth have taken less than ten. Estimates are that the fifth generation based on the bubble-memory will be developed in about three years. Unfortunately, there is no substitute for informed technical judgment for estimating the rate of obsolescence. In some cases of rapidly changing technology the only solution is to assume each change is merely a component of a larger investment, for the component could not justify the investment except in the larger context.

c. Mixed life assets.

Some investments involve assets of a mixed life. For instance, in building a steel mill the basic heavy machinery will have a

---

[1] Gordon Shillinglaw, *Cost Accounting: Analysis and Control*, 3rd ed. (Homewood, Ill.: Richard D. Irwin, 1972), p. 631.

life of about 40 years, while other machines will have lives of about 10 years. In this case it is suggested that the replacement of the shorter life investment be included under the "umbrella" investment of 40 years. To focus the analysis on the shorter life is a contrivance fraught with many theoretical problems concerned with estimating the value of the primary investment at year 10.

Residual value. Residual value is the economic worth of the asset at the end of its economic life. There are three basic measures of residual values:

a. Scrap.

In many examples, particularly where the economic life is expected to be determined by deterioration, the residual value is little more than the scrap value of the investment. However, it can also happen that relatively new equipment can be worth little more than scrap.

b. Market.

There is often a market for second-hand equipment with published prices classified by the age and condition of the equipment.

c. Earning power.

There are many examples whereby equipment becomes obsolete in one market but is economically viable in another. For instance, in the plastics industry technical advances usually mean faster cycle times for injection and blow molding equipment. In a high volume market area such as the United States the latest generation obsoletes its predecessor. But this displaced equipment is still the optimal equipment for a low volume market area like Brazil. Thus earning power of the equipment in this market is the residual value.

Except in areas of high technology, uncertainties over residual value and economic life are usually noncritical factors in the analysis of an investment proposal. Where the environment is highly uncertain the use of risk adjustment techniques, described later, can aid in measuring the impact of the uncertainty.

In the example used, the economic life of the asset was determined to be ten years based on engineering studies of comparable installations. The equipment is not subject to technological

EXHIBIT 9
Residual value ($000)

Item	Basis	Value
Equipment	Scrap (5% cost)	$ 325
Working capital	90% book	1,800
		$2,125
Add: Tax loss on working capital		100
		$2,225

change. Further, scrap value is estimated to be about 5 percent of that asset hardware value (excluding installation) and the accumulated working capital is redeemable at 90 percent of book value (see Exhibit 9).

The tax loss on working capital reflects the liquidation of the assets at less than book value a loss which is deductible against ordinary income.

4. Impact of taxes on capital expenditures. Federal taxes also play a significant role in the measurement of net cash flow. The significant tax considerations are the following:

Investment tax credit. The investment tax credit was first introduced in 1962 to encourage business expansion via increased capital spending. Under the investment tax credit program, businesses can deduct as a credit against their income tax liability a specified percentage of their new investment in eligible capital equipment. The credit was initially set at 7 percent of the amount of new investment in assets having a useful life of eight years or more (⅔ of 7 percent for lives of six or seven years, ⅓ of 7 percent for lives of four or five years, and zero for less than four years). The tax was suspended twice, in 1966 and 1969, and reinstated.

The current basic rate is 10 percent, and the Tax Reform Act of 1976 has extended the credit to assets acquired before 1981. The Act has described other provisions for (a) companies with Employee Stock Ownership Trusts (ESOTS), (b) used equipment, (c) vessels, and (d) movie and television films.

Not all expenditures qualify for the investment tax credit. Start-up costs, for instance, do not qualify. In the example being made here the credit is calculated as shown in Exhibit 10.

Corporate income taxes. The corporate income tax rate is 20 percent for the first $25,000 of taxable income, 22 percent for the second $25,000 and 48 percent for income over $50,000.

EXHIBIT 10
Calculation of investment tax credit ($000s)

	Cost	Credit
Engineering studies	$ 50	$ 5
Equipment plus installation costs of $550 thousand	7,050	$705
	$7,100	$710

Any additional revenues or cost reduction must, therefore, recognize the additional taxes which will be paid as an integral part of the investment proposal.

Accelerated depreciation.   As an incentive to business the tax laws permit the use of accelerated depreciation techniques. The two techniques most common to business are the sum-of-the-years' digits and double-declining balance. Depreciation is not a cash expenditure but is a tax deductible expense. Thus, the greater the depreciation charge the lower the corporate income tax.

Corporate capital gains and losses.   A full description of the corporate capital gains and losses is subject to many technical provisions. However, the following general description of the relevant aspects pertaining to depreciable property will support the example being constructed.

The sale of depreciable property for more than its book value can result in both a capital gain or ordinary income for tax purposes. If the sale is for less than its original cost then it is considered a recapture of depreciation and as such is treated as ordinary income. If the sale is greater than original cost then the excess is treated as a capital gain and subject to the lower capital gains tax rate of 30 percent.

Whenever the asset is sold for less than book value the loss is treated as a deduction against ordinary income without limitation.

Operating loss carry-back and carry-forward.   The 1976 Act extended the carry-forward provision by two years to seven years (formerly it was five years) against future profits.

This is particularly important in capital budgeting, for some investments give rise to substantial operating losses during the start-up phase. Unless there are adequate profits going either three years back or seven years forward in time, these benefits will be lost.

The impact of these tax regulations is shown in Exhibit 11, which summarizes the investment proposal example.

The data in this example is derived from the previous figures. The following should be noted:

a. Depreciation write-off in Year 11 reflects the difference between book and salvage value at that time.

b. Depreciation is included merely to calculate tax cash flow impacts and is then added back.

This example illustrates the general nature of the cash flows as one investment proposal and the major tax effects thereon. No matter how complex the investment proposal, the general principles illustrated here will be pertinent.

5. Related conceptual issues. In practice a number of conceptual issues tend to confound the preparer of capital expenditure proposals. The following include some of the more common misunderstandings:

Sunk and incremental costs. The acceptance of the concept of *sunk cost* is often more an emotional than an intellectual challenge. Capital budgeting is concerned with *incremental costs*. These related concepts hold that once an investment is made the only consideration is what additional expenditures have to be made in the future. Many an irrational decision is the result of being unable to stop looking back. To base an illustration on the foregoing example, if by Year 3 it appears that the final return on the investment is not going to be satisfactory it does not make sense to cancel the project after the investment has been made. The *incremental return* from that point is likely to be much higher than any alternative use of the equipment.

Acceptance of sunk cost should not be misconstrued as being an acceptance of bad decision making. The ideal is to evaluate proposals accurately *before* the investment is made.

Depreciation. Depreciation is relevant only inasmuch as it effects taxes. It is a noncash expense used for the purpose of accounting conventions to match the use of the asset against the associated revenue stream. In an economic sense the expense occurs when the cash transaction is made.

Allocation of fixed cost. Frequently investment proposals are "loaded" with fixed cost allocations to cover such items as corporate overhead, cafeteria service, plant maintenance, and many others. If these costs are truly fixed, meaning they will exist

EXHIBIT 11

Summary cash flow statement and tax impact ($000)

	(0)	(1)	(2)	(3)	(4)	(5)	(6)	(7)	(8)	(9)	(10)	(11)
								Year				
Investment												
Gross	$ 200	$ 3,200	$5,100	$ 1,300	$ 200							
Less: Investment tax credit	(20)	(300)	(390)									
Net	$ 180	$ 2,900	$4,710	$ 1,300	$ 200							
Operating cash flows												
Gross			$7,450	$10,310	$10,460	$10,460	$10,350	$10,350	$10,350	$10,350	$10,350	$10,350
Less: Depreciation			1,460	1,168	934	748	598	478	383	306	245	655
Net before taxes			$5,990	$ 9,142	$ 9,526	$ 9,712	$ 9,752	$ 9,872	$ 9,967	$10,044	$10,105	$ 9,695
Taxes (est. 50%)			(2,995)	(4,571)	(4,763)	(4,856)	(4,876)	(4,936)	(4,983)	(5,022)	(5,052)	(4,847)
Add: Depreciation			1,460	1,168	934	748	598	478	383	306	245	655
Net O.C.F.			$4,455	$ 5,739	$ 5,697	$ 5,604	$ 5,474	$ 5,414	$5,366	$ 5,328	$ 5,297	$ 5,502
Residual values												2,225
Net cash flow	$(180)	$(2,900)	$ (255)	$ 4,439	$ 5,497	$ 5,604	$ 5,474	$ 5,414	$ 5,366	$ 5,328	$ 5,297	$ 7,727

( ) = Negative.

regardless of the decision made on the particular proposal, then they should not impact the decision in any way.

Opportunity cost. The inability to accept the notion of opportunity cost is also a hindrance to good decision making. Opportunity cost is concerned with the alternative opportunity foregone by pursuing a particular course of action. An often cited dramatic example is that of the businessman who laments that he would be better off liquidating his assets and investing the proceeds in tax-free municipal bonds. Very often he is correct, but some emotional factors sway his decision not to pursue this course of action.

In developing and articulating capital expenditure proposals, the manager must be creative both in identifying investment opportunities and framing alternative approaches to these investments. Careful analysis and quantification of these investments and alternatives is equally important to prevent poor decisions before the expenditure is made and to help rank the other opportunities available to the business.

MEASUREMENT AND SELECTION OF INVESTMENT PROPOSALS

The capital investment proposal provides the basic information with which to evaluate the attractiveness of the investment. The next step is to establish a measurement methodology to help determine which proposals should be accepted and which rejected. The measures most commonly used are termed the basic and advanced concepts. The former includes simple return on investment, average rate of return, and payback method. The latter includes the internal rate of return and present value methods.

This section will evaluate the different methods of measurement and review the subject of the discount rate, which is critical to the application of the advanced concepts. Finally, the administrative and conceptual issues shaping the investment selection process will be discussed.

Basic concepts

Each of the three basic measures provide only an approximation of the economic return for the investment. While these approximations may suffice in some situations their flaws may lead to inaccurate conclusions regarding the attractiveness of the investment.

1. Simple return on investment. The simple return on investment is used to reflect the impact of the investment on the corporate financial statements:

$$\text{Return on investment} = \frac{\text{Average annual aftertax profit}}{\text{Net investment}}$$

For example, a five year project with average annual aftertax profits of $80 thousand and an investment of $1 million would show an 8 percent return.

This measure has significant drawbacks because it ignores the life of the investment and the uneven nature of profits. Furthermore, it ignores the decline of the asset value. These weaknesses are illustrated in the description of the average rate of return.

2. Average rate of return. The average rate of return is a minor improvement upon the simple return on investment, for it averages the investment in the project. In the example above, assuming straight line depreciation, the return would be:

$$\text{Average rate of return (\$000)} = \frac{80}{1,000 \div 2} = 16\%$$

Even as a balance sheet approximation this measure is flawed. Year by year measures of the rate of return would vary considerably, being lower in the first five years and higher in the second five.

Results obtained this way can be misleading. For example, suppose that there are two projects, each with an initial investment of $20,000 and a five year economic life. Both projects have the following profits and cash flows:

	Project A		Project B	
Year	*Book profit*	*Cash flow*	*Book profit*	*Cash flow*
1	$6,000	$10,000	$4,000	$8,000
2	5,000	9,000	4,000	8,000
3	4,000	8,000	4,000	8,000
4	3,000	7,000	4,000	8,000
5	2,000	6,000	4,000	8,000

In both cases the average return on investment is 40 percent; however, project A is preferable because the cash return is greater in the earlier years. This earlier cash return permits reinvestment and thus increased return.

3. Payback. One attempt to overcome the deficiency in the foregoing methods is the payback technique. Payback calculates the number of years required to recover the initial investment. Using the example of Project B above:

$$\text{Payback period} = \frac{20,000}{8,000} = 2.5 \text{ years}$$

When the flows are uneven the calculation is a little more difficult. For example, in Project A $1,000 of the original investment needs to be recovered by the beginning of the third year. The payback is, therefore, 2 years $+ \frac{1}{8} = 2$ years and 1½ months.

The payback method would result in selecting Project A in the example, which is the desired result. The payback method is still flawed because it fails to take account of the cash flows following the payback period. For instance, if Project B were to continue another three years or have substantially higher returns in the fourth and fifth years, payback would produce an incorrect result.

Much of the payback appeal, for it is used widely, stems from its measure of the liquidity of the investment and its simplicity. This is important to cash-poor companies who cannot have their money tied up for long periods. However, even here it is more constructive to view it as a constraint (no investments with a payback of less than four years would be considered) rather than a measure of profitability.

Advanced concepts

The weaknesses in the average return on investment and payback methods derive from their failure to quantify variations in the magnitude and timing of cash flows—a serious drawback in a society where capital productivity is a major ingredient for economic success. The advanced concepts of investment return measurement based on discounted cash flow techniques go a long way toward overcoming the deficiencies of the basic techniques.

The basis of the advanced concepts is the time value of money. Obviously, if one investment returns money earlier to an investor than does another, that investment is preferable because the money so released can in turn be reinvested.

For instance, an investor has the opportunity for an investment which offers a return of $1,000 at the end of one year. Assume for illustrative purposes that the investment is no more risky than putting his money in a bank where he can earn 6 percent interest. The maximum amount he would be willing to pay now for that investment, called the present value, is calculated as follows:

$$\text{Present value} = \frac{1,000}{1.06} = \$943$$

Obviously, if the investor has to invest *less* than $943 he will accept and—if greater—will not accept the investment.

The challenge, therefore, is to find a common measure of different cash flow streams. The discounted cash flow techniques most commonly used are the net present value method and the internal rate of return method.

1. Net present value method. The net present value method (*NPV*) discounts future cash flows to their present value using the required rate of return, sometimes called the cost of capital. Discount rates are discussed in the next section.

The *NPV* equation is:

$$NPV = \left[\frac{C_1}{1+R} + \frac{C_2}{(1+R)^2} + \frac{C_3}{(1+R)^3} \cdots \frac{C_n}{(1+R)^4} \right] - I$$

Here C_1 through C_n represent the project cash flows, I is the initial investment, R is the required rate of return, and N is the project life.

The shorthand form of this equation is:

$$NPV = \sum_{t=1}^{N} \frac{C_t}{(1+R)^t} - I$$

Fortunately, the equations do not have to be executed because present value tables are available for this purpose. Table 1 in the Appendix shows the present value of one dollar received at the end of N years using a variety of discount rates. For instance, the present value of a dollar received at the end of five years discounted at 10 percent is .621. Table 2 shows the value

EXHIBIT 12
Measurement of alternative project NPV

Year	Project A Net cash flow	Project A Present value factor (10%)	Project A Present value	Project B Net cash flow	Project B Present value factor (10%)	Project B Present value
0	$ 800	—	$(800)	$ 800	—	$(800)
1	800	0.91	728	300	0.91	273
2	300	0.83	249	300	0.83	249
3	300	0.75	225	800	0.75	600
	2,200			2,200		
Net present value			$ 402			$322

of a constant stream of one dollar per year for N years at R percent. The recent availability of small hand held calculators which can also compute these equations has made the job even easier.

Exhibit 12 illustrates the value of *NPV* measurement.

Both projects have the same initial investment and total cash flows. However, the variations in cash flow result in project A being the more attractive because of the greater cash flow in the first year.

2. Internal rate of return method. The internal rate of return method (*IRR*) calculates the discount rate which equates the present value of the expected cash outflows with the present value of the expected inflows. The *IRR* equation is shown below:

$$\sum_{t=0}^{N^1} \left[\frac{C_t}{(1 + R)^t} \right] = 0$$

Here, C_t is the cash flows, both inflows and outflows, for each time period, N is the project life and R is the discount rate that equates these flows to zero.

Solving for R is a process of trial and error. A discount rate on the table is picked and the net present value calculated. If the *NPV* is greater or less than zero, then another rate is picked and the calculation repeated. By this iterating process, the rate which brings the flows almost to zero (hitting zero exactly is not necessary) is identified. Again, computers are widely used for this purpose.

3. Differences between methods. A problem arises, however, with both the *IRR* and *NPV*. Because our focus with these advanced concepts is the productivity of capital, both calculation methods assume a reinvestment rate for the cash flows involved. The *IRR* assumes that funds are reinvested at the internal rate of return over the life of the project. The present value method assumes reinvestment at the same discount rate.

Thus the calculations are based on different reinvestment assumptions, neither of which may reflect the reinvestment opportunity available. The *IRR* is particularly suspect especially when the rate is high.

Notwithstanding these difficulties, the advanced concepts have largely displaced the basic measurement techniques because of their recognition of the time value of money.

Discount rates

The internal rate of return method calculates the intrinsic rate of return on the investment, while the net present value method determines whether or not the net value of the investment at time zero is positive after discounting future inflows and outflows. The former is often termed the expected rate of return and the latter the required rate of return. The questions remain, however, as to what is a satisfactory expected rate of return or how to determine the required rate of return. As the expected rate of return is referenced to the required rate of return, the question is directed to the latter.

Microeconomic theory holds that a firm should operate at the point where its marginal revenue is just equal to its marginal cost. In capital budgeting, marginal cost is the firm's cost of capital. Thus, if an investment is discounted at the cost of capital to the firm and the net present value is positive, then the project should be accepted, and if negative, the project should be rejected. This discount rate is sometimes referred to as the hurdle rate—for obvious reasons.

There are two fundamental questions to be resolved regarding this hurdle rate. First, how is the cost of capital calculated? Second, how should the cost of capital be adjusted to reflect differences in risk between alternative investment opportunities?

1. Cost of capital. The capital available to the firm is derived from two basic sources, debt instruments and equity. Preference stock is like debt instruments from an economic viewpoint and its cost is calculated in a similar manner. The component cost of both debt and equity is described below, together with a description of the weighted cost of capital.

Cost of debt. In its most common form the cost of debt is simple to calculate, for it is merely the tax adjusted interest rate on the debt. The general equation is:

$$\text{Cost of debt} = I(1 - T)$$

Here, I is the interest rate on the debt and T is the tax rate. For example, if a company borrows money at 8 percent, then the cost of debt using a 50 percent tax rate is:

$$8(1 - 0.5) = 4\%$$

It should be stressed that the cost of debt is concerned with incremental cost; thus, it ignores cost of past debt.

Cost of equity. The cost of equity is the rate of return stockholders require on the firm's common stock. The value of a share of common stock depends, ultimately, on the dividends paid on the stock. It is beyond the scope of this book to explain the complexities of capital market theory (for a detailed explanation read J. Fred Weston and Eugene T. Brigham's *Managerial Finance*, Dryden Press). The general equation for calculating the value of a share of common stock is:

$$P_0 = \frac{D_1}{R - g}$$

Here, P_0 is the price of the stock at time zero, R is the investor's required rate of return, and g is the growth rate in earnings. Solving this equation for R the result is:

$$R = \frac{D_1}{P_0} + g$$

Thus, the total return to stockholders is a combination of dividend yield and the growth rate in the value of their stock.

For example, a company pays a dividend of $1 and has a stock price of $20. If its earnings have been growing at the rate of 6 percent per year, then the cost of equity is:

$$R=\left(\frac{1}{20}\right)\% + 6 = 11\%$$

Using the growth rate of earnings avoids a complex and difficult-to-resolve discussion on the interrelationships between dividends, earnings, and the stock prices.

To some managers the cost of retained earnings is zero. However, unless the business manager can reinvest retained earnings at the opportunity cost to the company's stockholders, the firm's stock price will decline over the long term. Thus, the required rate of return must still be factored into their capital budgeting decision.

Weighted cost of capital. Because businesses finance their investments with a mix of debt and equity, it is necessary to calculate a weighted cost of capital. This is required notwithstanding that a particular investment will be financed entirely with debt, for such borrowing draws on the firm's total borrowing capacity. Otherwise, future investments will be supposedly financed entirely with higher cost equity. Capital accrues to the business, and only in exceptional circumstances to a particular investment.

Thus, when calculating discounted cash flows the cost of capital is weighted to reflect the mix between debt and equity. For instance, in a business which is financed by 50 percent debt and 50 percent equity, the weighted average cost of capital is:

	Cost	Weight	Net
Debt (after tax)	4%	0.5	2.0%
Equity	11	0.5	5.5
		1.0	7.5

This is a brief and simplified discussion of what is a difficult topic, subject to some controversy among both the business and academic communities. There are several theoretical difficulties with this measure resulting from the measure being biased by historical factors, and structural difficulties with the stock reflecting theoretical relationships between stock price and earnings performance. An alternative approach and an amplification of the cost of capital to reflect adjustment for financial risk is described below.

2. Risk and the cost of capital. An alternative approach to estimating the cost of capital for the firm is based on risk measurement. This technique holds that the required rate of return (*R*) for the firm is expressed by the equation:

$$R = A + B + C$$

Here *A* is the risk-free rate of return (based on the rate for long-term U.S. Treasury bonds), *B* is the premium for business risk, and *C* the premium for financial risk. The premium for business risk is caused by the relative dispersion of the probability distribution of possible future operating income.

The relationship between the required rate of return and business risk can be described by constructing the capital market line (CML). Exhibit 13 shows an example of this relationship. The vertical axis shows the required rate of return and the horizontal axis measures risk, shown here as the standard deviation of the rate of return. Weston & Brigham describe how a firm

EXHIBIT 13
Capital market line (CML)

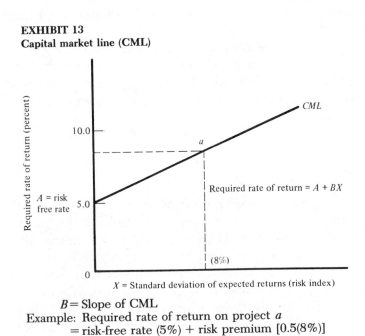

B = Slope of CML
Example: Required rate of return on project *a*
    = risk-free rate (5%) + risk premium [0.5(8%)]
    = 9%

can construct a CML.[2] The slope of the line relates a percentage increase in the standard deviation with an increase in the required rate of return.

Many companies employ a single measure of business risk throughout the organization. However, different business units have, obviously, different standard deviations of returns. Furthermore, different strategies also impact risk.

The strategic framework for the business unit, focusing on such factors as industry maturity, competitive position, and strategic thrust, can help management in establishing business risk premiums for the particular strategy of a given business unit. It should not be pretended that this can be done with any great precision; management judgment has to suffice rather than a mathematical solution. However, a reasonable attempt to reflect variations in risk by specifying multiple rates improves the quality of the capital budgeting decisions.

Financial risk is caused by the dispersion of expected future earnings available to common stockholders.

A financial risk premium should be applied to all investments regardless of business risk. The higher the financial leverage the greater the risk premium required. This risk can be illustrated by comparing two firms with equal total capital and earnings before interest and taxes (Exhibits 14A and 14B). The only difference in the two firms is that Company A has no debt while Company B has half debt (borrowed at 8 percent) and half equity.

EXHIBIT 14A
Effect of financial leverage

	Company A	*Company B*
Capital		
Debt	0	500
Equity	1,000	500
	1,000	1,000
Earnings		
EBIT	200	200
Interest	0	40
Taxes (50%)	100	80
Net earnings	100	80
Return on equity	10%	16%

---

[2] J. Fred Weston and Eugene F. Brigham, *Managerial Finance.*

934

EBIT	40	40
Interest	0	40
Taxes	20	0
	20	0
Return	2	0

Exhibit 14A looks particularly favorable to the stockholders of B. However, should earnings decline to 40, the result is shown in Exhibit 14B.

In addition to wiping out the return for Company B, the business may not have sufficient cash flow to service its debt—resulting in insolvency.

Ranking and selection

The discounted cash flow techniques provide a common basis of measurement. Management must then select among the various investments available. As mentioned before, economic theory of the firm holds that management should select those proposals where the marginal return exceeds marginal cost. Exhibit

EXHIBIT 15
Selection based on marginal cost of capital

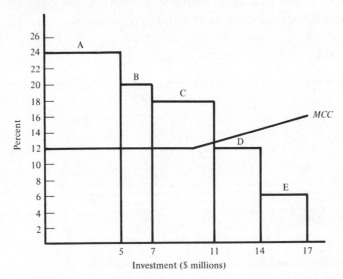

15 depicts this selection process. It should be noted that the marginal cost of capital increases as a function of abnormal capital requirements. It is self-evident that a company whose capital requirements double or triple in a given year from their usual requirements will have to pay more for those funds as a result of investor uncertainty about the ability of the company to manage such an abnormal increase. This could result in the less attractive project being cut off or postponed.

Mutually exclusive projects are generally those which are tactical in nature: two ways of doing the same job, and if one is selected, the other is not necessary. However, it may be that the method offering the better return requires the greater amount of initial investment. If capital is scarce—provided that the difference in return is not major—then it may be decided to select the project offering the lower return.

Interdependent projects are those bound together by strategic ties. Thus, if a given project is an integral part of a business strategy it may not be possible to reject that proposal without affecting the overall strategy. Care should be taken, however, to assure that the cumulative impact of such marginal investments does not go unnoticed and that the strategic wisdom is revised if necessary.

In order to avoid an administrative burden in capital budgeting, control limits should be set to permit delegation of decision making. Capital projects can be filtered on the basis of investment size so that only the most important reach the board for decision.

Finally, there should be an audit mechanism to follow up during and after the implementation to verify the quality of the data on which the decision was made. This can help in improving the quality of proposal submission.

DECISION MAKING UNDER CONDITIONS OF UNCERTAINTY

Because of the considerable measure of uncertainty surrounding capital budgeting data, several techniques have been devised to help decision makers cope with the problem. Some of these are briefly described below:

Sensitivity analysis

Sensitivity analysis is a way of systematically working through the impact of assumed changes in the key variables affecting the outcome of a project. Commonly referred to as "what if" questions are posed. These would include questions like "what if" sales were 10 percent less than projected or prices were 5 percent lower? It is a way of quantifying management's uncertainty regarding specific items of a project.

An elaboration of this technique approaches the project from the perspective of most likely, pessimistic, and optimistic assumptions. This approach attempts to set the parameters on the project.

Simulation analysis

Simulation analysis is a computer-based technique used to obtain the expected return and dispersion about this return for an investment return. Probability distributions are assigned to each of the major proposal determinants based on management's assessment of the probable outcomes. For instance, management believes that unit sales have the following probability distribution:

Unit sales	Probability
800	0.15
900	0.20
1,000	0.30
1,100	0.20
1,200	0.15

The computer selects a value at random from each of the distributions, combines it with other values selected from the other distributions and calculates a rate of return on the investment. The computer repeats this calculation several hundred times and records the number of times each rate of return is computed, creating a frequency distribution.

The resultant distribution measures the expected value, range, and standard deviation of return.

SUMMARY

Capital budgeting is an integral part of the process of management. It is a primary tool for the allocation of corporate resources, the consequences of which greatly affect the long-term prospects of the firm. The danger from the application of capital budgeting systems results from the tendency of the analytical techniques to assume greater importance than the business logic and data quality of the proposal itself.

The first objective, therefore, is to root the proposals in the strategic direction of the business. This will focus the allocation of resources and allow better understanding of the inherent business risk involved. Investment proposals prepared within the framework should consider the tactical options available. Each proposal and alternative should be rigorously developed to quantify the related cash flows. The quality of this analysis is vital to good decision making.

Of the measurement techniques available, those offering the best results are the internal rate of return and the net present value method. Although calculation of the appropriate required rate of return is subject to technical problems, a reasonable margin of error is preferable to the other available alternatives.

APPENDIX

TABLE 1
Present value of $1

Year	1%	2%	3%	4%	5%	6%
1	1.000	1.000	1.000	1.000	1.000	1.000
2	2.010	2.020	2.030	2.040	2.050	2.060
3	3.030	3.060	3.091	3.122	3.152	3.184
4	4.060	4.122	4.184	4.246	4.310	4.375
5	5.101	5.204	5.309	5.416	5.526	5.637
6	6.152	6.308	6.468	6.633	6.802	6.975
7	7.214	7.434	7.662	7.898	8.142	8.394
8	8.286	8.583	8.892	9.214	9.549	9.897
9	9.369	9.755	10.159	10.583	11.027	11.491
10	10.462	10.950	11.464	12.006	12.578	13.181
11	11.567	12.169	12.808	13.486	14.207	14.972
12	12.683	13.412	14.192	15.026	15.917	16.870
13	13.809	14.680	15.618	16.627	17.713	18.882
14	14.947	15.974	17.086	18.292	19.599	21.051
15	16.097	17.293	18.599	20.024	21.579	23.276
16	17.258	18.639	20.157	21.825	23.657	25.673
17	18.430	20.012	21.762	23.698	25.840	28.213
18	19.615	21.412	23.414	25.645	28.132	30.906
19	20.811	22.841	25.117	27.671	30.539	33.760
20	22.019	24.297	26.870	29.778	33.066	36.786
25	28.243	32.030	36.459	41.646	47.727	54.865
30	34.785	40.568	47.575	56.085	66.439	79.058

Year	7%	8%	9%	10%	12%	14%
1	1.000	1.000	1.000	1.000	1.000	1.000
2	2.070	2.080	2.090	2.100	2.120	2.140
3	3.215	3.246	3.278	3.310	3.374	3.440
4	4.440	4.506	4.573	4.641	4.770	4.921
5	5.751	5.867	5.985	6.105	6.353	6.610
6	7.153	7.336	7.523	7.716	8.115	8.536
7	8.654	8.923	9.200	9.487	10.089	10.730
8	10.260	10.637	11.028	11.436	12.300	13.233
9	11.978	12.488	13.021	13.579	14.776	16.085
10	13.816	14.487	15.193	15.937	17.549	19.337
11	15.784	16.645	17.560	18.531	20.655	23.044
12	17.888	18.977	20.141	21.384	24.133	27.271
13	20.141	21.495	22.953	24.523	28.029	32.089
14	22.550	24.215	26.019	27.975	32.393	37.581
15	25.129	27.152	29.361	31.772	37.280	43.842
16	27.888	30.324	33.003	35.950	42.753	50.980
17	30.840	33.750	36.974	40.545	48.884	59.118
18	33.999	37.450	41.301	45.599	55.750	68.394
19	37.379	41.446	46.018	51.159	63.440	78.969
20	40.995	45.762	51.160	57.275	72.052	91.025
25	63.249	73.106	84.701	98.347	133.334	181.871
30	94.461	113.283	136.308	164.494	241.333	356.787

TABLE 2
Present value of an annuity of $1

Year	1%	2%	3%	4%	5%	6%	7%	8%	9%	10%	11%	12%	14%	15%
1	.990	.980	.971	.962	.952	.943	.935	.926	.917	.909	.901	.893	.877	.870
2	.980	.961	.943	.925	.907	.890	.873	.857	.842	.826	.812	.797	.769	.756
3	.971	.942	.915	.889	.864	.840	.816	.794	.772	.751	.731	.712	.675	.658
4	.961	.924	.889	.855	.823	.792	.763	.735	.708	.683	.659	.636	.592	.572
5	.951	.906	.863	.822	.784	.747	.713	.681	.650	.621	.593	.567	.519	.497
6	.942	.888	.838	.790	.746	.705	.666	.630	.596	.564	.535	.507	.456	.432
7	.933	.871	.813	.760	.711	.665	.623	.583	.547	.513	.482	.452	.400	.376
8	.923	.853	.789	.731	.677	.627	.582	.540	.502	.467	.434	.404	.351	.327
9	.914	.837	.766	.703	.645	.592	.544	.500	.460	.424	.391	.361	.308	.284
10	.905	.820	.744	.676	.614	.558	.508	.463	.422	.386	.352	.322	.270	.247
11	.896	.804	.722	.650	.585	.527	.475	.429	.388	.350	.317	.287	.237	.215
12	.887	.788	.701	.625	.557	.497	.444	.397	.356	.319	.286	.257	.208	.187
13	.879	.773	.681	.601	.530	.469	.415	.368	.326	.290	.258	.229	.182	.163
14	.870	.758	.661	.577	.505	.442	.388	.340	.299	.263	.232	.205	.160	.141
15	.861	.743	.642	.555	.481	.417	.362	.315	.275	.239	.209	.183	.140	.123
16	.853	.728	.623	.534	.458	.394	.339	.292	.252	.218	.188	.163	.123	.107
17	.844	.714	.605	.513	.436	.371	.317	.270	.231	.198	.170	.146	.108	.093
18	.836	.700	.587	.494	.416	.350	.296	.250	.212	.180	.153	.130	.095	.081
19	.828	.686	.570	.475	.396	.331	.276	.232	.194	.164	.138	.116	.083	.070
20	.820	.673	.554	.456	.377	.319	.258	.215	.178	.149	.124	.104	.073	.061
25	.780	.610	.478	.375	.295	.233	.184	.146	.116	.092	.074	.059	.038	.030

Year	16%	18%	20%	21%	24%	26%	28%	32%	36%	40%	50%	60%	70%	80%	90%
1	.862	.847	.833	.826	.806	.794	.781	.758	.735	.714	.667	.625	.588	.556	.526
2	.743	.718	.694	.683	.650	.630	.610	.574	.541	.510	.444	.391	.346	.309	.277
3	.641	.609	.579	.564	.524	.500	.477	.435	.398	.364	.296	.244	.204	.171	.146
4	.552	.516	.482	.467	.423	.397	.373	.329	.292	.260	.198	.153	.120	.095	.077
5	.476	.437	.402	.386	.341	.315	.291	.250	.215	.186	.132	.095	.070	.053	.040
6	.410	.370	.335	.319	.275	.250	.227	.189	.158	.133	.088	.060	.041	.029	.021
7	.354	.314	.279	.263	.222	.198	.178	.143	.116	.095	.059	.037	.024	.016	.011
8	.305	.266	.233	.218	.179	.157	.139	.108	.085	.068	.039	.023	.014	.009	.006
9	.263	.226	.194	.180	.144	.125	.108	.082	.063	.048	.026	.015	.008	.005	.003
10	.227	.191	.162	.149	.116	.099	.085	.062	.046	.035	.017	.009	.005	.003	.002
11	.195	.162	.135	.123	.094	.079	.066	.047	.034	.025	.012	.006	.003	.002	.001
12	.168	.137	.112	.102	.076	.062	.052	.036	.025	.018	.008	.004	.002	.001	.001
13	.145	.116	.093	.084	.061	.050	.040	.027	.018	.013	.005	.002	.001	.001	.000
14	.125	.099	.078	.069	.049	.039	.032	.021	.014	.009	.003	.001	.001	.000	.000
15	.108	.084	.065	.057	.040	.031	.025	.016	.010	.006	.002	.001	.000	.000	.000
16	.093	.071	.054	.047	.032	.025	.019	.012	.007	.005	.002	.001	.000		
17	.080	.060	.045	.039	.026	.020	.015	.009	.005	.003	.001	.000	.000		
18	.069	.051	.038	.032	.021	.016	.012	.007	.004	.002	.001	.000	.000		
19	.060	.043	.031	.027	.017	.012	.009	.005	.003	.002	.000	.000			
20	.051	.037	.026	.022	.014	.010	.007	.004	.002	.001	.000	.000			
25	.024	.016	.010	.009	.005	.003	.002	.001	.000	.000					

34

Decision models and
mathematical modeling

*Gordon B. Harwood**
Kenneth C. Levine†

Decision models and mathematical modeling are closely related
to accounting in many areas of corporate activity. These include
both the areas of activity which are directly concerned with
the accounting process and those which are not related to the
accounting process *per se* but which involve the *use* of accounting data. Some mathematical decision models are so commonplace that they are often treated as if they were the reality
rather than as a symbolic abstraction serving as a stand-in for
reality. An example of a very common mathematical model is
that used to compute interest on a loan: $I = prt$. In this model
I is the amount of interest, p is the amount borrowed, r is the
annual interest rate, and t is the time (in years) for which the
loan will be outstanding. The amount of interest represented
by I is itself a symbol, in the form of numbers, which serves as
a stand-in for the actual dollar-flow which will be created as a
result of the loan. Symbolic, or mathematical, models have their
appeal principally because, in most instances, it is much easier
to manipulate surrogates for real life objects than the objects
themselves. For example, it is much easier to manipulate
symbols (for example, names or clock numbers) representing

* Associate Professor of Accounting, Georgia State University.
† Forecasting Manager, Coca-Cola USA.

employees on a given shift to form a shift work schedule than it would be to try out various configurations of the individuals themselves.

The use of mathematical decision models may be viewed as a twofold process; that is, (1) a model must be selected which accurately reflects the decision process to be followed, and (2) data which are relevant for use with the model must be identified. Every situation calling for a decision is enormously complex. The number of factors inherent in each decision is literally uncountable. In addition, every potential course of action starts a chain of cause-effect interaction which is almost endless, logically speaking. An example of this type of interaction is the macroeconomic multiplier effect which could be attributed to a tax rebate. So complex are even the so-called trivial decision situations that the mere human mind of the decision maker cannot grasp *all* the ramifications of the decision. Thus no model can portray a real-life situation faithfully to the smallest detail. But care must be taken to select or design a model where the portrayal of the real-life situation is at least reasonably accurate. Mathematical decision models which are closely related to accounting have been applied to the following problems: (1) financial forecasting,[1] (2) estimation of the bad debts allowance,[2] (3) cost-volume-profit analysis,[3] (4) the investigation of variances from standard cost,[4]

---

[1] See G. Benston, "Multiple Regression Analysis of Cost Beavhior," *The Accounting Review,* October 1966; and R. E. Jensen, "A Multiple Regression Model for Cost Control—Assumptions and Limitations," *The Accounting Review,* April 1967.

[2] See R. M. Cyert, H. J. Davidson, and G. L. Thompson, "Estimation of the Allowance for Doubtful Accounts by Markov Chains," *Management Science,* April 1962; and G. Schroderheim, "Using Mathematical Probability to Estimate the Allowance for Doubtful Accounts," *The Accounting Review,* July 1964.

[3] See A. Charnes and W. W. Cooper, *Management Models and Industrial Applications of Linear Programming* (John Wiley and Sons, Inc., 1961), ch. 9; Yuji Ijiri, *Management Goals and Accounting for Control* (North-Holland Publishing Co., 1965), ch. 2; R. Manes, "A New Dimension to Break-Even Analysis," *Journal of Accounting Research,* Spring 1966; G. Johnson and S. Simik, "Multiproduct C.V.P. Analysis Under Uncertainty," *Journal of Accounting Research,* Autumn 1971; J. S. H. Kornbluth, "Accounting in Multiple Objective Linear Programming," *The Accounting Review,* April 1974. Also see D. L. Jensen, "The Role of Cost in Pricing Joint Products; A Case of Production in Fixed Proportions," *The Accounting Review,* July 1974; R. S. Kaplan and U. P. Welam, "Overhead Allocation with Imperfect Markets and Nonlinear Technology," *The Accounting Review,* July 1974; K. El-Sheshai, G. B. Harwood, and R. H. Hermanson, "Cost Volume Profit Analysis with Integer Goal Programming," *Management Accounting,* October 1977.

[4] R. S. Kaplan, "Optimal Investigation Strategies with Imperfect Information," *Journal of Accounting Research,* Spring 1969.

(5) the selection of depreciation methods,[5] (6) capital budgeting,[6] (7) inventory decisions,[7] and (8) corporate financial modeling.[8] This is by no means an exhaustive listing, but it does provide a notion of the varied array of decisions which have been addressed in this manner.

The second part of the process of using mathematical models, as mentioned above, is the identification of data which are relevant to the particular model selected. As a general rule, data which are relevant to the process of deciding among alternative courses of action are data which would differ with the selection of one alternative as compared to the selection of another alternative. It is far easier to state the rule than to identify the specific differential data which are relevant in many actual cases. It is not possible to design a differential accounting system; that is, an accounting system whose output is differential data *per se.* The reason for this is that data which are differential in one context may well not be differential in the next context. Thus relevant (differential) data must be determined by special analysis of the accounting records in every situation. The subject of differential, or incremental, data is developed more fully in other chapters of this book, especially Chapter 25.

There are many benefits associated with mathematical modeling as a *process.* The most obvious benefit is the facilitation of a decision in the matter at hand, but some of the least obvious may be the most important. The modeling process requires decision makers to give full consideration to the objectives, alternatives, and significant variables in a situation as well as the interrelationships among all these factors. Such consideration in turn results in a broader understanding of the problem on the part of the decision makers. In many respects this broader understanding resembles hindsight, with the advantage of being avail-

---

[5] I. Reynolds, "Selecting the Proper Depreciation Policy," *The Accounting Review,* April 1961; also see Y. Ijiri and R. S. Kaplan, "Sequential Models in Probabilistic Depreciation," *Journal of Accounting Research,* Spring 1970; and R. P. Brief and J. Owen, "A Reformulation of the Estimation Problem," *Journal of Accounting Research,* Spring 1973.

[6] Harold Bierman, Jr. and Seymour Smidt, *The Capital Budgeting Decision* (New York: Macmillan Publishing Co., Inc., 1975).

[7] G. Hadley and T. Whitin, *Analysis of Inventory Systems* (Englewood Cliffs, N. J.: Prentice Hall, 1963).

[8] K. C. Levine, "Developing a Corporate Planning Model Without a Million Dollar Budget," *Managerial Planning,* July/August 1976, pp. 18–21.

able *before* the fact instead of afterwards. This is possible because a model provides a framework for testing the effects of alternative courses of action before they are actually implemented. All these considerations imply that a decision model should not be viewed solely as a machine for cranking out decisions quasi-automatically, but instead as a vehicle for enabling the manager to make more informed *subjective* decisions through a better understanding of the problem.

All mathematical models may be grouped into two broad categories for discussion purposes: (1) deterministic models and (2) stochastic models. *Deterministic models* are those in which the decision parameters are treated as constants. *Stochastic models* are those in which some decision parameters are permitted to vary over a range of values. Obviously stochastic models generally tend to be more complicated than deterministic models because of the variability associated with some of the decision parameters. The discussion which follows deals with linear programming and inventory control models in the deterministic context. Computer simulation is also discussed. Computer simulation models may be either deterministic or stochastic, and both aspects of this technique are covered in the discussion.

LINEAR PROGRAMMING

Linear programming (LP) is a mathematical decision model which is applicable in many different situations related to accounting. Programming in the LP context means *formulating* a program in the sense of formulating a plan. Examples of situations in which LP is applicable are:

a. *Planning shipments* from a number of different shipping points, such as factories or warehouses, to a number of different destinations, such as customers or field storage facilities. The objective is to ship needed quantities from shipping points having these quantities available *and* at the same time to incur the least possible total shipping cost.

b. *Planning blend proportions* of different raw materials entering into a final mixture. The objective is to observe prescribed minimum levels of contribution from each raw material *and* to incur the lowest possible total raw material cost at the same time. The mixing of livestock feed and the blending of gasoline are examples of this application. In the case of livestock feed certain minimum levels of the various nutrients which livestock require must be present in the end product. A given nutrient level may be achieved in several ways, each with a different total cost. LP can find the particular mixture which will minimize total cost. Gasoline blending is analogous in that minimum octane (antiknock) standards can be attained through various combinations of the different blend stocks. LP can find that combination which will result in the lowest total cost.

c. *Planning product mix* so as to maximize total contribution. Often situations exist in which productive facilities can be dedicated to the production of several different products. LP can find the particular combination of the various products which will be most profitable to the company.

Each of these situations exhibits certain characteristics which are found in all LP problems. That is, (1) there is an *objective*, usually in the form of maximizing a contribution or revenue function or minimizing a cost function, and (2) explicit limitations or *constraints* must be observed in attaining the objective. These situations also exhibit a certain conflict between the objective and the constraints. For example, the objective of maximizing total contribution in a product mix problem must be attained while holding resource costs to a minimum. If the cost of resources were no problem, total contribution might be increased without bound by raising resource usage *ad infinitum*. One other very important condition for the use of LP is that each unit of resource must make the same contribution to the objective function as every other unit, regardless of the level of activity. This condition amounts to the linearity condition, which gives LP its name. There are many actual business situations in which the linear model is a reliable one, though it may not correspond precisely to the situation.

Computer software for the solution of LP problems is readily available, even for use on very small computers. This fact relieves decision makers of the substantial computational burden which the use of LP decision models entails. The decision maker needs only to turn over the mathematical statement of the problem to data processing or other analytical personnel. These personnel in turn can consult computer users' manuals and convert the mathematical statement of the problem into the form required by the computer, then let the machine take over and provide the solution. The solution procedure which most computer procedures execute internally is the simultaneous solution of a set of linear equations. Normally there is an infinite number of solutions to such a system, only *one* of which optimizes the objective function. (Occasionally there can be multiple optimal solutions, but still only one optimal objective function *value.*) The specific solution technique usually followed is called the *Simplex algorithm.* This algorithm has the unique ability of summarily excluding from consideration the endless number of solutions which are *feasible* but have no chance of being *optimal.* Only those feasible solutions which also have a chance of being optimal are examined.

The use of a computer to solve LP problems suggests another responsibility which does remain with the decision maker, the importance of which cannot be overemphasized: that is, the correct formulation of the mathematical statement of the objective function and the constraints. A convenient sequence of steps to be followed in the formulation is:

1. Verbalize the objective.
2. Verbalize the constraints or limitations.
3. Identify the variables which are common to constraints and objective function.
4. Formulate the mathematical statement of the objective function.
5. Formulate the mathematical statement of the constraints.

Steps 1, 2, and 3 involve only verbalization and identification. No mathematical expressions are formed until steps 4 and 5 are reached.

An example involving the use of LP

The case of Dairy-O Distributors of Wisconsin will illustrate the use of LP in management decision making. Dairy-O manufactures frozen yogurt and ice cream. The yogurt is sold in bulk principally to hospitals but also to a few other institutional users such as restaurants and hotels. The ice cream is sold through several large retail grocery chains. Three distinct processes are involved in production: (1) batch-mixing both products in large vats in a mixing center in the plant, (2) packaging the products in liquid form, and (3) freezing the packaged products. The mixing process requires substantially more time for yogurt than for ice cream because of the extra time required for the yogurt bacteria culture. The packaging process requires less time for yogurt since all yogurt is sold in bulk. The freezing process is identical for both yogurt and ice cream so that this process does not affect the decision.

The plant operates 24 hours a day, 7 days a week. Because the different processes have differing time requirements, there are 60 hours during the week when the mixing vats in the mixing center are idle and 40 hours when the machinery in the packaging center is idle. Dairy-O's present customers have indicated that they will buy all the yogurt and ice cream which Dairy-O can manufacture. Present production schedules can be rearranged so that the idle time will fall in blocks corresponding in length to the blocks of time required for batches of ice cream and yogurt. Management is now faced with the decision as to what is the best way to utilize the plant time which is now idle.

This situation exhibits the linearity required for LP applications. Each batch of yogurt results in a constant contribution of $9, and each batch of ice cream results in a constant contribution of $7. This is the case regardless of the level of production. Each batch of yogurt requires 12 hours in mixing and 4 hours in packaging. Each batch of ice cream requires 4 hours in mixing and 8 hours in packaging. Stated in another way, the specific decision facing management is: How many additional batches of yogurt and ice cream can be produced with the idle time available in the plant in order to realize the greatest possible increase in contribution margin?

The variables which are common to the constraints and the objective function are (1) the number of batches of yogurt and (2) the number of batches of ice cream. In formulating the mathematical expressions for the constraints, X_1 will stand for the number of batches of yogurt to be made. X_2 will stand for the number of batches of ice cream to be made. The mathematical statement of the objective, which is to maximize total contribution margin, is:

$$\text{Maximize } \$9X_1 + \$7X_2 \tag{1}$$

The constraint for the mixing center is stated as follows:

$$12X_1 + 4X_2 \leq 60 \text{ hours.} \tag{2}$$

This says that 12 hours times the number of batches of yogurt produced, plus 4 hours times the number of batches of ice cream produced, may not exceed 60. Sixty is the total number of hours available in the mixing center.

The constraint for the packaging center is:

$$4X_1 + 8X_2 \leq 40 \text{ hours.} \tag{3}$$

This says that 4 hours times the number of batches of yogurt produced, plus 8 hours times the number of batches of ice cream produced, may not exceed 40. Forty is the total number of hours available in the packaging center.

Two final constraints are necessary to complete the system:

$$X_1 \geq 0 \tag{4}$$

and

$$X_2 \geq 0. \tag{5}$$

These constraints are called non-negativity constraints. They require that each variable in the system not be less than zero (negative). The idea of negative vats of yogurt, for example, would be senseless. Since non-negativity constraints are required in every LP system, the computer software provides for them automatically. Thus the non-negativity constraints in the LP system which is to be solved by computer do not have to be made explicit.

Expressions (1) through (3) comprise the LP problem to be turned over to EDP personnel to feed into the computer. That is:

$$\text{Maximize } \$9X_1 + \$7X_2$$

Subject to:

$$12X_1 + 4X_2 \leq 60 \text{ hours}$$
$$4X_1 + 8X_2 \leq 40 \text{ hours}$$

Graphing LP constraints

Graphs are very helpful in understanding LP problems. In real life, decisions may be so complex that the LP decision model requires thousands of constraints expressed in terms of thousands of different variables. Situations as complex as this cannot be

EXHIBIT 1
Graph of packaging center time constraint

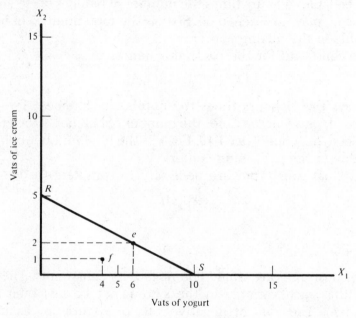

graphed, of course, because the physical space needed for a graph does not exist beyond 3 dimensions (variables). The Dairy-O case is simple enough to graph in only two dimensions. Understanding the graphical relationships in a simple case is helpful to decision makers because these same relationships may be generalized conceptually to more complex cases.

The graph of the constraint expressing the limited time available in the packaging center is shown in Exhibit 1. The point at which this line terminates on the horizontal axis was determined by computing the number of batches of yogurt (X_1) which could be made if all the available time in the packaging center were devoted to producing this one product. This number is determined by setting X_2 to zero in expression (3) and solving for X_1 as follows, just as if the expression were an equation:

$$4X_1 + 8(0) = 40$$
$$4X_1 = 40$$
$$X_1 = 10$$

Thus the point on the horizontal axis is 10. Similarly, the point at which the line terminates on the vertical axis is determined by computing the number of batches of ice cream (X_2) which could be made if all the available time in the packaging center were devoted to producing this one product. Following are the computations:

$$4(0) + 8X_2 = 40$$
$$8X_2 = 40$$
$$X_2 = 5$$

Thus the terminal point on the vertical axis is 5. The graph of the constraint is made by connecting these points with a straight line. The straight line reflects the linearity which must be present in LP constraints, as previously discussed.

What LP constraint graphs show

The graph of the LP constraint in Exhibit 1 has some important characteristics. The quantities of yogurt and ice cream associated with *any* point on the graph-line of the constraint will use up the entire amount of resource associated with the constraint (hours in the packaging center, in this case). For example, point *e* in Exhibit 1 corresponds to 6 batches of yogurt and 2 batches of ice cream. Substituting these values into the equation expressing the constraint produces the following computations:

$$4(6) + 8(2) = 40$$
$$24 + 16 = 40$$

These computations show that producing the two products in these proportions uses up the entire 40 hours in the packaging center.

Another important characteristic is borne out by Exhibit 1. That is, the quantities of yogurt and ice cream associated with any point within the space *under* the graph-line will use up an amount of time which is *less than* the total time available.

Thus these quantities will observe the less-than condition of the less-than-or-equal-to constraint. Point f, for example, is associated with 4 batches of yogurt and 1 batch of ice cream. Substituting these values for X_1 and X_2 into constraint (3) provides the following:

$$4(4) + 8(1) \leq 40$$
$$16 + 8 \ \leq 40$$

Since $16 + 8 = 24$, the less-than condition of the constraint is observed.

To be complete, the graph of a LP system must include all of the applicable constraints as well as the objective function. Exhibit 2 shows the graph of both the constraints in the Dairy-O case. Line R, S represents constraint (3), previously illustrated in Exhibit 1, and T, U represents constraint (2). The termination of these lines at the vertical and horizontal axes provides for the observance of the non-negativity constraints. Any point below the horizontal axis would imply that negative batches of

EXHIBIT 2
Graph of all constraints in Dairy-O case

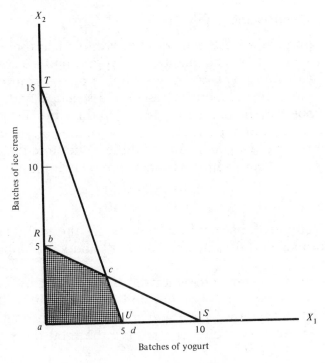

Batches of yogurt

ice cream could be produced. Any point left of the vertical axis would imply that negative batches of yogurt could be produced.

The shaded area in Exhibit 2 is the area which contains all feasible solutions. These are the solutions which observe all constraints. As explained before, all points in the graph-space area under line *R,S* provide feasible solutions to the objective which at the same time observe constraint (3). In order to observe *all* constraints a solution must lie in the graph-space area that *all* constraints have in common. It has been proven mathematically that the *optimal* feasible solution will coincide with the values of the variables associated with one of the *corners* of the area which all the constraints have in common.[9] (Disclosure of the proof is not necessary for our discussion.) The corners in Exhibit 2 are designated *a, b, c,* and *d*.

Proving the LP solution

The values of the variables at the corners of the solution area in Exhibit 2 are:

	Number of batches	
Corner	Yogurt (X_1)	Ice cream (X_2)
a 0		0
b 0		5
c. 4		3
d 5		0

The fact that none of the variables has a negative value shows that the non-negativity constraints have been observed. Whether or not conditions (2) and (3) are observed can be determined by substituting all pairs of values for X_1 and X_2 occurring at corners of the solution area into the constraints, as follows:

	Value of variable at corner		Condition (2)	Condition (3)
Corner	X_1	X_2	$12X_1 + 4X_2 \le 60$	$4X_1 + 8X_2 \le 40$
a 0		0	$0 + 0 \le 60$	$0 + 0 \le 40$
b 0		5	$0 + 20 \le 60$	$0 + 40 \le 40$
c 4		3	$48 + 12 \le 60$	$16 + 24 \le 40$
d 5		0	$60 + 0 \le 60$	$20 + 0 \le 40$

---

[9] In the case of multiple optimal solutions, the points of interest may not lie at a *corner* of this area, but they will always lie on its outer edge.

Since no pair of X_1, X_2 values results in using up more total hours than the maximum specified by each constraint, the constraints are properly observed.

The optimal solution is found by substituting each pair of X_1, X_2 corner values into the objective function. The pair of values which results in the highest value for the objective function is the optimal solution. This process is illustrated as follows:

	Value of variable at corner		Objective function $\$9X_1 + \$7X_2$
Corner	X_1	X_2	
a	0	0	$\$9(0) + \$7(0) = 0$
b	0	5	$\$9(0) + \$7(5) = \$35$
c	4	3	$\$9(4) + \$7(3) = \$57$
d	5	0	$\$9(5) + \$7(0) = \$45$

These computations show that $57 is the largest amount of increase in total contribution margin which may be brought about by using up the idle time in the mixing and packaging centers. This increase will occur when the quantities of the two products coincide with corner c. That is, when four more batches of yogurt and three more batches of ice cream are produced.

INVENTORY CONTROL

Another area in which mathematical decision models have considerable applicability is that of inventory control, particularly in companies where inventories constitute a sizeable investment. Aside from the investment in inventory, significant ancillary costs are incurred whenever inventories are maintained. The entire purchasing department operation of a company, for example, is carried on almost exclusively for the sake of having inventory on hand. All of the costs which are incurred for this purpose are collectively referred to as "*ordering costs.*" Exhibit 3 shows an accounting report detailing the purchasing department expenses of the Authier Company. The expenses in this report illustrate the typical purchasing department expenses incurred by most companies. Also included in the ordering costs of most companies are expenses incurred by the materials receiving department and part of the expenses incurred by the accounts payable department.

Another category of significant costs associated with having inventory on hand is "*carrying costs.*" These are the costs which must be borne by the company in carrying out "custodial" functions after the inventory arrives but before it is sold or placed in process. Custodial functions include such functions as storage and safekeeping. The costs associated with custodial functions

EXHIBIT 3

AUTHIER COMPANY
Purchasing Department Expenses
For the Year Ended December 31, 1979

Direct expenses:

Executive salaries	$55,000	
Buyers' salaries	35,000	
Expediters' salaries	19,000	
Clerical salaries	40,500	
Payroll fringe expenses	7,239	
Postage and supplies	1,125	
Depreciation on company cars	4,200	
Depreciation on office furniture and fixtures	2,700	
Total direct expenses		$164,764
Indirect expenses:		
Building occupancy expenses	$10,900	
General and administrative expenses	32,000*	
Total indirect expenses		42,900
Total purchasing department expenses		$207,664

* Includes Data Processing Department expenses of $7,200.

EXHIBIT 4

AUTHIER COMPANY
Warehouse Operating Expenses
For the Year Ended December 31, 1979

Direct expenses:

Warehouse management salaries	$42,000	
Receiving clerks' wages	38,438	
Pickers' wages	37,440	
Janitorial wages	7,200	
Payroll fringe expenses	7,800	
Postage and supplies	500	
Inventory spoilage expense	5,000	
Depreciation of furniture and fixtures	7,320	
Depreciation of autos and trucks	5,400	
Depreciation of warehouse building	12,332	
Other warehouse occupancy expenses	7,500	
Taxes and insurance on inventory	14,000	
Interest on borrowed funds	18,000*	
Total direct expenses		$202,930
Indirect expenses:		
General and administrative expenses		17,250†
Total warehouse operating expenses		$220,180

* Represents interest on average amount of borrowed funds tied up in inventory.
† Includes data processing department expenses of $10,250.

include such costs as warehouse salaries, depreciation on the warehouse building, and insurance on the inventory. Exhibit 4, which shows the warehouse operating expenses of the Authier Company, illustrates the different types of costs which are often incurred in this regard.

Ordering cost and carrying cost behavior

Ordering costs and carrying costs have their own distinctive behavior patterns, and these should be taken into consideration in making decisions involving inventory control. Total ordering costs tend to increase as the number of purchase orders issued by the company increases. For example, more file clerks are needed to keep the departmental files straight as more and more purchase orders are prepared. The same is true for other categories of ordering costs. Carrying costs behave just the opposite. Total carrying costs tend to *decrease* as the number of orders placed increases. Carrying costs behave this way because a larger number of orders placed means a lower quantity per order. The reason for this is that the *total* quantity ordered during the year is based on demand by customers and will remain unchanged. As a result, the average stock on hand will be lower and will require less attention in the way of custodial services. This will be reflected in lower costs. For example, the cost of wages for warehousemen to take charge of the stock is less than the cost would be if extensive quantities were maintained.

These cost behavior patterns are reflected in Exhibit 5. This graph brings out some important cost considerations related to inventory control. For instance, total costs arising from having inventory on hand decrease up to a point as the number of units ordered increases. Then total costs begin to increase. Point Q in Exhibit 5 is a crucial quantity. It is the quantity of goods ordered at which total ordering costs plus total carrying costs (that is, the total costs associated with having inventory) is minimal, as reflected by the downside peak on the total cost curve in Exhibit 5. Because the quantity is associated with minimal cost, it is called the Economic Order Quantity, or simply the EOQ. The flatness of the total cost curve in the vicinity of Q indicates that the EOQ can vary considerably in this range without significantly affecting total costs. Naturally management is

EXHIBIT 5
Graphic relationship of costs of inventorying goods

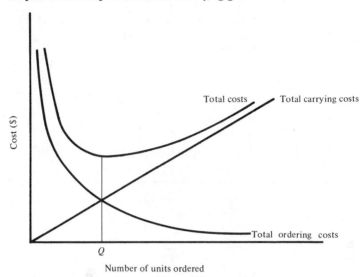

Number of units ordered

very interested in knowing the EOQ, but its determination is not always simple and straightforward.

A quantitative EOQ model

The area of inventory control has found considerable use for mathematical decision models, particularly to help in the determination of the EOQ. In all cases it is important to select a mathematical decision model which adequately portrays the situation being modeled. Because of the large variety of different circumstances which may surround EOQ decisions, several EOQ models have been developed. The EOQ model discussed in this section applies when the *rate of issuance* of inventory (either to customers through sales or to the production department for manufacturing activities) is *constant,* or nearly so. This model also requires that the stock level be replenished in full, right at the time the inventory balance reaches zero (or very close to that point). These requirements of the models are applicable in a large number of actual situations. Such is the case with the Authier Company mentioned previously, for example. Part

956

EXHIBIT 6
Authier Company's welding rod inventory behavior

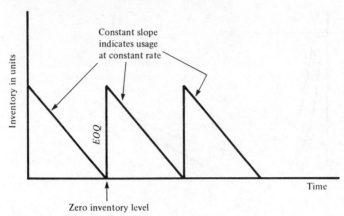

of Authier's operation is a large welding shop for repairing industrial equipment. A large part of the repair work is electric welding requiring the use of substantial quantities of welding rods, which are used up at a steady rate each day. Authier and the welding rod manufacturer's regional warehouses are both located in Atlanta. Thus Authier is able to obtain same-day delivery on large quantities of welding rods and orders welding rods at about the time their welding rod stock runs out. These relationships are shown graphically in Exhibit 6.

The EOQ model which applies in this situation is:[10]

$$\text{EOQ} = \sqrt{\frac{2AP}{RC}},$$

where

A = total annual usage (number of units)
P = incremental cost of placing an order
R = unit cost
C = incremental carrying cost as a percentage of average total inventory.

---

[10] This model is derived by differentiating a total cost function with respect to quantity. See, for example, C. M. Paik, *Quantitative Methods for Management Decisions* (New York: McGraw Hill Book, Co., 1973), p. 350.

As mentioned before, it is very important to identify the data which are relevant for use with a quantitative decision model. The cost data which are relevant for EOQ models are *incremental* cost data.

To illustrate the use of the EOQ formula given above, the following data are assumed for the Authier Company:

A = 12,000 units (in this case a unit is a box containing 5 dozen rods)
P = $30
R = $5
C = 10%

Thus,

$$\text{EOQ} = \sqrt{\frac{2(12,000)(\$30)}{0.10(\$5)}} = \sqrt{\frac{720,000}{0.5}} = \sqrt{1,440,000} = 1,200.$$

That is, orders placed for 1,200 boxes of welding rods at a time will result in the lowest possible total cost of having an inventory of welding rods. Since 12,000 boxes per year are required, the number of orders to be placed in a year's time is 10 (12,000 boxes in total ÷ 1,200 boxes per order).

The reorder point

Another decision which is closely related to the EOQ is the question of *when* to place orders for additional stock. This is known as the *reorder point (ROP)*. The ROP does not affect the EOQ. In fact, the determination of the ROP can only take place after the EOQ has been determined. The ROP can be expressed in terms of an interval of time. For example, in the illustration above it was determined that the EOQ for the Authier Company was 1,200 boxes of welding rods. Since the EOQ model employed assumes replacement is instantaneous when inventory level reaches zero (stockouts do not enter into the model) the time interval between orders is every 36½ days (365 days ÷ 10 orders per year).

More complicated models have been developed to apply under more complex circumstances. In some situations the assumption of instantaneous replacement is not realistic. In these cases management must make a conditioning decision before the ROP can be determined—that is, whether stockouts will or will not be allowed. This conditioning decision must take into consideration the probability of a stockout, which depends upon whether lead time and /or demand *during* lead time vary randomly. This decision must also take into consideration the expected cost/revenue trade-off which would occur as a result of a stockout.[11]

COMPUTER SIMULATION

The modeling techniques discussed up to this point assume that uncontrollable factors are known and can be represented by constants. Models of this type are classified as "deterministic" models. In some cases, factors such as unit sales, contribution margins, advertising levels, and unit costs are subject to random variation. Obviously, the presence of random variation in these factors affects the selection of an optimal decision strategy. Models which explicitly consider random variation are classified as "stochastic" models. Often the number of variables is so large and their interrelationships so complex that computer assistance is required. The final section of this chapter will synthesize the deterministic and stochastic approaches to mathematical modeling by analyzing a particular decision problem using both approaches.[12]

The case of the Food Mart grocery store in Oakland will be used as an illustration. The manager of Food Mart has noted that customers often leave the store without completing their purchases when confronted with long lines at the checkout counters. It is estimated that approximately 100 customers enter the store each eight-hour day and that it takes about five minutes for each of the two cashiers to service a customer, on the average. In order to reduce the long lines at the checkout counters the advisability of hiring an additional cashier is being considered.

---

[11] See Hadley and Whitin, Analysis of Inventory Systems for a dicussion of the complexities which may occur in inventory control decisions. Most complexities can be handled through appropriate variations in the basic EOQ model.

[12] See Billy E. Goetz, *Quantitative Methods: A Survey and Guide for Managers,* New York: McGraw-Hill Book Company, 1965. Also see E. E. Kaczka, "Computer Simulation," *Decision Sciences,* vol. 1, 1970, nos. 1 and 2, pp. 174–92.

The deterministic approach

Since 100 customers are expected per day on the average and each customer will be serviced by the cashier in approximately five minutes, 500 total cashier-minutes per day should be required. Since each cashier works eight hours or 480 minutes, this model indicates that one cashier should be able to service almost all of the customers, and two cashiers should be more than enough. These conclusions are based on the assumptions that customers enter and leave the store in a continuous stream throughout the day. These conclusions also assume that customers will wait in line as long as necessary to pay for their groceries, although the manager's observations indicate otherwise.

A second and more realistic approach would be to break down the day into homogeneous segments based on different customer frequencies and then fit cashier complements of appropriate sizes to each segment of the day. For example, if it can be assumed that 80 of the 100 customers reach the cashier between the hours of 10 A.M. and 1 P.M. with the remaining 20 customers evenly distributed throughout the day, then the day could be divided with two segments as follows:

Segment #1 (10 A.M.—1 P.M.):
80 customers × 5 minutes = 400 cashier-minutes required
3 hours = 180 minutes
400/180 = 2.22 cashiers needed

Segment #2 (9 A.M.—10 A.M.; 1 P.M.—5 P.M.):
20 customers × 5 minutes = 100 cashier-minutes required
5 hours = 300 minutes
100/300 = 0.33 cashiers needed

According to this approach, one cashier would suffice for the majority of the day (Segment 2), but more than two cashiers would be needed during the peak hours (Segment 1).

In a similar manner, if the expected demand can be further subdivided into hourly levels and if hourly part-time help is available, it is possible to determine the optimal level of cashiers during *each hour* of the day using this approach. If the two segments previously discussed represent the finest practicable partitioning, the following additional information will enable the analysis to be expanded to include cost considerations:

$4 per hour salary expense for cashiers
$7 average contribution per customer order

With these monetary parameters, a cost-benefit analysis to determine the optimal number of cashiers for each time period is possible as shown below for Segment 1 of the work day:

10 A.M. — 1 P.M. (3 hours = 180 minutes):

Case 1: *2 cashiers are employed:*

80 customers × 5 minutes = 400 minutes needed

$$2 \text{ cashiers} \times 180 \text{ minutes} = \frac{360 \text{ minutes available}}{40 \text{ minute deficit}}$$

40/5 = 8 customers lost on the average
8 customers × $7 = $56 lost contribution

Salary: 2 cashiers × 3 hours × $4.00 = $24

Total cost = Lost contribution + Salary expense
= $56 + $24 = $80

Case 2: *3 cashiers are employed:*

80 customers × 5 minutes = 400 minutes needed

$$3 \text{ cashiers} \times 180 \text{ minutes} = \frac{540 \text{ minutes available}}{140 \text{ minutes slack time}}$$
(therefore no lost contribution)

Salary: 3 cashiers × 3 hours × $4 = $36.

Total cost = Lost contribution + Salary expense
= $0 + $36 = $36

Based on this analysis, the store should hire three cashiers from 10 A.M. to 1 P.M. No matter how many cashiers are hired (within reasonable limits), there may still be queues, or waiting lines, since customers enter the store on a random basis in contrast to the average basis reflected in the analysis above. Therefore, some customers will be lost in addition to those reflected in the analysis. Besides the $7 lost contribution for each customer not completing his or her purchase, consideration must be given to any bad will created, which may in turn result in the permanent loss of a particular customer's repeat business. This factor can be quantified, or expressed in mathematical language in the deterministic analysis, if the analyst is able to predict the number of customers lost and the effect of the bad will generated, such as the present value of the average dollar contribution lost as a result of future business foregone.

Sensitivity analysis

In this instance, as is the case with many mathematical models, sensitivity analysis can vastly improve the value of the model. *Sensitivity analysis* is the determination of the effect which different values of the decision parameters will have on the ultimate decision criteria. The values of these parameters are allowed to vary within a relevant range of possibilities, and the effect on the model output is noted. If a very large effect is noted for a small change in a parameter value, the output of the model should be considered less reliable than in the case of an insignificant effect on the output.[13]

A complete sensitivity analysis is extremely tedious to perform by hand, as one would want to see the effect of a change in each assumption on the result of the model. If, for example, three values are to be tested for each of five assumptions in the model, 243, or 3^5, sensitivity tests are necessary. Fortunately, the computer provides a convenient way to solve this problem. By programming the basic model on the computer, numerous input values for each parameter can be tested in seconds with the aggregate results printed in tabular form for analysis.

To illustrate sensitivity analysis, suppose the Food Mart manager anticipates an increase in the hourly cashier's wage and wishes to know the effect of such an increase on the decision explained above concerning the number of cashiers in Segment 1 of the work day. He could rework the previous analysis based on the anticipated new salary rate to note the effect of the new rate on the prior decision. As an alternative method, he could use a break-even approach to the analysis; that is, he could find the wage rate which would cause the model to be indifferent

---

[13] In many cases, there may be multiple sensitive parameters in a decision model. In these cases, the sensitivity analysis will be valuable in determining what additional data should be sought before making a final decision.

between the alternative staffing complements under consideration. Using the information given above, the break-even approach is as follows:

$$\text{Total Cost} = \text{Lost Contribution} + \text{Salary Expense},$$

where salary expense = number of cashiers × 3 hours × hourly rate. Letting w stand for the hourly wage rate, the use of two cashiers results in total cost as follows:

$56 lost contribution + (2 cashiers × 3 hours' work each)w
$$= \$56 + 6w$$

The use of three cashiers results in total cost as follows:

$0 lost contribution + 3(3)(w) = \$0 + 9w$

Equating the decision costs,

$$9w = 56 + 6w$$
$$3w = 56$$
$$w = \frac{56}{3} = 18.67$$

These calculations show that a raise of more than $14.67 ($18.67 − $4.00) would be necessary to change the previous optimal decision.

The stochastic approach

As previously explained, deterministic models are those in which certain decision parameters are assumed to be constants. Of course, this assumption is made for simplification purposes because actual decision situations are often characterized by random variation. Assuming away random variation may have misleading and costly consequences. For example, Food Mart would have no problem in ordering milk for resale if 50 gallons are actually sold every day. If 50 gallons is the *average* number of gallons sold, the *actual* number might be 10, or 150, or some other number. In other words the average could be 50 gallons even though 50 gallons were never sold on any individual day. Thus it could be a serious mistake to order 50 gallons if actual sales were 10 gallons because the excess milk might spoil. It could also be a serious mistake to order 50 gallons if demand were 150 gallons because of the lost contribution which would result.

Expected value

To overcome this problem, a very simple stochastic process called an *expected-value model* can be developed. This type of model assumes that the number of customers per day is a random variable, described by a probability distribution or table showing each possible number in which customers may arrive and the probability of each number. Following is an example:

Number of customers per day	Probability
60	0.4
80	0.4
100	0.2

This probability distribution could have been derived from historical data, subjective judgment, or a combination of the two. The expected value of a random variable is a weighted average of all the possible values which the variable can assume. Each value is weighted by the probability that the value will occur. Based on the probability distribution of customers, the expected value is:

$$60(0.4) + 80(0.4) + 100(0.2) = 76$$

This means that in the long run the *average* daily number of customers will be 76. The *actual* number will never be 76, though; as the probability distribution shows, the actual number can only be 60, *or* 80, *or* 100.

Applying these concepts to the decision as to the number of cashiers which Food Mart should employ during the hours 10 A.M. to 1 P.M. daily results in the computations as to lost contribution shown in Exhibit 7. Based on the information in Exhibit 7, the *expected* lost contribution with 2 cashiers is computed as follows:

$$\$0(0.4) + \$56(0.4) + \$196(0.2) = \$61.60.$$

The expected lost contribution with three cashiers is computed as follows:

$$\$0(0.4) + \$0(0.4) + \$0(0.2) = \$0.$$

The cashier salary expense is $24 with two cashiers and $36 with three cashiers as shown on page 960 in the case of the deterministic simulation. Thus the *total* expected cost is $85.60

EXHIBIT 7

Expected value model for determining cashier complement from 10 A.M. to 1 P.M. daily

Number of customers	Two cashiers (cashier-minutes available = 360*)			Three cashiers (cashier-minutes available = 540†)		
	Cashier time required‡	Deficit in cashier time	Lost contribution§	Cashier time required‡	Deficit in cashier time	Lost contribution§
60	300	—	$ 0	300	—	$0
80	400	40	56	400	—	0
100	500	140	196	500	—	0

* 3 hours × 60 minutes × 2 cashiers = 360
† 3 hours × 60 minutes × 3 cashiers = 540
‡ Basis: 5 minutes per customer as assumed in deterministic example.
§ Deficit in cashier time ÷ 5 minutes per customer × $7 lost contribution per customer.

($61.60 + $24.00) with two cashiers and $36 ($0 + $36.00) with three cashiers. According to this analysis the lowest expected total cost would be incurred with three cashiers during the period in question. This corresponds to the indication derived from the deterministic simulation as previously explained. However, if the probabilities had been skewed more heavily toward smaller numbers of customers, this model might have reversed the prior decision.

In contrast to the single random variable in the preceding illustration, many decision situations are comprised of multiple random variables. For example, the expected-value analysis in the preceding situation does not take into account the possibility of variations in servicing time or shopping time per customer. As the number of random variables increases, the analysis becomes more cumbersome and time consuming. Once again, the computer may be used in solving this type of problem. After programming the general model on the computer, random numbers can be generated and transformed into events according to given probability distributions for each random variable. After a large number of computer runs it is possible to study the effect of variation on the model. This process is called "Monte Carlo" simulation.[14]

Monte Carlo simulation

As an illustration of Monte Carlo simulation the Food Mart model could be constructed in such a way that the number of customers entering the store, the shopping time per customer, and the cashier servicing time per customer all vary according to given probability distributions, such as:

Total number of customers arriving	Probability	Shopping time per customer (in minutes)	Probability	Cashier servicing time per customer (in minutes)	Probability
60	0.4	8	0.6	4	0.3
80	0.4	10	0.3	5	0.4
100	0.2	12	0.1	6	0.3

[14] Simulations can be performed manually; however, the availability of a computer transforms an extremely tedious task into a feasible one.

EXHIBIT 8

Computer simulation results based on Food Mart data and one cashier

Time	Present size of queue*	Number of customers arriving	Shopping time (in minutes)	Time entering checkout	Waiting time (in minutes)	Cashier servicing time (in minutes)	Time out
10:00—10:01	0	0	—	—	—	—	—
10:01—10:02	0	1	8	10:09	0	4	10:13
10:02—10:03	0	0	—	—	—	—	—
10:03—10:04	0	0	—	—	—	—	—
10:04—10:05	0	0	—	—	—	—	—
10:05—10:06	0	2	8†	10:13	0	5	10:18
			9†	10:14	4	4	10:22
10:06—10:07	0	1	8	10:14	8	6	10:28
10:07—10:08	0	0	—	—	—	—	—
10:08—10:09	0	0	—	—	—	—	—
10:09—10:10	0	1	12	10:21	7	5	10:33

(to 1 P.M.)

* The size of the queue, or number of customers waiting in line, will be zero until 10:14, when the third customer arrives at the checkout counter and has to wait for the second customer to be serviced.

† Data applicable to first and second customers entering the store during the one-minute period 10:05—10:06.

The computer can be programmed to select randomly the number of customers arriving minute after minute, the particular shopping time required by each customer, and the cashier servicing time (the amount of time required for each customer to check out) observing the distinct probability distribution for each variable. Different computer simulation runs can be performed to reflect results with different complements of cashiers.

Exhibit 8 provides detailed information concerning the first ten minutes' results of a computer simulation of the Food Mart cost based on one cashier. (In practice, similar information would be required for the entire three-hour period under study.) As previously explained, the number of customers arriving, the shopping time required by each customer, and the cashier servicing time for each customer are all randomly determined. The time entering the checkout is the time entering the store plus the shopping time for each customer. The time out is the time entering the checkout plus the sum of the waiting and servicing times. The waiting time is a function of the queue size and must be accumulated by totaling the servicing time of all customers in the queue prior to the customer under consideration.

In actually making a staffing decision, the summary statistics from computer simulation runs such as this must be taken into consideration. For the Food Mart case these statistics are given in Exhibit 9. As this illustration shows, in the simulation with one cashier almost half of the customers entering the store are still in line at the end of the time period with an average waiting time of approximately 2½ hours. In this case the arrival rate for new customers is greater than the cashier servicing rate, creating an "exploding queue," or a queue which will increase without bound. With two cashiers, there is no wait approximately 60 percent of the time. When someone does have to wait, the average delay is less than the time it takes to service one customer. There are never more than two people waiting in line. With three cashiers, only about 1 out of every 100 customers must wait. The average wait for these is almost one minute, and there is never more than one person waiting in line.

OTHER DECISION MODELS

Mathematical modeling has resulted in the development of other decision models which are also useful in various circum-

EXHIBIT 9
Summary statistics from computer simulation of Food Mart case for time period 10 A.M. to 1 P.M.

Number of cashiers	Total number of arrivals	Number of customers serviced	Customers in queue at 1 P.M.	Maximum queue length	Customers serviced without waiting	Percent of total serviced	Average waiting time
1	75	41	34	34	5	6.7	152.44
2	75	75	0	2	43	57.3	3.75
3	76	76	0	1	75	98.7	1.00

stances. Although it is not possible to discuss these in detail in this chapter, some other important models should at least be mentioned.

Learning curve models can be used in some cases to improve cost estimates. Intuitively it seems that workers should become more efficient at their jobs as they do them over and over. That is, workers should *learn* as they work, and the learning process should result in savings of some kind. An example of this would be savings in direct labor time (and hence dollars) per unit as the worker produces more and more units. Studies have shown that indeed some workers do tend to learn almost indefinitely in performing their jobs. In these cases, the variable cost per unit would not be constant but would decrease with successive units. The use of learning curves associated with a particular industry or job allows management to take into consideration the efficiencies brought about through the learning process when computing standard costs and preparing cost estimates.

Network analysis is another valuable decision model. Network analysis can be used to control the efficient use of labor and materials in projects calling for work to be done in a number of sequential steps. The building of an oil tanker is an example of such a project. Before the oil tanks can be welded into place within the hull of a tanker, certain structural work on the hull must be completed. Sequences of subtasks such as this can be identified throughout the entire project. Two closely related networking methods which are widely used are the *Program Evaluation and Review Technique (PERT)* and the *Critical Path Method (CPM)*. The shortening of total project time (and hence the lowering of costs) is one example of the control features provided by networking methods.

Another important decision tool is that provided by *statistical decision theory*. Decision theory provides a framework for analyzing decisions in situations of uncertainty. This model formally recognizes that the *payoff*, or dollar consequences, of such a decision results from the interaction of two factors: (1) the *decision*, or action selected by the decision maker and (2) *a state of the world* which occurs independently of the decision maker's action. The decision maker has *control* over the action which he selects, but he has *no control* over the state of the world, or simply "state," which occurs. In this framework, the use of expected values (as explained in a prior section of this paper) points out a course of action which will optimize the decision maker's preferences with respect to risk.

CONCLUSION

Decision models and mathematical modeling relate very closely to the work of accountants in many instances. Often decision models are concerned directly with decisions of an accounting nature. In many cases they are concerned with other areas of activity but are still related to accounting because they involve the use of accounting data. Regardless of the area of activity the value of a decision model stems as much from activities which are *tangential* to the actual decision as it does from the decision itself. This is so because the use of a model requires thorough examination of the problem under consideration and the fullest possible identification of the relevant factors. As a result the judgmental ability of the decision maker is sharpened with respect to the particular problem. In the final analysis decision models may enable managers to exercise the best possible judgment in the decision process because the use of a model forces them to obtain a better understanding of the problem than they would otherwise have obtained.

35

The learning curve:
Concepts and application

*Felix P. Kollaritsch**
Raymond B. Jordan†

INTRODUCTION

This chapter deals specifically with the nonlinear costs of the human phenomenon we call the *learning curve*. It will include the underlying assumptions of this concept, the methods of determining the cumulative and incremental average unit costs, and the specific uses and limitations of these costs. We shall also look at the way the learning curve is used in pricing and bidding, as well as specific industries and processes that use it.

All phases of management must be able to recognize curvilinear costs and measure them properly. Planning, decision making, controls, motivation, and performance measurement should be concerned with curvilinear costs. Their use will also explain to management many seemingly incomprehensible variances reported from operations. The learning curve can often reveal the causes of deviations that conventional variance analysis would not reveal.

DEFINITION OF LEARNING CURVE

The learning curve has to do with the ways people improve their performance of certain tasks. It may be defined as the

* Chairman and Professor of Accounting, The Ohio State University.
† Administrator-Cost Systems & Studies, General Electric Company. (Retired)

EXHIBIT 1

Cumulative and incremental unit cost with 80 percent learning curve on arithmetical graph paper

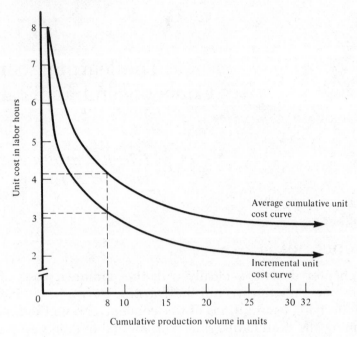

Cumulative production volume in units

ability of persons, under certain circumstances, to increase their efficiency or skill by a constant rate as the cumulative production quantity increases geometrically—that is, increases by doubling. In other words, the basic concept of the learning curve is that the cumulative average unit cost will decline by some constant percentage whenever the total quantity of produced units is doubled. Anyone who has repeatedly performed some specific task or operation knows that, in general, the time required to repeat the task is appreciably less than the time required to perform it originally.

The learning curve is called a curve because the various efficiencies, when plotted on standard graph paper (arithmetic scale), form a hyperbola, as in Exhibit 1. You may encounter other names used as synonyms for the learning curve—for example, manufacturing progress function, cost curve, production acceleration curve, improvement curve, and performance curve.

However, some of these terms are not true synonyms, since they have other meanings.

AVERAGE CUMULATIVE UNIT COST

Table 1 demonstrates the expected results of an 80 percent learning curve when the cumulative production quantity is doubled five times. We see in the table that the first unit produced required eight labor hours. Production of the second unit, using an 80 percent learning curve, reduced the average labor hours required to produce each unit to 6.4 hours—that is, 80 percent of the time required for the first unit. This reduction in labor hours per unit reflects an increase in efficiency, and, as Column 4 shows, the reduction of labor hours continued at this rate until the last lot of 16 units was produced—at which point the average number of hours required for each of the 32 units produced was down to 2.62 hours. These average times for various units are referred to as *average cumulative unit costs,* because the actual hours for all units produced are averaged in calculating the unit cost after each doubling of production.

The process of learning is not infinite, but ends with the achievement of a certain efficiency level, generally a certain production volume. In the discussion that follows we refer to each doubling of the units produced as a *lot.* In accounting literature, the term *batch* is also frequently used to identify lots. Table 1, for instance, deals with six lots, or batches.

TABLE 1
Average cumulative unit cost with 80 percent learning curve

(1) Lot number	(2) Units produced to double	(3) Cumulative production quantity	(4) Average cumulative unit hours*	(5) Cumulative total hours 3 × 4
1	1	1	8.00	8.00
2	1	2	6.40	12.80
3	2	4	5.12	20.48
4	4	8	4.10	32.80
5	8	16	3.28	52.48
6	16	32	2.62	83.84

* Amounts have been rounded to the nearest hundredth of an hour.

Experience has shown that learning has several phases. Phase I represents the gradual increase in production rate until the maximum expected rate (units per day, week, month or year) is reached. This phase is generally steep. Phase II represents the period during which the maximum rate is maintained. The learning rate during this period will gradually deteriorate because of the limitations of the equipment. Phase III takes place when the production rate begins to decrease due to a reduction in customer requirements. The learning rate during this period will eventually show costs increasing, a condition known in industry as *reverse learning*.

Average incremental unit cost

In order for the cumulative average cost to decrease with each doubling of the production quantity, the average incremental cost per unit must be lower than the average cumulative unit cost, as in Exhibit 1. This requirement can be proved with the information in Table 1 as follows:

```
2 units produced at 6.4 cumulative average = .......... 12.8 hours
1st unit produced (subtract) .......................... 8.0
2d unit produced (incremental cost) ................... 4.8 hours
Incremental cost improvement
   factor (4.8 hrs/8.0) ............................... 60%
```

Thus, if two units require an average of 6.4 hours per unit and the first unit was produced in 8 hours, the second unit must have been produced in 4.8 hours. This is the only combination that yields an average cumulative labor cost of 6.4 hours for the two units, given an original time of 8 hours.

Relating the incremental cost to the previous average cumulative unit cost gives us another constant, as we shall see, which has several important and special uses. The incremental cost constant (z) can be established by the following formulas:

$$z = 2X - 1.00$$

where X is the learning constant or learning rate, or

$$z = 1.00 - 2X',$$

where X' is the improvement rate.

For instance, the incremental cost constant for a learning curve of 80 percent could be calculated as follows:

$$z = (2 \text{ times } 0.8) - 1.00$$
$$= 0.60$$

or

$$z = 1.00 - (2 \text{ times } 0.2)$$
$$= 0.60$$

The incremental unit cost improvement factor is always found by doubling the learning curve improvement factor. For instance, with a learning curve of 80 percent, the improvement factor is 20 percent; the improvement factor for the incremental cost is therefore 40 percent; and the incremental cost curve is 60 percent. The incremental unit cost shows the actual efficiency achieved.

Table 2 demonstrates the expected average incremental unit cost for each of the six lots of Table 1. The *incremental average unit cost* of each lot is determined by multiplying the average cumulative unit cost of the preceding lot by the incremental cost curve constant (z). Thus, the second unit is produced in 4.8 hours (8.0 hours times 0.6) and the third and fourth units are produced at an average of 3.84 hours each (6.40 times 0.6).

Thus far, for illustrative purposes, we have demonstrated the behavior of the learning curve by including six lots representing the doubling of the quantity with each lot. In the real world, however, the doubling may take place over a long period of time. For example, 50 units may be made the first year, 75 the second, 125 the third, and so on. Such a buildup will indicate when learning should begin to change as the maximum rate is reached, maintained, and then lowered. In succeeding pages you will be shown how to operate in such an atmosphere.

First, however, two important observations should be made. A learning curve of 50 percent, for example, is impossible, since it implies that the second lot will be manufactured for nothing. This can be demonstrated by returning to our formula for (z), the incremental cost factor:

$$z = 100\% - (2 \text{ times improvement factor}), \text{ or}$$
$$z = 100 - (2 \text{ times } 50), \text{ thus}$$
$$z = 0$$

TABLE 2
Average cumulative and incremental unit costs with 80 percent learning curve

(1) Lot number	(2) Incremental units to double	(3) Cumulative production quantity	(4) Average unit cost Cumulative*	(5) Average unit cost Incremental†	(6) Total costs Incremental hours (2)×(5)	(7) Total costs Cumulative hours (3)×(4)
1	1	1	8.00	8.00	8.00	8.00
2	1	2	6.40	4.80	4.80	12.80
3	2	4	5.12	3.84	7.68	20.48
4	4	8	4.10‡	3.07	12.28	32.76
5	8	16	3.28‡	2.46	19.68	52.44
6	16	32	2.62‡	1.97	31.52	83.96

(80% relationships shown between successive cumulative average unit costs; 60% relationships shown between cumulative and incremental average unit costs.)

* From Table 1, Column 4.
† 60 percent of previous lot's average cumulative unit cost.
‡ Rounded.

The second observation is that learning stops when the rate equals 100 percent, and a rate in excess of 100 percent implies that cost is increasing. In general, a learning rate as high as 70 percent is suspect and has probably taken place because of the gradual buildup of the production rate until the maximum rate is reached. It should not be interpreted as indicative of a rate that can be maintained indefinitely, since, as previously mentioned, learning falls off after the maximum rate is reached.

Applications of the learning curve

The learning curve is generally applied to direct labor, since only people have the ability to learn. It also applies to completed parts which may be supplied by a vendor or subcontractor. Experience has shown that labor learning is generally steeper than materials learning (vendor or subcontracted parts), since the vendor's cost includes items which do not respond to learning, such as indirect costs, general and administrative expense, and profit. Some texts imply that certain expense items, such as supervisory costs and other overhead items, are affected by learning due to their relationship to direct labor. Such statements are true, but it would be impossible to calculate the overhead cost of a cost center using the principles of the learning curve, because overhead is a function of all of the activities which take place within the cost center. These activities generally include more than one product. The learning curve, on the other hand, may be applied to such losses as rejects and defective products, since people learn to work not only more quickly and efficiently, but also more carefully and skillfully.

As the use of machinery increases in relation to direct labor the potential for the learning curve is reduced, since the time to manufacture a specific part is limited by the maximum speed and feed of the particular machine. The advent of tape-controlled machines in recent years is an excellent example of this. American technology, however, does not sit still. Using the axiom that "there is always a better way," learning is possible even in the case of tape-controlled machines.

Since learning presupposes inexperience in performing an activity, the principles discussed here are applicable to several circumstances. These include new activities, old activities in which new employees are engaged, or old employees and old activities if these activities have been interrupted and relearning is needed.

Generally, one could say that the learning curve applies to "immature" cost values. It is especially important to organizations or industries that have a high rate of change in either product or process, or an excessive employee turnover rate. Up to now the learning curve has been used primarily in connection with product innovations, particularly in the home appliance industry, residential home construction, shipbuilding, the aerospace industry (where it is used the most due to its excellence as a negotiating tool), the armament industry, electronic equipment, and in various training programs in many industries. It is not applicable, however, to industries where the quantity is small, the cost is low, and repeat orders are never received.

Determination of specific cost values

There are several ways to establish cost values for the learning curve.

1. The most widely used is the basic formula for the learning curve, which can only be used when the cumulative average for a specific quantity is known.

2. The most practical is a variation of the basic formula so that the user can start at any point, lot, or cumulative average and perform calculations to find another point, lot, or cumulative average. The use of these formulas requires the use of logarithms if long-hand calculations are to be performed, since they employ an exponent less than one. For purposes of this chapter, however, mathematical tables have been provided, making the use of logarithms unnecessary. When the more complicated formula is used, which determines any point regardless of the start, a time-sharing computer program has been provided.

3. Another method is the use of log-log paper, which is extremely inaccurate and should be avoided if possible. Log-log plots, however, are a useful supplemental tool for showing management the results previously obtained by mathematical factors or by the time-sharing program.

Formula approach: Step and continuous functions

Formula I, the basic formula:

$$Y = KX^{-n},$$

where

> Y = the average cumulative man-hours, labor dollars, or material cost for X number of units;
> K = the theoretical value, or actual value (if known), of the first unit;
> n = the slope coefficient, exponent, or learning constant;
> X = the number of units produced.

Formula II, the logarithmic version of Formula I:

$$\log Y = \log K - n \text{ times } \log X,$$

where all symbols are the same as above.

Formula III, to locate the *xth* unit cost or hours when the cumulative average is known:

$$Yxth = (n + 1)KX^{-n},$$

where

> $Yxth$ = the cost of the Xth unit;
> $n + 1$ = the conversion factor arrived at by subtracting n from 1. The value of n is always negative, since the cost or number of hours is decreasing.
> All other symbols are the same as in Formula I.

Formula IV, to locate any unit cost, or hours of a specific unit or lot, when the cost or hours of another specific unit or lot is known, rather than the cumulative average:

$$Yd = \frac{K}{d}[L^c - (F - 1)^c]$$

where

> Yd = the cost or hours at unit or lot d;
> L = the cumulative unit number of the last unit of the lot;
> F = the cumulative unit number of the first unit of the lot;
> c = the conversion factor $n + 1$;

$K=$ the theoretical value of the first unit;

$d=$ the number of units in lot.

If d is an individual unit, its value is 1.

Formula V, to locate the theoretical cost of the first unit when the cumulative average is known:

$$K= Y/X^{-n},$$

where all symbols are as previously used.

Formula VI, to locate the theoretical value of the first unit when Formula IV is used:

$$K=(Yd)(d)/[(L^c-(F-1)^c)],$$

where all symbols are as in Formula IV.

Formula VII, to determine the value of the exponent n and the log of the learning percent for any learning curve:

$$n=\log \text{ of the learning percent}/\log 2.$$

Formula VIIA:

$$\log \text{ learning percent} = (n)(\log 2).$$

Formula VIII, to determine the total man-hours or cost when the cumulative average is known:

$$Tx= (X)(K)(X^{-n}),$$

where

$Tx =$ the total man hours required for X units.

Formula IX, to locate any unit cost or hours of a specific unit or lot when the cost or hours of another specific lot is known, rather than the cumulative average:

$$Yd=(K)[(X)(X^{-n}) - (X')(X'^{-n})]/d,$$

where

$X=$ the cumulative last unit of the lot;

$d= X - X'$ (the size of the lot);

$X=$ the last unit of the lot (L in Formula IV);

$X' =$ one less than the first unit of the lot ($F-1$ in Formula IV).

This formula allows the use of the tables from the Appendix. Formula IV can be used only with logarithms or the time-sharing computer program included later in the text.

Formula X, to locate the theoretical cost of the first unit when Formula IX is used:

$$K = (Yd \cdot d)/[(X \cdot X^{-n} - X' \cdot X'^{-n})]$$

For the mathematically inclined, $X \cdot X'$ is the same as L^c. When you multiply variables, you add the exponents. $1 + (-n) = c$.

Formula XI, to measure the slope coefficient, exponent, or learning constant between two points:

$$n = \frac{\log\left(\dfrac{\text{Cost 2}}{\text{Cost 1}}\right)}{\log\left(\dfrac{\text{Qty 2}}{\text{Qty 1}}\right)},$$

where

Qty 1 and Cost 1 are cost and cumulative quantity at one point;

Qty 2 and Cost 2 are cost and cumulative quantity at a second point;

Qty 2 does not have to be double Qty 1.

Note: If Qty 2 were double Qty 1, the learning percent may be derived rather simply by dividing Cost 2 by Cost 1. This is consistent with the learning curve definition.

Formula XII, to determine the slope coefficient, exponent, or learning constant using the method of least squares:

$$n = \frac{N\Sigma(X \cdot Y) - (\Sigma X)(\Sigma Y)}{N \cdot \Sigma(X^2) - (\Sigma X)^2},$$

where

N = number of lots for which cost or hours are available;

Σ = Sum of;

$X \cdot Y$ = Product of the log X and log Y;

X = log of the quantity of each lot (plot point or cumulative quantity);

$Y =$ log of cost at each point;
$X^2 =$ the square of the log of each quantity;
$(X)^2 =$ the square of the sum of the logs of the quantities.

Formula XIII, to locate the theoretical value of the first unit once the value of n has been derived by Formula XII:

$$\log K = \frac{\Sigma Y}{N} - \frac{n \cdot \log \Sigma X}{N}$$

$K =$ antilog of log K, and all previous terms have been explained.

Applying the formulas

The distinguishing factor in all learning curve calculations is the *learning curve constant,* sometimes called the *slope coefficient* or *exponent.* This is represented by (n) in each of the formulas and is the basis for the calculation of (c), the conversion factor, in Formulas IV and VI. Each learning curve percent has its own value for (n). When projections are made using the results of historical regression analysis there are an infinite number of values for (n), since learning curve results can be expressed to as many decimal points as the user desires, such as 81.0134. For purposes of this chapter, however, only whole numbers will be used in projections.

Demonstration problem 1: To derive the learning constant using Formula VII.

Derive constant for an 80 percent curve $\quad$ log 2 $\quad = 0.301030$
$n =$ log of the learning percent/log 2 $\qquad n = -0.096910/0.301030$
$n =$ log 0.8/log 2 $\qquad\qquad\qquad\qquad n = -0.321928$
log 0.8 $= 9.903090 - 10 = -0.096910$

The negative sign is always understood in expressing the value of (n).
The value of (c), the conversion factor $= 1 - 0.321928$ or 0.678072.

Values for (n) and (c) are shown in Table 3. If the reader desires values for (n) and (c) between 51 and 59, he may substitute into Formula VII.

Demonstration problem 2: To derive mathematical factors using Formula I.

Learning curve calculations have been simplified through the derivation of a series of mathematical factors using Formula I or its logarithmic version. The basic formulas have been used assuming the theoretical value of the first unit (K) is 1. Factors for learning percentages from 70–99 are contained in the Appendix. When made with a desk calculator or the new electronic hand calculators, a multitude of calculations may be made in a short time.

The factors contained in the Appendix were derived by using a high speed computer and Formula I. To demonstrate the derivation of the factors we will use the logarithmic version, Formula II.

$$\log Y = \log K - n \text{ times } \log X.$$

By assuming the value of K as 1, we eliminate the need for the log of K since the logarithm of 1 is zero.

To derive the factor for 32 units:

$$\log \text{factor } (32) = -0.321928 \text{ times } \log 32 \text{ and } \log 32 = 1.505150$$
$$= -0.321928 \text{ times } 1.505150$$
$$= -0.484550$$

Since this is a negative logarithm, we convert to positive,

$$= 9.51545 - 10$$
$$\text{antilog} = 0.327680 \text{ (checks with Appendix)}$$

Steps in using the mathematical factors

Situation 1: When the cumulative average value of X units is known, and it is desired to extrapolate beyond this point:

a. Divide cumulative average cost or hours by the factor for X from the Appendix to get the theoretical value of the first unit.
b. Select factor for X plus the additional number of units required. Designate this point as X'.
c. Multiply theoretical value of first unit from (a) by the factor from (c) to get the cumulative average for X' units.

d. Multiply X' times its cumulative average value and subtract X times the original cumulative average.

e. Divide the result by the additional quantity.

Situation 2: Same as 1 except only the value of the Xth unit is known.

a. Divide the Xth unit cost or hours by the appropriate conversion factor from Table 3. The result will be the cumulative average cost or hours for X units.

b. Proceed as in *Situation 1.*

Demonstration problem 3: The XY company, whose data appears in Tables 1 and 2, plans to produce 10 more units after the first 32 units have been produced. There will be no time lag between orders, and it is assumed that the learning will continue on an 80 percent curve. Determine the average cost for the additional 10 units and the new cumulative average cost. The cumulative average value for the first 32 units from the Tables is 2.62 hours.

Factors from the Appendix: 32 units = 0.327680 (See
Problem 2)
42 units = 0.300214.

Solution: Theoretical value of first unit = 2.62/0.327680 = 8.0 (checks with tables):

Cumulative average value for 42 units =

8 times 0.300214 = 2.40
Extended value for 42 units = 42 times 2.40 = 100.80
Extended value for 32 units = 32 times 2.62 =   83.84
Subtract   16.96
Average value of additional ten units =   1.70 hours.

Demonstration problem 4: A contract price based on an average cumulative 2.62 hours per unit was negotiated for 32 units (see Table 1). After four units were produced and delivered the remaining contract was cancelled. Determine the cost for the four delivered units, assuming that the work-in-process inventory for the incomplete units will be recovered through a separate negotiation. Assume an 80 percent curve.

Solution: Factors from Appendix: 4 units = 0.640000
32 units = 0.327680

Theoretical value of first unit = 2.62/0.327680 = 8.0 hours
Cumulative average value for 4 units = 8 times 0.64 = 5.12 (checks with tables).

TABLE 3
Slope *n* and conversion factor $1 + n$

Percent learning	n	1 + n	Percent learning	n	1 + n
60	0.736966	0.263034	80	0.321928	0.678072
61	0.713119	0.286881	81	0.304006	0.695994
62	0.689660	0.310340	82	0.286304	0.713696
63	0.666576	0.333424	83	0.268817	0.731183
64	0.643856	0.356144	84	0.251539	0.748461
65	0.621488	0.378512	85	0.234465	0.765535
66	0.599462	0.400538	86	0.217591	0.782409
67	0.577767	0.422233	87	0.200913	0.799087
68	0.556393	0.443607	88	0.184425	0.815575
69	0.535332	0.464668	89	0.168123	0.831877
70	0.514573	0.485427	90	0.152003	0.847997
71	0.494109	0.505891	91	0.136062	0.863938
72	0.473931	0.526069	92	0.120294	0.879706
73	0.454032	0.545968	93	0.104697	0.895303
74	0.434403	0.565597	94	0.089267	0.910733
75	0.415037	0.584963	95	0.074006	0.925994
76	0.395929	0.604071	96	0.058894	0.941106
77	0.377070	0.622930	97	0.043943	0.956057
78	0.358454	0.641546	98	0.029146	0.970854
79	0.340075	0.659925	99	0.014500	0.985500

Demonstration problem 5: To use the conversion factor, Formula III, to determine the cost of the *Xth* unit when the cumulative average is known.

In Formula III the conversion factor is the term $n + 1$ or c, for which values are shown in Table 3. KX^{-n} is the cumulative average cost of X units, with a theoretical first unit cost of K.

Determine the value of the 32d unit in which the cumulative average is 2.62, based on Table 1. The conversion factor for an 80 percent curve is 0.678072.

Unit $32 = (2.62)(0.678072) = 1.78$ (1.77655).

Due to the science of small numbers, this can be inaccurate due to rounding.

As a proof, let us use the factors from the Appendix to derive the hours for the 32d unit. We will be making use of Formula VIII in performing this exercise.

Since we already know the value of the first unit (8.0), we can derive the cumulative average for 31 units, then determine the value for the 32d unit using the procedure followed in Problem 3. We will round the answer to five decimal places to show the comparison. The factor for 31 units is 0.331046.

8 times 0.331046 = 2.648368 = unit cumulative average for
31 units.
The true value for 32 units = 8 times 0.327680 = 2.62144
32 units at 2.62144 = 83.88608
Subtract
31 units at 2.648368 = 82.09941
_____
1.78667

In general, it is found that the $n + 1$ factor becomes more accurate the farther out on the curve you go. The factor does not apply between units one and ten, when the cumulative average and unit curves are not parallel to each other.

Demonstration problem 6: To determine cost or hours of a specific lot when the cost or hours of another specific lot are known, not including the first unit.

a.   Formulas IX and X are used to solve this problem.
b.   The hours of units 9–16 from Table 2 are 2.46.
c.   Determine the hours for units 33–42. (See Problem 3.)

Step 1—Determine the theoretical cost of the first unit. (Ignore the fact that you already know that this value is 8 hours.)

Formula X: $K = (Yd)(d)/[(X)(X^{-n}) - (X')(X'^{-n})]$
$Yd = 2.46$
$d = 8$
$X = 16$
$X' = 8$

From the Appendix, the factor for $X^{-n} = 0.409600$, $X' = 0.512000$

$K = (2.46)(8)/[(16)(0.409600) - (8)(0.512000)]$
$= 19.68/2.4575$
$= 8.008$ hours.

Step 2—Apply Formula IX:

$K = 8$
$X = 42$
$X' = 32$
$X^{-n} = 0.300214$
$X'^{-n} = 0.327680$
$Yd = (K)[(X)(X^{-n}) - (X')(X'^{-n})]/d$
$= (8)[(42)(0.300214) - (32)(0.327680)]/10$
$= 1.70$ (checks with Problem 3)

Learning curve charts

Another relatively economical method of determining *average cumulative costs* for a given quantity, and/or *specific incremental unit costs* for a given unit, is the use of charts. In Exhibit 1 we saw the information from Tables 1 and 2 plotted on graph paper using an arithmetic scale. Exhibit 2 shows the same information plotted on log-log graph paper, which uses a geometric scale. The arithmetic scale produces a hyperbolic curve with a very steep slope that turns into a gradual decline, and then finally turns into what might appear to be a straight line if it were extended far enough.

The information from Tables 1 and 2 plotted on log-log graph paper results in a straight descending line for the cumulative average unit cost—because a constant improvement factor produces a geometric progression, rather than an arithmetic progression. The incremental unit cost line, although it appears to parallel the cumulative cost line, is actually asymptotic to it.

Depending on how carefully they are prepared and on their size, these charts can be used to approximate intermittent unit cost values. For instance, for eight units the cumulative average unit cost is about 4.1 hours and the incremental unit cost is

EXHIBIT 2

Cumulative and incremental unit cost with 80 percent learning curve on log-log graph paper

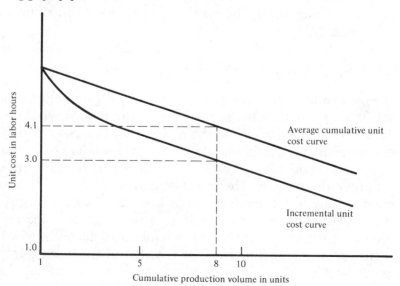

about 3 hours in Exhibits 1 and 2. The straight line of the log-log paper makes it easier to observe deviations of actual costs from those projected. It is also easier to recognize and interpret trends in actual cost figures. With the arithmetic scale curves, it is difficult to see the consistency of any improvement or regression. Also with the log-log technique, the learning curve for any number of units can be drawn from only two values. For example:

1. The cumulative average for X units, from which the cumulative value for $2X$ units may be derived by multiplying by the learning percent. The corresponding points on the unit or incremental curve may be drawn using the conversion factor.

2. If a point X on the incremental curve is known, the point at $2X$ may be determined by multiplying by the learning percent. The cumulative average line may be drawn by dividing by the conversion factor. The values selected, however, should be as far apart as possible, and the paper used should have as large a scale as possible.

Both factors will contribute to accuracy; the former permits the charting of a more nearly accurate slope, and the latter allows the information to be read easily. The fact that the charts can be read in either direction further enhances their use. A warning!! In using large numbers, such as hundreds of thousands, the width of the pencil contributes to inaccuracy.

ASSUMPTIONS

The learning curve is not applicable to all production situations. It is assumed to be useful for new operations where machines are not a major part of the production process. For example, tape-controlled machines do not lend themselves to learning unless a cost reduction program is initiated which will continue to improve the process. The improvement curve applies to purchased materials, although much of the cost progress is due to the use of an aggressive negotiator rather than true learning.

The next assumption is that the production will continue without any major interruptions. If for any reason the work is interrupted, as it would be during a strike, a shortage of supplies, or a power failure, the curve could possibly be deflected or assume a new slope. Unlearning takes place and relearning is necessary.

A further assumption is the continuity of the learning at a constant rate, even within the individual lots produced. It is not the same thing to assume that a constant improvement factor can be achieved with each doubling as it is to assume that this improvement is continuous and constant for each unit produced. They are entirely different assumptions. Experience in the jet engine business, for example, has shown that steep learning is achieved during the time period when production starts and continues until the maximum production rate is reached. At this point learning begins to level off, but does not become reversed (over 100 percent). Once the production rate begins to decline, however, learning changes rapidly and can show over 100 percent.

It is also assumed that the size of some specific production lot is known, from which to project costs and measure performance. It is not necessary to know the cost of the first unit or the first lot.

The last assumption is that the learning constant is a known quantity. Studies have shown that no industry, individual company, nor even specific products or processes can claim any one, unique learning constant. For years, however, literature on the learning curve has pointed out the characteristic 80 percent learning curve of the airframe industry. When actual data is observed, however, each aircraft model appears to assume its own learning rate, generally something other that the classic 80 percent.

Beware of industries reporting steep slopes. The amount of preplanning performed before putting the product into production will determine the steepness of the slope. The industry which shows the poorest slope may have the lowest cost because of the work done in the development shop before releasing the product for production.

FACTORS INFLUENCING THE LEARNING CURVE

The costs determined by the learning curve should always be subject to question, particularly if the control or decision involved is sensitive to the magnitude of the costs. The actual cost attained should also be questioned at any given time. Many factors other than learning may influence either of these costs. Any value, actual or estimated, is the result of the action and interaction of a complex conglomerate of factors. When the effects of each factor cannot be separated, they cannot be measured precisely. Let us look at some of these factors.

Sometimes the full benefits of the learning curve are not exploited because of management's unawareness of the facts. If, for instance, management believes erroneously that improvement stops with the fourth lot, the incentive to seek improvement beyond this point is virtually nonexistent.

Sometimes, for obvious reasons, cost estimators and pricing officers of corporations set up a very high initial labor cost and then proceed to prove a high learning curve. One must guard against such a practice, since it renders the curve and the information derived from it useless and has express negative effects on employees and the company. People tend to adjust to predictions that are easily achievable, and they resent capricious and impossible improvement forecasts.

The method of production—whether it emphasizes labor or machinery—will influence the slope of the learning curve, as will the complexity of the task involved. Also, the quality of employees is a factor to be considered. In times of an oversupply of workers, one can draw from a wealth of highly skilled laborers; in times of short labor supply, only less skilled employees may be available.

The learning curve is also applicable to group activities. Different crews may show different learning curve slopes. A crew with more experience will have a flatter learning curve and will start with a lower per-unit cost for the first lot. The employee turnover rate will influence the slope of the learning curve and the actual costs incurred. A company may never reach its maximum efficiency potential if it is always retraining new employees. Job assignments become an important factor. The fewer the interruptions, the greater the expected improvement in efficiency.

Other factors influencing the slope of the learning curve are changes in a product, the methods of production, designs, machinery, or the tools used. All have the effect of interrupting learning—either slowing it down or requiring entirely new learning because of new conditions. The frequency of such changes and their degree will have noticeable and measureable consequences on the slope and actual results of the learning curve. Frequent changes may result in no learning at all. Some product changes are brought about because products are put into production before their development is completed. Such circumstances make it impossible to schedule work, machinery, and men in a coordinated fashion for those parts still in development, since they are an unknown quantity. Modifications in designs or products, to be expected under those conditions, necessitate costly interruptions.

The amount of experience a particular company has in its field will also influence the learning curve. Experience generally results in the proper coordination of tools and machinery with the work to be performed and in the clarity of such factors as drawings of plans. The more experience a company has, the more helpful it can be to its employees. Management should insist on a careful job analysis and an analysis of the work involved before starting any new job. The experience necessary for efficient job analysis need not include the whole organization; it may be localized within one plant or department.

Also among factors influencing the learning curve are labor strikes, since they interrupt the learning process and result in unlearning. Another factor is the possible reclassification of certain expenses. The exclusion of direct labor costs, after reclassifying portions of them as indirect, will influence the results of the learning curve.

Wherever possible, the effects of these factors that affect the learning curve must be carefully separated from the data used to establish the curve. The effects of these factors must also be separated from the actual costs used to measure the real achievement. If these separations are not made, neither the projected costs nor the actual costs can be analyzed meaningfully.

USES OF THE LEARNING CURVE

The use of the learning curve in modern business has gone far beyond its first published use by T. P. Wright[1] in 1936. It

---

[1] T. P. Wright, "Factors Affecting the Cost of Airplanes," *Journal of Aeronautical Science*, February 1936, pp. 122–28.

now ranks equally in importance with all of our cost control and cost projection techniques.

The most frequently demonstrated use of the learning curve is in conjunction with establishing bid prices for contracts. Usually, the cumulative average unit cost for all the units to be produced for a given contract is used as the base for the price. If production is not interrupted, additional units beyond this quantity should be costed at the incremental costs incurred, and not at some continued cumulative average.

> *Demonstration problem 7:* The firm whose data are summarized in Tables 1 and 2 was asked to prepare a price for 16 units. It received this order and was asked to produce another 16 before the first 16 were finished, if it could reduce the price. Determine the cost to be considered for the order of the first 16 and the second 16.
>
> *Solution*
> First order—3.28 hours (cumulative average unit cost)
> Second order—1.97 hours (incremental average unit cost)

Many contracts include cancellation agreements, which permit stoppage of production. If cumulative average unit costs are used for the bid price and if production is stopped before the expected efficiency is reached, it would mean that the company involved had sold its previous production units at too low a price. The contractor must provide for these contingencies and make sure that he will be reimbursed for such losses. The loss can be measured by the difference between the cumulative average unit cost at the actual production level and the cumulative average unit cost at the contracted production level, times the number of units produced.

In planning the working capital requirements, the learning curve, where applicable, is indispensable. If a unit price is based on average cumulative unit costs, the revenues from the first few units may not cover the actual expenditures. For instance, if the price was based on the average cumulative unit cost of 2.62 hours (see Table 1) the first unit when produced and sold will cause a deficit of 5.38 hours (8.00 − 2.62). Provision must be made to cover these expenses, either through special pay arrangements with the contracting company or by loan arrangements with a bank.

Inventories of materials, work-in-process, and finished goods require careful planning. As employees become more efficient, production pace increases and more materials are needed. The work-in-process inventory turns over faster, and finished goods inventory grows at an accelerated place.

Using the learning curve is essential to the proper scheduling of work. It will show the manpower needed for certain production plans, and it will permit timely procurement of this manpower. The quantities produced and timing of deliveries are also influenced by the learning curve. For instance, in the example given in Tables 1 and 2, only one unit can be produced and delivered per 8-hour day (8 hours per unit) initially, but at maximum efficiency four units can be produced per 8-hour day (1.97 hours per unit).

Late deliveries by suppliers may cause production interruption and unlearning. Penalty clauses specifying amounts based on the higher costs due to such interruptions are not unusual.

To exercise control, learning curve techniques are indispensable. Variable norms can be established for each situation, and a comparison between these norms and actual expenses can be made. Specific or average incremental unit costs are used for this purpose. Used with training programs, the learning curve can measure the effectiveness of the program. The program should determine and eliminate those employees who lack the aptitude to meet the normal learning curve. We can also measure the progress which trainees make.

Other special decisions for which the learning curve may be used include make-or-buy decisions, especially if the outside manufacturer has reached the maximum on the learning curve. Decisions to speed up production would require adding new, inexperienced crews, and thus could involve higher than normal costs. At present, learning curve techniques are used most extensively in connection with defense contracts.

Very important to the public accountant is the valuation of the finished goods and work-in-process inventory. The CPA must determine whether or not the current work-in-process inventory can be completed at a cost below the stipulated selling price. In the early stages of learning this is not possible. The Securities and Exchange Commission wants disclosure of deferred manufacturing costs carried forward on a "learning curve" basis.[2] The

---

[2] See *Release No. 33–5492*, dated May 6, 1974.

Financial Accounting Standards Board is now considering this topic.

THE LEARNING CURVE AND
FINANCIAL REPORTING

The phenomenon of the learning curve can cause the results of operations to be grossly misstated if the following two conditions exist:

1. The contract(s) extends over several reporting periods;
2. The unit price is based on the cumulative average unit cost.

When these conditions exist, one can expect losses or extremely low income to be reported in the early periods of the contracts; these would be counterbalanced in later periods by extremely high profits.

Demonstration problem 8: The organization represented by the data in Table 1 contracted to sell 32 units for $15 per unit. Labor cost is $5 per hour and no other expenses are expected. Determine the profit per unit for the first and for the 20th unit, assuming that all 32 units will be sold.

Note: The factor for the 20th unit (using the Appendix) = (20) (0.3812080) − (19) (0.387555) = 0.261

Solution

	32 units sold	1st unit	20th unit
Revenue per unit	$15.00	$15.00	$15.00
Cost per unit			
Cumulative average 2.62 hrs · $5	13.10		
Incremental 8 hrs · $5		40.00	
Incremental 8 hrs · 0.261 · $5			10.44
Profit	$ 1.90		
Loss		($25.00)	
Profit			$ 4.56

Such reporting differences are surely undesirable. Among other things, they lead to erratic shifts in stock prices, loss of the confidence of investors, and accusations of excess profit. To correct the situation, part of the initial learning costs can be deferred as start-up costs, and thus charged to later periods that show lower labor costs. Thus, of the $40 cost of the first unit, $26.40 (the difference between the actual cost of $40 and the average cumulative unit cost of $13.10) should be deferred for later periods and units. The entry would be:

Deferred Production Expenses 26.40
    Work-in-Process Labor 26.40

For the 20th unit the finished goods inventory should be charged with an additional $2.66, the difference between the actual incremental cost of $10.44 and the average cumulative unit cost of $13.10.

Finished Goods 2.66
    Deferred Production Expenses 2.66

The procedure outlined would average the labor costs over the period of learning and reflect more realistically the accomplishments of this company. Exhibit 3 demonstrates graphically how such a deferring and averaging process can be accomplished.

EXHIBIT 3
Cost flows when cost difference due to learning is deferred

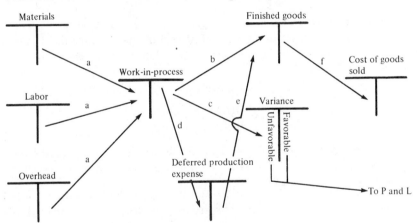

Note:
a. Actual costs.
b. Cumulative average unit cost for total anticipated production volume times the units finished during a given period.
c. Periodic actual costs less anticipated incremental costs of current production volume.
d. Excess of anticipated incremental unit cost of a given period over cumulative average unit cost (for total anticipated production volume).
e. Excess of cumulative average unit cost (for total anticipated production volume) over incremental unit cost of a given period.
f. Cumulative average unit cost (for total anticipated production volume) times the units sold during a given period.
g. Variance to P & L.

Source: Wayne J. Morse, "Reporting Production Costs that Follow the Learning Curve Phenomenon," *The Accounting Review,* October 1972, p. 765.

Using the time sharing program

The time sharing program has been written in the BASIC language, which is the acronym for BEGINNER'S ALL-PURPOSE SYMBOLIC INSTRUCTION CODE, the product of President Kemeny of Dartmouth College. Formulas I, IV, V and VI form the basis for the program and will be found on lines 705, 675, 315 and 345, respectively.

> *Demonstration problem 9:* The XYZ Corporation received a contract for 640 units of a jet engine used in a particular Navy fighter application. Due to Congressional pressure to reduce defense spending, the Navy has issued an amendment to the contract cutting the number to 160 units. 20 units have been manufactured. The cost of the 20th unit is $80,000 according to the contractor's cost system (job order). There was no previous production of this engine. The first 20 units were all manufactured in 1977. It will be necessary to renegotiate the contract. The learning curve is assumed to be 90 percent.
>
> *Required:*
> 1. Determine the theoretical cost of the first unit.
> 2. Determine the average unit cost of the remaining 140 units to be manufactured in accordance with the following schedule:
>
> > 1978—30 units
> > 1979—50 units
> > 1980—60 units
>
> Escalation factors will be applied separately by years through negotiation using applicable Department of Commerce Indices.

Note: All learning curve calculations are performed in constant dollars and escalated separately using various Government indices. Normally, material and labor would be calculated separately using experience applied to these cost elements. Expense would be applied in accordance with the contractor's projections taking into consideration shop load, and so forth, rather than with the use of the learning curve. Sophisticated programs are available which will apply the escalation, compute the expense, and bring the cost to selling price.

Input to the time sharing program

25 PRINT "SAMPLE PROGRAM INVOLVING THE XYZ
   CORPORATION"

30 DATA 3 (Three sets of data are to be inserted)
50 DATA 21,50,51,100,101,160 (The first and last units numbers
of the three sets)

Type RUN
When the computer asks, "F,L,S,Y=?" TYPE 20,20,90,80000
This means the base DATA is the 20th unit on a 90 percent
curve with a value of $80,000.

Computer output

SAMPLE PROBLEM INVOLVING THE XYZ CORPORATION
F,L,S,Y=? 20,20,90,80000
COST PROJECTIONS USING THE LOG-LINEAR CUMULA-
TIVE AVERAGE CURVE THEORY.
THE VALUE OF THE FIRST UNIT=148175.5
IMPROVEMENT CURVE ASSUMPTION 90 PERCENT
COST (HOURS) ASSUMPTION: UNITS 20 THROUGH 20
AVERAGE 80000

First unit	Last unit	Block	Average cost
21.0 .... 50.0		30.0	73612.013
51.0 .... 100.0		50.0	65406.003
101.0 .... 160.0		60.0	60052.569

TIME SHARING PROGRAM

115 REM READING IN THE NUMBER OF LOTS FOR
WHICH COST IS DESIRED
125 READ N1
135 IF N1=9E9 THEN 895
145 REM INSERTING BASIC ASSUMPTIONS AS TO COST
AND SLOPE OF A
155 REM SPECIFIC LOT, INDIVIDUAL UNIT OR CUMU-
LATIVE QUANTITY
165 PRINT "F,L,S,Y=";
175 INPUT F,L,S,Y
185 REM IDIOT PROOFING TO ASSURE THAT A SLOPE
OF 50 PERCENT OR LESS
195 REM HAS NOT BEEN USED
205 IF S < =50 THEN 845

225 LET N=L−F+1
235 IF N < 1 THEN 825
245 LET B=−(LOG(100)−LOG(S))/LOG(2) (Formula VII, B
used in place of *n*)
265 LET C=1 + B   (See Formula III)
305 IF F=1 THEN 345
315 LET A=(Y*N)/(L**C−(F−1)**C)   (Formula VI)
335 GO TO 435
345 LET A=Y/L**B   (Formula V)
435 PRINT
445 :####.#   #####.#   #####.#
#########.###
465 PRINT "COST PROJECTIONS USING THE LOG-LIN-
EAR CUMULATIVE AVERAGE";
475 PRINT "CURVE THEORY"
505 PRINT
515 PRINT "VALUE OF FIRST UNIT=";A
535 PRINT
545 PRINT "IMPROVEMENT CURVE ASSUMPTION";S;
"PERCENT"
550 PRINT
555 PRINT "COST(HOURS) ASSUMPTION: UNITS";F
"THROUGH";L;"AVERAGE";Y
575 PRINT
585 PRINT "FIRST", "LAST", " ", "AVERAGE"
595 PRINT "UNIT",UNIT",BLOCK",COST"
605 PRINT
615 FOR I= 1 TO N1
625 READ V,W
635 let X=W−V+1
645 IF X< 1 THEN 825
665 If V< =1 THEN 705
675 LET R=(A/X)*(W**C−(V−1)**C)   (Formula IV)
695 GO TO 795
705 LET R=A*(W**B)   (Formula I)
795 PRINT USING 445, V,W,X,R
805 NEXT I
815 STOP
825 PRINT "DATA DOES NOT CONFORM TO PRE-
SCRIBED FORMAT. PLEASE CHECK"
835 STOP

845 PRINT "SLOPE EQUAL TO OR LESS THAN 50 PER-
CENT. BEGIN AGAIN."

855 STOP

865 DATA 9E9

895 PRINT "THIS PROGRAM CALCULATES COSTS FROM
AN ASSUMED SLOPE WITH"

905 PRINT "A BASE QUANTITY (LOT, CUMULATIVE
AVERAGE OR INDIVIDUAL"

910 PRINT " UNIT) AND AN ASSUMED COST OR HOURS
USING THE LOG-LINEAR"

915 PRINT " CUMULATIVE AVERAGE CURVE THEORY"

950 PRINT "LINES 1–100 MAY BE USED FOR 'PRINT'
STATEMENTS DESCRIBING"

970 PRINT "THE EXERCISE AND TO INSERT DATA AS
FOLLOWS;"

975 PRINT "1. NUMBER OF LOTS FOR WHICH COST (OR
HOURS) IS REQUIRED"

980 PRINT" 2. FIRST AND LAST CUMULATIVE NUMBER
OF EACH LOT EQUAL"

985 PRINT"   TO THE NUMBER OF LOTS SHOWN IN 1.
IF AN INDIVIDUAL UNIT"

990 PRINT"   IS REQUIRED THE FIRST AND LAST UNIT
NUMBERS WILL BE"

995 PRINT"   IDENTICAL"

1000 PRINT "TYPE 'RUN' "

1050 PRINT   "COMPUTER   WILL   ASK   QUESTION,
'F,L,S,Y=?"

1060 PRINT "INSERT THE FIRST (F) AND LAST (L) CUMU-
LATIVE NUMBERS OF"

1070 PRINT " AN ASSUMED BASE."

1080 PRINT "IF BASE IS AN INDIVIDUAL UNIT, F AND L
ARE IDENTICAL. S AND"

1090 PRINT "Y ARE SLOPE (PCT) AND COST (OR HOURS)
RESPECTIVELY."

1100 PRINT "DEPRESS 'RETURN' KEY AND PROGRAM
WILL RUN TO COMPLETION"

1110 END

Key to Arithmetic Operations
  *= multiplication
  ** = raising to a power
  / = division

Historical linear regression

Until now we have been concerned with calculating cost from an assumed base point with an assumed learning rate. Assuming the learning rate without an attempt at justification can be dangerous. This section will be devoted to measuring historical performance in order to lend credence to future projections.

The following methods will be used:

1. The scattergram approach
2. The method of least squares (Formulas XII and XIII)
3. Measurements between two points (Formula XI)

The scattergram approach. The scatterback or "eyeball" method consists of plotting historical data on log-log paper. A line is drawn attempting to equalize the distances of the points above the line with the distances of the points below the line, which is called the *line of regression*. At times this can be very difficult if the points are widely scattered.

Once the line of regression has been established, the procedure is as follows:

1. Place a triangle in such a way that the hypotenuse (longest side) rests squarely along the line of regression.
2. Rest the left side of the triangle on a ruler or straight edge.
3. Keeping the straight edge in position (very important), slide the triangle until the hypotenuse passes through the top of the graph as the beginning of a cycle.
4. In accordance with the learning curve definition, the point where the triangle intersects the vertical (2) line (the doubling point) represents the learning percent. Thus, if the triangle passes through the vertical scale at (9), it will indicate a 90 percent curve.

We must first recompute the data to establish the correct plotting points for each of the lots shown in Table 4. (See Table

TABLE 4
The test case

		Cumulative	
Lot	*Cost*	*Quantity*	*Cost*
First 25	$125		
Next 35	115	60	$119.17
Next 50	107	110	114.64
Next 10	98	120	112.34

TABLE 5
The test case replotted

Lot	Plot	Cost
First 25	8.333	$125
Next 35	42.500	115
Next 50	85.000	107
Next 10	115.000	98

5.) As a rule of thumb the first lot, which includes the first unit, is plotted at the one-third point, while succeeding lots are plotted at the mid point. These data will also be used for the method of least squares.

Exhibit 4 is the scattergram showing that the triangle passes through the vertical (2) line at approximately the 95 percent point.

The method of least squares. Under the method of least squares, we are performing a calculation similar to the scatter-

EXHIBIT 4
The scattergram

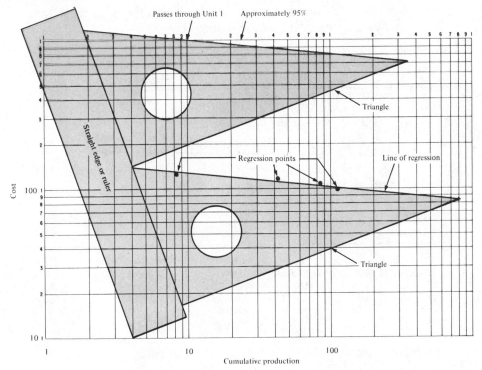

gram method with the exception that our measurement is more scientific than the "eyeball" method. Under the scattergram method we tried to draw a line such that the line appeared to be equidistant from the points. Under the least squares method, we are drawing an imaginary line between the points. The solution to the problem is the line with the lowest total, arrived at by squaring the distances of the points from the line of regression and finding the sum of these squares. The logarithmic version of the formula is used (Formula II).

$$\log Y_x = \log K - n \text{ times } \log X$$

Although the description of the least squares method implies that we must measure the distance from each point to the line of regression, the method calls for setting up the following columns in order to use Formulas XII and XIII:

Production	Cost				
X	Y_x	$\log X$	$\log Y_x$	$(\log X)(\log Y_x)$	$(\log X)^2$

Once the logarithmic columns have been completed and summed, the values will be inserted into Formula XII, in which $N =$ the number of points. (See Table 6.)

Formula XII:

$$n = \frac{(4)(13.32043) - (6.54652)(8.17822)}{(4)(11.48199) - 42.85692} = \frac{-.25716}{3.07104} = -0.08374$$

Formula VIIA:

Log learning percent $= (-0.08373)(0.30103) = 0.02521$
$$= 9.97479 - 10$$

Learning percent $= 94.4$ percent

TABLE 6
Least squares calculations

X	Y_x	$\log X$	$\log Y_x$	$(\log X)(\log Y_x)$	$(\log X)^2$
8.333	$125	0.98201	2.09691	1.94595	0.86120
42.500	115	1.62839	2.06070	3.35562	2.65165
85.00	107	1.92942	2.02938	3.91553	3.72266
115.00	98	2.06070	1.99123	4.10333	4.24648
		6.54652	8.17822	13.32043	11.48199

$(\Sigma X)^2 = 42.85692$ $\log 2 = 0.30103$

Formula XIII:

$$\log K = \frac{8.17822}{4} - \frac{(-0.08374)(6.54652)}{4} = 2.04456 + 0.13705$$

$$= 2.18161$$

$$K = 151.91$$

We now have a workable equation from which we may make projections:

$$\log Y_x = 2.18161 - (0.08374)(\log X)$$

Demonstration problem 10: To apply the formula:
Find the cost at unit 1,000 $\log 1{,}000 = 3.00000$
$\log Y_{1,000} = 2.18161 - (0.08374)(3) = 1.93039$
Unit $1{,}000 = \$85.19$

Measurement between two points. Occasionally the need arises to determine the learning between two known points, such as between the 750th and the 1020th units. It should be noted that these points should not be at the doubling point in order to use Formula XI. If the point is the doubling point, dividing the lower cost by the higher will determine the learning.

Demonstration problem 11: To measure the learning between two points:

$$\text{Formula XI } n = \frac{\log\left(\dfrac{\text{Cost 2}}{\text{Cost 1}}\right)}{\log\left(\dfrac{\text{Qty 2}}{\text{Qty 1}}\right)}$$

Given:
    750th unit $= \$47.50$
    1020th unit $=$ 44.75

$$\frac{44.75}{47.50} = 0.94210 \quad \log = 9.97410 - 10 = -0.02590$$

$$\frac{1020}{750} = 1.36 \quad \log = 0.13354$$

$$n = \frac{-0.02590}{0.13354} = -0.19395$$

With Formula VIIA:

log learning percent = −0.19395 times 0.30103 = −0.05838
Since this is a negative logarithm, we convert to positive = 9.94162−10
antilog = 87.4 percent.

Summary and conclusions

The learning curve is widely applicable. It is the indispensable tool for establishing prices, controlling costs, planning work loads, setting delivery schedules, and anticipating cash flows, working capital, and manpower needs. In the valuation of inventories, the learning curve must be considered. Penalty clauses, either for late delivery by a subcontractor or for early cancellation by the contractee, are based on unit cost differences determined by the use of the learning curve.

A multitude of cost values is needed for pricing, planning, controlling, motivating, and evaluating when the learning curve conditions prevail. Some are the cumulative average unit costs for a given production volume; some are specific incremental unit costs; others are average incremental unit costs. The multitude of available unit costs and the complexity of the subject are seldom fully understood.

APPENDIX

CUMULATIVE AVERAGE FACTORS BASED ON THE LOG-LINEAR CUMULATIVE AVERAGE CURVE THEORY

	70	71	72	73	74	75	76	77	78	79
1.	1.000000	1.000000	1.000000	1.000000	1.000000	1.000000	1.000000	1.000000	1.000000	1.000000
2.	0.700000	0.710000	0.720000	0.730000	0.740000	0.750000	0.760000	0.770000	0.780000	0.790000
3.	0.568180	0.581099	0.594124	0.607256	0.620493	0.633836	0.647283	0.660834	0.674488	0.688245
4.	0.490000	0.504100	0.518400	0.532900	0.547600	0.562500	0.577600	0.592900	0.608400	0.624100
5.	0.436845	0.451474	0.466356	0.481555	0.497010	0.512745	0.528759	0.545054	0.561631	0.578492
6.	0.397725	0.412580	0.427770	0.443297	0.459165	0.475377	0.491935	0.508842	0.526100	0.543713
7.	0.367397	0.382322	0.397632	0.413332	0.429425	0.445916	0.462809	0.480108	0.497819	0.515944
8.	0.343000	0.357911	0.373248	0.389017	0.405224	0.421875	0.438976	0.456533	0.474552	0.493039
9.	0.322822	0.337676	0.352984	0.368760	0.385012	0.401748	0.418975	0.436701	0.454934	0.473681
10.	0.305792	0.320546	0.335791	0.351535	0.367788	0.384559	0.401857	0.419692	0.438073	0.457009
11.	0.291157	0.305801	0.320960	0.336647	0.352871	0.369643	0.386975	0.404876	0.423359	0.442433
12.	0.278408	0.292932	0.307994	0.323607	0.339282	0.356533	0.373870	0.391808	0.410358	0.429533
13.	0.267174	0.281573	0.296529	0.312057	0.328171	0.344883	0.362208	0.380159	0.398752	0.417996
14.	0.257178	0.271449	0.286295	0.301732	0.317774	0.334437	0.351735	0.369683	0.388299	0.407596
15.	0.248208	0.262351	0.277085	0.292427	0.308392	0.324996	0.342257	0.360190	0.378813	0.398144
16.	0.240100	0.254117	0.268239	0.283982	0.299866	0.316406	0.333622	0.351530	0.370151	0.389501
17.	0.232725	0.246618	0.261127	0.276272	0.292072	0.308544	0.325709	0.343586	0.362194	0.381553
18.	0.225983	0.239750	0.254118	0.269195	0.284909	0.301311	0.318421	0.336260	0.354848	0.374208
19.	0.219780	0.234430	0.247719	0.262667	0.278295	0.294625	0.311677	0.329474	0.348037	0.367390
20.	0.214055	0.227588	0.241769	0.256620	0.272163	0.288419	0.305411	0.323163	0.341697	0.361037
21.	0.208768	0.222167	0.236235	0.250998	0.266455	0.282637	0.299568	0.317272	0.335773	0.355096
22.	0.203810	0.217118	0.231092	0.245752	0.261125	0.277233	0.294101	0.311755	0.330220	0.349522
23.	0.199201	0.212402	0.226274	0.240842	0.256131	0.272165	0.288970	0.306573	0.325000	0.344278
24.	0.194881	0.207982	0.221756	0.236233	0.251439	0.267399	0.284142	0.301692	0.320079	0.339331
25.	0.190835	0.203829	0.217507	0.231895	0.247019	0.262907	0.279586	0.297084	0.315430	0.334653
26.	0.187022	0.199917	0.213501	0.227802	0.242846	0.258662	0.275278	0.292723	0.311026	0.330219
27.	0.183425	0.196223	0.209716	0.223932	0.238897	0.254642	0.271195	0.288587	0.306847	0.326008
28.	0.180024	0.192729	0.206133	0.220264	0.235153	0.250828	0.267318	0.284656	0.302873	0.322001
29.	0.176803	0.189416	0.202733	0.216783	0.231596	0.247201	0.263630	0.280914	0.299087	0.318181
30.	0.173745	0.186269	0.199502	0.213472	0.228210	0.243747	0.260115	0.277346	0.295475	0.314534
31.	0.170833	0.183276	0.196425	0.210317	0.224982	0.240452	0.256760	0.273938	0.292025	0.311046
32.	0.168070	0.180423	0.193492	0.207307	0.221901	0.237305	0.253553	0.270678	0.288717	0.307706
33.	0.165433	0.177700	0.190690	0.204431	0.218954	0.234293	0.250482	0.267556	0.285550	0.304502
34.	0.162901	0.175098	0.188011	0.201679	0.216133	0.231408	0.247539	0.264561	0.282511	0.301427
35.	0.160493	0.172608	0.185446	0.199042	0.213429	0.228641	0.244714	0.261685	0.279591	0.298470
36.	0.158185	0.170222	0.182987	0.196512	0.210833	0.225983	0.242000	0.258920	0.276782	0.295624
37.	0.155972	0.167933	0.180626	0.194085	0.208338	0.223428	0.239389	0.256259	0.274077	0.292882
38.	0.153846	0.165735	0.178357	0.191747	0.205939	0.220969	0.236895	0.253695	0.271469	0.290238
39.	0.151803	0.163622	0.176175	0.189499	0.203628	0.218599	0.234451	0.251222	0.268953	0.287686
40.	0.149835	0.161587	0.174074	0.187333	0.201401	0.216314	0.232112	0.248835	0.266523	0.285219

APPENDIX (continued)

CUMULATIVE AVERAGE FACTORS BASED ON THE LOG-LINEAR CUMULATIVE AVERAGE CURVE THEORY

	70	71	72	73	74	75	76	77	78	79
41.	0.147947	0.152628	0.172049	0.185244	0.199252	0.214109	0.229854	0.246529	0.264175	0.282834
42.	0.146123	0.157739	0.170095	0.183229	0.197177	0.211978	0.227672	0.244299	0.261903	0.280526
43.	0.144365	0.155915	0.168209	0.181282	0.195172	0.209918	0.225560	0.242141	0.259703	0.278290
44.	0.142667	0.154154	0.166386	0.179399	0.193232	0.207924	0.223517	0.240051	0.257572	0.276123
45.	0.141027	0.152452	0.164623	0.177578	0.191355	0.205994	0.221537	0.238026	0.255505	0.274020
46.	0.139441	0.150805	0.162917	0.175815	0.189537	0.204124	0.219617	0.236061	0.253500	0.271980
47.	0.137906	0.149211	0.161265	0.174106	0.187774	0.202310	0.217755	0.234155	0.251553	0.269998
48.	0.136420	0.147667	0.159664	0.172450	0.186065	0.200550	0.215948	0.232303	0.249662	0.268072
49.	0.134980	0.146170	0.158111	0.170843	0.184406	0.198841	0.214192	0.230504	0.247824	0.266199
50.	0.133584	0.144718	0.156605	0.169283	0.182794	0.197180	0.212485	0.228755	0.246035	0.264376
51.	0.132230	0.143309	0.155142	0.167768	0.181229	0.195566	0.210826	0.227053	0.244295	0.262602
52.	0.130915	0.141941	0.153721	0.166295	0.179706	0.193997	0.209211	0.225397	0.242601	0.260873
53.	0.129638	0.140611	0.152339	0.164863	0.178225	0.192469	0.207639	0.223783	0.240950	0.259189
54.	0.128398	0.139318	0.150996	0.163470	0.176784	0.190982	0.206108	0.222212	0.239341	0.257546
55.	0.127191	0.138061	0.149688	0.162114	0.175381	0.189533	0.204616	0.220680	0.237772	0.255944
56.	0.126017	0.136837	0.148415	0.160793	0.174013	0.188121	0.203162	0.219185	0.236241	0.254381
57.	0.124875	0.135646	0.147176	0.159506	0.172680	0.186744	0.201743	0.217727	0.234747	0.252854
58.	0.123762	0.134485	0.145968	0.158252	0.171381	0.185401	0.200359	0.216304	0.233288	0.251363
59.	0.122678	0.133354	0.144790	0.157008	0.170113	0.184090	0.199007	0.214914	0.231863	0.249906
60.	0.121622	0.132251	0.143641	0.155834	0.168875	0.182810	0.197687	0.213557	0.230470	0.248482
61.	0.120592	0.131175	0.142520	0.154669	0.167667	0.181560	0.196398	0.212230	0.229109	0.247089
62.	0.119587	0.130126	0.141426	0.153531	0.166487	0.180339	0.195137	0.210932	0.227777	0.245726
63.	0.118605	0.129101	0.140358	0.152420	0.165334	0.179146	0.193905	0.209664	0.226477	0.244393
64.	0.117642	0.128100	0.139314	0.151334	0.164206	0.177979	0.192700	0.208422	0.225200	0.243087
65.	0.116714	0.127123	0.138294	0.150273	0.163104	0.176837	0.191521	0.207207	0.223952	0.241809
66.	0.115801	0.126167	0.137297	0.149235	0.162026	0.175720	0.190366	0.206018	0.222729	0.240557
67.	0.114908	0.125233	0.136322	0.148219	0.160971	0.174627	0.189236	0.204853	0.221532	0.239330
68.	0.114036	0.124320	0.135368	0.147225	0.159938	0.173556	0.188130	0.203712	0.220359	0.238127
69.	0.113182	0.123426	0.134435	0.146253	0.158927	0.172508	0.187045	0.202594	0.219208	0.236948
70.	0.112347	0.122552	0.133521	0.145301	0.157937	0.171481	0.185983	0.201497	0.218081	0.235791
71.	0.111530	0.121696	0.132627	0.144368	0.156967	0.170474	0.184941	0.200423	0.216975	0.234656
72.	0.110733	0.120858	0.131751	0.143454	0.156016	0.169487	0.183920	0.199368	0.215890	0.233543
73.	0.109947	0.120037	0.130892	0.142558	0.155084	0.168520	0.182918	0.198334	0.214825	0.232450
74.	0.109182	0.119233	0.130051	0.141680	0.154171	0.167571	0.181936	0.197319	0.213780	0.231377
75.	0.108429	0.118445	0.129226	0.140820	0.153274	0.166640	0.180971	0.196323	0.212754	0.230323
76.	0.107692	0.117672	0.128417	0.139975	0.152394	0.165726	0.180025	0.195345	0.211746	0.229288
77.	0.106970	0.116914	0.127624	0.139147	0.151532	0.164830	0.179095	0.194384	0.210756	0.228271
78.	0.106262	0.116171	0.126846	0.138334	0.150685	0.163949	0.178183	0.193441	0.209783	0.227272
79.	0.105565	0.115442	0.126083	0.137536	0.149853	0.163085	0.177286	0.192514	0.208828	0.226289
80.	0.104887	0.114727	0.125333	0.136753	0.149036	0.162236	0.176405	0.191603	0.207888	0.225323

CUMULATIVE AVERAGE FACTORS BASED ON THE LOG-LINEAR CUMULATIVE AVERAGE CURVE THEORY

	70	71	72	73	74	75	76	77	78	79
81.	0.104219	0.114025	0.124598	0.135984	0.148234	0.161401	0.175540	0.190708	0.206965	0.222373
82.	0.103563	0.113336	0.123875	0.135228	0.147446	0.160581	0.174689	0.189827	0.206056	0.223439
83.	0.102919	0.112659	0.123165	0.134486	0.146672	0.159776	0.173853	0.188962	0.205163	0.225220
84.	0.102288	0.111994	0.122468	0.133757	0.145911	0.158983	0.173030	0.188110	0.204284	0.221615
85.	0.101665	0.111341	0.121783	0.133040	0.145163	0.158204	0.172222	0.187273	0.203419	0.220725
86.	0.101055	0.110700	0.121110	0.132336	0.144427	0.157438	0.171426	0.186449	0.202558	0.219849
87.	0.100456	0.110069	0.120448	0.131643	0.143704	0.156685	0.170643	0.185638	0.201731	0.218986
88.	0.099867	0.109449	0.119798	0.130961	0.142992	0.155943	0.169873	0.184839	0.200906	0.218137
89.	0.099288	0.108840	0.119158	0.130291	0.142292	0.155214	0.169114	0.184054	0.200094	0.217300
90.	0.098719	0.108241	0.118529	0.129632	0.141603	0.154496	0.168368	0.183280	0.199294	0.216476
91.	0.098152	0.107651	0.117910	0.128983	0.140925	0.153789	0.167633	0.182518	0.198526	0.215664
92.	0.097608	0.107072	0.117300	0.128345	0.140257	0.153093	0.166909	0.181767	0.197730	0.214864
93.	0.097067	0.106501	0.116701	0.127716	0.139600	0.152407	0.166196	0.181028	0.196965	0.214076
94.	0.096534	0.105940	0.116111	0.127098	0.138953	0.151732	0.165494	0.180299	0.196212	0.213298
95.	0.096010	0.105387	0.115530	0.126488	0.138316	0.151067	0.164802	0.179581	0.195469	0.212532
96.	0.095494	0.104844	0.114958	0.125889	0.137688	0.150412	0.164120	0.178873	0.194736	0.211777
97.	0.094985	0.104308	0.114395	0.125298	0.137069	0.149767	0.163448	0.178176	0.194014	0.211032
98.	0.094486	0.103781	0.113840	0.124715	0.136460	0.149131	0.162786	0.177488	0.193302	0.210297
99.	0.093994	0.103262	0.113294	0.124142	0.135860	0.148503	0.162133	0.176810	0.192600	0.209572
100.	0.093509	0.102750	0.112755	0.123577	0.135268	0.147885	0.161489	0.176141	0.191908	0.208857
101.	0.093031	0.102246	0.112225	0.123020	0.134684	0.147276	0.160854	0.175481	0.191224	0.208151
102.	0.092561	0.101750	0.111702	0.122471	0.134109	0.146675	0.160228	0.174831	0.190550	0.207455
103.	0.092098	0.101260	0.111187	0.121929	0.133542	0.146082	0.159610	0.174189	0.189885	0.206768
104.	0.091641	0.100778	0.110679	0.121396	0.132983	0.145497	0.159001	0.173555	0.189228	0.206090
105.	0.091191	0.100303	0.110178	0.120869	0.132431	0.144921	0.158399	0.172930	0.188580	0.205420
106.	0.090747	0.099834	0.109684	0.120350	0.131887	0.144352	0.157806	0.172313	0.187941	0.204759
107.	0.090310	0.099372	0.109197	0.119838	0.131350	0.143790	0.157220	0.171704	0.187309	0.204106
108.	0.089878	0.098916	0.108717	0.119333	0.130820	0.143236	0.156642	0.171103	0.186686	0.203462
109.	0.089453	0.098467	0.108243	0.118835	0.130298	0.142689	0.156072	0.170509	0.186070	0.202825
110.	0.089034	0.098023	0.107776	0.118343	0.129782	0.142150	0.155508	0.169923	0.185462	0.202196
111.	0.088622	0.097586	0.107314	0.117858	0.129272	0.141617	0.154952	0.169344	0.184861	0.201575
112.	0.088212	0.097154	0.106859	0.117379	0.128770	0.141090	0.154403	0.168773	0.184268	0.200961
113.	0.087809	0.096729	0.106410	0.116906	0.128273	0.140571	0.153861	0.168208	0.183682	0.200354
114.	0.087412	0.096309	0.105967	0.116439	0.127783	0.140058	0.153325	0.167650	0.183103	0.199755
115.	0.087023	0.095894	0.105529	0.115979	0.127300	0.139551	0.152796	0.167099	0.182530	0.199162
116.	0.086633	0.095484	0.105097	0.115524	0.126822	0.139050	0.152273	0.166554	0.181965	0.198577
117.	0.086252	0.095080	0.104670	0.115074	0.126350	0.138556	0.151756	0.166016	0.181406	0.197998
118.	0.085875	0.094681	0.104249	0.114630	0.125883	0.138067	0.151246	0.165484	0.180853	0.197426
119.	0.085503	0.094287	0.103833	0.114192	0.125423	0.137585	0.150741	0.164958	0.180307	0.196860
120.	0.085135	0.093898	0.103422	0.113759	0.124968	0.137108	0.150242	0.164439	0.179767	0.196301

APPENDIX (continued)

CUMULATIVE AVERAGE FACTORS BASED ON THE LOG-LINEAR CUMULATIVE AVERAGE CURVE THEORY

	70	71	72	73	74	75	76	77	78	79
121.	0.084772	0.093514	0.103016	0.113331	0.124518	0.136636	0.149750	0.163925	0.179233	0.195747
122.	0.084416	0.093135	0.102615	0.112909	0.124074	0.136170	0.149262	0.163417	0.178705	0.195200
123.	0.084060	0.092760	0.102218	0.112491	0.123634	0.135710	0.148781	0.162915	0.178183	0.194650
124.	0.083711	0.092389	0.101827	0.112078	0.123200	0.135254	0.148304	0.162418	0.177666	0.194124
125.	0.083365	0.092023	0.101440	0.111670	0.122771	0.134804	0.147834	0.161927	0.177155	0.193594
126.	0.083024	0.091662	0.101058	0.111267	0.122347	0.134359	0.147368	0.161441	0.176650	0.193070
127.	0.082687	0.091304	0.100680	0.110868	0.121928	0.133919	0.146907	0.160961	0.176150	0.192552
128.	0.082354	0.090951	0.100306	0.110474	0.121513	0.133484	0.146452	0.160485	0.175656	0.192039
129.	0.082025	0.090602	0.099937	0.110084	0.121103	0.133053	0.146001	0.160015	0.175166	0.191532
130.	0.081700	0.090257	0.099572	0.109699	0.120697	0.132628	0.145556	0.159550	0.174682	0.191029
131.	0.081373	0.089916	0.099211	0.109318	0.120296	0.132207	0.145115	0.159089	0.174203	0.190532
132.	0.081061	0.089579	0.098854	0.108941	0.119899	0.131790	0.144678	0.158634	0.173729	0.190040
133.	0.080746	0.089245	0.098501	0.108569	0.119507	0.131378	0.144247	0.158183	0.173259	0.189553
134.	0.080436	0.088916	0.098152	0.108200	0.119119	0.130970	0.143820	0.157737	0.172795	0.189071
135.	0.080129	0.088590	0.097807	0.107835	0.118735	0.130566	0.143397	0.157295	0.172335	0.188593
136.	0.079825	0.088267	0.097465	0.107475	0.118354	0.130167	0.142979	0.156858	0.171890	0.188120
137.	0.079524	0.087948	0.097127	0.107118	0.117978	0.129772	0.142564	0.156425	0.171429	0.187652
138.	0.079227	0.087633	0.096793	0.106765	0.117606	0.129381	0.142154	0.155997	0.170983	0.187189
139.	0.078934	0.087321	0.096462	0.106415	0.117238	0.128994	0.141749	0.155573	0.170541	0.186730
140.	0.078643	0.087012	0.096135	0.106069	0.116873	0.128610	0.141347	0.155153	0.170103	0.186275
141.	0.078356	0.086706	0.095812	0.105727	0.116513	0.128231	0.140949	0.154737	0.169670	0.185825
142.	0.078071	0.086404	0.095491	0.105388	0.116156	0.127856	0.140555	0.154325	0.169240	0.185379
143.	0.077793	0.086105	0.095174	0.105053	0.115802	0.127484	0.140165	0.153918	0.168815	0.184937
144.	0.077511	0.085809	0.094860	0.104721	0.115452	0.127116	0.139779	0.153514	0.168394	0.184499
145.	0.077235	0.085516	0.094550	0.104393	0.115105	0.126751	0.139397	0.153114	0.167977	0.184065
146.	0.076963	0.085226	0.094242	0.104068	0.114762	0.126390	0.139018	0.152717	0.167563	0.183636
147.	0.076693	0.084939	0.093938	0.103746	0.114422	0.126032	0.138643	0.152325	0.167154	0.183210
148.	0.076425	0.084655	0.093637	0.103427	0.114086	0.125678	0.138271	0.151936	0.166748	0.182788
149.	0.076162	0.084374	0.093338	0.103111	0.113753	0.125327	0.137903	0.151551	0.166346	0.182370
150.	0.075900	0.084096	0.093043	0.102798	0.113423	0.124980	0.137538	0.151169	0.165948	0.181955
151.	0.075641	0.083820	0.092750	0.102489	0.113096	0.124636	0.137177	0.150790	0.165553	0.181545
152.	0.075384	0.083547	0.092461	0.102182	0.112772	0.124295	0.136819	0.150416	0.165162	0.181138
153.	0.075131	0.083277	0.092174	0.101878	0.112451	0.123957	0.136464	0.150044	0.164774	0.180734
154.	0.074879	0.083009	0.091889	0.101577	0.112133	0.123622	0.136112	0.149676	0.164390	0.180334
155.	0.074630	0.082744	0.091608	0.101279	0.111819	0.123291	0.135764	0.149311	0.164009	0.179938
156.	0.074384	0.082482	0.091329	0.100984	0.111507	0.122962	0.135419	0.148950	0.163631	0.179545
157.	0.074139	0.082222	0.091053	0.100691	0.111197	0.122636	0.135077	0.148591	0.163257	0.179155
158.	0.073898	0.081964	0.090780	0.100401	0.110888	0.122314	0.134738	0.148236	0.162886	0.178768
159.	0.073655	0.081709	0.090508	0.100114	0.110588	0.121994	0.134401	0.147884	0.162518	0.178385
160.	0.073421	0.081456	0.090240	0.099830	0.110287	0.121677	0.134068	0.147534	0.162153	0.178005

CUMULATIVE AVERAGE FACTORS BASED ON THE LOG-LINEAR CUMULATIVE AVERAGE CURVE THEORY

	80	81	82	83	84	85	86	87	88	89
1.	1.000000	1.000000	1.000000	1.000000	1.000000	1.000000	1.000000	1.000000	1.000000	1.000000
2.	0.800000	0.810000	0.820000	0.830000	0.840000	0.850000	0.860000	0.870000	0.880000	0.890000
3.	0.702104	0.716065	0.730127	0.744289	0.758552	0.772915	0.787377	0.801937	0.816596	0.831352
4.	0.640000	0.656100	0.672400	0.688900	0.705600	0.722500	0.739600	0.756900	0.774400	0.792100
5.	0.595637	0.613068	0.630786	0.648792	0.667086	0.685671	0.704547	0.723716	0.743178	0.762934
6.	0.561683	0.580012	0.598704	0.617760	0.637184	0.656978	0.677144	0.697685	0.718604	0.739905
7.	0.534490	0.553458	0.572855	0.592684	0.612950	0.633656	0.654808	0.676409	0.698463	0.720974
8.	0.512000	0.531441	0.551368	0.571787	0.592704	0.614125	0.636056	0.658505	0.681472	0.704969
9.	0.492952	0.512748	0.533085	0.553967	0.575402	0.597397	0.619962	0.643103	0.666829	0.691147
10.	0.476513	0.496585	0.517244	0.538497	0.560352	0.582820	0.605911	0.629633	0.653997	0.679012
11.	0.462111	0.482403	0.503321	0.524875	0.547078	0.569941	0.593474	0.617691	0.642601	0.668218
12.	0.449344	0.469810	0.490937	0.512741	0.535234	0.558431	0.582344	0.606986	0.632372	0.658514
13.	0.437916	0.458516	0.479814	0.501826	0.524566	0.548048	0.572289	0.597303	0.623105	0.649712
14.	0.427592	0.448301	0.469741	0.491928	0.514878	0.538608	0.563135	0.588475	0.614647	0.641667
15.	0.418199	0.438996	0.460554	0.482889	0.506020	0.529965	0.554744	0.580375	0.606876	0.634267
16.	0.409603	0.430467	0.452122	0.474583	0.497871	0.522006	0.547008	0.572898	0.599695	0.627422
17.	0.401683	0.422606	0.444342	0.466912	0.490337	0.514639	0.539840	0.565962	0.593028	0.621060
18.	0.394360	0.415326	0.437130	0.459792	0.483337	0.507788	0.533167	0.559500	0.586809	0.615120
19.	0.387555	0.408555	0.430415	0.453158	0.476808	0.501391	0.526932	0.553455	0.580987	0.609554
20.	0.381208	0.402234	0.424140	0.446952	0.470696	0.495397	0.521083	0.547780	0.575517	0.604320
21.	0.375267	0.396312	0.418257	0.441129	0.464955	0.489762	0.515580	0.542437	0.570362	0.599384
22.	0.369689	0.390747	0.412723	0.435647	0.459546	0.484450	0.510388	0.537391	0.565489	0.594714
23.	0.364436	0.385502	0.407504	0.430427	0.454436	0.479427	0.505475	0.532613	0.560872	0.590286
24.	0.359477	0.380546	0.402568	0.425575	0.449597	0.474666	0.500816	0.528078	0.556487	0.586078
25.	0.354784	0.375853	0.397891	0.420930	0.445004	0.470145	0.496387	0.523765	0.552313	0.582069
26.	0.350332	0.371398	0.393448	0.416516	0.440635	0.465841	0.492169	0.519654	0.548333	0.578244
27.	0.346102	0.367161	0.389219	0.412311	0.436472	0.461737	0.488143	0.515728	0.544529	0.574586
28.	0.342073	0.363124	0.385188	0.408300	0.432498	0.457817	0.484296	0.511974	0.540889	0.571084
29.	0.338231	0.359271	0.381337	0.404467	0.428697	0.454065	0.480612	0.508377	0.537400	0.567724
30.	0.334559	0.355587	0.377656	0.400798	0.425057	0.450471	0.477080	0.504926	0.534051	0.564498
31.	0.331045	0.352060	0.374125	0.397280	0.421565	0.447021	0.473688	0.501610	0.530831	0.561395
32.	0.327680	0.348678	0.370740	0.393904	0.418212	0.443705	0.470427	0.498421	0.527732	0.558406
33.	0.324453	0.345432	0.367488	0.390659	0.414987	0.440516	0.467288	0.495349	0.524745	0.555525
34.	0.321347	0.342311	0.364360	0.387537	0.411883	0.437443	0.464262	0.492387	0.521864	0.552743
35.	0.318362	0.339308	0.361349	0.384529	0.408891	0.434480	0.461343	0.489528	0.519082	0.550056
36.	0.315688	0.336414	0.358446	0.381628	0.406003	0.431620	0.458524	0.486765	0.516392	0.547457
37.	0.312717	0.333624	0.355645	0.378827	0.403215	0.428856	0.455798	0.484093	0.513789	0.544941
38.	0.310044	0.330930	0.352940	0.376121	0.400519	0.426183	0.453161	0.481506	0.511269	0.542503
39.	0.307462	0.328327	0.350325	0.373504	0.397911	0.423595	0.450607	0.478999	0.508825	0.540139
40.	0.304965	0.325810	0.347795	0.370971	0.395385	0.421088	0.448131	0.476569	0.506455	0.537845

APPENDIX (*continued*)

CUMULATIVE AVERAGE FACTORS BASED ON THE LOG-LINEAR CUMULATIVE AVERAGE CURVE THEORY

	80	81	82	83	84	85	86	87	88	89
41.	0.302552	0.323373	0.345345	0.368516	0.392936	0.418657	0.445730	0.474211	0.504154	0.535617
42.	0.300214	0.321013	0.342971	0.366137	0.390562	0.416298	0.443399	0.471920	0.501918	0.533451
43.	0.299748	0.318725	0.340668	0.363828	0.388257	0.414008	0.441135	0.469694	0.499745	0.531345
44.	0.295251	0.316505	0.338433	0.361587	0.386018	0.411282	0.438934	0.467530	0.497630	0.529295
45.	0.293619	0.314350	0.336262	0.359409	0.383842	0.409618	0.436792	0.465424	0.495572	0.527299
46.	0.291542	0.312256	0.334153	0.357292	0.381726	0.407513	0.434709	0.463373	0.493568	0.525355
47.	0.289537	0.310222	0.332102	0.355232	0.379667	0.405463	0.432679	0.461375	0.491614	0.523459
48.	0.287582	0.308242	0.330106	0.353227	0.377661	0.403466	0.430701	0.459428	0.489709	0.521609
49.	0.285672	0.306316	0.328163	0.351275	0.375708	0.401521	0.428773	0.457529	0.487850	0.519804
50.	0.283827	0.304441	0.326270	0.349372	0.373803	0.399623	0.426893	0.455675	0.486036	0.518041
51.	0.282023	0.302613	0.324426	0.347517	0.371946	0.397272	0.425052	0.453866	0.484264	0.516320
52.	0.280265	0.300832	0.322627	0.345708	0.370134	0.395965	0.423265	0.452099	0.482533	0.514637
53.	0.278553	0.299095	0.320873	0.343942	0.368365	0.394201	0.421514	0.450372	0.480841	0.512991
54.	0.276881	0.297400	0.319160	0.342219	0.366637	0.392477	0.419801	0.448684	0.479186	0.511382
55.	0.275251	0.295746	0.317488	0.340535	0.364948	0.390792	0.418131	0.447032	0.477567	0.509807
56.	0.273659	0.294130	0.315854	0.338889	0.363298	0.389144	0.416494	0.445417	0.475983	0.508265
57.	0.272104	0.292552	0.314258	0.337281	0.361684	0.387533	0.414894	0.443836	0.474432	0.506754
58.	0.270585	0.291009	0.312697	0.335707	0.360105	0.385956	0.413326	0.442288	0.472912	0.505275
59.	0.269100	0.289501	0.311170	0.334168	0.358560	0.384412	0.411792	0.440771	0.471424	0.503825
60.	0.267647	0.288026	0.309676	0.332662	0.357048	0.382900	0.410289	0.439285	0.469965	0.502403
61.	0.266227	0.286582	0.308214	0.331187	0.355566	0.381419	0.408816	0.437829	0.468534	0.501009
62.	0.264837	0.285169	0.306783	0.329743	0.354115	0.379967	0.407372	0.436401	0.467131	0.499641
63.	0.263476	0.283785	0.305380	0.328327	0.352692	0.378545	0.405956	0.435000	0.465755	0.498299
64.	0.262144	0.282430	0.304007	0.326940	0.351298	0.377150	0.404567	0.433626	0.464404	0.496981
65.	0.260839	0.281101	0.302660	0.325581	0.349931	0.375781	0.403205	0.432278	0.463078	0.495688
66.	0.259560	0.279800	0.301340	0.324247	0.348589	0.374438	0.401867	0.430954	0.461276	0.494417
67.	0.258306	0.278524	0.300046	0.322939	0.347273	0.373120	0.400555	0.429654	0.460497	0.493168
68.	0.257077	0.277272	0.298776	0.321655	0.345982	0.371826	0.399265	0.428377	0.459241	0.491942
69.	0.255872	0.276044	0.297529	0.320396	0.344713	0.370556	0.397999	0.427122	0.458006	0.490736
70.	0.254690	0.274839	0.296306	0.319159	0.343468	0.369308	0.396755	0.425889	0.456792	0.489550
71.	0.253529	0.273657	0.295105	0.317944	0.342245	0.368082	0.395532	0.424677	0.455599	0.488384
72.	0.252393	0.272496	0.293926	0.316751	0.341043	0.366877	0.394330	0.423485	0.454425	0.487237
73.	0.251272	0.271355	0.292768	0.315579	0.339862	0.365692	0.393149	0.422313	0.453271	0.486108
74.	0.250174	0.270235	0.291629	0.314427	0.338700	0.364527	0.391987	0.421160	0.452135	0.484998
75.	0.249095	0.269135	0.290511	0.313294	0.337559	0.363382	0.390843	0.420026	0.451017	0.483904
76.	0.248035	0.268053	0.289411	0.312181	0.336436	0.362255	0.389719	0.418910	0.449916	0.482828
77.	0.246994	0.266990	0.288330	0.311085	0.335332	0.361147	0.388612	0.417811	0.448833	0.481768
78.	0.245970	0.265945	0.287267	0.310008	0.334245	0.360056	0.387522	0.416729	0.447766	0.480724
79.	0.244963	0.264917	0.286221	0.308948	0.333176	0.358982	0.386449	0.415664	0.446715	0.479696
80.	0.243973	0.263906	0.285192	0.307906	0.332123	0.357925	0.385393	0.414615	0.445680	0.478682

CUMULATIVE AVERAGE FACTORS BASED ON THE LOG-LINEAR CUMULATIVE AVERAGE CURVE THEORY

	80	81	82	83	84	85	86	87	88	89
81.	0.242999	0.262911	0.284180	0.306879	0.331087	0.356884	0.384353	0.413582	0.444660	0.477683
82.	0.242041	0.261932	0.283183	0.305869	0.330067	0.355858	0.383328	0.412563	0.443655	0.476699
83.	0.241099	0.260969	0.282202	0.304873	0.329062	0.354848	0.382318	0.411560	0.442665	0.475729
84.	0.240171	0.260020	0.281236	0.303894	0.328072	0.353853	0.381323	0.410571	0.441688	0.474772
85.	0.239258	0.259086	0.280285	0.302928	0.327097	0.352873	0.380343	0.409596	0.440725	0.473828
86.	0.238358	0.258167	0.279348	0.301977	0.326136	0.351907	0.379376	0.408634	0.439775	0.472897
87.	0.237473	0.257261	0.278425	0.301040	0.325189	0.350954	0.378423	0.407686	0.438839	0.471979
88.	0.236601	0.256369	0.277515	0.300117	0.324255	0.350015	0.377483	0.406751	0.437915	0.471073
89.	0.235742	0.255490	0.276619	0.299207	0.323335	0.349089	0.376556	0.405829	0.437003	0.470179
90.	0.234895	0.254623	0.275735	0.298309	0.322428	0.348175	0.375642	0.404919	0.436104	0.469297
91.	0.234061	0.253769	0.274864	0.297425	0.321533	0.347274	0.374739	0.404021	0.435216	0.468426
92.	0.233239	0.252928	0.274006	0.296552	0.320650	0.346386	0.373849	0.403135	0.434339	0.467566
93.	0.232429	0.252098	0.273159	0.295691	0.319779	0.345509	0.372971	0.402260	0.433474	0.466717
94.	0.231630	0.251279	0.272324	0.294843	0.318920	0.344643	0.372104	0.401396	0.432620	0.465878
95.	0.230842	0.250472	0.271500	0.294005	0.318072	0.343789	0.371248	0.400544	0.431777	0.465050
96.	0.230065	0.249676	0.270687	0.293179	0.317236	0.342946	0.370403	0.399702	0.430944	0.464232
97.	0.229299	0.248891	0.269885	0.292363	0.316409	0.342114	0.369569	0.398871	0.430121	0.463424
98.	0.228543	0.248116	0.269094	0.291558	0.315595	0.341292	0.368745	0.398050	0.429308	0.462626
99.	0.227798	0.247352	0.268313	0.290763	0.314790	0.340481	0.367931	0.397239	0.428505	0.461837
100.	0.227062	0.246597	0.267542	0.289979	0.313995	0.339680	0.367128	0.396437	0.427711	0.461057
101.	0.226335	0.245852	0.266781	0.289204	0.313210	0.338888	0.366334	0.395646	0.426927	0.460286
102.	0.225619	0.245117	0.266029	0.288439	0.312435	0.338106	0.365549	0.394863	0.426152	0.459524
103.	0.224911	0.244391	0.265287	0.287684	0.311669	0.337334	0.364774	0.394090	0.425386	0.458771
104.	0.224213	0.243674	0.264554	0.286938	0.310912	0.336570	0.364008	0.393326	0.424629	0.458027
105.	0.223523	0.242966	0.263831	0.286201	0.310165	0.335816	0.363251	0.392570	0.423880	0.457290
106.	0.222842	0.242267	0.263116	0.285472	0.309426	0.335070	0.362502	0.391823	0.423140	0.456562
107.	0.222169	0.241577	0.262409	0.284753	0.308696	0.334334	0.361762	0.391085	0.422408	0.455842
108.	0.221505	0.240894	0.261711	0.284041	0.307975	0.333605	0.361031	0.390355	0.421684	0.455130
109.	0.220849	0.240220	0.261021	0.283339	0.307262	0.332885	0.360308	0.389632	0.420967	0.454425
110.	0.220201	0.239554	0.260340	0.282644	0.306557	0.332173	0.359592	0.388918	0.420259	0.453728
111.	0.219560	0.238896	0.259666	0.281957	0.305860	0.331469	0.358885	0.388212	0.419558	0.453038
112.	0.218927	0.238246	0.259000	0.281278	0.305170	0.330773	0.358185	0.387513	0.418865	0.452355
113.	0.218301	0.237603	0.258342	0.280607	0.304489	0.330084	0.357493	0.386821	0.418179	0.451680
114.	0.217683	0.236967	0.257691	0.279943	0.303815	0.329403	0.356808	0.386137	0.417500	0.451011
115.	0.217072	0.236339	0.257048	0.279286	0.303148	0.328729	0.356131	0.385460	0.416828	0.450350
116.	0.216468	0.235718	0.256412	0.278637	0.302488	0.328062	0.355461	0.384790	0.416163	0.449695
117.	0.215870	0.235103	0.255782	0.277995	0.301836	0.327403	0.354797	0.384127	0.415504	0.449046
118.	0.215280	0.234496	0.255159	0.277360	0.301191	0.326750	0.354141	0.383471	0.414853	0.448404
119.	0.214696	0.233895	0.254544	0.276731	0.300552	0.326104	0.353491	0.382821	0.414208	0.447768
120.	0.214115	0.233301	0.253934	0.276109	0.299920	0.325465	0.352848	0.382178	0.413559	0.447139

APPENDIX (*continued*)

CUMULATIVE AVERAGE FACTORS BASED ON THE LOG-LINEAR CUMULATIVE AVERAGE CURVE THEORY

	80	81	82	83	84	85	86	87	88	89
121.	0.213567	0.232713	0.253332	0.275494	0.299295	0.324832	0.352212	0.381542	0.412936	0.446515
122.	0.212982	0.232131	0.252736	0.274885	0.298676	0.324206	0.351581	0.380911	0.412310	0.445898
123.	0.212423	0.231556	0.252146	0.274283	0.298063	0.323586	0.350958	0.380287	0.411690	0.445286
124.	0.211870	0.230987	0.251562	0.273686	0.297456	0.322972	0.350340	0.379669	0.411076	0.444681
125.	0.211323	0.230423	0.250984	0.273096	0.296856	0.322365	0.349728	0.379057	0.410467	0.444080
126.	0.210281	0.229866	0.250412	0.272512	0.296262	0.321763	0.349122	0.378450	0.409864	0.443486
127.	0.210245	0.229314	0.249846	0.271933	0.295673	0.321167	0.348522	0.377850	0.409267	0.442897
128.	0.209715	0.228768	0.249285	0.271361	0.295090	0.320577	0.347928	0.377255	0.408676	0.442313
129.	0.209192	0.228227	0.248731	0.270793	0.294513	0.319993	0.347339	0.376665	0.408089	0.441735
130.	0.208671	0.227692	0.248181	0.270232	0.293942	0.319414	0.346756	0.376081	0.407509	0.441162
131.	0.208157	0.227162	0.247637	0.269676	0.293376	0.318840	0.346178	0.375503	0.406233	0.440594
132.	0.207643	0.226638	0.247099	0.269125	0.292815	0.318272	0.345606	0.374930	0.406363	0.440031
133.	0.207144	0.226118	0.246566	0.268580	0.292260	0.317710	0.345039	0.374362	0.405798	0.439473
134.	0.206645	0.225604	0.246037	0.268039	0.291710	0.317152	0.344477	0.373799	0.405237	0.438920
135.	0.206151	0.225095	0.245514	0.267504	0.291165	0.316600	0.343920	0.373241	0.404682	0.438372
136.	0.205662	0.224590	0.244996	0.266974	0.290625	0.316053	0.343368	0.372688	0.404132	0.437828
137.	0.205177	0.224091	0.244483	0.266449	0.290089	0.315510	0.342821	0.372139	0.403586	0.437289
138.	0.204693	0.223596	0.243974	0.265928	0.289559	0.314973	0.342279	0.371596	0.403045	0.436755
139.	0.204222	0.223105	0.243470	0.265413	0.289034	0.314440	0.341742	0.371057	0.402509	0.436225
140.	0.203752	0.222620	0.242971	0.264902	0.288513	0.313912	0.341209	0.370523	0.401977	0.435699
141.	0.203285	0.222139	0.242476	0.264395	0.287997	0.313388	0.340681	0.369994	0.401450	0.435178
142.	0.202823	0.221662	0.241986	0.263894	0.287486	0.312869	0.340158	0.369469	0.400927	0.434662
143.	0.202366	0.221190	0.241501	0.263396	0.286979	0.312355	0.339640	0.368948	0.400408	0.434149
144.	0.201912	0.220721	0.241019	0.262903	0.286476	0.311845	0.339124	0.368432	0.399894	0.433641
145.	0.201463	0.220258	0.240542	0.262415	0.285978	0.311340	0.338614	0.367920	0.399384	0.433137
146.	0.201018	0.219798	0.240069	0.261930	0.285484	0.310838	0.338108	0.367413	0.398878	0.432636
147.	0.200576	0.219342	0.239601	0.261450	0.284994	0.310341	0.337606	0.366909	0.398376	0.432140
148.	0.200137	0.218891	0.239136	0.260974	0.284508	0.309848	0.337108	0.366410	0.397878	0.431648
149.	0.199706	0.218443	0.238675	0.260502	0.284027	0.309359	0.336615	0.365914	0.397385	0.431159
150.	0.199276	0.217999	0.238219	0.260034	0.283549	0.308875	0.336125	0.365423	0.396895	0.430675
151.	0.198850	0.217559	0.237766	0.259570	0.283076	0.308394	0.335640	0.364935	0.396409	0.430194
152.	0.198428	0.217123	0.237317	0.259110	0.282606	0.307917	0.335158	0.364452	0.395926	0.429717
153.	0.198013	0.216691	0.236872	0.258653	0.282140	0.307444	0.334680	0.363972	0.395448	0.429243
154.	0.197595	0.216262	0.236431	0.258201	0.281679	0.306975	0.334206	0.363496	0.394973	0.428774
155.	0.197184	0.215837	0.235993	0.257752	0.281220	0.306509	0.333736	0.363023	0.394502	0.428307
156.	0.196775	0.215415	0.235559	0.257307	0.280766	0.306047	0.333269	0.362555	0.394034	0.427844
157.	0.196371	0.214997	0.235128	0.256865	0.280315	0.305589	0.332806	0.362089	0.393570	0.427385
158.	0.195970	0.214583	0.234701	0.256627	0.279868	0.305134	0.332346	0.361628	0.393110	0.426929
159.	0.195573	0.214171	0.234278	0.255993	0.279424	0.304683	0.331891	0.361170	0.392652	0.426476
160.	0.195173	0.213764	0.233857	0.255562	0.278983	0.304236	0.331438	0.360715	0.392199	0.426027

CUMULATIVE AVERAGE FACTORS BASED ON THE LOG-LINEAR CUMULATIVE AVERAGE CURVE THEORY

	90	91	92	93	94	95	96	97	98	99
1.	1.000000	1.000000	1.000000	1.000000	1.000000	1.000000	1.000000	1.000000	1.000000	1.000000
2.	0.900000	0.910000	0.920000	0.930000	0.940000	0.950000	0.960000	0.970000	0.980000	0.990000
3.	0.846206	0.861157	0.876224	0.891347	0.906585	0.921919	0.937347	0.952870	0.968487	0.984197
4.	0.810000	0.828100	0.846400	0.864900	0.883600	0.902500	0.921600	0.940900	0.960400	0.980100
5.	0.782987	0.803336	0.823982	0.844928	0.866173	0.887720	0.909568	0.931719	0.954174	0.976934
6.	0.761585	0.783653	0.806107	0.828952	0.852190	0.875823	0.899853	0.924284	0.949117	0.974355
7.	0.743945	0.767387	0.791297	0.815681	0.840544	0.865889	0.891721	0.918044	0.944862	0.972179
8.	0.729000	0.755571	0.778688	0.804357	0.830584	0.857375	0.884736	0.912673	0.941192	0.970299
9.	0.716065	0.741591	0.767733	0.794499	0.821897	0.849935	0.878620	0.907961	0.937966	0.968643
10.	0.704683	0.731035	0.758064	0.785783	0.814203	0.843334	0.873185	0.903767	0.935091	0.967165
11.	0.694553	0.721612	0.749422	0.777981	0.807305	0.837407	0.868297	0.899990	0.932496	0.965829
12.	0.685427	0.713124	0.741619	0.770926	0.801059	0.832032	0.863859	0.896555	0.930135	0.964611
13.	0.677135	0.705399	0.734512	0.764492	0.795355	0.827118	0.859797	0.893408	0.927967	0.963492
14.	0.669552	0.698323	0.727993	0.758584	0.790111	0.822595	0.856052	0.890503	0.925965	0.962458
15.	0.662565	0.691798	0.721976	0.753124	0.785260	0.818406	0.852581	0.887807	0.924105	0.961495
16.	0.656100	0.685750	0.716393	0.748052	0.780749	0.814506	0.849347	0.885293	0.922358	0.960596
17.	0.650082	0.680016	0.711187	0.743319	0.776535	0.810860	0.846319	0.882937	0.920740	0.959752
18.	0.644458	0.674848	0.706314	0.738884	0.772583	0.807438	0.843475	0.880723	0.919207	0.958957
19.	0.639181	0.669901	0.701735	0.734711	0.768863	0.804214	0.840794	0.878633	0.917760	0.958207
20.	0.634219	0.665242	0.697419	0.730778	0.765351	0.801167	0.838258	0.876654	0.916389	0.957493
21.	0.629533	0.660841	0.693337	0.727055	0.762025	0.798280	0.835852	0.874777	0.915086	0.956816
22.	0.625097	0.656671	0.689468	0.723522	0.758867	0.795536	0.833566	0.872990	0.913847	0.956171
23.	0.620888	0.652711	0.685791	0.720163	0.755861	0.792924	0.831386	0.871287	0.912663	0.955555
24.	0.616884	0.648943	0.682289	0.716961	0.752995	0.790430	0.829305	0.869659	0.911532	0.954965
25.	0.613068	0.645348	0.678947	0.713903	0.750256	0.788046	0.827314	0.868100	0.910448	0.954400
26.	0.609424	0.641914	0.675751	0.710978	0.747634	0.785762	0.825405	0.866605	0.909408	0.953857
27.	0.605938	0.638626	0.672690	0.708174	0.745120	0.783571	0.823572	0.865169	0.908408	0.953336
28.	0.602598	0.635473	0.669754	0.705483	0.742704	0.781465	0.821810	0.863788	0.907446	0.952833
29.	0.599392	0.632447	0.666933	0.702896	0.740382	0.779438	0.820114	0.862457	0.906518	0.952348
30.	0.596311	0.629536	0.664218	0.700405	0.738144	0.777485	0.818478	0.861173	0.905623	0.951880
31.	0.593347	0.626734	0.661603	0.698005	0.735987	0.775601	0.816899	0.859933	0.904758	0.951428
32.	0.590490	0.624032	0.659082	0.695688	0.733904	0.773781	0.815373	0.858734	0.903921	0.950990
33.	0.587734	0.621425	0.656646	0.693451	0.731891	0.772021	0.813896	0.857574	0.903110	0.950566
34.	0.585074	0.618906	0.654292	0.691287	0.729943	0.770317	0.812467	0.856449	0.902325	0.950154
35.	0.582501	0.616670	0.652015	0.689192	0.728057	0.768667	0.811081	0.855359	0.901563	0.949755
36.	0.580012	0.614111	0.649809	0.687162	0.726228	0.767066	0.809736	0.854301	0.900823	0.949367
37.	0.577602	0.611826	0.647671	0.685194	0.724454	0.765512	0.808431	0.853273	0.900104	0.948990
38.	0.575285	0.609610	0.645596	0.683283	0.722731	0.764003	0.807162	0.852274	0.899405	0.948623
39.	0.572928	0.607459	0.643582	0.681428	0.721057	0.762536	0.805928	0.851301	0.898724	0.948266
40.	0.570797	0.605370	0.641625	0.679624	0.719430	0.761109	0.804727	0.850355	0.898061	0.947918

APPENDIX (continued)

CUMULATIVE AVERAGE FACTORS BASED ON THE LOG-LINEAR CUMULATIVE AVERAGE CURVE THEORY

	90	91	92	93	94	95	96	97	98	99
41.	0.568659	0.603340	0.639722	0.677869	0.717846	0.759719	0.803558	0.849433	0.897415	0.947579
42.	0.566580	0.601165	0.637870	0.676161	0.716303	0.758366	0.802418	0.846533	0.896785	0.947248
43.	0.564557	0.599443	0.636067	0.674497	0.714800	0.757046	0.801307	0.847657	0.896170	0.946925
44.	0.562588	0.597571	0.634311	0.672876	0.713335	0.755759	0.800223	0.846801	0.895570	0.946600
45.	0.560669	0.595746	0.632598	0.671294	0.711905	0.754504	0.799165	0.845965	0.894983	0.946301
46.	0.558799	0.593967	0.630928	0.669751	0.710510	0.753277	0.798131	0.845148	0.894410	0.945999
47.	0.556975	0.592232	0.629298	0.668245	0.709147	0.752080	0.797121	0.844350	0.893850	0.945704
48.	0.555195	0.590538	0.627706	0.666774	0.707816	0.750909	0.796133	0.843569	0.893301	0.945416
49.	0.553458	0.588883	0.626151	0.665336	0.706511	0.749764	0.795167	0.842805	0.892765	0.945133
50.	0.551761	0.587267	0.624631	0.663930	0.705241	0.748644	0.794221	0.842057	0.892239	0.944856
51.	0.550105	0.585687	0.623145	0.662555	0.703995	0.747548	0.793295	0.841325	0.891724	0.944585
52.	0.548482	0.584141	0.621691	0.661209	0.702776	0.746474	0.792389	0.840607	0.891220	0.944319
53.	0.546896	0.582629	0.620268	0.659892	0.701582	0.745423	0.791500	0.839904	0.890725	0.944058
54.	0.545344	0.581149	0.618875	0.658602	0.700412	0.744392	0.790629	0.839214	0.890240	0.943802
55.	0.543825	0.579700	0.617511	0.657338	0.699266	0.743382	0.789775	0.838538	0.889764	0.943551
56.	0.542338	0.578281	0.616174	0.656099	0.698142	0.742392	0.788938	0.837874	0.889297	0.943305
57.	0.540881	0.576890	0.614863	0.654882	0.697040	0.741420	0.788116	0.837223	0.888838	0.943063
58.	0.539453	0.575526	0.613578	0.653693	0.695959	0.740466	0.787309	0.836583	0.888388	0.942825
59.	0.538053	0.574189	0.612318	0.652524	0.694898	0.739530	0.786517	0.835955	0.887945	0.942591
60.	0.536680	0.572878	0.611081	0.651377	0.693856	0.738611	0.785739	0.835338	0.887510	0.942362
61.	0.535333	0.571591	0.609867	0.650250	0.692833	0.737708	0.784974	0.834731	0.887083	0.942136
62.	0.534012	0.570328	0.608675	0.649144	0.691828	0.736821	0.784223	0.834135	0.886662	0.941914
63.	0.532715	0.569087	0.607505	0.648058	0.690840	0.735949	0.783484	0.833549	0.886249	0.941695
64.	0.531441	0.567869	0.606355	0.646990	0.689870	0.735092	0.782758	0.832972	0.885842	0.941480
65.	0.530190	0.566673	0.605225	0.645941	0.688916	0.734249	0.782043	0.832405	0.885442	0.941269
66.	0.528961	0.565497	0.604115	0.644909	0.687977	0.733420	0.781341	0.831846	0.885048	0.941060
67.	0.527753	0.564341	0.603023	0.643895	0.687054	0.732604	0.780649	0.831297	0.884660	0.940855
68.	0.526565	0.563204	0.601949	0.642897	0.686146	0.731801	0.779968	0.830756	0.884278	0.940653
69.	0.525392	0.562087	0.600893	0.641915	0.685253	0.731011	0.779298	0.830224	0.883902	0.940454
70.	0.524251	0.560987	0.599854	0.640948	0.684373	0.730233	0.778638	0.829698	0.883532	0.940258
71.	0.523122	0.559906	0.598831	0.639997	0.683507	0.729467	0.777987	0.829181	0.883166	0.940064
72.	0.522011	0.558841	0.597824	0.639061	0.682654	0.728713	0.777347	0.828672	0.882807	0.939874
73.	0.520918	0.557793	0.596833	0.638139	0.681814	0.727969	0.776716	0.828170	0.882452	0.939686
74.	0.519842	0.556762	0.595857	0.637230	0.680987	0.727237	0.776093	0.827675	0.882102	0.939500
75.	0.518782	0.555746	0.594896	0.636335	0.680171	0.726515	0.775480	0.827187	0.881757	0.939318
76.	0.517739	0.554745	0.593949	0.635453	0.679368	0.725803	0.774876	0.826705	0.881416	0.939137
77.	0.516711	0.553759	0.593016	0.634584	0.678575	0.725101	0.774279	0.826231	0.881081	0.938959
78.	0.515698	0.552788	0.592096	0.633728	0.677794	0.724409	0.773691	0.825762	0.880749	0.938783
79.	0.514701	0.551831	0.591189	0.632883	0.677024	0.723727	0.773111	0.825300	0.880422	0.938610
80.	0.513718	0.550887	0.590295	0.632050	0.676264	0.723053	0.772538	0.824844	0.880100	0.938439

CUMULATIVE AVERAGE FACTORS BASED ON THE LOG-LINEAR CUMULATIVE AVERAGE AVERAGE CURVE THEORY

	90	91	92	93	94	95	96	97	98	99
81.	0.512743	0.549957	0.589414	0.631229	0.675514	0.722389	0.771973	0.824394	0.879781	0.938270
82.	0.511793	0.549039	0.588544	0.630418	0.674775	0.721733	0.771416	0.823950	0.879467	0.938103
83.	0.510851	0.548135	0.587687	0.629619	0.674045	0.721086	0.770865	0.823511	0.879156	0.937938
84.	0.509922	0.547242	0.586841	0.628830	0.673325	0.720447	0.770322	0.823077	0.878849	0.937775
85.	0.509005	0.546362	0.586006	0.628051	0.672614	0.719817	0.769785	0.822650	0.878546	0.937614
86.	0.508101	0.545493	0.585182	0.627282	0.671912	0.719194	0.769255	0.822227	0.878247	0.937455
87.	0.507209	0.544636	0.584369	0.626524	0.671219	0.718579	0.768731	0.821809	0.877951	0.937298
88.	0.506329	0.543789	0.583566	0.625774	0.670535	0.717971	0.768214	0.821397	0.877658	0.937143
89.	0.505462	0.542954	0.582773	0.625034	0.669859	0.717371	0.767703	0.820989	0.877369	0.936989
90.	0.504602	0.542129	0.581990	0.624304	0.669191	0.716778	0.767198	0.820586	0.877084	0.936838
91.	0.503755	0.541315	0.581217	0.623582	0.668531	0.716193	0.766699	0.820188	0.876801	0.936688
92.	0.502919	0.540510	0.580454	0.622869	0.667879	0.715614	0.766206	0.819794	0.876522	0.936539
93.	0.502093	0.539716	0.579699	0.622164	0.667235	0.715041	0.765718	0.819404	0.876246	0.936392
94.	0.501278	0.538931	0.578993	0.621468	0.666598	0.714476	0.765236	0.819019	0.875973	0.936247
95.	0.500472	0.538156	0.578218	0.620780	0.665969	0.713916	0.764759	0.818639	0.875702	0.936103
96.	0.499676	0.537389	0.577490	0.620100	0.665347	0.713363	0.764287	0.818262	0.875435	0.935961
97.	0.498890	0.536632	0.576770	0.619427	0.664731	0.712816	0.763821	0.817889	0.875171	0.935821
98.	0.498113	0.535884	0.576059	0.618762	0.664123	0.712276	0.763360	0.817521	0.874910	0.935682
99.	0.497346	0.535144	0.575356	0.618105	0.663521	0.711741	0.762904	0.817156	0.874650	0.935544
100.	0.496585	0.534413	0.574661	0.617455	0.662926	0.711212	0.762452	0.816795	0.874394	0.935408
101.	0.495835	0.533690	0.573923	0.616812	0.662338	0.710688	0.762006	0.816438	0.874141	0.935273
102.	0.495093	0.532975	0.573293	0.616176	0.661756	0.710170	0.761564	0.816085	0.873890	0.935139
103.	0.494359	0.532268	0.572621	0.615547	0.661180	0.709658	0.761126	0.815735	0.873641	0.935007
104.	0.493634	0.531569	0.571956	0.614925	0.660609	0.709150	0.760693	0.815389	0.873395	0.934876
105.	0.492915	0.530877	0.571298	0.614309	0.660045	0.708648	0.760264	0.815046	0.873152	0.934746
106.	0.492205	0.530193	0.570647	0.613700	0.659487	0.708152	0.759840	0.814707	0.872911	0.934618
107.	0.491504	0.529516	0.570003	0.613097	0.658935	0.707660	0.759420	0.814371	0.872672	0.934490
108.	0.490813	0.528846	0.569365	0.612500	0.658388	0.707173	0.759004	0.814038	0.872435	0.934364
109.	0.490123	0.528183	0.568734	0.611909	0.657846	0.706691	0.758592	0.813708	0.872201	0.934239
110.	0.489443	0.527527	0.568110	0.611324	0.657310	0.706213	0.758184	0.813382	0.871969	0.934116
111.	0.488770	0.526878	0.567492	0.610745	0.656779	0.705740	0.757780	0.813058	0.871739	0.933993
112.	0.488104	0.526236	0.566880	0.610172	0.656254	0.705272	0.757380	0.812738	0.871511	0.933872
113.	0.487445	0.525600	0.566274	0.609604	0.655733	0.704808	0.756984	0.812420	0.871285	0.933751
114.	0.486793	0.524970	0.565674	0.609042	0.655218	0.704349	0.756591	0.812106	0.871061	0.933632
115.	0.486147	0.524346	0.565080	0.608486	0.654707	0.703894	0.756202	0.811794	0.870840	0.933514
116.	0.485508	0.523729	0.564492	0.607934	0.654201	0.703443	0.755817	0.811486	0.870620	0.933397
117.	0.484875	0.523118	0.563909	0.607388	0.653700	0.702996	0.755435	0.811180	0.870402	0.933281
118.	0.484248	0.522512	0.563332	0.606847	0.653200	0.702554	0.755056	0.810876	0.870186	0.933166
119.	0.483627	0.521913	0.562751	0.606311	0.652712	0.702115	0.754681	0.810576	0.869972	0.933051
120.	0.483012	0.521319	0.562194	0.605780	0.652224	0.701680	0.754309	0.810278	0.869760	0.932938

APPENDIX (*concluded*)

CUMULATIVE AVERAGE FACTORS BASED ON THE LOG-LINEAR CUMULATIVE AVERAGE CURVE THEORY

	90	91	92	93	94	95	96	97	98	99
121.	0.482403	0.520730	0.561633	0.605254	0.651741	0.701250	0.753941	0.809982	0.869550	0.932826
122.	0.481800	0.520148	0.561078	0.604733	0.651263	0.700823	0.753575	0.809689	0.869341	0.932714
123.	0.481203	0.519570	0.560527	0.604216	0.650788	0.700399	0.753213	0.809399	0.869134	0.932604
124.	0.480611	0.518998	0.559981	0.603704	0.650318	0.699980	0.752854	0.809111	0.868929	0.932495
125.	0.480024	0.518431	0.559440	0.603197	0.649852	0.699564	0.752498	0.808825	0.868726	0.932386
126.	0.479443	0.517869	0.558904	0.602694	0.649390	0.699152	0.752145	0.808542	0.868524	0.932278
127.	0.478857	0.517313	0.558373	0.602195	0.648932	0.698743	0.751795	0.808261	0.868324	0.932171
128.	0.478297	0.516761	0.557847	0.601701	0.648478	0.698337	0.751447	0.807983	0.868126	0.932065
129.	0.477731	0.516214	0.557325	0.601211	0.648027	0.697935	0.751103	0.807707	0.867929	0.931960
130.	0.477171	0.515672	0.556807	0.600725	0.647581	0.697537	0.750762	0.807433	0.867733	0.931856
131.	0.476615	0.515135	0.556294	0.600243	0.647138	0.697141	0.750423	0.807161	0.867540	0.931752
132.	0.476065	0.514602	0.555785	0.599765	0.646699	0.696749	0.750087	0.806891	0.867347	0.931650
133.	0.475519	0.514074	0.555281	0.599292	0.646263	0.696360	0.749754	0.806623	0.867157	0.931548
134.	0.474973	0.513550	0.554781	0.598822	0.645831	0.695974	0.749423	0.806358	0.866967	0.931446
135.	0.474442	0.513031	0.554285	0.598356	0.645403	0.695591	0.749095	0.806095	0.866779	0.931346
136.	0.473910	0.512516	0.553793	0.597894	0.644978	0.695211	0.748769	0.805833	0.866593	0.931246
137.	0.473382	0.512005	0.553305	0.597435	0.644556	0.694835	0.748446	0.805574	0.866408	0.931147
138.	0.472859	0.511499	0.552821	0.596981	0.644138	0.694461	0.748126	0.805316	0.866224	0.931049
139.	0.472340	0.510997	0.552341	0.596530	0.643723	0.694090	0.747808	0.805061	0.866042	0.930952
140.	0.471825	0.510499	0.551865	0.596082	0.643311	0.693722	0.747492	0.804807	0.865861	0.930855
141.	0.471312	0.510004	0.551393	0.595638	0.642902	0.693356	0.747179	0.804556	0.865681	0.930759
142.	0.470810	0.509514	0.550925	0.595197	0.642497	0.692994	0.746868	0.804306	0.865503	0.930664
143.	0.470305	0.509028	0.550460	0.594760	0.642094	0.692634	0.746559	0.804058	0.865326	0.930569
144.	0.469810	0.508546	0.549998	0.594327	0.641695	0.692277	0.746253	0.803812	0.865150	0.930475
145.	0.469315	0.508067	0.549541	0.593896	0.641299	0.691923	0.745949	0.803567	0.864972	0.930382
146.	0.468826	0.507592	0.549087	0.593469	0.640905	0.691571	0.745647	0.803325	0.864803	0.930289
147.	0.468340	0.507121	0.548636	0.593045	0.640515	0.691222	0.745347	0.803084	0.864631	0.930197
148.	0.467857	0.506653	0.548189	0.592624	0.640128	0.690875	0.745050	0.802844	0.864460	0.930105
149.	0.467379	0.506189	0.547745	0.592206	0.639743	0.690531	0.744754	0.802607	0.864290	0.930015
150.	0.466904	0.505729	0.547304	0.591792	0.639361	0.690189	0.744461	0.802371	0.864122	0.929924
151.	0.466432	0.505272	0.546867	0.591380	0.638982	0.689850	0.744170	0.802137	0.863954	0.929835
152.	0.465965	0.504818	0.546433	0.590972	0.638605	0.689513	0.743881	0.801904	0.863788	0.929746
153.	0.465500	0.504368	0.546002	0.590566	0.638232	0.689178	0.743593	0.801673	0.863623	0.929657
154.	0.465042	0.503921	0.545574	0.590163	0.637861	0.688846	0.743308	0.801444	0.863459	0.929570
155.	0.464582	0.503478	0.545150	0.589764	0.637492	0.688516	0.743025	0.801216	0.863296	0.929482
156.	0.464122	0.503037	0.544728	0.589367	0.637126	0.688189	0.742743	0.800989	0.863134	0.929396
157.	0.463673	0.502600	0.544310	0.588973	0.636763	0.687863	0.742464	0.800765	0.862974	0.929310
158.	0.463231	0.502166	0.543894	0.588581	0.636402	0.687540	0.742186	0.800541	0.862814	0.929224
159.	0.462787	0.501735	0.543481	0.588193	0.636044	0.687219	0.741911	0.800319	0.862655	0.929139
160.	0.462345	0.501307	0.543072	0.587807	0.635688	0.686901	0.741637	0.800099	0.862498	0.929055

REFERENCES

Andress, Frank J. "The Learning Curve as a Production Tool." *Harvard Business Review*, January–February 1954, pp. 87–97.

Berghell, A. B. "Production Engineering in the Aircraft Industry." New York: McGraw-Hill (1944).

Billon, S. A. "Industrial Learning Curve and Forecasting." *Management International Review* (Germany). 1966, pp. 65–79.

Boren, William H. "Some Applications of the Learning Curve to Government Contracts." *N.A.A. Bulletin*, October 1964, pp. 21–22.

Brennick, Ronald. "The Learning Curve for Labor Hours—For Pricing." *N.A.A. Bulletin*, June 1958, pp. 77–78.

Broadston, James A. "Learning Curve Wage Incentives." *Management Accounting (N.A.A. Bulletin.)*, vol. 49, section 1, August 1968, pp. 15–23.

Hirschmann, Winfred B. "Profit from the Learning Curve." *Harvard Business Review*, January–February 1964, pp. 125–39.

Jordan, Raymond B., "Learning How to Use the Learning Curve." *N.A.A. Bulletin*, January 1958, pp. 27–39.

_____. *How to Use the Learning Curve*. Boston, Mass.: Cahners, 1965.

Morse, Wayne J. "Reporting Production Costs that Follow the Learning Curve Phenomenon." *The Accounting Review*, October 1972, pp. 761–73.

Shroad, Vincent J. "Control of Labor Cost Through the Use of the Learning Curve." *N.A.A. Bulletin*, October 1964, pp. 15–20.

Summers, Edward L., and Welsch, Glenn A. "How the Learning Curve Model Can Be Applied to Profit Planning." *Management Services*, March–April 1970, pp. 45–50.

"The Learning Curve. Management Information, 156." *The Accountant*, January 14, 1967, pp. 47–48.

Taylor, Marvin L. "The Learning Curve—A Basic Cost Projection Tool." *N.A.A. Bulletin*, February 1961, pp. 21–26.

Wright, T. P. "Factors Affecting the Cost of Airplanes." *Journal of Aeronautical Science*, February 1936, pp. 122–28.

Wyer, Rolfe. "The Learning Curve Technique for Direct Labor Management." *N.A.A. Bulletin, Management Accounting*, July 1958, pp. 19–27.

Young, Samuel L. "Misapplications of the Learning Concept." *Journal of Industrial Engineering*, August 1966, pp. 410–15.

36

Input-output analysis

Werner G. Frank*
James Fella†

Origins of input-output analysis

Input-output analysis was developed to deal with the interrelationships between the activities of a group of entities or sectors within some overall system. These sectors are related in that the goods or services produced by one sector (outputs) are utilized as inputs to the activities carried out by one or more other sectors. Although the basic idea behind input-output analysis can be traced back at least as far as the 1750s to the work of the French economist François Quesnay, the development of this tool in its modern form was primarily the result of work done in the 1930s by Wassily Leontief, an economics professor at Harvard University. Leontief was awarded the Nobel prize in economics in 1973 for his important work in input-output analysis.

Macroeconomic applications. As input-output analysis was originally developed by economists, emphasis was placed on analyzing the activities of a national economy, and the sectors were defined as the various industries within that economy. Input-output analysis enabled economists to study how the economy

---

* Professor, University of Wisconsin—Madison.
† Director of Planning, Celanese Corporation.

would react to changes in a set of final demands by consumers, by government, for export, and for capital formation and inventory accumulation. (These final demands represent one way of measuring a country's total output, or gross national product.) Once this technique became better understood and more widely utilized, it was realized that input-output analysis could be applied to many different levels of interrelated economic activities simply by defining the sectors and the overall system in an appropriate way. Economists have applied input-output analysis to smaller economic systems such as a state, a geographic region or community, or a particular set of industries.

Applications to the firm.   Since the technique can be applied to any set of interrelated activities where the outputs produced by one sector are acquired as inputs to another sector, business firms have also applied input-output analysis to their own operations. Individual firms have related their own inputs and outputs to industry sectors in the economy, as well as constructing input-output models for their firm in which the sectors were defined as operating divisions or as production processes.

Input-output models assume that as outputs expand or contract, inputs will change proportionately. It is also necessary that the coefficients incorporated in the model reflect the relationships for the period under study. If these conditions can be accommodated, input-output models can be useful in certain financial planning situations. Plans developed using these models can then also serve as the basis for subsequent control of actual operations.

Explanation of input-output tables

Most input-output applications make use of three basic tables or matrices:

1. A *transaction* table, which shows the total dollar transactions (or physical transfers) between sectors.
2. A table of *direct* input requirements per dollar (or per unit) of output for each sector in the system.
3. A table which presents the *total* (direct plus indirect) requirements per dollar or unit of output to final demand sectors.

In each of these tables, the sectors in the system are listed both as rows and as columns. The columns of input-output tables represent the composition of each sector's purchases, while the rows reveal the distribution of each sector's sales. (See Table 1 for an illustration.)

In most input-output models, there exists one sector (usually referred to as the *primary input sector*) which only supplies inputs to the other sectors. In a macroeconomic input-output model of a national economy, this sector consists of the value-added component (labor, capital consumption, rent, interest, and profit) of an industry's total inputs. Similarly, a sector of *final demand* is included to which the various industries make sales, but which does not supply inputs. In a macroeconomic model, this sector of final demand includes purchases by consumers, the government, investment or inventory accumulations, and net exports.

Most input-output models in current use are characterized as *open* models. The term "open" refers to the fact that the final demand sector is not formally linked to the primary input sector. Input-output models may also be *static* or *dynamic* models. Static models depict relationships as of a given point in time, while dynamic models explicitly describe within the model how the relationships between sectors change over time. Such changes could occur as a result of improvements in technology, changes in relative prices, shifts in tastes, and so forth. Regardless of the type of model used, it is important that the model be representative of the time period under study. Because of the long intervals between the extensive government studies, most firms using economy-wide input-output models in their planning rely on commercial research and consulting firms to provide models incorporating estimated current and future parameter values.

The transaction table. The basic data for an input-output analysis is usually accumulated in a table which shows the total flows of resources between sectors for some period of time. Such a table is usually referred to as a *transaction table.* If each sector produces only a single output, these flows may be measured in terms of physical units. If the sector produces several types of outputs, in order to meet the requirement that only a single type of output be associated with each sector—the sector output may be measured in terms of dollars as a common denominator.

Because this is invariably the case in macroeconomic studies, such input-output studies work with data in dollar terms. Applications within a single firm, however, may find it possible to develop tables showing relationships between sectors in terms of physical flows of resources. If this approach is taken, an analysis initially carried out in physical units can subsequently be translated into dollars by applying appropriate unit costs to the physical measures.

To illustrate a transaction table, a portion of the 1967 input-output study of the U.S. economy carried out by the Bureau of Economic Analysis of the Department of Commerce will be described. This study involved approximately 370 industries, but for comparability with earlier studies and for ease in presentation, the published data were subsequently aggregated to 87 broader categories. Each of these categories or sectors may be related to industry definitions in terms of the Standard Industrial Classification (SIC) codes. The primary iron and steel manufacturing sector, for instance, includes firms whose output is classified as SIC codes 331 (blast furnaces and basic steel products), 332 (iron and steel foundries), 3391 (iron and steel forgings), and 3399 (primary metal products, n.e.c.).

A small portion of the interindustry transactions table for the 1967 U.S. economy is shown in Table 1. The *row* for the iron and steel industry, no. 37, shows where the outputs of that industry are distributed. This table indicates that in 1967 over $3 billion of output of this industry went to the heating, plumbing, and structural metal products industry. Most of the iron and steel industry's output went to various other industrial sectors within the economy. A much smaller portion went to final demand sectors directly. The transactions table indicates that approximately $0.5 billion of output went to satisfy the net export demand, and approximately $800 million went to various other sectors of final demand.

The *column* for the iron and steel industry in this transaction table indicates the composition of that industry's inputs. In 1967, for example, about $1.5 billion of inputs to the iron and steel industry came from the iron and ferroalloy ores mining industry, and over $600 million came from coal mining.

The direct requirements table. The second step in a typical input-output study is to develop the direct requirements table. Each column of this table shows the inputs required per dollar

TABLE 1
Portion of 1967 U.S. economy input-output transaction table (in millions of dollars)

Industry number and name (inputs)	Outputs*									Final Demand					
	1-36	37	38	39	40	41	42	43-87	1-87	Personal consumption expenditures	Net inventory change	Net exports	Government purchases	Total final demand	Total outputs
1-4. (Omitted)															
5. Iron and ferro-alloy ores mining		1,497													
6. (Omitted)															
7. Coal mining		644													
8-36. (Omitted)															
37. Primary iron and steel manufacturing					1,238	3,018	2,208	2,200	30,395	4	514	519	291	1,328	31,723
38-64. (Omitted)		6,017													
65. Transportation		1,420													
66-87. (Omitted)															
Total intermediate industry inputs, 1-87		19,336													
Value added		12,387													
Total inputs		31,723													

* Outputs
1-36 Omitted.
37-Primary iron and steel manufacturing. Column and row 37 do not foot because only 4 of the intermediate input sector rows and only 5 of the intermediate output sector columns are shown.
38-Omitted.
39-Metal containers.
40-Heating, plumbing, and structural metal products.
41-Stampings, screw machine, machine products, and bolts.
42-Other fabricated metal products.
43-87 Omitted.
Total intermediate industry outputs, 1-87.
Source: U.S. Department of Commerce, *Survey of Current Business* (Washington, D.C.: Government Printing Office, February 1974), pp. 38-43.

(or unit, if the analysis is being carried out in physical units) of that sector's output. Table 2 shows a portion of the direct requirements per dollar of output for the iron and steel industry. The values in this table are calculated by simply dividing the dollar transaction amounts in each column of Table 1 by the total dollar output of that sector. Table 2 indicates, for example, that each $1.00 of output from the iron and steel industry requires about $0.05 of input from the iron and ferroalloy ores mining industry. ($0.047 = $1.497 billion/$31.723 billion). Similarly, for each dollar of output, approximately $0.02 of coal ($644 million/$31.723 billion) and $0.045 of transportation services ($1.42 billion/ $31.723 billion) are required.

The total (direct and indirect) requirements table. While the direct requirements table shows the amount of each input directly acquired by each industry, it does not consider the fact that a given input may also be required by other industries which, in turn, supply that industry. Thus, although the iron and steel industry buys $0.045 worth of transportation services for each dollar of output, transportation is also a significant input to other industries providing inputs to the steel industry. To increase the output of the iron and steel industry by one dollar thus requires the transportation industry to also provide enough services to these various other industries. In addition, the output of the iron and steel industry is one of the inputs to the transportation industry. To generate one dollar of iron and steel output for final demand, net of any iron and steel output which its suppliers may require, the iron and steel industry must produce

TABLE 2
Portion of 1967 U.S. economy direct requirements per dollar of gross output table

Industry number and name *(inputs)*	*37. Primary iron and steel manufacturing*
5. Iron and ferroalloy ores mining	0.04717
7. Coal mining	0.02030
37. Primary iron and steel manufacturing	0.18966
65. Transportation	0.04477
All other intermediate industries	0.30763
Total intermediate industry input	0.60953
Value added	0.39047
Total inputs	1.00000

Source: U.S. Department of Commerce, *Survey of Current Business* (Washington, D.C.: Government Printing Office, February 1974), p. 46.

TABLE 3

Portion of 1967 U.S. economy total (direct and indirect) requirements per dollar of delivery to final demand

Industry number and name (inputs)	37. Primary iron and steel manufacturing
5. Iron and ferroalloy ores mining	0.06366
7. Coal mining	0.03160
37. Primary iron and steel manufacturing	1.27607
65. Transportation	0.08307

Source: U.S. Department of Commerce, *Survey of Current Business* (Washington, D.C.: Government Printing Office, February, 1974), p. 52.

more than one dollar of output. When all of these indirect relationships are also considered, the total requirements from the transportation industry to produce $1.00 of iron and steel output to final demand sectors increases from approximately $0.045 to somewhat more than $0.08. A portion of these direct plus indirect requirements for iron and steel manufacturing in the 1967 U.S. economy is shown in Table 3.

The usual way of computing the values in this table of total requirements per dollar of final demand is to use matrix algebra. The table, or matrix, of direct input coefficients, suitably adjusted, is "inverted," and the resulting matrix contains the required total input coefficients. (In mathematical terms, the direct coefficient matrix, $[D]$, is subtracted from an identity matrix, $[I]$, and the resulting $[I - D]$ matrix is inverted.) This matrix inversion, in essence, provides the solution for the set of simultaneous equations which relates the inputs to the outputs for every sector in the entire system. Because of the very large numbers of computations required to invert sizable matrices, computer routines are utilized to perform this calculation.

This table of total requirement coefficients is frequently used to evaluate the impact of alternative sets of final demand on the various sectors. Using an up-to-date table of input-output coefficients, multiplying this total requirements matrix by a set of final demands will provide the total output required of each industry in the system to support that set of demands. Once the level of output is established for each industry, the direct input-output coefficients for a given industry can then be used to determine the composition of inputs for that industry, if this is desired.

USE OF INPUT-OUTPUT ANALYSIS
IN PLANNING

Analyzing market potential

Since a transaction matrix shows in each row the distribution of sales (outputs) of a given industrial sector, a firm may be able to use such information to evaluate its market penetration by industry, relative to the overall sales made by the entire industry of which it is a part. In such an application, a firm would break down its own sales by industry using the same industrial categories appearing in an available input-output transaction table. Transaction table outputs to industrial segments not matched by the firm's sales could indicate an untapped market.

It must be remembered, however, that each industrial sector covers firms producing a fairly broad range of products. Differences between one firm's sales outputs and that of the entire industry may, accordingly, reflect differences in product mix as well as differences in penetration. Such product mix differences may be minimized by utilizing more detailed input-output tables incorporating finer breakdowns. In a Conference Board study, Elliott-Jones (Input-Output Analysis) illustrates how markets in the paper industry may be analyzed using the appropriate portions of a 478 sector input-output table for the U.S. economy.

Evaluating expansion alternatives

Firms considering expanding their operations may be interested in identifying those areas which complement their present activities in some particular way. Analysis of the merger prospects between North American Aviation and Rockwell involved the use of an input-output model to evaluate Rockwell's product mix in terms of growth prospects of various sectors in the economy (*Business Week*, Sept. 23, 1967). Management may wish to expand into industries which are related to their existing operations on the supply side, or they may wish to expand in such a way as to achieve a greater degree of vertical integration in terms of the chain of products going to ultimate consumers in the economy. Input-output tables serve as a natural place to begin in identifying such potential areas of interest. Since each column indicates purchases by a particular industry, this provides a way of identifying major possibilities for expansion on the supply side. On the other hand, if the interest is in expanding in the direction of upward vertical integration, analysis of data in the appropriate rows will reveal the major links in the chain leading to the ultimate consumer.

From a different perspective, management may be interested in moving into areas which have economic characteristics that are quite different from their present product line. Here, attention may be directed in an input-output table to those sectors which serve different segments of final demand, which are expected to grow at different rates, or which react in a different way to cyclical economic fluctuations. If acquisition efforts are directed toward these sectors, a more stable pattern of economic activity for the firm may be achieved.

Integrating macroeconomic planning with the firm's financial planning model

Many companies now utilize a formal planning model of their firm's operations in their annual budgeting and profit-planning process. These corporate financial planning models typically rely on forecasts of product sales as a key input variable. While sales forecasts may be generated in a variety of ways, refinements of the sales forecasting procedures often move in the direction of relating sales forecasts for the company's products to underlying basic factors in the general economy. One effective way of accomplishing this linkage is to use an input-output model. Russo (*Management Accounting,* vol. 58) describes how an input-output based sales forecast was used by a large chemical company to evaluate its projected financial requirements.

An input-output model is an attractive way of integrating a model of the firm to macroeconomic variables for several reasons. One desirable characteristic of most input-output models of the economy is that the definition of the final demand sectors corresponds to the components of gross national product: personal consumption expenditures, gross private domestic investment, net export of goods and services, and government purchases of goods and services. If forecasts of these components are developed, this set of forecasted final demands can be used as described on page 1024 to generate forecasts of the activity levels (total outputs) of each industry included as a sector in the input-output model. In addition, the implications of various alternative economic policies can be explored by using the input-output model as a simulation tool.

A variety of "what-if" type questions may be evaluated by relating a policy issue to its expected impact on final demand components. A possible change in tariffs, for example, may lead to the expectation that suggests that net exports will drop by 10 percent. This change in the net export component of final demand can then be evaluated by using a schedule of final demand incorporating this reduced export demand as input to the input-output model for the economy. An illustration of how Combustion Engineering used an input-output model to explore the sensitivity of its refractories-market forecasts to changes in key components of GNP is provided by Yost and Stowell (The Institute of Management Sciences, 17th International Conference.)

While a variety of macroeconomic forecasting models exists, an advantage of using a model based on input-output analysis is that such a model, by its very design, develops forecasts of industry levels of economic activity. This makes it possible to provide a simple linkage, through a share-of-the-industry-market parameter, to the sales of the firm. Other macroeconomic models typically only provide forecasts for the economy as a whole. Such forecasts by themselves may be inadequate since the state of the total economy and that of any particular industry may be quite different.

Developing an input-output model for a divisionalized firm

The applications in the previous sections of this chapter have all utilized data at the industry and national economy levels. In these models, the individual sectors consisted of industries, and the entire national economy was identified with the overall system. It is also possible to develop an input-output model at the firm level. In such a model, the individual sectors will consist of divisions within the firm and the overall system is represented by the firm as a whole. This type of model will be most useful where the activities of the firm are closely related, and significant amounts of internal transfers take place.

In such a model, each of the rows and columns represents a single division within the firm. The primary input sector would consist of purchases of materials, labor, and services from outside the firm. The final demand sector would typically represent purchases of the divisions' products by other firms. While the outside demand might be viewed as being composed of demand from a number of sources (outside sales might be determined by summarizing sales by customer, by geographic region, and so forth) for the purpose of using the input-output model, all outside demand for the output of a single division would be added together and treated as a single, composite amount. This corresponds to summing all the components of final demand for the economy (consumption by households, investment, net exports, and so forth) when dealing with a macroeconomic input-output model.

EXHIBIT 1
Activities of a hypothetical 3-division firm (divisionalized firm model)

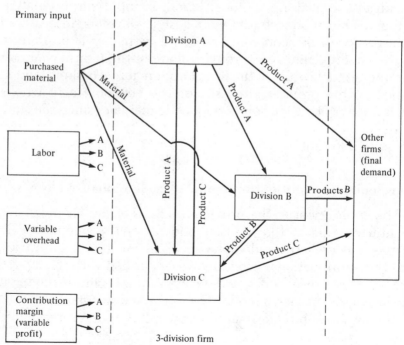

An input-output model for a hypothetical three-division firm is presented in Exhibit 1. In this example, all three divisions sell their products to outside firms. In addition, Division A's output is used as raw material by Divisions B and C. Division B also supplies part of its output to Division C, while C, in turn, manufactures a product which is utilized as one of the inputs to Division A. For notational convenience, the output of Division A is termed Product A, and similar notation is used for the other divisions.

As described on page 1020, the table of direct unit input-output coefficients for macroeconomic models must usually be derived from a transaction matrix. The value of each input-output coefficient is inferred from the total amount of each input factor used in a given period of time by a sector (industry) to produce its total output for that period. Although this same procedure can be followed by a firm in developing divisional input-output coefficients, often either prior analysis of the division's operations or budget targets will exist which can provide this information directly. The direct unit requirements table for this divisional model, obtained from such sources, is shown in Table 4.

The first column of Table 4 reveals that to produce $1.00 worth of Product A requires $0.10 of Product C, $0.20 of other raw materials purchased from outside companies, $0.40 of labor, and $0.20 of variable overhead. Each $1.00 of sales of Product A generates $0.10 of contribution margin (variable profit). In this model, the various elements of the primary inputs have been kept separate and treated as individual sectors, as opposed to the usual practice of summarizing these components in a

TABLE 4
Direct unit requirements per dollar of output (divisional firm model)

Inputs	Prod- uct A	Prod- uct B	Prod- uct C	Pur- chased material	Labor	Variable over- head	Contri- bution margin
1. Product A	0	0.2	0.3	0	0	0	0
2. Product B	0	0	0.1	0	0	0	0
3. Product C	0.1	0	0	0	0	0	0
4. Purchased material	0.2	0.3	0.1	0	0	0	0
5. Labor	0.4	0.2	0.3	0	0	0	0
6. Variable overhead	0.2	0.1	0.1	0	0	0	0
7. Contribution margin	0.1	0.2	0.1	0	0	0	0
Total	1.0	1.0	1.0	0	0	0	0

TABLE 5
Total requirements per dollar of sales to outside firms (divisionalized firm model)

Inputs	1. Product A	2. Product B	3. Product C	4. Purchased material	5. Labor	6. Variable overhead	7. Contribution margin
1. Product A	1.0330	0.2066	0.3306	0	0	0	0
2. Product B	0.0103	1.0021	0.1033	0	0	0	0
3. Product C	0.1033	0.0207	1.0330	0	0	0	0
4. Purchased material	0.2200	0.3440	0.2004	1	0	0	0
5. Labor	0.4463	0.2893	0.4628	0	1	0	0
6. Variable overhead	0.2180	0.1436	0.1800	0	0	1	0
7. Contribution margin	0.1157	0.2231	0.1570	0	0	0	1

single value-added primary input sector. While this latter practice is usually followed in developing macroeconomic models, it is often more useful to keep these individual components separate when developing input-output models at the level of the firm.

After the matrix of direct input-output coefficients shown in Table 4 has been developed, data from this matrix is used to generate the matrix of total (direct plus indirect) requirements coefficients. These total requirements coefficients are computed through a matrix inversion process in the same way that the corresponding coefficients for the macroeconomic input-output model was calculated (see page 1024). The total requirements coefficients for the divisional model are presented in Table 5.

The interpretation of the coefficients in this table of total input requirements is similar to that for the national economy model. The value in the first row of Column 2, for example, indicates that for each $1.00 of Product B sold at outside firms or accumulated in ending inventory (valued at selling price), about $0.21 of Product A will need to be manufactured. Although only $0.20 of Product A goes directly into Product B (this figure appears in the corresponding location of Table 4), an additional amount is indirectly required. This additional requirement arises from the fact that slightly more than one dollar of Product B must be produced for each dollar's worth of sales. Product A requires inputs of Product C, which in turn requires inputs of Product B as well as Product A. The requirements of Product C account for the additional indirect requirements of Product A reflected in the $0.21 direct plus indirect requirements figure.

In developing the corporate profit plan for this divisionalized firm, total sales dollar forecasts for Products, A, B, and C would initially be established. If inventories of any of the products are to be built up during the year, or if some existing inventories are to be liquidated, the sales figures would be adjusted for these planned inventory changes, valued at market prices. These adjusted sales figures can then be used to calculate the total level of each division's activity required to support these desired levels of output. If $100,000 of Product A and $200,000 of Products B and C are to be sold during the period covered by the planning horizon, the total input requirements necessary are shown in Table 6.

TABLE 6
Total dollar requirements for profit plan (divisionalized firm model)

I.	Total planned sales to outside firms:	
	Product A..	$100,000
	Product B..	200,000
	Product C..	200,000
	Total	$500,000
II.	Gross divisional output required (at market price):	
	Product A..	$210,744
	Product B..	222,107
	Product C..	221,074
III.	Total input requirements:	
	Purchased materials...	$130,889
	Labor...	195,041
	Variable overhead	86,467
	Contribution margin	87,603
		$500,000

The total amount of Product A required, $211,000 (rounded) is calculated by multiplying in turn each of the total (direct plus indirect) input-output coefficients given in the first row of Table 5 by the corresponding final demand for that product, and then summing these individual results:

$$(1.033) \ (\$100,000) + (0.2066) \ (\$200,000)$$
$$+ (0.3306) \ (\$200,000) = \$211,000 \ (\text{rounded})$$

While this involves only straightforward arithmetic, the computations for a system containing many sectors are tedious to perform. For convenience, the calculations may be relegated to the computer by making use of a standard matrix multiplication routine. (In mathematical terms, the desired vector of total requirements is calculated by postmultiplying the appropriate inverse containing the direct plus indirect unit coefficients by the specified vector of final demands.) Once the total outputs of each division are obtained, individual inputs for each division may be obtained by using the direct coefficients given in Table 4. This breakdown is shown in Table 7.

Once the direct and total input coefficients have been determined, it is comparatively simple to evaluate alternative schedules of final demand, especially if programmed matrix arithmetic routines on a computer are utilized. This makes it feasible to perform various types of sensitivity analyses. If there is particular

TABLE 7
Divisional inputs required for profit model (divisionalized firm model)

Inputs	Division A	Division B	Division C
1. Product A	—	$ 44,422	$ 66,322
2. Product B	—	—	22,107
3. Product C	$ 21,074	—	—
4. Purchased material	42,149	66,632	22,107
5. Labor	84,298	44,421	66,322
6. Variable overhead	42,149	22,211	22,108
7. Contribution margin	21,074	44,421	22,108
Total	$210,744	$222,107	$221,074

uncertainty about the value of certain sales forecasts or of the value of some of the input-output coefficients, these values can be varied systematically over the range of interest and the results on the profit plan can be observed. Similarly, instead of relying on a single most likely estimate, optimistic and pessimistic estimates may be made and the input-output analysis may be repeated using these extreme values. The results obtained under these more unlikely conditions may nevertheless provide useful insights as to where potential bottlenecks could arise. Being forewarned of the possibilities of such troublesome areas allows management to respond more quickly and in a more appropriate fashion should these contingencies arise.

The illustration described above does not specify how the sales forecasts for the divisions' products are being generated. It would also be possible to relate the divisional model of the firm to an industry model of the economy to provide these sales forecasts. An analysis at the economy level of the type described on pages 1025 and 1026 would provide information about forecasted demands at the industry level. Using share-of-the-market parameters, these industry demands can be translated into demand for each division's products, which would then serve as the final demand schedule required for the divisional input-output model.

Another approach to developing an input-output model for a corporation was followed by Celanese (*Sales Management,* vol. 99). The sectors in their model were defined in terms of the company's major product groups, and data for the matrix was obtained by analyzing the firm's sales, purchases, and intracom-

pany transfers. Firms have also used these models as a preliminary stage in moving toward an optimizing (linear programming)
model.

Establishing cost standards for a complex
production process

In certain environments, such as the chemical industry, the
development of cost standards is especially difficult because the
production process is not a straightforward linear progression
of production operations where the output of each successive
operation becomes the input to the next. For many of the individual operations, the output may be utilized in several alternative production streams. For this reason, there may be no single
fixed sequence of operations. Moreover, the outputs of certain
processes may be recycled downstream, where they are utilized
in some operation occurring earlier in the overall production
process. Additionally, losses may occur within a given process,
so that not all of the potential output of a particular production
process will be available for use in other processes or for sale
to outside customers. These conditions make it difficult to establish reliable yield and cost standards on an *a priori* basis.

In these circumstances, the input-output model provides a
useful way of describing the production operations in a way
which is consistent with the accountant's concepts of unit physical and dollar standards. The input-output framework can be
used to accumulate data on the physical flow of resources into,
and product flow out of, each of the individual production processes for some period of time when the plant is operating in
a satisfactory fashion. This information is then placed in a suitably
constructed transaction table or matrix, and the direct and total
unit requirement coefficients are then computed in the same
way as was done for the input-output models described earlier
in the chapter. The values obtained in these input-output tables
represent the desired physical standards for this application.

In the previous applications, the input-output analysis was
carried out entirely in financial terms. While an analysis in dollar
terms may be necessary if the basic data is only available in
dollars, or if the sectors considered are broadly defined so that
the use of the dollar as a common denominator is required,

measurement for input-output models is not restricted to dollar measures. The analysis may be carried out in terms of physical units if this is desirable, and the results later translated into dollar terms by the application of suitable unit prices.

To illustrate an input-output analysis of several interrelated production operations which is carried out in physical terms, a simplified application will be described and illustrated in Exhibit 2. The Adams Co. manufactures two products, P1 and P2. The production of P1 begins in Department 1 and the semifinished output is transferred to Department 2 where it is completed. Some loss of the product occurs in both departments. While semifinished P1 has no commercial market, it is used, along with other purchased raw materials, in the manufacture of Product P2.

EXHIBIT 2
Activities of Adams Company for a period of standard operations

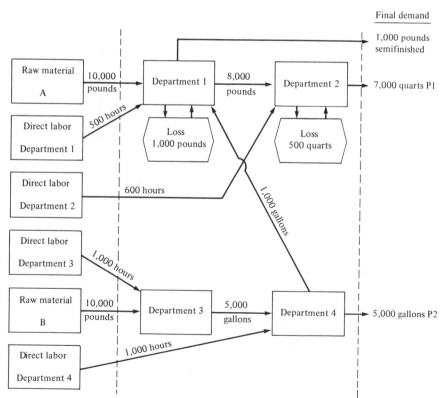

TABLE 8
Transaction matrix, Adams Company

Input \ Output	3. Semifinished P1	5. Product P1	8. Semifinished P2	10. Product P2	Inventory increase and outside sales	Total
1. Raw material A	10,000					10,000 lbs.
2. Direct labor—Department 1	500					500 hrs.
3. Semifinished P1	1,000	8,000			1,000	10,000 lbs.
4. Direct labor—Department 2		600				600 hrs.
5. Product P1		500			7,000	7,500 qts.
6. Raw material B			10,000			10,000 lbs.
7. Direct labor—Department 3			1,000			1,000 lbs.
8. Semifinished P2				5,000		5,000 gal.
9. Direct labor—Department 4				1,000		1,000 hrs.
10. Product P2	1,000				5,000	6,000 gals.

Note. Only nonzero elements and columns shown.

Production of P2 begins in Department 3. The output of processing occurring in this department is transferred to Department 4 where it is mixed with semifinished P1, and processed to yield P2. Losses involved with the production of P2 are negligible. P2, in addition to being produced for sale to outside customers, is used along with other raw materials in Department 1.

If there is extensive engineering knowledge of the nature of the production processes involved in the manufacture of P1 and P2, this information may be used to construct the table of direct input-output coefficients. If the process is relatively new, however, such information may not be available. In these circumstances, records of the total amounts of actual inputs used and outputs obtained for a period of standard operations can be used to generate this direct requirements table. Only prime cost inputs (material and direct labor) are shown in this illustration, although the analysis could be extended to include other input factors. Normal processing losses are shown in this diagram as special sectors or categories with arrows leading in both directions to indicate that some of the production (output) of a given sector has also been consumed (used as input) in the processing taking place in that sector.

Table 8 summarizes the flows shown in Exhibit 2 in the form of a transactions table. The direct unit requirements table, which shows the direct input-output coefficients, is obtained by dividing each entry in a given column by the total gross output of that sector. This information is shown in Table 9. While these direct requirements coefficients are useful if the focus is only on the activities of a single department, it is difficult to derive cost standards for departments because of the interrelationships and feedback which exists between the various departments. This problem can be solved by using information from the total requirements (inverse) matrix, which is shown in Table 10. Since the total requirements matrix takes into account all the relationships inherent in the overall system, it provides cumulative totals from which a set of consistent dollar standards may be derived.

The unit costs of Products P1 and P2 in both the semifinished stage and the finished form are most easily computed by multiplying the elements in the appropriate column of the total requirements (inverse) matrix (Table 10) by the corresponding unit cost for each element, and then summing these individual prod-

TABLE 9
Direct unit requirements, Adams Company

Input	3. Semi-finished P1 (per pound)	5. Product P1 (per quart)	8. Semi-finished P2 (per gallon)	10. Product P2 (per gallon)
1. Raw material	1.0 lb.			
2. Direct labor—				
Department 1	0.05 hrs.			
3. Semifinished P1	0.1 lb.	1.067		0.167
4. Direct labor—				
Department 2		0.08		
5. Product P1		0.067		
6. Raw material B			2.0	
7. Direct labor—				
Department 3			0.2	
8. Semifinished P2				0.83
9. Direct labor—				
Department 4				0.17
10. Product P2	0.1			

Note. Only nonzero elements and columns shown.

ucts. (In mathematical terms, a unit-cost row vector of input prices is multiplied by the inverse matrix.) If the unit costs of the primary inputs are $2, $5, 0, $8, 0, $1, $6, 0, $8, and 0 (zeros represent sectors which are *not* primary inputs), the result of this calculation for semifinished P1 (Sector 3) is $3 per unit, as shown below:

Outside (primary) units	Unit cost	Physical requirements (from Col. 3, Table 10)	Total component cost per unit of semifinished P1
Raw material A	$2/lb.	1.132 lbs.	$2.264
Direct labor—Department 1	$5/hr.	0.0566 hrs.	0.283
Raw material B	$1/lb.	0.1887 lbs.	0.189
Direct labor—Department 3	$6/hr.	0.0189 hrs.	0.113
Direct labor—Department 4	$8/hr.	0.0189 hrs.	0.151
Total unit cost			$3.000

While it is convenient to derive these unit costs using the physical requirements from the inverse matrix, for internal use within the accounting department a more conventional presentation is to cost out a product using only those inputs going directly into the product. Once the product costs have been established, the direct input coefficients (Table 9) can be used to develop unit cost standards. These computations are shown in Table 11. As can be seen, the $3.00 unit cost presented in

TABLE 10
Total unit physical requirements (inverse) matrix, Adams Company

Input	1. Raw material–P1	2. Direct labor–1	3. Semi-finished P1	4. Direct labor–2	5. Product P1	6. Raw material–P2	7. Direct labor–3	8. Semi-finished P2	9. Direct labor–4	10. Product P2
1. Raw material P1	1.0	•	1.132	•	1.294	•	•	•	•	0.189
2. Direct labor—1		1.0	.057		0.065					0.009
3. Semifinished P1			1.132		1.294					0.189
4. Direct labor—2				1.0	0.086					
5. Product P1					1.071					
6. Raw material P2			0.189		0.216	1.0		2.0		1.698
7. Direct labor—3			0.019		0.022		1.0	0.2		0.170
8. Semifinished P2			0.094		0.108			1.0		0.849
9. Direct labor—4			0.019		0.022				1.0	0.170
10. Product P2			0.113		0.129					1.019

Note. Only nonzero elements, rounded, shown.

TABLE 11
Unit product costs, Adams Company

Input	Semifinished P1	Product P1	Semifinished P2	Product P2
1. Raw material A at $2/lb.	$2.00	.	.	.
2. Direct labor—Department 1 at $5/hr.	0.25			
3. Semifinished P1 at $3/lb.	0.30*	$3.20		$0.50
4. Direct labor—Department 2 at $8/hr.		0.64		
5. Product P1 at $3/lb.		0.2743†		
6. Raw material B at $1/lb.			$2.00	
7. Direct labor—Department 3 at $6/hr.			1.20	
8. Semifinished P2 at $3.20/gal......				2.67
9. Direct labor—Department 4 at $8/hr.				1.33
10. Product P2 at $4.50/gal.	0.45			
Total unit cost	$3.00	$4.1143	$3.20	$4.50

* Represents 10% of gross output lost.
† Represents loss of 6.67% of gross output.

the first column of Table 11 is identical with the unit cost derived above from the total physical requirements matrix.

A case history of a similar application in a chemical company is described by Arnoff (*Management Accounting,* vol. 51). In this application, a highly complex process of product flows involving much branching and recycling was traced through a series of process cost centers and holding centers using a variation of input-output analysis to arrive at product costs. In a quite different environment, Cleverly (*Health Services Research,* vol. 10) describes how input-output analysis was used to develop a budget system for a 210-bed general hospital. Twenty-seven departments or product centers were incorporated in the model. Costs derived from this model could then be used for pricing and output decisions, as well as for planning and cost control.

EXTENSIONS OF INPUT-OUTPUT ANALYSIS FOR CONTROL

Use of input-output models in performance evaluation

A very desirable feature inherent in the use of a formal model for planning is that it then becomes possible to use the plans generated by the model to evaluate subsequent performance. While a plan or budget generated by any procedure is useful to some extent as a basis for evaluating actual results, if that plan originates in an informal, unstructured way, actual results must, of necessity, be compared to the original fixed budget or plan. There is no systematic and objective way of later adjusting such plans to reflect changes in assumptions which are no longer appropriate.

A key advantage in using flexible budgets to evaluate performance is that the original budgets can be restated to show what should have been accomplished given the level of activity which actually took place. These flexible budgets are typically used to eliminate the effect of volume differences when evaluating production managers, since volume is considered to be uncontrollable by this group of managers. This same approach can be applied to achieve flexibility in any dimension which is not deemed to be the responsibility of a given manager if a method exists to adjust the plan for differences in that factor. Input-output models provide such a method of adjusting for departures in the levels of basic economic factors as they are reflected in the final demand for the economy.

If actual factors for these final demand components differ from the values assumed in establishing the firm's original operating and profit plans, a revised set of plans can be developed to serve as the benchmarks for comparing the results of actual operations. A firm with a significant national market might develop its quarterly sales forecasts, for example, by applying target share-of-market percentages to total industry demands. The industry demands could be computed using an input-output model incorporating certain estimates for the various factors included in the final demand for GNP—personal consumption expenditures, governmental expenditures, net exports, and capital expenditures. (This procedure was described on pp. 1026–27). Instead of comparing actual operating results with this initial plan, however, the plan can be adjusted by using the *actual* values for the GNP components, as they have materialized during the quarter. In this way, managers of the firm are evaluated against the background of economic conditions actually prevailing during the period in question, and the effects of forecasting errors relating to these macroeconomic factors can be eliminated from the performance evaluation. This approach was taken by Combustion Engineering in evaluating profit center performance (Yost and Stowell, T.I.M.S. 17th International Conference).

Although the above example described performance evaluation in terms of an input-output model at the level of the national economy, the same approach can be used at any level. Most planning applications of input-output analysis require that an appropriate set of final output demands be specified. These planning models naturally lend themselves to developing at a later date alternative plans which incorporate the actual levels of final outputs for a given period. These revised plans, having eliminated the effect of final demand forecasting errors, can then be used in evaluating performance for that period.

LIMITATIONS AND CAUTIONS IN THE USE OF INPUT-OUTPUT ANALYSIS

Assumptions of the input-output model

Since a model, by definition, is a simplification of some real-world set of phenomena, it will not capture every detail. Input-output models, similarly, rely on certain assumptions in order to achieve a useful representation with a minimum of structure. Accountants wishing to apply input-output analysis should be aware of these assumptions. If an application is carried out in which these assumptions are severely violated, the information produced by the model is likely to contain significant error and to be of limited value.

The static input-output model assumes that:

1. The direct input-output coefficients developed at one point in time will be applicable to a later application.
2. Over some relevant range, an increase (or decrease) in the output of each sector in the system will result in a proportionate increase (or decrease) in each of the inputs to the sector.
3. Although the activities carried out by each sector may have many different inputs, each sector must have only a single output. Alternatively, if a sector produces several different outputs, the mix of these outputs is assumed to be constant.

The first assumption involves the stability of the input-output coefficients over time. If there has been a significant time lag since the set of input-output coefficients was determined, these coefficients may no longer represent the current input-output relationships. These changes may reflect improvements in the production technology itself, or differences which have resulted from changes in relative prices. This is especially a problem if the national economy input-output tables prepared by the U.S. Department of Commerce are to be utilized. There is a lag of several years between the time the data is collected and the issuance of these input-output tables. Moreover, since these tables are not issued for every year, the latest set of tables may relate to a year in which the general economic conditions were quite different from those prevailing in the year of a proposed application. This particular problem is likely to be less severe for input-output models based on data for an individual firm. In these circumstances, the firm's own information system can be relied upon to provide more current data.

Several alternative approaches exist to deal with this problem. One commonly used procedure is to extrapolate the values of a series of coefficients relating to prior years into the future. Often a trend may be seen in the pattern of the coefficients over time, and this trend may then be projected. In other cases, knowledge of changes in the technology of specific production processes utilized in a particular industry may be used to estimate directly the future values of input-output coefficients for that industry. The most elaborate approach for dealing with this problem is to construct a *dynamic input-output model.* Here a formal model is developed which explicitly describes the functional relationships between the variation in the values of the input-output coefficients and the passage of time. If the application involves an economy-wide input-output model, commercial sources may be used to provide models incorporating more current input-output coefficients.

The second assumption incorporated in input-output models, the proportionality of changes in inputs and the corresponding outputs, restricts the use of these models to applications where the resources consumed (along with their total costs) vary directly with the outputs produced. At the firm level, this suggests that inputs be limited to items such as direct materials, direct labor, and other factors typically considered within the category of variable costs. It also limits the application of input-output models to a relevant range of activities over which significant economies (or diseconomies) of scale are not present.

The third assumption requires that each sector produce only a single output, or alternatively that it produce a constant mix of products. This assumption can normally be satisfied by the appropriate design of the input-output model for applications within the firm. In these situations, the accountant can break down the sectors in such a way that this condition will be met. Divisions, departments, product lines, production processes, and so forth, may be grouped together or divided into separate sectors to accomplish this. Where this cannot be done because of existing data limitations, a given product output mix must be established for those sectors which generate several different outputs, and input-output coefficients must be established for this particular mix. A change in product mix would then call for a suitable revision in the input-output coefficients.

While none of these assumptions are likely to hold in a strict sense, in many cases the departures will not be so serious as to impair significantly the usefulness of the results. It should also be noted that similar assumptions apply to other accounting techniques, such as break-even analysis and standard costs—techniques which are among the most widely used and effective in cost accounting.

37

Zero base budgeting:
From the ground up

Robert A. Bonsack*
Thomas F. Rowan†

Zero base budgeting (ZBB), the hottest 1970s buzzword in financial management circles, rose to prominence on the coattails of its most famous advocate, Jimmy Carter. The business community's reaction to the new concept in management was to ask: How does ZBB work and how does it apply to my organization? The purpose of this chapter is to provide both an overview of the mechanics of ZBB as it was originally published and implemented and more importantly, a discussion of the many considerations involved in adapting ZBB to different business environments. The following discussion is therefore grouped into sections dealing with:

The origin of ZBB.

The ZBB concept.

Mechanics of ZBB.

Applying ZBB.

Implementing ZBB.

Closing.

The closing paragraphs present the authors' prediction with respect to the role ZBB will ultimately take in the conduct and

---

* Principal, Peat, Marwick, Mitchell & Co.

† Manager, Peat, Marwick, Mitchell & Co.

control of business and how it will fare compared to other "modern management tools."

ORIGINS OF ZBB

ZBB, as it's known today, was developed in 1968 by Peter A. Pyhrr, then Manager of Staff Control at Texas Instruments (TI). As Manager of Staff Control, Mr. Pyhrr's responsibilities included preparing the annual operating budget for the Staff and Research Divisions. Knowing that cuts would be required in the 1969 budget, Mr. Pyhrr requested that managers identify a portion of their proposed budgets that could be cut. For example, if a 10 percent budget cut was identified by a department slated for a 5 percent cut, upper management reviewing committees would have the opportunity to choose what would be cut to meet the budget's ceiling.

Mr. Pyhrr's special ingredient for preparing the operating budget created a new awareness among TI's management. Ironically, senior executives realized that they knew more about the projects cut from the proposed budget than they knew about projects included in the approved budget. This awareness was attributable to the close review given the projects at or near the budget cutoff.

Subsequently, a series of meetings was held to review the approved projects of each department. Three basic problems were identified during these reviews:

1. Realistic goals and objectives had not been established in advance of the budget.
2. Basic operating decisions having direct budget impact had not been made.
3. Budget cuts tended to be arbitrary ("Everyone must cut 5 percent") and not necessarily in accordance with changing workloads.

To address these problems, Pyhrr essentially formalized a basic preexistent budgeting philosophy that has since become known as zero base budgeting. ZBB was used at TI to prepare the 1970 budget for the Staff and Research Divisions, and was expanded throughout all divisions of TI for the 1971 budget.

Pyhrr's ZBB experience at TI was published in the December

1970 issue of the *Harvard Business Review*. His article was read by the Georgia Governor, Jimmy Carter. The concept's immediate appeal to Governor Carter resulted in Pyhrr's eventual departure from TI to help install ZBB in the State of Georgia for fiscal 1973.

To date, ZBB has been adopted by numerous state and local agencies, as well as by several firms in the private sector. At President Carter's direction, the ZBB approach is being pilot tested at the federal level, and he has committed himself to the very formidable task of implementing ZBB across the federal government.

THE ZBB CONCEPT

As its name suggests, ZBB is a "from the ground up" approach that may be used to prepare proposed budgets. Using the ZBB approach requires a thorough review, analysis, and justification of *all* activities the budget proposes to fund.

The ZBB approach differs from the so-called traditional budgeting approach in that it focuses far more attention on the justification of current spending levels. Under the traditional approach, management reviews and related budget adjustments tend to focus on the new (incremental) projects, while the much larger budget base (representing current spending) receives disproportionately less, if any, attention.

The ZBB approach is designed to remedy this imbalance by requiring that all current activities be reevaluated on a merit basis before inclusion in the proposed budget. An underlying assumption of ZBB is that budget ceilings do exist; therefore, not all proposed projects or spending levels can be funded.

Accordingly, there is a need to weigh programs and projects, both current and proposed, against one another to prioritize each within the confines of the budget ceiling. Pyhrr's ZBB technique includes a method for reducing the proposed budget to discrete component units so that they may be analyzed, reviewed, and ultimately prioritized by using a ranking system.

MECHANICS OF ZBB

The mechanics of the ZBB process establish a very basic and logical approach that:

- Forces evaluation of all projects.
- Forces participation by multiple levels of management.
- Provides top management with well-defined alternatives and consequences
- Provides a comprehensive framework within which to make budgeting decisions.

ZBB is highly applicable to people-intensive functions, such as overhead areas, where the relationship of costs to volume is not well defined. For example, proposed expenditures in the selling, research, and administrative areas are at least partially subjective and independent of volume levels in the short term. Whether three or four research technicians are required to support development is largely judgmental.

Conversely, ZBB does not apply to the production area with regard to direct manufacturing costs because these costs are directly related to volume. If each widget contains five pounds of rubber and requires two labor hours to produce, then a budgeted volume of 100 widgets dictates that 500 pounds of rubber and 200 labor hours will be required. There are no alternatives to these direct manufacturing costs, hence the ZBB technique is inapplicable here.

The mechanics of the ZBB process can be easily understood and applied to a variety of business organizations. These mechanics can best be summarized in the following steps:

1. Establish "decision units." Decision units are defined as discrete activities which can be separately reviewed, analyzed, and assigned dollar costs. Decision units are often established at the department level (such as Personnel) or for major activities within a department (such as recruiting, training, personnel and administration). Examples of common decision unit topics can be found in Exhibit 1.

For illustrative purposes, assume that the recruiting activity is identified as a decision unit. This example will be used in discussing the remaining three steps.

2. Develop "decision packages." The next step is to review, analyze, and justify the decision unit. First, a written decision package is developed that focuses on the decision unit and includes key information such as:

- The purpose of the decision unit activity.
- The consequences of not performing the activity.

EXHIBIT 1
Examples of common decision unit topics

General and administrative	*Marketing/sales*
Cafeteria services	Advertising
Janitorial services	Customer services
Mail	Entertainment expense
Security services	Leased cars
Telephone service	Order processing
Travel	Promotional programs
	Public relations

Data processing	*Accounting/finance*
Data input	Accounts payable
File back-up	Accounts receivable
Operations	Cost accounting
Program maintenance	Credit
Programming	Internal audit
Public relations	Payroll

Personnel	*Research and development*
Benefits program	Documentation
Employee relations	New product development
Recruiting	Technical service
Salary administration	
Training	

- A measure of performance of the activity.
- Alternative courses of action.
- Costs and benefits of the activity.

The key to ZBB lies in the identification and evaluation of alternatives for each activity. Under this concept, two types of alternatives should be considered: (1) different ways of performing the same activity, and (2) different levels of effort in performing the same activity. Pursuing the example of recruiting as a decision unit, assume that currently four full-time recruiters are employed at an annual cost of $100,000, and that time spent by functional supervisors in recruiting is moderate. Further assume that, on the average, the recruiting process takes eight weeks from start to finish. Alternative approaches to the recruiting effort might include:

- Eliminating full-time recruiters and using an outside agency.
- Eliminating full-time recruiters and shifting their work to functional supervisors.
- Maintaining the present approach.

Assume that it is decided to maintain the present approach, since no suitable outside agency is available and functional supervisors could not effectively absorb the entire recruiting effort. However, assume that, by increasing the degree of participation of functional supervisors from moderate to heavy, the full-time recruiting staff can be reduced by one person, thereby reducing the annual recruiting cost from $100,000 to $80,000. Under this approach, average recruiting time is estimated to increase to twelve weeks. This reduction of one recruiter represents an alternative level of effort for the recruiting function.

Another level of effort might be represented by the addition of one more recruiter (making a total of five) at an annual cost of $15,000. Under this alternative, participation by functional supervisors would be reduced from moderate to light, and average recruiting time would be reduced from the present eight weeks to six weeks. The decision packages formed for these alternatives might be summarized as follows:

a. *Recruiting function (1 of 3) cost—$80,000.* Three recruiters needed for minimum coverage of hiring requirements. Necessitates increased involvement of functional supervisors and increase hiring time from eight to twelve weeks.

b. *Recruiting function (2 of 3) cost—$20,000 (present level).* One recruiter needed to maintain present coverage of recruiting requirements. Permits maintenance of present eight-week hiring time with no increase in functional supervisor participation.

c. *Recruiting function (3 of 3) cost—$15,000.* One additional (new) recruiter needed to decrease average hiring time from eight to six weeks and reduce participation of functional supervisors from moderate to light.

Using this approach gives management reviewing committees the opportunity to make budget funding decisions with specific knowledge of the consequences of each alternative. In this example management may: disapprove all packages (eliminating the recruiting function); approve package *a* at a cost of $80,000; approve packages *a* and *b* at a cost of $100,000; or approve all packages (*a, b* and *c*) at a cost of $115,000.

3. **Rank the decision packages.** After developing all decision packages in a certain area, the manager responsible assigns a numerical ranking to each package. The manager's decision

packages are forwarded to the next higher management level for review and consolidation with other packages.

At some point in the review process, it is common that a committee be formed to assign rankings. Committee members would usually represent the different functional departments which submit decision packages. In a committee situation, a voting scale is used for ranking decision packages. It is advisable to use an even number of points on the voting scale so that there is no middle group. For example, a scale of five points would tend to attract many votes of three and would fail to assign the priorities desired.

Exhibit 2 (a ranking mechanism) is an example of a voting scale that could be used. Care should be taken to keep the voting process simple so that the decision packages receiving the most points are assigned the highest priority.

4. Select and approve decision packages and finalize the budget. When all decision packages have been ranked and

EXHIBIT 2
A ranking mechanism

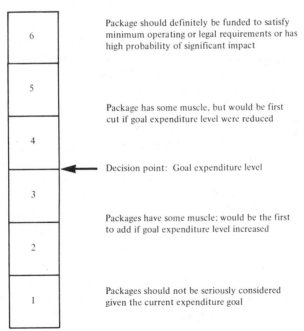

6	Package should definitely be funded to satisfy minimum operating or legal requirements or has high probability of significant impact
5	
4	Package has some muscle, but would be first cut if goal expenditure level were reduced
	← Decision point: Goal expenditure level
3	
2	Packages have some muscle; would be the first to add if goal expenditure level increased
1	Packages should not be seriously considered given the current expenditure goal

Source: Peter A. Pyhrr, *Zero Base Budgeting* (New York: Wiley, 1973), p. 90.

have flowed upward to the highest reviewing level, the budget is established and finalized. The approved budget consists of those decision packages whose final ranking and approved funding is within the budget ceiling set by top management. (It is safe to assume that there is always a budget ceiling, whether it be close to or far larger than current spending levels.)

One advantage of the ZBB technique is that projects not within the approved funding level can be readily implemented if funds become available during the year.

APPLYING ZBB

Several factors and their impact on ZBB effectiveness should be considered in adapting the concept to a particular environment. Tailoring ZBB to fit a particular business environment will be affected by the following factors:

Public versus private business

The majority of ZBB installations have been in local, state, and federal government due to the emphasis given the technique by Jimmy Carter. Obviously, ZBB is applicable to both public and private organizations, although ZBB "experts" believe the opportunities for ZBB's payoff is greater in the public sector.

The logic to support the applicability of ZBB in government (or other nonprofit organizations) is sound. Typically, budgets are made up of programs or projects which are "funded" to a prescribed dollar level. The middle management philosophy is typified by the idea that if the funds allocated to a program, project, or department are not spent in a given fiscal year, they are forever lost. Thus, the emphasis is on spending all funds allotted.

In the private sector, financial planning and budgets are typically not fund-oriented. Budgets tend to be tied to the level of revenue generation anticipated, the volume of activity (sales, production, and so forth), and to profit level goals. The motivation (often tied to bonus plans) is to keep costs low and maximize profits. A private company tends to run "leaner" than a public or fund-oriented organization and management tends to be more cost conscious.

Major cost reductions resulting from ZBB implementation have occurred in companies such as International Harvester, Southern California Edison, Playboy Enterprises, and General Radio. Typical modifications of the basic ZBB process made by its industrial (profit-motivated) users are:

A nonzero base. Some companies have concluded that there is a valid "minimum level of effort" below which further cost reduction would imply elimination of an essential function. Therefore, in order to concentrate the analytical work on what some might call "discretionary spending" and also to reduce the numbers of decision packages to be prepared, a level such as 50 to 60 percent of the previous year's budget level is defined as the base point. Those activities considered by management to be essential to ongoing operations, and which represent the first 50 to 60 percent of the department's spending, are accepted as being essential and as being performed as cost effectively as possible. Those ranked above the 60 percent level are challenged, analyzed, ranked, and justified by using standard ZBB decision criteria.

Those who challenge this approach express concern that the clever manager who wishes to hide a "pet" function or protect his empire can hide a nonessential function or person in this base 60 percent. That is true. One solution is to require that every second or third year each major department fully analyze its activities down to the zero base.

Applying ZBB to selected departments. Applying ZBB selectively based on a preliminary evaluation of the potential for cost reduction may be the most effective way to maximize the benefits and minimize the administrative costs associated with the ZBB process. By identifying those departments or functions which have historically accounted for the majority of overhead spending, the budgeting effort may be minimized. In most cases there will be relatively few departments identified. The age old "80–20" rule suggests that the largest percentage of cost will be concentrated in a small percentage of the organization. Apply the ZBB techniques in these departments. Once having identified overhead "fat" in this fashion, it may not be necessary to apply ZBB at any higher levels in the organization.

EXHIBIT 3

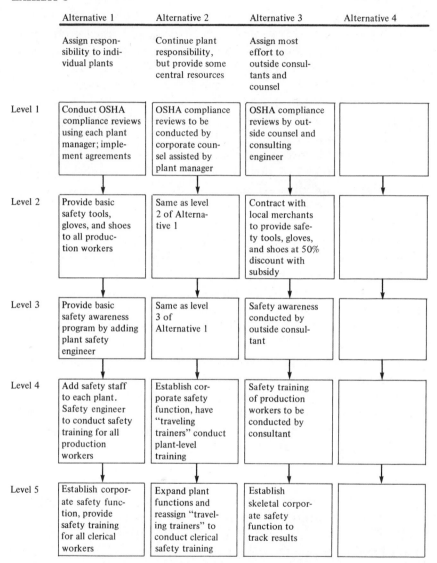

	Alternative 1	Alternative 2	Alternative 3	Alternative 4
	Assign responsibility to individual plants	Continue plant responsibility, but provide some central resources	Assign most effort to outside consultants and counsel	
Level 1	Conduct OSHA compliance reviews using each plant manager; implement agreements	OSHA compliance reviews to be conducted by corporate counsel assisted by plant manager	OSHA compliance reviews by outside counsel and consulting engineer	
Level 2	Provide basic safety tools, gloves, and shoes to all production workers	Same as level 2 of Alternative 1	Contract with local merchants to provide safety tools, gloves, and shoes at 50% discount with subsidy	
Level 3	Provide basic safety awareness program by adding plant safety engineer	Same as level 3 of Alternative 1	Safety awareness conducted by outside consultant	
Level 4	Add safety staff to each plant. Safety engineer to conduct safety training for all production workers	Establish corporate safety function, have "traveling trainers" conduct plant-level training	Safety training of production workers to be conducted by consultant	
Level 5	Establish corporate safety function, provide safety training for all clerical workers	Expand plant functions and reassign "traveling trainers" to conduct clerical safety training	Establish skeletal corporate safety function to track results	

Replacing decision packages with an alternative matrix. A technique suggested by Logan M. Cheek in his book, *ZBB Comes of Age,* designed to eliminate much of the formal decision package paperwork, is the use of a matrix to display and analyze the alternatives to be considered for any particular function.[1] Notes, calculations, and background research may still fill a file cabinet, but the final display to be used for management evaluation is a matrix displaying on one axis the alternative courses of action or services to be rendered, and on the other axis, the alternative levels of effort required or available. The cost of each combination is shown in the body of the matrix. Exhibit 3 is an example of an alternative matrix.

Considering cyclical ZBB. Should management decide that full scope ZBB be used in all departments throughout the organization, consideration should be given to cyclical analysis in order to ease the administrative burden. A schedule is developed so that each department does a full ZBB analysis every third year and more traditional line-item budget analysis in the interim years.

Current budgeting and financial reporting practices

The existence of formalized, well-designed budgeting, accounting, and financial reporting systems has a great deal to do with how, or even *if,* ZBB should be implemented. One major company has developed, over a long period of years, a comprehensive planning and management system based on "management by objectives" (MBO). The system encompasses the budgeting process and requires each department manager to reevaluate, analyze, and rejustify each function each year. It is, in effect, ZBB by a different name.

Implementation of ZBB is in many respects a "systems decision" in that management must decide whether ZBB is to replace or supplement current procedures. If current financial reports include a "budget" column for comparison to actual performance, the origin of the budget data should be reviewed.

If financial planning and performance reporting have tradi-

---

[1] Logan M. Cheek, *Zero Base Budgeting Comes of Age,* AMACOM, Division of American Management Associations, 1977.

tionally been weak, informal, or nonexistent, then some form of ZBB coupled with strengthening of the accounting and reporting systems should be considered.

Management style and motivation

The top management of any organization, whether public or private, small or large, can be characterized as having a particular "style." Their philosophies of management, their technical orientation, the functional disciplines through which they passed and their personalities, all contribute to their "style" of managing the organization. They can be autonomous, dictatorial, democratic, passive, do-it-yourselfers, delegators, engineers, marketers, financiers, and so on, and on, and each will have a different outlook toward budgeting or financial planning.

Some will see it as a powerful control tool, others as a necessary evil. Some will support it strongly, others may give it "lip service" and delegate the responsibility. Some may insist on its application, but not understand its shortcomings; some may reject it for lack of understanding its strengths.

An awareness of what drives, motivates, and excites top management could be helpful in guiding the ZBB efforts. The interest in, and consideration of, ZBB can develop for several reasons ranging from curiosity over a new "in" management tool to profound concern over the financial well-being of the company.

In the governmental environment, demands for increased services, offset by equal demands for reduced taxes, provides an incentive for applying ZBB. In the case of Playboy Enterprises, a $9 million drop in after-tax profits in one year provided the motivation.

Size of the organization

The size of an organization, whether public or private, can bear on how ZBB is applied. In a small, owner-managed firm two important ingredients necessary for full ZBB implementation could be the lack of adequate professional management skills and lack of sufficient administrative time. By applying the techniques suggested above, the small organization may be able to realize the full benefit of ZBB. The process may be further modified by concentrating the analytical effort higher in the organization structure. In the smallest of companies, the owner-manager may complete the entire budget analysis alone, using subordinate department heads as resources for detailed functional information only. The owner-manager may choose to do final ranking and decide what functions or level of effort should be budgeted and approved.

IMPLEMENTING ZBB

The major determinant of a successful ZBB implementation in any given environment is the manner in which it is introduced. An ill-planned introduction, insensitive to the current organizational climate, can have disastrous and perhaps irreversible effects. A common-sense approach to administering the introduction is essential. If the technique is abruptly imposed without explanation to, or participation by, operating management, substantial animosity and resistance will severely hinder progress. The following paragraphs discuss several pitfalls to be avoided in implementing ZBB.

Strategic planning

In order for department heads to define the various functions and activities for which they are responsible, and to thereby develop recommended levels of effort and resource allocations, they must receive guidance from senior management. This guidance must take the form of strategic plans and assumptions regarding the course of business in the near term, articulation of company goals and objectives which can be translated to departmental goals and objectives, and overall budget parameters which indicate a level of "budgeting ceiling" which management has in mind for the coming year.

There must be a business planning system in place in order to provide this type of direction. Without consistent parameters for department managers working in the program, the results will be inconsistent, incomplete, and unresponsive to the needs of the company.

Training and education

Top management and department heads must be exposed to and understand the scope, objectives, mechanics, and pitfalls of ZBB before it is introduced or adapted. The rules must be clear and they should support both the concept and the approach. Outside consulting assistance and attendance at technical seminars are effective in providing this tutorial support.

Once the details of the ZBB mechanics have been worked out, further procedural training is needed for those who will participate in the program.

Top management commitment

The direction and guidance discussed above will not be provided without involvement by key senior executives. They must make a commitment to the ZBB concept and program in the form of a recognizable portion of their time and expertise if the program is to succeed. They must also make available the necessary resources to implement and operate the system and must participate in the program throughout its cycle, from initiation to performance evaluation.

Customize techniques

Every organization is different. Financial planning and control techniques must be customized to meet the unique needs of the organization. A "textbook" approach to ZBB will usually fail after considerable investment of valuable resources.

Systems integration

The ZBB process will provide budget data for selected segments (usually the overhead areas) of an organization. Other accounting and planning systems provide control information for the rest of the company. These data must be integrated and utilized in the overall accounting and financial control and reporting systems if management is to realize the benefits of ZBB and be in a position to measure operating performance. The introduction and implementation of ZBB therefore implies significant systems and procedure review and/or refinement.

Implementation steps

The following steps provide a simple, effective process for the organization to follow when implementing ZBB:

1. Fix responsibilities. Any project of the magnitude of ZBB requires the fixing of responsibilities for the various steps among all concerned individuals and groups, for example, the chief executive; department, division, and section heads; accounting staff; and outside consultants if employed. More specifically, the responsibility for preparation of a budget calendar should probably be assigned to the budget staff, and the responsibility for approval of that calendar should be assumed by the chief executive. These responsibilities should be fixed at the beginning of the process, defined in writing, and then adhered to during the budget preparation.

2. Develop a budget calendar. With a normal, ongoing budget process, the budget calendar might begin about six months prior to the beginning of the next fiscal year. For the first year under ZBB, however, more time will be required and the budget process, rather than starting during the seventh month of the fiscal year, needs to be initiated in the third or fourth month of the year. This schedule would provide department heads additional time to become familiar with the ZBB process and to prepare competent decision packages. Also, time will be required for ranking and for evaluation of the recommended budget by the chief executive. In subsequent years, the organization should be able to return to the calendar of its former budget process.

3. Define policies and procedures. Before departments are able to prepare decision packages, several preliminary questions must be answered. Should a zero base be used? Should the "minimum level of effort" concept be used? At what spending levels should the units of submitting packages be stated? These are usually stated in percentages of current expenditures, e.g., 50 percent, 60 percent, 70 percent. The decision should obviously consider the economic condition during the budget year. The tighter the situation, the lower the levels should be set.

What ZBB forms are to be used? During the first year, a three- to four-page decision package form may be required. (This can be reduced in complexity and length in subsequent years) The decision package form should include budgetary and accounting decisions regarding such matters as level of expense detail to be required in the decision packages, the procedure for handling capital-project items, the approach to handling salary increases, methods for recognizing allocated items, and minimum and maximum dollar size of packages. All of these decisions should be incorporated in a budget manual to be distributed to department heads and other key officials at the orientation session (Step 5).

4. Consider a pilot-project approach. The organization should consider implementing ZBB by having only selected departments install the system in the first year on a pilot-project basis. The advantages of the pilot-project approach are that the initial effort is reduced and it enables the organization to work out the "bugs" so that full implementation can proceed in a more orderly fashion. The disadvantages are that individual departments do not relish the idea of serving as guinea pigs, that little practical advantage is gained by segregating one or two departments from the rest, and that no ranking of packages can be accomplished with a pilot since there is no company-wide mechanism to be ranked against. Further, a pilot-project approach can be used in an attempt to satisfy an officer with a "we gave it a try and, see, it didn't work" response.

5. Conduct an orientation seminar. Training of senior management and departmental personnel is an important preliminary step. This should be used to present the history, concepts, principles, and terminology of ZBB to stress the value of departmental goals, objectives, and work load measures.

The opening seminars can also be used to describe where ZBB is now being used and what benefits have resulted. Finally, ask the department heads to take time following the seminar to consider and then establish or reconfirm their department's goals, objectives, and work load measures.

6. Define decision units. At this point, the organization is ready to define its decision units. The department heads should define their decision units following instructions from senior management. Management should then review and suggest changes. The end result should be a reasonable number of decision units that reflect the way the company is organized to provide its services and products.

7. Conduct training workshops for personnel who will be preparing the budget. The next step is to train people for their role in formulating decision units and packages, and in ranking. This training should be provided for all management, including the lower-level supervisors. One of the strengths of ZBB is the involvement of personnel who are at the operating level, but who have not taken part previously in budget preparation.

The training workshop should last approximately four to six hours. The principles of ZBB should be discussed, but this should be followed by specific exercises in working with ZBB decision packages in order to give the participants a "hands on" feeling for their tasks. The workshop should also provide instructions for the completion of every block on the ZBB forms. In contrast to the orientation seminar, which is more general, the purpose of the training workshops is to impart specific information in order that the department managers can prepare the ZBB packages.

8. Prepare decision packages.   Following the training session, departmental managers should be given reasonable time to consider alternative approaches to providing the functions for which they are responsible, to decide how these services should be provided in the ensuing year, and to develop the decision packages. These instructions should be part of a budget manual containing illustrative completed forms.

9. Rank decision packages in the department.   In small organizations the ranking can be done entirely by the department head. In larger organizations with sections below the department level, the section heads will first rank all of their packages; the department head will then combine them into an overall departmental ranking for all sections in the department.

10. Audit of decision packages by accounting staff.   The first step for the budget staff is to review the packages for completeness and adherence to the instructions. This can be facilitated by using a decision package check sheet that lists each block in the ZBB form and specifies the kind of response that should be in each block. Also, since a computer is often used in the budget preparation process, photocopies of the decision package forms can be sent to the data processing center, and the computer can be used to check the calculations.

11. Analysis of decision packages by accounting staff.   While the decision packages and departmental ranking sheets can go directly to the chief executive or his designated group for a company-wide ranking, it is advisable to have the budgeting staff first review each package. They should be alert to certain recurring problems:

a. Departmental personnel may attempt "gamesmanship"—by ranking packages out of order. Packages that are obvious necessities are ranked low with the thought in mind that they will have to be funded even if they miss the cutoff line.

b. The packages may include too small or too large dollar amounts for useful analysis. These can usually be detected by identifying more than one level of service that has been compressed into a single package.

c. There may be obvious discrepancies in expenditure or work load estimates that do not correspond to personnel estimates to accomplish the same level of service.

12. Estimate revenues for the new year. During the time the department heads and budgeting staff are preparing and analyzing the decision packages, revenue estimates for the new year should be finalized. Preliminary estimates can be made early to give general guidance to the preparation of decision packages, that is, the percentages of the current year's spending at which to develop the packages. As the year moves on, the revenue estimates for the new year should be sharpened so that by the time the departmental rankings and reviews are completed, the budgeting staff is able to submit a fairly accurate estimate of next year's revenues.

13. Consolidated ranking of decision packages. The tasks of ranking all decision packages across the complete spectrum of a company has probably brought as much criticism to ZBB as any other single step. No doubt it is difficult for a single chief executive, or even a team, to rank all the packages, particularly if there are several thousand. This very problem is the one which gave rise to the concepts of pilot runs, minimum levels of effort, and cyclical ZBB.

14. If the organization is a government unit

a. *Hold a training session for the governing body.* The chief executive should conduct a briefing session with whatever legislative body is going to review the budget prior to its submission. The purpose is to acquaint the members with the new process that was used to develop the budget they will receive, to explain what the document will look like and how they can benefit from this format, and otherwise to set the stage for their consideration of the budget document. If the council initiated the entire process, it would be well also to have a session with the group at the beginning of the process.

b. *Submit budget to the governing body.* At this point the chief executive submits his budget to the governing body. It is built from the unit-wide rankings of expenditures requests and the revenue estimates. The chief executive might consider supplementing this basic recommendation with some of the documentation used to develop the budget. It would provide a foundation in case the governing body wanted to hold hearings with departments.

c. *Review and adoption of the budget by the governing body:* The role of the governing body in the budget process should be planned from the beginning. If its expectations have been properly considered and met, the review and adoption of the budget by the governing body should go quite smoothly.

15. Subsequent years. ZBB is still new and there is no logic that requires an organization to follow the first year's procedures precisely in subsequent years. Indeed, the first city to adopt ZBB changed its emphasis each year for the first four years. Thus, after the first year the budget staff should evaluate the process and adopt modifications for improvement. Forms can generally be simplified. Analytical effort can be concentrated on internal administrative services and policies affecting the entire organization, such as wage and salary programs, data processing, telephone costs, or vehicle management—or on one functional area, for example, the marketing area, which may seem to merit attention. Still another approach is to place emphasis on other methods of performing the service in question. This is rarely addressed adequately in the first year or two, even though it deserves substantial attention.

CONCLUSION

The birth of ZBB resulted from the need to reduce spending in order to remain competitive and maintain profit levels. The approach taken was one of pure logic—analyze what is being done now and explore alternative ways to do it for less in the future. To the extent that this is done objectively and relative priorities are clear, that *is* ZBB.

Many companies have done this for years. It has been called many things, usually business planning or just "budgeting." However, this is the first time it has been given a separate name and formalized to this degree. The name chosen was an unfortunate one, since the real value and strength of the process is in its support of the planning function. "Budgeting" is too frequently relegated to a lowly accounting function and dealt with as a necessary evil.

The principle concepts of ZBB—analyzing each function and challenging its effectiveness and value—is sound. Every organization, whether public or private, large or small, new or old, would benefit from this type of scrutiny on a regular basis. Every organization should adapt these concepts and integrate them into its business planning process. Whether ZBB as a "management tool"—as a "package"—will survive, only time will tell.

One author suggested that as the 1950s was the decade of network program planning and control techniques (CPM, PERT) and the 60s was the decade of management by objectives (MBO) and program budgeting (PPBS), so the 70s will be known as the ZBB decade. These earlier techniques went through a cycle of introduction, growth, acceptance, panacea, disappointment, and practical application, and today are used quite effectively by many organizations. ZBB will no doubt behave the same way. It will find its proper place among other management tools, recognized as a homogenous group of concepts for planning and management which, when appropriately applied and integrated with other management systems and techniques, will provide benefits to the knowledgeable and prudent user.

PART
EIGHT

*Emerging trends and
challenges in managerial
and cost accounting*

38

Current versus historical costs

Edward V. McIntyre*
William J. Ihlanfeldt†

Historical cost financial statements have served management and the financial community since the inception of modern financial reporting; however, these statements also have been the target of numerous criticisms through time, particularly during periods of prolonged inflation. Individual accountants and professional bodies have suggested a variety of alternative methods of accounting which address various aspects of the financial reporting problems created by inflation. The current setting is one of experimentation with methods of inflation accounting and controversy concerning the very foundations of financial reporting. This chapter reviews and analyzes several of the more prominent inflation accounting proposals, with particular emphasis on a replacement cost model, and contrasts certain features of these methods with conventional historical cost statements. To provide an initial perspective, the chapter begins with a brief summary of the development of historical cost accounting, the financial reporting problems related to inflation, and the principal methods that have been suggested for coping with these problems.

* Professor of Accounting, Florida State University.

† Manager, Accounting Research and Policy, Shell Oil Company.

HISTORICAL COST ACCOUNTING
AND INFLATION ACCOUNTING

The precise origin of modern double-entry record keeping is unknown but the earliest text on the subject is believed to have been published by Fra Luca Pacioli, an Italian mathematician who lived from 1445 to 1520. In a special supplement to a book on mathematics, Pacioli described the dual entry bookkeeping procedures that had been employed by merchants in Venice perhaps as far back as the 13th century. Some of the basic procedures and concepts described by this Franciscan monk are still employed today. Our accounting methodology therefore has its roots in antiquity but the information stored within the accounts is largely a product of the current century.

Prior to the mid-1800s nearly all of the world's commerce related to farming or to the operation of privately owned shops. This was particularly true in the United States. Accounting was based as much on barter as on cash, which was in short supply and of unstable value. Historical cost accounting, as we think of it today, therefore evolved with monetary transactions which in turn were necessitated by the great industrial growth and the advent of multiple ownership of business enterprises.

The first modern text on accounting was written by Thomas Jones in 1840[1] and emphasized the financial statements resulting from double-entry accounting procedures. During this era educators were advocating more standardized practices through the use of what was then described as scientific bookkeeping or the science of accounts. Although there was great flexibility and diversity in practice, entries and financial results were based largely on the amounts involved in actual transactions. This common feature became the foundation for much of today's generally accepted accounting principles.

The first attempt in the United States to present a set of national standards for accounting practice was developed by members of the national CPA organization in cooperation with government agencies. While these rules were based on historical costs, they were not enforceable and not uniformly applied. During the inflationary spiral that preceded the 1929 market crash

---

[1] Gary John Previts, "The Accountant in Our History: A Bicentennial Overview," *Journal of Accountancy*, July 1976.

there were substantial departures—some of which were grossly deceptive—from historical cost constraints. Abuses of this nature and the lack of sufficient disclosures led Congress to enact the Securities Act of 1933 and in 1934 to adopt legislation which created the Securities and Exchange Commission (SEC). These laws were among the earliest "New Deal" enactments and were designed to protect the interests of investors and the public by requiring certain disclosures and by prohibiting fraud and manipulative practices. In general the ensuing rules adhered closely to historical cost accounting concepts to provide data with a high degree of objectivity and verifiability.

The historical cost concept views the business cycle as progressing from cash to goods to cash. Profit is thereby the difference between cash outlays and subsequent receipts, without regard to the cost of replacement goods that will be acquired in the next business cycle.

Many accountants believe it more appropriate to view the business cycle as starting and ending with goods—goods to cash to goods. Proponents of this view argue that this method more accurately reflects the economic conditions required to maintain a going business. When prices and the economy are stable the two views provide similar results. However, during periods of high inflation or rapidly changing prices the two views produce significantly different financial statements. It is during such periods that pressures mount to abandon or greatly modify historical cost concepts.

Most criticisms of conventional historical-cost financial statements prepared in inflationary periods center around three points:

1. Historical costs are said to be understated and not representative of the current sacrifices of using existing resources. A corollary to this proposition is that dividends, ostensibly paid from earnings, may be distributions of capital.
2. Operating profits include holding gains and losses, which may contribute to misleading inferences about the success of a firm's past operating activities.
3. Reported assets and liabilities are a miscellany of current values, past costs, and unamortized past costs of varying dates. The interpretation and usefulness of aggregations of

such heterogeneous amounts (total assets, net worth) have been called into question.

Of the principal methods that have been suggested as alternatives to the historical cost model, three are based on value measures—current selling prices (exit values), current replacement costs (entry values), and discounted present values of cash flows. A fourth proposal, general price-level adjusted historical cost, does not report current values, but restates historical cost balances in constant dollars. Most of the proposals under present consideration are applications, partial applications, or combinations of the preceding reporting systems.

Recent reporting requirements of the Securities and Exchange Commission have focused attention on replacement cost accounting, and in this chapter we compare replacement cost (hereafter, RC) accounting with historical cost (HC) accounting. We also consider general price-level adjustments (GPLA) and, briefly, exit value accounting. Comparison of the three systems provides a fuller understanding of all accounting models.

Discounted cash flows provide the foundation for capital budgeting analysis and thus have appeal as a basis for financial statements; however, implementation problems make this method the least likely candidate for widespread adoption. The principal difficulty in constructing present value statements stems from the joint nature of cash flows. When cash flows are attributable to the interaction of multiple resources used in combination, the valuation of individual assets requires rather arbitrary allocations of estimated future cash flows to specific items on the balance sheet. Because of the substantial problems encountered in attempting to apply present value techniques simultaneously to all assets held by a firm, no further discussion of this method will be presented.

The analysis begins with a review of efforts by the accounting profession and the SEC to implement some form of inflation accounting, up to, and including, the current situation as of this writing. Subsequent sections examine the primary characteristics of RC financial statements, their relationship to general price-level adjusted statements and to exit value statements, and their uses and limitations.

We believe that accountants in all areas of practice have a

stake in understanding RC accounting. The information that could be produced by such a system is potentially very useful to management, but, as with other methods, it is also subject to a number of limitations. Substantial controversy has arisen over the relative costs and benefits of RC information. At the very least, the topic warrants the serious study of anyone involved with the accounting process.

EFFORTS BY THE PROFESSION TO DEAL WITH INFLATION

For the most part, the accounting profession, while recognizing the limitations of HC accounting, has strongly defended HC as the basis of financial statements. The HC concept is concerned primarily with actual transactions. As indicated earlier it views the business cycle as progressing from cash to goods to cash. This view is in keeping with the age-old business objective of buying cheap and selling dear. It is a simple, well-understood concept that represents a general view of business success. Not so well understood, perhaps, is the fact that the accounting model has not remained static and that several departures from the cost principle have been adopted to provide more useful information. The most common examples are accounts receivable, which are carried at a transaction price less an allowance for doubtful accounts, and inventories and marketable securities, which are carried at the lower of cost or market.

HC has proven its usefulness over time as a recognized foundation for analyzing results and performance. Inherent in HC data are controls and disciplines that contribute to the objective and verifiable (auditable) nature of financial statements. Many accountants believe that these qualities are vital to the credibility of the financial reporting process and, further, they believe that HC statements possess these attributes to a much greater extent than would alternative statements based on some measure of current value.

Some of the strongest arguments for HC are based on practical considerations. To HC advocates, the advantages of preparing financial statements on the basis of actual transactions and in an objective and verifiable (auditable) manner far outweigh the advantages attributed to the theoretically appealing, but largely untried, current value concepts. On the other hand, there is general agreement that the relevance of the HC financial statements suffers during, and for many years following, periods of prolonged or severe inflation. For example, when the rate of inflation began to increase in the late 1960s and the erosion of the purchasing power of the dollar became more apparent, the HC approach came under increasing criticism for failing to convey a meaningful picture to the reader of financial statements.

In June 1969, the Accounting Principles Board (APB) released their *Statement No. 3* entitled "Financial Statements Restated for General Price-Level Changes" which gave general guidance for the voluntary presentation of supplementary financial statements restated for price-level changes. The need for such statements was summarized in the following paragraphs:

> General price-level financial statements take into account changes in the general purchasing power of money. These changes are now ignored in preparing financial statements in the United States. In conventional financial statements the individual asset, liability, stockholders' equity, revenue, expense, gain, and loss items are stated in terms of dollars of the period in which these items originated. Conventional financial statements may be referred to as "historical-dollar financial statements."
>
> The basic difference between general price-level and historical-dollar financial statements is the unit of measure used in the statements. In general price-level statements, the unit of measure is defined in terms of a single specified amount of purchasing power—the general purchasing power of the dollar at a specified date. Thus, dollars which represent the same amount of general purchasing power are used in general price-level statements whereas dollars which represent diverse amounts of general purchasing power are used in historical-dollar statements.
>
> The cost principle on which historical-dollar statements are based is also the basis of general price-level statements. In general, amounts shown at historical cost in historical-dollar statements are shown at historical cost restated for changes in the general purchasing power of the dollar in general price-level statements. The amount may be restated, but it still represents cost and not a current value. The process of restating historical costs in terms of a specified amount of general purchasing power does not introduce any factors other than general price-level changes. The amounts shown in general price-level financial statements are

not intended to represent appraisal values, replacement costs, or any other measure of current value. (See Appendix D for further discussion.)

The general purchasing power of the dollar—its command over goods and services in general—varies, often significantly, from time to time. Changes in the general purchasing power of money are known as inflation or deflation. During inflation, the general purchasing power of money declines as the general level of prices of goods and services rises. During deflation, the general purchasing power of money increases as the general level of prices falls. The general purchasing power of money and the general price level are reciprocals.

In December 1974, the Financial Accounting Standards Board (FASB), as successor to the APB, published an Exposure Draft covering "Financial Reporting in Units of General Purchasing Power," stating that:

The proposal is not a new one, and much has been written on the subject. Despite a 1969 recommendation of the Accounting Principles Board, few enterprises in the United States have reported financial information expressed in units of general purchasing power, and many of those directly involved in financial accounting and reporting are unfamiliar with general purchasing power accounting.

Expressing financial information in units of general purchasing power should not be confused with the proposal that financial statements reflect changes in the specific prices ("current values") of goods held or obligations owed by an enterprise while they are held or owed. Proponents of current value accounting suggest various measures of current value including selling price, replacement price, and the present value of future cash flows. Some advocate the adoption of current value accounting rather than general purchasing power accounting, and general purchasing power accounting has sometimes been suggested as a means of approximating current values. Although both the general level of prices and most specific prices tend to move in the same direction in a period of inflation or deflation, general purchasing power accounting and current value accounting are proposals with different objectives, and each should be evaluated on its own merits. This Exposure Draft relates only to the proposal for general purchasing power accounting, and its adoption would not in any way preclude FASB consideration of current value accounting.

The Board is taking action now on general purchasing power

accounting because techniques for restating financial information in terms of units of general purchasing power are well developed, and the feasibility of applying them has been demonstrated in a number of field tests. Reporting current values would be a significant departure from the historical cost basis of accounting, and much work remains to be done in considering the concepts and implementation issues related to that proposal. Current value accounting is within the scope of another project presently on the Board's agenda, "Conceptual Framework for Accounting and Reporting."

Because general purchasing power accounting was relatively untested, the FASB provided an extended exposure period for the draft and requested business enterprises to experiment with the recommended procedures. The Financial Executives Institute and the American Petroleum Institute arranged for approximately 100 companies to participate in a field test which included the preparation of price-level adjusted financial statements for the previous three fiscal years. These were submitted to the FASB in July 1975, along with comments on any conceptual or implementation problems that had been encountered. Opinions and evaluations by the participants were divided. In the ensuing months the FASB held several meetings with selected companies and different industry groups to better understand the results and problems of price-level restatements.

In a move away from GPLA statements and towards RC, the SEC issued, in March 1976, *Accounting Series Release 190* requiring generally that all registrants with inventories and gross plant investments aggregating $100 million and amounting to more than 10 percent of their total assets must disclose:

> . . . either in a footnote or in a separate section of the financial statements, the current cost of replacing inventories and productive capacity and the amount of cost of sales and depreciation if they had been computed on the basis of replacement costs. The rule is applicable to annual financial statements covering periods beginning after December 25, 1975, and thus will require disclosures in 1976 statements.
>
> While the Commission noted that it was not requiring a change in the fact of the basic financial statements which are prepared on the basis of historical costs, it did recognize that the new rule

would require companies subject to it to produce on a supplemental basis significantly different data than currently available.

These data based on current replacement costs, may represent the first step toward a revised system of accounting based on current values. The commission specifically stated that it did not intend to require fundamental changes in basic financial statements beyond requiring the disclosures set forth in the rule, since it is believed that any such change should be initiated by the Financial Accounting Standards Board which is currently studying the conceptual framework of financial statements. The data required based on current replacement cost should provide useful input to the Board as it considers this matter.

In June 1976, the FASB announced that it had decided to defer further consideration "at this time" of a Statement on Financial Reporting in Units of General Purchasing Power. In explaining its action, the Board stated:

> In deciding to defer further consideration at this time, the Board has not reached a conclusion about the merits of providing financial information stated in terms of units of general purchasing power. The Board has only concluded that general purchasing power information is not now sufficiently well understood by preparers and users and the need for it is not now sufficiently well demonstrated to justify imposing the cost of implementation upon all preparers of financial statements at this time. The current effort being undertaken by the largest corporations to provide the current replacement cost data required by SEC *Accounting Series Release No. 190* and the further consideration that will necessarily be given to financial measures in units of general purchasing power in connection with the Board's conceptual framework project were important factors in deferring further consideration rather than attempting to reach a final judgment at this time.

The various pronouncements and recommendations by standard setting and regulatory agencies provide ample evidence that historical cost financial statements do not provide sufficient information during periods of high inflation. However, none of the proposals for dealing with the problem have received widespread industry support in the United States. This opposition appears to be particularly strong against proposals which would change or are perceived to jeopardize the historical cost concept in the basic financial statements. Recent developments to distinguish financial statements more clearly from the broader area of financial reporting may reduce this opposition and encourage greater experimentation with supplemental disclosures.

Financial reporting versus financial statements

Much of the debate in the past concerning the appropriate way to report the effects of inflation has focused on which, if any, current value measurement technique should be substituted for historical cost as the *primary* basis of *financial statements*. A related and critical issue has been whether the audited "financial statements," *per se,* are the appropriate vehicle to use in portraying the effects of inflation on the enterprise. When historical cost statements did not handle the effects of a severe inflationary period very well, the focus turned almost automatically to consideration of changes to the basic financial statements. Recently, however, there appears to be growing support for reporting the effects of inflation as supplementary information while retaining HC as the primary basis of financial statements. The term "financial reporting" has been employed in this context to refer to a broad information set which would include supplementary financial data, such as RC, in addition to the audited HC financial statements.

Report of the study group on objectives of financial statements (Trueblood report)

In a report issued in October 1973, the prestigious Study Group gave support to expanded financial reporting by concluding in part:

> The Study Group believes that the objectives of financial statements cannot be best served by the exclusive use of a single valuation basis. The objectives that prescribe statements of earnings and financial position are based on the user's need to predict, compare, and evaluate earning power. To satisfy these information requirements, the Study Group concludes that different valuation bases are preferable for assets and liabilities. That means that financial statements might contain data based on a combination of valuation bases.

The report goes on to say:

> The quantifications produced by applying each of these valuation bases vary in reliability, precision, and cost of application. These factors should be weighed in the process of choosing the appropriate basis or combination of bases for fulfilling financial statement objectives as they relate to each of the assets or liabilities under consideration.

FASB Discussion Memorandum on conceptual framework

In June 1974, the FASB issued a Discussion Memorandum (D/M) entitled "Conceptual Framework for Financial Accounting and *Reporting*" (emphasis added), which exposed the Trueblood Report for full public debate. The D/M included the following pertinent paragraph:

> It seems eminently clear that an abrupt and immediate implementation of all the proposed objectives of financial statements as stated in the Objectives Study is not realistic and indeed was not contemplated by the Study Group. Rather, the Study Group states that objectives developed in the Study can be looked upon as "attainable in stages within a reasonable time" and urges that its conclusions be considered as "an initial step in developing objectives important for the ongoing refinement and improvement of accounting standards and practices."

Although the FASB broadened the scope of its D/M to include "reporting," as well as accounting, the D/M did not really distinguish "financial statements" from "financial reporting." However, responses to the D/M and remarks made at the public hearing held in September 1974, introduced concern over this distinction. The principal concern was that the proposed objectives appeared to cover a far broader subject than just financial statements. Many of the concerned parties felt that if the FASB would expand their definition of financial reporting, certain objectives of the Study Group might be achieved outside the primary (HC) financial statements and thus be accepted more readily by a significant part of the accounting and financial community. To illustrate this concern, consider objective seven of the Trueblood Report and several respondents' comments.

> OBJECTIVE SEVEN: An objective is to provide a statement of financial position useful for predicting, comparing, and evaluat-

ing enterprise earning power. This statement should provide information concerning enterprise transactions and other events that are part of incomplete earnings cycles. Current values should also be reported when they differ significantly from historical costs. Assets and liabilities should be grouped or segregated by the relative uncertainty of the amount and timing of prospective realization or liquidation. (Page 36)

The following comments illustrate the concern of one respondent to the FASB's Discussion Memorandum:

> The D/M makes little, if any, distinction between financial statements and financial reports. We perceive these to be quite different things which have different characteristics and different purposes. It is essential that the FASB recognize this difference and not attempt to enunciate one objective applicable to different things. The financial statements presently are the balance sheet, income statement, statement of shareholders' equity, and statement of changes in financial position and the notes thereto. Financial statements are independently verifiable because they are susceptible to established standards of measurement and disclosure. As historical documents, financial statements are also a useful starting or reference point for those users who wish to predict the future. Since financial reports can include a very wide range of information, their preparation requires more judgment than financial statements and . . . it is self evident that they are subject to different standards or qualitative characteristics. Clearly the quality of independent verifiability is different from the conventional financial statements and the annual report or the various other media loosely classified as finanical reports.

Comments by the Financial Executives Institute on this D/M included the following:

> We believe that financial reporting, in the broadest sense, provides substantial information outside the formal structure of financial statements. The inherent difficulty of evaluating future events, for example, illustrates potential difficulties regarding the attestation function. Thus, as a possible solution, the FASB might specify that certain types of information and explanatory data presented outside the formal financial statements need not be audited, but should be reviewed by auditors as to reasonableness and consistency with the financial statements.

An important part of the FASB's current project on a Conceptual Framework for Financial Accounting and Reporting (D/M dated December 2, 1976) are the following questions:

1. How should the basic elements of accounting be measured? For example, for assets should the measure be historical cost? Current replacement cost? Current selling price? Net cash flows expected in the due course of business? Present value of expected cash flows?

2. Should the basic measuring unit of accounting—the dollar— be adjusted for changes in its general purchasing power over time, or should those changes be ignored, or should information about the changes be reported supplementally?

Although the board has not yet reached any decisions on these issues, in their news release dated March 31, 1978 the FASB formally adopted the point of view that disclosures related to the effects of inflation should be reported as supplemental information. The news release stated that:

> The FASB has decided that any major changes in measurement concepts needed to show the effects of inflation on business enterprises should be introduced as supplemental disclosures rather than by changing the basic financial statements. To implement that decision, the board has authorized its staff to undertake work on both measurement concepts and possible types of supplemental disclosures of inflation effects consistent with those concepts.
>
> One reason for the Board's preference for the supplemental disclosure route to introduce new measurement concepts is that it provides an opportunity for preparers, auditors, and users of financial statements to gain experience under less rigid guidance than would be required if the changes were to be made immediately in the basic financial statements themselves. That experience may provide a basis for a subsequent board decision to change the measurements in the basic statements, or it could suggest that no such change should be made. Another advantage to the supplemental disclosure route is that it permits introduction of changes in the financial reports of selected business enterprises, for example the larger or more widely held companies, without suggesting that the basic financial statements of large and small companies should be based on different underlying concepts.

Recognition of this distinction may open the way for a more productive dialogue on how accountants can best deal with the problem of inflation. Advocates of HC who have feared that a move to current value may cause an untimely and radical change in the basis of financial statements would presumably be more willing to report current values as information supplemental to the HC financial statements. Such a procedure would provide a basis for testing the merit of current value information, while preserving the established framework of HC financial statements.

The remainder of this chapter discusses one of many proposals that are being made for dealing with the financial reporting problems created by inflation. It is a replacement cost concept that envisions a complete accounting model rather than the partial disclosures currently required by the SEC. Although the following discussion often contrasts RC financial statements with HC financial statements, we are not suggesting that a choice must be made between the two methods for purposes of *financial reporting*. As our earlier discussion suggested, various types of financial data may be necessary for effective disclosure. Because the *actual* benefits of RC financial statements are not well established, it is the authors' view also that such statements should be regarded essentially as supplemental data.

CURRENT REPLACEMENT COST ACCOUNTING

Operating profit and holding gains

One of the principal advantages claimed for current RC financial statements is that income would be divided into two segments: *operating profit* and *holding gains and losses.*

Operating profit is computed as the difference between sales revenue and the current cost of replacing resources used up in the production of current revenues. As such, it is a measure of a firm's ability to obtain revenues in excess of the current costs of production, which is generally considered to be a necessary condition for a firm to remain in business. It also has been asserted that RC operating income is the amount that could be distributed as dividends without impairing a firm's productive capacity. Undoubtedly, RC operating income provides a better shield for maintaining capital than does HC operating income, but, as we will show later, RC income will not fully shelter a firm's "real" capital.

Another advantage claimed by some advocates of RC accounting is that RC operating income has greater predictive power than other income numbers (it can be used to predict more successfully variables of interest, such as cash flow from future operations). The empirical support for this view at present is rather scant.

The second component of RC income is *holding gains and losses.* This portion of income is the change in the replacement cost of assets and liabilities over the reporting period. Holding gains are sometimes referred to generally as realizable cost savings, or in specific applications they have been identified as inventory profits. An increase in replacement costs represents the benefit to a firm of having acquired assets in advance of a price increase, or of having issued debt at an interest rate lower than the current rate.

A simple inventory example will illustrate the separation of operating profit and holding gains. Suppose that a company purchased (or produced) two units of inventory, the first at a cost of $100 and the second at a cost of $110. The first unit was sold for $150 when the RC was $116 per unit. At the end of the period the RC of a unit of inventory was $118. Gross margin figures for RC and several commonly-used inventory methods are shown in Table 1.

The holding gain on each unit is the difference between its original cost and the current replacement cost when the unit is sold, or at the end of period if the unit is unsold. In this example the holding gains are $16 on the first unit and $8 on the second unit.

As can be seen from the following analysis, only under RC computations is the entire holding gain removed from the gross margin. Note also that only with RC could the gross margin

TABLE 1

	RC	Fifo	Average cost	Lifo
Sales	$ 150	$ 150	$ 150	$ 150
Cost of goods sold	(116)	(100)	(105)	(110)
Gross margin	$ 34	$ 50	$ 45	$ 40

TABLE 2

	RC	Fifo	Average cost	Lifo
Sales	$ 150	$ 150	$ 150	$ 150
Current cost of goods sold	(116)	(116)	(116)	(116)
Amount of holding gain included in gross margin	0	16	11	6
Gross margin	$ 34	$ 50	$ 45	$ 40

be distributed and sufficient funds retained to replenish inventory (Table 2).

Lifo is the most successful of conventional methods in removing holding gains, but even Lifo fails to eliminate all of the holding gains because it does not cost all units sold at their current replacement costs at the time of sale. Thus historical-cost inventory techniques include a portion of the current period's holding gains in operating profit of the current period, and the balance of these gains in operating profit of subsequent periods when currently produced units are eventually sold. In contrast, RC income would report as a nonoperating item all holding gains of the period. This result is accomplished by valuing ending inventory, as well as cost of goods sold, at replacement costs. Journal entries to convert HC income to RC income for the preceding example would be as follows (assuming Fifo is used for HC reporting):

$$
\begin{array}{lr}
\text{Inventory } (118-110) & 8 \\
\text{Cost of goods sold } (116-100) & 16 \\
\quad \text{Inventory holding gains} & 24 \\
\end{array}
$$

By the above entry, ending inventory is valued at $118, the end of the period RC, and cost of goods sold is valued at $116, the current RC when the unit was sold. Note that even if we change our assumption concerning which unit is sold, the ending inventory, cost of goods sold, and total holding gains remain unchanged. If Lifo was used for HC reporting, the journal entry to record RC would be:

$$
\begin{array}{lr}
\text{Inventory } (118-100) & 18 \\
\text{Cost of goods sold } (116-110) & 6 \\
\quad \text{Inventory holding gains} & 24 \\
\end{array}
$$

A similar entry would adjust average costing to identical replacement cost amounts.

The issue of comparability

Interestingly, claims have been made on both sides of the comparability issue. Supporters of RC accounting assert that it would improve comparability, while detractors claim exactly the opposite. The computations of the previous section show that RC statements *potentially* improve comparability, both within firms and across firms. To the extent that the RC of inventory is uniquely determinable, variations caused by the use of different inventory methods among divisions or firms would disappear. This conclusion also holds in varying degrees for other classes of assets and liabilities.

In practice, however, firms often will have to rely on traditional accounting methods to approximate replacement cost and to isolate holding gains and operating profits. Consider the computations related to a depreciable asset. Unless a firm can obtain market estimates of the asset in its existing condition at the beginning of the year and at the end of the year, it will be necessary to approximate the asset's RC by estimating its RC new, and deducting allowances for depreciation. Even if beginning and end-of-year market estimates can be obtained, the net change includes the effects of both appreciation (assuming increasing replacement costs) and depreciation from use, obsolescence, and so forth. Appreciation is a holding gain and depreciation is an operating expense. In the absence of some improbable comparisons of market values, a depreciation calculation is required to partition the net change into the two components.

As an illustration of the preceding points, assume that a firm owns a depreciable asset that was purchased three years ago for $1,000. The asset has an estimated useful life of ten years and is being depreciated on a straight-line basis. For the fourth year, HC depreciation is $100, and beginning and ending book values are $700 and $600, respectively. Assume further that there is no active second-hand market for this type of asset and that its current cost is estimated by applying a U.S. Government price index for comparable machinery to the asset's book value. This index had a value of 120 when the asset was purchased, 150 at the beginning of the current year, and 164 at the end of the year. RC of the asset is estimated to be $700 (150/120) = $875 at the beginning of the year and $600 (164/120) =

$820 at the end of the year. Depreciation can be estimated as $\frac{1}{10}$ of the average replacement cost (new) during the year. Assuming that the price index increased at an even pace over the year, the depreciation calculation would be

$$\frac{1}{10}\left[\frac{\$1,000(150/120) + \$1,000(164/120)}{2}\right] =$$

$$\frac{1}{10}\left(\frac{\$1,250 + \$1,367}{2}\right) = \$131.$$

The holding gain can be computed as the difference between depreciation and the net change in the assets. The holding gain is thus equal to [$131 − ($875 − $820)] = $76. An alternative, but equivalent, set of calculations is to compute a holding gain for the first six months on the asset's beginning RC, compute depreciation on the mid-year value, and then compute a holding gain for the second six months on the newly depreciated RC. These computations are shown in Table 3. The assumed mid-year value of the price index is $(150 + 164)\frac{1}{2} = 157$.

Returning to the issue of comparability, we see that certain aspects of RC accounting could improve the comparability of accounting information, even for accounts such as plant and equipment. Consider, for example, two divisions (or two firms) operating with similar assets, except that Division One acquired the bulk of its plant and equipment a number of years prior to Division Two. Given increasing replacement costs, Division One will have a larger amount of holding gains included in historical-cost operating profit than will Division Two. The commin-

TABLE 3

RC, beginning of year	$ 875
Holding gain, first six months:	
$\$875\left(\dfrac{157 - 150}{150}\right)$	41
Depreciation on mid-year value (there are seven depreciable years remaining):	
$(\$875 + \$41)\dfrac{1}{7}$	(131)
Holding gain, second six months:	
$(\$875 + \$41 - \$131)\left(\dfrac{164 - 157}{157}\right)$	35
RC, end of year	$ 820

gling of holding gains and operating profits may obscure the relative operating efficiency of the two divisions. By separating holding gains and operating profits, and by deducting from current revenues the current costs of resources used, RC accounting potentially can improve comparisons of the two divisions. Further, measures of division performance, such as Return on Investment or Residual Income, should be more comparable when the investment bases are measured at current replacement costs. For each division, RC numbers give more current, and therefore potentially more comparable, measures of income to investment than do HC amounts.

On the other hand, comparability is reduced when firms or divisions use different procedures, assumptions, and price data in estimating current RC. We have also seen that separation of holding gains and depreciation will usually require a choice of depreciation method, which reintroduces a familiar source of variation among financial statements of divisions and firms. Even when similar estimating methods are used, differences in simplifying assumptions may produce dissimilar results. Suppose that in the previous example we had computed depreciation on the ending RC rather than on the average or mid-year RC. The calculations would be as follows:

RC, beginning of year .... $ 875
Holding gain for the year:
$$875 \left(\frac{164 - 150}{150} \right)$$ 82
Depreciation on ending RC:
($875 + $82) 1/7 .... (137)
RC, end of year .... $ 820

The balance sheet values and total income for the year have not changed; however, depreciation and holding gains each have been increased by the same amount, shifting operating profit to holding gains.

Thus we see that RC accounting offers the possibility of greater comparability in accounting numbers, but implementation differences reduce the possible advantage. Whether the net result is a general increase or decrease in comparability is still an open question. Further experimentation with replacement costs should provide information needed to answer the question more precisely.

GENERAL PRICE LEVEL ADJUSTMENTS AND CAPITAL MAINTENANCE CONSIDERATIONS

To fully understand RC accounting it is necessary to compare RC statements to general price level adjusted (GPLA) statements. General price level (GPL) adjustments to financial statements have been proposed both as an alternative to, and as a supplement to, replacement costs. We will discuss both applications, beginning with GPLA-HC statements and a comparison with RC statements.

General price-level adjusted historical cost statements

HC financial statements adjusted for changes in the GPL are generally considered to retain most of the features of conventional HC statements, since the purpose of the adjustment is to restate HC amounts in constant dollars. The procedure calls for restating nonmonetary assets, owners' equity, and revenues and expenses to end-of-year dollars as measured by some general index, such as the Consumer Price Index or the Gross National Product Implicit Price Deflator. Monetary assets and liabilities are already stated in current dollars so no adjustment of these amounts is needed. However, because the dollar amounts of these items do not change during inflation, holders of cash and other monetary assets suffer losses in general purchasing power, and debtors experience a gain in general purchasing power. These purchasing power gains and losses are reported in GPLA financial statements.

GPLA–HC versus RC statements

To compare GPLA statements with RC statements, we use a highly simplified set of financial statements. The simplifying assumptions are warranted because they permit us to examine the principal characteristics of the two systems without becoming bogged down in computational details. Additional and more detailed illustrations of the adjustment procedures are contained in a number of the references listed at the end of the chapter.

The data for the example are as follows:

1. Sales are $200 and all sales occur at the end of the year.
2. The firm holds a $300 cash balance through the year.

3. The firm maintains a constant balance of $200 in a noninterest-bearing liability account. Further, we assume that there is no change in the RC of this liability during the year.
4. The only noncash asset held by the firm is the depreciable asset used in the preceding example. The RC of the asset and the related RC income statement amounts are as previously described.
5. The only expense for the year is depreciation.
6. The general price level index had a value of 130 when the depreciable asset was purchased, 145 at the beginning of the current year, and 154 at the end of the year. The mid-year value was 149.

The data are summarized in the HC statements in Exhibit 1. The exhibit also shows RC and GPLA statements for purpose of comparison and analysis.

EXHIBIT 1
Comparison of HC, GPLA, and RC financial statements

Balance sheet (beginning of year)	HC	RC	GPLA*
Cash	$ 300	$ 300	$ 300
Equipment	700	875	781
Total	$1,000	$1,175	$1,081
Liabilities	$ 200	$ 200	$ 200
Owners' equity	800	975	881
Total	$1,000	$1,175	$1,081
Income statement			
Sales	$ 200	$ 200	$ 200
Depreciation	(100)	(131)	(119)
Operating income	100	69	81
Holding gain	0	76	0
Purchasing power loss	0	0	(6)
Net income	$ 100	$ 145	$ 75
Balance sheet (end of year)			
Cash	$ 500	$ 500	$ 500
Equipment	600	820	711
Total	$1,100	$1,320	$1,211
Liabilities	$ 200	$ 200	$ 200
Owners' equity:			
Beginning balance	800	975	881
Price level adjustment	0	0	55
Net income	100	145	75
Total	$1,100	$1,320	$1,211

* Presentations of comparative GPLA statements often report all statements in end-of-current-year dollars. If this procedure had been followed in this example, all amounts in the GPLA beginning balance sheet, including cash, would have been multiplied by 154/145. This computation is not necessary for the present analysis, therefore it is omitted.

Preparation of GPLA–HC statements

Amounts in the GPLA statements were determined in the following manner. Beginning and ending equipment balances were computed in exactly the same way as were the RC balances, except that the general price index was used instead of the specific price index. Depreciation also is calculated in a similar fashion. The computations are shown in Table 4.

Depreciation of $115 is computed using mid-year dollars and is "rolled forward" to $115 (154/149) = $119 in the income statement. In the GPLA statements all amounts are reported in constant, end-of-year dollars. Note that the increase in the equipment balance of $22 + $23 is *not* considered to be a holding gain in GPLA statements. The adjustment is simply a restatement of existing balances in the new measuring unit—end-of-year dollars. GPL adjustments are a revision of the measurement scales and not an assessment of value. For this reason, holding gains and losses on nonmonetary assets will never be included as a separate item in GPLA financial statements.

TABLE 4

Beginning balance: 700\left(\frac{145}{130}\right)$ .... $ 781

Price-level restatement, first six months:

781\left(\frac{149-145}{145}\right)$ 22

Depreciation on mid-year value:

($781 + $22) $\frac{1}{7}$ .... (115)

Price-level restatement, second six months:

($781 + $22 − $115) $\left(\frac{154-149}{149}\right)$ 23

Ending balance: 600$\left(\frac{154}{130}\right)$ .... $ 711

On the other hand, purchasing power gains and losses on monetary items always appear in GPLA statements because the measuring unit is changing, but the amounts of monetary assets and liabilities are, by definition, stated in current dollars. It is, of course, a well-recognized phenomenon that holders of cash and other monetary assets lose purchasing power in periods of inflation while debtors gain by paying debts in dollars of reduced value. The firm in the present example holds net monetary assets of $300 cash − 200 liability = $100, and therefore experiences a net purchasing power loss of $6, calculated as follows: $100 (154/145) − $100 = $106 − $100 = $6. In other words, the firm's net monetary assets would have had to increase to $106 by the end of the year for the firm to keep pace with inflation. Since the net balance remained at $100, the firm experienced a $6 loss.

In comparison, observe that the RC statements show no purchasing power loss. The usual interpretation of RC increments (and decrements) is that a change in value has occurred. Changes in the monetary unit are ignored and thus implicitly assumed to be zero. Under these assumptions, purchasing power gains and losses on monetary items will not be reported in RC financial statements.

The restated beginning balance in the GPLA owners' equity account of $881 + $55 = $936 is computed by multiplying the beginning owners' equity of $881 by 154/145, the relative increase in the GPL. With the adjustment to owners' equity, all amounts in the income statement and balance sheet are stated in constant, end-of-year dollars. All amounts were adjusted upwards except sales, cash, and liabilities. Sales were assumed to occur on the last day of the year and therefore were already stated in current dollars. Cash and liabilities are always expressed in year-end dollars and cannot be adjusted upwards. This restriction is precisely the cause of the net loss of purchasing power.

Comparison of GPLA and RC statements

The differences between GPLA financial statements and RC statements are cited both as strengths and weaknesses of the former. The chief criticisms of GPL adjustments is that they do not report current values of assets and liabilities. Financial statements, although stated in constant dollars, are still a composite of dissimilar amounts for similar items. Consider two shares of stock, one purchased for $100 when the general price level index was 100 and the second purchased for $120 when the same index was 110. The current value of the index is 115. Under GPLA accounting the first share would be reported at $100 (115/100) = $115, and the second share would be reported at $120(115/110) = $125. The two shares of stock are identical, but they are reported at different amounts. Further, it is quite likely that the current cost of the two shares is significantly different from either reported amount.

A related argument is that since GPLA assets and liabilities are not reported at current costs, expenses do not reflect the current opportunity cost of using resources. Advocates of historical cost, however, turn these criticisms around and argue that they are advantages of both HC and GPLA statements. They argue that since GPLA statements are still essentially HC statements, the former possess most of the attributes and advantages of the latter. As mentioned earlier, supporters of HC accounting argue in particular that HC statements, and therefore also GPLA statements, possess a higher degree of "objectivity" than do RC statements. HC advocates believe that this greater objectivity contributes significantly to the credibility and usefulness of HC financial statements. A lack of precision in the specific (and operational) definition of "objectivity" has contributed to the disagreement among accountants on this point.

An interesting perspective on the relationship between HC statements, GPLA statements, and RC statements is provided by considering the effects of RC and GPL adjustments on the lifetime income of a firm. RC adjustments will not change a firm's reported lifetime income (as compared to HC income) because all holding gains and losses will eventually be fully offset by higher or lower expense charges. GPL, on the other hand, will permanently change a firm's lifetime income. In periods of inflation, GPL adjustments will increase book values of nonmonetary assets and therefore increase future expenses; however, the credit side of the increase is a capital adjustment factor, not income. Additionally, GPLA statements recognize purchasing power gains and losses that are never recognized in HC statements. Thus RC statements change the timing and classification of income, but they do not change lifetime income. GPLA statements change the timing and classification of income *and* the amount of lifetime income. From this perspective, GPLA accounting seems a greater departure from HC accounting than does RC accounting. We note in passing that RC adjustments, since they are timing differences, would seem to call for deferred income tax accruals, while GPL adjustments, being permanent differences, would not.

An additional criticism of GPLA accounting is that firms with large amounts of liabilities could report large increases in income because of purchasing power gains without corresponding increases in cash flows. A response to this criticism is that the dollar is an unstable measuring unit, and GPL accounting attempts to remedy this problem by accounting for units of constant purchasing power. When a firm pays liabilities in "cheaper" dollars than those borrowed, it does realize a gain in purchasing power.

Capital maintenance factors

A capital maintenance factor is implicit in every measure of income; it distinguishes return *on* capital from return *of* capital. Explicit recognition of the capital maintenance factor helps in understanding the impact of inflation on any system of accounting.

The key to understanding the capital maintenance assumption behind any income number is to look at the adjustment for inflation which is made to the owners' equity accounts. Since income is the increase in owners' equity (assuming no capital contributions or withdrawals, as we will do for the remainder of the discussion), any upward adjustment to owners' equity for inflation reduces income by the same amount. Income becomes that part of the increment to owners' equity which is over and above the increase needed to keep pace with inflation. The mix of resources in the price index used to adjust the equity accounts therefore determines the nature of the owners' capital that would be maintained if income were completely distributed to owners.

No adjustment for inflation is made to HC financial statements, thus the total increment to owners' equity is HC income. Accelerated depreciation, Lifo inventory, and other accounting techniques may temporarily reduce HC income and provide a partial shield against unknowing distributions of "real" capital, but, over time, the capital shielded or maintained by HC accounting is simply the number of dollars invested.

In contrast, GPLA statements define capital in terms of units of general purchasing power (GPP). GPLA income could be fully distributed without impairing the general purchasing power of the dollar balance reported for owners' equity as of the beginning of the period.[2] The fact that most firms increase or decrease capital rather than maintain a given level of capital is irrelevant, just as it is irrelevant to the measurement of income whether management intends to distribute all of a period's income, or some greater or lesser amount. A capital maintenance concept is required for the accounting construct of income.

An analysis of the RC statements in Exhibit 1 shows that there is no restatement of beginning owners' equity to adjust for inflation. From this observation we see that the capital maintained after distributions of RC net income is the beginning number of dollars of owners' equity and *not* the amount required to replace existing assets. This conclusion is confirmed by our earlier analysis that showed lifetime RC income to be equal to lifetime HC income.

In our earlier example we saw that if RC gross margin were distributed sufficient funds would be available to replace inventory. Holding gains could not be distributed if replacement were to be made from existing funds. Retention of holding gains is a *necessary*, but not *sufficient*, condition for the replacement of operating assets without additional borrowing or investment. Stated another way, even if only RC operating profit were distributed, existing capacity could not be replaced without raising additional external funds. To see this, simply consider RC depreciation charges to income. With continually increasing RC, the cumulative RC depreciation charges will be less than the cost to replace at the time of replacement. Only if depreciation were taken on estimated future RC, or if funds equal to current RC depreciation were invested at a rate equal to, or greater than, the rate of increase in RC and the resulting earnings were not distributed, would funds be available for replacement of the initial depreciable equipment.

To achieve a RC concept of capital maintenance all assets and liabilities must be adjusted to their replacement costs *and* a purchasing power gain or loss on net monetary items must

---

[2] This statement assumes that net assets reported in GPLA statements are not overstated, that is, not reported at an amount in excess of their value. Given the lower-of-cost-or-market rule and the conservative nature of HC accounting, this assumption would appear usually to be net. However, note that since GPLA–HC statements do not record values, it is impossible to determine precisely whether sufficient value has been retained to meet GPP capital maintenance requirements.

be recognized. The purchasing power gain or loss would be measured by reference to a firm-specific index based upon the mix of specific resources held and used by the firm. An equivalent procedure producing the same result (the same net income) is to adjust beginning owners' equity by such a firm-specific index.

The equivalency of these two sets of procedures can be ascertained by reviewing the comparable computations in the GPLA statements in Exhibit 1. The GPLA income statement shows an item by item analysis of the effects of changes in the GPL on income. Alternatively, income can be computed as the change in net assets, less the adjustment to owners' equity. The alternative computation is shown below:

```
Net GPLA assets, end of year:
    $1,211 − $200 ...................................    $1,011
Net GPLA assets, beginning of year:
    $1,081 − $200 ...................................     (881)
    Net change .....................................      130
    Less adjustment to owners' equity ..............      (55)
    GPLA net income ................................    $   75
```

Upon reflection it becomes clear that the two methods of adjustment are, of course, identical. Adjusting nonmonetary items by a given index, and recognizing a purchasing-power gain or loss on monetary accounts, is, in total, an adjustment to net assets or owners' equity.

The preceding analysis shows that if we were to construct financial statements using a firm-specific price index in exactly the same manner that we used a GPL index in preparing GPLA statements, we would achieve a RC concept of capital maintenance. RC financial statements as usually constructed (and as illustrated in this chapter) do not employ such a complete adjustment procedure, and therefore they do not utilize a RC capital maintenance concept nor do they shield sufficient funds for replacement of all assets. RC *operating* income provides a partial shield, but RC *net* income contains exactly the same concept of capital maintenance as does HC net income. Further, even if a firm-specific index were used to adjust owners' equity and to produce a RC capital maintenance concept, replacement of existing assets would still require an increase in liabilities proportionate to the upward adjustment to owners' equity. Capital maintenance adjustments are just what the term implies—adjustments to (owners') capital. But since assets are financed by owners' capital *and* debt, proportionate increases in *both* capital and debt would be needed to assure replacement of assets subject to increasing costs. The point of this discussion is to demonstrate that reliance on either a RC operating income concept or a RC capital maintenance concept is not sufficient to guarantee that adequate resources will be available for replacement of assets without the need for additional investment or borrowing.[3]

Selection of a purchasing power index

The preceding discussion also shows that the type of index applied to owners' equity determines the implied concept of capital maintenance. The capital maintenance factor also can be interpreted as a scale correction to adjust the beginning owners' equity balance to its equivalent value in end-of-year dollars. But what is the appropriate measure of the change in the value of the dollar? What market basket is relevant to a given firm, or perhaps to all firms, to measure the impact of inflation? Or, asked another way, what type of owners' capital should be maintained before income is reported? Some relevant possibilities are listed below, together with the related price index.

1. Purchasing power over all goods in the economy (GNP implicit price deflator).
2. Purchasing power over selected consumer goods (consumer price index).
3. Purchasing power over the specific resources used by a firm (firm-specific index).
4. Purchasing power over resources used by a given industry (industry-specific index).
5. Purchasing power over investment goods in general (broad-based index of price movements in investment goods in the relevant economic sector).

---

[3] Note also that by using a firm-specific index as a capital maintenance adjustment, increments in the RC of assets would be considered restatements of capital rather than holding gains. Thus firms whose principal business is comprised of holding activities (investment firms of various types) would report little, if any, income under this procedure.

6. Maintenance of the initial number of dollars of capital (no adjustment to HC statements required).

Explicit consideration of the capital maintenance aspects of any accounting system should assist in interpreting the income numbers produced by the system. Such considerations also should provide a useful tool in judging and comparing alternative methods of measuring and reporting income.

Combining GPLA and RC adjustments

As we have seen, RC financial statements only provide for maintenance of original dollar capital and ignore changes in the value of the dollar itself. For these reasons, a number of accountants and economists have suggested combining GPL and RC adjustments. Such GPLA–RC statements would (1) calculate holding gains as the change in the estimated replacement costs of assets and liabilities, (2) deflate holding gains for the amount of increase necessary to keep pace with the increase in the GPL, (3) report "real" holding gains separately from RC operating profit, (4) report balance sheet amounts at current replacement costs, and (5) yield an income measure that includes general purchasing power gains and losses on monetary accounts. Exhibit 2 illustrates this system, using the data of Exhibit 1.

The amounts in Exhibit 2 were computed as follows:

1. The beginning and ending balance sheets are essentially the same as the RC balance sheets shown in Exhibit 1, except that the total increment to owners' equity is no longer considered to be entirely income. Beginning owners' equity is restated to end-of-year dollars by adding $61 to the beginning balance of $975. The restated opening balance is $975 (154/145) = $1,036. The remainder of the change in net assets, or owners' equity, is net income of $84. From these calculations we see that the capital maintenance factor in GPLA–RC statements is the same as in GPLA statements (general purchasing power). Net income is the increase in the replacement costs of net assets *after* net assets have been augmented for the decrease in the general purchasing power of the dollar. Note that all GPL adjustments are based on the beginning RC balances.

EXHIBIT 2
GPLA-RC financial statements

Balance sheet
(beginning of year)

Cash..............................	$ 300
Equipment..........................	875
Total	$1,175
Liabilities	$ 200
Owners' equity	975
Total	$1,175

Income statement

Sales..............................	$ 200
Depreciation	(135)
Operating income	65
Real holding gain	25
Purchasing power loss...................	(6)
Net income	$ 84

Balance sheet
(end of year)

Cash..............................	$ 500
Equipment..........................	820
Total	$1,320
Liabilities	$ 200
Owners' equity:	
Beginning balance	975
Price level adjustment	61
Net income	84
Total	$1,320

2. As before, sales are already stated in end-of-year dollars and no adjustment is necessary.

3. Current RC depreciation of $131 was computed on the average, or mid-year, RC value. Since GPLA statements are in constant end-of-year dollars, RC depreciation is "rolled forward" to $131(154/149) = $135. The depreciation is still based on average RC, but is restated to its equivalent amount in end-of-year dollars.

4. The "real" holding gain of $25 is the difference between the increase in RC of equipment of $76, computed earlier, and the increase needed to keep pace with inflation generally. Adjustments of the latter type have been termed fictional gains because increases in asset values that just match changes in the GPL do not increase general purchasing power. An analogous situation is a bond that yields 8 percent when the inflation rate is 6 percent. The "real" rate of return on the bond is 8 percent − 6 percent = 2 percent, and

the 6 percent portion is a fictional or illusory gain. The fictional gain on equipment was computed in the following manner.

Price level restatement, or fictional gain,
  during first six months:
    $875 (149 − 145/145) .... $24+
Price level restatement, or fictional gain,
  during second six months:
    ($875 + $41 − $131) (154 − 149/149) .... 26+
    Total $51

The fictional gain for the second six months is based on the RC at mid-year, after adding the holding gain for the first six months and deducting depreciation. The real holding gain is the $76 increase in RC less the $51 fictional gain.

5. The purchasing power loss of $6 is the same loss computed and reported in the GPLA statements of Exhibit 1. Although our highly-simplified example does not show it, GPLA–RC statements would usually report two types of adjustments to liabilities and noncash monetary assets. Changes in the interest rate could change the RC cost of these items and produce holding gains or losses independent of changes in the GPL. In this event, liabilities and noncash monetary assets would be listed at their current RC, holding gains and losses would be reported based on changes in replacement costs of these assets and liabilities, and general purchasing power gains and losses also would be calculated by applying changes in the GPL index to RC balances.

USES OF RC FINANCIAL STATEMENTS

The most comprehensive RC financial statements, for the purpose of disclosing the impact of inflation on a firm, are GPLA–RC statements. Accordingly, the ensuing discussion will focus on GPLA–RC statements. General references to RC will be in the context of this dual system of reporting, although some of the following comments are applicable equally to either RC or GPLA–RC statements.

The potential usefulness of GPLA–RC statements lies in their contribution to the evaluation of current operations. The existence of RC operating profit indicates that in the current period, revenues exceeded the current costs of replacing resources consumed in the production of revenues. A sufficient level of operating profit should usually be a reliable signal for the continuation of production. By comparison, HC statements, by including holding gains in operating profits, may encourage firms to continue or expand production in areas where the margin of revenues over current costs would not justify such a decision. Evaluations of relative profitability also could be more reliable when operating earnings are compared to assets valued at their current costs. Return on investment percentages based on the amortized historical costs of assets will usually be higher and may contribute to overly optimistic evaluations of current operating methods.

As we have seen, GPLA–RC income statements also include holding gains and losses, but report them separately from operating profits and deflate them for rises in the GPL. In fact, GPLA–RC statements will report holding gains in current statements that will be realized only later in HC statements. HC income spreads or smoothes holding gains over time by reporting expenses at less than their current costs. While this smoothing procedure may give a useful picture of overall results over time, advocates of RC accounting believe that separation of the two components of income permits a more detailed and accurate analysis.

Recall that GPLA–RC statements also reveal the impact of inflation (as captured in the index employed) on a firm's lending and borrowing policies. This information may call for and provide a sharper evaluation of these activities. The "bottom line" of the GPLA–RC income statement is a number that approximates the increase in purchasing power produced by the firm during the year. Depending upon the GPL index used, this income number provides a summary figure that can be interpreted *roughly* as an index of management's ability to increase the firm's, or owners', command over goods and services in the economy.

Some replacement cost techniques have become common practice and are used regularly by corporate management without a conscious awareness of doing so. Product pricing is probably one of the more frequently occurring examples. If the product has been purchased for resale or if it is a major, high cost item, the replacement cost will generally be one of the dominant considerations in establishing a desired selling price. On the other hand, if the product is manufactured, the price setter may anticipate further labor and material costs but most likely will not consider the replacement cost of the productive facilities. This can be a costly omission, particularly if equipment replacement is likely in the foreseeable future. Knowledge of replacement costs and the operating costs and characteristics of new facilities can provide a different perspective on the adequacy of existing prices. This knowledge is also helpful in estimating the operating economics of competitors and provides a sound basis for setting pricing goals.

Any long-range strategic planning also will be enhanced by previously developed replacement cost information, particularly if it incorporates the latest technological improvements. The potential economic benefits of such replacements may suggest a different allocation of capital or a different sequence or timing of investments. Replacement costs reflect current cost levels but they can be readily modified for future periods by applying estimated price changes or estimated inflation rates for the intervening period.

Replacement cost or current value information is useful in monitoring property tax assessments. Taxing authorities frequently base their assessments on historical costs supplied by the company. A general price index is usually applied to the data to approximate either a current cost or current value. Well-founded replacement cost information will not only verify the validity of such assessments but may also serve as a basis for obtaining reassessments when warranted.

The determination of insurance values is also greatly enhanced by having complete and current replacement cost information available. In the event of insurable losses such information may be very beneficial in negotiating a settlement with the carrier.

There are also a broad range of profit center evaluations and financial ratio analyses that are particularly well-suited to replacement cost or current value concepts. Some of the more significant applications are as follows:

1. Maintenance as percent of gross replacement cost. Due to the rapidly changing cost of productive facilities it is sometimes difficult to compare the operating performance of units which are of different size and age. A more equitable comparison of maintenance expense can be made if it is related to the replacement cost of the assets employed. Similar comparisons can be made for other expenses which are affected by the amount of assets employed.

2. **Financial ratios.** Analyses of financial ratios which are based on current values or replacement costs can frequently provide a helpful perspective. We have already mentioned the use of RC in comparing return on investment rates of units with assets of widely different ages. Other financial management ratios in which current value or replacement cost procedures can be useful are asset turnover rates, net income margins, and other interunit comparisons of profit or expense.

LIMITATIONS OF RC AND PROBLEMS OF IMPLEMENTATION

As we have seen, RC accounting has many potential advantages during periods of high inflation or rapidly changing costs. Its superiority over historical costs in reporting the effects of inflation is clearly illustrated in simplified examples. Unfortunately, when these concepts are applied to actual large and complex industrial enterprises, the problems encountered are usually substantial.

One of the most frequently cited problems with replacement cost accounting concerns the subjectivity of the exercise, particularly in estimating the replacement cost of productive facilities. Numerous sequential judgments are required and each may have a profound impact on the end result. The first judgment required is whether to estimate the replacement cost of identical facilities (usually referred to as *a reproduction cost*) or to estimate the *replacement cost* of the firm's productive capacity. The latter recognizes technological change, is more representative of what would actually happen if indeed the facilities were replaced, and is therefore usually recommended. For most companies the two approaches will yield greatly different answers.

The second major judgment area concerns the form and location of replacement. Will larger, more economical facilities replace smaller ones? Obviously, this would be the normal means of replacement for a growing company, but the operating costs of such facilities might differ significantly. In addition to operating efficiencies, the modern facilities might also be capable of producing higher quality products, or in some instances even different products. For example, a modern oil refinery is capable of converting a greater proportion of the crude oil to higher value products than a refinery which is a few years old. Revenues as well as operating costs would therefore be different if such productive facilities were actually replaced. Opponents of replacement cost reporting question the propriety of deducting a depreciation charge based on the cost of new facilities without considering all of the other changes that would result from such replacements. On the other hand, if all such changes were built into an estimate, the end result would bear little resemblance to the existing company.

When a firm intends to replace in kind, the interpretation and use of RC statements are fairly straightforward. But, given technological change, exact replacement in kind of many types of assets is probably a rare event for most firms. If RC is defined as the cost of equivalent services or capacity, rather than the cost of identical assets, the concept would seem still to have some relevance to the evaluation of continuing production. However, the greater the technological differences between replacement assets and existing capacity, the more "iffy" the computations become, and at some extreme the relevance of the data is called into question. This limitation also becomes apparent when one considers the interpretation of assets listed on the balance sheet at the replacement costs of assets that differ significantly from present assets in technology, capacity, required resource mix, and so forth. These considerations suggest that RC financial statements are more useful when some stability in technology is present. In rapidly changing environments the usefulness of RC, defined as the cost of equivalent services, would seem to diminish accordingly. Other measures of asset value may become more useful in these circumstances. We will return to this consideration in later sections of the chapter.

After determining the *form of replacement,* additional problems may occur in determining the *cost.* Direct pricing is often impossible for large companies, not only because of the magnitude of the task but also because market prices are not available for their unique operating processes and equipment. In such circumstances it becomes necessary to rely upon some combination of appraisals, engineering estimates, or indexing of historical costs. Unfortunately, widely different answers can be obtained from equally authoritative sources. For example, there are many indices published in the United States which are purported to reflect changing costs within a specific industry. Some also contain allowances for technological advances. Because of the different weighting of components and assessments of the impact of technological change, some of these indices vary significantly.

Another criticism of most replacement cost proposals is that they fail to recognize *leverage effects*. Most companies strive to maintain certain debt/equity ratios, and a portion of the higher replacement costs that are incurred in the future will be financed with debt. This policy reduces the need for retention of funds equal to the total replacement cost of existing assets.

Finally, there are also objections to the notional concept of instantaneous total replacement of assets, since this concept implies that replacement actually will occur and that the company will remain indefinitely in the existing lines of business.

EXIT VALUES AS AN ALTERNATIVE TO REPLACEMENT COSTS

Because the relevance of RC computations becomes questionable when replacement either will occur in substantially different form or will not occur at all, the search for a useful measure of current value turns to other measurement bases. One such basis advocated by a number of accountants and at least one prominent accounting firm is exit value (EV). The following paragraphs provide a brief discussion of EV accounting.

The essence of EV accounting is that assets and liabilities are valued at their current exit (market) values, and net income is the change in net assets so valued. GPL adjustments may be imposed on an EV system, just as with HC and RC accounting systems. The mechanics of EV accounting are quite similar to those of RC accounting, except that exit values rather than entry values are used. As with RC accounting, EV accounting changes the timing of income recognition, but not the amount of lifetime income, and when GPL adjustments are used also, the implied capital maintenance policy is general purchasing power.

EV is usually taken to mean a current liquidation price, but not a distress sale price. In the case of inventory some accountants have suggested that, because of the cost of waiting and risk-bearing, exit value is something less than the final selling price in the normal selling market. Presumably, exit value of inventory would refer to a sale in the entry market (i.e., the markets in which a firm *acquires* inventory, raw material, etc.), and this market value would then approximate the RC of the inventory. This procedure allows a margin to be earned at the time of sale; if inventory were valued at final selling price, the sale itself would have no influence on revenue recognition.

Some accountants would not attempt to partition EV income into operating income and holding gains and losses, primarily to avoid the accounting allocations needed to do so. In its purest form, EV accounting values all assets and liabilities by reference to market prices, thus avoiding the usual accounting allocations involved in choices of inventory, depreciation, and other accounting methods.

Supporters of EV statements argue that neither HC nor RC statements show the value of the specific assets held and used by the firm. Such values, they argue, are not shown by the unamortized HC of assets nor by the RC of equivalent services, but by the value, measured in the market place, of the specific assets and liabilities held by the firm. On the other hand, opponents of EV have questioned the relevance of exit values of assets that the firm does not intend to sell. As an illustration of the point in contention, consider a comparison of HC accounting and EV accounting for a $1,000 bond purchased at par as an investment by a firm that intends to hold the bond until it matures in five years. If the coupon rate of the bond is 8 percent, HC statements will report an 8 percent return in each of the five years, regardless of changes in the market rate of interest and market value of the bond. If the interest rate dropped to 6 percent during the year, EV statements would report a gain due to the increase in the bond's market value, and a 6 percent yield in subsequent periods as long as the interest rate remained unchanged at 6 percent. If the bond is held to maturity, the average (geometric mean) annual return is, in fact, 8 percent, regardless of changes in the market rate. HC advocates argue that this averaging process provides information more relevant to the evaluation of management's actions. EV supporters point out, however, that management's continuing decision to hold the investment actually yielded more than 8 percent the first year and less than 8 percent in subsequent years. They argue further that a series of returns that averages 8 percent is not the same as a series of constant 8 percent returns, and that evaluations would be improved if the differences in these two series were revealed.

In the preceding illustration, one could argue that the firm had the option to sell the bond, even though it elected not to do so. For other classes of assets, particularly large chunks of productive capacity, sale often is simply not a feasible alternative, and the relevance of EV for these assets has been questioned. To the extent that EV provides some measure of the "economic worth" of resources held and used by a firm, these values still may be relevant to the evaluation of a firm, even for assets for which immediate liquidation has been ruled out.

A related problem concerns a firm's ability to obtain market values for certain classes of assets, particularly special-purpose assets. Presumably, as long as an asset has the ability to produce future cash flows, it will be saleable under some set of conditions. However, these conditions may not be easily obtained by potential buyers, or conditions for sale may not be encountered frequently enough to allow regular financial statement presentation. In the case of special-purpose assets for which no apparent current resale market exists, a strict EV system would seem to call for a zero valuation. Yet these assets clearly may have substantial value to the firm, and zero values for such assets seem to send a misleading set of signals. As Professor Carl Devine has observed, if new special-purpose assets are drastically written down due to inactive or nonexistent resale markets, income will be significantly depressed just when prospects may be brightest for the firm. Moreover, future income statements will be relieved of the charges resulting from use of the assets, which implies that their use is cost free. If there genuinely are no alternative uses of an asset, its opportunity cost is correctly reckoned to be zero, but the utility of the resulting income number for evaluation and prediction is suspect.

Exit values are not unambiguous even when resale markets exist for a given class of assets. If various markets exist, geographically or otherwise, which market should be tapped regularly for periodic financial reporting? For what combination of assets should market values be obtained? Aggregate asset values will usually vary depending upon the combination in which they are sold. A key and a lock sold separately will have little value. If the appropriate level of aggregation is the firm itself, the danger of circularity exists. The best measure of the aggregate net assets may be the market values of all shares of stock outstanding (assuming a reasonably active market for the stock). Net income would then be equal to the change in net assets, which presumably influence stock prices, which are then used as the determinant of income.[4]

AN ECLECTIC APPROACH
AS AN ALTERNATIVE

In some circumstances the choice between RC and EV may be of little consequence because the difference between the two may be only a nominal broker's margin (as in the preceding bond example). Or, differences in the two methods may disappear in the estimating procedures. If, for example, a specific index number is used to estimate RC or EV, the result may serve as a reasonable approximation of either quantity.

However, in numerous cases we can expect that the replacement (construction) costs of assets or equivalent services will differ significantly from resale values of existing assets, and a choice between methods is required if some measure of current value is desired. Particularly bothersome are the relevance of RC when replacement will be in substantially different form, if at all, and the relevance of the EV of assets for which no readily available resale markets exist. Unfortunately, the limitations of RC and EV in these situations do not necessarily increase the relevance of HC. Earlier sections reviewed the limitations of HC financial statements in periods of inflation.

A reconsideration of the objectives of alternatives to HC accounting suggests that a selective use of RC and EV (and possibly other) concepts may, in certain circumstances (such as those specified in the preceding paragraph), meet these objectives bet-

---

[4] The problem of specifying the appropriate level of aggregation to use in determining EV somewhat parallels the allocation (disaggregation) problem inherent in HC accounting.

ter than any single system. A common feature of RC and EV accounting is that they both attempt to replace the older HC of resources held and used by a firm with some measure of current economic worth. Advocates of both systems believe that the financial condition of a firm is better revealed by a balance sheet that uses some measure of current worth, and that income statements based on changes in current worth provide a better report card on the current performance of management. An eclectic approach, choosing one measure or the other as the most relevant measure of current worth in given circumstances, may overcome some of the more serious deficiencies of all systems of reporting. For example, when replacement will be in substantially different form, exit values may be more relevant than either RC or HC. When no exit values can readily be obtained for certain assets, estimated cost to replace may be a useful approximation of current worth. In other circumstances, HC may provide a satisfactory estimate of current worth.

Numerous business firms have experimented with RC or EV, either voluntarily or to meet imposed reporting requirements. It seems reasonable to expect continuing experimentation and use of these alternative accounting systems. Such experience should help establish the conditions under which each type of information is most relevant and useful.

The preceding discussion has not considered the cost of implementing RC or EV information systems. Evidence on the additional cost of these systems is varied. Some firms report minimum and/or acceptable levels of cost, while many feel that the cost is too great and outweighs the benefits of the information. In either case, costs can be expected to decrease with repeated applications.

SUMMARY

In this chapter we have examined several methods of inflation accounting, with particular emphasis on RC accounting. Since the SEC has required certain RC disclosures for fiscal years ending after December 25, 1976, many firms now have limited experience with partial disclosure of RC data. Although there are a few notable exceptions to the common view, it does not seem unfair to state that in general, industry has been almost unanimous in its opposition to RC disclosure for shareholder's reports, registration statements, and other reports to the general public. Presumably, this opposition stems from concerns about the limitations of RC data and problems of implementation as discussed in earlier sections of this chapter.

However, even the most vocal opponents of value accounting generally concede that something needs to be done to disclose the impact of inflation, and many people have suggested further experimentation to develop the most useful procedures. Such experimentation hopefully will demonstrate the validity (or lack thereof) of advantages claimed for many techniques that have been and are currently being proposed. It is entirely possible that the ultimate resolution may encompass several of what at present appear to be conflicting methodologies. It is also likely that different procedures may be needed for different purposes, since there is no one definition of "value" nor one unique form of replacement for which a single number could be generated that would suffice for all types of economic decisions. The recent distinction by the FASB between financial statements and financial reporting may facilitate experimentation by assuring industry that HC financial statements will not precipitously be replaced by alternative value-based statements.

The cost accountant can play a leading role in this experimentation and in the development of reporting concepts. Internal reports to management can more easily explain the subjective judgments involved, and the effect of alternative judgments and procedures will be more readily apparent. Many of the concerns relative to external reporting would either not apply or be of lesser importance for data submitted to a well-informed member of management. Greater freedom can therefore be exercised in such experimentations. Information which is proven useful to management should also provide a sound basis for useful disclosures to shareholders and investors.

REFERENCES

American Accounting Association (AAA), Committee to Prepare a Statement of Basic Accounting Theory, *A Statement of Basic Accounting Theory*, AAA, Sarasota, Florida, 1966.

American Institute of Certified Public Accountants (AICPA), *Objectives of Financial Statements*, New York, 1973.

———, "Financial Statements Restated for General Price Level Changes," *Statement of the Accounting Principles Board No. 3*, New York, 1969.

———, Accounting Research Division, *Reporting the Financial Effects of Price-Level Changes*, Accounting Research Study No. 6, New York, 1963.

Bruns, W. J., Jr., and Vancil, R. F. *A Primer on Cost Replacement Accounting*. Glen Ridge, N.J.: Thomas Horton and Daughters, 1976.

Chambers, R. J. *Accounting, Evaluation, and Economic Behavior*. Englewood Cliffs, N.J.: Prentice-Hall, 1966.

Davidson, S., Stickney, C. P. and Weil, R. J. *Inflation Accounting, A Guide for the Accountant and the Financial Analyst*, New York: McGraw-Hill, 1976.

Edwards, E. O., and Bell, P. W. *The Theory and Measurement of Business Income*. Berkeley and Los Angeles, University of California Press, 1961.

Financial Accounting Standards Board (FASB), *Conceptual Framework for Financial Accounting and Reporting: Elements of Financial Statements and Their Measurement*, FASB Discussion Memorandum, Stamford, Conn., December 2, 1976.

———, *Conceptual Framework for Accounting and Reporting: Consideration of the Report of the Study Group on the Objectives of Financial Statements*, FASB Discussion Memorandum, Stamford, Conn., June 6, 1974.

Hendriksen, E. S. *Accounting Theory*, 3rd ed. Homewood, Ill.: Richard D. Irwin, Inc., 1977 (especially Chapter 7).

Largay, J. A., and Livingstone, J. L. *Accounting for Changing Prices: Replacement Costs and General Price Level Adjustments*. Santa Barbara, Calif.: Wiley/Hamilton, 1976.

Revsine, L. *Replacement Cost Accounting*. Englewood Cliffs, N.J.: Prentice-Hall, 1973.

Sterling, R. R. "Relevant Financial Reporting in an Age of Price Changes." *Journal of Accountancy*, February 1975, 42–51.

———, *Theory of the Measurement of Enterprise Income*. Lawrence, Kans.: The University Press of Kansas, 1970.

39

Accounting and reporting for segment performance evaluation

Donald C. Haley†
*Charles W. Plum**

In an uncertain and expanding economy where a business entity must deal with increased competition, proliferating government regulation and constraints, and altering life styles and social mores, a successful enterprise doesn't just happen. These transforming conditions have emphasized the need for planned and coordinated action. Besides these environmental changes, inter- and intraentity modifications have also made organization segmentation highly desirable by managerial decision makers. When a business expands it becomes increasingly difficult to manage the more complex organization. As a result, top decision makers find that by dividing the entity into manageable parts with responsible managers, the principal functions of planning, controlling, and evaluating may be better attained. Thus, more meaningful and timely information upon which to base decisions and measure performance has become the essential ingredient for successful operations.

PROS AND CONS OF SEGMENTATION

The NAA Committee on Research (NACA *Bulletin*, vol. 36) states:

---
† Controller, The Standard Oil Company (Ohio).

* Professor of Accounting, Texas A & M University.

. . . experience has shown that the executive who receives too much detail is not necessarily well informed because he becomes confused by details and is unable to visualize the trends and broad aspects which are more important than the individual items. Moreover, if the executive actually studies and analyzes the figures, valuable time is consumed at a task which can be delegated in large part.

This describes the main advantage of segmentation: spreading the volume of recurring operating decisions among many executives, which allows top management more time for strategic planning.

Other major benefits from partitioning an enterprise into smaller units are:

1. Separate evaluation of profitability rates, degrees of risk, and opportunities for growth. Decision makers are better able to determine whether additional investment of money, time, or managerial talent is needed or justified in a particular segment. If the components are healthy, then logically the combined action will produce a more successful and profitable entity.

2. Prompt decisions when action is necessary because of environmental changes. Timely segment information will permit organizations to adapt more quickly and efficiently, for example, to changes in market demand and to new or revised government regulations.

3. Greater freedom to make decisions and thereby to impact results. Although varying degrees of decentralized management exist under differing levels of authority and responsibility within most segmented organizations, there will be more incentive for improving the performance of segments.

4. A mechanism for checking a producing segment whose unit variable production costs exceed the prevailing "willing buyer—willing seller" prices. Where an arms-length market price is the basis for recording and reporting intersegment sales, it may be possible to highlight economic activities which might be impossible to emphasize in a centralized environment. Similarly, an identical check is present for a receiving segment under the arms-length market concept.

Offsetting these advantages are several negative factors which in most cases do not cancel the "pluses."

Depending upon the degree of each segment's autonomy, a decision benefiting one segment will not always enhance another. In fact, it can be to the other's detriment. In such dysfunctional decisions the benefit to the entity must be predominant.

Unless consideration is given to the design of measurement performance techniques, segment managers may compete for the use of centralized services such as computer facilities. A manager may attempt to overutilize such services, believing that he will be assisted in making better decisions that will lead to outperforming other segments. Thus, long-range goals of the entity may be sacrificed to improve a short-run showing for the segment.

Finally, there may be a requirement for more managerial time in some functions. Intracompany sale and purchase pricing is an example. In a centralized organization where a transfer price exists between segments and all sales and purchases are required to be made only within the company, managers are not compelled to spend time evaluating prices in outside markets. In a decentralized environment, collecting and evaluating this extra information will result in additional costs.

While there are other potential disadvantages, it is realistic that "there is no such thing as a free lunch." Managers should therefore always rely on the traditional yardstick of "cost versus benefit."

SEGMENT ORGANIZATION

It is important to remember that while accounting systems are impacted by segment organization of any type or degree, it is not the internal or external reporting requirements that control organizational structure. Rather, companies determine the ultimate organization based on operational and managerial effectiveness, which then requires accounting systems to provide information needed for performance evaluation.

It is obvious that the current business world has concluded that operations, except for planning and control, must be in parts of some kind. Every enterprise possesses some degree of segmentation unless the activity is confined to one product line, manufactured at one location, and distributed in a narrow geographical market to only one class of customer. Accordingly, there are as many organization patterns as there are business enterprises, since it would be impossible to find "identical twins."

The factors that impact the final decision on organizational structure are endless. Consequently, organizational structures are never static; they are under continual evaluation as the impact of the previously mentioned transforming external conditions and internal modifications result in reassessment as to the best means of achieving alternative goals and objectives.

Exhibit 1 illustrates the organization alternatives which can dictate the structure of the accounting system to fulfill internal

EXHIBIT 1
Segment organization alternatives

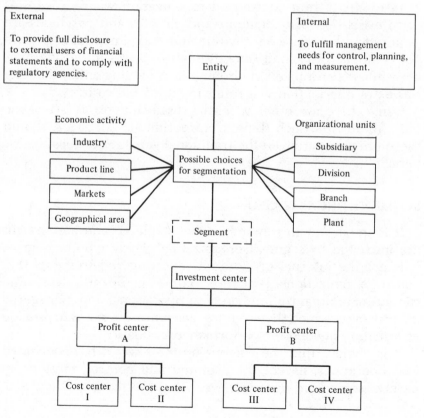

and external reporting requirements. Each alternate can have many modifications, variations, and divisions. The end result can be a combination of any of these economic activities and organizational units.

The relationship between a company's organization philosophy and its accounting function is demonstrated in Appendix A at the end of the chapter (Securities and Exchange Commission public record).

IMPACT OF EXTERNAL REPORTING REQUIREMENTS ON SEGMENT ACCOUNTING

Segment accounting, for the most part, is merely an extension of generally accepted accounting principles applied to components on less than a total enterprise basis. As organizations increased in size and were subdivided, natural developments were the recording, accumulating, and reporting of revenues and costs relating to each subdivision. Thus, segment accounting for internal management purposes emerged and gained wide acceptance.

Only in the last ten years have companies felt the effects of external inquiries into the fractionalized operations.[1] Professor Joel Dirlam of Rhode Island University was one of the first to assert publicly that both antitrust authorities and investors would benefit from operational information of diversified firms on a segmented basis. In 1965, Professor Dirlam recommended to the Subcommittee on Anti-Trust and Monopoly of the Senate Committee on the Judiciary that the Securities Exchange Act of 1934 be amended to require a registrant to disclose revenues and profits for each area of its operations.

In subsequent years, various regulatory and quasi-regulatory agencies have established their own rules regarding segment disclosure. These rules naturally have impacted the procedural phases of accounting. Currently, there are three organizations which decree requirements for segment disclosure:

---

[1] A summarized history of segment reporting is contained in Charles W. Plum and Daniel W. Collins, "Business Segment Reporting," *The Modern Accountant's Handbook,* James Don Edwards and Homer A. Black eds. (Homewood, Ill.: Dow Jones–Irwin, Inc., 1976).

1. Financial Accounting Standards Board (FASB).
2. Securities and Exchange Commissions (SEC).
3. Federal Trade Commission (FTC).

In addition, the Cost Accounting Standards Board (CASB) and Federal Energy Agency (FEA) promulgate rules which in some cases impact segment accounting, even though this was not an original objective of the regulations.

These external reporting requirements vary among agencies in differing degrees. The design of an accounting and reporting system to comply with the regulations of one or more of the groups and to still provide information useful for internal purposes is a continuing challenge to accounting management.

Until segment reporting for large firms became a generally accepted accounting principle under the new FASB rules, many companies considered financial results by segments as confidential information. Even though disclosure of operations is now required, important data is often obscured by different policies relative to common cost allocations, transfer pricing and, most importantly, definitions of a segment.

The concepts of objectivity and verifiability become more significant with segment information now being subject to examination by independent accountants. A key question is "When does a segment exist?"

Requirements of the Financial Accounting Standards Board and the Securities and Exchange Commission

Aside from a few minor exceptions on disclosure practices, there are no significant differences between the *Financial Accounting Standards Board* (FASB) *Statement No. 14* and the Securities and Exchange Commission (SEC) requirements for accounting and reporting segment information. The core concept as determined by the board is:

> The information required to be reported . . . is a disaggregation of the consolidated financial information included in the enterprise's financial statements. The accounting principles underlying the disaggregated information should be the same accounting principles as those underlying the consolidated information, except that most intersegment transactions that are eliminated from

consolidated financial information are included in segment information.[2]

Certain cost accounting principles which have been adopted
by the total entity naturally apply to segment accounting. Before
considering the effects of *Statement No. 14* on cost accounting,
a few terms should be mentioned.

The Board decided, with later concurrence by the SEC, that
"determination of an enterprise's industry segments must depend to a considerable extent on the judgment of the management of the enterprise."[3]

The *Statement* really considers segments in terms of "industry
segments." An *industry segment* is defined as "a component
of an enterprise engaged in providing a product or service or
a group of related products and services primarily to unaffiliated
customers for a profit."[4] By "unaffiliated customers" is meant
"customers outside the enterprise."[5] Thus, vertically integrated
segments, whose principal transactions are of an internal nature,
would not fall within this definition. Therefore, no disaggregation
of information would be required. After much research the
Board concluded that:

> Many enterprises presently accumulate information about reve-
> nue and profitability on a less-than-total enterprise basis for inter-
> nal planning and control purposes. Frequently, that type of in-
> formation is maintained by profit centers for individual products
> and services. . . . The term "profit center" is used to refer only
> to those components of an enterprise that sell primarily to outside
> markets and for which information about revenue and profitabil-
> ity is accumulated. An enterprise's existing profit centers . . .
> represent a logical starting point for determining the enterprise's
> industry segments. If an enterprise's existing profit centers cross
> industry lines, it will be necessary to disaggregate its existing
> profit centers into smaller groups of related products and services.
> . . . If an enterprise operates in more than one industry but does
> not presently accumulate any information on a less-than-total-

---

[2] *Financial Accounting Standards Board, Statement No. 14,* "Financial Reporting
for Segments of a Business Enterprise" (Stamford, Conn., December 1976), par. 6.

[3] Ibid., par. 12.

[4] Ibid., par. 10(a).

[5] Ibid.

enterprise basis . . . it shall disaggregate its operation along industry lines. . . .[6]

While the FASB in effect "delegated" much of the authority
for determination of segments to company managements, it did
issue some guidelines. A segment is deemed to be significant
and thus "reportable" if any one of the following tests is satisfied:

Its revenue (including both sales to unaffiliated customers and
intersegment sales or transfers) is 10 percent or more of the combined revenue (sales to unaffiliated customers and intersegment
sales or transfers) of all of the enterprise's industry segments.

The absolute amount of its operating profit or operating loss is
10 percent or more of the greater, in absolute amount, of:

1. The combined operating profit of all industry segments that
   did not incur an operating loss, or
2. The combined operating loss of all industry segments that
   did incur an operating loss.

Its identifiable assets are 10 percent or more of the combined
indentifiable assets of all industry segments.[7]

The *Statement* requires disclosure of the following information:

Revenue:
1. Sales to unaffiliated customers and
2. Transfers to other segments.
Operating profit or loss.
Other related data:
1. Method of intersegment pricing,
2. Methods of allocating common costs, and
3. Depreciation, depletion, and amortization.

Since the *Statement* only requires disclosures of revenues and
operating profit or loss, *operating costs and expenses are hidden
elements in the segment report.* No detail of costs and expenses
is required except for depreciation, depletion, and amortization
of property, plant, and equipment.

In arriving at operating profit or loss, the *Statement* specifies,
"None of the following shall be added or deducted, as the case

---

[6] Ibid., par. 13.
[7] Ibid., par. 15.

may be, in computing the operating profit or loss of an industry segment: revenue earned at the corporate level and not derived from the operations of any industry segment; general corporate expenses; interest expense; domestic and foreign income taxes; equity in income or loss from unconsolidated subsidiaries and other unconsolidated investees; gain or loss on discontinued operations (as defined in *APB Opinion No. 30,* "Reporting the Results of Operations"); extraordinary items; minority interest; and the cumulative effect of a change in accounting principles (see *APB Opinion No. 20,* "Accounting Changes").

The Board further mandated that "If the enterprise elects to present net income or a measure of profitability between operating profit or loss and net income, the nature and amount of each category of revenue or expense that was added or deducted and the methods of allocation, if any, shall be disclosed."[8]

The above information requires an accounting system that provides the proper handling of three significant cost accounting problems:

1. Identification of traceable costs.
2. Allocation of common costs.
3. Determination of transfer prices and the effect of those prices on the receiving segment.

The Exposure Draft of *Statement No. 14* proposed two levels of profitability: (1) "Profit or Loss Contribution," and (2) "Operating Profit or Loss." The former definition called for revenue less directly traceable expenses only. The second level required subtracting both directly traceable and allocated expenses from revenue. In the final statement the Board selected only the *operating profit and loss* concept since a fine line often exists between those expenses directly traceable and those (generally of an administrative nature) to be allocated, even if the allocation procedure is on a reasonable basis.

Traceable costs are not actually defined in the statement; however, the term does connote those costs that can be assigned directly to an organization unit or a product. "All other costs," the *Statement* continues, "that are not directly traceable to an industry segment shall be allocated on a reasonable basis."[9]

---

[8] Ibid., par. 25.
[9] Ibid., par. 10(d).

The influence of *Statement No. 14,* effective for years beginning after December 15, 1976, on cost accounting is difficult to ascertain due to the emphasis on disclosure of revenues and operating profits. A limited review of 1977 stockholder annual reports revealed an insignificant number of companies disclosing cost and expense information. Appendix B includes examples of disclosures of this information in 1976 (before *Statement No. 14*) and 1977 reports. Because of the higher priority normally assigned to other information, it is doubtful that cost and expense reporting will be more extensive unless additional guidelines are issued and further disclosure is mandated.

While external reporting spotlights revenues and operating profits, internal data for an organization unit usually include extensive cost information, whether the unit is a segment, line of business, investment center, profit center, or cost center. Similarly, cost information is presented whether the enterprise setup emphasizes economic activity or organization (legal or location). Due to the wide variations of data needs, it is impossible to delineate even the minimum contents for an internal report. Appendix C is an example of top management monthly statements of segment results.

The Federal Trade Commission

The Federal Trade Commission (FTC) Line-of-Business (LOB) report demands much more information than is required by *Financial Accounting Standards Board Statement No. 14.* The purpose of the LOB report is to enable FTC to publish aggregated financial data for manufacturing industries. There probably has been no single reporting development that has caused as much furor as the LOB report.

The LOB segment categories are much narrower and greater in number than those promulgated by FASB. This could easily require substantial changes in many companies' normal accounting and reporting structure for investment or profit centers. The cost of preparing the LOB report has been substantial for some companies.

Rather than labeling the components of a business as segments, FTC has selected Lines of Business. It defines a *Line-of-Business* as "The consolidation of all basic components of the

EXHIBIT 2

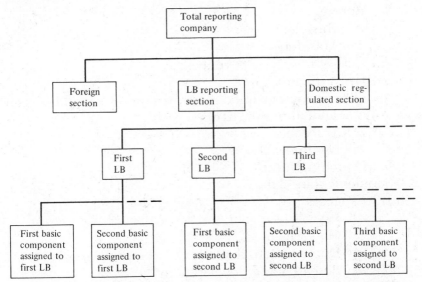

Source: Federal Trade Commission, "Annual Line-of-Business Report Program" (Washington, D.C.: U.S. Government Printing Office), 1974.

LB reporting section which have the same primary activity. An exception is described for certain vertically related operations."[10] A *primary activity* is defined as an "industry category from the Industry Category List which accounts for the largest percentage of net operating revenues. The term may be used for the whole company or some part of it, for example, basic component or LB."[11]

The industry category list contains over 250 manufacturing categories plus nonmanufacturing categories. Data for Lines-of-Business with less than $10 million in net operating revenues may be combined.

The makeup of a line-of-business is best explained by Exhibit 2.

When the line-of-business has been determined, the following revenue and expense data is reportable for each business (in addition to other financial data):

---

[10] See Federal Trade Commission, "Annual Line-of-Business Report Program" (Washington, D.C.: U.S. Government Printing Office, 1974).

[11] Ibid.

A. Profit and loss summary.
  1. Revenue.
     a. Outside.
     b. Transfers.
  2. Cost of operating revenue.
  3. Gross margin.
  4. Other expenses (media advertising, other selling, general and administrative).
     a. Traceable.
     b. Nontraceable.
  5. Operating income.
B. Supplementary data.
  1. Expenses.
     a. Payroll.
     b. Materials used.
     c. Depreciation, depletion, and amortization.
     d. Research and development.
  2. Inventory cost method (last-in, first-out; first-in, first-out; average; other).
  3. Depreciation method (straight-line, sum-of-years digits, double-declining balance, other).
  4. Transfer price method (market, cost plus markup, cost, other).

The above information requires an accounting system that provides the proper recording of significant revenue and cost transactions and allocations. Whereas FASB does not require the segregation disclosure of costs and expenses, FTC demands the reporting of costs applicable to operating revenue in addition to other traceable and nontraceable expenses.

The Commission has defined *traceable* as "Those costs and assets which a company can directly attribute to a line of business or which can be assigned to a line of business by use of a reasonable allocation method developed on the basis of operating level realities."[12] Otherwise, costs and expenses are nontraceable.

The FTC began collecting limited data for 1973 and, after substantial revisions, companies were requested to file reports for 1974–76. The agency is considering further changes in cer-

---

[12] Ibid.

tain terms and concepts in its rules that will still be different from those in FASB *Statement No. 14.*

As is often the case with government reports, the LOB report is nothing more than a "form fill-out exercise" once the underlying data have been classified under the definitions of the Federal Trade Commission. The LOB report is not useful for internal purposes and has no value to stockholders, creditors, and analysts. Appendix D contains only the summary portions of the report. The mere idea of this LOB requirement being extended beyond the 400 companies included in the first survey is quite frightening.

INTERSEGMENT TRANSFERS

Goods and services are often exchanged between segments as sales and purchases. Their exchange price affects important decisions concerning resource allocations as well as reported profits of each segment. It is imperative that the transfer pricing method guide managers toward decisions that will be optimal for the entire concern as well as the segment. This is as important to the "transferee" segment as to the "transferor."

The transfer pricing procedure should:

1. Result in a reasonable measure of the producing manager's performance.
2. Represent a logical cost for goods and services to the recipient division manager.
3. Be a guide toward profitable decisions by division managers.
4. Provide incentive to managers for maximization of corporate rather than divisional profits.
5. Enable decision makers to judge the performance of each segment and form conclusions regarding further investment in that segment.[13]

There are a multitude of transfer price concepts with each having unlimited variations. The procedure ultimately selected must relate to an individual company's circumstances. In reality, a "customer tailored" system is required.

---

[13] Robert Reon Irish, *The Measurement of Divisional Performance in Terms of Accounting Data,* an unpublished doctoral dissertation, the University of Texas (Austin, 1970), p. 152.

A common transfer price is "*unit cost*" or "*cost plus*" (some arbitrary percentage or fixed fee). The production cost becomes the basis for the price to the consuming segment. This method is simple and easy to administer. It has the disadvantage, however, of a "buyer" segment's performance depending partly on an allied "seller" division over which it probably has no control. Further, there is no incentive for the producing segment to reduce costs since it knows that the transfer price will recover all costs.

In some cases transfer prices are *arbitrarily resolved by upper management.* The ineffectiveness of this approach should be evident. Questions concerning (1) make or buy and (2) sell internally or on the competitive market cannot be objectively answered when transfers are recorded at some arbitrary price. There would be an incentive for the producer to sell outside the firm if the intersegment price is lower than the market price and an incentive for the buyer to procure supplies from outside if the internal price is too high. Arbitrary transfer prices also reduce the cost consciousness of managers, especially when the item can be obtained from the outside for less than from the producing division.

Many firms base their internal pricing systems on *external competitive prices,* particularly if the same product is sold to unaffiliated customers. It is the most objective basis since it normally reflects competitive conditions. The producer/seller welcomes arms-length prices since it incurs lower selling and administrative costs when dealing with an internal segment. The purchasing segment considers the price as equitable since it is no greater than outside sources would have charged. Segment profit under competitive prices also provides better information concerning make versus buy and alternative uses for productive capacity. In some instances efficiency of the producing segment can be measured by the market price technique. However, this concept requires a well-defined market at the point of transfer. It also involves continuous monitoring of market prices, accompanied by additional difficulty in determining the actual total production cost, since profit is usually added at each transfer point.

Another method of recording internal transfers is by *negotiation between selling and buying segments.* Each segment has a voice in determining the transfer price. This procedure takes executive time and lacks a check on efficiency that an outside market provides. Other problems arise if the buying segment fills its requirements both from internal and external sources. The buying segment would be in a better negotiating position with the outside supplier if it had some knowledge of its affiliated producing segment's costs. Unless by management edict, the producing segment will not likely give data that will enable the buying segment to better negotiate with the outside, since it would probably result in lower internal transfer prices. This method is used only when others are not suitable or practical and no established market exists.

No method is satisfactory by itself. All have disadvantages which can often be eliminated by adapting a method to best fill a firm's needs. A well designed system would make it advantageous for all segments to share data so that the best outside price may be obtained. Unless the firm's internal pricing system gives incentives that will further corporate objectives, the system will likely fail to achieve goal congruence.

ALLOCATION OF COMMON COSTS

Common costs are expenditures that cannot be traced to any single segment, but which are shared. There are two classifications of common costs: (1) those which attach to a product and are inventoriable and (2) those which are noninventoriable and are considered period costs. Inventoriable common costs (usually manufacturing overhead) are associated with the manufacturing function and relate to cost of goods sold, as well as to finished goods and work-in-process inventories.

A management interested in operating results by components (from cost center to segment/line of business) cannot escape the difficult issue of allocating common costs. Proponents of allocation contend that analysis of income and all costs by segments provides a better understanding of the elements which make up overall profit. Those opposed to allocation argue that questionable and misleading conclusions can result from inherent subjective judgments in assigning common costs.

Most firms allocate common manufacturing costs first to divisions or profit centers. This costing technique is used because, under absorption accounting, it is necessary to allocate manufacturing overhead to units of production in order to match costs with revenues.

As to "period" or noninventoriable expense (generally of a general and administrative or corporate overhead nature), allocation practices vary widely—from no allocation to complete apportionment. These expenses are often distributed to segments on some arbitrary basis, such as sales, payroll, asset ratios, ability to bear, or a combination of these bases. These subjective methods assume that the use of central services relates to the resulting cost allocation, which is often not true. Proponents of allocation contend that full costs, including corporate overhead, are useful as a guide to pricing decisions. They argue that exclusion of some common costs may cause management to overlook the recovery of all expenses in the marketplace.

It is not possible to state that a certain basis should be used in all cases to allocate a particular common cost. Management should choose an equitable basis which is measurable without undue expense. Some guidelines in arriving at such a basis, when little or no demonstrable relationship exists between a cost and benefit, are:

1. Cost Accounting Standards Board (CASB) guidelines for determining methods by which costs are to be allocated to cost objectives. In some instances these guidelines have applicability to segment or division allocations.
2. Scatter charts may be helpful in measuring an activity and its related cost. A factor which serves as a good measure of activity for controlling a cost is usually also a basis for allocating that cost.
3. Time studies and job analyses of particular activities of employees may provide insight into what factors influence costs and the relationship to individual segment activities.
4. Searching inquiries for factors likely to influence costs of the function should be made. Inquiries should pertain to:
    a. What is the segment set up to do?
    b. What are the steps taken to accomplish this result?
    c. Are they repetitive individually or in groups?
    d. Can any of these repeated operations be segregated to products or to customers, thus pointing to a proper allocation basis?

Under the contribution margin concept, common costs are normally not allocated. This method reflects the results of managers' decisions and actions since only those costs that are controllable by the manager (based on corporate policy) are charged against the segment's operating revenue. The result reported is the segment's contribution toward the entity's fixed corporate expenses and profit.

An inadequate contribution from a segment may indicate a need for more effective supervision, better cost control, or elimination of certain products. A long-term decline in contribution margin may indicate that rising costs are not being matched by product price increases.

It is difficult to use the contribution margin method where divisions are highly interdependent and where an assignment of revenues and costs to divisions cannot be made objectively.

What method should be used to evaluate whether a division's return is adequate? Should general and administrative expenses be allocated to evaluate division performance? If the entity is considering whether to sell a segment, only those general and administrative expenses that will not be incurred after disposal should be allocated. If management is determining prospective return on a new investment or segment, only those incremental expenses that will be incurred should be allocated to the new operation. By these methods, the total entity's return on investment (ROI) will not be the weighted average of the segments' ROI, since some expenses will affect only total entity return.

EVALUATION CONSIDERATIONS

The *residual income* method of analysis[14] is often used in performance evaluation. Different decisions will be induced depending on whether return on investment (ROI) or residual income is chosen. *Residual income* is defined as operating income less "imputed interest" on segment assets. The imputed interest rate should be the cost of capital to the firm, plus an adjustment for the risk which the segment adds to the entity. A segment that adds a high degree of risk to the enterprise should be

---

[14] Used extensively throughout the Residual Income portion of this chapter was Charles T. Horngren, *Accounting for Management Control* (Englewood Cliffs, N.J.: Prentice Hall, Inc., 1974).

charged a higher imputed interest rate than one which involves less uncertainty. The Capital Asset Pricing Model is often used to compute the risk-adjusted interest rate.

The following example demonstrates the difference between the residual income and the return on investment approaches to measuring performance.

		Division 1	Division 2
1.	Operating income	$ 25,000	$ 25,000
2.	Assets	100,000	100,000
3.	Imputed interest (15%) (line 2 multipled by rate)		15,000
4.	Residual income (line 1 minus line 3)		10,000
5.	Return on investment (line 1 divided by line 2)	25%	

If the objective is to maximize residual income, the manager of Division 2 will accept all projects as long as the return exceeds the imputed interest rate on investment. An objective of maximizing ROI will induce managers of highly profitable segments to reject projects that will yield less than its current return even though they might increase profits for the entity. The manager of Division 1 would not accept a return of 20 percent on a new investment even though that return exceeds the 15 percent cost of capital charged to Division 2. Another limitation of ROI is that, in order to maximize or reach an ROI objective, a manager may extend the use of older and less efficient plants when replacement should be considered. Investment measured by the historical cost of the older plant retained is lower than if investment were measured on a replacement cost basis. In spite of these limitations, ROI is easy to compute and to understand.

Some firms judge all their segments by a standard rate of return. M. K. Evans, in the *NACA Bulletin* of August 1955, comments on how a uniform rate obscures the issue. His observation, which is still appropriate, was:

A standard rate of return cannot be applied uniformly to all profit units. Differences in age of assets, depreciation policies, inventory valuation methods, etc., make this impossible. Although useful for appraisal of long-term performance, profit potentialities and long-term planning, return on assets standards are not usable as a measure of short term performance.

SUMMARY

The increasing complexity of business is an incentive for many managements to divide their entities into manageable parts, or "segments," for performance evaluation. This partitioning and subdividing of recurring operating decisions among many executives provides top management with better controls and more time for corporate planning. The type of segmentation of an enterprise differs among organizations and is determined by top management based upon many internal factors, with no two patterns being similar.

The broadened scope of operations of many companies has increased the need of financial statement users for additional information. Presently three organizations, *FASB, SEC,* and *FTC* require reporting of segment information of various degrees in reports to the public. However, operating costs and expenses are hidden elements in these segment reports except for depreciation, depletion, and amortization expense.

Meaningful segment reporting requires a system that provides the proper handling of three significant cost accounting considerations: (1) identification of traceable costs, (2) allocation of common costs, and (3) determination of transfer prices and the effect of those prices on the receiving segment. It is imperative that these items be resolved in a manner that will guide managers toward decisions that will be optimal for the entire company as well as for the segment.

Accounting systems must be designed to provide decentralized management, often with differing levels of authority and responsibility, separate evaluations of profitability rates, degrees of risk, and opportunities for growth. Generally accepted cost accounting principles which have been adopted by the total entity will, as a general rule, apply to individual segment accounting.

FASB *Statement No. 14* prescribes guidelines and requirements for disclosing segment information to external users. However, management requires additional data and analysis of segments for evaluating corporate performance. The residual income analysis and the return on investment are two methods widely used by management for segment performance and project evaluations.

APPENDIX A: Relationship between a company's organizational philosophy and its accounting function

The following comments were furnished at the request of the Securities and Exchange Commission relative to the sale of certain assets by two subsidiaries of The Standard Oil Company (Ohio) to American Petrofina, Inc. in 1973.

ASSETS TO BE SOLD

American Petrofina has agreed to buy (1) marketing properties in North Carolina, South Carolina, Georgia, and Florida (service stations, bulk plants, terminal facilities, offices and office buildings, warehouses, and so forth), (2) Port Arthur refinery, (3) all or specified undivided interests in certain pipelines, and (4) capital stock interest in two corporations.

SOHIO'S EXTERNAL REPORTING

The Standard Oil Company (Ohio) in its annual report to stockholders and 10–K report to the Securities and Exchange Commission discloses income in three lines of business:

A. Petroleum.
B. Coal.
C. Other (each individually less than 10 percent of sales and income before taxes).

This disclosure has been in effect since the 1968 report to stockholders when it was stated "Sohio continues to be primarily an integrated petroleum company." In reporting this information, the Company followed that recommendation of a Financial Executives Research Foundation study which proposed that "companies which operate almost completely within a single broadly-defined industry or which are highly integrated should not be expected to fractionalize themselves for reporting purposes." The disclosure also meets the requirements of Item 1 (*c*) for the 10-K report as adopted in Release 9000 under the Securities Exchange Act of 1934 effective for fiscal years ending on or after December 31, 1970.

SOHIO'S INTERNAL ACCOUNTING

Prior to the public reporting, the Company had studied alternative measures of performance for internal control purposes. Ernst & Ernst recommended to Sohio in 1963 that profit performance and return on investment in the *petroleum line of business* should be measured in only three segments:

A. Oil and gas—Exploration for and production of crude oil and gas.
B. Marketing and refining—Purchase, transportation and refining of crude oil and transportation and selling of products and services.
C. Foreign crude oil purchases and sales.

Since that date, internal reporting at the profit level and calculations of return on investment have followed this pattern.

Within the Marketing and Refining segment, directed by the Executive Vice President, are several departments which are essentially cost centers. The department functions in Sohio are:

A. Marketing
B. Refining
C. Transportation
D. Supply and distribution

The Marketing and Refining segment is coordinated by a Planning and Control staff reporting to the Executive Vice President. Its responsibility is to plan and monitor the operations of the four operating departments. In evaluating performance in these four departments, the essential criterion is cost control rather than profitability. We found that determination of paper profits at departmental levels within *natural* business segments was costly and complex, and completely disproportionate to any benefits. Furthermore, optimization of profit involves the entire

Marketing and Refining segment, sometimes to the detriment of a single operating department.

Sohio's internal record-keeping and reporting has thus been geared toward cost control at the departmental level and profit measurement only for the natural business segment. The only income statement prepared is for the total Marketing and Refining segment with these elements:

Sales
Cost and Expenses
    Crude oil
    Crude oil transportation
    Refining processing
    Product transportation
    Product distribution
    Selling
    Administrative
    Depreciation
Operating Income

An example of refining department accountability describes the next level of reporting. The Vice President—Refining has no profit objective nor goal in terms of dollars. He is not responsible at any of the four refineries for:

A. Level of crude oil processed (barrels per day).
B. Cost of crude oil.
C. Mix of crude oil to be processed (high sulphur versus low sulphur, and so forth).
D. Mix of product to be produced (gasoline versus distillates, and so forth).

He is accountable for:

A. Operating costs per barrel processed.
B. Product yield based upon predetermined level and crude oil type.

Therefore, all reporting based on historical records is confined to volumes and operating costs. The department is not charged for crude oil cost nor is given credit for value of production.

This does not infer that studies for refinery expansions are made which ignore these elements. Studies are based on future crude oil costs and product realizations, not on historical data.

As one further step, since the refining department does not record income for product delivered to the marketing function, neither is the marketing department accountable for cost of products sold. Marketing is responsible for sales volumes by trade channels, product prices and distribution and selling cost (cents per gallon). An operating profit figure for the total marketing function or any part thereof is not available in our financial records.

Sohio's Board of Directors and Management Committee are only furnished income statements for the total marketing and refining segment integrating the four departments and supplemented by operating statistics for the individual functions. We believe this control of profit and return on investment at the segment level and control of costs at the department level is effective for our management.

INFORMATION ON OPERATION OF ASSETS TO BE SOLD

In this transaction Sohio is not disposing of a line of business or even a viable business segment. *The sale involves certain unrelated assets of a nonintegral nature in three operating departments (Marketing and Refining) in one line of business (Petroleum) and a part of two subsidiaries (BP Oil and Sohio Pipe Line).* None of the assets has a complete relationship with any other.

Without detailing in this letter all of the individual assets of the Marketing and Refining Departments to be sold, the significant point is that production at the Port Arthur Refinery is not directly related to the marketing properties being disposed of. Only a fraction of that refinery's production is supplied directly to the entire BP East Coast marketing territory. Furthermore, over one half of the sales volume in the Southeastern region is supplied from sources other than the Port Arthur refinery.

To further emphasize the separate identity of the individual properties in the transaction, the disposal of transportation facilities includes:

	Ownership to be sold (percent)	Size (inches)	Approximate length (miles)
West Texas Pipeline			
Midland to Port Arthur	100%	10	510
Bronte Gathering System			
to West Texas Pipeline	100	2–6	11
Neches Pipeline System			
Port Arthur—Union Oil			
Refining	50	3–6	24
Neale Gathering System			
to Neale Pipeline	30	2–6	50
East Texas Pipeline			
Longview to Port Arthur	30	10	186

These assets comprise only a part of the entire Sohio Pipe Line system located in other states and serving completely different territories. The above lines do not deliver *all* of the Port Arthur refinery's crude oil requirements. Furthermore, all crude from the lines is *not* processed at Port Arthur.

Since the sale involves only individual assets in each of three operating departments, and only a part of a business segment, it is impossible to furnish an historical statement of earnings as if these assets represented a viable business. In our opinion, any estimated statement would be misleading and would require a disclaimer by us as to the substance of the figures. Also our independent accountants have advised us they would be unable to express an opinion on such a statement. Too many arbitrary assumptions would be necessary. Also operating results for the Southeastern Marketing Region would be impossible to assemble since the present division and regional alignment is not comparable with prior years due to boundaries having continually changed. Also making impossible any historical comparison is a significant withdrawal from the Carolinas by BP in 1972 as the first step in a planned withdrawal program from the southeastern market. The present package includes only a small remainder of the original Carolinas' marketing operation. You will recall these assets have moved from Sinclair to Atlantic Richfield to BP to Sohio since 1968.

We are attaching to this letter estimated summaries of operations on each of the asset groups. The summaries are based on certain arbitrary assumptions as to revenues and costs and on statistics available in Sohio's records. We emphasize the summaries should not be combined since they show operating results of unrelated asset groups. They have been furnished at your request so that you are informed as to the maximum information available based on historical operating statistics and the afore-mentioned arbitrary assumptions. Because the opportunity for misinterpretation of these summaries is present, Sohio would be obliged to disclaim that the summaries are a fair presentation of operating results for the assets to be purchased by Petrofina.

APPENDIX B: Cost information disclosure to stockholders

Continental Oil Company–1976

Business Area Income and Per-Share Data (millions of dollars, except per-share amounts)

	Annual		1976 Quarters				1975 Quarters			
	1976	1975	4th	3rd	2nd	1st	4th	3rd	2nd	1st
Contributions to Income: [1]										
Petroleum exploration and production:										
United States operations	167.9	155.0	41.9	40.7	43.0	42.3	40.6	37.6	30.9	45.9
International operations	4.9	(34.7)	(.8)	.8	.1	4.8	(14.0)	(7.2)	(9.8)	(3.7)
Hudson's Bay Oil and Gas Company .	40.7	35.1	12.4	8.8	8.5	11.0	8.4	8.9	8.9	8.9
Subtotal	213.5	155.4	53.5	50.3	51.6	58.1	35.0	39.3	30.0	51.1
Petroleum refining, marketing, and transportation:										
United States operations	25.9	9.1	9.6	7.9	7.3	1.1	(4.3)	11.1	8.0	(5.7)
International operations	34.8	12.3	4.6	11.4	3.6	15.2	(16.7)	3.5	11.7	13.8
Subtotal	60.7	21.4	14.2	19.3	10.9	16.3	(21.0)	14.6	19.7	8.1
Petroleum	274.2	176.8	67.7	69.6	62.5	74.4	14.0	53.9	49.7	59.2
Coal	174.5	142.0	43.3	29.9	41.1	60.2	64.8	16.5	37.5	23.2
Chemicals	60.2	32.2	15.7	15.7	16.6	12.2	5.3	8.2	7.2	11.5
Minerals	(12.4)	(11.7)	(2.8)	(3.6)	(3.2)	(2.8)	(3.9)	(3.3)	(2.8)	(1.7)
Corporate										
Foreign exchange gain (loss) [2]	15.3	13.0	(5.6)	2.0	1.9	17.0	(4.2)	23.5	3.5	(9.8)
Other	(51.8)	(21.4)	(21.4)	(6.4)	(5.9)	(18.1)	2.0	(16.2)	(5.9)	(1.3)
Total	460.0	330.9	96.9	107.2	113.0	142.9	78.0	82.6	89.2	81.1
Per Common Share: [3]										
Net income [4]	4.38	3.25	.90	1.00	1.08	1.40	.77	.81	.87	.80
Dividends	1.15	1.00	.30	.30	.30	.25	.25	.25	.25	.25
Market price—high	40.88	37.50	38.63	39.75	40.88	35.00	34.88	37.50	35.00	23.25
—low	29.75	20.25	33.00	35.00	33.25	29.75	27.50	29.75	21.88	20.25

(1) Income of business areas includes the after-tax operating income of wholly owned operations and Conoco's equity in net income of majority owned subsidiaries and of affiliates accounted for on an equity basis. Transfer prices on sales between business areas are based on the Company's estimates of market values. Corporate items include corporate administrative expense, interest expense and income, a portion of foreign currency exchange adjustments, investment tax credits, and other items of a general nature not allocated to the business areas

(2) The portion of foreign currency exchange adjustments included in corporate consists primarily of gains and losses on translation of debt payable in foreign currencies and on forward exchange contracts.

(3) Amounts give retroactive effect to the share-for-share stock distribution declared in May 1976.

(4) Based on weighted-average number of Common shares outstanding.

Business Area Investment

Business area investment at year-end 1976 totaled $2,970.5 million, an increase of 9.8% from the prior-year level as summarized in the following table. Business area investment consists of net property, plant, and equipment plus investments and advances. For majority owned subsidiaries, only Conoco's share of these items is included.

Business Area Investment (millions of dollars at December 31)	1976	1975	% Change
Petroleum exploration and production:			
United States operations	856.7	759.5	12.8
International operations	292.0	218.2	33.8
Hudson's Bay Oil and Gas Company	247.2	230.7	7.2
Subtotal	1,395.9	1,208.4	15.5
Petroleum refining, marketing, and transportation:			
United States operations ...	381.4	364.2	4.7
International operations	284.7	300.5	(5.3)
Subtotal	666.1	664.7	.2
Petroleum	2,062.0	1,873.1	10.1
Coal	686.3	626.4	9.6
Chemicals	134.1	126.9	5.7
Minerals	20.5	17.3	19.1
Corporate	67.6	61.2	10.3
Total	2,970.5	2,704.9	9.8

APPENDIX B (*continued*)

Continental Oil Company–1977

Note 11–Segment information

Selected financial data by industry segment and geographic area are presented, in accordance with the provisions of Statement of Financial Accounting Standards No. 14, on pages 32 and 33.

The petroleum segment for Continental includes all petroleum operations except those of Hudson's Bay Oil and Gas Company Limited (HBOG), a 52.9%-owned Canadian subsidiary whose operations are principally in the petroleum industry. Transfer prices between industry segments and geographic areas are based on Continental's estimates of market values. Corporate revenue comprises principally interest income and other nonoperating revenue, including a portion of foreign currency exchange gains and losses. Income taxes of individual industry segments and geographic areas represent the approximate effect of the income or loss of each segment or area on the consolidated provision for income taxes, exclusive of U.S. investment tax credits. U.S. investment tax credits are reported in Corporate as utilized and were generated by the following segments:

Net income for each industry segment and geographic area includes after-tax operating profit of wholly owned operations, Continental's equity in net income of majority owned subsidiaries and of affiliates accounted for on an equity basis, and dividends from other affiliates. Corporate net income comprises nonallocated items of wholly owned operations, including administrative expenses, interest expense and income, a portion of foreign currency exchange gains and losses (primarily on translation of debt payable in foreign currencies and on forward exchange contracts), and U.S. investment tax credits.

Identifiable assets are those identified with the industry segment or geographic area based on operations or location. Corporate assets consist primarily of cash and marketable securities of wholly owned operations and investments in and advances to nonconsolidated subsidiaries.

	1977	1976
	($000)	
Petroleum	$10,895	$10,674
Chemicals	1,897	2,910
Coal	12,028	7,910
Minerals	442	243
Corporate	397	606
	$25,659	$22,343

	Geographic areas						
	United States	Canada	Europe	Other (1)	Corporate	Adjustments and eliminations	Consolidated
1977:				($000)			
Revenue(2):							
Total, excluding interarea transfers	$5,758,285	$315,738	$1,953,971	$ 948,252	$ 42,278	$ —	$9,018,524
Interarea transfers	2,410	27,876	6,695	1,219,330	—	(1,256,311)	—
	$5,760,695	$343,614	$1,960,666	$2,167,582	$ 42,278	$(1,256,311)	$9,018,524
Income:							
Net income	$ 360,863	$ 61,430	$ (3,993)	$ 33,762	$ (72,276)	$ 840	$ 380,626
Equity in net income of nonconsolidated affiliates (included in net income above)	$ 8,373	$ 520	$ 4,765	$ 5,394	$ 14,174	$ —	$ 33,226
Identifiable assets at December 31:							
Consolidated operations	$3,568,872	$747,634	$ 968,102	$ 658,110	$ 748,425	$ (226,544)	$6,464,599
Investments in and advances to nonconsolidated affiliates:							
Equity basis companies	19,223	1,608	51,974	13,521	68,445	—	154,771
Cost basis companies	1,841	256	3,714	20	28	—	5,859
	$3,589,936	$749,498	$1,023,790	$ 671,651	$ 816,898	$ (226,544)	$6,625,229
1976:							
Revenue(2):							
Total, excluding interarea transfers	$5,309,911	$278,258	$1,749,610	$ 898,130	$ 80,995	$ —	$8,316,904
Interarea transfers	2,101	31,215	1,753	984,052	—	(1,019,121)	—
	$5,312,012	$309,473	$1,751,363	$1,882,182	$ 80,995	$(1,019,121)	$8,316,904
Income:							
Net income	$ 395,104	$ 60,711	$ 17,809	$ 26,752	$ (46,383)	$ 2,203	$ 456,196
Equity in net income of nonconsolidated affiliates (included in net income above)	$ 13,083	$ 322	$ 6,092	$ 2,892	$ 12,983	$ —	$ 35,372
Identifiable assets at December 31:							
Consolidated operations	$3,231,950	$632,674	$ 884,748	$ 585,989	$1,076,160	$ (130,303)	$6,281,218
Investments in and advances to nonconsolidated affiliates:							
Equity basis companies	18,346	1,578	38,243	11,361	52,507	—	122,035
Cost basis companies	2,037	242	3,858	15	29	—	6,181
	$3,252,333	$634,494	$ 926,849	$ 597,365	$1,128,696	$ (130,303)	$6,409,434

(1) Principally eastern hemisphere other than Europe, including marine transportation operations.
(2) Excludes equity in net income of nonconsolidated affiliates in the amounts of $33,226,000 in 1977 and $35,372,000 in 1976.

APPENDIX B (*continued*)

Continental Oil Company–1977

Note 11 – Segment information (continued from page 31)

	Petroleum Continental	HBOG	Chemicals	Coal	Minerals	Corporate	Adjustments and eliminations	Consolidated
				($000)				
1977:								
Revenue[1]:								
Total, excluding intersegment transfers	$6,982,394	$315,589	$454,410	$1,214,467	$ 9,386	$ 42,278	$ —	$9,018,524
Intersegment transfers	118,198	27,876	49,849	—	—	—	(195,923)	—
	$7,100,592	$343,465	$504,259	$1,214,467	$ 9,386	$ 42,278	$(195,923)	$9,018,524
Income:								
Operating profit	$1,087,628	$182,961	$ 96,488	$ 142,273	$(28,486)	$ (165,594)	$ —	$1,315,270
Equity in net income of nonconsolidated affiliates	8,386	518	7,166	2,982	—	14,174	—	33,226
Income tax (expense) savings	(845,381)	(95,151)	(48,164)	(32,976)	14,196	84,176	—	(923,300)
Minority interest and other	632	(40,876)	(948)	1,654	—	(5,032)	—	(44,570)
Net income	$ 251,265	$ 47,452	$ 54,542	$ 113,933	$(14,290)	$ (72,276)	$ —	$ 380,626
Identifiable assets at December 31:								
Consolidated operations	$3,503,191	$714,248	$263,080	$1,218,136	$ 41,733	$ 748,425	$ (24,214)	$6,464,599
Investments in and advances to nonconsolidated affiliates:								
Equity basis companies	24,776	1,592	47,500	12,458	—	68,445	—	154,771
Cost basis companies	5,293	256	(173)	455	—	28	—	5,859
	$3,533,260	$716,096	$310,407	$1,231,049	$ 41,733	$ 816,898	$ (24,214)	$6,625,229
Capital additions:								
Consolidated operations[2]	$ 492,344	$100,886	$ 28,598	$ 195,324	$ 11,131	$ 8,939	$ —	$ 837,222
Investments in and advances to nonconsolidated affiliates	14,745	14	716	—	—	—	—	15,475
	$ 507,089	$100,900	$ 29,314	$ 195,324	$ 11,131	$ 8,939	$ —	$ 852,697
Depreciation, depletion, and amortization expense	$ 216,928	$ 42,153	$ 12,105	$ 70,002	$ 3,781	$ 2,365	$ —	$ 347,334
1976:								
Revenue[1]:								
Total, excluding intersegment transfers	$6,315,201	$246,233	$398,337	$1,266,688	$ 9,450	$ 80,995	$ —	$8,316,904
Intersegment transfers	92,969	31,215	45,188	—	—	—	(169,372)	—
	$6,408,170	$277,448	$443,525	$1,266,688	$ 9,450	$ 80,995	$(169,372)	$8,316,904
Income:								
Operating profit	$ 959,821	$149,979	$105,743	$ 230,272	$(24,776)	$ (136,552)	$ —	$1,284,487
Equity in net income of nonconsolidated affiliates	5,257	321	8,680	8,131	—	12,983	—	35,372
Income tax (expense) savings	(726,254)	(74,725)	(52,749)	(66,891)	12,351	83,268	—	(825,000)
Minority interest and other	494	(34,854)	(1,337)	3,116	—	(6,082)	—	(38,663)
Net income	$ 239,318	$ 40,721	$ 60,337	· $ 174,628	$(12,425)	$ (46,383)	$ —	$ 456,196
Identifiable assets at December 31:								
Consolidated operations	$3,176,320	$630,471	$218,811	$1,150,436	$ 32,990	$1,076,160	$ (3,970)	$6,281,218
Investments in and advances to nonconsolidated affiliates:								
Equity basis companies	13,296	1,564	43,410	11,258	—	52,507	—	122,035
Cost basis companies	5,623	242	(173)	460	—	29	—	6,181
	$3,195,239	$632,277	$262,048	$1,162,154	$ 32,990	$1,128,696	$ (3,970)	$6,409,434
Capital additions:								
Consolidated operations[2]	$ 534,038	$ 84,832	$ 16,588	$ 147,142	$ 5,502	$ 6,226	$ —	$ 794,328
Investments in and advances to nonconsolidated affiliates	1,769	125	991	—	—	—	—	2,885
	$ 535,807	$ 84,957	$ 17,579	$ 147,142	$ 5,502	$ 6,226	$ —	$ 797,213
Depreciation, depletion, and amortization expense	$ 218,058	$ 35,206	$ 15,052	$ 61,128	$ 2,145	$ 2,073	$ —	$ 333,662

(1) Excludes equity in net income of nonconsolidated affiliates in the amounts of $33,226,000 in 1977 and $35,372,000 in 1976.
(2) Capital expenditures and additions to assets leased under capital leases.

APPENDIX B (*continued*)

SANTA FE INDUSTRIES, INC. and SUBSIDIARY COMPANIES

STATEMENT OF INCOME FOR THE YEAR

	1977	1976
	(In Thousands)	
Revenues and Sales		
Transportation	$1,450,044	$1,226,795
Natural resources	159,709	144,396
Forest products	99,712	71,992
Real estate and construction	140,918	150,843
Total revenues and sales	1,850,383	1,594,026
Operating Expenses		
Transportation	1,335,644	1,139,071
Natural resources	84,191	65,962
Forest products	76,775	58,918
Real estate and construction	120,965	136,994
Total operating expenses	1,617,575	1,400,945
Operating Income	232,808	193,081
Interest and Other Income—Net (Note 10)	35,396	21,580
Interest Expense	49,725	46,400
Income Before Federal Income Tax	218,479	168,261
Federal Income Tax (Note 5)		
Currently payable	10,700	26,200
Deferred	49,300	21,600
Total federal income tax	60,000	47,800
Net Income	$ 158,479	$ 120,461

APPENDIX B (*continued*)

SANTA FE INDUSTRIES, INC. and SUBSIDIARY COMPANIES

CONTRIBUTION BY BUSINESS GROUPS (In Millions)

	1977 (6)	1976	1975	1974	1973	1972	1971	1970	1969	1968
REVENUES AND SALES										
Transportation										
Rail	$1,349.0	$1,153.0	$1,042.5	$1,075.7	$ 951.1	$834.9	$783.2	$757.9	$722.2	$676.4
Truck	59.8	45.5	35.2	39.2	34.9	28.4	25.0	25.0	26.9	24.3
Pipeline	41.3	28.3	23.3	16.6	13.5	9.8	6.3	1.4	.5	.2
Air freight forwarding (1)					7.4	5.2	3.0	.4		
Natural Resources										
Petroleum	149.8	140.8	137.5	112.3	59.3	46.8	43.0	38.8	35.2	31.6
Hard minerals (2)	9.9	3.6	7.3	5.4	4.1	2.8	2.2	2.2	2.4	2.4
Forest Products	99.7	72.0	49.0	34.0	32.4	23.0	18.7	14.7	17.4	15.4
Real Estate and Construction (3)	140.9	150.8	137.4	139.9	116.2	21.9	15.4	19.3	14.4	13.3
TOTAL	$1,850.4	$1,594.0	$1,432.2	$1,423.1	$1,218.9	$972.8	$896.8	$859.7	$819.0	$763.6
INCOME (LOSS) BEFORE FEDERAL INCOME TAX AND EXTRAORDINARY ITEMS										
Transportation										
Rail (4)	$ 61.4	$ 47.5	$ 51.2	$ 76.8	$ 84.6	$ 88.0	$ 80.0	$ 47.2	$ 54.3	$ 37.4
Truck	1.6	(.6)	(1.6)	(.9)	(1.0)	(.7)	(.7)	.2		(.1)
Pipeline	11.9	3.2	(.1)	(5.0)	(6.3)	(7.3)	(8.0)	(5.7)	.1	
Air freight forwarding (1)					(1.6)	(1.4)	(1.4)	(.2)		
Natural Resources										
Petroleum	63.0	75.0	82.3	71.6	32.3	22.3	21.2	19.1	17.8	16.7
Hard minerals (2)	8.8	3.0	1.3	.5	.8	.9	1.0	1.1	1.0	.5
Forest Products	21.9	11.9	5.1	5.2	7.0	4.4	2.8	1.7	5.2	3.3
Real Estate and Construction (3)	19.8	13.2	6.4	7.7	13.2	9.8	4.2	9.6	7.5	7.5
Interest and Other Income—Net	35.4	21.6	12.3	19.9	22.2	9.9	9.5	9.9	9.2	3.9
Unallocated Interest Expense (5)	(5.3)	(6.5)	(6.8)	(6.8)	(6.8)	(6.7)	(6.7)	(6.7)	(6.7)	(2.8)
TOTAL	$ 218.5	$ 168.3	$ 150.1	$ 169.0	$ 144.4	$119.2	$101.9	$ 76.2	$ 88.4	$ 66.4

(1) Operations which commenced in 1970 were discontinued in December 1973.
(2) Prior to 1976, also includes certain other natural resources activities.
(3) Results since 1972 include Robert E. McKee, Inc., purchased in January 1973.
(4) Represents operating income less interest expense of The Atchison, Topeka and Santa Fe Railway Company and subsidiary companies (see page 39) and consolidating adjustments relating to rail operations. For years prior to 1974 also includes that portion of operating income of The Santa Fe Trail Transportation Company which relates to rail operations.
(5) Interest on 6¼% Subordinated Debentures due 1998.
(6) See Note 14 to the financial statements for a reconciliation to operating income in accordance with Financial Accounting Standards Board Statement 14.

APPENDIX B (*continued*)

Note 14: Supplemental Information on Business Segments

Summarized below is the information required by FASB Statement 14, "Financial Reporting for Segments of a Business Enterprise" for the year 1977. Revenues and sales and contribution to income before federal income tax for the transportation and natural resources segments of Santa Fe are summarized in greater detail in the table appearing on page 36. A detailed description of the operations of each segment is presented beginning on page 4 of this Annual Report.

	Transportation	Natural Resources	Forest Products	Real Estate and Construction	Corporate	Consolidated
				(In Millions)		
Revenues and sales	$1,450.1	$159.7	$99.7	$140.9	$	$1,850.4
Interest and other income—net (Note 10)					35.4	35.4
	$1,450.1	$159.7	$99.7	$140.9	$ 35.4	$1,885.8
Operating income and interest and other income-net, before general corporate expense	$ 117.4	$ 76.4	$23.3	$ 20.2	$ 35.4	$ 272.7
Allocation of general corporate expense	(2.9)	(.9)	(.4)	(.3)		(4.5)
Interest expense	(39.6)	(3.7)	(1.0)	(.1)	(5.3)	(49.7)
Contribution to income before federal income tax	$ 74.9	$ 71.8	$21.9	$ 19.8	$ 30.1	$ 218.5
Identifiable assets	$2,505.0	$255.3	$95.7	$142.1	$295.0	$3,293.1
Capital expenditures	$ 195.4	$124.0	$12.3	$ 2.9		$ 334.6
Depreciation, depletion and amortization expense	$ 75.6	$ 26.0	$ 5.4	$ 1.9		$ 108.9

Interest and other income-net includes gains on sale of operating properties under threat of condemnation which have not been allocated to the transportation and forest products segments since the gains have not been reported as operating income in the statement of income. Intersegment sales are immaterial. No one customer accounts for 10% of consolidated revenues and sales. Corporate assets consist primarily of temporary and other investments.

APPENDIX B (*continued*)

Household Finance Corporation
and Consolidated Subsidiaries

Statements of Income
All amounts other than per share data are stated in thousands of dollars.

	Year Ended December 31	1977	1976
Income From Finance Business			
Revenues:			
Finance charges—Note 2		$538,796	$494,467
Insurance premiums and commissions		66,727	59,970
Investment and other income—Notes 2 and 5		31,083	22,800
Total revenues		636,606	577,237
Expenses:			
Salaries and fringe benefits		119,045	112,608
Other operating expenses		102,772	92,894
Provision for credit losses		70,081	63,362
Provision for insurance claims		44,624	40,887
Interest:			
Long-term—Note 7		137,613	118,489
Short-term—Note 6		35,830	35,263
Total expenses		509,965	463,503
Income Before Unrealized Foreign Exchange Gains (Losses) and Provision for Taxes on Income		126,641	113,734
Unrealized Foreign Exchange Gains (Losses)		(35,314)	1,274
Income Before Provision for Taxes on Income		91,327	115,008
Provision for United States and Foreign Taxes on Income—Note 10:			
Current		26,896	52,353
Deferred		11,953	(1,914)
Total provision for taxes on income		38,849	50,439
Income From Finance Business		52,478	64,569
Income From Merchandising Business		53,062	42,320
Income From Manufacturing Business		19,164	18,315
Income From Rental and Leasing Business		14,001	8,750
Net Income		$138,705	$133,954
Earnings Per Common Share			
Primary		$2.90	$2.87
Fully diluted		2.71	2.62

The accompanying Summary of Significant Accounting Policies and Notes to Financial Statements are an integral part of these statements.

APPENDIX B (*continued*)

Household Finance Corporation
and Consolidated Subsidiaries

Balance Sheets
All amounts are stated in thousands of dollars.

	December 31	1977	1976
Assets			
Cash—Note 6		$ 30,483	$ 25,303
Investments in Securities—Note 1		282,313	249,659
Receivables—Note 2:			
Consumer—less unearned charges, 1977—$637,119; 1976—$535,043		2,837,245	2,635,921
Commercial		73,778	22,997
Total finance receivables		2,911,023	2,658,918
Less: Credit loss reserves		(122,472)	(110,560)
Insurance policy and claim reserves applicable to finance receivables		(115,017)	(107,483)
Finance receivables—net		2,673,534	2,440,875
Revolving credit accounts purchased from Merchandising Subsidiaries		50,383	66,771
Receivables—net		2,723,917	2,507,646
Investments in Subsidiaries:			
Merchandising		407,447	375,385
Manufacturing		108,432	103,268
Rental and leasing		176,952	163,023
Other—Note 5		48,575	9,941
Total investments in subsidiaries		741,406	651,617
Property and Equipment—less accumulated depreciation and amortization, 1977—$33,340; 1976—$33,528		40,151	24,517
Other Assets—Notes 4 and 5		91,924	69,738
		$3,910,194	$3,528,480
Liabilities and Shareholders' Equity			
Short-Term Debt—Note 6		$ 647,584	$ 558,801
Accounts Payable and Other Liabilities—Note 4		114,060	100,984
Insurance Policy and Claim Reserves— applicable to risks other than finance receivables		81,040	42,665
United States Federal and Foreign Taxes on Income—Note 10		8,544	17,811
Senior Long-Term Debt—Note 7		1,784,450	1,705,670
Senior Subordinated Long-Term Debt—Note 7		197,400	99,888
Shareholders' Equity—Notes 7, 8, and 9		1,077,116	1,002,661
		$3,910,194	$3,528,480

The accompanying Summary of Significant Accounting Policies and Notes to Financial Statements are an integral part of these Balance Sheets.

APPENDIX B (*continued*)

Merchandising Subsidiaries
of Household Finance Corporation

Statements of Income
All amounts are stated in thousands of dollars.

	Year Ended December 31	1977	1976
Net Sales and Revenues		**$2,846,930**	$2,521,400
Costs and Expenses			
	Cost of sales, buying, and occupancy—Note 6	**2,258,363**	1,994,295
	Selling and administrative	**470,485**	429,467
	Interest—Notes 2 and 4	**16,862**	16,290
	Total costs and expenses	**2,745,710**	2,440,052
Income Before Provision For Taxes on Income		**101,220**	81,348
Provision for Taxes on Income			
	Current	**45,250**	42,211
	Deferred	**2,908**	(3,183)
	Total provision for taxes on income	**48,158**	39,028
Net Income		**$ 53,062**	$ 42,320

Balance Sheets
All amounts are stated in thousands of dollars.

	December 31	1977	1976
Assets			
	Current Assets:		
	Cash—Note 3	**$ 15,080**	$ 24,959
	Notes and accounts receivable—less allowance for doubtful accounts, 1977—$11,707; 1976—$15,560—Note 2	**113,783**	96,214
	Inventories	**504,619**	439,561
	Prepaid expenses	**7,049**	6,700
	Total current assets	**640,531**	567,434
	Property and Equipment—Note 6:		
	Land and buildings	**131,776**	126,007
	Equipment and improvements	**253,230**	226,053
	Less accumulated depreciation and amortization	**(165,604)**	(156,541)
	Property and equipment—net	**219,402**	195,519
	Other Assets:		
	Cost of investments in acquired businesses in excess of net assets at acquisition	**8,822**	8,822
	Other	**16,364**	17,385
	Total other assets	**25,186**	26,207
		$ 885,119	$ 789,160
Liabilities and Shareholder's Equity			
	Current Liabilities:		
	Short-term debt	**$ 15,000**	$ 11,755
	Current maturities of long-term debt	**7,806**	6,852
	Accounts payable and other liabilities	**291,767**	258,404
	Dividend payable	**10,500**	9,000
	Federal taxes on income:		
	Current	**7,616**	12,833
	Deferred	**12,200**	11,900
	Total current liabilities	**344,889**	310,744
	Long-Term Debt—Notes 4 and 6	**120,783**	93,131
	Deferred Federal Taxes on Income	**12,000**	9,900
	Shareholder's Equity—Note 4	**407,447**	375,385
		$ 885,119	$ 789,160

The accompanying Notes to Financial Statements are an integral part of these statements.

APPENDIX B (*continued*)

Manufacturing Subsidiaries
of Household Finance Corporation

Statements of Income
All amounts are stated in thousands of dollars.

Year Ended December 31	1977	1976
Net Sales and Revenues	**$209,310**	$206,157
Costs and Expenses		
Manufacturing	**146,567**	144,032
Selling and administrative	**25,644**	23,113
Interest	**219**	96
Total costs and expenses	**172,430**	167,241
Income Before Unrealized Foreign Exchange Gains (Losses) and Provision for Taxes on Income	**36,880**	38,916
Unrealized Foreign Exchange Gains (Losses)	**274**	(1,109)
Income Before Provision for Taxes on Income	**37,154**	37,807
Provision for Taxes on Income—Note 5	**17,990**	19,492
Net Income	**$ 19,164**	$ 18,315

Balance Sheets
All amounts are stated in thousands of dollars.

December 31	1977	1976
Assets		
Current Assets:		
Cash	**$ 3,054**	$ 1,200
Marketable securities	**4,160**	7,663
Accounts receivable—less allowance for doubtful accounts, 1977—$634; 1976—$526	**31,757**	32,246
Account and note receivable from sale of assets	**140**	2,511
Inventories	**57,032**	48,176
Prepaid expenses	**887**	640
Total current assets	**97,030**	92,436
Property and Equipment—Note 2	**27,077**	25,270
Other Assets:		
Cost of investments in acquired businesses in excess of net assets at acquisition	**8,859**	8,859
Note receivable	**1,155**	1,260
Other	**493**	423
Total other assets	**10,507**	10,542
	$134,614	$128,248
Liabilities and Shareholder's Equity		
Current Liabilities:		
Short-term debt	**$ 4,000**	$ 176
Accounts payable	**9,203**	9,253
Taxes on income	**6,977**	9,586
Accrued and other liabilities	**6,002**	5,965
Total current liabilities	**26,182**	24,980
Shareholder's Equity	**108,432**	103,268
	$134,614	$128,248

The accompanying Notes to Financial Statements are an integral part of these statements.

APPENDIX B (*concluded*)

Rental and Leasing Subsidiaries
of Household Finance Corporation

Statements of Income
All amounts are stated in thousands of dollars.

Year Ended December 31	1977	1976
Revenues—Note 3	**$201,072**	$173,832
Expenses		
Direct operating	**100,686**	89,534
Depreciation of revenue-earning assets—Notes 1 and 3	**33,327**	37,231
Selling and administrative	**28,748**	21,057
Interest	**13,530**	10,996
Total expenses	**176,291**	158,818
Income Before Provision for Taxes on Income	**24,781**	15,014
Provision for Taxes on Income—Note 7		
Current	**(2,273)**	(5,620)
Deferred	**13,053**	12,225
Total provision for taxes on income	**10,780**	6,605
Income From Continuing Operations	**14,001**	8,409
Income from Discontinued Operations—Note 2		656
Net Income	**$ 14,001**	$ 9,065

Balance Sheets
All amounts are stated in thousands of dollars.

December 31	1977	1976
Assets		
Cash—Note 4	**$ 1,714**	$ 4,903
Trade Receivables—less allowance for doubtful accounts, 1977—$3,369; 1976—$2,935	**23,226**	20,083
Other Assets and Prepaid Expenses	**4,918**	3,240
Investment in Direct Financing Leases—less unearned income, $7,534—Notes 3, 4, and 11	**59,717**	
Revenue-Earning Assets—less accumulated depreciation, 1977—$33,270; 1976—$43,487—Notes 3, 4, and 11	**203,681**	184,273
Property and Equipment—less accumulated depreciation and amortization, 1977—$9,194; 1976—$7,864	**23,542**	20,109
Receivable from Household—Note 7	**8,624**	6,624
Cost of Investments in Acquired Businesses in Excess of Net Assets at Acquisition	**11,934**	12,436
	$337,356	$251,668
Liabilities and Shareholder's Equity		
Accounts Payable and Accrued Liabilities	**$ 28,275**	$ 23,985
Vehicle Obligations—Note 4	**204,162**	156,959
Other Notes Payable—Note 5	**14,350**	7,209
Deferred Taxes on Income—Note 7	**23,642**	10,589
Shareholder's Equity	**66,927**	52,926
	$337,356	$251,668

The accompanying Notes to Financial Statements are an integral part of these statements.

APPENDIX C: Top management monthly reporting of segment results

Income by business segments and subsegments (millions of dollars)

| | Ten months | | | October | |
| | 1977 | | | | |
	Budget	Actual	1976 Actual	1977 Actual	1976 Actual
Petroleum					
Domestic					
Oil and gas—Lower 48					
Marketing and refining					
Alaska					
Asset sales, other					
Total					
Foreign (Iran)					
Total					
Coal					
Chemicals and plastics					
Industrial chemicals					
Nitrogen chemicals					
Plastics					
Future developments, other					
Total					
Royalties					
Other					
Uranium					
Oil Shale/Inns/Corporate					
Total					
Income before interest and income taxes					
Net interest expense					
Income before taxes					
Income taxes					
Net income					
Earnings per share					

APPENDIX C (*continued*)

Industrial chemicals

	Operating income (in millions)		
	1977		*1976*
	Budget	*Actual*	*Actual*
9 Months			
October			
10 Months			

DISCUSSION

Operating income review	*Ten months 1977 vs.*		*October 1977 vs.*	
Favorable (unfavorable)	*Budget*	*1976*	*Budget*	*1976*
	(in millions)		(in millions)	
Gross margin analysis				
Acrylo —Volume				
—Margin				
Catalyst—Volume				
—Margin				
Barex				
Total Gross Margin				
Selling, general and administrative				
Other				
Total variance				

Operating statistics	*Ten months*			*October*		
	1977		*1976*	*1977*		*1976*
	Budget	*Actual*	*Actual*	*Budget*	*Actual*	*Actual*
Acrylo						
Sales—mil. lbs.						
Realized—¢/lb.						
Manufacturing cost—¢/lb.						
Catalyst						
Sales—mil. lbs.						
Realized—$/lb.						
Manufacturing cost—$/lb.						
Barex						
Sales—mil. lbs.						
Realized—$/lb.						
Manufacturing cost—$/lb.						

APPENDIX C (concluded)

Nitrogen chemicals

Operating income (in millions)

	October 1977 vs.		
	1977		*1976*
	Budget	*Actual*	*Actual*
9 Months			
October			
10 Months			

DISCUSSION

Operating income review

	Ten months 1977 vs.		
	1977		*1976*
	Budget	*Actual*	*Actual*
Favorable (unfavorable)			
Plant sales —Volume			
—Margin			
Retail sales—Volume			
—Margin			
Total Gross Margin			
Selling, general and administrative			
Other			
Total variance			

Operating Statistics

	October		
	1977		*1976*
	Budget	*Actual*	*Actual*
Nitrogen produced —M Tons NH$_3$			
Nitrogen plant sales —M Tons NH$_3$			
Ammonia manufacturing cost—$/ton			
Natural gas cost —$/mcf			
Retail sales —M tons material			
Realized prices:			
Anhydrous ammonia —Ind. $/ton			
—Whsle. $/ton			
—Direct $/ton			
Urea—Wholesale $/ton NH$_3$			

APPENDIX D: Federal Trade Commission line of business form

Control No. (1-3)	FTC Use Only (4-8)		FINANCIAL AND STATISTICAL DATA FOR LINES OF BUSINESS PROFIT AND LOSS SUMMARY	Schedule III(A) Sheet ____ of ____
		3	1	

		(9-10)	(30-34)	(38-42)	(46-50)	Combined LB Totals
1.	Primary Activity Code	01	(27-34)	(35-42)	(43-50)	
2.	Revenues From Outsiders	02				
3.	Transfers — Other LBs	03				
4.	Transfers — For. Sect.	04				
5.	Transfers — Dom. Reg. Sect.	05				
6.	Total Net Operating Revenues & Transfers	06				
7.	Cost of Operating Revenues	07				
8.	Gross Margin	08				
	Other Expense — Traceable		(27-34)	(35-42)	(43-50)	
9.	Media Advertising	09				
10.	Other Selling	10				
11.	Gen'l & Admin.	11				
12.	Total Traceable Other Expense	12				
13.	Contribution Margin	13				
	Other Expense — Non-Traceable					
14.	Media Advertising	14				
15.	Other Selling	15				
16.	Gen'l & Admin.	16				
17.	Total Non-Traceable Other Expense	17				
18.	Operating Income	18				

APPENDIX D: Federal trade commission line of business form (*continued*)

Control No. (1-3)	FTC Use Only (4-8)			FINANCIAL AND STATISTICAL DATA FOR LINES OF BUSINESS SUPPLEMENTARY DATA	Schedule III (C) Sheet ___ of ___
		3	3		

		(30-34)	(38-42)	(46-50)	(54-58)	(62-66)
33. Primary Activity Code						

		(9-10)	(27-34)	(35-42)	(43-50)	(51-58)	(59-66)
34.	Payrolls	34					
35.	Materials Used	35					
36.	Deprec., Depl., & Amort. on PP & E	36					
	Applied R & D Activities						
37.	Billed to Fed. Govt.	37					
38.	Billed to Other Outsiders	38					
39.	Cost of Company R & D	39					
	Percentage of Ending Inventory Valued According To:						
40.	Lifo	40					
41.	Fifo	41					
42.	Average	42					
43.	Other — Specify	43					
	Percentage of gr. PP & E Deprec., Depl., & Amort. According To:		(27-34)	(35-42)	(43-50)	(51-58)	(59-66)
44.	Straight Line	44					
45.	Sum of Years Digits	45					
46.	Double Declining Balance	46					
47.	Other — Specify	47					
	Percentage of gr. PP & E Acquired						
48.	During Last 5 years	48					
49.	Between 5 & 10 Years Ago	49					
50.	Between 10 & 20 Years Ago	50					
51.	Over 20 Years Ago	51					
	Percentage of Transfers Valued At:						
52.	Market	52					
53.	Cost Plus Markup	53					
54.	Cost	54					
55.	Other — Specify	55					

REFERENCES

Dearden, John, *Cost Accounting and Financial Control Systems.* Reading, Mass.: Addison Wesley Publishing Co., 1973.

Federal Trade Commission "Annual Line-of-Business Report Program." Washington, D.C., March 27, 1974.

Ferrara, William L., "Accounting for Performance Evaluation and Decision-Making." *Management Accounting,* December 1970, pp. 13–19.

Financial Accounting Standards Board, Exposure Draft, "Financial Reporting for Segments of a Business Enterprise," Stamford, Connecticut, September 1975.

Financial Accounting Standards Board, Statement No. 14, "Financial Reporting for Segments of a Business Enterprise," Stamford, Connecticut, December 1976.

Horngren, Charles T., *Accounting for Management Control.* Englewood Cliffs, N.J.: Prentice-Hall, Inc., 1974.

———, *Cost Accounting—A Managerial Emphasis*, 4th ed. Englewood Cliffs, N.J.: Prentice-Hall, Inc., 1977.

Irish, Robert Reon, "The Measurement of Divisional Performance in Terms of Accounting Data," an unpublished Ph.D. dissertation, The University of Texas, Austin, Texas, 1970.

Mautz, R. K., Financial Reporting by Diversified Companies, New York; Financial Executives Research Foundation, 1968.

NAA Research Report Series. New York: National Association of Accountants No. 28, "Presenting Accounting Information to Management," December 1954.

Plum, Charles W., & Collins, Daniel W., "Business Segment Reporting" in *The Modern Accountant's Handbook*, ed. James Don Edwards and Homer A. Black. Homewood, Ill.: Dow–Jones Irwin, Inc., 1976; pp. 469–511.

Rappaport, Alfred, & Lerner, Eugene M., A Framework for Financial Reporting by Diversified Companies, NAA Research Study, New York, 1969.

Rappaport, Alfred & Lerner, Eugene M., Segment Reporting for Managers and Investors, NAA Research Study, New York, 1972.

Securities and Exchange Commission, SEC Docket vol. 12, no. 14, "Industry and Homogeneous Geographic Segment Reporting," Washington, D. C., May 24, 1977. pp. 340–61.

Skousen, Karl Frederick, "Accounting Aspects of Non-Inventoriable Common Costs in Diversified Companies," an unpublished Ph.D. dissertation, University of Illinois; Urbana, Illinois, 1968.

Solomons, David, Divisional Performance: Measurement and Control, Financial Executives Research Foundation, New York, 1965.

40

Control of
computer resources

*Peter B. B. Turney**
Donald A. Watne†

INTRODUCTION

Scope

The rapid increase in data processing expenditures over the last 25 years has created a significant and special control situation for management. The significance of computer resources relates to the size of data processing expenditures and to the impact these resources have upon the operations of the entire organization. Control of computer resources is a special situation because of the unique characteristics of data processing technology and the developmental nature of control techniques in a new area.

This chapter demonstrates a variety of techniques for achieving good control over computer resources. The presentation of several control techniques rather than a single solution is inevitable. First, the concept of control is, in part, a behavioral one, and the behavioral aspects of organizations are still not well understood. Second, the appropriateness of any control technique is a function of the type and purpose of the organization in question. Organizations are complex and vary in many ways.

* Associate Professor of Accounting, Portland State University.
† Assistant Professor of Accounting, Portland State University.

Consequently, it is difficult to generalize about appropriate control techniques. Third, the control of computer resources is a developing area and our understanding of the control problem is still evolving.

The general approach in this chapter is to demonstrate the application of both traditional control techniques and specific data processing controls. The traditional techniques are organizational and accounting controls as applied to the computer function. The specific data processing controls are techniques developed by data processing to meet their own special needs.

This introduction includes a section defining the scope of computer resources and the meaning of control as applied to computer resources. The second section discusses the special problems of data processing that affect the control of computer resources. The first part of that section covers unique supply problems in data processing. The second part identifies unique demand problems for computer services.

The third section, the major section of the chapter, outlines the techniques for controlling computer resources. The section is in three parts: the planning and control of data processing development, planning and control of the computer resources, and management audit and review.

In recognition of the evolution of computer control techniques, the last section discusses the application of two advanced resource management techniques, simulation and normative models, to the control of computer resources.

Definitions

Computer resources. This section defines the scope of computer resources. This is necessary because the types and location of resources included in the definitions will affect the type and variety of control techniques required. Accordingly, this section identifies major classes of computer resources and their physical location within the company.

Five major categories of computer resources can be found in the data processing budget.

1. Personnel expenditures cover operating and data preparation activities (central or remote), application software development, and administrative expenditures.

2. Expenditures for purchased software.
3. Hardware expenditures covering the central CPU, core storage, peripheral devices, remote computer (stand-alone or tele-processing units), terminals, and even programmable calculators (hand-held and desk-top).
4. Data processing supplies include punched cards, paper, disc packs, and similar items.
5. Overhead covers space and miscellaneous administrative requirements.

In addition to items listed in the current period's budget, there are previously expensed computer resources still providing service. These resources include the application program library, magnetic tape and disc packs, and fully amortized or expensed hardware items.

For the purposes of this chapter computer resources are defined to include all the above categories of resources, and all items with the exception of hand-held programmable calculators.

Regardless of the physical location of computer resources in the company, they should be included in a master plan for controlling computer resources. Computer resources may be centralized in one data processing (DP) or management information system (MIS) department. Alternatively, each division or operating department might have its own DP or MIS organization. As a third alternative, in combination with one or both of the above, computer resources may be located under the control of user departments. These alternative locations affect the responsibility and accountability for the resources, but not the need for adequate control.

Control. The utilization of computer resources should have identifiable objectives that are intended to help achieve the overall goals of the company. These objectives may be defined in general terms as *information support objectives* for the company, and more specifically as support objectives for particular functions such as accounting, for divisions or departments, and for user applications. The computer resources themselves—the personnel, hardware, and so on are the inputs required to accomplish these objectives.

The control of computer resources is related to both the accomplishment of these objectives and the use of the resources themselves. Control over the accomplishment of data processing objectives relates to the effectiveness of computer resources. Control in this sense is the assurance that the outputs resulting from the use of computer resources are consistent with the stated objectives.

Control over the use of computer resources refers to the efficiency with which the inputs, the computer resources, are converted into data processing outputs. Control in this sense is the assurance that computer resources are used efficiently in the process of creating these outputs.

For the purposes of this chapter control over computer resources covers both the effectiveness and efficiency with which they are used. The value of control techniques should be judged by the degree to which effectiveness and efficiency are accomplished.

SPECIAL PROBLEMS

Unique supply problems

Behavior and traceability of data processing costs. In most areas the key to controlling efficiency rests on the ability to trace costs to those segments of the company which are responsible for them via the decisions they make. Data processing is not unique in this respect. A thorough understanding of the behavior and traceability of data processing costs is an essential prerequisite to the efficient use of computer resources.

The uniqueness of data processing technology, however, limits the precision with which we can measure the efficient use of computer resources. The proportionately high ratios of fixed to variable DP costs, and joint to separable DP costs, make it difficult to relate the decisions to incur these costs to the particular applications or outputs that result. Consequently, the measurement of the efficiency with which computer resources are used can be only partially determined via cost measures.

Acquisition and proliferation of hardware. Although the acquisition of equipment for the central data processing facility and some remote tele-processing sites may be under data processing budgetary control, the uncontrolled proliferation of computer equipment is still possible. This proliferation has been experienced by organizations in a variety of installations. The following are examples of uncontrolled proliferation:

Word processing. Equipment is sometimes sold in conjunction with the central computer facility utilizing specialized software, but often provided as stand-alone hardware with self-supporting software. In the latter form, the equipment may be regarded as just so many typewriters.

Calculators. Many sophisticated desk-top calculators are difficult, if not impossible, to distinguish from small computers. In addition to typical computer features such as removable storage, stored programs, and a choice of perhaps APL or BASIC programming languages, they may even have tele-processing couplers so that complex problems can be transferred to the central data processing CPU.

Terminals. Various analytical subunits in the organization, such as engineering and financial analysis, may subscribe to numerous time-sharing service bureaus for access to data banks and specialized analytical routines necessary to their work.

All too frequently, not all reasonable alternatives are evaluated in the determination of whether specialized equipment or enhancements to the central processing facility will best serve the needs of the organization. Some subunits may be able to cost justify equipment acquisitions serving only their purposes on a decentralized basis, while a more efficient utilization of resources could be provided by expansion of the central facility through a combination of more core, enhanced software, additional terminals, and other improvements. Often the decentralization of facilities is the best alternative, but many times it is the least efficient choice. Too often, because of a lack of internal communication, decentralization occurs by default.

Hardware economies of scale. Hardware economies of scale may significantly enhance the cost effectiveness of user applications. These economies may be realized through major improvements in the system configuration, or through somewhat subtle changes in components of the system and its operating environment.

Major improvements in the system configuration include upgrades from one model to the next within a particular series, or conversion to a completely new series. These enhancements may be required simply to process the ever-increasing volume of base applications. Other applications which could not be cost justified with the previous computer model may be efficient with the larger or more sophisticated configuration. Consequently, management must continually reexamine potential applications because of changes in efficiency.

Hardware economies of scale may result not only from major upgrades from one computer model to another, but also from more subtle changes in peripheral equipment, software availability, and even alternative rental and purchase options. Utilized at capacity, the faster the printer or the bigger the central processing unit, the lower the cost of writing a line or executing an instruction. Software improvements may significantly improve throughout, for example, by handling multiple tasks such as computing while printing the output of a previous job from a disc or tape file. To improve their competitive position, vendors may make changes in their rental or purchase policies which may substantially enhance the efficiency of some or all applications.

Capacity adjustment in large steps.   Since computer facilities cannot be expanded on a continuum, but only in discrete steps, careful planning of capacity changes is necessary. Planning can reduce the size of these jumps in capacity, determine the optimum time at which to increase capacity, and provide a lead time in which potential dislocations can be minimized.

It is frequently possible to smooth computer capacity increases by reducing the size of the adjustment steps.[1] It is not always necessary to perform a major upgrade to a new computer model. It may be adequate, for example, to make changes in peripheral equipment. In addition, the effective capacity of a system can be increased via software enhancements and adjustments in staffing levels.

Long-range planning permits determination of the optimum time at which to enhance the capabilities of the computer resources. This determination requires the analysis of factors that affect the demands on components of the system. These factors include anticipated increases in volume for existing applications,

---

[1] Peter B. B. Turney, "A Systems Approach to Adjusting Computer Capacity," *Management Adviser,* vol. 11, no. 6, July–August, 1974, pp. 32–35.

the conversion of additional applications, and the effects of numerous ongoing modifications.

The lead times required for some system enhancements virtually dictate a comprehensive planning effort. Substantial time may be required to locate and train necessary personnel. Although some equipment can be acquired off-the-shelf, other components may require lead times of 18 months or more. A long-range plan spanning a period of from three to five years should be a requirement of every computer organization.

Rapid technological change. Anticipation of technological change is important in determining the basic feasibility of an application and its efficiency. Although such anticipation may contribute to long-range planning, it is not always possible to outguess the computer industry, which is famous for the rapidity with which it embraces technological improvements.

Technological change relates not only to major leaps in computer capabilities as we have moved from one entire computer generation to another, but also to specific enhancements within a particular generation or class of computers.

Not knowing when the next significant enhancements will be available, management is well-advised to practice contingency planning. Alternative scenarios of potential technological changes, incorporated into long-range planning, should adequately prepare management to capitalize on any of several breakthroughs.

During the 1960s many organizations wrongly concluded that significant enhancements to the central processing unit would not be forthcoming for several years, while certainly tremendous strides would be made in the performance of peripheral equipment. As a consequence, CPUs were often purchased outright, while peripheral equipment was acquired on lease. The computer manufacturers, perhaps because of the actions taken by their customers, continued to announce the availability of ever more powerful and cost effective CPUs, while relatively minor improvements occurred in peripheral devices.

Unique demand problems

Difficulty in quantifying benefits. The quantification of data processing outputs in financial terms would greatly facilitate the measurement of data processing effectiveness. Market prices of data processing services, for example, might be used as a measure of the gross value of these services to the company.

The net value of these services would then be computed by deducting the cost of providing the services from their market price. A ranking of projects by their net value would be a basis for selecting those projects that contribute the most to the achievement of data processing objectives.

Unfortunately, the measurement of data processing outputs via actual or surrogate market prices is most difficult. Market prices of data processing services may be available for basic accounting and clerical applications, but generally not for unique, complex, or sophisticated systems. In addition, the benefits derived from sophisticated systems are usually intangible and indeterminate. It would be difficult to quantify these benefits as a substitute for market prices.

Consequently, it is generally difficult to measure the effectiveness of computer resources via the relation of costs and benefits. Accordingly, the choice among competing applications and the evaluation of data processing performance must be based upon noneconomic as well as economic factors.

Demand cycles. The existence of short-run cycles in the demand for data processing services may have a significant impact on the efficient use of computer resources. These cycles will vary from computer center to computer center, depending on the nature of the demand. In a university computer center, for example, most jobs will be small and short-lived. A corporate MIS, on the other hand, will generally service fewer but large jobs. In each particular situation there will be variations in demand that will create daily, weekly, and monthly cycles.

These cycles may create periodic over- and under utilization of facilities. Consequently, the management of these cycles has important implications for efficiency. It is economically infeasible to provide computer resources that can meet peak demand levels. Thus, it is necessary to formulate methods of smoothing demand or diverting excessive loads. (Management techniques to smooth demand are discussed under the heading *Control of Short-Run Demand.*)

Rapid growth of demand. The growth in demand for data processing services has been quite dramatic in the last 25 years.

Rapid technological advances in hardware and software have opened up opportunities for new and improved uses of the computer.

These advances in data processing technology have been motivated by the search for cost reductions and for new and advanced computer applications. Cost reductions have been quite dramatic, particularly for the central processing unit. There has been an average decrease in the cost of computers of 20 percent per year, on a declining balance, since the first UNIVAC I was installed in 1952. In addition, advanced computer applications, utilizing mass storage technology and other advances, are becoming more complicated and diverse.

Inevitably the task of evaluating and controlling the contribution that these new uses or methods of operation provide to the company becomes more and more difficult.

PLANNING AND CONTROL OF COMPUTER RESOURCES

Planning and control of data processing development

The planning and control of data processing development will be addressed from two vantage points. The first will be from the standpoint of the initial planning for the data processing project. The second aspect will be a review of data processing project control. The initial planning of data processing development and the review of data processing project control will benefit from analyses performed by the cost accountant.

Planning data processing development

Formulating the master development plan. Data processing development is best undertaken through the formulation of, and adherence to, a master development plan. To be successful, these plans require the active participation of all levels of personnel within the organization, the division of the project into phases, and the involvement of the cost accountant.

The users and data processing personnel should determine jointly what is to be accomplished by the proposed application.

Because there are always varying degrees of accomplishment, priorities must be established. Initially the users should specify everything that they would like the proposed application to do, from absolute necessities to those features which would be appreciated but are not required. After such an initial specification, priorities can be assigned to each of the proposed features.

The development may have to be done in phases of short- and long-range plans where projects are complex. Short-range plans may incorporate those features with the highest priorities, either because of their value to the user or because some aspect of software development or hardware implementation must precede another aspect. Long-range plans will incorporate activities of future phases, and may provide guidance for analyzing alternative courses of action within the short-range plans because of their subsequent effect on future development.

The cost accountant may be able to aid the master plan formulation aspect of data processing development through his analytical contributions in the area of cost-benefit analysis. The accountant's perspective on overall contribution to the efficient operation of the organization will assist in setting priorities, in defining what should be done during which phases, and even in determining what applications should be considered.

Content of master development plan. The master development plan consists of several components. These include:

1. A specification of organizational goals and objectives.
2. An analysis of the capabilities of the organization for undertaking the activity.
3. A review of what developments may occur in hardware, software, and human resource aspects of the data processing environment in the future which will affect attainment of goals.
4. Components of the specific system development plan.

An analysis of organizational goals and objectives may require an appraisal of several facets. These may include:

1. An appraisal of how the proposed system will contribute toward achieving the broader goals of the organization.
2. How these goals mesh with the stated objectives of the subject data processing project.

3. What internal organizational constraints, such as management attitudes, must be dealt with.
4. What environmental factors external to the organization will impinge on goal attainment.
5. How the overall structure of the data processing system will interface with and establish a framework for incorporation of the contemplated system.

Capabilities of the organization for undertaking the activity will include an assessment of hardware, system and application software, personnel, and physical facilities. This assessment will review not only the quality and quantities of each of these components, but also relative costs of the new undertaking and potential effects on projects currently underway.

Technological enhancements and personnel development are future developments which must be taken into account in the master plan. In addition to improved performance which might be anticipated from future hardware and software, improved quality of new personnel through improvements in the educational process may also contribute to the feasibility of a phase of the project.

Components of the specific system development plan, comprising both short- and long-range aspects, include an identification of who is to do what, by when, with which resources, and subject to what cost and time constraints. Identifying "who" may necessitate the preparation of a detailed personnel schedule. The "what," the determination of tasks, includes an assignment by task to all of these individuals. "When" requires that their activities be planned for applicable time periods. Resource allocations will ensure that the personnel have the tools available with which to do their jobs. Establishing cost and time constraints will provide management with a very important tool for monitoring the progress of the project, in terms of both the financial and time constraints established.

The short-range plan will usually contain a very detailed specification of the components listed above, while the long-range plan may provide broad guidelines. As the project progresses, new short-range plans will have to be made and the long-range plan updated. Modifications may have to be made for various reasons, including the appearance of the previously anticipated future developments. The organization itself may change, necessitating a comprehensive review of the entire project. The dynamic nature of planning must be appreciated; a philosophy that a plan is static and once made must be adhered to in every detail will often result in disaster.

Data processing project control

Effective project control is necessary to ensure that the developed master plan is brought to fruition. Management cannot step back after participating in the development of the master plan and expect that simply because their desires are known they will actually be met. Project control requires the continuation of management involvement.

Project control entails not only a determination of whether the specified application functions as designed, but also whether it is implemented within the desired time frame, that budgeted costs were not exceeded, and that the quality of performance equals or exceeds that anticipated. To wait until completion of the project for such a determination will usually ensure that one of the time, cost, or quality objectives fails miserably to be achieved.

Data processing project control will be discussed from two aspects. The first will review criteria to evaluate the suitability of project management techniques, followed by an evaluation of various techniques based on the specified criteria. The second will review feasibility studies and their relationship to project control.

Project management. Several criteria can be used to analyze whether a particular project management system is suitable.

Criteria oriented toward assessing whether the project management system is adhering to a previously established time schedule include:

1. The ability to determine the current status of the project.
2. The ease with which project status can be updated.
3. The ability to forecast ahead to final and interim project completion dates.
4. The capability for simulating alternative courses of action.

Criteria oriented toward cost determination include:

1. The ability to determine current costs of the project.
2. The ease with which cost information can be incorporated into the project management system.
3. The ability to determine final costs of the project.
4. The capability for simulating the effect on costs of alternative courses of action.

Quality control criteria for a project management system include:

1. A means for interim evaluation of the performance and functional ability of completed segments.
2. A technique for assessing the impact of changes in project costs and the time schedule on application quality.
3. A system of approvals for project acceptance.

Inherent in the criteria for the subcomponents described above is that the project management system be reliable in its accumulation, analysis, and dissemination of information; that its implementation in terms of ease of understanding and operation not be too demanding; and that it have universality of application in that all components of the project can be controlled by one system and that all management levels are able to use it.

Several techniques have been proposed and utilized for project management control systems, among them the following:[2]

Gantt charts: Bar charts showing planned and actual performance for those computer resources which management desires to control.

Milestone charts: Completion dates for major activities are specified with columns representing days, weeks, months, quarters, years, or some other time frame provided to indicate planned completion time and actual completion time.

Critical path method (CPM): Basic elements include a flow diagram or network depicting the sequence of anticipated

---

[2] For an excellent review of these techniques see J. N. Holtz, "An Analysis of Major Scheduling Techniques in the Defense Systems Environment," in David T. Cleland and William R. King, eds., *Systems, Organizations, Analysis, Management: A Book of Readings* (New York: McGraw-Hill Book Company, 1969), pp. 317–55. Copyright © 1969. Used with permission of McGraw-Hill Book Company.

activities, critical time paths specifying which activities must be completed on time or the entire project will be in jeopardy, the float or scheduling leeway for activities not on the critical path, and a time/cost function for analyzing the incremental costs of speeding up activities.

Program evaluation and review technique (PERT): Similar to CPM in the utilization of networks, critical paths, and a time/cost function, except PERT provides for more information in the treatment of scheduling uncertainties through the specification of optimistic, pessimistic, and most likely completion times.

Each of these project management systems, and others available but not listed, should be analyzed in terms of the criteria specified above to determine their suitability. An analysis of the four techniques reviewed above is presented in Exhibit 1.

Feasibility studies. Feasibility studies contribute important information to the subsequent project management phase, in addition to fulfilling their basic purpose of determining whether a proposed application should be undertaken. Significant problems in completing the feasibility study include estimating benefits and the appropriate treatment of costs.

The information utilized by the project management control system will come from the analyses performed during the feasibility study phase of the project. It is important, therefore, that the written documentation not be limited to the benefit/cost information calculated to justify the project. The documentation should include:

a. The feasibility analyses undertaken with respect to anticipated completion times for the entire project and interim checkpoints.
b. Those acceptance tests specified to determine if the project has met its stated objectives, which can also be utilized for quality control purposes.
c. Provision for segregating project costs and benefits for post-audit reviews as well as ongoing project monitoring.

Perhaps the most difficult aspect of the feasibility study will be the determination of benefits to be derived from the data

EXHIBIT 1
Evaluation of selected project management techniques

Criteria	Gantt charts	Milestone charts	Critical path method	Program evaluation and review techniques
Time status				
Current	Simple and effective	Simple and effective	Good to excellent	Good to excellent
Update	Simple and effective	Simple and effective	Good capability	Good capability
Forecast	Effective for simple projects where few interrelationships among activities exist	Effective for simple projects where few interrelationships among activities exist	Excellent capability	Excellent capability
Simulate	No significant capability	No significant capability	Excellent capability	Excellent capability
Cost status				
Current	No significant capability	No significant capability	No significant capability	No significant capability
Update			No significant capability	No significant capability
Forecast			Good for determining effects of completing project on a "crash" basis	Very good for determining effects of completing project based on most likely, pessimistic, and optimistic times
Simulate				
Quality status				
Interim evaluation	No significant capability	No significant capability	No significant capability	No significant capability
Change assessment				
Acceptance				

Other				
Information reliability	Simplicity affords reliability	Simplicity affords reliability	Numerous estimates required may introduce significant errors	Numerous estimates required may introduce significant errors
System implementation	Easy	Easy	Difficult to explain	Difficult to explain
Universality of application	Effective for specific project phase, less useful for multiple phases	Effective for specific project phase, less useful for multiple phases	Very good for specific project phases	Very good for specific project phases

processing application. In some cases these benefits can be readily quantified; in others perhaps they can only be listed qualitatively without recourse to quantification.

Techniques to quantify benefits include a direct estimation of benefits through cost reduction or other readily identifiable changes, and indirect estimation by having the users specify the value of the application to them through various means. These can include estimates of the worth of the information in terms of enhancing their job performance and a range of amounts they would pay to obtain the information, including maximums, minimums, and most likely estimates. In addition, users could estimate the potential effect on their operations if the information is partially or completely unavailable.

The costs of the proposed application are usually analyzed in terms of two major components. One component represents those one-time costs which, once incurred, will not be faced again. The second component includes the ongoing annual operating costs.

One-time costs may include, in addition to equipment and software—personnel training, physical site preparation, file conversion, parallel operations, and perhaps relocation of non-EDP personnel displaced by the computer application. Ongoing costs include rental of equipment and software, personnel, maintenance, operating supplies, continuing staff education, physical site utilities and rental, teleprocessing charges, fidelity and other insurance, incremental costs of internal and external auditing, and certainly others not included here.

The analyses of both one-time and ongoing costs include problems of segregating fixed and variable costs plus the treatment of separable versus joint costs. These problems are discussed in detail in a subsequent section.

After determining benefits and costs, annual savings or incremental revenues can be calculated. The time value of money should be incorporated in investment calculations by use of techniques such as net present value or internal rate of return.

Those projects which cannot be justified based upon the quantified calculations, perhaps can still be justified through incorporation of the expected intangible benefits. These would simply be enumerated as benefits in the feasibility study with a recognition that although nonquantifiable, they justify the project.

PLANNING AND CONTROL OF THE COMPUTER ORGANIZATIONS AND OPERATIONS

The requirements of planning and control of the computer organizations and operations will be discussed at these different levels: organizations, management control, and operational control. Each of these management levels requires a different focus in order to achieve an efficient D.P. department. In addition, to achieve effective as well as efficient use of computer resources, the means of achieving quality control will also be discussed.

Organization of the data processing function

Responsibility for data processing. Corporate management control over the data processing function requires that the top computer executive report directly to an executive with overall corporate responsibilities. The particular corporate executive chosen for data processing responsibility, however, varies from company to company. In a 1967 study of manufacturing companies, 35 percent of the top computer executives in the companies surveyed reported to the controller, 19 percent fo the vice president of finance, 12 percent to the president, and 12 percent to the executive or senior vice president.[3]

The particular executive chosen depends on several factors. These factors include the centralization or decentralization of data processing, the general level of development of information systems, and the support of top management for information systems development.

Although the 1967 study found that 58 percent of top computer executives reported to a financial executive, there appears to be a trend towards treating data processing as a nonaccounting function. In particular there is a trend towards establishing information systems responsibility at the vice-presidential level. This trend reflects the growth and evolution of information systems away from purely accounting functions.

Organization for control. Different organizational formats for data processing are generally variants on two major types

---

[3] Neil T. Dean, "Computer Comes of Age," *Harvard Business Review,* January–February 1968.

EXHIBIT 2
Organization of the data processing department

A. Project organization for data processing

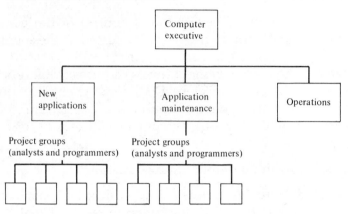

B. Matrix organization for data processing

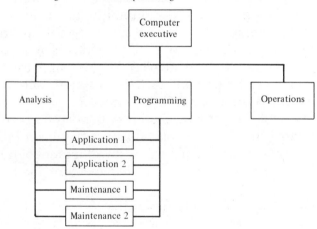

of organization structure, the project organization and the matrix organization (see Exhibit 2). The *project organization* assigns responsibility for each application to a project leader, who then organizes a group of analysts and programmers under his control to work on the project. The *matrix organization* assigns organizational responsibility to the functions of analysis, programming, and operations. Analysts and programmers are then assigned to a particular project, either new applications or application maintenance, where they will work under a project leader to whom they have no functional responsibility.[4]

There are advantages and disadvantages to both forms of organization. The project organization reduces communication problems by focusing solely on the project. On the other hand, programmers and analysts are moved from one project to another as each task is completed; their responsibility lines are therefore changing frequently. The matrix organization is a project organization superimposed on a functional organization. It has the advantage of identifying clear and permanent functional reporting responsibilities while providing project control. It has the disadvantage of being more complex to administer because of the problems of coordinating people with different functional responsibilities.

Centralization issue. The issue of centralization of computer resources continues to be a controversial and complicated one. The topic has been dealt with extensively in computer texts and journals and the reader is referred to these sources.[5]

There are several levels upon which one may centralize or decentralize: the hardware/operations function, the systems analysis function, the programming function, and the systems management function. In each of these areas it is possible to locate centrally, locally—or a combination of the two (the mixed strategy).

The main argument for centralization is an economic one, and the main argument in favor of decentralization is improved user service. The issue of economies of scale is most controversial. It is generally agreed that large computers cost relatively less per computation than small computers. Empirical studies have supported Grosch's law that computer system performance is proportional to the square of the cost.[6] On the other hand, recent

---

[4] For a complete discussion of DP project control, see the section entitled *Data Processing Project Control.* See the section entitled *Organizational Quality Control* for a discussion of the internal control aspects of organization.

[5] See, for example, F. Warren McFarland, Richard L. Nolan, and David P. Norton, *Information Systems Administration* (New York: Holt, Rinehart and Winston, Inc., 1973) pp. 485–519; also Donald H. Sanders, *Computers and Management* (New York: McGraw-Hill, 1970), pp. 269–74.

[6] William F. Sharpe, *The Economics of Computers* (New York: Columbia University Press, 1967).

technological developments in minicomputers have made distributed processing cost-effective. In addition, large computers require complicated operating systems and increased communication costs. It is possible that these factors offset the relative cost advantage of the hardware.

The issue of user service relates to the location of the systems analysis function. The location of systems analysts in user departments may make the analysts more responsive to the user's needs. On the other hand, it may be more difficult to support and train a group of specialists at the local level.

The issue of centralization/decentralization is likely to be resolved for each company by the specific organizational characteristics of the company. These characteristics relate to size, organization structure, and management philosophy. A small company will have no choice but to centralize. A large company has a wider choice of alternatives. The organization structure, divisional or functional, may affect the centralization decision. The most important factor, however, will be management's philosophy regarding the relative advantages of centralization and decentralization as tools for management control.

Management control

Recognition of cost behavior. Control over computer resources requires an understanding of the cost behavior of these resources, including the traceability and avoidability of these costs. Traceability means the tracing or identification of costs to those segments of the company which are responsible for their incurrence. Avoidability relates to the ability to avoid or cease incurring costs via decision responsibility. An understanding of cost traceability and avoidability is important in any cost control situation. It is particularly important in the area of computer resources, because the newness of the technology creates uncertainty as to the nature of the underlying cost function.

The *traceability* of computer resources costs to individual applications or users is difficult because of the large proportion of costs that are incurred jointly to benefit groups of users. A recent study of computer resources cost behavior indicated that only 42 percent of MIS department costs was traceable to

EXHIBIT 3
MIS department cost traceability

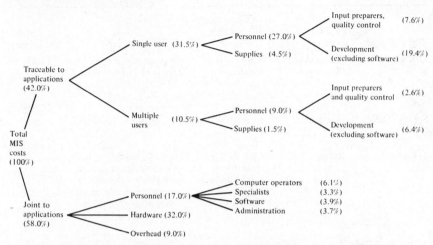

Source: Peter B. B. Turney and Charles Purdy, "An Accounting Analysis of Management Information System Costs: A Case Study," *Management Datamatics* vol. 14, no. 6, December 1975, p. 228.

applications.[7] Of this 42 percent, a further portion representing multiple user applications was not traceable to each individual user. The results of this study are summarized in Exhibit 3.

The distinction between traceable and joint costs is not sufficient because not all traceable costs possess identical characteristics of variability. It is therefore necessary to classify computer resource costs by a second criterion, that of avoidability. The classification of costs by *avoidability* distinguishes between costs by their decision variability (decision relevance). The costs of developing applications, for example, are traceable costs that are incurred before the applications can provide service to the user. When the application has been developed, the development costs are sunk (unavoidable). On the other hand, certain traceable costs are incurred each time the user receives service. These costs can be avoided by cessation of service. Exhibit 4 reproduces a summary of computer resource cost behavior by traceability and avoidability.

---

[7] Peter B. B. Turney and Charles Purdy, "An Accounting Analysis of Management Information System Costs: A Case Study," *Management Datamatics*, vol. 14, no. 6, December 1975, pp. 221–30.

EXHIBIT 4
MIS cost behavior

Type of cost	Traceable or joint (to applications)	Avoidable after implementation or sunk	Constituent	Relative importance
Development ...	Traceable	Sunk	Applications personnel	11.1%
Variable	Traceable	Avoidable	Data processing supplies, input data, and quality control personnel	16.2%
Step-variable ...	Traceable	Avoidable	Program maintenance and conversion personnel	14.6%
Systems	Joint	Sunk or jointly avoidable	Software, hardware operations, specialists in operations department, administrative personnel, building and overhead	58.0%
Total				100.0%

Source: Peter B. B. Turney and Charles Purdy, "An Accounting Analysis of Management Information System Costs: A Case Study," *Management Datamatics* Vol. 14, no. 6, December 1975, p. 228.

A sound knowledge of the traceability and avoidability of computer costs is necessary for developing rational charge-out schemes and for determining relevant costs for management decisions. Many companies charge users for a share of the cost of computer resources. The method of calculating the charge to the user should be based upon traceability and avoidability. (Charge-out methods are more fully discussed under *Control Through Pricing* later in this section). In addition, there are many decisions made in data processing that require knowledge of the incremental or avoidable costs of the decision. These decisions include application make or buy decisions, retain or drop decisions for applications, and computer resource acquisition decisions.

Budgetary control. The data processing budget has both a planning and a control function and should be designed to support these two functions. From a planning standpoint, the budget represents a detailed financial plan for data processing for the next accounting period. As a control tool, the budget represents a spending commitment for computer resources for the next accounting period. The information in the budget should be structured to support these two functions.

As a planning tool, the budget reflects the financial impact of the first year of the corporate long-term plan for data processing. As such it represents the next period's commitment of computer resources to help achieve corporate data processing objectives. The budget also reflects the immediate economic constraints on the allocation of scarce corporate resources to data processing.

From a control standpoint, the data processing budget is an imprecise measure of efficiency. Unlike a budget for a manufacturing department, it is difficult to set engineered standards that measure efficient operation. One possible exception is the setting of standards for routine clerical operations such as key-punching. In other areas it is not possible to measure precisely the relationship between inputs and outputs.

Consequently, the data processing budget must serve a more limited function, that of assigning responsibility for limiting spending on computer resources to the level of the budget. The key to controlling costs in this situation is the participation in the budgeting process and the determination of cost levels.

The information in the budget should be presented in a format to support the above functions. Two levels of detail should be possible, a summary budget for top management and a more detailed budget for data processing management. In either case, the major categories of the budget should be as follows:

a. Major line items by cost behavior (fixed versus variable, and joint versus separable).
b. Cost center.
c. User.

The delineation of major line items by cost behavior facilitates rational decision making. Cost classification by cost center—for example, operations versus systems and programming—assigns costs by functional responsibility. Cost classification by projects permits project control. Cost classification by user facilitates cost charge-out.

It is necessary to accumulate actual costs during the budget period to permit comparison between budgeted and actual costs. A chart of accounts for an MIS department that would support such a budgeting system is reproduced in Exhibit 5.

EXHIBIT 5

Chart of accounts for an MIS department

80—*THE MIS DEPARTMENT*
81—COMPUTER OPERATIONS COST CENTER
100—Personnel
  —110— Computer operators
  —120— Input data preparers
  —121— Project #1
    —1 User #1 (sole user)
    —2 User #2, 3 . . . (joint users)
  —122— Project #2
  130— Quality control,
  131— Project #1
    —1 User #1
    —2 Users #2, 3 . . .
  —132— Project #2
  —140— Specialists
200—Hardware
  —210— Central processing unit
  —211— Depreciation
  —212— Rental
  —213— Maintenance
  —220— Tape drive #3
300—Supplies
  —310— Punched cards and/or tape
  —311— Project #1
    —1 User #1
  —320— Magnetic tape and/or discs
  —321— Project #1
    —1 User #1
  —330— Output paper
  —331— Project #1
    —1 User #1
—400—Building
—500—Overhead
(if allocation to cost centers is desired)

82—SYSTEMS & PROGRAMMING, OPERATIONS, RESEARCH, SOFTWARE COST CENTERS (cost centers are combined and project/user subclassifications omitted for brevity)
  —100—Personnel
  —110— Applications development (S&P)
  —120— Applications maintenance
  —130— Applications conversion
  —140— Operations research
  —150— Software development
  —400—Building
  —500—Overhead
(if allocation to cost centers is desired)
83—ADMINISTRATION COST CENTER
  —100—Personnel
  —110— Administrative
  —120— Clerical
  —200—Supplies
  —400—Building
  —500—Overhead   (could include total cost allocated to MIS department if not re-allocated to MIS department cost centers)

Source: Peter B. B. Turney and Charles Purdy, "An Accounting Analysis of Management Information System Costs: A Case Study," *Management Datamatics*, vol. 14, no. 6, December 1975, p. 229.

Control through pricing. The purpose of charging users for a portion of the cost of computer resources is an attempt to decentralize effectiveness and efficiency decisions to the users of data processing services. There is some controversy whether users should be charged at all, and, if they should, which method of charging is most appropriate.

The assumption behind charging for computer resources is that the user will be forced to make effectiveness and efficiency judgments when the cost of computer services affects his budget. The user will have difficulty, however, in making anything more than imperfect decisions because of the difficulty in measuring the outputs of his services in financial terms. Consequently, the use of a charge-out system will be imperfect at the best and should be used as only one of several means for evaluating effectiveness and efficiency.

Alternative approaches to the charge-out of computer costs can be grouped into four major categories:

1. No charge.
2. Partial charge-out.
3. Full cost charge-out.
4. Decision-relevant charge-out.

The first method reflects a decision on the part of the company *not to charge out* the costs of its computer services. In some cases this may be done to avoid the problems inherent in calculating the charge-out price. In other cases it reflects a corporate strategy of encouraging use of the data processing facilities, since the computer services are a "free good" to the user.

Partial charge-out methods are used to influence the selective use of computer resources. There are two major types of partial charge-out. In the first, users are charged for the systems and programming costs of developing new services. Computer system costs are charged to corporate overhead. This approach has the dual purpose of encouraging more extensive use of the computer facilities for which there is no charge, while policing the investment of funds in projects to develop new services. In the second type, users are not charged for any direct costs of the development or use of applications. They are charged only for computer system overhead. This approach has the dual

EXHIBIT 6
Charge-out of computer costs

Charge-out approach	Centralized versus decentralized control	Corporate strategy	Relevant costs for decentralized decisions
No charge	Centralized	Computer services a "free good"	Not applicable
Partial charge-out	Decentralized	Encouragement of selective use of computer resources	Incomplete at best
Full cost charge-out ..	Decentralized	Full cost recovery	No
Decision relevant ..... charge-out	Decentralized	Effective and efficient decentralized decisions	Yes

purpose of encouraging systems development and restricting use of available system capacity.

The third method, the full cost approach, *charges the user for all the costs of computer resources.* A usual procedure is to convert all computer costs into an average usage rate where costs are recovered from the users according to the number of hours of time for which each user is accountable. This approach appears to be the most popular in practice.[8]

The fourth approach is the *decision-relevant method.* In this approach the costs of computer services are grouped according to decision relevance and a charge-out price is developed for each of the four cost groups. Three of these groups are direct costs: the development costs of application systems and programming, the incremental costs of application maintenance and conversion, and the variable costs of ongoing application use. A separate charge is made to the user for each of these direct costs. The fourth group of costs, the joint computer system costs, are allocated to each user and charged on a periodic lump-sum basis.

The choice among these alternatives depends upon management's philosophy regarding decentralization and their objective in decentralizing. The noncharge-out method implies that effectiveness and efficiency are controlled centrally. The charge-out methods, alternatively, decentralize decision making in different ways. Of the alternatives presented, only the decision-relevant

---

[8] Norman R. Nielsen, "Flexible Pricing: An Approach to the Allocation of Computer Resources," Proceedings *AFIPS 1968 Fall Joint Computer Conference,* vol. 33, pt. 1, Wayne, Penn.: MDI Publications, pp. 521–31.

approach provides the necessary economic information for effectiveness and efficiency decisions.[9] Exhibit 6 summarizes the major characteristics of each method.

Operational control

The control of DP operations will be approached from two perspectives, performance standards and the control of short-run demand. Performance standards refer to both engineered standards and scheduling techniques. Control of short-run demand encompasses the utilization of priority schemes.

Performance standards.   *Engineered standards* provide an effective means of monitoring performance by defining precisely the volume of work which a specific unit can be expected to accomplish. Engineered standards include time and motion studies of keypunch and key verification activities to determine the quantity of cards each station should be able to process in a given period of time. Engineered standards, established with sophisticated computer system monitoring devices which determine throughput capabilities, have also been used for performance evaluation of DP hardware and software.

Scheduling techniques can also be utilized to specify performance standards. Operational control in general can be maintained over both computer equipment and personnel by defining which applications should be processed when, and how long they should take. More precise control can be maintained over multiple computer operators by creating specific activity schedules for each of them.

Control of short-run demand.   Priority charging schemes can be used to dampen short-run fluctuations in demand and to encourage balanced use of the components of the computer system capacity. Priority schemes generally depend upon pricing mechanisms.

Priority schemes are necessary because a user can influence the availability of system capacity in two ways. First, he can run his programs on the system and reduce the general availability of the system for other users. Consequently, it is not unusual

---

[9] For further discussion of charge-out methods see Peter B. B. Turney, "Transfer Pricing Information Systems," *Management Information Systems Quarterly*, vol. 1, March 1977, pp. 27–35.

for computer centers to suffer cycles in demand depending upon the popularity of the time of day, week, or month. Second, he may be more or less efficient in his use of different components of the system via the design and writing of his programs. Available computer capacity is not simply a function of computer size, but also a function of the complex interaction of the different parts of the total system. A user can affect the balance in this complex system in many ways. A new application, for example, may require excessive channel time and create bottlenecks in what otherwise is a balanced system.

Priority schemes can be designed to smooth demand cycles and to encourage balanced use of the system. These schemes generally rely upon establishing different priority levels, each priority defining a level of service (turnaround time) and a price for each level of service. If this price is further subdivided by a hardware component, it is possible to balance the demand for the system. In addition, priority pricing schemes can be run in coordination with charge-out systems.[10]

Quality control

Quality control in the management of computer resources is multifaceted. It involves control of the effectiveness of computer output. Quality control involves control over the quality of output. It is important that the cost accountant understand its ramifications because of the benefits which may be realized by the organization through good quality control, the costs which must be incurred to achieve it, and the special techniques which must be understood and utilized to implement and practice it.

Benefits to the organization from practicing good quality control techniques include:

1. The goodwill of customers or clients who need not contend with erroneous billings and other communications.
2. Minimizing disruption to operations through computer down-time, computer-generated errors, and untimely reports.

---

[10] For a full discussion of priority schemes and their use in charge-out systems see Peter B. B. Turney, "An Accounting Study of Cost Behavior and Transfer Pricing of Management Information Systems," unpublished Ph.D. dissertation, University of Minnesota, 1972.

3. Enhanced productivity of employees freed from having to track down errors and make the necessary adjustments to records.

Several types of costs may be incurred to provide effective quality control. These costs may arise from:

1. The extended time required to write computer programs because of the inclusion of various input, processing, and output controls.
2. The additional costs of providing physical facilities to house the electronic data processing system and its related equipment and staff because of provision for physical safeguards.
3. The special efforts required by the systems analysts to develop an adequate audit trail that might otherwise be barely visible or nonexistent.
4. Numerous other techniques and procedures that contribute to the quality of computer output.

To even consider quality control benefits and costs for inclusion in analyses of computer projects and operations requires that the cost accountant be familiar with applicable procedures, techniques, and facilities. By asking the relevant questions the cost accountant can ascertain that no significant quality control considerations and related costs or benefits have been overlooked in the preparation of project proposals and operations analyses.

The following discussion should be considered a checklist of quality control practices. Comprehensive explanations can be found in the references cited at the end of the chapter.

Control over effectiveness of output. The effectiveness of computer output can be measured in terms of the level achieved in satisfying its objectives. Several techniques can be utilized to determine such achievement. These include a qualitative evaluation of the appropriateness of the subject output, a quantification of its relative worth, and finally a determination of its effectiveness.

Effectiveness analyses of computer output must start with the user. Is the report satisfying the requirements of the user? With what level of satisfaction? Simply obtaining that information from the user may be an extremely difficult task. Some firms have halted selectively all computer output of a certain class or to a certain class of user and begun redistribution only after specific request for it. Although this technique may be valuable in determining whether the basic report is even necessary, it is not of much use in improving a needed report.

A technique adopted by some cost accountants to determine the benefits derived from a computer report is to query the user as to how much he would pay to receive it. Although there may be no intention of charging users based upon the worth of a particular report to a user, such an approach may provide valuable insights on the relative merits of output.

Once the cost accountant knows the relative worth of the computer output in question, attention can then be directed toward the effectiveness of that output. To enhance its effectiveness the worth of the report provides some guidelines as to the costs that could be incurred for improvement, or simply to justify its initial preparation. Although this type of analysis will challenge the most astute accountant, the tools of cost-benefit analysis are no less applicable to analyzing the effectiveness of computer output than they are to the initial determination of computer acquisition.

Control over quality of output

1. Organizational quality control. The data processing function should be organized so as to separate the duties of personnel. This permits both the specialization of tasks and the accompanying increase in efficiency, and the establishment of a system of checks and balances necessary for quality control.[11] The quality of work performed by the data processing staff will be enhanced by encouraging the development of expertise in systems design and analysis, programming, documentation, library functions, and operations, among others. In addition, separation of duties is a key aspect of a strong system of internal control, which in turn contributes to reduction in input, processing, and output errors.

Separation of duties usually entails two major divisions within the data processing unit. First, operations are segregated from programming and related systems design. As a key deterrent to fraud and embezzlement, programmers should never be al-

---

[11] See section entitled *Organization for Control* for a more detailed discussion.

lowed to operate the computer. Computer operators allowed to program acquire skills to manipulate programs and data file content in conjunction with their assigned task of computer operation.

Second, it is necessary to separate the functions of program maintenance and the file library. The separation of program maintenance ensures that modifications to programs receive the necessary approvals before execution. The separation of the file library function provides safeguards on access to program files as well as data files.

2. Audit trail. An *audit trail* is defined as the ability to trace a source document forward to a summarized total and a summarized total back to a source document. An audit trail is not only required by the internal and external auditors, but also by Internal Revenue Service regulations. In a manual system it is usually highly visible and incorporated into journals, ledgers, and workpapers. Such visibility is frequently lacking in a computerized system and significant effort may be required to provide for it.

Lack of visibility of an audit trail in an electronic data processing system may be the result of:

a. The elimination or reduction of source documents, often because of cathode ray tube input devices.

b. Lack of provision for transaction listings or journals.

c. Impossibility of reading the magnetic medium files without using the computer and a program.

d. Difficulty of access to information, especially since the source documents may no longer be a component of the processing cycle.

e. Unavailability of amounts leading up to summarized values because ledger summaries previously showing such amounts may be replaced by master files which may not contain them.

f. Lack of printouts which may be prepared on an exception basis only, with a subsequent loss of historical printed information.

g. Difficulty of observing the sequence of records and processing because much of it is contained within the computer system.

The effort to provide for an adequate audit trail may be expended only with active management involvement. Computer personnel typically concern themselves primarily with getting an application running. Once it is running, they prefer to move on to the next project. The audit trail may be incorporated into the program with the unyielding support of management.

3. *Control over data preparation and input.* An important element of quality control is control over data preparation and input. Such control has two major aspects: source authorization and conversion to machine readable form. Only properly authorized data should be processed by the computer. Data once properly authorized should not be subject to additions, modifications, or deletions during the conversion process. There are techniques which exist for both aspects.

Authorization over the origination of data requires that the functions of initiating the data be segregated from approval of such initiation. Documents prepared by a clerk, for example, require supervisory approval before submission to the processing stream. Initiation and authorization, in addition, require separation from the recording function. This control procedure dictates, for example, that data processing department personnel should never be allowed to generate source data.

Data conversion to machine readable form requires the inclusion of numerous control elements. Once authorized data has been received by the computer center, that data should not be lost, suppressed, added to, duplicated, or otherwise improperly changed.

Techniques for control over data preparation and input include:

Procedural controls on data creation (for example, specially designed forms to promote accuracy, sequential numbering of source documents, turnaround documents, and access control to direct input equipment).

Data authorization (for example, forms designed for signatures or initials, internal control group reviews of documents, and computer-programmed authorization).

Data conversion (for example, key verification, turnaround documents, and check digits).

Transmission to computer (for example, transmittal controls such as logs, route slips, control totals, and external file labels).

Input validation (for example, validation tests such as computer programmed tests of codes, characters, fields, transactions, combinations of fields, missing data, check digit, sequence, and limit or reasonableness; error detection, correction, and resubmission procedures; control totals such as hash, financial, and document; and internal file labels).

4. Programmed control over processing. Programmed controls over processing are designed to ensure that all transactions are processed as authorized, that no authorized transactions are omitted, and that no unauthorized transactions are added. These controls are often deemed to take the place of the visual checks normally made in a manual system by the personnel displaced by the computer.

There are several techniques that provide programmed control over processing. One control technique is oriented toward the loss or nonprocessing of data and incorporates the type of control totals discussed under input controls. A second technique provides a cross-check on program logic for arithmetic calculations and includes limit and reasonableness tests, crossfooting checks, and overflow tests. A third technique provides file checks to ascertain that postings have been made to the correct files and utilizes such features as internal and external file labels. A fourth technique specifies procedures to monitor changes to permanent files as part of file maintenance operations to maintain the integrity of files.

Comprehensive program controls may represent a substantial part of the cost of developing a program. The expenditure may be only a fraction of the disruptive cost of computer errors to the organization, errors which they can reduce. This is particularly true because large programs are sufficiently complex that latent errors may not show up for weeks, months, or even years. The assumption that if input data are correct and the program is properly debugged and tested, no errors in processing will be made, is rarely a valid one.

5. Output and distribution control. Output controls have two major objectives: to assure the accuracy of processing results and to assure that only authorized personnel receive the output.

Control over the accuracy of output data includes techniques such as reconciling output data with the previously established input control totals, reviewing the output data for reasonableness, and controlling input data rejected by the computer during processing for distribution to appropriate personnel for correction and resubmission.

Distribution of output to authorized users involves two facets. One aspect simply provides for proper distribution. The second is a continuing reexamination of user data needs and ascertaining that reports are actually needed and utilized.

Computer output distribution is controlled through utilization of a list of authorized recipients. This list must be reviewed periodically to add new users and, just as important, to eliminate others no longer entitled to receive the output.

The continuing reexamination of user needs may result in selective curtailment of output reports. These reports should be redistributed only upon specific request to the data processing department. This technique has been utilized by some companies to reduce their output volume by 40 to 60 percent.

6. *Hardware features for control over equipment.* Hardware features for control over equipment are provided by the computer vendors to minimize errors caused by electronic circuitry and to reduce problems caused by operator errors. Familiarity with available features not only provides assurance to the accountant that hardware errors are almost nonexistent, but also ensures that numerous options and alternatives are incorporated where necessary into cost-benefit analyses of computer acquisition and operations.

Equipment control features for monitoring hardware performance include:

a. Parity checks (to detect the loss of electronic pulses as data is moved through the computer).
b. Duplicate processes (dual reading of data or reading after writing).
c. Echo checks (signals from peripheral equipment to the CPU that mechanisms for performing an operation have been activated).
d. Validity checks (ascertain that a valid data code is utilized).
e. Equipment check (photoelectric sensing in card readers to determine that photoelectric cells are on and working).
f. Boundary protection (prevents one program from interfer-

ing with another when computer is operating in multipro-gramming mode).

g. Interlock (prevents one device or operation from interfering with another such as locking a terminal keyboard until CPU is ready for input).

h. File protection rings (ring must be in place on tape reel before data can be written on tape).

7. Preventing destruction of and misuse of data files and programs. The misuse and destruction of data files can represent an enormous cost to an organization. The impact may range from additional personnel costs to the reconstruction of a file and the complete termination of operations of the organization. These benefits can be provided by an adequate prevention program. The type and scope of such a program involves a careful analysis of related costs and benefits.

An adequate prevention program should include the following:

a. Procedures to protect data files and programs range from preventing loss to begin with, to facilitating the recovery from losses. These procedures include physical safeguards, procedural controls, retention and reconstruction plans, file restrictions for remote access, approval and documentation of program and file changes, and various types of insurance.

b. Physical safeguards to provide fire protection, security protection, off-premises storage of backup files and programs, and environmental control.

c. Procedural controls to eliminate operator errors include labels and file protection rings.

d. Librarianship function provides custody and recordkeeping of file and data libraries.

e. Retention and reconstruction plans that specify source document retention, magnetic tape cycling procedures such as the son-father-grandfather retention cycle, requirements for periodic dumps from disc packs to tape reels for backup purposes, provision for and testing of backup computer facilities, and file reconstruction procedures for recreating files with a minimum of time and effort.

f. Control of remote access files with techniques such as passwords, a catalog of eligible users, and scrambled data fields.

g. Program and file changes allowed only with proper authorization and maintenance of a log recording all changes.

h. Detailed specifications for procedures to be followed for program testing and program changes.

i. Provision of insurance as a means of financing massive reconstruction efforts. Service bureau users should ascertain that adequate insurance is maintained to protect users. In-house systems, at a minimum, should utilize fire insurance and fidelity insurance on key employees.

MANAGEMENT AUDIT AND REVIEW

Computer resource control should incorporate two types of audits. One type is referred to as a post audit, or completion review, and attempts to determine whether a project meets its stated objectives. The second type is referred to as an operations audit, or performance evaluation audit, and attempts to determine whether computer resources are being utilized at maximum efficiency. Both of these audits can provide valuable information for the cost accountant.

Post audit

Once a project has been completed it is necessary to determine whether it was performed according to plan. Any departures may be valuable for determining the effect on ongoing operations in terms of budgeting and other considerations. In addition, any departures from plan may provide important information in planning the next project. The cost accountant may benefit by incorporating the information in his analyses of operations affected by the project, and in improved cost analyses for subsequent projects.

Unfortunately, once a project has been completed and incorporated into ongoing operations, it is sometimes next to impossible to ferret out relevant information for the post-audit review. To enhance performance of the post-audit review, it may be necessary to specify unique interim reporting requirements to provide the necessary information. Incremental volume, cost, and other information may have to be collected for subsequent analysis during the post-completion review.

Operations audit

Performance evaluation to analyze the efficiency of computer resource utilization is typically an inherent part of the mission of internal audit groups. The cost accountant may be called upon to assist in, or he may benefit from the results of, analyses performed by the internal auditors through improvements in his data base.

The efficiency aspect of performance evaluation is basically an intensive cost analysis. Is the organization maximizing the utilization of its resources? What is being produced for the dollars expended? Could it be done more cheaply?

The assimilation by the cost accountant of comparative information and presentation to the data processing group may provide some standards toward which the computer staff can strive. The cost accountant will examine not only trends and ratios within his own organization, but also statistical information from external sources, such as competitors and industry groups, environmental and other local considerations, regional and national information from various data processing societies and publications, and perhaps even international information, if relevant.

FUTURE DEVELOPMENTS

Computers can be utilized very effectively in the control of computer resources. Such an application is usually within the context of resource management models. Numerous models are available from which to choose. Some of these are currently used by relatively sophisticated resource management groups, while others are expected to be adopted in the not-too-distant future.

Resource management models fall into two general categories: simulation models and normative models. The former type of models allow the user to analyze alternative scenarios of computer configurations, operating environments, and other "what if?" aspects of computer resource management. Normative models provide insight into what "should" management do to optimize the allocation of computer resources. Although both types of models can be used to address the same issue, the outputs of simulation models are deemed to be oriented toward questions of what "could" or "would" happen, while normative models are expected to infer what "should" happen.

Simulation models

Various types of simulation models have been applied to the analysis and management of computer resources. These include queuing simulation models and others incorporating Monte Carlo techniques.

An example of a queuing simulation model is GPSS, an IBM-developed interpretive simulation programming language. To determine the optimum central processing unit, peripheral equipment, and tele-processing network for an on-line system serving tellers and their customers in a multi-state utility, GPSS was used by one of the authors for a comprehensive analysis of the entire system. Given the desired mean wait time of customers as they arrived to pay their bills, ask questions, and so forth, it was relatively easy to model the effects of alternative terminals, line speeds, disc versus tape versus data cell storage devices, the quantities of alternative hardware configurations, and so forth. The effort could not have been justified for a small computer system, but for larger systems the technique may be invaluable, as it was in this instance.

In addition to queuing models, such as GPSS, simulation models incorporating Monte Carlo techniques have been applied to the analysis of feasibility and operations of data processing installations. Instead of single values, the output of the analyses will be a probability distribution of likely occurrences.

The feasibility model may be used to calculate net present values or discounted cash flow return on investment amounts based on anticipated benefits and related costs of a new installation, or modifications to an existing one. The feasibility model has been used for the analysis of appropriation requests for computer resource capital expenditures.

An operations model may be used to analyze alternative computer schedules incorporating the probability of various work loads or changes in priorities. The operations model has been used for the preparation of annual flexible budgets.

Normative models

A normative model familiar to cost accountants is the linear programming model. Although often applied to production to optimize the allocation of production resources, raw material, personnel, and so forth, this same model has also been used to optimize the allocation of computer resources. More sophisticated versions of the linear programming model include decomposition models and goal programming models.

The complexity of distributed data processing with decentralized decision making by geographically disbursed operations supervisors may benefit from a recent advance in applied mathematical programming techniques. Decomposition algorithms have been developed to deal specifically with decentralized operations.[12] A price-directed version has application for analyzing the effects of alternative charge-out (transfer pricing) schemes. A version based on direct allocation of computer resources, incorporating components of a bid model, is an alternative to transfer pricing. Both of these models can function as excellent planning tools for optimizing the allocation of computer resources. Cost accountants already familiar with linear programming techniques should experience little difficulty in applying these more sophisticated models.

Goal programming models may also prove invaluable to the cost accountant experiencing difficulty in quantifying all of the benefits and costs necessitated by the linear programming models.[13] Application of goal programming models requires specification of the priorities associated with accomplishing various tasks. The priorities must be quantified, but this is often easier than the quantification of benefits associated with computer projects and operations.

---

[12] For a discussion of these techniques see R. M. Burton, W. W. Damon, and D. W. Loughbridge, "The Economics of Decomposition: Resource Allocation versus Transfer Pricing," *Decision Sciences* vol. 5, 1974, pp. 298–302.

[13] For a discussion of this technique see Lang M. Lee, "Goal Programming for Decision Analysis of Multiple Objectives," *Sloan Management Review*, vol. 14, Winter 1972–73, pp. 15–16.

CONCLUSION

The control of computer resources is a complex and difficult control situation. This is partly because of the particular characteristics of data processing, and partly because of the developmental nature of control in a new area. Particular characteristics include the pervasive impact data processing has on all aspects of the corporate organization, problems related to cost behavior and technology, and the difficulty of evaluating potential and growing demands. The developmental nature of control in a new area generates uncertainty, both in the application of traditional accounting and organizational control techniques and in the use of specific data processing controls that are still being evolved.

The approach of this chapter is to discuss the control of computer resources via accounting and organizational control techniques, and via specific data processing controls. Accounting and organizational questions include the role of centralized versus decentralized control, the role of the budget, and the possible use of pricing techniques. Specific data processing controls include quality control techniques, such as programmed control over processing, and hardware features for control over equipment.

The planning and control of computer resources follows three major stages:

1. Planning and control of data processing development covers the data processing master development plan and data processing project control.
2. Planning and control of the computer organization and operations includes the organization of the data processing department, management control of the data processing department, operational control within the department, and quality control over the output of the department.
3. The final stage requires management audit and review via post audit and operations audit.

The control of computer resources will continue to evolve in the future. This will occur as our understanding of the usefulness of accounting and organizational techniques in this area improves. It will continue as data processing controls are either improved or developed to meet the needs of new systems. Finally, it is expected that advanced resource management techniques will gain greater acceptance as feasible data processing controls.

REFERENCES

Anthony, Robert N., and Dearden, John. *Management Control Systems.* Homewood, Ill.: Irwin, 1976.

Burton, R. M., Damon, W. W., and Loughbridge, D. W. "The Economics of Decomposition: Resource Allocation versus Transfer Pricing." *Decision Sciences* vol. 5, 1974.

Churchman, C. West. *The Design of Inquiring Systems.* New York: Basic Books, Inc., 1971.

Dantzig, George B., and Wolfe, Phillip. "Decomposition Principles for Linear Programs." *Operations Research,* vol. 8, 1960, p. 1.

_____. "The Decomposition Algorithm for Linear Programs." *Econometrica,* vol. 29, no. 4, October 1961, p. 4.

Davis, Gordon B. *Auditing and EDP,* New York: AICPA, 1968.

_____. *Management Information Systems.* New York: McGraw-Hill, 1974.

Holtz, J. N. "An Analysis of Major Scheduling Techniques in the Defense Systems Environment," in David T. Cleland and William R. King, eds., *Systems, Organizations, Analysis, Management: A Book of Readings.* New York: McGraw-Hill Book Company, 1969, pp. 317–55.

Ijiri, Yuji. *Management Goals and Accounting for Control.* Amsterdam: North-Holland Publishing Company, 1965.

Joslin, Edward O., and Bassler, Richard A. *Management Data Processing.* Alexandria: College Readings, 1976.

Kornai, J., and Liptak, T. "Two Level Planning." *Econometrica,* vol. 33, January 1965, p. 1.

Lee, Sang M. "Goal Programming for Decision Analysis of Multiple Objectives." *Sloan Management Review,* vol. 14, Winter 1972–73.

McFarland, F. Warren, Nolan, Richard L., and Norton, David P. *Information Systems Administration.* New York: Holt, Rinehart and Winston, 1973.

Porter, W. Thomas, and Perry, William E. *EDP, Controls and Auditing,* 2d ed. Belmont, California: Wadsworth Publishing Company, Inc., 1977.

1192

Sanders, Donald H. *Computers and Management.* New York: McGraw-Hill, 1970.

Ten Kate, A. "A Comparison between Two Kinds of Decentralized Optimality Conditions in Nonconvex Programming." *Management Science* vol. 18, August 1972, p. 12.

Turney, Peter B. B. "A Systems Approach to Adjusting Computer Capacity," *Management Adviser,* vol. 11, no. 4 (July–August 1974), pp. 32–35.

———. "Transfer Pricing Management Information Systems." *Management Information Systems Quarterly,* vol. 1, no. 1, March 1977, pp. 27–35.

———, and Purdy, Charles. "An Accounting Analysis of Management Information System Costs: A Case Study." *Management Datamatics,* vol. 14, no. 6, December 1975, pp. 221–30.

———, and Uyar, Kivlcim M. "Profit Center Control for Corporate Management Information Systems: An Organizational Analysis." *Management International Review,* vol. 14, nos. 4–5, 1974, pp. 91–104.

41

Costs and forecasting

Doyle Z. Williams*
Wig B. DeMoville†
Larry D. Franklin‡

For most firms in a competitive business environment, sound managerial planning is essential. Forecasting techniques provide management with valuable tools to utilize in the exercise of the planning function. Managerial planning has long-range strategic aspects and short-range operational objectives. Each may benefit from appropriate forecasting techniques. When operational plans are formalized in a budget and the budget is used for part of the evaluation of performance, the accuracy of the forecasts on which the budget is based may have considerable behavioral impact. Forecasts also aid the planning function when they provide input to decision models. Thus it may be said that forecasts play an important role in the managerial process by assisting management to fulfill its responsibilities regarding planning, controlling, and decision making.

Forecasting techniques can serve management's needs best when they are carefully selected, well understood, and properly used. Although many writers have attempted to distinguish such terms as forecast, projection, and prediction as well as risk and

* Professor and Chairman, Department of Accounting, University of Southern California.

† Assistant Professor of Accounting, University of Wisconsin-Milwaukee.

‡ Senior Vice President and Treasurer, Harte-Hanks Communications, Inc.

uncertainty, this chapter utilizes the terms within each group interchangeably. This chapter will focus on the selection process before turning its attention to a taxonomy of forecasting methods and a discussion of various forecasting models. Finally, the implementation of a forecasting function will be considered. There are many different forecasting models, but this chapter focuses only on those which tend to be well defined and which have been tested in practice.

SELECTION OF THE APPROPRIATE FORECASTING TECHNIQUE

Forecasting techniques are extremely varied in nature and have been developed to meet different managerial needs. The forecaster, who is assumed in the discussion which follows to be responsible for selecting the appropriate forecast method, must ascertain several factors before making a choice among methods. Certain factors must be obtained from the person who is to use the forecast and other factors must be ascertained from the model(s) under consideration. As suggested by Wheelwright and Makridakis (*Forecasting Methods for Management*), and Chambers, Mullick, and Smith (*Harvard Business Review*, vol. 49), the forecaster may find it useful to pose the following questions to management and to the forecast model.

Questions to ask of management

What is the purpose of the forecast? This question is the most important question to be asked of management, and it is important that both the manager and the forecaster understand its implications and the importance of the answer. The answer entails some specification of how the forecast will be used. The use to be made of the forecast usually specifies the power and accuracy that will be required of the model. Occasionally the answer to this question will obviate the necessity of asking any of the remaining questions, for all of these questions are highly interrelated and are meant to ensure that the forecaster has as much information as possible upon which to make his decision regarding model selection. The forecaster should be certain to understand how much accuracy is required by management before proceeding to the next question.

When is the forecast required? The answer to this question establishes the lead time available for developing the forecast. Long lead times for important forecasts may allow the forecaster time to develop a model for the situation, or short lead times may limit the models which might be used. In general, the forecaster should encourage management to anticipate its forecast needs so that the number of forecasts with short lead times will be small.

What is the time horizon of the forecast? Since the power of forecasting models is dependent upon the time period to be forecast, this question also serves to narrow the field of models from which the forecaster can choose. The answer to the question should specify not only how far into the future the forecast is to be, but also the number of future periods to be forecast.

Are the data for the forecast available? For certain forecasts, especially those of a recurrent nature, the data will probably be a part of the information system of the firm. Other types of forecasts may require data to be gathered before the forecast is made. The forecaster should also be aware that even though data may be available, they may not be in a usable form. For example, the degree of aggregation or the lack of equal time intervals between recordings may render them unusable. Before choosing a forecasting technique, the forecaster may need to inspect the data personally, and to verify that they have not been distorted.

Has the pattern of the data been determined? Some forecasting techniques require that the data pattern be known, and some techniques are best suited for certain types of data patterns. For example, decomposition models are often highly effective for seasonal data but inefficient for trend data with no seasonal or cyclical pattern. If the data pattern has not been determined, the forecaster may have to determine it prior to the selection of the appropriate model.

How much detail is required to be forecast? The method of data analysis preparatory to forecasting and perhaps the model(s) to be used will depend upon whether aggregated or disaggregated variables are being forecast. For example, does management desire a forecast of all production costs or only those for the milling department? Often, the purpose of the forecast will clarify this point, but the forecaster should ask the question whenever management's desires are not clearly understood.

What technology is available for the forecast? This question has two entirely different implications. On the one hand it is concerned with the technology to be utilized by the firm itself. That is, for forecasts with intermediate to long-term time horizons, the forecaster needs to know whether or not management is contemplating a change in technology. On the other hand, the forecaster needs to know what technology may be utilized by the forecast. May experts and technology outside the forecaster's own department be utilized?

What models are available for forecasting? This question is more pertinent to consultation than to in-house forecasts. If a consultant is the forecaster and is to be confined to the forecast models available within the firm, the consultant needs to know the set of models available. In special situations, the consultant-forecaster may be called upon to develop one or more forecast models for the firm to utilize.

Questions to ask of the model

How accurate is the model? The question can only be answered in a relative sense based on the forecaster's knowledge of the model's characteristics and the pattern of the data to be forecast. The forecaster should attempt to match the characteristics of the model with management's purpose for the forecast. The forecaster should be aware of the necessity of making trade-offs between the costs of forecasting and the benefit to be derived from the information. If a relatively unsophisticated, low-cost model will provide forecasts of sufficient accuracy for management's purpose, subsequent actions will be dysfunctional if the forecaster utilizes a high-cost method to obtain even greater accuracy.

Is the term of the forecast model suitable for management's time horizon? Very few forecast methods are equally good for various time horizons. Most tend to be good for short-term forecasts, fair for intermediate forecasts, and poor for long-range forecasts, or vice versa. The few models which are good for all terms are not necessarily superior for any term. Thus, knowledge of the model's time characteristic is indispensable to the selection of the most appropriate model.

What quantity of data is required by the model? Although some qualitative techniques require virtually no past data, most forecasting models use parameters estimated on past data. The forecaster needs to match the data requirements of the model against the availability of data. For forecasts of an ongoing nature, the forecaster can request that data be gathered for use in a particular model and utilize a different model until there is a sufficient amount of data collected to allow use of a better model.

What is the cost associated with using the model? The costs associated with utilizing a model are normally of three types: model operating costs, model maintenance costs, and information acquisition and storage costs. The information costs are self explanatory although they may be difficult to isolate and/or allocate. Some models such as Box-Jenkins may have high operating costs but low maintenance and information-related costs, whereas other models such as multiple regression models may have relatively low operating costs but high costs in other areas. The operating costs are those associated with the computer or other mechanical equipment and with the marginal costs of the forecaster. The maintenance costs are those associated with updating the model through parameter reestimation. The forecaster needs to consider all of the relevent costs, particularly in a small firm where only a limited number of models may be used.

All of the foregoing questions and the associated answers combine to aid the forecaster in selecting the appropriate forecasting technique for the particular situation. As the forecaster gains experience, it may be appropriate to ask fewer questions or additional questions. An ability to communicate with forecast users, and expertise at forecasting will determine, in part, the forecaster's contribution to the organization's ability to plan for the future and to attain its objectives successfully.

CLASSIFICATION OF SELECTED FORECASTING TECHNIQUES

In order for the answers to the questions suggested in the previous section to be of value, the forecaster and the manager must be familiar with the characteristics of various forecasting techniques. Chambers, *et al.* (*Harvard Business Review*, vol. 49, 501) noted that:

> In virtually every decision he makes, the executive today considers some kind of forecast. Sound predictions of demands and trends are no longer luxury items, but a necessity, if the manager is to cope with seasonality, sudden changes in demand levels, price-cutting maneuvers of the competition, strikes, and large swings of the economy. Forecasting can help him deal with these troubles; but it can help him more, the more he knows about the general principles of forecasting, what it can and cannot do for him currently, and which techniques are suited to his needs of the moment.[1]

Various classification schemes have been devised which vary in their degree of complexity and in the characteristics which they use to differentiate between forecast models. The following discussion blends the features of the classification charts used by Wheelwright and Makridakis (*Forecasting Methods*) and by Chambers, *et al.* (*Harvard Business Review*, vol. 49). Forecasting models may be classified first into one of two *genres*: qualitative or quantitative. The former is often referred to as technological forecasting whereas the latter may be further subdivided into explanatory and time-series models.

Qualitative forecasting methods

Although qualitative forecasting methods may utilize historical data of various types, they are characterized by a much greater degree of human judgment than quantitative forecasts. Often such judgmental approaches are necessitated by a scarcity of data. Wheelwright and Makridakis (*Forecasting Methods*, 177) have suggested that qualitative techniques tend to be used in two types of situations:

> First is to forecast *when* a given new process or product becomes widely adopted . . . The second situation that might require a

---

[1] John C. Chambers, Satinder K. Mullick, and Donald D. Smith, "How to Choose the Right Forecasting Technique," *Harvard Business Review*, July–August 1971. Copyright © 1971 by the President and Fellows of Harvard College; all rights reserved.

qualitative approach to forecasting would be one aimed at predicting *what* new developments and discoveries will be made in a specific area.

Each qualitative method is an attempt to "bring together in a logical, unbiased, and systematic way all information and judgments which relate to the factors being estimated." (Chambers, *et al., Harvard Business Review,* vol. 49, 506.) Each employs one or more experts to prepare or help to prepare the forecasts; thus these methods tend to be relatively expensive. Recent studies indicate that "more than 70 percent of the middle and large corporations in the United States are currently using qualitative forecasting and/or long-range planning methods." (Wheelwright and Makridakis, *Forecasting Methods,* 179.)

These methods often focus on the technological feasibility of accomplishing a given task rather than on its economic viability. Although estimates of costs and revenues may also be indicated, they are usually of secondary importance. Since technological advancement is often closely related to social pressures and political decisions, the experts responsible for technological forecasts may pay attention to these factors as well as to developments in technology. G. M. Folie (*Australian Accountant,* vol. 43) discusses several factors of importance to technological forecasting. These models include: the Delphi method, the morphological research method, the relevance tree method, logistic and S-curves, and time independent comparison methods. To this list could be added approaches such as: market surveys, the executive panel, and the visionary forecast.

These nonstatistical methods tend to be associated with long time horizons and some of them require considerable time for the forecast to be developed. Their results are usually fairly easy to understand. It has been recommended that the following areas may also be suitable to technological forecast methods:

1. To predict the behavior of the national economy, especially the phases of the business cycle.
2. To analyze the demand prospects in new and established markets.
3. To ascertain whether the availability and cost of credit tend to stimulate or depress sales.

4. To determine whether the economic strength of the competition is apt to intensify or diminish.

5. To aid strategic planning by studying the future social and economic environment, identifying important opportunities and threats posed by economic and technological progress, and estimating the probability and likely impact of legislative action. (Folie, *Australian Accountant*, vol. 43, 88–89)

Quantitative methods

Quantitative methods are characterized by the application of a mathematical model which relates the variable to be forecast to either some independent variable(s) or to its own previous values. The former is a common quality of explanatory models and the latter is found in time-series models. The time horizon of the forecast, the pattern of the data utilized for the model, the type of model, its cost, accuracy, and applicability vary considerably from model to model. Such variation provides the forecaster and management with a wide range of models from which to choose the proper method for the purpose and needs at hand.

Explanatory models

Explanatory models are based on the proposition that the item to be forecast is a function of one or more independent variables. Changes in value in the independent variables are said to explain changes in the dependent variable (the variable being forecast). If the relationship is such that changes in the independent variable values are believed to *cause* changes in the dependent variable, then the model may be referred to as causal rather than explanatory. The different terminology employed has no effect, however, on the mathematical aspects of the model or its associated characteristics. In general, most explanatory models do not work well for time horizons of less than three months, but intermediate to long-term time horizons may produce fairly good results.

Some explanatory models, such as the large scale econometric models, have the ability to predict turning points with some degree of accuracy. However, their cost tends to be relatively high and the time required to develop the forecast may be in excess of one month. The development time alone makes them unsuitable for short-term forecasts.

Explanatory and/or causal models includes the following types of forecast models: simple and multiple regression, econometric models, input/output models, Bayesian forecasts, and material requirements planning. Some writers have included life-cycle analysis employing S-curves as a type of explanatory model.

Time-series models

Although all quantitative forecasting models make assumptions about data patterns, the time-series models incorporate the assumption that the underlying pattern revealed by an analysis of the variable's historical values can be used to forecast its future values. Traditionally, the patterns of interest were identified as horizontal, trend, cyclical, and seasonal. Recently methods have been developed which utilize patterns of autocorrelations to develop the parameters of the time-series model.

In general, time-series models are well-suited to short and intermediate term forecasts, but they are not statistical in nature. The cost of utilizing time-series models varies, but most time-series models offer the advantage of requiring little developmental time. These characteristics make most time-series models quite suitable for such short-term forecasts as inventory needs, production runs, sales, and so forth.

Table 1 presents a classification of various forecasting models along with their characteristics. The table blends the classification tables of Wheelwright and Makridakis (*Forecast Methods*) and Chambers, *et al.* (*Harvard Business Review*, vol. 49) Many categories, such as cost and accuracy, present scaled measures which range from zero to ten, where zero is the smallest and ten is the highest, permitting comparisons among models. The data in the regression column indicate simple regression first followed by multiple regression. In some cells of the table the data given are conflicting because the two sources were in disagreement.

TABLE 1
Qualitative methods

Characteristics	Delphi method	Morphological	Relevance tree	Logistics and S-curves
Time horizon:				
Short term				
0–3 months	Fair to very good	na	na	Poor
Medium term				
3 months–2 years	Fair to very good	na	na	Good to fair
Long term				
2 years and more	Fair to very good	NA	NA	Good to fair
Accuracy:				
Predicting turning	Fair to good	NA	NA	Poor to fair
Points	0	0	0	0
Predicting pattern	5	5	5	5
Costs:				
Developmental	5	9	8	5
Storage	4	NA	NA	NA
Running	9	NA	NA	NA
Dollar estimate of computer cost	$2,000+	NA	NA	$1,000+
Time required to obtain forecast	2 months+ 4	10	10	1 month+ 5
Type of model:				
Statistical				
Nonstatistical	X	X	X	
Mixed				X

na = not applicable
NA = not available

Characteristics	Market surveys	Executive panel	Visionary forecast
Time horizon:			
Short term 0–3 months	Excellent	Poor to fair	Poor
Medium term 3 months–2 years	Good	Poor to fair	Poor
Long term 2 years and more	Fair to good	Poor	Poor
Accuracy:			
Predicting turning Points	Fair to very good	Poor to fair	Poor
Predicting pattern	NA	NA	NA
Costs:			
Developmental	NA	NA	NA
Storage	NA	NA	NA
Running	NA	NA	NA
Dollar estimate of computer cost	$5,000+	$1,000+	$100+
Time required to obtain forecast	{ 3 months+	2 weeks+	1 week+
	NA	NA	NA
Type of model:			
Statistical	X		
Nonstatistical		X	X
Mixed			

TABLE 1 (*continued*)
Quantitative methods

Characteristics	Explanatory models		Input/output
	Regression	Econometrics	
Time horizon:			
Short term			
0–3 months	Good to very good	Good to very good	na
Medium term			
3 months–2 years	Good to very good	Very good to excellent	Good to very good
Long Term			
2 years or more	Poor	Good	Good to very good
Accuracy:			
Predicting turning	Very good	Excellent	Fair
Points	0–4	4	0
Predicting pattern	5–8	8	6
Costs:			
Developmental	3–6	8	10
Storage	6–8	9	10
Running	3–6	8	10
Dollar estimate of computer cost	$100	$5,000+	$50,000–$100,000
Time required to obtain forecast	{ Depends on ability to identify relationships	2 months+	6 months+
	2.5–6	9	10
Type of model:			
Statistical	XX	X	
Nonstatistical			X
Mixed			
Pattern:			
Horizontal			X
Trend	XX	X	X
Seasonal			
Cyclical			
Data requirements	Mathematical: 2 more than the number of independent variables. 30–34 per independent variable	Same as regression	Dependent on type Few thousand

Time-series models

Characteristics	Multiplicative (decomposition)	Moving average	Exponential smoothing	Adaptive filtering
Time horizon:				
Short term 0–3 months	Good to excellent	Poor to good	Fair to very good	Very good to excellent
Medium term 3 months–2 years	Fair to good	Poor	Poor to good	Fair to very good
Long term 2 years and more	Fair	Very poor	Very poor	Fair
Accuracy:				
Predicting turning	Fair	Poor	Poor	Fair
Points	3	0	0	6
Predicting patterns	5	2	3.5	7
Costs:				
Developmental	4	1	0.5	4
Storage	7	1	0	7
Running	4	1	0	7
Dollar estimate of computer cost	NA	0.005	0.005	NA
Time required to obtain forecast	{ 1–2 days / 3	{ 1 day / 1	0.5	4
Type of model:				
Statistical	X	X	X	X
Nonstatistical				
Mixed				
Pattern:				
Horizontal	X	X simple form only	X simple form only	X
Trend	X	X linear form only	X linear form only	X
Seasonal	X			X
Cyclical	X			X
Data requirements	5 seasons	2 years if seasonal 10–20 observations	Same as moving average 3 observations	5 seasons

TABLE 1 (*concluded*)
Quantitative models

Characteristics	*Census II (X-11)*	*Time-series models* Foran	*Box-Jenkins*
Time horizon:			
Short-term			
0–3 months	Very good to excellent	Good to excellent	Very good to excellent
Medium term			
3 months–2 years	Good	Good	Poor to good
Long term			
2 years and more	Very poor	Poor	Very poor
Accuracy:			
Predicting turning	Very good	Fair	Fair
Points	8	7	8
Predicting pattern	7	7	10
Costs:			
Developmental	6	5	8
Storage	8	8	7
Running	7	6	10
Dollar estimate of computer cost	$10	NA	$10
Time required to obtain forecast	{ 1 day 5	NA 5	1 day 7
Type of Model:			
Statistical			X
Nonstatistical			
Mixed	X	X	
Pattern:			
Horizontal	X	X	X
Trend	X	X	X
Seasonal	X	X	X
Cyclical	X	X	X

FORECASTING TECHNIQUES

This section briefly discusses selected forecasting techniques. Qualitative forecasting models are discussed first, followed by a discussion of explanatory models and time-series models, respectively. These discussions provide general descriptions of each model's characteristics, but it is strongly recommended that the forecaster consult more detailed references before attempting to utilize any of these models.

Qualitative forecasting methods

The *Delphi method* has achieved perhaps greater popularity than any other qualitative method. The method was developed at the RAND Corporation by Olaf Helmer (*Social Technology*) and others. It has two advantages over most other qualitative methods. First, the members of the panel of experts do not have to meet together; in fact, the method is designed to avoid the social pressures and personality biases which often characterize small group behavior by obtaining opinions without the experts' meeting together physically. Second, the method allows the results to be presented as a range of values rather than a single point estimate.

The method requires a person to act as coordinator of a panel of persons chosen for their knowledge about the area of interest. The coordinator then elicits from each panel member the response(s) to selected questions. It is imperative that the questions be unambiguous. The Delphi method often works best where the panel is not too large (5 to 15 members) and where the number of questions and allowable responses are limited in number.

From the initial responses, the coordinator compiles a list which is then returned to the experts. The experts are asked to explain the reasons for the divergent items. Divergent items are usually defined as those whose frequency places them in the upper or lower quartile of response frequencies. At this point, many experts revise their estimates toward the middle range while others may offer substantial justification for their original position.

A revised frequency list and the reasons given for divergent items are sent to panel members. Each member is given the opportunity to revise his or her opinion. At the end of several rounds, the panel has usually narrowed the range of estimates considerably and achieved some consensus. Interesting applications of this technique are discussed in Smil (*Long Range Planning*, vol. 50) and DeMoville (*Management Accounting*, vol. 59).

The morphological method was developed by Zwicky (*Monographs on Morphological Research*, no. 1) while working in the field of jet engines. The method "concerns itself with the development and the practical application of basic methods which will allow us to discover and analyze the structural or morphological interrelations among objects, phenomena and concepts, to explore the results gained for the construction of a sound world." (Zwicky, *Monographs*, no. 1, 275.) The method involves a systematic way of thinking about problems and discovering solutions. There are five essential steps to Zwicky's method:

1. The problem must be explicitly formulated and defined.
2. All parameters that may enter into the solution must be identified and characterized.
3. A multidimensional matrix (the morphological box) containing all identified parameters is constructed.
4. All solutions of the morphological box should be examined for their feasibility and analyzed and evaluated with respect to the purposes to be achieved.
5. The best solutions identified in step 3 (sic) should be analyzed, possibly in an additional morphological study, according to their feasibility and the resources and means available. (Wheelwright and Makridakis, *Forecasting Methods*, pp. 186–87.)

The method can swiftly become unwieldy if the parameters and their components are numerous. For example, if there are three parameters, each of which has five components, the morphological box would contain 125 combinations (5x5x5). The aim of the method is to reduce the number of alternatives to be considered and to assess the likelihood of each alternative occurring. The chief advantage of the morphological method is that it may enumerate combinations which were unidentified previously.

The relevance tree method originated in decision theory where it was characterized by quantitative analysis. Its purpose as a qualitative forecasting technique is usually to identify what technological developments are necessary to achieve a long-range goal. The method was initiated by the Honeywell Corporation. (Sigford and Parvin, *IEEE Transactions on Engineering Management,* vol. 12.) After the tree is developed, a panel of experts may be asked to vote (usually by secret ballot) to determine the relative importance of each item in the tree. The votes are averaged and the results indicate which paths of the tree have the greatest relevance for attaining the specified goal.

Logistics and S-curves are based on the observation that many phenomena are characterized by a slow start, a steep growth, and then a plateau. Not only do many technological developments follow such a pattern but also many product life-cycles are adequately described by an S-curve. By plotting the variable to be forecast on a vertical axis and time on a horizontal axis, expert opinion may be used to determine the shape of the curve. For example:

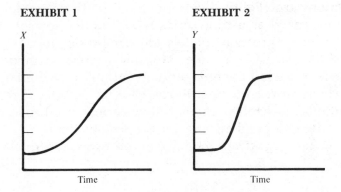

EXHIBIT 1

X

Time

EXHIBIT 2

Y

Time

If the horizontal scales are the same, Exhibit 1 illustrates a variable which has a comparatively slower start and rate of growth than the one in Exhibit 2. However, since the shape of such curves is extremely subjective, "in the business setting the S-curve approach may be of limited usefulness." (Wheelwright and Makridakis, *Forecast Methods,* p. 182.)

Time-Independent Technological Comparisons are quite similar to the S-curve approach except that the development in one area is used as a basis for predicting developments in another area. Chambers, *et al.*, (*Harvard Business Review*, vol. 49) present an example of projecting color-TV sales on the basis of black and white TV sales. Gerstenfeld (*Journal of Business*, vol. 44) discusses additional applications of time-independent comparisons.

Market-based surveys, questionnaires, and variants of executive panels also constitute qualitative forecasting methods. Each of these methods as well as those discussed above are strongly influenced by opinion and are usually employed in instances where little or no historical data are available. Companies which utilize such methods are usually those which are also involved in intensive long-range planning efforts.

Quantitative forecasting methods—explanatory models

Regression models are probably the most widely known of all the explanatory models. A useful distinction may be made between simple and multiple regression models because their assumptions are slightly different. Each of those models may be characterized as a time-series model under special restrictions. Simple regression models are time-series models if the independent variable is time. Multiple regression models are time-series models if the independent variables are dummy variables which represent time. In the case of multiple regression, a mixed model—explanatory and time-series—is possible if only some of the independent variables represent time.

The *simple regression* model may be expressed mathematically as

$$Y = f(X) \tag{1}$$

Such an expression states that Y is a function of X. That is, Y is caused by or explained by X. The model is linear if the power of X is one and nonlinear in high-order models. The discussion which follows is based on the assumption that the functional relationships are linear.

A linear relationship can be expressed as

$$Y = a + bX + e \tag{2}$$

The right-hand portion of the equation means that the value of Y is explained by a constant term (a), a multiple (b) of X, and an error term (e). The expected value of Y is

$$E(Y) = a + bX \qquad (3)$$

That is, the expected value of the error term is zero in an appropriately determined linear expression.

Three statistical assumptions are made regarding the error terms of regression equations, and one assumption is made regarding the relationship of the independent variable and the error term in simple regression. These assumptions are presented in Table 2.

TABLE 2
Regression assumptions

1. The error term has an expected value (that is, mean) of zero and constant variance.
2. The error terms are normally distributed.
3. The error terms are independent of each other.
4. The error term is independent of the value of the independent variable.

For a more complete treatment of these statistical assumptions, an introductory statistics text should be consulted.

The process of determining the values of a and b should be accomplished by the method of least squares unless the purpose of the forecast requires neither accuracy nor the development of confidence intervals. At the sacrifice of accuracy and reliability, other methods of determining model parameters may be used. Such methods include the free-hand method and the high-low method. (Mason, *Statistical Techniques in Business and Economics.*)

Because the significance of the model's parameters can be determined in statistical terms, the model is said to be statistical. More specifically, statistical methods can provide confidence limits for the model and for the value of b. They can determine whether or not the value of b is significantly different from zero. Correlation analysis may also be undertaken to measure the percentage of total variation which is explained by the model. The coefficient of determination for a simple regression equation is known as r^2 and is determined as

$$r^2 = \frac{\Sigma(Y_p - \overline{Y})^2}{\Sigma(Y_a - \overline{Y})^2} \tag{4}$$

Y_p is the predicted value for a particular time; Y_a is the actual value of Y which was observed, and $\overline{Y}$ is the mean or average value of Y. Thus, the numerator of (4) determines the amount of variation provided by the prediction model, and the denominator represents the total variation. The relationship of these two values determines the amount of variation explained by the model. The correlation coefficient r is merely the square root of r^2.

The regression approach is of little value for forecasting if the value of the independent variable is not known at the time the forecast is to be made. Thus, leading indicators or variables under the control of management should be used as independent variables. If the regression equation to be used is $Y = 2 + 4X$, and if the value of X is determined to be 3, the resulting forecast is $Y = 14 = 2 + 4(3)$.

In addition to ascertaining that the statistical and mathematical assumptions of the model are satisfied, the forecaster should be certain that the parameters were obtained from a sufficiently large sample and that the forecast value or the value of X does not exceed the range of obtained historical values used to determine the model's parameters. Should the sample of historical data have been too small or the value used for X be unrepresentative, the results of the model may be unreliable.

Multiple regression is quite similar to simple regression. It relates the changes in two or more independent variables to changes in the dependent variable by the method of least squares. The model may be represented as

$$Y = b_0 + b_1X_1 + b_2X_2 \ldots b_nX_n + e \tag{5}$$

Like simple regression, the model in prediction form is

$$Y = b_0 + b_1X_1 + b_2X_2 \ldots b_nX_n \tag{6}$$

In addition to the assumptions in Table 2, the multiple regression model adds the assumptions in Table 3.

TABLE 3
Additional assumptions of multiple regression

1. The independent variables are not dependent upon each other.
2. The independent variables are linearly related to the dependent variable.

The first assumption in Table 3 is seldom strictly met, and as long as the model does not contain gross violations of the assumption, the model will perform adequately. If the independent variables have strong covariance, the *b* terms will not have dependable explanatory power although the model itself may provide good forecasts. The problem of covariance between the independent variables is known as multicollinearity. Multicollinearity, its causes, and its treatments is usually discussed in advanced texts on statistics or forecasting. Neter and Wasserman (*Applied Linear Statistical Models*), Pindyck and Rubinfeld (*Econometric Models and Economic Forecasts*), and Benston (*The Accounting Review*, vol. 41) *inter alios* have stressed the absolute necessity of checking the assumptions of the regression model. Benston has written,

> It is all too easy to "crank out" numbers that seem useful but actually render the whole program, if not deceptive, worthless ... it is necessary to remember that it is a tool, not a cure-all. Where the desired conditions prevail, multiple regression can provide valuable information. ... (p. 672.)

Wheelwright and Makridakis (*Forecast Methods*) have suggested that seven basic steps be followed in implementing a multiple regression forecast model:

1. Formulate the problem.
2. Choose the economic and other relevant indicators.
3. Initiate test runs to obtain a correlation matrix.
4. Study the correlation matrix for indications of multicollinearity.
5. Decide upon the best model from among the individual regressions.
6. Check the validity of the regression assumptions.
7. Prepare a forecast. (pp. 113–14.)

Since multiple regression models require a considerable quantity of data and amount of time to develop, they tend to be utilized for longer term forecasts which require considerable accuracy.

Econometric models are seldom developed by an individual firm because of the high costs associated with developing and maintaining such models. The best known econometric models are associated with the Wharton School of Finance and the Brookings Institute. These are multi-equation models of the United States economy. It has been said that:

the great advantage of an econometric model is indirect. It can be used to predict the direction and extent of change of the overall economic activity or any of its components. This information can then become input required to estimate the independent variables of a single equation forecasting model. (Wheelwright and Makridakis, *Forecast Methods*, p. 140.)

An econometric model is characterized by a series of equations which must be solved simultaneously. The large scale econometric models employ hundreds of equations and utilize highly sophisticated mathematical techniques such as two-stage and three-stage least squares methods. The complexity of parameter estimation exceeds that found in multiple regression. Further discussion of econometric models, their theory, and their applications may be found in Johnston (*Econometric Methods*), Klein (*An Introduction to Econometrics*), and Pindyck and Rubinfeld (*Econometric Models*).

Input/output models are similar to econometric models in that they consider the economy or a section of the economy. The approach is somewhat similar to that associated with accounting for inventories; that is, input plus beginning balance should equal output plus ending balance. The model may be useful as a planning device where the technology of the economic sector of interest is fairly constant and where a firm's market share does not fluctuate radically. Yost and Stowell (*Information for Decision Making*) discuss an interesting application of input/output models in the industrial wholesale industry. One aspect of using such models is that management is forced to give consideration to factors external to the firm. Thus, the technique has more value for planning than for forecasting purposes. (For further details concerning the use of input/output analysis, see Chapter 36.)

Materials Requirement Planning (MRP) is a method of inventory control which acts like a forecasting device. The basic premise is that if one knows the output expected of a production system and the associated time schedule, the required materials may be planned by utilizing the production schedule and the lead time for the required items. The output expected, of course, may be the orders received or the result of another forecast. The method resembles the input/output model in that it recognizes the necessity of a certain material input to produce a given output. However, it does not involve the macroeconomy nor the high cost associated with input/output models. Some firms have reported significant reductions in carrying costs by using MRP as a method of inventory control.

Bayesian decision making is also a type of forecasting method which may be appropriate under certain circumstances. Bayesian statistics is basically the process of combining prior expectation with sample information to arrive at posterior expectations or forecasts. It is somewhat analogous to the smoothing techniques for time-series data which are presented in the next section. Smoothing techniques usually adjust forecasts by a certain prespecified percentage of the realized error. The adjustment process in Bayesian forecasts, in certain circumstances, depends upon the relative size of the variances of the prior probability distribution and sample probability distribution respectively. For example, with a prior distribution which is normal, Schlaifer (*Statistics for Business Decision*) has noted, "The total information contained in (the posterior mean) is the sum of the information contained in (the prior mean) and the information contained in (the sample mean)" (p. 305). The quantity of information summarized by the prior distribution and sample distribution are related by the inverse of their variances respectively. That is, total information (I) is the sum of $1/S_p^2$ plus $1/S_s^2$ where S is the standard deviation symbol and the subscripts p and s identify the prior distribution and sample distribution of the means respectively. Additional information on Bayesian statistics is found in Thompson (*Statistics for Decisions*).

The Bayesian process can be used to update expectations based on historical results (Empirical Bayes) with sample information. Since the sample information could be the actual results for a time period, the Bayesian approach can be a method of continually updating forecasts. Since the exact mathematical approach is dependent upon the shape of the prior and sample distributions, the reader is advised to consult other sources such as Raiffa and Schlaifer (*Applied Statistical Decision Theory*).

Quantitative methods—time-series models

Time-series models attempt to forecast the value of the variable of interest on the basis of its observed historical pattern.

1216

The basic assumption underlying all time-series models is that the pattern revealed by historical observations will continue through the time horizon of the forecast. This assumption tends to limit the use of most time-series models to short and intermediate terms.

Because the values of many economic variables are serially correlated over time, the time-series model is often a useful substitute for regression models since the latters' assumptions are violated by the presence of serial correlation, especially in the error terms. The four types of time-series patterns which are often identified are: horizontal, trend, seasonal, and cyclical. A horizontal pattern implies that the forecast variable is relatively insensitive to the passage of time. A trend pattern will reveal a general increase or decrease in the value of the forecast variable over time. A seasonal pattern suggests that, within a year's duration, peaks and troughs, increases and or decreases occur at regular intervals. Cyclical patterns resemble seasonal patterns but their duration exceeds one year. Exhibit 3 represents each of these patterns graphically.

The multiplicative model is the classical economic time-series model. It may be represented as

$$Y = TSCI \tag{7}$$

where the right-hand terms are trend, seasonal, cyclical, and irregular respectively. Since these parameters are determined

EXHIBIT 3

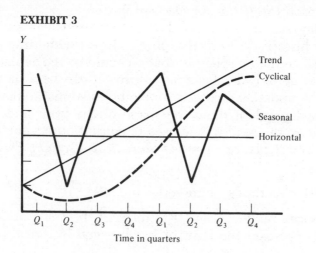

Time in quarters

by decomposing a series of historical observations, the model is often called a decomposition model. Although there are many procedures for isolating the terms of the multiplicative model, one method is a four-step process. The steps may be summarized as follows:

1. Determine the seasonal factor by calculating a twelve-month moving average. Obtain the ratio of the actual monthly value to the moving average and then average the ratios for each month to obtain a seasonal index for each month. The seasonal index is often a medial average or modified mean. (cf. Mason, *Statistical Techniques*, p. 215.)

2. Determine the trend factor by fitting a straight line to the moving average values.

3. Determine the cyclical factor by dividing the moving average series by the trend value.

4. Forecast for the desired time period by specifying the time period of interest in the trend equation and then multiplying trend times seasonal times cyclical to obtain the forecast.

By definition, the irregular element is random and cannot be forecast by itself; however, since its value was neither determined nor eliminated in the four steps above, it is present but unidentifiable in the final forecast. Some writers have suggested that the irregular element is eliminated or compensated for by utilizing the modified mean approach mentioned in step one (cf. Mason, *Statistical Techniques*). However, the seasonal indexes are by definition summed to equal 1,200. If they do not, and if the difference is material, a correction factor is employed (Mason, *Statistical Techniques*, p. 221). The effect of these procedures on the irregular factor is indeterminate. Although the classical decomposition or multiplicative model presented here uses a straight-line approach to dealing with trends, there are other methods available for dealing with the trend factor. Some of these alternative approaches will be discussed in this section on time-series models.

The multiplicative process may be programmed for computer use. Empirical results have suggested that the model is fairly accurate (Wheelwright and Makridakis, *Forecast Methods*, p. 96). The model does have certain disadvantages, however. First, it is a nonstatistical model; that is, the method neither provides confidence limits for the forecasted values nor permits tests of significance of the model's parameters. The model requires considerable data during the developmental stage and the updating process, if updating is necessary, is fairly expensive. Wheelwright and Makridakis (*Forecast Methods*, p. 97) suggest that managers have expressed a growing preference for regression over decomposition models.

The moving average model attempts to smooth the effect of random fluctuations in the time-series. The process of making forecasts with the moving average model is quite simple and the costs of using the model are low; thus this model, as well as other lower-order smoothing techniques, is suitable for use with individual small products. That is, if a manager has several hundred items and wishes to forecast each item individually, the smoothing methods, such as the moving average and exponential smoothing, might serve the purpose.

The moving average model may be represented as

$$E(Y_{t+1}) = \frac{\Sigma\ Y_t + Y_{t-1} + Y_{t-2}\ .\ .\ .\ Y_{t-n+1}}{n} \tag{8}$$

which is the same as

$$E(Y_{t+1}) = 1/n \sum_{i=1}^{n} Y_i \tag{9}$$

The number of periods, n, can be any size, but three-month, five-month and twelve-month averages are common. The larger the value of n, the greater the smoothing effect. The t subscripts indicate time. Equations (8) and (9) make it clear that the moving average method assigns equal weight to each value in the time series; that is, each historical observation contained in the moving average receives a weight of $1/n$th. The memory of the model is limited to the number of time periods being averaged, which means that the number of data items stored is equal to n. The model adapts to changes in trend very slowly and does not work well with seasonal data. However, if a decomposition model has been developed for the time series, the moving average method may be used to replace the trend, if any, present in the deseasonalized data. Since the deseasonalized data results from a moving average, such an approach is a higher-order moving average model.

Exponential smoothing models may be used to improve upon the moving average technique. The exponential smoothing model only requires that the last period predicted value (Y_t) and the last observed value (X_t) be stored. Furthermore, this model gives greater weight to more recent observations. The exponential smoothing model may be represented as

$$Y_{t+1} = Y_t + \alpha(X_t - Y_t) \tag{10}$$

Since Y_t is the previous forecasted value of the series, the model basically says that the new forecast will be equal to the old forecast plus a proportion of the error ($X_t - Y_t$) in the old forecast. The value assigned to alpha (α) determines the speed with which the model will respond to change just as the size of n in (8) and (9) determines the response rate of the moving average model. Since Y_t was determined in the same manner as (10), the model has an infinite memory with the older error terms receiving less and less weight. Brown (*Smoothing, Forecasting, and Prediction*) has recommended that alpha values between .01 and .3 be chosen. Values of alpha in excess of 0.3 do not accomplish the desired smoothing effect very well and cause the model to respond too much to random fluctuations. If the data require a value of alpha larger than 0.3, there are probably better models that could be used. Like the moving average model, the exponential model is not well suited to data containing seasonality, but it may work quite well with deseasonalized data.

The adaptive smoothing model has been proposed by Trigg and Leach (*Operational Research Quarterly,* vol. 18) as a variation on the exponential smoothing model which avoids some of the problems which may occur because alpha is set at a constant value. Their method employs an adaptive response rate or tracking signal which allows the model to be self-correcting.

The tracking signal is defined as:

$$\text{Tracking signal} = \frac{\text{Smoothed error}}{\text{Smoothed absolute error}} \tag{11}$$

According to Trigg and Leach (*Operational Research Quarterly,* vol. 18, p. 54), "As each error becomes available, the equations:

New smoothed error

$$= (1 - \lambda) \text{ old smoothed error} + \lambda \text{ error} \tag{12}$$

New smoothed absolute error

$$= (1 - \lambda) \text{ old smoothed error} + \lambda \text{ absolute error} \quad (13)$$

are applied. The tracking signal is the ratio of these two quantities." When the forecast is under control, the value of the tracking signal will fluctuate around zero, but when biased errors occur, the signal will move toward $+1$ or -1. Thus, it is recommended that alpha be set equal to the modulus of the tracking signal. The use of this method in initializing exponential smoothing models is particularly recommended for it allows the value of alpha to be determined by the data. Trigg and Leach (*Operational Research Quarterly*, vol. 18, p. 59) note that "The method obviates the dilemma of determining the optimal value of alpha. However, it does leave the problem of determining the best value of λ to be used in calculation of the tracking signal." Thus, although not without problems, their method offers an improvement over the unadjusted exponential smoothing model.

Adaptive filtering models also resemble the moving average and exponential models. However, unlike them, adaptive filtering models do not require the user to prespecify the value of the weights to be used. According to Wheelwright and Makridakis (*Operational Research Quarterly*, vol. 24), "The real power of adaptive filtering comes in having a rule that can be used to adjust the weights after each computation *that guarantees that the error will always decrease and will never increase*" (p. 56). The rule to which they refer is:

$$W_{j+1} = W_j + 2ke_jX_j \quad (14)$$

where W_{j+1} is the revised weight vector; W_j is the old weight vector; k is the learning constant; e_j is the forecast error using the old weights; and X_j is the vector of past observations. The objective is to minimize the squared error of the forecast.

Adaptive filtering is not without its own particular set of problems. The forecaster must determine the number of weights which he is interested in using and must select the value of the learning constant. Wheelwright and Makridakis (*Operational Research Quarterly*, vol. 24) suggest that the forecaster may wish to examine the rate of change in W_{j+1} for each iteration and to adjust the value of k. It has also been suggested that convergence to the "best" values for the weights may be aided by initializing the weights according to the autocorrelation function (Wheelwright and Makridakis, *Forecast Methods,* p. 62).

Wheelwright and Makridakis (*Operational Research Quarterly,* vol. 24, p. 56) conclude that "in practice adaptive filtering which adapts the weights to the specific time series in question will always do as well if not better than either moving averages, exponential smoothing or any other technique which uses a relationship between the weights that is independent of the properties of the time series in question." The advantages of adaptive filtering are that it combines greater accuracy with the low-cost features of exponential smoothing and moving averages. It does not require as much data as regression analysis and is more accurate than many seasonal time-series models. On certain time series, it is even more accurate than regression. Its disadvantages are that it is not suitable for long-term forecasting and that it is more costly than moving averages and exponential smoothing. It is also a nonstatistical model.

Time-series regression models are often used with time-series data for forecasting purposes. The regression model in this form has no explanatory value; it is merely a forecasting tool. The form of the model remains unchanged from equations (3) and (6) but many of the assumptions are relaxed. In equation (3) the independent variable is time. In equation (6) the independent variables are usually dummy variables representing months of the year or quarters. Each dummy variable has the value of zero or one depending upon the time period being forecast. For example, the equation

$$Y_q = 2.9 + 6.4X_1 + 9.2X_2 + 3.4X_3 + 12.1X_4$$

could represent a time-series regression model for quarterly data. If the firm were interested in forecasting the second quarter, the values of X_1, X_3, and X_4 would be zero and the value of X_2 would be one. The forecast of Y_2 would 12.1. The model can be adjusted to contain a seasonality factor if so desired (cf. Makridakis and Wheelwright, *Interactive Forecasting,* pp. 180 ff).

Census II was developed by Julius Shiskin (*National Bureau of Economic Research*) during the 1950s. The model is a refinement upon the multiplicative model of (7), and relatively inexpensive computer programs and instructions may be obtained from the Census Bureau. Census II uses statistical procedures and an improved method to adjust for seasonal and irregular elements. The model is also easily manipulated to incorporate the personal judgment of management. Since the model has been widely used, its accuracy and validity have been empirically established. Further information in summary form may be obtained from Wheelwright and Makridakis (*Forecast Methods*, pp. 97–98).

The Foran System, developed by McLaughlin (*Short Term Forecasting*), is similar to Census II but has the ability to incorporate independent variables other than time. Its output is a number of forecasts and associated reliability levels. Thus the user is able to select from among several alternatives.

Autoregressive integrated moving average models, which are more commonly referred to as *Box-Jenkins models*, are the last of the time-series models to be considered in this chapter. The Box-Jenkins models are the most sophisticated of the time-series models. They are statistical models capable of forecasting with seasonal or nonseasonal data. The general Box-Jenkins model is

$$Y_t = \phi_1 Y_{t-1} + \phi_2 Y_{t-2} \ldots \phi_p Y_{t-p} + \phi_t - \theta_1 \phi_{t-1} - \theta_2 \phi_{t-2} - \ldots - \theta_q e_{t-q} \quad (15)$$

The general model can be used to fit any stationary time series. The user's job is basically that of determining that the data is stationary, and of specifying the values of p and q.

Mabert and Radcliffe (*Financial Management*, vol. 3) identify two basic reasons for the Box-Jenkins methodology leading to better forecasts than most other methods:

> First, using traditional approaches, the forecaster would more or less arbitrarily select a specific forecasting model. . . . Using this broad model (equation 15), the forecaster eliminates inappropriate models until the most suitable one remains. Second, the specific form of a given model to be used has traditionally been the result of a trial-and-error procedure. In contrast, Box and Jenkins present a rational, structured approach to the determination of a specific model (p. 60).

Box and Jenkins (*Applied Statistics*, vol. 17, p. 96) claim that (15) "supplies too rich a class of models to permit immediate estimation." They suggest that the sample autocorrelation function be used to identify "a subset of models worthy to be entertained." *(Applied Statistics,* vol. 17, p. 96.) The identification process is the subject of one chapter in Box and Jenkins *(Time-Series Analysis, Forecasting and Control)* and is discussed by Mabert and Radcliffe *(The Accounting Review,* vol. 49), *inter alios.*

Following the identification process, the user systematically follows an estimation process to establish parameter values for the identified models and a diagnostic checking process to ascertain whether or not the tentatively identified model produces estimated residuals that are uncorrelated random deviations.

Stationarity is an important assumption underlying many forecasting techniques including regression. Box and Jenkins have defined stationarity as follows:

> A series is strictly stationary if its properties are completely unaffected by a shift in the time origin. In particular a stationary series varies about some *fixed* mean. . . . It exhibits no change in mean and no drift *(Applied Statistics,* vol. 17, p. 93).

If the original series is not stationary, the data may be transformed (usually through differencing) to produce a stationary series. A model with data in first difference form with 1 ϕ and 1 θ would be a *p,d,q,* model of order (1,1,1). Most economic series will be stationary at their first or second difference if the initial series is nonstationary.

Since Box-Jenkins models tend to do their best with short to intermediate time horizons and since their computer utilization costs are high, management may wish to use such a sophisticated technique with only those forecasts where great accuracy is desired and where the opportunity cost of an incorrect decision is high.

Extensive treatment of the Box-Jenkins models is found in Box and Jenkins *(Time Series Analysis, Forecasting and Control),* Nelson *(Applied Time Series Analysis for Managerial Forecasting),* and Pindyck and Rubinfeld *(Econometric Models).* Box-Jenkins techniques may also be used to correct for several types of violations which may be present in regression models. Thus, the manager determined to use a regression model might well consider a mixed model consisting of regression and autoregressive integrated moving averages. The Box-Jenkins part of such a mixed model is usually applied to the error terms of the regression in order to reduce their magnitude.

USAGE OF FORECASTING MODELS

Any discussion of managerial uses of forecasting models may emphasize a descriptive approach, a normative approach, or both. For a handbook such as this, both approaches are appropriate. Recently, Wheelwright and Clarke (*Harvard Business Review*, vol. 54) reported the results of a judgmental sampling of companies with substantial commitments to forecasting. Their results are probably typical of forecasting usage in large companies.

Wheelwright and Clarke (*Harvard Business Review*, vol. 54) made the following observations based upon inferences from their sample results. The forecasting function tends to be centralized in companies having $500 million or less in sales revenue. Decentralized forecasting functions, however, may be found in some firms whose revenue is under $20 million, but above that point decentralization takes place rapidly. As the amount and diversity of products increase, the amount of data to be collected and the number of forecasts to be made can also be expected to increase; thus decentralization of the forecast function in large corporations is sensible.

Wheelwright and Clarke also discovered that over 50 percent of the 127 companies which responded to their questionnaire utilized seven of the eight methods listed in their questionnaire. Only 40 percent of the respondents had utilized Box-Jenkins models. The eight methods listed included three qualitative methods: jury of executive opinion, sales force composite, and customer expectations. Of the five quantitative models, two were explanatory—regression analysis and econometric models. The time-series models listed were Box-Jenkins, time-series smoothing, and index numbers. The latter method is a variant of the decomposition method. The percentage of use was highest for the jury of executive opinion (82 percent), and the largest percentage of ongoing use was associated with regression analysis (91 percent).

Four problems were identified by respondents as barriers to successful application of forecasts:

1. Lack of effective communication between users and preparers of forecasts.
2. Lack of skills required for effective forecasting.
3. Disparity in user-preparer perceptions of the company's forecasting status and needs.
4. Failure to plan a progressive set of actions to realize the company's full potential for forecasting (Wheelwright and Clarke, *Harvard Business Review*, vol. 54, pp. 47–48).

The identification of such problems provides the transition from a descriptive focus to that of a normative focus. Wheelwright and Makridakis (*Forecast Methods*) have identified three factors that determine an organization's preparedness for forecasting:

1. The attitude of top management.
2. The attitude of middle management.
3. The competence of the forecasting staff (p. 224).

Of the *barriers* to successful application of forecasts, number four relates to top management's attitude, number two addresses the skills or competency of the forecasting staff, and numbers three and four are related to the communication at different corporate levels between each other and the forecasting staff. Although the behavioral aspect of corporate relationships is beyond the scope of this chapter, it should be emphasized that the success of the forecasting function relies upon the backing of top management and its willingness to use forecast information in the decision-making process. Generally speaking, it is necessary for management to have an understanding of forecast techniques if it is to be completely behind the efforts of the forecasting staff.

Since data collection is crucial to the forecasting function, the backing of corporate management is necessary to provide partial assurance that data are correctly collected at the appropriate time and in sufficient detail. The data should be internally verified for accuracy. The more accurate the data are, the more faith management and the forecasting staff will have in the result. Thus, the information system of the firm needs to consider the data needs of the forecast function.

Top and middle management involvement

The quality, accuracy, and usefulness of a forecast is directly related to the support of top management and its participation in providing input. Top and middle management participation provides commitment to the concept of forecasting and the forecast.

Top management's participation may start with approving the broad, general assumptions that are to be used in the forecasting process for the economy, industry, and finally, the company. Assumptions should be made and documented about variables beyond the control of management. By a postaudit comparison of forecasted and actual results, it can be determined if an assumption was missed and the degree to which this missed assumption caused the forecast to be high or low. Examples would be the assumption that there will be no wage-price controls during the next 12 months or 3 years, mortgage rates will be within plus or minus 200 basis points of current levels, unemployment will not exceed 6 percent, and retail sales will grow at 7 percent. If any of these assumptions are incorrect, the actual performance can be above or below forecast.

Wage-price controls affect payroll expense. In the publishing business, for example, payroll is 45 percent of total expenses. Therefore, if there are wage-price controls, there will certainly be a deviation from forecast. Also in the publishing business, mortgage rates and unemployment rates affect classified advertising revenues, and retail sales affect retail advertising revenues.

Middle managers make even more specific assumptions about their departments. For example, it may be assumed that a new shopping center will open on a certain date, or it may be assumed that the pending request for capital dollars for new machinery will be approved and that the machinery will be installed by a certain date. It may also be appropriate to assume that there will be no strikes at plants of principal suppliers of raw materials. The effect of missing these assumptions on departmental performance relative to the budget is obvious.

While assumptions are made about variables that cannot be controlled, significant effort must be made to gather the most reliable data possible about the variables under discussion. There are numerous sources for obtaining information before making assumptions about economic variables and labor situations in particular industries. For example, *Business Cycle Developments, Survey of Current Business,* and the *Federal Reserve Bulletin* provide useful macroeconomic data on a monthly basis.

Documentation and distribution of assumptions are essential so that everyone involved in the forecasting process is looking through the same glass as to those variables that could affect the ability to meet the forecast. Otherwise, one manager may plan with recession in mind while another is planning with boom in mind. Further, documenting assumptions preserves the credibility of the plan when something happens beyond the control of management. If there are certain assumptions that are extremely critical to the ability to meet a forecast, then there may be a need for backup plans or contingency plans if it becomes apparent that an assumption is missed.

Finally, the forecasting staff should be led by a person who can communicate the results to management and who can supervise the staff activities. Preferably, this person will have competency in the technical aspects of forecasting as well. In addition, persons with computer expertise should either be on the forecasting staff or accessible to it. It may be possible in some firms to form *ad hoc* committees combining the expertise from various sections of the company to attack particular forecasting problems; such a group should not, however, be the forecasting staff per se.

Forecasting time horizon

Long-range forecasting in any significant level of detail is becoming less and less useful, particularly if the forecasting system is so cumbersome that a forecast cannot be effectively updated on a timely basis. However, industries with rapid technological turnover may still utilize qualitative forecasting techniques advantageously.

There are a number of factors affecting the credibility of long-range planning. Some of the more significant ones are:

1. The level of government regulations. There is no way to predict the likely effect on one's business of legislation that will be passed next week or next month, much less next

year. Perfect examples are tax bills, the EPA, OSHA, and EEO.

2. The inability to predict overall inflation, much less industry inflation. Newsprint prices, for example, increased 3 percent per year for 25 years and then doubled in 36 months. Currently, prices are increasing at 7 percent per year with the industry operating at 70 percent capacity. Inflation, likewise, has been much more punitive in the construction industry than it has been overall.

3. The effect of international economics on domestic economics. This variable most directly affects the availability of capital and the cost of energy.

4. Changing values of society—women working, single member families, and so forth.

The changing environment makes it essential to have a dynamic forecasting system rather than a static system, to document carefully the underlying assumptions, and to have all levels of management involved in the forecasting process.

In any case, a firm should plan carefully before implementing a forecast function. The development of a successful forecasting function within an organization is a result of continued effort on the part of management and the forecasting staff. In companies where management is truly interested in improving the decision-making process and is willing to invest the effort necessary to understand the techniques of forecasting, and where the forecaster is able to understand the information needs of management, the usage of forecast information should be considerable, and the profit structure of the firm should reflect the results of improved decisions.

REFERENCES

Benston, G. J. "Multiple Regression Analysis of Cost Behavior." *The Accounting Review*, vol. 41, October 1966, pp. 657–72.

Box, G. E. P. and Jenkins, G. M. "Some Recent Advances in Forecasting and Control." *Applied Statistics*, vol. 17, 1968, pp. 91–109.

———— *Time Series Analysis, Forecasting and Control.* San Francisco: Holden Day, 1970.

Brown, R. G. *Smoothing, Forecasting, and Prediction of Discrete Time Series.* Englewood Cliffs, N.J.: Prentice-Hall, 1962.

Chambers, J. C., Mullick, S. K., and Smith, D. D. "How to Choose the Right Forecasting Technique." *Harvard Business Review*, vol. 49, July–August, 1971, pp. 45–74; reprinted in *Harvard Business Review on Management*, New York: Harper & Row, 1975, pp. 501–28.

DeMoville, W. "Capital Budgeting in Municipalities." *Management Accounting*, vol. 59, July 1977, pp. 17–20 ff.

Folie, G. M. "Role of Forecasting in the Decision-Making Process." *Australian Accountant*, vol. 43, March 1973, pp. 86–89.

Gerstenfeld, A. "Technological Forecasting." *Journal of Business*, vol. 44, January 1971, p. 10–18.

Helmer, O. *Social Technology.* New York: Basic Books, 1966.

Johnston, J. *Econometric Methods.* New York: McGraw-Hill, 1972.

Klein, L. R. *An Introduction to Econometrics.* Englewood Cliffs, N.J.: Prentice-Hall, 1965.

Mabert, V. A. and Radcliffe, R. C. "Forecasting—A Systematic Modeling Methodology." *Financial Management*, vol. 3, Autumn 1974, pp. 59–67.

Makridakis, S. and Wheelwright, S. C. *Interactive Forecasting.* Palo Alto, Calif.: The Scientific Press, 1977.

Mason, R. D. *Statistical Techniques in Business and Economics*, 4th ed. Homewood, Ill.: Richard D. Irwin, Inc., 1978.

McLaughlin, R. L. and Boyle, J. J. *Short Term Forecasting.* American Marketing Association, 1968.

Nelson, C. R. *Applied Time Series Analysis for Managerial Forecasting.* San Francisco: Holden Day, 1973.

Neter, J. and Wasserman, W. *Applied Linear Statistical Models.* Homewood, Ill.: Richard D. Irwin, Inc., 1974.

Pindyck, R. S. and Rubinfeld, D. L. *Econometric Models and Economic Forecasts.* New York: McGraw-Hill, 1976.

Raiffa, H. and Schlaifer, R. "Applied Statistical Decision Theory." Division of Research, Graduate School of Business Administration, Harvard University, Boston, 1961.

Schlaifer, R. *Introduction to Statistics for Business Decisions.* New York: McGraw-Hill, 1961.

Shiskin, J. "Electronic Computers and Business Indicators." *National Bureau of Economic Research*, occasional paper 57.

Sigford, J. V. and Parvin, R. H. "Project PATTERN: A Methodology for Determining Relevance in Complex Decision-Making." *IEEE Transactions on Engineering Management*, vol. 12, no. 1, March 1965, pp. 9–13.

1230

Vaclavsmil. "Energy and the Environment—A Delphi Forecast." *Long Range Planning,* vol. 50, December 1972, pp. 27–32.

Thompson, G. E. *Statistics for Decisions: An Elementary Introduction.* Boston: Little, Brown & Co., 1972.

Trigg, D. W. and Leach, A. G. "Exponential Smoothing with an Adaptive Response Rate." *Operational Research Quarterly,* vol. 18, no. 1, pp. 53–59.

Wheelwright, S. C. and Clarke, D. C. "Probing Opinions." *Harvard Business Review,* vol. 54, November–December 1976, pp. 40–42 ff.

_____ and Makridakis, S. "An Examination of the Use of Adaptive Filtering in Forecasting." *Operational Research Quarterly,* vol. 24, Winter 1973, pp. 55–64. (London).

_____. *Forecasting Methods for Management.* New York: John Wiley & Sons, 1973.

Yost, S. W. and Stowell, C. E. "Using Input/Output Analysis for Evaluation Profit Center Performance." *Information for Decision Making: Quantitative and Behavioral Dimensions,* 2d ed., ed. A. Rappaport. Englewood Cliffs, N.J.: Prentice-Hall, Inc., 1975, pp. 275–92.

Zwicky, F. "Morphology of Propulsive Power." *Monographs on Morphological Research No. 1.* Pasadena: Society for Morphological Research, 1962.

42

The Cost Accounting
Standards Board

*Gary F. Bulmash**
Louis I. Rosen†

The creation of the Cost Accounting Standards Board (CASB, or Board) added a significant new dimension to the procurement of negotiated national defense contracts and subcontracts. This organization, unique in its political and legal concept, was created to deal specifically with the cost accounting requirements of negotiated national defense contracts and subcontracts. This chapter provides the reader with a foundation for successfully dealing with the Board's regulations and Cost Accounting Standards (CAS, or Standards). No attempt is made to describe the overall environment of government procurement with all of its administrative requirements. That is a topic worthy of a textbook. The following material is oriented to providing an introduction for the accounting practitioner who engages a client who is, or becomes, a government contractor, and who obtains a contract subject to CASB requirements.

Note: The views expressed are those of the authors and do not necessarily represent the views of the Cost Accounting Standards Board.

* Assistant Professor, The American University.

† Staff, The Cost Accounting Standards Board.

BACKGROUND

The CASB was established on August 15, 1970, by Public Law 91–379.[1] The passage of this law consummated a long process of Congressional hearings and research, including a feasibility study conducted by the U.S. General Accounting Office pursuant to Public Law 90–370.

The Report on the Feasibility of Applying Uniform Cost Accounting Standards to Negotiated Defense Contracts (The Feasibility Study) involved participation by the accounting profession, government agencies, defense contractors, professional organizations, and academia. Although many witnesses opposed creation of a "CASB" or a similar organization, Congress felt that The Feasibility Study's conclusions proved that cost accounting standards were feasible and desirable and should be promulgated by a "new mechanism" outside of the Defense Department (DOD). Existing cost principles for negotiated defense contracts had been provided by the DOD in Part 2, Section XV of the Armed Services Procurement Regulation (ASPR).

PRIMARY OBJECTIVES

The price of negotiated government contracts is based on either the projected cost of performance or the actual cost incurred as determined by the contractors' cost accounting systems. Thus, cost accounting to a significant extent establishes the number of dollars to be exchanged between the buyer (government) and seller (company). It is this particular function of determining the number of dollars to be exchanged which not only distinguishes CASB pronouncements from financial accounting standards, but also creates an intense and vocal interest in the Board's research and promulgation and administrative processes.

Public Law (P.L.) 91–379 establishes the CASB's primary task as the promulgation of Cost Accounting Standards to achieve "uniformity and consistency" in cost accounting principles followed by contractors and subcontractors under negotiated national defense contracts, and to provide for the written disclosure of contractor cost accounting practices. The CASB is authorized

---

[1] U.S., Congress, *An Act to Amend the Defense Production Act of 1950*, Public Law 91–379, 91st Congress; 1970, 50 U.S.C., pp. 2151–2167.

to make, promulgate, amend, and rescind rules and regulations to implement Standards.

The Board views "uniformity" as relating to comparability of results among two or more contractors in similar circumstances. The Board recognizes that absolute uniformity of accounting practices is not a practical objective due in large part to problems in defining like circumstances. The term "consistency" pertains to the comparability of results among various time periods for a given contractor, again assuming similar circumstances. Such consistency within an entity aids in comparing estimates with actual results. It is the Board's view that increased uniformity and consistency in accounting serve to improve understanding and communication among the contracting parties, to reduce disagreements, and to facilitate equitable contract settlements.[2]

The CASB also considers fairness as one of its objectives. Fairness results when a Standard shows neither bias nor prejudice to either party involved in the contract.[3]

As part of the promulgation of Standards, the Board is required to consider the probable costs, including inflationary effects, compared to the probable benefits.

The Board recognizes that Standards are only a part of the contracting process and are not a substitute for effective contract negotiation.

ORGANIZATION

The CASB is an agent of the Congress, independent of the executive branch of government. The Chairman of the CASB is the Comptroller General of the United States. P.L. 91–379 directs him to appoint four members. Of these four, two are to be from the accounting profession, one is to be representative of industry, and one is to be from a department or agency of the federal government. The law also specifies that of the two from the accounting profession one member shall be particularly knowledgeable about cost accounting problems of small business.

---

[2] Cost Accounting Standards Board, *Restatement of Objectives, Policies and Concepts,* May 1977, pp. 1–2.

[3] Ibid., p. 3.

The research and administrative tasks of the CASB are performed by a full-time professional staff currently numbering 21. The staff is directed by an Executive Secretary. The professional staff includes people from industry, government, and academia, among whom are attorneys and certified public accountants. In addition to the full-time professional staff, outside consultants also serve from time to time. Input from these staff members, other government agencies, contractors, and the general public is considered by the Board in reaching a final decision on a Standard. All of these comments, however, are only advisory to the Board members.

PROCEDURES

The process of developing Standards involves extensive library and empirical research.[4] There are detailed studies of the subjects with participation by various interested parties. The research steps generally include the following:

1. **Selection of topics.**   Subjects are selected for research after considering the nature and magnitude of the costing problems inherent in the subjects and their relationship to other Cost Accounting Standards. Selection of a subject does not necessarily mean that a Standard is forthcoming.

2. **Research of concepts and existing practices.**   A review of accounting concepts and existing practices entails examining available literature, discussions with representatives of professional and industry organizations, and reviewing the treatment of the cost of government contracts. The latter review includes examining government procurement regulations and court and Board of Contract Appeals decisions. Contractor Disclosure Statements filed with the CASB are also reviewed. Personal interviews and plant visits are an integral part of the review of existing practices.

3. **Analysis of alternatives.**   Having identified relevant issues by the research discussed above, the staff helps the Board develop analytical discussions of these issues. The staff prepares questions to elicit opinions and additional empirical data on the subject matter.

---

[4] Ibid., pp. 15–17.

4. Draft of a Standard. A draft of a Standard is prepared by the staff after analyzing the problems, practices, and alternatives. The draft usually includes a request for information concerning the potential cost of implementation.

5. Federal Register proposal. A proposed Cost Accounting Standard is published in the *Federal Register* for comment. The proposal is also mailed to individuals and organizations on a Board-maintained mailing list. The Board reviews all responses and modifies the proposed Standards as warranted. Major revisions may involve republication for further comment. Comments may result in staff visits to government agencies or contractors.

6. Promulgations. The Standard as finally revised is promulgated and published in the *Federal Register.*

7. Submission to Congress. At the time of promulgation, Standards are sent to Congress along with an evaluation of probable costs and benefits. The Standard becomes effective unless Congress, within 60 days of continuous session, adopts a concurrent resolution disapproving the proposed Standard.

8. Continuous review. The Board keeps continuously informed on operations of Standards in actual contract situations. Where necessary, the Board will publish interpretations of Standards. Industry representatives are encouraged to maintain contact with the Board for this purpose.

CONTRACTORS AND CONTRACTS SUBJECT TO CAS

General

Two of the most important questions which accountants using the Board's regulations will face are:

1. What companies and contracts are subject to CASB regulations?
2. How does a contractor or contract become subject to these regulations?

Public Law 91–379 requires that Cost Accounting Standards shall be applied to:

> . . . all negotiated prime contract and subcontract national defense procurements with the United States in excess of $100,000

other than contracts or subcontracts where the price negotiated is based on (1) established catalog or market prices of commercial items sold in substantial quantities to the general public or (2) prices set by law or regulation.

The law authorized the Board to exempt additional classes or categories of defense contractors or subcontractors when appropriate and consistent with the purposes of the law.

Classes of contracts exempted by CASB action

Section 331.30 (4 CFR 331.30)[5] of the Board's regulations exempts classes of contracts from the Board's requirements. The active exemptions in this section each represent a type of class of contract. The most widely applicable is the exemption of all contracts of $500,000 or less except those performed by a contractor who has also received a contract of more than $500,000. Once a contractor receives a contract subject to CAS in excess of $500,000, he must follow Cost Accounting Standards requirements on *all* contracts in excess of $100,000 which are of the type subject to CAS.

The Board recently promulgated and placed before the Congress a proposal establishing significant new contract coverage thresholds. If accepted by the Congress, the proposal will exempt from all CASB requirements all contracts with small businesses and will limit compliance to CAS 401 and CAS 402 for those business units having less than $10 million in covered contracts which constitute less than 10 percent of the business unit's total sales.

Waivers

The Board has also used its authority to

1. Waive CAS requirements for certain individual contracts.
2. Limit disclosure of accounting practices to larger defense contractors.
3. Limit the application of some individual Standards either by exempting certain categories of contractors or by estab-

---

[5] This is Title 4 of the Code of Federal Regulations.

lishing a dollar threshold for the application of Standards.
4. Exempt certain classes of contractors from the requirement
    to comply with Standards on the condition that they accept
    application of the disclosure regulations.

The Board has stated that it will grant a waiver for individual
contracts only in rare and unusual cases. A waiver would be
justified only if (1) the administrative burden is grossly disproportionate to the benefits which could be expected, or (2) failure
to grant an exemption would prevent the orderly and economical acquisition on a timely basis of supplies or services essential
to the needs of the government. The procedure and requirements for seeking a waiver are in paragraph 331.30(c) (4 CFR
331.30) of the Board's regulations.

Application of CAS to nondefense contracts

In addition to the contracts subject to Cost Accounting Standards as per the requirements of P.L. 91–379, the General Services Administration (GSA), as a matter of administrative policy,
has required CAS to be applied to some but not all nondefense
contracts. The regulations related to nondefense contracts are
found in the Federal Procurement Regulation, Section 1–3.1203,
particularly paragraphs (a)(1), (a)(2), (a)(4) and (h)(1). As applied
to nondefense contracts, the GSA has seen fit to include additional exemptions for contracts awarded to educational institutions, state and local governments, hospitals, and certain fixed-
price contracts.

Cost Accounting Standards contract clause

A contractor becomes subject to the rules, regulations, and
Standards of the Cost Accounting Standards Board by entering
into a contract which is subject to the Cost Accounting Standards
clause. Both the ASPR (Section 3–1203) and the Federal Procurement Regulation (paragraph 1–3.1203(a)(3) provide that a notice
shall be inserted in all solicitations which are likely to result in
negotiated contracts exceeding $100,000, unless the proposal
is exempt under the existing provisions.

For a contract to become exempt under the provisions of

paragraph 331.30(c) (4 CFR 331.30), no contractual action is required on the part of the contractor except in the use of the $500,000 exemption. To claim the exemption for a contract of $500,000 or less, the contractor is required to make the positive act of checking a box. ASPR Section 3–1203 requires inclusion of the solicitation notice found in Section 7–2003.67 in all solicitations expected to result in award of a CAS-type contract.

Rights and obligations under the Cost Accounting Standards clause

The Cost Accounting Standards clause which is found in Section 331.50 (4 CFR 331.50) sets out the rights and obligations of the parties with respect to CASB requirements. These rights and obligations are as follows:

Disclosure practices
1. As a condition precedent to contracting, the contractor is required to disclose his cost accounting practices. Further, the practices disclosed must be those currently in use and must conform to the cost accounting practices used on all other CAS contracts.

Consistently follow practices
2. The contractor must consistently follow his disclosed practices and must use the disclosed practices to accumulate and record cost data on this contract. [This requirement is also tied to CAS 401 which requires a contractor to use his disclosed practices not only in accumulating and reporting costs, but also in estimating costs for the contract.]

Comply with CAS
3. The contractor agrees to comply with all Cost Accounting Standards in effect, from the date of award of the contract (or if the contractor had submitted costs and pricing data, the date of final agreement on price as shown on the contractor's signed certificates of current costs or pricing data). Further, the contractor agrees to comply with all future Standards on a prospective basis from the date of applicability to this contract.

Mandatory change in cost accounting practice
4. The contractor agrees to an equitable adjustment as provided in the changes clause of the contract, if contract cost is affected

by a change in cost accounting practice required for the first-time adoption of a Cost Accounting Standard.

Other changes in cost accounting practice

5. All changes in a contractor's cost accounting practice other than those caused by the impact of the first time a Standard becomes applicable to the contractor shall be negotiated with the contracting officer to determine the terms and condition under which the change shall be implemented. [The key is that the requirements of P.L. 91–379 and of subparagraph 331.50(a)(4)(B) require that no agreement shall be made under this provision that will increase costs paid by the United States. The Board in Section 331.70 (4 CFR 331.70) provides a definition and measurement of increased costs.]

Price adjustment for failure to comply

6. The contractor agrees that in instances of failure to comply with Cost Accounting Standards or to follow his disclosed cost accounting practices (a factual determination in each case) he shall agree to an adjustment of the contract price or cost allowance if such failure results in any increased costs paid by the United States. The agreement shall provide for the recovery of the increased costs, together with any interest thereon computed at the rate determined by the Secretary of the Treasury pursuant to P.L. 92–41 (85 Stat. 97) or 7 percent per annum, whichever is less, from the time the payment by the United States was made to the time the adjustment is effective.

Disputes

7. The parties agree that where they fail to agree as to whether there has been a noncompliance and any cost adjustment is demanded, such failure shall be a dispute concerning a question of the fact within the meaning of the disputes clause of this contract.

Access to records

8. Any authorized representative of the Head of the Cost Accounting Standards Board or the Comptroller General of the United States shall have the right to examine documents, papers, or records related to compliance with the requirements of the Cost Accounting Standards clause.

Subcontracts

9. The contractor is obligated to include in all negotiated subcontracts the substance of this clause except for the requirements related to using the disputes clause. All negotiated subcon-

tracts must include the CAS clause, except those where the priced negotiated is not based on established catalog or market prices, commercial items sold in substantial quantities to the public, or prices set by law or regulation or those exempt by reason of Section 331.30(b) [4 CFR 331.30(b)] of the Board's regulations.

Interpretations

Section 331.70 Interpretations (4 CFR 331.70) of the Board's regulations provide a description and measurement of *"increased cost"* as used in the CASB contract clause. This provision is intended to aid in the application of the requirements of the contract clause to specific contracts in a variety of circumstances. The guidelines are to be used for measuring the cost impact of changes in cost accounting practices and for measuring the cost impact of noncompliance with Cost Accounting Standards or a contractor's disclosed or established cost accounting practices.

Increased cost paid by the United States is described as a situation where the cost paid by the government is greater than if the contractor had followed either his disclosed cost accounting practices or applicable Cost Accounting Standards. With respect to fixed-price contracts, the increase in cost is based on the difference in cost resulting from changing practices used in estimating costs for the contract and the practices used in accumulating and reporting such contract costs. This may be seen as the difference between the price that was negotiated and the price that would have been negotiated had the same practices been used. The measurement of increased costs and the administration of any contract cost or price adjustment necessary may be negotiated and settled, notwithstanding the fact that experience may subsequently establish that the actual impact of the change differed from that agreed to.

Section 331.70 also provides that a *"set-off"* procedure is available as part of the implementation of contractor-initiated changes. Where costs as a result of a change in cost accounting practice shift from one CAS contract to another, the cost increases or decreases may be netted in determining the final amount of any contract cost or price adjustment necessary. The

Board recognized that the number of contracts involved may be large and may involve procurements through various procurement agencies and any number of administrative contracting officers. In light of this, the Board has urged, and the contracting agencies have established, procedures so that a contractor who has contracts with different agencies will settle with a single procurement official the impact of proposed changes to all contracts of a particular contractor. This has become known as "the single face of the government concept" as applied to Cost Accounting Standards.

RECENT PROPOSALS TO AMEND CASB RULES AND REGULATIONS

The Board has recently proposed three additions to its administrative regulations. The first of these is the definition of *"cost accounting practice."*

A "cost accounting practice" is any accounting method or technique which is used for measurement of cost, assignment of cost to cost accounting periods, or allocation of cost to cost objectives.

(1) Measurement of cost encompasses accounting methods and techniques used in defining the components of cost, determining the basis for cost measurement, and establishing criteria for use of alternative cost measurement techniques. Examples of cost accounting practices which involve measurement of costs are:

- (*i*)   The use of either historical cost, market value, or present value;
- (*ii*) The use of standard cost or actual cost; or
- (*iii*) The designation of those items of cost which must be included or excluded from tangible capital assets or pension cost.

Accounting practices related to measurement of cost do not include the determination of the price paid by the enterprise for a given component of cost.

(2) Assignment of cost to cost accounting periods refers to a method or technique used in determining the amount of cost to be assigned to individual cost accounting periods. Examples of cost accounting practices which involve the assignment of cost to cost accounting periods are requirements for the use of accrual basis accounting or cash basis accounting.

(3) Allocation of cost to cost objectives includes both direct and indirect allocation of cost. Examples of cost accounting practices involving allocation of cost to cost objectives are the accounting methods or techniques used to accumulate cost, to determine whether a cost is to be directly or indirectly allocated, to determine the composition of cost pools, and the selection and composition of the appropriate allocation base.

The second of these proposed regulations provides a definition of *"a change in cost accounting practice."*

(i) A "change to either a disclosed cost accounting practice or an established cost accounting practice" is any alteration in a cost accounting practice, whether such practices are covered by a Disclosure Statement or not, as defined in paragraph (h) of this section.

(1) The initial adoption of a cost accounting practice for the first time a cost is incurred or a function is created is not a change in cost accounting practice. The partial or total elimination of a cost or the cost of a function is not a change in cost accounting practice. As used here, function is an activity or group of activities that is identifiable in scope with a purpose or end to be accomplished.

(2) If the express provisions of any law of the United States compel a contractor to alter a cost accounting practice, such alteration shall not be a change in cost accounting practice for purposes of paragraphs (a)(4) and (a)(5) of the Cost Accounting Standards clause (4 CFR 331.50).

(3) When a Cost Accounting Standard which has been applied by a contractor subsequently requires the contractor to alter a cost accounting practice in order to remain in compliance, that alteration shall not be a change in cost accounting practice for purposes of paragraphs (a)(4) and (a)(5) of the Cost Accounting Standards clause (4 CFR 331.50).

These proposed definitions provide a base line for the contractor, his accountant, and the procurement agencies to evaluate proposed changes to a contractor's accounting system as to whether these changes must be processed as a "change in cost accounting practice" under the requirements of the CAS contract clause.

In addition to the above proposals, the Board has recently promulgated criteria for determining "materiality." These criteria are to be applied whenever the words *significant* or *material* are used, and they also provide guidelines for dealing with materiality decisions as they apply to price or cost adjustments to contracts. The Board has stated that it will continue to provide more specific guidance on materiality in any Standard or regulation where it deems it appropriate. The guidance is also to be used in situations in which an existing Standard uses the words "significant" or "material." These criteria for *"materiality"* are:

a. In determining whether amounts of cost are material or immaterial, the following criteria shall be considered where appropriate; no one criterion is necessarily determinative.

1. The absolute dollar amount involved. The larger the dollar amount, the more likely it is to be material.
2. The amount of contract cost compared with the amount under consideration. The larger the proportion of the amount under consideration to contract cost, the more likely it is to be material.
3. The relationship between a cost item and a cost objective. Direct cost items, especially if the amounts are themselves part of a base for allocation of indirect costs, will normally have more impact than the same amount of indirect costs.
4. The impact on government funding. Changes in accounting treatment will have more impact if they influence the distribution of costs between government and nongovernment cost objectives than if all cost objectives have government financial support.
5. The cumulative impact of individually immaterial items. It is appropriate to consider whether such impacts (*a*) tend to offset one another, or (*b*) tend to be in the same direction and hence to accumulate into a material amount.
6. The cost of administrative processing of the price adjustment modification shall be considered. If the cost to process exceeds the amount to be recovered, it is less likely the amount will be material.

DISCLOSURE STATEMENT

As noted in a previous section, subparagraph 331.50(a)(1), (4 CFR 331.50) requires a contractor to submit a Disclosure Statement which discloses in writing his cost accounting practices. Section 351 (4 CFR 351) of the Board's regulations provides the requirements for this form and the form itself. The Board has two forms, one applicable to a wide variety of contractor organizations and a special form for universities.

The requirement to file a Disclosure Statement has been limited to large defense contractors. The limitations have generally been based on dollar amounts of negotiated national defense prime contracts and subcontracts. For fiscal years following fiscal year 1975 the requirement to file a Disclosure Statement is applied to any company which as a whole had defense prime contracts and subcontracts subject to Cost Accounting Standards of $10 million awarded in the prior year.

The regulations provide that the Disclosure Statement must be submitted in advance. However, provision is made for a post-award submission in Section 331.60(4 CFR 331.60) of the Board's regulations. Such submission is permitted only where it is authorized in writing by the contracting officer and shall be based on a written determination that the authorization is (1) essential to the national defense, (2) necessary because of the public exigency, or (3) necessary to avoid undue hardship. The postaward submission is not to exceed 90 days after the contract award. The Board has stated that it will provide confidential treatment for Disclosure Statements when specifically requested to do so.

The requirement to submit a Disclosure Statement may be waived at the secretarial level on the basis that it is impractical to secure a Disclosure Statement. Such waiver must be reported to the Board within thirty days.

A Disclosure Statement must be filed for each profit center, division, or similar organizational unit which has a covered contract, or for any other division, corporate group office or profit center whose costs included in the total price of any covered contract exceed $500,000, except as provided in [4 CFR 331.30(b)].

Once a Disclosure Statement is submitted a copy is retained by the procuring contracting officer and a copy is sent to the Board. The procurement agency will initially review the Disclosure Statement to determine its adequacy: whether it is current, accurate, and complete. A second review will be made for compliance with the provisions of ASPR Section XV and the requirements of the Board.

The Disclosure Statement provides a common framework for

the description of the accounting practices to be used by contractors in the accounting for contract costs. It provides a means for better understanding contract cost estimates and the subsequent reports of actual costs. In completing a Disclosure Statement a contractor must identify what he considers to be direct costs of contracts, and disclose his method of applying these costs to contracts. The contractor must also disclose his method of distinguishing direct costs from indirect costs and his method of allocating indirect costs to contracts. The Disclosure Statement form itself is a combination of objective answers, descriptive codes, and continuation sheets for a more detailed description of accounting practices and is divided into eight separate parts for information regarding the cost accounting practices of contractors. These eight parts are:

Part I—General Information

Part II—Direct Costs

Part III—Direct versus Indirect

Part IV—Indirect Costs

Part V—Depreciation and Capitalization Practices

Part VI—Other Costs and Credits

Part VII—Deferred Compensation and Insurance Costs

Part VIII—Corporate or Group Expenses

COST ACCOUNTING STANDARDS

Introduction to Standards

The Cost Accounting Standards Board has described a Cost Accounting Standard as follows:

> A Cost Accounting Standard is a statement formally issued by the Cost Accounting Standards Board that (1) enunciates a principle or principles to be followed, (2) establishes practices to be applied, or (3) specifies criteria to be employed in selecting from alternative principles and practices in estimating, accumulating, and reporting costs of contracts subject to the rules of the Board. A Cost Accounting Standard may be stated in terms as general or as specific as the Cost Accounting Standards Board considers necessary to accomplish its purpose.

The above statement provides insight as to the scope of the Board's work and establishes expectations as to the content of Standards. The definition also has the effect of precluding arguments that Standards should deal only with broad principles rather than with the methods and techniques of accounting for the costs of Government contracts.

Relationship to the existing Armed Services Procurement Regulation

As pointed out earlier, Standards are applicable only to certain contracts. Also, the Standards promulgated to date do not cover the entire spectrum of costs which must be accounted for in the performance of CAS contracts. This apparent void in accounting regulations is filled by the Armed Services Procurement Regulation (ASPR). It contains accounting principles applicable to both non-CAS contracts and costs as yet not covered by Standards. The obligation to follow the ASPR requirements for non-CAS contracts and costs not yet covered by Standards is agreed to as part of the contract clauses included in national defense procurements.

To the extent that there is an overlap in coverage between Cost Accounting Standards and ASPR requirements, the requirements of a Standard must be followed on CAS-covered contracts. As a result, today the accounting for contracts subject to Standards is a mixture of CASB requirements and ASPR requirements.

Administration and implementation of CASB requirements

The administration of, and audit for compliance with, CASB requirements is performed by the various procurement agencies and the Defense Contract Audit Agency (DCAA). The procurement agencies are responsible for including the CAS clause in qualifying contracts. The administrating and contracting officers of these agencies are responsible for decisions regarding a contractor's compliance with the requirements of both the Disclosure Statement and Standards. The same contracting officers also make decisions as to the cost impact of both Standards and contractor-proposed changes in their cost accounting systems.

The DCAA as part of its audit function reviews the Disclosure Statement for adequacy (current, accurate, and complete), and for compliance with the requirements of the Standards. The auditor forwards his conclusion to the appropriate contracting officer for consideration in the contracting officer's decisions regarding compliance and disclosure. Similarly, when a contractor proposes a change in his cost accounting practices or implements a new Standard, the auditor reviews the proposed accounting and the cost impact analysis and submits his evaluation to the contracting officer.

Both the procurement agencies and the DCAA have established a network of CASB specialists to facilitate the administration of the Board's requirements.

Format of Standards

The Board uses the same format for all of its Standards. A Standard must be read in its entirety, and any one section must be interpreted and implemented in the context of the entire Standard. The contents of each Standard are as follows:

General Applicability—establishes the universe of contracts to which the Standard applies.

Purpose—describes the areas of accounting involved and the Board's objectives.

Definitions—reprint Part 400 of the Board's regulations of terms prominent in that particular Standard.

Fundamental Requirement—states the broad principles or practices used in accounting for the costs covered by the Standard.

Techniques for Application—provide criteria to select alternative practices to implement concepts contained in the "Fundamental Requirement" Section. The "Techniques" will, as compared with the "Fundamental Requirement," usually narrow available accounting options.

Illustrations—provide examples of how the Standard is to operate in specific cases.

Exemptions—exclude certain classes of contracts from coverage of this Standard.

Effective Date—provides the date on which the Standard can first take effect per the requirements of P.L. 91–379.

Appendices—may also be included where warranted.

Prefatory comments

Standards are prefaced with analytical comments to provide additional insight into the research and significant factors leading to the Standard. These prefatory comments include summaries of comments received from the public when the Standard was initially published and reasons why significant changes were made, or not made. The prefatory comments aid users in applying the Standard.

Standards promulgated

To date, fifteen Standards have been promulgated by the CASB. These Standards are incorporated into the Cost Accounting Standards Board Regulations, Subchapter G, Parts 401 through 415. Summaries are included herein to aid the reader in using these Standards. Summaries, however, are not a substitute for reading the entire Standard.

Part 401—Consistency in estimating, accumulating, and reporting costs

This Standard promotes consistency among cost accounting practices used in estimating costs for a proposal and cost accounting practices used in accumulating and reporting such costs. Consistency provides an important basis for control over costs and aids in establishing accountability for costs in a manner agreed to by the contracting parties.

The Standard requires that costs be presented in sufficient detail that the estimate of any significant cost element can be compared with the actual cost accumulated and reported. The Standard applies to the classification of elements or functions of cost as direct or indirect, the indirect cost pools to which each element or function of cost is charged or proposed to be charged, and the methods of allocating indirect costs to the contract.

Part 402—Consistency in allocating costs incurred for the same purpose

This Standard requires that costs incurred for the same purpose in like circumstances be allocated on only one basis to any contract. All costs incurred for the same purpose, in like circumstances, are either direct costs or indirect costs with respect to final cost objectives, such as a contract. This Standard prevents double counting in instances in which the same cost items are allocated both directly and indirectly to a cost objective.

A contractor's Disclosure Statement must set forth his cost accounting practices regarding the distinction between direct and indirect costs. The Standard allows a direct cost of minor dollar amount to be treated as an indirect cost for practical reasons provided that the treatment is consistently applied and that the results are substantially the same as would be obtained if such cost had been treated as a direct cost.

Part 403—Allocation of home office expenses to segments

This Standard establishes criteria for allocating home office expenses to segments of the organization. Such segments might be divisions, product departments, plants, or other subdivisions of an organization which report directly to a home office. These criteria are based on the beneficial or causal relationship between home office expenses and the receiving segments and require that:

1. Expenses must be identified for direct allocation to segments to the maximum extent practical.
2. Significant nondirectly allocated expenses must be accumulated into homogeneous pools and allocated on bases reflecting the relationship of the expenses to the segments concerned.
3. Any remaining or residual expenses must be allocated to all segments.

An important goal of Step 2 above is to minimize the amount of home office expenses classified as residual. These residual expenses should be limited to expenses of managing the organization as a whole.

Residual home office expenses should be allocated to segments by means of a base representing the total activity of the segments. Where the residual expenses exceed a certain percentage of an organization's operating revenues a three-factor formula, based on payroll dollars, operating revenue, and assets, must be used to allocate the residual expenses to the segments.

The Standard provides criteria for allocating specific groups of home office expenses. For example, central payments or accruals should be assigned directly to segments or allocated on the basis on which the payments are made.

The Standard is applicable initially to those contractors who received net awards of negotiated national defense prime contracts during federal fiscal year 1971 totaling more than $30 million. Educational institutions are exempt from the requirements of this Standard.

Part 404—Capitalization of tangible assets

The Standard requires that contractors establish and consistently apply written capitalization policies satisfying criteria provided in the Standard. The contractor's policy shall designate economic and physical characteristics for capitalization of tangible assets, including a minimum service life criterion not to exceed two years and a minimum acquisition cost criterion not to exceed $500. The contractor's policy may cite other characteristics which are pertinent to capitalization decisions.

The acquisition cost of tangible capital assets, purchase price plus any costs necessary to prepare the asset for use, should be capitalized. Fair value is the purchase price used for donated assets. The cost of constructed assets to be capitalized includes all indirect costs—manufacturing and general and administrative—allocable to such assets in accordance with the requirements of this Standard.

The contractor's policy may designate higher minimum dollar limitations than above, if reasonable, for a group of items necessary to outfit an operational unit—an original complement of low cost equipment; that is, items which individually are small in amount, but in the aggregate represent a material investment.

Betterments and improvements which extend the life or increase the productivity of the asset should be capitalized if the contractor's established capitalization criteria are met. Repairs and maintenance costs are expensed if they either restore the asset to, or maintain it at its normal or expected service life or production capacity.

Part 405—Accounting for unallowable costs

The Standard provides for contractor identification of costs specifically described as unallowable when the costs first became defined or authoritatively designated as unallowable, and the cost accounting treatment accorded to such costs. This Standard does not govern allowability of costs. Allowability is a function of the appropriate procurement or reviewing authority.

Unallowable costs, either expressly unallowable by law or regulation, or determined unallowable by the contracting officer, must be identified by the contractor in any billing, claim, or proposal applicable to a Government contract. Unallowable costs are subject to the same cost accounting principles governing cost allocability as allowable costs.

The Standard also addresses directly associated costs and indirect costs allocable by means of a base containing unallowable costs. Directly associated costs—costs generated solely because certain other costs were incurred—must be separately identified when related to an unallowable cost. Where unallowable costs normally would be part of a contractor's regular indirect cost allocation base, they should remain as part of that base.

Part 406—Cost accounting period

This Standard provides criteria for selecting time periods to be used as cost accounting periods for contract costing purposes. A contractor should use its fiscal year (the same accounting period for which annual financial statements are regularly prepared) as the cost accounting period, except where an indirect function exists only part of the year, a different period is used as an established practice of the contractor, or a short transitional period is needed when a fiscal year is changed.

A contractor is required to follow consistent practices in selecting cost accounting periods in which any types of expense and any types of adjustment to expense are accumulated and allocated. The same cost accounting period should be used for accumulating costs in an indirect cost pool as for establishing the pool's allocation base, except where there is mutual agreement and the conditions specified in the Standard are satisfied.

Part 407—Use of standard costs for direct material and direct labor

This Standard provides criteria for determining when standard costs may be used and how standard costs are to be used for estimating, accumulating, and reporting costs of direct material and direct labor, including disposing of variances from standard costs. Standard costs may be used when they are entered into the books of account; standard costs and related variances are appropriately accounted for at the level of the production unit; and practices concerning setting, revising, and use of standards and disclosing of variances are stated in writing and consistently followed.

The Standard provides criteria for a contractor concerning standards setting, variance allocation, and categorization and groupings of items or costs based on the concept of homogeneity.

Variances between actual and standard cost should be disposed of annually by either allocating them to cost objectives or, where immaterial, including them in appropriate indirect cost pools.

Part 408—Accounting for costs of compensated personal absence

This Standard provides for uniformity in the measurement of costs of vacation, sick leave, holidays, and other compensated personal absence for a cost accounting period. Its purpose is to increase the probability that the measured costs are allocated to the proper cost objectives. The costs of compensation for personal absence shall be assigned to the cost accounting period or periods in which the employee's right to receive it was earned. The key test is that entitlement is presumed to be earned at the same time and in the same amount as the employer becomes liable to compensate the employee for such absence, if the employer terminates the employee's employment for reasons unrelated to employee performance. In the absence of a determinable liability, entitlement is presumed to be earned in the cost accounting period in which it is paid. The Standard provides a means of handling transitional accounting adjustments where a change to accrual accounting for compensated personal absence is required.

The costs of compensated personal absence for an entire cost accounting period should be allocated pro rata on an annual basis among the final cost objectives of that period. This pro rata basis should reflect the total compensated personal absence costs and the total of the allocation base for the entire cost accounting period.

Educational institutions and contracts with state and local governments are exempt from this Standard.

Part 409—Depreciation of tangible capital assets

This Standard provides criteria and guidance for assigning costs of tangible capital assets to cost accounting periods and for allocating such costs to cost objectives within these periods. The Standard is based on the concept that depreciation costs identified with cost accounting periods and benefiting cost objectives therein, should be a reasonable measure of the expiration of the tangible asset's service potential. This Standard does not cover assets subject to depletion.

The Standard requires that depreciation be assigned to cost accounting periods by a method reflecting the pattern of service consumption over the asset's life. When estimating service lives and likely pattern of service consumption, the contractor may consider quantity, quality, and timing of expected output; repair and maintenance costs and timing thereof; standby or incidental use; and technical or economic obsolescence of the asset or of the product it is producing. Tangible capital assets may be treated individually or by combining two or more assets into a group. Service life to be used for an original complement of low-cost equipment should be based on service consumption of the complement as a whole. Service lives used must be supported by the contractor's experience.

Estimated residual value reduces an asset's depreciation base; however, for tangible personal property, a residual value need be used only where it is in excess of 10 percent of the asset's capitalized cost. Changes in estimated service life, residual value, or depreciation method are assigned to current and future cost accounting periods, not retroactively. The annual depreciation cost shall be allocated directly to cost objectives only if such charges are made on the basis of usage and if depreciation of like assets used for similar purposes is charged in a like manner. If tangible capital assets are part of an organizational unit whose cost is reallocated to other cost objectives, the depreciation thereon may be charged directly to the organizational unit. Otherwise, depreciation costs are included in appropriate indirect cost pools. Material gains and losses on disposition of depreciable assets shall be assigned to the cost accounting period in which they occur and shall be allocated in the same manner as the depreciation cost of the asset. Immaterial gains and losses may be included in an appropriate indirect cost pool.

The Standard provides for a phasing-in of certain requirements over a period of time. Educational institutions and contracts with state and local governments are exempt. Exemption from this Standard is available where compensation for use of tangible capital assets is based on use allowances.

Part 410—Allocation of business unit general and administrative expenses to final cost objectives

This Standard provides criteria for the allocation of Business Unit General and Administrative (G&A) expenses to final cost objectives and for the allocation of the expenses of home office services received by a segment to cost objectives of that segment. The Standard defines G&A expenses and provides that G&A expenses shall be grouped in a separate indirect cost pool and allocated only to final cost objectives by using a cost input base. This requirement effectively eliminates the use of a cost of sales allocation base. The Standard also provides a transition methodology for change from a cost of sales base to a cost input base.

Guidelines for selecting a particular cost input base in given circumstances are provided. Other expenses may be combined with G&A expenses where the same allocation base is appropriate for both groups of expenses.

Part 411—Accounting for acquisition cost of material

This Standard provides criteria for the measurement and allocation of material costs to specific contracts. The cost of material may be allocated directly to a cost objective, provided that the material is specifically identified with that contract at the time of the purchase. Inventory costing methods shall be applied in a manner which results in a systematic and rational costing of the issues of materials to cost objectives. Where the amount of ending inventory is a significant amount in comparison to the total material cost in an indirect cost pool, an asset shall be established by reducing the indirect cost pools.

Part 412—Composition and measurement of pension cost

The Standard provides guidance for identifying and measuring the components of pension costs and establishes the basis on which pension costs shall be assigned to a cost accounting period. The Standard also requires that for defined benefit plans actuarial cost methods must be used, and each actuarial assumption used to measure pension cost must be specifically identified and supported. Pension costs are allocable to the cost objectives of a cost accounting period to the extent that the liquidation of the liability for such costs can be compelled or liquidation is actually effected in that period.

This Standard establishes the parameters and criteria for amortization of unfunded actuarial liabilities. The validity of the actuarial assumptions may be evaluated as an aggregate rather than on an assumption-by-assumption basis. The pension cost of a cost accounting period is assignable only to that period. For any portion of the pension cost not funded in a period, no amounts for interest "freezing payments" on that portion not funded in the period shall be a component of the pension cost of any future cost accounting period. Information identifying the actuarial gains and losses that have occurred since the last determination of gains and losses must be compiled.

Part 413—Adjustment and allocation of pension cost

This Standard provides guidance for measuring and assigning actuarial gains and losses to cost accounting periods and provides the bases on which pension costs shall be allocated to the segments of an organization. Actuarial gains and losses must be calculated annually by using a valuation method which takes into account the unrealized appreciation and depreciation of all pension fund assets. The base to be used to allocate pension cost to segments shall be representative of the factors on which the pension benefits are based. A separate allocation for a segment is required where certain conditions exist that would materially affect the amount of pension cost allocated to a segment.

Any recognized asset valuation method that provides equivalent recognition of appreciation and depreciation of assets may be used. However, the total asset value produced by the method shall fall within a corridor, from 80 to 100 percent of the market value of the assets determined as of the valuation date. Actuarial gains and losses are to be amortized over a 15-year period with equal annual installments.

Where separate allocation of pension costs to a segment is required, appropriate records dealing with allocation of assets, income, and expenses for that segment shall be maintained. Where a segment is closed, the Standard requires that a determination be made of the differences between the actuarial liability for the segment and the market value of the asset allocated to the segment. This difference represents an adjustment of previously determined pension cost.

Part 414—Cost of money as an element of facilities capital

The Standard provides a technique for measuring and allocating the imputed cost of a contractor's investment in facilities capital. The investment base used for purposes of computing this cost is the historical net book value of the contractor's facilities capital used for contract costing purposes. The interest rate to be applied to this base is derived from the semiannual interest rate established by the Secretary of Treasury pursuant to Public Law 92–41. Through a series of forms and procedures the Standard allocates capital to the various indirect cost pools, assigns a cost to the capital, and then expresses this cost as a rate using the allocation base for the indirect cost pool.

The Standard provides for the identification, measurement, and allocation of these costs to contracts. The Standard does not establish how this cost shall be expressed in Government contract pricing. This is the responsibility of the procurement agencies.

Part 415—Accounting for cost of deferred compensation

The Standard provides guidance for the measurement and assignment of the cost of deferred compensation. The cost of deferred compensation shall be assigned to the cost accounting period in which the contractor incurred an obligation to compensate the employee. This represents a change from the existing contract accounting, which provides that the cost is not recognizable until paid. Criteria for identifying when a contractor shall be deemed to have incurred an obligation for the cost are provided. If all the criteria are not met, then the cost shall be recognized in the cost accounting period in which the award is paid. The Standard provides a means for adjusting the cost for these plans in which interest rates may fluctuate in accordance with a particular plan or index. Where future services are required to obtain the award, the Standard requires that the amount of award be prorated among the periods of future service. The cost of awards made in the stock of a contractor shall be based on the market value of the stock on the measurement date— the first date on which the number of shares awarded is known. The cost of stock options shall be the amount by which the market value of the stock exceeds the option price on the measurement date.

Statements of the CASB

The Board has issued two broad policy and operating statements—in 1973, the *Statement of Operating Policies, Procedures and Objectives,* and in 1977, the *Restatement of Objectives, Policies and Concepts.* The statements represent a significant effort by the Board to provide an insight and orientation to the Board's work for those coming into contact with its pronouncements. The statements also describe the Board's operating policy, including its relationship to other authoritative bodies. A major aspect of the statements in terms of accounting theory is the inclusion of the Board's cost allocation concepts.

Cost allocation concepts

Cost Accounting Standards provide criteria for the allocation of the cost of resources used to cost objectives. For contract costing purposes, the Board generally adheres to the concept of full costing, including G&A expenses and all other indirect costs. Allocation bases are devices used to associate cost with the final cost objectives when such costs are not directly identifiable with those cost objectives. These bases portray a reasonable measure of the beneficial or causal relationship between these costs and cost objectives.

The Board has established a hierarchy for allocating costs as a basic framework for the allocation Standards issued by the Board. The Board expressed preference for direct identification of costs where the beneficial or causal relationship is clear and exclusive and the amount of resource used is readily and economically measurable.

In those instances where the units of resource are not directly identifiable with final cost objectives, the cost of the resource should be grouped in logical and homogeneous pools and allocated to cost objectives in accordance with the hierarchy for allocating costs. *Homogeneity* means that the cost of functions allocated by a single base have the same or a similar relationship to the cost objectives for which the functions are performed; the grouping results in a better identification of costs to cost objectives. Unlike functions may have the same or a similar relationship to cost objectives and may be allocated over the same base. Also, where the final output is the same or similar, all indirect functions attributable to the output may be grouped.

The Board has stated that the preferable allocation techniques for distributing homogeneous pools of cost, in descending order, are:

1. A measure of the activity of the function represented by the pool of costs.
2. A measurement of the output of the function.
3. A surrogate, if needed, may be used. This generally is a measure of the activity of the cost objective receiving the service and should vary in proportion to the services received.

Pooled costs, which cannot be readily allocated on measures of specific beneficial or causal relationship, generally represent the entire activity being managed and should be allocated by using a measure of the total activity. This hierarchy from direct identification to activity being managed provides a framework for determining the type of allocation base which shall be used in specific circumstances. It also provides a framework for evaluating the Board's allocation Standards.

Other research

In addition to the Standards already promulgated, other areas have been enumerated representing ongoing research in progress by the CASB staff for possible development into Standards. These areas of research are as follows:

1. Allocation of manufacturing, engineering, and comparable overhead.
2. Distinguishing between direct and indirect costs.
3. Accounting for costs of service centers.
4. Accounting for insurance costs.
5. Allocation of material-related costs.
6. Independent research and development and bid and proposal costs.
7. Indirect costs of colleges and universities.
8. Accounting for contract termination.
9. Accounting for intracompany transfers.
10. Cost of money as an element of the cost of operating capital.
11. Joint product costing.

SOURCES OF INFORMATION

This chapter has introduced the reader to the operations of the CASB and its regulations. For more detailed data about CASB matters, interested parties may refer to Title 4 of the Code of Federal Regulations (CFR) or the publication *Cost Accounting Standards Board-Standards, Rules and Regulations* published by the Government Printing Office.

Persons interested in current CASB research and other matters should contact the Board at 441 G Street, N.W., Washington, D.C. 20548. The Board maintains a mailing list to keep interested parties informed.

Index